DESCENDANTS OF CHRISTEN CHRISTNER

Christner

Table of Contents

DESCENDANTS OF CHRISTEN CHRISTNER

BOOK I

SWITZERLAND TO AMERICA

COMPILED BY

DR. DORAINE EASTER DORMAN

Published by BERLIN AREA HISTORICAL SOCIETY
             400 VINE STREET
             BERLIN, PA 15530

ISBN- 978-0-9886458-2-0 Book I
ISBN- 978-0-9886458-3-7 Book II

Dedication

This book is dedicated to
my wonderful and supportive husband
who has endured my time writing
the Christner Genealogy for the past few years.
Thank you Kenny and I love you very much!

Forward

If it wasn't for our ancestors we would not need a history book. Thanks to the people before me who decided to write down and keep track of our ancestors, we have now compiled the information up to the year 2013. The last book that I found was written in February 1960. So between the last book and to present day there was a lot of ground to cover. Also, a lot of the information was not verified. So from the beginning of when Christen Christner's descendants came from Switzerland to Pennsylvania, I have collected and compiled the data. I went through almost every cemetery that I could find in the US and Canada for Christner's and was able to add data that is listed here. The end is just the beginning in the never ending quest for information about our ancestors.

Going back to when I was 14 years old and the oldest of 4 girls, my mother was dying of brain cancer. One day I asked her who her grandparents were. I wrote it down and stuck it in the Bible that she saved up with her green stamps for my 10th birthday. She died 2 years later when I was 16. After a long career in law enforcement and the Army Reserve, I pulled it out and really started studying it. I had no clue on how to get started. One day in Office Depot I found the huge box of CD's that was the first addition of Family Tree Maker. As they direct you to put in what you know, which was not much at the time, I would sit and start putting in names. When I made it to 2000 names I was over joyed. Now, 15 years later I have over 54,000 names in my tree, of which over 14,250 are Christner descendants.

I would like to thank the people who worked on the Christner genealogy before me, who had a lot of work already completed. Those people are: Steven Carl Christner, Jay Lewis Christner, Donna Christner Reece, Tom Christner, Chris Christner, Dora Lue Gilliam, Connie Yokum, and Sheri Christner Kirshbaum. If I missed anyone, please accept my apology. A special thank you to Stewart Saylor.

Any corrections or additions, with proof can be emailed to Dr. Doraine Dorman at (ancestortrunk@gmail.com).

Thank you again everyone who contributed to our wonderful family history.

Dr. Doraine Dorman
November 2013

Descendants of Christen Christner

Generation No. 1

1. Christen[1] Christner[1] was born 1695 in Oberdiessbach, Bern, Canton, Switzerland[1], and died 1734 in Switzerland[1,2]. He married **Barbara Burkhard[2]** Abt. 1716 in Oberdiessbach, Bern, Switzerland. She was born 1699 in Oberdiessbach, Bern, Canton, Switzerland, and died 1735 in Switzerland[2].

Notes for Christen Christner:
Was a known Anabaptist or Täufer and lived at Oberdiessbach formally known as Diessbach which means this/these brook ober means upper. The Castle at Oberdiessbach was built by Niklaus von Diesbach 1546.

From here on back the family name was spelled Christnener

Täufer was the term for a follower of Christ but not the doctrines of the State approved Church. Täufer's could not own land or be buried in a cemetery or own any possessions, if that isn't enough to discourage you the next step is to be burned at the stake or tied to the end of a pole, taken out on the river and held under the water until death.

Notes for Barbara Burkhard:
Both Christian and Barbara are from Oberdiessbach Switzerland some say they were married in Oberdiessbach.

Children of Christen Christner and Barbara Burkhard are:

2		i.	Christina[2] Christner, born 1717 in Oberdiessbach, Bern, Canton, Switzerland.
3		ii.	Jacob Christner, born 1719 in Oberdiessbach, Bern, Canton, Switzerland.
+	4	iii.	Christian Christner, born 1721 in Oberdiessbach, Bern, Canton, Switzerland; died 1812 in Windstein, Bas-Rhin, Alsace, France.
5		iv.	Magdalena Christner, born 1724 in Oberdiessbach, Bern, Canton, Switzerland.
6		v.	Barbara Christner, born 1724 in Oberdiessbach, Bern, Canton, Switzerland.
7		vi.	Saloma Christner, born 1730 in Oberdiessbach, Bern, Switzerland.
8		vii.	Johannes Christner, born 1732 in Oberdiessbach, Bern, Canton, Switzerland; died 27 Feb 1794 in Windstein, Alsace, France.

Notes for Johannes Christner:
John moved to Alsace, France year unknown.

He remained single. It is believed this is the Han's that wrote the letter that came to America in 1770. This was our Han's the immigrant's uncle.

More About Johannes Christner:
Fact 1 (2): Died single

9		viii.	Elisbeth Christner, born 1738 in Oberdiessbach, Bern, Canton, Switzerland.

Generation No. 2

4. Christian[2] Christner (Christen[1])[2,3] was born 1721 in Oberdiessbach, Bern, Canton, Switzerland[4], and died 1812 in Windstein, Bas-Rhin, Alsace, France[4,5]. He married **(1) Barbara Burkhard**[6,7]. She was born 1725 in Oberdiessbach, Luzern, Switzerland[7,8], and died in Switzerland[8,9]. He married **(2) Agnes Scheck**[10]. She was born in Weilheim, Tubingen, Baden-Wuerttemberg, Germany[10].

Notes for Christian Christner:
Christian moved to the Forest of the Normanvillars which is northeast of Montbeliard, France and southeast of Belfort. This is a forest and swamp/ponds area ruled by the Lords of Florimont. Today the area is called Les Mennonites. Later to Windstein, Alsace, France around 1752 to 1762. We do not know who Christian married.

Our name was also spelled several different ways at this time (Christen & Christener).

He was a Täufer. Täufer was the term for a follower of Christ but not the doctrines of the State approved Church. Täufer's could not own land or be buried in a cemetery or own any possessions, if that isn't enough to discourage you the next step is to be burned at the stake or tied to the end of a pole, taken out on the river and held under the water until death.

This can be studied further in the book (page 89) Bernese Anabaptists by Delbert Gratz.

Amish and Amish Mennonite Genealogies; Hugh F. Gingerich and Rachel W. Kreider; Publication: Pequea Publishers, Gordonville, PA 17529; CH, p 56;

Child of Christian Christner and Barbara Burkhard is:

+ 10   i.   Anna[3] Christner, born 1745 in Oberdiessbach, Bern, Canton, Switzerland; died 1824 in Elklick Twp., Somerset Co., PA.

Children of Christian Christner and Agnes Scheck are:

+ 11   i.   Johannes John Hans[3] Christner, born 08 Nov 1749 in Oberdiessbach, Bern, Switzerland; died 28 Sep 1833 in Elk Lick Twp., Somerset Co., PA.

+ 12   ii.   Christian Christner Jr., born 1750 in Oberdiessbach, Bern, Switzerland; died in Windstien, Alsace, France.

Generation No. 3

    10. Anna[3] Christner (Christian[2], Christen[1])[11] was born 1745 in Oberdiessbach, Bern, Canton, Switzerland, and died 1824 in Elklick Twp., Somerset Co., PA[11]. She married **(1) Ulrich Schrag Schrock**[11] 1765 in Berne Canton, Switzerland[12]. He was born 1740 in Berne Canton, Switzerland[12], and died 1795 in Somerset Co., PA[12,13]. She married **(2) John Hochstetler Sr**[14,15] Aft. 1787 in Somerset Co., PA. He was born 01 Jan 1730 in Echery, Nr St Marie Aux Mines, Alsace, Switzerland (France)[16], and died 15 Apr 1805 in Elk Lick Twp., Somerset Co., PA.

Notes for Anna Christner:
Amish and Amish Mennonite Genealogies; p. 56, CH1

Birth: 1745
Death: Apr. 7, 1824 - Somerset Co., PA

Married first to Uli Schrock, with whom she had 8 children, including John Schrock, Barbara, Anna Hershberger, Freni Schrock and Mary Maust. Married secondly to John Hochstetler Sr., original owner of the farm on which this cemetery is located.

Spouse: John Hochstetler (_____ - 1805)

Inscription: "1824 7AP AHO"

Burial: Old Joel Hershberger Farm Cemetery, Elk Lick Twp., Somerset Co., PA
Plot: #22 in Bender Survey (1934)
Find A Grave Memorial# 15541167

Notes for Ulrich Schrag Schrock:
Amish and Amish Mennonite Genealogies; p. 391, SK2

Came to america in 1769 (his brother Hanes in 1766). Uli came with Joseph (Schantz) Johns Ulrich came to America on the ship Nancy and Sukey Sept 1, 1769. (his brother Hanes in 1766) . Uli came with Joseph & Franie (Schantz) Johns they were brother & sister, Franie married John Hans Christner born 1749.

More About Ulrich Schrag Schrock:
Immigration: 01 Sep 1770, From Switzerland to Philadelphia, PA[17]

Notes for John Hochstetler Sr:
Amish and Amish Mennonite Genealogies; CH1, p. 56; HS1, p. 122

Will dated March 15, 1805.

Birth: 1 Jan 1730
Death: Apr. 11, 1805 - Somerset Co., PA

Original tombstone reads: "1805 H H 11 APRIL" (HH for Hans Hochstetler).

Born ca. 1735 in Europe, probably along the Rhine, son of Jacob Hochstetler. Immigrated to the America with his parents in 1738 on the ship Charming Nancy and settled in Bern Twp., Berks Co., PA. As a young married man, he witnessed an Indian attack on his parents' home, where his mother, sister and brother were killed and his father and two other brothers were taken prisoner.

John was married to Catherine, daughter of Amish Bishop Jacob Hertzler, and eventually removed to Somerset Co., PA. Father of Jacob, John, Catherine, Joseph, David, Henry, Daniel and Jonathan Hochstetler, Freni Yoder and Anna Miller. Married secondly to Anna Christner, widow of Uli Schrock.

John was buried on his home farm, one mile southwest of Summit Mills, PA. The farm was owned by Joel Hershberger shortly before 1934 when a survey of the cemetery was taken and is generally referred to by that name. It is also known as the historic Hochstetler/Yoder Cemetery.

John's original tombstone was removed for safekeeping to the restored "Little House" (Grossdaddy Haus) on his home farm. When the house was destroyed by a tornado in 1998, the tombstone was recovered and saved. The present Memorial Marker was placed in 1978 by the late Paul V. Hostetler.

Photos from HHH Newsletter, Goshen, IN

Note: The burial place of John's father, Jacob, is unknown. There was some speculation that he may have been buried on his last farm, but that is unproven at this time.

Parents: Mrs. Jacob Hochstetler (____ - 1757)

Spouses:
Catherine Hertzler Hochstetler (____ - 1800)
Anna Christner Hochstetler (1745 - 1824)

Children:
John Hochstetler (____ - 1813)
Jacob Hochstetler (1752 - 1813)
Anna Hochstetler Miller (1764 - ____)
Joseph Hochstetler (1768 - 1823)
Henry Hochstetler (1773 - 1846)

Burial: Old Joel Hershberger Farm Cemetery, Elk Lick Twp., Somerset Co., PA
Plot: #26 in Bender Survey (1934)
Find A Grave Memorial# 15540776

More About John Hochstetler Sr:
Burial: Old Joel Hershberger Farm Cemetery, Elk Lick Twp., Somerset Co., PA[18]
Residence: 1800, Elk Lick, Somerset Co., PA[18]

Children of Anna Christner and Ulrich Schrock are:

13   i.   Anna[4] Schrock[19], born 1760 in Connellsville, Fayette Co., PA[19]; died 1810[19].

                    Notes for Anna Schrock:
                    Amish and Amish Mennonite Genealogies; p. 391, SK23

14   ii.   Barbara Schrock[19], born 1762[19]; died 1767[19].

                    Notes for Barbara Schrock:
                    Amish and Amish Mennonite Genealogies; p. 391, SK22

15   iii. John Hans Schrag Schrock[19], born 10 Mar 1766 in Alsace, France[19]; died 28 Aug 1843 in Cambria Co., PA[19]. He married Barbara Yoder; born 11 Apr 1787; died 30 Sep 1877 in Elkhart Co., IN.

                    Notes for John Hans Schrag Schrock:
                    Amish and Amish Mennonite Genealogies; p. 391, SK21

16   iv. Anna Schrock[19], born 1774 in Elk Lick Twp., Somerset Co., PA[19]; died 1824 in Somerset Co., PA[19]. She married Jonathan Hochstetler[20]; born Bet. 1776 - 1777 in Northkill, Hamburg, Berks Co., PA[20]; died 08 May 1823 in Berlin, Holmes Co., OH.

                    Notes for Jonathan Hochstetler:
                    He inherited the family book Egyptian Mysteries. (Do not know what this is or what it is about). His 2nd wife was a Anna Christner.

                    More About Jonathan Hochstetler:
                    Burial: Holmes Co., OH[20]
                    Residence: 1810, Elk Lick, Somerset Co., PA[20]

17   v.   Veronica Frany Schrock[21], born 1786 in Somerset Co., PA[21].

                    Notes for Veronica Frany Schrock:
                    Amish and Amish Mennonite Genealogies; p. 391, SK27

18   vi. Mary Schrock[21], born 04 Mar 1787 in Somerset, Somerset Co., PA[21]; died 24 Nov 1855 in Somerset Co., PA[21].

                    Notes for Mary Schrock:
                    Amish and Amish Mennonite Genealogies; p. 391, SK28

                    Mary married Joseph Maust born 1763 and died 1845
                    DJH3311

Child of Anna Christner and John Hochstetler is:

19   i.   Jonathan[4] Hochstetler[22], born Bet. 1776 - 1777 in Northkill, Hamburg, Berks Co., PA[22]; died 08 May 1823 in Berlin, Holmes Co., OH. He married Anna Schrock[23]; born 1774 in Elk Lick Twp., Somerset Co., PA[23]; died 1824 in Somerset Co., PA[23].

                    Notes for Jonathan Hochstetler:
                    He inherited the family book Egyptian Mysteries. (Do not know what this is or what it is about). His 2nd wife was a Anna Christner.

                    More About Jonathan Hochstetler:
                    Burial: Holmes Co., OH[24]
                    Residence: 1810, Elk Lick, Somerset Co., PA[24]

11. Johannes John Hans[3] Christner (Christian[2], Christen[1])[25,26,27] was born 08 Nov 1749 in Oberdiessbach,

Bern, Switzerland[28,29,30,31,32,33], and died 28 Sep 1833 in Elk Lick Twp., Somerset Co., PA[34]. He married **Veronica Frany (Schantz) Johns**[35,36,37,38,39] 1771 in Somerset Co., PA. She was born 1751 in Switzerland[40,41,42,43,44], and died 23 Sep 1833 in Elk Lick Twp., Somerset Co., PA[45].

Notes for Johannes John Hans Christner:
Amish and Amish Mennonite Genealogies; JH2, p. 157; CH2, p. 56

John came to America age 38 on Oct 29, 1770 via the ship Sally. The captain of the ship was John Osmond. They first went to Rotterdam Holland, then Cowes England where the permit was applied for to take the immigrants to Englands new country. The arrived at Philadelphia, PA. John had to work his passage off and there is know record of him till April 24, 1775 when he and his wife had land dated. Land was surveyed Feb 26 1785 by Vickory Deputy Surveyor General Estate #37 on Tub Mill Run then Brothers Twp.,Bedford Co., PA 192 acres.

1790 census John, wife, 6 boys, 1girl
1795 Somerset Co., organized from part of Brothers Valley
1796 only Christner family in Co.
Got patent on land named "White OAK PLAINS"
1779 1horse, 2 cows,land
1783 2 horses, 2 cows, 2 sheep, land
1784 2horses, 2 cows, 2sheep, land,dwelling
1790 no slaves 9 members in family
1794 first family in Co. to have wooden FLoors in Co.
1800 both over 45 7 sons, 2 daughters
1810 parents living with son John Jr. Jr age 34, wife Mary C. Mast/Maust

John had a sister Ann who married Uly Schrag/Schrock. She brought a letter written May 16 1770. No news only scripture. The letter was written after John had left Switzerland and in the letter the father says his sister will give him all the family news when she arrives.

It is believed Hans's father being a Täufer had to leave Oberdiessbach Switzerland and move to Windstein, Alsace, France (1752 to 1762) where very few law authorities lived. They arrived at Philadelphia, PA the permit was applied for to take the immigrants to Englands new country. It is believed Hans's father being a Täufer had to leave Oberdiessbach Switzerland and move to Windstein, Alsace, France (1752 to 1762) where very few law authorities lived. They arrived at Philadelphia Pa. John had to work his passage off and there is no record of him till April 24, 1775 when he and his wife had land dated and deeded. Land was surveyed Feb 26, 1785 by Vickory Deputy Surveyor General Estate #37 on Tub Mill Run then Brothers Twp., Bedford Co. 192 acres.

John Hans Christner died in 1816. He and Frany are believed to be buried on the original tract of land at a site near where the caboose sits on the hill overlooking the Compton/Brenneman farm near West Salisbury. The stones marking the site are no longer in evidence. As a part of the Somerset County 1995 Bicentennial celebration, John and Frany'sdescendants erected a stone memorial in the cemetery of the Maple Glen Church of the Brethren at Savage on the southwest side of Mt. Davis along Christner Hollow Road. Some of John's descendants who attended the church are buried next to the memorial.

Had 192 acres dated and warranted on Tub Mill Run, Bedford Co. , PA 1775. (now Somerset Co.)

From The Laurel Messenger, Aug. 1964, pg. 132:
Joseph Johns, the founder of Johnstown, was a native of Switzerland. He, and a sister named Frannie Johns came to this country about 1758, when he was nineteen years of age and first located in Berks Co., PA where he and Franie Holly were married.

Joseph's sister, Frannie Johns married Hans John Christner. They located in what is now Elk Lick Twp., Somerset County. On 24 April 1775 John Christner was warrented a 192.5 acre tract on Negro Mt. slope, in Brothersvalley Township. The patent named it "White Oak Plains". Their children were Peter, Eli, Jonas, David, Joseph, Benjamin, Christian, Gabriel, John and Daniel.

Christner Cemetery 150 feet left of the caboose. Caboose at the Compton Farm. Elk Lick, Somerset Co, PA

Buried under the caboose. First Christner farm Look for Caboose N39°44.942 X W79°7.304 about 1200 Oakdale Road Salisbury, PA 15558 or North of Springs Road (St.Rd.669) on Oak Dale Road.

The Descendants of John J. Christner, privately published 1961, February 1961, p 4.

More About Johannes John Hans Christner:
Arrival: 1770, Philadelphia, PA[46,47]
Burial: Compton Cemetery, orginal homestead, Elklick Twp., Somerset Co., PA
Military service: Paid Federal Supply Tax for the Revolutionary War/
Residence: 1810, Elk Lick, Somerset Co., PA[48]

Notes for Veronica Frany (Schantz) Johns:
Amish and Amish Mennonite Genealogies; JH2, p. 157; CH2, p. 56

Frany/Franie (Schantz) Johns:

Frany and her brother Joseph Schantz Johns (born 1750) came to America on the ship Nancy and Suckey September 1, 1769. They settled in Berks Co., PA. Joseph married Freni Holly. Joseph was the founder of Johnstown, PA. He plotted out the town, but because of the age of this record.

Because of the age of this record, we will include a little bit of Joseph Johns history that we know in hopes it will help someone else in later searches.

Joseph Johns and Freni Holly had a son Joseph II born Jan 19, 1792. He married Anna Nancy Blough and she was born Aug 26 1799.

Some of this info came from the Laurel Messenger Feb 1981.

Fannie Frannie Freny Frany Freni are all nicknames for Veronica as the german pronunciation uses an F sound instead of a V as in Furronica. (roll the R's) so like many languages if you add a Y sound to the end of a name you have a nickname. Example Johnny, Dickie or Dicky, Bobby.

Last names had the same problem, Schantz became Johns as you can play with the word in german it will sound like (chaunts) the a is ah.

Both Sides of the Ocean: Amish-Mennonites from Switzerland to America by J. Virgil Miller, p. 119

Frany Veronica and her brother Joseph Schantz Johns (born 1750) came to America on the ship Nancy and Sukey Sept 1, 1769. They settled in Berks Co., PA. Frany brought the 1548 Froschauer Bible with her. The bible is at Goshen College Goshen,Indiana. The Bible was given to the College by Levi D. Christner (born 8/20/1897) this is Frany's 3rd. great grandson. Freny's brother Joseph married Freni Veronica Holly.Joseph was the founder of Johnstown, PA. He plotted out the town. Because of the age of this record,we will include a little bit of Joseph Johns history that we know in hopes it will help someone else in later searches, Joseph Johns and Freni Veronica Holly had a son Joseph II born Jan 19, 1792. He married Anna Nancy Blough and she was born Aug 26, 1799.

Some say his name was (Michael) Schantz & he was a preacher to the Amish/Mennonites in Smithville, OH. Frany Veronica Holly is the daughter of Johannes Holly and Freny ?

Veronica was a popular name with the early Christner family. Veronica was the woman who gave Jesus a cloth to wipe his face while he carried the cross. This name comes from the fourteen Stations of the Cross, including the extra-biblical character, Veronica, who wipes Jesus' bloody face with her veil which retains the image of his face imprinted upon it, left as a gift for her and for Christians to contemplate forever. This is a medieval Roman Catholic Holdover from their early religion. Origin of the name Veronica This was legend, NOT recorded in scripture. It was a small step from vera icon (true Image) to Veronica.Read The Acts of Pilate & Gospel of Nicodemus for more information.

Fannie Frannie Freny Frany Freni are all nicknames for Veronica as the german pronunciation uses an F sound instead of a V as in Furronica. (roll the R's) so like many languages if you add a Y sound to the end of a name you have a nickname. Example Johnny, Dickie or Dicky, Bobby.

Last names had the same problem, Schantz became Johns as you can play with the word in german it will sound like (chaunts) the a is ah.

The Descendants of John J. Christner, privately published 1961, February 1961, p 4.

Joseph Johns/ Schantz, the founder of Johnstown, was also a native of Switzerland. He, and a sister named Frainie, came to this country about 1768, when he was nineteen years of age and first located in Berks county where he and Frainie Holley were married. Joseph Johns/Schantz later bought a farm near Berlin. He appears on the 1779 assessment list with 200 acres of land. This farm was sold in 1793 and on September 13, 1793 he bought land called the Campbell tract, on which most of the city of Johnstown is now situated (1896) Joseph's sister, Frainie Johns/Schantz married John hanns christner by 1775. They located in what is now Elk Lick township, Somerset county. The 192 acre warranted tract of land was also described as being on Negro Mountain slope in Brothers Valley township. The patent name it "White Oak Plains." It has been said that John settled here because it reminded him of his homeland. By the time Somerset county was born, they were listed as the county's only Christner fammily, having 7 boys and 2 girls. Christner Road on top of Negro Moutain still bears the family name even today.

The original Christner homestead of John Hans and Frainie was located in Elk Lick Twp. Near the end of John Hans life, the homestead farm was sold to his son John Jr. John and Frainie lived with John Jr. and family until their deaths. This farm was sold by the descendents of John Jr. to Phines Compton in 1845. There was a large Christner cemetery on the property. There were approximately 45 gravesites. Headstones and markers of this cemetery are gone today. The Comptons permitted some mining on the property. At one time, the headstones and markers were removed and piled on the property. No sign of the cemetery remains today. This was the burial site of John Hans, Frannie, and many of the early family members. Today, the remains of the Compton Mill are still located on the original property. Much of the cited information is from an article by Levi D. Christner and Morman records.   Rev. David A. Christner

More About Veronica Frany (Schantz) Johns:
Burial: Compton Cemetery, orginal homestead, Elk Lick Twp., Somerset Co., PA
Nickname: Frany/Franie

Children of Johannes Christner and Veronica Johns are:

+	20	i.	Christian J.[4] Christner, born 21 Jun 1774 in Somerset Co., PA; died Sep 1845 in Holmes Co., OH.
+	21	ii.	John J. Christner Jr., born 08 Jun 1776 in Elk Lick Twp., Somerset Co., PA; died 20 Sep 1845 in Elk Lick Twp., Somerset Co., PA.
+	22	iii.	Peter Christner, born 30 Sep 1779 in Elk Lick Twp., Somerset Co., PA; died 05 Apr 1839 in Elk Lick Twp., Somerset Co., PA.
+	23	iv.	David Christner, born 30 Aug 1781 in Elk Lick Twp., Somerset Co., PA.
+	24	v.	Joseph "Zep" Christner, born 19 Aug 1783 in Elk Lick Twp., Somerset Co., PA; died May 1850 in Garrett, Somerset Co., PA.
+	25	vi.	Benjamin Christner, born 13 Sep 1785 in Elk Lick Twp., Somerset Co., PA; died 01 Mar 1854 in Etobicoke Twp., York Co., Toronto, Ontario, Canada.
	26	vii.	Magdalena Christner, born 21 Jan 1790 in Elk Lick Twp., Somerset Co., PA; died 1800.
	27	viii.	Barbara Christner, born 16 Oct 1792 in Elk Lick Twp., Somerset Co., PA; died 1890.

Notes for Barbara Christner:
Barbara never married. She lived in OH with her brother Zeps son. Don't know which son. Birth maybe Nov.16, 1791.

+	28	ix.	Jonas Christner, born 11 Feb 1794 in Elk Lick Twp., Somerset Co., PA; died 1849 in Essex, Ontario, Canada.

12. Christian[3] Christner Jr. (Christian[2], Christen[1]) was born 1750 in Oberdiessbach, Bern, Switzerland, and died in Windstien, Alsace, France. He married **Margarete Stucki Stubi**. She was born 1754 in Switzerland or Alsace France.

Notes for Christian Christner Jr.:
Amish and Amish Mennonite Genealogies; CH, p. 56;

Christian moved to the Forest of the Normanvillars which is northeast of Montbeliard, France and southeast of Belfort. This is a forest and swamp/ponds area ruled by the Lords of Florimont. Today the area is called Les Mennonites. This can be studied further in the book (page 89) Bernese Anabaptists by Delbert Gratz or Windstein Alsace France around 1752 to 1762. We do not know which area first they are only 100 miles apart. We do not know who Christian married. Our name was also spelled several different ways at this time (Christen & Christener).

Notes for Margarete Stucki Stubi:
Sometimes the name is spelled Stubi or Stuby.

Children of Christian Christner and Margarete Stubi are:

+	29	i.	Barbe[4] Christner, born 1770 in Windstein, Alsace, France; died 05 Mar 1829 in Neuhofen, Germany.
+	30	ii.	Catherine Christner, born 1772 in Windstein Alsace France or Switzerland; died 07 Jul 1840 in Dambach, Alsace, France.
+	31	iii.	Maria Anna Christner, born 1773; died in Rannsbrunnerhaf.
+	32	iv.	Peter Christner, born 1775 in Guenstelhof, near Windstein, Alsace, France; died 1826 in Burgwalden, Augsburg, Bayern, Germany.
+	33	v.	John Johann Christner, born 13 Dec 1780 in Florimont, Alsace, France; died 25 May 1871 in Wilmont Twp., Waterloo Co., Ontario, Canada.

Generation No. 4

20. Christian J.[4] Christner (Johannes John Hans[3], Christian[2], Christen[1])[49] was born 21 Jun 1774 in Somerset Co., PA[49], and died Sep 1845 in Holmes Co., OH[49]. He married **Barbara Holly Hooley** 1802 in Somerset Co., PA. She was born 06 Nov 1780 in Berlin Twp., Somerset Co., PA, and died 1850 in Holmes Co., OH.

Notes for Christian J. Christner:
Amish and Amish Mennonite Genealogies; CH21, p. 56

Da Ault Bauverei - The Old Family Farm, Holmes Co., OH

Christian J. & wife Barbara & family moved to Holmes Co., OH in 1824.

Before Christian and Barbara moved to Holmes Co., they lived in Ontario, Canada. They lived in Etobicoke Twp., York Co., Canada. This is now inside the city of Toronto. The 1856 map has Christner Mill. If you look it up, it's where the streets Scarlett, Lawrence, Royal York, and Weston come together on the Humber River.

After John Holly's (Barbara Holly's brother) Death the Christner Mill at York Twp. Ontario, Canada was operated for the benefit of his widow.

The Christner Mill was started by Christian J. Christner (born 1774) a 1st cousin to Veronica Frenika Johns. The mill was on the west bank of the Humber River north of the St. Philips Church at Weston.

By 1779 the Christners, Hollys, and Troyers were all located in Somerset Co., PA. About 1790, John and Christian Troyer, Sons of Michael traveled to Ontario Canada and settled There. Later, Christian Troyer returned to Somerset Co., PA and tried to persuade others to migrate to Canada. Christian bought a 158 acre farm on June 13, 1798 in Elk Lick Twp., Somerset Co., PA. from John and Barbara Fike, so it had to be after that before going to Canada.

A document from Canada gives the names of some of these immigrants. Included are Christian and John Troyer, David Holly Sr., David Holly Jr., John Holly, Christian Christner, and other well known Amish/Mennonite names. Christian Christner's wife Barbara was a Holly. By 1824 they moved to Holmes Co., OH. Christian

Christner is listed as a landowner of German Twp. (now Clark Twp.) in 1825. German township is now known as Clark Twp. This area is comprised of the land around Charm, Farmerstown and Walnut Creek. Christian purchased the 1/4 section on which the cemetery on the present Daniel Miller farm is located. This cemetery was the final resting spot for the early Ohio Christners. Christian purchased this land on March 10, 1825. In 1834, Christian sold his land to his son John. The farm is just south of Walnut Creek on Township road 70 which was the old Walnut Creek-Charm road. N40°30.5000' by W81°44.4500' Buried in the cemetery on the Daniel Miller farm are: Christian and Barbara (Holly) Christner, Christian's son John who died young on December 27, 1838, Magdalena Honderich Christner Miller (first the wife of John C. and then the wife of Issac Miller), Isaac Miller, the Honderichs (Magdalena's parents), and other family members. The farm has been passed down in the Miller family until this day.

The Descendants of John J. Christner, privately published February 1961, p. 4.

More About Christian J. Christner:
Burial: Daniel Miller Farm South of Walnut Creek OH N40°30.5000' by W81°44.4500'

Notes for Barbara Holly Hooley:
Amish and Amish Mennonite Genealogies; CH21, p. 56; HL291, p. 118

Barbara lived with granddaughter Sarah Sipe Mishler in Berlin Twp., Holmes Co., OH in 1850 & was 69 years old. Barbara is the daughter of David and Catherine Gindlesperger Hulley. Some spellings are Hooley & Holly

After John Holly's (Barbara Holly's brother) Death the Christner Mill at York Twp., Ontario, Canada was operated for the benifit of his widow. The Christner Mill was started by Christian J. Christner (born 1774) a 1st cousin to Veronica Frenika Johns. The mill was on the west bank ot the Humber River north of the St. Philips Church at Weston.

The Descendants of John J. Christner, privately published February 1961, p. 4.

More About Barbara Holly Hooley:
Burial: Daniel Miller Farm South of Walnut Creek OH

Children of Christian Christner and Barbara Hooley are:

+ 34   i.   Elizabeth[5] Christner, born 15 Jul 1803 in Somerset Co., PA; died Jul 1849 in Summit Twp., Somerset Co., PA.

+ 35   ii.   Joseph C. Christner, born 23 Oct 1805 in Somerset Co., PA; died 01 Sep 1881 in Lagrange Co., IN.

   36   iii.   Gabriel Christner[50,51], born 02 May 1808 in Elk Lick, Somerset Co., PA[51]; died 15 Oct 1886 in Milford, Somerset Co., PA[51,52]. He married Susan Walters[53] in Fayette Co, PA; born 15 Jul 1813; died 17 Aug 1899[53].

> Notes for Gabriel Christner:
> Amish and Amish Mennonite Genealogies; CH213, p. 56
>
> Gabril granted a tract of land in Holmes Co., OH from the Government in 1835 - Section 17 Twp. 9 Range 6 (Hardy Twp.) Transfered Land in 1845 to Daniel Christner. The deed was dated September 8, 1835 and signed by President Andrew Jackson.
>
> Union Center Cemetery records have Susan Wife of G. Christner died Aug 17 1899 age 86 years 1 month 2 days. This would make her born July 15, 1813 and in the proper age range to be the wife of Gabril, but this is unconfirmed.
>
> More About Gabriel Christner:
> Residence: 1840, Fayette Co., PA[54]
>
> Notes for Susan Walters:
> Birth: Jan. 27, 1813
> Death: Aug. 17, 1899
> Somerset Co., PA

Children:
John C. Christner (1841 - 1921)

Inscription: 86y 1m 2d - w/o of G

Burial: Center Lutheran Church Cemetery, Summit Twp., Somerset Co., PA
Find A Grave Memorial# 6700737

More About Susan Walters:
Burial: Union Center Cemetery

+ 37   iv.   John J. Christner, born 15 Nov 1810 in Holmes Co., OH; died 27 Dec 1838 in Holmes Co., OH.
   38   v.   Jonas Christner[55], born 26 Aug 1813 in Connellsville, Fayette Co., PA; died 1871.

        Notes for Jonas Christner:
        Amish and Amish Mennonite Genealogies; CH215 p. 56

+ 39   vi.   Veronica Fannie Christner, born 12 Oct 1816 in Holmes Co. OH.
+ 40   vii.   Daniel Christner, born 14 Nov 1819 in Holmes Co., OH; died 1871.

21. John J.[4] Christner Jr. (Johannes John Hans[3], Christian[2], Christen[1])[55,56] was born 08 Jun 1776 in Elk Lick Twp., Somerset Co., PA, and died 20 Sep 1845 in Elk Lick Twp., Somerset Co., PA. He married **Mary Catherine Maust**[57] 31 Oct 1802 in Somerset Co., PA, daughter of Jacob Maust and Barbara Fike. She was born 1781 in Bernville, Berks Co., PA, and died 05 Sep 1855 in Elk Lick Twp., Somerset Co., PA.

Notes for John J. Christner Jr.:
Amish and Amish Mennonite Genealogies; CH22, pp. 56, 64; MS339, p. 324, 328

1810 US Census - PA; John and Mary were married

1820 US Census - PA; John and Mary have 6 children.

In 1838 John, Jr. deeded 14 acres to Samuel Compton.

In 1845 John's heirs sold the estate of 484 acres in Elk Lick Twp. to Phinias Compton for $4,000.00.

John Jr. & Mary Maust kept the parents until their death & lived on the original homestead. John Jr.'s heirs sold the farm & two adjoining tracts totaling 484 acres to Phineas Compton for $40 00 in 1845. The Compton family still owns the property (2002). The census of 1810 John Jr. and Mary were already married.

In 1838 John Jr. deeded 14 acres to Samuel Compton John Jr. heirs sold this (estate #37) property and 2 other adjoining tracts totaling 484 acres in Elk lick Twp as a whole to Phinias Compton for $4,000.00.

1845 Will probated Sept 20, 1845 - dated Aug 18, 1845.
We are missing 2 children. The only records we have are of 4 children.

In census of 1820 has 6 children In 1838 John Jr deeded 14 acres to Samuel Compton John Jr. heirs sold this (estate #37) property and 2 other adjoining tracts totaling 484 acres in Elk lick Twp as a whole to Phinias Compton for $4,000.00 in 1845.

Will probated Sept 20 1845//dated Aug 18 1845.
We are missing one child. The only records we have are of 5 children.

The Descendants of John J. Christner, self published February 1961, p. 4.

More About John J. Christner Jr.:
Burial: Sep 1845, Compton Farm, Elk lick Twp., Somerset Co., PA - Buried 150 feet left of the caboose caboose
Census: 1810, PA - Elklick Twp., Somerset Co., PA

Will: 18 Aug 1845, Probated 20 September 1845

Notes for Mary Catherine Maust:
Mary is the daughter of Jacob Maust and Barbara Fike Jacob got land Somerset Co., PA deed Vol. 18 page 223 in 1838 that Jacob Mosht got in 1806, 103 acres. This land bordered land of Ebenezer Griffith and vacant mountain land.

The Descendants of John J. Christner, privately published February 1961, p. 4.

More About Mary Catherine Maust:
Burial: Sep 1855, Compton Farm, Elk lick Twp., Somerset Co., PA - Buried 150 feet left of the caboose caboose

Children of John Christner and Mary Maust are:
+ 41   i.   John[5] Christner III, born 1805 in Somerset Co., PA.
+ 42   ii.   Veronica Fannie Christner, born Jan 1810 in Somerset Co., PA; died 1845.
   43   iii.   Samuel Christner, born 13 Oct 1810 in Elk Lick Twp., Somerset Co., PA; died 28 Dec 1833 in Elk Lick Twp., Somerset Co., PA.

           Notes for Samuel Christner:
           Christner Burial Gound: Situated in Elk Lick Twp., Somerset Co., PA on the Phineas Compton Farm, north west of the building on top of the hill.

           More About Samuel Christner:
           Burial: Buried 150 feet left of the caboose caboose/Compton Cemetery, orginal homestead, Elk Lick Twp., Somerset Co., PA

+ 44   iv.   Jacob C. Christner, born 16 Aug 1816 in Somerset, Somerset Co., PA; died 20 Jul 1881 in Garrett, Somerset Co., PA.

     22. Peter[4] Christner (Johannes John Hans[3], Christian[2], Christen[1])[58,59,60] was born 30 Sep 1779 in Elk Lick Twp., Somerset Co., PA, and died 05 Apr 1839 in Elk Lick Twp., Somerset Co., PA[61,62]. He married **Susanna Burkholder**[62,63] 1801 in Somerset Co., PA. She was born 10 Feb 1781 in Elk Lick Twp., Somerset Co., PA[64,65], and died 1820 in Elklick Twp., Somerset Co., PA[65].

Notes for Peter Christner:
Peters will is in deed book #16 page 464. It was actually written after his death Peter son of John Hans married Susanna Burkholder. Joseph "Zep" son of John Hans married Barbara Burkholder.

Susanna and Barbara are sisters. Susannas Father John sold 136.5 acres to Peter.

The Descendants of John J. Christner, privately published 1961, February 1961, p 4.

Amish and Amish Mennonite Families; CH23; p. 56

More About Peter Christner:
Burial: Compton Cemetery, orginal homestead, Elklick Twp., Somerset Co., PA
Residence: 1830, Somerset Co., PA[66]

Notes for Susanna Burkholder:
Susanna is the daughter of John Burkholder and Elizabeth Vought.

Susanna and Barbara are sisters and they married brothers Peter and Joseph Christner.

Amish and Amish Mennonite Families; CH23; p. 56

Children of Peter Christner and Susanna Burkholder are:
   45   i.   Christian[5] Christner[66], born 1799[66]; died 1836 in Ontario, Canada[66].
+ 46   ii.   John Christner, born 1802 in Somerset, Somerset Co., PA; died Feb 1863 in Indian Head, Saltlick Twp.,

Fayette Co., PA.

47   iii.   Jonathan Christner[66], born 1811[66]. He married Mary.

Notes for Jonathan Christner:
PA census of 1840 Jonathan and Mary were living in Elk Lick Twp., PA.

PA census of 1850 Jonathan and Mary were living in Holmes Co., OH.

+   48   iv.   Levi Christner, born 1813 in Elk Lick, Somerset Co., PA; died 04 Nov 1882 in Bullskin Twp., Fayette Co., PA.

+   49   v.   Lydia Christner, born 1820 in Somerset, Somerset Co., PA; died 25 Nov 1899 in Somerset Co., PA.

23. David[4] Christner (Johannes John Hans[3], Christian[2], Christen[1])[67,68,69] was born 30 Aug 1781 in Elk Lick Twp., Somerset Co., PA[70,71]. He married **Elizabeth Mishler**[72,73,74,75,76,77] Bef. 1805 in Somerset Co., PA[78]. She was born 1798 in Somerset Co., PA[79,80], and died 1840 in Somerset Co., PA[81,82,83].

Notes for David Christner:
David had 5 children, son born 1806, maybe married Susanna, daughter born 1813, daughter born 1815, Jesse which we know, and daughter born 1825. This info from book Amish and Amish Mennonite Genealogies. David Married a black woman -- they moved to Conemaugh Twp. before 1830. His wife is buried at Maple springs Church of the Brethren Somerset Co., PA.

The Amish and Amish Mennonite Genealogies book lists Davids wife as Elizabeth Mishler. The book does not give Elizabeth's Mother or Grandmother's name. She could of been black as all of Davids children are listed as mulatto in the census. It is a possibility that Elizabeth parents were from black heritage and it was not recognized on the census.

Amish and Amish Mennonite Genealogies; CH24; p. 56

More About David Christner:
Residence: 1850, Conemaugh, Somerset, PA[84,85]

Notes for Elizabeth Mishler:
Amish and Amish Mennonite Genealogies; CH24, p. 56; MH323, p. 261

Elizabeth is the daughter of Joseph and Elizabeth (Hulley) Mishler.

She was a black woman. The book does not give Elizabeth's Mother or grandmother's name and she could of been black as all of Davids children are listed as mulatto in the census. It is a possibility that Elizabeth parents were from black heritage and it was not recognized on the census.

More About Elizabeth Mishler:
Burial: Maple Springs Church of the Brethern, Somerset Co., PA

Children of David Christner and Elizabeth Mishler are:

+   50   i.   Susan[5] Christner, born 1806.

+   51   ii.   David Christner, born 1806 in Somerset Co., PA; died 1849 in Somerset Co., PA.

+   52   iii.   Barbara Shoemaker, born 1813 in Somerset Co., PA.

+   53   iv.   Jessie Christner, born 1818 in Somerset, Somerset Co., PA; died in Conemaugh, Somerset Co., PA.

54   v.   Daughter Christner, born 1825.

24. Joseph "Zep"[4] Christner (Johannes John Hans[3], Christian[2], Christen[1])[86,87,88,89,90,91,92,93,94,95] was born 19 Aug 1783 in Elk Lick Twp., Somerset Co., PA[96,97,98,99,100,101,102,103,104], and died May 1850 in Garrett, Somerset Co., PA[105,105,106,107,108,109]. He married **Barbara "Peggy" Burkholder**[110,111,112,113,114,115,116,117,118] Bet. 1806 - 1808 in Somerset Co., PA[119]. She was born 1789 in Somerset, Somerset Co., PA[120], and died 1850 in Somerset, Somerset Co., PA[121,122,123,124,125,126,127,128].

Notes for Joseph "Zep" Christner:
This info comes from Dora Lue, Laura Paulitick and Connie Yokum. Connie can find no records of a Christner ever marrying a Faust. Zep owned the farm that later was owned by his great grandson Earl of the referred to Earl Christner Farm and Christner Cemetery at Garrett, PA on Johnson Road and Phillippi Road. Part of the cemetery is under the road.

The Descendants of John J. Christner, privately published 1961, February 1961, p. 4.

Amish and Amish Mennonite Genealogies; CH25, p. 57

More About Joseph "Zep" Christner:
Burial: Earl Christner Farm Lower Section
Residence: 1860, Summit, Somerset, Pennsylvania USA[128,128]

Notes for Barbara "Peggy" Burkholder:
Barbara was the daughter of John Burkholder and Elizabeth Vought. Susanna and Barbara are sisters and they married brothers Peter and Joseph Christner. Barbara being Lutheran provided the path away from being Amish thru her son Christian.

More About Barbara "Peggy" Burkholder:
Residence: 1850, Summit, Somerset, Pennsylvania USA[128,129,130,131,132,133,134,135,136]

Children of Joseph Christner and Barbara Burkholder are:

+ 55   i.   Abraham D.[5] Christner, born 30 Sep 1802 in Elk Lick, Somerset Co., PA; died 04 Mar 1879 in Earl Christner Farm, Garrett, Somerset Co., PA.
+ 56   ii.   Mary Christner, born 16 Jan 1808 in Somerset, Somerset Co., PA; died 1879 in Somerset Co., PA.
+ 57   iii.   Elizabeth Christner, born 01 Apr 1810 in Summitt Twp., Somerset Co., PA; died 1879 in Somerset Co., PA.
+ 58   iv.   Christian Christner, born 1811 in Elk Lick Twp., Somerset Co., PA; died 09 Mar 1888 in Somerset Co., PA.
+ 59   v.   Gabriel Christner, born 08 May 1812 in Elk Lick Twp., Somerset Co., PA; died 15 Oct 1886 in Pleasant Hill Cemetery, Milford Twp., Somerset Co., PA/Somerset Co., PA.
+ 60   vi.   Jr. Joseph Christner Jr., born 17 May 1813 in Elk Lick Twp., Somerset Co., PA; died 07 Jan 1897 in Elk Lick Twp., Somerset Co., PA.
+ 61   vii.   Jonas Yone Christner, born 14 Sep 1816 in Summitt, Somerset Co. PA; died 26 Jan 1881 in Garrett, Somerset Co., PA.
   62   viii.   Susanna Christner[137,138], born 1817 in Somerset, Somerset Co., PA[139]; died 1870 in Somerset Co., PA[140,141]. She married Jacob C. Schrock Bet. 1821 - 1865; born 07 Feb 1802 in Somerset Co., PA; died 22 Jan 1884 in Somerset Co., PA.

     Notes for Susanna Christner:
     Amish and Amish Mennonite Genealogies; CH258, p. 57

     More About Susanna Christner:
     Residence: 1880, Summit, Somerset Co., PA[142]

     Notes for Jacob C. Schrock:
     Amish and Amish Mennonite Genealogies; SK151, p. 395

+ 63   ix.   Moses C. Christner, born 28 Jan 1819 in Elk Lick Twp., Somerset Co., PA; died 18 Dec 1898 in Cashion, Lockridge, Logan Co., OK.
+ 64   x.   Eve Christner, born 21 Oct 1821 in Summitt, Somerset Co., PA; died 1901 in Somerset Co., PA.

25. Benjamin[4] Christner (Johannes John Hans[3], Christian[2], Christen[1])[143,144,145,146,147] was born 13 Sep 1785 in Elk Lick Twp., Somerset Co., PA[148,149], and died 01 Mar 1854 in Etobicoke Twp., York Co., Toronto,

Ontario, Canada[150,151]. He married **Margaret McKenzie**[152,153,154] 1810 in Etobicoke Twp., York Co., Ontario, Canada[154]. She was born 1789 in Scotland[155,156,157], and died 1858 in Etobicoke Twp. York Co., Toronto, Ontario, Canada[158,159,160].

Notes for Benjamin Christner:
Amish and Amish Mennonite Genealogies; CH26, p. 56;

Benjamin lived in Ontario Canada close to his brother Christian. We dont no for how long. Benjamin purchased a parcel of land from Kings College in 1837.

Will - April 1 1854 Probate Court York Co.,Ontario Canada (RG22 series 6-2,c10,lds film 1312943).

1851 Census Ontario,York, Etobicoke page 87.

Birth: 13 Sep 1785
Death: Mar 1, 1854

Burial: Saint Philips Churchyard Cemetery, Etobicoke, Ontario, Canada

More About Benjamin Christner:
Burial: St. Phillip's Anglican Churchyard, Etobicoke Twp., York Co. Ontario, Canada
Nickname: Bentz
Residence: 1852, York Co., Canada West (Ontario), Canada[161,162]

More About Margaret McKenzie:
Burial: St. Phillips Church Cemetery across from the Humber River Etobicoke Twp. Toronto CA

Children of Benjamin Christner and Margaret McKenzie are:

	65	i.	Frenika[5] Christner. She married (1) Jacob Holly.
+	66	ii.	Solomon McKenzie Christner, born 1811 in Somerset Co., PA; died 28 Oct 1878 in Painesville, Lake Co., OH.
	67	iii.	Helen Christner[162], born 1813 in Etobicoke, York, Ontario, Canada[162].
	68	iv.	Moses Christner[162], born 1815 in Etobicoke, York, Ontario, Canada[162].
+	69	v.	Barbara Christner, born 1817 in Etobicoke, York, Ontario, Canada; died in Canada.
	70	vi.	Hannah Christner[162], born 1818 in Etobicoke, York, Ontario, Canada[162].
	71	vii.	Susan Christner[162], born 1821 in Etobicoke, York, Ontario, Canada[162].
	72	viii.	Nancy Christner[162], born 1822 in Etobicoke, York, Ontario, Canada[162].
	73	ix.	Aaron Christner, born 28 Jun 1824; died 07 Aug 1835.

More About Aaron Christner:
Burial: St. Phillip's Anglican Churchyard, Etobicoke Twp., York Co. Ontario, Canada

+	74	x.	Mary Jane Christner, born 08 Feb 1829 in Etobicoke Twp., York Toronto, Ontario Canada; died 31 Jul 1911.

28. Jonas[4] Christner (Johannes John Hans[3], Christian[2], Christen[1])[163] was born 11 Feb 1794 in Elk Lick Twp., Somerset Co., PA, and died 1849 in Essex, Ontario, Canada. He married **Margaret Phillips** 01 Oct 1817 in York, Etobicoke , Ontario, Canada.

Notes for Jonas Christner:
Amish and Amish Mennonite Genealogies, CH29, p 56

Benjamin (brother) & Levi (nephew) Christner were sponsors for the marriage of Jonas Christner and Margaret Phillips.

Notes for Margaret Phillips:
She was married to Jonas before 1817 but found out it was not legal so remarried Him. They lived in Etobicoke Twp., Ontario, Canada area.

Children of Jonas Christner and Margaret Phillips are:

75	i.	Laverin Lazarus[5] Christner.
76	ii.	Soloman Christner.
77	iii.	William Christner.
78	iv.	Jonas Christner Jr..

29. Barbe[4] Christner (Christian[3], Christian[2], Christen[1]) was born 1770 in Windstein, Alsace, France, and died 05 Mar 1829 in Neuhofen, Germany. She married **(1) Pierre/Peter Hirschberger.** He was born 1770 in Elsasshaus, and died 14 May 1829 in Neuhofen, Germany. She married **(2) Peter Hersberger Hirschberger.** He was born 1770 in Elsasshaus, and died 14 May 1829 in Neuhoffen, Alsace France.

Notes for Barbe Christner:
Neuhofen, could be in Germany or Austria.

Child of Barbe Christner and Peter Hirschberger is:

79	i.	Catherine Hersberger[5] Hirschberger, born in Windstien, Alsace, France. She married Jean Kreemer 04 Feb 1813 in Dambach, Alsace France; born in neuf Grange, Dept. Moselle.

30. Catherine[4] Christner (Christian[3], Christian[2], Christen[1]) was born 1772 in Windstein Alsace France or Switzerland, and died 07 Jul 1840 in Dambach, Alsace, France. She married **Michael Mueller**[164] 1809. He was born in Dambach, Bas-Rhin, Alsace, France[164], and died 1813 in Wissembourg, Bas-Rhin, Alsace, France[164].

Children of Catherine Christner and Michael Mueller are:

80	i.	Barbara[5] Mueller. She married Joseph Bachman.
81	ii.	Michel Mueller. He married Jacobina Bernart.
82	iii.	Pierre Mueller. He married Elisabeth Steinmann.

31. Maria Anna[4] Christner (Christian[3], Christian[2], Christen[1]) was born 1773, and died in Rannsbrunnerhaf. She married **Jean Johannes Guth** 1797 in Windstein, Alsace, France. He was born 1773 in Gunstalhof near Windstein, Alsace, France, and died 1828 in Rannsbrunnerhaf near Eppenbrunn Palatinate.

Children of Maria Christner and Jean Guth are:

83	i.	Georg[5] Guth, born in Rannsbrunnerhaf; died in Dorsterhof in Lorraine France.

          Notes for Georg Guth:
          Great Grandfather of Historian Hermann Guth

84	ii.	Johannes Guth, born 1798 in Gunstelhof.

          Notes for Johannes Guth:
          Was the first Guth to live on the Barenbrunnerhof near Dahn. He died there and his descendants still live there.

+ 85	iii.	Peter Guth, born 09 Feb 1806; died 24 Jun 1886 in Washington, IL.

32. Peter[4] Christner (Christian[3], Christian[2], Christen[1])[165] was born 1775 in Guenstelhof, near Windstein, Alsace, France[165], and died 1826 in Burgwalden, Augsburg, Bayern, Germany[165]. He married **Magdalena Guth**[165,166] Abt. 1794. She was born in Guenstelhof, near Windstein, Alsace, France[167], and died 1822[167,168].

Notes for Peter Christner:
Peter moved to Bravaria in 1809. Peter's descendants still live on farms on the shores of the Ammersee near Munich Germany. The family has been farmers and Millers for over 150 years. Peter moved to Bavaria 1809.

Notes for Magdalena Guth:
Maybe Spelled Madeleine.

Children of Peter Christner and Magdalena Guth are:

	86	i.	Jean[5] Christner, born 1795 in Alsace, France; died 1822 in Alsace, France.
+	87	ii.	Christian Christner, born 1796 in Alsace, France; died 1836 in Wilmot Twp., Ontario, Canada.
+	88	iii.	Peter Christner II, born 04 Feb 1798 in Guenstelhof, Alsace, France; died 30 Dec 1880 in Marshall, Henry Co., IA.
+	89	iv.	Josef Christner, born 29 Apr 1809 in Windstein, Alsace, France; died 1871 in Germany.

33. John Johann[4] Christner (Christian[3], Christian[2], Christen[1]) was born 13 Dec 1780 in Florimont, Alsace, France, and died 25 May 1871 in Wilmont Twp., Waterloo Co., Ontario, Canada. He married **Maria Mary Luckenbill** 26 Aug 1806. She was born 27 Mar 1784 in Lorraine, Alsace, France, and died 08 Mar 1841.

Notes for John Johann Christner:
OBITUARY - Gospel Harold - 1871

On the 25th of May, in Wilmot Twp., Waterloo Co., Ontario of the infirmities of old age, John Christener, aged 90 years, 5 months and 15 day. He was buried on the 31st on which occasion funeral discourses were delivered by Moses Bowman, from Rev. 2:17, and Geo Schmitt, from Deut. 32:29. He was a native of Florimont, Upper Alsace, and emigrated with his family to Canada, in 1826, where his wife died 30 years ago. He was a member of the Mennonite Church for about 70 years.

John emigrated to Canada about 1825. His name in France was Johann. He was listed as an Anabaptist of Florimont which is just north of Switzerland near Montbeliard France in a swamp called les Mennonites.

Birth: Jun 21, 1815
Death: Apr 6, 1907

April 25, 1907, page 159

Volume XLIV, Number 17 Christner - Christian Christner was born in upper Alsace, Germany, Jun 21, 1815. Emigrated to this country in the year 1825. After suffering but a short time he passed peacefully away in New Hamburg, Ontario, Canada on Apr 6, 1907, 91 Y., 9 M., 15 D. His wife preceded him 23 years, after which he moved to New Hamburg where he resided with two of his daughters until death. He was a member of the Mennonite church. He leaves to mourn his departure four sons and six daughters. Two of his daughters became members of the same church. Funeral services were conducted by Amos S. Cressman, from Psa 90:12 and Noah Stauffer, from Rev. 20:6. The services were held in our Amish Brethren's place of worship, Steinman's M. H.

Parents:
John Christner (1780 - 1871)
Maria Lugebiehl Christner (1784 - 1841)

Spouse: Anna Honsberger Christner (1825 - 1884)

Children:
Daniel Christner (1846 - 1915)
Enos Christner (1850 - 1936)
Catherine Christner (1854 - 1918)
Abraham Christner (1856 - 1872)
Leah Christner Shantz (1858 - 1914)
Christian H. Christner (1860 - 1939)

Burial: Christner Cemetery, Waterloo Co., Ontario, Canada

More About John Johann Christner:
Burial: 31 May 1871
Immigration: 1825, Canada from Germany

Notes for Maria Mary Luckenbill:
Maria (Mary) and John emigrated to Canada about 1825   He name maybe spelled Luckinbill or Luginbuhl.

Birth: Mar. 27, 1784
Death: Mar. 8, 1841

Spouse: John Christner (1780 - 1871)

Children:
Barbara Christner Müller (1812 - 1860)
Christian Christner (1815 - 1907)
Peter L. Christner (1817 - 1899)
Veronica Christner Bechtel (1820 - 1907)

Burial: Christner Cemetery, Waterloo Co., Ontario, Canada

More About Maria Mary Luckenbill:
Immigration: 1825, Canada from Germany

Children of John Christner and Maria Luckenbill are:

	90	i.	Verena Veronica⁵ Christner.
+	91	ii.	Barbara Christner, born 21 Nov 1812 in Lepuix Delle near Florimont, Belfort, Alsace, France; died 15 Oct 1860.
+	92	iii.	Christian Christner, born 21 Jun 1815 in Lepuix Delle near Florimont, Alsace, France; died 06 Apr 1907 in New Hamburg, Wilmot Twp., Waterloo Co., Ontario, Canada.
+	93	iv.	Peter L. Christner, born 12 Oct 1817 in Lepuix Delle near Florimont, Belfort, Alsace, France; died 28 Jan 1899 in Waterloo, New Hamburg, Ontario, Canada.
+	94	v.	Veronica Luckenbill Christner, born 28 Sep 1820 in Lepuix Delle near Florimont, Belfort, Alsace, France; died 21 Apr 2007 in Waterloo Co., Ontario, Canada.

Generation No. 5

34. Elizabeth⁵ Christner (Christian J.⁴, Johannes John Hans³, Christian², Christen¹)[169] was born 15 Jul 1803 in Somerset Co., PA, and died Jul 1849 in Summit Twp., Somerset Co., PA. She married **Andrew Sipe**[169,170,171] 1822 in Holmes Co., OH[172,173]. He was born 05 May 1798 in Somerset, Somerset Co., PA, and died 30 Jul 1877 in Eden, Lagrange Co., IN[174,175].

Notes for Elizabeth Christner:
Amish and Amish Mennonite Genealogies; CH211, p. 56; SI8, p. 389

1850 Census - Summit Twp., Somerset Co., PA
Elizabeth Christner - age 45 died of Malaria.

The Descendants of John J. Christner, privately published 1961, February 1961, p. 4.

More About Elizabeth Christner:
Cause of death (Facts Pg): Malaria
Residence: Ligonier, Noble Co., IN

Notes for Andrew Sipe:
Amish and Amish Mennonite Genealogies;
Page: CH211, page 56; SI8, p 389, 390

Andrew and Elizabeth lived in Holmes Co., OH and then later moved to Legioner, IN. They sold their land in Holmes Co. in 1842 to Joseph Christner.

DEED Transfer: Lagrange Co., IN - Vol 26, Page 602; Andrew Sipe to Straus Brothers 1876 80 acres.

At this time Andrew was listed as a widower and there was a wheat growing crop which was reserved by Andrew. This was October 30, 1876. Andrew is the son of Peter and Barbara Troyer Sipe.

Peter and Barbara came from Germany to the Meyersdale area in 1783 Andrew and Elizabeth lived in Holmes Co., OH and then later in Ligioner, IN. and maybe buried there.

Andrew is the son of Peter and Barbara Troyer Sipe. Peter and Barbara came from Germany to the Meyersdale area in 1783. Andrew and Elizabeth lived in Holmes Co., OH and then later in Ligonier, IN. They sold their land in Holmes Co., OH in 1842 to Elizabeth's brother Joseph Christner. DEED TRANSFER Lagrange Co., IN VOL 26 PAGE 602. Andrew Sipe to Straus Brothers 1876 80 acres. At this time Andrew was listed as a widower,also that there was a growing wheat crop which was reserved by Andrew in Oct 30 1876. They lived in the Ligonier, IN.

More About Andrew Sipe:
Burial: 1877, .N41°31.492 x W85°34.396 - Row 2 Plot15/Maple Grove Cemetery, Topeka, Lagrange Co., IN

Children of Elizabeth Christner and Andrew Sipe are:

+ 95 i. Elizabeth "Betsy"[6] Sipe, born 1824 in Holmes Co., OH; died 22 Oct 1905 in Nappanee, Elkhart Co., IN.
+ 96 ii. Sarah Sipe, born 03 Aug 1826 in Holmes Co., OH; died 25 Sep 1890 in Row5 plot 4.
  97 iii. Barbara Sipe, born 09 Sep 1829 in Holmes Co., OH.
  98 iv. Benjamin Sipe, born 26 Sep 1831 in Holmes Co., OH.

      Notes for Benjamin Sipe:
      Amish and Amish Mennonite Genealogies, Hugh F. Gingerich and Rachel W. Kreider, SI84, p. 390

  99 v. Veronica Fanny Sipe, born 01 Apr 1834 in Holmes Co., OH.
  100 vi. Anna Sipe, born 24 Oct 1836 in Holmes Co., OH. She married Shilling.
  101 vii. Leah Sipe, born 26 Oct 1838 in Holmes Co., OH.
  102 viii. Mary Sipe, born 30 Apr 1841 in Holmes Co., OH; died 24 Dec 1909. She married Joseph Z. Hochstetler; born 11 Nov 1837 in Bellefontaine OH.

      Notes for Mary Sipe:
      Mary married Joseph Z.Hochstetler

  103 ix. William Levi Sipe, born 03 Jun 1844 in Holmes Co., OH; died 13 Jun 1916. He married (1) Matilda J 1864; born 23 Jun 1843; died 16 Jul 1884. He married (2) Susie H 1885; born 24 May 1862; died 22 Mar 1908.

      More About William Levi Sipe:
      Burial: Eden Cemetery 1/2 mile west of Topeka Indiana Lagrange Co. IN

      More About Matilda J:
      Burial: Eden Cemetery 1/2 mile west of Topeka Indiana Lagrange Co. IN

      Notes for Susie H:
      William Levi Sipe is buried west of Topeka IN 1/2 mile with his first wife since he all ready had a headstone there with his name on it.

      More About Susie H:
      Burial: Ligonier IN. just North of US 6 close (West of) to Mausoleum's

35. Joseph C.[5] Christner (Christian J.[4], Johannes John Hans[3], Christian[2], Christen[1])[176,177,178] was born 23 Oct 1805 in Somerset Co., PA[179,180], and died 01 Sep 1881 in Lagrange Co., IN[180,181]. He married **Mary Maria J. Miller**[182,183,184,185] 08 Jan 1827 in Holmes Co., OH. She was born 23 Feb 1809 in Somerset, Somerset Co., PA[186,187,188], and died 02 Aug 1869 in Holmes Co., OH[189,190,191].

Notes for Joseph C. Christner:
Amish and Amish Mennonite Genealogies; CH212 p. 56, ML6132, p. 283

Joseph and Mary lived in Holmes Co., OH in 1819. In his last years he moved to Lagrange Co., IN. I think that Mary moved there also. The census of 1850 has them listed in Holmes Co., OH. They sold there farm in 1855. Joseph was a cooper. Info about his farm on wifes notes. Joseph was a miller and cooper (a maker of wooden Barrels)Info about his farm on wifes notes. Maybe born August 23 And Maybe had two more children Frannie born 1824 and Jacob born 1831.

The Descendants of John J. Christner, privately published 1961, February 1961, p 4.

More About Joseph C. Christner:
Burial: Miller Amish Cemetery, Lagrange, Lagrange Co., IN
Occupation: Cooper/
Residence: 1850, Mechanic, Holmes Co., OH[192]

Notes for Mary Maria J. Miller:
Mary was married to Joseph C. Christner b. 1805. Mary is the daughter of Jonathan Miller (b. Mar 7, 1789 and d. Sep 18, 1867) and Magdalina Kauffman (b. Sept 9, 1785 and d. Aug 16, 1862) Jonathan and Magdalina were married in 1806 in PA. Mary had at least one sister Veronica (b. Oct 13, 1807) Jonathan Millers father was Christian Schmidt Miller.

Joseph and Mary lived in Holmes Co., OH. They bought the farm in 1842 from his brother in law Andrew Sipe married to Joseph's sister Elizabeth. The census of 1850 has them in Mechanic Township Holmes Co., Ohio. They sold the farm in 1855. In the 1860 census it has them in German Township Holmes Co., OH. Joseph moved to Lagrange Co., IN but maybe after Mary died?

Amish and Amish Mennonite Genealogies, CH212, p. 56; ML6132, p. 283

Joseph and Mary lived in Holmes Co., OH in 1819. In his last years he moved to Lagrange Co., IN. I think that Mary moved there also. The census of 1850 has them listed in Holmes Co., OH. They sold there farm in 1855. Mary is the aughter of Jonathan Miller(b. Mar 7, 1789 and d. Sept 18, 1867)and Magdalina Kauffman (b. Sept 9, 1785 and d. Aug 16, 1862) Jonathan and Magdalina were married in 1806 in PA. Mary had at least one sister Veronica (b. Oct 13, 1807)Jonathan Millers father was Christian Schmidt Miller. Joseph and Mary lived in Holmes Co., Ohio in 1819. In his later years he moved to Lagrange Co., IN. I think Mary moved also. The census of 1850 has them in Holmes Co., OH. They sold the farm in 1855.

The Descendants of John J. Christner, privately published 1961, February 1961, p. 4.

More About Mary Maria J. Miller:
Residence: 1850, Mechanic, Holmes Co., OH[193,194]

Children of Joseph Christner and Mary Miller are:

	104	i.	Fannie[6] Christner, born 1824.
+	105	ii.	John J. Christner, born 24 Nov 1827 in Berlin, Holmes Co., OH; died 03 Jul 1893 in Honeyville, Lagrange Co., IN.
+	106	iii.	Elizabeth J. Christner, born 01 Sep 1829 in Holmes Co., OH; died 16 Oct 1903 in Elkhart, Elkhart Co., IN.
	107	iv.	Jacob Christner, born 1831.

37. John J.[5] Christner (Christian J.[4], Johannes John Hans[3], Christian[2], Christen[1])[195,196] was born 15 Nov 1810 in Holmes Co., OH[196], and died 27 Dec 1838 in Holmes Co., OH[196]. He married **Magdalene Honderich**[196], daughter of Christian Honderich and Magdalene. She was born 02 Aug 1809 in Waldeck, Germany[196], and died 04 Apr 1894 in Holmes Co., OH[196].

Notes for John J. Christner:
Da Ault Bauverei = The Old Family Farm, Holmes Co., OH

John and Magdalena purchased the Walnut Creek homestead from Christian (the Ohio pioneer) in 1834. During their stay at the farm, Magdalena's parents came to live with them. Magdalena's parents are buried at the homestead plot. John died very young at 29 yrs. old. John is also buried at the homestead plot. Magdalena later remarried to Isaac Miller buried in the homestead plot. After Isaac's death, Magdalena lived with John H. Schrock and his wife Elizabeth (Christner) Schrock (her daughter) in her old age. Both Isaac and Magdalena Honderich Christner Miller are buried in the homestead plot.

Amish and Amish Mennonite Genealogies; CH214 p. 56, 57; HN5, p. 121

The Descendants of John J. Christner, privately published 1961, February 1961, p 4.

More About John J. Christner:
Burial: Daniel Miller Farm South of Walnut Creek OH

Notes for Magdalene Honderich:
Magdalena Christner later married Isaac Miller. Isaac was a brother to John Broad Run and Christian (SCHMIDT) Miller. Broad Run Miller married a Catherine Yoder. Isaac Miller was single until the age of 65.

More About Magdalene Honderich:
Burial: Walnut Creek A.M. Mennonite Cemetery, Walnut Creek, Holmes Co., OH

Children of John Christner and Magdalene Honderich are:

    108   i.   Mary[6] Christner, born 10 Jan 1833 in Holmes Co., OH; died 10 Oct 1840.

                        More About Mary Christner:
                        Burial: Daniel Miller Farm South of Walnut Creek OH

+   109   ii. Barbara Christner, born 10 Jan 1834 in Holmes Co., OH; died 22 Jan 1912.
+   110   iii. Joseph J. Christner, born 15 Dec 1835 in Holmes Co., OH; died 01 Jan 1908 in Baltic, Tuscarawas Co., OH.
+   111   iv. Elizabeth Christner, born 25 Oct 1837 in Holmes Co., OH; died 29 Apr 1922 in Holmes Co., OH.

39. Veronica Fannie[5] Christner (Christian J.[4], Johannes John Hans[3], Christian[2], Christen[1])[197] was born 12 Oct 1816 in Holmes Co. OH. She married **David Lantz** Bef. 1856 in Holmes Co., OH. He was born 17 May 1795 in Lancaster Co., PA.

Notes for Veronica Fannie Christner:
The Descendants of John J. Christner, privately published 1961, February 1961, p. 99

Amish and Amish Mennonite Genealogies; CH216 p. 56

More About Veronica Fannie Christner:
Nickname: Fanny

Notes for David Lantz:
The Descendants of John J. Christner, privately published February 1961, p. 99.

David is Old Order Amish.

Amish and Amish MennoniteGenealogies, p. 254, LZ39

More About David Lantz:
Religion: Amish/

Children of Veronica Christner and David Lantz are:
+   112   i.   Philip[6] Lantz, born 22 Aug 1857 in Holmes Co., OH; died 04 Oct 1924 in Lagrange Co., IN.

40. Daniel[5] Christner (Christian J.[4], Johannes John Hans[3], Christian[2], Christen[1])[197,198] was born 14 Nov 1819 in Holmes Co., OH[199,200,201], and died 1871. He married **(1) Juliet Julie**. She was born 1824. He married **(2) Nancy Anna Quier** 17 Mar 1842 in Holmes Co., OH by Joel Hall, JP. She was born 13 Dec 1818 in Somerset Co., PA, and died 06 May 1903 in Elkhart, Elkhart Co., IN.

Notes for Daniel Christner:
GABRIL, (Daniel's Brother) Granted a tract of land in Holmes Co., OH from the government 1835 section 17 Twp., 9 range 6 (Hardy Twp.) transferred land in 1845 to Daniel Christner. The deed was dated Sept 8, 1835 and signed by President Andrew Jackson.

Amish and Amish Mennonite Genealogies; CH216, p., 56

More About Daniel Christner:
Residence: 1880, Bourbon, Marshall Co., IN[202]

Notes for Nancy Anna Quier:
Nancy moved from Holmes Co., OH in 1819 to one mile E. Goshen, Elkhart Co., IN. 1820 she moved to Marshal Co., IN. 1881 she moved to Nappanee, Elkhart Co., IN. 1882 she moved to Elkhart, Elkhart Co., IN (207 Kuzy Street).

Amish and Amish Mennonite Genealogies, Hugh F. Gingerich and Rachel W. Kreider, CH217 p. 56

Obituary:

Christner-on the 8th of May, 1903 in the city of Elkhart, IN of the infirmities of old age, Nancy Quier Christner, aged 84 Y, 4M, 23D. She was born in Somerset Co., PA on the 13th of Dec, 1818. Funeral services were held in the Mennonite M.H. in Elkhart on the 9th inst. Funeral services were conducted by J.S. Hartzler. She leaves a brother, sister, a foster son and a number of friends to mourn her death.

James was a foster son of Nancy and Daniel. He owned the burial lots (5) that he and his mother are on. Section 1 lot 30 - extreme northeast corner close to Hively and the fence Just west of James's stone is a stone for William Quier b.1861- d.1938 and Mary b. 1865 - d.1914 Nancy Anne would have been about 43 years old when William was born.

NANCYS PARENTS ARE ADAM QUIER AND FANNY TROYER. Nancy used her middle name Anna more than her first name of Nancy.

More About Nancy Anna Quier:
Burial: Prarier Street Cemetery, Elkhart, Elkhart Co., IN

Children of Daniel Christner and Juliet Julie are:
    114   i.   Elizabeth[6] Christner, born 1846 in Holmes Co., OH.
    115   ii.   Hetty Christner, born 1848 in Holmes Co., OH.

Child of Daniel Christner and Nancy Quier is:
    116   i.   James B.[6] Grant, born 1847; died 1912.

        Notes for James B. Grant:
        James was a foster son of Nancy and Daniel. He owned the burial lots (5) that he and his mother are on. Section 1 lot 30 = extreme northeast corner close to Hively and the fence. Elkhart Indiana

        More About James B. Grant:

Burial: Prairie St. Cemt., Elkhart, In. 400 E. Hively Ave.

41. John[5] Christner III (John J.[4], Johannes John Hans[3], Christian[2], Christen[1])[203,204] was born 1805 in Somerset Co., PA[205,206]. He married **Barbara Shoemaker**[207] 1836 in Somerset Co., PA[207], daughter of David Christner and Elizabeth Mishler. She was born 1813 in Somerset Co., PA[208,209,210,211,212].

Notes for John Christner III:
Amish and Amish Mennonite Genealogies; p. 56-57, CH222

More About John Christner III:
Residence: 1850, Elk Lick, Somerset Co., PA[213,214]

Notes for Barbara Shoemaker:
Amish and Amish Mennonite Genealogies; p. 57

Spelled - Shoemaker or Shumaker

More About Barbara Shoemaker:
Residence: 1850, Elk Lick, Somerset Co., PA[215,216]

Children of John Christner and Barbara Shoemaker are:

+	117	i.	Mary[6] Christner, born 06 Aug 1836 in Somerset, Somerset Co., PA; died 28 Dec 1904.
+	118	ii.	Christina Christner, born 1838 in Somerset Co., PA; died 1931 in Garrett Co., MD.
+	119	iii.	Mary Catherine Christner, born 1840 in Somerset Co., PA; died 12 Nov 1932 in Akron, Summit Co., OH.
+	120	iv.	Jacob Christner, born 1841 in Somerset Co., PA; died 16 Aug 1891 in Harrison Co., WV.
	121	v.	Rebecca Christner[217,218], born 1843 in Somerset Co., PA[218].

Notes for Rebecca Christner:
Amish and Amish Mennonite Genealogies; p. 57, CH2225

+	122	vi.	Sarah Ellen "Helena" Christner, born 04 Jul 1845 in Somerset Co., PA; died 02 Jun 1938 in Long Stretch, Garrett Co., MD.
+	123	vii.	Veronica "Frany" Christner, born 03 Aug 1845 in Somerset Co., PA; died 10 Jul 1934 in Avilton, Garrett Co., MD.
	124	viii.	Anna Christner[219,220], born 1858 in Garrett Co., MD[220].

Notes for Anna Christner:
Amish and Amish Mennonite Genealogies; p. 57, CH2229

42. Veronica Fannie[5] Christner (John J.[4], Johannes John Hans[3], Christian[2], Christen[1]) was born Jan 1810 in Somerset Co., PA, and died 1845. She married **Henry Ransberger**.

Notes for Veronica Fannie Christner:
Amish and Amish Mennonite Genealogies; CH223, p. 56

Fannie was born before 1810 but no date is available. Compton Cemetery, Meyersdale, Somerset Co., PA.

More About Veronica Fannie Christner:
Burial: Compton Cemetery Meyersdale PA

Notes for Henry Ransberger:
Henry is the son of Elias and Catherine _____ Ransberger.

Amish and Amish Mennonite book says Franie was the 2nd wife of Henry. Some spell it Ramsberger. Some have John Ramesberger. Death date for Fanny or John of April 20, 1841. Burial at Van Sickle Cemetery, Wharton Twp., Fayette Co., PA.

More About Henry Ransberger:
Burial: Van Sickle Cemetery Wharton Twp. Fayette Co. PA

Children of Veronica Christner and Henry Ransberger are:
125   i.   Martha[6] Ransberger.
126   ii. Mary Ransberger.
127   iii. Elizabeth Ransberger.
128   iv. Samuel H. Ransberger.

44. Jacob C.[5] Christner (John J.[4], Johannes John Hans[3], Christian[2], Christen[1])[221] was born 16 Aug 1816 in Somerset, Somerset Co., PA[222,223], and died 20 Jul 1881 in Garrett, Somerset Co., PA[223]. He married **(1) Julia Rumiser**. She was born 03 Jan 1831 in Connellsville, Fayette Co., PA, and died 11 Feb 1909 in or Nov. 11, 1909. He married **(2) Julia Ohler** Bet. 1841 - 1844 in Somerset Co., PA[224]. She was born Apr 1835 in Somerset Co., PA, and died 03 Mar 1910.

Notes for Jacob C. Christner:
There are 15 children and the last date of birth for a child that I have is 1878. This is 3 years before Jacobs death and there is four more children to be born yet. Maybe some of these kids do not belong in this family or the death date is wrong. Jacob married Julian Rumiser and his brother Abe married Elizabeth Rumiser. Julian and Elizabeth may be sisters.

This info came from Connie Yokum. Question the death date. There are 15 children and the last date of birth for a child that I have is 1878. This is 3 years before Jacobs death and there is four more children to be born yet. Maybe some of these kids do not belong in this family or the death date is wrong. Jacob married Julian Rumiser and his brother Abe married Elizabeth Rumiser. Julian and Elizabeth may be sisters.   Could be another wife Julie Ohler some spell it Julianna and Rumizer some have the first 4 children with the first wife Second Wife born 1/3/1831 Died 2/11/1909.

Amish and Amish Mennonite Genealogies; CH224, p. 56;

More About Jacob C. Christner:
Burial: St. Paul (Fritz) Lutheran Cemetery, Brothersvalley, Somerset Co., PA[225]
Military service: Connellsville, Fayette Co., PA[226]

Notes for Julia Rumiser:
This is 1st wife of Jacob. The birth dates of the children indicated a second wife as the first wife would of been in her late 60's when some were born. Info from Amish and Amish Mennonite Genealogies. We have no info on her last name or parents. This is quite confusing as both wives were Julian or Julyann orJulianna. Some spell her last name as Rumizer.

Amish and Amish Mennonite Genealogies; CH224, p. 56;

More About Julia Rumiser:
Burial: Pine Hill Cemetery Somerset Co., PA

Notes for Julia Ohler:
This is the 2nd wife of Jacob. The birth dates of the children indicated a second fe as the first wife would of been in her late 60's when some were born. Info is from Amish and Amish Mennonite Genealogies. We have no info on her last name or parents. This is quite confusing as both wives were Julian or Julyann or Julianna.

Amish and Amish Mennonite Genealogies; CH224, p. 56;

More About Julia Ohler:
Residence: 1900, Summit Twp., Somerset Co., PA[227]

Children of Jacob Christner and Julia Rumiser are:

129   i.   Sarah[6] Christner[228,229], born 28 Jul 1842 in Somerset Co., PA; died 02 Nov 1924 in Somerset Co., PA. She married Cornelius Klink[229] 1862 in Somerset Co., PA; born 09 Jan 1843[229]; died 28 Mar 1911[229].

Notes for Sarah Christner:
Birth: Jul., 1842
Death: 1924

Spouse: Cornelius Klink (1843 - 1911)

Children:
Joseph C. Klink (1867 - 1938)
Calvin C. Klink (1874 - 1947)
Reuben Klink (1877 - 1974)
Marianne Klink (1879 - 1934)
Alonzo Klink (1883 - 1951)

Burial: Delilah Younkin Cemetery, Upper Turkeyfoot, Somerset Co., PA
Find A Grave Memorial# 65910804

More About Sarah Christner:
Burial: N39°46.230' BY W79°12.200'/Maple Glen Cemetery, Elk Lick Twp., Somerset Co., PA
Residence: 1902, Nicolay, Fayettte Co., PA - per John Christner's Obit.

Notes for Cornelius Klink:
Birth: Jan., 1843
Death: Mar. 28, 1911
Upper Turkeyfoot, Somerset Co., PA

Spouse: Sarah Christner Klink (1842 - 1924)

Children:
Joseph C Klink (1867 - 1938)
Calvin C Klink (1874 - 1947)
Reuben Klink (1877 - 1974)
Marianne Klink (1879 - 1934)
Alonzo Klink (1883 - 1951)

Note: Son of Jemima Rugg Klink, Grandson to Priscilla Rugg.

Burial: Delilah Younkin Cemetery, Upper Turkeyfoot, Somerset Co., PA
Find A Grave Memorial# 65910759

+   130   ii.   Elizabeth Christner, born 07 Feb 1844 in Connellsville, Fayette Co., PA; died 04 Dec 1918 in Republic, Fayette Co., PA.

+   131   iii.   John (Invalid John) Christner, born 05 Mar 1847 in Summit Twp., Somerset Co., PA; died 01 Apr 1908 in Somerset Co., PA.

+   132   iv.   Jacob (Lumix Jake) Christner, born 1848.

Children of Jacob Christner and Julia Ohler are:

133   i.   Tena Tenia[6] Christner. She married John Logson.

Notes for Tena Tenia Christner:
See notes for George Kendall. This was his real mother.

134   ii.   Catherine Christner, born 1855. She married Andrew Wakefoos.

135   iii.   Anna Maria Christner[230], born 1856 in Connellsville, Fayette Co., PA[230]; died 1870.

Notes for Anna Maria Christner:
Amish and Amish Mennonite Genealogies; CH2246, p. 58;

More About Anna Maria Christner:

Residence: 1860, Summit Twp., Somerset Co., PA[230]

136	iv.	Malinda Christner, born 1859.
+ 137	v.	Mary Elizabeth Christner, born 1861; died 15 Dec 1897.
+ 138	vi.	Samuel Christner, born Aug 1863 in Somerset, Somerset Co., PA; died 16 Aug 1909 in Meyersdale, Somerset Co., PA.
+ 139	vii.	Caroline (Carrie) Christner, born 1866; died 1943.
+ 140	viii.	Franklin Grant Christner, born 04 May 1866 in Connellsville, Fayette Co., PA; died 1967 in Brownsville, Fayette Co., PA.
141	ix.	Jerome Christner, born 1869 in Connellsville, Fayette Co., PA; died 1951 in Meyersdale, Somerset Co., PA.

Notes for Jerome Christner:
Jerome never married. He was a Coal miner.
1910 soundex PA he was living at his brothers widows house. Samuel Christner's widow Lydia & four of her daughters.

More About Jerome Christner:
Burial: Meyersdale Cemetery, Meyersdale, Somerset Co., PA

142	x.	Emma Christner, born Jun 1871 in Connellsville, Fayette Co., PA[231]. She married George Beal.

Notes for Emma Christner:
May not be Jacob's daughter.

More About Emma Christner:
Residence: 1900, Summit Twp., Somerset Co., PA[231]

143	xi.	Veronica Christner[232], born Abt. 1873 in Somerset, Somerset Co., PA[232].
144	xii.	Amy Veronica Christner, born 1873.
+ 145	xiii.	Frank Christner, born 21 Mar 1875 in Somerset Co., PA; died 15 Mar 1946 in Glade City, Somerset Co., PA.
146	xiv.	Dinah Christina Christner, born 1878.

46. John[5] Christner (Peter[4], Johannes John Hans[3], Christian[2], Christen[1])[233,234,235,236,237] was born 1802 in Somerset, Somerset Co., PA[238,239], and died Feb 1863 in Indian Head, Saltlick Twp., Fayette Co., PA[240,241]. He married **Susannah Griffith**[241,242] 1822 in Connellsville, Fayette Co., PA, daughter of Ebenezer Griffith and Rachel. She was born 07 Mar 1797 in Elk Lick Twp., Somerset Co., PA[242], and died 05 Apr 1881 in Indian Head, Salt Lick Twp, . Fayette Co., PA[242].

Notes for John Christner:
John was a farmer (402 Acres) and a pioneer merchant. He had a sawmill and Tannery at Indian Head, Salt Lick Twp., Fayette Co., PA. The deed to his land lists John & Gabriel as residents of Somerset Co., PA.

More About John Christner:
Occupation: Farmer and Pioneer Merchant/
Residence: 1850, Salt Lick, Fayette, PA[243]

More About Susannah Griffith:
Burial: Luthern Good Hope Cemetery

Children of John Christner and Susannah Griffith are:

+ 147	i.	Isabella A.[6] Christner, born 1823 in Connellsville, Fayette Co., PA; died 19 Aug 1892 in Saltlick Twp., Fayette Co., PA.
+ 148	ii.	Deliah Christner, born 08 Nov 1824 in Somerset Co., PA; died 25 Oct 1905.
+ 149	iii.	Peter Christner, born 08 Apr 1826 in Somerset Co., PA; died 23 Nov 1914 in Silver Lake, Kosciusko Co., IN.
+ 150	iv.	Cain Christner, born 02 Aug 1827 in Somerset, Somerset Co., PA; died 25 Sep 1911 in Connellsville,

Fayette Co., PA.

+ 151 v. Samuel Christner, born 18 Sep 1829 in Somerset, Somerset Co., PA; died 08 Nov 1913 in Connellsville, Fayette Co., PA.

+ 152 vi. Urias Christner, born Mar 1831 in Somerset, Somerset Co., PA; died 03 Oct 1902 in Indian Head, Saltlick Twp., Fayette Co., PA.

+ 153 vii. Uriah Christner, born 01 Mar 1831 in Somerset, Somerset Co., PA; died 03 Oct 1902 in Indian Head, Saltlick Twp., Fayette Co., PA.

+ 154 viii. Mahala A. Christner, born 19 Jan 1833 in Somerset, Somerset Co., PA; died 28 Dec 1910 in Mt. Pleasant, Westmoreland Co., PA//.

+ 155 ix. Priscilla Christner, born Dec 1835 in Somerset, Somerset Co., PA; died 1918 in Connellsville, Fayette Co., PA.

  156 x. Cornelius Christner, born 1836 in Somerset, Somerset Co., PA. He married Susanna.

+ 157 xi. Mary Magdalena Christner, born 10 Jun 1841 in Connellsville, Fayette Co., PA; died 09 Mar 1924 in Connellsville, Fayette Co., PA.

+ 158 xii. Cyrus John Christner, born 06 Apr 1842 in Fayette Co., PA; died 20 Oct 1916 in Bullskin Twp., Fayette Co., PA.

+ 159 xiii. Jacob G. Christner, born 18 Feb 1846 in Somerset Co., PA; died 26 May 1917 in Connellsville, Fayette Co., PA.

+ 160 xiv. Joseph Christner, born 22 May 1847 in Somerset, Somerset Co., PA; died 1937 in Connellsville, Fayette Co., PA.

48. Levi⁵ Christner (Peter⁴, Johannes John Hans³, Christian², Christen¹)[243,244,245,246] was born 1813 in Elk Lick, Somerset Co., PA[247], and died 04 Nov 1882 in Bullskin Twp., Fayette Co., PA[247,248]. He married **(1) Katherine Younkin**[248,249] in Somerset Co., PA. She was born 26 Jun 1817 in Turkeyfoot, Somerset Co., PA[250,251], and died 01 Apr 1883 in Upper Turkeyfoot Twp, Somerset Co., PA[252,253]. He married **(2) Mary Warrick** 1860. She was born Abt. 1817[254].

Notes for Levi Christner:
Levi was possabbly the first Amish in the family to break from tradition. He was a farmer and when he died he was taken to Elk Lick Twp., in Somerset to be buried with the Burkholder Family. Levi's mother was a Burkholder and that is why he is probably buried in the Burkholder cemetery.

Birth: 1813
Death: 4 Nov 1882

Note: Not inscribed, said to contain body of Levi Christner.

Burial: Burkholder Burial Ground, Garrett, Somerset Co., PA
Find A Grave Memorial# 5782923

More About Levi Christner:
Census: 07 Jun 1880, Bullskin Twp., Fayette Co., PA[255]
Occupation: 07 Jun 1880, farmer/[255]
Residence: 1860, Springfield, Fayette Co., PA[256]

Notes for Katherine Younkin:
Katherine Younkin Wife of Levi Christner.

I believe there are 2 Katherine Younkins born in Somerset area around 1817. I'm not even sure that birthdate is correct yet. Some people incorrectly have Mary Warrick as the mother of a few of the Christner kids. Elvina's obituary in The Daily Courier (Connellsville, PA) states that Katherine was her mother. All death records of Children spell her name with a K and not the C that most people have. I have nothing but a hunch, but I believe she probably died around the time of last Daughter Elvina's birth in 1862. She would have been in her early 40's and may have had a hard pregnancy because of her age. She does not appear on the 1870 Bullskin Census with Levi. Levi already has Mary with him at this time. I suppose there may be a scandal with Mary and Katherine left him but that seems doubtfull as there is evidence that Levi remained in good stead with friends and family of Katherine's. Also the family stands somewhat allied with Mary Warrick in Estate Documents after Levi's death in 1882. Katherine is nowhere to be found in those documents. I beleve the Katherine Younnkin that died in

Somerset in 1883 is a different Katherine Younkin.

More About Katherine Younkin:
Residence: 1850, Springfield, Fayette, PA[257]

Notes for Mary Warrick:
maybe spelled Warrek

Children of Levi Christner and Katherine Younkin are:

+	161	i.	Clarissa[6] Christner, born 1840 in Connellsville, Fayette Co., PA; died 01 Jan 1918 in Springfield, Fayette Co , PA.
	162	ii.	Mary J. Christner, born 1841.

Notes for Mary J. Christner:
Mary may be a twin to Susanna.

	163	iii.	Susanna Christner[258], born 1841[258].

Notes for Susanna Christner:
Susanna may be a twin to Mary J.

+	164	iv.	Elias Christner, born 15 Nov 1844 in Bullskin Twp., Fayette Co., PA; died 29 Jul 1923 in Bullskin Twp., Fayette Co., PA.
+	165	v.	Charles Christner, born Sep 1845 in Springfield, Fayette Co., PA; died 28 Jul 1931 in Mt. Pleasant, Westmoreland Co., PA.
	166	vi.	Lydia Ann Christner, born Mar 1848 in Wooddale, Bullskin, Fayette Co., PA[259]; died 21 Jan 1931 in Connellsville, Fayette Co., PA. She married Cossell.
	167	vii.	Rachel Christner, born 1849.
+	168	viii.	Rufus Christner, born Feb 1851 in Springfield, Fayette Co., PA; died 18 Sep 1925 in Davistown, Fayette Co., PA.
+	169	ix.	Elvina Belle Christner, born 12 May 1862 in Springfield Twp., Fayette Co., PA; died 28 Nov 1956 in Akron, Summit Co., OH.

Children of Levi Christner and Mary Warrick are:

+	170	i.	Rufus[6] Christner.
	171	ii.	Soloman Christner.
+	172	iii.	Louvena Christner, born Jul 1844.
+	173	iv.	Elijah H. Christner, born 05 Jul 1856 in Springfield, Fayette Co., PA; died 05 Jul 1856 in Bullskin Twp., Fayette Co., PA.

49. Lydia[5] Christner (Peter[4], Johannes John Hans[3], Christian[2], Christen[1])[260,261] was born 1820 in Somerset, Somerset Co., PA[262], and died 25 Nov 1899 in Somerset Co., PA[263,264]. She married **Jacob Wiltrout** 1837 in Elk Lick, Fayette Co., PA[265]. He was born Abt. 1816 in PA[265], and died 16 Sep 1894 in PA[265].

More About Lydia Christner:
Residence: 1860, Springfield, Fayette Co., PA[266]

More About Jacob Wiltrout:
Residence: 1880, Connellsville, Fayette Co., PA[267]

Children of Lydia Christner and Jacob Wiltrout are:

	174	i.	Priscilla[6] Wiltrout[267], born 1838 in PA[267]; died 1899[267].
	175	ii.	Drucilla Wiltrout[267], born Dec 1840 in Saltllick, Fayette Co., PA[267].
	176	iii.	Gabriel Wiltrout[267], born 16 Nov 1842 in Saltlick Twp., Fayette Co., PA[267].

More About Gabriel Wiltrout:
Residence: 1860, Springfield, Fayette Co., PA[267]

177	iv.	Mary Wiltrout[267], born 1845 in Saltlick Twp., Fayette Co., PA[267].
178	v.	Magdalena Wiltrout[267], born 05 Sep 1848 in Gibson, Cameron Co., PA[267]; died 15 May 1906 in Connellesville, Fayette Co., PA[267].
179	vi.	Alford C. Willtrout[267], born 1855 in Saltlick Twp., Fayette Co., PA[267].

More About Alford C. Willtrout:
Residence: 1880, Connellsville, Fayette Co., PA[267]

50. Susan[5] Christner (David[4], Johannes John Hans[3], Christian[2], Christen[1])[268] was born 1806[268]. She married **(1) George Deitz**.   She married **(2) George Dietz**[269]. He was born 1807.

Notes for Susan Christner:
Susan and her husband George and all the children are listed in the 1850 census as mulatto George is a laborer and so is son Samuel.

In the 1860 census all of Susan's children are listed as Christners. I do not know why they all changed there last names. Some children are also listed as white instead of mulatto, could this have been the reason?

The Amish and Amish Mennonite book says that George Deitz married Veronica Coblentz,could be that George left his first wife and remarried and that is why the children changed their name back to Christner.

Amish and Amish Mennonite Genealogies; CH242, p. 57

Notes for George Deitz:
Census 1840 Jenner township PA has George as a negro. I believe Susanna is a sister of George Deitz. She was most likely negro.

Notes for George Dietz:
1840 census Jenner Twp., PA has George listed as a negro. I belive Susanna is a sister of George Deitz. She was most likely negro.

1850 Census - PA
Susan and her husband George and all the children are listed as mulatto.

1860 Census - PA
Susan's children are listed as Christner's in this census. Not sure why they all changed their last names. Some children are listed as White in this census and not mulatto - this could be the reason why the name change.

Amish and Amish Mennonite Families

This book indicates that George Dietz married Veronica Coblentz. It could be that George left his first wife and remarried and that is why the children changed their name back to Christner.

More About George Dietz:
Census: 1840, Jenner Twp., PA - George is listed as Negro
Occupation: Laborer/

Children of Susan Christner and George Dietz are:

180	i.	Elizabeth Deitz[6] Christner, born 1830.

Notes for Elizabeth Deitz Christner:
1850 census she is Elizabeth Deets a Mulatto.
1860 census she is Elizabeth Christner.
1860 census Joseph McCelvia/McKelsey age 7 and Franklin Risher/Richer age 2 are listed with Elizabeth.
1870 census these boys are still listed with Elizabeth. These may be sons of hers or 2 boys she just took to raise. There is no information that either child went by the name of Christner.

181   ii.   Samuel Deitz Christner, born 1832.

Notes for Samuel Deitz Christner:
1850 census he is listed as mulatto and his name is Deets.
1860 he is listed as Samuel Christner as mulatto
1870 census he is not listed at all

+   182   iii.   George Deitz Christner, born 1840.
    183   iv.   Lavenia Deitz Christner, born 1846.

Notes for Lavenia Deitz Christner:
1850 census she is Lavenia Deets and mulatto
1860 census she is Lavenia Christner and mulatto
1870 census she is not listed

51. David[5] Christner (David[4], Johannes John Hans[3], Christian[2], Christen[1])[270,271] was born 1806 in Somerset Co., PA[272], and died 1849 in Somerset Co., PA[272]. He married **Susanna Dietz**. She was born 1806 in Connellsville, Fayette Co., PA.

Notes for David Christner:
I believe Susanna is a sister of George Deitz.

Amish and Amish Mennonite Genealogies; CH241, p. 57

Notes for Susanna Dietz:
Amish and Amish Mennonite Genealogies; CH241, p. 57

I belive Susanna is a sister of George Deitz. She was most likely negro.

Children of David Christner and Susanna Dietz are:
+   184   i.   Elizabeth[6] Christner, born 21 Mar 1830 in Somerset Co., PA.
+   185   ii.   Samuel Christner, born 11 Oct 1833 in Jenner Twp., Somerset Co., PA; died 16 Mar 1918 in Somerset Co., PA.
+   186   iii.   Susanna Deitz Christner, born 13 Sep 1836 in Somerset Co., PA; died 19 Dec 1925 in Scottdale, Westmoreland Co., PA.
    187   iv.   George C. Christner[273], born 11 Aug 1840 in Somerset Co., PA; died 18 Jun 1888. He married Mary Gint; born 02 Mar 1845 in Somerset, Somerset Co., PA; died 21 Feb 1926.

Notes for George C. Christner:
Enlisted as a Private in the Infantry on March 17, 1864 in Company C. Also in the Army as a Private in the 54th Regiment PA Volunteers.

Enlisted at Chambersburg, PA for 3 years. Captured in action at High Bridge, VA. April 6, 1865. Parolled at Appomattex Court House VA. April 9, 1865. Wounded at Battle of Wilderness May 6, 1865. Discharged May 31, 1865. He had a son.

Birth: Aug. 11, 1840
Death: Jun. 18, 1888

Company C, 54th Regiment, Pennsylvania Infantry.

Burial: Saint James Lutheran Church Cemetery, Boswell, Somerset Co., PA
Plot: Center Section, Row 8

More About George C. Christner:
Burial: St. James Cemetery 2 miles North of Boswell
Cause of Death: Disease of left lung
Residence: 1870, Conemaugh, Somerset, PA[274]

More About Mary Gint:
Residence: 1900, Conemaugh, Somerset, PA[275]

33

188   v.   Lavina Christner, born 1846 in Somerset Co., PA.

52. Barbara⁵ Shoemaker (David⁴ Christner, Johannes John Hans³, Christian², Christen¹)²⁷⁶ was born 1813 in Somerset Co., PA²⁷⁷,²⁷⁸,²⁷⁹,²⁸⁰,²⁸¹. She married **John Christner III**²⁸²,²⁸³ 1836 in Somerset Co., PA²⁸⁴, son of John Christner and Mary Maust. He was born 1805 in Somerset Co., PA²⁸⁴,²⁸⁵.

Notes for Barbara Shoemaker:
Amish and Amish Mennonite Genealogies; p. 57

Spelled - Shoemaker or Shumaker

More About Barbara Shoemaker:
Residence: 1850, Elk Lick, Somerset Co., PA²⁸⁶,²⁸⁷

Notes for John Christner III:
Amish and Amish Mennonite Genealogies; p. 56-57, CH222

More About John Christner III:
Residence: 1850, Elk Lick, Somerset Co., PA²⁸⁷,²⁸⁸

Children are listed above under (41) John Christner III.

53. Jessie⁵ Christner (David⁴, Johannes John Hans³, Christian², Christen¹) was born 1818 in Somerset, Somerset Co., PA²⁸⁹,²⁹⁰, and died in Conemaugh, Somerset Co., PA²⁹¹,²⁹². He married **Veronica Schantz**²⁹³,²⁹⁴ 1839 in Somerset Co., PA²⁹⁵. She was born 1815 in Somerset Co., PA²⁹⁶, and died 25 Oct 1900 in Conemaugh, Somerset Co., PA²⁹⁷,²⁹⁸.

Notes for Jessie Christner:
When Jessie Christner was born in 1818 in Somerset, PA his father, David, was 36 and his mother, Elizabeth, was 20. He married Veronica Schantz in 1839 in his hometown. He had four children by the time he was 29. He died in Conemaugh, PA.

1850 census Jessie is listed as mulatto. He can read and write. He lived in Conemaugh Twp., PA

In the 1850 census and Jesse's father David is living with them.

Amish and Amish Mennonite Genealogies; CH244, p. 57

More About Jessie Christner:
Residence: 1850, Conemaugh, Somerset, PA²⁹⁸

Notes for Veronica Schantz:
1850 census Faney is listed as white, She can not read and write.

Amish and Amish Mennonite Genealogies; CH244, p. 57

More About Veronica Schantz:
Residence: 1850, Conemaugh, Somerset, PA²⁹⁸

Children of Jessie Christner and Veronica Schantz are:
189   i.   Elizabeth⁶ Christner²⁹⁸,²⁹⁹,²⁹⁹, born 1840 in Somerset Co., PA³⁰⁰,³⁰¹; died 23 Apr 1903 in Elkhart Co., IN³⁰¹,³⁰². She married Jeremiah Yoder³⁰²,³⁰²; born 1840³⁰²; died in IN³⁰².

               Notes for Elizabeth Christner:
               1850 census Elizabeth is listed as mulatto. She can read and write.

More About Elizabeth Christner:
Residence: 1850, Conemaugh, Somerset, PA[303]

More About Jeremiah Yoder:
Residence: 1880, Clay, Lagrange Co., IN[304]

+ 190 ii. David Christner, born May 1841 in Connellsville, Fayette Co., PA; died 11 Feb 1918 in Elkhart Co., IN.
+ 191 iii. John Christner, born 10 Apr 1842 in Somerset Co., PA; died 26 Jan 1928 in Waterford, IN.
+ 192 iv. Harriet "Hattie" Christner, born 02 Apr 1847 in Connellsville, Fayette Co., PA; died 29 Jun 1911 in Bloomington, Monroe Co., IN.

55. Abraham D.[5] Christner (Joseph "Zep"[4], Johannes John Hans[3], Christian[2], Christen[1])[305,305,306,307,308,309,310,311,312,313,314,315] was born 30 Sep 1802 in Elk Lick, Somerset Co., PA[316,317,318,319,320], and died 04 Mar 1879 in Earl Christner Farm, Garrett, Somerset Co., PA[321,321,321,322]. He married **(2) Mary (Maria) Hoover**[323,324] 1827 in Somerset Co., PA[325,325]. She was born 18 Mar 1806 in Garrett, Summit Twp., Somerset Co., PA[325,325], and died 18 Apr 1881 in Pine Hill, Somerset Co., PA[325,325]. He married **(3) Elizabeth Rumiser** 16 Apr 1829 in Somerset, Somerset Co., PA. She was born 15 Jul 1803 in Somerset, Somerset Co., PA[326], and died 25 Jun 1849 in Somerset, Somerset Co., PA.

Notes for Abraham D. Christner:
Buried on the hill near Bixbie Creek on old Earl Christner farm owned in 1997 by Tinkeys.

On April 28, 1832 Christian Burkholder sold 200 acres in Elk Lick for $100.00 to Abraham Christner. The land is on Phillippi Road just south of the Center Luthern Church Near Garrett PA. This farm was first owned by Christian Burkholder's father John.

Amish and Amish Mennonite Genealogies; CH, CH251, pp. 56, 57

In the somerset census of 1850 Abe was listed as a widower. Abe was a general laborer. Abe married Elizabeth Rumiser and his brother Jacob married Julian Rumiser. Elizabeth and Julian may be sisters. His son Henry was his estate exec. March 31 1881.

He had the reputation of a great woodsman having killed more Deer and Wolves then any others of his generation.

In the somerset census of 1850 Abe was listed as a widower. Abe was a general laborer. Abe married Elizabeth Rumiser and his brother Jacob married Julian Rumiser. Elizabeth and Julian may be sisters. His son Henry was his estate exec. March 31 1881.

He had the reputation of a great woodsman having killed more Deer and Wolves then any others of his generation.

Birth: 31 Oct 1802
Death: Mar 30, 1881

Inscription: aged 77Y 9M 30D

Burial: Maple Glen Church of the Brethren Cemetery, Somerset Co., PA
Find A Grave Memorial# 69215165

More About Abraham D. Christner:
Burial: Earl Christner Farm, Garrett, Somerset Co., PA[327]
Occupation: Farmer[328]
Residence: 1850, Summit, Somerset Co., PA[329]

Notes for Mary (Maria) Hoover:

35

Birth: 1806
Death: 1881

Burial: Maple Glen Church of the Brethren Cemetery, Somerset Co., PA

More About Mary (Maria) Hoover:
Burial: Maple Glen Church of the Brethren Cemetery, Somerset Co., PA
Residence: 1870, Summit Twp., Somerset Co., PA[330]

Notes for Elizabeth Rumiser:
Some people spell it Rumizer.

Buried in Mable Glen Cemetery, next to Samuel, her son, Somerset Co., PA

More About Elizabeth Rumiser:
Burial: Mable Glen Cemetery, nxt to Samuel, her son, PA
Residence: 1860, Walnut Creek, Holmes Co., OH[331]

Child of Abraham D. Christner is:

+	193	i.	Lydia Lucinda[6] Christner, born 15 Jan 1846 in Somerset Co., PA; died 16 Feb 1875 in PA.

Children of Abraham Christner and Mary Hoover are:

+	194	i.	Mary[6] Christner, born 1831 in Somerset Co., PA.
+	195	ii.	Julianna Christner, born 08 Nov 1832 in Somerset Co., PA.
+	196	iii.	Tyrannus Christner, born 12 May 1834 in Somerset Co., PA; died 18 Oct 1905.
	197	iv.	Veronica Christner[332], born 12 May 1834 in Somerset Co., PA[332]; died 1905.
+	198	v.	Herman Christner, born 23 Dec 1836 in Summit Twp., Somerset Co., PA; died 23 Mar 1898 in Summit Twp., Somerset Co., PA.
+	199	vi.	Susanna Christner, born 12 Nov 1838 in Somerset Co., PA; died 04 Mar 1926.
	200	vii.	Elam Christner[332], born 03 Sep 1840 in Somerset Co., PA[332]; died 1844 in Somerset Co., PA[332].

Notes for Elam Christner:
Some say this is a girl named Elon who froze to death.

+	201	viii.	Freeman L. Christner, born 29 Dec 1842 in Somerset Co., PA.
+	202	ix.	Henry A. Christner, born 30 Dec 1842 in Somerset Co., PA; died 09 Nov 1914 in Salisbury, Somerset Co., PA.
+	203	x.	Elizabeth Christner, born 06 Oct 1845 in Somerset Co., PA; died 15 Jan 1922 in Fairhope Township, Somerset Co., PA.
+	204	xi.	Elias Christner, born 30 Mar 1848 in or Nov. 3, 1848; died 18 Mar 1876 in Summit Twp., Somerset Co., PA.
+	205	xii.	Joanna Christner, born 30 Nov 1848 in Somerset Co., PA.

Children of Abraham Christner and Elizabeth Rumiser are:

+	206	i.	Sally Sarah[6] Christner, born 22 Mar 1832 in Somerset Co., PA; died 19 Jul 1879 in Addison Twp., Somerset Co., PA.
	207	ii.	Elizabeth Christner, born 18 Jul 1835 in Somerset Co., PA; died 29 Jun 1862. She married David Faust.

Notes for Elizabeth Christner:
Both Elizabeth and Sally had children. Birthday maybe 1836. Maybe married Daniel Fawcit.

	208	iii.	Susan Christner[333,334], born 1838 in Somerset Co., PA[335,336]. She married Joseph Jacob White.

More About Susan Christner:
Residence: 1870, Summit Twp., Somerset Co., PA[337]

+	209	iv.	Samuel A. Christner, born May 1840 in Somerset Co., PA; died 08 Jan 1913 in Somerset, Somerset Co., PA.

56. Mary[5] Christner (Joseph "Zep"[4], Johannes John Hans[3], Christian[2], Christen[1])[338,339,340,341,342] was born 16 Jan 1808 in Somerset, Somerset Co., PA[342,343], and died 1879 in Somerset Co., PA[344]. She married **Matthias Judy**[345,346,347] 1840 in Somerset Co., PA. He was born 04 Jul 1813 in Summit, Somerset Co., PA[348,349], and died 20 Jun 1878 in Connellsville, Fayette Co., PA[350,351,352].

Notes for Mary Christner:
The John Burkholder history has 5 more children Susan, Mary, Elizibeth, Elizabeth, Lila but no Nelson or Minerva.
Amish and Amish Mennonite Genealogies; CH252, p. 57

The John Burkholder history has 5 more children Susan, Mary, Elizabeth, Elizabeth, Lila, but no Nelson or Minerva.

More About Mary Christner:
Residence: 1850, Summit, Somerset, Pennsylvania USA[352]

More About Matthias Judy:
Residence: 01 Jun 1840, Elk Lick Twp., Somerset Co., PA[353]

Children of Mary Christner and Matthias Judy are:

+ 210   i.   Barbara Bevvy[6] Judy, born 12 May 1838 in Somerset Co., PA; died 30 Oct 1895 in Summit Twp., Somerset Co., PA.

+ 211   ii.   Christina Dinah Judy, born 08 Jul 1839 in Somerset Co., PA; died 28 Nov 1908 in Shickley, Fillmore Co., NE.

   212   iii.   Delilah Judy[353], born 03 Apr 1847 in Somerset Co., PA[353]. She married Adam Walter.

         Notes for Delilah Judy:
         Delilah may be a twin to Samuel.

         More About Delilah Judy:
         Residence: 1930, Meyersdale, Somerset Co., PA[353]

   213   iv.   Samuel Judy[353], born Apr 1849 in Somerset Co., PA[353]; died Aft. 1930 in Laramie Co, Wyoming[353]. He married Lydia Burkholder.

         More About Samuel Judy:
         Residence: 1930, Election District 10, Laramie, Wyoming[353]

   214   v.   Nelson Judy, born 1852.
   215   vi.   Minerva Judy[353], born Mar 1862 in Somerset Co., PA[353]; died 1944[353].

         More About Minerva Judy:
         Christening: 07 Feb 1869, Somerset Co., PA[353]
         Residence: 1930, Summit, Somerset Co., PA[353]

57. Elizabeth[5] Christner (Joseph "Zep"[4], Johannes John Hans[3], Christian[2], Christen[1])[354,355,356,357,358,359,360,361] was born 01 Apr 1810 in Summitt Twp., Somerset Co., PA[362,363,364,365,366,367], and died 1879 in Somerset Co., PA[368,369,370,371,372,373,374]. She married **(1) John Henry Craig**. She married **(2) Matthias Judy**[375,376,377] Abt. 1833 in Somerset Co., PA[378]. He was born 04 Jul 1813 in Summit, Somerset Co., PA[379,380], and died 20 Jun 1878 in Connellsville, Fayette Co., PA[381,382,383]. She married **(3) Lazarus Hostetler**[384,385,386,387] 1833 in Somerset Co., PA[388]. He was born 23 Dec 1810 in Elk Lick Twp., Somerset Co., PA[389,390,391], and died 05 Dec 1883 in Trent, Fayette Co., PA[391,392,393].

Notes for Elizabeth Christner:
Amish and Amish Mennonite Genealogies; CH253, p. 57

The John Burkholder history has 5 more children Susan, Mary, Elizabeth, Lila but no Nelson or Minerva.

More About Elizabeth Christner:
Residence: 1870, Milford, Somerset Co., PA[394]

More About Matthias Judy:
Residence: 01 Jun 1840, Elk Lick Twp., Somerset Co., PA[394]

Notes for Lazarus Hostetler:
Amish and Amish Mennonite Genealogies; HS1234, p. 127

Lazarus is the son of John and Magdalena Lehman Hostetler. John either died or is buried 4 miles west of Trent, PA.

More About Lazarus Hostetler:
Residence: 1870, Jefferson, Somerset Co., PA[395,396]

Children of Elizabeth Christner and Matthias Judy are:

216   i.   Roseann[6] Judy[397], born 05 Jun 1833 in Somerset Co., PA[397]; died 1923[397].

> More About Roseann Judy:
> Residence: 1920, Summit, Somerset Co., PA[397]

217   ii.   Susanna Judy[397], born 05 Mar 1836 in Somerset Co., PA[397].

> More About Susanna Judy:
> Residence: 1850, Summit, Somerset Co., PA[397]

218   iii.   Mary Anne Judy[397], born 29 Jan 1840 in Somerset Co., PA[397].

> More About Mary Anne Judy:
> Residence: 1850, Summit, Somerset Co., PA[397]

+ 219   iv.   Elizabeth Judy, born 15 Mar 1842 in Somerset Co., PA; died 12 Mar 1923.

220   v.   Lavina Judy[397], born 22 Mar 1845 in Somerset Co., PA[397].

> More About Lavina Judy:
> Residence: 1850, Summit, Somerset Co., PA[397]

Children of Elizabeth Christner and Lazarus Hostetler are:

+ 221   i.   Gabriel[6] Hostetler, born 12 Aug 1834 in Jefferson, Somerset, Pennsylvania, United States; died 10 Mar 1892 in Trent, Somerset Co., PA.

222   ii.   Rosanah Hostetler[398,399], born 30 Oct 1837 in Jefferson, Somerset Co., PA[400,401]; died 29 Apr 1902 in Milford, Somerset Co., PA[402]. She married Jacob Pletcher[403]; born 19 Jun 1836 in PA[403]; died 17 Oct 1914 in Somerset Co., PA[403].

> Notes for Rosanah Hostetler:
> Birth: Oct. 30, 1837 - Somerset Co., PA
> Death: Apr. 28, 1902 - Somerset Co., PA
>
> Spouse: Jacob Pletcher (1836 - 1914)
>
> Children:
> Infant Daughter Pletcher
> Elizabeth Pletcher Ritter (1863 - 1890)
> Josiah Pletcher (1864 - 1944)
> Jeremiah Pletcher (1865 - ____)
> Amanda Pletcher Ritter (1867 - 1889)
> William Nelson Pletcher (1869 - 1949)
> Jemima Pletcher Bearl (1872 - 1952)

Burial: Saint Johns Centennial United Brethren Cemetery
Somerset, Somerset Co., PA
Find A Grave Memorial# 31109146

More About Rosanah Hostetler:
Residence: 1870, Middlecreek, Somerset, PA[404]

Notes for Jacob Pletcher:
Birth: Jun 19, 1836
Death: Oct. 17, 1914

Obituary: Pletcher, Jacob - Meyersdale Commercial, Nov. 5, 1914

"Jacob Pletcher" Seventy-eight years old, died Saturday morning at his home in Somerset, and was
buried Monday afternoon when services were conducted by Rev. H. A. Buffington of the U. B. Church.
Mr. Pletcher was a veteran of the Civil War fighting on the Union side, and resided for many years in
Middlecreek Township. He leaves a widow.

Parents:
Samuel Pletcher (1798 - 1886)
Elizabeth Nedrow Pletcher (1812 - 1892)

Spouses:
Rosanah Hochstetler Pletcher (1837 - 1902)
Mary E. Pyle Pletcher (1851 - 1925)

Children:
Infant Daughter Pletcher
Elizabeth Pletcher Ritter (1863 - 1890)
Josiah Pletcher (1864 - 1944)
Jeremiah Pletcher (1865 - ____)
Amanda Pletcher Ritter (1867 - 1889)
William Nelson Pletcher (1869 - 1949)
Jemima Pletcher Bearl (1872 - 1952)

Burial: Saint Johns Centennial United Brethren Cemetery, Somerset, Somerset Co., PA
Find A Grave Memorial# 39561200

More About Jacob Pletcher:
Burial: Somerset; Somerset County, Pennsylvania[405]
Residence: 1910, Age in 1910: 73; Marital Status: Married; Relation to Head of House: Self; Relation to
Head of House: Head/Somerset, Somerset, Pennsylvania[405]

+ 223   iii. Jonathan Hostetler, born 07 Oct 1840 in Somerset Co., PA; died 10 Mar 1892 in Trent, Somerset Co.,
PA.

224   iv. Mary Hostetler[406,407], born 07 Oct 1841 in Somerset Co., PA[408,409]; died 05 May 1876 in New Lexington,
Somerset Co., PA[410,411]. She married Israel Lyons.

More About Mary Hostetler:
Residence: 1860, Jefferson, Somerset Co., PA[411]

225   v. John Hostetler[412], born 1848 in Somerset Co., PA[412]; died 1890[412]. He married Besty Reese; died 1890.

226   vi. Joanna Hochstetler[413], born 1848 in Somerset, Somerset Co., PA[413].

More About Joanna Hochstetler:
Residence: 1860, Jefferson, Somerset Co., PA[413]

227   vii. Jacob C. Hostetler[413], born 20 Oct 1850 in Garrett, Somerset Co., PA[414,415]; died 11 Nov 1892 in
Cassville, Cass Co., IN[416,417]. He married Annie Saylor 23 Mar 1873 in Brethern Church, Trent, PA;
born Sep 1856 in PA[418]; died Bet. 1900 - 1910 in Trent, Somerset Co., PA[418].

More About Annie Saylor:
Residence: 1900, Age: 43; Marital Status: Married; Relation to Head of House: Wife/Middlecreek,

Somerset, Pennsylvania[418]

+ 228   viii.   Jeremiah Hostetler, born 1853 in Jefferson, Somerset Co., PA; died in Trent, Somerset Co., PA.

58. Christian[5] Christner (Joseph "Zep"[4], Johannes John Hans[3], Christian[2], Christen[1])[419,420,421,422,422] was born 1811 in Elk Lick Twp., Somerset Co., PA[423,424], and died 09 Mar 1888 in Somerset Co., PA[425]. He married **Susanna Walters**[426] 1836. She was born 26 Jun 1813 in Brothersvalley Twp., Somerset Co., PA[426,427], and died 17 Aug 1899 in Somerset, Somerset Co., PA[428,429].

Notes for Christian Christner:
This info from Connie Yokum: Christian was elected to the first council of Center Luthern Church Summit Township, Somerset Co., PA in January 20, 1850. This was the first break away from the Amish his mother Barbara was Lutheran.

Some say he died 3/9/1888. He was a farmer and a Democrat. In 1868 Summit Twp., Somerset Co., PA. Tax List he had 175 Acres + one horse + two cows.

Amish and Amish Mennonite Genealogies; CH254, p. 57

More About Christian Christner:
Burial: 09 Oct 1888, Earl Christner Farm, Garrett, Somerset Co., PA
Residence: 1870, Summit Twp., Somerset Co., PA[430]

Notes for Susanna Walters:
Susan is the daughter of Fredrick and Elizabeth Barndt Walter
Some spell it Susanna Walter also called Lucy Ann maybe birthday 3/26/1813.

Birth: Jan 27, 1813
Death: Aug 17, 1899 - Somerset Co., PA

Inscription: 86y 1m 2d
w/o of G

Burial: Center Lutheran Church Cemetery, Summit Twp., Somerset Co., PA

More About Susanna Walters:
Burial: Center Church, Luthern, Summit Twp., Summit Twp., Somerset Co., PA
Residence: 1870, Summit Twp., Somerset Co., PA[430]

Children of Christian Christner and Susanna Walters are:
229   i.   Eva[6] Christner.

                 Notes for Eva Christner:
                 This female child may not even belong in this family.There is also info that
                 Eva may be Elvie, being a male child. There is no info on birth or death. Eva
                 could be a grandchild also.

+ 230   ii.   Zachariah Christner, born 21 Apr 1837 in Summit Twp., Somerset Co., PA; died 1917 in Londonderry Twp., Bedford Co., PA.
   231   iii.   Louise A. Christner[431], born 1840[431].
+ 232   iv.   Susanna Lucy Anne Christner, born 21 Mar 1840 in Somerset Co., PA; died 1926 in Jenner, Somerset Co., PA.
+ 233   v.   John C. Christner, born 16 Jul 1842 in Connellsville, Fayette Co., PA; died 14 Dec 1921 in Summit Twp., Somerset Co., PA.
+ 234   vi.   Caroline Christner, born 1843.
   235   vii.   Samuel Christner[431], born 23 Jan 1849 in Garrett, Somerset Co., PA[431].

59. Gabriel[5] Christner (Joseph "Zep"[4], Johannes John Hans[3], Christian[2], Christen[1])[432,433,434,435,436,437,438,439] was born 08 May 1812 in Elk Lick Twp., Somerset Co., PA[440,441,441], and died 15 Oct 1886 in Pleasant Hill Cemetery, Milford Twp., Somerset Co., PA/Somerset Co., PA[441,442,443,444]. He married **(1) Magdalena Dickey**[445,446,447,448] 1838. She was born 08 Apr 1816 in Elk Lick Twp., Somerset Co., PA[449,450,451,452,453,454], and died 07 Nov 1878 in Donegal, Westmoreland Co., PA[454,455,456,457,458,459]. He married **(2) Elizabeth Peterson** 24 Sep 1888. She was born 1831.

Notes for Gabriel Christner:
Andrew Trapp built a saw mill at the mouth of Back Run about 1800. Trapp operated the mill for a number of years and then it was operated by his son Andrew. The son Andrew sold the mill to brothers John and Gabriel Christner. Andrew Trapp died in 1824. His son carried on the business for about 8 or 10 years. Gabriel and John kept it a few years longer.

We figure they owned this mill around 1832 - 1834. Gabriel came to the county just before the civil war. He devoted his attention to farming and dealing in stock and agricultural implements. He sold some of these farm tools at the mill. He lived in Milford Township and later in Fayette Twp., PA.

In his will he gave $500.00 to his second wife Elizabeth and the real and personal property sold and divided among legal heirs. Named only are Amos E. and Nelson B. Christner. Deed Record, Vol. 71 page 436-437 Registered October, 1886 Andrew Trapp built a saw mill at the mouth of Back Run about 1800. Trapp operated the mill for a number of years and then it was operated by his son Andrew. The son Andrew sold the mill to brothers John and Gabriel Christner. Andrew Trapp died in 1824. His son carried on the business for about 8 or 10 years.Gabriel and John kept it a few years longer.

We figure they owned this mill around 1832/34. Gabriel came to the county just before the civil war. He devoted his attention to farming and dealing in stock and agricultural implements. He sold some of these farm tools at the mill. He lived in Milford Township and later in Fayette Twp., PA.
In his will he gave $500.00 to his second wife Elizabeth and the real and personal property sold and divided among legal heirs. Named only are Amos E. and Nelson B. Christner. Deed Record Vol. 71 page 436-437 Registered October, 1886.

Birth: 08 May 1812
Death: Oct. 15, 1886

Burial: Pleasant Hill Cemetery, Somerset Co., PA

More About Gabriel Christner:
Burial: Pleasant Hill Cemetery, Milford Twp., Somerset Co., PA
Residence: 1860, Jefferson, Somerset Co., PA[460,461,462,463,464]

Notes for Magdalena Dickey:
Magdalena is the daughter of George Dickey born Oct 5, 1791 and Mary_____born Mar 8, 1790 Magdalena is the 3rd child of 11.

Birth: 1816
Death: Nov. 7, 1878

Burial: Berger Cemetery, Westmoreland Co., PA

More About Magdalena Dickey:
Burial: Berger Cemetery, Donegal, Westmoreland Co., PA[465]
Residence: 1850, Milford, Somerset Co., PA[466]

Children of Gabriel Christner and Magdalena Dickey are:

236	i.	Silas[6] Christner[467,468,469,470], born 1842 in Somerset Co., PA[470,470]; died Aft. 1920 in Blue River, Henry Co., IN[470].
237	ii.	Hannah Christner[471], born 1843 in Somerset, Somerset Co., PA[472].
+ 238	iii.	Amos Dickey Christner, born 24 Jan 1845 in Westmoreland Co., PA; died 26 Dec 1931 in Mt. Pleasant, Westmoreland Co., PA.
+ 239	iv.	David Christner, born 1848 in Somerset Co., PA.
+ 240	v.	Reverend Nelson Brown Christner, born 22 Jul 1851 in Donegal, Westmoreland Co, PA; died 29 Jul 1904 in Somerset Co., PA.

60. Jr. Joseph[5] Christner Jr. (Joseph "Zep"[4], Johannes John Hans[3], Christian[2], Christen[1])[473,474,474,475,476,477] was born 17 May 1813 in Elk Lick Twp., Somerset Co., PA[478,478,479], and died 07 Jan 1897 in Elk Lick Twp., Somerset Co., PA[479,480]. He married **(1) Barbara**. She was born 11 Jun 1811, and died 03 Jan 1891. He married **(2) Mary Salome Keim**[480,480] 26 Nov 1836 in Somerset Co., PA[481]. She was born 29 Oct 1818 in Elk Lick Twp., Somerset Co., PA[482], and died 01 Jan 1882 in Salisbury, Somerset Co., PA[482].

Notes for Jr. Joseph Christner Jr.:
Amish and Amish Mennonite Genealogies; CH255, p. 57

Birth: 1814
Death: Jan 7, 1897 - Summit Mills, Somerset Co., PA

Spouse: Mary Keim Christner (1818 - 1882)

Children: Samuel J. Christner (1847 - 1937)

Burial: Lichty Burial Ground, Summit Mills, Somerset Co., PA
Find A Grave Memorial# 87026355

More About Jr. Joseph Christner Jr.:
Burial: Lichty Burial Ground, Elk Lick Twp., Fayette Co., PA
Christened: Dunkard
Residence: 1860, Elk Lick, Somerset Co., PA[482]

Notes for Mary Salome Keim:
Birth: Oct 28, 1818 - Somerset Co., PA
Death: 1882

Parents:
John Sign Keim (1792 - 1887)
Barbara Livengood Keim (1789 - 1883)

Inscription: Mary, wife of Joseph Christnor, daughter of John Keime

Note: Stone was leaning forward at about 45 degree angle.

Burial: Lichty Cemetery, Somerset, Somerset Co., PA

More About Mary Salome Keim:
Burial: Lichty Burial Ground Cemetery
Residence: 1850, East Hanover, Dauphin, PA[482]

Children of Joseph Christner and Mary Keim are:

241	i.	Louisiana[6] Christner, born 08 Sep 1837 in Somerset, Somerset Co., PA[483]; died 1840 in Somerset, Somerset Co., PA[483].
+ 242	ii.	Elizabeth Christner, born 17 Jan 1839 in Elk Lick, Somerset Co., PA; died 16 Sep 1936 in Omaha, Douglas Co., NE.
+ 243	iii.	Katherine Christner, born 08 Oct 1840 in Salisbury, Somerset Co., PA; died 03 Jul 1925 in Columbus,

			Colorado Co., TX.
244		iv.	John Christner, born 19 Dec 1842; died 24 May 1922 in Omaha, Douglas Co., NE. He married Mary Shoemaker.

Notes for John Christner:
Info from Hochstetler and Stutzman book - 13367.

Notes for Mary Shoemaker:
13367 The birth date for Mary may not be right. This would make her 29 years older than her husband. She was from Negro Mt.

| 245 | | v. | Abraham Christner[184,185,186], born 07 Mar 1845 in Somerset Co., PA[486,487,488]; died 1860 in Somerset Co., PA[488,488]. |

More About Abraham Christner:
Residence: 1850, Elk Lick, Somerset Co., PA[489]

+	246	vi.	Samuel J. "Matlick Sam" Christner, born 19 Apr 1847 in Elk Lick, Somerset Co., PA; died 01 Feb 1937 in Meyersdale, Somerset Co., PA.
+	247	vii.	Sarah Christner, born 21 Mar 1850; died in Rocky Ford, Otero Co., CO.
+	248	viii.	Susannah Christner, born 27 Jun 1851 in Elklick, Somerset Co., PA; died 06 Mar 1881 in Meyersdale, Somerset Co., PA.
+	249	ix.	Henry J. Christner, born 17 Sep 1853 in Elk Lick, Somerset Co., PA; died 24 Dec 1916 in Salisbury, Somerset Co., PA.
	250	x.	Carrie B. Christner, born 1854; died 17 Jul 1880. She married S. A. Handwork.

Notes for Carrie B. Christner:
Some info shows that Joseph and Mary only had 12 children. Carrie may not belong with this family.

+	251	xi.	Jeremiah Christner, born 20 Dec 1855.
+	252	xii.	Sevilla Christner, born 03 May 1858 in Salisbury, Somerset Co., PA; died Feb 1943 in Hood River, Hood River Co., OR.
+	253	xiii.	Harvey Christner, born 21 Jul 1860 in Salisbury, Elklick Twp., Somerset Co., PA.

61. Jonas Yone[5] Christner (Joseph "Zep"[4], Johannes John Hans[3], Christian[2], Christen[1])[490,491,492,493,494] was born 14 Sep 1816 in Summitt, Somerset Co., PA[494], and died 26 Jan 1881 in Garrett, Somerset Co., PA[494,495,496,497]. He married **(1) Margaret Wiltrout** 1842. She was born 23 May 1817 in Somerset Co., PA, and died 02 Dec 1858 in Somerset Co., PA. He married **(2) Rebecca Mankemeyer**[497,498] 1858 in Somerset Co., PA[498]. She was born 1839 in Prussia[498], and died 19 Sep 1892 in Meyersdale, Somerset Co., PA[499]. He married **(3) Caroline Frederica Mankemyer**[500] 1858[500]. She was born 29 Mar 1839 in Prussia or Hanover, Germany[500], and died 19 Sep 1892 in Meyersdale, Somerset Co., PA[500].

Notes for Jonas Yone Christner:
Jonas was a tanner. The 1870 census list Jonas as unmarried. 1st wife probably died in or soon after child birth of the 13th child.This info comes from Connie Yokum and some from Paul son of Uriah J.

Tombstone says Dec.13 1813. Burial at Garrett Somerset Co., PA on the Earl Christner Farm.

The first grocery store (1865) in Garrett was owned by Jonas Christner. It was at Jackson Street where the Fire Hall now stands.

The 1886 Summit Twp., Somerset Co PA. tax list has him taxed for 135 acres of good land (at Garrett, PA) + 2 horses + 1 cow + 1 carriage + Sawmill. main source of income listed 1868 for tax purposes were Farmer & Sawmill. Jonas had 135 acres listed at $675.00 taxable when his brother Christian had 175 acres taxable at $700.00.

Amish and Amish Mennonite Genealogies; CH257, p. 57

More About Jonas Yone Christner:

Burial: Earl Christner, Farm, Garrett, PA Upper Section
Residence: 1880, Summit Twp., Somerset Co., PA[501,502]

Notes for Margaret Wiltrout:
May have died in Oct 1869 or Wiltsout.

Amish and Amish Mennonite Genealogies; CH257, p. 57

Notes for Rebecca Mankemeyer:
Amish and Amish Mennonite Genealogies; CH257, p. 57

More About Rebecca Mankemeyer:
Residence: 1880, Summit Twp., Somerset Co., PA[503]

Notes for Caroline Frederica Mankemyer:
Caroline was the daughter of Ludwig Mankameyer .She later married Alton Coleman on April 18, 1887. Ludwig was born Nov 24, 1809 died Sept 18, 1870 and buried at the Luthern Cemetery, Mt. Carmel Larimer Twp., Somerset Co., PA. Ludwig married Hannah, she was born April 1, 1804 and died Mar 15, 1877, buried with Ludwig.Children of Ludwig and Hannah Christian born Sept 15, 1833, Fredricka (Caroline) Born 1839 Adolph, born 1852 was a preacher. Paul Christner grandson of Caroline Fredricka says Fredrika was born in Prussia. Censes info from 1930 indicates Hanover Germany. Caroline buried at White Oak Church Cemetery Meyersdale, Somerset Co., PA.

Birth: Mar. 26, 1839
Death: Sep. 19, 1892 - Somerset Co., PA

2nd w/o Alton
53y 5m 24d

Spouse: Alton Coleman (1848 - 1895)

Burial: Union Cemetery, Meyersdale, Somerset Co., PA

More About Caroline Frederica Mankemyer:
Burial: Union Cem, Somerset Co, PA, Coleman Plot

Children of Jonas Christner and Margaret Wiltrout are:

254   i. Carolyn/Carolina Reca[6] Christner, born 1839[504]; died 1871.

     More About Carolyn/Carolina Reca Christner:
     Residence: 1860, Summit Twp., Somerset Co., PA[504]

255   ii. Lydia Christner, born 25 Jun 1841; died 1850.
256   iii. Cornelius Christner, born 07 Jun 1843 in Somerset Co., PA.
+ 257   iv. Dinah Christina Christner, born 1846.
258   v. Sevilla Christner, born 31 Dec 1851 in Somerset Co., PA. She married Phineas Cavenaugh; born 1835.

     Notes for Sevilla Christner:
     She is still in the 1920 census at Somerset Co., PA.

259   vi. Mary Christner, born 27 Mar 1855.
260   vii. Nathaniel Christner, born 1858 in Somerset Co., PA.

     Notes for Nathaniel Christner:
     Nathaniel went west. Gladys Tolbert told me he settled in Wyoming and his saddle is in the Fort Laramie Museum. It maybe his son Jonas's saddle. He may be buried near Worland.

Children of Jonas Christner and Rebecca Mankemeyer are:

	261	i.	Christina[6] Christner[505], born 1846 in Somerset, Somerset Co., PA[505].
	262	ii.	Albert Christner[505], born 22 May 1860 in Somerset Co., PA[505]; died 1870 in Somerset Co., PA[505].

More About Albert Christner:
Residence: 1860, Summit Twp., Somerset Co., PA[505]

+	263	iii.	Urias Jonas Christner, born 04 May 1865 in Union Center, Meyersdale, Somerset Co., PA; died 03 Feb 1943 in Meyersdale, Somerset Co., PA.
	264	iv.	Nathaniel Christner[505], born Dec 1865 in Somerset Co., PA[505]; died 01 Feb 1926 in Cane Creek, Lincoln Co., AR[505].

More About Nathaniel Christner:
Residence: 1920, Cane Creek, Lincoln Co., AR[505]

	265	v.	Rufus Christner[505], born 1867 in Somerset Co., PA[505]; died 1943 in Somerset Co., PA[505].

More About Rufus Christner:
Residence: 1910, Summit Twp., Somerset Co., PA[505]

	266	vi.	Jonas Christner[505], born 1869 in Somerset Co., PA[505].

More About Jonas Christner:
Residence: 1930, Spoon Buttes, Goshen, Wyoming[505]

+	267	vii.	Charles Christner, born 08 Dec 1876 in Garrett, Somerset Co., PA; died 07 Jun 1934 in Lincoln, Lancaster Co., NE.
	268	viii.	Franklin Christner[505], born 1878[505].
	269	ix.	Samuel Christner[505], born 1879 in Somerset Co., PA[505].

More About Samuel Christner:
Residence: 1880, Summit Twp., Somerset Co., PA[505]

	270	x.	Irvin Christner[505,506,507,508], born 08 Feb 1879[509,510,511]; died Oct 1964[512,513,514].

Notes for Irvin Christner:
The Mankamyer Family doesn't recognize this name?

More About Irvin Christner:
Residence: Elkhart, Elkhart Co., IN[515]
Social Security Number: 555-22-9594/[516,517]
SSN issued: CA[518,519]

	271	xi.	Joseph Christner[520], born 1882[520].

Notes for Joseph Christner:
The Mankamyer Family doesn't recognize this name?

Children of Jonas Christner and Caroline Mankemyer are:

+	272	i.	Calvin M.[6] Christner, born 29 Apr 1863 in Larimer, Somerset Co., PA; died 08 Sep 1947 in Larimer, Somerset Co., PA.
+	273	ii.	Rufus J. Christner, born 15 Sep 1866 in Somerset Co., PA; died 1943 in Somerset Co., PA.
+	274	iii.	Jonas H. Christner Jr., born Oct 1869 in Somerset Co., PA; died in Thayer Co., NE.
	275	iv.	Elenor Christner[520], born 1872[520]; died 1880[520].

Notes for Elenor Christner:
The Mankamyer Family doesn't recognize this name?

63. Moses C.[5] Christner (Joseph "Zep"[4], Johannes John Hans[3], Christian[2], Christen[1])[521,522,523,524,525] was born 28 Jan 1819 in Elk Lick Twp., Somerset Co., PA[526,527], and died 18 Dec 1898 in Cashion, Lockridge,

Logan Co., OK. He married **Mary Ann Nicklow**[528,529,530,531,532,533,534] 1838 in Garrett, Somerset Co., PA[535]. She was born 23 Dec 1822 in Somerset, Somerset Co., PA[535,536,537,538,539], and died 20 Feb 1904 in Garrett, Somerset Co., PA[540,541,542,543,544,545].

Notes for Moses C. Christner:
Amish and Amish Mennonite Genealogies; CH259; p. 59

Moses and Mary migrated to Oklahoma and homesteaded in Logan Co. in 1889. The homestead sold around 1900 after his death. Oil wells were drilled on the land and produced oil. There is a Christner Cemetery located 2 and 1/2 miles of Lockridge, OK on the south side of the road. The homestead was in the southeast part of Logan Co., OK.

Mary NICKLOW, b. 25 Dec. 1822 England, d. 1904 Garrett PA. m. Moses Christner. Daughter-in-law of Joseph "Zep" and Barbara Burkholder. Family Legend says she was a baby when they came to USA. Also everyone in Family remembers her last name different. Have a half a dozen or so spellings. Very petite lady, I would say from her photo about 4 Ft. Tall.

She is listed on all census as b. in PA, except the 1900 OK census, (after she was widowed) which lists b. England.

Moses Christner is buried in the Christner Cemetery near Lockridge, OK. A couple of years or so after his death Mary returned to Garrett, PA to live with daughter Ruena. Where she died in 1904.

Any info on Mary and her siblings or her parents would be appreciated. I think she had a brother William. Dora Moses and Mary migrated to Oklahoma and homesteaded in Logan Co in 1889. The homstead was sold around 1900 after his death. Oil wells were drilled on the land and it produced oil. Christner Cemetary is located 2 and 1/2 miles E. of Lockridge Oklahoma on the S. side of the road. The homestead is in the southeast part of Logan Co.

Birth: 28 Jan 1819
Death: Dec. 18, 1898

Age 79 yrs, 10 mos, 20 dys.

Burial: Christner Cemetery, Oklahoma Co., OK
Find A Grave Memorial# 30951532

More About Moses C. Christner:
Burial: Oklahoma Co., OK[546]
Census: 12 Jun 1860, Brothersvalley Twp, Somerset Co., PA[547]
Occupation: 1890, Farmer/Stella, Muddy Pt Twp, Richardson Co, NE[548,549,550,551]
Residence: 01 Jul 1863, Conemaugh, Somerset Co., PA[552]

Notes for Mary Ann Nicklow:
There may be some confusion as to where Mary is buried. I have notes as to her being buried in Garrett, PA and also buried in Stella Richardson Co., NE. Her tombstone is in Ridgeview Cemetery, north of Highland Cemetery, North of Garrett, PA. Soon after you drive in on the right side. Mary and her son Richard moved back to Garrett, Somerset Co., PA after her husband died.

Amish and Amish Mennonite Genealogies; CH259; pp. 57, 59

From: fivesquirrels@peakonline.com (Dora Gillilan) 12/6/01

Mary NICKLOW, b. 25 Dec. 1822 England, d. 1904 Garrett PA. m. Moses Christner. Daughter-in-law of Joseph "Zep" and Barbara Burkholder. Family Legend says she was a baby when they came to America. Also everyone in Family remembers her last name different. Have a half a dozen or so spellings. Very petite lady, I would say from her photo about 4 Ft. Tall.

She is listed on all census as b. in PA, except the 1900 OK census, (after she was widowed) which lists b. England.

Moses Christner is buried in the Christner Cemetery near Lockridge, OK. A couple of years or so after his death Mary returned to Garrett, PA to live with daughter Ruena. Where she died in 1904.

Any info on Mary and her siblings or her parents would be appreciated. I think she had a brother William.

Dora

Burial: February 23, 1904 - Old Cemetery, Garrett, Somerset Co., PA

More About Mary Ann Nicklow:
Burial: Old Ridgeview Cemetery, Garrett Union Garrett, Somerset Co., PA
Census: 12 Jun 1860, Brothersvalley Twp, Somerset Co., PA[553,554,555,556]
Residence: 1890, Township 15, Logan Co., OK[557]

Children of Moses Christner and Mary Nicklow are:

+ 276   i.   Mary Ann[6] Christner, born 11 Mar 1841 in Brothersvalley, Somerset Co., PA; died 10 Feb 1909 in Black Twp, Rockwood, Somerset Co., PA.

+ 277   ii.   Jacob M. Christner, born 21 Apr 1843 in Elk Lick Twp., Somerset Co., PA; died 09 Feb 1875 in Garrett, Somerset Co., PA.

+ 278   iii.   Adeline Polly Christner, born 02 Feb 1845 in Garrett, Summit Twp., Somerset Co., PA; died 08 Jul 1921 in Lockridge, Logan Co., OK.

+ 279   iv.   Rena Christner, born 15 Dec 1847 in Brothersvalley, Somerset Co., PA; died 1921 in Brothersvalley, Somerset Co., PA.

+ 280   v.   Joseph M. Christner, born 10 Mar 1849 in Brothersvalley, Somerset Co., PA; died 18 Oct 1907 in Guthrie, Logan Co., OK.

   281   vi.   Simon Christner, born 1852; died 1856.

Notes for Simon Christner:
Simon died infancy.

More About Simon Christner:
Burial: Garrett Borough, Somerset Co., PA

+ 282   vii.   Nelson "Nels" Christner, born 14 Jan 1854 in Garrett, Summit Twp., Somerset Co., PA; died 01 Jul 1925 in Oklahoma City, Oklahoma Co., OK.

+ 283   viii.   Alexander Christner, born 04 Apr 1856 in Garrett, Summit Twp., Somerset Co., PA; died 02 Dec 1947 in Strasburg, Adams Co., CO.

+ 284   ix.   Leah Christner, born 17 Apr 1858 in Garrett, Summit Twp., Somerset Co., PA; died 09 Nov 1930 in Northampton, Somerset Co., PA.

+ 285   x.   Katherine Ann Christner, born 11 Jul 1860 in Somerset Co., PA; died May 1938 in Marysville, Marshall Co., KS.

+ 286   xi.   George Washington Christner, born 14 Feb 1862 in Brothersvalley, Somerset Co., PA; died 14 Jan 1931 in Willard, Logan Co., CO.

+ 287   xii.   Richard W. Christner, born 14 Jan 1867 in Garrett, Somerset Co., PA; died 1950 in Garrett, Somerset Co., PA.

   288   xiii.   Madison Christner[558,559], born 1869 in Garrett, Somerset Co., PA[560,561]; died 1876 in Garrett, Somerset Co., PA[562,563].

Notes for Madison Christner:
Birth: 1869
Death: 1876

Inscription: 7 Years

Burial: Ridgeview Cemetery, Garrett, Somerset Co., PA
Madison died of Diptheria.

More About Madison Christner:
Burial: Summit Twp., Somerset Co., PA

   289   xiv.   Simon Christner[564,565], born 1870 in Garret, Somerset Co., PA[566,567]; died 1870 in Garret, Somerset Co.,

PA[568,569].

64. Eve[5] Christner (Joseph "Zep"[4], Johannes John Hans[3], Christian[2], Christen[1])[570,571,572,573,574,575,576,577] was born 21 Oct 1821 in Summitt, Somerset Co., PA[577], and died 1901 in Somerset Co., PA. She married **Jonathan Judy** 1834[578]. He was born 04 Nov 1815 in Brothers Valley, Twp, Somerset Co., PA, and died 1885 in Somerset Co., PA[578,579].

Notes for Eve Christner:
Amish and Amish Mennonite Genealogies; CH256, p. 57

Laurel Messenger - The Judy Family History
Author: Eber Cockley and Capt. Will Judy; February 1961, p. 5

More About Eve Christner:
Burial: Ridgeview Cemetery, Beachdale, Somerset Co., PA
Residence: 1880, Brothersvalley, Somerset Co., PA[580]

Notes for Jonathan Judy:
Jonathan resided in Brothervalley, Somerset Co., PA. Jonathan operated a saw mill. He was German Baptist and a republician.

Buried: Ridgeview Cemetery, Beachdale, Somerset Co., PA

More About Jonathan Judy:
Residence: 1880, Brothers Valley, Somerset Co., PA[581]

Children of Eve Christner and Jonathan Judy are:

> 290   i.   Jacob[6] Judy, born 1844.
>
> > Notes for Jacob Judy:
> > Jacob may be a twin to Mary Polly.
>
> 291   ii.   Mary Polly Judy, born 1844; died 1900. She married Jonathan Schrock 23 Nov 1861 in Somerset Co., PA.
>
> > Notes for Mary Polly Judy:
> > Mary may be a twin to Jacob.
>
> + 292   iii.   Cornelius Judy, born 21 Jan 1846 in Brothervalley, Somerset Co., PA; died 24 Jul 1917 in Age: 71/Garrett, Somerset Co., PA.
> 293   iv.   John W. Judy[581], born 1847 in VA[581]; died Aft. 1920[581].
>
> > More About John W. Judy:
> > Residence: 1870, Brothersvalley, Somerset Co., PA[581]
>
> + 294   v.   John Judy, born 14 Aug 1848 in Garrett, Somerset Co., PA; died 1925 in Thayer Co., NE.
> + 295   vi.   Jerome Henry Judy, born 14 May 1852 in Garrett, Somerset Co., PA; died 31 May 1922 in Garrett, Somerset Co., PA.
> 296   vii.   William Judy, born 1855. He married Lena Brown.
>
> > Notes for William Judy:
> > William may be a twin to Caroline.
>
> 297   viii.   Caroline Judy, born 1856.
> 298   ix.   Ellen Malinda Judy, born 1857. She married Herman Vogel.
>
> > Notes for Ellen Malinda Judy:
> > Ellen or Melinda married Herman Vogel.

66. Solomon McKenzie[5] Christner (Benjamin[4], Johannes John Hans[3], Christian[2], Christen[1])[582,583,584,585,586,587] was born 1811 in Somerset Co., PA[588,589,590,591], and died 28 Oct 1878 in Painesville, Lake Co., OH[592,593,594,595]. He married **Elizabeth Chevens**[596,597,598,599,600] Nov 1831 in St. James, Toronto, Peel, Ontario[600]. She was born 1811 in England[601,602,603,604,605], and died 17 May 1875 in Painesville, Lake Co., OH[606,607,608,609].

More About Solomon McKenzie Christner:
Arrival: 1871, New Hamburg, Ontario, Canada[610,611,612,613]
Residence: 1852, York Co., Canada West (Ontario), Canada[614]

More About Elizabeth Chevens:
Residence: 1871, Grey South, Ontario, Canada[615,616]

Children of Solomon Christner and Elizabeth Chevens are:

	299	i.	Benjamin[6] Christner[616], born 1832 in Etobicoke, York, Ontario, Canada[616].
+	300	ii.	John Smith Christner, born 1834 in Etobicoke, York, Ontario, Canada.
+	301	iii.	William Henry Christner, born 07 Oct 1837 in Weston Etobicoke, York, Ontario, Canada; died 14 Mar 1923 in Fullerton, Orange Co., CA.
+	302	iv.	Jane Elizabeth Christner, born 01 Feb 1839 in Etobicoke, York, Ontario, Canada; died 04 Dec 1903 in Pleasant Dale, Seward, NE.
+	303	v.	Mary Ann Christner, born 1840 in Etobicoke, York, Ontario, Canada; died 30 Oct 1914 in Colorado Springs, El Paso Co., CO.
	304	vi.	Victoria Christner[617], born 1845 in Etobicoke, York, Ontario, Canada[617]; died 07 Oct 1911 in Roblin, Manitoba, Canada[617]. She married Joseph Anderson 28 Mar 1867 in Osprey, Grey, Ontario, Canada.

More About Victoria Christner:
Residence: 1861, Osprey Township, Grey, Ontario, Canada[617]

	305	vii.	Susannah Christner, born 1846 in Etobicoke, York, Ontario, Canada.
+	306	viii.	Moses Isaac Christner, born 1853 in Etobicoke, York, Ontario, Canada; died 07 Sep 1917 in Tacoma, Pierce Co., WA.
	307	ix.	Aaron Christner[618], born 1854 in Etobicoke, York, Ontario, Canada[618].
+	308	x.	Richard Christner, born 1856 in Etobicoke, York, Ontario, Canada; died 22 Jun 1938 in Fort Smith, Sebastian Co., AR.
	309	xi.	Richard Henry Christner[618], born 04 Mar 1869 in CA[618]; died 12 Oct 1941 in Fort Smith, Sebastian Co., AR[618].

Notes for Richard Henry Christner:
Birth: May 3, 1869
Ontario, Canada
Death: Dec. 7, 1948
Port Huron, St. Clair Co., MI

Burial: Lakeside Cemetery, Port Huron, St. Clair Co., MI

More About Richard Henry Christner:
Arrival: 1888[618]
Residence: 1910, Port Huron Ward 11, St Clair, Michigan[618]

69. Barbara[5] Christner (Benjamin[4], Johannes John Hans[3], Christian[2], Christen[1])[619] was born 1817 in Etobicoke, York, Ontario, Canada[619], and died in Canada[620]. She married **Robert Harvey**[620]. He was born 1808 in Nottingham Eng[620], and died 05 Mar 1899 in Death Certificate: old age/Muskoka, Oakley Twp, Ontario, Canada[620].

Children of Barbara Christner and Robert Harvey are:

| | 310 | i. | Edward[6] Harvey[620], born Aug 1836 in Canada[620]; died 26 Apr 1927 in Veneta, Lane, Oregon, United States[620]. |
| | 311 | ii. | Hannah Margaret Harvey[620], born 17 Jul 1838 in Ontario, Canada[620]; died 16 Mar 1917 in Bronchitis; Death Record/Artemesia, Grey, Ontario, Canada[620]. |

More About Hannah Margaret Harvey:
Residence: 1911, Grey East, Ontario, Canada[620]

312   iii. Peter Benjamin Harvey[620], born 1842 in York, , Ontario, Canada[620]; died 11 Jan 1926 in Perry Sound, , Ontario, Canada[620].
313   iv. John Franklin Harvey[620], born 1852 in Canada[620].
314   v. George Harvey[620], born 1854 in Ontario, Canada[620].

74. Mary Jane[5] Christner (Benjamin[4], Johannes John Hans[3], Christian[2], Christen[1])[621] was born 08 Feb 1829 in Etobicoke Twp., York Toronto, Ontario Canada[621], and died 31 Jul 1911. She married **William Irvine Jr.** 20 Aug 1846 in St. Andrews Presbyterian. He was born 26 Dec 1824 in Quebec City, Canada, and died 1872 in Weston, Canada.

More About Mary Jane Christner:
Burial: Riverside Cemetery by Lawrence Ave. & Royal York Road Toronto CA.

Notes for William Irvine Jr.:
He was the Weston village Blacksmith.

More About William Irvine Jr.:
Burial: Necropolis Cemetery Toronto, Canada

Children of Mary Christner and William Irvine are:
+ 315   i. Eliza[6] Irvine, born 1847.
+ 316   ii. William Irvine, born 1848; died 1906.
+ 317   iii. James Irvine, born 11 Aug 1850; died 28 Nov 1921 in Weston, Canada.
+ 318   iv. Alex Irvine, born 1851.
+ 319   v. Benjamin Irvine, born 20 Jan 1854; died 24 Feb 1928.
   320   vi. Mary Irvine, born 1856; died 29 Nov 1925.
+ 321   vii. Susan Jen Irvine, born 1858.
+ 322   viii. Samual Irvine, born 1860.
+ 323   ix. Art Irvine, born 1862.
   324   x. Tom Irvine, born 1864.

85. Peter[5] Guth (Maria Anna[4] Christner, Christian[3], Christian[2], Christen[1]) was born 09 Feb 1806, and died 24 Jun 1886 in Washington, IL. He married **Susanna Oyer** in Niederhof Lorraine France. She was born 05 Apr 1809, and died 12 Dec 1888 in Washington, IL.

Children of Peter Guth and Susanna Oyer are:
   325   i. Christian[6] Guth.
   326   ii. Elizabeth Guth.
   327   iii. John Guth.
   328   iv. Joseph Guth.
   329   v. Peter Guth Jr..
   330   vi. Anna Guth, born 20 Aug 1836 in Washington IL; died 25 Aug 1921 in Shickley NE. She married (1) Jacob Rediger 20 Feb 1856 in Tazewell Co. IL. She married (2) Christian G. Roth 07 Mar 1867.

87. Christian[5] Christner (Peter[4], Christian[3], Christian[2], Christen[1])[622,623,624] was born 1796 in Alsace, France[625,626,627], and died 1836 in Wilmot Twp., Ontario, Canada[628,629]. He married **Elizabeth**[630,631] 1816 in Alsace, France[631]. She was born 1796 in Germany[632,633], and died 1862 in Wayland, Henry Co., IA.

Notes for Christian Christner:
Christian & Elizabeth plus their five oldest children emigrated to Canada about 1828 Baden, Wilmot Twp., Waterloo Co., Ontario, Canada this is north of Lake Erie. This was called the German Block. It's about 55 miles west southwest of Toronto, Canada. He maybe born 1799.

Christian was killed by a falling tree. He cut a tree which fell on a larger tree so he cut the big tree which must have kicked back and killed him.

For a complete history of Christian and his family read Homer Walter Christner's book "Our Immigrants". Christian and Elizabeth Christner's Family at Goshen College, Goshen, IN.

Homer Walter Christner is the author of the book Our Immigrants, Christian and Elizabeth Christner's family Published by H. Walter Christner 2912 E. Forest Lake Drive Sarasota,FL 34232 Well written Many stories & pictures about family of Christian the Immigrant to Canada. His grandfather Christian (2) was a brother of John Han's Christner Immigrant to PA. Both came from Alsace France.John Hans Christner had a son Christian J. b.1774 who also lived in Humber River Etobicoke Twp. York Co.Toronto Canada area around 1811 to 1824. This is only about 50 miles west from Nith River at New Hamburg, Kitchener Ontario Canada where Christian b1796 lived.
The book can be seen at Goshen College Goshen Indiana. Homer Walter Christner changed his name to H. Walter Christner or Walter H. Christner.

Christian and Elizabeth immigrated to Canada about 1828 to Wilmot Twp., Ontario, Canada.

More About Christian Christner:
Arrival: 1807, New Hamburg, Ontario, Canada[634,635]
Immigration: 1828, Wilmot Twp., Ontario, Canada
Residence: Ontario, Canada[635]

Notes for Elizabeth:
Christian and Elizabeth immigrated to Canada about 1828 to Wilmot Twp., Ontario, Canada.

After her husband died they became very poor. Elizabeth and the children walked to Elkhart Co., IN. They had a horse and wagon but the load was to much for the horse so they had to help push the wagon at the bad spots to help the poor horse. At Detroit they built a log raft (to get across the Detroit River) which started to come apart as they cross into the US after this she walked to Wayland, IA.

Baden, Wilmot Twp., Waterloo Co., Ontario, Canada this is north of Lake Erie. This was called the German Block. It's about 65 miles west southwest of Toronto Canada

For the rest of this story and a complete history of Elizabeth and her family read H. Walter Christner's book Our Immigrants. Christian and Elizabeth Christner's Family at Goshen College, Goshen, IN.

More About Elizabeth:
Burial: Sommers Cemetery next to her daughter Magdalena & her son in law Nicholas Roth
Immigration: 1828, Wilmot Twp., Ontario, Canada
Residence: 1860, Tippecanoe, Henry Co., IA[635]

Children of Christian Christner and Elizabeth are:

    331   i.   Elizabeth[6] Christner[635], born 1820 in Alsace, France[635]; died 1839 in Canada[635]. She married Nicholas Roth 1838; born 1822; died 15 Jul 1862 in North of Wayland, IA.

                     More About Elizabeth Christner:
                     Burial: Sommers Cemetery north of Wayland, IA

                     More About Nicholas Roth:
                     Burial: Sommers Cemetery north of Wayland, IA

+   332   ii.   Magdalena Christner, born 21 Oct 1821 in Alsace, France; died 09 Mar 1898 in Wayland, Henry Co., IA.

+   333   iii. Peter C. Christner, born 30 Jun 1823 in Alsace, Lorraine, France; died 11 Nov 1894 in Miami Co., IN.

+   334   iv. Catherine Christner, born 04 Oct 1824 in Bavaria Germany; died 25 Jan 1905.

+   335   v.   Jacob Christner, born 11 Apr 1828 in Wurttemberg Germany or Alsace, France; died 24 Mar 1893 in Elkhart, Elkhart Co., IN.

+	336	vi.	Daniel S. Christner, born 11 Apr 1830 in Nith River New Hamburg, Ontario, Canada; died 24 Oct 1897 in Hays Center, Hays Co., NE.
	337	vii.	Mary Christner[635], born Aft. 1830 in Nith River New Hamburg, Ontario, Canada.
	338	viii.	Christian Christner[635], born 1834 in Nith River New Hamburg, Ontario, Canada[635].

Notes for Christian Christner:
Christian never married and was some what crippled. The other brothers and sisters gave him the family trunk. Was he left behind with neighbors?

More About Christian Christner:
Burial: Geiger Mennonite Church Cemetery, New Hamburg, Ontario, Canada

88. Peter[5] Christner II (Peter[4], Christian[3], Christian[2], Christen[1])[636,637] was born 04 Feb 1798 in Guenstelhof, Alsace, France[638], and died 30 Dec 1880 in Marshall, Henry Co., IA[639,640]. He married **Veronica "Fanny" Christner**[640] 10 Jul 1821. She was born 1805 in Bavaria, Germany[640,641], and died Aft. 25 Aug 1870 in Henry Co., IA[642,643].

Notes for Peter Christner II:
Amish and Amish Mennonite Families; CHB; p. 60

OBITUARY - Herald of Truth - Volume XVIII, Number 2 - February, 1881
Christner- December 30th, 1880, in Marshall, Henry Co., IA of dropsy of the heart, Bro. Peter Christner, at the great age of 81 years, 10 months and 26 days. He was a brother in the Amish church. Funeral services by S. T. Miller and Sebastian Gerig, from 1 Cor. 15.

All of the info from this family comes from the A and A/M book The owned a 100 acre farm about a mile east of Tavistock, Ontario Canada but sold it in 1855.

More About Peter Christner II:
Cause of Death: Dropsy of the heart
Religion: Amish/
Residence: 1870, Trenton, Henry Co., IA[644,645]

Notes for Veronica "Fanny" Christner:
Amish and Amish Mennonite Families; CHB; p. 60

More About Veronica "Fanny" Christner:
Residence: 1870, Trenton, Henry Co., IA[646,647]

Children of Peter Christner and Veronica Christner are:

| + | 339 | i. | John B.[6] Christner, born 09 Jun 1829 in Lorraine, Alsace, France/; died 10 Sep 1922 in Lagrange Co., IN. |
| | 340 | ii. | Magdalena Christner[647], born 29 Sep 1831 in Alsace/Lorraine, France; died 16 Mar 1912 in Daviess Co, IN[647]. She married John S. Wagler 1852 in Tavistock, Ontario, Canada; born 08 Nov 1820 in Alsace/Lorraine, France; died 17 Apr 1908 in Daviess Co., IN. |

Notes for Magdalena Christner:
Maybe died Feb 29,1912 maybe born Germany in Sep 22 1831.

She came to America (Canada, New Hamburg) with her parents in 1847.

Amish and Amish Mennonite Families; CHB2; p. 60

Notes for John S. Wagler:
John moved to Daviess Co., IN in 1871.

Amish and Amish Mennonite Families; WFH p. 52; CHB1, p. 60

+ 341   iii. Peter Christner III, born 13 Jul 1833 in Alsace, Lorraine, France; died 09 Nov 1912 in Elmira, Aurora, Lane Co., OR.

+ 342   iv. Jacob Christner, born 20 Jun 1838 in Bavaria, Germany; died 06 Mar 1904 in Henry Co., IA.

   343   v. Elizabeth Christner[648], born 24 Apr 1839 in Alsace, France/Alsace, France/Germany[648]; died 06 Jan 1913 in Trenton, Henry Co., IA[648]. She married Joseph Roth 20 Jan 1859; born 1828 in France; died 06 Jul 1882.

     Notes for Elizabeth Christner:
     ROTH - Elizabeth (Christner) Roth was born in Germany, April 24, 1839; died Jan. 6, 1913; aged 73y. 8m. 12d. She came to Canada with her parents when 8 years old. When 15 years of age they came to Henry Co., IA on the farm where she died. She was a member of the A.M. Church since a young girl. She was married to Joseph Roth Jan. 20, 1859. To this union were born 11 children. Three sons and the husband have gone before, and 3 sons, 5 daughters, and 20 grandchildren remain to mourn her departure. She came to America (Canada, New Hamburg) with his parents in 1847.

     Birth: Apr. 24, 1839
     Death: Jan. 6, 1913

     Spouse: Joseph Roth (1828 - 1882)

     Burial: Roth Cemetery, Trenton, Henry Co.,
     Find A Grave Memorial# 66386824

     Notes for Joseph Roth:
     Birth: 1828, France
     Death: Jul. 6, 1882

     Per Mt Pleasant Library records he was born in Alsace, France. He aged 54 years.

     Spouse: Elizabeth Christner Roth (1839 - 1913)

     Burial: Roth Cemetery, Trenton, Henry Co., IA
     Find A Grave Memorial# 66386775

89. Josef[5] Christner (Peter[4], Christian[3], Christian[2], Christen[1]) was born 29 Apr 1809 in Windstein, Alsace, France, and died 1871 in Germany. He married **Katharina Oesch** 1838. She was born 06 Apr 1817 in Unterweilbach, Germany, and died 24 Feb 1894 in Deutenhausen, Germany.

Notes for Josef Christner:
He moved to Bavaria in 1823. Josef was born and died in Germany.

Child of Josef Christner and Katharina Oesch is:
+ 344   i. Josef[6] Christner, born 1844; died 1927.

91. Barbara[5] Christner (John Johann[4], Christian[3], Christian[2], Christen[1]) was born 21 Nov 1812 in Lepuix Delle near Florimont, Belfort, Alsace, France, and died 15 Oct 1860. She married **Christian Müller**. He was born 04 Jul 1813 in Bern, Switzerland, and died 15 Jan 1883.

Notes for Barbara Christner:
Birth: Nov. 21, 1812
Death: Oct. 15, 1860

Parents:
John Christner (1780 - 1871)
Maria Lugebiehl Christner (1784 - 1841)

Spouse: Christian Müller (1813 - 1883)

Burial: Christner Cemetery, Waterloo Co., Ontario, Canada

Notes for Christian Müller:
Birth: Jul 4, 1813 - Bern, Switzerland
Death: Jan 15, 1883

Spouse: Barbara Christner Müller (1812 - 1860)

Burial: Christner Cemetery, Waterloo Co., Ontario, Canada

Child of Barbara Christner and Christian Müller is:
+   345   i.   Christian[6] Guth, born 24 Feb 1833 in Burgwalden, Germany; died 26 Sep 1889 in Kokomo, Howard
                     Co., IN.

92. Christian[5] Christner (John Johann[4], Christian[3], Christian[2], Christen[1])[649] was born 21 Jun 1815 in
Lepuix Delle near Florimont, Alsace, France, and died 06 Apr 1907 in New Hamburg, Wilmot Twp., Waterloo
Co., Ontario, Canada[650,651]. He married **Nancy Anna Honsberger**[652]. She was born 15 May 1825 in Wilmot
Twp., Waterloo Co., Ontario, Canada.[652], and died 20 Mar 1884 in New Hamburg, Wilmot Twp., Waterloo Co.,
Ontario, Canada[653,654].

Notes for Christian Christner:
Birth: Jun. 21, 1815
Death: Apr. 6, 1907

April 25, 1907, page 159
Volume XLIV, Number 17 Christner - Christian Christner was born in upper Alsace, Germany, June 21, 1815.
Emigrated to this country in the year 1825. After suffering but a short time he passed peacefully away in New
Hamburg, Ont., on April 6, 1907, 91 Y., 9 M., 15 D. His wife preceded him 23 years, after which he moved to
New Hamburg where he resided with two of his daughters until death. He was a member of the Mennonite
church. He leaves to mourn his departure four sons and six daughters. Two of his daughters became members of
the same church. Funeral services were conducted by Amos S. Cressman, from Psa 90:12 and Noah Stauffer,
from Rev. 20:6. The services were held in our Amish Brethren's place of worship, Steinman's M. H.

Parents:
John Christner (1780 - 1871)
Maria Lugebiehl Christner (1784 - 1841)

Spouse: Anna Honsberger Christner (1825 - 1884)

Children:
Daniel Christner (1846 - 1915)
Enos Christner (1850 - 1936)
Catherine Christner (1854 - 1918)
Abraham Christner (1856 - 1872)
Leah Christner Shantz (1858 - 1914)
Christian H. Christner (1860 - 1939)

Burial: Christner Cemetery, Waterloo Co., Ontario, Canada
Find A Grave Memorial# 51254235

More About Christian Christner:
Burial: Abt. 09 Apr 1907, Christner Cem, Waterloo Co, Ontario, Canada[655,656]
Immigration: 1825, Canada after his marriage to a farm near New Hamburg, Ontario, Canada
Residence: 1891, Waterloo Co., Ontario, Canada[656]

Notes for Nancy Anna Honsberger:

Nancy's mothers name maybe Janzen.

Birth: Mar. 15, 1825
Death: Mar. 20, 1884

Herald of Truth - Volume XXI, Number 7 - APRIL 1,1884, page 108-109

CHRISTNER - On the 20th of March, near New Hamburg, Waterloo Co., Ont., Sister Anna, wife of Christian Christner, aged 59 years and 5 days. She was buried in their family burying-ground on the 23d. She leaves a husband and 10 children to mourn their loss. Funeral services were held by Amos Cressman from Phil. 1 21-24, and by Noah Stauffer, from Matt. 25:10. A large number of friends and relatives were present.

Spouse: Christian Christner (1815 - 1907)

Children:
Daniel Christner (1846 - 1915)
Enos Christner (1850 - 1936)
Catherine Christner (1854 - 1918)
Abraham Christner (1856 - 1872)
Leah Christner Shantz (1858 - 1914)
Christian H. Christner (1860 - 1939)

Burial: Christner Cemetery, Waterloo Co., Ontario, Canada

More About Nancy Anna Honsberger:
Burial: Abt. 23 Mar 1884, Christner Cem, Waterloo Co, Ontario, Canada[657,658]
Residence: 1871, Wilmot Twp., Waterloo Co., Ontario, Canada[659,660]

Children of Christian Christner and Nancy Honsberger are:

+   346   i.   Daniel[6] Christner, born 08 Nov 1846 in New Hamburg, Wilmot Twp., Waterloo Co., Ontario, Canada; died 17 Feb 1915 in Kitchener, Ontario, Canada.

+   347   ii.   Mary Christner, born 14 Mar 1848 in New Hamburg, Ontario, Canada.

+   348   iii.   Enos H. Christner, born 21 Feb 1850 in New Hamburg, Wilmot Twp., Waterloo Co., Ontario, Canada; died 11 Mar 1936 in New Hamburg, Wilmot Twp., Waterloo Co., Ontario, Canada.

    349   iv.   John Christner, born 26 Jan 1852 in Wilmot Twp., Waterloo Co., Ontario, Canada[660]; died 09 Jul 1940 in Los Angeles Co., CA[660]. He married Louisa Beckner[660].

             Notes for John Christner:
             Maybe born near DeWitt, NE.

    350   v.   Catharine Christner, born 12 Feb 1854 in New Hamburg, Ontario, Canada; died 17 Feb 1918 in New Hamburg, Ontario, Canada.

             Notes for Catharine Christner:
             Birth: Feb. 12, 1854
             Death: Feb. 17, 1918

             Parents:
             Christian Christner (1815 - 1907)
             Anna Honsberger Christner (1825 - 1884)

             Burial: Christner Cemetery, Waterloo Co., Ontario, Canada

    351   vi.   Abraham Christner[661,662,663], born 19 Aug 1856 in New Hamburg, Ontario, Canada[663,664]; died 29 Feb 1872 in Waterloo Co., Ontario, Canada[665].

             Notes for Abraham Christner:
             Birth: Aug. 19, 1856
             Death: Feb. 29, 1872

Parents:
Christian Christner (1815 - 1907)
Anna Honsberger Christner (1825 - 1884)

Burial: Christner Cemetery, Waterloo Co., Ontario, Canada

More About Abraham Christner:
Residence: 1871, New Hamburg, Ontario, Canada[665,666]

+ 352   vii.   Leah Christner, born 15 Sep 1858 in New Hamburg, Ontario, Canada; died 15 Sep 1914 in Waterloo, Onatario, Canada.
+ 353   viii. Christian H. Christner, born 25 Mar 1860 in New Hamburg, Ontario, Canada; died 13 Apr 1939 in Medford, OR.
+ 354   ix.   Annie Christner, born 08 Apr 1862 in New Hamburg, Ontario, Canada.
   355   x.   Barbara Christner, born 29 May 1864 in New Hamburg, Ontario, Canada; died 27 Sep 1947 in Los Angeles, Los Angeles Co., CA.

            Notes for Barbara Christner:
            Dress Maker in DeWitt, NE.

   356   xi.   Lydia Christner, born 02 Oct 1867.

            Notes for Lydia Christner:
            Maybe born Omaha, NE.

   357   xii.   Lydia Christner, born 03 Feb 1878; died 08 Jul 1879 in Summit Twp., Somerset Co., PA.

            Notes for Lydia Christner:
            Maybe born Omaha, NE.

93. Peter L.[5] Christner (John Johann[4], Christian[3], Christian[2], Christen[1]) was born 12 Oct 1817 in Lepuix Delle near Florimont, Belfort, Alsace, France, and died 28 Jan 1899 in Waterloo, New Hamburg, Ontario, Canada[667]. He married **(1) Catherine Nahrgang**[668]. She was born 29 Apr 1828 in Germany[669], and died 24 Dec 1915[670]. He married **(2) Magdalena Amanda Eby**.

Notes for Peter L. Christner:
Birth: Oct. 12, 1817
Death: Jan. 28, 1899

Parents:
John Christner (1780 - 1871)
Maria Lugebiehl Christner (1784 - 1841)

Spouse: Catharine Nahrgang Christner (1828 - 1915)

Children:
Isaac Christner (1849 - 1927)
Mary Ann Christner (1851 - 1912)
Elizabeth Christner Otto (1853 - 1928)
Barbara Christner (1853 - 1868)
Lucinda Christner Zimmerman (1858 - 1900)
Cyrus Christner (1860 - 1924)
Chris N Christner (1862 - 1917)
John Manly Christner (1867 - 1874)

Burial: Wilmot Mennonite Cemetery, Waterloo Co., Ontario, Canada

More About Peter L. Christner:
Residence: 1852, Waterloo Co., Ontario, Canada[671]

Notes for Catherine Nahrgang:
Birth: Apr 24, 1828
Death: Dec 24, 1915

Spouse: Peter L. Christner (1817 - 1899)

Children:
Isaac Christner (1849 - 1927)
Mary Ann Christner (1851 - 1912)
Elizabeth Christner Otto (1853 - 1928)
Barbara Christner (1853 - 1868)
Lucinda Christner Zimmerman (1858 - 1900)
Cyrus Christner (1860 - 1924)
Chris N. Christner (1862 - 1917)
John Manly Christner (1867 - 1874)

Burial: Wilmot Mennonite Cemetery, Waterloo Co., Ontario, Canada

More About Catherine Nahrgang:
Arrival: 1832[671,672,673]
Residence: 1911, Waterloo South, Ontario, Canada[674,675,676]

Children of Peter Christner and Catherine Nahrgang are:

358	i.	Christopher[6] Christner[677].
359	ii.	Caroline Christner[677].
360	iii.	Menno Christner[677,678], born 1849 in Canada[678].
361	iv.	Isaac Christner[679], born 25 Dec 1849; died 07 Jun 1927. He married Elizabeth Binkle; born 12 Mar 1861; died 23 Sep 1943.

  Notes for Isaac Christner:
  Birth: Dec 25, 1849
  Death: Jun 7, 1927

  Son of Catharine (Nahrgang) and Peter Christner

  Parents:
  Peter L. Christner (1817 - 1899)
  Catharine Nahrgang Christner (1828 - 1915)

  Spouse: Elizabeth Binkle Christner (1861 - 1943)

  Burial: Riverside Cemetery, Waterloo Co., Ontario, Canada

  Notes for Elizabeth Binkle:
  Birth: Mar 12, 1861
  Death: Sep 23, 1943

  Daughter of Henrietta and Christian Binkle

  Spouse:
  Isaac Christner (1849 - 1927)

  Burial: Riverside Cemetery, Waterloo Co., Ontario, Canada

362	v.	Barbara Christner[679], born 19 Jul 1853 in New Hamburg, Waterloo, Co., Ontario, Canada[679]; died 26 Aug 1868 in New Hamburg, Waterloo, Co., Ontario, Canada[679].

Notes for Barbara Christner:
Birth: Jul. 19, 1853
Death: Aug. 26, 1868

Parents:
Peter L. Christner (1817 - 1899)
Catharine Nahrgang Christner (1828 - 1915)

Burial: Wilmot Mennonite Cemetery, Waterloo Co., Ontario, Canada

+   363   vi.   Elizabeth Christner, born 19 Jul 1853; died 24 Apr 1928.

+   364   vii.   Lucinda Christner, born 19 Oct 1858 in New Hamburg, Waterloo, Co., Ontario, Canada; died 17 Feb 1900 in New Hamburg, Waterloo, Co., Ontario, Canada.

   365   viii.   Mary Ann Christner[679], born 02 Dec 1860 in New Hamburg, Waterloo, Co., Ontario, Canada[679]; died 17 Apr 1924 in New Hamburg, Waterloo, Co., Ontario, Canada[679].

   366   ix.   Cyrus Christner[679,680], born 12 Dec 1860 in Wilmot Twp., Ontario, Canada[680]; died 17 Apr 1924 in Cause of death listed as hemorrhage into abdominal cavity. Informant brother-in-law Simon Shantz/Waterloo Co., Ontario, Canada[680].

Notes for Cyrus Christner:
Birth: Dec. 12, 1860
Death: Apr. 17, 1924

Parents:
Peter L. Christner (1817 - 1899)
Catharine Nahrgang Christner (1828 - 1915)

Burial:Wilmot Mennonite Cemetery, Waterloo Co., Ontario, Canada

More About Cyrus Christner:
Residence: 1911, Waterloo South, Ontario, Canada[680]

+   367   x.   Christopher N. Christner, born 06 Mar 1862 in New Hamburg, Waterloo, Co., Ontario, Canada; died 23 Oct 1917 in New Hamburg, Waterloo, Co., Ontario, Canada.

   368   xi.   John Manley Christner[681], born 24 Aug 1867 in New Hamburg, Waterloo, Co., Ontario, Canada[681]; died 03 Mar 1874 in New Hamburg, Waterloo, Co., Ontario, Canada[681].

Notes for John Manley Christner:
Birth: Oct. 25, 1867
Death: May 3, 1874

Parents:
Peter L. Christner (1817 - 1899)
Catharine Nahrgang Christner (1828 - 1915)

Burial: Wilmot Mennonite Cemetery, Waterloo Co., Ontario, Canada

Child of Peter Christner and Magdalena Eby is:

+   369   i.   Aaron[6] Christner, born 21 Oct 1843 in Waterloo Co., New Hamburg, Ontario, Canada; died 10 Jun 1902 in Harrison Twp., Elkhart Co., IN.

94. Veronica Luckenbill[5] Christner (John Johann[4], Christian[3], Christian[2], Christen[1]) was born 28 Sep 1820 in Lepuix Delle near Florimont, Belfort, Alsace, France, and died 21 Apr 2007 in Waterloo Co., Ontario, Canada. She married **Noah Shoemaker Bechtel** 13 Mar 1841 in Waterloo, Ontario, Canada[682]. He was born 22 Sep 1818 in Montgomery, Montgomery, PA[682], and died 02 Sep 1901 in Waterloo Co., Ontario, Canada[683].

Notes for Veronica Luckenbill Christner:
Birth: Sep. 28, 1820
Death: Apr. 21, 1907

Daughter of John & Maria (Luckebihl) Christner. Wife of Noah S. Bechtel.

Parents:
John Christner (1780 - 1871)
Maria Lugebiehl Christner (1784 - 1841)

Spouse: Noah S. Bechtel (1818 - 1901)

Children:
Menno Bechtel (1842 - 1902)
Mary Bechtel Hunsperger (1846 - 1894)
Isaac C Bechtel (1854 - 1918)
Noah C. Bechtel (1856 - 1951)
Esther Bechtel Snyder (1863 - 1940)

Burial: Mannheim Mennonite Cemetery, Waterloo Co., Ontario, Canada

More About Veronica Luckenbill Christner:
Arrival: Oct 1825, The family settled in Canada/Waterloo Co., Ontario, Canada[683]
Residence: 1891, Waterloo South, Ontario, Canada[683,684,685]
Widowed: Sep 1901, Death of Noa/Waterloo Co., Ontario, Canada[685]

Notes for Noah Shoemaker Bechtel:
Birth: Sep. 22, 1818
Death: Sep. 2, 1901

Parents:
George B. Bechtel (1777 - 1851)
Mary Shoemaker Bechtel (1793 - 1840)

Spouse: Veronica Christner Bechtel (1820 - 1907)

Children:
Menno Bechtel (1842 - 1902)
Mary Bechtel Hunsperger (1846 - 1894)
Isaac C. Bechtel (1854 - 1918)
Noah C. Bechtel (1856 - 1951)
Esther Bechtel Snyder (1863 - 1940)

Burial: Mannheim Mennonite Cemetery, Waterloo Co., Ontario, Canada

More About Noah Shoemaker Bechtel:
Arrival: Abt. Jan 1841, St Agatha, Wilmot, Waterloo, Ontario, Canada[685,686]
Occupation: 02 Sep 1901, Farmer/[686]
Residence: 1861, Waterloo, Wilmot, Ontario, Canada[686]

Children of Veronica Christner and Noah Bechtel are:
+   370   i.   Menno[6] Bechtel, born 29 Jul 1842 in Waterloo, Wilmot Twnp, Ontario, Canada; died 19 Sep 1902 in Cardiac Disease/Waterloo Co., Wilmot Twp., Ontario, Canada.
    371   ii. Leah Bechtel[686], born 26 Apr 1844 in Waterloo, Wilmot Township, Ontario, Canada[686]; died 26 Nov 1929 in Huron South, Hay Twnp, Ontario, Canada[686].

              More About Leah Bechtel:
              Residence: 1891, Huron South, Ontario, Canada[686]

    372   iii. Mary Maria Bechtel[686], born 19 May 1846 in Waterloo Co., Ontario, Canada[686]; died 13 Aug 1894[686].
    373   iv. Moses Bechtel[686], born 23 Feb 1848 in Canada[686]; died 07 Jul 1941[686].

374 v.   Catharine (Catharina?) Bechtel[686], born 19 Feb 1850 in Waterloo Co., Ontario, Canada[686]; died 28 Jun 1884 in New Hamburg, , Ontario, Canada[686].

More About Catharine (Catharina?) Bechtel:
Residence: 1871, Ontario, Canada[686]

375 vi. Christian Bechtel[686], born 19 Aug 1852 in Waterloo Co., Ontario, Canada[686]; died 28 Feb 1854 in Wilmot, Waterloo, Ontario, Canada[686].

More About Christian Bechtel:
Burial: 28 Feb 1854, Shantz Mennonite Cemetery   Wilhelm Cemetery ??/Waterloo Co, Wilmot Twnp, Ont Cda[686]

376 vii. Isaac Bechtel[686], born 11 Jul 1854 in Wilmot, Waterloo Co., Ontario, Canada[686]; died 18 Nov 1918 in 64y 4m 7d - Date of Death from Death Register./Waterloo, Ontario, Canada[686].

More About Isaac Bechtel:
Residence: 1911, Waterloo South, Ontario, Canada[686]

377 viii. Noah (Nohale) Bechtel[686], born 20 Nov 1856 in Waterloo, Wilmot, Ontario, Canada[686]; died 1951 in Canada[686].

More About Noah (Nohale) Bechtel:
Burial: Mannheim Mennonite Cemetery/[686]

+ 378 ix. Veronica "Fanny" Christner Bechtel, born 04 Mar 1859 in Waterloo Co., Ontario, Canada; died 18 Apr 1935 in Pandora, Putnam Co., OH.

379 x.   Lydia Bechtel[686], born 01 May 1861[686]; died 20 May 1937 in RR2 Petersburg, Wilmot Twp, Ontario, Canada[686].

380 xi. Esther Hettie Bechtel[686], born 05 Dec 1863 in Wilmot, Waterloo Co., Ontario, Canada[686]; died 04 Jun 1940 in Waterloo Co., Ontario, Canada[686].

More About Esther Hettie Bechtel:
Residence: 1871, Waterloo Co., Ontario, Canada[686]

Generation No. 6

95. Elizabeth "Betsy"[6] Sipe (Elizabeth[5] Christner, Christian J.[4], Johannes John Hans[3], Christian[2], Christen[1])[687] was born 1824 in Holmes Co., OH[688], and died 22 Oct 1905 in Nappanee, Elkhart Co., IN. She married **Soloman Hamsher**. He was born 01 Feb 1829 in NY[688], and died 22 Oct 1905 in Nappanee, Elkhart Co., IN.

Notes for Elizabeth "Betsy" Sipe:
Amish and Amish Mennonite Genealogies; p. 389; SI81

More About Elizabeth "Betsy" Sipe:
Nickname: Betsy

Notes for Soloman Hamsher:
They Lived at Bourbon, IN and Walnut Creek, OH where he was a Township Clerk.

Children of Elizabeth Sipe and Soloman Hamsher are:
381 i.   John F.[7] Hamsher, born 24 May 1855 in Luck, Elkhart Co., IN[689]; died 08 Jan 1916 in Etna Green, Kosciusko Co., IN[689]. He married Saloma Stahley[689] 09 Jun 1901 in Nappanee, Elkhart Co., IN[689]; born 26 Aug 1881 in Shelbyville, Shelby Co., IL[689].

Notes for John F. Hamsher:
He was from Nappanee, IN.   He was Dunkard Amish.

More About Saloma Stahley:
Residence: 1912, Etna Green, Indiana[689]

+ 382   ii.   Andrew Hamsher, born 22 Oct 1866 in Bourbon, Marshall Co., IN; died 10 Oct 1953 in Walnut Creek, Holmes Co., OH.

96. Sarah[6] Sipe (Elizabeth[5] Christner, Christian J.[4], Johannes John Hans[3], Christian[2], Christen[1])[690] was born 03 Aug 1826 in Holmes Co., OH, and died 25 Sep 1890 in Row5 plot 4. She married **Samuel Mishler** 13 Aug 1846 in Holmes Co. OH. He was born 06 Apr 1822 in Somerset Co., PA, and died 30 Nov 1897 in Eden Twp., Lagrange Co., IN.

Notes for Sarah Sipe:
Sarah married Samuel Mishler in Holmes Co., OH. 1850 census has Barbara (Holly) Christner living with Sarah. Barbara is listed as 69 years old. Barbara is the grandmother of Sarah. Sarah had the first marked grave (Sarah Mishler) in the Christner Cemetery

Amish and Amish Mennonite Genealogies; SI82, p. 390

More About Sarah Sipe:
Baptism (LDS): 14 Nov 1987, IFALL[691]
Burial: Christner Cemetery, Honeyville, Lagrange Co., IN
Endowment (LDS): 07 Jan 1988, IFALL[691]
Record Change: 19 Sep 2005
Sealed to parents (LDS): 20 Feb 1988, IFALL[691]

More About Samuel Mishler:
Burial: Christner Cemetery Honeyville IN N 41°34.500-W 85°35.900 Row5 Plot 3

Children of Sarah Sipe and Samuel Mishler are:
    383   i.   Drusilla[7] Mishler, born 08 Oct 1847.
+ 384   ii.   Andrew S. Mishler, born 03 Apr 1850 in Holmes Co., OH; died 24 Feb 1897 in Newbury Township, Honeyville, Lagrange Co., IN.
    385   iii. Jeremiah Mishler, born 18 Jun 1853.
    386   iv. Elizabeth Mishler, born 21 Aug 1856.
    387   v.   David Mishler, born 25 Aug 1859.
    388   vi. Anna Mishler, born 12 Feb 1866.

105. John J.[6] Christner (Joseph C.[5], Christian J.[4], Johannes John Hans[3], Christian[2], Christen[1])[692,693] was born 24 Nov 1827 in Berlin, Holmes Co., OH[693,694], and died 03 Jul 1893 in Honeyville, Lagrange Co., IN[695,696]. He married **(1) Susanna Mast**[697,698,699,700] 21 Aug 1849 in Holmes Co., OH - Married by Bishop Abraham A. Troyer. She was born 01 Dec 1829 in Holmes Co., OH[701,702], and died 02 Jan 1859 in Charm, Holmes Co., OH[702]. He married **(2) Susanna Stutzman**[703,704,705] 21 Aug 1859 in Berlin, Holmes Co., OH. She was born 01 Dec 1829 in Millersburg, Holmes Co., OH, and died 04 Jun 1909 in Topeka, Lagrange Co., IN.

Notes for John J. Christner:
Amish and Amish Mennonite Genealogies; CH2121, pp. 57, 60, 65

John and Susie lived in Holmes Co., OH and owned the farm known as the Old Bishop Samuel Miller Farm. In 1863 John and his 2nd wife moved to In. Came to Warsaw by train, someone brought them up to Bonnieville Mills by wagon. The next morning John and the older boys drove their cattle to Honeyville using a horse and buggy. The old buildings were about 700 feet west of Christner Cemetery. south of Honeyville, IN marked by large pile of stones. These buildings were just west of the Christner Cemetery. John died after raking hay . He began to feel ill and went to the shade tree, then from the shade to the house and finally in the house and was found dead by suppertime in bed. Sons Joseph and David. John gave land to start the first one room school in Eden Township and the Christner Cemetery, Lockridge, Logan Co., OK.

Bonnyville Mill an over night resting camp for the first Christner in Indiana. My Grandfather's Grandfather moved to Indiana from Holmes Co., OH in 1863. His name is John J Christner born November 24 1827. He married Susie Mast. They had 6 children-all sons. My Great Grandfather Joseph J - Noah - David J - John J - Abraham J - and Christian. Susie Mast died January 2 - 1859. John then married Susanna Stuzman they had 4 girls Mary - Elizabeth - Annie - Emma

John Hans Christner had a son Christian J Christner married to Barbara Holly. Christian and Barbara moved to Holmes Co. Ohio in 1820. They had lived in Berlin Township Pennsylvania plus a short time in Canada. His Grandson is the John that that moved to Indiana.

When John and Susie lived in Holmes Co., OH they owned the farm known as the Old Bishop Samuel Miller Farm. John and his second wife Susanna came to Indiana by the way of train to Warsaw Indiana. (Maybe around May 1864) They moved with farm implements, cattle, horses, wagons, furniture, pots and pans, dishes, grapevines, hops and ten kids. What a trip. Are we there yet? Are we there yet?They first came to Bonneyville Mills close to Bristol IN. N41°43.1483' by W85°45.9157'. After resting the night John and the older sons drove their cattle to Honeyville, Indiana using a horse and buggy. John built a house 700 feet west of the Christner Cemetery marked by a large pile of stones at (N41° 34.500 - W85° 36.150). The Hops are still growing on a fence line west of the site of the old house. John died June 5, 1893 after raking hay in this field. He began to feel ill and went to a shade tree. Not feeling better he made his way to the shade of the house. His next move was to his bedroom where he was found dead at supper time. John gave land to build the first one room school in Eden Township, Lagrange Co., IN.

Rev. Harvey Hostetler, "Descendants of Jacob Hochstetler" (Elgin, IL: Brethren Publishing House, 1912) [reprint, Berlin, OH: Gospel Book Store, 1977], p. 446.

Birth: Nov. 24, 1827
Death: Jul. 7, 1893

John J. Christner was married (1) 21 Aug 1849 to Susie Mast. She was born Dec. 1, 1829 and died Jan 2, 1859. Seven children were born of this marriage. John J. married (2) 21 Aug 1859 (same date as his first marriage) to Susanna Stutzman at Berlin, Ohio. Four children were born of this marriage. Bontrager, David R. etal.

Spouse: Susanna Christner (1829 - 1909)

Children:
Joseph J. Christner (1851 - 1925)
John J. Christner (1855 - 1946)
Annie Schrock (1863 - 1949)

Burial: Christner Cemetery, Honeyville, Lagrange Co., IN

The Descendants of John J. Christner, privately published 1961, February 1961, p 4.

More About John J. Christner:
Burial: N 41°34.500-W 85°35.900 Row 5 plot10/Ira Christner Farm, Christner Cemetery, Honeyville, Lagrange Co., IN
Death Certificate: Book H-12 on page 132, Lagrange Co., IN
Occupation: Farmer/
Residence: 1880, Eden, Lagrange Co., IN[706,707]

Notes for Susanna Mast:
Susie Mast was the daughter of Jacob Mast and Magdalena Miller. Susie was married to William Miller before she married John Christner and she had a son Jacob born between 1840 and 1850 possibily 1848. Jacob died about the age of 2. No death info on William Miller.

Susies family history recorded book Joseph J. Mast and Mary Miller 1814 to 1958.

Bonnyville Mill an over night resting camp for the first Christner in Indiana. My Grandfather's Grandfather moved to Indiana from Holmes Co., OH in 1863. His name is John J Christner born November 24 1827. He married Susie Mast. They had 6 children-all sons. My Great Grandfather Joseph J. - Noah - David J - John J - Abraham J - and Christian. Susie Mast died January 2 - 1859. John then married Susanna Stuzman they had 4 girls Mary - Elizabeth - Annie - Emma; John Hans Christner had a son Christian J Christner married to Barbara Holly. Christian and Barbara moved to Holmes Co., OH in 1820. They had lived in Berlin Twp., PA plus a short time in Canada. His Grandson is the John that that moved to Indiana.

When John and Susie lived in Holmes Co., OH they owned the farm known as the Old Bishop Samuel Miller Farm. John and his second wife Susanna came to Indiana by the way of train to Wabash Indiana. (Maybe around May 1864) They moved with farm implements, cattle, horses, wagons, furniture, pots and pans, dishes, grapevines, hops and ten kids. What a trip. Are we there yet? Are we there yet? They first came to Bonneyville Mills close to Bristol, IN. N41°43.1483' by W85°45.9157'. After resting the night John and the older sons drove their cattle to Honeyville, IN using a horse and buggy. John built a house 700 feet west of the Christner Cemetery marked by a large pile of stones at (N41° 34.500 - W85° 36.150). The Hops are still growing on a fence line west of the site of the old house. John died June 5 1893 after raking hay in this field. He began to feel ill and went to a shade tree. Not feeling better he made his way to the shade of the house. His next move was to his bedroom where he was found dead at supper time. John is my (Steven Carl Christner) only Great Great Grandfather since my mother is also a Christner. John gave land to build the first one room school in Eden Township, Lagrange, IN.

Birth: Dec. 1, 1829
Death: Jun. 4, 1909

Spouse: John J Christner (1827 - 1893)

Children: Annie Schrock (1863 - 1949)

Inscription: Susanna Christner Wife of John Christner born Dec. 1, 1829 and died June 4, 1909

Burial: Christner Cemetery, Honeyville, Lagrange Co., IN

The Descendants of John J. Christner, privately published February 1961, p. 4.

More About Susanna Mast:
Residence: 1850, Mechanic, Holmes Co., OH[708]

Notes for Susanna Stutzman:
Amish and Amish Mennonite Genealogies; CH2121, p. 60

Died 4 June 1909 - 79 yrs 6 mo 2da
Lived with her daughter Annie, the Isaac Schrock's in her last years.

More About Susanna Stutzman:
Burial: row 5 plot11/Christner Cemetery, Honeyville, Lagrange Co., IN
Cause of Death: Dropsy

Children of John Christner and Susanna Mast are:
+   389   i.   Joseph J.[7] Christner, born 19 Feb 1851 in Holmes Co., OH; died 09 Jan 1925.
     390   ii. Noah Christner[709], born 24 Aug 1852 in Holmes Co., OH; died 24 Aug 1865 in Lagrange, Lagrange Co., IN[709,710,711].

              Notes for Noah Christner:
              Amish and Amish Mennonite Genealogies; CH21211, p. 60

              The Descendants of John J. Christner, privately published 1961, p. 4.

+   391   iii. David J. Christner, born 31 Dec 1853 in Millersburg, Holmes Co., OH; died 13 Nov 1927 in Topeka, Lagrange Co., IN.
+   392   iv. John J. Christner, born 25 Nov 1855 in Holmes Co., OH; died 08 Oct 1946 in Row 1 Plot 6 from south to north.
+   393   v.   Abraham J. Christner, born 08 Dec 1856 in Millersburg, Holmes Co., OH; died 13 Dec 1931 in

Honeyville, Lagrange Co., IN.

394   vi.   Magdalena Christner, born 25 Dec 1857 in Holmes Co., OH[712]; died 23 Oct 1860 in Holmes Co., OH[712].

Notes for Magdalena Christner:
Amish and Amish Mennonite Genealogies; CH21216, p. 60

The Descendants of John J. Christner, privately published 1961, p. 4.

More About Magdalena Christner:
Burial: Daniel Miller Farm, Walnut Creek, Holmes Co., OH

395   vii.   Christian Christner[713,714], born 02 Jan 1859 in Holmes Co., OH; died 18 Aug 1859 in Holmes Co., OH[714].

Notes for Christian Christner:
Amish and Amish Mennonite Genealogies;

This farm is located 2 1/2 miles east and 1/4 mile north of Charm, Holmes Co., OH. His mother died in child birth for Christian. He is buried Daniel Miller Farm South of Walnut Creek, OH. He died and was buried at the same time as his father was published for his second marriage.

The Descendants of John J. Christner, privately published 1961, p. 4.

More About Christian Christner:
Burial: Daniel Miller Farm, Charm, Holmes Co., OH

+ 396   viii.   Mary Christner, born 26 Aug 1860 in Shipshewana, Lagrange Co., IN; died 03 Sep 1922 in Shipshewana, Lagrange Co., IN.

397   ix.   Elizabeth Christner[715,716], born 19 Dec 1862 in Holmes Co., OH[717]; died 20 Sep 1881 in Elkhart Co., IN[717]. She married Cornelius M. Hostetler 17 Feb 1881 in IN; born 06 Jan 1858 in Nappanee, Elkhart Co., IN.

Notes for Elizabeth Christner:
The Descendants of John J. Christner, privately published 1961, pp. 4, 36.

Birth may have been at Holmes Co., OH since her Father didn't leave Holmes Co., OH until 1863. Some say Nappanee, IN.

Amish and Amish Mennonite Genealogies; CH21219, p. 60

Herald of Truth - Volume XVIII, Number 11 - November, 1881, Page 197, 198

HOCHSTETLER - Sept. 20th, in Elkhart Co., IN Sister Elizabeth, wife of Cornelius Hochstetler, and daughter of John and Susanna Christner, aged 19 years, 9 months and 3 days; was a faithful sister in the Amish Mennonite church, and lived in wedlock 7 months and 3 days. Buried the 21st in Manasseh Hochstetler's burying-ground. Funeral services conducted by John Schlabach, from the 5th chapter of John.

More About Elizabeth Christner:
Burial: Manasseh Hochstetler's Burying ground

Notes for Cornelius M. Hostetler:
The Descendants of John J. Christner, privately published February 1961, p. 36.

Cornelius and Elizabeth were only married 7 months before she died. Cornelius then married Barbara Helmuth Feb 28. 1884 and had 15 children.

+ 398   x.   Anna Christner, born 20 May 1863 in Holmes Co., OH; died 27 Mar 1949 in Topeka, Lagrange Co., IN.

+ 399   xi.   Emma J. Christner, born 22 Sep 1865 in Topeka, Lagrange Co., IN; died 15 Mar 1901 in Topeka, Lagrange Co., IN.

106. Elizabeth J.[6] **Christner** (Joseph C.[5], Christian J.[4], Johannes John Hans[3], Christian[2], Christen[1])[718,719,720] was born 01 Sep 1829 in Holmes Co., OH[721,722], and died 16 Oct 1903 in Elkhart, Elkhart Co., IN[722]. She married **Daniel J. Frey**[723,724] 05 Jan 1851 in Holmes Co., OH[725], son of John Frey and Barbara Farmwald. He was born 14 Jun 1827 in Holmes Co., OH[725], and died 27 Aug 1878 in Lagrange Co., IN.

Notes for Elizabeth J. Christner:
Amish and Amish Mennonite Genealogies

They lived in Holmes Co., OH until 1866 when they moved to Lagrange Co., IN.   She died of paralysis.

The Descendants of John J. Christner, privately published 1961, February 1961, p. 52.

More About Elizabeth J. Christner:
Causes of Death: Paralysis
Religion: Old Order Amish/
Residence: 1920, Johnstown Ward 8, Cambria Co., PA[725]

Notes for Daniel J. Frey:
The Descendants of John J. Christner, privately published February 1961, p. 52.

Daniel was an ordained minister, Old Order Amish and a farmer. His parents imigrated from Germany. Daniel died of cancer.

Amish and Amish Mennonite Genealogies;

More About Daniel J. Frey:
Causes of Death: Cancer
Census: 01 Aug 1860, 1860 Federal Census/German Twp., Holmes Co., OH[726,727]
Occupation: Ordained Minister - O. O. Amish and Farmer/
Religion: Old Order Amish/
Residence: 1920, Johnstown Ward 8, Cambria Co., PA[728]

Children of Elizabeth Christner and Daniel Frey are:
+	400	i.	Mary D.[7] Frey, born 20 Feb 1852 in Holmes Co., OH; died 18 Sep 1935.
+	401	ii.	Barbara D. Frey, born 13 Dec 1854 in Holmes Co., OH; died 22 Dec 1929.
+	402	iii.	John D. Frey, born 16 Jul 1857 in Holmes Co., OH; died 27 Jan 1934 in Lagrange Co., IN.
+	403	iv.	Joseph D. Frey, born 16 Jul 1857 in Holmes Co., OH; died 27 Mar 1945 in Haven, Reno Co., KS.
+	404	v.	Samuel D. Frey, born 19 May 1860 in Holmes Co., OH; died 11 Feb 1938.
+	405	vi.	Noah D. Frey, born 11 Apr 1863 in Farmerstown, Holmes Co., OH; died 20 Feb 1928 in Lagrange Co., IN.
+	406	vii.	Daniel D. Frey Jr., born 31 Mar 1866 in Holmes Co., OH; died 25 Feb 1947.
+	407	viii.	Elizabeth D. Frey, born 11 May 1869 in Lagrange Co., IN; died 04 Nov 1958 in Goshen, Elkhart Co., IN.

109. Barbara[6] **Christner** (John J.[5], Christian J.[4], Johannes John Hans[3], Christian[2], Christen[1]) was born 10 Jan 1834 in Holmes Co., OH, and died 22 Jan 1912. She married **Solomon S. Miller** 18 Mar 1860. He was born 09 May 1828 in Charm OH, and died 05 May 1880.

Notes for Barbara Christner:
Miller - Barbara S. Miller (nee Christner) was born in Holmes Co., OH Jan 10, 1834; died Jan. 22, 1912; aged 78 y. 12 d. She was married to Solomon S. Miller Mar 18, 1860. To this union were born 1 son and 7 daughters. Husband, 3 sons and 2 daughters preceded her to the spirit world. She lived as widow 31 y. 8 m. 17 d. She leaves 1 sister, 5 daughters, 1 step-son, 1 step daughter, 25 grandchildren and a host of friends. She was buried at the Walnut Creek A. M. Church, of which she was a faithful member. Services by M. A. Mast (Heb. 11:24) and S. H. Miller (Psa. 39:4, 5).
Farmers close to Charm, OH.

More About Barbara Christner:
Burial: Walnut Creek A.M. Church Cemetery Holmes Co, OH

Notes for Solomon S. Miller:
Solomon is the son of Simon and Elizabeth Gnagey Miller of Walnut Creek, OH.

Simon is the son of Broad Run John Miller DBH book 12.

A and A/M book says Solomon was 1st married to Mary Hershberger.

More About Solomon S. Miller:
Burial: Walnut Creek A.M. Church Cemetery Holmes Co, OH

Children of Barbara Christner and Solomon Miller are:
+   408   i.   Martha[7] Miller.
     409   ii.   Elizabeth Miller. She married William J. Mullet.
     410   iii.   Malinda Miller. She married George Flinner.
     411   iv.   Sarah Miller. She married Alexander Stutzman.
+   412   v.   Lydia Ellen Miller, born 13 Jun 1865 in Charm, Holmes Co., OH; died 20 Feb 1934 in Walnut Creek, Holmes Co., OH.

110. Joseph J.[6] Christner (John J.[5], Christian J.[4], Johannes John Hans[3], Christian[2], Christen[1])[729,730] was born 15 Dec 1835 in Holmes Co., OH[731,732,733], and died 01 Jan 1908 in Baltic, Tuscarawas Co., OH[734,735]. He married **Sarah Gerber**[736,737,738] 02 Oct 1856. She was born 31 Jan 1837 in Somerset, Somerset Co., PA[739], and died 09 Nov 1923 in Baltic, Tuscarawas Co., OH[739,740].

Notes for Joseph J. Christner:
Birth: Dec. 15, 1835
Death: Jan. 1, 1908

Burial: Amish Mennonite Cemetery, Walnut Creek, Holmes Co., OH

Joseph had a brick yard at Baltic, OH. The Brick yard is at N40°26.828 by W81°41.590 North East side of Baltic, OH off State Road 93. He maybe have had a child Magdalena born 1858.

More About Joseph J. Christner:
Burial: Walnut Creek, Mennonite, Walnut Creek, OH
Residence: 1860, Walnut Creek, OH, United States[741]

Notes for Sarah Gerber:
Birth: Jan. 31, 1837
Death: Nov. 9, 1923

Burial: Amish Mennonite Cemetery, Walnut Creek, Holmes Co., OH

Sarah is the daughter of Jacob Gerber and Elizabeth Miller. She was from the Walnut Creek, OH area. She may had a child Magdalena born 1858.

Obituary:
Christner - Sarah daughter of Jacob and Elizabeth Miller Gerber was born Jan. 31, 1837, at Strasburg, OH; died Nov. 9, 1923; aged 86 y. 9 m. 8 d. On Oct. 2, 1856, she was married to Joseph Christner of Walnut Creek, OH who preceded her in death. To this union were born 5 sons and 5 daughters, 3 daughters having preceded her to the great beyond. She leaves 5 sons (Jacob, John, Henry, Harvey, and William), and 2 daughters (Amanda, and Katie, wife of Emanuel Gerber); also 2 brothers (Jerry and Nathaniel), 5 sisters (Mrs. Katie Kuhns, Fanny Blosser, Lydia Deardorf, Elizabeth Hostetler, and Mary Haas), 40 grandchildren, 50 great-grandchildren, and a host of friends. She spent the declining days of her life with her daughter, Mrs. Emanuel Gerber, at whose home

she passed away. Her last sickness, arteriosclerosis, lasted only a few days. She was a lifelong member of the Walnut A. M. Church, excepting a few years when she lived in NE. Services at the Walnut A. M. Church. Burial in cemetery nearby. Services were conducted by Lester Hostetler and S. H. Miller. Texts, I Cor. 15:57 and Job 3:17.

More About Sarah Gerber:
Burial: Amish Mennonite Cemetery, Walnut Creek, Holmes Co., OH
Residence: 1900, Bucks, Tuscarawas Co., OH[741]

Children of Joseph Christner and Sarah Gerber are:

	413	i.	Jacob J.[7] Christner. He married Mary Jane Stautz.
+	414	ii.	Elizabeth "Lizzie" Christner, born 14 Mar 1860 in Holmes Co., OH; died 20 Jan 1916 in Beaver Crossing, Seward Co., NE.
+	415	iii.	Fanny Christner, born 01 Feb 1864 in OH.
+	416	iv.	Franica Christner, born 01 Feb 1864 in OH; died 07 Apr 1921 in Tuscarawas Co., OH.
+	417	v.	Jacob J. Christner, born 26 Apr 1866 in OH; died 08 May 1939 in Holmes Co., OH.
+	418	vi.	Catherine Ann Christner, born 11 Apr 1868 in Sugarcreek, Holmes Co., OH; died 31 Dec 1955 in Sugarcreek, Holmes Co., OH.
+	419	vii.	John Christner, born Mar 1871 in OH; died 23 Oct 1954 in OH.
+	420	viii.	William J. Christner, born 17 Apr 1873 in Holmes Co., OH; died 28 Apr 1952 in Streetsboro, OH.
	421	ix.	Henry Christner[742,743], born 19 Jun 1875 in Union Co., OH[743,744]; died 22 May 1957 in Coshocton, Coshocton Co., OH[745]. He married Phoebe Scaar 23 Apr 1904; born 05 May 1876 in OH; died 13 Mar 1942 in Baltic, Tuscarawas Co., OH.

Notes for Henry Christner:
Birth: Jun 19, 1875 - Holmes Co., OH
Death: May 22, 1957 - Coshocton Co., OH

Spouse: Phebe Scarr Christner (1876 - 1942)

Burial: West Lawn Cemetery, Baltic, Tuscarawas Co., OH

Obituary: Services for Henry Christner 81, who died Wednesday morning at Country Memorial Hospital as a result of a stroke, will be held at 2 pm (EST) Saturday at the Zion Evangelical and Reformed Church of Baltic. Rev. E. O. Agrolica will officate and burial will be in West Lawn Cemetery, Baltic. He was born in Holmes County June 19, 1875, a son of Joseph and Sarah Gerber Christner and was married to Phoebe Scarr who died in 1942. The only close suvivor is one brother Harvey Christner, Baltic. A retired farner, he had made his home with Mr. & Mrs. Elmer Ott, Baltic in recent months.
Friends may call at the Haley Funeral Home in Baltic from 7 - 9 pm Friday and the Church Saturday from 1 until 2 pm.

More About Henry Christner:
Burial: Baltic West Lawn Cemetery Holmes Co. OH
Residence: 1900, Bucks, Tuscarawas Co., OH[745]

Notes for Phoebe Scaar:
Birth: May 5, 1876 - OH
Death: Mar 13, 1942 - Baltic, Tuscarawas Co., OH

Spouse: Henry Christner (1875 - 1957)

Burial: West Lawn Cemetery, Baltic, Tuscarawas Co., OH

Beside her tombstone (Right side) is a matching smaller stone with Katie Scarr 1854--1930 and on the left side is a matching stone with Callie Scarr 1871--1952

More About Phoebe Scaar:
Burial: Baltic West Lawn Cemetery Holmes Co. OH

| + | 422 | x. | Harvey C. Christner, born 07 Jul 1880 in OH; died 15 Apr 1970 in Dover, Tuscarawas Co., OH. |

111. Elizabeth[6] Christner (John J.[5], Christian J.[4], Johannes John Hans[3], Christian[2], Christen[1])[746] was born 25 Oct 1837 in Holmes Co., OH[746], and died 29 Apr 1922 in Holmes Co., OH[746]. She married **John H. Schrock**[746] 28 Mar 1861 in Holmes Co., OH[746]. He was born 20 Mar 1839 in Holmes Co., OH[746], and died 21 Sep 1927 in Holmes Co., OH[746].

Notes for Elizabeth Christner:
She maybe died Oct. 29, 1922. She lived with her brother Joseph J. and Sarah Gerber until her marriage in 1861 at the age of 24. They owned a farm close to Sugarcreek, OH. Painted on the barn was the name Die Heimat.

Schrock - Elizabeth (Christner) Schrock was born Oct. 25, 1837; died Apr. 29, 1922; aged 84 y. 6 m. 4 d. She was married to John H. Schrock, Mar. 28, 1861. To this union were born 5 sons and 4 daughters. One son and 1 daughter preceded her in death. She leaves husband, 4 sons, 3 daughters, 35 grandchildren, 10 great-grandchildren, and a host of relatives and friends. She was a member of the Walnut Creek A. M. Church where services were held May 2, 1922. Services conducted by Cosan Mast, S. H. Miller, and D. M. Friedt, Texts, Psa. 90; II Cor. 4:18; II Tim. 4:6-8. Burial in cemetery near church.

More About Elizabeth Christner:
Burial: 02 May 1922, Walnut Creek A.M. Mennonite Cemetery Holmes Co, OH
Residence: 1920, Walnut Creek, Holmes Co., OH[746]

More About John H. Schrock:
Burial: Walnut Creek Mennonite Cemetery Holmes Co, OH
Residence: 1920, Walnut Creek, Holmes Co., OH[746]

Children of Elizabeth Christner and John Schrock are:

423 i. Alexander J.[7] Schrock[746], born 16 May 1862 in Holmes Co., OH[746]; died 18 Mar 1948 in Holmes Co., OH[746]. He married Malinda; born 15 Jul 1866; died 14 May 1959.

    More About Alexander J. Schrock:
    Burial: Walnut Creek A.M. Mennonite Cemetery Holmes Co, OH

    More About Malinda:
    Burial: Walnut Creek A.M. Mennonite Cemetery Holmes Co, OH

424 ii. Henry J. Schrock, born 1864 in Holmes Co., OH; died 1933. He married Eliza Ann; born 1872; died 1945.

    More About Henry J. Schrock:
    Burial: Walnut Creek A.M. Mennonite Cemetery Holmes Co, OH

    More About Eliza Ann:
    Burial: Walnut Creek A.M. Mennonite Cemetery Holmes Co, OH

425 iii. William J. Schrock[746], born 16 Dec 1868 in Holmes Co., OH[746]; died 13 Feb 1957 in Dover, Tuscarawas Co., OH[746]. He married (1) Mary L. Weaver. He married (2) Frances Mast 15 Jan 1893; born 14 Nov 1873; died 16 Nov 1921.

    Notes for William J. Schrock:
    Frances is the daughter of Benjamin and Amanda Gerber Mast of OH.

    More About William J. Schrock:
    Burial: Walnut Creek A.M. Mennonite Cemetery Holmes Co, OH
    Residence: 1920, Walnut Creek, Holmes Co., OH[746]

    More About Frances Mast:
    Burial: Walnut Creek A.M. Mennonite Cemetery Holmes Co, OH

426 iv. Mattie Shrock[746], born 16 Dec 1868 in Holmes Co., OH[746]; died 22 May 1942 in Sugarcreek, Holmes Co., OH[746].

427 v. Willard Schrock, born 1869 in Holmes Co., OH; died 1970. He married Alta; born 1898; died 1993.

More About Willard Schrock:
Burial: Walnut Creek A.M. Mennonite Cemetery Holmes Co, OH

More About Alta:
Burial: Walnut Creek A.M. Mennonite Cemetery Holmes Co, OH

+ 428 vi. Amanda Carrie Schrock, born 18 Nov 1870 in Licking Co., OH; died 11 Jun 1948 in Wawpecong, Miami County, Indiana - Buried - Memorial Park Cemetery, Kokomo, Howard County, Indiana.

429 vii. Angeline Schrock[747], born Abt. 1876 in Walnut Creek, Holmes Co., OH[747]. She married Benjamin Troyer.

More About Angeline Schrock:
Residence: 1880, Walnut Creek, Holmes Co., OH[747]

430 viii. Allen J. Schrock, born 14 Nov 1879 in Holmes Co., OH; died 29 May 1949.

More About Allen J. Schrock:
Burial: Walnut Creek A.M. Mennonite Cemetery Holmes Co, OH

112. Philip[6] Lantz (Veronica Fannie[5] Christner, Christian J.[4], Johannes John Hans[3], Christian[2], Christen[1]) was born 22 Aug 1857 in Holmes Co., OH, and died 04 Oct 1924 in Lagrange Co., IN. He married **Barbara Schrock**[748,749] 14 Apr 1886 in Honeyville, Lagrange Co., IN[749]. She was born 05 Jul 1867 in Johnson Co., IA[750,751], and died 08 Dec 1958[751].

Notes for Philip Lantz:
The Descendants of John J. Christner, privately published February 1961, p. 99.

More About Philip Lantz:
Religion: Old Order Amish/

Notes for Barbara Schrock:
The Descendants of John J. Christner, privately published February 1961, p. 99.

Children of Philip Lantz and Barbara Schrock are:
431 i. Clara[7] Lantz, born 25 Jun 1888 in Middlebury, Elkhart Co., IN; died 30 Mar 1909. She married Noah Brandonberger.

Notes for Clara Lantz:
The Descendants of John J. Christner, privately published February 1961, p. 100.

Notes for Noah Brandonberger:
The Descendants of John J. Christner, privately published February 1961, p.100.

+ 432 ii. Edward Lantz, born 27 Mar 1891 in Topeka, Lagrange Co., IN.
433 iii. Enos Lantz, born 30 Jan 1893. He married Clara Yoder.

Notes for Enos Lantz:
The Descendants of John J. Christner, privately published February 1961, p. 100.

Notes for Clara Yoder:
The Descendants of John J. Christner, privately published February 1961, p. 100.

+ 434 iv. Ezra Lantz, born 27 Dec 1895; died Dec 1976 in Lagrange Co., IN.
+ 435 v. Earl Lantz, born 19 Jan 1898.
+ 436 vi. Carrie Lantz, born 08 Sep 1902.

113. Magdalena Mattie[6] Lantz (Veronica Fannie[5] Christner, Christian J.[4], Johannes John Hans[3], Christian[2], Christen[1])[752] was born 01 Jun 1860 in Holme Co., OH[752], and died 03 Mar 1938 in Lagrange, Lagrange Co., IN[752]. She married **Simon L. Miller**[752] 24 Nov 1881. He was born 28 Jan 1860 in Elkhart,

Elkhart Co., IN[752], and died 03 Dec 1930 in Lagrange, Lagrange Co., IN[752].

Notes for Magdalena Mattie Lantz:
The Descendants of John J. Christner, privately published February 1961, pp. 99, 102.

More About Magdalena Mattie Lantz:
Residence: 1910, Wilcox, Newaygo Co., MI[752]

Notes for Simon L. Miller:
The Descendants of John J. Christner, privately published February 1961, p. 102.

More About Simon L. Miller:
Residence: 1910, Wilcox, Newaygo Co., MI[752]

Children of Magdalena Lantz and Simon Miller are:

    437   i.   Enos[7] Miller, born 04 Sep 1882; died 07 Mar 1909.

    Notes for Enos Miller:
    The Descendants of John J. Christner, privately published February 1961, p. 102.

    Birth: 4 Sep 1882
    Death: Mar. 7, 1909

    26 year-old son of S. & M. D.

    Burial: Miller Amish Cemetery, Lagrange, Lagrange Co., IN
    Find A Grave Memorial# 66674511

+   438   ii.   Phineas S. Miller, born 04 Sep 1882; died 03 Nov 1953.
+   439   iii. Milo S. Miller, born 25 May 1885 in Mercer, PA; died 24 Aug 1967.
+   440   iv. Elizabeth Ann Miller, born 17 Jun 1887 in Lagrange Co., IN; died 05 Feb 1985.
    441   v.   Barbara S. Miller, born 23 Sep 1889 in Millersburg, Holmes Co., OH[753]. She married Noah M. Gingerich 11 Feb 1915 in Lagrange Co., IN[753]; born 29 Dec 1889 in Holmes Co., OH[753].

    Notes for Barbara S. Miller:
    The Descendants of John J. Christner, privately published February 1961, pp. 102, 104.

    More About Barbara S. Miller:
    DBH Book: 4354/[753]

    Notes for Noah M. Gingerich:
    The Descendants of John J. Christner, privately published February 1961, p.104.

    More About Noah M. Gingerich:
    DBH Book: 4354/[753]
    Religion: Old Order Amish/[753]

+   442   vi. Sarah Hershberger, born 23 Sep 1889 in Millerburg, Holmes Co., OH.
+   443   vii. Amos S. Miller, born 24 Mar 1892 in Topeka, Lagrange Co., IN.
+   444   viii. Levi S. Miller, born 23 Jun 1896 in Topeka, Lagrange Co., IN; died 12 Nov 1989.
+   445   ix. Fannie Elmina Miller, born 30 Mar 1900 in White Cloud, Newaygo Co., MI; died 11 Oct 1968.
+   446   x.   Edna Mae Miller, born 18 Jan 1906 in Nappanee, Elkhart Co., IN; died 09 Jun 1990 in IN.

117. Mary[6] Christner (John[5], John J.[4], Johannes John Hans[3], Christian[2], Christen[1])[754,755,756,757] was born 06 Aug 1836 in Somerset, Somerset Co., PA[757,758,759,760], and died 28 Dec 1904[761,762,763]. She married **Josephus Reckner**[763,764] 06 Feb 1868 in Allegany Co., MD[765]. He was born 11 Feb 1823 in PA[765], and died 11 Aug 1925 in Dayton, Greene Co., OH[765].

Notes for Mary Christner:
Amish and Amish Mennonite Genealogies; p. 57; CH2221

More About Mary Christner:
Burial: Maple Glen Cemetery, Elk Lick Twp., Somerset Co., PA
Residence: 1850, Elk Lick, Somerset Co., PA[766]

More About Josephus Reckner:
Residence: 1900, Elk Lick Township (West Part), Somerset, Pennsylvania[767]

Child of Mary Christner and Josephus Reckner is:
+   447   i.   Charles O.[7] Reckner, born 27 Jun 1867 in MD; died 22 Mar 1951 in Salisbury, Somerset Co., PA.

118. Christina[6] Christner (John[5], John J.[4], Johannes John Hans[3], Christian[2], Christen[1])[768,769] was born 1838 in Somerset Co., PA[770], and died 1931 in Garrett Co., MD[771,772,773]. She married **Henry Poleman**[774,774] 28 Oct 1863 in Allegany County Maryland[774], son of Frederick Poleman and Catherine Revling. He was born 1841 in VA[774], and died 1918 in Garrett Co., MD[774,774].

Notes for Christina Christner:
Amish and Amish Mennonite Genealogies; p. 57, CH2222

More About Christina Christner:
Residence: 1930, Avilton, Garrett, Maryland[774]

Notes for Henry Poleman:
Amish and Amish Mennonite Genealogies; p. 57

More About Henry Poleman:
Residence: 1910, District 3, Garrett, MD[774]

Children of Christina Christner and Henry Poleman are:
   448   i.   Charles Henry[7] Poleman, born 01 Apr 1864 in MD[775]; died 21 Jun 1950 in Garrett Co., MD[775]. He
                  married Annie V. Glotfelty 30 Mar 1891 in Garrett Co., MD; born 15 Jun 1872 in Garrett Co., MD; died
                  1932.

                  More About Charles Henry Poleman:
                  Burial: Trinity U.C.C. Cemetery, New Germany, Maryland[775]
                  Residence: 1930, Grantsville, Garrett, Maryland[776]

   449   ii.   Floyd A. Poleman[776], born 01 Apr 1864 in MD[776]; died 21 Jun 1950 in Grantsville, Garrett Co, MD[776].

                  More About Floyd A. Poleman:
                  Residence: 1910, District 3, Garrett, MD[776]

   450   iii. Richard Thomas Poleman[777], born 1866[777]; died 03 Jan 1881 in Diptheria/[777].
   451   iv.   Jerome G. Poleman[777], born 1874[777].
   452   v.   Albetty Poleman[777], born 1876[777].
   453   vi.   Jacob Poleman[777], born 1878[777].

119. Mary Catherine[6] Christner (John[5], John J.[4], Johannes John Hans[3], Christian[2], Christen[1])[778,779,780,781] was born 1840 in Somerset Co., PA[782,783], and died 12 Nov 1932 in Akron, Summit Co., OH[784]. She married **William F. Garlitz**[784] 16 Jan 1861 in Allegany Co., MD[784]. He was born 06 May 1839 in Garrett Co., MD[784], and died 12 Feb 1917 in St. Micheals Church, West Salisbury, Somerset Co., PA/West Salisbury, Somerset Co., PA[784].

Notes for Mary Catherine Christner:
Amish and Amish Mennonite Genealogies; p. 57; CH2223

More About Mary Catherine Christner:
Residence: 1930, Akron, Summit Co., OH[784]

More About William F. Garlitz:
Residence: 1910, Occupation; Teamster; General delivery/Elk Lick, Somerset Co., PA[784]

Children of Mary Christner and William Garlitz are:

454   i.   Barbara Ellen[7] Garlitz[785,786], born 24 Jun 1861 in Avilton, Garrett Co., MD[786]; died 19 Dec 1933 in Salisbury, Somerset Co., PA[786,787].

More About Barbara Ellen Garlitz:
Residence: 1930, Salisbury, Somerset Co., PA[788]

455   ii.   Ada Anna Florence Garlitz[788], born 20 Sep 1864 in MD[788]; died 1911 in Elk Lick, Somerset[788].

More About Ada Anna Florence Garlitz:
Residence: 1870, District 5, Allegany, Maryland, United States[788]

456   iii.   Henrietta Garlitz[788], born 20 Sep 1867 in MD[788].

More About Henrietta Garlitz:
Residence: 1910, Salisbury, Somerset Co., PA[788]

457   iv.   John C Garlitz[788], born Abt. 1870 in MD[788].

More About John C Garlitz:
Residence: 1920, Elk Lick, Somerset Co., PA[788]

458   v.   Mary Viola Garlitz[788], born 08 Nov 1878 in MD[788].

More About Mary Viola Garlitz:
Residence: 1880, Elk Lick, Somerset Co., PA[788]

120. Jacob[6] Christner (John[5], John J.[4], Johannes John Hans[3], Christian[2], Christen[1])[789,790,791,792,793,794,795] was born 1841 in Somerset Co., PA[796,797,798,799], and died 16 Aug 1891 in Harrison Co., WV[800]. He married **Frances Atlanta Reger**[801] 19 Apr 1865 in Upshur Co., WV[802]. She was born 13 Jan 1847 in Lewis, Upshur Co., WV[802,803,804], and died 19 Jan 1909 in Monongahalia, Marion Co., WV[805,806].

Notes for Jacob Christner:
Jacob Christner came to Buckhannon, VA as a private in the Third Maryland Infantry. It was there that he met and married Frances Atlanta Reger, the daughter of Riley Reger, who was reportedly was imprisoned and subsequently died at Camp Chase in Ohio for his sympathy with the Confederacy. Jacob's death record indicaties that he was killed by a train. The enumeration of Civil War Veterans lists Jacob as living in the Adamnston, Harrison County and indicaties that he had been "shot through the left lung."

Birth: 1843
Death: 1891

Burial: Hepzibah Cemetery, Hepzibah, Harrison Co., WV

Amish and Amish Mennonite Genealogies; p. 57, CH2224

More About Jacob Christner:
Burial: 18 Aug 1891, Hepzibah Cemetary, Harrison Co.WV
Cause of Death: Killed by a Train
Military service: 1864-1865 Company A 3rd MD Infantry/
Occupation: Laborer/
Residence: 1880, Coal, Harrison Co., WV[807]

Notes for Frances Atlanta Reger:
Birth: Jan. 13, 1847
Death: Jan. 18, 1909

Burial: Hepzibah Cemetery, Hepzibah, Harrison Co., WV

More About Frances Atlanta Reger:
Burial: 20 Jan 1909, Hepzibah Cemetary, Harrison Co.WV
Cause of Death: nephritis
Residence: 1880, Coal, Harrison Co., WV[808,809,810]

Children of Jacob Christner and Frances Reger are:

+ 459   i.   John Riley[7] Christner, born 01 Mar 1867 in West Moreland Co. PA; died 13 Jul 1944 in Clarksburg, Harrison Co., WV.

   460   ii.   Minnie Mae Christner[811], born 01 Mar 1869 in Frostburg, Allegany Co., MD[811]; died 31 Mar 1951 in Monoghelia, Marion Co., WV[811]. She married Jefferson Jackson Flanigan; born 01 Jul 1864 in WV; died 17 Sep 1949 in Monoghelia, Marion Co., WV.

         More About Minnie Mae Christner:
         Burial: 04 Apr 1951, Woodlaw Cemetery
         Cause of Death: Heart Attack
         Residence: 1880, Coal, Harrison Co., WV[811]

         More About Jefferson Jackson Flanigan:
         Burial: 19 Sep 1949, Woodlaw Cemetery
         Cause of Death: Arterioscleroic Heart Disease
         Occupation: Coal Miner/

   461   iii.   Sarah Christner[811,812], born Abt. 1872 in Marion Co., WV[812].

         More About Sarah Christner:
         Residence: 1880, Coal, Harrison Co., WV[813]

   462   iv.   Missouri Christner[813], born 02 Oct 1872 in Harrison Co., WV[813]; died 03 Jun 1951 in Marietta, Washington Co., OH[813]. She married (1) Alexander Theobald; born 14 Feb 1874; died 05 May 1952 in Marietta, OH. She married (2) Jefferson Danley 29 Apr 1891; born 1864 in Marion Co., WV; died 02 Mar 1926 in Harrison Co., WV.

         More About Missouri Christner:
         Burial: Marietta, OH

+ 463   v.   Nora Delia Christner, born 02 Jun 1873 in Harrison Co., WV; died 01 Sep 1964 in Clarksburg, Harrison Co., WV.

+ 464   vi.   Alfred Christner, born 24 Oct 1876 in Harrison Co., WV; died 10 Dec 1947 in Fairmont, Marion Co., WV.

   465   vii.   Alpha Christner[813,814], born 1877 in WV[815,816].

         More About Alpha Christner:
         Residence: 1880, Coal, Harrison Co., WV[817,818]

   466   viii.   Fannie Christner[819,820], born 1878 in WV[821]; died 24 Feb 1889 in Adamston, Harrison Co., WV[822].

         Notes for Fannie Christner:
         Birth: 1878
         Death: 1889

         Burial: Hepzibah Cemetery, Hepzibah, Harrison Co., WV

         More About Fannie Christner:
         Burial: 26 Feb 1889, Age: 9/United States[822]
         Race: White/[822]
         Residence: 1880, Coal, Harrison Co., WV[823]

467   ix.   Francis Christner[823], born 1881 in Harrison Co., VA[823]; died 1889 in Harrison Co., VA[823].

More About Francis Christner:
Burial: Hepzibah Cemetary, Harrison Co.WV

468   x.   Leondus Christner, born 02 May 1883 in Coal, Harrison Co., WV[824]; died 1900 in Monoghelia, Marion Co., WV.

Notes for Leondus Christner:
Birth: 1881
Death: 1890

Burial: Hepzibah Cemetery, Hepzibah, Harrison Co., WV
Find A Grave Memorial# 68783958

More About Leondus Christner:
Burial: Hepzibah Cemetary, Harrison Co.WV
Cause of Death: Fell from Railroad Bridge while Playing at age 8

+   469   xi.   James Hoy Christner, born 28 Jun 1886 in Harrison Co., WV; died 13 Oct 1950 in Mannington, Marion Co., WV.

122. Sarah Ellen "Helena"[6] Christner (John[5], John J.[4], Johannes John Hans[3], Christian[2], Christen[1])[825] was born 04 Jul 1845 in Somerset Co., PA[826], and died 02 Jun 1938 in Long Stretch, Garrett Co., MD[827,828,829]. She married **John L. McKenzie**[830] 16 Jun 1865 in Allegany Co., MD. He was born 17 Jun 1839 in Greenville Twp., Somerset Co., PA, and died 23 Feb 1921 in Garrett Co., MD[831].

Notes for Sarah Ellen "Helena" Christner:
Birth: 4 Jul 1845
Death: 2 Jun 1938

Sarah Ellen Christner (1845-1938 d/o John & Barbara)

Spouse: John L. Mckenzie (1839 - 1921)

Children:
Mary Olive Mckenzie Mckenzie (1866 - 1931)
James Harris Mckenzie (1873 - 1959)

Burial: Saint Anns Cemetery, Avilton, Garrett Co., MD
Find A Grave Memorial# 43649696

More About Sarah Ellen "Helena" Christner:
Burial: Maple Glen Cemetery, Elk Lick Twp., Somerset Co., PA
Residence: 1920, Johnsons, Garrett, MD[832,833]

Notes for John L. McKenzie:
Birth: Jun. 17, 1842 - PA
Death: Feb. 23, 1921 - MD

John L. McKenzie - 17 Jun 1842 PA - 23 Feb 1921 MD
s/o Samuel J. MCKENZIE and Sarah Ann "Sally" WORKMAN

He married 1865 Sarah Ellen Christner (1845-1938 d/o John & Barbara)

Parents:
Samuel McKenzie (1824 - 1888)
Sarah Ann Workman McKenzie (1821 - 1893)

Spouse: Sarah Ellen Christner McKenzie

Children:
Mary Olive Mckenzie Mckenzie (1866 - 1931)
James Harris Mckenzie (1873 - 1959)

Burial: Saint Anns Cemetery, Avilton, Garrett Co., MD
Find A Grave Memorial# 43649670

Obituary: The Cumberland Evening Times, February 24, 1921
John McKenzie of Avilton died yesterday morning at 5 o'clock. He is survived by three sons and three daughters.
Funeral will take place Friday at 11 o'clock from St. Ann's Catholic Church.

He was buried on 25 Feb 1921 in St. Ann's Catholic Cemetery, Avilton, Garrett Co., MD.

More About John L. McKenzie:
Residence: 1900, Johnson, Garrett, MD[834]

Children of Sarah Christner and John McKenzie are:

470	i.	Lauretta[7] McKenzie.
471	ii.	Virginia Agnes McKenzie[835].
+ 472	iii.	Mary Olive McKenzie, born 03 Jun 1866 in MD; died 24 Feb 1931.
473	iv.	Henrietta Anna McKenzie[835], born 03 Jun 1868 in MD.

    More About Henrietta Anna McKenzie:
    Residence: 1900, Election Distrists 9, 11, Johnsons, The Elbow, Garrett, Maryland[835]

474	v.	Francis Leo McKenzie, born 15 Feb 1870 in Garrett Co., MD; died 14 Mar 1948 in Orange, Orange Co., TX[836].

    Notes for Francis Leo McKenzie:
    Birth: 1870
    Death: 1948

    Burial: Evergreen Cemetery, Orange, Orange Co., TX
    Find A Grave Memorial# 77036955

    Obituary: Meyersdale Republican, March 25, 1948

    Mrs. Milton Younkin received word last week of the death of her brother, Frank McKenzie, a native of Garrett County, who died at his home at Orange, TX, Sunday, march 14. A shipyard carpenter, mr. McKenzie had resided in Texas for 50 years. He visited here about 13 years ago fo rthe last time. He was the son of the late John and Sara McKenzie. Internment took place at Orange. Surviving are four sisters - Mrs. Milton Younkin, Grantsville, Mrs. Ruth Carey, Orange, Mrs. Allen Baker, Frostburg and Mrs. Bruce Robinson, Hancock and by four brothers - John McKenzie, Tyrone, PA; Joseph McKenzie, Cumberland; Jacob McKenzie, Frostburg and James McKenzie, Mt. Zion.

+ 475	vi.	George Thomas McKenzie, born 25 Mar 1871; died 01 Oct 1927 in Bolair, Webster Co., WV.
476	vii.	George W. McKenzie, born 13 Apr 1872.
+ 477	viii.	James Harris McKenzie, born 03 Jul 1873 in MD; died 13 Apr 1959 in Frostburg, Allegany Co., MD.
+ 478	ix.	Samuel Gregory McKenzie, born 03 Nov 1877 in Garrett Co., MD; died 05 Mar 1947 in Frostburg, Allegany Co., MD.
479	x.	John Simon McKenzie[837], born 29 Apr 1881 in New Germany, Garrett Co., MD[837]; died 11 Nov 1956 in Frostburg, Allegany Co., MD[837].

    Notes for John Simon McKenzie:
    He died of heart disease according to death certificate.

    More About John Simon McKenzie:
    Residence: 1910, District 9, Garrett, Maryland[837]

+ 480 xi. Emma Theresa McKenzie, born 07 Apr 1884 in Pine Grove, MD; died 07 Dec 1961 in Meyerstown, Somerset Co., PA.
+ 481 xii. Ruth McKenzie, born 29 Mar 1886 in Pine Grove, MD; died 08 Sep 1952 in Orange Co., TX.
+ 482 xiii. Jacob Henry McKenzie, born 15 Apr 1888 in Garrett Co., MD; died 06 Nov 1972 in Hagerstown Washington Co., MD.
   483 xiv. Joseph Tecumseh McKenzie[837], born 27 May 1890 in Garrett Co., MD[837,838]; died 20 Dec 1966 in Frostburg, Allegany Co., MD[839,839]. He married Anna Schwerzer; born 02 Jan 1883 in Westernport, Allegany Co., MD[840]; died 03 Jan 1930 in Westernport, Allegany Co., MD[840].

Notes for Joseph Tecumseh McKenzie:
Obituary: The Cumberland Evening Times - 21 Dec 1966

GRANTSVILLE - Joseph T. McKenzie, 76 died yesterday at Miners Hospital, Frostburg. A native of Garrett Co., he was a son of the late John and Sarah Ellen Christner McKenzie. His wife, Anna Schwerzer Mckenzie, preeceded him in death. He is survived by a son, William J. McKenzie, Frostburg; daughter Mrs. Teresa Garlilz, Lancoming; a brother Jacob McKenzie, Frostburg; two sisters, Mrs. Elizabeth Baker and Mrs. Lela Robison both of Frsotburg; four grandchildren and three great-granschildren. He was a member of St. Ann;s Church, Avilton where a requiem mass will be celebrated on Friday at 10 am Rev. Fabian Kekich, OFM, cap will be celebrant and internment will be in the church cemetery. The body is at the Newman Funeral Home where friends will be received today from 7 to 9 pm and tomorrow from 2 to 4 and 7 to 9 pm. the rosary will be recited there tomorrrow at 8:30 pm.

Obituary: Meyersdale Republican -Dec 29, 1966

Joseph T. McKenzie, 76 Grantsville, died at Miners Hospital, Frostburg. A native of Garrett Co., he was a son of the late John and Sarah Ellen Christner McKenzie. His wife the former Anna Schwerzer, preeceded him in death. Surviving are a son, William J. McKenzie, Frostburg; a daughter Mrs. Teresa Garlilz, Lancoming; a brother Jacob McKenzie, Frostburg; two sisters, Mrs. Elizabeth Baker and Mrs. Lela Robison both of Frostburg; four grandchildren and three great-granschildren. He was a member of St. Ann;s Church, Avilton on Friday morning by Rev. Fabian Kebich OFM, Cap. Internment was made in the church cemetery.

Death certificate states name of spouse as Swartz.

More About Joseph Tecumseh McKenzie:
Residence: 1910, District 9, Garrett, Maryland[841]
Social Security Number: 210-09-7953/[842]
SSN issued: Pittsburgh, Allegheny Co., PA[842]

   484 xv. Elizabeth G. McKenzie[843,843], born 14 Apr 1892 in Garrett Co., MD[843,843]; died 02 Jan 1969 in Norfolk, Princess Anne Co., VA[843]. She married Allen E. Baker[844]; born 1901 in Garrett Co., MD[844]; died 03 Oct 1958 in Cumberland, Allegany Co., MD[844].

Notes for Elizabeth G. McKenzie:
Obituary:
FROSTBURG - Mrs. Elizabeth G. Baker, 76 formerly of West College Avenue, died yesterday at Norfolk hospital. She had been in failing heath the past year. Born in Garrett Co., she was a daughter of the late John and Sarah Christner McKenzie and was the widow of Allen E. Baker. She was a member of the Church of the Nazarene. Surviving are a daughter, Mrs. Hugh Mason, Virginia Beach, VA; a son Mervin Carey, Detroit, MI.

More About Elizabeth G. McKenzie:
Residence: 1920, Johnsons, Garrett Co., MD[845]

   485 xvi. Ulalia Agnes McKenzie, born 19 Jul 1894.
   486 xvii. Eulalia Agnes McKenzie[845], born 19 Jul 1894 in Long Stretch, MD[845]; died 04 Feb 1989 in Cumberland, Allegany Co., MD[845].

More About Eulalia Agnes McKenzie:
Residence: 1910, District 9, Garrett, Maryland[845]

123. Veronica "Frany"[6] Christner (John[5], John J.[4], Johannes John Hans[3], Christian[2], Christen[1]) was born

03 Aug 1845 in Somerset Co., PA[846], and died 10 Jul 1934 in Avilton, Garrett Co., MD[846]. She married **Jacob Patrick McKenzie**[847] 12 Mar 1866 in St. Michael's Church, Frostburg, Garrett Co., MD. He was born 05 Mar 1844 in Greenville Twp., Somerset Co., PA, and died 28 Feb 1921 in Morgantown, Monongalia Co., WV[848].

More About Veronica "Frany" Christner:
Residence: 1850, Elk Lick, Somerset Co., PA[849]

Children of Veronica Christner and Jacob McKenzie are:
    487   i.   Anne Elizabeth[7] McKenzie, born 16 Sep 1867; died 1868[850].
    488   ii.   Patrick McKenzie, born 1880.
    489   iii. John William McKenzie, born 1886.

130. Elizabeth[6] Christner (Jacob C.[5], John J.[4], Johannes John Hans[3], Christian[2], Christen[1])[851,852,853,854,855,856,857,857,858,859,860,861] was born 07 Feb 1844 in Connellsville, Fayette Co., PA[862], and died 04 Dec 1918 in Republic, Fayette Co., PA[863,864,865]. She married **Henry C. Diehl**[865,866,867,868] 1863 in Stated[869,869,870,870,871]. He was born 22 Feb 1842 in Cove, Allegany Co., MD[872,872,873,873,873,874,875,876,877,878,879,880,881], and died 10 Mar 1918 in Republic, Fayette Co., PA[882,883].

Notes for Elizabeth Christner:
Birth: Feb. 7, 1844 - PA
Death: Dec. 4, 1918 - Republic, Fayette Co., PA

Obituary:
Mrs. Elizabeth Diehl, aged 74 years, widow of H. C. Diehl, died at her home at Republic on Dec 4 from a complication of diseases. She is survived by the following children: Mrs. Emma Taylor, Mrs. Emma Hennessey and George Diehl, Republic; Mrs. Laura Hawkins, Donora; Mrs. Mary Johnson, Mill Run; Samuel and William Diehl, Meyersdale; Mrs. Amanda Hampshire and Mrs. Ellen Newcomer, Connellsville. She is also survived by four sisters and three brothers. She is grandmother of 51 grandchildren, and 24 great grandchildren. Mrs. Diehl was a resident, of Morgan Valley for a number of years and was widely and favorably known and loved by all her friends. Her husband died last March. Brief funeral services were held Sunday. Interment was made in Park Place Cemetery, Uniontown." The Daily Courier, Connellsville, PA, Wednesday, Dec 11, 1918.

Spouse: Henry C. Diehl (1842 - 1918)

Children: Laura C. Diehl Hawkins (1865 - 1959)

Burial: Park Place Cemetery, Uniontown, Fayette Co., PA
Plot: Up against fence on school side

Some say born Feb. 07, 1844 however the 1850 census has her listed as 3/12 so she would be 3 months old in 1850 at the time of the census. 1900 census has her & Henry married 33 years that would be 1867--after her 2nd child was born.

Amish and Amish Mennonite Genealogies; CH2242, p. 58;

More About Elizabeth Christner:
Burial: 06 Dec 1918, Park Place Cemetery, Uniontown, Fayette Co., PA[884,885]
Cause of Death: Pnemonia & Influenza
Census: 1850, Elk Lick Twp., Somerset Co., PA
Death Certificate: 04 Dec 1918, File # 182539 - died of pnemonia and influenza at the age of 74 yrs, 9 months and 27 days.
Residence: 1880, Addison Twp., Somerset Co., PA[886]

Notes for Henry C. Diehl:
Birth: Feb. 22, 1842
Death: Mar. 11, 1918
Republic, Fayette Co., PA

Spouse: Elizabeth Christner Diehl (1844 - 1918)

Children: Laura C. Diehl Hawkins (1865 - 1959)

Burial: Park Place Cemetery, Uniontown, Fayette Co., PA
Plot: Up against fence on school side

1900 Census - States that they have been married for 33 years.

OBITUARY: The Daily Courier, Connellsville, PA, 11 March 1918, p. 3.
Henry C. Diehl, aged 76, died Monday morning (March 11, 1918) at his home at Republic after a lingering illness. He is survived by his wife and one sister, Mary Swartzwelder, West Salisbury, and nine sons and daughters.

Surviving also are 50 grandchildren and 20 great grandchildren. The sons and daughters are William Diehl, Samuel Diehl, W. Salisbury; George Diehl, Republic; Mrs. Laura Hawkins, Donora; Mrs. Mary Johnson, Mill Run; Mrs. Ellen Newcomer, Mrs. Amanda Hampshire, Connellsville; Mrs. Edna Taylor, Thompson No. 1; Mrs. Emma Hennessey, Allison. Funeral services will be held Wednesday morning at the home. The funeral party will come to Uniontown on a special West Penn car, interment being made in Park Place Cemetery.

More About Henry C. Diehl:
Burial: 13 Mar 1918, Park Place Cemetery, Uniontown, Fayette Co., PA[887]
Census: 1850, Elk Lick Twp., Somerset Co., PA
Death Certificate: 13 Mar 1918, PA - file # 25599 died from broncho pnemonia
Residence: 1900, Upper Tyrone Twp., Fayette Co., PA[888]

Children of Elizabeth Christner and Henry Diehl are:

+ 490   i.   William Henry[7] Diehl, born 31 Mar 1864 in Cove, Garrett Co., MD; died 31 May 1935 in West Salisbury, Somerset Co., PA.

+ 491   ii.   Laura Catherine Diehl, born 23 Sep 1865 in Somerset Co., MD; died 03 Nov 1959 in South Union Twp., Uniontown, Fayette Co., PA.

   492   iii.   Mary Diehl[889], born 14 Jul 1867 in Grantsville, Garrett Co., MD[889]; died 11 Jun 1955 in Mill Run, Normalville, Fayette Co., PA[889]. She married (1) Burton Johnson. She married (2) Wade Henry Johnson Nov 1901 in Connellsville, Fayette Co., PA; born 1872 in Connellsville, Fayette Co., PA; died Abt. 1918 in Mill Run, Fayette Co., PA.

          Notes for Mary Diehl:
          Obituary: The Daily Courier, Connellsville, PA - 13 Jun 1955

          Mrs. Mary Diehl Johnson, 87, died suddenly at her home at Normalville at 8 o'clock Saturday evening. Born in Grantsville, MD, July 14, 1867, she was a daughter of the late Mr. and Mrs. Henry C. Diehl. Surviving are four sons, Clyde Fulmer of Normalville, William H. Fulmer of Canton, OH and Burton and Gilbert Johnson of Normalville; a daughter, Miss Laura Fulmer of Pittsburgh; two brothers, Samuel Diehl of Tyrone and George Diehl of Cleveland, OH and three sisters, Mrs. Laura Hawkins of New Salem, Mrs. Edna Taylor of Orient and Mrs. Emma Hennessey of Republic. The funeral service will be held at the Brooks Funeral home in East Green Street at 1 o'clock Tuesday afternoon. Burial will take place in Hill Grove Cemetery.

          More About Mary Diehl:
          Burial: 14 Jun 1955, Hill Grove Cemetery, Connellsville, Fayette Co., PA

          More About Wade Henry Johnson:
          Burial: Hill Grove Cemetery, Connellsville, Fayette Co., PA

+ 493   iv.   Ida C. Diehl, born Aug 1867 in PA.
   494   v.   John Diehl[890], born Jan 1870 in Frostburg, Allegany Co., MD[891,891,892]; died 1880[893].
+ 495   vi.   Ellen Diehl, born 21 Jun 1871 in Addison, Fayette Co., PA; died 17 Jun 1945 in Connellsville, Fayette Co., PA.
   496   vii.   Matilda Diehl[894,894], born Abt. 1872 in PA[894,894].

More About Matilda Diehl:
Residence: 1880, Hatfield, Montgomery Co., PA[894]

+ 497   viii.   Margaret Elizabeth Diehl, born 1873 in Frostburg, Allegany Co., MD; died Feb 1894 in PA.
+ 498   ix.   Amanda Alice Diehl, born 31 Jan 1877 in Listonburg, Addison Twp., Somerset Co., PA; died 03 Apr 1950 in Connellsville, Fayette Co., PA.
   499   x.   Lucinda Diehl[894], born Dec 1877[895,896,897]. She married Thomas Hennessey; born 1879 in Connellsville, Fayette Co., PA; died 01 May 1938 in Republic, Fayette Co., PA.

More About Lucinda Diehl:
Residence: 1880, Addison Twp., Somerset Co., PA[898]

Notes for Thomas Hennessey:
The Daily Courier, 2 May 1938, Thomas Hennessey obituary.

More About Thomas Hennessey:
Burial: 03 May 1938, St. Joseph's Cemetery, Connellsville, Fayette Co., PA

+ 500   xi.   Samuel Diehl, born 27 Sep 1878 in Connellsville, Fayette Co., PA; died 31 Dec 1948.
+ 501   xii.   Edna Diehl, born Oct 1879 in Somerset Co., PA; died 03 Oct 1960 in Republic, Fayette Co., PA.
   502   xiii.   Edna Diehl[899,899], born 1880 in Frostburg, Allegany Co., MD[899,899]; died 11 Jun 1955 in Normalville, Fayette Co., PA[899,899].
   503   xiv.   Emma Susan Diehl[899], born Jul 1882 in Connellsville, Fayette Co., PA[899,899]; died 16 Jun 1965 in Uniontown, Fayette Co., PA[900,901,901]. She married Thomas Hennessey 1901 in Bullskin Twp., Fayette Co., PA; born 1879 in Connellsville, Fayette Co., PA; died 01 May 1938 in Republic, Fayette Co., PA.

Notes for Emma Susan Diehl:
U.S. Federal Census, 1900 Connellsville, Fayette Co., PA, ED 8, sheet 14
Residence: 1918 According To Henry C. Diehl's Obit She Lived In Allison, PA
Residence: 1935 According To Wm. H. Diehl's Obit, she Lived In Connellsville, Fayette Co., PA.

Obituary: The Daily Courier, Connellsville, PA - 18 Jun 1965

Mrs. Emma Susan Hennessey, 84, Republic, died at 9:30 pm Wednesday in Uniontown Hospital. She was a member of the First Christian Church of Republic. Surviving are four sons: Thomas, Donald and Edward of Republic and George of Cardale; a duaghter Mrs. Elizabeth Murray of Republic; 10 grandchildren and two brothers. She was the widow of Thomas Hennessey.

More About Emma Susan Diehl:
Burial: 20 Jun 1965, Lafayette Memorial Park, Brier Hill, Fayette Co., PA[901]

Notes for Thomas Hennessey:
The Daily Courier, 2 May 1938, Thomas Hennessey obituary.

More About Thomas Hennessey:
Burial: 03 May 1938, St. Joseph's Cemetery, Connellsville, Fayette Co., PA

+ 504   xv.   Samuel Cleveland Diehl, born 06 Mar 1885 in Listonburg, Addison Twp., Somerset Co., PA; died 06 Aug 1975 in Johnstown, Cambria Co., PA.
+ 505   xvi.   George Oscar Diehl, born 14 Aug 1888 in Somerset, Somerset Co., PA; died 22 Mar 1970 in Cleveland, Cuyahoga Co., OH.

131. John (Invalid John)[6] Christner (Jacob C.[5], John J.[4], Johannes John Hans[3], Christian[2], Christen[1]) was born 05 Mar 1847 in Summit Twp., Somerset Co., PA[902], and died 01 Apr 1908 in Somerset Co., PA. He married **Elizabeth Ann Kretchman** 04 May 1871 in Somerset Co., PA by Rev.A.Coplin. She was born 09 May 1849 in Somerset Co., PA, and died 03 Jul 1919 in Somerset Co., PA.

Notes for John (Invalid John) Christner:
Obituary: Meyersdale Republican
John Christner was born March 5, 1847, and died April 1, 1908, aged 61 years and 26 days. He was the son of Jacob and Julia (Hensel) Christner, who for these many years have passed the shores of time. Mr. Christner was

married May 4, 1871, to Eliza Kretchman, a daughter of Reuben Kretchman and followed farming as long as he was able to work. For the last fourteen years he was lying in bed suffering with rheumatism, which afFLection he pariently bore with christian fortitude.

In 1868 he united with the Reformed Church and remained a loyal and sonsistent member. The deceased is survived by his widow, a brother, Jacob Christner, of Garrett: Mrs. Cornelius Klink, of Nicolay, Fayette Co., and Mrs. Henry Deal of Connellsville, PA.

The funeral was well attended at St. Paul, (Keim) where internment was made in the Reformed Cemetery. The Scripture chosen for the occassion read as follows: "for my yoke is easy and my burden light." St. Mat. 3:29?

"The Whilhelms and the Wilhelm Charge." page 180

He was an invalid with rheumatism for at least 14 years. Belonged to the Reformed Church. He and Elizabeth were very active in their church and
attended regularly.

Amish and Amish Mennonite Genealogies; p. 57, Ch2221

More About John (Invalid John) Christner:
Burial: St. Paul Reformed Church Cemetery
Census: 1850, Elk Lick Twp., Somerset Co., PA

Notes for Elizabeth Ann Kretchman:
Elizabeth is the daughter of Reuben Kretchman and Elizabeth Hochstedler. John and Elizabeth had no children of their own. They adopted Alice Evora Bockes. Alice never went by the surname of Christner and she married Daniel Klink. Eliza (sister of Lewis) served as a foster mother to Homer Klink. This info came from Bernice A. Yoder, R1, Salisbury, PA and J. Hochstetler book 6000.

Birth: May 9, 1849
Death: Jul 3, 1919

Mrs. Eliza Kretchman Christner died at her home in Summit township on Thursday, July 3, from a complication of diseases, including cancer, from which she had suffered long and patiently, death coming to her as a welcome change from mortal ills to the bliss of immortality. She was a daughter of the late Reuben Kretchman and was born May 9, 1849, being 70 years, 1 month and 24days old at the time of her death. On May 4, 1871, she was married to John Christner, who died April 1, 1908, after having been bedfast for 14 years. The couple had no children, but had one adopted daughter, who is now Mrs. Daniel Klink. After the death of her husband Mrs. Christner continued to line on the farm which was their joint property, remaining quite active until about one year ago, when the hand of affliction was laid heavily upon her, but she bore her sufferings with Christian fortitude and abiding faith in the Great Physician, who would in his own appointed time make her whole. She was a devout member of St. Paul's Reformed church and never absent from any of the services unless prevented from attendance by sickness. She was scrupulously honest and kindness personified. She died as she lived, at peace with the loved and honored by all who knew her. Funeral services, conducted by her pastor, Rev. L. N. Wilson, were held at St. Paul's church, at 10 o'clock Saturday morning, July 5; interment in St. Paul Cemetery. Mrs. Christner is survived by one brother, N. J. Kretchman, of York, Pa., and four sisters, Mrs. Jacob Nicholson of Kansas; Mrs. Abraham Hay, Rockwood; Mrs. Mortimore Welfley, Akron, O; Mrs. Samuel Bittner, Rockwood. Three of her brothers and one sister are deceased, namely, Lewis A., Samuel and Josiah Kretchman and Mrs. Wesley McClintock. On July 12, 1917 she made a will bequeathing her farm to Homer Klink, the 19-year-old son of the foster daughter, Mrs. Daniel Klink, on condition that he shall not dispose of the land during his lifetime; her personal property to Mrs. Alice Klink (wife of Daniel Klink), and $525 in trust to her nephew, Ed R. Hay, who is to erect a monument in her memory with the money. Mrs. Klink is named as her executor.

Burial: Saint Paul Reformed Church Cemetery, Elk Lick Twp., Somerset Co., PA

More About Elizabeth Ann Kretchman:
Burial: Saint Paul Reformed Church Cemetery, Elk Lick Twp., Somerset Co., PA

Child of John Christner and Elizabeth Kretchman is:

506   i.   Alice Evora[7] Bockes. She married Daniel Klink.

> Notes for Alice Evora Bockes:
> In John's will -- Alice Evora Bockes girl we brought up, too receive and dispose of property after wife's death. probate April 9, 1908.

132. Jacob (Lumix Jake)[6] Christner (Jacob C.[5], John J.[4], Johannes John Hans[3], Christian[2], Christen[1]) was born 1848. He married **Caroline Christner**[903] 1869, daughter of Christian Christner and Susanna Walters. She was born 1843.

Notes for Jacob (Lumix Jake) Christner:
1920 census has him living with his daughter Sadie & Peter Klink at Orchard Street, Berlin, Somerset Co., PA.

Notes for Caroline Christner:
1920 Census has Cariline living with her daughter Sadie & Sadie's husband Peter Klink on Orchard Street, Berlin, Somerset Co., Pennsylvania. She was 74 at the time.

More About Caroline Christner:
Christened: 23 Jun 1849

Children of Jacob Christner and Caroline Christner are:

     507   i.   Amanda[7] Christner[904].
+ 508   ii.   Elizabeth Christner, born Mar 1868 in PA; died Nov 1947 in Meyersdale, Somerset Co., PA.
     509   iii.   Saloma Christner, born 1874. She married Samuel Bockes 22 Feb 1893; born 20 Nov 1870.
     510   iv.   Susan "Sadie" Christner, born 1875; died 06 Jan 1939 in Somerset, Somerset Co., PA. She married Peter Klink.

> Notes for Susan "Sadie" Christner:
> Obituary - The Dailey Courier - Connellsville, Fayette Co., PA - 10 Jan 1939
> MRS. PETER KLINK DEAD
> SOMERSET - Jan 10 - Mrs. Susan Christner Klink, 59, wife of Peter Klink of Berlin died Friday in Somerset Community Hospital.

     511   v.   Susan Christner, born 1879.

137. Mary Elizabeth[6] Christner (Jacob C.[5], John J.[4], Johannes John Hans[3], Christian[2], Christen[1])[905,905] was born 1861, and died 15 Dec 1897[905,905]. She married **John Gray**[906,907,907]. He was born 01 Sep 1846 in Connellsville, Fayette Co., PA[908], and died 1925 in Larmier Twp., Somerset Co., PA[909,909,910].

Notes for Mary Elizabeth Christner:
May not be Jacob's daughter.
Amish and Amish Mennonite Genealogies; CH2248, p. 58;

Notes for John Gray:

More About John Gray:
Burial: Fritzes Church, near Garrett, Somerset Co., PA
Residence: 1920, Elk Lick, Somerset Co., PA[911]

Children of Mary Christner and John Gray are:

     512   i.   Thomas[7] Gray, born 18 Mar in Meyersdale, Somerset Co., PA.
     513   ii.   William Harry Gray[911], born 02 Sep 1882 in Meyersdale, Somerset Co., PA[911]; died 26 Feb 1963 in Meyersdale, PA[911].

> More About William Harry Gray:
> Residence: 1930, Summit, Somerset Co., PA[911]

514   iii.   Ida Susan Gray[911], born 04 Jul 1886 in Meyersdale, Somerset Co., PA.

+ 515   iv.   George Harrison Gray, born 03 May 1890 in Meyersdale, Somerset Co., PA; died 13 Dec 1969 in Garrett, Somerset, PA.

516   v.   Catherine Nora Gray, born 29 Jun 1892 in Meyersdale, Somerset Co., PA; died 21 Apr 1980 in Berlin, Somerset Co., PA. She married George W. Shaffer 1911 in Cumberland Allegany Co., MD.

Notes for Catherine Nora Gray:
Burial: Fritzes Church, near Garrett, Somerset Co., PA

More About Catherine Nora Gray:
Burial: Fritzes Church, near Garrett, Somerset Co., PA

517   vi.   Emma Margaret Gray, born 02 Jun 1896 in Meyersdale, Somerset Co., PA; died 03 Apr 1934.

138. Samuel[6] Christner (Jacob C.[5], John J.[4], Johannes John Hans[3], Christian[2], Christen[1]) was born Aug 1863 in Somerset, Somerset Co., PA, and died 16 Aug 1909 in Meyersdale, Somerset Co., PA. He married **Lydia Dale** 14 Feb 1886 in Sand Patch, Somerset Co., PA. She was born Nov 1864 in Larimer Twp., Somerset Co. PA, and died 1939.

Notes for Samuel Christner:
Coal Miner of Larimer Twp., Somerset Co., PA.

The Daily Courier - Connellsville, Fayette Co., PA, Page 1, Man Meets Death in Train Cut - 16 Aug 1909

Samuel Christner Caugt by A Train on the Baltimore & Ohio Near Meyersdale

Meyersdale - Aug 16, 1909 - Samuel Christner aged about 48 years was run over by a train in the deep cut just west of this place and horribly mangled. The remains were picked up and removed to Reiegh's Mortuary where they were prepared for burial.

Christner, who for some time had been living apart from his family and was drinking heavily. It was kow that he was intoxicated shortly before the accident occurred and with several companions had been drinking all day.

Deceased is surived by his wife and several children and four brothers, all who reside near town.

More About Samuel Christner:
Burial: Meyersdale Cemetery, Meyersdale, Somerset Co., PA
Residence: 1900, Summit Township (South Part), Somerset, PA[912]

Notes for Lydia Dale:
1920 census has Lydia's daughter, Nora & a grandson of Lydia's Harry P. age 16, living with her at 323 Salisbury Street, Meyersdale, Somerset Co., PA. All were born in PA.

More About Lydia Dale:
Burial: Meyersdale Cemetery, Meyersdale, Somerset Co., PA
Residence: 1920, Meyersdale, Somerset Co., PA[912]

Children of Samuel Christner and Lydia Dale are:

518   i.   William D.[7] Christner, born Dec 1884 in Summit Twp., Somerset Co., PA; died 05 Dec 1901.

Notes for William D. Christner:
I realize that William is born 2 years before the marriage of his parents. This may be an incorrect birth date or he may not belong in this family.

More About William D. Christner:
Burial: Meyersdale Cemetery, Meyersdale, Somerset Co., PA

+ 519   ii.   Nora Christner, born Mar 1887 in Summit Twp., Somerset Co., PA.
+ 520   iii.   Susan Christner, born 29 Jul 1889 in Summit Twp., Somerset Co., PA; died 10 Jan 1972.
   521   iv.   Gertrude Christner, born 09 Apr 1891 in Summit Twp., Somerset Co., PA; died Jan 1978 in Somerset, Somerset Co., PA[913]. She married Lloyd N. Blubaugh[914]; born 12 Feb 1894 in PA[915,916]; died May 1979 in Somerset, Somerset Co., PA[917].

> More About Gertrude Christner:
> Social Security Number: 205-16-0282/[918]
> SSN issued: Connellsville, Fayette Co., PA[918]

> More About Lloyd N. Blubaugh:
> Residence: [919]
> Social Security Number: 170-18-0870/[920]
> SSN issued: PA[920]

   522   v.   Robbie Christner, born 08 Apr 1895; died 02 Jul 1896.

> Notes for Robbie Christner:
> Robbie was a coal miner.

> More About Robbie Christner:
> Burial: Meyersdale Cemetery, Meyersdale, Somerset Co., PA

   523   vi.   Maggie Christner, born 12 May 1897 in Garrett, Somerset Co., PA; died 12 May 1897 in Lagrange Co., IN.

> More About Maggie Christner:
> Burial: Union Cemetery, Summitt Twp., Somerset Co., PA

   524   vii.   Sadie Emma Christner, born Jan 1899. She married Archibald Thomas Gray in Cumberland, Allegany Co., MD.

> Notes for Sadie Emma Christner:
> The Daily Courier - 8 Dec 1917 - Licensed to Wed

> Archibald Thomas Gray and Sadie Emma Christner both of Myeresdale were granted a license to wed in Cumberland.

> Notes for Archibald Thomas Gray:
> The Daily Courier - 8 Dec 1917 - Licensed to Wed

> Archibald Thomas Gray and Sadie Emma Christner both of Myeresdale were granted a license to wed in Cumberland.

139. Caroline (Carrie)[6] Christner (Jacob C.[5], John J.[4], Johannes John Hans[3], Christian[2], Christen[1])[921] was born 1866, and died 1943. She married **Peirce Kendall**. He was born 1862 in Connellsville, Fayette Co., PA[921].

More About Caroline (Carrie) Christner:
Residence: 1910, Summit, Somerset Co., PA[921]

More About Peirce Kendall:
Residence: 1910, Summit, Somerset Co., PA[921]

Children of Caroline Christner and Peirce Kendall are:
+ 525   i.   George[7] Kendall, died Oct 1964.
   526   ii.   Gertrude Kendall, born 1896 in Connellsville, Fayette Co., PA[921].

> More About Gertrude Kendall:
> Residence: 1910, Summit, Somerset Co., PA[921]

140. Franklin Grant[6] Christner (Jacob C.[5], John J.[4], Johannes John Hans[3], Christian[2], Christen[1])[922,923,924,925,926,927,928,929,930,931,931] was born 04 May 1866 in Connellsville, Fayette Co., PA[932,933,934,935,936,937,938,939,940,941,941], and died 1967 in Brownsville, Fayette Co., PA[942,943,944,945,946,947]. He married **(1) Susan Grim**. She was born 1870. He married **(2) Lillian B. Gould**[948,949,950,951,952] 1890[953,954]. She was born 16 Apr 1869 in Connellsville, Fayette Co., PA[955,956,957], and died 01 Nov 1918[958,959,960,961].

More About Franklin Grant Christner:
Residence: 1930, Franklin, Fayette Co., PA[962,963,964,965,966,967,968,969]

More About Susan Grim:
Namesake: Used Christner Name but we can not find marrage documents/

Notes for Lillian B. Gould:
Birth: Apr. 16, 1869 - PA
Death: Nov. 1, 1918

Inscription: Mother

Burial: Redstone Cemetery, Brownsville, Fayette Co., PA

More About Lillian B. Gould:
Occupation: She had a take in Laundry or clothes washing service/
Residence: 1900, Bridgeport Borough, Fayette Co., PA[970,971,972,973,974]

Child of Franklin Christner and Susan Grim is:

+ 527   i.   Mason Franklin[7] Christner, born 24 Apr 1891 in Bullskin Twp., Fayette Co., PA; died 04 Mar 1958 in Connellsville, Fayette Co., PA.

Children of Franklin Christner and Lillian Gould are:

   528   i.   Francis J.[7] Christner[974,975,976], born Sep 1887 in Connellsville, Fayette Co., PA[977,978,979].

                 More About Francis J. Christner:
                 Residence: 1910, South Union, Fayette Co., PA[980,981,982]

   529   ii.   Charles Henry Christner[983,984,985], born 21 Feb 1894 in Connellsville, Fayette Co., PA[986,987,988]; died 13 Feb 1957 in Johns Hopkins Hosp., Baltimore, Baltimore Co., MD[988]. He married Blanche S.

                 Notes for Charles Henry Christner:
                 Birth: 1894
                 Death: 1957

                 Spouse: Blanche S Christner (1900 - 1996)

                 Inscription: In loving memory

                 Burial: Redstone Cemetery, Brownsville, Fayette Co., PA

                 More About Charles Henry Christner:
                 Residence: 1930, Franklin, Fayette Co., PA[988,989,990]

                 Notes for Blanche S:
                 Birth: 1900
                 Death: 1996

                 Spouse: Charles H. Christner (1894 - 1957)

                 Inscription: In loving memory

                 Burial: Redstone Cemetery, Brownsville, Fayette Co., PA

530   iii.   Samuel Raymond Christner[991,992], born Dec 1897 in Connellsville, Fayette Co., PA[993]; died 1961.

        More About Samuel Raymond Christner:
        Residence: 1900, Bridgeport Borough, Fayette Co., PA[993,994]

531   iv.   Infant Christner[995], born Feb 1900 in Connellsville, Fayette Co., PA[995].

        More About Infant Christner:
        Residence: 1900, Bridgeport Borough, Fayette Co., PA[995]

+ 532   v.   George West Christner, born 22 Feb 1900 in Brownsville, Fayette Co., PA; died Jun 1971 in Dover, York Co., PA.

+ 533   vi.   James Allen Christner, born 30 Aug 1902 in Connellsville, Fayette Co., PA; died 24 Apr 1998 in Anchorage, Anchorage Co., Alaska.

534   vii.   Annie S. Christner[995], born 1906 in Connellsville, Fayette Co., PA[995]. She married Thomas Kurek.

535   viii.   Edna L. Christner[996,997,998], born 1908 in Connellsville, Fayette Co., PA[999,1000,1001]; died 18 Jan 1968 in Brownsville, Fayette Co., PA[1002,1003,1004]. She married (1) John Carroll. She married (2) Sylvester.

        More About Edna L. Christner:
        Residence: 1910, South Union, Fayette Co., PA[1005,1006,1007]

145. Frank[6] Christner (Jacob C.[5], John J.[4], Johannes John Hans[3], Christian[2], Christen[1])[1008,1009] was born 21 Mar 1875 in Somerset Co., PA[1010], and died 15 Mar 1946 in Glade City, Somerset Co., PA[1010]. He married **Margaret Mae "Maggie" Pletcher**[1010]. She was born 12 Aug 1890 in Meyersdale, Somerset Co., PA[1010], and died 13 May 1931 in Meyersdale, Somerset Co., PA[1011].

Notes for Frank Christner:
Birth: Mar. 21, 1875 - Somerset Co., PA
Death: Mar. 16, 1946 - Somerset Co., PA

Obituary: FRANK CHRISTNER - Meyersdale Republican, March 21, 1946

Frank Christner, retired miner, aged 70, died at his home in Glade City, Friday night, March 15. He was born in Somerset County on March 21, 1875, a son of Jacob and Kathryn (Ohler) Christner. Surviving are seven children: Clyde, Meyersdale R.D.; Mrs. Marie Housel, Meyersdale R.D. 3; Mrs. Emma Housel, Meyersdale R.D. 2; George and John Christner, Mrs. Dorothy Ohler and Mrs. Margaret Albright, Baltimore. He was a brother of Jerome Christner, Somerset, and Mrs. Tennie Logsdon, Hyndman. Funeral services were held at 2 p.m., Tuesday, at the Konhaus Funeral Home. Interment was made in Pine Hill Cemetery, Brothersvalley Township, under the direction of H. R. Konhaus.

Spouse: Margaret Mae Pletcher Christner (1890 - 1931)

Children: Sadie Marie Christner Housel (1911 - 2007)

Burial: Pine Hill Cemetery, Berlin, Somerset Co., PA

More About Frank Christner:
Burial: Mar 1946, Pine Hill Cemetery, Brothersvalley Twp., Somerset Co., PA[1012]
Residence: 1880, Larimer, Somerset Co., PA[1013]

Notes for Margaret Mae "Maggie" Pletcher:
Birth: Aug. 12, 1890
Somerset Co., PA
Death: Mar. 14, 1931

Wife of Frank Christner, daughter of Amos Pletcher and Elizabeth Sleesman.

Spouse: Frank Christner (1875 - 1946)

Children: Sadie Marie Christner Housel (1911 - 2007)

Burial: Pine Hill Cemetery, Berlin, Somerset Co., PA

More About Margaret Mae "Maggie" Pletcher:
Residence: 1900, Summit Twp., Somerset Co., PA[1014]

Children of Frank Christner and Margaret Pletcher are:

+ 536   i.   Sadie Marie[7] Christner, born 24 Mar 1911 in Pine Hill, Somerset Co., PA; died 05 Jun 2007 in Meyersdale, Somerset Co., PA.

+ 537   ii.   Margaret M. Christner, born 25 Nov 1912 in Berlin, Somerset Co., PA; died 1994 in Trenton, Mercer Co., NJ.

+ 538   iii.   Clyde Franklin Christner, born 15 Mar 1915 in Brothersvalley Twp., Somerset Co., PA; died 01 Oct 1988 in Trenton, Mercer Co., NJ.

+ 539   iv.   George L. Christner, born 07 Jul 1917; died 02 Mar 1948 in Baltimore, Baltimore Co., MD.

+ 540   v.   John W. Christner, born 07 May 1920 in Berlin, Somerset Co., PA; died 03 Oct 1987 in Laurel Crest Manor, Somerset Co., PA.

+ 541   vi.   Emma Catherine Christner, born 06 Jul 1923 in Somerset, Somerset Co., PA; died 30 Sep 1980.

+ 542   vii.   Dorothy Caroline Christner, born 08 Oct 1926 in Brothersvalley Twp., Somerset Co., PA; died 16 Apr 1996 in Pittsburgh, Allegheny Co., PA.

   543   viii.   Albert James Christner, born 04 May 1931 in Somerset Co., PA[1015]; died 04 May 1931 in Somerset Co., PA[1015].

147. Isabella A.[6] Christner (John[5], Peter[4], Johannes John Hans[3], Christian[2], Christen[1]) was born 1823 in Connellsville, Fayette Co., PA[1016,1017,1018], and died 19 Aug 1892 in Saltlick Twp., Fayette Co., PA[1019]. She married **Isaac Hart Miller** 1838 in Fayette Co, PA[1019]. He was born 1820 in Saltlick Twp., Fayette Co., PA[1019], and died 1857 in Saltlick Twp., Fayette Co., PA[1019].

More About Isabella A. Christner:
Residence: 1900, Quemahoning Township (South Part), Somerset Co., PA[1019]

Children of Isabella Christner and Isaac Miller are:

   544   i.   Isaac[7] Miller[1019], born 1839 in Fayette Co, PA[1019].
   545   ii.   William Miller, born 1840.
   546   iii.   John Miller, born 1841; died 1915[1019].

       More About John Miller:
       Residence: 1910, Saltlick, Fayette, PA[1019]

   547   iv.   Jacob C. Miller[1020,1021,1022], born 1844 in Connellsville, Fayette Co., PA[1023,1024,1025].
   548   v.   Susanna Miller[1026,1027,1028], born 1846 in Connellsville, Fayette Co., PA.
   549   vi.   Freeman C. Miller[1029,1030,1031], born 14 Aug 1850 in Connellsville, Fayette Co., PA; died 16 Mar 1939 in Saltlick Twp., Fayette Co., PA[1032]. He married Malinda Echard[1033]; born 30 Aug 1851 in Saltlick Twp., Fayette Co., PA[1033]; died 29 Feb 1916 in Saltlick Twp., Fayette Co., PA[1033].

       More About Freeman C. Miller:
       Burial: Eutsey Cemetery, White, Saltlick Twp., Fayette Co., PA

       More About Malinda Echard:
       Burial: Eutsey Cemetery, White, Saltlick Twp., Fayette Co., PA
       Residence: 1910, Harrisburg Ward 8, Dauphin, PA[1033]

   550   vii.   Priscilla Miller[1034,1035,1036], born Sep 1853 in Connellsville, Fayette Co., PA; died 07 Jun 1933[1037,1038,1039].
   551   viii.   Deliah Miller, born 1854 in Connellsville, Fayette Co., PA; died 09 Dec 1939 in Fayette Co, PA[1040].
   552   ix.   Rachel Miller, born 1856.
   553   x.   Mary Ellen Miller[1041,1042,1043], born 1858 in Connellsville, Fayette Co., PA; died Bet. 1859 - 1952.
   554   xi.   Harmon C. Miller[1044,1045,1046], born 1859 in Connellsville, Fayette Co., PA.
   555   xii.   Eliza Miller[1047], born 1862 in Fayette Co, PA[1047].
   556   xiii.   Lisa Miller[1047], born 1862 in Saltlick Twp., Fayette Co., PA[1047].

557   xiv.   Albert Miller[1048,1049,1050], born 1864 in Connellsville, Fayette Co., PA.

148. Deliah[6] Christner (John[5], Peter[4], Johannes John Hans[3], Christian[2], Christen[1])[1051] was born 08 Nov 1824 in Somerset Co., PA, and died 25 Oct 1905. She married **(1) Joseph Berg**.

Children of Deliah Christner and Joseph Berg are:
+   558   i.   John R.[7] Berg.
    559   ii.   Nancy Berg, born 1844.
    560   iii.   Susan Berg, born 1846.
    561   iv.   Elizabeth Berg, born 1848.
    562   v.   Mary Berg, born 1850.
    563   vi.   Rebecca Berg, born 1852.
    564   vii.   Benjamin Berg, born 1852.
    565   viii.   Harriet Berg, born 1859.
    566   ix.   Joseph Berg, born 1864.
    567   x.   Sarah Berg, born 1867.
    568   xi.   George Berg, born 1870.

149. Peter[6] Christner (John[5], Peter[4], Johannes John Hans[3], Christian[2], Christen[1])[1052,1053] was born 08 Apr 1826 in Somerset Co., PA[1053], and died 23 Nov 1914 in Silver Lake, Kosciusko Co., IN[1054,1055]. He married **(1) Harriet Sipe**[1056,1057] 1848 in Salt Lick Twp. Fayette Co. PA. She was born 19 Sep 1830 in Mill Run, Fayette Co., PA[1058,1059], and died Feb 1859[1060,1061]. He married **(2) Magdaline Martha Gingery** 18 Oct 1862 in Wayne Co., OH[1061]. She was born 30 Jun 1835 in Wayne Co., OH, and died 21 Jun 1922 in Silver Lake, Kosciusko Co., IN.

Notes for Peter Christner:
Peter bought a farm in Saltlick Twp., Fayette Co., PA January 20, 1849. He sold this farm on December 21, 1855.

Obituary for Peter Christner from the Akron News, Akron, IN.

In 1863 they moved from Wayne Co.,OH to Wabash Co., IN where they purchased a farm and where he has lived for over 52 years in the same neighborhood Christner was one of the pioneers of northern Indiana when this country was an unbroken forest and hard work and true manliness not only provided comfort and happiness for those in his household, but also a great factor in making the community an enjoyable and desirable one. Yet the attractions of this life gradually decreased and he was waiting for the welcome message of "well done". Considering his age he had comparatively good health. He had made his peace with God and man and expressed his willingness many times to the family that he was ready to go. He was baptized under the labor of Rev. Swinehart and was a member of the Eel River Brethren Church. He leaves to mourn his aged companion, two sons, and four daughters, thirty grandchildren and several great grandchildren, three brothers, three sisters, and many friends, who hold him in sacred memory. The funeral services took place fro South Pleasent Wednesday afternoon Conducted by Rev. Swihart of Roann IN. and Leckrone of Silver Lake, IN in the presence of a large concourse of friends and relatives. Farwell dear father, sweet thy rest, Weary with years and worn with pain, Farewell, till in some happy place WE shall behold thy face again. Tis ours to miss thee, all our years and tender memories of thee keep. Thine in the Lord to rest, for so, He giveth his his beloved sleep. Precious Father, you have left us, Yes, forever more. But we hope to meet you again, On that bright and happy shore. Lonely the house, and sad the hours since our dear one has gone, But oh! a brighter home than ours IN heaven, is now his own.

From the Silver Lake Record Nov. 26, 1914 Vol.29 number 50 Kosciusko Co., IN. Death was sudden. Peter Christner passed away at home Monday afternoon at an advanced age. He died without a struggle. Had been husking corn and was as usual ate hearty dinner then sat down to rest death came without warning. Monday shortly after the noon hour, Peter Christner, aged about eighty years, died very suddenly at his home, three miles south and two miles west of town. Mr Christner had been in his usual health and had been husking corn Monday forenoon. He quit work at the usual time for dinner and after attending to some chores about the barn went to the house to partake of the noonday meal. Seated at the table, he ate Hearty and after completing the meal he remarked to his wife that he didn't believe he would care for any supper as he had ate such a Hearty meal, as he was quite hungry. After talking to his wife Mr. Christner arose from the dinner table, and went to another room to rest for a short time as had been his habit, before going out to his work and Mrs. Christner began her household duties. Some little time had passed and Mrs. Christner asked her husband a question and getting no response went to the aged gentleman and after speaking tried to arouse the husband, who seamed to be asleep. Failing in an attempt to even get him to open his eyes Mrs. Christner hastened to a neighbor for assistance and a physician was telephoned for. From all appearances the aged gentleman had died immediately after being seated in the chair and indications are that he passed away without a struggle. Mr. Christner was well known to the people of this locality as he was among the early settlers to locate in this country when the community was one vast wilderness The funeral was held at the South Pleasent Church, three miles south of town, Wednesday afternoon and was attended by a large concourse of friends and old neighbors. Internment was made in the cemetery near by.

Peter Christner   4/8/1826-11/23/1914

I have found conflicting information about Peter Christner. His Obituary from the Akron News on Friday 11/27/1914 states:

Peter Christner, son of John & Anna Christner, was borne in Sommerset Co., PA 4/8/1826 and departed this life at his home in Silver Lake, Indiana 11/23/1914, at the age of 88 years, 7 months, & 15 days. In or about the year of 1848 he was united in marriage to Miss Harriet Sipe, and to this union was born 5 children, 1 son & 4 daughters. Annias, Mary, Malinda, Anna, & Francis. The mother and 1 daughter Francis, preceded the father to the Spirit world. The father then provided a comfortable home for his 4 surviving children.

October 5, 1862 he married Miss Martha Gingery of Wayne Co., OH and 2 children were born, Winfield & Alice. In 1863 they moved from Wayne Co., OH to Wabash Co., IN. They purchased a farm where Peter has lived for over 32 years in the same neighborhood. He leaves to mourn his aged companion. 2 sons, 4 daughters, 30 grandchildren, 3 brothers, 3 sisters, and many friends. The funeral services took place from South Pleasant on Wednesday afternoon, where he is buried. The funeral director was Ed Case.

However, the Certificate of Death Registration from the Wabash County Health Department states:

That his date of death was 11/28/1914. The cause of death was Chronic Valvular Heart Lesian. That Peter was born in Pennsylvania. The name of his father was James Christner, who was born in Pennsylvania and the name of his mother was Susan Griffen Christner, who also was born in Pennsylvania. That Peter was buried in South Pleasant Cemetery, 11/30/1914, with E.A. Case of Akron the Funeral Home. I have not been able to locate any marker.

For the date of Peter's death, I am inclined to believe the Akron News Report, as the paper was published on 11/27/1914, stating that Peter died on 11/23/1914 for Peter's obituary to be in there at that date, he would have to have died prior to that, not on 11/30/1914.   Sheri Christner Krichbaum

Burial:
Christner Cemetery, Wawpecong, Miami Co., IN
Plot: Space K7

More About Peter Christner:
Burial: 25 Nov 1914, South Pleasant Cemetery, Wabash Co., IN
Residence: 1900, Silver Lake Village, Kosciusko Co., IN[1062]

Notes for Harriet Sipe:
Her Christening was June 19, 1831 at Sanner Church Milford Twp., Somerset Co., PA.

More About Harriet Sipe:
Residence: 1870, Spring Garden, York, PA[1063]

Notes for Magdaline Martha Gingery:
Martha Gingery Christner 1838-6/21/1922

From the Obituary of Martha Christner we know that she passed away at her home in the south part of Silver Lake, Indiana about 3 a.m. Wednesday. She had been an invalid for a number of years and for the past several weeks her condition had been very critical suffering from complications. She was survived by one son Winfield Christner of Silver Lake, and one daughter Mrs., Mason Grogg of Akron. The funeral was held on Thursday afternoon at 2 p.m. and internment was at South Pleasant Cemetery, Wabash County. This Silver Lake newspaper was called The Record.

From the Kosciusko County Court House, her death record states that Martha died on 6/21/1922 in Silver Lake, Indiana. That she was born in Ohio. Her residence was Silver Lake, Indiana. Her age was 86 years, 11 months, and 22 days. Her occupation was housewife, she was widowed. The name of her father was Peter Gluerry (?), whose birthplace was Germany and the name of her mother was Ompa Hendricks, also born in Germany. The date of her burial was 6/22/1922 in South Pleasant Cemetery. The Coroner was J.M. Amiss, the undertake was E.T. Baber and the cause of death was Enility and Emaciation and injury to her right hip. The duration being 15 years. I have not been able to locate any marker. She went by the name Martha.
Sheri Christner Krichbaum

More About Magdaline Martha Gingery:
Burial: 22 Jun 1922, South Pleasant Cemetery, Wabash Co., IN
Cause of Death: Enility & Emaciation & injury to right hip   Duration=15 years

Children of Peter Christner and Harriet Sipe are:
+   569   i.   Ananias Sipe[7] Christner, born 26 Jul 1850 in Saltlick Twp, Fayette Co PA; died Jan 1930 in Lost Springs, Marion Co., KS.
    570   ii.   Mary Elizabeth Christner, born 12 Aug 1852. She married John Henry Craig.
    571   iii.   Indiana Christner, born 17 Sep 1854[1064]; died 07 Apr 1916. She married William Baker.

            Notes for Indiana Christner:
            Some of the info that we have from 1870 Wabash Co., IN census list this woman as Indiana Christner, maybe she shortened it to Anna.

    572   iv.   Malinda Christner, born 07 Feb 1856; died 23 May 1942. She married Samuel Hammond Sparks 1871 in Lost Springs, Marion Co., KS.
    573   v.   Francis Christner, born 03 May 1858; died 20 Apr 1905. She married Davis.

Children of Peter Christner and Magdaline Gingery are:
+   574   i.   Winfield Scott[7] Christner, born 23 Sep 1863 in Wabash Co., IN; died 11 May 1947 in Silver Lake, Kosciusko Co., IN.
+   575   ii.   Alice D. Christner, born 13 Apr 1871 in Wabash, Wabash Co., IN; died 21 Nov 1961 in North Manchester, IN.

150. Cain[6] Christner (John[5], Peter[4], Johannes John Hans[3], Christian[2], Christen[1])[1065,1066] was born 02 Aug 1827 in Somerset, Somerset Co., PA[1067], and died 25 Sep 1911 in Connellsville, Fayette Co., PA[1067]. He married **Christina Elizabeth Hart**[1067] 11 Apr 1852 in Connellsville, Fayette Co., PA[1067]. She was born 03 Jul 1831 in Saltlick Twp., Fayette Co., PA[1067], and died 08 Mar 1905 in Indian Head, Saltlick Twp., Fayette Co., PA[1067].

Notes for Cain Christner:
Cain was a blacksmith and a gun smith. This info came from Connie Yokum 1340 E. Warwick, Miamisburg, OH Phone 513-859-7776 Robert Weimer info has birth Aug 1, 1827 death Sept 29, 1911 and marriage as April 11, 1852.

Robert Weimer found this letter. A letter written by Cain Christner in Fayette Co. PA. to his grandson Cain Weimer in Wabash Co., IN Circa November 1, 1905. The following are the last four pages. I don't know what happened to the first four pages.

Well you wish to know about that little anvil indeed Cain if I had it yet I would make present to you if you wish to have it, but it went with the rest of my things I had to sell and give em away I give somethings away and some that ware sold dident fetch much our kitchen stove with eleven joints of stove pipe on it fetch 75 cents the heating stove in the room also eleven joints pipe on it fetch 100 my Buggy fetch 100 my two horse waggon with one wheel broke down fetch a quarter dollar four waggon wheels that your pap filled them before he went to Kansas the first time he filld them for Sol Schaffer I got them of Sol he had got the howns and axels put in his other waggon then I got thee wheels of him I allowed him twelve dollars for the wheels well the fetch 20 cents thats the way most of the things went except the cow and the mare the fetch all the wer worth and hay fetch 11 dollars a tun wheat 86 per bushel cow 40 dollars mare 42 corn 40 cents for single bushel them are all the articles that fetch what the wer worth the other things all went nearly for nothing a Beauro that i paid 12 doll fetch 3 dol a Corner Cubbard that I paid 11 dol fetch 5 doll I give some bedsteads away I give a coalstove without pipe for a quarter dol I have never been to a salr in my life that things went so low the blacksmith tools brought about twelve altogether I dident sell them all on a lump that is the way it goes sometimes well Cain tell uncle Peter Delila Berg is dead and buried she was buried last week she was within a few weeks eighty one years old if Peter lives until next April he will be eighty if I live until next August i will be seventy nine brother Sam is about seventy six Well Cain as you belong into our family I will give you a short history of our family I was 25 and granmother was 21 when we got married we wer married just one year when we had the first baby well we lived together fifty three years Raised four children the wer all over eighteen when the got married now we have thirty one granchildren living and four or five of em dead I am only counting the living ones and thirty geat granchildren counting your baby but yours is not the youngest one there is one Younger yet then yours no more at present but remain ever your granfather.

Buried: Sparks Cemetery, Indian Head, Fayette Co., PA

More About Cain Christner:
Burial: Sparks Cemetery, Indian Head, Fayette Co., PA
Residence: 1910, Saltlick, Fayette, PA[1067]

More About Christina Elizabeth Hart:
Burial: Sparks Cemt., Indian Head, Pa.
Residence: 1880, Saltlick Twp., Fayette Co., PA[1067]

Children of Cain Christner and Christina Hart are:

+   576   i.   Clarissa[7] Christner, born 12 Apr 1853 in Indian Head, Saltlick Twp., Fayette Co., PA; died 20 May 1930 in Connellsville, Fayette Co., PA.

+   577   ii.   Mary Christner, born 29 Jul 1855 in Saltlick Twp., Fayette Co., PA; died 08 Apr 1933 in Glendo, Platte Co., WY.

+   578   iii.   Susana Susannah Christner, born 02 May 1857 in Connellsville, Fayette Co., PA; died 12 Dec 1945 in Connellsville, Fayette Co., PA.

+   579   iv.   Priscilla Christner, born 17 Mar 1863 in Saltlick Twp., Fayette Co., PA; died 18 May 1916 in Disco, Wabash Co., IN.

       580   v.   Isaiah Christner[1067], born 21 Nov 1867 in Connellsville, Fayette Co., PA[1067]; died 12 Sep 1870 in Connellsville, Fayette Co., PA.

               More About Isaiah Christner:
               Burial: Old Luthern Cemetery, Indian Head, Fayette Co., PA

151. Samuel[6] Christner (John[5], Peter[4], Johannes John Hans[3], Christian[2], Christen[1]) was born 18 Sep 1829 in Somerset, Somerset Co., PA, and died 08 Nov 1913 in Connellsville, Fayette Co., PA. He married **Rachel Berg** 03 Oct 1853. She was born 04 Feb 1834 in Pittsburgh, Allegheny Co., PA[1068].

Notes for Samuel Christner:
Newspaper clipping - Oct 3, 1913

Mr. and Mrs. Samuel Christner living about a mile E. of Hammondville celebrated their 60th wedding anniversary on Fri. Mr. Christner is the fourth child of 13, born in Somerset Co., PA Sept 18, 1829 and came to Fayette Co., PA as a young boy. He was a carpenter. Samuel died about a month after this was written.

Sam & Rachel had a grandson living with them along with Sarah ----Rhuel --Winfields son

Fayette Co., PA - Marriages

page 20
Samuel CHRISTNER, son of John and Susan Christner, laborer, residence Saltlick Twp., and Rachel BERG, daughter of D. and Mary Berg
marriage 10-20-1853 at Saltlick Twp., legal ceremony by Peter Dumbauld of Saltlick Twp., registered 12-14-1853.   P.A. Johns

More About Samuel Christner:
Christened: Dunkard
Residence: 1900, Bullskin Twp., Fayette Co., PA[1069]

Notes for Rachel Berg:
Rachel is the daughter of David Berg. Information is from a newspaper clipping written in Oct 3, 1913 that Rachel was the 2nd child of 10 children and her father was a well known miller. 1920 census has Rachael living with her son Warren.

More About Rachel Berg:
Residence: 1900, Bullskin Twp., Fayette Co., PA[1069]

Children of Samuel Christner and Rachel Berg are:
+   581   i.   Winfield Scott[7] Christner, born 18 Sep 1854 in Bullskin Twp., Fayette Co., PA; died 07 Nov 1934 in Pittsfield, Washtenaw Co., MI.
     582   ii.   Sarah Christner, born Oct 1857 in Connellsville, Fayette Co., PA[1070,1071,1072]; died 1957.

                      Notes for Sarah Christner:
                      Sarah never married.

                      More About Sarah Christner:
                      Burial: Mt.Joy, Fayette Co., PA
                      Residence: 1910, Bullskin Twp., Fayette Co., PA[1073]

+   583   iii.   Warren Christner, born 26 Apr 1861 in Bullskin Twp., Fayette Co., PA; died 07 Jul 1934 in Bullskin Twp., Fayette Co., PA.
     584   iv.   David A. Christner, born 04 Mar 1867; died 29 Jan 1885.

                      Notes for David A. Christner:
                      David died as a young man. He may not have married.

                      More About David A. Christner:
                      Burial: Salt Lick, Fayette PA

     585   v.   Mary Christner, born 1869. She married C. H. Lee.

152. Urias[6] Christner (John[5], Peter[4], Johannes John Hans[3], Christian[2], Christen[1])[1074] was born Mar 1831 in Somerset, Somerset Co., PA[1075], and died 03 Oct 1902 in Indian Head, Saltlick Twp., Fayette Co., PA[1075,1075]. He married **Susanna Christner**[1076], daughter of Abraham Christner and Mary Hoover. She was born 12 Nov 1838 in Somerset Co., PA[1076], and died 04 Mar 1926[1076].

Notes for Urias Christner:
Name: Pvt Uriah Christner
Birth Date: 1 Mar 1831
Age at Death: 71
Death Date: 3 Oct 1902
Burial Place: Fayette Co., PA

More About Urias Christner:
Residence: Jun 1880, Saltlick Twp., Fayette Co., PA[1077,1078]

Notes for Susanna Christner:
Susan never married. Susan worked most of her life for Bernard (Barney) Miller.
Susan may of also worked for Adam Handwerk.

More About Susanna Christner:
Burial: Miller Burial, Grounds
Residence: 1850, Elk Lick, Somerset, PA[1079]

Children of Urias Christner and Susanna Christner are:

586   i.   Jeremiah[7] Christner[1080], born 1858 in Connellsville, Fayette Co., PA[1080].

    More About Jeremiah Christner:
    Residence: 1880, Saltlick Twp., Fayette Co., PA[1080]

587   ii.   Levi Christner[1080], born 1870 in Connellsville, Fayette Co., PA[1080,1081].

    More About Levi Christner:
    Residence: 1880, Saltlick Twp., Fayette Co., PA[1082]

588   iii. Malinda Christner[1082], born 1875 in Connellsville, Fayette Co., PA[1082].

    More About Malinda Christner:
    Residence: 1880, Saltlick Twp., Fayette Co., PA[1082]

589   iv. Samuel Christner[1082], born 1877 in Connellsville, Fayette Co., PA[1082].

    More About Samuel Christner:
    Residence: 1880, Saltlick Twp., Fayette Co., PA[1082]

590   v.   Jacob Christner[1082], born 1879 in Connellsville, Fayette Co., PA[1082].

    More About Jacob Christner:
    Residence: 1880, Saltlick Twp., Fayette Co., PA[1082]

153. Uriah[6] Christner (John[5], Peter[4], Johannes John Hans[3], Christian[2], Christen[1])[1083,1084,1085,1086] was born 01 Mar 1831 in Somerset, Somerset Co., PA[1086], and died 03 Oct 1902 in Indian Head, Saltlick Twp., Fayette Co., PA[1087,1088]. He married **Susannah Bungard**[1089] 07 Aug 1856 in Fayette Co., PA[1090,1091,1092,1093], daughter of Jacob Bungard and Mahala Christner. She was born 03 Mar 1838 in Fayette Co., PA[1093], and died 10 Feb 1916 in Fayette Co., PA[1093].

Notes for Uriah Christner:
Birth: Mar. 1, 1831
Death: Oct. 3, 1902

Uriah Christner
Enlisted on 9/30/1864 as a Private.
On 9/30/1864 he was drafted into "G" Co. PA 199th Infantry
He was transferred out on 2/13/1865
On 2/13/1865 he transferred into "A" Co. PA 97th Infantry (date and method of discharge not given)

b. 1 Mar 1831
d. 3 Oct 1902

Burial: Dan Snyder Cemetery, Fayette Co., PA

U.S. Civil War Soldiers, 1861-1865
Name: Uriah Christner

Side: Union
Regiment State/Origin: Pennsylvania
Regiment Name: 97 Pennsylvania Inf.
Regiment Name Expanded: 97th Regiment, Pennsylvania Infantry
Company: A
Rank In: Private
Rank In Expanded: Private
Rank Out: Private
Rank Out Expanded: Private
Alternate Name: Uriah/Christian
Film Number: M554 roll 19

More About Uriah Christner:
Burial: Oct 1902, Dan Snyder Cemetery, Fayette Co., PA[1093]
Military service: Served during Civil War-Co. A 97th Bat.[1093]
Residence: 1900, Saltlick Twp., Fayette Co., PA[1094]

More About Susannah Bungard:
Baptised: 15 Jun 1838, Good Hope Lutheran Church, Saltlick Twp., Fayette Co., PA
Burial: Feb 1916, Daniel Snyder Cemetery, White, Fayette Co., PA
Residence: 1910, Fayette, PA[1094]

Children of Uriah Christner and Susannah Bungard are:

591	i.	Jeremiah[7] Christner[1095], born 1858[1095].
+ 592	ii.	Sophia Christner, born 06 Mar 1860 in Bullskin Twp., Fayette Co., PA; died 22 Aug 1930 in Connellsville, Fayette Co., PA.
593	iii.	Rachel Christner[1096,1097,1098,1099], born 1862 in Bullskin Twp., Fayette Co., PA[1100,1101,1102].
594	iv.	Sarah B. Christner[1103,1104,1105,1106,1107], born 25 Sep 1863 in Saltlick Twp., Fayette Co., PA[1108]; died 06 Nov 1895[1108].

> More About Sarah B. Christner:
> Burial: Nov 1895, Dan Snyder Cemetery, White, Fayette Co., PA[1108]

595	v.	John Christner[1109,1110,1111], born 1867 in Bullskin Twp., Fayette Co., PA[1112,1113,1114].
+ 596	vi.	Levi Christner, born 13 Jul 1869 in Bullskin Twp., Fayette Co., PA; died 03 Aug 1947.
597	vii.	Malinda Christner[1115,1116,1117,1118], born 24 Mar 1874 in Indian Head, Fayette Co., PA; died 1952 in Uniontown, Fayette Co., PA. She married Oliver Witt[1119,1120,1121]; died Feb 1952 in Bullskin Twp., Fayette Co., PA.

> Notes for Malinda Christner:
> Mrs. Malinda Christner Witt, 78, of Indian Head, died at 6:30 A.M. Thursday at Uniontown. She was born at Indian Head, March 24, 1874, a daughter of the late Uriah and Susannah Bungard Christner, and lived all her life in the Indian Head community. Surviving are nephews and nieces. Her Husband, Oliver Witt died February, 1952.
>
> Burial: Sparks Cemetery, Indian Head, Fayette Co., PA
>
> More About Malinda Christner:
> Burial: Sparks Cemetery, Indian Head, Fayette, PA[1122,1123,1124]

598	viii.	Samuel Christner[1125,1126,1127,1128,1129], born 23 Oct 1876 in Bullskin Twp., Fayette Co., PA[1130,1131,1132]; died 03 May 1944 in Los Angeles Co., CA[1133].
599	ix.	Jacob Christner[1134,1135,1136], born 1879 in Bullskin Twp., Fayette Co., PA[1137,1138,1139].

154. Mahala A.[6] Christner (John[5], Peter[4], Johannes John Hans[3], Christian[2], Christen[1]) was born 19 Jan 1833 in Somerset, Somerset Co., PA, and died 28 Dec 1910 in Mt. Pleasant, Westmoreland Co., PA//. She married **Jacob Bungard**. He was born 16 Jan 1813 in Fayette Co., PA, and died 21 Nov 1892 in Saltlick Twp.Fayette Co.PA.

More About Jacob Bungard:
Burial: 23 Nov 1892, Saltlick Twp.Fayette Co.PA

Children of Mahala Christner and Jacob Bungard are:

	600	i.	Nancy[7] Bungard, born 17 Oct in Connellsville, Fayette Co., PA; died Bef. 1880 in Bullskin Twp., Fayette Co., PA.
+	601	ii.	Susannah Bungard, born 03 Mar 1838 in Fayette Co., PA; died 10 Feb 1916 in Fayette Co., PA.
	602	iii.	Samuel C. Bungard, born 22 Jul 1852 in Saltlick Twp.Fayette Co PA; died 1936 in Mt. Pleasant, Westmoreland Co., PA. He married (1) Annie Sheetz. He married (2) Anna "Annie" Sheets 25 Sep 1888 in Connellsville, Fayette Co., PA; born 12 Nov 1864 in Bullskin Twp., Fayette Co., PA; died 1946 in Mt. Pleasant Twp., Westmoreland Co., PA.

More About Samuel C. Bungard:
Burial: Mt. Pleasant Cemetery, Mt. Pleasant, Westmoreland Co., PA

More About Anna "Annie" Sheets:
Burial: Mt. Pleasant Cemetery, Mt. Pleasant, Westmoreland Co., PA

	603	iv.	Lucinda Bungard, born 26 Aug 1854 in Saltlick Twp., Fayette Co., PA. She married Samuel Echard; born 1846 in Connellsville, Fayette Co., PA.
+	604	v.	Josiah C. Bungard, born 12 Mar 1856 in Saltlick Twp., Fayette Co., PA; died 28 Mar 1944 in White, Fayette Co., PA.
	605	vi.	Sarah Bungard, born 21 Jan 1858 in Springfield Twp., Fayette Co., PA; died 09 Mar 1947 in Uniontown, Fayette Co., PA. She married Allen Trump 04 Nov 1880 in Connellsville, Fayette Co., PA; born 1849 in Connellsville, Fayette Co., PA; died 25 Dec 1927 in Uniontown, Fayette Co., PA.

More About Sarah Bungard:
Burial: Park Place Cemetery, Uniontown, Fayette Co., PA

More About Allen Trump:
Burial: Park Place Cemetery, Uniontown, Fayette Co., PA

	606	vii.	Priscilla Bungard, born 06 Jun 1860 in Bullskin Twp., Fayette Co., PA. She married James W. Kinnear 04 Aug 1887 in Bullskin Twp., Fayette Co., PA; born 1852 in Connellsville, Fayette Co., PA.
	607	viii.	Noah Bungard, born 09 Aug 1862 in Bullskin Twp., Fayette Co., PA.
+	608	ix.	Malinda Bungard, born 11 Apr 1863 in Connellsville, Fayette Co., PA; died 15 May 1944 in Davistown, Fayette Co., PA.
+	609	x.	Isaiah Bungard, born 23 Aug 1864 in Bullskin Twp., Fayette Co., PA; died 1944 in Westmoreland Co., PA.
	610	xi.	Elizabeth Bungard, born 18 Apr 1866 in Connellsville, Fayette Co., PA.
+	611	xii.	Sophia Bungard, born 28 Jun 1868 in Indian Head, Saltlick Twp., Fayette Co., PA; died 1953 in Bullskin Twp., Fayette Co., PA.
	612	xiii.	Minnie Mahala Bungard, born 11 Nov 1873 in Bullskin Twp., Fayette Co., PA; died 16 Jul 1874 in Bullskin Twp., Fayette Co., PA.
	613	xiv.	Henry Jacob Bungard, born 11 Nov 1873 in Connellsville, Fayette Co., PA; died 1941 in Mt. Pleasant, Westmoreland Co., PA.
+	614	xv.	Alice Bungard, born 20 Aug 1875 in Saltlick Twp., Fayette Co., PA; died 1956 in Mt. Pleasant, Westmoreland Co., PA.

155. Priscilla[6] Christner (John[5], Peter[4], Johannes John Hans[3], Christian[2], Christen[1]) was born Dec 1835 in Somerset, Somerset Co., PA[1140], and died 1918 in Connellsville, Fayette Co., PA. She married **John R. Berg** 1861 in They raised 5 childeren. John served in the 168th PA. Infantry, Company B in the Civil War./, son of Joseph Berg and Deliah Christner.

More About Priscilla Christner:
Residence: 1910, Mount Pleasant, Westmoreland, PA[1140]

Children of Priscilla Christner and John Berg are:

	615	i.	Emma[7] Berg, born 1863.
	616	ii.	Grant Berg, born 1864.

617 iii. Elmer Berg, born 1865.

618 iv. Robinson Berg, born 1869; died 1938. He married Mary Janet; born 1870; died 1933.

      More About Robinson Berg:
      Burial: Mt Joy Cemetery, Mt. Pleasant, Westmoreland Co., PA

157. Mary Magdalena[6] Christner (John[5], Peter[4], Johannes John Hans[3], Christian[2], Christen[1]) was born 10 Jun 1841 in Connellsville, Fayette Co., PA, and died 09 Mar 1924 in Connellsville, Fayette Co., PA. She married **George A. Brown**. He was born 01 Jun 1839, and died 24 Mar 1929.

Child of Mary Christner and George Brown is:

619 i. Charles John[7] Brown, born 05 Apr 1886; died 03 Nov 1973.

      Notes for Charles John Brown:
      Charles married Emma French born July 3, 1889 died Feb 14, 1977.

158. Cyrus John[6] Christner (John[5], Peter[4], Johannes John Hans[3], Christian[2], Christen[1]) was born 06 Apr 1842 in Fayette Co., PA[1141], and died 20 Oct 1916 in Bullskin Twp., Fayette Co., PA[1141]. He married **Rachel Eicher**[1142,1143] 1863. She was born 1844 in Saltlick Twp., Fayette Co., PA[1144], and died 17 Nov 1909[1145,1146].

Notes for Cyrus John Christner:
Cyrus John/John Cyrus and Rachel lived in Fayette Co., PA settling at Indian Head. There is records that show John and Rachel had 9 children. I don't have any info on the last 3.

Birth: 1842
Death: 1916

Burial: Mount Olive Cemetery, Connellsville, Fayette Co., PA
Find A Grave Memorial# 91719089

More About Cyrus John Christner:
Census: 16 Jun 1880, Bullskin Twp., Fayette Co., PA[1147]
Occupation: 16 Jun 1880, coal miner/[1147]
Residence: 1900, Upper Tyrone Township, Precinct 2, Fayette Co., PA[1148]

Notes for Rachel Eicher:
Records indicate that Rachel and Cyrus had 9 children. We don't have that many, but do know that son Samuel was the 4th born.

Birth: 1843
Death: 1909

Burial: Mount Olive Cemetery, Connellsville, Fayette Co., PA
Find A Grave Memorial# 91719113

More About Rachel Eicher:
Census: 16 Jun 1880, Bullskin Twp., Fayette Co., PA[1149]
Residence: 1900, Upper Tyrone Township, Precinct 2, Fayette Co., PA[1150]

Children of Cyrus Christner and Rachel Eicher are:

620 i. Alice Ann[7] Christner[1151,1152,1152], born Feb 1864 in Fayette Co., PA[1152].

      More About Alice Ann Christner:
      Census: 16 Jun 1880, Bullskin Twp., Fayette Co., PA[1153]

+ 621 ii. Richard E. Christner, born Nov 1867 in Connellsville, Fayette Co., PA; died 1948.

622   iii.   Marcellus Christner[1153], born 04 Aug 1870 in Connellsville, Fayette Co., PA[1153]; died 27 Apr 1950 in Lakeland, Polk Co., FL[1153]. He married Almeda Reed 26 Aug 1922; born 29 Aug 1879 in Scottdale, Westmoreland Co., PA; died 17 Jun 1969 in Pittsburgh, Allegheny Co., PA.

More About Marcellus Christner:
Census: 1880, Bullskin Twp., Fayette Co., PA Film #T91129, page 34C[1153]
Residence: 16 Jun 1880, Bullskin Twp., Fayette Co., PA[1153]

+   623   iv.   Samuel E. Christner, born 12 Sep 1872 in Pennsville, Bullskin Twp., Fayette Co., PA; died 11 Jul 1937 in Connellsville, Fayette Co., PA.

624   v.   Victor Christner[1153], born 15 Nov 1875 in Pennsville, Bullskin Twp., Fayette Co., PA[1154]; died 18 May 1943 in Near Wesley Chapel, East Huntingdon Township, Westmoreland Co., PA[1154].

More About Victor Christner:
Burial: Mt. Olive Cemetery, Bullskin Twp., Fayette Co., PA[1154]
Census: 18 Jun 1880, Bullskin Twp., Fayette Co., PA[1155]
Residence: 1930, East Huntingdon, Westmoreland Co., PA[1156]

625   vi.   Lawerence Christner[1157], born 1879[1157].

More About Lawerence Christner:
Census: 16 Jun 1880, Bullskin Twp., Fayette Co., PA[1157]

159. Jacob G.[6] Christner (John[5], Peter[4], Johannes John Hans[3], Christian[2], Christen[1])[1158,1159] was born 18 Feb 1846 in Somerset Co., PA[1160,1161], and died 26 May 1917 in Connellsville, Fayette Co., PA[1162]. He married **Sarah Davis**[1162] 1865[1163]. She was born Jan 1844 in Connellsville, Fayette Co., PA[1164], and died 01 Oct 1919.

Notes for Jacob G. Christner:
Birth: Feb 16, 1846 - Fayette Co., PA
Death: May 26, 1917 - Fayette Co., PA

Spouse: Sara Davis Christner (1844 - 1919)

Burial: Mount Joy Church Of The Brethren Cemetery, Mount Pleasant, Westmoreland Co., PA
Find A Grave Memorial# 88321150

More About Jacob G. Christner:
Burial: Mt.Joy
Military service: 25 Aug 1862, Pittsburgh, Allegheny Co., PA[1165,1166]
Residence: 1910, Mt. Pleasant Boro Ward 3, Westmoreland Co., PA[1167]

Notes for Sarah Davis:
Birth: Jan 21, 1844
Death: Oct 1, 1919

Spouse: Jacob G. Christner (1846 - 1917)

Burial: Mount Joy Church Of The Brethren Cemetery, Mount Pleasant, Westmoreland Co., PA
Find A Grave Memorial# 88321414

More About Sarah Davis:
Burial: Mt.Joy
Residence: 1910, Mt. Pleasant Boro Ward 3, Westmoreland Co., PA[1167]

Children of Jacob Christner and Sarah Davis are:
+   626   i.   Amos D.[7] Christner, born Apr 1866 in Davistown, Fayette Co., PA; died 1941.
+   627   ii.   Anna Elizabeth Hoffmeyer, born Jun 1868 in Connellsville, Fayette Co., PA; died 1955 in Pittsburgh, Allegheny Co., PA.
+   628   iii. Nelson D. Christner, born 1871 in Connellsville, Fayette Co., PA; died 1959.

629   iv.   Henry Christner, born 1876 in Twin.

          Notes for Henry Christner:
          May be a twin to John.

          More About Henry Christner:
          Residence: 1880, Saltlick Twp., Fayette Co., PA[1168]

630   v.   John Christner, born 1876 in Twin.

          Notes for John Christner:
          May be a twin to Henry.

          More About John Christner:
          Residence: 1880, Saltlick Twp., Fayette Co., PA

160. Joseph⁶ Christner (John⁵, Peter⁴, Johannes John Hans³, Christian², Christen¹) was born 22 May 1847 in Somerset, Somerset Co., PA[1169], and died 1937 in Connellsville, Fayette Co., PA. He married **(1) Susan**. She was born Feb 1856 in Connellsville, Fayette Co., PA. He married **(2) Frances Miller**. She was born 25 May 1841 in Fayette Co, PA[1170], and died 26 Jun 1888 in Fayette Co, PA[1170].

Notes for Frances Miller:
Had nick name of Francina Frannie.

More About Frances Miller:
Burial: Hopewell Cemetery, Saltlick Twp., Fayette Co., PA

Children of Joseph Christner and Frances Miller are:
+ 631   i.   Keturah May⁷ Christner, born 26 Aug 1871 in Pittsburgh, Allegheny Co., PA; died 24 Jun 1957 in Poplar Grove, Connellsville, Fayette Co., PA.
+ 632   ii.   Frank Homer Christner, born 07 Jun 1873 in Wilkinsburg, Allegheny Co., PA; died 30 Mar 1951.
   633   iii.   Almon M. Christner[1171,1172,1173], born 09 May 1875 in Connellsville, Fayette Co., PA[1174,1175,1176]; died Jul 1977 in Windber, Somerset Co., PA[1177]. He married Florence M; born 09 Jan 1886[1178]; died Mar 1977 in Windber, Somerset Co., PA[1178].

          Notes for Almon M. Christner:
          SS# 344-01-5437 Iss. IL last zip 15963

          Birth: 1875
          Death: 1977

          Spouse: Florence M. Christner (1886 - 1977

          Burial: Cerro Gordo Cemetery, Cerro Gordo, Piatt Co., IL
          Find A Grave Memorial# 92320696

          More About Almon M. Christner:
          Residence: 1900, Connellsville, Fayette, PA[1179]
          Social Security Number: 344-01-5437[1180]
          SSN issued: IL[1180]

          Notes for Florence M:
          Birth: 1886
          Death: 1977

          Spouse: Almon M. Christner (1875 - 1977)

          Burial: Cerro Gordo Cemetery, Cerro Gordo, Piatt Co., IL

More About Florence M:
Social Security Number: 318-56-9211/[1181]
SSN issued: IL[1181]

634   iv.   Cora Christner, born Aug 1877[1182].

Notes for Cora Christner:
1900 census Cora servant to Christ Medaia.
1910 soundex PA has her living at home with father & stepmother.

635   v.   Lottie Jane Christner, born 18 Mar 1880 in Saltlick Twp., Fayette Co., PA; died 18 Mar 1880 in Salt Lick Twp., Fayette Co., PA.

636   vi.   Laura B. Christner, born Jul 1881; died 1952. She married Jacob R. Berg 24 Jun 1900; born 1875; died 1955.

More About Laura B. Christner:
Burial: Mt Joy Cemetery, Mt. Pleasant, Westmoreland Co., PA

More About Jacob R. Berg:
Burial: Mt Joy Cemetery, Mt. Pleasant, Westmoreland Co., PA

637   vii.   Oakie Christner, born 17 Mar 1886 in Pittsburgh, Allegheny Co., PA[1183]; died 01 Dec 1981 in Ventura, Ventura Co., CA[1184]. She married Strawn Robbins 25 Dec 1909 in Fayette Co., PA; born Jan 1887 in Connellsville, Fayette Co., PA.

Notes for Oakie Christner:
We are not sure if Oakie is male or female.

More About Oakie Christner:
Occupation: School Teacher/
Social Security Number: 577-84-3841/[1185]

More About Strawn Robbins:
Occupation: Bricklayer/

161. Clarissa[6] **Christner** (Levi[5], Peter[4], Johannes John Hans[3], Christian[2], Christen[1])[1186,1187,1188] was born 1840 in Connellsville, Fayette Co., PA[1189], and died 01 Jan 1918 in Springfield, Fayette Co , PA[1190]. She married **(1) George W. Brooks.** She married **(2) John Andrew Kooser**[1191]. He was born 23 Jun 1824 in Mill Run, Fayette, PA, United States[1191], and died 25 Nov 1885[1192,1193].

More About Clarissa Christner:
Residence: 1880, Springfield, Fayette Co , PA[1194]

Notes for John Andrew Kooser:
John maybe buried at Normalville Cemetery, Fayette Co., PA with Clarrisa Christner and George W. Brooks.

More About John Andrew Kooser:
Burial: Normalville Cem
Residence: 1880, Springfield, Fayette Co , PA[1194]

Children of Clarissa Christner and John Kooser are:

638   i.   Ella[7] Kooser[1194], born 12 Dec 1861 in Mill Run, Fayette Co., PA[1194]; died 23 Mar 1938 in Scottdale, Westmoreland Co., PA[1194].

639   ii.   William F. Kooser[1194], born 1863 in Mill Run, Fayette Co., PA[1194]; died 21 Jan 1938 in New Brighton, Beaver Co., PA[1194].

640   iii.   Kate Kooser[1194], born 1865[1194].

641   iv.   Isaac N. Kooser[1194], born 1872[1194].

+ 642   v.   Marguerite Kooser, born 1875 in Millrun, Fayette Co., PA; died in Pittsburgh, Allegheny Co., PA.

164. Elias[6] **Christner** (Levi[5], Peter[4], Johannes John Hans[3], Christian[2], Christen[1])[1195,1196,1197,1198,1199] was born 15 Nov 1844 in Bullskin Twp., Fayette Co., PA[1200,1201,1202,1203,1204], and died 29 Jul 1923 in Bullskin Twp., Fayette Co., PA[1205,1206]. He married **Phoebe Nicholson**[1207,1208] 1869. She was born 09 Jan 1853 in Connellsville, Fayette Co., PA[1209,1210,1211,1212,1213], and died 27 Mar 1921 in Bullskin Twp., Fayette Co., PA[1214].

Notes for Elias Christner:
Elias Christner was born on November 15, 1844 in Bullskin Twp., Fayette Co., PA. He appeared on the census on August 15, 1860 in Springfield Twp., Fayette Co., PA. He was a Farm Laborer on June 4, 1870. He appeared on the census on June 4, 1870 in Pennsville, Bullskin Twp., Fayette Co., PA. He appeared on the census in 1880 in Bullskin Twp., Fayette, PA. He appeared on the census on June 21, 1900 in Bullskin Twp., Fayette Co., PA. He appeared on the census on April 20, 1910 in Bullskin Twp., Fayette Co., PA. He appeared on the census on January 21, 1920 in Bullskin Twp., Fayette Co., PA. He died on July 29, 1923 in Bullskin Twp., Fayette Co., PA. He was buried on July 31, 1923 in Mt Olive Cemetery, Connellsville, Fayette Co., PA.

He was married to Pheobe Nicholson (daughter of William Nicholson) about 1869. Pheobe Nicholson was born on January 9, 1853 in PA. She appeared on the census on June 4, 1870 in Pennsville, Bullskin Township, Fayette, PA. She appeared on the census in 1880 in Bullskin Twp, Fayette, PA. She appeared on the census on June 21, 1900 in Bullskin Twp, Fayette, PA. She appeared on the census on April 20, 1910 in Bullskin Twp, Fayette, PA. She appeared on the census on January 21, 1920 in Bullskin Twp, Fayette, PA. She died on March 27, 1921 in Bullskin Twp, Fayette, PA. She was buried on March 29, 1921 in Mt Olive Cemetery, Connellsville, Fayette Co, PA.

Birth: Nov. 15, 1844 - Fayette Co., PA
Death: Jul. 29, 1923 - Fayette Co., PA

Son of Levi Christner and Catherine (Younkin) Christner.

Spouse: Phoebe Ncholson Christner (1835 - 1921)

Children: Bertha May Christner Newell (1870 - 1932)

Burial: Mount Olive Cemetery, Connellsville, Fayette Co., PA
Find A Grave Memorial# 114025892

More About Elias Christner:
Burial: 31 Jul 1923, Mt. Olive Cemetery Connellsville Fayette Co. PA.[1214,1215,1216]
Census: 04 Jun 1870, Pennsville, Bullskin Twp., Fayette Co., PA[1216,1217,1218]
Occupation: 20 Apr 1910, farmer on a general farm/[1219,1220,1221]
Residence: 1900, Bullskin Twp., Fayette Co., PA[1222]

Notes for Phoebe Nicholson:
Pheobe Nicholson (daughter of William Nicholson) about 1869. Pheobe Nicholson was born on January 9, 1853 in PA. She appeared on the census on June 4, 1870 in Pennsville, Bullskin Township, Fayette, PA. She appeared on the census in 1880 in Bullskin Twp, Fayette, PA. She appeared on the census on June 21, 1900 in Bullskin Twp, Fayette, PA. She appeared on the census on April 20, 1910 in Bullskin Twp, Fayette, PA. She appeared on the census on January 21, 1920 in Bullskin Twp, Fayette, PA. She spelled her name (or some one did) Febie on the 1920 census. She died on March 27, 1921 in Bullskin Twp, Fayette, PA. She was buried on March 29, 1921 in Mt. Olive Cemetery, Connellsville, Fayette Co, PA.

Birth: Jan. 9, 1835 - PA
Death: Mar. 27, 1921 - Fayette Co., PA

Phoebe was the daughter of William Nicholson. She died in Bullskin Twp. Burial was on March 29, 1921.

Spouse: Elias Christner (1844 - 1923)

Children: Bertha May Christner Newell (1870 - 1932)

Inscription: Wife of E. Christner

Burial: Mount Olive Cemetery, Connellsville, Fayette Co., PA
Find A Grave Memorial# 86401941

More About Phoebe Nicholson:
Burial: 29 Mar 1921, Mt. Olive Cemetery, Connellsville, Fayette Co., PA[1223]
Census: 04 Jun 1870, Pennsville, Bullskin Twp., Fayette Co., PA[1223,1224,1225]

Children of Elias Christner and Phoebe Nicholson are:
+   643   i.   Bertha May[7] Christner, born 25 Feb 1870 in Bullskin Twp., Fayette Co., PA; died 02 Apr 1932 in BullskinTwp., Fayette Co., PA.
+   644   ii.   Braden Hurst Christner, born 01 Jun 1873 in Connellsville, Fayette Co., PA; died Dec 1936.

      165. Charles[6] Christner (Levi[5], Peter[4], Johannes John Hans[3], Christian[2], Christen[1])[1226,1227,1228,1228,1229,1230,1231,1232,1233,1234,1235,1236] was born Sep 1845 in Springfield, Fayette Co., PA[1237,1238,1239,1239,1240], and died 28 Jul 1931 in Mt. Pleasant, Westmoreland Co., PA[1241,1242,1243,1244]. He married **Sarah Jane Glenn**[1245,1246,1247,1248,1249,1250,1251] 1869[1252,1252,1253]. She was born 25 Mar 1850 in Connellsville, Fayette Co., PA[1254,1255,1256,1257,1258], and died 17 Oct 1933 in Connellsville, Fayette Co., PA[1259,1260,1261,1262,1263,1264].

Notes for Charles Christner:
It is important to note that the family believed that Walter had been beaten to death by the Police in Mt. Pleasant. Apparently his body was in very bad shape when they saw him afterwards. Walter could be mean and arrogant and liked to fight according to my grandfather. Nobody ever took him to be depressed. My grandfather had a disdain for law enforcement until the day he died. It's pretty amazing that his son and two of his grandkids would go on to be high ranking members of Law Enforcement agencies. Pap didn't agree with our career choice, but loved us anyway. Shows what kind of man Charles Christner Sr. was!

Charles worked at the coke ovens in the area and owned a farm in Prittstown, PA.
Information provide by Chris Christner.

More About Charles Christner:
Residence: 1930, Mt. Pleasant, Westmoreland Co., PA[1265]

More About Sarah Jane Glenn:
Burial: Redstone Cemetery, Brownsville, Fayette Co., PA[1266]
Residence: 1920, East Huntingdon, Westmoreland Co., PA[1267]

Children of Charles Christner and Sarah Glenn are:
     645   i.   Elmer E.[7] Christner[1268,1269,1269], born 1868 in Fayette Co., PA[1269,1269,1270].

                   Notes for Elmer E. Christner:
                   1920 Census has Elmer still living with Parents at 52 years old.

                   More About Elmer E. Christner:
                   Residence: 1920, East Huntingdon, Westmoreland Co., PA[1270]

+   646   ii.   Martha (Mattie) Christner, born 01 Nov 1869 in Prittstown, Fayette Co., PA; died 30 Jun 1952 in Prittstown, Fayette Co., PA.
+   647   iii.   Corriabell "Cora B" Christner, born Nov 1872 in Connellsville, Fayette Co., PA; died Bet. 1930 - 1940.
+   648   iv.   Elizabeth Christner, born Jan 1876 in Fayette Co., PA.
     649   v.   William H. Christner[1271,1271], born 1877 in Connellsville, Fayette Co., PA[1271,1271].

More About William H. Christner:
Residence: 1880, Upper Tyrone, Fayette Co., PA[1271,1271]

650   vi.   Maggie L. Christner[1271,1271], born 1879 in Connellsville, Fayette Co., PA[1271,1271].

More About Maggie L. Christner:
Residence: 1880, Upper Tyrone, Fayette Co., PA[1271,1271]

651   vii.   Levi Christner[1271,1271], born 1880 in Connellsville, Fayette Co., PA[1271,1271].

More About Levi Christner:
Residence: 1880, Upper Tyrone, Fayette Co., PA[1271,1271]

+ 652   viii.   Gertrude Christner, born Aug 1882 in Saltlick Twp., Fayette Co., PA; died Jun 1934 in Ligonier, Westmoreland Co., PA.

+ 653   ix.   Walter Joseph Christner, born 21 Jun 1885 in Prittstown, Fayette Co., PA; died 01 Apr 1934 in Mt Pleasant, Westmoreland Co., PA.

+ 654   x.   George Washington Christner, born 28 Jan 1887 in Prittstown, Fayette Co., PA; died 15 Dec 1948 in Hammondville, PA.

655   xi.   Sadie Christner[1271], born Jan 1894 in Saltlick Twp., Fayette Co., PA[1271].

168. Rufus[6] Christner (Levi[5], Peter[4], Johannes John Hans[3], Christian[2], Christen[1])[1272,1273,1274,1275] was born Feb 1851 in Springfield, Fayette Co., PA[1276], and died 18 Sep 1925 in Davistown, Fayette Co., PA[1277]. He married **Luteria Cease**[1278]. She was born Apr 1845 in Fayette Co., PA[1278,1279], and died 30 Sep 1914[1280,1281].

Notes for Rufus Christner:
1880 census Summit Twp., Somerset Co., PA on the farm of Earl Christner Southwest of the buildings about 50 rods on the hill above a spring along road leading from Garrett to Cross Roads Church is a cemetery. There is a stone marked Franklin Christner born Jan 8, 1878 Aged 6 MO Son of Rufus.

Birth: 1851
Death: 1925

Burial: Mount Olive Cemetery, Connellsville, Fayette Co., PA
Find A Grave Memorial# 91658725

Also Christian Christner died 10 1888 aged 77-3--17
Abraham Christner died March 4, 1879 71--5--4
Jonas Christner died Jan 26, 1881 67--4---12

The Daily Courier - Connellsville, PA
18 Sep 1925
Rufus Christner Ends Life with Bullet at Davistown; Had Been in Poor Health Act Committed in Bathroom While Daughter is at Work in Garden.

Rufus Christner, 73 years old, a farmer of Davistown in the Indian Creek Valley, yesterday afternoon, killed himself in the bathroom of his home. While his daughter was outside in the garden, he secured a flobert rifle and going to the bathroom placed it against his right temple and pulled the trigger. He had been in ill health for several years.

The bullet entered his brain and caused instant death. Coroner S. A. Baliz and County Detective A. W. Bell viewed the body.

Mr. Christner was a widower, his wife having died a number of year ago. He is survived by the following sons and daughters, william, Edward, and Miss Hattie, all of Indian Head; Mrs. S. B. Howard of Milcroft, Mrs. J. B. Brown of Mount Pleasant; and Solomon Christner of Scottdale.

The funeral service will be held Sunday morning at 9 o'clock at the home and later at the Mount Olive Church od

Pennsville. Interment will be made in the church cemetery in charge of funeral Director C. B. Brooks of Indian Head.

More About Rufus Christner:
Census: 07 Jun 1880, Bullskin Twp., Fayette Co., PA[1281]
Occupation: 07 Jun 1880, farm laborer/[1281]
Residence: 1910, Saltlick Twp., Fayette Co., PA[1282]

Notes for Luteria Cease:
1880 census has Luteria sister living with them Hattie Cease born 1862.

Birth: 1845
Death: 1919

Burial: Mount Olive Cemetery, Connellsville, Fayette Co., PA
Find A Grave Memorial# 91658744

More About Luteria Cease:
Census: 07 Jun 1880, Bullskin Twp., Fayette Co., PA[1283]
Residence: 1900, Saltlick Twp., Fayette Co., PA[1284]

Children of Rufus Christner and Luteria Cease are:

656   i.   Solomon[7] Christner.

657   ii.   Burton Christner[1285], born Abt. 1871 in Connellsville, Fayette Co., PA[1285]; died 18 Feb 1883.

    Notes for Burton Christner:
    Birth:
    Death: Feb. 18, 1883

    Inscription: Aged 11 years 9 mon's & 26 days

    Burial: Mount Olive Cemetery, Connellsville, Fayette Co., PA
    Find A Grave Memorial# 89594763

    More About Burton Christner:
    Residence: 1880, Bullskin Twp., Fayette Co., PA[1285]

+   658   iii.   William S. Christner, born 1873; died 1973.

659   iv.   Lucy Ann Christner, born 1875.

660   v.   Edgar Haze Christner[1286,1287,1288], born 02 Nov 1876 in PA[1289,1290,1291].

    More About Edgar Haze Christner:
    Census: 07 Jun 1880, Bullskin Twp., Fayette Co., PA[1292]
    Residence: 1900, Saltlick, Fayette, PA[1293]

661   vi.   Edith Mable Christner, born 1878.

662   vii.   Harriet Christner[1294,1295], born Jul 1884 in Connellsville, Fayette Co., PA[1296,1297]; died 04 Mar 1931 in Connellsville, Fayette Co., PA.

    Notes for Harriet Christner:
    Obituary: The Daily Courier - Connellsville, PA - 4 March 1931

    MISS HATTIE CHRISTNER DIES FOLLOWING STROKE
    Special to The Courier
    Mount Pleasant, March 4 - Miss Hattie Christner, 47 years old, died this morning at 9:30 o'clock at the home of her Aunt Mrs. John Brown in North Church Street, following a stroke of paralysis. Miss Christner a daughter of the late Ruus Christner of Indian Head, had been living at the home of Mr. and Mrs. William Christner of Indian Head. Two weeks ago she came to the Brown home on a visit a week ago she suffered a stroke.

More About Harriet Christner:
Residence: 1900, Saltlick Twp., Fayette Co., PA[1298,1299]

+   663   viii.   Charles F. Russell Christner, born 08 Sep 1887 in Pittsburgh, Allegheny Co., PA; died Dec 1918.

169. Elvina Belle[6] Christner (Levi[5], Peter[4], Johannes John Hans[3], Christian[2], Christen[1])[1300] was born 12 May 1862 in Springfield Twp., Fayette Co., PA[1300], and died 28 Nov 1956 in Akron, Summit Co., OH[1301]. She married **John W. Cramer**[1302,1303] 19 Oct 1882[1304]. He was born 25 Jun 1855 in Middlecreek Twp., Somerset Co., PA[1304,1305], and died 11 Jan 1922 in Dickerson Run, Fayette Co., PA[1305].

Notes for Elvina Belle Christner:
Birth: 1862
Death: 1956

Burial: Dickerson Run-Union Cemetery, Dickerson Run, Fayette Co., PA
Find A Grave Memorial# 54388016

More About Elvina Belle Christner:
Residence: 1920, Franklin, Fayette Co., PA[1306,1307]

Notes for John W. Cramer:
Birth: 1855
Death: 1922

Burial: Dickerson Run-Union Cemetery, Dickerson Run, Fayette Co., PA
Find A Grave Memorial# 54388335

More About John W. Cramer:
Residence: 1910, Franklin, Fayette Co., PA[1307,1308]

Children of Elvina Christner and John Cramer are:
664   i.   Charles Levi[7] Cramer[1309], born 12 Jun 1883 in Milford, Somerset Co., PA[1309]; died 03 Oct 1968 in Rockwood, Somerset Co., PA[1309].

         More About Charles Levi Cramer:
         Residence: 1930, Middlecreek, Somerset, PA[1309]

665   ii.   Georgia Hair Cramer[1309], born 26 Aug 1885 in Milford, Somerset Co., PA[1309]; died Oct 1986 in Tarentum, Allegheny Co., PA[1309].

         More About Georgia Hair Cramer:
         Residence: 1910, Fayette, PA[1309]

666   iii. Edgar H. Cramer[1309], born 30 Aug 1887 in Somerset Co., PA[1309]; died 06 Nov 1968 in Thompson No. 1/Republic, Fayette, PA, United States of America[1309].

         More About Edgar H. Cramer:
         Burial: Nov 1968, DICKERSON RUN CEMETERY/Fayette Co., PA[1309]
         Residence: 1930, Dunbar, Fayette, PA[1309]

667   iv.   Della Mae Cramer[1309], born Oct 1889 in Milford, Somerset Co., PA[1309]; died 10 Nov 1957 in Flatwoods, Fayette Co., PA[1309].

         More About Della Mae Cramer:
         Burial: 1957, Dickerson Run UNION CEMETERY[1309]
         Residence: 1930, Vanderbilt, Fayette Co., PA[1309]

+   668   v.   Elmer E. Cramer, born 27 May 1893 in Rockwood, Somerset Co., PA; died 09 Dec 1936 in Browntown, WV.
     669   vi.   Lucy E. Cramer[1309], born 17 May 1895 in Milford, Somerset Co., PA[1309]; died 16 Dec 1976 in East

Cleveland, Cuyahoga Co., OH[1309].

More About Lucy E. Cramer:
Residence: Cleveland Heights, Cuyahoga, Ohio, United States[1309]

670   vii.   Orpha M. Cramer[1309], born 03 Jun 1897 in Milford, Somerset Co., PA[1309]; died 23 Apr 1978 in Cleveland, Cuyahoga, Ohio, United States of America[1309].

More About Orpha M. Cramer:
Residence: South Euclid, Cuyahoga, Ohio, United States[1309]

671   viii.   Lydia Blanche Cramer[1309], born 09 Aug 1899 in Rockwood, Somerset Co., PA[1309]; died 04 May 1974 in Elyria, Lorain, Ohio[1309].

More About Lydia Blanche Cramer:
Residence: Lorain, Ohio, United States[1309]

672   ix.   Olive F. Cramer[1309], born 01 Jun 1902 in Franklin, Fayette Co., PA[1309]; died 20 Jul 1975 in Akron, Summit Co., OH[1309].

More About Olive F. Cramer:
Residence: Nov 1956, Evanston, Illinois[1309]

673   x.   Ruby M. Cramer[1309], born 01 Jun 1902 in Dickerson Run, Fayette Co., PA[1309]; died 22 Jan 1977 in Connellsville, Fayette Co., PA[1309].

More About Ruby M. Cramer:
Residence: 1910, Franklin, Fayette Co., PA[1309]

674   xi.   Gladys A. Cramer[1309], born 21 Sep 1906 in Dickerson Run, Fayette Co., PA[1309]; died 18 Nov 1971 in Barberton, Summit, Ohio, United States of America[1309].

More About Gladys A. Cramer:
Residence: Norton, Summit Co., OH[1309]

170. Rufus[6] Christner (Levi[5], Peter[4], Johannes John Hans[3], Christian[2], Christen[1])

Children of Rufus Christner are:
675   i.   Donald[7] Christner.
676   ii.   Erma Christner.
677   iii.   William Christner. He married Elsie Freeman.

172. Louvena[6] Christner (Levi[5], Peter[4], Johannes John Hans[3], Christian[2], Christen[1]) was born Jul 1844[1310]. She married **John Cramer**. He was born Aug 1834 in OH[1310].

Child of Louvena Christner and John Cramer is:
678   i.   Frank[7] Cramer[1310], born Jan 1875 in IL[1310].

173. Elijah H.[6] Christner (Levi[5], Peter[4], Johannes John Hans[3], Christian[2], Christen[1])[1311,1312,1313] was born 05 Jul 1856 in Springfield, Fayette Co., PA[1314], and died 05 Jul 1856 in Bullskin Twp., Fayette Co., PA[1314]. He married **Minerva Louverna Theakston**[1315,1315,1316]. She was born 28 Oct 1861 in Connellsville, Fayette Co., PA[1316,1317,1318,1318,1319], and died 18 Sep 1907 in Bullskin Twp., Fayette Co., PA[1320].

Notes for Elijah H. Christner:
Birth: 5 Jul 1856
Death: Jul. 5, 1856

Burial: Greenlick Cemetery, Fayette Co., PA
7 Children plus maybe 2 sets of twins

Buried with wife Minerva no death date on stone.

More About Elijah H. Christner:
Residence: 1880, Bullskin Twp., Fayette Co., PA[1320,1321,1321,1322]

Notes for Minerva Louverna Theakston:
Birth: Oct. 28, 1861
Death: Sep. 18, 1907

Burial: Greenlick Cemetery, Fayette Co., PA

More About Minerva Louverna Theakston:
Burial: Aft. 18 Sep 1907, Greenlick Cemetery/Bullskin Twp., Fayette Co., PA[1323,1324]
Residence: 1880, Bullskin Twp., Fayette Co., PA[1325,1326,1326,1327]

Children of Elijah Christner and Minerva Theakston are:

679   i.   Ned[7] Christner.

+ 680   ii.   Minnie L. Christner, born 01 May 1879 in Mt. Pleasant, Westmoreland Co., PA; died 05 Dec 1961 in Charleroi, PA.

+ 681   iii.   Mary Mae Christner, born Mar 1882 in Pittsburgh, Allegheny Co., PA; died 1962.

+ 682   iv.   Harry Cramer Christner, born 04 Mar 1882; died 19 Jul 1971 in Mt. Pleasant, Westmoreland Co., PA.

683   v.   Carl Christner[1328,1328,1329], born Aug 1888 in twin/Pittsburgh, Allegheny Co., PA[1330,1330,1331].

         More About Carl Christner:
         Residence: 1900, Bullskin Twp., Fayette Co., PA[1332,1333]

684   vi.   Carroll H. Christner, born 1889 in Scottdale, Westmoreland Co., PA. He married Emma Jane Boyer 05 Jan 1914 in Connellsville, Fayette Co., PA; born 1898.

         Notes for Carroll H. Christner:
         The Daily Courier - 12 Dec 1918 - Connellsville, Fayette Co., PA
         Divorce Notices
         E. D. Brown Attorney

         Emma J. Christner vs Carroll H. Christner in the Court of Common Pleas of Fayette Co., PA. No. 158 (unreadable) September Term. 1918

         To Caroll H. Christner Respondent

685   vii.   Gerald Christner[1334,1334,1335], born 17 Aug 1890 in Wooddale, Fayette Co., PA[1335].

         More About Gerald Christner:
         Residence: 1900, Bullskin, Fayette Co., PA[1336,1336]

686   viii.   Mable Christner[1336,1336], born Apr 1893 in Connellsville, Fayette Co., PA[1336,1336]. She married Howard Weight.

         More About Mable Christner:
         Residence: 1900, Bullskin, Fayette Co., PA[1336,1336]

182. George Deitz[6] Christner (Susan[5], David[4], Johannes John Hans[3], Christian[2], Christen[1]) was born 1840. He married **Mary**. She was born 03 Mar 1845, and died 21 Feb 1925 in Pittsburgh, Allegheny Co., PA.

Notes for George Deitz Christner:
1850 and 1860 census George is listed as mulatto. 1870 census he is listed as white. He must of been light enough to pass for white. 1850 he is George Deets, 1860 and 1870 he is George Christner. 1870 census lists wife Mary as white. George (a mulatto) is born George Deets or Deitz and why he has changed his name to his mothers name, Christner is unclear.

Notes for Mary:
Mary is listed as white in the 1870/80 census. We know George is a Mulatto.

She was buried as Mary Christner.

Child of George Christner and Mary is:
+   687   i.   Jacob "Deets/Deitz" R.[7] Christner, born 05 Oct 1863 in Trenton, Henry Co., IA; died 25 Sep 1933 in Henry Co., IA.

184. Elizabeth[6] Christner (David[5], David[4], Johannes John Hans[3], Christian[2], Christen[1]) was born 21 Mar 1830 in Somerset Co., PA. She married **Risher**.

Children of Elizabeth Christner and Risher are:
     688   i.   Joseph[7] McKelvey, born May 1854 in Connellsville, Fayette Co., PA; died 18 Apr 1905 in Jenner Twp., Somerset Co., PA. He married Mary C.
+   689   ii.   William Franklin Frank Risher, born 13 Dec 1856 in Connellsville, Fayette Co., PA; died 20 Dec 1943 in Johnstown, Cambria Co., PA.

185. Samuel[6] Christner (David[5], David[4], Johannes John Hans[3], Christian[2], Christen[1])[1337,1338] was born 11 Oct 1833 in Jenner Twp., Somerset Co., PA[1339,1340], and died 16 Mar 1918 in Somerset Co., PA[1341,1342]. He married **Barbara Miller**[1343] 18 Aug 1859 in No certificate, John Howard J.P.. She was born 26 Feb 1839 in Jenner Twp., Somerse Co., PA[1343], and died 25 Jan 1911 in Garrett, Somerset Co., PA.

Notes for Samuel Christner:
Civil war records of Samuel:
5 feet 9 inches tall 160 pounds black hair black eyes dark complexion. shot in the left hip at the battle of the Wilderness in Virginia. Samuel is a mulatto 1870 census, Samuel can't read or write.

Military records show birth Dec 14 1833 - Death Feb. 16, 1918. Some say birth at October 11, 1833. Death certificate does not add up correctly. Died from Carcinoma of the Face. Loss of right eye, rheumatism and hearing.

Enlisted 3/17/1864 mustered out 7/15/1865 as a private Company C PA. Volunteers   54th Regiment Infantry Length of service l year 3 months 29 days.

Birth: Oct. 11, 1833
Death: Mar. 16, 1918
Somerset Co., PA

Veteran 1861-1865

Spouse: Barbara Miller Christner (1839 - 1911)

Children: John Christner (1866 - 1932)

Burial: Jenners Baptist Church Cemetery, Jenners, Somerset Co., PA
Find A Grave Memorial# 65739403

More About Samuel Christner:
Burial: Baptist Church Cemetery, Jenner Twp, 1 mile Northwest of Boswell, PA
Cause of Death: Carcinoma of the Face
Residence: 1900, Jenner Township (East Part), Somerset Co., PA[1343]

Notes for Barbara Miller:
Barbara is the daughter of Soloman Miller and Annie Thomas Miller

Soloman born Nov 30, 1797 and died June 11, 1869 buried Jeremiah Miller Cemetery, Conemaugh Twp., PA. Annie born Oct 11, 1809 and died Sept 15, 1881 buried same as Soloman. Robert W. Shaffer states her tombstone has Barbria on it.

Birth: Feb. 26, 1839
Death: Jan. 25, 1911 - Somerset Co., PA

Parents: Solomon G. Miller (1797 - 1869)

Spouse: Samuel Christner (1833 - 1918)

Children: John Christner (1866 - 1932)

Burial: Jenners Baptist Church Cemetery, Jenners, Somerset Co., PA
Find A Grave Memorial# 65739444

More About Barbara Miller:
Burial: Baptist Church, Boswell, Jenner Twp, PA
Residence: 1900, Jenner Township (East Part), Somerset Co., PA[1343]

Children of Samuel Christner and Barbara Miller are:

690	i.	Levi[7] Christner, born 1859 in Somerset Co., PA; died 1898 in before.
691	ii.	Mary Polly Christner, born 1861 in Somerset Co., PA; died 03 Nov 1882.
692	iii.	Susan Christner, born 24 Jun 1862 in Somerset Co., PA; died 17 Apr 1897 in Somerset Co., PA.

Notes for Susan Christner:
CHRISTNER - On the 17th of April 1897 in Somerset Co., PA Susan, daughter of Samuel and Barbara Christner, aged 34 years, 9 months and 24 days. She was buried on the 19th at the Baptist church. Funeral services by Samuel Zimmerman and Levi A. Blough. Her tombstone states birth as 1856, Census 1864, I think they are both wrong. Steven Carl Christner.

More About Susan Christner:
Burial: 19 Apr 1897, Baptist Church

+ 693	iv.	John Christner, born 05 Apr 1868 in Jenner Twp., Somerset Co., PA; died 1932 in Conner, Jenner Twp., Somerset Co., , PA.
694	v.	Lydia Christner, born 08 Apr 1868 in Somerset Co., PA.
695	vi.	Catherine Christner, born 18 Apr 1870 in Somerset Co., PA.

Notes for Catherine Christner:
Catherine's father is a mulatto and her mother is white, but the children are listed as mulatto 1870 census.

+ 696	vii.	Jesse Christner, born 10 Jan 1872 in Jenner, Somerset Co., PA; died 25 Jun 1941 in Johnstown, Cambria Co., PA.
697	viii.	Fannie Christner, born 07 Mar 1874 in Somerset Co., PA; died 30 Mar 1961. She married Irvin C. Shaffer 01 Feb 1892.
698	ix.	Lizzie Christner, born 14 Mar 1876 in Somerset Co., PA.
699	x.	Franklin Christner, born 08 Jan 1878; died Jun 1878.

Notes for Franklin Christner:
On his tombstone it says son of Rufus.

More About Franklin Christner:
Burial: Christner Cemetery Top of the Hill   Earl Christner Farm

700	xi.	Franklin Christner, born 24 Jan 1879 in Somerset Co., PA.
+ 701	xii.	David Christner, born 30 Dec 1883 in Somerset Co., PA; died 1945.

186. Susanna Deitz[6] Christner (David[5], David[4], Johannes John Hans[3], Christian[2], Christen[1]) was born 13 Sep 1836 in Somerset Co., PA[1344], and died 19 Dec 1925 in Scottdale, Westmoreland Co., PA[1345]. She married **George Washington Lowry**. He was born 17 Apr 1840 in Middlecreek Twp. Somerset Co., PA[1346,1347], and died 27 Oct 1897 in Middlecreek Twp. Somerset. Co. Pa..

Notes for Susanna Deitz Christner:
1850 census she is Susan Deets and mulatto.
1860 census she is Susan Christner and mulatto.
1870 census she is not listed.

More About Susanna Deitz Christner:
Burial: Middle Church of the Brethern Middlecreek Twp. Somerset. Co. Pa.
Residence: 1850, Milford, Somerset Co., PA[1348]

Notes for George Washington Lowry:
He got $1.50 Relief Voucher on April 8, 1864 from the Somerset Co., PA Commissioners.

More About George Washington Lowry:
Burial: Middle Church of the Brethern Middlecreek Twp. Somerset. Co. Pa.
Residence: 1880, Springfield, Fayette Co., PA[1349]

Children of Susanna Christner and George Lowry are:

+ 702   i.   Louisa Ellen[7] Lowry, born 25 Dec 1860 in Somerset Co., PA; died 11 Mar 1954 in Somerset Co., PA.
+ 703   ii.   Albert W. Lowry, born 03 Mar 1862 in Somerset Co., PA.
   704   iii.   Arthur Franklin Lowry, born 03 Sep 1865 in Middle Creek Twp., Somerset Co., PA; died 09 Feb 1866 in Middle Creek Twp., Somerset Co., PA.
+ 705   iv.   Amos Herbert Lowry, born 07 Nov 1866 in Middle Creek Twp., Somerset Co., PA; died in PA.
+ 706   v.   Cora Estelle Lowry, born 31 Dec 1870 in Somerset Co., PA; died 06 Sep 1937 in Aspenwall, PA..
+ 707   vi.   Ida Mae Lowry, born 31 Dec 1870 in Somerset Co., PA; died 1899 in Somerset Co., PA.
+ 708   vii.   Anna B. Lowry, born 15 Aug 1872 in Somerset Co., PA; died 16 Mar 1950.
   709   viii.   Maggie Lowry, born 16 Jul 1874 in Somerset Co., PA; died 01 May 1875 in Middle Creek Twp., Somerset Co., PA.
+ 710   ix.   John E. Lowry, born 06 Feb 1876 in Somerset Co., PA; died 06 Feb 1961 in Milford Twp., Somerset Co., PA.
   711   x.   William Prosper Lowry, born 02 Jun 1878 in Middle Creek Twp., Somerset Co., PA; died 02 Apr 1893 in Middle Creek Twp., Somerset Co., PA.

190. David[6] Christner (Jessie[5], David[4], Johannes John Hans[3], Christian[2], Christen[1])[1350] was born May 1841 in Connellsville, Fayette Co., PA[1351], and died 11 Feb 1918 in Elkhart Co., IN[1352]. He married **(1) Elizabeth Brumbaugh**[1353]. She was born May 1841 in Connellsville, Fayette Co., PA[1353], and died 23 Apr 1903 in Goshen, Elkhart Co., IN[1353]. He married **(2) Jane Snyder**[1353] 21 Jun 1882 in Goshen, Elkhart Co., IN[1353]. She was born Dec 1861 in IN[1353], and died 1929 in Goshen, Elkhart Co., IN[1353].

Notes for David Christner:
1850 census David is listed as malatto. He can read and write

More About David Christner:
Residence: 1917, Rt. 5, Goshen, IN[1353]

More About Elizabeth Brumbaugh:
Residence: 1900, Elkhart Township (Excl. Goshen City), Elkhart, Indiana[1353]

More About Jane Snyder:
Residence: 1920, Goshen Ward 1, Elkhart, Indiana[1353]

Child of David Christner and Elizabeth Brumbaugh is:
   712   i.   William[7] Christner[1353], born Jul 1872 in Goshen, Elkhart Co., IN[1353].

More About William Christner:
Residence: 1930, Elkhart, Elkhart Co., IN[1353]

191. John[6] Christner (Jessie[5], David[4], Johannes John Hans[3], Christian[2], Christen[1])[1354,1355,1356] was born 10 Apr 1842 in Somerset Co., PA[1357], and died 26 Jan 1928 in Waterford, IN[1357]. He married **Susan Mary Malissa Wogoman** 16 Nov 1871 in Goshen, Elkhart Co., IN[1358]. She was born 13 Sep 1852 in Elkhart Co., IN, and died 20 Aug 1889 in Goshen, Elkhart Co., IN[1359].

Notes for John Christner:
1850 census John is listed as mulatto. He can read and write. 1900 census said he can't. wwe have two & three year differences in birth dates in various census. I am going to use the information in the family bible but it is not a proven fact.some say he was born April 10 1845. He built his own house south of Violet Cemetery in Waterford Mills (Goshen, IN). On a Indian camp ground 300 feet south of County Road 40   N41°32.55 x W85° 50.115

More About John Christner:
Burial: 28 Jan 1928, Saturday at Violett Cem. Goshen IN N41°.32.857xW85°50.122
Description: 5'3", dark complexion, auburn hair, hazel eyes/[1360,1361]
Military service: 74th Indiana Volunteers General Sherman Civil War/
Residence: 1910, Elkhart, Elkhart Co., IN[1362]

More About Susan Mary Malissa Wogoman:
Residence: 1880, Elkhart, Elkhart Co., IN[1363,1364]

Children of John Christner and Susan Wogoman are:

713	i.	Rebecca Frances[7] Christner[1364], born 21 Jul 1872 in Goshen, Elkhart Co., IN[1364].

More About Rebecca Frances Christner:
Residence: 1880, Elkhart, Elkhart Co., IN[1364]

+ 714	ii.	Cora Alice Christner, born 23 Sep 1873 in Goshen, Elkhart Co., IN; died 18 Nov 1953 in Goshen, Elkhart Co., IN.
+ 715	iii.	Jesse Calvin Christner, born 02 Nov 1874 in Goshen, Elkhart Co., IN.
+ 716	iv.	Harry Christner, born 13 Sep 1876 in Goshen, Elkhart Co., IN; died 09 Aug 1964 in Waterford Mills, Goshen, Elkhart Co., IN.
717	v.	Jennie Christner[1364], born Aug 1878 in IN[1364].

More About Jennie Christner:
Residence: 1900, Elkhart Township (Excl. Goshen City), Elkhart, Indiana[1364]

| 718 | vi. | Mary Jane Christner[1364], born 25 Aug 1878 in Goshen, Elkhart Co., IN[1364]. |

More About Mary Jane Christner:
Residence: 1880, Elkhart, Elkhart Co., IN[1364]

| + 719 | vii. | Martha M. Christner, born 16 Oct 1879 in Goshen, Elkhart Co., IN. |
| 720 | viii. | Lilly May Christner, born 06 Apr 1881 in Goshen, Elkhart Co., IN[1364]. |

More About Lilly May Christner:
Residence: 1900, Elkhart Township (Excl. Goshen City), Elkhart, Indiana[1364]

| + 721 | ix. | Matilda Garnetta Christner, born 18 Apr 1884 in Goshen, Elkhart Co., IN. |
| 722 | x. | Emma Blanch Christner[1365,1366], born 22 Sep 1886 in Goshen, Elkhart Co., IN[1366]. She married Wines in Milford Indiana. |

More About Emma Blanch Christner:
Residence: 1900, Elkhart, Elkhart Co., IN[1367]

| + 723 | xi. | Mable Persilla Christner, born 18 Nov 1888 in Goshen, Elkhart Co., IN; died 16 Nov 1918. |

192. Harriet "Hattie"[6] Christner (Jessie[5], David[4], Johannes John Hans[3], Christian[2], Christen[1])[1368,1369,1370,1371] was born 02 Apr 1847 in Connellsville, Fayette Co., PA[1372], and died 29 Jun 1911 in Bloomington, Monroe Co., IN[1373,1374,1375]. She married **(1) John A. Whetstone**[1376] 27 Apr 1868 in Elkhart Co., IN[1376]. He was born 30 Aug 1829 in Schuylkill Co., PA[1376], and died 27 Feb 1889 in Norton, Norton Co., KS[1376]. She married **(2) John W. Leasa**[1376] 1890 in Elkhart Co., IN[1377,1378]. He was born Sep 1864 in VA[1379], and died Aft. 1920 in Boulder, Boulder Co., CO[1379,1380].

Notes for Harriet "Hattie" Christner:
1850 census Harriet is listed as malatto. She is age 1. Her picture does not show that she is part black.

More About Harriet "Hattie" Christner:
Residence: 1910, Hoyt, Morgan Co., CO[1381]

More About John A. Whetstone:
Residence: 1900, Townships 157-159-Ranges 66-68, Towner, ND[1382]

More About John W. Leasa:
Residence: 1910, Hoyt, Morgan Co., CO[1383]

Children of Harriet Christner and John Whetstone are:

724   i.   Benjamin Franklin[7] Whetstone[1384], born 06 Jun 1868 in St Joseph Co., IN[1384]; died 27 Feb 1943 in Green Mountain Cemetary/Boulder, Boulder Co., CO[1385]. He married Anna G; born 1868 in VA[1386]; died 24 Nov 1934 in Boulder, Boulder Co., CO[1386].

        Notes for Benjamin Franklin Whetstone:
        Birth: 1868
        Death: Feb. 27, 1943

        Burial: Green Mountain Cemetery, Boulder, Boulder Co., CO.
        Find A Grave Memorial# 11114671

        More About Benjamin Franklin Whetstone:
        Residence: 1880, Leota, Norton Co., KS[1387]

        More About Anna G:
        Burial: Boulder, Boulder Co., CO[1388]
        Residence: 1920, Spokane, Spokane, Washington[1389]

725   ii.   Samuel A Whetstone Whetstine[1390], born 31 Aug 1870 in St Joe, De Kalb Co., IN[1390,1391]; died 01 Mar 1947 in Longmont, Boulder Co., CO[1392].

        More About Samuel A Whetstone Whetstine:
        Residence: 1936, Longmont, Colorado[1393]

+ 726   iii.   Ellen Mary (Lesh) Kolkhorst Whetstone, born 06 Apr 1875 in IN; died 06 Apr 1962 in Longmont, Boulder Co., CO.

727   iv.   Fannie (Thornburg) Whetstone Whetstine[1394], born 09 Aug 1882 in Norton, Norton Co., KS[1394]; died 01 Sep 1944 in Longmont, Boulder Co., CO[1394].

        More About Fannie (Thornburg) Whetstone Whetstine:
        Residence: 1920, Anderson Ward 1, Madison, Indiana[1395]

728   v.   Edna Mae (Little) Whetstone Whetstine[1396], born 16 May 1884 in Norton, Kansas, United States[1396]; died 20 Feb 1959 in Greeley, Weld, Colorado, United States[1396].

        More About Edna Mae (Little) Whetstone Whetstine:
        Residence: 1930, Hoyt, Morgan Co., CO[1397]

729   vi.   George Whetstone Whetstine[1398], born 04 Sep 1886 in Norton, Norton Co., KS[1398]; died 19 Apr 1936 in

Longmont, Boulder Co., CO[1398].

More About George Whetstone Whetstine:
Residence: 1936, Longmont, Colorado[1399]

730 vii. Charles Whetstone Whetstine[1400], born 29 Jul 1888 in Norton, Norton Co., KS[1400]; died 13 Jun 1970 in Greeley, Weld, Colorado, United States of America[1400].

More About Charles Whetstone Whetstine:
Residence: 1910, Fort Collins Ward 4, Larimer, Colorado[1401]

Child of Harriet Christner and John Leasa is:
731 i. Amanda Pearl[7] Leasa[1402], born 22 Nov 1893 in Goshen, Elkhart Co., IN[1402]; died 10 Nov 1982 in Longmont, Boulder Co., CO[1402].

More About Amanda Pearl Leasa:
Residence: 1930, West Longmont, Boulder, Colorado[1402]

193. Lydia Lucinda[6] Christner (Abraham D.[5], Joseph "Zep"[4], Johannes John Hans[3], Christian[2], Christen[1])[1403] was born 15 Jan 1846 in Somerset Co., PA[1403], and died 16 Feb 1875 in PA. She married **John Koontz**. He was born 1841.

Notes for Lydia Lucinda Christner:
Birth: 15 Jan 1846
Death: Feb. 16, 1875

Inscription: aged 20Y 1M 1D

Burial: Maple Glen Church of the Brethren Cemetery, Somerset Co., PA

Amish and Amish Mennonite Genealogies;

Lydia or Lucinda not sure of the name married John Koontz. Records shows Lydia born 1845 and another record shows Lucinda born Jan 15, 1846 and died Feb 16, 1875. Lydia had a son Edward who also died 1875 and it may have been from child birth.

More About Lydia Lucinda Christner:
Burial: N39°46.230' BY W79°12.200'/Maple Glenn Cemetery, Elk Lick Twp., Somerset Co., PA

Child of Lydia Christner and John Koontz is:
732 i. Edward[7] Koontz, born 1875; died Feb 1875.

More About Edward Koontz:
Burial: PA, next to Lucinda

194. Mary[6] Christner (Abraham D.[5], Joseph "Zep"[4], Johannes John Hans[3], Christian[2], Christen[1])[1403] was born 1831 in Somerset Co., PA. She married **Adam Handwerk**.

Notes for Mary Christner:
Amish and Amish Mennonite Genealogies;

Notes for Adam Handwerk:
Susan daughter of Abraham and Mary Hoover Christner never married but she worked as a servant to Adam.

Amish and Amish Mennonite Genealogies, By Hugh F. Gingerich and Rachel W. Kreider, Pequea Publishers, Gordonville, PA 17529, 1986

Child of Mary Christner and Adam Handwerk is:

733   i.   Lydia[7] Handwerk. She married Jacob P. Kinsinger 09 Jan 1875.

Notes for Lydia Handwerk:
Lydia married Jacob P. Kinsinger Jan 9 1875

195. Julianna[6] Christner (Abraham D.[5], Joseph "Zep"[4], Johannes John Hans[3], Christian[2], Christen[1])[1404,1405] was born 08 Nov 1832 in Somerset Co., PA[1406]. She married **(1) Domer**. She married **(2) Peter Kesler**[1407]. He was born Abt. 1823 in PA[1407]. She married **(3) Daniel Lowry**. He was born 1827 in Summit Twp. Somerset Co., PA, and died 1887 in Garrett, Somerset Co., PA. She married **(4) Eichner** 07 Nov 1852.

Notes for Julianna Christner:
Julianna married a Domer and then Peter Kesler (Kessler) Peter born 1823.

More About Julianna Christner:
Residence: 1880, Summit Twp., Somerset Co., PA[1408]

More About Peter Kesler:
Race: White[1409]
Residence: 1880, Age: 57; Marital Status: Married; Relation to Head of House: Self/Summit, Somerset, Pennsylvania, United States[1409]

Notes for Daniel Lowry:
He divorced and married Tyrannus Christner later? His death Date maybe before 1880, like maybe 1877?

Children of Julianna Christner and Peter Kesler are:

734   i.   Catherine[7] Kessler, born 1849 in Northampton Twp., Somerset Co., PA.
735   ii.   Simon Kessler, born 1851 in Northampton Twp., Somerset Co., PA.
736   iii.   Elizabeth Kessler, born 1853 in Northampton Twp., Somerset Co., PA.

Notes for Elizabeth Kessler:
1860 census has her listed as insane.

737   iv.   Deliah Kessler, born 1855 in Northampton Twp., Somerset Co., PA.
738   v.   Sarah Kessler, born 1857 in Northampton Twp., Somerset Co., PA.
739   vi.   Wesley Kessler, born 1859 in Northampton Twp., Somerset Co., PA.

More About Wesley Kessler:
Residence: 1880, Summit Twp., Somerset Co., PA[1410]

740   vii.   Emaline Emma Kessler, born 1867 in Northampton Twp., Somerset Co., PA.

More About Emaline Emma Kessler:
Residence: 1880, Summit Twp., Somerset Co., PA[1410]

741   viii.   Lydia E. Kessler, born 1869 in Northampton Twp., Somerset Co., PA.

More About Lydia E. Kessler:
Residence: 1880, Summit Twp., Somerset Co., PA[1410]

742   ix.   Herman Kessler, born 1871 in Northampton Twp., Somerset Co., PA.

More About Herman Kessler:
Residence: 1880, Summit Twp., Somerset Co., PA[1410]

196. Tyrannus[6] Christner (Abraham D.[5], Joseph "Zep"[4], Johannes John Hans[3], Christian[2], Christen[1])[1411] was born 12 May 1834 in Somerset Co., PA[1411], and died 18 Oct 1905. She married **(1) Conrad Eicher** 07 Nov 1852. She married **(2) Daniel Lowry** 1859 in Summett PA. He was born 1827 in Summit Twp. Somerset Co., PA, and died 1887 in Garrett, Somerset Co., PA.

Notes for Tyrannus Christner:
Tyrannus//Toranacy/Tryann - Ed Surkosky Found this for me in August 2003. I was at the center on Thurs. I found Tyrannus Christner Lowry Eichnor's Estate Papers (93 pgs.). She died btwn. 4 and 5 p.m., October 18, 1905. Her heirs are listed as J. H. Lowry, Garrett, PA; Jennie Weaver, Garrett, PA; Julia Domer, Meyersdale, PA; Polly Baer, Meyersdale, PA; Samuel Lowry, Meyersdale, PA; Susan M. Benny, Pittsburg, PA; Sadie Goe, Franklin, PA and A. J. Lowry, Garrett, PA.

Tyrannus ran a small grocery store in Garrett until she had a house built around 1893. She then took in boarders. Apparently Allen J. Lowry helped build the house. Her estate sold the house for $ 3,505.+.

A. J. Lowry presented notes purportedly signed by Tyrannus for $ 500 and $ 1500 and wanted paid. The heir protested that with existing debts of his mother that would exhaust the estate. Everything dragged on until a hearing was held on October 31, 1907 before Harvey Berkley at Somerset. 18 pgs. of testimony were taken. The witnesses were 1. Polly Baer (daughter); 2. Mrs. Husband (niece); 3. Mrs. Annie Smith (sister); 4. Mahlon Christner (nephew); 5. Lewis Christner (nephew); 6. Squire A. J. McKenzie; 7. Jonathan P. Growall (lumber dealer); 8. Francis Christner (nephew); 9. F. E. Judy (general Merchandise); 10. S. P. Burkholder (laborer), and 11. Albert Christner (nephew).

Allen was strongly supported by his sister Mrs. Goe, and she pressured Susan Benney. The heirs finally agreed to pay him $ 1500. From what I saw he apparently spent some money on the house and additional expenses. The land the house was built on was his mothers. He lived with his mother off and on over the years. It was believed that the mother's signature was forged on the two notes. It sounded like he tried to recover some expenses and presented the notes which he may have fabricated to justify his case. Anyway he got 1500.

All the rest of the heirs, including him, got what as left $101.96 and 1/4 cents!

This was found the following at Somerset:
Eichnor, Conrad, #61 - 1886; Eichnor, George, #43 - 1882; Eichnor, Tyrannus, #67 - 1905. I looked up Tyrannus and found 93 pages,18 of which were testimony at a hearing, 2 1/2 pgs. of testimony by my great-grandmother, Pollie Baer and confirmed her 8 heir as being all children of her and Daniel Lowry.

I decided to check out George and Conrad. George's was about 6 pgs. and it included a page of his wife's renunciation of the estate. Her name was Julian Eichnor. Then I went to Conrad's. Disappointment. His estate papers are missing and were never microfilmed. About an hour later one of the volunteers suggested that I look in the Orphan's Court Records.

"Estate of Conrad Eichnor, Dec.". This is just a financial accounting, But the first paragraph opens "First and Final Account of Tyrannus Eichnor Admst. of Conrad Eichnor dec. and Trustee for the sale of his real estate. Accountant charges herself with amt. of App. filed 6 Jany. 1886.......Amt. realized fr. sale of lots Nos. 257 & 258 sold to J.M. Olinger being in one enclosure ---- 300.00.........Accountant claims credit for the following payments & Amt. taken by Widow and set apart for her out of lot 257 & 258 ---- $ 300.00." I conclude that the Admst., Accountant, and Widow are one and the same ---- Tyrannus Christner Lowry Eichnor ? What do you think? The Hostetler Book, pub. 1912, has Barbara Hostetler Baer, # 65, dated at born 1830 and died 1894. This is in error. She was born in 1840 and died 1904. I have verified this from her Civil War Pension papers, obituary and her tombstone. The book goes on to list her husband and children. Her son, William H. was married to " Polly (sic) Lowery, dau. of Daniel Lowery who d. in 1887, at Garrett, PA and Tyrannus Christner, who died in 1905.", pg. 81. The 1870 census lists Daniel (head of house)and Tyrannus and their children. The 1880 census lists Tyrannus (head of house) and her children. The box that designates widowed or divorced are the same and it was checked. The disc was digital could not make out which was designated. So Tyrannus was married a second time in the 1880's.

The Hostetler book said Daniel died in 1887 and I cannot find any burial record. He must not have had a

113

tombstone. When putting Orphan's Court film back, I saw the 1880 census. So I thought I would check out the film which may have better resolution. It did. The widowed/divorced box captions were quite clear - widowed = / and divorced = D. The box was checked! Therefore Daniel Lowry/Lowery died before 1880. The listing in the Hostetler book is in error and could be 1877? It would fit. Now the only thing left is to confirm when Daniel died and where he is buried and when Tyrannus married Conrad. It took me years to find the aforementioned facts. I hope it doesn't as long to find out the marriage death dates.   Ed Surkosky

More About Tyrannus Christner:
Burial: Union Cemetery Meyersdale PA.

Notes for Conrad Eicher:
His name maybe spelled Eichnor, but have not found a grave for him.

Notes for Daniel Lowry:
He divorced and married Tyrannus Christner later? His death Date maybe before 1880, like maybe 1877?

Children of Tyrannus Christner and Conrad Eicher are:
    743   i.   Julian[7] Lowry, born 1854.

             Notes for Julian Lowry:
             These children never used the name of Eichner

    744   ii. Susan Lowry, born 1857.

             Notes for Susan Lowry:
             These children never used the name of Eichner

+   745   iii. Jonas Henry Lowry, born 1858; died 1919.

Children of Tyrannus Christner and Daniel Lowry are:
    746   i.   Julia Ann[7] Lowrey, born 1854.
    747   ii. Susan Lowrey, born 1856.
    748   iii. Jonas Lowrey, born 1857.
+   749   iv. Mary "Pollie" Lowry, born 1860 in Somerset Co., PA; died 1931.
    750   v.   Mary Pollie Lowry, born 1860 in Somerset Co., PA; died 1931. She married William Henry Baer 06 Dec 1885; born 18 Sep 1863 in Meyersdale, Somerset Co., PA; died 1947.

             Notes for Mary Pollie Lowry:
             Pollie married William Henry Baer Dec 6 1885
             She didn't like her name (Mary) so she changed it to Pollie

             More About Mary Pollie Lowry:
             Burial: Union Cemetery Meyersdale PA.

             More About William Henry Baer:
             Burial: Union Cemetery Meyersdale PA.

    751   vi. Samuel Lowery, born 1862 in Somerset Co., PA.
    752   vii. Elizabeth S. C. Lowery, born 1864 in Somerset Co., PA.
    753   viii. Annie M. Lowery, born 1865 in Somerset Co., PA; died 1883.

             Notes for Annie M. Lowery:
             Large stone buried with her mother Tyrannus Christner Eichner 1834 - 1905.

             More About Annie M. Lowery:
             Burial: Union Cemetery Meyersdale PA.

    754   ix. John A.B. Lowery, born Nov 1869 in Somerset Co., PA.

198. Herman[6] Christner (Abraham D.[5], Joseph "Zep"[4], Johannes John Hans[3], Christian[2], Christen[1])[1411,1412,1413,1414,1415] was born 23 Dec 1836 in Summit Twp., Somerset Co., PA[1415,1416,1417,1418,1419], and died 23 Mar 1898 in Summit Twp., Somerset Co., PA[1419,1420,1421]. He married **(1) Susanna Ringer**[1422,1423,1424]. She was born 30 Nov 1834 in Black Twp., Somerset Co., PA[1425,1426], and died 05 Nov 1897 in Garrett, Somerset Co., PA[1427]. He married **(2) Sadie Mary White**.

Notes for Herman Christner:
Birth: 23 Dec 1836
Death: Mar. 23, 1898

Burial: Center Lutheran Church Cemetery, Summit Twp., Somerset Co., PA

Harmon or Herman - This info is a combination of things from Robert C. Christner, Tom Christner R.R.#1 Garrett Connie Yokum and Laura Pauletick. All agree that Harmon/Herman 1st son Lewis had a mother named Sadie Mary White. There seems to be no other record for Sadie. Harmons youngest son Francis told his son Robert C. that he had a sister Annie who died in infancy. She is buried right beside the road about 400 feet from the Allen Decker house on the right side of the road as you come towards Garrett. There were native stones and lilies to mark the graves, but the road has been widened and it is now gone. There is no dates for Annie so we don't know where she fits in among the children.
Harmon or Herman committed suicide by cutting his throat. He was very despondent about the death of his wife.

More About Herman Christner:
Burial: Center Lutheran Church Cemetery, Summit Township, Somerset Co., PA
Residence: 1880, Summit Twp., Somerset Co., PA[1428]

Notes for Susanna Ringer:
Birth: 30 Nov 1834
Death: Nov. 5, 1897

Inscription: w/o of H.

Burial: Center Lutheran Church Cemetery, Summit Twp., Somerset Co., PA

More About Susanna Ringer:
Burial: Center Church, Union, Pa. or Pleasent Hill, Cem, Somerset Co, PA
Residence: 1880, Summit Twp., Somerset Co., PA[1429,1430,1431]

Children of Herman Christner and Susanna Ringer are:
755   i.   Annie[7] Christner.

                Notes for Annie Christner:
                Annie died in infancy and there is no dates available. Her death and burial is recorded in the notes of Harmon her father.

756   ii.   Clarissa Christner, born 14 Sep 1861 in Summit Twp., Somerset Co., PA[1431]; died 10 Feb 1941. She married William Martin 14 Sep 1890 in Stonycreek.

                More About Clarissa Christner:
                Residence: 1880, Summit Twp., Somerset Co., PA[1431]

                Notes for William Martin:
                Maybe son of John H. & Mary.

757   iii. Ellen Mary Christner[1431], born 17 Sep 1862 in Summit Twp., Somerset Co., PA[1431]; died 1937 in Berlin, Somerset Co., PA. She married (1) William Morgan; born Abt. 1860 in Pittsburgh, Allegheny Co., PA[1432]. She married (2) Silas Sylvester Lane 22 May 1886 in Garrett, Somerset Co., PA maybe March 22 1886; born 1851; died 1907.

More About Ellen Mary Christner:
Burial: Berlin, Somerset Co., PA
Race: White/[1432]
Residence: 1880, Summit Twp., Somerset Co., PA[1433]

More About William Morgan:
Race: White/[1434]
Residence: 1930, Age: 70; Marital Status: Married; Relation to Head of House: Head/Garrett, Summit Twp., Somerset Co., PA[1434]

Notes for Silas Sylvester Lane:
Silas is the son of Jacob and Mary_____Lane. His first wife died August 13, 1883.

He was a harness Maker of Berlin Borough, PA.

More About Silas Sylvester Lane:
Residence: Garrett, Somerset Co., PA

+   758   iv.   Mahlon Christner, born 15 Sep 1865 in Summit Twp., Somerset Co., PA; died 24 Apr 1932 in Summit Garret Somerset Co., PA.
+   759   v.   Amanda Christner, born 13 Oct 1867 in Garrett, Summit Twp., Somerset Co., PA; died 28 Mar 1932 in Somerset, Somerset Co., PA.
+   760   vi.   Albert Paul. Christner Sr., born 20 Jan 1870 in Summit Twp. Somerset PA; died Jul 1952 in Garrett, Somerset Co., PA.
+   761   vii. William H. Christner, born 21 Jun 1874 in Summit Twp., Somerset Co., PA; died 31 Mar 1930 in Flint, Genesee Co., MI.
+   762   viii. Sadie Christner, born 16 Apr 1876 in Summit Twp., Somerset Co., PA; died 06 May 1955 in Cumberland, Allegany Co., MD.
+   763   ix.   Francis A. "Wash" Christner, born 24 Jan 1878 in Summit Twp., Somerset Co., PA; died 13 Jun 1928.

Child of Herman Christner and Sadie White is:
+   764   i.   Lewis[7] Christner, born 20 Aug 1860 in Elk Lick Twp., Somerset Co., PA; died 14 Dec 1941 in Garrett, Somerset Co., PA.

199. Susanna[6] Christner (Abraham D.[5], Joseph "Zep"[4], Johannes John Hans[3], Christian[2], Christen[1])[1435] was born 12 Nov 1838 in Somerset Co., PA[1435], and died 04 Mar 1926[1435]. She married **Urias Christner**[1436], son of John Christner and Susannah Griffith. He was born Mar 1831 in Somerset, Somerset Co., PA[1437], and died 03 Oct 1902 in Indian Head, Saltlick Twp., Fayette Co., PA[1437,1437].

Notes for Susanna Christner:
Susan never married. Susan worked most of her life for Bernard (Barney) Miller.
Susan may of also worked for Adam Handwerk.

More About Susanna Christner:
Burial: Miller Burial, Grounds
Residence: 1850, Elk Lick, Somerset, PA[1438]

Notes for Urias Christner:
Name: Pvt Uriah Christner
Birth Date: 1 Mar 1831
Age at Death: 71
Death Date: 3 Oct 1902
Burial Place: Fayette Co., PA

More About Urias Christner:
Residence: Jun 1880, Saltlick Twp., Fayette Co., PA[1439,1440]

Children are listed above under (152) Urias Christner.

201. Freeman L.[6] **Christner** (Abraham D.[5], Joseph "Zep"[4], Johannes John Hans[3], Christian[2], Christen[1]) was born 29 Dec 1842 in Somerset Co., PA. He married **(1) Louisa Pleiffer Pifer**. He married **(2) Mary Snyder**.

Notes for Freeman L. Christner:
Freeman froze to death. He may have had a son Eli Christner who froze to death. Inquest at house of Freeman Christner of Jenner Twp. PA. on March 18, 1876.

Children of Freeman Christner and Louisa Pifer are:
+   765   i.   William[7] Christner, born Feb 1869 in Somerset Co., PA.
+   766   ii.   Hiram P. "Hiry" Christner, born May 1870 in Connellsville, Fayette Co., PA.

202. Henry A.[6] **Christner** (Abraham D.[5], Joseph "Zep"[4], Johannes John Hans[3], Christian[2], Christen[1])[1441] was born 30 Dec 1842 in Somerset Co., PA[1441,1442], and died 09 Nov 1914 in Salisbury, Somerset Co., PA[1442,1442]. He married **(1) Sarah**. She was born 15 Dec 1842[1442], and died 09 Nov 1914 in Somerset Co., PA[1442]. He married **(2) Sarah Hawn**. She was born 15 Dec 1841 in Connellsville, Fayette Co., PA, and died Mar 1920 in Somerset Co., PA.

Notes for Henry A. Christner:
Birth: Dec 30, 1842
Death: Nov 9, 1914

Obituary: Meyersdale Commercial, Nov. 19, 1914
Henry A. Christner, aged 71 years and 10 months, died at his home near Savage Post Office, November 9, of pneumonia and was buried Thursday at Maple Glen. He is survived by his widow, who was Miss Sarah Hahn.

Spouse: Sarah Christner (1842 - _____)

Burial: Maple Glen Church of the Brethren Cemetery, Somerset Co., PA
Find A Grave Memorial# 69215168

Amish and Amish Mennonite Genealogies;

1850 US Census for Somerset Co., PA
List Abraham as a widower.

Farmer - Executor to his fathers will

More About Henry A. Christner:
Burial: 12 Nov 1914, Maple Glen Cemetery, Elk Lick Twp., Somerset Co., PA
Occupation: Farmer/
Residence: 1880, Addison Twp., Somerset Co., PA[1443,1444,1444]

Notes for Sarah Hawn:
Birth: Dec. 15, 1842
Death: Sep. 11, 1917

Christner, Sister Sarah, nee Hawn born in Somerset Co., PA Dec 15, 1842, died Sept 11, 1917 aged 74 years, 8 months and 26 days. She was married to Henry Christner, who preceded her in death nearly three years ago. She had a kind disposition, and in her younger days was a great benefit to the community in which she lived. She lived a consistent Christian life until her death. Surviving her are a daughter and six grandchildren, besides a number of great-grandchildren. Services in the Maple Glen church bu Bro. O. S. Davis, assisted by Bro. L. A. Peck. Text, Eccles. 12:7 (Mrs. P. S. Davis, Springs, PA)
Gospel Messsenger - Vol. 66, No. 39, Sept 29, 1917, p. 622

Spouse: Henry A. Christner (1842 - 1914)

Burial: Maple Glen Church of the Brethren Cemetery, Somerset Co., PA
Find A Grave Memorial# 69215169

Sarah & Henry died the same day maybe problem of date check out at Cemetery. Checked the Cemetery but they never carved her death date in her stone.

More About Sarah Hawn:
Burial: Maple Glen Church of the Brethren Cemetery, Somerset Co., PA

Child of Henry Christner and Sarah Hawn is:
+   767   i.   Margaret[7] Christner, born Jul 1864 in Pittsburgh, Allegheny Co., PA.

203. Elizabeth[6] Christner (Abraham D.[5], Joseph "Zep"[4], Johannes John Hans[3], Christian[2], Christen[1])[1445] was born 06 Oct 1845 in Somerset Co., PA[1445], and died 15 Jan 1922 in Fairhope Township, Somerset Co., PA[1445]. She married **Soloman Shumaker**[1445] 04 Nov 1883[1445]. He was born 06 Feb 1837 in Southampton Township, Somerset Co., PA[1445], and died 11 Mar 1914 in Southampton Township, Somerset Co., PA[1445].

Notes for Elizabeth Christner:
Reformed Church of Fairhope PA. She died at her son Wilson's Home. At one time she lived in Garrett, PA.

More About Elizabeth Christner:
Burial: Comp or Komps Cemetery
Census: 15 Apr 1910, Fairhope Township, Somerset Co., PA[1445]

Notes for Soloman Shumaker:
Veteran of the Civil war - Union Army Company K, 82 Regment, PA Volunteers Funeral at Komps Reformed Church. He lived near Fairhope, PA. He was sick for five years and bed ridden for three years with several diseases.

More About Soloman Shumaker:
Census: 15 Apr 1910, Fairhope Township, Somerset Co., PA[1445]
Military: Civil War[1445]
Occupation: Bet. 1870 - 1910, was a Farmer/Southampton Township, Somerset Co., PA[1445]

Children of Elizabeth Christner and Soloman Shumaker are:
     768   i.   Anna Elizabeth[7] Shumaker.

                      Notes for Anna Elizabeth Shumaker:
                      Died as infant

     769   ii.   Christour Shumaker[1445].

                      More About Christour Shumaker:
                      Baptism: 04 Mar 1883[1445]

+   770   iii.   Wilson Milton Shumaker, born 02 Sep 1878 in Rairhope, Southampton Township, Somerset Co., PA; died 30 Oct 1956 in 28 Virginia Ave..
     771   iv.   William Howard Shumaker[1445], born 02 Sep 1883 in Southampton Township, Somerset Co., PA[1445].

                      Notes for William Howard Shumaker:
                      He lived at Fairhope, PA.

                      More About William Howard Shumaker:
                      Census: 14 Apr 1930, Somerset, Somerset Co., , PA[1445]
                      Description: 1918, being medium height and build with blue eyes and brown hair/Somerset Co., PA[1445]
                      Occupation: Bet. 1930 - 1942, was a Mail Carrier for the Post Office/Somerset, Somerset Co., , PA[1445]

204. Elias[6] **Christner** (Abraham D.[5], Joseph "Zep"[4], Johannes John Hans[3], Christian[2], Christen[1]) was born 30 Mar 1848 in or Nov. 3, 1848, and died 18 Mar 1876 in Summit Twp., Somerset Co., PA. He married **Susan Long**.

Notes for Elias Christner:
Elias was a twin to Joanna. He froze to death near Jennerville, PA . Some say Born Nov 3, 1848.

Birth: Nov 30, 1848
Death: Mar 18, 1876

Burial: Ridgeview Cemetery, Garrett, Somerset Co., PA

Children of Elias Christner and Susan Long are:
+   772   i.   Martha MO[7] Christner, born 1870.
+   773   ii.   Louise Christner, born 25 Nov 1874 in Garrett, Somerset Co., PA.
       774   iii.   Mary M. Christner, born 1877 in Connellsville, Fayette Co., PA[1446].

205. Joanna[6] **Christner** (Abraham D.[5], Joseph "Zep"[4], Johannes John Hans[3], Christian[2], Christen[1])[1447] was born 30 Nov 1848 in Somerset Co., PA[1447]. She married **Jess Herman Smith**.

Notes for Joanna Christner:
Joanna or Johanna was a twin to Elias. Maybe born November 30, 1848.

Children of Joanna Christner and Jess Smith are:
+   775   i.   Francis M.[7] Smith, born 07 Jun 1879 in Glencoe Somerset Co., PA; died 1940 in 938 Lemon St. Dale.
+   776   ii.   William Harrison Smith, born 26 Aug 1888 in Northampton TWP.; died 21 Apr 1965 in Somerset Co., PA.

206. Sally Sarah[6] **Christner** (Abraham D.[5], Joseph "Zep"[4], Johannes John Hans[3], Christian[2], Christen[1]) was born 22 Mar 1832 in Somerset Co., PA, and died 19 Jul 1879 in Addison Twp., Somerset Co., PA. She married **Anthony A. Shoemaker** Apr 1849 in Somerset, Somerset Co., PA. He was born 04 May 1829 in Black Twp., Somerset PA, and died 06 May 1901 in Black Twp., Somerset Co., PA.

Notes for Sally Sarah Christner:
Maple Glen Church Cemetery. Her Headstone reads (wife of Anthony d. 19 Jul 1879 46 years 3 months and 27 days. Some have her death date at 7/19/1875--40y 3 mon 27 days or her birthday maybe March 22, 1833.

More About Sally Sarah Christner:
Burial: Maple Glen Church Cemetery

More About Anthony A. Shoemaker:
Burial: Sanner Cemetery Black Twp Somerset PA

Children of Sally Christner and Anthony Shoemaker are:
       777   i.   Lydia[7] Shoemaker.
       778   ii.   Lydia Shoemaker, born 25 Feb 1850 in Addison Twp., Somerset Co., PA; died 28 Nov 1910.
       779   iii.   Jacob Shoemaker, born 23 Mar 1851 in Addison Twp., Somerset Co., PA; died 13 Feb 1935 in Addison Twp., Somerset Co., PA. He married Mary A. Folk 1871 in Elk Lick Twp. Somerset, PA.

                         More About Jacob Shoemaker:
                         Burial: Maple Glen Cemetery Savage, PA

+   780   iv.   Mary A. Shoemaker, born 24 Nov 1852 in Addison Twp., Somerset Co., PA; died 25 Jan 1918.

781   v.   Abraham Shoemaker, born 17 Jul 1856 in Addison Twp., Somerset Co., PA; died 13 Sep 1926. He married (1) Wanda ?? Amanda 1878 in Addison Twp., Somerset Co., PA. He married (2) Elizabeth Baker Hoover 14 Oct 1897 in Rockwood, PA.

782   vi.   Samuel A. Shoemaker, born 15 May 1858 in Addison Twp., Somerset Co., PA; died 01 Jan 1917 in Black Twp., Somerset Co., PA. He married Amanda Catharine Humbert 1880 in Somerset, Somerset Co., PA.

Notes for Samuel A. Shoemaker:
Sam went into Rockwood on new years eve to celebrate the New Year & on his way home he sat down on the railroad tracks & passed out from his drinking. Sometime during the night the train hit & killed him. (as told to Warren Shumaker).

More About Samuel A. Shoemaker:
Burial: Sanner Cemetery Black Twp Somerset PA

783   vii.   Susannah Shoemaker, born 19 Jan 1860 in Addison Twp., Somerset Co., PA; died 07 Apr 1928 in Somerset, Somerset Co., PA. She married Solomon M Gnagey 29 Apr 1894 in Meyersdale, Somerset Co., PA.

784   viii.   Jonas Anthony Shoemaker, born 03 Jul 1866 in Addison Twp., Somerset Co., PA; died 05 Feb 1937 in Black Twp., Somerset Co., PA. He married Emma Jane Humbert 02 Apr 1893 in Milford Station Somerset, PA.

Notes for Jonas Anthony Shoemaker:
They lived on Purdum or Locke in Kokomo IN. in 1916. When they moved back to PA. Shelbert stayed, he was 17 years old. (Warren Shumaker)

More About Jonas Anthony Shoemaker:
Burial: Sanner Cemetery Black Twp Somerset PA

209. Samuel A.[6] Christner (Abraham D.[5], Joseph "Zep"[4], Johannes John Hans[3], Christian[2], Christen[1]) was born May 1840 in Somerset Co., PA, and died 08 Jan 1913 in Somerset, Somerset Co., PA. He married **(1) Lucinda**. She was born 1846. He married **(2) Elizabeth**. She was born Mar 1842 in Connellsville, Fayette Co., PA, and died 1909.

Notes for Samuel A. Christner:
Sam was the postmaster of Savage Post office Negro Mountain.

Sam had first wife Lucinda born 1846 died after 1870. Death maybe before August 1886. Sam and his wife Elizabeth sold land for $10.00 in 1894 for a cemetery located at State Road 2002 and Christner Hollow Road (N39°46.200'- - W79°12.200') Know called Maple Glen Church of the Brethren Cemetery.

Samuel A. Christner left all his estate to Mary Ann Turney except for Mary Martha Christner got $1.00 as did Norman B. his son. 1910 soundex PA has his daughter Mary Ann Turney & his sistner in law Susan White (age 72) living at Samuel's home.

Birth: 1840
Death: 1913

Burial: Maple Glen Church of the Brethren Cemetery, Somerset Co., PA

More About Samuel A. Christner:
Burial: Maple Glen Church of the Brethren Cemetery, Somerset Co., PA
Residence: 1910, Elk Lick, Somerset Co., PA[1448]

Notes for Lucinda:
Birth: 1846
Death: Feb. 16, 1875

Inscription: aged 20Y 1M 1D

Burial: Maple Glen Church of the Brethren Cemetery, Somerset Co., PA

Notes for Elizabeth:
She my have a daughter Mary Ann Turney before being married to Samuel A. Christner as he left all his estate to Mary Ann Turney except for Mary Martha Christner got $1.00 as did Norman B. his son.

More About Elizabeth:
Burial: Maple Glen Church of the Brethren Cemetery, Somerset Co., PA

Children of Samuel Christner and Lucinda are:

785   i.   Mary Martha[7] Christner, born Mar 1864 in Frostburg, Allegany Co., MD. She married (1) Turney Or Furney. She married (2) Michael B. Zimmerman 19 Aug 1886 in Somerset Co., PA; born 1853.

        Notes for Mary Martha Christner:
        Mary was 13 years younger than her husband. 1910 soundex PA has her living with her father Samuel A. Christner she is listed as Mary Turney.

        Notes for Michael B. Zimmerman:
        Michael is the son of George and Mary_____Zimmerman. Both of his parents were dead by 1886. He was a farmer of Somerset Twp., PA . His former wife died on April 23, 1885. Michael was able to get consent from Samuel A. Christner the brides father. Michael even got two witnesses to the consent, Charles C. Shafer and Austin S. Keel.

786   ii.   Savilla Christner, born Mar 1870 in Somerset, Somerset Co., PA[1448]; died 1888.

        Notes for Savilla Christner:
        Birth: 1870
        Death: 1888

        Burial: Maple Glen Church of the Brethren Cemetery, Somerset Co., PA

        More About Savilla Christner:
        Burial: Maple Glen Cemetery, Elk Lick Twp., Somerset Co., PA

210. Barbara Bevvy[6] Judy (Mary[5] Christner, Joseph "Zep"[4], Johannes John Hans[3], Christian[2], Christen[1])[1449,1450] was born 12 May 1838 in Somerset Co., PA[1450,1451], and died 30 Oct 1895 in Summit Twp., Somerset Co., PA[1451,1452]. She married **John C. Christner**[1453], son of Christian Christner and Susanna Walters. He was born 16 Jul 1842 in Connellsville, Fayette Co., PA[1453], and died 14 Dec 1921 in Summit Twp., Somerset Co., PA.

Notes for Barbara Bevvy Judy:
Barbara was the daughter of Matthias Judy and Elizabeth Christner. Her Father is Zep.

This record is very confusing. It looks as if there are 3 sets of twins in this family. The info came from Cary Christner of Meyersdale, PA.

More About Barbara Bevvy Judy:
Residence: 1880, Garrett, Somerset Co., PA[1454]

Notes for John C. Christner:
John may have been married a 3rd time to Ylona Kovac on 4/5/1905 or to Nancy Tressler 5/4/1905? John's 2nd wife was Samantha J. Nicklow and she was married to a Tressler and had a son Walter G. Tressler that she shares a tombstone with. The 1910 soundex PA has Grace Christner age 16 & no first name Tressler age 18 living with Samantha in Somerset Co., PA & no one else in the household.

Birth: Jul. 16, 1842
Death: Jan. 14, 1921

79y 6m 2d

Burial: Ridgeview Cemetery, Garrett, Somerset Co., PA

More About John C. Christner:
Residence: 1920, Summit Twp., Somerset Co., PA[1455]

Children of Barbara Judy and John Christner are:

787   i.   Jonas[7] Christner.

            Notes for Jonas Christner:
            Jonas birthdate the same as brother John. Cheyenne They may be twins.

788   ii.   Henry Christner[1456], born Abt. 1862 in PA[1456].

            More About Henry Christner:
            Residence: 1880, Garrett, Somerset Co., PA[1456]

+ 789   iii. Rudolph Christner, born Nov 1864 in Somerset Co., PA; died 1939.
   790   iv.   Henry Christner, born 1865.
   791   v.   Jonas Christner, born 12 Nov 1866; died 22 Jan 1882 in Summit Twp., Somerset Co., PA.

            Notes for Jonas Christner:
            Birth: Nov. 12, 1866
            Death: Jan. 22, 1882

            15y 2m 10d birthday calculated
            s/o J & B

            Burial: Ridgeview Cemetery, Garrett, Somerset Co., PA

            Jonas birthdate the same as brother John. Cheyenne They may be twins.

            More About Jonas Christner:
            Burial: Garrett, Summit Twp., Somerset Co., PA

   792   vi.   Cheyenne Christner, born 12 Nov 1866.
+ 793   vii. Sevilla Christner, born Nov 1870 in Somerset Co., PA; died in Somerset Co., PA.
   794   viii. Wilson Christner, born 1871; died 26 Feb 1876 in Summit Twp., Somerset Co., PA.

            Notes for Wilson Christner:

            More About Wilson Christner:
            Burial: Summit Twp., Somerset Co., PA

795   ix.   Mary Ann Christner[1457], born 1874[1457]. She married Harvey Hoover 21 Nov 1897 in !!!!First
             Cousins!!!!; born 1865.

            Notes for Mary Ann Christner:
            Mary has the same birth year as brother Wilson. They may be twins.

            Notes for Harvey Hoover:
            Laborer

796   x.   Polly Christner, born 1877; died 02 May 1892 in Summit Twp., Somerset Co., PA.

            More About Polly Christner:
            Burial: May 1892, Summit Twp., Somerset Co., PA

797   xi.   Norman Christner, born 08 Sep 1878; died 08 Apr 1880 in Summit Twp., Somerset Co., PA.

More About Norman Christner:
Burial: Garrett, Summit Twp., Somerset Co., PA

211. Christina Dinah[6] Judy (Mary[5] Christner, Joseph "Zep"[4], Johannes John Hans[3], Christian[2], Christen[1])[1458,1459] was born 08 Jul 1839 in Somerset Co., PA[1459,1460], and died 28 Nov 1908 in Shickley, Fillmore Co., NE[1460]. She married **John George Walter**[1460] 1862 in Garrett, Somerset Co., PA[1460]. He was born 25 Dec 1841 in Somerset Co., PA[1460], and died 17 May 1912 in Shickley, Fillmore Co., NE[1460].

Notes for Christina Dinah Judy:
Dinah married John Walters.

More About Christina Dinah Judy:
Burial: Shickley, Fillmore Co., NE[1460]
Residence: 1880, Garrett, Somerset Co., PA[1461]

More About John George Walter:
Burial: Shickley, Fillmore Co., NE[1462]
Residence: 1930, Age in 1930: 88; Marital Status: Married; Relation to Head of House: Head/East Stroudsburg, Monroe, PA[1462]

Children of Christina Judy and John Walter are:

798   i.   Ellen[7] Walter[1462], born 19 Oct 1861 in Garrett, Somerset Co., PA[1462]; died 07 Apr 1933 in Ong, Clay Co., NE[1462].

More About Ellen Walter:
Burial: Shickley, Fillmore Co., NE[1462]
Residence: 1880, Age: 18; Marital Status: Single; Relation to Head of House: Daughter/Garrett, Somerset Co., PA[1462]

799   ii.   Eliza Angeline Walter[1462], born 07 Jun 1865 in Garrett, Somerset Co., PA[1462]; died 07 Feb 1939 in Humboldt, Richardson Co., NE[1462].

More About Eliza Angeline Walter:
Burial: Davenport, Thayer County, NE, USA[1462]
Residence: 1880, Age: 15; Marital Status: Single; Relation to Head of House: Daughter/Garrett, Somerset Co., PA[1462]

800   iii.   Jackson Walter[1462], born 01 Oct 1867 in Garrett, Somerset Co., PA[1462]; died 27 Apr 1933 in Geneva, Fillmore Co., NE[1462].

More About Jackson Walter:
Burial: Geneva, Fillmore County, NE, USA[1462]
Residence: 1920, Age: 52; Marital Status: Married; Relation to Head of House: Head/Bryant, Fillmore, NE[1462]

801   iv.   Nathaniel W Walter[1462], born 29 Oct 1869 in Somerset Co., PA[1462]; died 08 Feb 1934 in Shickley, Fillmore Co., NE[1462].

More About Nathaniel W Walter:
Burial: Shickley, Fillmore Co., NE[1462]
Residence: 1910, Davenport, Thayer, NE, USA[1462]

802   v.   Edward Samuel Walter (S)[1462], born 10 Apr 1872 in Garrett, Somerset Co., PA[1462]; died 09 Jun 1963 in Davenport, Thayer Co., NE[1462].

More About Edward Samuel Walter (S):

Burial: Davenport, Thayer County, NE, USA[1462]
Residence: 1880, Age: 8; Marital Status: Single; Relation to Head of House: Son/Garrett, Somerset Co., PA[1462]

803   vi.   Seward J. Walter[1462], born 28 Oct 1873 in Garrett, Somerset Co., PA[1462]; died Feb 1949 in Gering, Scottsbluff Co., NE[1462].

More About Seward J. Walter:
Residence: 1880, Age: 6; Marital Status: Single; Relation to Head of House: Son/Garrett, Somerset Co., PA[1462]

804   vii.   Susie Caroline Walters[1462], born 10 Feb 1877 in Garrett, Somerset Co., PA[1462]; died 13 Jan 1951 in Geneva, Fillmore Co., NE[1462].

More About Susie Caroline Walters:
Burial: Geneva, Fillmore County, NE, USA[1462]
Residence: 01 Apr 1940, Momence, Fillmore, NE, United States[1462]

805   viii.   Lila Irene Walter[1462], born 11 Feb 1878 in Garret, Somerset Co, PA USA[1462]; died 08 Jul 1956 in Scotts Bluff, Scotts Bluff Co., NE[1462].

More About Lila Irene Walter:
Residence: 1935, Lyman, Scotts Bluff, NE[1462]

806   ix.   Anna F Walter[1462], born Abt. 1880 in PA[1462].

More About Anna F Walter:
Residence: 01 Jun 1915, Age: 35; Relationship: Wife/Colonie, Albany, New York, United States[1462]

807   x.   Daniel Ruben Walter[1462], born 22 Aug 1884 in Stella, Richardson Co., NE[1462]; died 28 Apr 1959 in Warren Memorial Hospital/Friend, Saline Co., NE[1462].

More About Daniel Ruben Walter:
Residence: 1935, Davenport, Thayer Co., NE[1462]

219. Elizabeth[6] Judy (Elizabeth[5] Christner, Joseph "Zep"[4], Johannes John Hans[3], Christian[2], Christen[1])[1463] was born 15 Mar 1842 in Somerset Co., PA[1463], and died 12 Mar 1923[1463]. She married **Benjamin Bockes**.

More About Elizabeth Judy:
Residence: 1900, Summit, Somerset Co., PA[1463]

Child of Elizabeth Judy and Benjamin Bockes is:
808   i.   Samuel[7] Bockes, born 20 Nov 1870. He married Saloma Christner 22 Feb 1893; born 1874.

221. Gabriel[6] Hostetler (Elizabeth[5] Christner, Joseph "Zep"[4], Johannes John Hans[3], Christian[2], Christen[1])[1464,1465,1466,1467] was born 12 Aug 1834 in Jefferson, Somerset, Pennsylvania, United States[1467,1468,1469,1470], and died 10 Mar 1892 in Trent, Somerset Co., PA[1471]. He married **Magdalena Bitinger**[1472,1473] 12 Aug 1851. She was born 16 May 1834 in Pennsylvania, United States[1473], and died 22 Nov 1902 in Jackson, Jackson, Ohio, United States[1473].

More About Gabriel Hostetler:
Residence: 1900, Canton Ward 7, Stark, Ohio[1474,1475]

More About Magdalena Bitinger:
Residence: 1900, Canton Ward 7, Stark, Ohio[1476,1477]

Children of Gabriel Hostetler and Magdalena Bitinger are:
809   i.   Delilah[7] Hostetler[1478], born 30 Nov 1852 in Middlecreek, Somerset Co., PA[1478]; died 23 Aug 1889 in Wooster, Wayne Co., OH[1478].

| 810 | ii. | Samuel Hostetler[1478], born 05 Dec 1852 in Middlecreek, Somerset Co., PA[1478]; died in Coronado, San Diego Co., CA[1478]. |
| 811 | iii. | Conrad Hostetler[1478], born 28 May 1854 in Middlecreek, Somerset Co., PA[1478]; died 18 Oct 1923 in Cuyahoga Co., OH[1478]. |

More About Conrad Hostetler:
Residence: 1880, Canaan, Wayne Co., OH[1478]

812	iv.	William Bittinger Hostetler[1478], born 18 Aug 1855 in Middlecreek, Somerset Co., PA[1478]; died 1900[1478].
813	v.	Elizabeth Hochstetler[1478], born 29 Aug 1857 in Middlecreek, Somerset Co., PA[1478].
814	vi.	Catherine Hostetler[1478], born 08 Mar 1859 in Middlecreek, Somerset Co., PA[1478].
815	vii.	Lucinda Hostetler[1478], born 22 Oct 1860 in Middlecreek, Somerset Co., PA[1478]; died 1910 in Canaan, Wayne Co., OH[1478].
816	viii.	Mary Hostetler[1478], born 30 Nov 1865 in Middlecreek, Somerset Co., PA[1478]; died 24 Mar 1876 in Canaan, Wayne Co., OH[1478].
+ 817	ix.	Aaron Hostetter, born 16 Nov 1867 in Canaan, Wayne Co., OH; died 24 Jun 1938 in Canton, Stark Co., OH.
818	x.	John Hostetler[1478], born 15 Mar 1869 in Canaan, Wayne Co., OH[1478].
819	xi.	Emma Jane Hostetler[1478], born 31 Dec 1872 in Canaan, Wayne Co., OH[1478].

223. Jonathan⁶ Hostetler (Elizabeth⁵ Christner, Joseph "Zep"⁴, Johannes John Hans³, Christian², Christen¹)[1479,1480] was born 07 Oct 1840 in Somerset Co., PA[1480,1481], and died 10 Mar 1892 in Trent, Somerset Co., PA[1482]. He married **Catherine Grim**[1482]. She was born 20 Feb 1838 in PA[1482], and died 15 Jan 1912 in Somerset Co., PA[1482].

More About Catherine Grim:
Residence: 1910, Jefferson, Somerset, Pennsylvania[1482]

Children of Jonathan Hostetler and Catherine Grim are:

| 820 | i. | Rolla G⁷ Hostetler[1482], born 12 Mar 1865 in Trent, Somerset Co., PA[1482]; died 1926 in Trent, Somerset Co., PA[1482]. |

More About Rolla G Hostetler:
Burial: 1926, Barons Cemetery/Middle Creek, Somerset, Pennsylvania[1482]
Residence: 1910, Middlecreek, Somerset, Pennsylvania[1482]

| 821 | ii. | Buel G Hostetler[1482], born 22 Sep 1866 in Trent, Somerset Co., PA[1482]; died 1924 in Milford, Somerset, Pennsylvania[1482]. |

More About Buel G Hostetler:
Burial: 1924, Middle Creek Cemetery/Middlecreek, Somerset, Pennsylvani[1482]
Residence: 1920, Milford, Somerset, Pennsylvania[1482]

| 822 | iii. | Cora Hostetler[1482], born 11 Jan 1870 in Trent, Somerset Co., PA[1482]; died 1932 in Somerset Co., PA[1482]. |

More About Cora Hostetler:
Burial: 1932, Bakersville Lutheran Cemetery/Jefferson, Somerset, Pennsylvania[1482]
Residence: 1930, Donegal, Westmoreland, Pennsylvania[1482]

| 823 | iv. | Harvey Hostetler[1482], born 19 Jun 1874 in Trent, Somerset Co., PA[1482]. |

More About Harvey Hostetler:
Residence: 1930, Summit, Somerset, Pennsylvania[1482]

| 824 | v. | Wesley Hostetler[1482], born 15 Feb 1876 in Trent, Somerset Co., PA[1482]. |

More About Wesley Hostetler:
Residence: 12 Sep 1918, Somerset Co., PA[1482]

228. Jeremiah⁶ Hostetler (Elizabeth⁵ Christner, Joseph "Zep"⁴, Johannes John Hans³, Christian²,

Christen[1])[1483,1484,1485] was born 1853 in Jefferson, Somerset Co., PA[1486,1487], and died in Trent, Somerset Co., PA[1488]. He married **Amanda Sanner**[1489]. She was born 01 Mar 1859 in Somerset Co., PA[1489], and died 21 Mar 1915[1489].

More About Jeremiah Hostetler:
Residence: 1870, Jefferson, Somerset Co., PA[1490]

More About Amanda Sanner:
Residence: 1930, Frackville, Schuylkill, PA[1491]

Children of Jeremiah Hostetler and Amanda Sanner are:

825   i.   Elizabeth[7] Hostetler[1491].
826   ii.   Mary Hostetler[1491].
827   iii.   Robert Hostetler[1491], born 27 Mar 1879 in Summit, Somerset Co., PA[1491]; died 1954 in Connellsville, Fayette Co., PA[1491].

                More About Robert Hostetler:
                Residence: 1900, Garrett Borough, Somerset, PA[1491]

828   iv.   Hiram H Hostetler[1491], born 27 Jun 1883 in Black Twp., Somerset Co., PA[1491]; died 07 Oct 1958[1491].

230. Zachariah[6] Christner (Christian[5], Joseph "Zep"[4], Johannes John Hans[3], Christian[2], Christen[1])[1492] was born 21 Apr 1837 in Summit Twp., Somerset Co., PA[1492], and died 1917 in Londonderry Twp., Bedford Co., PA[1492]. He married **Magdalene "Maggie" Hoover**[1492] 1860. She was born 04 Jul 1840 in Summit Twp., Somerset Co., PA[1492], and died 27 Jan 1917 in Londonderry Twp., Bedford Co., PA[1492].

Notes for Zachariah Christner:
Zacharia operated a lime kiln in 1890 at the junction of highway 219 and 653
Laurel Messenger Nov 1966 Born in Garrett PA moved to Summit Township PA after 1870 moved to Scottdale PA. and Point Pleasant PA. Retired in Canton Ohio 919 South Main Street from 1901 to 1905 from 1905 to 1908 lived at 1409 Navarre street. In 1909 moved back to Hyndman PA. for there last days they owned a farm and orchard. The farm had two tenant house's. Theodore and Generva moved into one of the tenant homes. The agreement was that they should pay $300. for the house and if the older generation died before the amount was paid, the debt was forgiven. After the death of his wife he moved to his son Austin's farm (this was Zachariah's) at Meyersdale PA. He died later in the year of 1917. From various sources, we learned that it was Carrie that promoted the idea that her father Theodore wanted to be buried between his father Zachariah and his mother Magdalena. Theodore was originally buried per that request, but Generva was greatly bothered by the fact that Theodore would not be buried with his own immediate family in the large plot purchased by Generva for the family. He was later reintered in the Madly Cemetery next to Generva.

Birth: Apr. 21, 1837
Summit Twp., Somerset Co., PA
Death: 1918
Hyndman, Bedford Co., PA

Spouse: Magdalena M. Hoover Christner (1840 - 1917)

Children: Theodore Christner (1875 - 1947)

Burial: Hyndman Cemetery, Hyndman, Bedford Co., PA

More About Zachariah Christner:
Burial: Hyndman Cemetery PA.
Religion: Luthern/

Notes for Magdalene "Maggie" Hoover:
1900 census she was living with her daughter MO & son-in-law George Judy

1910 soundex PA has she was living with her daughter Jennie & Nathan Berkett

Birth: Jul. 4, 1840 - Summit Twp., Somerset Co., PA
Death: Jan. 27, 1917 - Hyndman, Bedford Co., PA

Spouse: Zachariah Christner (1837 - 1918)

Children: Theodore Christner (1875 - 1947)

Burial: Hyndman Cemetery, Hyndman, Bedford Co., PA

More About Magdalene "Maggie" Hoover:
Burial: Hyndman Cemetery PA.
Christened: 23 Jun 1849

Children of Zachariah Christner and Magdalene Hoover are:

+ 829   i.   Austin George[7] Christner, born 01 Oct 1863 in Somerset, Somerset Co., PA; died 1933 in Summit Twp., Somerset Co., PA.

   830   ii.   Clara Ann Carrie Christner, born 1866.

         Notes for Clara Ann Carrie Christner:
         Little is presently known about Carrie Ann except that she lived with her parents when they retired to Canton,OH from 1901 to 1909. From various sources, we learned that it was Carrie that promoted the idea that her brother Theodore wanted to be buried between his father Zachariah and his mother Magdalena. Theodore was originally buried per that request, but Generva was greatly bothered by the fact that Theodore would not be buried with his own immediate family in the large plot purchased by Generva for the family. He was later reintered in the Madly Cemetery next to Generva. Oral tradition through KO Myers put Jennie in a negative Position. some say trouble maker. She got sister Carrie to have Theodore in the wrong grave see Theodore's note's.

+ 831   iii.   MO Christner, born 1868.
+ 832   iv.   Washington Christner, born Aug 1871 in Connellsville, Fayette Co., PA.
+ 833   v.   George Washington Christner, born Aug 1871; died 1941.
+ 834   vi.   Wilson William Christner, born 29 Sep 1873 in PA.
+ 835   vii.   Theodore "Dorrie" Christner, born 18 Mar 1875 in Summit Twp., Somerset Co., PA; died 1947 in Hyndman, Bedford Co., PA.

   836   viii.   Jennie Christner, born 1878. She married (1) Nathan Burkett. She married (2) Tom Pollard.

         Notes for Jennie Christner:
         She lived in Cumberland, MD. Oral tradition through KO Myers put Jennie in a negative Position. some say trouble maker. She got sister Carrie to have Theodore in the wrong grave see Theodore's note's.
         1910 soundex Bedford PA has her father Zacharia living with her.

232. Susanna Lucy Anne[6] Christner (Christian[5], Joseph "Zep"[4], Johannes John Hans[3], Christian[2], Christen[1]) was born 21 Mar 1840 in Somerset Co., PA, and died 1926 in Jenner, Somerset Co., PA[1493]. She married **John Hoover**. He was born 1833 in Garrett, Somerset Co., PA, and died 1896.

Notes for Susanna Lucy Anne Christner:
Birth: 1840
Death: 1926

Spouse: John Hoover (1833 - 1896)

Inscription: Wife

Burial: Center Lutheran Church Cemetery, Summit Twp., Somerset Co., PA

More About Susanna Lucy Anne Christner:
Burial: Center Church, Luthern, Southwest of Garrett PA.

Christened: 06 Jun 1849, Mt. Zion Hays Reformed Somerset PA

Notes for John Hoover:
He has a son (John A. Jr.b-1880-d-1921) buried with him but we don't know if this was Susanna Lucy's Child.

Birth: Oct. 18, 1833
Somerset Co., PA
Death: Sep. 14, 1896
Somerset Co., PA

Spouse: Lucy Ann Christner Hoover (1840 - 1926)

Children: Tena Hoover Phillippi (1867 - 1950)

Inscription: G.A.R.

Burial: Center Lutheran Church Cemetery, Summit Twp., Somerset Co.,

More About John Hoover:
Burial: Center Church, Luthern, Southwest of Garrett PA.

Children of Susanna Christner and John Hoover are:

	837	i.	John[7] Hoover Jr..
	838	ii.	Melinda Hoover, born 1862.
	839	iii.	Alfred Hoover, born 1864.
	840	iv.	Jefferson Hoover, born 1865.
	841	v.	Ellen Hoover, born 1866.
+	842	vi.	Tena Hoover, born 07 Oct 1867; died 20 Dec 1950 in Garrett, Someret Co., PA.
	843	vii.	Dinah Hoover, born 1868.

233. John C.[6] Christner (Christian[5], Joseph "Zep"[4], Johannes John Hans[3], Christian[2], Christen[1])[1494] was born 16 Jul 1842 in Connellsville, Fayette Co., PA[1494], and died 14 Dec 1921 in Summit Twp., Somerset Co., PA. He married **(1) Barbara Bevvy Judy**[1495,1496], daughter of Matthias Judy and Mary Christner. She was born 12 May 1838 in Somerset Co., PA[1496,1497], and died 30 Oct 1895 in Summit Twp., Somerset Co., PA[1497,1498]. He married **(2) Samantha J. Nicklow**[1499] 1899. She was born 1865 in Connellsville, Fayette Co., PA[1499].

Notes for John C. Christner:
John may have been married a 3rd time to Ylona Kovac on 4/5/1905 or to Nancy Tressler 5/4/1905? John's 2nd wife was Samantha J. Nicklow and she was married to a Tressler and had a son Walter G. Tressler that she shares a tombstone with. The 1910 soundex PA has Grace Christner age 16 & no first name Tressler age 18 living with Samantha in Somerset Co., PA & no one else in the household.

Birth: Jul. 16, 1842
Death: Jan. 14, 1921

79y 6m 2d

Burial: Ridgeview Cemetery, Garrett, Somerset Co., PA

More About John C. Christner:
Residence: 1920, Summit Twp., Somerset Co., PA[1499]

Notes for Barbara Bevvy Judy:
Barbara was the daughter of Matthias Judy and Elizabeth Christner. Her Father is Zep.

This record is very confusing. It looks as if there are 3 sets of twins in this family. The info came from Cary Christner of Meyersdale, PA.

More About Barbara Bevvy Judy:
Residence: 1880, Garrett, Somerset Co., PA[1500]

Notes for Samantha J. Nicklow:
She was blind. She was the sister of William Lincoln Nicklow he Died June 20 1938. John may have been married a 3rd time to Ylona Kovac on 4/5/1905 or to Nancy Tressler 5/4/1905? John's 2nd wife was Samantha J. Nicklow and she was married to a Tressler and had a son Walter G. Tressler that she shares a tombstone with. The 1910 soundex PA has Grace Christner age 16 & no first name Tressler age 18 living with Samantha in Somerset Co. PA & no one else in the household.

Birth: 1865
Death: unknown

Note: Death date written as 19--

Burial: Highland Cemetery, Garrett, Somerset Co., PA

More About Samantha J. Nicklow:
Burial: Highland Cemetery, Garrett, Somerset Co., PA
Residence: 1930, Ursina, Somerset, PA[1501]

Children are listed above under (210) Barbara Bevvy Judy.

Child of John Christner and Samantha Nicklow is:
844   i.   John Cheyenne[7] Christner[1501], born Feb 1901 in Somerset, Somerset Co., PA[1501]; died May 1962 in Meyersdale, Somerset Co., PA.

           Notes for John Cheyenne Christner:
           John (Cheyenne) died in a automobile accident South of Meyersdale, PA.

           More About John Cheyenne Christner:
           Burial: Highland Cemetery, Garrett, Somerset Co., PA

234. Caroline[6] Christner (Christian[5], Joseph "Zep"[4], Johannes John Hans[3], Christian[2], Christen[1])[1502] was born 1843. She married **(1) Jonathan Hoover.** She married **(2) Jacob (Lumix Jake) Christner** 1869, son of Jacob Christner and Julia Rumiser. He was born 1848.

Notes for Caroline Christner:
1920 Census has Cariline living with her daughter Sadie & Sadie's husband Peter Klink on Orchard Street, Berlin, Somerset Co., Pennsylvania. She was 74 at the time.

More About Caroline Christner:
Christened: 23 Jun 1849

Notes for Jacob (Lumix Jake) Christner:
1920 census has him living with his daughter Sadie & Peter Klink at Orchard Street, Berlin, Somerset Co., PA.

Children of Caroline Christner and Jonathan Hoover are:
845   i.   Harvey[7] Hoover, born 1865. He married Mary Ann Christner[1503] 21 Nov 1897 in !!!!First Cousins!!!!; born 1874[1503].

           Notes for Harvey Hoover:
           Laborer

           Notes for Mary Ann Christner:
           Mary has the same birth year as brother Wilson. They may be twins.

846 ii. Amanda Christner, born 1868. She married Benjamin Harden Jr. 18 Jun 1886 in Alleghany Co., MD; born 1865.

      Notes for Amanda Christner:
      She didn't use the Hoover name.

      Notes for Benjamin Harden Jr.:
      Benjamin was from Alleghany Co., MD when he married Amanda. He worked on the railroad. They moved to Greenville Twp., PA.

      Marriage Notes for Amanda Christner and Benjamin Harden:
      Some source had January 19, 1886 but marriage register in Somerset PA had June 18, 1886.

Children are listed above under (132) Jacob (Lumix Jake) Christner.

238. Amos Dickey[6] Christner (Gabriel[5], Joseph "Zep"[4], Johannes John Hans[3], Christian[2], Christen[1])[1504,1505,1506,1507,1508,1508,1509,1510] was born 24 Jan 1845 in Westmoreland Co., PA[1511], and died 26 Dec 1931 in Mt. Pleasant, Westmoreland Co., PA[1512,1513,1514]. He married **Samantha C. Pile** 07 May 1871[1515]. She was born 15 Jan 1854 in Connellsville, Fayette Co., PA[1516], and died 03 Feb 1930 in Connellsville, Fayette Co., PA[1516].

Notes for Amos Dickey Christner:
Amos is the son of Gabriel Christner and Madalena or Magdalena Dickey. He had a nickname of Duky. Amos lived on a farm 6 miles west of Somerset PA on the route to Centerville PA. His neighbor was The Groundhog Glory Church of God.

It is believed that he preached at the Middle Creek Dunkard Church. Now known as The Middlecreek Church of The Brethren. The farm where he lived was later owned by AL Bruner. 1920 Census at age 74 he was living with his wife at Westmoreland County, Mt Pleasant Boro, West Main Street PA.

More About Amos Dickey Christner:
Burial: Mt.Joy, Fayette Co., PA
Residence: 1920, Age: 74; Marital Status: Married; Relation to Head of House: Head/Mount Pleasant Ward 1, Westmoreland, PA[1517]

More About Samantha C. Pile:
Residence: 1920, Mount Pleasant Ward 1, Westmoreland, PA[1518]

Children of Amos Christner and Samantha Pile are:
847 i. Jeanette[7] Christner, born 24 Feb 1872; died 13 Mar 1917. She married Albert Charles Snively; born 26 Nov 1869 in PA[1519]; died 02 Dec 1940 in Greensburg, Westmoreland Co., PA[1519].

      Notes for Jeanette Christner:
      Birth: 1872
      Death: 1918

      Burial: Saint Clair Cemetery, Greensburg, Westmoreland Co., PA
      Find A Grave Memorial# 97412489

      More About Jeanette Christner:
      Residence: 1910, Age: 38; Marital Status: Married; Relation to Head of House: Wife/Irwin Ward 2, Westmoreland, PA[1520]

      Notes for Albert Charles Snively:
      Birth: 1869
      Death: 1940

Burial: Saint Clair Cemetery, Greensburg, Westmoreland Co., PA
Find A Grave Memorial# 97412468

More About Albert Charles Snively:
Residence: 1920, Mount Pleasant Ward 1, Westmoreland, PA[1521]

848   ii.   Dorsey N. Christner, born 16 Sep 1873 in Pittsburgh, Allegheny Co., PA; died 29 Jun 1956.

More About Dorsey N. Christner:
Residence: 1880, Age: 6; Marital Status: Single; Relation to Head of House: Son/Mt. Pleasant, Westmoreland Co., PA[1522]

849   iii.   Lloyd M. Christner, born 27 Feb 1876 in Connellsville, Fayette Co., PA[1523]; died 13 Feb 1979. He married Elizabeth Hartzell; born 1886 in PA.

Notes for Lloyd M. Christner:
Birth: 1875
Death: 1980

Note: Same stone as Elizabeth O. Christner

Burial: Saint Johns Union Cemetery, Mount Pleasant, Westmoreland Co., PA

1920 census he is living at Westmoreland Co., PA, Mt. Pleasant Boro, 923 West Main Street

More About Lloyd M. Christner:
Burial: Mount Pleasant, Westmoreland County, PA, USA[1524]
Residence: 01 Apr 1940, Age: 64; Marital Status: Married; Relation to Head of House: Head/Mt. Pleasant, Westmoreland Co., PA[1524]
Social Security Number: 200-40-8915/[1525]
SSN issued: PA[1525]

Notes for Elizabeth Hartzell:
Birth: 1885
Death: 1969

Note: Same stone as Lloyd M. Christner

Burial: Saint Johns Union Cemetery, Mount Pleasant, Westmoreland Co., PA

Wife of Lloyd M.

Burial: Union Cemetery, New Centerville, Somerset Co., PA

+ 850   iv.   Emma D. Christner, born 11 Jan 1877.
+ 851   v.   Laura Ellen Christner, born 30 Aug 1877 in Somerset Co., PA; died 20 Sep 1973 in Age: 95 Years/Danbury, Fairfield Co., CT.
+ 852   vi.   Clarence Herbert Christner, born 05 Jul 1881 in Westmoreland Co., PA; died in Pittsburgh, Allegheny Co., PA.
    853   vii.   Stuart Christner[1526], born 24 Nov 1884 in Pittsburgh, Allegheny Co., PA[1526].

Notes for Stuart Christner:
Never Married

More About Stuart Christner:
Residence: 1910, Age: 25; Marital Status: Single; Relation to Head of House: Son/Mt. Pleasant Boro Ward 1, Westmoreland Co., PA[1526]

+ 854   viii.   Isa Olive Christner, born 19 Mar 1889 in Milford, Somerset Co., PA; died Aug 1978 in Scottdale, Westmoreland Co., PA.
+ 855   ix.   Barton Roy Christner, born 04 Apr 1892 in Connellsville, Fayette Co., PA; died 18 Jul 1963.

239. David[6] **Christner** (Gabriel[5], Joseph "Zep"[4], Johannes John Hans[3], Christian[2], Christen[1])[1527,1528,1529] was born 1848 in Somerset Co., PA[1530]. He married **Libbie J. Christner**[1531]. She was born Abt. 1857 in NY[1531].

Notes for David Christner:
Amish and Amish Mennonite Genealogies

More About David Christner:
Christened: 23 Jun 1849
Residence: 1880, Mcpherson, McPherson, Kansas, United States[1531]

More About Libbie J. Christner:
Residence: 1880, Mcpherson, McPherson, Kansas, United States[1531]

Child of David Christner and Libbie Christner is:
  856   i.   Lulu May[7] Christner[1531], born Abt. 1878 in NY[1531].

               More About Lulu May Christner:
               Residence: 1880, Mcpherson, McPherson, Kansas, United States[1531]

240. Reverend Nelson Brown[6] **Christner** (Gabriel[5], Joseph "Zep"[4], Johannes John Hans[3], Christian[2], Christen[1])[1532,1533,1534] was born 22 Jul 1851 in Donegal, Westmoreland Co, PA[1535,1536,1537], and died 29 Jul 1904 in Somerset Co., PA[1538,1539,1540]. He married **Mary Amanda Wissinger**[1541,1542] 12 Mar 1870 in Jones Hill, PA[1542]. She was born 14 Jul 1850 in Westmoreland Co., PA[1543,1544], and died 18 Nov 1921 in Butler Co., PA[1545,1546].

Notes for Reverend Nelson Brown Christner:
This info came from "TWO CENTURIES OF THE CHURCH OF THE BRETHERN OF WESTERN PA"
Nelson B. located in Somerset Co about 1880 and purchased a farm from Henry Mull Nelson was a farmer and a minister in the German Baptist Church. Nelson was also a school teacher at the Old Mud School House, Cook Twp., Westmoreland Co., PA. His ministry took him to PA and to Tennessee.

Others say Nelson B. Christner Residences were:
1860------With parents in Jefferson Twp. Somerset Co. PA
1870's--Living in Bullskin Twp. Fayette Co. PA.Elected to the ministry intheIndianCreek Congragation Church of the Brethern maybe County Line Church,Champion, PA
1877---Purchases land in My. Pleasant Twp., Westmoreland Co., PA
1880---Residing in Springfield Twp., Fayette Co., PA
1887---Purchases land on Cox's Creek -- Nelson B. residing in Miford Twp., PA
1892---Nelson B. sells his land on Cox's Creek, Nelson B. Living in Washington Co., PA.
1898---Nelson B. living in Milford Twp., PA.

More About Reverend Nelson Brown Christner:
Burial: 31 Jul 1904, Pleasant Hill Cemetery, New Centerville, Somerset Co, PA
Cause of Death: Consumption
Residence: 1900, Civil District 8, Washington, TN[1547,1548,1549]

Notes for Mary Amanda Wissinger:
Birth: 1850
Death: 1921

Burial: Pleasent Hill Cemetery, New Centerville, Somerset Co., PA

More About Mary Amanda Wissinger:
Burial: Pleasent Hill Cemetery, New Centerville, Somerset Co., PA
Residence: 1880, Springfield Twp., Fayette Co., PA[1549,1550]

Children of Nelson Christner and Mary Wissinger are:

857   i.   Norman Wissinger[7] Christner[1551], born 21 Jul 1871 in Donegal, Westmoreland Co, PA[1551]; died 21 Mar 1915 in McKeesport, Allegheny Co., PA[1551]. He married Elizabeth Schmidt.

More About Norman Wissinger Christner:
Burial: Grandview Cemetery, McKeesport, Allegheny Co., PA
Residence: 1880, Springfield Twp., Fayette Co., PA[1551]

858   ii.   William R. Christner[1551], born 14 Oct 1872 in Saltlick Twp., Fayette Co., PA[1551]; died 19 Jun 1888 in Milford Twp., Somerset Co., PA.[1551].

Notes for William R. Christner:
Maybe born in February 14 1873. He drowned while swimming at Cox's Creek in Milford Twp., Somerset Co., PA.

More About William R. Christner:
Burial: Pleasent Hill Cemetery, Somerset Co., PA
Residence: 1880, Springfield Twp., Fayette Co., PA[1551]

859   iii.   Harry Urbane Christner[1551], born 31 Mar 1874 in Bullskin Twp., Fayette Co., PA[1551]; died 16 Feb 1949 in San Bernadino Co., CA[1552]. He married Elizabeth M.[1552]; born Nov 1878 in Pittsburgh, Allegheny Co., PA[1553].

More About Harry Urbane Christner:
Residence: 1900, Derry, Westmoreland Co., PA[1553]

More About Elizabeth M.:
Residence: 1900, Derry, Westmoreland Co., PA[1553]

+   860   iv.   Gabriel Dickey "Milton" Christner, born 18 Aug 1876 in Donegal, Westmoreland Co., PA; died 17 Jul 1962 in McKeesport, Allegheny Co., PA.

861   v.   Bertha Belle Christner[1554], born 01 Feb 1879 in Mt.Pleasant Twp, Westmoreland Co, PA[1554]. She married R. O. Boggs.

More About Bertha Belle Christner:
Burial: Butler Co., PA
Residence: 1900, Civil District 8, Washington Co., TN[1554]

862   vi.   Ivy M. Christner[1554], born 22 Oct 1880 in Bakersville, Somerset Co., PA[1554]; died 09 Nov 1880[1554].

Notes for Ivy M. Christner:
Buried in Dickey Cemetery, Springfield Twp., Fayette Co., PA.

Ivy M. dau of N. B. and M. A. Christner died Nov 9, 1880 aged 15 days.

More About Ivy M. Christner:
Burial: Dickey Cemetery, Springfield Twp., Fayette Co., PA

863   vii.   Infant Christner[1554], born 13 Dec 1881[1554]; died 17 Dec 1881[1554].

More About Infant Christner:
Burial: Bakersville, Somerset Co., PA

864   viii.   Mary L. Christner[1554], born 24 Mar 1883 in Bakersville, Somerset Co., PA[1554]; died 15 Dec 1883 in Bakersville, Somerset Co., PA[1554].

More About Mary L. Christner:
Burial: Bakersville, Somerset Co., PA

865   ix.   Ida May Christner[1554], born 05 Oct 1884 in Bakersville, Somerset Co., PA[1554]; died 23 Jul 1904[1554].

More About Ida May Christner:
Burial: 24 Jul 1904, Pleasent Hill Cemetery, Somerset Co., PA
Cause of Death: Consumption
Residence: 1900, Civil District 8, Washington Co., TN[1554]

866   x.   Annie Estelle Christner[1554], born 24 Oct 1886 in Milford, Somerset Co., PA[1554]; died 29 Dec 1900[1554].

Notes for Annie Estelle Christner:

More About Annie Estelle Christner:
Burial: Pleasant Hill, Cem, Somerset Co, PA or State of Tenn.
Residence: 1900, Civil District 8, Washington Co., TN[1554]

867   xi.   Cora Belinda Christner[1554], born 10 Sep 1889 in Milford, Somerset Co., PA; died 15 Nov 1902[1554].

More About Cora Belinda Christner:
Burial: TN
Residence: 1900, Civil District 8, Washington Co., TN[1554]

868   xii.   Infant Christner[1554], born 10 Sep 1889 in Milford, Somerset Co., PA[1554].

Notes for Infant Christner:
This male child is a twin to Cora.

More About Infant Christner:
Burial: Pleasant Hill Cemetery, Somerset Co., PA

869   xiii. Edna Rebecca Christner[1555,1556], born 13 Oct 1893 in Odell, Washington Co., PA[1557,1558]; died 16 Oct 1909 in Connellsville, Fayette Co., PA[1559,1560].

Notes for Edna Rebecca Christner:
Birth: 1893
Death: 1909

Burial: Pleasant Hill Cemetery, Somerset Co., PA
Find A Grave Memorial# 88019442

More About Edna Rebecca Christner:
Burial: Pleasant Hill Cemetery Somerset Co., PA
Residence: 1900, Civil District 8, Washington Co., TN[1561,1562]

242. Elizabeth[6] Christner (Joseph[5], Joseph "Zep"[4], Johannes John Hans[3], Christian[2], Christen[1])[1563] was born 17 Jan 1839 in Elk Lick, Somerset Co., PA[1563], and died 16 Sep 1936 in Omaha, Douglas Co., NE[1563]. She married **Henry Miller** 14 May 1857 in Salisbury, Somerset Co., PA[1563]. He was born 20 Dec 1833 in Bavaria, Germany, and died 1928 in Omaha, Douglas Co., NE[1563].

More About Elizabeth Christner:
Residence: 1920, Bryant, Fillmore Co., NE[1563]

Notes for Henry Miller:
Henry is the son of Adam and Anna Miller. Henry and Elizabeth lived at 4709 Cass St. in Omaha, NE.

13339 Hochstedler/Stutzman

More About Henry Miller:
Arrival: Bet. 1850 - 1857[1563]
Christened: English, Luthern
Residence: 1880, Gilletts Grove, Clay Co., IA[1563]

Children of Elizabeth Christner and Henry Miller are:

870   i.   Nancy[7] Miller, born 14 Jun 1859 in Salisbury, Somerset Co., PA; died in Omaha, Douglas Co., NE[1563]. She married Henry C. Negus 01 Jan 1878; born 1852; died 1925.

Notes for Nancy Miller:

More About Nancy Miller:
Residence: 1930, Omaha, Douglas, NE[1563]

871   ii.   Jeremiah Miller, born 13 Apr 1861; died 31 Jul 1924 in Shickley, NE[1563]. He married (1) Christina Schram. He married (2) Lena Rohweder 15 Jun 1893.

Notes for Jeremiah Miller:
Jeremiah married Lena Rohweder on June 15 1893.
He later married Christiana Schram

More About Jeremiah Miller:
Residence: 1880, Gilletts Grove, Clay Co., IA[1563]

872   iii.   Mary Ann Miller, born 13 May 1862; died May 1865 in Salisbury, Somerset Co., PA[1563].

More About Mary Ann Miller:
Residence: United States[1563]

+ 873   iv.   Amanda Miller, born 27 Aug 1864; died 1903 in Lincoln, Lancaster Co., NE.
874   v.   Sarah C. Miller, born 20 Dec 1867 in Somerset, Somerset Co., PA[1563]; died in Omaha, Douglas Co., NE[1563]. She married Harry B. Kerlin 24 Mar 1887.

Notes for Sarah C. Miller:

More About Sarah C. Miller:
Residence: 1880, Gilletts Grove, Clay Co., IA[1563]

243. Katherine[6] Christner (Joseph[5], Joseph "Zep"[4], Johannes John Hans[3], Christian[2], Christen[1]) was born 08 Oct 1840 in Salisbury, Somerset Co., PA, and died 03 Jul 1925 in Columbus, Colorado Co., TX[1564]. She married **Chauncey F. Beal**[1564] 02 Dec 1860. He was born 14 Nov 1836 in Somerset Co., PA[1564], and died 19 Apr 1905 in East Columbia, Texas, USA[1564].

More About Katherine Christner:
Burial: Texas Columbia Cemetery

Notes for Chauncey F. Beal:
13361 Hochstedler/Stutzman

Children of Katherine Christner and Chauncey Beal are:
875   i.   Christiana[7] Beal, born 26 Nov 1861; died 18 Jan 1863.
876   ii.   Dahlgren Beal, born 27 Mar 1864; died 04 Jul 1865.
+ 877   iii.   Savilla Beal, born 10 Aug 1866; died 15 Dec 1896 in Enid, Garfield Co., OK.
878   iv.   Albert Beal, born 06 Mar 1871 in Howard Lake, MN. He married Ruth Hagemever[1565] 26 Nov 1901 in TX; born Abt. 1876 in TX[1565].

Notes for Albert Beal:
Albert was a road worker.

More About Ruth Hagemever:
Race: White[1565]

Residence: 1910, Age: 34; Marital Status: Married; Relation to Head of House: Wife/Justice Precinct 2, Brazoria, Texas, USA[1565]

879   v.   Ezra Beal, born 11 Feb 1874; died 09 Apr 1876.

246. Samuel J. "Matlick Sam"[6] Christner (Joseph[5], Joseph "Zep"[4], Johannes John Hans[3], Christian[2], Christen[1]) was born 19 Apr 1847 in Elk Lick, Somerset Co., PA[1566], and died 01 Feb 1937 in Meyersdale, Somerset Co., PA. He married **(1) Mary A. Shoemaker**[1567], daughter of Anthony Shoemaker and Sally Christner. She was born 24 Nov 1852 in Addison Twp., Somerset Co., PA[1567], and died 25 Jan 1918[1567]. He married **(2) Adaline Florence Wagner** 03 Jul 1877 in Somerset, Somerset Co., PA[1567]. She was born Aug 1850 in Somerset, Somerset Co., PA[1568], and died 05 May 1944 in Meyersdale, Somerset Co., PA[1568,1569].

Notes for Samuel J. "Matlick Sam" Christner:
Information from Mrs. Roy Linderman Meyersdale, PA is the daughter of Matlick Sam.

Birth: Apr 19, 1847 - PA
Death: Feb 1, 1937 - Meyersdale, Somerset Co., PA

The son of Joseph Christner, Jr. and Mary Salome Keim.

He married Ada Florence Wagner in 1878.

Parents:
Joseph Christner (1814 - 1897)
Mary Keim Christner (1818 - 1882)

Spouse: Ada Florence Wagner Christner (1850 - 1944)

Burial: St. Paul's Wilhelm Cemetery, Meyersdale, Somerset Co., PA
Find A Grave Memorial# 114109997

More About Samuel J. "Matlick Sam" Christner:
Residence: 1930, Clarksburg, Harrison Co., WV[1570]

Notes for Adaline Florence Wagner:
Obituary: Meyersdale Republican, May 11, 1944

Mrs. Ada Florence Christner, born Aug. 18, 1850, in Garrett Co., MD died May 5, 1944 at the home of her son-in-law and daughter, Mr. and Mrs. Roy Lindeman, of Meyersdale, at the age of 93 years, 8 months and 17 days.

Mrs. Christner was a daughter of Peter and Rachael Newman Wagner. Her husband was Samuel J. Christner who died six years ago. She is survived by three sons and three daughters, namely, Hattie, wife of William Corley of Boynton; Mrs. Mae Peck of Waterloo, Iowa; Florence, wife of Ray Lindeman, Meyersdale; George of Ypsilanti, Mich.; Irvin of Huntingdon, PA and Clyde of Johnstown.

Prior to the funeral, Mrs. Christner's body was taken to the home of Mr. and Mrs. William Corley in Boynton and from there to the St. Paul Evangelical and Reformed Church at the village of St. Paul, where funeral services were conducted last Sunday by Rev. Ira S. Monn.

Interment was in the church cemetery near by, under the direction of Mortician Stanley M. Thomas of Salisbury.

Birth: 1850 - MD
Death: 1944

The daughter of Peter Wagner and Rachael Newman.

She married Samuel J. Christner in 1878.

Spouse: Samuel J. Christner (1847 - 1937)

Burial: St. Paul's Wilhelm Cemetery, Meyersdale, Somerset Co., PA
Find A Grave Memorial# 114110336

More About Adaline Florence Wagner:
Residence: 1930, Clarksburg, Harrison Co., WV[1570]

Child of Samuel Christner and Mary Shoemaker is:

+ 880   i.   Norman B.[7] Christner, born 13 Oct 1867 in Addison, Somerset Co., PA; died 02 Nov 1943 in Meyersdale, Somerset Co., PA.

Children of Samuel Christner and Adaline Wagner are:

   881   i.   Martha[7] Christner[1570], born 1877[1570].
+ 882   ii.   George Calvin Christner, born 24 Aug 1878 in Elk Lick, Somerset Co., PA; died 12 Jan 1965 in Brevard Co., FL.
+ 883   iii.   Hattie Christner, born Nov 1880 in Spring City, Berks, PA.
+ 884   iv.   Irvin F. Christner, born 08 May 1883 in Connellsville, Fayette Co., PA.
+ 885   v.   Cornelia Mae Christner, born 28 May 1885 in Elklick Twp., Bedford (now Somerset) Co., PA; died 07 Nov 1964 in Waterloo, Black Hawk Co., IA.
+ 886   vi.   Florence B. Christner, born Dec 1889 in Somerset, Somerset Co., PA; died 1963 in Meyersdale, Somerset Co., PA.
+ 887   vii.   Clyde Evans Christner, born 06 Aug 1894 in Meyersdale, Somerset Co., PA; died Apr 1963 in OH.

247. Sarah[6] Christner (Joseph[5], Joseph "Zep"[4], Johannes John Hans[3], Christian[2], Christen[1])[1571,1572] was born 21 Mar 1850, and died in Rocky Ford, Otero Co., CO[1573]. She married **John A. Hochstedler** 21 Nov 1869 in By Samuel Compton. He was born 13 Nov 1845 in Summit Mills, Somerset Co., PA[1574], and died 26 Jan 1918 in Rocky Ford, Otero Co., CO[1575].

Notes for Sarah Christner:
Sarah was married by Samuel Compton J.P. Some have her born 1848. She may have died at Rocky Ford, CO.

More About Sarah Christner:
Residence: 1880, Elk Lick, Somerset Co., PA[1576]

Notes for John A. Hochstedler:
John is the son of Adam and Mary (Miriam) Miller Hochstedler.
John was a farmer. John and Sarah were married by Samuel Compton.

More About John A. Hochstedler:
Christened: German Baptist
Residence: 1880, Elk Lick, Somerset Co., PA[1576]

Children of Sarah Christner and John Hochstedler are:

   888   i.   Clara Belle[7] Hochstedler, born 11 Jan 1879; died in Denver, Denver Co., CO[1576].

       More About Clara Belle Hochstedler:
       Residence: 1880, Elk Lick, Somerset Co., PA[1576]

   889   ii.   Mary Ellen Hochstedler, born 14 Oct 1880 in Summit Mills, Somerset Co., PA[1576]; died 07 Jun 1926 in Empire, Stanislaus Co., CA[1577]. She married Edwin O. Heiny 22 Feb 1904 in Rock Ford, CO.

       More About Mary Ellen Hochstedler:
       Residence: 1920, Precinct 18, Otero, Colorado[1578]

   890   iii.   Charles Russell Hochstedler, born 08 Jan 1883 in Somerset Co., PA; died in Fillmore, Ventura Co.,

CA[1578]. He married Ruth Forrester 26 Mar 1916 in CA.

248. Susannah[6] **Christner** (Joseph[5], Joseph "Zep"[4], Johannes John Hans[3], Christian[2], Christen[1]) was born 27 Jun 1851 in Elklick, Somerset Co., PA, and died 06 Mar 1881 in Meyersdale, Somerset Co., PA. She married **Samuel Briskey** 16 Jun 1878. He was born 01 Oct 1851 in Elklick Twp., Somerset Co., PA, and died 16 Mar 1921 in Meyersdale, Somerset Co., PA.

Notes for Susannah Christner:
Birth date maybe June 22, 1851 or Susanna.

Notes for Samuel Briskey:
Samuel is the son of William Briskey and Susan Fullem Briskey.

Child of Susannah Christner and Samuel Briskey is:

891   i.   Olive May[7] Briskey, born 01 Dec 1879 in Elklick Twp., Somerset Co., PA; died 05 Jun 1955. She married George Christian Haer[1579] 01 Jun 1905 in Garrett, Somerset Co., PA; born 12 May 1880 in Sumit Twp., Somerset, Pennsylvania[1579]; died Jan 1950[1579].

            Notes for Olive May Briskey:

            More About George Christian Haer:
            Fact 5: PA[1579]

249. Henry J.[6] **Christner** (Joseph[5], Joseph "Zep"[4], Johannes John Hans[3], Christian[2], Christen[1])[1580] was born 17 Sep 1853 in Elk Lick, Somerset Co., PA[1580], and died 24 Dec 1916 in Salisbury, Somerset Co., PA[1581]. He married **Charlotte "Lottie" Wagner**[1582] 11 Dec 1881 in Berlin, Somerset Co., PA. She was born 28 Jun 1854 in Elk Lick, Somerset Co., PA[1583], and died 03 Dec 1934 in Elk Lick, Somerset Co., PA[1584].

Notes for Henry J. Christner:
Salisbury Somerset County Star 28 Dec. 1916

The sudden calling of Mr. Henry Christner, of Boynton, from this life to the life beyond the grave, caused much sorrow to his wife, children, grandchildren and a host of friends.

Mr. Christner was at his work, in Bedford Co. digging coal when on last Friday, December 22nd, he was stricken with paralysis. He became unconscious and never recovered from it. His son- in- law, Mr. F. G. Argenbright, who was working with him, brought him home on Saturday, where early on Monday morning he passed quietly to his rest.

The funeral was held at his late residence on Wednesday afternoon at two o'clock, conducted by the Rev. Ira S. Monn, pastor to the family and of the deceased. Interment was made in the I. O. O. F. Cemetery, Salisbury.

The United Mine Workers turned out en-mass, thus paying a beautiful tribute to a brother workman. their ceremony at the grave was beautiful, very touching and greatly significant of the great brotherhood of man, which brotherhood is coming to be more and more felt throughout the world.

The deceased leaves to mourn his loss a wife, two sons and one daughter, also four grandchildren as well as many friends.

History of Bedford and Somerset Counties, Pennsylvania; Bedford County by E. Howard Blackburn; Somerset County by William H. Welfley; v.3, Pub. The Lewis Publishing Company, New York/Chicago 1906, pg. 259

Henry J. CHRISTNER

Henry J. Christner, a merchant of West Salisbury, is descended from ancestors who were among the early settlers of Elk Lick township. His grandfather and father were both Joseph Christner, the latter a native of Somerset county and a farmer. He was a German Baptist. He was a Democrat for forty years before his death, at the age of eighty-four. He married Mary Keim, by whom he had twelve children, all living in 1906 but three. Mary (Keim) Christner died at the age of fifty-three.

Henry J. Christner, third son of Joseph Christner, was born September 17, 1853, in Elk Lick township, and until the age of nineteen attended the public schools for a term of three months annually. He assisted his father in the labors of the farm and in the management of the sawmill until 1875, and then for a short time was employed by the neighboring farmers. Afterward he worked in the mines until 1887, when he again sought and found employment among the farmers. In 1903, in company with his wife, he bought the grocery and feed business of Joseph Patton, of West Salisbury, and has since carried on the business at that place. Since 1904 he has held the office of assistant postmaster of West Salisbury, and for one term served as assessor of Elk Lick township. He is an adherent of the Democratic party and a member of the Reformed church.

Mr. Christner married Charlotte Wagner, daughter of Peter Wagner, of Elk Lick township, and they are the parents of three children: Florence Ruth (Mrs. Frank Argenbright), Harry Buford, and Herbert Eugene.

---laborer--13377 B. Hochstedler C. Stutzman book

More About Henry J. Christner:
Burial: old I.O.O.F Cemetery in Salisbury PA
Christened: Reformed
Residence: 1910, Elk Lick, Somerset Co., PA[1585]

Notes for Charlotte "Lottie" Wagner:
Obituary: Meyersdale Republican 6 Dec. 1934

Charlotte Wagner Christner, widow of Henry Christner, died at the home of her daughter, Mrs. Florence Ruth Wallace, in Huntingdon, PA last Monday afternoon at the age of 80 years, 5 months and 5 days. She was born in Garrett County, MD June 28, 1854, but most of her life was spent in Elk Lick Township, Somerset County, PA where on December 11, 1881, she became the wife of Henry Christner, who for many years worked on farms and in mines of Elk Lick. For several years he was also engaged in the merchandising business in the village of West Salisbury, and later became a resident of Boyton, where he died about fifteen years ago. Mrs. Christner's death was brought about by infirmities of old age.

She was one of the thirteen children born to the late Peter and Rachael (Newman) Wagner and was the mother of three children - Harry of Detroit, MI, Hubert of Boyton, PA and Mrs. Ruth Wallace of Huntingdon, PA all of whom survive. She is also survived by two sisters and one brother--- Ada Florence, wife of Samuel J. Christner of Meyersdale; Mrs. Cornelia Beutman, of Scalp Level, PA and A. Carr Wagner of Salisbury. She is also survived by eleven grandchildren and six great grandchildren. In addition to the bereaved relatives, Mrs. Christner's death is also mourned by a large circle of friends residing in Somerset Co., PA and elsewhere, who held her high esteem.

The funeral service was held in Huntingdon, and the burial took place in the Odd Fellows' Cemetery at Salisbury, Thursday afternoon, the 6th inst.

1920 Census has Charlotte living with her daughter Florence Ruth (Christner) Argenbright.

More About Charlotte "Lottie" Wagner:
Burial: old I.O.O.F Cemetery in Salisbury PA
Residence: 1930, Huntingdon, Huntingdon, PA[1586]

Children of Henry Christner and Charlotte Wagner are:
+   892   i.   Florence Ruth[7] Christner, born 10 Mar 1883 in Salisbury, Elk Lick Twp., Somerset C., PA; died 06 Jul 1975 in Jackson Co., MI.
+   893   ii.   Harry Buford Christner, born 23 Dec 1889 in West Salisbury, Somerset Co., PA; died 29 Jul 1953 in Detroit, Wayne Co., MI.
+   894   iii. Hubert Eugene Christner, born 02 Mar 1892 in West Salisbury, Somerset Co., PA; died 15 Mar 1971 in

Meyersdale, Somerset Co., PA.

251. Jeremiah[6] Christner (Joseph[5], Joseph "Zep"[4], Johannes John Hans[3], Christian[2], Christen[1]) was born 20 Dec 1855. He married **Rosanna**. She was born 10 Dec 1857 in Connellsville, Fayette Co., PA, and died 19 Apr 1904 in Summit Twp., Somerset Co., PA.

Notes for Jeremiah Christner:
Jerry died in a railroad accident before 19 Apr 1904 and his wife and children died in a house fire.

More About Jeremiah Christner:
Burial: Garrett Union Cemetery Somerset Co., PA.

Notes for Rosanna:
Rosanna's husband Jerry died in a railroad accident and she and children died in a house fire.

There is a Lucinda Meyers 8/17/1882 -- 4/19/1904 buried with them. Mother of Richard?

There is a Annie Meyers 6/24/1893 -- 4/19/1904 buried with them. Daughter of Jerry and wife of Richard Meyers

Birth: Dec. 10, 1857
Death: Apr. 19, 1904

Rosanna burned to death in a house fire - Wife of Jerry Christner.

Burial: Ridgeview Cemetery, Garrett, Somerset Co., PA

Children of Jeremiah Christner and Rosanna are:

895   i.   Pansy[7] Christner, born 22 Jun 1900; died 19 Apr 1904.

                Notes for Pansy Christner:
                Birth: Jan. 13, 1904
                Death: Apr. 19, 1904

                Daughter of Lucinda Meyers

                Note: died in a house fire

                Burial: Garrett Union Cemetery, Somerset Co., PA

                More About Pansy Christner:
                Burial: Garrett Union Cemetery Somerset Co., PA.

896   ii.   Ellen Christner, born 24 Feb 1901 in Garrett, Somerset Co., PA; died 19 Apr 1904 in Garrett, Somerset Co., PA.

                Notes for Ellen Christner:
                A horror that may or may not be connected with the strike situation at Garrett was the burning to death of two women and four children in their homes at that place. The victims were Mrs. Rosanna Meyers, her two daughters, Lucinda and Annie, aged 30 and 8 years respectively, and her son, Richard, aged 5 years. The two other victims were young children of Lucinda who was unmarried. The house was a one and one half story log building and the women and children were sleeping in the upper story. Mr. Meyers and Jonas Sullivan, a boarder, were asleep on the first floor. They were awakened by the smoke and the noise made by the fire and had barely time to save their lives by rushing from the building. The victims in the upper story perished without help and their bodies were all reduced to ashes. The origin of the fire is unknown. Meyers, the head of the household, was a miner and until recently he worked for the Somerset Coal company.

                Burial: Ridgeview Cemetery, Garrett, Somerset Co., PA

Another listing on Find A Grave

Birth: Jun. 22, 1901
Death: Apr. 19, 1904

Daughter of Lucinda Meyers

Note: died in a house fire

Burial: Garrett Union Cemetery, Somerset Co., PA

More About Ellen Christner:
Burial: Garrett Union Cemetery Somerset Co., PA.

252. Sevilla[6] Christner (Joseph[5], Joseph "Zep"[4], Johannes John Hans[3], Christian[2], Christen[1])[1587,1588] was born 03 May 1858 in Salisbury, Somerset Co., PA, and died Feb 1943 in Hood River, Hood River Co., OR[1588,1589]. She married **Urias A. Newman** 23 Dec 1875 in Summit Mills, PA. He was born 06 Jul 1848 in Pittsburgh, Allegheny Co., PA[1589], and died 1923 in Hood River, Hood River Co., OR[1590].

More About Sevilla Christner:
Residence: 1900, Eagle & Lincoln Townships, Black Hawk Co., IA[1591,1592]

Notes for Urias A. Newman:
N.A. is the son of George and Mary Ringler Newman
This could also be Urias A.

More About Urias A. Newman:
Christened: German Reformed
Residence: 1900, Eagle & Lincoln Townships, Black Hawk Co., IA[1593,1594]

Children of Sevilla Christner and Urias Newman are:

> 897   i.   Mary Arminta[7] Newman, born 28 Jul 1878 in Elklick Twp., Somerset Co., PA. She married Wilson Fike 13 May 1897.
>
>   Notes for Mary Arminta Newman:
>   Mary married Wilson Fike May 13 1897

+ 898   ii.   Earl Nevin Newman, born 06 Jun 1886 in St.Paul, PA; died 17 Oct 1959 in Wenatchee, Chelan Co., WA.

> 899   iii.   Carl DeForrest Newman, born 05 Apr 1893. He married Leona Hugill 14 Nov 1913.
>
>   Notes for Carl DeForrest Newman:
>   Carl married Leona Hugill Nov 14 1913

> 900   iv.   Zoe Hortense Newman, born 18 Feb 1898[1595]. He married R. K. Imholz.
>
>   Notes for Zoe Hortense Newman:
>   Joe married R.K. Imholz

253. Harvey[6] Christner (Joseph[5], Joseph "Zep"[4], Johannes John Hans[3], Christian[2], Christen[1]) was born 21 Jul 1860 in Salisbury, Elklick Twp., Somerset Co., PA. He married **Isabelle Boyer** Abt. 1882.

Notes for Harvey Christner:
--13389 B. Hochstedler C. Stutzman book.

Child of Harvey Christner and Isabelle Boyer is:
+   901   i.   Arthur Grover[7] Christner, born 29 Nov 1884 in Salisburg, Elklick Twp., Somerset Co., PA.

257. Dinah Christina[6] Christner (Jonas Yone[5], Joseph "Zep"[4], Johannes John Hans[3], Christian[2], Christen[1]) was born 1846. She married **Jacob Wought Wright Vought**.

Notes for Dinah Christina Christner:
Dinah was listed orginally as a male child Christian. Connie told me the child was Dinah and the religion was Christian. Possibly Dinah could also be Carolyn/Carolina and then there would be a male child Christian. No answers to these questions yet.

Child of Dinah Christner and Jacob Vought is:
     902   i.   Annie Wought[7] Wright Vought.

263. Urias Jonas[6] Christner (Jonas Yone[5], Joseph "Zep"[4], Johannes John Hans[3], Christian[2], Christen[1])[1596,1597,1598] was born 04 May 1865 in Union Center, Meyersdale, Somerset Co., PA[1599], and died 03 Feb 1943 in Meyersdale, Somerset Co., PA[1600,1601]. He married **Sevilla Catherine Coleman**[1602,1603,1604] 06 Feb 1896 in Meyersdale, Somerset Co., PA. She was born 06 Mar 1878 in Larimer, Somerset Co, PA[1605,1606,1607], and died 09 Apr 1937 in Meyersdale, Somerset Co., PA[1608].

Notes for Urias Jonas Christner:
Urias and his family has been one of the biggest challenges of the entire Christner family tree. Paul Jacob wrote to me that their were 2 children that died on Oct 20, 1909. We believe these children may have been Uba and Maggie. These names come up in this history but there is no other info on them. Some records indicate that Urias and Sevilla had 15 children, if this is true then all this would be correct with Uba and Maggie. In 1900 Urias built a brick home in Plumb Bottom, Meyersdale, PA. While he was butchering in November his daughter Edith age 2 wandered away and drowned in Flaughterty Creek. Urias couldn't live there anymore and in 1916 traded his farm for one known as Sandspring Mountain. In 1922 the Meyersdale Water Co. bought this farm. In 1930 Urias bought the Sam Meese farm in Greenville Twp., MD. The family moved by wagon and it took 12 hours. Urias farm consisted of 272 acres. His son Paul says his father worked for one year without wages to learn the building trade. When the depression came in 1930 Urias sold fat cattle for $40.00 each and pigs for $5.00 each. Urias paid $6100.00 for their farm of 272 acres. He had borrowed $1100.00 and never saw the day he could pay it back. After he died in 1943 and the farm was sold for $4700.00. In 1937 Urias's wife died in April and his daughter Myrtle shot herself in Oct. The Funerals could not be paid until after the farm was sold in 1943. The 1900 census has a birthday of August 1867 for Urias.

OBIT: Urias J. CHRISTNER, 1943, Greenville Township, Somerset County, PA - Meyersdale Republican, February 4, 1943

Urias J. Christner, 77, died at his home in Greenville Township Saturday evening, Jan. 30. He was born in Garrett, the son of the late Jonas and Caroline Mankameyer Christner. Six sons and three daughters survive: Orlin Christner, Pittsburgh; Carl, Meyersdale; Stewart, Canonsburg; Urie, Aliquippa; Paul, Meyersdale; Harry, U.S. Army in Africa; Mrs. Freda Forest, Meyersdale; Mrs. Eula Kapphan, Mt. Washington; Mrs. Lucy Wright, Salisbury.

Also surviving are three brothers and one sister: Carl Christner, Sand Patch; Rufus, Garrett; Jonas, Farrington, Wyoming; Mrs. Ada Wetzel, Omaha, NE. Funeral services were held Tuesday at 2 p.m. at Main Street Brethren Church, Meyersdale, with Rev. Kenneth Ashman, pastor, officiating. Burial in the Meyersdale Union Cemetery directed by H. R. Konhaus, local mortician.

More About Urias Jonas Christner:
Residence: 1910, Meyersdale, Somerset Co., PA[1609]

Notes for Sevilla Catherine Coleman:
Sevilla is the daughter of Alton Coleman and Mary Ann Bittner.

More About Sevilla Catherine Coleman:
Burial: Union Cemetery, Meyerdale, Sumerset Co, PA[1610,1611]
Residence: 1900, Meyersdale, Somerset Co., PA[1612]

Children of Urias Christner and Sevilla Coleman are:

903   i.   Orlin R.[7] Christner, born 21 Jun 1896 in Meyersdale, Somerset Co., PA[1613]; died 13 Aug 1978 in Volusia Co., FL[1614]. He married Jessie Mae Jiccolus.

Notes for Orlin R. Christner:
OBIT: Orlin R. CHRISTNER, 1978, native of Meyersdale, Somerset County, PA - The Republic, August 17, 1978

Orlin R. Christner, 82, of Deltona, FL died August 13 following a long illness. Born in Meyersdale, he was the son of Urias and Sevilla (Coleman) Christner. He is survived by his widow, Jessie Mae; two sisters: Mrs. Ula Kapphan, Pittsburgh, and Mrs. Lucy Wright, Frostburg, Md.; and one brother, Paul of Salisbury. He was a conductor for the B & O Railroad, stationed in the Pittsburgh office for 43 years before his retirement. He was also a WWI veteran and a member of the Pittsburgh American Legion. Funeral services were conducted by the Stephen Baldauff Funeral Home in Deltona, FL.

More About Orlin R. Christner:
Burial: Deltona Memorial Gardens, Deltona, Volusia Co., FL
Residence: 1930, Pittsburgh, Allegheny, PA[1614]

+ 904   ii.   Ora Christner, born 15 Jan 1898 in Connellsville, Fayette Co., PA; died 15 Nov 1927 in Meyersdale, Somerset Co., PA.

905   iii.   Leo Christner, born Jul 1899 in Connellsville, Fayette Co., PA.

+ 906   iv.   Karl J. Christner, born 14 Jul 1899 in Meyersdale, Somerset Co., PA; died 04 Sep 1967 in Meyersdale, Somerset Co., PA.

+ 907   v.   Stewart A. Christner, born 21 Feb 1901 in Connellsville, Fayette Co., PA; died 13 Sep 1969 in Connellsville, Fayette Co., PA.

+ 908   vi.   Freda Christner, born 19 Nov 1902 in Meyersdale, Summit Twp., Somerset Co., PA; died 03 Jun 1978 in Meyersdale, Somerset Co., PA.

909   vii.   Vera Christner, born 06 Jan 1905; died 1906.

Notes for Vera Christner:
Vera drowned at age 2 in the river at Meyersdale, Somerset Co., PA.

More About Vera Christner:
Burial: Union Cemetery, Meyersdale, Somerset Co., PA

+ 910   viii.   Ula Christner, born 19 Aug 1906 in PA; died 11 Nov 1980 in Pittsburgh, Allegheny Co., PA.

911   ix.   Edith Christner[1615,1615], born 13 May 1908[1615]; died 1910[1615].

Notes for Edith Christner:
Edith died of the flu in the autumn.

Buried: Union Cemetery, Meyersdale, Somerset Co., PA
Coleman Plot

More About Edith Christner:
Burial: Union Cemetery, Meyersdale, Somerset Co., PA

912   x.   Twin Infants Christner[1616], born 20 Oct 1909; died 1927 in Meyersdale, Somerset Co., PA[1616].

+ 913   xi.   Lucy Catherine Christner, born 26 Mar 1912 in Meyersdale, Somerset Co., PA; died 20 Oct 2001.

+ 914   xii.   Urias Bud Christner, born 20 Jul 1914 in Meyersdale, Somerset Co., PA; died 12 Jan 1974 in Sewickley Valley Hospital.

+ 915   xiii.   Paul Jacob Christner, born 22 Jul 1916 in Meyersdale, Somerset Co., PA; died 24 Mar 1988 in

Salisbury, Somerset Co., PA.

916   xiv.   Harry Edison Christner, born 01 Jun 1918; died 01 Aug 1944 in Normandy, France.

Notes for Harry Edison Christner:
Sgt. Harry Christner Hq. Co 26th infantry killed during WWII. One note says he is buried in Normandy, France. Grave 136 7-plot A Marigny Cemetery # 1.
Some notes say he is buried in Brittany American Cemetery, St James (Manche) France. Plot M, Row 3, Grave 6.

Memorial placed for Harry in Union Cemetery, Meyersdale, Somerset Co., PA
ID# 13001976
Rank of Sergeant.
US Army, 26th Inf Reg, 1st Inf Div.
Died Tuesday Aug 1st 1944.

Award: Purple Heart.

More About Harry Edison Christner:
Burial: Marigny Cemetery #1, Normandy, France

917   xv.   Myrtle Larue Christner, born 11 Aug 1919; died 09 Oct 1937.

Notes for Myrtle Larue Christner:
Myrtle never married and died from a self inflicked gun shot wound.

More About Myrtle Larue Christner:
Burial: Union Cem, Meyersdale, PA, Christner Plot

267. Charles[6] Christner (Jonas Yone[5], Joseph "Zep"[4], Johannes John Hans[3], Christian[2], Christen[1])[1617] was born 08 Dec 1876 in Garrett, Somerset Co., PA[1617], and died 07 Jun 1934 in Lincoln, Lancaster Co., NE. He married **Goldie Fern Raffensparger** 20 Jun 1901 in Belleville, Republic Co., IA, daughter of George Raffensparger and Amanda Miller. She was born 28 Dec 1883 in Spencer, IA, and died 28 Sep 1973 in Orange Co., CA.

Notes for Charles Christner:
Charles & his son Dale plus another man went hunting. They got out of their Ford model T automobile. The auto came out of parking gear and started to roll down a hill. Charles tried to stop the auto from rolling down the Mountain side with all the strength he could muster up and in doing so ruptured something in his stomach. Being a Christner he didn't go to the doctor because he will just tough it out by himself, well he got gangrene and died.

More About Charles Christner:
Burial: Wyuka Cemetery (free ground space 334) Lincoln NE.
Cause of Death: Gangrene
Christened: Presbyterian

Notes for Goldie Fern Raffensparger:
B.Hochstedler book 13356 C. Stutzman--------Goldie Raffensparger mother Amanda Miller had a mother Elizabeth Christner married to Henry Miller
Elizabeth Christner Miller is the daughter of Joseph Christner, Jr. and Mary Keim.

Children of Charles Christner and Goldie Raffensparger are:
     918   i.   Ariel E.[7] Christner, born 10 Aug 1904.
+   919   ii.   Leta M. Christner, born 18 Oct 1906 in Monroe, NE.
     920   iii.   Fern A. Christner, born 18 Oct 1908.
+   921   iv.   Dale Wilber Christner, born 07 Nov 1909 in Monroe, NE; died 30 Sep 1992 in Hi Desert Medical Center, Joshua Tree, CA.

272. Calvin M.[6] Christner (Jonas Yone[5], Joseph "Zep"[4], Johannes John Hans[3], Christian[2], Christen[1])[1618] was born 29 Apr 1863 in Larimer, Somerset Co., PA[1618,1619], and died 08 Sep 1947 in Larimer, Somerset Co., PA[1620,1621]. He married **(1) Sarah Dietle**[1622,1623] 08 Oct 1887 in Greenville, Somerset Co., PA[1624]. She was born Mar 1865 in Connellsville, Fayette Co., PA[1625], and died Mar 1920 in Somerset, Somerset Co., PA. He married **(2) Eleanora Weimer**[1626,1627] 30 May 1916 in Somerset, Somerset Co., PA[1628]. She was born 19 Jul 1863 in Larimer, Somerset Co., PA[1628,1629], and died 16 Jan 1936 in Somerset, Somerset Co., PA[1630,1631].

Notes for Calvin M. Christner:
Birth: 1863
Death: 8 Sep 1947

Burial: Temple Cemetery, Meyersdale, Somerset Co., PA
He was a School Teacher.

Obituary: Meyersdale Republican, September 18, 1947

Calvin M. Christner, 84, died Monday, Sept. 8, at the home of his son-in-law and daughter, Mr. and Mrs. Milton Shuck, in Larimer Township, after an illness of 10 months.

Born April 29, 1863, he spent all of his life in Somerset County, employed as a school teacher and a mail carrier. A life-long member of the Church of the Brethren, Mr. Christner was awarded a medal for serving 50 years as a Sunday School officer.

Mr. Christner was married three times - first to Sarah Deitle, who died 31 years ago. To this union were born nine children, two of whom died in infancy.

Later he married Eleanor Weimer, who died 11 years ago, after which he married Etta Miller Mort. After she passed away, he made his home with his son-in-law and daughter, where he died.

He is survived by the following children: Mrs. Eli (Linnie) Weimer, Mrs. Milton (Mary) Shuck, Clarence C. and Walter C., all of Sand Patch; Miss Margaret and Miles E. of Johnstown, and Mrs. Joseph (Sadie) Lint, Holsopple. Also surviving are two brothers and a sister, Jonas, Torrington, Wyo., Rufus, Garrett, and Mrs. Ada Wetzel, Omaha, NE, and 24 grandchildren and 13 great-grandchildren.

He was a kind and loving father and is sadly missed. Funeral services were conducted Thursday afternoon in St. John's Evangelical Church, White Oak, Rev. J. E. Jones of the Hostetler Church of the Brethren and Rev. A. F. Richards of the Evangelical United Brethren Church officiating.

Pallbearers were Harvey and John Geiger, Harvey Petenbrink, Frank Bittner, William Mankamyer and Samuel Baer. Interment was made in the Church Cemetery.

memorial # 43260962

More About Calvin M. Christner:
Residence: 1880, Summit Twp., Somerset Co., PA[1632]

Notes for Sarah Dietle:
Birth: 1865
Death: 1916

Burial: Temple Cemetery, Meyersdale, Somerset Co., PA

More About Sarah Dietle:
Residence: 1910, Larimer, Somerset, PA[1633]

Marriage Notes for Calvin Christner and Sarah Dietle:
one source has October 23, 1887

Notes for Eleanora Weimer:
Birth: Jul 19, 1863 - Somerset Co., PA
Death: Jan 16, 1935 -
Somerset, Somerset Co., PA

Burial: White Oak Cemetery, Wittenberg, Somerset Co., PA

More About Eleanora Weimer:
Residence: 1880, Larimer, Somerset Co., PA[1634]

Children of Calvin Christner and Sarah Dietle are:
+   922   i.   Linda[7] Christner, born Dec 1888 in Somerset Co., PA.
+   923   ii.   Mary Etta Christner, born Mar 1894 in Connellsville, Fayette Co., PA; died 20 Apr 1972 in Summit
                  Twp., Somerset Co., PA.
+   924   iii. Clarence Cadalso Christner, born 09 Oct 1895 in Summit, Somerset Co., PA; died 1971.
+   925   iv.   Walter C. Christner, born 14 Jan 1899 in Meyersdale, Somerset Co., PA; died 27 Dec 1975 in
                  Meyersdale, Somerset Co., PA.
     926   v.   Margaret Katherine Christner, born 07 Feb 1902 in Larimer Twp., Somerset Co., PA[1635]; died 07 Nov
                  1966 in Johnstown, Cambria Co., PA[1635].

                  Notes for Margaret Katherine Christner:
                  Obituary: Margaret Katherine Christner, 1966, native of Somerset County, PA - Meyersdale Republican,
                  November 17, 1966

                  Miss Margaret Katherine Christner, 64, Johnstown, died Nov 7, in Johnstown Memorial Hospital. Born
                  Feb 6, 1902, in Larimer Twp., she was a daughter of the late Calvin and Sarah (Dietle) Christner.

                  Surviving are three brothers and a sister; Clarence, Walter and Mrs. Mary Shuck, all of Meyersdale RD;
                  and Miles of Johnstown. She was a member of St. Paul's EUB Church and Johnstown Business and
                  Professional Women's Club, and served as supervisor of cafeterias in the Johnstown school system.
                  Funeral service was held at John Henderson Funeral Home, Johnstown on Thursday afternoon, with Rev.
                  Dwayne Carter officiating. Interment was made in Grandview Cemetery, Johnstown.

                  More About Margaret Katherine Christner:
                  Residence: 1910, Larimer, Somerset, PA[1635]

+   927   vi.   Sadie Sarah Christner, born 31 Oct 1903 in Larimer Twp., Somerset Co., PA; died 1951 in Hollsopple,
                  Conemaugh Twp., Somerset Co., PA.
     928   vii. Willard Christner, born 30 Mar 1906 in Connellsville, Fayette Co., PA; died 01 Oct 1906.

                  Notes for Willard Christner:
                  Birth: Mar. 30, 1906
                  Death: Oct. 1, 1906

                  Note: Christner, Willard, (no photo available), 30 Mar 1906 - 01 Oct 1906, WPA RECORD

                  Burial: Temple Cemetery, Meyersdale, Somerset Co., PA

+   929   viii. Miles E Christner, born 1908 in Connellsville, Fayette Co., PA.

273. Rufus J.[6] Christner (Jonas Yone[5], Joseph "Zep"[4], Johannes John Hans[3], Christian[2], Christen[1])[1636] was
born 15 Sep 1866 in Somerset Co., PA[1636], and died 1943 in Somerset Co., PA[1636]. He married **Susan
Marker**[1636,1637] 14 Nov 1895 in Rockwood, Somerset Co., PA. She was born 20 Apr 1879 in Black
Twp.Somerset Co., PA[1638], and died 03 Nov 1925 in Somerset, Somerset Co., PA[1638,1639].

Notes for Rufus J. Christner:
Rufus was a coal miner. He may have had a daughter Lula Mae born -- 5/6/1914 - died 9/30/1914. 1920 census
has living at Garrett, PA on Layfette (yes that is how they spelled it) Street with Ralph 22, James 21, Foster 19,
Bruce 16, and Viola R. 3½ living at home with both parents.

Obituary: Rufus Christner 1949, Garrett, Somerset County, PA

Rufus Christner passed away at his home in Garrett Oct. 2, 1949, at 12:30 p.m. He was born Sept. 15, 1867, and was 82 years old at the time of his death. He was preceded in death by his wife Susan (Marker) Christner and a son James. The following children survive: Foster, El Paso, TX; Mrs. Allan Halley, Denver, CO; Ralph of St. Paul and Bruce at home. A sister, Mrs. William Wetzell of Omaha, NE and a brother, Jonas Christner of Ferrington, WY also survive.

Services were held Oct. 4, at the Konhaus Funeral Home, Meyersdale, in charge of Rev. A. J. Replogle. Interment at Center Church.

Mr. Christner was a member of the (Dunkard) Brethren Church. He was in good health until about a week before his death and kept his keen mind until he died. He was a quiet man much admired by the neighboring children and will be greatly missed by them.

Meyersdale Republican, October 6, 1949

Birth: 1867
Death: 1940

Burial:
Center Lutheran Church Cemetery, Summit Twp., Somerset Co., PA

More About Rufus J. Christner:
Burial: Center Church, Luthern, Southwest of Garrett PA.
Residence: 1930, Garrett, Somerset Co., PA[1640]

Notes for Susan Marker:
They were Lutheran. The Center Church Cemetery is a Lutheran Cemetery and this may have been where they attended church.

Birth: 20 Apr 1879
Death: Nov. 3, 1925

Parents:
Jacob M. Marker (1845 - 1927)
Sarah Meyers Marker (1849 - 1923)

Inscription: 46y 6m 14d

Burial: Center Lutheran Church Cemetery, Summit Twp., Somerset Co., PA

More About Susan Marker:
Burial: Center Church, Luthern, Southwest of Garrett PA.
Residence: 1920, Garrett, Somerset Co., PA[1640]

Children of Rufus Christner and Susan Marker are:
    930   i.   Christina[7] Christner.

                    Notes for Christina Christner:
                    Christina & Ruth Christner are not in the 1900 Census with the parents, Maybe belong with other parents.

    931   ii.   Ruth Christner.

                    Notes for Ruth Christner:

Christina & Ruth Christner are not in the 1900 Census with the parents. Maybe belong with other parents.

+ 932   iii.   Ralph Christner, born 27 Feb 1897 in Coal Run, Somerset Co., PA; died 16 Mar 1985 in Akron, Summit Co., OH.

933   iv.   James Christner[1641], born Aug 1898 in Connellsville, Fayette Co., PA; died 1933.

Notes for James Christner:
Son of Rufus & Fredericka was a note I found but failed to write down where the note came from. don't know which Fredericka it is but probley not Caroline Fredericka Mankemyer(1892) because she died before he was born.

Birth: 1898
Death: 1933

Burial: Center Lutheran Church Cemetery, Summit Township, Somerset Co., PA

More About James Christner:
Burial: Center Church, Luthern, Union, Pa.
Residence: 1920, Garrett, Somerset Co., PA[1641]

934   v.   Foster Christner[1642,1643,1644,1645], born 28 Jul 1900 in Connellsville, Fayette Co., PA; died 19 Sep 1978[1646].

Notes for Foster Christner:
Foster moved to Texas.SS#;453-32-2801 iss TX Last address Simi Valley CA.93065

Birth: Jul. 28, 1900
Death: Sep. 19, 1978

PVT, US ARMY

Burial: Fort Bliss National Cemetery, El Paso, El Paso Co., TX
Plot: K, 0, 557
Find A Grave Memorial# 490323

More About Foster Christner:
Burial: 22 Sep 1978, TX[1647]
Military service: 19 Aug 1942, Fort Bliss El Paso, Texas[1647,1648]
Residence: El Paso, TX[1648]
Social Security Number: 453-32-2801/[1649]
SSN issued: TX[1649]

935   vi.   Bruce Christner[1650], born 26 Apr 1905 in Garrett, Somerset Co., PA; died 23 Feb 1973 in Garrett, Somerset Co., PA[1650].

Notes for Bruce Christner:
Birth: Apr 26, 1905
Death: Feb 22, 1973

Burial: Center Lutheran Church Cemetery, Summit Twp., Somerset Co., PA

Bruce lived at Garrett, Somerset Co., PA.

SS# 193-10-0873 Iss.PA Last zip 15542

Obituary: Meyersdale Republican, March 1, 1973
Bruce Christner, 67 of Garrett, died Feb 22, 1973. Born Apr 26, 1905 in Garrett, he was a son of the late Rufus and Susan (Marker) Christner.

Surviving are a brother, Ralph, Meyersdale RD 1; Foster of Salinas, CA; and a sister, Ruth Christner of Denver, CO; also three nieces and three nephews. Funeral service was held Monday morning in Konhaus Funeral Home, Meyersdale, with Rev. Phennicie officiating. Internment in Center Church

Cemetery, Summit Twp., Somerset Co., PA.

Pvt. WWII

More About Bruce Christner:
Residence: 1920, Garrett, Somerset Co., PA[1650]

936   vii.   Lula Mae Christner, born 06 May 1914; died 30 Sep 1914.

Notes for Lula Mae Christner:
Birth: May 6, 1914
Death: Sep 30, 1914

Burial: Center Lutheran Church Cemetery, Summit Township., Somerset Co., PA

937   viii.   Viola R. Christner, born 1916 in Connellsville, Fayette Co., PA.

274. Jonas H.[6] Christner Jr. (Jonas Yone[5], Joseph "Zep"[4], Johannes John Hans[3], Christian[2], Christen[1])[1651] was born Oct 1869 in Somerset Co., PA[1651], and died in Thayer Co., NE. He married **Ellenora**[1651]. She was born Feb 1875 in PA[1651].

More About Jonas H. Christner Jr.:
Residence: 1930, Spoon Buttes, Goshen, Wyoming[1651]

More About Ellenora:
Residence: 1930, Spoon Buttes, Goshen, Wyoming[1651]

Children of Jonas Christner and Ellenora are:
938   i.   Emma B.[7] Christner, born Mar 1894 in NE; died Oct 1896 in NE.
939   ii.   Lester Christner, born 14 Oct 1896 in NE[1652].

More About Lester Christner:
Residence: Goshen, Wyoming[1652]

940   iii.   Nate Christner, born Feb 1898 in NE.

276. Mary Ann[6] Christner (Moses C.[5], Joseph "Zep"[4], Johannes John Hans[3], Christian[2], Christen[1])[1653,1654,1655,1656] was born 11 Mar 1841 in Brothersvalley, Somerset Co., PA[1657], and died 10 Feb 1909 in Black Twp, Rockwood, Somerset Co., PA[1658,1659,1660,1661]. She married **Israel Pritts**[1662,1663,1664,1665,1666,1667] 10 May 1857 in Somerset, Somerset Co., PA[1668]. He was born 09 Dec 1837 in Black Twp., Somerset Co., PA[1669], and died 13 Mar 1904 in Rockwood, Somerset Co., PA[1670,1671].

Notes for Mary Ann Christner:
Amish and Amish Mennonite Genealogies
By Hugh F. Gingerich and Rachel W. Kreider
Pequea Publishers, Gordonville, PA 17529
1986; CH2591; p. 59

Birth: Mar. 11, 1841
Death: Feb. 10, 1909

Inscription: "His Wife"

Burial: Hauger Church Cemetery, Blackfield, Somerset Co., PA

More About Mary Ann Christner:
Burial: Hauger Cemetery, Rockwood, Somerset Co., PA[1671]

Census: 12 Jun 1860, Brothersvalley Twp, Somerset Co., PA[1672,1673,1674,1675]
Residence: 1870, Summit, Somerset Co, PA[1676,1677]

Notes for Israel Pritts:
Birth: Dec. 9, 1837
Death: Mar. 13, 1904
Somerset Co., PA

Co. E. 93 Regt. PA Vol. GAR

Burial: Hauger Church Cemetery, Blackfield, Somerset Co., PA
Civil War Soldiers, 1861-1865

Name: Israel Pritts
Side: Union
Regiment State/Origin: PA
Regiment Name: 93 Pennsylvania Infantry
Company: E
Rank In: Private
Film Number:
M554 roll 97

More About Israel Pritts:
Burial: Hauger Cemetery, Rockwood, Somerset Co., PA[1678]
Civil: Pittsburgh, Allegheny Co., PA[1679]
Description: 1895, his civil war enlistment card said: he was 5 feet 6 inches, black hair, dark complexion and brown eyes./PA[1680]
Military service: 1865, Pittsburgh, Allegheny Co., PA[1680]
Occupation: Abt. 1900, Irvin was a day laboree and a coal miner/Pittsburgh, Allegheny Co., PA[1680]
Residence: 01 Jul 1863, Brothers Valley, PA, United States[1680,1681]

Children of Mary Christner and Israel Pritts are:

+   941   i.   Harrison Simon[7] Pritts, born 13 Oct 1859 in Black Twp., PA; died 11 Mar 1948 in Rockwood (Wilson Creek), Somerset, PA.
+   942   ii.   Catherine Amanda Pritts, born 24 Feb 1862 in Summit, Somerset Co., PA; died 21 May 1926 in Connellsville, Fayette Co., PA.
+   943   iii. Jacob Lewis Pritts, born 09 May 1865 in Somerset Co., PA; died 30 Mar 1894 in Somerset Co., PA.
+   944   iv.   Irene Milissa Pritts, born 22 May 1869 in Somerset, Somerset Co., PA; died 04 Dec 1953 in Rockwood, Somerset Co., PA.
+   945   v.   Irvin Franklin Pritts, born 05 Oct 1871 in Somerset, Somerset Co., PA; died 23 Jun 1950 in Somerset, Somerset Co., PA.
+   946   vi.   Caroline "Carrie" Earl Pritts, born 30 Apr 1874 in Somerset, Somerset Co., PA; died 16 Jul 1930 in Connellsville, Fayette Co., PA.
     947   vii. Lavina "Irene" Pritts[1682], born Oct 1876 in PA[1682].
+   948   viii. Ida Masouri Pritts, born 17 Oct 1876 in Somerset, Somerset Co., PA; died 03 Dec 1903 in Somerset, Somerset Co., PA.
     949   ix.   William Miltion Pritts, born 09 Feb 1880 in Connellsville, Fayette Co., PA; died 25 May 1881 in Connellsville, Fayette Co., PA.

          Notes for William Miltion Pritts:
          Birth: unknown
          Death: May 25, 1881

          Son of I & M Pritts

          Inscription: Aged 1y 3m 16d

          Burial: Ridgeview Cemetery, Garrett, Somerset Co., PA
          Find A Grave Memorial# 51243193

More About William Miltion Pritts:
Burial: Garrett Union Cem, Somerset, PA[1683]

277. Jacob M.[6] Christner (Moses C.[5], Joseph "Zep"[4], Johannes John Hans[3], Christian[2], Christen[1])[1684,1685,1686] was born 21 Apr 1843 in Elk Lick Twp., Somerset Co., PA[1687,1688], and died 09 Feb 1875 in Garrett, Somerset Co., PA[1689,1690]. He married **Mary Ann Walter** 18 Feb 1869 in by John Yorty. She was born 17 Feb 1847 in Summitt Twp., Somerset Co., PA., and died 25 Sep 1911 in Davenport, Thayer Co., NE.

Notes for Jacob M. Christner:
Jacob enlisted in the service Aug 11 1862 in Berlin, PA. He was in the 142 PA Regiment. Volunteers Army. Company F. He was wounded in the leg at the battle of Wilderness in May 1864. Discharged May 29 1865 near Washington, D.C. US archives Pension file 1880 Jun 25----erf #307,845. Jacob died of jaundice.

He listed his profession as a stone mason in the 1870 census.

Amish and Amish Mennonite Genealogies, CH2592; p. 59

More About Jacob M. Christner:
Burial: Old Cemetery, Garrett, Somerset Co., PA.
Cause of death (Facts Pg): Jaundice
Census: 12 Jun 1860, Brothersvalley Twp, Somerset Co., PA[1690]
Fact 1: Occupation: Stone Mason
Military service: Civil War, 142 Reg., PA, Vol. Army, Company F. Wounded from a gunshot to the leg at the Battle of Wilderness in May 1864. Discharged 29 May, 1865 near Washington, DC. Sources U. S. Archives Pension File 1880 Jun 25 --erf#307, 845./
Residence: 1880, Larimer, Somerset, PA[1690]

Notes for Mary Ann Walter:
Mary is the daughter of Baltger or Baltzer Walter or Walters and Hannah_____. Her parents were from Thayer Co., NE.

Name: Mary Ann Walter
Surname: Walter
Sex: F
Birth: 11 February 1847 in Somerset Co., PA
Death: 25 SEP 1911 in Davenport, Thayer Co., NE

Ealser Walter's Family Bible - Record was copies from pages torn from the Bible. Photocopy in possession of Pat Geary, Harrisonburg, VA.

More About Mary Ann Walter:
Burial: Stella, NE
Cause of Death: Diabetes Mellitus

Children of Jacob Christner and Mary Walter are:
+   950   i.   Laura Virginia[7] Christner, born 29 Dec 1869; died 27 Apr 1942.
+   951   ii.   Geneive Rebecca Christner, born 01 Oct 1871 in Garrett, Somerset Co., PA; died 01 Jun 1943 in Boulder, Boulder Co., CO.
+   952   iii.   Hannah Bell Christner, born 02 Oct 1873 in Garrett, Somerset Co., PA; died 09 Jun 1952 in Denver, Denver Co., CO.
+   953   iv.   Warren Jacob (Grant) Christner, born 29 Aug 1875 in Garrett, Somerset Co., PA; died 17 May 1940 in Willard, Logan Co., CO.

278. Adeline Polly[6] Christner (Moses C.[5], Joseph "Zep"[4], Johannes John Hans[3], Christian[2], Christen[1])[1691,1692,1693] was born 02 Feb 1845 in Garrett, Summit Twp., Somerset Co., PA[1694,1695,1696], and died 08

Jul 1921 in Lockridge, Logan Co., OK[1697,1698,1699]. She married **Ananias Lenhart**[1700,1701] 1870 in Somerset Co., PA[1702]. He was born 14 Sep 1850 in Somerset, Somerset Co., PA[1703], and died 14 Nov 1923 in Lockridge, Logan Co., OK[1704].

Notes for Adeline Polly Christner:
Amish and Amish Mennonite Genealogies; CH2593; p. 59

Adaline was raised in the Luthern church but attended Cashion Christian Church after moving to Oklahoma. Adaline and Ananias homesteaded 1 mile north of Lockridge in Logan Co. They moved from Garrett, PA to NE and then to OK. This was done in a covered wagon. When they came to Oklahoma they brought with them many musical instruments and they played for many dances in the area. There first home was made of sod.

Birth: 1845
Death: 1921

Spouse: Annanias Lenhart (1850 - 1923)

Burial: Christner Cemetery, Oklahoma Co., OK
Find A Grave Memorial# 37054948

More About Adeline Polly Christner:
Burial: Christner Cemetery, Oklahoma Co., OK
Residence: 1910, Spring Creek, Logan Co., OK[1705,1706]

Notes for Ananias Lenhart:
Ananias is the son of Benjamin and Elizabeth Foust Lenhart. Ananias and Adeline bought a homestead 1 mile N of Lockridge, OK in Spring Creek Twp. They built a home that was the showplace of the community. The farm passed to son Madison and is now owned by his son Herb (1979).

Vol. II Pub. by the Committee for the Logan Coungty HIstory 1980, Logan County OK. Lockridge- Lockridge was a name coined for the little community on the St. Louis, El Reno and Western Railroad when that line was laid from El Reno to Guthrie in 1902-1903.

The name "Lockridge" was derived from the names of the four counties that abut each other near the site: Logan, Canadian, Oklahoma, and Kingfisher. The town was just 300 yards north of the Oklahoma county line, on land originally homesteaded by Annais and Adeline Lenhart. The site was on a ridge, hence the latter part of the name for the shipping point.

John Lenhart and his father built a store near the railrad in 1903, a two story structure for general merchandise. Mac Wilson soon opened a grocery store, as did Willis Green. A blacksmith shop and a hotel also were soon built.

At its peak, Lockridge had five general stores, a drug store, the Railsback hardware store, and two saloons in addition to the other businesses previously mentioned. A telephone comapny was added early, as was a post office Nov. 7, 1903. The post office continued in operation unol Nov. 30, 1928.

As was usual for a rail stop in an agricultural community, there were two elevators in the town, a depot for the railroad, and a cotton gin. There was no bank at the beginning; Mr. Lenhart filled the role of "banker" advancing credit to customers when needed from one crop year to the next. Shorlty, however, he saw the need for a bank, and built a separate building to house the Farmers Guarantee Bank.

There were about 500 people in the town at its heyday, around 1911. That year saw wheat and other crop prices fall, and the beginning of the end for the town. Morgan's Creamery opened about 1920 in the town. A garage and service station were also operated.

In 1922, the railroad asked to discontinue the line, but the rails stayed and a gasoline-powererd engine "doodle-bug" continued to carry the mail from Guthrie. Two trains were put back on to handle the wheat crop in 1924, but this did not last.

The nearest school was a little distance, so the townspeople started thier own subscription school, which they maintained for a time. People of the Protestant faith used the school as a setting for Sunday School classes, and occasional services of visiting ministers. Most Protestants attended church in Cashion, nearby.

Catholics of the community had a church, St. Patricks, a mile south and a half-mile west of the town, and a cementery alongside it. The church stood many years. Protestants were buried in the Christner Cementery, 2 1/2 miles each and just across the Oklahoma county line.

The railroad tracks that gave birth to the town were taken up in 1925. Morgan's Creamery, operated by the Douglas family, closed about the same time. Several other small businesses continued to operate in the town until the mid '30s, and the town used to have street dances Saturday nights under the store front canopies in an effort to attract interest.

Birth: 1850
Death: 1923

Spouse: Adaline Lenhart (1845 - 1921)

Burial: Christner Cemetery, Oklahoma Co., OK
Find A Grave Memorial# 37054970

More About Ananias Lenhart:
Burial: Christner Cemetery, Guthrie, Logan Co., OK
Residence: 1920, Spring Creek, Logan Co., OK[1706]

Children of Adeline Christner and Ananias Lenhart are:

+ 954   i.   John Joseph[7] Lenhart, born 16 Mar 1871 in Somerset Co., PA; died 1948 in Guthrie, Logan Co., OK.

+ 955   ii.   Charles Wallace Lenhart, born 23 Jan 1872 in Somerset Co., PA; died 1940 in OK.

   956   iii.   William Harrison Lenhart[1707,1708], born 23 Mar 1874 in Somerset Co., PA[1709]; died 1942 in OK[1709]. He married Mary Jane Casey.

         Notes for William Harrison Lenhart:
         Mary is the sister of Ellen who married William's brother Matt.

         More About William Harrison Lenhart:
         Residence: 1880, Sherman, Furnas Co., NE[1710]

   957   iv.   George Washington Lenhart[1711,1712], born 22 Feb 1876 in Somerset Co., PA[1713]; died 1959 in OK[1713]. He married Olive Walters.

         More About George Washington Lenhart:
         Residence: 1880, Sherman, Furnas Co., NE[1714]

   958   v.   Madison Willard (Matt) Lenhart[1715], born 30 Jan 1879 in Sherman, Furnas, NE, USA[1716]; died 1966 in Oklahoma City, Oklahoma Co., OK[1716]. He married Ellen Lenora Casey.

         More About Madison Willard (Matt) Lenhart:
         Residence: 1880, Sherman, Furnas Co., NE[1716]

+ 959   vi.   Emma Elizabeth Lenhart, born 25 Mar 1881 in Wilsonville, Furnas Co., NE; died 24 Feb 1975 in Guthrie, Logan Co., OK.

   960   vii.   Moses Ananias Lenhart[1717,1718], born 28 Feb 1883 in Wilsonville, Furnas Co., NE[1718]; died Jul 1976 in Oklahoma City, Oklahoma Co., OK[1718]. He married Mazie Myrtle Pugh.

+ 961   viii.   James Blaine Lenhart, born 02 Nov 1885 in Humbolt, Richardson Co., NE; died 06 Apr 1961 in Hawthorne, Los Angeles Co., CA.

279. Rena[6] Christner (Moses C.[5], Joseph "Zep"[4], Johannes John Hans[3], Christian[2], Christen[1])[1719] was born 15 Dec 1847 in Brothersvalley, Somerset Co., PA[1719,1720], and died 1921 in Brothersvalley, Somerset Co., PA[1721,1722]. She married **William Lenard Hoover** 1869 in Somerset Co., PA[1723]. He was born 13 Feb 1852 in Somerset Co., PA[1723], and died 13 Sep 1913 in Somerset Co., PA[1723].

Notes for Rena Christner:
Amish and Amish Mennonite Genealogies; CH2594; p. 59

Some spell her name Ruena. Rena's Grandaughter Verda Brant Herboldheimer had the 1548 Froschauer Bible that is in the Goshen College Historical Library. It was donated in 1971 by Levi D. Christner. Levi born 1897 & died 1984. There is another story, the Bible was thrown into a fire and a little girl saved it from the fire. We don't know how it got to an auction in Lagrange Co., IN. It does not look like it was ever in a fire. It is very old and looks that way.

Birth: 1849
Death: 1921

Burial: Highland Cemetery, Garrett, Somerset Co., PA
Find A Grave Memorial# 78282858

More About Rena Christner:
Burial: Highland Cemetery, Garrett, Somerset Co., PA
Residence: 1910, Garrett, Summit Twp., Somerset Co., PA[1723]

Notes for William Lenard Hoover:
Owned Lime Kilns on Ridge Road.

More About William Lenard Hoover:
Burial: Highland Cemetery, Garrett, Somerset Co., PA

Children of Rena Christner and William Hoover are:
+   962   i.   Ida Victoria[7] Hoover, born 07 Dec 1869 in Brothersvalley Twp., Somerset Co., PA; died 19 Dec 1944 in Garrett, Somerset Co., PA.
     963   ii.   Charles Franklin Hoover[1723], born 21 Dec 1877 in Somerset Co., PA[1723]; died 22 Oct 1899 in Somerset Co., PA[1723].

           More About Charles Franklin Hoover:
           Burial: Highland Cemetery, Garrett, Somerset Co., PA
           Residence: 1900, Lockport city, Niagara, New York[1723]

280. Joseph M.[6] Christner (Moses C.[5], Joseph "Zep"[4], Johannes John Hans[3], Christian[2], Christen[1])[1724,1725,1726,1727,1728,1729,1730] was born 10 Mar 1849 in Brothersvalley, Somerset Co., PA[1731], and died 18 Oct 1907 in Guthrie, Logan Co., OK[1732]. He married **Ida Belle Pritts**[1733,1734,1735,1736,1737,1738,1739] 1882. She was born 11 Jan 1867 in Brotheresvalley, Somerset, PA[1740], and died 14 Apr 1946 in Guthrie, Logan Co., OK[1741].

Notes for Joseph M. Christner:
Amish and Amish Mennonite Genealogies, CH2595; p. 59

This info came from dora Lue Gilliam, Kingfisher, OK Joseph belonged to the Odd Fellows Joes home was across the road from his brother Nelson. Nelson Nels Christner, his brother, married Joseph's wife's sister. They married sisters. It was Joe who gave 2 acres of his land for the Christner Cemetary. Joe told his children that he was 14 when the battle of Gettysburg happened and he could hear it. In 1896 a tornado hit their home and destroyed it. This happened at night and there were 4 children upstairs asleep.

Birth: Mar. 10, 1849

Death: Oct 18, 1907

Burial: Christner Cemetery, Oklahoma Co., OK

More About Joseph M. Christner:
Burial: Christner Cemetery, Guthrie, Logan Co., OK[1742,1743]
Residence: 1860, Brothersvalley, Somerset Co., PA[1744]

Notes for Ida Belle Pritts:
Birth: 1867
Death: 1946

Burial: Christner Cemetery, Oklahoma Co., OK

More About Ida Belle Pritts:
Burial: Christner Cemetery, Guthrie, Logan Co., OK[1745,1746]
Residence: 1930, Red Rock, Noble Co., OK[1747]

Children of Joseph Christner and Ida Pritts are:

964   i.   Grace[7] Christner[1748], born 09 Mar 1883 in Marysville, Marshal Co., KS[1748]; died 07 Apr 1883 in Marysville, Marshal Co., KS[1748].

Notes for Grace Christner:
Died in infancy.

965   ii.   Susan Christner, born 09 Mar 1884[1749]; died 15 May 1885 in Marysville, Marshal Co., KS.

966   iii.   Dora Christner[1750], born 05 Aug 1885 in Marysville, Marshall Co., KS[1750]; died 05 Aug 1885 in Marysville, Marshall Co., KS[1750].

Notes for Dora Christner:
Died in infancy.

+ 967   iv.   Mary Christner, born 27 Mar 1887 in Marysville, Marshall Co., KS; died 27 Feb 1973 in Longmont, Boulder Co., CO.

968   v.   Moses Christner, born 27 Mar 1887; died 07 Dec 1890 in OK.

Notes for Moses Christner:
Moses was a twin to Mary.

Birth: Mar. 27, 1887
Death: Dec. 7, 1890

Inscribed "Moses - son of J.M. and Ida B. Christner";

Burial: Christner Cemetery, Oklahoma Co., OK

More About Moses Christner:
Burial: Christner Cemetery, Oklahoma Co., OK

+ 969   vi.   Jacob J. Christner, born 11 Aug 1888 in Marysville, Marshal Co., KS; died 07 Feb 1960 in Bellevue, Sarpy Co., NE.

+ 970   vii.   Kate Christner, born 27 Jan 1890 in Guthrie, Logan Co., OK; died 18 Feb 1974 in Ponca, Kay Co., OK.

+ 971   viii.   Archie B. Christner, born 22 Sep 1892 in Lockridge, Logan Co., OK; died 08 Nov 1962 in Los Angeles, Los Angeles Co., CA.

+ 972   ix.   Sampson Samuel Christner, born 16 Aug 1893 in Downs, Kingfisher Co., OK; died 04 Mar 1919 in Oklahoma City, Oklahoma Co., OK.

+ 973   x.   Lauretta Christner, born 17 Apr 1895 in Oklahoma City, Oklahoma, Oklahoma, United States; died 03 Feb 1946 in Denver, Denver, CO.

974   xi.   Alice Christner, born 15 Jul 1897; died 1923 in Tulare Co., CA.

Notes for Alice Christner:

Birth: 1897
Death: 1923

Burial: Tulare Cemetery, Tulare, Tulare Co., CA

+ 975   xii.   Nannie Christner, born 15 Aug 1899 in Lockridge, Logan, OK; died 30 Dec 1979 in Brea, Los Angeles Co., CA.

+ 976   xiii.   Annie Christner, born 15 Aug 1899 in OK; died 15 Jun 1976 in Hawthorne, CA.

   977   xiv.   Elvira Christner[1751], born 13 Oct 1901 in Oklahoma Territory, OK[1751,1752]; died 10 Sep 2002 in El Monte, Los Angeles Co., CA[1752]. She married Roy Stonum[1753]; born 13 Dec 1900 in IL[1753]; died Jun 1974 in El Monte, Los Angeles Co., CA[1753].

       More About Elvira Christner:
       Residence: 1920, Guthrie Ward 4, Logan Co., OK[1753]
       Social Security Number: 564-16-1491/[1754]
       SSN issued: CA[1754]

+ 978   xv.   Pearl Christner, born 22 Dec 1903 in OK; died 28 Nov 1989 in Norwalk, Los Angeles, California, USA.

   979   xvi.   Charles Christner, born 22 Dec 1903; died 01 May 1974.

       Notes for Charles Christner:
       Charles is a twin to Pearl.

       Birth: Aug. 16, 1893
       Death: Mar. 4, 1919

       Burial: Christner Cemetery, Oklahoma Co., OK

       More About Charles Christner:
       Burial: 12 row, Christner Cem, near Cashion Oklahoma

+ 980   xvii.   Daisy Victoria Christner, born 16 Apr 1905 in OK; died 16 Jan 1992 in Arkansas City, Cowley Co., KS.

282. Nelson "Nels"[6] Christner (Moses C.[5], Joseph "Zep"[4], Johannes John Hans[3], Christian[2], Christen[1])[1755,1756,1757,1758,1759,1760] was born 14 Jan 1854 in Garrett, Summit Twp., Somerset Co., PA[1761,1762,1763,1764,1765], and died 01 Jul 1925 in Oklahoma City, Oklahoma Co., OK[1766,1767]. He married **Sarah Catherine Pritts**[1768,1769,1770,1771,1772,1773,1774] 16 Jul 1884 in NE[1775]. She was born 02 Feb 1870 in Garrett, Somerset Co., PA[1776,1777,1778], and died 19 Oct 1939 in Guthrie, Logan Co., OK[1779,1780].

Notes for Nelson "Nels" Christner:
Amish and Amish Mennonite Genealogies; CH2596; p. 59

Early in life Nelson joined the Lutheran Church in Garrett Co., PA. He farmed in PA and NE and came to Oklahoma in the fall of 1889. He bought a homestead 1 1/2 miles north of Lockridge in Logan Co. Sarah and two sons came in the spring of 1890. They raised wheat, oats, corn and cotton. Nelson worked in the winter months on the Fort Smith railroad and later in a cotton gin in Lockridge. The Chisholm Trail ran through their farm. Nelson and the family saw several tornadoes go thru their farm and in May 1908 were at the cellar door and watched it take 2 of the neighbors homes. The family has kept most of the oil rights on the homestead having sold the surface rights in 1956. Joseph, Nelsons brother lived down the road in Oklahoma Co. They married sisters.

Birth: 1854
Death: 1925 - OK

Burial: Christner Cemetery, Oklahoma Co., OK
Find A Grave Memorial# 89066751

More About Nelson "Nels" Christner:
Burial: [1781]
Residence: 13 Jun 1885, Muddy, Richardson Co., NE[1782,1783]

Notes for Sarah Catherine Pritts:
Sarah Catherine Pritts Christner grew up in Somerset Co, PA. She traveled to Nebraska and then Colorado with her husband Nelson and small children before coming to Oklahoma in 1890. She had fourteen children. One died in infancy. She helped her husband on the farm, with the animals, chickens and gardening and sold milk, cream, eggs and garden produce. She attended church at Cashion Christian Church, Kingfisher Co, OK.

Notes for Iris Dean Davis Deurmyer
Iris grew up on the family homestead, attended Cashion Public Schools for twelve years, and graduated from Cashion High School. She attended Central State University, Edmond, OK. majoring in special education. After marrying Richard "Deon" Deurmyer, she moved to Eugene, OR. and was a homemaker and teacher of special needs children for her church.

She moved to Mangum, OK, commuted to Southwestern Oklahoma State University, and became youth pastor for First United Methodist Church. She works with various mission groups, going on mission trips in the states and overseas. She is an ordained pastor of International Pentecostal Holiness Church and serves as pastor of a church in rural western Oklahoma. Rev Deurmyer is host to missionaries and sponsors revivals and prayer groups in several communities. She enjoys gardening, camping, teaching children, spending time with her granddaughter, acting in community theatre, and writing. She writes skits for performance in church settings, and is a published author of short stories and poems.

Birth: 1870
Death: Oct 1939

Burial: Christner Cemetery, Oklahoma Co., OK

More About Sarah Catherine Pritts:
Burial: Christner Cemetery, Oklahoma Co., OK[1784]
Residence: 1910, Spring Creek, Logan Co., OK[1785]

Children of Nelson Christner and Sarah Pritts are:

981   i.   Ulyses[7] Christner, born 24 Sep 1885 in Connellsville, Fayette Co., PA; died 1885 in Infancy.

982   ii.   Arthur Jacob Christner, born 21 Jan 1887 in Connellsville, Fayette Co., PA; died 15 Oct 1956 in Sterling, Logan Co., CO[1786].

Notes for Arthur Jacob Christner:
When Arthur's father, Nelson,"Nels", died in 1925, Arthur left his home and farming operation in Colorado to return to the family home to help his mother run the Christner homestead and provide for the younger children. Arthur never married. After his mother died, he continued operating the farm. When a fire destroyed the farmhouse in 1940, he paid for the materials to have another house built on the old foundation. He continued living and working on the farm along with his sister Gladys and her children until his death.

It was said that Arthur could and would do the work of at least 2 men. He helped neighbors at harvest time, thrashing wheat and harvesting crops. Arthur assisted his brother Roy and several young farmers establish their farms. He continued using his team of Clydesdales for many decades. The huge family garden and the larger garden by the west creek were maintained using a horse and hand cultivator. Produce was taken to market using horses and wagons. In his last years he continued to milk his cows by hand although he had to walk with the help of crutches due to arthritis in his knees. He went to visit family and friends in Colorado, but died in his sleep the first night he arrived in Sterling, Colorado in 1956.

Arthur never married. He took care of his mother and the younger children. He was a farmer.

Birth: Jan. 21, 1887
Death: Oct. 15, 1956

Burial: Christner Cemetery, Oklahoma Co., OK

More About Arthur Jacob Christner:
Burial: Christner Cemetery, Oklahoma Co., OK

Residence: 1930, Spring Creek, Logan Co., OK[1786]

983   iii.   Ray Nelson Christner, born 17 Dec 1888 in NE[1786]; died 09 May 1955 in Little Rock, Pulaski Co., AR[1786].

Notes for Ray Nelson Christner:
Ray was in the Navy during WWI and WWII. He joined the Navy in 1910. He was a Chief Petty Officer Chief Boatswain's Mate G). He served 21 years active and 12 years reserves. When he reired he moved to Allison, AR and gardened on a steep hillside plot. He died in the Veterans Hospital in Little Rock, AR after a short illness.

Birth: Dec. 17, 1888
Death: May 9, 1955

Burial: Christner Cemetery, Oklahoma Co., OK

More About Ray Nelson Christner:
Residence: 1930, Spring Creek, Logan Co., OK[1786]

+   984   iv.   Sidney Lewis Christner, born 30 Aug 1890 in Lockridge, Logan Co., OK; died 12 Jan 1970 in Oklahoma City, Oklahoma Co., OK.

+   985   v.   Earl Harrison Christner, born 16 Sep 1892 in Lockridge, Logan Co., OK; died 13 Aug 1958 in North Platte, Lincoln Co., NE.

+   986   vi.   Musetta Christner, born 20 Oct 1894 in Lockridge, Logan Co., OK; died 06 Aug 1928 in Cashion, Kingfisher Co., OK.

+   987   vii.   Dewey Guy Christner, born 25 Jan 1897 in Lockridge, Logan Co., OK; died 01 Dec 1971 in Guthrie, Logan Co., OK.

+   988   viii.   Jeanette "Nettie" Christner, born 25 Oct 1898 in Lockridge, Logan Co., OK; died 16 Jan 1963 in Fort Collins, Laramie Co., CO.

+   989   ix.   Ermit Theodore "Erm" Christner, born 06 Nov 1900 in Lockridge, Logan Co., OK; died 14 Dec 1979 in Minco, Grady Co., OK.

+   990   x.   Elva O. Christner, born 06 Dec 1902 in Lockridge, Logan Co., OK; died 30 Aug 1993 in Oklahoma City, Oklahoma Co., OK.

+   991   xi.   Alma Christner, born 28 Dec 1905 in Lockridge, Logan Co., OK; died 09 Aug 1991 in Guthrie, Logan Co., OK.

+   992   xii.   Verdell Christner, born 04 Apr 1908 in Lockridge, Logan Co., OK; died 29 Oct 1994 in Edmond, Logan Co., OK.

+   993   xiii.   Gladys Irene Christner, born 12 Jan 1910 in OK; died 24 Oct 1981 in Mangum, Greer Co., OK.

+   994   xiv.   Roy M. Christner, born 19 Sep 1913 in Lockridge, Logan Co., OK; died 15 Apr 1993 in Oklahoma City, Oklahoma Co., OK.

283. Alexander[6] **Christner** (Moses C.[5], Joseph "Zep"[4], Johannes John Hans[3], Christian[2], Christen[1])[1787,1788,1789,1790,1791] was born 04 Apr 1856 in Garrett, Summit Twp., Somerset Co., PA[1792,1793,1794,1795,1796], and died 02 Dec 1947 in Strasburg, Adams Co., CO[1797,1798,1799]. He married **Ellen Louise "Nellie" Gilbert**[1800,1801] 1881 in Stella, Richardson Co., NE. She was born 27 Jan 1865 in IL[1802], and died 1914 in Strasburg, Adams Co., CO[1802].

Notes for Alexander Christner:
Amish and Amish Mennonite Genealogies; CH2597; p. 59

Birth: Apr. 4, 1856
Death: Dec. 2, 1947

Inscription: "In Loving Memory"

Burial: Mount View Cemetery, Bennett, Adams Co., CO

More About Alexander Christner:
Burial: Mount View Cemetery, Bennett, Adams Co., CO[1803]
Census: 1920, Estes Park, Larimer Co., CO[1804]

Residence: 1900, Cedar & Spring Creek Townships, Logan Co., OK[1805]

More About Ellen Louise "Nellie" Gilbert:
Burial: Lyons Cemetery, Lyons, Boulder Co.Colorado[1806]
Residence: 1910, Noland, Boulder, Colorado[1806]

Children of Alexander Christner and Ellen Gilbert are:
+   995   i.   Josephine[7] Christner, born 06 Jun 1881 in Stella, Richardson Co., NE; died 21 Nov 1925 in Guthrie,
                    Logan Co., OK.
     996   ii.   Florence "Flossie" Christner[1806], born 25 Nov 1883[1806]; died Abt. 1916 in Lyons, Boulder Co., CO[1806].
                    She married Jr. Johnny L. Wilson Jr.; died in Lyons, Boulder Co., CO.

                    More About Florence "Flossie" Christner:
                    Burial: Lyons Cemetery, Lyons, Boulder Co., CO

+   997   iii.   Philo Leroy (Roy P) Christner, born 11 Jan 1886 in Oxford, Crowley Co., KS; died 21 Feb 1954 in
                    Denver, Arapahoe Co., CO.

284. Leah[6] Christner (Moses C.[5], Joseph "Zep"[4], Johannes John Hans[3], Christian[2],
Christen[1])[1807,1808,1809,1810,1811] was born 17 Apr 1858 in Garrett, Summit Twp., Somerset Co., PA[1812,1813,1814,1815],
and died 09 Nov 1930 in Northampton, Somerset Co., PA[1816]. She married **Paul Ackerman**[1817,1818,1819,1820]
1878[1821]. He was born 04 Oct 1855 in Summit Twp., Somerset Co., PA[1822,1823,1824], and died 04 May 1910 in
Northampton Twp., Somerset Co., PA[1824].

Notes for Leah Christner:
Amish and Amish Mennonite Genealogies; CH2598; p. 59

More About Leah Christner:
Burial: 11 Nov 1930, Mt.Lebanon Cemetery, Northampton Twp., Somerset Co., PA
Residence: 1880, Northampton, Somerset Co., PA[1824,1825]

More About Paul Ackerman:
Residence: 1880, Northampton, Somerset Co., PA[1826,1827]

Children of Leah Christner and Paul Ackerman are:
+   998   i.   Eva Geneva Idella[7] Ackerman, born 1880 in Northampton, Somerset Co., PA; died 1920.
     999   ii.   Irving C. Ackerman[1828,1829,1830], born 19 Aug 1891[1831,1832]; died 12 Nov 1996 in Flushing, Queens,
                    NY[1833].

                    More About Irving C. Ackerman:
                    Residence: 1930, Meyersdale, Somerset Co., PA[1834]
                    Social Security Number: 065-05-4239/[1835]
                    SSN issued: NY[1835]

    1000   iii.   Harry Ackerman[1836,1837], born 1893 in Connellsville, Fayette Co., PA[1838].

                    More About Harry Ackerman:
                    Residence: 1920, Mount Oliver, Allegheny Co., PA[1838]

    1001   iv.   Dennis Ackerman[1838], born 1896 in Connellsville, Fayette Co., PA[1838].
    1002   v.   Samuel Ackerman[1838], born 1901 in Connellsville, Fayette Co., PA[1838].
    1003   vi.   Mahlon P. Ackerman[1838], born 1903 in Connellsville, Fayette Co., PA[1838].

                    More About Mahlon P. Ackerman:
                    Residence: 1930, Northampton, Somerset Co., PA[1838]

285. Katherine Ann[6] Christner (Moses C.[5], Joseph "Zep"[4], Johannes John Hans[3], Christian[2], Christen[1])
was born 11 Jul 1860 in Somerset Co., PA[1839,1840], and died May 1938 in Marysville, Marshall Co., KS[1841,1842].

She married **John Henry Otto**. He was born 21 Sep 1858, and died 1899 in Marysville, Marshall Co., KS.

Notes for Katherine Ann Christner:
Amish and Amish Mennonite Genealogies, CH2599; p. 59

More About Katherine Ann Christner:
Burial: Marysville, Marshall Co., KS

More About John Henry Otto:
Burial: Marysville, Marshall Co., KS

Children of Katherine Christner and John Otto are:

| 1004 | i. | Irvin Leroy[7] Otto, born 10 Jul 1882; died 1952 in Marysville, Marshal Co., KS. He married Edna S. Meyer. |

1005 ii. Nettie Janette Otto, born 23 Jun 1884; died 1918 in Marysville, Marshal Co., KS. She married Michael Herboldshiemer.

Notes for Nettie Janette Otto:
Nettie married Mike Herboldshiemer

1006 iii. Clayton Henry Otto, born 15 Aug 1886; died 1958 in Marysville, Marshal Co., KS. He married Alice Burket.

Notes for Clayton Henry Otto:
Clayton married Alice Burket

286. George Washington[6] Christner (Moses C.[5], Joseph "Zep"[4], Johannes John Hans[3], Christian[2], Christen[1])[1843,1844,1845,1846,1847] was born 14 Feb 1862 in Brothersvalley, Somerset Co., PA[1848,1849,1850,1851], and died 14 Jan 1931 in Willard, Logan Co., CO[1852,1853,1854]. He married **(1) Mabel Jones**[1855,1856,1857] 1899 in Marysville, Marshall Co., KS. She was born 1865 in England[1858,1859], and died 1890 in Lockridge, Logan Co., OK[1860]. He married **(2) Elizabeth Betty Blackwell Reed**[1861] 1902 in Fayette Co., PA. She was born 1871 in VA.

Notes for George Washington Christner:
Information from Dora Lue Gillilan. George lived near old Yoder coal station south of Garrett, PA. He migrated to Colorado later. He is buried in Prairie Lawn Cemetery, Willard, Logan Co., CO.

More About George Washington Christner:
Burial: Prairie Lawn Cemetery, Willard, Logan Co.., CO
Residence: 1910, Somerset Co., PA[1862]

Notes for Mabel Jones:
She died from Typhoid Fever. She was taken to Canada after her mother died by an unknown lady and somehow ended up in Marysville, Kansas working for Kate (Christner) Otto and thats how George Christner met her. She named her two sons with middle names of Gilbert and Jones, so is her fathers name Gilbert Jones? She had three sisters Bessie (also her daughters name) and Rose and Elsie.

More About Mabel Jones:
Burial: Christner Cemetery, Oklahoma Co., OK[1863]
Cause of Death: Typhoid Fever

Notes for Elizabeth Betty Blackwell Reed:
She had still born twins in 1914.

More About Elizabeth Betty Blackwell Reed:

Residence: 1870, Age in 1870: 1/Fort Chiswell, Wythe, Virginia, United States[1864]

Children of George Christner and Mabel Jones are:

+ 1007   i.   Irvin Gibert[7] Christner, born 24 Aug 1889 in OK; died 27 Mar 1961 in Sterling, Logan Co., CO.

    1008   ii.   Harry Jones Christner, born 26 Mar 1895 in Lockridge, Logan Co., OK[1864]; died 23 Apr 1978 in Cashion, Kingfisher Co., OK[1865]. He married Mary Stella Ekstein 14 Dec 1916 in Willard, Co.; born 27 Jan 1899 in Davenport, Neb.; died 11 Dec 1991 in Kingfisher Hospital, Kingfisher, Kingfisher Co., OK.

Notes for Harry Jones Christner:
Last address Cashion OK 73016 SS#;440-14-6442 Iss OK

Birth: Mar. 26, 1895
Death: Apr. 23, 1978

Inscription: TOGETHER FOREVER

Burial: Cashion Cemetery, Cashion, Kingfisher Co., OK
Find A Grave Memorial# 7809288

More About Harry Jones Christner:
Burial: Cashion, Kingfisher Co., OK[1866]
Residence: 01 Apr 1940, Age: 45; Marital Status: Married; Relation to Head of House: Head/Sterling, Logan Co., CO[1866]

Notes for Mary Stella Ekstein:
Mary is the daughter of George and Adele Lewis Ekstein. She was a housewife and took in two girls to rear Florence and Edna Womach around 1920.Mary and Harry moved to Cahsion Colorado in 1926, in 1938 moved to Sterling, Colorado and back to Cashion in 1975.

Birth: Jan. 27, 1899
Death: Dec. 11, 1991

Burial: Cashion Cemetery, Cashion, Kingfisher Co., OK
Find A Grave Memorial# 7809289

More About Mary Stella Ekstein:
Burial: 14 Dec 1991, Cashion Cem, Cashion, Oklahoma

+ 1009   iii.   Bessie Vera Christner, born 16 Feb 1898 in OK; died 23 Jul 1979 in Cashion, Kingfisher Co., OK.

Children of George Christner and Elizabeth Reed are:

    1010   i.   Robert B.[7] Reed, born 1887 in VA.
    1011   ii.   James H. Reed, born 1888 in VA.

287. Richard W.[6] Christner (Moses C.[5], Joseph "Zep"[4], Johannes John Hans[3], Christian[2], Christen[1])[1867,1868,1869] was born 14 Jan 1867 in Garrett, Somerset Co., PA[1870], and died 1950 in Garrett, Somerset Co., PA[1870,1871,1872]. He married **(1) Amanda**. She was born 1860, and died 15 Jul 1894. He married **(2) Louisa "Dillie" Verbena Brant** 11 Apr 1902. She was born 25 Aug 1875 in Somerset Co., PA[1872], and died 1951 in Somerset Co., PA[1872].

Notes for Richard W. Christner:
Some have birthday as1867 and 1864.
1900 census - 1867. He and his wife Amanda moved to Garrett Somerset Co. PA. with his mother after her husband died. The 1900 census has Richard enumerated with his brother in law, William L. Brant - Garrett - as boarder, he was married to Rena Christner.

Birth: 1866
Death: 1950

Burial: Highland Cemetery, Garrett, Somerset Co., PA

More About Richard W. Christner:
Burial: Highland Cemetery, Garrett, Somerset Co., PA
Residence: 1920, Summit, Somerset Co., PA[1872]

Notes for Amanda:
Birth:
Death: Jul. 15, 1894

Inscription: Aged 34y 2m

Burial: Ridgeview Cemetery, Garrett, Somerset Co., PA

Notes for Louisa "Dillie" Verbena Brant:
Maybe spelled Delia Brant -----------.

1910 soundex PA has her bithday as 1868.
1920 census has 1876 & Tillie V.

Birth: 1866
Death: 1950

Burial: Highland Cemetery, Garrett, Somerset Co., PA

More About Louisa "Dillie" Verbena Brant:
Burial: Highland Cemetery, Garrett, Somerset Co., PA
Residence: 1910, Summit, Somerset Co, PA[1873]

Children of Richard Christner and Louisa Brant are:
1012 i. Violet[7] Christner[1874], born 18 Jun 1903 in Connellsville, Fayette Co., PA[1874]; died 25 Apr 1972 in Somerset Co., PA[1874]. She married Mason.

More About Violet Christner:
Burial: Highland Cemetery, Garrett, Somerset Co., PA

1013 ii. Florence Christner[1875], born 29 May 1905 in Garrett, Somerset Co., PA[1875,1876]; died May 1985 in Pennsauken, Camden Co., NJ[1876]. She married John Robertson; born 11 Oct 1901 in Sunbury, Northumberland Co., PA; died 06 Nov 1985 in Camden, Camden Co., NJ.

Notes for Florence Christner:
Birth: May 29, 1905 - Garrett, Somerset Co., NJ
Death: May 22, 1985 - Camden, Camden Co., NJ

Obituary: ROBERTSON - Daily American, May 24, 1985
Florence E. Robertson, 78, Camden, N.J., died May 22, 1985 in Camden, N.J. She was born in Garrett, lived there for 35 years, and moved to Pennsauken, N.J. She is survived by her husband John E. and several nieces and nephews. Graveside services will be held Saturday at Rockwood Cemetery, Rockwood. Viewing and services were held in Pennsauken, N.J.

Spouse: John E. Robertson (1901 - 1985)

Burial: Rockwood IOOF Cemetery, Rockwood, Somerset Co., PA
Find A Grave Memorial# 96353257

More About Florence Christner:
Residence: 1910, Summit, Somerset Co., PA[1877]
Social Security Number: 158-38-2490/[1878]
SSN issued: NJ[1878]

Notes for John Robertson:
Birth: Oct 11, 1901 - Sunbury, Northumberland Co., PA
Death: Nov 6, 1985 - Camden, Camden Co., NJ

Obituary: ROBERTSON - Daily American, November 8, 1985

John E. Robertson, 84, died Nov. 5, 1985, in Camden, NJ. A resident of Pennsauken, NJ he was born in West Sunbury, and was a former Somerset County resident. Son of James and Lelia Robertson. Husband of the late Florence. He is survived by two brothers, Harry of Jenners and Robert of Indiana, PA; one sister, Mary Fetterman, also of Indiana, PA; and several nieces and nephews. He was a member of Somerset Masonic Lodge 358, F&AM. Graveside services will be noon Monday at Rockwood I.O.O.F. Cemetery. Viewing Sunday evening at the Inglesby Funeral Homes, 2426 Cove Rd, Pennsauken, NJ.

Spouse: Florence E. Robertson (1905 - 1985)

Burial: Rockwood IOOF Cemetery, Rockwood, Somerset Co., PA
Find A Grave Memorial# 96353216

+ 1014 iii. Mabel Christner, born 09 May 1907 in Connellsville, Fayette Co., PA; died 19 May 1985 in Lima, Allen Co., OH.

  1015 iv. Emma D. Christner[1879], born Abt. 1910 in Connellsville, Fayette Co., PA[1879].

  More About Emma D. Christner:
  Residence: 1910, Summit, Somerset Co., PA[1879]

+ 1016 v. Blanche Beloye Christner, born 10 Mar 1910 in Garrett, Somerset Co., PA; died 01 Oct 1980 in Berlin, Somerset Co., PA.

  1017 vi. Theal E. Christner[1879], born 06 Feb 1914 in Chongqing, Chongqing Shiqu, Chongqing, China[1879]; died 1971 in Somerset, Somerset Co., PA[1879].

  Notes for Theal E. Christner:
  Birth: 1914
  Death: 1971

  Burial: Highland Cemetery, Garrett, Somerset Co., PA

  More About Theal E. Christner:
  Residence: 1920, Summit, Somerset Co., PA[1880]

292. Cornelius[6] Judy (Eve[5] Christner, Joseph "Zep"[4], Johannes John Hans[3], Christian[2], Christen[1])[1881,1882] was born 21 Jan 1846 in Brothervalley, Somerset Co., PA[1882], and died 24 Jul 1917 in Age: 71/Garrett, Somerset Co., PA[1883]. He married **Henrietta Dorthea Hoffman**[1884] 18 Sep 1873 in Somerset Co., PA[1885]. She was born 10 Feb 1851 in Garrett, Somerset Co., PA[1886], and died 14 Feb 1912 in Beachdale, Brothersvalley Twp., Somerset Co., PA[1887].

Notes for Cornelius Judy:
Cornelius married Henrietta Huffman Sept 18, 1873. She was born Feb 1851. Cornelius bought a farm in 1904 (146 acres) which contained alot of coal and was leased to the Somerset Coal Co and worked on a royalty. The farm was near Althouse, PA. Cornelius and Henrietta were German Baptist. He was a democrat.

He is buried: Beachdale Cemetery, Brothersvalley Twp., Somerset Co., PA

More About Cornelius Judy:
Burial: Somerset County, PA, USA[1887]
Residence: 1900, Age: 54; Marital Status: Married; Relation to Head of House: Head/Brothersvalley, Somerset, PA[1887,1888]

More About Henrietta Dorthea Hoffman:

Burial: Somerset Co., PA*1888*
Residence: 1850, Age: 3/Kensington Ward 5, Philadelphia, Pennsylvania*1888*

Children of Cornelius Judy and Henrietta Hoffman are:

    1018   i.   Alice[7] Judy*1889*, born 24 Aug 1875 in Brothersvalley, Somerset Co., PA*1889*; died 08 Jul 1964 in FL*1889*.

        More About Alice Judy:
        Residence: 1880, Age: 4; Marital Status: Single; Relation to Head of House: Daughter/Brothers Valley, Somerset Co., PA*1889*

    1019   ii.   Henry Wilson Judy*1889*, born Oct 1877 in Pittsburgh, Allegheny Co., PA*1889*; died 26 Jun 1969 in Meyersdale, Somerset, PA, USA*1889*.

        More About Henry Wilson Judy:
        Residence: 1900, Age: 22; Marital Status: Single; Relation to Head of House: Son/Brothersvalley, Somerset, PA*1889*

+   1020   iii.   Bertha Idella "Della" Judy, born 12 Feb 1880 in Pittsburgh, Allegheny Co., PA; died 12 Nov 1980 in Somerset, Co., PA.

+   1021   iv.   Elias F. Judy, born 27 Mar 1884 in Pittsburgh, Allegheny Co., PA; died 11 Mar 1973 in Garrett, Somerset Co., PA.

    1022   v.   Babe Judy*1889*, born Jul 1890 in Pittsburgh, Allegheny Co., PA*1889*.

        More About Babe Judy:
        Residence: 1900, Age: 10; Marital Status: Single; Relation to Head of House: Son/Brothersvalley, Somerset, PA*1889*

294. John[6] Judy (Eve[5] Christner, Joseph "Zep"[4], Johannes John Hans[3], Christian[2], Christen[1])*1890* was born 14 Aug 1848 in Garrett, Somerset Co., PA*1890*, and died 1925 in Thayer Co., NE*1890*. He married **Eliza J Swarner***1890* 1874*1890*. She was born Jul 1855 in PA*1890*.

Notes for John Judy:
John married Eliza Swan/Swana.

More About John Judy:
Residence: 1920, Angus, Nuckolls, Nebraska*1890*

More About Eliza J Swarner:
Residence: 1930, Edgar, Clay, Nebraska*1890*

Children of John Judy and Eliza Swarner are:

    1023   i.   John C[7] Judy*1890*, born Apr 1881 in PA*1890*.

        More About John C Judy:
        Residence: 1900, Blaine, Nuckolls, Nebraska*1890*

    1024   ii.   Hattie B Judy*1890*, born Sep 1883 in PA*1890*.

        More About Hattie B Judy:
        Residence: 1900, Blaine, Nuckolls, Nebraska*1890*

    1025   iii.   Maggie B Judy*1890*, born Oct 1886 in PA*1890*.

        More About Maggie B Judy:
        Residence: 1900, Blaine, Nuckolls, Nebraska*1890*

    1026   iv.   Minnie M Judy*1890*, born Oct 1888 in PA*1890*.

        More About Minnie M Judy:
        Residence: 1900, Blaine, Nuckolls, Nebraska*1890*

1027   v.   George Arthur Judy*1890*, born 30 Dec 1891 in NE*1890*; died Jun 1967 in Oak, Nuckolls Co., NE*1890*.

              More About George Arthur Judy:
              Residence: 1900, Blaine, Nuckolls, Nebraska*1890*

1028   vi.   Verda M Judy*1890*, born Sep 1898 in NE*1890*.

              More About Verda M Judy:
              Residence: 1900, Blaine, Nuckolls, Nebraska*1890*

1029   vii.   Earl Judy*1890*, born Abt. 1900 in NE*1890*.

              More About Earl Judy:
              Residence: 1920, Angus, Nuckolls, Nebraska*1890*

295. Jerome Henry⁶ Judy (Eve⁵ Christner, Joseph "Zep"⁴, Johannes John Hans³, Christian², Christen¹)*1891* was born 14 May 1852 in Garrett, Somerset Co., PA*1891*, and died 31 May 1922 in Garrett, Somerset Co., PA*1891*. He married **Barbara Ellen Burkholder***1891* 29 Jul 1880 in Garrett, Somerset Co., PA*1891*, daughter of William Burkholder. She was born 13 Mar 1860 in Garrett, Somerset Co., PA*1891*, and died 31 Mar 1928 in Garrett, Somerset Co., PA*1891*.

Notes for Jerome Henry Judy:
Jerome attended Berlin Normal School and became a teacher. He taught for 1 year at Brothers Valley School. In 1880 he formed a partnership with a couisin Samuel and operated a general store (formerly store of Frank Enos) under the name of J. H. & S. Judy. In 1886 he opened a general store in Garrett and in 1890 bought out the older store of Samuel Judy. Jerome was also treasurer of the Garrett Water Co. and a director in the First National Bank of Garrett. He was also a councilman for Garrett, PA.

Children of Jerome Judy and Barbara Burkholder are:
    1030   i.   Frank Ervin⁷ Judy*1891*, born 07 Dec 1880 in Garrett, Somerset Co., PA*1891*; died 14 Jun 1927*1891*.
+ 1031   ii.   Albert Barton Judy, born 02 Mar 1888 in Garrett, Somerset Co., PA; died 1960 in Garrett, Somerset Co., PA.
    1032   iii.   Charles H. Judy*1891*, born 13 Sep 1890*1891*; died 14 Apr 1891*1891*.
    1033   iv.   William Lewis Judy*1891*, born 20 Sep 1891 in Garrett, Somerset Co., PA*1891*; died Abt. 1974 in Chicago, Cook Co., IL*1891*.
    1034   v.   Anna B. Judy*1891*, born 30 Nov 1894 in Garrett, Somerset Co., PA*1891*.
    1035   vi.   Verda May Judy*1891*, born 23 Aug 1897 in Garrett, Somerset Co., PA*1891*; died 17 Mar 1899 in Garrett, Somerset Co., PA*1891*.
    1036   vii.   Richard Thomas Judy*1891*, born 19 Feb 1901 in Garrett, Somerset Co., PA*1891*.
    1037   viii. Harry Albert Judy*1891*, born Mar 1903*1891*; died Jun 1971 in Chicago, Cook Co., IL*1891*.

300. John Smith⁶ Christner (Solomon McKenzie⁵, Benjamin⁴, Johannes John Hans³, Christian², Christen¹)*1892* was born 1834 in Etobicoke, York, Ontario, Canada*1892*. He married **Sarah Margaret** 1857 in Osprey, Grey, Ontario, Canada. She was born Nov 1844 in Ont*1893*.

More About John Smith Christner:
Residence: 1880, Perry, Lake Co., OH*1894*

More About Sarah Margaret:
Residence: 1900, Big Blue Precinct, Saline, NE*1895*

Children of John Christner and Sarah Margaret are:
    1038   i.   Frederick Willace⁷ Christner, born 1858 in Grey, York, Ontario, Canada.
    1039   ii.   George M. Christner*1895*, born Oct 1871 in Grey, York, Ontario, Canada*1895*.

              More About George M. Christner:
              Residence: 1900, Big Blue Precinct, Saline, NE*1895*

1040   iii.   James H. Christner, born 1875 in Grey, York, Ontario, Canada.

1041   iv.   Maggie M. Christner, born 1878 in Grey, York, Ontario, Canada.

301. William Henry[6] Christner (Solomon McKenzie[5], Benjamin[4], Johannes John Hans[3], Christian[2], Christen[1])[1896,1897] was born 07 Oct 1837 in Weston Etobicoke, York, Ontario, Canada[1898,1899], and died 14 Mar 1923 in Fullerton, Orange Co., CA[1900,1901]. He married **Mary Ann Fowler**[1901] 09 Sep 1868 in Osprey, Grey, Ontario, Canada[1901]. She was born 12 Jun 1850 in Yorkshire - East Riding, United Kingdom[1901,1902], and died 08 Sep 1912 in Douglas Co., MO[1903].

Notes for William Henry Christner:
Birth: Oct. 7, 1837
Death: Mar. 14, 1923
Douglas Co., MO

Spouse: Mary Ann Fowler Christner (1850 - 1912)

Burial: Shiloh Cemetery, Douglas Co., MO
Find A Grave Memorial# 60496649

More About William Henry Christner:
Residence: 1880, Painesville, Lake Co., OH[1903,1904]

Notes for Mary Ann Fowler:
Birth: Jun. 12, 1850
Kingston upon Hull, East Riding of Yorkshire, England
Death: Sep. 8, 1912
Douglas Co., MO

Born in Hull, Yorkshire County, England. The daughter of Thomas & Elizabeth (Lambert) Fowler. The wife of W. H. Christner. Died in Clay Township, Douglas County, Missouri. [Bio info courtesy of Pat Thomas, #47094871]

Family links:
Spouse:
W. H. Christner (1837 - 1923)

Inscription:
"his wife"

Note: Shared gravestone

Burial:
Shiloh Cemetery, Douglas Co., MO
Find A Grave Memorial# 60496593

More About Mary Ann Fowler:
Residence: 1910, Clay, Douglas, MO[1905]

Children of William Christner and Mary Fowler are:

+   1042   i.   Elizabeth Amelia[7] Christner, born 29 Aug 1869 in Grey, York, Ontario, Canada; died 10 Oct 1940 in Lincoln, Lancaster Co., NE.

     1043   ii.   Mary Ellen Christner[1905], born 24 Jul 1871 in Collingwood, Twp., Gray, Ontario, Canada[1905]; died 24 Sep 1958 in Westminster, Orange Co., CA[1905]. She married (1) Frank L. Cox 02 Feb 1894. She married (2) John J. Smith 25 Dec 1901.

More About Mary Ellen Christner:
Residence: 1880, Painesville, Lake Co., OH*1905*

1044   iii.   Nellie Smith*1905*, born Abt. 1873 in Canada*1905*.

More About Nellie Smith:
Arrival: 1875*1905*
Residence: 1920, Placentia, Orange, California*1905*

1045   iv.   William Thomas Christner*1905*, born 03 Jan 1873 in Canada*1905*; died 30 Jan 1934.

More About William Thomas Christner:
Residence: 1880, Painesville, Lake Co., OH*1905*

+   1046   v.   Sarah Etta Christner, born 30 May 1874 in Canada; died 17 Jan 1939.
+   1047   vi.   Frederick Walter Christner, born 14 Aug 1876 in Canada; died 10 Jan 1945 in San Luis Obispo, CA.
+   1048   vii.   Rosa Mae Christner, born 27 Jul 1878 in Painesville, Lake Co., OH; died Apr 1974 in Lincoln, Lancaster Co., NE.
1049   viii.   Charles Christner*1905*, born 05 Aug 1880 in Painesville, Lake Co., OH*1905*; died 12 Apr 1929 in Fullerton, Orange Co., CA*1905*. He married Lena Faye McCleary 15 Aug 1918 in Mulberry, KS.
+   1050   ix.   Lena Belle Christner, born 28 Jun 1882 in Painesville, Lake Co., OH; died 31 Aug 1954 in Lindsay, Tulare Co., CA.
1051   x.   James Lambert Christner*1905*, born 28 Jun 1882 in Painesville, Lake Co., OH*1905*; died Aug 1882 in Painesville, Lake Co., OH*1905*.
1052   xi.   Benjamin Franklin Christner*1905*, born 05 Jul 1883 in Painesville, Lake Co., OH*1905*; died 26 Feb 1962 in Lindsay, Tulare Co., CA*1905*. He married (1) Pearl Foster 04 Jul 1917 in Douglas Co., MO. He married (2) Emily Newton 26 Mar 1937 in Las Vegas, NV.

More About Benjamin Franklin Christner:
Residence: 1910, Clay, Douglas, MO*1905*

+   1053   xii.   Grace Estelle Christner, born 07 Oct 1884 in Painesville, Lake Co., OH; died 13 Jun 1967 in Lindsay, Tulare Co., CA.
1054   xiii.   George Arthur Christner*1905*, born 08 Jul 1886 in Crete, Saline Co., KS*1905*; died 08 Mar 1887*1905*.
1055   xiv.   Herbert Fowler Christner*1905*, born 05 Aug 1888 in Crete, Saline Co., NE; died 18 Sep 1922 in CA*1905*. He married Rachel Ann Yearwood 14 Nov 1911 in Ellensburg, WA.

More About Herbert Fowler Christner:
Residence: 1910, Clay, Douglas, MO*1905*

1056   xv.   Ruth Edna Christner*1905*, born 23 Sep 1890 in Crete, Saline Co., KS*1905*; died 10 Sep 1986 in Lovington, Lea Co., NM*1905*. She married Charles Sidney Frank Garnand 29 Nov 1917 in Pittsburgh, Crawford Co., KS.

More About Ruth Edna Christner:
Social Security Number: 585-74-2967/*1906*
SSN issued: New Mexico*1906*

1057   xvi.   Harry Edward Christner*1907*, born 20 Feb 1892 in Crete, Saline Co., KS*1907*; died 12 Oct 1892*1907*.
1058   xvii.   Carrie Luella Christner*1907*, born 03 Oct 1894 in Brookville, Saline Co., NE*1908*; died 13 May 1986 in Lindsay, Tulare Co., CA*1909*. She married Oliver Millburn Rogers 23 Dec 1918 in Brookville, KS.

More About Carrie Luella Christner:
Social Security Number: 549-76-8425/*1910*
SSN issued: CA*1910*

+   1059   xviii.   Bertha Ida Christner, born 02 Dec 1896 in Olathe, Douglas Co., MO; died Dec 1986 in Pittsburg, Crawford Co., KS.

302. Jane Elizabeth⁶ Christner (Solomon McKenzie⁵, Benjamin⁴, Johannes John Hans³, Christian², Christen¹)*1911* was born 01 Feb 1839 in Etobicoke, York, Ontario, Canada*1911*, and died 04 Dec 1903 in Pleasant Dale, Seward, NE*1911*. She married **Joseph Merrill** 27 Sep 1858 in Osprey, Grey, Ontario, Canada. He was born

1832.

Notes for Jane Elizabeth Christner:
Census showes her in Canada in 1871, Painesville, Ohio in 1880, Saline Co., NE in 1890.

More About Jane Elizabeth Christner:
Residence: 1880, Painesville, Lake Co., OH[1911]

Child of Jane Christner and Joseph Merrill is:
+   1060   i.   William John[7] Merrill, born 02 Mar 1860; died 01 Jun 1927 in Southeastern NE.

303. Mary Ann[6] Christner (Solomon McKenzie[5], Benjamin[4], Johannes John Hans[3], Christian[2], Christen[1])[1911,1912,1913] was born 1840 in Etobicoke, York, Ontario, Canada[1914,1915], and died 30 Oct 1914 in Colorado Springs, El Paso Co., CO[1916,1917,1918]. She married **William Henry Merrill**[1918,1919] 24 Oct 1859 in Osprey, Grey, Ontario, Canada. He was born 01 Mar 1837 in Nantwich, Cheshire, England[1920,1921], and died 27 Aug 1918 in Wauneta, Chase Co., NE[1921,1922].

Notes for Mary Ann Christner:
Birth: 1841 - Canada
Death: Oct. 30, 1914 - Colorado Springs, El Paso Co., CO

Spouse: William H. Merrill (1837 - 1917)

Children:
Benjamin Christner Merrill (1864 - 1941)
Martha Marcella Merrill Bressie (1867 - 1955)
William Henry Merrill (1869 - 1916)
Herbert Franklin Merrill (1871 - 1949)
Jessie Amanda Merrill Carpenter (1882 - 1951)

Burial: Riverside Cemetery, Wauneta, Chase Co., NE
Plot: 39-2-3
Find A Grave Memorial# 37222621

More About Mary Ann Christner:
Arrival: 1875[1923,1924,1925]
Burial: Riverside Cemetery, Wauneta, Chase, Nebraska[1925]
Residence: 1900, Precinct I, Seward, Nebraska[1925,1926,1927]

Notes for William Henry Merrill:
Birth: Mar 1, 1837 - England
Death: Aug 27, 1917

Spouse: Mary Ann Christner Merrill (1841 - 1914)

Children:
Benjamin Christner Merrill (1864 - 1941)
Martha Marcella Merrill Bressie (1867 - 1955)
William Henry Merrill (1869 - 1916)
Herbert Franklin Merrill (1871 - 1949)
Jessie Amanda Merrill Carpenter (1882 - 1951)

Burial: Riverside Cemetery, Wauneta, Chase Co., NE
Plot: 39-2-6
Find A Grave Memorial# 37222648

More About William Henry Merrill:
Arrival: 1875[1928,1929]
Burial: Riverside Cemetery, Wauneta, Chase, Nebraska[1929]
Residence: 1900, Precinct I, Seward, Nebraska[1929,1930,1931]

Children of Mary Christner and William Merrill are:

+ 1061   i.   Benjamin Christner[7] Merrill, born 07 Jun 1864 in Ontario, Canada; died 08 Jul 1941 in Hayes Co., NE.
+ 1062   ii.   William Henry Merrill Jr., born 12 May 1869 in Ontario, Canada; died 15 Oct 1916 in railroad accident/Railroad, York Co., PA.
   1063   iii.   Herber Franklin Merrill[1932], born 13 May 1871 in Grey, Ontario, Canada[1932]; died 01 Jul 1949 in Wauneta, Chase Co., NE, United States[1932].

         Notes for Herber Franklin Merrill:
         Birth: 1871
         Death: 1949

         Parents:
         William H. Merrill (1837 - 1917)
         Mary Ann Christner Merrill (1841 - 1914)

         Burial: Riverside Cemetery, Wauneta, Chase Co., NE
         Plot: 39-2-5
         Find A Grave Memorial# 37222591

         More About Herber Franklin Merrill:
         Arrival: 1873[1932]
         Residence: 1910, Wallace, Lincoln, NE[1932]

   1064   iv.   Norman Merrill[1932], born Oct 1883 in NE[1932]; died 04 Mar 1954 in Lafayette, Yamhill, Oregon, USA[1932].

         More About Norman Merrill:
         Residence: 1900, P Precinct, Seward, NE[1932]

+ 1065   v.   Jessie Amanda Merrill, born 17 Oct 1885 in NE; died 07 Mar 1951 in Riverside, Burt Co., NE.

306. Moses Isaac[6] Christner (Solomon McKenzie[5], Benjamin[4], Johannes John Hans[3], Christian[2], Christen[1])[1933,1934,1935] was born 1853 in Etobicoke, York, Ontario, Canada[1935], and died 07 Sep 1917 in Tacoma, Pierce Co., WA[1935,1936,1937]. He married **Manila Sarah 'Sally' Bradley**[1938,1939] 10 Dec 1874 in Meaford, Grey, Ontario, Canada. She was born 21 Jul 1853 in Ontario, Canada[1940], and died 14 Jun 1934 in Seattle, King Co., WA[1940].

More About Moses Isaac Christner:
Arrival: 26 Mar 1910, Huntingdon, Quebec[1941,1942]
Residence: 1861, Grey, Canada West, Canada[1943,1944,1945]

More About Manila Sarah 'Sally' Bradley:
Arrival: 1893[1945]
Residence: 1930, Seattle, King Co., WA[1945]

Children of Moses Christner and Manila Bradley are:
   1066   i.   Benjamin Bradley[7] Christner[1945], born 20 Oct 1875 in Painesville, Lake Co., OH[1945]; died 18 Oct 1935 in McNeil Island, Pierce Co., WA[1945]. He married Margaret Otis[1945] 1908 in Pierce Co., WA[1945]; born 1871 in New Brunswick, Canada[1945]; died 19 Sep 1952 in Seattle, King Co., WA[1945].

         More About Benjamin Bradley Christner:
         Residence: 1930, University Place, Pierce, Washington[1945]

         More About Margaret Otis:

Arrival: 1874[1945]
Residence: 1910, Regents Park, Pierce, Washington[1945]

+ 1067   ii.   William Arthur Christner, born 09 Sep 1879 in Painesville, Lake Co., OH; died 18 Sep 1946 in Golden Gate National Cemetery, Marin, CA.

308. Richard[6] Christner (Solomon McKenzie[5], Benjamin[4], Johannes John Hans[3], Christian[2], Christen[1])[1946] was born 1856 in Etobicoke, York, Ontario, Canada[1946], and died 22 Jun 1938 in Fort Smith, Sebastian Co., AR[1946]. He married **Anna Marie Beyerle**[1947] 14 Mar 1884 in OH[1947]. She was born 06 May 1861 in West Point, Lee Co., IA[1947], and died 27 Dec 1935 in Fort Smith, Sebastian Co., AR[1947].

More About Richard Christner:
Residence: 1861, Grey, Canada West, Canada[1948]

Children of Richard Christner and Anna Beyerle are:
   1068   i.   Myrtle Marion[7] Christner[1949], born 12 Mar 1886 in NE[1949]; died 22 Jun 1974 in Fort Smith, Sebastian Co., AR[1949].
   1069   ii.   Charles Harold Christner[1949], born 07 Aug 1889 in Lincoln, Johnson Co., NE[1949]; died 06 Jul 1936 in Portland, Multnomah Co., OR[1949].

315. Eliza[6] Irvine (Mary Jane[5] Christner, Benjamin[4], Johannes John Hans[3], Christian[2], Christen[1]) was born 1847. She married **C. Peacock**.

Children of Eliza Irvine and C. Peacock are:
+ 1070   i.   Elizabeth[7] Peacock.
   1071   ii.   Millicent Peacock.
   1072   iii.   Millicent Peacock.

316. William[6] Irvine (Mary Jane[5] Christner, Benjamin[4], Johannes John Hans[3], Christian[2], Christen[1]) was born 1848, and died 1906. He married **Annie Oathwaite**.

More About William Irvine:
Burial: Riverside Cemetery by Lawrence Ave. & Royal York Road Toronto CA.

Children of William Irvine and Annie Oathwaite are:
   1073   i.   Alice[7] Irvine.
   1074   ii.   Art Irvine.
   1075   iii.   Bob Irvine.
   1076   iv.   Eddie Irvine.
   1077   v.   Art Irvine.
   1078   vi.   Will Irvine.

317. James[6] Irvine (Mary Jane[5] Christner, Benjamin[4], Johannes John Hans[3], Christian[2], Christen[1]) was born 11 Aug 1850, and died 28 Nov 1921 in Weston, Canada. He married **(1) Emily Dixon** 1883. She died 1883 in Emily & Infant died in Childbirth. He married **(2) Jane Ross Foster** 24 Nov 1886 in Toronto, Canada.

More About James Irvine:
Burial: Riverside Cemetery by Lawrence Ave. & Royal York Road Toronto CA.

Children of James Irvine and Jane Foster are:
+ 1079   i.   Frank O.[7] Irvine, born 1889; died 1960 in IL.
+ 1080   ii.   May Adelaide Irvine, born 05 Nov 1894 in Weston, York Co., Canada; died 24 Mar 1984.
+ 1081   iii.   Harry Foreman Irvine, born 08 Aug 1897 in Weston, York Co., Canada; died 27 Dec 1953.
   1082   iv.   Alex M. Irvine, born 08 Mar 1903 in Weston, York Co., Canada; died 26 Jul 1964. He married Janet Skelton 26 Dec 1929 in Toronto, Canada.

More About Alex M. Irvine:
Burial: Riverside Cemetery by Lawrence Ave. & Royal York Road Toronto CA.

318. Alex[6] **Irvine** (Mary Jane[5] Christner, Benjamin[4], Johannes John Hans[3], Christian[2], Christen[1]) was born 1851. He married **Evelyn Taylor**.

Children of Alex Irvine and Evelyn Taylor are:
1083	i.	Amy[7] Irvine.
1084	ii.	Art Irvine.
1085	iii.	Charlie Irvine.
1086	iv.	George Irvine.
1087	v.	Art Irvine.
1088	vi.	Bob Irvine.

319. Benjamin[6] **Irvine** (Mary Jane[5] Christner, Benjamin[4], Johannes John Hans[3], Christian[2], Christen[1]) was born 20 Jan 1854, and died 24 Feb 1928. He married **Cora Grover** 01 Jan 1891.

Children of Benjamin Irvine and Cora Grover are:
1089	i.	Don[7] Irvine.
1090	ii.	Emily Irvine.
1091	iii.	Gordon Irvine, born 1921.

321. Susan Jen[6] **Irvine** (Mary Jane[5] Christner, Benjamin[4], Johannes John Hans[3], Christian[2], Christen[1]) was born 1858. She married **Fred Hill**.

Children of Susan Irvine and Fred Hill are:
1092	i.	Art[7] Hill.
1093	ii.	Bessie Cora Hill.
1094	iii.	Fred Hill, died in Drowed with brother in Humber River @ 1900.
1095	iv.	Gertie Hill.
1096	v.	Jack Hill, died in Drowed with brother in Humber River @ 1900.
1097	vi.	Reg Hill.

322. Samual[6] **Irvine** (Mary Jane[5] Christner, Benjamin[4], Johannes John Hans[3], Christian[2], Christen[1]) was born 1860. He married **Elizabeth Rowntree**.

Children of Samual Irvine and Elizabeth Rowntree are:
1098	i.	Chrissy[7] Irvine.
1099	ii.	Evelyn Irvine.
1100	iii.	Horace Irvine.
1101	iv.	Mabel Irvine.
1102	v.	Ross Irvine.
1103	vi.	David Irvine.
1104	vii.	Olive Irvine.

323. Art[6] **Irvine** (Mary Jane[5] Christner, Benjamin[4], Johannes John Hans[3], Christian[2], Christen[1]) was born 1862. He married **May**.

Children of Art Irvine and May are:
1105	i.	Jack[7] Irvine.
1106	ii.	Jean Irvine.
1107	iii.	Marjory Irvine.

332. Magdalena[6] **Christner** (Christian[5], Peter[4], Christian[3], Christian[2], Christen[1])[1950] was born 21 Oct 1821 in Alsace, France[1950], and died 09 Mar 1898 in Wayland, Henry Co., IA[1951]. She married **Joseph Schlatter** 06

Sep 1840 in Wilmot Twp., Ontario, Canada[1951]. He was born 05 May 1812 in Richwiller, Haut-Rhin, Alsace, France[1951], and died 14 Apr 1876 in Wayland, Henry Co., IA[1951].

Notes for Magdalena Christner:
Magdalena and Joseph migrated to Wayland, IA.

More About Magdalena Christner:
Burial: Sommers Cemetery north of Wayland, IA
Residence: 1895, Marion Township, Washington Co., IA[1951]

More About Joseph Schlatter:
Burial: Sommers Cemetery north of Wayland, IA

Children of Magdalena Christner and Joseph Schlatter are:

1108   i.   Christian C[7] Schlatter[1951], born 02 Mar 1842 in S Easthope Twp, 1654328, Ontario, Canada[1951]; died 01 Dec 1926 in Born in Ontario, Canada[1951].

More About Christian C Schlatter:
Arrival: 1855[1951]
Residence: 1920, Jefferson, Henry Co., IA[1951]

1109   ii.   Joseph Schlatter[1951], born Abt. 1844 in Canada[1951].

More About Joseph Schlatter:
Residence: 1880, Marion, Washington Co., IA[1951]

1110   iii.   Katrina "Katy" Schlatter[1951], born 08 Aug 1846 in Perth, Ontario, Canada[1951]; died 05 Jan 1929 in Wayland, Henry Co., IA[1951].

More About Katrina "Katy" Schlatter:
Residence: 1900, Wayland City, Henry, Iowa[1951]

1111   iv.   Fannie Schlatter[1951], born May 1848 in Canada[1951].

More About Fannie Schlatter:
Arrival: 1855[1951]
Residence: 1880, Marion, Washington Co., IA[1951]

1112   v.   Mary Schlatter[1951], born 1850 in S Easthope Twp, 1654328, Ontario, Canada[1951]; died 20 Oct 1933[1951].

More About Mary Schlatter:
Arrival: 1856[1951]
Residence: 1930, Jefferson, Henry Co., IA[1951]

1113   vi.   John Schlatter[1951], born 25 Jun 1851 in Hamburg, Ontario, Canada[1951]; died 1877[1951].
1114   vii.   Barbara Schlatter[1951], born 1853 in IA[1951].
1115   viii.   Benjamin C Slatter[1951], born 28 Jun 1854 in Wayland, Henry Co., IA[1951]; died 21 Apr 1914 in Filer, Twin Falls, Idaho, USA[1951].

More About Benjamin C Slatter:
Burial: Apr 1914, Kearney, Buffalo, NE, USA[1951]
Residence: 1910, Center, Buffalo, NE[1951]

1116   ix.   Nicholas C Schlatter[1951], born 16 Oct 1856 in IA[1951]; died 28 Aug 1941 in Alameda, California[1951].

More About Nicholas C Schlatter:
Residence: 1910, San Francisco Assembly District 35, San Francisco, California[1951]

1117   x.   George Peter Schlatter[1951], born Apr 1859 in IA[1951]; died 22 Jul 1929 in Kalispell, Flathead, Montana, USA[1951].

More About George Peter Schlatter:
Residence: 1920, Kalispell Ward 2, Flathead, Montana[1951]

1118   xi.   Jacob C Schlatter[1951], born 30 Jan 1861 in Henry Co., IA[1951]; died 17 Jul 1936 in Wayland, Henry Co., IA[1951].

More About Jacob C Schlatter:
Residence: 01 Jan 1925, Wayland[1951]

333. Peter C.[6] **Christner** (Christian[5], Peter[4], Christian[3], Christian[2], Christen[1])[1952,1953] was born 30 Jun 1823 in Alsace, Lorraine, France[1954,1955], and died 11 Nov 1894 in Miami Co., IN[1955,1956]. He married **(1) Sarah Troyer**[1956]. She was born 17 Aug 1831 in Holmes Co., OH[1956], and died 17 Mar 1893 in Miami Co., IN[1956]. He married **(2) Barbara Egli**, daughter of Christian Egli and Catherine Stahley. She was born 1831 in Germany, and died 1852 in Elkhart Co., IN.

Notes for Peter C. Christner:
For a complete history of Peter and his family read H. Walter Christner's book "Our Immigrants". Christian and Elizabeth Christner's Family at Goshen College Goshen, IN.

Lived just south of Waupecong, Miami Co. Indiana on 160 acre farm. Donated the land for the Christner Cemetery at N40°33.880' by W86°02.000' in Miami County Indiana just northeast of Kokomo, IN. County road 500 east and Cr.1400 south.

Birth: Mar. 12, 1823
Death: Nov. 11, 1894

Burial: Christner Cemetery, Wawpecong, Miami Co., IN
Plot: Space K7

More About Peter C. Christner:
Burial: N40°33.889'byW86°02.0'Lot17/Christner Cemetery Miami Co., IN
Residence: 1880, Clay, Miami Co., IN[1956]

Notes for Sarah Troyer:
Sarah is the daughter of Samuel and Magdalena Hochstedler Troyer.

Birth: Aug. 17, 1831
Death: Mar. 17, 1893

Burial: Christner Cemetery, Wawpecong, Miami Co., IN
Plot: Space K8

More About Sarah Troyer:
Burial: N40°33.889'byW86°02.0' Lot18/Christner Cemetery, Miami Co., IN
Residence: 1880, Clay, Miami Co., IN[1956]

Notes for Barbara Egli:

Children of Peter Christner and Sarah Troyer are:
1119   i.   Anna[7] Christner[1956], born 28 Aug 1869 in Miami Co., IN. She married Ephraim J. S. Miller 30 Mar 1882; born 23 Jul 1859.

More About Anna Christner:
Residence: 1880, Clay, Miami Co., IN[1956]

+ 1120   ii.   John Christner, born 06 Nov 1870 in Miami Co., IN; died 13 Apr 1941 in Age at Death: 72/Wawpecong,

Miami County, Indiana - Buried - Kokomo Memorial Park Cemetery, Kokomo, Howard County, Indiana.

Children of Peter Christner and Barbara Egli are:

+   1121   i.   Christian C "Chris"[7] Christner, born 02 Aug 1849 in Elkhart, Elkhart Co., IN; died 19 Oct 1926 in Wayland, Henry Co., IA.

+   1122   ii.   Lydia Christner, born 29 Jun 1851 in Elkhart, Elkhart Co., IN; died 19 Aug 1882 in Miami, Miami Co., IN.

334. Catherine[6] Christner (Christian[5], Peter[4], Christian[3], Christian[2], Christen[1])[1957] was born 04 Oct 1824 in Bavaria Germany, and died 25 Jan 1905[1957]. She married **Nicholas Roth**. He was born 1822, and died 15 Jul 1862 in North of Wayland, IA.

Notes for Catherine Christner:
Catherine married Nicholas Roth after her sister Elizabeth died. After Nicholas died Catherine moved to Oregon.

Roth - Catharine Roth (nee Christner) was born in Bavaria, Germany, Oct. 4, 1824; died near Albany, Ore., Jan. 25, 1905; aged 80 Y., 3 M., 21 D. She came with her parents to Canada at the age of six years. She was married to Nicholas Roth, who preceded her to the spirit world a number of years ago. She is survived by six sons, two daughters, 45 grandchildren and 47 greatgrandchildren. Her remains were laid to rest in the Knox Butte cemetery. Funeral services were conducted by L. J. Yoder in English, from Psa. 106:8, and Christian Gerig in German, from Isa. 35:10. Deceased was a member of the Amish Mennonite Church.

More About Catherine Christner:
Burial: Knox Butte Cemetery Oregon

More About Nicholas Roth:
Burial: Sommers Cemetery north of Wayland, IA

Children of Catherine Christner and Nicholas Roth are:
     1123   i.   Benedict[7] Roth, born 1841; died 1861.
     1124   ii.   Christian Roth, born 1847; died 1927.
     1125   iii.   Nicholas Roth Jr., born 1847; died 1907.
     1126   iv.   Jacob Roth, born 1850; died 1928.
     1127   v.   Barbara Roth, born 1852; died 1925.
     1128   vi.   Katherine Roth, born 1854; died 1934.
     1129   vii.   Daniel Roth, born 1857; died 1939.
     1130   viii.   Joseph Roth, born 1858. He married Mary Breuy.
     1131   ix.   John C. Roth, born 1861; died 1943.

335. Jacob[6] Christner (Christian[5], Peter[4], Christian[3], Christian[2], Christen[1])[1958,1959,1960,1961] was born 11 Apr 1828 in Wurttemberg Germany or Alsace, France[1962], and died 24 Mar 1893 in Elkhart, Elkhart Co., IN[1963,1964]. He married **(1) Elizabeth Borntrager**[1965] 14 Nov 1850 in Goshen, Elkhart Co., IN[1965]. She was born 08 May 1833 in Somerset Co., PA[1965], and died 01 Apr 1851 in Elkhart Co., IN[1965]. He married **(2) Elizabeth Walter**[1965,1966] 14 Aug 1851 in Lagrange Co., IN[1967]. She was born 01 Feb 1826 in Holmes Co., OH, and died 14 Dec 1894 in Elkhart, Elkhart Co., IN[1968]. He married **(3) Anna Kennel**[1969,1970] 28 Feb 1886 in Wellesley, Ontario, Canada/[1971]. She was born 19 Mar 1837 in Lewis Co., NY[1972], and died 25 Jun 1910 in Pigeon, Huron Co., MI[1973,1974].

Notes for Jacob Christner:
For a complete history of Jacob and his family read H. Walter Christner's book Our Immigrants. Christian and Elizabeth Christner's Family at Goshen College, Goshen, IN.

CHRISTNER - On the 31st of March, 1893, in Clinton Twp., Elkhart Co., Ind., of consumption, Bro. Jacob Christner, aged 64 years, 11 months and 20 days. He was a faithful brother in the A.M. church. He leaves his wife and seven children to mourn his departure. He greatly desired to depart this life and be at rest with his Savior. He was buried in the Union graveyard. Funeral services by J.E. Bontreger and D.J. Hochstetler.

Amish and Amish Mennonite Genealogies; CHC5, p. 61

OBITUARY - Herald of Truth , Vol. XXX, No. 8, April 15, 1893 - Page 134, 135
Christner - On the 31st of March, 1893, in Clinton Twp., Elkhart Co., Ind., of consumption, Bro. Jacob Christner, aged 64 years, 11 months and 20 days. He was a faithful brother in the A.M. church. He leaves his wife and seven children to mourn his departure. He greatly desired to depart this life and be at rest with his Savior. He was buried in the Union graveyard. Funeral services by J.E. Bontreger and D. J. Hochstetler.

Birth: Apr 11, 1828 - France
Death: Mar 31, 1893 - Elkhart Co., IN

Spouses:
Elizabeth Bontrager Christner (1833 - 1851)
Elizabeth Walter Christner (1826 - 1881)

Children: Jacob Christner (1862 - 1939)

Inscription: 64y 11m 2d

Burial: Clinton Union Cemetery, Millersburg, Elkhart Co., IN
Plot: Section 2 Row 10 Space 9

More About Jacob Christner:
Burial: N41°34.072'xW85°44.270'/Clinton Union Cemetery, Clinton Twp., Elkhart Co., IN - Row 10, plot 12
Cause of Death: Consumption
Religion: A.M. Church/
Residence: 1880, Clinton, Elkhart Co., IN[1975,1976]

Notes for Elizabeth Borntrager:
Elizabeth's grandmother was Barbara (Shantz) Johns. Shantz was the original (German) name for Johns. Elizabeth died with her baby the first year of their marriage. Jacob then married Elizabeth Walter (an aunt through the Borntrager's) to his first wife, Elizabeth Borntrager.
Elizabeth is the daughter of Joseph and Barbara Yoder Bontrager
Elizabeth's last name was (modern spelling is Bontrager) Borntrager.

Birth: May 8, 1833 - Somerset Co., PA
Death: Apr 1, 1851

1st wife of Jacob Christner. Died in childbirth with J. C.

Spouse: Jacob Christner (1828 - 1893)

Burial: Clinton Union Cemetery, Millersburg, IN
Plot: Section 2 Row 10 Space 12

More About Elizabeth Borntrager:
Burial: Clinton Union Cemetery, Clinton Twp., Elkhart Co., IN - Row 10, plot 12

Notes for Elizabeth Walter:
Amish and Amish Mennonite Genealogies; CHC5, p. 61

Elizabeth is the daughter of Samuel and Veronica Bontrager Walter.

Elizabeths death date is listed in the same book 2 different places and 2 different dates 1.1884,2.1894 the headstone says Dec.14 1881 58y 10m 14d   another birth date of February 01, 1826 still another of Jan. 30 1826

CHRISTNER. On the 16th of December, in Clinton township, Elkhart Co., IN, Elizabeth, wife of Jacob Christner, aged 59 years, 10 months and 14 days. Funeral services were held by J. L. Miller and J. C. Barntreger from John 5 : 20--29. Sister Christner was a faithful member in the Amish Mennonite Church, and often confessed that she had peace with God and all men, and desired to take her leave of this world. She kindly admonished her children, and spoke words of comfort to her sorrowing husband.

Birth: Feb 1, 1826 - Holmes Co., OH
Death: Dec 14, 1881

2nd wife of Jacob Christner

Spouse: Jacob Christner (1828 - 1893)

Burial: Clinton Union Cemetery, Millersburg, Elkhart Co., IN
Plot: Section 2 Row 10 Space 10

More About Elizabeth Walter:
Burial: N41°34.072'xW85°44.270'/Clinton Union Cemetery, Clinton Twp., Elkhart Co., IN - Row 10, plot 10
Residence: 1860, Clinton, Elkhart Co., IN*1977*

Notes for Anna Kennel:
Anna was 1st married to Jacob Albrecht some say her & Jacob Christner had Children ????
She came from Waterloo Co., Ontario Canada to Elkhart Co. Indiana but after Jacob Christner's death she moved back to Canada. Maybe born June 25. Jacob Christner's family lived in the Kitchener, Waterloo Co., Ontario Canada until his fathers death from a tree he felled in an incorrect manner.

Child of Jacob Christner and Elizabeth Borntrager is:
    1132   i.   J.C.[7] Christner, born 01 Apr 1851 in Elkhart Co., IN; died 01 Apr 1851 in Elkhart Co., IN.

        Notes for J.C. Christner:
        This child (son) and its mother both died on the same day.

        More About J.C. Christner:
        Burial: Clinton Union Cemetery Co Rd. 34 Elkhart Co Indiana

Children of Jacob Christner and Elizabeth Walter are:
+   1133   i.   Susanna[7] Christner, born 10 Jun 1852 in Elkhart, Elkhart Co., IN; died 23 Nov 1881 in Clinton, Elkhart Co., IN.
+   1134   ii.   Elizabeth Christner, born 19 Jul 1853 in Elkhart Co., IN; died 03 Nov 1917 in Haven, Reno Co., KS.
+   1135   iii. Samuel Christner, born 12 Nov 1854 in Elkhart Co., IN; died 20 Oct 1937 in Nursing home at Eureka, IL.
+   1136   iv. Frances Frany Christner, born 23 Apr 1856 in Goshen, Elkhart Co., IN; died 24 May 1934 in Goshen, Elkhart Co., IN.
+   1137   v.   Mary Christner, born 06 Apr 1858 in Elkhart Co., IN; died 22 Mar 1923 in Elkhart Co., IN.
+   1138   vi. Barbara Christner, born 06 Apr 1860 in Elkhart Co., IN; died 25 Apr 1921 in Elkhart Co., IN.
     1139   vii. Joseph Christner*1978*, born 18 Jun 1861*1978*; died 16 May 1862*1978*.

        Notes for Joseph Christner:
        Tombstone says 6 years 28 days death May 16, 1862 this would make his birth date April 18, 1856, that would almost make Frances Frany Christner (his sister) a late twin.

        More About Joseph Christner:
        Burial: Clinton Union Cemetery, Elkhart Co., IN N41°34.072'xW85°44.270'

+   1140   viii. Jacob J. Christner, born 23 Sep 1862 in Middlebury, Elkhart Co., IN; died 06 Feb 1939 in Johnson Co.,

IA.

+ 1141 ix. David J. Christner, born 10 Mar 1865 in Elkhart, Elkhart Co., IN; died 10 Apr 1941 in Shelbyville, Bedford Co., OH.

+ 1142 x. Joseph Christner, born 10 Mar 1865 in Elkhart, Elkhart Co., IN; died 10 Apr 1941 in Shelbyville, Bedford Co., OH.

1143 xi. David Christner, born 10 Mar 1865[1979]; died 10 Apr 1941[1979]. He married Lovina D; born 25 Jul 1868; died 25 May 1938.

Notes for David Christner:
Amish and Amish Mennonite Genealogies; CHC59, p. 61

Birth: Mar. 10, 1865
Death: Apr. 10, 1941
IL

Spouse: Lovina D. Christner (1868 - 1938)

Burial: Mount Hermon Cemetery, Shelbyville, Shelby Co., IL
Find A Grave Memorial# 75101647

More About David Christner:
Burial: Shelbyville, Shelby County, Illinois, USA[1979]

Notes for Lovina D:
Amish and Amish Mennonite Genealogies; CHC59, p. 61

Birth: Jul. 25, 1868
Death: May 25, 1938

Spouse:
David J. Christner (1865 - 1941)

Burial: Mount Hermon Cemetery, Shelbyville, Shelby Co., IL
Find A Grave Memorial# 75101699

336. Daniel S.[6] Christner (Christian[5], Peter[4], Christian[3], Christian[2], Christen[1])[1980] was born 11 Apr 1830 in Nith River New Hamburg, Ontario, Canada[1980,1981,1982], and died 24 Oct 1897 in Hays Center, Hays Co., NE[1983]. He married **Magdalena Mattie Miller**[1984] 1854 in Pulaski, Davis Co., IA. She was born 06 Mar 1835 in Ontario, Canada[1985,1986,1987,1988], and died 07 Aug 1912 in Hays Center, Hays Co., NE[1988].

Notes for Daniel S. Christner:
Daniel migrated to Iowa 1870 census he is at Montgomery Twp., Hickory Co., MO than Hays Co., NE.

For a complete history of Daniel and his family read H. Walter Christner's book "Our Immigrants". Christian and Elizabeth Christner's Family at Goshen College, Goshen, IN.

More About Daniel S. Christner:
Residence: 1880, Perry, Lake Co., OH[1989]

More About Magdalena Mattie Miller:
Arrival: 1853[1990]
Census: 1851, Waterloo County, Ontario, Canada[1990]
Residence: 1910, High Ridge, Hayes, Nebraska[1990,1991,1992]

Children of Daniel Christner and Magdalena Miller are:

1144 i. Catherine[7] Christner.

1145 ii. William Christner.

+ 1146 iii. Elizabeth Christner, born 11 Sep 1856 in Pulaski, Davis Co., IA; died 08 Aug 1898 in Altmota, Whitman Co., WA.

1147 iv. Nancy Christner, born 28 Oct 1857 in Pulaski, Davis Co., IA; died 09 Jun 1921 in Waumeta, Chase Co.,

NE. She married Thompson.

+ 1148   v.   John Hubert Christner, born 12 Jan 1860 in Pulaski, Davis Co., IA; died 30 Mar 1941 in Hidalgo, TX.

+ 1149   vi.   Michael M. Christner, born 02 Jan 1862 in Pulaski, Davis Co., IA; died 26 Mar 1946 in Pulaski, Davis Co., IA.

+ 1150   vii.   Daniel Lincoln Christner, born 15 May 1863 in Pulaski, Davis Co., IA; died 13 Jul 1954 in Orland, Glenn Co., CA.

   1151   viii.   Magdalina Christner, born 15 May 1863 in Pulaski, Davis Co., IA; died 03 Mar 1865[1993].

+ 1152   ix.   Pheobe Or Philipine Christner, born 17 Apr 1865 in Pulaski, Davis Co., IA; died 04 May 1932 in Holdridge, Phelps Co., NE.

+ 1153   x.   Joseph J. Christner, born 25 Jan 1868 in or Sept. 1868 Quincy, Hickory Co., MO; died 10 Jan 1959.

   1154   xi.   Catherine Christner, born 04 Nov 1869 in Quincy, Hickory Co., MO; died 25 Jan 1948[1994].

   1155   xii.   William Christner, born 27 Feb 1872 in Quincy, Hickory Co., MO; died 03 Dec 1934 in Lincoln, Lancaster Co., NE.

+ 1156   xiii.   Leah Christner, born 14 Apr 1874 in Quincy, Hickory Co., MO; died 23 Mar 1932 in Hamlet, Hayes Co., NE.

+ 1157   xiv.   Mary C. Christner, born 30 Sep 1876 in Pulaski, Davis Co., IA; died 05 May 1968 in Springfield, MO.

339. John B.[6] **Christner** (Peter[5], Peter[4], Christian[3], Christian[2], Christen[1])[1995,1996] was born 09 Jun 1829 in Lorraine, Alsace, France/[1997], and died 10 Sep 1922 in Lagrange Co., IN. He married **Rachel Miller**[1998,1999] 1855. She was born 21 Nov 1837 in Somerset Co., PA[2000], and died 11 Sep 1924 in Lagrange Co., IN[2000].

Notes for John B. Christner:
He came to America (Canada, New Hamburg) with his parents in 1847.

Had a farm at the end of the road east from Griner (Greiner) Church in Indiana.

Amish and Amish Mennonite Families; CHB1; p. 60

More About John B. Christner:
Amish and Amish Mennonite: CHB1+/[2001]
Arrival: 1848[2002,2003,2004,2005]
Burial: Bontrager North Cemetery Lagrange Co.IN
Residence: 1852, Ontario Co., Canada West (Ontario), Canada[2006]

Notes for Rachel Miller:
Rachel is the daughter of Christian and Margaret Borntrager Miller.

Amish and Amish Mennonite Families; CHB1;DMB247; p. 60

More About Rachel Miller:
Burial: Bontrager North Cemetery Lagrange Co.IN
Residence: 1910, Middlebury, Elkhart Co., IN[2007]

Children of John Christner and Rachel Miller are:

+ 1158   i.   Joseph B. "Just"[7] Christner, born 06 May 1857 in Henry Co., IN; died 17 May 1937 in Kent Co., DE.

   1159   ii.   Veronica Frany Fanny Christner, born 24 Mar 1859 in Henry Co., IN; died 16 Jun 1911 in Lagrange Co., IN. She married (1) Daniel J. Hershberger; born 12 Nov 1854 in Lagrange Co., IN; died 27 Oct 1880 in Lagrange Co., IN. She married (2) John Baumgardner; born 29 Mar 1861 in IN; died 31 Dec 1903.

       Notes for Veronica Frany Fanny Christner:
       Amish and Amish Mennonite Families; CHB12; p. 60

       Birth: Mar. 24, 1859
       Death: Jun. 16, 1901

       Burial: Pashan Cemetery, Shipshewana, Lagrange Co., IN
       Find A Grave Memorial# 82851175

Notes for Daniel J. Hershberger:
Title: Amish and Amish Mennonite Families
Author: Hugh F. Gingerich and Rachel W. Kreider, 1986; HB4782, CHB1; p. 60

Daniel is the son of Joseph and Barbara Blough Hershberger.

Notes for John Baumgardner:
Title: Amish and Amish Mennonite Families
Author: Hugh F. Gingerich and Rachel W. Kreider, 1986; BG4h; CHB1; p. 60

John is the son of John and Hannah Shepherd Baumgardner.

Birth: Mar. 29, 1861
Death: Dec. 31, 1903

Burial: Pashan Cemetery, Shipshewana, Lagrange Co., IN
Find A Grave Memorial# 82851144

+ 1160   iii.   John E. Christner, born 01 May 1861 in Henry Co., IN; died 22 Feb 1939 in Newbury, Lagrange Co., IN.

+ 1161   iv.   Margaret Christner, born 25 Oct 1865 in or 1863 Trenton, Henry Co., IN; died 15 Oct 1929 in Goshen, Elkhart Co., IN.

+ 1162   v.   Peter J. Christner, born 18 Mar 1867 in Lagrange Co., IN; died 31 Jan 1948 in Three Rivers, St Joseph Co., MI.

   1163   vi.   Eli Christner[2008], born 03 Oct 1869 in Lagrange Co., IN; died 03 Feb 1882 in Clay, Lagrange Co., IN[2008].

Notes for Eli Christner:
Amish and Amish Mennonite Families; CHB16; p. 60

Birth: 3 Oct 1869
Death: Feb. 9, 1882

Burial: Bontrager North Cemetery, Lagrange Co., IN
Find A Grave Memorial# 82398172

More About Eli Christner:
Burial: N41°40.560xW85°37.884/Bontrager North Cemetery, Lagrange Co., IN
Residence: 1880, Clay, Lagrange Co., IN[2008]

   1164   vii.   Lydia Christner[2009], born 24 Apr 1872 in Lagrange Co., IN; died 03 Sep 1872 in Lagrange Co., IN.

Notes for Lydia Christner:
Amish and Amish Mennonite Families; CHB17; p. 60

More About Lydia Christner:
Amish and Amish Mennonite: CHB17/[2009]

+ 1165   viii.   Sarah Christner, born 07 Aug 1873 in Lagrange Co., IN; died 05 Mar 1964 in Elkhart Co., IN.

+ 1166   ix.   Samuel J. Christner, born 17 Dec 1875 in Lagrange Co., IN; died 05 Nov 1971 in Shipshewana Lagrange Co., IN.

   1167   x.   David J. Christner, born 22 Jan 1880 in Lagrange Co., IN; died 29 Jun 1882 in Lagrange Co., IN.

Notes for David J. Christner:
CHRISTNER - Jan 29th near Middlebury, Lagrange Co., IN of diphtheria, David, son of John and Rachel Christner, aged 1 year, 6 months and 7 days. Buried the 31st. Funeral sermon by David S. Kauffman and John E. Borntreger. Text, Mark 10: 18-19.

Amish and Amish Mennonite Families; CHB1a; p. 60

More About David J. Christner:
Burial: Bontreger North Cem. on 250N east of 1100W Lagrange Co. Indiana N41°40.560xW85°37.890

+ 1168   xi.   Edward J. Christner, born 28 Oct 1883 in Lagrange Co., IN; died 12 Nov 1960 in Huntington Park, Los Angeles Co., CA.

341. Peter⁶ Christner III (Peter⁵, Peter⁴, Christian³, Christian², Christen¹)²⁰¹⁰,²⁰¹¹ was born 13 Jul 1833 in Alsace, Lorraine, France²⁰¹², and died 09 Nov 1912 in Elmira, Aurora, Lane Co., OR²⁰¹². He married **Barbara Haus/Haas** 12 Jan 1858 in Henry Co.. IA. She was born 25 Sep 1828 in Lorraine, France²⁰¹³, and died 30 Jan 1898 in Elmira, Lane Co., OR²⁰¹⁴,²⁰¹⁵.

Notes for Peter Christner III:
Amish and Amish Mennonite Families; CHB3; p. 60

Family History of Christian Schmucker and Catherine Christner, p. 9

He came to America (Canada, New Hamburg) with his parents in 1847.

Church History of Eugene, Oregon By S. G. Shetler

Ben Miller and family and Peter Mishler, who had been members of the Forks Amish/Mennonite Church near Middlebury, IN located near Hubbard, OR. About 1887 Bishop Jonathan Smucker from the Indiana-Michigan A. M. Conference came to Hubbard and organized a congregation. The membership consisted of two families named, together with Joseph Maurer and family, Peter Christner and wife, L. J. Yoder and wife, the last two families named having been members of the Old Order Amish Church. Peter Christner had been ordained minister in the church of which he had been a member in Howard Co., IN. At the organization of the congregation, Peter Mishler was ordained bishop by Bishop Christner.

In a few years, a number of these families began to move to Eugene, OR out of which grew another congregation. For several years, Peter Mishler, who lived at Woodburn, OR went to Eugene to preach and then moved there also. Among the early families to move there were L. J. Yoder, Peter Christner, J. D. Mishler, Soloman Miller and others.

Peter Christner preached at Elmira, Oregon and later at the Zion Cave, near Hubbard, Oregon. Finally he settled in the foot hills of the Cascade Mountains and preached for the Swiss Mennonites.

Birth: Jul. 13, 1833, Germany
Death: Nov. 9, 1912
Aurora, Clackamas Co., OR

Gospel Herald - Volume V, Number 37 - December 12, 1912 - page 590, 591

Peter Christner was born July 13, 1833, at Byer, Germany; died near Aurora, Oreg., Nov. 9, 1912; aged 79 y. 3 m. 27 d. He was married to Barbara Hass, Jan. 12, 1858, in Henry Co., IA. There were born to this union 10 children. Wife and 3 children preceded him to the spirit world. He leaves to mourn his departure 7 children, 23 grandchildren, and 40 great grandchildren. Bro. Christner preached in the Mennonite Church for 53 years. Funeral services conducted at the Bethel Church. A. P. Troyer and Christian Geiger preached; the former in English, text Psa. 90:12; the latter in German on II Cor. 5:1. The remains were laid to rest in the Bear Creek Cemetery, according to his request.

Spouse: Barbara Haus Christner (1828 - 1898)

Children:
Mattie Christner Miller (1862 - 1929)
Christian C. Christner (1871 - 1945)

Inscription: Age 79 Yrs. 3 Ms. 27 Days

Burial: Bear Creek Cemetery, Molalla, Clackamas Co., OR

More About Peter Christner III:

Arrival: 1854, Age: 21/*2016,2017*
Burial: Bear Creek Cemetery, Molalla, Clackamas Co., OR*2017*
Residence: 1852, Ontario Co., Canada West (Ontario), Canada*2018*

Notes for Barbara Haus/Haas:
Family History of Christian Schmucker and Catherine Christner, p. 9

Obituary: Herald of Truth - March 1898
CHRISTNER - Near Elmira, Lane Co., Oregon, on the 30th of Jan. 1898, of consumption, Barbara, wife of bishop Peter Christner, aged 69 years, 3 mos., and 15 days. She was born in France, Oct. 15, 1828; lived in matrimony with her surviving husband 40 years. She was a member of the Amish Mennonite Church 57 years; was the mother of ten children and grandmother to twenty-four. She was buried in the Inman cemetery on the 31st. Funeral services were conducted at the house by J. D. Mishler from 1 Thess. 4:13-18, and at the church by Rev. Howard from Heb. 9:27.
Spelled Hass by some.

Birth: Sep. 25, 1828 - France
Death: Jan. 30, 1898 - OR

Spouse: Peter Christner (1833 - 1912)

Children:
Mattie Christner Miller (1862 - 1929)
Christian C. Christner (1871 - 1945)

Burial: Inman Cemetery, Elmira, Lane Co., OR

More About Barbara Haus/Haas:
Burial: Inman Cemetery, Elmira, Lane Co., OR
Cause of Death: Consumption

Children of Peter Christner and Barbara Haus/Haas are:

+   1169   i.   Veronica Fannie[7] Christner, born 04 Mar 1859 in Wayland, Henry Co., IA; died 18 Jan 1894 in Peach Orchard, Clay Co., AR.

+   1170   ii.   Catherine Christner, born 09 Mar 1860 in Henry Co., IA; died 26 Nov 1933 in Nappanee, Elkhart Co., IN.

+   1171   iii.   Jacob Christner, born 30 Mar 1861 in Henry Co., IA; died 1933.

+   1172   iv.   Magdalena "Mattie" Christner, born 21 Jul 1862 in Trenton, Henry Co., IA; died 28 Mar 1929 in Hubbard, Marion Co., OR.

     1173   v.   Joseph Christner*2019,2019*, born 05 Mar 1865 in Henry Co., IA; died Jan 1938 in Portland, Multnomah Co., OR*2019*.

                    Notes for Joseph Christner:
                    It is belived that Joseph died single.

     1174   vi.   Peter Christner, born 28 Apr 1867 in Henry Co., IA; died 1929. He married Ella Eash.

                    Notes for Peter Christner:
                    Family History of Christian Schmucker and Catherine Christner, p. 9

                    Notes for Ella Eash:
                    Family History of Christian Schmucker and Catherine Christner, p. 9

     1175   vii.   Noah Christner, born 06 Nov 1869 in Hickory Co., MO; died 1950. He married Emma Schlumberger.

                    Notes for Noah Christner:
                    Family History of Christian Schmucker and Catherine Christner, p. 9

+ 1176   viii.   Christian S. Christner, born 13 Feb 1871 in Wheatland, Hickory Co., MO; died 09 Jan 1945 in Molalla, Clackamas Co., OR.

342. Jacob[6] **Christner** (Peter[5], Peter[4], Christian[3], Christian[2], Christen[1])[2020,2021,2022,2023] was born 20 Jun 1838 in Bavaria, Germany[2024], and died 06 Mar 1904 in Henry Co., IA[2024]. He married **Barbara Egli**[2024,2025] 18 Oct 1860. She was born 02 May 1839 in Alsace, Lorraine, France[2026], and died 03 Apr 1915 in Trenton, Henry Co., IA[2026].

Notes for Jacob Christner:
Birth: Jun 20, 1836
Death: Mar 6, 1904

Jacob is father to Benjamin E. Christner, grandfather to Luther Hansel Christner, Great grandfather to Benjamin Richard Christner.

Spouse: Barbara Egli Christner (1835 - 1915)

Children:
Magdalena Christner Hirschy (1861 - 1943)
Jacob E. Christner (1863 - 1933)
Christian E. Christner (1868 - 1951)
Enos Christner (1879 - 1951)
Amos Christner (1883 - 1968)

Burial: Sugar Creek Cemetery, Wayland, Henry Co., IA

HERALD OF TRUTH, Vol. XLI, No. 13, March 24, 1904 - pp. 103,104
CHRISTNER - Jacob Christner was born in Bavaria, Germany, in 1836. He came with his parents to Canada in 1847 and moved to Iowa in 1855. He was married to Barbara Egli, Oct. 18, 1860. Bro. Christner died March 6, 1904, aged 67 Y., 8 M., 25 D. He leaves a wife, seven sons and two daughters to mourn his departure, one son having preceded him to the spirit world. Buried in the Sugar Creek cemetery, Henry Co., IA. Services by S. Gerig and D. Graber in German and S.M. Musselman in English from Phil. 1:21 and Thess. 4:13-18.

More About Jacob Christner:
Burial: Sugar Creek Church Cemetery Henry Co., Wayland Co., IA
Residence: 1895, Wayne, Henry Co., IA[2026]

Notes for Barbara Egli:
Obituary: Gospel Herald-VolII, Number 5-April 29, 1915-pages 76,77

Christner - Barbara Egli Christner was born in Alsace, Germany, May 21, 1839; died at the home of her daughter, Mrs. Jacob Hirschey, April 3, 1915; aged 75 y. 10 m. 12 d.; came to Canada with her parents when 8 years of age; moved with her parents to Iowa when 16 years old; united with the Amish Mennonite Church in her youth, of which she was a faithful member till death. Oct. 18, 1860, she was united in marriage to Jacob Christner, who preceded her to the spirit world 11 years ago. To this union were born 8 sons and 2 daughters of whom 1 son died in infancy. Nine children, 36 grand-children, 6 great-grandchildren, 3 brothers, and 1 sister with a host of friends remain to mourn her loss. Funeral services were conducted at the Sugar Creek Church near Wayland, Iowa, by S. Gerig (German), Simon Gingerich (English). Texts, Heb. 13:14; II Cor. 5:1,2. The remains were laid to rest in the cemetery nearby.

Birth: May 21, 1835
Death: Apr 3, 1915

Mother of Benjamin E. Christner

Spouse: Jacob Christner (1836 - 1904)

Children:
Magdalena Christner Hirschy (1861 - 1943)
Jacob E Christner (1863 - 1933)
Christian E Christner (1868 - 1951)
Enos Christner (1879 - 1951)
Amos Christner (1883 - 1968)

Burial: Sugar Creek Cemetery, Wayland, Henry Co., IA

More About Barbara Egli:
Burial: Sugar Creek Church Cemetery Henry Co., Wayland Co., IA[2026]
Immigration: 1848, Came to America/[2027]
Residence: 1900, Wayne Township, Henry Co., IA[2027]

Children of Jacob Christner and Barbara Egli are:

	1177	i.	Mary[7] Christner. She married Gisser.
+	1178	ii.	Magdalena "Lena" Christner, born 08 Jun 1861 in Henry Co., IA; died 19 Apr 1943 in IA.
+	1179	iii.	Jacob E. Christner, born 27 Aug 1863 in Henry Co., IA; died 25 Sep 1933 in Henry Co., IA.
+	1180	iv.	Christian E. Christner, born 20 Jan 1868 in Trenton, Henry Co., IA; died 02 Dec 1951 in Wayland, Henr Co., PA.
+	1181	v.	Benjamin E. Christner, born 04 Feb 1877 in Trenton, Henry Co., IA; died 06 Jan 1919 in Trenton, Henry Co., IA.
	1182	vi.	Enos Christner[2027], born 16 Dec 1879 in Trenton, Henry Co., IA[2027]; died 24 Dec 1951 in Henry Co., IA[2027]. He married Nettie M. Stone[2027] 18 Dec 1907[2027]; born 10 Feb 1886 in IA[2027]; died 15 Nov 1972 in Wayland, Henry Co., IA[2027].

More About Enos Christner:
Residence: 1930, Brighton, Washington Co., IA[2027]

More About Nettie M. Stone:
Residence: 1920, Jefferson, Henry Co., IA[2027]

| | 1183 | vii. | Amos Christner, born 27 Mar 1883 in Henry Co., IA; died Aug 1968 in Washington, Washington Co., IA. |

344. Josef[6] Christner (Josef[5], Peter[4], Christian[3], Christian[2], Christen[1]) was born 1844, and died 1927. He married **Elise Ingold Eyer**. She was born 1836, and died 1904.

Notes for Josef Christner:
Josef lived near Munich Germany.

Child of Josef Christner and Elise Eyer is:

| + | 1184 | i. | Christian[7] Christner, born 1876; died 1960. |

345. Christian[6] Guth (Barbara[5] Christner, John Johann[4], Christian[3], Christian[2], Christen[1]) was born 24 Feb 1833 in Burgwalden, Germany, and died 26 Sep 1889 in Kokomo, Howard Co., IN. He married **Pheobe Ehrismann**. She was born 11 Mar 1835, and died 04 May 1904 in Kokomo, Howard Co., IN.

Child of Christian Guth and Pheobe Ehrismann is:

| + | 1185 | i. | Jacob[7] Good, born 28 Mar 1870; died 25 May 1937 in Kokomo, Howard Co., IN. |

346. Daniel[6] Christner (Christian[5], John Johann[4], Christian[3], Christian[2], Christen[1])[2028,2029,2030,2031,2032,2033] was born 08 Nov 1846 in New Hamburg, Wilmot Twp., Waterloo Co., Ontario, Canada[2034,2035,2036,2037,2038], and died 17 Feb 1915 in Kitchener, Ontario, Canada. He married **(1) Mary "Polly" Shantz**. She was born 21 Apr 1856 in Wilmot Twp., Waterloo Co., Ontario, Canada[2039,2040,2041], and died 21 Apr 1884 in Waterloo Co.,

Ontario, Canada[2042]. He married **(2) Hannah Feick**[2043]. She was born 17 Apr 1853 in Ontario, Canada[2044,2045], and died 07 Jul 1923 in Canada.

Notes for Daniel Christner:
Birth: Nov. 8, 1846
Death: Feb. 8, 1915

Parents:
Christian Christner (1815 - 1907)
Anna Honsberger Christner (1825 - 1884)

Spouses:
Mary Shantz Christner (1856 - 1884)
Hannah Feick Christner (1853 - 1923)

Burial: Wilmot Centre Cemetery, Waterloo Co., Ontario, Canada

More About Daniel Christner:
Residence: 1891, Waterloo South, Ontario, Canada[2045]

Notes for Mary "Polly" Shantz:
Birth: Apr. 21, 1856
Death: Apr. 21, 1884

Death caused by inflamation after childbirth of her last child (un-named daughter born Apr 20, 1884).

Parents:
Joseph Y. Shantz (1815 - 1900)
Elizabeth Stauffer Shantz (1820 - 1898)

Spouse: Daniel Christner (1846 - 1915)

Burial: Wilmot Mennonite Cemetery, Waterloo Co., Ontario, Canada

More About Mary "Polly" Shantz:
Residence: 1911, Oxford North, Ontario, Canada[2046,2047,2048]

More About Hannah Feick:
Residence: 1891, Waterloo South, Ontario, Canada[2049]

Children of Daniel Christner and Mary Shantz are:
     1186   i.   Ira[7] Christner, born Abt. 1877 in Ontario, Canada[2050].

                           More About Ira Christner:
                           Residence: 1891, Waterloo South, Ontario, Canada[2050]

     1187   ii.   David Christner[2051], born 10 Sep 1878 in Waterloo Co., Ontario, Canada[2051].

                           More About David Christner:
                           Residence: 1891, Waterloo South, Ontario, Canada[2052]

+   1188   iii.   Ida Christner, born 29 Jun 1880 in Wilmot Twp, Waterloo Co, Ontario, Canada..
     1189   iv.   Eldon Christner, born Abt. 1882 in Ontario, Canada[2053].

                           More About Eldon Christner:
                           Residence: 1891, Waterloo South, Ontario, Canada[2053]

Children of Daniel Christner and Hannah Feick are:

1190   i.   John[7] Christner.

1191   ii. John Christner[2054], born Abt. 1890 in Ontario, Canada[2054].

More About John Christner:
Residence: Detroit, Wayne, Michigan[2054]

1192   iii. Minnie Christner, born Jun 1892 in Ontario, Canada[2055].

More About Minnie Christner:
Residence: 1911, Oxford North, Ontario, Canada[2055]

347. Mary[6] Christner (Christian[5], John Johann[4], Christian[3], Christian[2], Christen[1]) was born 14 Mar 1848 in New Hamburg, Ontario, Canada. She married **James Hastings**.

Children of Mary Christner and James Hastings are:
1193   i.   Allan[7] Hastings.
1194   ii. Annie Hastings.
1195   iii. Jennie Hastings.
1196   iv. Oliver Hastings.
1197   v.   Roy Hastings.

348. Enos H.[6] Christner (Christian[5], John Johann[4], Christian[3], Christian[2], Christen[1])[2056,2057,2058,2059,2060] was born 21 Feb 1850 in New Hamburg, Wilmot Twp., Waterloo Co., Ontario, Canada[2061], and died 11 Mar 1936 in New Hamburg, Wilmot Twp., Waterloo Co., Ontario, Canada[2061]. He married **Hannah Adeline Feick**[2062,2063,2064] 16 Mar 1887 in Waterloo Co., Ontario, Canada[2065]. She was born 16 Jan 1867 in Ontario, Canada[2066], and died 14 Nov 1924 in New Hamburg, Ontario, Canada.

Notes for Enos H. Christner:
He was a farmer lived 2 miles north of New Hamburg, Ontario, Canada.

Birth: Feb. 21, 1850
Death: Mar. 11, 1936

Parents:
Christian Christner (1815 - 1907)
Anna Honsberger Christner (1825 - 1884)

Spouse: Hannah "Adeline" Feick Christner (1866 - 1924)

Children:
Ada Louisa Christner (1891 - 1988)
Charles Albert Christner (1894 - 1982

Burial: Riverside Cemetery, Waterloo Co., Ontario, Canada
Find A Grave Memorial# 51257892

More About Enos H. Christner:
Burial: Abt. 14 Mar 1936, Riverside Cem, New Hamburg, Wilmot Twp, Waterloo Co, Ontario, Canada[2067]
Residence: 1911, Waterloo South, Ontario, Canada[2068,2069]

Notes for Hannah Adeline Feick:
Birth: Jan. 16, 1866
Death: Nov. 14, 1924

Adeline was born Jan 16, 1866 according to the 1901 census.

Spouse: Enos Christner (1850 - 1936)

Children:
Ada Louisa Christner (1891 - 1988)
Charles Albert Christner (1894 - 1982)

Burial: Riverside Cemetery, Waterloo Co., Ontario, Canada

More About Hannah Adeline Feick:
Burial: Riverside Cem, New Hamburg, Wilmot Twp, Waterloo Co, Ontario, Canada[2070]
Residence: 1891, Wilmot, Waterloo South, Ontario, Canada[2071]

Children of Enos Christner and Hannah Feick are:

1198   i.   Alexander[7] Christner[2072,2073,2074,2075], born 28 Feb 1888 in Waterloo Co., Ontario, Canada[2076,2077]; died 18 May 1982. He married Idella May Schweitzer; born 10 May 1890; died 05 Sep 1980.

Notes for Alexander Christner:
Birth: Feb. 28, 1888
Death: May 18, 1982

Spouse: Idella May Schweitzer Christner (1890 - 1980)

Burial: Lingelbach Cemetery, Perth, Ontario, Canada
Find A Grave Memorial# 13906488

More About Alexander Christner:
Residence: 1891, Wilmot, Waterloo South, Ontario, Canada[2077]

Notes for Idella May Schweitzer:
Birth: May 10, 1890
Death: Sep. 5, 1980

Daughter of Rebecca (Rupp) and William Schweitzer. Idella's stone says her birthday is the 10th. I did find her birth record (#026647) dated May 8th 1910

Parents:
William Henry Schweitzer (1865 - 1923)
Rebecca Rupp Schweitzer (1863 - 1934)

Spouse: Alexander F Christner (1888 - 1982)

Burial: Lingelbach Cemetery, Perth, Ontario, Canada
Find A Grave Memorial# 13906520

More About Idella May Schweitzer:
Residence: 1911, Perth North, Ontario, Canada[2078]

1199   ii.   Ada Louisa Christner[2079,2080], born 18 May 1891 in Waterloo Co., Ontario, Canada[2081,2082,2083,2084]; died 1988 in New Hambug, Ontario, Canada[2085,2086]. She married Henry Thomas Hopwood.

Notes for Ada Louisa Christner:
Birth: May 18, 1891
Death: Dec. 27, 1988

Parents:
Enos Christner (1850 - 1936)
Hannah "Adeline" Feick Christner (1866 - 1924)

Burial: Riverside Cemetery, Waterloo Co., Ontario, Canada
Find A Grave Memorial# 51266178

More About Ada Louisa Christner:
Arrival: 03 Aug 1915, Port Huron, St. Clair Co., MI[2087]

Residence: 1911, Waterloo South, Ontario, Canada[2088, 2089]

+ 1200   iii.   Charles Albert Christner, born 12 Jul 1894; died 1982.

352. Leah[6] Christner (Christian[5], John Johann[4], Christian[3], Christian[2], Christen[1])[2090] was born 15 Sep 1858 in New Hamburg, Ontario, Canada[2090], and died 15 Sep 1914 in Waterloo, Onatario, Canada[2090]. She married **David S. Shantz** 11 Oct 1883 in Wilmot Township, Ontario, Canada[2090], son of David Shantz and Barbara Stouffer. He was born 23 Jun 1859 in Wilmot Ontario[2090, 2091], and died 21 Aug 1950 in Waterloo CO., On, Can[2092].

Notes for Leah Christner:
Shantz - Leah Christner, beloved wife of David S. Shantz, died in Waterloo Co., Ontario, Sept. 15, 1914; aged 55 y. 11 m. 17 d. She was the mother of 10 children and leaves to mourn a loving husband, 6 sons and 2 daughters, 2 sons having preceded her. She was a faithful member of the Mennonite Church for many years. She was of a kind and loving disposition. Her place in the church is vacant, but much more in the home. "What is home without a mother?" We feel to sympathize with the bereaved family, but we believe that our loss is her eternal gain. According to our views this mother could not have been spared, but the Bible teaches us, "For my thoughts are not your thoughts, neither are your ways my ways, saith the Lord." "For as the heavens are higher than the earth, so are my ways higher than your ways, and my thoughts than your thoughts." Funeral was held Sept. 19 and was perhaps the largest ever held at this place. Services at the house by Orphen Wismer and at the church by Bish. Jonas Snyder and Manasseh Hallman. Text. Matt. 25:6; Phil. 1:23. Interment in Shantz's Cemetery. May God comfort the bereaved.

More About Leah Christner:
Burial: Shantz Cemetery
Residence: 1911, Waterloo South, Ontario, Canada[2092]

Notes for David S. Shantz:
David's father was also David

More About David S. Shantz:
Burial: Waterloo County, Ontario, Canada[2092]
Residence: 1911, Waterloo South, Ontario, Canada[2092]

Children of Leah Christner and David Shantz are:
   1201   i.   Oliver[7] Shantz.
   1202   ii.   Harvey Shantz, born 1885 in Ontario[2092].

     More About Harvey Shantz:
     Residence: 1901, Wilmot, Waterloo (South/Sud), Ontario, Canada[2092]

   1203   iii.   Elmer Shantz[2092], born 1886 in Ontario[2092].

     More About Elmer Shantz:
     Residence: Abt. 1916, 30, 2, W5, None[2092]

   1204   iv.   Cummin Shantz[2092], born 1888 in Canada English[2092]; died 25 Mar 1967 in Minneapolis, Hennepin, Minnesota, United States of America[2092].

     More About Cummin Shantz:
     Arrival: 1915[2092]
     Burial: Minneapolis, Hennepin County, Minnesota, USA[2092]
     Civil: 08 Aug 1918[2092]
     Residence: Illinois, Indiana, Wisconsin, Iowa[2092]
     Social Security Number: 468-12-5434/[2092]
     SSN issued: Minnesota[2092]

   1205   v.   Elroy Shantz[2092], born 1889 in Ontario[2092].

More About Elroy Shantz:
Residence: 1911, Waterloo South, Ontario, Canada[2092]

1206   vi.   Wesley Shantz, born 06 Nov 1890 in Waterloo, Ontario, Canada[2092]; died Feb 1977 in Orlando, Orange, Florida, United States of America[2092].

More About Wesley Shantz:
Arrival: 1915[2092]
Residence: 1930, Detroit, Wayne, Michigan[2092]
Social Security Number: 376-05-7921/[2092]
SSN issued: Michigan[2092]

1207   vii.   David Oliver Shantz[2092], born 27 Oct 1892 in Waterloo, Ontario, Canada[2092]; died 25 Dec 1991 in Wayne, Wayne, Michigan[2092].

More About David Oliver Shantz:
Residence: 1901, Wilmot, Waterloo (South/Sud), Ontario, Canada[2092]
Social Security Number: 382-05-5577/[2092]
SSN issued: Michigan[2092]

1208   viii.   Barbara Ann Shantz[2092], born 14 Nov 1894 in Waterloo, Ontario, Canada[2092].

More About Barbara Ann Shantz:
Residence: 1911, Waterloo South, Ontario, Canada[2092]

1209   ix.   Melvin Howard Shantz[2092], born 01 Feb 1897 in Waterloo, Ontario, Canada[2092]; died 30 Jun 1903 in Waterloo[2092].

More About Melvin Howard Shantz:
Residence: 1901, Wilmot, Waterloo (South/Sud), Ontario, Canada[2092]

1210   x.   Floyd Stauffer Shantz[2092], born 14 Feb 1899 in Waterloo, Ontario, Canada[2092]; died 28 Feb 1899 in Waterloo[2092].

More About Floyd Stauffer Shantz:
Residence: Ontario, Canada[2092]

1211   xi.   Luella May Shantz[2092], born 09 Apr 1903 in Waterloo, Ontario, Canada[2092]; died Jan 1991[2092].

More About Luella May Shantz:
Residence: 1911, Waterloo South, Ontario, Canada[2092]

353. Christian H.[6] Christner (Christian[5], John Johann[4], Christian[3], Christian[2], Christen[1]) was born 25 Mar 1860 in New Hamburg, Ontario, Canada[2093], and died 13 Apr 1939 in Medford, OR[2094,2095]. He married **Elizabeth Beckner**[2096,2097] 30 Dec 1896 in DeWitt, NE[2097]. She was born 29 Jun 1874 in Mount Forest, Ontario, Canada[2097], and died 05 Feb 1953 in Eugene, Lane Co., OR[2098].

Notes for Christian H. Christner:
Birth: Mar. 25, 1860
Death: 1939

Parents:
Christian Christner (1815 - 1907)
Anna Honsberger Christner (1825 - 1884)

Spouse: Elizabeth Beckner Christner (1874 - 1953)

Children: Robert G. Christner (1912 - 2001)

Burial: Siskiyou Memorial Park, Medford, Jackson Co., OR

Find A Grave Memorial# 59794502

More About Christian H. Christner:
Burial: Medford, Jackson Co., OR[2099]
Immigration: 1889[2100]

Notes for Elizabeth Beckner:
Birth: Jun. 29, 1874
Death: 1953

Daughter of Margaret (Wiederholdt) and Heinrich Boeckner Boeckner/Beckner

Spouse: Christian H. Christner (1860 - 1939)

Children: Robert G. Christner (1912 - 2001)

Burial: Siskiyou Memorial Park, Medford, Jackson Co., OR
Find A Grave Memorial# 59794503

More About Elizabeth Beckner:
Burial: Siskiyou Memorial Park[2100]

Children of Christian Christner and Elizabeth Beckner are:
    1212   i.   Lucille[7] Christner[2100], born 30 Aug 1899 in Great Bend, KS[2100]; died 08 Feb 1901 in Great Bend, KS[2100].
    1213   ii. Harry C. Christner[2100], born 17 Dec 1901 in Great Bend, KS[2100].
    1214   iii. Robert G. Christner[2100], born 13 Oct 1912 in Los Angeles Co., CA[2100,2101]; died 16 Mar 2001 in Eugene, Lane Co., OR[2101,2102].

        More About Robert G. Christner:
        Social Security Number: 543-05-7392/[2103]
        SSN issued: OR[2103]

354. Annie[6] Christner (Christian[5], John Johann[4], Christian[3], Christian[2], Christen[1]) was born 08 Apr 1862 in New Hamburg, Ontario, Canada. She married **Cummin Rennie**.

Children of Annie Christner and Cummin Rennie are:
    1215   i.   Essie[7] Rennie.
    1216   ii. Herbert Rennie.
    1217   iii. Percy Rennie.

363. Elizabeth[6] Christner (Peter L.[5], John Johann[4], Christian[3], Christian[2], Christen[1])[2104] was born 19 Jul 1853, and died 24 Apr 1928. She married **Christian Otto**. He was born 23 Aug 1846, and died 08 May 1911.

Notes for Elizabeth Christner:
Birth: Jul. 19, 1853
Death: Apr. 24, 1928

Parents:
Peter L. Christner (1817 - 1899)
Catharine Nahrgang Christner (1828 - 1915)

Spouse: Christian Otto (1846 - 1911)

Children:
Sidney Otto (1887 - 1930)
Milton Otto (1889 - 1956)

Burial: Riverside Cemetery, Waterloo Co., Ontario, Canada

Notes for Christian Otto:
Birth: Aug. 23, 1846
Death: May 8, 1911

He was born Aug 25, 1846 if you use his death date and accumulated age as indicated on the gravestone.

Children of Elizabeth Christner and Christian Otto are:

1218   i.   Sidney[7] Otto, born 07 May 1887; died 26 Mar 1930.

> Notes for Sidney Otto:
> Birth: May 7, 1887
> Death: Mar 26, 1930
>
> Parents:
> Christian Otto (1846 - 1911)
> Elizabeth Christner Otto (1853 - 1928)
>
> Burial: Riverside Cemetery, Waterloo Co., Ontario, Canada

+   1219   ii.   Milton Otto, born 27 Aug 1889 in Ontario, Canada; died 24 May 1956.

364. Lucinda[6] Christner (Peter L.[5], John Johann[4], Christian[3], Christian[2], Christen[1])[2104,2105] was born 19 Oct 1858 in New Hamburg, Waterloo, Co., Ontario, Canada[2106], and died 17 Feb 1900 in New Hamburg, Waterloo, Co., Ontario, Canada[2106]. She married **Christian Zimmerman**[2107,2108] 25 Dec 1878 in Waterloo Co., Ontario, Canada[2109]. He was born 22 Aug 1848 in Sebringville, Ontario, Canada[2110], and died 17 Aug 1934 in Yamhill Co., OR[2110].

Notes for Lucinda Christner:
Birth: Oct. 19, 1858
Death: Feb. 17, 1900

Parents:
Peter L. Christner (1817 - 1899)
Catharine Nahrgang Christner (1828 - 1915)

Burial: Wilmot Mennonite Cemetery, Waterloo Co., Ontario, Canada

More About Lucinda Christner:
Residence: 1891, Waterloo South, Ontario, Canada[2111]

Notes for Christian Zimmerman:
Birth: Aug. 22, 1848
Death: Aug. 17, 1934

The Telephone Register, McMinnville, Oregon Thursday, Aug. 23, 1934

RITES HELD FOR C. ZIMMERMAN - Yamhill Pioneer Dies Here Friday

YAMHILL, Aug. 23 - Christian Zimmerman, 85, father of Senator Peter Zimmerman, independent candidate for governor, died Friday of heart trouble at the McMinnville hospital where he was received Thursday for treatment for his heart. He was born in Canada, Aug. 22, 1848. He lost his father at the age of 3 and his mother when he was 9. He made his home with his married brother until 17 years of age, when he went to Minnesota with his brother, Peter. Soon afterwards he came to Washington territory where he was engaged in the lumber industry near Everett, WA until 1881, when he returned to Ontario, Canada.

On March 29, 1882 he married Louisa Nolte at Sebringville, Ontario. A year later he came west again to find a satisfactory location for a home. He purchased a portion of the J.J. Burton donation land claim near Yamhill, and returned to Ontario to bring his wife and baby boy to their new home. He later purchased many adjoining acres and established an outstanding Christian home, where six more children were born. The three daughters died in infancy.

He was an ardent Christian worker in the Wesleyan Methodist church all his younger years. For this organization he built a church in this community. He was always ready to give financial and moral support to any movement that was for the betterment of his fellowman. He was especially interested in the temperance movement and in home missions.

Christian Zimmerman was one of a family of seven children three brothers and two sisters having preceded him in death. He leaves his widow; a brother, Phillip Zimmerman of Spring Valley, Minn.; four sons, B. Frank of Seattle, Wash.; George S., Peter C., of Yamhill, and Edward O. of Beaverton, and thirteen grandchildren.

Spouse: Louise Nolte Zimmerman (1857 - 1938)

Children:
Benjamin Frank Zimmerman (1883 - 1947)
George Samuel Zimmerman (1885 - 1976)
Peter Chris Zimmerman (1887 - 1950)
Catherine Zimmerman (1888 - 1888)
Mary Zimmerman (1889 - 1889)
Emma Zimmerman (1889 - 1889)
Edward O Zimmerman (1890 - 1985)

Note: Born Sebringville, Ontario, Canada

Burial: Yamhill-Carlton Cemetery, Yamhill, Yamhill Co., OR
Find A Grave Memorial# 17604878

Children of Lucinda Christner and Christian Zimmerman are:

   1220   i.   Catherine[7] Zimmerman.
   1221   ii.   Diana Zimmerman[2111], born 16 Oct 1878 in Oxford, Ontario, Canada[2111].

               More About Diana Zimmerman:
               Residence: 1891, Waterloo South, Ontario, Canada[2111]

   1222   iii. Manly Zimmerman[2111,2112], born 18 Feb 1881 in South Easthope Twp., Ontario, Can.[2112]; died 07 Oct
               1927 in Wilmot Twp., Ontario, Can.[2112]. He married Nancy Gardner Schaefer[2112] 22 Jun 1908 in Baden,
               Ontario, Can.[2112]; born 31 Dec 1881 in Baden, Ontario, Can.[2112]; died 22 Oct 1959 in New Hamburg,
               Ontario, Can.[2112].

               More About Manly Zimmerman:
               Burial: 11 Oct 1927, Riverside Cemetery, New Hamburg, Ont., Can.[2112]
               Residence: 1891, Waterloo South, Ontario, Canada[2113,2114]

               More About Nancy Gardner Schaefer:
               Burial: 26 Oct 1959, Riverside Cemetery, New Hamburg, Ont., Can.[2114]

   1223   iv.   Benjamin Frank Zimmerman[2115], born 1883[2115]; died 31 Aug 1947 in Age: 64/[2115].

               Notes for Benjamin Frank Zimmerman:
               Birth: 1883
               Death: Aug. 31, 1947

               Parents:
               Christian Zimmerman (1848 - 1934)
               Louise Nolte Zimmerman (1857 - 1938)

Burial: Evergreen Washelli Memorial Park, Seattle, King Co., WA
Find A Grave Memorial# 17746506

More About Benjamin Frank Zimmerman:
Burial: Seattle, King County, Washington, USA[2115]

+   1224   v.   George Samuel Zimmerman, born 26 Feb 1885 in Yamhill Co., OR; died 25 Sep 1976 in Age: 91/.
    1225   vi.   Peter Christian Zimmerman[2116], born 17 Aug 1887; died 28 Oct 1950 in Yamhill Co., OR[2116]. He
                  married Ethel Frances Petty 1929[2116]; born 1896[2116]; died 1980 in Portland City, Multnomah Co.,
                  OR[2116].

                  Notes for Peter Christian Zimmerman:
                  Birth: Aug. 17, 1887
                  Death: Oct. 28, 1950

                  Parents:
                  Christian Zimmerman (1848 - 1934)
                  Louise Nolte Zimmerman (1857 - 1938)

                  Note: Husband to Ethel Frances Petty

                  Burial: Yamhill-Carlton Cemetery, Yamhill, Yamhill Co., OR
                  Find A Grave Memorial# 17359462

                  More About Peter Christian Zimmerman:
                  Occupation: Was a state senator in Orgeon, also ran (unsuccessfully) for governor in 1934.[2116]

    1226   vii. Mary Zimmerman, born 06 Jan 1889; died 26 Jan 1889 in Yamhill Co., OR.

                  Notes for Mary Zimmerman:
                  Birth: Jan. 6, 1889
                  Death: Jan. 26, 1889 - Yamhill Co., OR

                  Parents:
                  Christian Zimmerman (1848 - 1934)
                  Louise Nolte Zimmerman (1857 - 1938)

                  Burial: Yamhill-Carlton Cemetery, Yamhill, Yamhill Co., OR
                  Find A Grave Memorial# 17416898

    1227   viii. Emma Zimmerman, born 06 Jan 1889 in Yamhill Co., OR; died 01 Feb 1889 in Yamhill Co., OR.

                  Notes for Emma Zimmerman:
                  Birth: Jan. 6, 1889 - Yamhill Co., OR
                  Death: Feb. 1, 1889 - Yamhill Co., OR

                  Parents:
                  Christian Zimmerman (1848 - 1934)
                  Louise Nolte Zimmerman (1857 - 1938)

                  Burial: Yamhill-Carlton Cemetery, Yamhill, Yamhill Co., OR
                  Find A Grave Memorial# 17416902

    1228   ix.   Edward O. Zimmerman, born 10 Jun 1890. He married Cecil F. Deach; born 1901; died 1993.

                  Notes for Edward O. Zimmerman:
                  Birth: Jun. 10, 1890 - Yamhill, Yamhill Co., OR
                  Death: Jul. 18, 1985 - Loma Linda, San Bernardino Co., CA

                  News-Register, McMinnville, Oregon, Monday, July 22, 1985

Services for longtime Yamhill resident Edward O. Zimmerman of Redlands, CA will be held at 10:30 a.m. Tuesday in United Methodist Church of Yamhill. Officiating will be the Rev. Rick Hohnbaum and the Rev. Robert Kuykendall.

Mr. Zimmerman died July 18, 1985, in Loma Linda, CA. He was 95. Interment will be in Yamhill-Carlton Pioneer Cemetery.

Born June 10, 1890 in Yamhill he was the son of Christian and Louisa Nolte Zimmerman. He grew up and attended school in Yamhill.

Mr. Zimmerman graduated from Oregon Agricultural College (now Oregon State University) in 1915 with a degree in mining engineering. He earned a second degree in electrical engineering in 1917.

He served in the Army during World War I.

He and Cecil F. Deach were married May 8, 1921 in Yamhill.

The Zimmermans lived in Yamhill until they moved to Beaverton, where they lived from 1931 to 1934. They moved back to Yamhill and lived there until they moved to Redlands, CA in 1979 to be near their family.

Mr. Zimmerman worked as an electrical engineer for Portland Public Utility District. He also farmed most of his life in Yamhill and worked for Zimmerman Grain Co.

He was a member of United Methodist Church of Yamhill, American Legion and World War I Veterans. He also served for many years on both the Cove Orchard and Yamhill school boards and Yamhill Volunteer Fire Department.

Survivors include his wife, Cecil F. Zimmerman of Redlands; three sons, Martin Zimmerman of Madras, Edward Zimmerman of Renton, WA and Orin Zimmerman of Menlo Park, CA; two daughters, Elnor Kuykendall of Seattle; and C. Jeanette DeShazer of Redlands, 15 grandchildren; and nine great-grandchildren.

Arrangements are by Macy & Son Funeral Directors, McMinnville.

Parents:
Christian Zimmerman (1848 - 1934)
Louise Nolte Zimmerman (1857 - 1938)

Spouse: Cecil F. Deach Zimmerman (1901 - 1993)

Burial: Yamhill-Carlton Cemetery, Yamhill, Yamhill Co., OR
Find A Grave Memorial# 11911027

Notes for Cecil F. Deach:
Birth: 1901
Death: 1993

Spouse: Edward O Zimmerman (1890 - 1985)

Burial: Yamhill-Carlton Cemetery, Yamhill, Yamhill Co., OR
Find A Grave Memorial# 82146952

367. Christopher N.[6] **Christner** (Peter L.[5], John Johann[4], Christian[3], Christian[2], Christen[1])[2117] was born 06 Mar 1862 in New Hamburg, Waterloo, Co., Ontario, Canada[2117], and died 23 Oct 1917 in New Hamburg, Waterloo, Co., Ontario, Canada[2117]. He married **Ellen Clyde Brash**[2118,2119]. She was born 03 Dec 1872 in Blandford Township, Oxford Co., Ontario, Canada[2120], and died 05 Jul 1932 in Wilmot Twp., Waterloo Co., Ontario Canada[2121].

Notes for Christopher N. Christner:
Birth: Mar. 6, 1862
Death: Oct. 23, 1917

Parents:
Peter L. Christner (1817 - 1899)
Catharine Nahrgang Christner (1828 - 1915)

Spouse: Ellen Clyde Brash Christner (1873 - 1932)

Children: Katie Ann Christner Lederman (1899 - 1993)

Burial: Wilmot Mennonite Cemetery, Waterloo Co., Ontario, Canada
Find A Grave Memorial# 51276786

Notes for Ellen Clyde Brash:
Birth: Dec. 3, 1873
Death: Jul. 5, 1932

Daughter of Marion (Ferguson) and William Brash

Spouse: Chris N. Christner (1862 - 1917)

Children: Katie Ann Christner Lederman (1899 - 1993)

Burial: Wilmot Mennonite Cemetery, Waterloo Co., Ontario, Canada

More About Ellen Clyde Brash:
Burial: on Bleams Road; Wilmot Twp., Waterloo Co., Ontario Canada[2121]

Children of Christopher Christner and Ellen Brash are:

1229	i.	Marion[7] Christner. She married Hewitt.
1230	ii.	Alfred B Christner[2122], born 28 Sep 1897 in Wilmot Twp., Waterloo County, Ontario Canada[2122]; died 26 Jan 1990 in New Hamburg, Waterloo County, Ontario Canada[2122]. He married Elizabeth Craig[2122] 19 Nov 1927 in Bright, Blandford Twp., Oxford County, Ontario Canada[2122]; born 1897 in Blandford Township, Oxford County, Ontario Canada[2122]; died 1991 in New Hamburg, Waterloo County, Ontario Canada[2122].
+ 1231	iii.	Kathryn "Katie" Ann Christner, born 26 Jul 1899 in Wilmot Twp., Waterloo Co., Ontario Canada; died 30 Jan 1993 in New Hamburg, Waterloo Co., Ontario Canada.

369. Aaron[6] Christner (Peter L.[5], John Johann[4], Christian[3], Christian[2], Christen[1])[2123,2124,2125,2126,2127,2128,2129] was born 21 Oct 1843 in Waterloo Co., New Hamburg, Ontario, Canada[2130,2131,2132,2133], and died 10 Jun 1902 in Harrison Twp., Elkhart Co., IN[2134]. He married **Anna Elizabetha Pletcher**[2135,2136,2137] 07 Dec 1873 in Elkhart Co., IN. She was born 02 Jul 1853 in Crawford Co., OH[2138,2139], and died 21 Sep 1933 in Osceola, Elkhart Co., IN.

Notes for Aaron Christner:
Birth: Oct. 21, 1843 - Waterloo Co., Ontario, Canada
Death: 1902 - Elkhart Co., IN

Aaron Christner, possible son of Solomon McKenzie Christner & his wife Elizabeth Chevens Christner

Married 1873 Elizabeth aka Anna Elizabetha Pletcher daughter of Christian Pletcher & his 1st wife Mary Schneider Pletcher.

2nd Christian married Mary C. Enders Pletcher.

Spouse: Elizabeth A. Pletcher Christner (____ - 1933)

Children: Charles F. Christner (1877 - 1965)

Burial: Olive Cemetery, Wakarusa, Elkhart Co., IN

1. Census - 1900 Harrison Twp., Elkhart Co., IN 56, Oct 1843 Canada
2. Obituary - Wakarusa Tribune, 14 Jun 1902
3. Indiana State Library - WPA Death Records; Goshen Book H-14 p.10
4. Indiana State Library - WPA Marriage Records; Elkhart Co., IN; Bk 4 p. 139

More About Aaron Christner:
Burial: N41°36.414XW86°01.353/Olive Cemetery, Wakarusa, Elkhart Co., IN
Residence: 1861, Gore, Kent, Canada West, Canada[2140]

Notes for Anna Elizabetha Pletcher:
After her husband died she lived with her daughter Iva Grippen Scott. During her lifetime the family planned to get to get together for a birthday celebration on the Sunday nearest July 2nd. Many funny things happened on those occasions, like the time everyone took apple pie or the time the chicken waded through the vanilla tart pie.Recalling these incidents makes our reunions very interesting. After grandma died the family continued to get together during the summer but not on a set date.

Birth: Jul. 2, 1853 - Crawford Co., OH
Death: Sep. 21, 1933 - Elkhart Co., IN

Wife of Aaron Christner, daughter of Christian Pletcher and Mary Schneider

Burial: Olive Cemetery, Wakarusa, Elkhart Co., IN

Name: Anna Elizabetha Pletcher
Surname: Pletcher
Given Name: Anna Elizabetha
Sex: F
Birth: 2 Jul 1853 in ,Crawford Co., OH
Christening: 3 Sep 1853 St Mark Methodist,Crawford Co., OH
Death: 21 Sep 1933 in Osceola, Elkhart Co., IN
Burial: Olive Cemetery, Elkhart Co., IN

More About Anna Elizabetha Pletcher:
Burial: N41°36.414XW86°01.353/Olive Cemetery West Elkhart Co., IN
Residence: 1880, Harrison, Elkhart Co., IN[2141,2142]

Marriage Notes for Aaron Christner and Anna Pletcher:
Some have marrage date July 7 1873

Children of Aaron Christner and Anna Pletcher are:
    1232   i.   Mary Alberta[7] Christner[2143], born 19 Jul 1869 in Elkhart Co., IN[2143]; died Jul 1957 in Elkhart Co., IN. She married William Detweiler 01 Jan 1890 in Elkhart Co., IN.

            More About Mary Alberta Christner:
            Residence: 1880, Harrison, Elkhart Co., IN[2143]

+   1233   ii.   John Melvin Christner, born 10 Mar 1875 in Elkhart Co., IN; died 15 Feb 1944 in Elkhart, Elkhart Co., IN.

    1234   iii.   Clara Christner[2144], born Sep 1876 in IN[2144].

            More About Clara Christner:
            Residence: 1900, Harrison, Elkhart Co., IN[2144]

+   1235   iv.   Charles Franklin Christner, born 11 Sep 1877 in Elkhart Co., IN; died 10 Sep 1965 in Goshen, Elkhart Co., IN.

+ 1236   v.   Henry Edward Christner, born 31 Dec 1878 in Elkhart Co., IN; died 24 Mar 1956 in Union, Cass Co., MI.

  1237   vi.   William Irvin Christner[2144,2145], born 08 Feb 1880 in Elkhart Co., IN[2146,2147]; died Apr 1965 in Kalamazoo, MI. He married Nellie Zimmerman 28 Dec 1901 in Elkhart Co., IN; born Abt. 1882 in IN[2148].

        More About William Irvin Christner:
        Burial: Los Angeles Co., CA
        Residence: 1880, Harrison, Elkhart Co., IN[2149]
        Social Security Number: 555-22-9594/[2150]
        SSN issued: CA[2150]

        More About Nellie Zimmerman:
        Burial: Los Angeles Co., CA
        Residence: 1920, Los Angeles Assembly District 72, Los Angeles Co., CA[2151]

  1238   vii. Christian Talmer Christner, born 29 Nov 1882 in Elkhart Co., IN; died 14 Jun 1883 in Locke Twp., Elkhart Co., IN.

        More About Christian Talmer Christner:
        Burial: Olive Cemetery, Wakarusa, Elkhart Co., IN

+ 1239   viii. Sarah Mandella Christner, born 12 Jul 1884 in Elkhart Co., IN; died 13 Jan 1921 in Goshen, Elkhart Co., IN.

  1240   ix.   Dellie Christner[2152], born 12 Jul 1884 in Elkhart, IN[2153,2154]. She married David C. Rathbun[2155] 11 Apr 1914 in Elkhart, IN[2155].

        More About Dellie Christner:
        Residence: 1900, Harrison, Elkhart Co., IN[2156]

+ 1241   x.   Orange Vandever Eugene Christner, born 06 Mar 1889 in Elkhart Co., IN; died 15 Sep 1966 in Elkhart, Elkhart Co., IN.

  1242   xi.   Orrin Christner[2156], born Mar 1890 in IN[2156].

        More About Orrin Christner:
        Residence: 1900, Harrison, Elkhart Co., IN[2156]

+ 1243   xii. Iva Madgerene Christner, born 03 Dec 1892; died 18 Sep 1982 in Kalamazoo, MI.

370. Menno[6] Bechtel (Veronica Luckenbill[5] Christner, John Johann[4], Christian[3], Christian[2], Christen[1])[2157] was born 29 Jul 1842 in Waterloo, Wilmot Twnp, Ontario, Canada[2157], and died 19 Sep 1902 in Cardiac Disease/Waterloo Co., Wilmot Twp., Ontario, Canada[2157]. He married **Isabella Shirk**. She was born 21 Sep 1847, and died 07 Sep 1919.

Notes for Menno Bechtel:
Birth: Jul. 29, 1842
Death: Sep. 19, 1902

Son of Noah S. & Veronica (Christner) Bechtel. Husband of Isabella Shirk.
Menno's birthdate is confirmed in the 1901 census. It appears his accumulated age, as stated on the gravestone, may be off by 1 day.

Parents:
Noah S. Bechtel (1818 - 1901)
Veronica Christner Bechtel (1820 - 1907)

Spouse: Isabella Shirk Bechtel (1847 - 1919)

Children:
Leah Bechtel (1868 - 1886)

Allan Bechtel (1870 - 1942)
Sarah Bechtel Borman (1871 - 1894)
Miranda Bechtel (1876 - 1962)
Eden Bechtel (1885 - 1886)
Milton Bechtel (1887 - 1933)
Winnie E Bechtel Bish (1895 - 1977)

Burial: Shantz Mennonite Church Cemetery, Waterloo Co., Ontario, Canada

More About Menno Bechtel:
Burial: 19 Sep 1902, Shantz Mennonite Church Cemetery/Waterloo Co., Wilmot Twp., Ontario, Canada[2157]
Occupation: 19 Sep 1902, Contractor/Wentworth, Ontario, Canada[2157]
Residence: 29 Jul 1902, Ontario, Canada[2157]

Notes for Isabella Shirk:
Birth: Sep. 21, 1847
Death: Sep. 7, 1919

Daughter of John & Magdalena (Grody) Scherch. Wife of Menno Bechtel.
Isabella's birthdate is confirmed by the 1901 census. This birthdate and the deathdate as indicated on the gravestone agree with the accumulated age - also on the gravestone.

Spouse: Menno Bechtel (1842 - 1902)

Children:
Leah Bechtel (1868 - 1886)
Allan Bechtel (1870 - 1942)
Sarah Bechtel Borman (1871 - 1894)
Miranda Bechtel (1876 - 1962)
Eden Bechtel (1885 - 1886)
Milton Bechtel (1887 - 1933)
Winnie E Bechtel Bish (1895 - 1977)

Burial: Shantz Mennonite Church Cemetery, Waterloo Co., Ontario, Canada

Children of Menno Bechtel and Isabella Shirk are:
    1244   i.   Leah[7] Bechtel.
+ 1245   ii.   Allan Bechtel, born 08 Mar 1870 in Waterloo Co., Ontario, Canada; died 26 Jul 1942.
    1246   iii.   Sarah (Bechtel) Borman[2158], born 25 Dec 1871 in Waterloo, Ontario, Canada[2158]; died 05 Feb 1894 in Waterloo, Ontario, Canada[2158].

           More About Sarah (Bechtel) Borman:
           Residence: Ontario, Canada[2158]

    1247   iv.   Maranda Bechtel[2158], born 1876 in Ontario, Canada[2158].

           More About Maranda Bechtel:
           Residence: 1901, Berlin (Town/Ville), Waterloo (North/Nord), Ontario, Canada[2158]

    1248   v.   Milton Bechtel[2158], born 1887 in Ontario, Canada[2158].

           More About Milton Bechtel:
           Residence: 1901, Berlin (Town/Ville), Waterloo (North/Nord), Ontario, Canada[2158]

    1249   vi.   Lora Bechtel[2158], born 1889 in Ontario, Canada[2158].

           More About Lora Bechtel:
           Residence: 1901, Berlin (Town/Ville), Waterloo (North/Nord), Ontario, Canada[2158]

1250   vii.   Winney Bechtel[2158], born 1895 in Ontario, Canada[2158].

More About Winney Bechtel:
Residence: 1901, Berlin (Town/Ville), Waterloo (North/Nord), Ontario, Canada[2158]

378. Veronica "Fanny" Christner[6] Bechtel (Veronica Luckenbill[5] Christner, John Johann[4], Christian[3], Christian[2], Christen[1])[2159] was born 04 Mar 1859 in Waterloo Co., Ontario, Canada[2159,2160], and died 18 Apr 1935 in Pandora, Putnam Co., OH[2160]. She married **John S. Geiger**[2161] 29 Nov 1881 in New Hamburg, Ontario, Canada[2161]. He was born 11 Jun 1858 in Pandora, Putnam Co., OH[2161], and died 09 May 1945 in Pandora, Putnam Co., OH[2161].

More About Veronica "Fanny" Christner Bechtel:
Residence: 1930, Riley, Putnam Co., OH[2161]

More About John S. Geiger:
Residence: 1880, Putnam Co., OH[2161]

Children of Veronica Bechtel and John Geiger are:
1251   i.   Hattie[7] Geiger[2161], born 07 Oct 1882 in Pandora, Putnam Co., OH[2161]; died 20 May 1967 in Hancock Co., Hancock, Ohio, United States[2161].

More About Hattie Geiger:
Residence: 1900, Pandora Village, Putnam Co., OH[2161]

1252   ii.   Elton Bechtel Geiger[2161], born 25 May 1884 in OH[2161]; died 17 Nov 1966 in Decatur, Macon, Illinois, United States[2161].

More About Elton Bechtel Geiger:
Residence: 1900, Pandora Village, Putnam Co., OH[2161]

1253   iii.   Mary Avon Geiger[2161], born 21 Mar 1886 in OH[2161]; died 21 Feb 1920[2161].

More About Mary Avon Geiger:
Residence: 1900, Pandora Village, Putnam Co., OH[2161]

1254   iv.   Walter Bechtel Geiger[2161], born 11 Dec 1888 in OH[2161]; died 21 Nov 1963 in Pandora, Putnam, Ohio, United States[2161].

More About Walter Bechtel Geiger:
Residence: 1900, Pandora Village, Putnam Co., OH[2161]

1255   v.   Grover Giger[2161], born Abt. 1891 in OH[2161].

More About Grover Giger:
Residence: 1900, Pandora Village, Putnam Co., OH[2161]

1256   vi.   Milon Bechtel Geiger[2161], born 30 Aug 1892 in Pandora, Putnam Co., OH[2161]; died 01 Nov 1972 in Escondido, San Diego, California, USA[2161].

More About Milon Bechtel Geiger:
Residence: 1900, Pandora Village, Putnam Co., OH[2161]

1257   vii.   Lydia Bechtel Geiger[2161], born 11 Aug 1894 in OH[2161]; died 08 Nov 1981 in MI[2161].

More About Lydia Bechtel Geiger:
Residence: 1900, Pandora Village, Putnam Co., OH[2161]

1258   viii.   Elmer R. Geiger[2161], born 10 Sep 1897 in Pandora, Putnam Co., OH[2161]; died 27 Feb 1961 in Lima Memorial Hospial, Pandora, Putnam Co., OH[2161].

More About Elmer R. Geiger:
Residence: 1900, Pandora Village, Putnam Co., OH[2161]

Generation No. 7

382. Andrew[7] Hamsher (Elizabeth "Betsy"[6] Sipe, Elizabeth[5] Christner, Christian J.[4], Johannes John Hans[3], Christian[2], Christen[1])[2162] was born 22 Oct 1866 in Bourbon, Marshall Co., IN[2163,2164], and died 10 Oct 1953 in Walnut Creek, Holmes Co., OH[2165,2166]. He married **(1) Sarah Ann Gardner**[2166] 1889 in Holmes Co., OH[2166]. She was born 16 Nov 1872 in Walnut Creek, Holmes Co., OH[2166], and died 24 Mar 1890 in Walnut Creek, Holmes Co., OH[2166]. He married **(2) Amanda Hochstetler**[2167] 15 Feb 1890 in Trail, Ohio, United States[2167]. She was born 16 Mar 1870 in Trail OH, and died 12 Oct 1957 in Walnut Creek, Holmes Co., OH[2167].

Children of Andrew Hamsher and Amanda Hochstetler are:

1259	i.	Iva[8] Hamsher[2167], born 21 Feb 1891 in Trail, Holmes Co., OH[2167]; died 11 Aug 1891 in Trail, Holmes Co., OH[2167].
+ 1260	ii.	Milo Hamsher, born 27 Jul 1893 in Trail, Holmes Co., OH; died 22 May 1974 in Dover, Tuscarawas Co., OH.
1261	iii.	Melvin Hamsher[2167], born 03 Sep 1895 in Strasburg, Tuscarawas Co., OH[2167]; died 16 Sep 1962 in Millersburg, Holmes Co., OH[2167].

More About Melvin Hamsher:
Residence: 1910, Holmes Co., OH[2167]

1262	iv.	Sadie Hamsher[2167], born 05 Sep 1897 in Nappanee, Elkhar Co., IN[2167]; died 16 Mar 1951 in Walnut Creek, Holmes Co., OH[2167].
1263	v.	DeEtta Hamsher[2167], born 24 Sep 1900 in Trail, Holmes Co., OH[2167].
1264	vi.	Wallace Hamsher[2167], born 24 Jun 1903 in Trail, Holmes Co., OH[2167]; died 03 Sep 1974 in Sarasota Co., FL[2167].
1265	vii.	Tressie Hamsher[2167], born 13 Aug 1905 in Trail, Holmes Co., OH[2167].
1266	viii.	Paul A. Hamsher[2167], born 08 Dec 1909 in Walnut Creek, Holmes Co., OH[2167]; died 28 Apr 1991 in Cleveland, Cuyahoga Co., OH[2167].

384. Andrew S.[7] Mishler (Sarah[6] Sipe, Elizabeth[5] Christner, Christian J.[4], Johannes John Hans[3], Christian[2], Christen[1]) was born 03 Apr 1850 in Holmes Co., OH[2168], and died 24 Feb 1897 in Newbury Township, Honeyville, Lagrange Co., IN[2168]. He married **Sarah Hershberger**[2168]. She was born 13 May 1846 in Topeka, Lagrange Co., IN[2168], and died 25 May 1920 in Lagrange Co., IN[2168].

More About Andrew S. Mishler:
Alt. Marriage: 18 Apr 1875, Alt. Marriage/[2168]
Census: 25 Jun 1880, Newbury Township, Honeyville, Lagrange Co., IN[2168]

More About Sarah Hershberger:
Census: 22 Jul 1860, Middlebury Township, Elkhart Co., Indiana[2168]

Child of Andrew Mishler and Sarah Hershberger is:

+ 1267	i.	Malinda[8] Mishler, born 15 Jan 1887 in Lagrange Co., IN; died Aft. 1952 in Millersburg, Elkhart Co., IN.

389. Joseph J.[7] Christner (John J.[6], Joseph C.[5], Christian J.[4], Johannes John Hans[3], Christian[2], Christen[1])[2169,2170,2171,2172] was born 19 Feb 1851 in Holmes Co., OH[2173,2174,2175], and died 09 Jan 1925[2176,2177,2178,2179]. He married **(1) Francheon Nichelson**[2180]. He married **(2) Sarah Gerber**[2181,2182,2183]. She was born 31 Jan 1837 in Somerset, Somerset Co., PA[2184], and died 09 Nov 1923 in Baltic, Tuscarawas Co., OH[2184,2185]. He married **(3) Amanda Folk**[2186,2187,2188] 06 Nov 1874 in Holmes Co., OH[2189]. She was born 23 Jan 1857 in OH[2190,2191,2192], and died 27 Feb 1920[2193,2194,2195].

Notes for Joseph J. Christner:
Amish and Amish Mennonite Genealogies;

Newspaper clipping, the week of Mar 29 1888 nine pieces of meat were stolen from his Smokehouse.

His farm was at Honeyville IN. N41°34.841xW85°36.322

Joseph J. Christner became a recluse for five years after his wife, Amanda died. He would sit on a chair in his bedroom barely coming out to use the restroom. The first summer after Amanda died his sons, Ira, Eli, Abe, & Joe all went as a group to encourage him to join them by sitting on the wagon while they work the fields. He lasted until noon lunch, after which he refused to go back out. He was in good physical shape but the loss of his wife was more then he could bear.

Birth: Feb. 19, 1851
Death: Jan. 9, 1925

Parents: John J. Christner (1827 - 1893)

Children:
Clara Christner (1879 - 1886)
Mary A. Christner (1881 - 1960)
Lydia Eash (1884 - 1943)
Abraham A. Christner (1889 - 1959)

Spouse: Amanda Folk Christner (1857 - 1920)

Burial: Christner Cemetery, Honeyville, Lagrange Co., IN

The Descendants of John J. Christner, privately published 1961, February 1961, p. 4.

More About Joseph J. Christner:
Burial: Jan 1925, Row 4, plot 22/Christner Cemetery, Honeyville, Lagrange Co., IN

Notes for Sarah Gerber:
Birth: Jan. 31, 1837
Death: Nov. 9, 1923

Burial: Amish Mennonite Cemetery, Walnut Creek, Holmes Co., OH

Sarah is the daughter of Jacob Gerber and Elizabeth Miller. She was from the Walnut Creek, OH area. She may had a child Magdalena born 1858.

Obituary:
Christner - Sarah daughter of Jacob and Elizabeth Miller Gerber was born Jan. 31, 1837, at Strasburg, OH; died Nov. 9, 1923; aged 86 y. 9 m. 8 d. On Oct. 2, 1856, she was married to Joseph Christner of Walnut Creek, OH who preceded her in death. To this union were born 5 sons and 5 daughters, 3 daughters having preceded her to the great beyond. She leaves 5 sons (Jacob, John, Henry, Harvey, and William), and 2 daughters (Amanda, and Katie, wife of Emanuel Gerber); also 2 brothers (Jerry and Nathaniel), 5 sisters (Mrs. Katie Kuhns, Fanny Blosser, Lydia Deardorf, Elizabeth Hostetler, and Mary Haas), 40 grandchildren, 50 great-grandchildren, and a host of friends. She spent the declining days of her life with her daughter, Mrs. Emanuel Gerber, at whose home she passed away. Her last sickness, arteriosclerosis, lasted only a few days. She was a lifelong member of the Walnut A. M. Church, excepting a few years when she lived in NE. Services at the Walnut A. M. Church. Burial in cemetery nearby. Services were conducted by Lester Hostetler and S. H. Miller. Texts, I Cor. 15:57 and Job 3:17.

More About Sarah Gerber:
Burial: Amish Mennonite Cemetery, Walnut Creek, Holmes Co., OH
Residence: 1900, Bucks, Tuscarawas Co., OH[2196]

Notes for Amanda Folk:
Amanda Folks mother was Susie Kaser. Susie had 3 children while she was single. Amanda had one brother Eli, she also had 2 half brothers Ferrel and Ira Zaug or Zaugg.

Ira Zaugg's wife is buried at Eden Cemetery, Topeka, Indiana N41°32.392xW85°33.948 row 11 -- plot16

Eva Zaugg died Oct.2 1904--25 years old. Amanda was raised at Vistula, IN by preacher Jacob Miller son of Jonathan Miller. When Jacobs wife died he married an english women (non-amish) and she was mean and abusive to Amanda. Preacher Jacob Miller buried at Vistula Indiana Cemetery. Amanda named her son Ira after her half brother.

Amanda was eating breakfast, had only eaten part of her egg, went to the rocking chair in the living room and died there.

Birth: Jan. 23, 1857
Death: Feb. 27, 1920

Children: Clara Christner (1879 - 1886)

Spouse: Joseph J. Christner (1851 - 1925)

Burial: Christner Cemetery, Honeyville, Lagrange Co., IN

The Descendants of John J. Christner, privately published 1961, February 1961, p 4.

More About Amanda Folk:
Burial: Christner Cemetery Honeyville, Lagrange Co., IN - row 4, plot 23 - N 41°34.529-W 85°35.895

Child of Joseph Christner and Sarah Gerber is:
+   1268   i.   Amanda[8] Christner, born 24 Oct 1861 in Holmes Co., OH; died 10 Mar 1947 in Chappell, Deuel Co., NE.

Children of Joseph Christner and Amanda Folk are:
+   1269   i.   John D.[8] Christner, born 28 Oct 1875 in Honeyville, Lagrange Co., IN; died 29 May 1942 in Shipshewana, Lagrange Co., IN.
     1270   ii.   Clara Christner[2197,2198], born 07 Aug 1878 in Honeyville, Lagrange Co., IN[2198]; died 22 Aug 1886 in Lagrange, Lagrange Co., IN[2199,2200,2201].

                   Notes for Clara Christner:
                   Clara and Carrie were twins. Clara lived less then one day. Page 13 Christner Book.

                   Daughter of Joseph J. Christner and Amanda (Folk) Christner.

                   Their children:
                   Clara, Aug 7, 1879, died Aug. 22, 1886
                   Bontrager, David R. etal, The Descendants of John J. Christner, privately published 1961, fam 6 p 4.

                   Parents:
                   Joseph J. Christner (1851 - 1925)
                   Amanda Folk Christner (1857 - 1920)

                   Inscription: Clara Dau of Joseph J. and A. Christner Died Oct 22, 1886 Aged 7 y. 2 M. 15 AD

                   Burial: Christner Family Cemetery, Honeyville, Lagrange Co., IN

                   The Descendants of John J. Christner, privately published February 1961, p. 4.

+   1271   iii. Annie J. Christner, born 29 Aug 1879 in Holmes Co., OH; died 18 Sep 1957.
     1272   iv.   Mary A. Christner[2202,2203], born 31 Dec 1881 in Holmes Co., OH; died 13 Aug 1960 in Row 3 Plot 22.

Notes for Mary A. Christner:
Mary never married but she did earn $200.00 a year to keep house for her Father.

Birth: Dec. 31, 1881
Death: Aug. 13, 1960

Parents: Joseph J. Christner (1851 - 1925)

Inscription: Dau of Joseph & Amanda Christner

Burial: Christner Cemetery, Honeyville, Lagrange Co., IN

The Descendants of John J. Christner, privately published 1961, February 1961, p 4.

More About Mary A. Christner:
Burial: Christner Cemetery, Honeyville, Lagrange Co., IN

+ 1273   v.   Lydia J. Christner, born 08 Dec 1884 in Honeyville, Lagrange Co., IN; died 24 Nov 1943 in Rome City, Noble Co., IN.

+ 1274   vi.   Noah J. Christner, born 12 Apr 1887 in Honeyville, Lagrange Co., IN; died 12 Mar 1947.

+ 1275   vii.   Abraham A. Christner, born 19 Mar 1889 in Honeyville, Lagrange Co., IN; died 12 May 1959 in Lagrange, Lagrange Co., IN.

   1276   viii.   Joseph Joe Christner[2204,2205], born 25 Nov 1891 in Honeyville, Lagrange Co., IN[2206,2207]; died 07 Sep 1942[2208,2209].

Notes for Joseph Joe Christner:
Joe never married. He had cancer Abe and his brother Joe owned the Honeyville Store.

Birth: 1891
Death: 1942

Burial: Christner Cemetery, Honeyville, Lagrange Co., IN

The Descendants of John J. Christner, privately published 1961, February 1961, p. 4.

More About Joseph Joe Christner:
Burial: Row 4 plot 21/Christner Cemetery, Honeyville, Lagrange Co., IN
Causes of Death: Cancer
Nickname: Joe

+ 1277   ix.   Eli J. Christner, born 19 Aug 1894 in Millersburg, Elkhart Co., IN; died 31 May 1972 in Topeka, Lagrange Co., IN.

   1278   x.   Mary A. Christner, born 05 Feb 1897; died 1979.

Notes for Mary A. Christner:
Mary never married but she did earn $200.00 a year to keep house for her dad.

Birth: Feb. 5, 1897
Death: 1979

Spouse: Abraham A Christner (1889 - 1959)

Burial: Christner Cemetery, Honeyville, Lagrange Co., IN

The Descendants of John J. Christner, privately published 1961, February 1961, p. 4.

+ 1279   xi.   Ira J. Christner, born 27 May 1897 in Honeyville, Lagrange Co., IN; died 21 Aug 1982 in Carl Christner Home, Lagrange Co., IN.

+ 1280   xii.   Bessie Amanda Christner, born 09 Dec 1899 in Goshen, Elkhart Co., IN; died 01 Oct 1966.

391. David J.[7] Christner (John J.[6], Joseph C.[5], Christian J.[4], Johannes John Hans[3], Christian[2],

Christen[1])[2210,2211,2212,2213,2214,2215] was born 31 Dec 1853 in Millersburg, Holmes Co., OH[2216,2217,2218,2219,2220], and died 13 Nov 1927 in Topeka, Lagrange Co., IN[2221,2222,2223]. He married **Elizabeth C. Berlincourt**[2224,2225] 11 Jan 1880[2226,2227,2228]. She was born 14 Jan 1857 in Elkhart Co., IN[2229,2229], and died 24 Jul 1929 in Lagrange Co., IN[2230,2231,2232].

Notes for David J. Christner:
His farm was in Honeyville, LaGrange Co., IN. The west fence line was 950W. The South fence line was 500S. The east fence line was 900W. The North fence line was the south edge of the Christner Cemetery. He died from Paralysis. His burial at Miller Cemetery, LaGrange Co., IN. N41°35.324'xW85°28.927' Row7 Plot 37, Short row north of the south entrance, between rows 7 & 8. This cemetery is located at County Roads 300S and 300W -- 3 miles south & 3 miles west of the Lagrange Co. Court House.

Birth: Dec. 31, 1853
Death: Nov. 13, 1928

Spouse: Elizabeth Christener (1857 - 1929)

Burial: Miller Amish Cemetery, Lagrange, Lagrange Co., IN
Plot: lot 37, short row between 7/8

The Descendants of John J. Christner, privately published 1961, pp. 4, 17.

Amish and Amish Mennonite Genealogies; CH21213, p. 60

More About David J. Christner:
Burial: Miller Cemetery, Lagrange Co., IN N41°35.324'xW85°28.927' Row7 Plot 37
Cause of Death: Stroke
Residence: 1870, Eden, Lagrange Co., IN[2233]

Notes for Elizabeth C. Berlincourt:
The Descendants of John J. Christner, privately published February 1961, p. 17.

Birth: Jan. 14, 1857
Death: Jul. 24, 1929

Spouse: David Christner (1853 - 1928)

Burial: Miller Amish Cemetery, Lagrange, Lagrange Co., IN

Elizabeth's parents were Cyrus Berlincourt & Annie Houshover Elizabeth & David J. had a son that died in infancy no name or date of birth 1881-buried at N.41 Deg.34.526 x W.85 Deg.35.725 Old Christner Cemetery East of the Christner Cemetery out by the road.Honeyville, Lagrange Co., IN. Cyrus is the son of Joseph P. and Elizabeth Berlincourt. Joseph died 1839, Elizabeth died 1868. Cryus came to America age 12 with his mother,settling in Wayne Co., Ohio. Cryus born in Monible, Switzerland July 10, 1831 and died 1900.

Anna born Nov 22 1829 in Wayne Co., OH died July 23, 1914. Cryus and Anna came to Locke Twp., Nappanee, Elkhart Co., IN in 1853. They owned a farm of 120 acres in Locke Twp. There is a ditch named for the family in t in the town of Nappanee, IN. The ditch started on Cyrus's farm west of the town of Nappanee, IN. Cryus's will Book 6 page 445 Elkhart Co. court house Goshen, IN.

Cryus had remarkable psychophysical powers.

Elizabeth died in her sleep. Her burial is next to her husband at Miller Cemetery, LaGrange Co, IN. N41°35.324'xW85°28.927' Row7 Plot 38, Short row north of the south entrance, between rows 7 & 8. This cemetery is located at County Roads 300S and 300W -- 3 miles south & 3 miles west of the Lagrange County Court House.

More About Elizabeth C. Berlincourt:
Burial: N41°35.324'xW85°28.927' Row7 Plot 38/Miller Cemetery, Lagrange Co., IN
Residence: 1920, Clearspring, Lagrange Co., IN[2234,2235,2236]

Children of David Christner and Elizabeth Berlincourt are:
+   1281   i.   Cornelius D.[8] Christner, born 22 Jan 1883 in Topeka, Lagrange Co., IN; died 15 Sep 1954 in IN.

     1282   ii.   Joseph David Christner, born 19 Sep 1884 in Topeka, Lagrange Co., IN[2237]; died 02 Jan 1954 in San Joaquin Co., CA[2238]. He married Lydia Bechtold[2239]; born 03 Jul 1889 in SD[2240,2241]; died 21 Dec 1972 in San Joaquin Co., CA[2241,2242].

Notes for Joseph David Christner:
The Descendants of John J. Christner, privately published 1961, pp. 17, 18.

Moved to California as a young man right after his girlfriend left him in Indiana. He had no children. He married Lydia Bechtold in California. He was a man that took no back talk from anyone. Strong willed and enthusiastic.

Birth: Sep 19, 1884 - IN
Death: 1934
California, USA - CA

Spouse: Lydia B Bechthold Christner (1889 - 1972)

Burial: Lodi Memorial Cemetery, Lodi, San Joaquin Co., CA
Find A Grave Memorial# 21760852

More About Joseph David Christner:
Other-Begin: San Joaquin County[2243]
Residence: 1942, San Joaquin Co., CA[2244]

Notes for Lydia Bechtold:
The Descendants of John J. Christner, privately published 1961, p. 18.

Birth: Jul 3, 1889 - Hutchinson Co., SD
Death: Dec 21, 1972 - CA

Parents:
Henry Bechthold (1860 - 1953)
Willhelmina Klauss Bechthold (1862 - 1936)

Spouse: Joseph David Christner (1884 - 1934)

Burial: Lodi Memorial Cemetery, Lodi, San Joaquin Co., CA
Find A Grave Memorial# 21760832

More About Lydia Bechtold:
Residence: 1920, Elkhorn, San Joaquin Co., CA[2244]

+   1283   iii.   Eddranis D. Christner, born 10 May 1886 in Topeka, Lagrange Co., IN; died 27 Aug 1963 in IN.
+   1284   iv.   Mary Ann Christner, born 12 Jan 1888 in Honeyville, Lagrange Co., IN; died 20 Jan 1958 in IN.
+   1285   v.   David D. Christner, born 08 Jun 1889 in Topeka, Lagrange Co., IN; died 25 Nov 1948 in Lagrange Co., IN.
+   1286   vi.   Katie D. Christner, born 22 Feb 1891 in Topeka, Lagrange Co., IN; died 28 Mar 1959 in Lagrange, Lagrange Co., IN.
+   1287   vii.   Emma D. Christner, born 18 Apr 1893 in Topeka, Lagrange Co., IN; died 15 Apr 1928 in IN.
     1288 viii.   Unnamed Infant Christner, born 21 Apr 1895.
+   1289   ix.   Levi D. Christner, born 20 Aug 1897 in Topeka, Lagrange Co., IN; died 08 Nov 1985 in Elklick Twp., Bedford (now Somerset) Co., PA.

392. John J.[7] Christner (John J.[6], Joseph C.[5], Christian J.[4], Johannes John Hans[3], Christian[2], Christen[1])[2245,2246] was born 25 Nov 1855 in Holmes Co., OH[2247,2248], and died 08 Oct 1946 in Row 1 Plot 6 from south to north. He married **Mary D. Miller**[2249,2250,2251] 02 May 1878 in Lagrange Co., IN[2252]. She was born 28 Feb 1860 in Berlin, Holmes Co., OH[2252,2253,2254], and died 01 Mar 1947[2255,2256,2257].

Notes for John J. Christner:
The Descendants of John J. Christner, privately published February 1961, pp. 4, 26

Amish and Amish Mennonite Genealogies; CH21214, p. 60

He was old order amish. He moved here from Holmes Co., OH. Some records show that he was born in 1854. John told a story to Levi D. Christner his nephew about the trip from Warsaw to Bonnieville Mills. Joe, Noah, and David would get off the wagon and run along beside the wagon. The driver did not know the boys had gotten off the wagon and moved the horses at a faster pace. The boys got quite a ways behind and had to really run to catch up with the wagon. Johnnie was really afraid that his brothers were getting lost.

At age 80 Johnnie (as he was known) Buried a one hundred foot long landfill or trash dump by hand shovel plus a large rock that many of the neighbors would kid him about how an old man could do this. If you want to see what he buried it's still down there. Dig three feet deep at N41°34.9269' by W85°36.4006' East and West on the north side of County road 400S 300 to 400 feet east of 950 W. LaGrange Co., IN.

John J. Christner (born Nov 25,1855) Unearthed a stone near Christner Cemetery, Honeyville, IN N 41°34.500 - W 85°35.900. He liked the shape and weight for a horse hitching post. In the winter of 1878 he fashioned a pin and ring on the family forge, then set about drilling a hole in the top of the stone. He drilled a hole with two sticks, a small rope, and some powdered abrasive. One stick was shaped like a bow. With the rope making one turn around the other stick, the bow is held horizontal and the other stick vertical. Pulling and pushing with one hand while holding a wooden cupping block on the top of the vertical stick. Abrasive is kept at the bottom of the vertical stick. This wears a hole in the stone. This stone is so hard; John soon discovered this would be a lengthy endeavor. He persevered until he had the job completed. Very few people are able to finish a job that develops into much more then they had envisioned. I (Steven Carl Christner) have moved this stone to several places, each time I am amazed by it's weight and hardness. This stone has been touched by most of our relatives because they tied there horse up to it. I have moved it one last time to Christner Cemetery Honeyville, IN N 41°34.500-W 85°35.900 on Sep 13 of 2003.

Birth: Nov 25, 1855
Death: Oct 8, 1946

Parents: John J Christner (1827 - 1893)

Spouse: Mary Christner (1860 - 1947)

Children:
Magdalena Christner (1884 - 1885)
Andrew Christner (1893 - 1896)

Burial: Christner Cemetery, Honeyville, Lagrange Co., IN

More About John J. Christner:
Burial: Oct 1946, Christner Cemetery, Honeyville, Lagrange Co., IN
Cause of Death: Intestinal Hemorrage
Residence: 1880, Eden, Lagrange Co., IN[2257]

Notes for Mary D. Miller:
Amish and Amish Mennonite Genealogies; CH21214, p. 60

Mary is the daughter of David S. Miller and Katie Gingerich.

The Descendants of John J. Christner, privately published February 1961, p. 26.

Birth: Feb. 28, 1860
Death: Mar. 2, 1947

Spouse: John J. Christner (1855 - 1946)

Children:
Magdalena Christner (1884 - 1885)
Andrew Christner (1893 - 1896)

Inscription: Wife of J.J. Christner

Burial: Christner Cemetery, Honeyville, Lagrange Co., IN

More About Mary D. Miller:
Burial: Christner Cemetery, Honeyville, Lagrange Co., IN
Cause of Death: Stroke
Residence: 1930, Eden, Lagrange Co., IN[2257]

Children of John Christner and Mary Miller are:
+   1290   i.   Katherine[8] Christner, born 17 Mar 1879 in Millersburg, Elkhart Co., IN; died 01 Oct 1962 in Row 2 plot
                     7.
      1291   ii. Magdalena "Mattie" Christner, born 18 Jan 1884 in Topeka, Lagrange Co., IN[2258]; died 28 Aug 1885 in
                     Topeka, Lagrange Co., IN[2258].

                     Notes for Magdalena "Mattie" Christner:
                     The Descendants of John J. Christner, privately published February 1961, p. 26.

                     Birth: Jan. 18, 1884
                     Death: Aug. 28, 1885
                     Lagrange Co., IN

                     Parents:
                     John J. Christner (1855 - 1946)
                     Mary Christner (1860 - 1947)

                     Inscription: Magdalena dau of J.J. & M. Christner Died Aug. 28, 1885 Aged 1 Y. 7 M. 10 D.

                     Burial: Christner Family Cemetery, Honeyville, Lagrange Co., IN

                     More About Magdalena "Mattie" Christner:
                     Burial: N41°34.503byW85°35.599/Old Christner Cemetery, Honeyville, Lagrange Co., IN

      1292   iii. Joseph Christner[2259,2260,2261,2262], born 16 Apr 1886[2263]; died 04 Sep 1888 in Lagrange Co., IN[2264,2265].

                     Notes for Joseph Christner:
                     The Descendants of John J. Christner, privately published February 1961, p. 26.

                     More About Joseph Christner:
                     Burial: OrvilleChristner, Farm/Lagrange Co., IN

+   1293   iv. Lydia M. Christner, born 04 Nov 1888 in Honeyville, Lagrange Co., IN; died 15 Jan 1990 in Honeyville,
                     Lagrange Co., IN.
      1294   v.   Andrew Christner[2266], born 28 Aug 1893[2266]; died 05 Jan 1896 in Honeyville, Elkhart Co., IN.

                     Notes for Andrew Christner:
                     The Descendants of John J. Christner, privately published February 1961, p. 26.

                     OBITUARY - Herald of Truth, Vol. XXXIII, No. 4, February 15, 1896, Page 61, 62, 63
                     CHRISTNER - On the 6th of January, 1896, Andrew, son of John and Maria Christner, aged 2 years, 4

months and 9 days. Funeral services by Eli E. and Manassas J. Borntreger.

Birth: Aug. 28, 1893
Death: Jan. 5, 1896

15 Feb 1896 - CHRISTNER - On the 6th of January, 1896, Andrew, son of John and Maria Christner, aged 2 years, 4 months and 9 days. Funeral services by Eli E. and Manassas J. Borntreger. Herald of Truth, Vol. XXXIII, No. 4 pg 61-63

Parents:
John J. Christner (1855 - 1946)
Mary Christner (1860 - 1947)

Inscription: Son of J.J. & M. Christner

Burial: Christner Cemetery, Honeyville, Lagrange Co., IN

More About Andrew Christner:
Burial: Christner Cemetery, Honeyville, Lagrange Co., IN

+   1295   vi.   Mary M. Christner, born 15 Aug 1901 in Lagrange Co., IN; died 28 Dec 1999 in Honeyville, Lagrange Co., IN.

393. Abraham J.[7] Christner (John J.[6], Joseph C.[5], Christian J.[4], Johannes John Hans[3], Christian[2], Christen[1])[2267] was born 08 Dec 1856 in Millersburg, Holmes Co., OH[2267], and died 13 Dec 1931 in Honeyville, Lagrange Co., IN. He married **Magdalena Miller**[2268,2269,2270] 29 Jan 1882 in Elkhart Co., IN. She was born 08 Jul 1856 in Holmes Co., OH[2271,2272,2273], and died 06 Jun 1926 in Millersburg, Elkhart Co., IN[2274,2275].

Notes for Abraham J. Christner:
Amish and Amish Mennonite Genealogies; CH212145, p. 60

The Descendants of John J. Christner, privately published February 1961, pp. 4, 30.

Abraham was a farmer all his life in Honeyville IN (N41°34.691'by W85°36.500). He was a very enterprising man and bought a farm for his daughter Mattie (Honeyville-N41°34.074'by W85°36.918) & his daughter Elizabeth (he bought in 1919) at Clearspring Twp. The farm went from Elizabeth to her sister Mary Nan (Christner) Glick. This farm was a favored land of the Potawatomi Indians & this is the location of a Clearspring (N41°33.800'byW85°28.500) giving the township the namesake of Clearspring Twp. This farm is located next to Dr. David Rogers Park. Abraham was found dead on the floor of his bedroom.

Birth: Jan. 23, 1857
Death: Feb. 27, 1920

Children: Clara Christner (1879 - 1886)

Spouse: Joseph J. Christner (1851 - 1925)

Burial: Christner Cemetery, Honeyville, Lagrange Co., IN

More About Abraham J. Christner:
Burial: Christner Cemetery, Honeyville, Lagrange Co., IN
Residence: 1880, Eden, Lagrange Co., IN[2276]

Notes for Magdalena Miller:
The Descendants of John J. Christner, privately published February 1961, p. 30.

Parents of Magdalena are Levi Miller and Fannie Chupp. Her Aunt Katie Chupp lived with Abraham & Magdalena. Katie was deaf because of a childhood illness but Magdalena taught her how to talk and write

English. She earned a living by weaving rugs on a large wooden loom. Abraham built a loom room at the east end of of the wood shed, near the wash house. Most of this info from Maggie Glick. She died from Asthma.

Birth: Jul. 8, 1865
Death: Jun. 6, 1926

Spouse: Abraham J Christner (1856 - 1931)

Children: Amelia Christner (1900 - 1901)

Inscription: Wife of A. J. Christner

Burial: Christner Cemetery, Honeyville, Lagrange Co., IN

More About Magdalena Miller:
Burial: Christner Cemetery, Honeyville, Lagrange Co., IN
Cause of Death: Asthma

Children of Abraham Christner and Magdalena Miller are:

1296   i.   Fannie A.[8] Christner[2277], born 25 Dec 1882 in Honeyville, Lagrange Co., IN[2277,2278,2279]; died 26 Oct 1918 in Newton Co., IN[2280,2281,2282].

           Notes for Fannie A. Christner:
           The Descendants of John J. Christner, privately published February 1961, p. 30.

           She died from the Influenza Epidemic after WWI. At the time of her death she was taking care of others with the Influenza. She never married.
           She died from the Influenza Epidemic after WWI .

           Birth: Dec 25, 1882
           Death: Oct 26, 1918

           Inscription: Dau of A & M Christner

           Burial: Christner Cemetery, Honeyville, Lagrange Co., IN

           More About Fannie A. Christner:
           Burial: row 5 plot 14/Christner Cemetery, Honeyville, Lagrange Co., IN
           Causes of Death: Influenza

1297   ii.   Katie Ann Christner[2283,2284], born 22 Jan 1885 in Honeyville, Lagrange Co., IN[2285,2286,2287]; died 06 May 1897 in Kokomo, Howard Co., IN[2288].

           Notes for Katie Ann Christner:
           The Descendants of John J. Christner, privately published February 1961, p., 30.
           Katie had T.B. She was named after her mothers Aunt Katie Chupp.

           More About Katie Ann Christner:
           Burial: Kokomo, Howard Co., IN
           Causes of Death: Tuberlocus

1298   iii.   Levi Christner[2288,2289], born 16 Mar 1886[2290]; died 17 Dec 1886 in Honeyville, Lagrange Co., IN[2290,2291,2292].

           Notes for Levi Christner:
           The Descendants of John J. Christner, privately published February 1961, p. 30.
           Levi is buried on the Orville Christner farm in Honeyville, IN. The grave yard is about 3/8 mile south of the Honeyville school and 100 yards east of the road.

           More About Levi Christner:

Burial: Orville Christner Farm, Honeyville, Lagrange Co., IN

+ 1299   iv.   Nathan Christner, born 26 Nov 1887 in Millersburg, Elkhart Co., IN; died 05 Nov 1964 in Aurora, NE.
+ 1300   v.   Daniel A. Christner, born 04 Aug 1889 in Lagrange Co., IN; died 29 Sep 1976 in Shipshewana, Lagrange Co., IN.
+ 1301   vi.   Mattie A. Christner, born 19 Sep 1891 in Honeyville, Lagrange Co., IN; died 20 Oct 1975 in Goshen, Elkhart Co., IN.
+ 1302   vii.   John A. Christner, born 16 Jan 1895 in Millersburg, Elkhart Co., IN; died 02 Apr 1965 in IN.
+ 1303   viii.   Elizabeth A. Christner, born 18 Sep 1897 in Lagrange Co., IN; died 30 Dec 1992 in Goshen. Elkhart Co., IN.
   1304   ix.   Amelia Christner[2293], born 07 Jan 1900[2293]; died 23 Jan 1900[2293].

Notes for Amelia Christner:
The Descendants of John J. Christner, privately published February 1961, p. 30.

Birth: Jan. 7, 1900
Death: Jan. 23, 1901

Abraham Christner married Magdalena Miller; Their children Amelia, Feb 7, 1900, died Jan 21, 1901 Bontrager, David R. etal.

The Descendants of John J. Christner, privately published February 1961, family 211 page 30.

Parents:
Abraham J Christner (1856 - 1931)
Mattie Christner (1865 - 1926)

Inscription: Amelia, Dau of A.J. & M. Christner, Died Jan. 23, 1900 Aged (remainder below grade)

Note: There is a conflict in the birth/death dates; neither is recorded in the Lagrange Co. vital records.

Burial: Christner Cemetery, Honeyville, Lagrange Co., IN

+ 1305   x.   Mary Nan Christner, born 28 Sep 1903 in Millersburg, Elkhart Co., IN; died 20 Jan 1975 in Goshen, Elkhart Co., IN.
+ 1306   xi.   Soloma Christner, born 31 May 1905 in Millersburg, Elkhart Co., IN; died 18 Feb 1998 in Orrville, Wayne Co., OH.

396. Mary[7] Christner (John J.[6], Joseph C.[5], Christian J.[4], Johannes John Hans[3], Christian[2], Christen[1])[2294,2295] was born 26 Aug 1860 in Shipshewana, Lagrange Co., IN, and died 03 Sep 1922 in Shipshewana, Lagrange Co., IN[2295]. She married **Tobias D. Kemp** 27 May 1880 in IN[2295]. He was born 21 Mar 1861, and died 18 Feb 1933 in Elkhart Co., IN.

Notes for Mary Christner:
The Descendants of John J. Christner, privately published February 1961, pp. 4, 35.

Amish and Amish Mennonite Genealogies; CH21219, p. 60

Birth: Aug. 26, 1860
Death: 1922

Spouse: Tobias Kemp (1861 - 1933)

Burial: Yoder Cemetery, Shipshewana, Lagrange Co., IN

More About Mary Christner:
Cause of Death: Cancer

Notes for Tobias D. Kemp:

The Descendants of John J. Christner, privately published February 1961, p. 35.

Tobias is the son of Daniel and Elizabeth Yoder Kemp.

There is a very good spring 1/2 mile Northeast of their home at N41°37.992 x W85° 35.958. Their home/farm was at N41° 37.700 x W85° 36.417 in a long lane. He was a Amish farmer.

Birth: Mar. 21, 1861
Death: Feb. 18, 1933

Spouse: Mary Kemp (1860 - 1922)

Burial: Yoder Cemetery, Shipshewana, Lagrange Co., IN

More About Tobias D. Kemp:
Cause of Death: Pnemonia

Children of Mary Christner and Tobias Kemp are:
     1307   i.   Not Named[8] Kemp, born 14 May 1891; died 14 May 1891.

                       Notes for Not Named Kemp:
                       The Descendants of John J. Christner, privately published February 1961, p. 35.

+   1308   ii. Bertha Kemp, born 10 Jul 1894 in Shipshewana, Lagrange Co., IN; died 07 Dec 1936.

398. Anna[7] Christner (John J.[6], Joseph C.[5], Christian J.[4], Johannes John Hans[3], Christian[2], Christen[1])[2296] was born 20 May 1863 in Holmes Co., OH[2296], and died 27 Mar 1949 in Topeka, Lagrange Co., IN[2296]. She married **Issac C. Schrock** 18 Jan 1883. He was born 04 Mar 1862 in Elkhart Co., IN, and died 02 Mar 1932 in Lagrange Co., IN.

Notes for Anna Christner:
Amish and Amish Mennonite Genealogies; CH2121a, p. 60

The Descendants of John J. Christner, privately published February 1961, pp. 4, 37.

Annie moved to Indiana with her parents age 3 weeks old. At the time of her death she had 187 Great Grand Children.

Birth: May 20, 1863
Death: Mar. 27, 1949

Parents:
John J. Christner (1827 - 1893)
Susanna Christner (1829 - 1909)

Spouse: Isaac C. Schrock (1862 - 1932)

Inscription: Annie Schrock wife of Isaac C. Schrock B. May 20, 1863 D. Mar. 27, 1949 A. 85Y 10MO. 7D.

Burial: Christner Cemetery, Honeyville, Lagrange Co., IN
row 6 plot 15

More About Anna Christner:
Burial: Christner Cemetery, Honeyville, Lagrange Co., IN
Residence: 1880, Eden, Lagrange Co., IN[2296]

Notes for Issac C. Schrock:
The Descendants of John J. Christner, privately published February 1961, p. 36.

Issac is the son of Cornelius and Magdelena Bontrager Schrock Issac is a brother to Harry.

11074HOCHSTEDLER/STUTZMAN Issac died from a heart attack during work.

Grandpa Schrock was a horse man and raised registered Percheron horses. Dad had two of these mares as his first team of horses, Babe and Ruth. They had fancy registered names also. There were big pictures of beautiful horses on the inside of the doors of the gray shop. The little barn to the south of the big barn was where he kept his stallions. That barn was well built and unique. A west part and an east part with hay mangers built across the outside corners so you could push the hay down from the mow without going in to the horses. In the middle, between these two parts, was a hallway with a ladder going up to the mow and an oats bin. There were mangers built on either side of this hall on the horse side so they could be fed from this hallway. As far back as I can remember, this barn was no longer used for horses, but for sheep, sows with baby pigs. Grandma Schrock also used it for her setting hens. She would take potato crates and fill them with straw for a nest and set her hens on the eggs in a nest. She kept water there and ears of corn for the hens. Once when some chicks had hatched she gathered them in her apron and was just coming out of the gate of the yard when a load of company came to visit her and met her there with her apron full of chicks. She would bring these chicks in and had small cages where she kept these chicks in her chicken yard till they were grown.

Grandmother's chicken house, out house, the wood-house and wash-house were also built that summer of 1928; I think. Also the pump house and metal milk house. I was then born December 6, 1928 and have no memories of 1929, 1930 and 1931,1932.

The morning of March 2, 1932, Grandpa Schrock walked out the east lane and north to the home of Will Beechy's. There was an old building there made of logs, which had a door which didn't close right and he wanted to saw off along the bottom of this door so they could close it. I think he lay on the ground to saw this off and the exertion caused him to have a heart attach and died there while sawing off the bottom of that door.

Grandpa Isaac Schrock died on March 2 and was buried on March 4, on his 70th birthday. Grandpa became a widow at the age of 68. I have a memory of Grandpa's body lying on the lounge in the daudy house in the evening. The double bedroom doors were also both open. Menno Eash stood at the head of the lounge holding an oil lamp and there were people around. I suppose this was the first evening. All I remember of the funeral was that Mother took me upstairs in the daudy house to rock me. She gave me one of the pasteboard kitties which were on Grandma's bureau and were to advertise spools of thread. I suppose I was tired of trying to hold still these several days and she wanted to rock me to sleep. I suppose I was naughty.

Another memory I have of Grandpa Schrock was when he was in the Elkhart Hospital to have hernia surgery. We went to visit him one evening at the hospital. On a shelf beside his bed he had a white paper bag containing chocolate drops and he gave us some of that candy. Also, when he came home from the hospital, he walked in the yard using a cane to walk.

He would sometimes come over in our house to stay with Anna and me while Mother went milking. He would hold both of us on his lap and rock us and sing. One song I remember was, "Old King Cole was a merry old sole and a merry old soul was he. He called for his pipe and he called for his bowl and he called for his fiddlers three." Also, "Four and twenty blackbirds baked in a pie, When the pie was opened the birds began to sing, 'Wasn't that a dandy dish to set before the King."

Issac C. Schrock had a white beard and rather stocky build.

Birth: Mar. 4, 1862
Death: Mar. 2, 1932

Spouse: Annie Schrock (1863 - 1949)

Burial: Christner Cemetery, Honeyville, Lagrange Co., IN

row 6 plot 14

More About Issac C. Schrock:
Burial: 04 Mar 1932, Christner Cemetery, Honeyville, Lagrange Co., IN
Cause of Death: Heart Attack
Religion: Old Order Amish/

Children of Anna Christner and Issac Schrock are:
+ 1309   i.   Eli I.[8] Schrock, born 11 Sep 1885 in Topeka, Lagrange Co., IN.
+ 1310   ii.   Amos I. Schrock, born 13 Feb 1887 in Topeka, Eden Twp., Lagrange Co., IN; died 02 Nov 1944 in of accute Nephritis.
+ 1311   iii.   Cornelius I. Schrock, born 01 Dec 1888 in Topeka, Lagrange Co., IN; died Jul 1969 in Phoenix, Maricopa Co., AZ.
+ 1312   iv.   Susanna I. Schrock, born 13 Dec 1888 in Topeka, Lagrange Co., IN; died 26 Nov 1983 in Wolcottville, Lagrange Co., IN.
+ 1313   v.   Levi I. Schrock, born 22 Oct 1891 in Topeka, Lagrange Co., IN; died 21 Aug 1971 in Row 6 plot 16.
+ 1314   vi.   Mary I. Schrock, born 28 Mar 1894 in Topeka, Lagrange Co., IN; died 29 Mar 1946 in Lagrange, Lagrange Co., IN.
+ 1315   vii.   John I. Schrock, born 26 May 1896 in Topeka, Lagrange Co., IN; died 31 Aug 1952 in Lagrange Co. IN of Cancer.
+ 1316   viii.   Andrew I. Schrock, born 07 May 1898 in Lagrange Co., IN.
+ 1317   ix.   Lydia I. Schrock, born 01 Nov 1900 in Topeka, Lagrange Co., IN.
+ 1318   x.   Amanda I. Schrock, born 18 Nov 1902 in Topeka, Lagrange Co., IN; died 15 Feb 1929 in Scarlet Fever.
+ 1319   xi.   Ammon I. Schrock, born 20 Dec 1904 in Topeka, Lagrange Co., IN; died 20 Apr 1994 in Manatee Co., FL.
+ 1320   xii.   Fanny I. Schrock, born 03 Sep 1907 in Topeka, Lagrange Co., IN; died 09 Aug 1953.

399. Emma J.[7] Christner (John J.[6], Joseph C.[5], Christian J.[4], Johannes John Hans[3], Christian[2], Christen[1])[2296,2297] was born 22 Sep 1865 in Topeka, Lagrange Co., IN[2298], and died 15 Mar 1901 in Topeka, Lagrange Co., IN[2299,2300,2301]. She married **John E. Christner**[2302,2303] 1883 in by David Kauffman Lagrange Co, IN, son of John Christner and Rachel Miller. He was born 01 May 1861 in Henry Co., IN[2304,2305], and died 22 Feb 1939 in Newbury, Lagrange Co., IN[2306,2307,2308,2309].

Notes for Emma J. Christner:
Amish and Amish Mennonite Families; CH2121b, CHB1; p. 60

The Descendants of John J. Christner, privately published 1961, pp. 4, 46.

Birth: Sep. 24, 1865
Death: Mar. 15, 1901

Inscription: Wife of John E. Christner, aged 35 Y 5 M 21 D

Burial: Christner Cemetery, Honeyville, Lagrange Co., IN
Row 5 plot 18

More About Emma J. Christner:
Burial: Christner Cemetery, Honeyville, Lagrange Co., IN
DBH Book: 11086/[2310,2311]
Religion: Old Order Amish/
Residence: 1900, Eden, Lagrange Co., IN[2312]

Notes for John E. Christner:
Amish and Amish Mennonite Families; CHB13; p. 60

The Descendants of John J. Christner, privately published February 1961, p. 46.

He was Old Order Amish.

John E. is the son of John B.(Hans) Christner and Rachel Miller. John B. was born in Alsace-Lorraine France June 9, 1829. Rachel was born in Somerset Co., PA on Nov 21, 1837. John B and Rachel were married in 1855.

Birth: May 1, 1861
Death: Feb. 22, 1939

Burial: Forks Yoder Cemetery, Lagrange Co., IN

More About John E. Christner:
Amish and Amish Mennonite: CHB13/[2313]
Burial: Yoder Cemetery, Forks, Lagrange Co., IN
Occupation: Farmer/
Religion: Old Order Amish/
Residence: 1930, Newbury, Lagrange Co., IN[2314]

Children of Emma Christner and John Christner are:

+	1321	i.	Elmer J.[8] Christner, born 12 Oct 1886 in Topeka, Lagrange Co., IN; died 26 Nov 1917 in Goshen, Elkhart Co., IN.
+	1322	ii.	Samuel J. Christner, born 27 Mar 1888 in Topeka, Lagrange Co., IN; died 14 Dec 1980 in Scott, Kosciusko Co., IN.
+	1323	iii.	Susie J. Christner, born 04 Mar 1890 in Topeka, Lagrange Co., IN; died 11 Aug 1981.
+	1324	iv.	Mary J. Christner, born 05 Dec 1892 in Topeka, Lagrange Co., IN; died 14 Jan 1979 in Shipshewana, Lagrange Co., IN.
+	1325	v.	Amanda J. Christner, born 01 Jun 1895 in Topeka, Lagrange Co., IN; died 18 Oct 1981 in Shipshewana, Lagrange Co., IN.
+	1326	vi.	Levi J. Christner, born 10 Jun 1897 in Topeka, Lagrange Co., IN; died 06 Aug 1984 in Lagrange, Lagrange Co., IN.
+	1327	vii.	Amos J. Christner, born 06 Apr 1899 in Wolcottville, Lagrange Co., IN; died 06 Oct 1963.

400. Mary D.[7] Frey (Elizabeth J.[6] Christner, Joseph C.[5], Christian J.[4], Johannes John Hans[3], Christian[2], Christen[1])[2315] was born 20 Feb 1852 in Holmes Co., OH, and died 18 Sep 1935[2315,2316,2317,2318]. She married **Jonathan Schlabach**[2319,2320] 17 Sep 1871[2321]. He was born 03 May 1850 in Becks Mills, Holmes Co., OH[2322,2323,2324], and died 26 Oct 1922 in Emma, Lagrange Co., IN.

Notes for Mary D. Frey:
The Descendants of John J. Christner, privately published February 1961, p 52.

More About Mary D. Frey:
Residence: 1930, Age: 78; Marital Status: Widowed; Relation to Head of House: Mother/Elkhart, Elkhart Co., IN[2324]

Notes for Jonathan Schlabach:
The Descendants of John J. Christner, privately published February 1961, p. 52.

Birth: 1850
Death: 1922

Burial: Miller Cemetery, Shipshewana, Lagrange Co., IN
Find A Grave Memorial# 82703171

More About Jonathan Schlabach:
Residence: 1900, Age: 50; Marital Status: Married; Relation to Head of House: Head/Clearspring, Lagrange Co., IN[2324]

Children of Mary Frey and Jonathan Schlabach are:

+ 1328   i.   Elizabeth Lizzie[8] Schlabach, born 20 Oct 1872 in Topeka, Lagrange Co., IN; died 07 May 1927.
+ 1329   ii.   Joseph J. Schlabach, born 23 Dec 1874 in Lagrange Co., IN; died 30 May 1951 in Anderson, Indiana.
+ 1330   iii.   Jacob J. Schlabach, born 13 Mar 1877 in Topeka, Lagrange Co., IN.
+ 1331   iv.   Daniel J. Schlabach, born 17 Apr 1879 in IN.
+ 1332   v.   Barbara J. Schlabach, born 31 Dec 1881 in Emma, Lagrange Co., IN; died Mar 1975 in Elkhart, Elkhart Co., IN.
+ 1333   vi.   Anna J. Schlabach, born 19 Apr 1884 in Lagrange Co., IN.
+ 1334   vii.   Ezra J. Schlabach, born 20 Mar 1887 in Topeka, Lagrange Co., IN; died Oct 1975 in Topeka, Lagrange Co., IN.
+ 1335   viii.   Eleanora Schlabach, born 04 Mar 1892.

401. Barbara D.[7] Frey (Elizabeth J.[6] Christner, Joseph C.[5], Christian J.[4], Johannes John Hans[3], Christian[2], Christen[1])[2325,2326,2326] was born 13 Dec 1854 in Holmes Co., OH[2326,2326], and died 22 Dec 1929[2327,2328,2328,2329]. She married **Benedict Miller** 17 Dec 1874[2330,2331,2331]. He was born 11 Aug 1853 in Holmes Co., OH[2332,2333,2333], and died 05 Mar 1926 in Lagrange Co., IN[2334,2335,2335].

Notes for Barbara D. Frey:
The Descendants of John J. Christner, February 1961, pp. 52, 60.

More About Barbara D. Frey:
Residence: 1920, Clearspring, Lagrange Co., IN[2335]

Notes for Benedict Miller:
The Descendants of John J. Christner, privately published February 1961, p. 60.

More About Benedict Miller:
Religion: Old Order Amish/
Residence: 1920, Clearspring, Lagrange Co., IN[2335]

Children of Barbara Frey and Benedict Miller are:

   1336   i.   Mary[8] Miller[2335,2335], born 02 Oct 1876[2335,2335]; died 20 Feb 1877[2335,2335].

         Notes for Mary Miller:
         The Descendants of John J. Christner, privately published February 1961, p. 60.

+ 1337   ii.   Daniel B. Miller, born 24 Apr 1878 in Lagrange, Lagrange Co., IN; died 14 Mar 1944.
+ 1338   iii.   Joseph B. Miller, born 01 Aug 1880 in Lagrange Co., IN; died 23 Mar 1936 in Lagrange Co., IN.
+ 1339   iv.   Elizabeth B. Miller, born 31 Jan 1885 in Lagrange Co., IN.
+ 1340   v.   Noah B. Miller, born 25 Feb 1891 in South Bend, St Joseph, IN.

402. John D.[7] Frey (Elizabeth J.[6] Christner, Joseph C.[5], Christian J.[4], Johannes John Hans[3], Christian[2], Christen[1])[2336,2337] was born 16 Jul 1857 in Holmes Co., OH[2338,2339,2340], and died 27 Jan 1934 in Lagrange Co., IN[2340]. He married **(1) Lizzie J. Troyer**. She was born 19 Oct 1859, and died 01 Dec 1907 in White Cloud, Newaygo Co., MI[2340]. He married **(2) Mary D. Yoder**. She was born 02 Mar 1882.

Notes for John D. Frey:
The Descendants of John J. Christner, privately published February 1961, pp. 52, 82.

John is a twin to Joseph.

More About John D. Frey:
Religion: Old Order Amish/
Residence: 1880, Clear Spring, Lagrange Co., IN[2341]

Notes for Lizzie J. Troyer:
The Descendants of John J. Christner, privately published February 1961, p. 82.

Children of John Frey and Lizzie Troyer are:

	1341	i.	Lizzie[8] Frey, born 19 Nov 1881; died 19 Nov 1881.

Notes for Lizzie Frey:
The Descendants of John J. Christner, privately published February 1961, p. 82.

+	1342	ii.	Simon J. Frey, born 18 Dec 1882 in Holmes Co., OH; died 1956 in Goshen, Elkhart Co., IN.
	1343	iii.	Joseph J. Frey, born 24 Feb 1884. He married Fannie Kaser 27 Jan 1910; born 30 Aug 1889.

Notes for Joseph J. Frey:
The Descendants of John J. Christner, privately published February 1961, pp. 82, 83.

Notes for Fannie Kaser:
The Descendants of John J. Christner, privately published February 1961, p. 83.

	1344	iv.	William Frey, born 12 Sep 1885; died 12 Sep 1885.

Notes for William Frey:
The Descendants of John J. Christner, privately published February 1961, p. 82.

+	1345	v.	Elmer J. Frey, born 26 Oct 1888.
+	1346	vi.	Sarah J. Frey, born 22 Oct 1891.
	1347	vii.	Cornelius Frey, born 03 Jul 1893; died 03 Jul 1893.

Notes for Cornelius Frey:
The Descendants of John J. Christner, privately published February 1961, p. 82.

	1348	viii.	Robert Frey, born 03 Jul 1893; died 03 Jul 1893.

Notes for Robert Frey:
The Descendants of John J. Christner, privately published February 1961, p. 82.

	1349	ix.	Hosanna Frey, born 24 Jun 1896; died 24 Jun 1896.

Notes for Hosanna Frey:
The Descendants of John J. Christner, privately published February 1961, p. 82.

+	1350	x.	Andrew J. Frey, born 10 Jun 1897 in Muskegon, MI.
	1351	xi.	John Frey, born 18 Oct 1904; died 20 Oct 1904.

Notes for John Frey:
The Descendants of John J. Christner, privately published February 1961, p. 82.

Children of John Frey and Mary Yoder are:

+	1352	i.	Daniel J.[8] Frey, born 19 Aug 1915.
+	1353	ii.	Willard J. Frey, born 03 Feb 1918.
+	1354	iii.	Samuel J. Frey, born 13 Jan 1920 in Lagrange Co., IN; died 27 Oct 1999 in Auburn, Dekalb Co., IN.

403. Joseph D.[7] Frey (Elizabeth J.[6] Christner, Joseph C.[5], Christian J.[4], Johannes John Hans[3], Christian[2], Christen[1])[2342,2343] was born 16 Jul 1857 in Holmes Co., OH[2343], and died 27 Mar 1945 in Haven, Reno Co., KS. He married **Barbara Hochstetler**[2343] 24 Jan 1878[2344]. She was born 09 Jan 1856 in Elkhart Co., IN[2345], and died 02 Nov 1914 in Reno Co., KS[2345].

Notes for Joseph D. Frey:

The Descendants of John J. Christner, privately published February 1961, pp. 52, 65, 72.

Joseph is a twin to John.

Amish and Amish Mennonite Genealogies; HS19bc, FR233

More About Joseph D. Frey:
Alt. Birth: 16 Jul 1857[2345]
Religion: Old Order Amish/

Notes for Barbara Hochstetler:
The Descendants of John J. Christner, privately published February 1961, pp. 65, 72.

More About Barbara Hochstetler:
Alt. Birth: 09 Jan 1856[2345]

Children of Joseph Frey and Barbara Hochstetler are:
+   1355   i.   Elizabeth J.[8] Fry, born 24 Jan 1879 in Emma, Lagrange Co., IN; died 23 Aug 1933 in Yoder, KS.
+   1356   ii.   Mary J. Fry, born 24 Aug 1880 in Kalona, Washington Co., IA; died 13 Oct 1964.
+   1357   iii.   John J. Fry, born 02 Jul 1882 in Lagrange Co., IN; died 13 Dec 1966 in Shipshewana, Lagrange Co., IN.
+   1358   iv.   Daniel J. Fry, born 24 Jan 1884 in Lagrange Co., IN; died 24 Nov 1911 in Haven, Reno Co., KS.
+   1359   v.   Amos J. Fry, born 20 Nov 1885 in Lagrange Co., IN; died 29 Nov 1967 in Reno Co., KS.
+   1360   vi.   Fannie J. Fry, born 21 Mar 1887 in Lagrange Co., IN; died 07 Sep 1934.
    1361   vii.   David J. Fry, born 01 Mar 1888; died 25 Aug 1888.

> Notes for David J. Fry:
> The Descendants of John J. Christner, privately published February 1961, p. 66.

+   1362   viii.   Enos J. Fry, born 14 Apr 1890 in Lagrange Co., IN; died 29 May 1966 in Lagrange Co., IN.
+   1363   ix.   Manileus J. Fry, born 13 Nov 1891; died 10 Jan 1919.
+   1364   x.   Barbara Ann Fry, born 03 May 1893 in Haven, Reno Co., KS; died 06 Sep 1975 in ID.
+   1365   xi.   Noah J. Fry, born 03 Nov 1894 in Haven, Reno Co., KS; died 22 Aug 1977 in Lagrange Co., IN.
+   1366   xii.   Mattie Fry, born 11 Mar 1896 in Hutchinson, Reno Co., KS.

404. Samuel D.[7] Frey (Elizabeth J.[6] Christner, Joseph C.[5], Christian J.[4], Johannes John Hans[3], Christian[2], Christen[1])[2346] was born 19 May 1860 in Holmes Co., OH[2346], and died 11 Feb 1938[2347]. He married **Lovina Hershberger** 20 Jan 1897. She was born 15 May 1866.

Notes for Samuel D. Frey:
The Descendants of John J. Christner, privately published February 1961, pp. 52, 84.

Dave Pottinger moved Sam's house from the east edge of Emma Indiana to the southwest of (300 feet) the Honeyville Store about 1980. Levi Christner's wife Goldie used her inheritance to buy a china cupboard, china cabinet, & sink all hand made by Sam.

More About Samuel D. Frey:
Occupation: Carpenter/
Religion: Old Order Amish/
Residence: 1880, Clear Spring, Lagrange Co., IN[2348]

Notes for Lovina Hershberger:
The Descendants of John J. Christner, privately published February 1961, p. 84.

Children of Samuel Frey and Lovina Hershberger are:
    1367   i.   Harvey[8] Fry.

> Notes for Harvey Fry:

The Descendants of John J. Christner, privately published February 1961, p. 84.

+ 1368   ii.   Noah S. Frye, born 23 Jul 1891 in Wolcottville, Lagrange Co., IN.
   1369   iii.   Jonas Fry, born 16 Mar 1894; died 03 Mar 1904.

           Notes for Jonas Fry:
           The Descendants of John J. Christner, privately published February 1961, p. 84.

+ 1370   iv.   Henry S. Frye, born 26 Jul 1896 in Topeka, Lagrange Co., IN; died 05 Oct 1947 in Lagrange Co., IN.
+ 1371   v.   Cassie S. Fry, born 02 Aug 1899 in Topeka, Lagrange Co., IN.
   1372   vi.   Joseph Fry, born 28 Jun 1902; died 02 Aug 1905.

           Notes for Joseph Fry:
           The Descendants of John J. Christner, privately published February 1961, p. 84.

405. Noah D.[7] **Frey** (Elizabeth J.[6] Christner, Joseph C.[5], Christian J.[4], Johannes John Hans[3], Christian[2], Christen[1])[2348] was born 11 Apr 1863 in Farmerstown, Holmes Co., OH[2348], and died 20 Feb 1928 in Lagrange Co., IN. He married **(1) Mary Ann Hostetler** 18 Sep 1884 in By John Yoder. She was born 18 Feb 1864.

Notes for Noah D. Frey:
The Descendants of John J. Christner, privately published February 1961, pp. 52.

Fred Mishler was raised by Noah Fred Married Mary I. Schrock.

More About Noah D. Frey:
Residence: 1880, Clear Spring, Lagrange Co., IN[2348]

Child of Noah Frey and Mary Hostetler is:
   1373   i.   Fred[8] Fry.

406. Daniel D.[7] **Frey Jr.** (Elizabeth J.[6] Christner, Joseph C.[5], Christian J.[4], Johannes John Hans[3], Christian[2], Christen[1])[2348] was born 31 Mar 1866 in Holmes Co., OH[2348], and died 25 Feb 1947[2349]. He married **Mary Ellen Miller** 25 Dec 1887 in By Abraham A Troyer. She was born 09 May 1866 in Holmes Co. OH, and died 23 Dec 1950.

Notes for Daniel D. Frey Jr.:
The Descendants of John J. Christner, privately published February 1961, pp. 52, 87.

More About Daniel D. Frey Jr.:
Record Change: 26 Jan 2003
Religion: Old Order Amish/
Residence: 1880, Clear Spring, Lagrange Co., IN[2350]

Notes for Mary Ellen Miller:
The Descendants of John J. Christner, privately published February 1961, p. 87.

Children of Daniel Frey and Mary Miller are:
   1374   i.   William D.[8] Frey, born 30 Sep 1888; died 24 Jun 1900.

           Notes for William D. Frey:
           The Descendants of John J. Christner, privately published February 1961, p. 87.

   1375   ii.   Jacob D. Frey, born 21 Jan 1890; died 24 Aug 1890.

           Notes for Jacob D. Frey:
           The Descendants of John J. Christner, privately published February 1961, p. 87.

+	1376	iii.	Elizabeth D. Frey, born 22 Jan 1891 in Lagrange Co., IN.
+	1377	iv.	Catherine D. Frey, born 08 Jul 1892 in Monroe, IN.
	1378	v.	Mary Frey, born 30 Dec 1893; died 10 Jun 1905.

Notes for Mary Frey:
The Descendants of John J. Christner, privately published February 1961, p. 87.

+	1379	vi.	Daniel D. M. Frey, born 13 Sep 1895 in Emma, Lagrange Co., IN; died 21 Oct 1972.
+	1380	vii.	Anna D. Frey, born 12 Apr 1899 in Topeka, Lagrange Co., IN; died 05 Oct 1982 in Lagrange Co., IN.
+	1381	viii.	Barbara D. Frey, born 30 Mar 1902.
+	1382	ix.	John D. Frey, born 24 Jun 1903.
+	1383	x.	Joseph D. M. Frey, born 04 May 1905.
	1384	xi.	Infant Frey, born 12 Mar 1910.

407. Elizabeth D.[7] Frey (Elizabeth J.[6] Christner, Joseph C.[5], Christian J.[4], Johannes John Hans[3], Christian[2], Christen[1])[2351,2352,2353] was born 11 May 1869 in Lagrange Co., IN[2354,2355], and died 04 Nov 1958 in Goshen, Elkhart Co., IN[2355]. She married **Rudolph D. Borntrager** 30 Jan 1890 in Lagrange Co., IN[2356]. He was born 21 Feb 1871 in Eden, Lagrange Co., IN[2357,2357], and died 04 Nov 1958.

Notes for Elizabeth D. Frey:
The Descendants of John J. Christner, privately published February 1961, pp. 52, 93.

Birth: May 11, 1869
Death: Mar. 24, 1949

Burial: Miller Amish Cemetery, Lagrange, Lagrange Co., IN

More About Elizabeth D. Frey:
Identifier Number: 22979
Religion: Old Order Amish/
Residence: 1880, Clear Spring, Lagrange Co., IN[2358]

Notes for Rudolph D. Borntrager:
The Descendants of John J. Christner, privately published February 1961, p. 93.

Birth: Feb. 21, 1871
Death: Nov. 4, 1958

Burial: Miller Amish Cemetery, Lagrange, Lagrange Co., IN

Children of Elizabeth Frey and Rudolph Borntrager are:

+	1385	i.	Daniel R.[8] Borntrager, born 18 Nov 1890 in Ligonier, Noble Co., IN.
+	1386	ii.	Susan R. Borntrager, born 25 Oct 1892 in Haven, Reno Co., KS; died 15 Jan 1919.
+	1387	iii.	Henry R. Borntrager, born 07 Nov 1893 in Goshen, Elkhart Co., IN; died 16 Apr 1957 in Goshen, Elkhart Co., IN.
+	1388	iv.	Samuel R. Borntrager, born 28 Nov 1896 in Curryville, Pike Co., MO.
+	1389	v.	Mary Borntrager, born 28 Sep 1899 in Haven, Reno Co., KS; died 26 Nov 1983.
+	1390	vi.	Harvey R. Borntrager, born 15 Jun 1901 in Haven, Reno Co., KS; died 02 Dec 1991 in Haven, Reno Co., KS.
	1391	vii.	Uriah R. Borntrager, born 27 Mar 1904 in Yoder, Reno Co., KS[2359]; died 21 Oct 1904 in Yoder, Reno Co., KS[2359].

Notes for Uriah R. Borntrager:
The Descendants of John J. Christner, privately published February 1961, p. 93.

| | 1392 | viii. | Infant Son Borntrager, born 12 Apr 1906; died 14 Apr 1906. |

Notes for Infant Son Borntrager:
The Descendants of John J. Christner, privately published February 1961, p. 93.

1393   ix.   Infant Borntrager, born 02 May 1907; died 05 May 1907.

        Notes for Infant Borntrager:
        The Descendants of John J. Christner, privately published February 1961, p. 93.

+   1394   x.   Clemens R. Borntrager, born 23 Nov 1909 in Medford, WI.

408. Martha[7] Miller (Barbara[6] Christner, John J.[5], Christian J.[4], Johannes John Hans[3], Christian[2], Christen[1]) She married **Benjamin D. Miller** 14 Jan 1883.

Notes for Benjamin D. Miller:
He had a farm between Charm and Walnut Creek, OH about 1/2 mile from Christian Christner's farm referred to as the Dan Miller Farm. He is the Grandfather of J. Virgil Miller. This was in German Twp. which now is Clark Twp., Holmes Co., OH.

Child of Martha Miller and Benjamin Miller is:
+   1395   i.   Ura R.[8] Miller.

412. Lydia Ellen[7] Miller (Barbara[6] Christner, John J.[5], Christian J.[4], Johannes John Hans[3], Christian[2], Christen[1])[2360] was born 13 Jun 1865 in Charm, Holmes Co., OH[2360,2361,2362], and died 20 Feb 1934 in Walnut Creek, Holmes Co., OH[2363]. She married **Nathaniel J Hershberger**[2363,2364,2365,2366] 01 Jan 1891 in Walnut Creek, Holmes Co., OH[2367,2368]. He was born 02 Jan 1860 in Walnut Creek, Holmes Co., OH[2369,2370,2371,2372], and died 31 Mar 1923 in Walnut Creek, Holmes Co., OH[2373,2374].

More About Lydia Ellen Miller:
Residence: 1900, Walnut Creek, Holmes Co., OH[2375]

More About Nathaniel J Hershberger:
Residence: 1920, Walnut Creek, Holmes, Ohio[2376,2377]

Children of Lydia Miller and Nathaniel Hershberger are:
1396   i.   Amanda[8] Hershbergen[2377], born Sep 1884 in OH[2377].

        More About Amanda Hershbergen:
        Residence: 1900, Walnut Creek, Holmes Co., OH[2377]

1397   ii.   Lavina Hershbergen[2377], born Apr 1885 in OH[2377].

        More About Lavina Hershbergen:
        Residence: 1900, Walnut Creek, Holmes Co., OH[2377]

1398   iii.   Leonard Hershberger[2378], born 12 Apr 1892 in Walnut Creek, Holmes Co., OH[2378]; died 07 Feb 1983 in Walnut Creek, Holmes Co., OH[2378].

        More About Leonard Hershberger:
        Other-Begin: Holmes Co.[2378]
        Residence: Holmes Co., OH[2378]
        Social Security Number: 283-03-8973/[2378]
        SSN issued: OH[2378]

1399   iv.   Daniel N Hershberger[2378,2379,2380], born 05 Mar 1894 in Walnut Creek, Holmes Co., OH[2381,2382,2383]; died 16 Jul 1970 in Home, Holmes, Ohio[2384].

        More About Daniel N Hershberger:
        Other-Begin: Holmes Co.[2384]
        Residence: 1900, Walnut Creek, Holmes Co., OH[2385,2386]

1400   v.   Lloyd George Hershberger[2386,2387,2388], born 07 Dec 1896 in Walnut Creek, Holmes Co., OH[2389,2390,2391]; died Nov 1972 in Louisville, Stark, Ohio[2392].

More About Lloyd George Hershberger:
Other-Begin: Holmes Co.[2392]
Residence: 1900, Walnut Creek, Holmes Co., OH[2393,2394]
Social Security Number: 274-07-0812/[2394]
SSN issued: OH[2394]

1401   vi.   Verna Hershberger[2394,2395,2396], born 11 Dec 1899 in Walnut Creek, Holmes Co., OH[2397,2398,2399]; died 23 Jun 1969 in Goshen, Elkhart Co., IN[2400].

More About Verna Hershberger:
Residence: 1900, Walnut Creek, Holmes Co., OH[2401]

1402   vii.   Infant Hershberger[2402], born 21 Dec 1902 in Walnut Creek, Holmes Co., OH[2402]; died 28 Jan 1903 in Walnut Creek, Holmes Co., OH[2402].

1403   viii.   Ray Hershberger[2402,2403], born 14 Jun 1905 in Walnut Creek, Holmes Co., OH[2404,2405].

More About Ray Hershberger:
Residence: 1910, Walnut Creek, Holmes Co., OH[2405]

414. Elizabeth "Lizzie"[7] Christner (Joseph J.[6], John J.[5], Christian J.[4], Johannes John Hans[3], Christian[2], Christen[1])[2406] was born 14 Mar 1860 in Holmes Co., OH[2406], and died 20 Jan 1916 in Beaver Crossing, Seward Co., NE[2406]. She married **William J. Stutzman** 20 Oct 1881. He was born 07 Jan 1859 in Walnut Creek, Holmes Co., OH[2407], and died 09 Nov 1929 in Chappell, Deuel Co., NE[2407].

Notes for Elizabeth "Lizzie" Christner:
Stutzman - Elizabeth Stutzman (Christner) was born Mar. 14, 1860 in Holmes Co., OH; died at her home near Beaver Crossing, NE, Jan. 20, 1916; aged 55 y. 10 m. 6 d. She was married to W. J. Stutzman Oct. 20, 1881. To this union were born 9 children, 2 having preceded her to the spirit world in infancy. She leaves to mourn her departure, husband, 4 sons, 3 daughters, 12 grandchildren, mother, 3 sisters, 5 brothers, besides other relatives and friends. She accepted her Savior in her youth, became a member of the Amish Mennonite Church, and remained a faithful member. Her health had been failing for about a year, caused form heart trouble. Death was due to an attack of pneumonia from which she suffered only 8 days. But bore all her suffering patiently.

More About Elizabeth "Lizzie" Christner:
Cause of Death: Pneumonia
Religion: Amish/Mennonite
Residence: 1910, Clinton, Oscoda, Michigan[2408]

More About William J. Stutzman:
DBH Book: 10976/[2409]

Children of Elizabeth Christner and William Stutzman are:
1404   i.   Irwin[8] Stutzman[2409], born 06 Mar 1882 in Sugarcreek, Tuscarawas Co., OH[2409].

More About Irwin Stutzman:
DBH Book: 10977/[2409]

1405   ii.   Harry W Stutzman[2409], born 28 Apr 1883 in Walnut Creek, Holmes Co., OH[2409].

More About Harry W Stutzman:
DBH Book: 10980/[2409]

1406   iii.   Minnie Stutzman[2409], born 05 Dec 1884 in Milford, Seward Co., NE[2409].

More About Minnie Stutzman:
DBH Book: 10982/[2409]

1407   iv.   Katie Stutzman[2409], born 03 Apr 1886 in Milford, Seward Co., NE[2409].

        More About Katie Stutzman:
        DBH Book: 10984/[2409]

1408   v.   Sarah Stutzman[2409], born 30 Nov 1888 in Chappell, Deuel Co., NE[2409].

        More About Sarah Stutzman:
        DBH Book: 6440/[2409]

1409   vi.   Ray Stutzman[2409], born 28 Dec 1893 in Chappell, Deuel Co., NE[2409].

        More About Ray Stutzman:
        DBH Book: 10985/[2409]

1410   vii.   George Stutzman[2409], born 21 Jan 1895 in Chappell, Deuel Co., NE[2409]; died 04 Dec 1914 in NE[2409].

        More About George Stutzman:
        DBH Book: 10976/[2409]

415. Fanny[7] Christner (Joseph J.[6], John J.[5], Christian J.[4], Johannes John Hans[3], Christian[2], Christen[1]) was born 01 Feb 1864 in OH[2410]. She married **Henry Gerber**[2410] 1885[2410]. He was born Oct 1859 in OH[2410,2410], and died 05 Apr 1932 in Tuscarawas Co., OH[2410].

Notes for Fanny Christner:
Fanny and her sister Katie Ann married brothers in Holmes Co., OH.

More About Fanny Christner:
Residence: 1910, Wayne, Tuscarawas Co., OH[2410]

Notes for Henry Gerber:
Henry is a brother to Emanual. These brothers married sisters Fanny and Katie Ann.

More About Henry Gerber:
Residence: 1900, Age: 40; Marital Status: Married; Relation to Head of House: Head/Walnut Creek, Holmes Co., OH[2410]

Children of Fanny Christner and Henry Gerber are:
1411   i.   Clarence[8] Gerber[2410,2410], born 15 Jul 1885 in Barrs Mills, OH[2410,2410]; died 19 May 1961 in Indiana Co., PA[2410,2410].

        More About Clarence Gerber:
        Residence: 1910, Holmes Co., OH[2410]

1412   ii.   Curtis A. Gerber[2410,2410], born 07 Apr 1887 in Holmes Co., OH[2410,2410]; died 09 May 1964 in Home[2410,2410].

        More About Curtis A. Gerber:
        Residence: 1910, Berlin, Holmes Co., OH[2410]

1413   iii.   Maurice Edward Gerber[2410,2410], born 28 Jan 1892 in Crawford Twp., Coshocton Co., OH[2410,2410]; died 12 Sep 1928 in OH[2410,2410].

        More About Maurice Edward Gerber:
        Residence: Tuscarawas Co., OH[2410]

1414   iv.   Owen Gerber[2410,2410], born 15 Oct 1893 in Coshocton Co., OH[2410,2410]; died 24 Jan 1953[2410].

        More About Owen Gerber:

Residence: 1920, Wayne, Tuscarawas Co., OH[2410]

1415 v. Alma M Gerber[2410], born Oct 1897 in OH[2410].

   More About Alma M Gerber:
   Residence: 1920, Milton, Wayne Co., OH[2410]

1416 vi. Renos Bryan Gerber[2410,2410], born 20 Dec 1899 in Holmes Co., OH[2410,2410]; died 25 Jun 1984 in Dalton, OH[2410,2410].

   More About Renos Bryan Gerber:
   Residence: 1930, Sugar Creek, Stark Co., OH[2410]

1417 vii. Cora Edna Gerber[2410,2410], born 09 Mar 1902 in OH[2410,2410]; died 17 Dec 1988 in Navarre, Stark Co., OH[2410,2410].

   More About Cora Edna Gerber:
   Residence: 1930, Sugar Creek, Stark Co., OH[2410]

416. Franica[7] Christner (Joseph J.[6], John J.[5], Christian J.[4], Johannes John Hans[3], Christian[2], Christen[1])[2410,2411] was born 01 Feb 1864 in OH[2412,2413], and died 07 Apr 1921 in Tuscarawas Co., OH[2414]. She married **Henry Gerber**[2414] 1885[2414]. He was born Oct 1859 in OH[2414,2414], and died 05 Apr 1932 in Tuscarawas Co., OH[2414].

More About Franica Christner:
Residence: 1920, Age: 55; Marital Status: Married; Relation to Head of House: Wife/Wayne, Tuscarawas, Ohio[2414]

Notes for Henry Gerber:
Henry is a brother to Emanual. These brothers married sisters Fanny and Katie Ann.

More About Henry Gerber:
Residence: 1900, Age: 40; Marital Status: Married; Relation to Head of House: Head/Walnut Creek, Holmes Co., OH[2414]

Children of Franica Christner and Henry Gerber are:

1418 i. Alice Minerva[8] Gerber[2414,2414], born 23 Apr 1889 in Berlin, Delaware Co., OH[2414,2414]; died 01 Dec 1947 in Navarre, Stark Co., OH[2414].

   More About Alice Minerva Gerber:
   Residence: 1900, Walnut Creek, Holmes Co., OH[2414]

1419 ii. Earl W. Gerber[2414], born 17 Nov 1895 in Baltic, OH[2414,2414]; died 30 Oct 1962 in Indiana Co., PA[2414,2414].

   More About Earl W. Gerber:
   Residence: 1900, Age: 4; Marital Status: Single; Relation to Head of House: Son/Walnut Creek, Holmes Co., OH[2414]

1420 iii. Alma Mable Gerber[2414], born 09 Oct 1897 in Holmes Co., OH[2414].

   More About Alma Mable Gerber:
   Residence: 1900, Age: 2; Marital Status: Single; Relation to Head of House: Daughter/Walnut Creek, Holmes Co., OH[2414]

417. Jacob J.[7] Christner (Joseph J.[6], John J.[5], Christian J.[4], Johannes John Hans[3], Christian[2], Christen[1])[2415,2416] was born 26 Apr 1866 in OH[2417], and died 08 May 1939 in Holmes Co., OH[2418]. He married **Martha 'Mary' Jane Stantz**[2419]. She was born 02 Jan 1865 in Holmes Co., OH[2419], and died 02 Feb 1915 in Walnut Creek Twp., Holmes Co., OH[2419].

Notes for Jacob J. Christner:
Birth: 1866
Death: 1939

Spouse: Mary Jane Stantz Christner (1865 - 1915)

Burial: East Lawn Cemetery, Sugarcreek, Tuscarawas Co., OH

More About Jacob J. Christner:
Burial: East Lawn Cemetery in Sugarcreek OH
Residence: 1900, Bucks, Tuscarawas Co., OH[2420]

Notes for Martha 'Mary' Jane Stantz:
Birth: Jan. 2, 1865
Death: Feb. 9, 1915

AGED 50Y 1M 7D

Spouse: Jacob J Christner (1866 - 1939)

Burial: East Lawn Cemetery, Sugarcreek, Tuscarawas Co., OH

More About Martha 'Mary' Jane Stantz:
Burial: East Lawn Cemetery, Sugarcreek, Tuscarawas Co., OH[2421]

Child of Jacob Christner and Martha Stantz is:
    1421   i.   Mildred M.[8] Christner[2421,2422], born 13 Jul 1899 in Holmes Co., OH[2422,2423]; died 05 May 1973 in Sugarcreek Twp., Tuscarawas Co., OH[2424,2425]. She married Karl Edward Warnes[2426,2427,2428] 1940; born 12 Jul 1890 in OH[2428,2429,2430]; died 15 Feb 1892 in Holmes Co., OH[2431].

        More About Mildred M. Christner:
        Social Security Number: 273-62-9725/[2432]
        SSN issued: OH[2432]

        Notes for Karl Edward Warnes:
        Ohio Obituary Index, 1830's - 2009, Rutherford B. Hayes Presidential Center

        Name: Karl E Warnes
        Nickname: Kap
        Birth Date: 1890
        Death Date: 15 Feb 1982
        Age at Death: 91
        Death Place: Sugarcreek, OH
        Spouse: Mildred Christner
        Parents: William
        Newspaper: Wooster Daily Record, Wooster, Ohio
        Newspaper Date: 16 Feb 1982
        Newspaper Page: p. 27, col. 1
        Newspaper Repository: Wayne County Public Library (Wooster); Wayne County Public Library (Wooster)
        Notes: East Lawn Cemetery; Sugarcreek Tuscarawas Co., OH

418. Catherine Ann[7] Christner (Joseph J.[6], John J.[5], Christian J.[4], Johannes John Hans[3], Christian[2], Christen[1])[2433] was born 11 Apr 1868 in Sugarcreek, Holmes Co., OH, and died 31 Dec 1955 in Sugarcreek, Holmes Co., OH[2433]. She married **Emanuel Gerber** 13 Mar 1892. He died 1934.

Notes for Catherine Ann Christner:

Gerber, Catherine (Katie Ann), daughter of the late Joe and Sarah (Garver) Christner, was born in Holmes Co., OH April 11, 1868; departed this life Dec 31, 1955, at the home of a son Harry, Sugarcreek, OH with whom she and a daughter had been residing, following an extended illness, being bedfast about 4 years; aged 87 y. 8 m. 20 d. In her late teens she made a confession of Christ and became a member of the Walnut Creek Mennonite Church, retaining her membership here until her death. On Mar 13, 1892, she was untied in marriage to Emanuel Gerber, who predeceased her in 1934. All five children born to this union survive her passing (Elmer, Lloyd, Ada, and Harry of the same community, and Wilbur, Wooster, OH). Also surviving are 17 grandchildren, 22 great-grandchildren, 2 brothers (Harvey and Henry both of Baltic, OH), besides many other friends and relatives. Funeral services conducted at the Walnut Creek Church on Jan. 3 were in charge of Venus Hershberger, Alvin W. Miller, and Paul R. miller, with burial in the church cemetery.

Katie Ann and her sister Fanny married brothers from Holmes Co., OH maybe called Kelly born 19 Jun 1875.

More About Catherine Ann Christner:
Burial: Walnut Creek Mennonite Church Holmes Co, OH
Residence: 1880, Precinct O, Seward Co., NE[2433]

Children of Catherine Christner and Emanuel Gerber are:
> 1422   i.   Ada[8] Gerber.
> 1423   ii.   Elmer Gerber.
> 1424   iii.   Wilbur Gerber.
> 1425   iv.   Lloyd Gerber.
> + 1426   v.   Harry Gerber, born 04 May 1900 in Bars Mills, OH; died 19 Oct 1990 in Baltic, Tuscarawas Co., OH.

419. John[7] Christner (Joseph J.[6], John J.[5], Christian J.[4], Johannes John Hans[3], Christian[2], Christen[1])[2433] was born Mar 1871 in OH[2433], and died 23 Oct 1954 in OH[2433]. He married **Ida Kaser**. She was born 1883, and died 1965 in N40°26.587 by W81°42.567 NW of Baltic on 651 Port Washington Highway.

More About John Christner:
Burial: Baltic West Lawn Cemetery Holmes Co. OH
Residence: 1900, Bucks, Tuscarawas Co., OH[2433]

More About Ida Kaser:
Burial: Baltic West Lawn Cemetery Holmes Co. OH
Christened: Brethern

Child of John Christner and Ida Kaser is:
> 1427   i.   Infant[8] Christner.
>
> > Notes for Infant Christner:
> > Birth: Apr 7, 1909
> > Death: Apr 7, 1909
> >
> > Note: Son of John Christner and Ida Ellen Kaser Christner
> >
> > Burial: Amish Mennonite Cemetery, Walnut Creek, Holmes Co., OH

420. William J.[7] Christner (Joseph J.[6], John J.[5], Christian J.[4], Johannes John Hans[3], Christian[2], Christen[1])[2433,2434] was born 17 Apr 1873 in Holmes Co., OH[2435,2436], and died 28 Apr 1952 in Streetsboro, OH. He married **Mary Elizabeth Hershberger**[2436] 24 May 1896. She was born 31 May 1876 in Walnut Creek, Holmes Co., OH[2436], and died 25 Nov 1962 in Ravenna, Portage Co., OH[2436].

Notes for William J. Christner:
Christner, -- William J., son of the late Joseph and Sarah (Gerber) Christner, was born in Trail, Ohio, April 17, 1873; passed away at his home in Streetsboro, April 28, 1952; aged 79 y. 11 d. In his youth he accepted Christ as his Saviour, uniting with the Mennonite Church. He was always a faithful and regular attendant at the services. On May 24, 1896, he was united in marriage to Mary Elizabeth Hershberger. Surviving are his wife, 3 sons (Wade,

Youngstown, OH and Floyd, and Rollie, Kent, Ohio), 5 daughters (Velma-Mrs. Dan Stuckey, Stryker, Ohio; Malinda-Mrs. Ernie Bontrager, Beulah-Mrs. Noah Schrock, Kent, Ohio; Lorene-Mrs. Frank Johnson, Middletown, Ohio; and Elvesta-Mrs. Lloyd Grieser, Stryker, Ohio), 28 grandchildren, 13 great-grandchildren, 3 brothers (John, Henry, and Harvey, all of Baltic, Ohio), and a sister (Mrs. Katie Ann Gerber, Sugarcreek, Ohio). His parents, 4 sisters, 1 brother, 1 son (who died in infancy), and 1 daughter (Niva-Mrs. John G. Miller) preceded him in death. Funeral services were held at the Plainview Church, Aurora, Ohio, in charge of Eugene Yoder and Elmer Stoltzfus.

I found a William J. Christner b.11/1/1903◇d. 8/25/1966 married to a Hazel N. b. 9/5/1901◇d. 6/30/1976 burial Baltic West Lawn Cemetery, Holmes Co., OH close to Henry Christner & Phoebe Scaar & John Christner & Ida N40°26.597 by W81° 42.628

More About William J. Christner:
Religion: Mennonite/
Residence: 1880, Precinct O, Seward Co., NE[2437]

Notes for Mary Elizabeth Hershberger:
Christner, Mary Elizabeth, daughter of Abraham and Catherine (Mast) Hershberger, was born near Walnut Creek, OH May 31, 1876; died at the Robinson Memorial Hospital, Ravenna, OH Nov. 25, 1962; aged 86 y. 5 m. 25 d. On May 24, 1896, she was married to William J. Christner, who died in April, 1952. Also preceding her in death were 2 daughters and one infant son. Surviving are 4 daughters (Velma-Mrs. Dan Stuckey, Beulah-Mrs. Noah Schrock, Lorene-Mrs. Frank Johnson, and Elvesta-Mrs. Lloyd Grieser), 3 sons (Wade, Floyd, and Rollie), 29 grandchildren, and 62 great-grandchildren. She was a member of the Mennonite Church. Funeral services were con-ducted at the Plainview Church, Nov. 29, in charge of Eugene Yoder and Elmer Stoltzfus.

More About Mary Elizabeth Hershberger:
Residence: 1930, Streetsboro, Portage Co., OH[2438]

Children of William Christner and Mary Hershberger are:

+ 1428   i.   Niva[8] Christner, born 20 Dec 1896 in Tuscarawas Co., OH; died 13 Apr 1947.
+ 1429   ii.   Velma Christner, born 26 Apr 1898 in Baltic, Tuscarawas Co., OH; died 25 Mar 1987 in Achbold, OH.
+ 1430   iii.   Malinda Leona Christner, born 20 Dec 1899 in Baltic, Tuscarawas Co., OH; died 19 Oct 1962 in Streetsboro, Portage Co., OH.
+ 1431   iv.   Beulah Fern Christner, born 06 Feb 1901 in Tuscarawas Co., OH; died 10 Mar 1999 in Stryker, OH, USA.
    1432   v.   William Wade Christner, born 10 Oct 1904; died 1976. He married Thelma B. Osborne.

Notes for William Wade Christner:
I found a William J. Christner b.11/1/1903 - d. 8/25/1966 married to a Hazel N. b. 9/5/1901 - d. 6/30/1976 burial Baltic West Lawn Cemetery, Holmes Co., OH close to Henry Christner & Phoebe Scaar & John Christner & Ida. N40°26.597 by W81° 42.628.

Burial - 1976 in Cornersburg Cemetery, Row 03, Canfield Twp., Mahoning Co. OH
"Father"

Spouse: Thelma B. Osborne Christner (1906 - 1953)

Burial: Cornersburg Cemetery, Cornersburg, Mahoning Co.,
Plot: Row 03

Notes for Thelma B. Osborne:
Birth: Sep. 19, 1906 - OH
Death: Aug. 14, 1953 - Youngstown, Mahoning Co., OH

Inscription: "Mother"
Death Certificate for Thelma B. Christner - file no. 54788

Parents:
Charles Osborne (1865 - 1932)
Esther Ellen Sanders Osborne (1872 - 1939)

Spouse: W. Wade Christner (1903 - 1976)

Burial: Cornersburg Cemetery, Cornersburg, Mahoning Co., OH
Plot: Row 03

1433   vi.   Floyd Lester Christner[2439], born 14 Jan 1907 in Walnut Creek, Holmes Co., OH[2439]; died 06 Jun 1965 in Portage Co., OH[2439].

1434   vii.   Rollie Herbert Christner[2440], born 15 Aug 1909 in Walnut Creek Twp., Holmes Co., OH[2440]; died 03 Nov 2005 in St. Petersburg, Pinellas Co., FL[2440]. He married Thelma I; born 27 Apr 1909; died 03 Aug 1992.

Notes for Rollie Herbert Christner:
Birth: Aug. 15, 1909
Death: Nov. 3, 2005

Note: SGT US ARMY; WORLD WAR II

Burial: Florida National Cemetery, Bushnell, Sumter Co., FL
Plot: Sec 112, Site 2182

More About Rollie Herbert Christner:
Other-Begin: Bradenton, Manatee Co., FL[2440]
Social Security Number: 280-10-2846/[2440]
SSN issued: OH[2440]

Notes for Thelma I:
Birth: Apr. 27, 1909
Death: Aug. 3, 1992

MSGT, US ARMY

Burial: Florida National Cemetery, Bushnell, Sumter Co., FL
Plot: 112, 0, 2182
Buried with husband Rollie Herbert Christner

1435   viii.   Lorene Christner, born 09 Apr 1916 in Walnut Creek, Holmes Co., OH[2441]; died 28 Nov 1995 in Middletown, Butler Co., OH[2441]. She married Frank Johnson.

More About Lorene Christner:
Residence: 1930, Streetsboro, Portage Co., OH[2441]

1436   ix.   Elvesta M. Christner, born 1919 in OH[2442]; died 11 Mar 2013[2443]. She married Lloyd J. Grieser[2444]; born 01 Mar 1918 in OH[2444].

Notes for Elvesta M. Christner:
Grieser, Elvesta, age 94 years, of Archbold, OH passed away March 11, 2013. Short Funeral Home, Archbold, OH.

Published in Toledo Blade on March 13, 2013

More About Elvesta M. Christner:
Residence: 01 Apr 1940, Stryker, Williams Co., OH[2444]

More About Lloyd J. Grieser:
Residence: 01 Apr 1940, Stryker, Williams Co., OH[2444]

422. Harvey C.[7] Christner (Joseph J.[6], John J.[5], Christian J.[4], Johannes John Hans[3], Christian[2], Christen[1])[2445,2446,2447] was born 07 Jul 1880 in OH[2447,2448,2449], and died 15 Apr 1970 in Dover, Tuscarawas Co., OH[2450,2451,2451]. He married **Amanda Elizabeth Lower**[2451,2451] 12 Nov 1903 in Coshcocton, OH[2451,2451]. She was born 11 Mar 1881 in Crawford, Coshocton Co., OH[2451], and died 26 Apr 1949 in Baltic, Tuscarawas Co., OH[2451,2451].

226

Notes for Harvey C. Christner:
Birth: Jul 7, 1880
Death: Apr 4, 1970

Spouse: Amanda Christner (1881 - 1949)

Burial: Brethren Cemetery, Baltic, Tuscarawas Co., OH

More About Harvey C. Christner:
Residence: 1942, World War 2 Draft Registration, Tuscarawas Co., OH[2451]
Social Security Number: 280-48-8061/[2452]
SSN issued: OH[2452]

Notes for Amanda Elizabeth Lower:
Birth: Mar 10, 1881
Death: Apr 26, 1949

Spouse: Harvey Christner (1880 - 1970)

Burial: Brethren Cemetery, Baltic, Tuscarawas Co., OH

More About Amanda Elizabeth Lower:
Residence: 1920, Bucks, Tuscarawas Co., OH[2453,2453]

Children of Harvey Christner and Amanda Lower are:
+   1437   i.   William J.[8] Christner, born 01 Nov 1904 in Coshocton, Coshocton Co., OH; died 25 Aug 1966 in Dover, Tuscarawas Co., OH.
    1438   ii.   Pearl May Christner[2453,2453], born 05 Mar 1905 in Crawford, Coshocton Co., OH[2454,2455,2456,2456]; died 19 Mar 1989 in Walnut Creek, Holmes Co., OH[2456,2456]. She married Hugo B. Miller[2457] 31 Mar 1923 in Sugar Creek, Tuscarawas Co., OH[2457]; born 04 Apr 1897 in OH[2457]; died 09 Nov 1990 in Sugar Creek, OH[2457].

      More About Pearl May Christner:
      Residence: 1920, Bucks, Tuscarawas Co., OH[2458,2458]

      Notes for Hugo B. Miller:
      Birth: Apr. 4, 1897
      Death: Nov. 9, 1990

      Burial: East Lawn Cemetery, Sugarcreek, Tuscarawas Co., OH
      Find A Grave Memorial# 28591685

      More About Hugo B. Miller:
      Residence: 1917, World War 1 Draft Registration, Canton, Stark Co., OH[2459]

428. Amanda Carrie[7] Schrock (Elizabeth[6] Christner, John J.[5], Christian J.[4], Johannes John Hans[3], Christian[2], Christen[1])[2460] was born 18 Nov 1870 in Licking Co., OH[2461], and died 11 Jun 1948 in Wawpecong, Miami County, Indiana - Buried - Memorial Park Cemetery, Kokomo, Howard County, Indiana[2461]. She married **John Christner**[2461] 06 May 1893, son of Peter Christner and Sarah Troyer. He was born 06 Nov 1870 in Miami Co., IN, and died 13 Apr 1941 in Age at Death: 72/Wawpecong, Miami County, Indiana - Buried - Kokomo Memorial Park Cemetery, Kokomo, Howard County, Indiana[2461].

Notes for Amanda Carrie Schrock:
Birth: 1870
Death: Jun. 11, 1948

Burial: Kokomo Memorial Park Cemetery, Kokomo, Howard Co., IN
Plot: Sec: Memorial

More About Amanda Carrie Schrock:
Residence: 1910, Clay Township, Miami Co., IN[2461]

Notes for John Christner:
Amish

More About John Christner:
Religion: Amish/
Residence: 1900, Clay Township, Miami Co., IN[2462]

Children of Amanda Schrock and John Christner are:

+ 1439   i.   Bertha[8] Christner, born 18 Dec 1892; died Apr 1977 in Kokomo, Howard Co., IN.
+ 1440   ii.   Harry Irvin Christner, born 18 Aug 1894; died 22 Feb 1971.
   1441   iii.   Laura Christner, born 06 Aug 1896.
   1442   iv.   Mabel Christner, born 21 Feb 1898.

> More About Mabel Christner:
> Residence: 1910, Clay, Miami Co., IN[2463]

   1443   v.   William L. Christner, born 07 May 1901; died 09 May 1968 in Sharpsville, Tipton Co., IN[2464]. He married Lela E; born 1897; died 25 Aug 1983.

> Notes for William L. Christner:
> Birth: 1901
> Death: May 9, 1968
>
> Spouse: Lela E Christner (1897 - 1983)
>
> Inscription: Aged 67 years
>
> Burial: Sharpsville Cemetery, Sharpsville, Tipton Co., IN
> Section 4, Row 8, #20
>
> More About William L. Christner:
> Social Security Number: 308-09-2079/[2464]
> SSN issued: IN[2464]
>
> Notes for Lela E:
> Birth: 1897
> Death: Aug. 25, 1983
>
> Spouse: William L Christner (1901 - 1968)
>
> Burial: Sharpsville Cemetery, Sharpsville, Tipton Co., IN
> Section 4, Row 8, #20

   1444   vi.   Mary Christner, born 10 Mar 1903.
+ 1445   vii.   Raymond Russell "Friz" Christner, born 11 Dec 1905 in Waupecong, IN; died Apr 1976 in Bradford, Miami Co., OH.
   1446   viii.   Mildred Christner, born 23 Jul 1909.

432. Edward[7] Lantz (Philip[6], Veronica Fannie[5] Christner, Christian J.[4], Johannes John Hans[3], Christian[2], Christen[1]) was born 27 Mar 1891 in Topeka, Lagrange Co., IN. He married **Lizzie Ann Yoder** 07 Apr 1921 in Madison Co., OH. She was born 09 Aug 1896.

Notes for Edward Lantz:
The Descendants of John J. Christner, privately published February 1961, p. 100.

Notes for Lizzie Ann Yoder:

The Descendants of John J. Christner, privately published February 1961, p. 100.

Children of Edward Lantz and Lizzie Yoder are:

+	1447	i.	Treva[8] Lantz, born 15 Jul 1922 in Goshen, Elkhart Co., IN; died 22 Sep 2009 in Indianapolis, Marion Co., IN.
+	1448	ii.	Delbert Lantz, born 01 May 1924.
+	1449	iii.	Virgil Lantz, born 25 Mar 1926; died 29 Sep 1958.
+	1450	iv.	Floyd Lantz, born 04 Dec 1927.
+	1451	v.	Barbara Ellen Lantz, born 12 Mar 1930 in Topeka, Lagrange Co., IN.
	1452	vi.	Harlan Lantz, born 14 Jun 1934.

Notes for Harlan Lantz:
The Descendants of John J. Christner, privately published February 1961, p. 99.

+	1453	vii.	Omar Lantz, born 11 Apr 1936.

434. Ezra[7] Lantz (Philip[6], Veronica Fannie[5] Christner, Christian J.[4], Johannes John Hans[3], Christian[2], Christen[1])[2465] was born 27 Dec 1895[2465], and died Dec 1976 in Lagrange Co., IN[2465]. He married **Ina Marie Troyer**[2465] 10 Apr 1919[2465]. She was born 26 Dec 1901[2466,2467], and died Aug 1984 in Shipshewana, Lagrange Co., IN[2468].

Notes for Ezra Lantz:
The Descendants of John J. Christner, privately published February 1961, p. 100.

Notes for Ina Marie Troyer:
The Descendants of John J. Christner, privately published February 1961, p. 101.

More About Ina Marie Troyer:
Social Security Number: 303-70-3352[2468]
SSN issued: IN[2468]

Children of Ezra Lantz and Ina Troyer are:

+	1454	i.	Truman Lavoid[8] Lantz, born 11 Jan 1921; died 16 Jul 1999 in Lagrange Co., IN.
+	1455	ii.	Gladys Barbra Lantz, born 27 Dec 1923.
+	1456	iii.	Irma Arlene Lantz, born 23 Mar 1925.
	1457	iv.	Robert Lee Lantz, born 24 May 1933. He married Mary Cathrine Miller 31 Oct 1952; born 07 Jan 1936.

Notes for Robert Lee Lantz:
The Descendants of John J. Christner, privately published February 1961, p. 101.

Notes for Mary Cathrine Miller:
The Descendants of John J. Christner, privately published February 1961, p. 101.

+	1458	v.	Glendon Ezra Lantz, born 02 Nov 1934.

435. Earl[7] Lantz (Philip[6], Veronica Fannie[5] Christner, Christian J.[4], Johannes John Hans[3], Christian[2], Christen[1]) was born 19 Jan 1898. He married **Luella Yoder** 12 Feb 1922. She was born 02 May 1904.

Notes for Earl Lantz:
The Descendants of John J. Christner, privately published February 1961, p. 101.

More About Earl Lantz:
Religion: Conservative Amish/
Residence: Topeka, Lagrange Co., IN

Notes for Luella Yoder:
The Descendants of John J. Christner, privately published February 1961, p. 101.

Children of Earl Lantz and Luella Yoder are:

+	1459	i.	Harold[8] Lantz, born 03 Mar 1923.
+	1460	ii.	Dorothy Ellen Lantz, born 24 Dec 1927.
+	1461	iii.	Kenneth Lantz, born 22 May 1930.
	1462	iv.	Marrietta Lantz, born 28 Sep 1940. She married Larry Richard Schrock 02 Aug 1959; born 19 Jul 1939.

Notes for Marrietta Lantz:
The Descendants of John J. Christner, privately published February 1961, p. 101.

Notes for Larry Richard Schrock:
The Descendants of John J. Christner, privately published February 1961, p. 101.

436. Carrie[7] Lantz (Philip[6], Veronica Fannie[5] Christner, Christian J.[4], Johannes John Hans[3], Christian[2], Christen[1]) was born 08 Sep 1902. She married **Peter Lichti** 24 Oct 1926. He was born 25 Aug 1900.

Notes for Carrie Lantz:
The Descendants of John J. Christner, privately published February 1961, p. 102.

Notes for Peter Lichti:
The Descendants of John J. Christner, privately published February 1961, p. 102.

More About Peter Lichti:
Religion: Conservative Amish/
Residence: Wellesley, Ontario, Canada

Children of Carrie Lantz and Peter Lichti are:

    1463   i.   Abner Leroy[8] Lichti, born 08 Mar 1927.

                   Notes for Abner Leroy Lichti:
                   The Descendants of John J. Christner, privately published February 1961, p. 102.

    1464   ii.   Arlene Lichti, born 02 Nov 1928.

                   Notes for Arlene Lichti:
                   The Descendants of John J. Christner, privately published February 1961, p. 102.

    1465   iii.   Anna Mae Lichti, born 11 Jan 1930.

                   Notes for Anna Mae Lichti:
                   The Descendants of John J. Christner, privately published February 1961, p. 102.

    1466   iv.   Alice Marie Lichti, born 26 Jun 1933.

                   Notes for Alice Marie Lichti:
                   The Descendants of John J. Christner, privately published February 1961, p. 102.

438. Phineas S.[7] Miller (Magdalena Mattie[6] Lantz, Veronica Fannie[5] Christner, Christian J.[4], Johannes John Hans[3], Christian[2], Christen[1]) was born 04 Sep 1882, and died 03 Nov 1953. He married **Elizabeth Anderson** 08 Feb 1906 in By Valentine Hochstetler at Nappenee, IN. She was born 22 Nov 1884.

Notes for Phineas S. Miller:
The Descendants of John J. Christner, privately published February 1961, p. 102.

Notes for Elizabeth Anderson:
The Descendants of John J. Christner, privately published February 1961, p. 102.

Children of Phineas Miller and Elizabeth Anderson are:

+	1467	i.	Emma Marie[8] Miller, born 07 May 1907; died 19 Feb 1994.
+	1468	ii.	Ammon Leo Miller, born 07 Oct 1909; died 16 Nov 1960.
+	1469	iii.	Alvin Elias Miller, born 22 Jan 1913.
+	1470	iv.	Magdalena Opal Miller, born 03 Apr 1915; died 23 Sep 1997 in Maricopa Co., AZ.
	1471	v.	Willard Ivan Miller, born 11 Jun 1918; died 23 Nov 1929.

Notes for Willard Ivan Miller:
The Descendants of John J. Christner, privately published February 1961, p. 102.

+	1472	vi.	Harold Marvin Miller, born 06 Jul 1921 in Nappanee, Elkhart Co., IN.
+	1473	vii.	Ruby Elizabeth Miller, born 20 Jul 1924.

439. Milo S.[7] Miller (Magdalena Mattie[6] Lantz, Veronica Fannie[5] Christner, Christian J.[4], Johannes John Hans[3], Christian[2], Christen[1]) was born 25 May 1885 in Mercer, PA, and died 24 Aug 1967[2469]. He married **Emma E. Miller**[2469] 14 Mar 1912. She was born 02 Jun 1888 in Nappanee, Elkhart Co., IN[2469].

Notes for Milo S. Miller:
The Descendants of John J. Christner, privately published February 1961, pp. 102, 103.

Notes for Emma E. Miller:
The Descendants of John J. Christner, privately published February 1961, p. 103.

Children of Milo Miller and Emma Miller are:
	1474	i.	Amos M.[8] Miller, born 30 Dec 1913 in IN[2470]; died 08 Dec 1996 in Washington Co., OH[2470].

Notes for Amos M. Miller:
The Descendants of John J. Christner, privately published February 1961, p. 103.

+	1475	ii.	Mahlon M. S. Miller, born 13 Aug 1915 in Middlefield, OH; died 03 Feb 2002 in Geauga Co., OH.
+	1476	iii.	Henry M. Miller, born 20 Sep 1922 in Nappanee, Elkhart Co., IN; died 18 Jul 2000 in Riceville, Howard Co., IA.
+	1477	iv.	Levi M. Miller, born 26 Jun 1925 in Stoneboro, PA.
+	1478	v.	Ida M. Miller, born 19 Jun 1931 in Mercer, PA.
+	1479	vi.	Owen M. Miller, born 19 Jun 1931 in Mercer, PA.
	1480	vii.	Mattie M. Miller, born 19 Jun 1931 in Mercer, PA. She married Daniel N. Yoder 25 Apr 1950; born 29 Sep 1924.

Notes for Mattie M. Miller:
The Descendants of John J. Christner, privately published February 1961, p. 103.

Notes for Daniel N. Yoder:
The Descendants of John J. Christner, privately published February 1961, p. 104.

440. Elizabeth Ann[7] Miller (Magdalena Mattie[6] Lantz, Veronica Fannie[5] Christner, Christian J.[4], Johannes John Hans[3], Christian[2], Christen[1])[2471,2472,2473] was born 17 Jun 1887 in Lagrange Co., IN[2474,2475,2476], and died 05 Feb 1985[2477]. She married **Samuel J. Christner**[2478,2479,2480] 12 Oct 1907, son of John Christner and Emma Christner. He was born 27 Mar 1888 in Topeka, Lagrange Co., IN[2481,2482], and died 14 Dec 1980 in Scott, Kosciusko Co., IN[2483].

Notes for Elizabeth Ann Miller:
The Descendants of John J. Christner, privately published February 1961, pp. 47, 102.

More About Elizabeth Ann Miller:
Residence: 1920, Scott, Kosciusko Co., IN[2483,2484]

Notes for Samuel J. Christner:
The Descendants of John J. Christner, privately published February 1961, pp. 46, 47.

More About Samuel J. Christner:
Residence: 1920, Scott, Kosciusko Co., IN[2485,2486]

Children of Elizabeth Miller and Samuel Christner are:
+   1481   i.   Emma S.[8] Christner, born 12 Aug 1916 in Topeka, Lagrange Co., IN.
+   1482   ii.   Levi S. Christner, born 06 Jul 1920 in Topeka, Lagrange Co., IN; died 10 Feb 2011 in Decatur, Adams Co., IN.
+   1483   iii. Edna S. Christner, born 06 Jan 1925 in Nappanee, Elkhart Co., IN.
+   1484   iv.   Sylvia S. Christner, born 20 Oct 1927 in Nappanee, Elkhart Co., IN.
+   1485   v.   Ida S. Christner, born 21 Jul 1933 in Berne, Adams Co., IN.

442. Sarah[7] Hershberger (Magdalena Mattie[6] Lantz, Veronica Fannie[5] Christner, Christian J.[4], Johannes John Hans[3], Christian[2], Christen[1]) was born 23 Sep 1889 in Millerburg, Holmes Co., OH. She married **Noah J. Miller** 11 Feb 1915. He was born 29 Dec 1889.

Notes for Sarah Hershberger:
The Descendants of John J. Christner, privately published February 1961, p. 102.

More About Noah J. Miller:
Religion: Old Order Amish/

Children of Sarah Hershberger and Noah Miller are:
+   1486   i.   Ervin N.[8] Gingerich, born 06 Jan 1916 in Millerburg, Holmes Co., OH.
+   1487   ii.   Alvin N. Gingerich, born 17 Mar 1918 in Millerburg, Holmes Co., OH.
+   1488   iii. Edna Gingerich, born 20 Apr 1920 in Millerburg, Holmes Co., OH.
+   1489   iv.   Mary Gingerich, born 11 Jul 1922 in Millerburg, Holmes Co., OH.
+   1490   v.   Ernest N. Miller, born 29 Nov 1923.
+   1491   vi.   Fannie Gingerich, born 28 Apr 1924 in Millerburg, Holmes Co., OH; died 14 Feb 1975 in Holmes Co., OH.
+   1492   vii. Emma Gingerich, born 27 Dec 1926 in Sugarcreek, Tuscarawas Co., OH.
+   1493   viii. Mahlon Gingerich, born 12 Mar 1929 in Millerburg, Holmes Co., OH.
    1494   ix.   Moses Gingerich[2487], born 19 Jun 1931[2487].

                 More About Moses Gingerich:
                 Residence: Millersburg, OH[2487]

443. Amos S.[7] Miller (Magdalena Mattie[6] Lantz, Veronica Fannie[5] Christner, Christian J.[4], Johannes John Hans[3], Christian[2], Christen[1]) was born 24 Mar 1892 in Topeka, Lagrange Co., IN[2488]. He married **Edna Yoder** 10 Jan 1918. She was born 27 Aug 1897.

Notes for Amos S. Miller:
The Descendants of John J. Christner, privately published February 1961, pp. 102, 105.

More About Amos S. Miller:
Residence: 1910, Wilcox, Newaygo Co., MI[2488]

Notes for Edna Yoder:
The Descendants of John J. Christner, privately published February 1961, p. 105.

Children of Amos Miller and Edna Yoder are:
    1495   i.   Ora[8] Miller, born 25 Oct 1918; died 31 May 1943.

                 Notes for Ora Miller:
                 The Descendants of John J. Christner, privately published February 1961, p. 105.

                 He contracted T.B. in C.P.S. camp in 1942 and dies in May 31, 1943.

1496 ii. Infant Miller, born Dec 1921; died Dec 1921.

      Notes for Infant Miller:
      The Descendants of John J. Christner, privately published February 1961, p. 105.

+ 1497 iii. Cletus Miller, born 01 Feb 1924 in Topeka, Lagrange Co., IN.
+ 1498 iv. Anna Miller, born 08 Feb 1927 in Topeka, Lagrange Co., IN.

444. Levi S.[7] Miller (Magdalena Mattie[6] Lantz, Veronica Fannie[5] Christner, Christian J.[4], Johannes John Hans[3], Christian[2], Christen[1])[2488] was born 23 Jun 1896 in Topeka, Lagrange Co., IN[2489], and died 12 Nov 1989[2490]. He married **Anna S. Miller**[2491] 20 Jan 1921, daughter of John Christner and Elizabeth Miller. She was born 26 Jan 1899 in Lagrange Co., IN[2491], and died 21 Jun 1973.

Notes for Levi S. Miller:
The Descendants of John J. Christner, privately published February 1961, p. 102.

More About Levi S. Miller:
Burial: Amish Cemetery/Saling, Audrain, Missouri, USA[2492]
Find A Grave Link: Memorial# 27751113/[2492]
Residence: 1910, Wilcox, Newaygo Co., MI[2493]

Children of Levi Miller and Anna Miller are:
+ 1499 i. Ellis L.[8] Miller, born 27 May 1923 in Lagrange Co., IN; died 09 May 2000 in Fort Wayne, Allen Co., IN.
  1500 ii. Ivan Miller[2494], born 08 Nov 1924[2494]; died 14 Jan 1935[2494].

      More About Ivan Miller:
      Burial: Christner Cemetery/Honeyville, Lagrange Co., IN[2494]

+ 1501 iii. Edna Lucy Miller, born 29 Dec 1926 in Lagrange Co., IN; died 11 Sep 1999 in Clark, Randolph Co., MO.
  1502 iv. Infant Miller[2494], born 25 Feb 1930 in Lagrange Co., IN[2494]; died 25 Feb 1930 in Lagrange Co., IN[2494].
  1503 v. Mattie Elizabeth Miller[2494], born 13 Oct 1931[2494]; died 10 Jun 2010[2494]. She married Jake Swartz 13 Jan 1955; born 23 Dec 1935 in Hazleton, IA.

      Notes for Mattie Elizabeth Miller:
      The Descendants of John J. Christner, privately published February 1961, p. 106.

      More About Mattie Elizabeth Miller:
      SSN issued: Maryland, USA[2494]

      Notes for Jake Swartz:
      The Descendants of John J. Christner, privately published February 1961, p.106.

+ 1504 vi. Fannie L. Miller, born 01 Jul 1934.
  1505 vii. Calvin Miller, born 07 Apr 1936.
  1506 viii. Ida L. Miller, born 15 Dec 1939. She married Norman G. Yutzy 22 Jan 1959; born 05 Aug 1938.

      Notes for Ida L. Miller:
      The Descendants of John J. Christner, privately published February 1961, p. 106.

      Notes for Norman G. Yutzy:
      The Descendants of John J. Christner, privately published February 1961, p. 106.

  1507 ix. Ora L. Miller, born 18 Sep 1941. He married Martha Edna Bontrager 23 Feb 1960.

      Notes for Ora L. Miller:
      The Descendants of John J. Christner, privately published February 1961, p. 106.

      Notes for Martha Edna Bontrager:
      The Descendants of John J. Christner, privately published February 1961, p.106.

+ 1508   x.   Alma L. Miller, born 03 Sep 1957.

445. Fannie Elmina[7] Miller (Magdalena Mattie[6] Lantz, Veronica Fannie[5] Christner, Christian J.[4], Johannes John Hans[3], Christian[2], Christen[1])[2495,2496] was born 30 Mar 1900 in White Cloud, Newaygo Co., MI[2496], and died 11 Oct 1968[2496]. She married **Willis E. Miller**[2497] 20 Feb 1921, son of Ezra Miller and Annie Christner. He was born 29 Jan 1899 in Shipshewana, Lagrange Co., IN[2498], and died 14 Sep 1980 in Shipshewana, Lagrange Co., IN[2498].

Notes for Fannie Elmina Miller:
The Descendants of John J. Christner, privately published February 1961, pp. 7, 102.

More About Fannie Elmina Miller:
Residence: 1910, Wilcox, Newaygo Co., MI[2499]

Notes for Willis E. Miller:
Willis married Fannie Elmina Miller Feb 20, 1921.

Willis married a 2nd time to Elizabeth Bontrager Christner 1969
Elizabeth died July 25 1983

Elizabeth born June 12 1905 and her 1st husband was Amos J. Christner.

Children of Fannie Miller and Willis Miller are:
+ 1509   i.   Orva Eldon[8] Miller, born 29 Jan 1922; died Feb 1971.
   1510   ii.   Arlene Miller, born 30 Dec 1923; died 27 Oct 1949.

       Notes for Arlene Miller:
       The Descendants of John J. Christner, privately published February 1961, p. 8.

+ 1511   iii.   Orla Vernon Miller, born 01 Apr 1925 in Lagrange Co., IN; died 07 Jan 1993 in Fort Wayne, Allen Co., IN.
   1512   iv.   Glen Edvin Miller, born 23 May 1926; died 19 Mar 1927.

       Notes for Glen Edvin Miller:
       The Descendants of John J. Christner, privately published February 1961, p. 8.

+ 1513   v.   Ruby Ellen Miller, born 07 Jul 1927 in Lagrange Co., IN; died 07 Apr 2006 in Shipshewana, Elkhart Co., IN.
   1514   vi.   Floyd Miller[2500], born 06 Apr 1930[2500]; died 21 Sep 1946[2500].

       Notes for Floyd Miller:
       The Descendants of John J. Christner, privately published February 1961, p. 8.

   1515   vii.   Amos Miller, born 28 Nov 1932. He married Grace Jean Moehing 23 Feb 1957.

       Notes for Amos Miller:
       The Descendants of John J. Christner, privately published February 1961, p. 8.

       Notes for Grace Jean Moehing:
       The Descendants of John J. Christner, privately published February 1961, p. 8.

   1516   viii.   Raymond Miller, born 06 Mar 1935; died 09 Mar 1935.

       Notes for Raymond Miller:
       The Descendants of John J. Christner, privately published February 1961, p. 8.

+ 1517   ix.   Mary Magdalene Miller, born 03 Feb 1936 in Shipshewanna, Lagrange Co., IN; died 09 Jun 1998 in Goshen, Elkhart Co., IN.

1518   x.   Edna Mae Miller, born 04 Jun 1939. She married Ervin Schlabach Jr 22 May 1958.

                Notes for Edna Mae Miller:
                The Descendants of John J. Christner, privately published February 1961, p. 8.

                More About Edna Mae Miller:
                Residence: 01 Apr 1940, Van Buren, Lagrange Co., IN[2501]

                Notes for Ervin Schlabach Jr:
                The Descendants of John J. Christner, privately published February 1961, p. 8.

446. Edna Mae[7] Miller (Magdalena Mattie[6] Lantz, Veronica Fannie[5] Christner, Christian J.[4], Johannes John Hans[3], Christian[2], Christen[1]) was born 18 Jan 1906 in Nappanee, Elkhart Co., IN, and died 09 Jun 1990 in IN[2502]. She married **(1) Rayman J. (Ray) Miller**[2503] 26 Dec 1925, son of Jonas Miller and Elizabeth Farmwald. He was born 25 Mar 1906 in Holmes Co., OH[2503]. She married **(2) John Miller** 26 Dec 1925. He was born 25 Mar 1906.

Notes for Edna Mae Miller:
The Descendants of John J. Christner, privately published February 1961, pp. 102, 106.

More About Edna Mae Miller:
Residence: 1930, Providence, Providence, Rhode Island[2504]

Notes for John Miller:
The Descendants of John J. Christner, privately published February 1961, p. 106.

Children of Edna Miller and Rayman Miller are:
+   1519   i.   Wilma[8] Miller, born 13 Sep 1926.
+   1520   ii.   Ada Marie Miller, born 28 Apr 1931.
    1521   iii. Alvin Miller, born 29 Apr 1933.

                Notes for Alvin Miller:
                The Descendants of John J. Christner, privately published February 1961, p. 107.

Child of Edna Miller and John Miller is:
    1522   i.   Melvin[8] Miller, born 31 Mar 1929. He married Gertrude Miller 24 Aug 1958; born 07 May 1937.

                Notes for Melvin Miller:
                The Descendants of John J. Christner, privately published February 1961, p. 107.

                Notes for Gertrude Miller:
                The Descendants of John J. Christner, privately published February 1961, p. 107.

447. Charles O.[7] Reckner (Mary[6] Christner, John[5], John J.[4], Johannes John Hans[3], Christian[2], Christen[1])[2505,2506,2507,2508] was born 27 Jun 1867 in MD[2509,2510,2511,2512], and died 22 Mar 1951 in Salisbury, Somerset Co., PA[2513,2514]. He married **Bertha Annie Tipton**[2514,2515] 1890[2515], daughter of John Tipton and Elizabeth Grimes. She was born 25 Dec 1872 in PA[2515,2516], and died 08 Nov 1941 in PA[2517].

More About Charles O. Reckner:
Residence: 1920, Elk Lick, Somerset, Pennsylvania[2518,2519]

More About Bertha Annie Tipton:
Residence: 1910, Jenner, Somerset, Pennsylvania[2520,2521]

Children of Charles Reckner and Bertha Tipton are:
    1523   i.   Eva E.[8] Reckner[2521,2522], born Mar 1890 in PA[2523,2524].

More About Eva E. Reckner:
Residence: 1900, Age: 10; Marital Status: Single; Relation to Head of House: Daughter/Elk Lick, Somerset, Pennsylvania[2525,2526]

1524   ii.   William Charles Reckner[2527,2528], born 27 May 1892 in PA[2529,2530]; died Jan 1963[2531].

More About William Charles Reckner:
Residence: 1910, Jenner, Somerset, Pennsylvania[2532,2533]

1525   iii.   Ella E. Reckner[2533,2534], born Jun 1894 in PA[2535,2536].

More About Ella E. Reckner:
Residence: 1910, Jenner, Somerset, Pennsylvania[2536,2537]

1526   iv.   James E. Reckner[2537,2538], born Feb 1896 in PA[2539,2540].

More About James E. Reckner:
Residence: 1910, Jenner, Somerset, Pennsylvania[2540,2541]

1527   v.   George Lee Reckner[2541,2542], born 14 Nov 1898 in PA[2543,2544].

More About George Lee Reckner:
Residence: 1910, Jenner, Somerset, Pennsylvania[2544,2545]

1528   vi.   Harry Rickner[2546], born 1899 in PA[2546].

More About Harry Rickner:
Residence: 1910, Jenner, Somerset, Pennsylvania[2546]

1529   vii.   Laurena Rickner[2546], born 1904 in PA[2546].

More About Laurena Rickner:
Residence: 1910, Jenner, Somerset, Pennsylvania[2546]

1530   viii.   Theodore R. Reckner[2547,2548], born 28 Jan 1904 in PA[2548,2549]; died 13 Dec 1990[2550,2551].

More About Theodore R. Reckner:
Residence: 1910, Age in 1910: 6; Marital Status: Single; Relation to Head of House: Son/Jenner, Somerset, Pennsylvania[2551,2552]

1531   ix.   Florence May Reckner[2553], born 28 Jan 1904 in PA[2553,2554]; died May 1975 in Jerome, Somerset Co., PA[2555].

More About Florence May Reckner:
Residence: 1920, Elk Lick, Somerset, Pennsylvania[2556]

1532   x.   Albert Rickner[2556], born 1907 in PA[2556].

More About Albert Rickner:
Residence: 1910, Jenner, Somerset, Pennsylvania[2556]

1533   xi.   John J. Reckner[2557,2558], born 1910 in PA[2559,2560]; died 1939 in Salisbury, Somerset Co., PA[2561].

More About John J. Reckner:
Residence: 1930, Age: 20; Marital Status: Married; Relation to Head of House: Brother-in-law/Conemaugh, Somerset, Pennsylvania[2561,2561,2562]

1534   xii.   Leroy Robert Reckner[2563], born 03 Jul 1912 in Jenners, Comerset Co., PA[2563]; died 22 Nov 1982 in Johnstown, Cambria Co., PA[2563].
1535   xiii.   Ethel Reckner[2563], born 29 Aug 1914 in Sailsbury, Somerset Co., PA[2563]; died 30 Mar 2011 in Somerset, Somerset Co., PA[2563].
1536   xiv.   Franklin A. Reckner[2563], born 08 Sep 1917 in Salisbury, Somerset Co., PA[2563]; died 28 May 1993 in Johnstown, Cambria Co., PA[2563].

More About Franklin A. Reckner:
Residence: 1910, Age in 1910: 3; Marital Status: Single; Relation to Head of House: Son/Jenner, Somerset, Pennsylvania[2563]

459. John Riley[7] Christner (Jacob[6], John[5], John J.[4], Johannes John Hans[3], Christian[2], Christen[1]) was born 01 Mar 1867 in West Moreland Co. PA, and died 13 Jul 1944 in Clarksburg, Harrison Co., WV. He married **(1) Ollie V. Goodwin** 25 Nov 1889 in Harrison Co., WV. She was born 10 Dec 1870 in Doddridge Co., WV, and died 29 May 1897 in Marion Co., WV. He married **(2) Jessie L. Cheuvrant** 25 Feb 1901 in ,M.P. Parsonage Fairmont, WV. She was born 1883 in Doddridge Co., WV.

Notes for John Riley Christner:
As a child, Noreita remembers her grandfather Rile growing a garden even though he had only one arm. At times, he was prone to over indulge in alcohol and his father-in-law , Asa N. Payne, would go to Clendenin to get him out of jail. Evidently this happened to him during his early years. He managed most daily task very well with one arm. He always grew tobacco and would hang it to dry under the front porch of the boarding house facing Elk River. As it would dry, he would twist it into a roll of approximately six inches. Because Noreita had a bad case of the colic, he would spend the "night shift" rocking her.

More About John Riley Christner:
Burial: 15 Jul 1944, Greenlawn Cemetery, Clarksburg, WV
Cause of Death: Prostate Cancer: Secondary-Structure of Urethra

Notes for Ollie V. Goodwin:
Ollie was only 16 at the time of her marriage to John

More About Ollie V. Goodwin:
Burial: 30 May 1897, Shaver Hill MonongahWV

Children of John Christner and Ollie Goodwin are:
+   1537   i.   Charles[8] Christner, born 01 Mar 1895 in Monoghelia, Marion Co., WV; died 10 Dec 1970 in Pearce Hospital, Salina, IL.
+   1538   ii.   Pearl Ada Christner, born 12 Apr 1897 in Monoghelia, Marion Co., WV; died 20 Aug 1981 in Milton Cabell Co. WV.

463. Nora Delia[7] Christner (Jacob[6], John[5], John J.[4], Johannes John Hans[3], Christian[2], Christen[1])[2564] was born 02 Jun 1873 in Harrison Co., WV[2564], and died 01 Sep 1964 in Clarksburg, Harrison Co., WV. She married **Guy Danley**.

More About Nora Delia Christner:
Burial: 03 Sep 1964, Greenlawn Cemetary Clarksburg Harrison Co. WV
Residence: 1880, Coal, Harrison Co., WV[2564]

Child of Nora Christner and Guy Danley is:
+   1539   i.   Carl[8] Danley, born 14 Aug 1895 in Clarksburg, Harrison Co., WV; died 17 Apr 1967 in Clarksburg, Harrison Co., WV.

464. Alfred[7] Christner (Jacob[6], John[5], John J.[4], Johannes John Hans[3], Christian[2], Christen[1])[2565,2566,2567,2568] was born 24 Oct 1876 in Harrison Co., WV[2569,2570,2571], and died 10 Dec 1947 in Fairmont, Marion Co., WV[2572,2573,2574]. He married **Clara Anna Yost**[2575,2576]. She was born 31 Mar 1881 in Wetzel Co. WV[2577,2578,2579], and died 13 Oct 1974 in Fairmont, Marion Co., WV[2580,2581].

Notes for Alfred Christner:
Birth: 24 Oct 1876
Death: Dec. 10, 1947

Burial: Grafton National Cemetery, Grafton, Taylor Co., WV
Plot: B, 0, 1526

More About Alfred Christner:
Burial: 12 Dec 1947, Grafton National Cemetery, Grafton, Taylor Co., WV
Cause of Death: Coroonary Thrombosis
Occupation: Electrician/
Residence: 1930, Eagle, Harrison Co., WV[2581,2582]

Notes for Clara Anna Yost:
Birth: Mar. 31, 1881
Death: Oct. 13, 1974

PVT, US ARMY

Burial: Grafton National Cemetery, Grafton, Taylor Co., WV
Plot: B, 0, 1527

More About Clara Anna Yost:
Burial: 15 Oct 1974, Grafton National Cemetery, Grafton, Taylor Co., WV
Residence: 1900, Fairmont, Marion Co., WV[2583,2584]
Social Security Number: 234-96-4298/[2585]
SSN issued: WV[2585]

Children of Alfred Christner and Clara Yost are:

	1540	i.	Ralph[8] Christner.
	1541	ii.	Irene Christner, born 13 Mar 1903; died 13 Oct 1975. She married Donald Weichart.
	1542	iii.	Hazel Christner, born 21 Apr 1906 in WV[2586]; died 26 Feb 1939 in Lewis, Upshur Co., WV[2587]. She married Doyle McCoy.

More About Hazel Christner:
Residence: 1920, Glenwood, Harrison Co., WV[2588]

	1543	iv.	Kenneth Christner[2589,2590,2591], born 17 Oct 1907 in Brandonville, Preston Co., WV[2592]; died 15 Jun 1970 in Warren, Trumbull Co., OH[2592]. He married Anna Mori.

More About Kenneth Christner:
Residence: 1930, Fairmont, Marion Co., WV[2592]

+	1544	v.	Ruby Christner, born 15 Jul 1913; died 20 Feb 1994 in Fairmont, Marion Co., WV.
+	1545	vi.	Horace Alfred Christner, born 15 Jan 1916 in Clarksburg, Harrison Co., WV; died 02 Jan 1994 in Capistrano, Orange Co., CA.
	1546	vii.	Lucille Christner, born 18 Aug 1918. She married Charles Brewer.
	1547	viii.	Maxine Christner, born 1920. She married Clarence Lowe.

469. James Hoy[7] Christner (Jacob[6], John[5], John J.[4], Johannes John Hans[3], Christian[2], Christen[1])[2593,2594,2595] was born 28 Jun 1886 in Harrison Co., WV[2596,2597], and died 13 Oct 1950 in Mannington, Marion Co., WV[2598]. He married **(1) Ada Claudia Boggess**[2599] 25 Feb 1909 in Fayette Co., PA. She was born 21 May 1883 in Eagle, Harrison Co., WV[2599], and died 1939 in Fairmont, Marion Co., WV[2600]. He married **(2) Eva Blanche Lowe**[2601] 16 Aug 1924 in Harrison Co., WV. She was born 18 Sep 1900 in Harrison Co., WV[2601], and died 18 Feb 1952 in Mannington, Marion Co., WV.

Notes for James Hoy Christner:
Birth: 1886
Death: 1950

Spouse: Eva Blanche Christner (1900 - 1952)

Children: Alfred Hoy Christner (1927 - 1992

Burial: Mannington Cemetery, Mannington, Marion Co., WV
Find A Grave Memorial# 93903650

Name: James Hoy Christner
Birth Date: 28 Jun 1886
Death Date: 13 Oct 1950
Death Place: Mannington, Marion, WV
Burial Date: 15 Oct 1950
Burial Place: WV
Cemetery Name: Mannington
Death Age: 64 years 4 months 15 days
Occupation: Coal Miner
Race: White
Marital Status: Married
Gender: Male
Father Name: Jacob Christner
Mother Name: Atlanta Reggar
FHL Film Number: 834819

More About James Hoy Christner:
Burial: 15 Oct 1950, Mannington Cemetery, Marion Co., WV
Cause of Death: Cancer of the Prostate
Occupation: Miner/
Residence: 1930, Fairmont, Marion Co., WV[2601,2602]

More About Ada Claudia Boggess:
Burial: Boggess Cemetery, Falls Mills, Marion Co., WV[2602]
Residence: 1910, Schuylkill, Schuykill Haven, PA[2602]

Notes for Eva Blanche Lowe:
Birth: 1900
Death: 1952

Spouse: James Hoy Christner (1886 - 1950)

Children: Alfred Hoy Christner (1927 - 1992)

Burial: Mannington Cemetery, Mannington,Marion Co., WV
Find A Grave Memorial# 93903678

More About Eva Blanche Lowe:
Burial: 20 Feb 1952, Mannington Cemetery, Marion Co., WV
Residence: Akron, Summit, OH, United States[2603]

Children of James Christner and Eva Lowe are:
+   1548   i.   Nora[8] Christner, born 13 Oct 1919; died 16 Apr 1990 in Republic, Ferry Co., WA.
+   1549   ii.   Lee Edward Christner, born 01 Jul 1921 in Harlan, KY; died 24 Mar 1984 in Fairmont, Marion Co., WV.
    1550   iii.   Roy Christner, born 17 May 1922 in Barracksville, Marion Co., WV; died 04 Mar 1993 in Canton, Stark Co., OH. He married Ruby Starkey 14 Oct 1946 in Marion Co., WV; born 22 Aug 1918 in Mannington, Marion Co., WV; died 17 Aug 1991 in Canton, Stark Co., OH.

             More About Roy Christner:
             Burial: Canton, Stark Co., OH

             More About Ruby Starkey:

Burial: Canton, Stark Co., OH

1551 iv. Viola Frances Christner, born 03 Aug 1925 in Dakota, Marion Co., WV; died 29 Oct 1927 in Fairmont, Marion Co., WV.

More About Viola Frances Christner:
Burial: 01 Nov 1927, Jones Cemetary Fairmont Marion Co. WV
Cause of Death: Aortic Insufficiency

+ 1552 v. Alfred Hoy Christner, born 28 Aug 1927 in Dakota, Marion Co., WV; died 12 Jul 1992 in Fairmont, Marion Co., WV.

+ 1553 vi. Mary Jo Christner, born 18 Oct 1930 in Barracksville, Marion Co., WV; died Mar 1957 in Fairmont, Marion Co., WV.

472. Mary Olive[7] McKenzie (Sarah Ellen "Helena"[6] Christner, John[5], John J.[4], Johannes John Hans[3], Christian[2], Christen[1]) was born 03 Jun 1866 in MD[2604], and died 24 Feb 1931[2605,2606]. She married **Lewis Joseph McKenzie**[2607,2608] 08 Feb 1887[2609]. He was born 21 Mar 1863 in Garrett Co., MD[2610], and died 12 Sep 1934 in Frostburg, Allegany Co., MD[2611].

Notes for Mary Olive McKenzie:
Birth: Jun. 3, 1866 - MD
Death: Feb. 24, 1931

Mary Olive MCKENZIE - 03 JUN1866 MD - 24FEB1931

She married Lewis Joseph McKenzie (1863-1934 s/o Isadore & Harriett)

Parents:
John L. Mckenzie (1842 - 1921)
Sarah Ellen Christner Mckenzie

Spouse: Lewis Joseph Mckenzie (1863 - 1934)

Children: John Lewis McKenzie (1901 - 1984)

Burial: Saint Anns Cemetery, Avilton, Garrett Co., PA
Find A Grave Memorial# 43649902

More About Mary Olive McKenzie:
Residence: 1920, Johnsons, Garrett Co., MD[2612]

Notes for Lewis Joseph McKenzie:
Birth: 1863
Death: 1934

Lewis Joseph Mckenzie
(1863-1934 s/o Isadore & Harriett)

Parents:
Isadore J McKenzie (1820 - 1907)
Harriet E Garlitz McKenzie (1835 - 1887)

Spouse: Mary Olive Mckenzie Mckenzie (1866 - 1931)

Children: John Lewis McKenzie (1901 - 1984)

Burial: Saint Anns Cemetery, Avilton, Garrett Co., MD
Find A Grave Memorial# 43649930

More About Lewis Joseph McKenzie:
Residence: 1920, Age: 56; Marital Status: Married; Relation to Head of House: Head/Johnsons, Garrett Co., MD[2613]

Children of Mary McKenzie and Lewis McKenzie are:

+ 1554   i.   Dorothy[8] McKenzie, born in MD; died in MD.
+ 1555   ii.   Edward Joseph McKenzie, born 02 Aug 1887 in MD; died 29 Aug 1957 in Frostburg, Allegany Co., MD.
  1556   iii. James Francis McKenzie[2614], born 08 Jul 1889[2614,2615]; died 29 May 1982[2616].

          More About James Francis McKenzie:
          Social Security Number: 221-10-1052/[2617]
          SSN issued: Delaware[2617]

+ 1557   iv.   Rose Blanche McKenzie, born 17 Jan 1891 in Union District, Grant Co., WV; died 30 Dec 1969 in Akron, Summit Co., OH.
+ 1558   v.   Leonard Clarence McKenzie, born 27 Jan 1893 in Eckhart, Allegany Co., MD; died 25 Jan 2011 in Cumberland, Allegany Co., MD.
  1559   vi.   Elizabeth Cecelia McKenzie[2618], born 03 Jul 1895[2618]; died 13 Jul 1960 in Garrett Co., MD[2618].
  1560   vii. Edith Sarah McKenzie[2618], born 15 Jun 1897[2618]; died 09 Oct 1919 in Garrett Co., MD[2618].
  1561   viii. Ruth Gertrude McKenzie[2618], born 15 Sep 1899[2618]; died 09 Mar 1986 in Akron, Summit Co., OH[2618].
  1562   ix.   John Lewis McKenzie[2618], born 31 Jan 1901[2618]; died 19 Sep 1984 in Akron, Summit Co., OH[2618].
+ 1563   x.   Thomas Patrick McKenzie, born 25 Jan 1906 in MD; died 17 Nov 1991 in Cumberland, Allegany Co., MD.

475. George Thomas[7] McKenzie (Sarah Ellen "Helena"[6] Christner, John[5], John J.[4], Johannes John Hans[3], Christian[2], Christen[1])[2619] was born 25 Mar 1871[2619], and died 01 Oct 1927 in Bolair, Webster Co., WV[2619]. He married **Anna Louisa (Annie) Carey**. She was born 16 May 1886 in Garrett Co., MD[2619,2620], and died Jun 1969 in Hyattsville, Prince Georges Co., MD[2621].

Notes for George Thomas McKenzie:
Thomas McKenzie Slain With Axe, in Webster Co., WV,
To be Burned (sic: Buried) Near Frostburg

The body of Thomas McKenzie, aged 51, who was murdered with an axe near his home on the Samuel Hill Farm, near Cam Caesar in Webster County, W. Va. was brought to the home of his mother, Mrs. John McKenzie in Garret county, a mile off the National Highway and six miles west of Frostburg, where burial will take place tomorrow. Mrs. McKenzie, 37, widow of the slain man and Seymour Smith, 28, are in Webster county jail at Webster Springs, charged with murder. The body was found about a third of a mile from the McKenzie home. A short distance from the body was discovered a double-bitted axe with blood on the handle. McKenzie's head had been hacked with an axe. There was one big gash in the forehead and three back of his head, one of which penetrated his skull. Mrs. McKenzie and Smith disclaim all knowledge of McKenzie's death. They say McKenzie left home early Saturday morning with a lantern in his hand. He later returned and placed the lantern on the front porch. Cumberland Evening Times, October 4, 1927
****
FINGER PRINTS THOUGHT CLUE IN M'KENZIE MURDER
Widow of Former Garrett Co. Man and Young Smith Held on Slaying Charge
Mrs. Annie McKenzie, widow of Thomas McKenzie, formerly of Garrett county, Md., near Frostburg, and Seymour Smith, youth, engaged to the oldest daughter of the McKenzies, were held Saturday on the charge of murder of Thomas McKenzie, following a hearing at Webster Springs, W.Va., and were remanded to jail for the action of the January Court. Laboratory examination of finger prints on a blood stained axe handle are being made. A chestnut leaf, supposed to be stained with human blood, was found between the McKenzie home and the laurel bush where the dead man's body was suspended. This, the authorities contend, tends to establish that the man was slain at his home and his body carried to the laurel bush.

SUICIDE THEORY SCOUTED

Little credence is put in the suicide theory. His body had been terribly mutilated, apparently by the axe found nearby, and was suspended by the chain from a laurel bush, with his hands tightly clasping a branch. There were four wounds in the head, any one of which might have been fatal, doctors say. Bloodhounds followed an alleged trail from the scene of the body's finding in the bedside of Smith in the McKenzie home where he was spending the weekend, and he was aroused by the bloodhounds licking his face, officers said. The McKenzies were married when he was 37 and she 17. They have nine children. The authorities say they have evidence that they quarreled frequently. Mckenzie was a lumberman and farmer. Smith, a railroad worker, was not his hired man, as was first reported. The body of McKenzie was brought to his former home, six miles west of Frostburg on the National Highway, for burial. Mrs. McKenzie, a former Garrett county woman, is said to have recently come into possession of a goodly sum of money from her father in Maryland. Cumberland Evening Times, October 10, 1927

He was buried on 27 Oct 1927 in Garrett Co., Maryland.

George Thomas MCKENZIE and Anna Louisa (Annie) CAREY were married about 1909. Anna Louisa (Annie) CAREY (daughter of James CAREY and Ada Louisa BLOCHER) was born on 16 May 1886 in Garrett Co., Maryland. She died on 19 Jun 1969 in Washington, D. C.. Webster Springs, W. Va., May 2 - The pedigree of bloodhounds and their trustworthiness in trailing human beings today entered into testimony at the trial of Mrs. Annie L. McKenzie, charged with the slaying of her husband, Thomas McKenzie, native of Garrett county, Md., a few miles west of Frostburg. According to state witnesses, the dogs owned by Deputy Sheriff O. D. Martin followed a scent from McKenzie's mutilated body to the bedside of Seymour Smith, 27, farmhand in the McKenzie home. The state alleges McKenzie was killed in his home and his body dragged to nearby woods. Martin testified his dogs were purebred animals and that they had been trained to trail only human beings. He was questioned closely by defense attorneys. Three blocks of wood cut from the floor of the McKenzie home were submitted as evidence yesterday. The wood is believed by authorities to contain blood stains from the slaying of McKenzie, a lumberman. A blood-stained ax and dyed cloth also were submitted and expert testimony on these articles was to be introduced later. Sheriff A. L. Gregory. Dr. J. D. Dodrill, E. L. Cutlip and Magistrate J. J. Morrison of Arcola were witnesses yesterday. The Cumberland Evening Times, May 2, 1928

LIFE SENTENCE FOR MURDER APPEALED;
WOMAN CONVICTED OF SLAYING HUSBAND ASKS
ERROR IN SUPREME COURT
Annie L. McKenzie of Webster Springs, sentenced several months ago in the Webster county circuit court to life imprisonment for the murder of her husband, Thomas McKenzie on October 1, 1927, petitioned the supreme court for a writ of error and supersedeas in the decision of the lower court. The petition was taken under advisement. William R. Offutt of Oakland, MD, who presented the application, contended in his oral argument to the court, "that the evidence which the state produced in the lower courts is not sufficient to sustain the verdict." Mrs. McKenzie was found guilty of murder in the first degree by the jury in the case which recommended mercy. Seymour Smith, jointly charged with Mrs. McKenzie of the crime was found guilty of murder in the second degree by the lower court. No application in behalf of Smith was filed. At the trial in the lower court, it was brought out that Smith, suitor of Ruby McKenzie, eldest daughter of Mrs. McKenzie and the murdered man, spent the night on which McKenzie was murdered at McKenzie's house. McKenzie was last seen alive at 5:30 o'clock Saturday morning, October 1, 1927, when he called Mrs. McKenzie. His body was found about 4:30 o'clock Saturday evening wedged in a laurel tree which grew about 2000 feet from the house. He had been knocked in the head with an axe or hatchet. Smith and Mrs. McKenzie were arrested and charged with the crime. The state, during the trial in the lower court, attempted to prove that a liason existed between Smith and Mrs. McKenzie. Charleston (WV) Daily Mail, November 13, 1928

SLAYER RELEASED, WILL BE RETRIED
Mrs. Anna McKenzie, Webster County, Now on Own Recognizance
WEBSTER SPRINGS - Jan 8 - (AP) Mrs. Anna L. McKenzie, 44 years old was released from the county jail yesterday on her own recognizance after having served two years of a life sentence in connection with the murder of her husband, Thomas McKenzie at Bolair in September, 1927. Mrs. McKenzie has been granted a new trial by the state supreme court. At her first trial, Mrs. McKenzie had been sentenced to life imprisonment in the state penitentiary but had never been removed to that institution from the county jail. Charleston Daily Mail, January 8, 1930.

Obituary:
The Cumberland Evening News
June 20, 1969

Mrs. Annie C. McKenzie, 83 of 6107 Osborn Road, Hyattsville and former resident of Star Route Frostburg, died yesterday at Cafritz Hospital, Washington, where she was admitted June 2. Born in Garrett County, she was the daughter of the late James and Ada Blocher Carey. Her husband, Thomas McKenzie, died in 1927. Surviving are six dauthers , Mrs. Vera McClure, Upper Glade, WV; Mrs. Ruby Cottrill, Hyattsville; Mrs. Myrtle Woodring, Bolair, WV; Mrs. Rhoda Murphy, Hyattsville, with whom she resided; Mrs. Nora Alt, Flintstone and Mrs. Georgia hildreth, Macon, GA; three sons, Daniel McKenzie, Bolair, WV; Norvel McKenzie, Star Route, Frostburg; one brother, Allen Carey, Star Route Frostburg,. She was buried in Blocher Cemetery, Grantsville, Garrett Co., MD.

Birth: 1871
Death: 1927

Spouse: Annie L McKenzie (1886 - 1969)

Burial: Blocher Cemetery, Garrett Co., MD
Find A Grave Memorial# 37695876

Notes for Anna Louisa (Annie) Carey:
FROSTBURG - Mrs. Annie C. McKenzie, 83, of 6107 Osborn Road, Hyattsville, and former resident of Star Route Frostburg, died yesterday at Cafritz Hospital, Washington, where she was admitted June 2. Born in Garrett County, she was the daughter of the late James and Ada (Blocher) Carey. Her husband, Thomas McKenzie, died in 1927. Surviving are six daughters, Mrs. Vera McClure, Upper Glade, W. Va.; Mrs. Ruby Cottrill, Hyattsville; Mrs. Myrtle Woodring, Bolair, W. Va.; Mrs. Rhoda Murphy, Hyattsville, with whom she resided; Mrs. Nora Alt, Flintstone; and Mrs. Georgia Hildreth, Macon, Ga.; three sons, Daniel McKenzie, Bolair, W. Va.; Norvel McKenzie, Star Route, Frostburg, and Melvin McKenzie, Keyser; two sisters, Mrs. George Robison, Cumberland; and Mrs. George Meese, Star Route, Frostburg; one brother, Allen Carey, Star Route, Frostburg; 24 grandchildren and 50 great-grandchildren. The body will be returned to the Durst Funeral Home, Frostburg. The Cumberland Evening Times, June 20, 1969 She was buried in Blocher Cemetery, Grantsville, Garrett Co., Maryland.

Birth: 1886
Death: 1969

Spouse: G. Thomas McKenzie (1871 - 1927)

Burial: Blocher Cemetery, Garrett Co., MD
Find A Grave Memorial# 37695882

More About Anna Louisa (Annie) Carey:
Residence: 1910, Falling Spring, Greenbrier Co., WV[2621]
Social Security Number: 578-62-9784/[2622]
SSN issued: District of Columbia[2622]

Children of George McKenzie and Anna Carey are:
1564	i.	George[8] McKenzie.
+ 1565	ii.	Verna Virginia McKenzie, born 11 Jun 1909 in WV; died 12 Jan 1999 in Upper Glade, Webster Co., WV.
1566	iii.	Ruby McKenzie[2623], born 10 Oct 1910 in WV[2623]; died 19 Oct 2003 in Allegany Co., MD[2623]. She married Bartlett Cottrell 09 Dec 1929 in Cowan, Webster Co., WV; born 1909 in Cowan, Webster Co., WV.
1567	iv.	Myrtle Catherine McKenzie, born 1912 in WV. She married Clarence Woodring[2624] 26 Nov 1930 in Webster Co., WV; born 03 Oct 1908 in Wirt Co., WV[2624]; died 04 Jan 1988 in Cowen, Webster Co., WV[2624].

More About Clarence Woodring:
Social Security Number: 232-26-9293/[2624]
SSN issued: North Carolina or West Virginia[2624]

1568   v.   Daniel Freeman McKenzie[2625], born 19 Dec 1913[2626,2627]; died 25 Dec 1989 in Staunton, Staunton Co.,
              VA[2628,2629]. He married Arlene McAvoy[2629] 08 Nov 1938 in Nicholas Co., WV[2629]; born 19 Jul 1918 in
              Webster Co., WV[2629,2630]; died 23 Jun 1985 in Webster Co., WV[2631].

       More About Daniel Freeman McKenzie:
       Social Security Number: 235-05-8337/[2632]
       SSN issued: WV[2632]

       More About Arlene McAvoy:
       Social Security Number: 234-58-6776/[2633]
       SSN issued: WV[2633]

1569   vi.   Rhoda Renee McKenzie[2634], born 17 Nov 1916 in WV[2634]; died 06 Apr 2006 in Sun City, Hillsborough
              Co., FL[2634]. She married Kilpatrick.
1570   vii. Norvell Lee McKenzie, born 28 Jan 1918 in Webster Co., WV[2635]; died 24 Jun 1997 in Frostburg,
              Allegany Co., MD.

       Notes for Norvell Lee McKenzie:
       Obituary: Cumberland Times News - 25 Jun 1997

       FROSTBURG - Norvel Lee McKenzie, 79 of 17631 National Pike, Frostburg, (Garrett County), MD,
       died Tuesday, June 24, 1997 at Sacred Heart Hospital, Cumberland. Born Jan 28, 1918 in webster Co.,
       WV, he was the son of the late George Thomas and Annie (Carey) McKenzie. he also was preceded in
       death by two brothers, Melvin and Dan McKenzie and one sister, Nora Mae Alt. Mr. McKenzie was
       formerly employed in the Warp Knitting Department of the Celanese Corporation and was a farmer. He
       was a United States Army Veteran of World War II and a member of the American Legion and VFW,
       both of Frostburg and Mount Zion United Methodist Church. Surviving are five sisters, Verna McClure,
       Upper Glade, WV; Ruby Cottrill, Cowen, WV; Myrtle Woodring, Bolair WV; Rhoda Kilpatrick, Sun
       City, FL and Georgia Hildreth, Alexandria, VA. Friends will be received at the Newman Funeral Home,
       Grantsville on Friday from 2 to 6 pm. Services will be conducted at the funeral home on Saturday at 10
       am witht he Rev. Warren Friend officiating. Internment will be in Blocher Cemetery.

       More About Norvell Lee McKenzie:
       Social Security Number: 217-10-4072/[2635]
       SSN issued: MD[2635]

1571   viii. Norma/Nora Mae McKenzie[2636], born 01 Dec 1920 in Webster Co., WV[2636]; died 19 Jul 1990[2636,2637].
1572   ix.   Melvin Noah McKenzie[2638], born 01 Dec 1920 in Webster Co., WV[2638,2639]; died 03 Dec 1974 in Keyser,
              Mineral Co., WV[2640,2641].

       More About Melvin Noah McKenzie:
       Social Security Number: 220-10-9002/[2641]
       SSN issued: MD[2641]

477. James Harris[7] **McKenzie** (Sarah Ellen "Helena"[6] Christner, John[5], John J.[4], Johannes John Hans[3],
Christian[2], Christen[1])[2642,2643] was born 03 Jul 1873 in MD[2644,2645], and died 13 Apr 1959 in Frostburg, Allegany
Co., MD[2645]. He married **Jeanetta Genettie Frances Jenny Painter**[2645] 02 Aug 1901 in Tucker, WV[2645]. She
was born 03 Sep 1888 in Elkins, Randolph Co., WV[2645], and died 17 Feb 1977 in Frostburg, Allegany Co.,
MD[2645].

Notes for James Harris McKenzie:
Death - Accidental (Struck by car) - The Cumberland Evening Times, April 14, 1959

He was born on 3 Jul 1873 in Maryland and died on 13 Apr 1959 in Frostburg, Allegany Co., Maryland. James
Harris McKenzie, 85, Frostburg, died last night in Miners Hospital where he was admitted last week after being
struck by an automobile. McKenzie was seriously injured last Tuesday afternoon when he was struck by a car
operated by Francis H. Lutz, Baltimore. The accident occurred along U.S. Route 40, about one mile west of

Frostburg. State Police, who investigated, said Mr. McKenzie resided in the area of the accident and was crossing the highway when he was struck. Police said McKenzie apparently failed to see the Lutz car and walked into the path of the vehicle. He sustained a compound fracture of the right leg, fractured shoulder and multiple lacerations of his face and forehead. Mr. McKenzie was the son of the late John and Sarah (Christner) McKenzie. He was a member of St. Michael's Catholic Church. Survivors include his widow, Mrs. Jeanette (Painter) McKenzie; nine daughters, Mrs. Robert Wiley, Los Angeles, Calif.; Mrs. John McKenzie, Akron; Mrs. Harold Wampler, Manassas, Va.; Mrs. William Beechie, Vale Summit; Mrs. Evelyn Leary, Baltimore; Mrs. Beulah McKenzie, Akron; Mrs. Charles Yoder, Glen Burnie; Mrs. Warren Snyder, Pittsburgh; and Mrs. Joy Perkins, Midland; five sons, Lawrence, James, Frank and Edgar McKenzie, all of Frostburg, and Glen McKenzie, Eckhart. Also surviving are three sisters, Mrs. Emma Younkin, Washington; Mrs. Elizabeth Baker, Frostburg, and Mrs. Eulah Robison, Eckhart; two brothers, Jacob McKenzie, Frostburg, and Joseph McKenzie, Avilton; 49 grandchildren and 25 great-grandchildren. The body will be at the Durst Funeral Home in Frostburg after 7 p.m. today. The family will receive friends at the funeral home today from 7 to 9 p.m. and tomorrow from 2 to 4 and 7 to 9 p.m.

James Harris MCKENZIE and Jeanetta PAINTER were married. Jeanetta PAINTER was born about 1889 in Elkins, Randolph Co., West Virginia. She died on 17 Feb 1977 in Oakland, Garrett Co., Maryland. FROSTBURG - Mrs. Jeanetta F. McKenzie, 88, of RD 2, died yesterday at Cuppett-Weeks Nursing Home, Oakland, where she had resided 16 months. Born in Elkins, she was a daughter of Adam and Barbara Painter, and was the widow of James H. McKenzie. She was a member of St. Michael's Catholic Church. Surviving are eight daughters, Mrs. Fred Wiley, Los Angeles, Cal.; Mrs. Agnes McKenzie, Mrs. Beulah McKenzie, Akron, Ohio; Mrs. Leota Wampler, LaVale; Mrs. Jeanetta Yoder, Glen Burnie; Mrs. Mabel Beechie, Vale Summit; Mrs. Imogene Snyder, Export, Pa.; and Mrs. Joy Perkins, Midland; three sons, James McKenzie, Brunswick; Glenn McKenzie, Eckhart, and Edgar McKenzie, Lonaconing; 49 grandchildren, and 63 great-grandchildren. The body is at the Durst Funeral Home, where friends will be received from 7 until 9 p.m. A Christian wake service will be held there today at 7:30 p.m. Mass of Christian Burial will be celebrated tomorrow at 11 a.m. at St. Michael's Catholic Church. Interment will be in Mt. Zion Cemetery, Route 40, Garrett County.

The Cumberland Evening Times, February 18, 1977

More About James Harris McKenzie:
Residence: 01 Apr 1940, Garrett Co., MD[2645,2645,2646]

More About Jeanetta Genettie Frances Jenny Painter:
Residence: 01 Apr 1940, Garrett Co., MD[2647]

Children of James McKenzie and Jeanetta Painter are:

1573   i. Freda Alta[8] McKenzie[2647], born 17 Sep 1904 in Davis, Tucker Co., WV[2647]; died 28 Nov 1998 in Westminster, Orange Co., CA[2647].

        More About Freda Alta McKenzie:
        Residence: 1930, Los Angeles, Los Angeles, California[2647]

1574   ii. Leota Beatrice McKenzie[2647], born 07 Apr 1905 in Avilton, Garrett Co., MD[2647]; died 24 Apr 1981 in Cumberland, Allegany Co., MD[2647].

        More About Leota Beatrice McKenzie:
        Residence: 1920, Johnsons, Garrett Co., MD[2647]

1575   iii. Agnes Mae Barbara McKenzie[2647], born 18 Aug 1907 in Frostburg, Allegany Co., MD[2647]; died 15 Jun 2001 in Akron, Summit Co., OH[2647].

        More About Agnes Mae Barbara McKenzie:
        Residence: 1920, Johnsons, Garrett Co., MD[2647]

1576   iv. Mabel F Mckenzie[2647], born 07 Jan 1911 in Garrett Co., MD[2647]; died 17 Mar 1989 in Cumberland, Allegany Co., MD[2647].

        More About Mabel F Mckenzie:
        Residence: 1920, Johnsons, Garrett Co., MD[2647]

1577   v.   Lawrence Leo Mckenzie[2647], born 14 Jul 1912 in Garrett Co., MD[2647]; died 02 Jan 1976 in Baltimore, Baltimore Co., MD[2647].

More About Lawrence Leo Mckenzie:
Residence: 1920, Johnsons, Garrett Co., MD[2647]

1578   vi.   Beulah L. Mckenzie[2647], born 08 Apr 1916 in Elkins, Randolph Co., WV[2647]; died 08 Jun 2000 in Canton, Stark Co., OH[2647].

More About Beulah L. Mckenzie:
Residence: 1920, Johnsons, Garrett Co., MD[2647]

1579   vii.   Jeanetta Elizabeth McKenzie[2647], born 06 May 1918 in MD[2647]; died 05 Jul 2009 in Mt Airy, MD[2647].

More About Jeanetta Elizabeth McKenzie:
Residence: 1920, Johnsons, Garrett Co., MD[2647]

1580   viii.   Glen Robert Mckenzie Sr Pvt[2647], born 13 Mar 1920 in Avilton, Garrett Co., MD[2647]; died 05 Dec 2007 in Lonaconing, Allegany Co., MD[2647].

More About Glen Robert Mckenzie Sr Pvt:
Residence: Bet. 1935 - 1993, Frostburg, MD[2647]

1581   ix.   James Kenneth McKenzie Sr[2647], born 20 Nov 1921 in Grantsville, Garrett Co., MD[2647]; died 14 Jan 1993 in Meyersdale, Somerset Co., PA[2647].

More About James Kenneth McKenzie Sr:
Residence: 01 Apr 1940, Garrett Co., MD[2647]

1582   x.   Frank Clement McKenzie Sr[2647], born 08 Dec 1923 in Frostburg, Allegany Co., MD[2647]; died 18 May 1970 in Morgantown, Monongalia Co., WV[2647].

More About Frank Clement McKenzie Sr:
Residence: 01 Apr 1940, Garrett Co., MD[2647]

1583   xi.   Edgar Lewis Mckenzie[2647], born 29 Dec 1925 in Garrett Co., MD[2647]; died 16 Oct 1999 in Lonaconing, Allegany Co., MD[2647].

More About Edgar Lewis Mckenzie:
Residence: 01 Apr 1940, Garrett Co., MD[2647]

478. Samuel Gregory[7] McKenzie (Sarah Ellen "Helena"[6] Christner, John[5], John J.[4], Johannes John Hans[3], Christian[2], Christen[1])[2648] was born 03 Nov 1877 in Garrett Co., MD[2648], and died 05 Mar 1947 in Frostburg, Allegany Co., MD[2648]. He married **Caroline Jenkins**. She was born 01 Sep 1866, and died Sep 1922 in Dayton, Montgomery Co., OH.

Notes for Samuel Gregory McKenzie:
He born on 3 Nov 1877 in Garrett Co., Maryland. He died due to a cerebral hemorrhage on 5 Mar 1947 in Frostburg, Allegany Co., Maryland. Death Certificate courtesy of Don Kagle He was buried on 8 Mar 1947 in St. Ann's Catholic Cemetery, Avilton, Garrett Co., Maryland.

Samuel Gregory MCKENZIE and Caroline JENKINS were married. Caroline JENKINS died in Sep 1922 in Dayton, Montgomery Co., Ohio. Mrs. Grant McKenzie, aged 56, formerly of Cumberland, died at her late home, 256 Maple street, Dayton, OH of complication of diseases. The funeral took place Thursday at 2 o'clock with service at the home. Mrs. McKenzie is survived by her husband, Grant McKenzie, one daughter, Mrs. Meta Hiltner; two sons, Roy McKenzie, of Dayton, O., and Ervin McKenzie, Cumberland, and Mrs. William Fuller, of Cumberland, who is a sister. The Cumberland Evening Times, October 3, 1922 Samuel Gregory MCKENZIE and Caroline JENKINS

More About Samuel Gregory McKenzie:
Residence: 1910, District 9, Garrett, Maryland[2648]

Notes for Caroline Jenkins:
Caroline JENKINS died in Sep 1922 in Dayton, Montgomery Co., OH. Mrs. Grant McKenzie, aged 56 formerly of Cumberland, died at her late home, 256 Maple street, Dayton, OH of complication of diseases. The funeral took place Thursday at 2 o'clock with service at the home. Mrs. McKenzie is survived by her husband, Grant McKenzie, one daughter, Mrs. Meta Hiltner; two sons, Roy McKenzie, of Dayton, OH and Ervin McKenzie, Cumberland, and Mrs. William Fuller of Cumberland, who is a sister. The Cumberland Evening Times, October 3, 1922.

Children of Samuel McKenzie and Caroline Jenkins are:
- 1584   i.   Harry Roy[8] McKenzie.
- 1585   ii.   Meta McKenzie.
- 1586   iii. Sanford Ervin McKenzie[2649], born 28 Oct 1891 in Cumberland, Allegany Co., MD[2649]; died 11 Jul 1948 in Cumberland, Allegany Co., MD.

> More About Sanford Ervin McKenzie:
> Residence: 1942, Allegany, Maryland[2649]

480.   Emma Theresa[7] McKenzie (Sarah Ellen "Helena"[6] Christner, John[5], John J.[4], Johannes John Hans[3], Christian[2], Christen[1])[2650,2651] was born 07 Apr 1884 in Pine Grove, MD[2652], and died 07 Dec 1961 in Meyerstown, Somerset Co., PA[2653]. She married **Milton Younkin**. He died 12 Feb 1933.

Notes for Emma Theresa McKenzie:
Obituary: The Cumberland Evening Times, December 8, 1961

GRANTSVILLE - Mrs. Emma Younkin, 77, of here, died yesterday in Meyersdale (Pa.) Community Hospital. She had been in ill health five years. A native of Garrett County, she was a daughter of the late John and Sarah (Christner) McKenzie. Her husband, Milton Younkin, preceded her in death. Mrs. Younkin was a member of St. Stephen's Catholic Church. Surviving are two daughters, Mrs. Rozella Long, Baltimore, and Sister Eileen, St. Therese's Hospital, Waukegan, Illinois; two brothers, Jacob, Frostburg, and Joseph McKenzie, Lonaconing; two sisters, Mrs. Bessie Baker, Frostburg, and Mrs. Eleleh Robison, Lonaconing, and two grandchildren. A requiem mass will be celebrated tomorrow at 10 a.m. at St. Stephen's Church by Rev. Conrad Raffel. Burial will be in Grantsville Cemetery. The body is at the residence, where the rosary will be recited today at 8 p.m.

More About Emma Theresa McKenzie:
Residence: 1900, Election Distrists 9, 11, Johnsons, The Elbow, Garrett, MD[2653]

Children of Emma McKenzie and Milton Younkin are:
- 1587   i.   Eileen[8] Younkin.
- 1588   ii.   Bernard C. Younkin[2653], born 1907 in MD[2653]; died 13 Feb 1933 in Frostburg, Allegany Co., MD[2653].

> Notes for Bernard C. Younkin:
> Obituary: The Cumberland Evening Times, February 14, 1933
>
> The funeral of Bernard C. Younkin, 26; who died Sunday night in Miners' Hospital, Frostburg, from a fractured skull, when struck by a falling pole, will be held at 9 o'clock Wednesday morning from St. Stephen's Catholic Church here. Burial will be In Grantsville cemetery. He was a member of the Grantsville Fire Department and Woodmen of the World Camp at Grantsville. Younkin, with several others, was helping in the erection of poles for a private electric light line from the National Highway to the lodge of Marshall Pressman, Frostburg, along the Castleman River. A 35-feet pole being raised with pike poles slipped and began to fall. Younkin stumbled and fell as he stepped to the side, and the toppling pole struck him back of the head. He was brought to the hospital about 5 o'clock and died several hours later. He is survived by his parents, Mr. and Mrs. Milton Younkin; two sisters, Rosella, at home, and Sister Eileen, St. Monica's convent, Milwaukee, WI.

- 1589   iii. Rozella Younkin, born Abt. 1916.

481. Ruth[7] McKenzie (Sarah Ellen "Helena"[6] Christner, John[5], John J.[4], Johannes John Hans[3], Christian[2], Christen[1])[2654] was born 29 Mar 1886 in Pine Grove, MD[2654,2655], and died 08 Sep 1952 in Orange Co., TX[2656,2657]. She married **Grover Francis Carey**. He was born 24 Sep 1887[2657], and died 1919[2657].

Notes for Ruth McKenzie:
Obituary: The Cumberland Evening Times, September 9, 1952

FROSTBURG - Mrs. Grover Carrie, 66, of Orange, Texas, died yesterday. A native of Garrett County, she was a daughter of the late John and Sarah McKenzie. Survivors include four brothers, James, John and Jacob McKenzie, all of Frostburg, and Joseph McKenzie, Cumberland, and three sisters, Mrs. Alan Baker, Frostburg; Mrs. Milton Younkin, Grantsville, and Mrs. Bruce Robeson, Fllntstone. Services will be conducted there tomorrow.

More About Ruth McKenzie:
Burial: Orange Co., TX[2657]
Residence: 1900, Election Distrists 9, 11, Johnsons, The Elbow, Garrett, Maryland[2658]

More About Grover Francis Carey:
Residence: Garrett, Maryland[2659]

Child of Ruth McKenzie and Grover Carey is:
  1590   i.   Enid Carol Carey[8] Gholson[2660], born 06 Aug 1917 in Frostburg, Allegany Co., MD[2660]; died 06 Jul 2002 in Beaumont, Jefferson Co., Texas[2660].

            More About Enid Carol Carey Gholson:
            Burial: 11 Jul 2002, Orange, Orange Co., Texas[2660]
            Event: 11 Jun 1934, in a taxi by a Justice Of The Peace in front of the Harris Co. Court House/Houston, Harris Co., Texas[2660]

482. Jacob Henry[7] McKenzie (Sarah Ellen "Helena"[6] Christner, John[5], John J.[4], Johannes John Hans[3], Christian[2], Christen[1])[2661,2662,2663] was born 15 Apr 1888 in Garrett Co., MD[2663], and died 06 Nov 1972 in Hagerstown Washington Co., MD[2663]. He married **Lucy McKenzie** 23 May 1909 in St. Michael's Catholic Church, Frostburg, Allegany Co., MD[2664]. She was born 31 Dec 1884 in Garrett Co., MD[2664], and died 27 Jul 1915 in Johnson, Garrett Co., MD[2664].

Notes for Jacob Henry McKenzie:
Jacob H. McKenzie, 84, of Grantsville, died Nov. 6, 1972, in Western Maryland State Hospital in Hagerstown. Born in Garrett County, Md., he was a son of the late John and Sarah E. (Christner) McKenzie. His wife the former Lucy McKenzie, preceded him in death. Surviving are two sons, James H. Frankhauser, Keyser, W. Va.; and Cecil B. McKenzie, Cumberland; a daughter, Mrs. Uleleh Krause, Grantsville; eight grandchildren, 13 great-grandchildren, three great-great-grandchildren and a sister, Mrs. Lela Robinson, Eckhart, Md. Funeral service was conducted Wednesday afternoon in Newman Funeral Home, Grantsville, with Rev. Paul Lovejoy officiating. Interment in St. Ann's Catholic Cemetery. Meyersdale Republican, November 9, 1972

GRANTSVILLE - Jacob H. McKenzie, 84, of here, died yesterday at the Western Maryland State Hospital in Hagerstown. Born in Garrett County, he was a son of the late John and Sarah E. (Christner) McKenzie. His wife, Lucy (McKenzie) McKenzie, preceded him in death. He is survived by two sons, James H. Frankhauser, Keyser, and Cecil B. McKenzie, Cumberland; a daughter, Mrs. Uleleh Krause, Grantsville; a sister, Mrs. Lela Robinson, Eckhart; eight grandchildren, 12 great-grandchildren and three great-great-grandchildren. The body is at the Newman Funeral Home, here, where friends will be received today from 2 to 4 and 7 to 9 p.m. Services will be conducted Wednesday at 2 p.m. at the funeral home by Rev . Paul Lovejoy. Interment will be in St. Ann's Catholic Cemetery. The Cumberland News, November 7, 1972
He was buried in St. Ann's Catholic Cemetery, Avilton, Garrett Co., Maryland.

Jacob Henry MCKENZIE and Lucy Alice MCKENZIE were married on 23 May 1909 in St. Michael's Catholic Church, Frostburg, Allegany Co., Maryland. Lucy and Jacob Henry are firs cousins and needed special permission to marry. Lucy Alice MCKENZIE (daughter of Francis Patrick MCKENZIE and Sarah Margaret GARLITZ) was born on 30 Dec 1883 in Garrett Co., Maryland. Death Certificate lists 1883, which is different from Christening record. She was christened on 27 May 1885 in St. Michael's Catholic Church, Frostburg, Allegany Co., Maryland. WESTERN MARYLAND CATHOLICS 1819-1851
MCKENZIE, LUCIAM ALICIAM of Francis McKenzie & Sarah Maragaretha Garlitz b 31 December 1884 in Garrett Co., MD; c 27 May 1885 Sponsors Thomas Beane & Sarah Anna McKenzie by Fr. V.F. Schmitt p 270 (married to Jacob H.
McKenzie on May 23 1909 by Fr. S. Cuddy p. 270)
She died of a bowel obstruction on 27 Jul 1915 in Johnson, Garrett Co., Maryland.

McKENZIE - 28 Jul 1915 - Mrs. Jacob McKenzie, aged 31 years, died yesterday at her home on National Pike near Johnson, Garrett Co. from an illness of 6 days from stomach trouble. She was formerly Miss Lucy McKenzie, both families being old residents of this section. She was mother of 6 children, ranging in age from 3 months to 6 years. Also surviving are 4 brothers and 5 sisters: Olin, Noah, George, and Peter of Garrett Co; and Anna and Laura at home; Mrs. Robert Walker of Salisbury, Pa.; Mrs. Richard McKenzie of Garrett Co.; and Mrs. Edward Lynch of WV. Burial services in Garrett Co. Cumberland Times obituary transcription, AlleganyCoGenWeb

Mrs. Robert Walker received the sad news on Tuesday morning of the sudden death of her sister, Mrs. Jacob McKenzie, of near Frostburg. [NOTE: Obituary located in the Salisbury column.] Meyersdale Commercial, July 29, 1915

More About Jacob Henry McKenzie:
Residence: Allegany, MD[2664]

More About Lucy McKenzie:
Residence: 1910, District 9, Garrett, MD[2664]

Children of Jacob McKenzie and Lucy McKenzie are:
  1591   i.   Luella Alice[8] McKenzie.
  1592   ii.   Ulela C. McKenzie[2664], born 1909 in MD[2664].

                  More About Ulela C. McKenzie:
                  Residence: 1910, District 9, Garrett, MD[2664]

  1593   iii.   Sarah Ellen McKenzie[2664], born 10 Nov 1910 in MD[2664]; died 23 Jul 1965[2664].

                  More About Sarah Ellen McKenzie:
                  Residence: 1920, Johnsons, Garrett, MD[2664]

  1594   iv.   Cecil Benedict McKenzie[2664], born 07 Apr 1915[2665]; died 30 Nov 1977 in Cumberland, Allegany Co., MD[2666].

                  Notes for Cecil Benedict McKenzie:
                  Birth: Apr. 7, 1915
                  Death: Nov. 30, 1977

                  Burial: - Saint Anns Cemetery, Avilton, Garrett Co., MD
                  Find A Grave Memorial# 74570760

                  More About Cecil Benedict McKenzie:
                  Other-Begin: Cumberland, Allegany, Maryland, United States of America[2667]
                  Social Security Number: 216-14-5738/[2667]
                  SSN issued: MD[2667]

490. William Henry[7] Diehl (Elizabeth[6] Christner, Jacob C.[5], John J.[4], Johannes John Hans[3], Christian[2],

Christen[1])[2668,2669,2670,2671,2671,2671,2672,2673] was born 31 Mar 1864 in Cove, Garrett Co., MD[2674,2675,2676,2677], and died 31 May 1935 in West Salisbury, Somerset Co., PA[2677,2678,2678,2678]. He married **Fredericka Gerke**[2679,2680,2681,2682] 03 May 1890 in Morgan Station, Upper Tyrone Twp., Fayette Co., PA. She was born 01 Jul 1871 in Connellsville, Fayette Co., PA[2683,2684], and died 13 Apr 1955 in West Saisbury, Somerset Co., PA.

Notes for William Henry Diehl:
Name: William Henry Diehl
Sex: M
Birth: 31 Mar 1864 in Cove, MD
Death: 31 May 1935 in West Salisbury, Elklick Twp., Somerset Co., PA
Burial: 3 June 1935 I.O.O.F. Cemetery, Salisbury, PA
Occupation: retired coal miner, carpenter

Obituary:

William H. Diehl, a citizen of West Salisbury for about 45 years, died very suddenly at his home in that village on Friday morning, May 31, 1935, at the age of 71 years and 2 months. He was the son of the late Henry C. Diehl and Elizabeth Christner Diehl, and was born in the Cove of Garrett Co., MD, where he also grew to manhood. His death was brought on by complications which resulted from an accident which befell him in November 1929, while employed in coal mine, at which time his back was badly injured. He never fully recovered from his injuries, and was never able to do much work after the day he was injured.

Mr. Diehl was a good and useful citizen, and in addition to working in the mines for many years, he also at intervals worked at the stone mason trade.

His wife who survives him; was Fredericka Gurke, a resident of Fayette Co., PA, before her marriage. Eight children born to Mr. And Mrs. Diehl also survive, as follows: Henry of West Salisbury; Minnie wife of Ernest Holler, of Boyton, William J. of Salisbury; Edna, wife of Miles Glotfelty, of Pittsburgh; Margaret wife of Leon Brown, of Salisbury, Edith, George and Earl, at home. She is also survived by two brothers, George of Republic and Samuel of Jerome, and three sisters; Mrs. Laura Hawkins. Mrs. Emma Henessy and Mrs. Andrew Taylor, of Republic; Mrs. Smith Newcomer and Mrs. C. H. Hampshire of Connellsville; Mrs. Henry Johnson of Mill Run; also by a number of grandchildren. The funeral services was held at the Diehl residence in West Salisbury, last monday at 2:00 pm, conducted by Rev. E. V. May, pastor of the Meyersdale and Salisbury Methodist Episcopal Churches. Bring a member of the local tribe of the Improved Order of Red Men, Mr. Diehl's brethren of that fraternal organization participated in the funeral rites in the I.O.O.F. Cemetery in Salisbury, where his remains were interred. The burial arrangements were in charge of Mortician W. C. Price of Meyersdale.

More About William Henry Diehl:
Burial: 03 Jun 1935, IOOF Cemetery, Salisbury, Somerset Co., PA
Causes of Death: Heart disease, likely coronary thromboses
Death Certificate: 31 May 1935, Elk Lick Twp., Somerset Co., PA - file # 51721 from heart disease, likely cornoney thrombosis
Mariage: 03 May 1890, G. A. Firgan, Pastor
Occupation: Coal Miner & Carpenter/
Residence: 1910, Elk Lick, Somerset Co., PA[2685]

More About Fredericka Gerke:
Burial: 16 Apr 1955, IOOF Cemetery, Salisbury, Somerset Co., PA
Residence: 1910, Elk Lick, Somerset Co., PA[2685]

Children of William Diehl and Fredericka Gerke are:
+ 1595   i.   Henry C.[8] Diehl, born 08 Mar 1891 in Connellsville, Fayette Co., PA; died 17 Nov 1968 in Meyersdale, Somerset Co., PA.
+ 1596   ii.   Elizabeth Wilhelmina Diehl, born 28 Jul 1893 in Connellsville, Fayette Co., PA; died 29 Mar 1955 in Meyersdale, Somerset Co., PA.
   1597   iii.   Minnie Diehl[2686], born 1894 in Connellsville, Fayette Co., PA[2686].

     More About Minnie Diehl:

Residence: 1910, Elk Lick, Somerset, PA[2686]

+ 1598   iv.   William James Diehl, born 28 Jan 1896 in Connellsville, Fayette Co., PA; died 13 Apr 1974 in Cumberland, Allegany Co., MD.

+ 1599   v.   Edna May Diehl, born 25 Aug 1898 in Connellsville, Fayette Co., PA; died 26 Mar 1991 in Monroeville, Allegheny Co., PA.

+ 1600   vi.   Edith Mary Diehl, born 24 Dec 1904 in W. Salisbury, Somerset Co., PA; died 19 Dec 1985 in Boynton, Somerset Co., PA.

+ 1601   vii.   Marguerite Christianna Gerke Diehl, born 16 Oct 1908 in W. Salisbury, Somerset Co., PA; died 11 Oct 1994 in W. Salisbury, Somerset Co., PA.

+ 1602   viii.   George Edward Diehl, born 31 Mar 1911 in W. Salisbury, Somerset Co., PA; died 09 Oct 2002 in Meyersdale, Somerset Co., PA.

+ 1603   ix.   Earl Robert Diehl, born 16 Aug 1914 in W. Salisbury, Somerset Co., PA; died 18 Sep 1977 in Salisbury, Somerset Co., PA.

491. Laura Catherine[7] Diehl (Elizabeth[6] Christner, Jacob C.[5], John J.[4], Johannes John Hans[3], Christian[2], Christen[1])[2687] was born 23 Sep 1865 in Somerset Co., MD[2687], and died 03 Nov 1959 in South Union Twp., Uniontown, Fayette Co., PA[2688]. She married **Lemuel J. Hawkins** 26 Apr 1905 in Clarksburg, Harrison Co., WV. He was born Dec 1877 in Bridgeport, Harrison Co., WV, and died 23 Jul 1913 in Memorial Hospital, Mongehelia, Allegheny Co., PA.

Notes for Laura Catherine Diehl:
Residence: 1918 According to Henry C. Diehl's obit she lived in Donora, Fayette Co., PA.

Birth: Sep. 23, 1865 - Somerset Co., PA
Death: Nov. 3, 1959 - Uniontown, Fayette Co., PA

Obituary: The Evening Standard, Uniontown, PA, 4 Nov 1959.

Laura Catherine Hawkins, aged 94 years of New Salem Road died at 2:45 p.m. Tuesday, November 3, 1959. She was born September 23, 1865 in Somerset County and was the widow of Lynn Hawkins. She was a member of the Pleasant View Presbyterian Church. Surviving are one daughter, Mr. Clara Donovan of Seguine, Texas; two brothers, Samuel Diehl, Jerome, PA; George Diehl, Cleveland, OH; two sisters, Mrs. Emma Hennessy and Mr. Edna Taylor, both of Republic; five grandchildren; twelve great grandchildren and five great great grandchildren. Friends will be received at the C.B. Dearth Botis Funeral Home, New Salem, after 7 p.m. today and until Friday at 2 p.m. the hour of service with Rev. George F. Conley, her pastor officiating. Burial will be in the Lafayette Memorial Park.

Parents:
Henry C. Diehl (1842 - 1918)
Elizabeth Christner Diehl (1844 - 1918)

Children: Clara Elizabeth Donavan (1885 - 1967)

Note: No headstone

Burial: LaFayette Memorial Park, Brier Hill, Fayette Co., PA
Plot: St. Matthew section, 183-1
Find A Grave Memorial# 63819558

More About Laura Catherine Diehl:
Burial: 06 Nov 1959, Lafayette Memorial Park, Brier Hill, Fayette Co., PA[2689]
Cause of death (Facts Pg): Arterial Sclerosis
Death Certifica: Copy in file
Residence: 1880, Addison Twp., Somerset Co., PA[2690]

Notes for Lemuel J. Hawkins:
Residence in 1935 Republic, Fayette Co., Pa According To Obit Of Wm. H. Diehl

Title: WV Birth Archives
Note: www.wvculture.org/vrr/va

More About Lemuel J. Hawkins:
Burial: Parkersburg, Wood Co., WV[2691]
Residence: 1900, Clarksburg (Part), Harrison Co., WV[2692]

Child of Laura Diehl and Lemuel Hawkins is:
+   1604   i.   Clara Elizabeth[8] Hawkins, born 15 Apr 1885 in Mountain Lake Park, Garrett Co., MD; died 02 Dec 1967 in Indiana, Indiana Co., PA.

493.   Ida C.[7] Diehl (Elizabeth[6] Christner, Jacob C.[5], John J.[4], Johannes John Hans[3], Christian[2], Christen[1])[2693,2693] was born Aug 1867 in PA[2694]. She married **Horace Harris A. Kuhns**[2695] 1886[2695], son of Leon Kuhns and Juliana. He was born 17 Feb 1861 in Connellsville, Fayette Co., PA[2695].

More About Ida C. Diehl:
Residence: 1900, South Whitehall, Lehigh Co., PA[2696]

More About Horace Harris A. Kuhns:
Residence: 1930, Allentown, Lehigh, Pennsylvania, USA[2696]

Child of Ida Diehl and Horace Kuhns is:
     1605   i.   May[8] Kuhns[2697], born Abt. 1883 in Connellsville, Fayette Co., PA[2697].

                    More About May Kuhns:
                    Residence: 1920, Allentown Ward 8, Lehigh Co., PA[2697]

495.   Ellen[7] Diehl (Elizabeth[6] Christner, Jacob C.[5], John J.[4], Johannes John Hans[3], Christian[2], Christen[1])[2698,2699,2699,2699,2700] was born 21 Jun 1871 in Addison, Fayette Co., PA, and died 17 Jun 1945 in Connellsville, Fayette Co., PA[2701,2701]. She married **Smith Newcomer**[2702] 08 Aug 1891 in Connellsville, Fayette Co., PA[2702]. He was born 01 Nov 1866 in Everson, Fayette Co., PA[2702], and died 21 Nov 1956 in Connellsville, Fayette Co., PA[2702].

Notes for Ellen Diehl:
Residence: 1918 According To Henry C. Diehl's Obit She Lived In Connellsville, Fayette Co., PA
Residence: 1935 Connellsville, Fayette Co., PA According To Obit Of Wm. H. Diehl

Obituary: The Daily Courier, Connellsville, PA, 18 Jun 1945. p. 2
Mrs. Ellen Newcomer, 73 years, 11 months and 26 days old, wife of Smith Newcomer of 276 1/2 East Fairview Avenue died 5:30 o'clock Sunday evening at her home.
She was born June 21, 1871 at Addison and was a member of te central Methodist Church. Besides her husband, she is survived by the following children: E. D. Newcomer, Mammoth; Mrs. Mae Rowe, Phillips; Mrs. Viola Henderson, Jersey City, NJ; Mrs. Bessie Graham, East Connellsville and Harry Newcomer, detroit, MI. there are two brothers and five sisters, Samuel Diehl, Jerome; George Diehl, Republic; Mrs. Laura Hawkins, Uniontown; Mrs. Emma Hennessey, Republic; Mrs. Edna Taylor, Orient; Mrs. Mary Johnson, Mill run; and Mrs. Amanda Hampshire, Connellsville; also 17 grandchildren and nine great-grandchildren. Two grandsons in the armed forces are James Arthur Graham, somewhere in England and Dwight Henderson in the South Pacific.
The funeral service will be held at 2 o'clock Wednesday afternoon at the charles A. McCormick funeral home in South Pittsburgh street with Rev. Howard W. Jamison, pastor of the central Methodist Church officiating.
Internment will be made in Westmoreland Memorial Park at Greensburg.

More About Ellen Diehl:
Burial: 20 Jun 1945, Westmoreland Memorial Park, Greensburg, Westmoreland Co., PA[2703]
Social Security Number: 172-36-8823/

Notes for Smith Newcomer:
Obituary: The Daily Courier, Connellsville, PA, 23 Nov 1956

Smith Newcomer, 90 of 276 1/2 East Fairview Ave., died Wednesday evening in Connellsville State hospital after a lingering illness. He was born at Everson Nov. 1, 1866, a son of the late Benjamin F. and Mary Anderson Newcomer and had lived in Connellsville since 1915. Prior to that he resided at Morgan Station, near Broad Ford. He was amember of the Central methodist Church.

Surviving are three daughters, Mrs. William (Mae) Rowe of Uniontown, Mrs. Viola Henderson of Jersey City, NJ and Mrs. Arthur (Besie) Graham of East Connellsville; two sons, Earl of Mammoth and Harry of Detroit, MI; 17 grandchildren; 29 great-grandchildren; two brothers, George W. of Connellsville and William of Rockwood and three sisters. Mrs. George (Daisey) Porter of Scottdale, Mrs. Walter (Pearl) Shaner of Bethelem and Mrs. R. J. (Bertha) Foster of St. Petersburg, FL. He was proceed in death by his wife, Ellen Diehl Newcomer, Jun 17, 1945.

The funeral service will be held at 2 o'clock Sunday afternoon at the Brooks Funeral Home at 111 East Green St. with the Rev. C. R. Wick officiating. Internment will be in Westmoreland County Memorial Park.

More About Smith Newcomer:
Burial: 25 Nov 1956, Westmoreland Co. Memorial Park, Greensburg, Westmoreland Co., PA[2704]

Children of Ellen Diehl and Smith Newcomer are:
1606	i.	Earl Diehl[8] Newcomer, born 28 Oct 1891 in Morgan, Fayette Co., PA; died Mar 1969 in Mammoth, Westmoreland Co., PA. He married Helen.
1607	ii.	May Newcomer, born Dec 1893 in Morgan, Fayette Co., PA; died May 1976 in Akron, Summit Co., OH. She married William Rowe.
1608	iii.	Allie Newcomer, born May 1897 in Morgan, Fayette Co., PA.
1609	iv.	Bessie Newcomer, born 08 Apr 1900 in Morgan, Fayette Co., PA; died 21 May 1985 in Lemont Furnace, Fayette Co., PA.

497. Margaret Elizabeth[7] Diehl (Elizabeth[6] Christner, Jacob C.[5], John J.[4], Johannes John Hans[3], Christian[2], Christen[1])[2705,2705] was born 1873 in Frostburg, Allegany Co., MD[2705,2705,2705], and died Feb 1894 in PA. She married **William Perry**.

Child of Margaret Diehl and William Perry is:
| 1610 | i. | Elizabeth[8] Diehl[2706,2706], born 1894 in Connellsville, Fayette Co., PA. |

498. Amanda Alice[7] Diehl (Elizabeth[6] Christner, Jacob C.[5], John J.[4], Johannes John Hans[3], Christian[2], Christen[1])[2707,2708,2709,2710,2711,2712,2713,2714] was born 31 Jan 1877 in Listonburg, Addison Twp., Somerset Co., PA[2715,2716,2717,2718,2719,2720,2721], and died 03 Apr 1950 in Connellsville, Fayette Co., PA[2721,2721,2721,2722,2723,2724,2724,2725,2726,2727,2728,2729,2730,2731]. She married **Charles Henry Hampshire**[2732,2733,2734,2735,2736,2737,2738] 19 Aug 1897 in New Harven, Broadford, Fayette Co., PA[2739,2739,2740,2741]. He was born 21 Jul 1874 in Casparis, Fayette Co., PA[2742,2743,2744,2744,2745,2746,2747,2748,2749,2750,2751,2752], and died 02 Nov 1943 in Connellsville, Fayette Co., PA[2753,2753,2754,2755].

Notes for Amanda Alice Diehl:
The Daily Courier - Connellsville, PA
8 Nov 1939

MRS. HAMPSHIRE BREAKS HIP

Mrs. Charles Hampshire of Vine Street is a patient at the Connellsville State Hospital for treatment of a fractured hip, suffered Sunday morning when she fell down the stairs of her home. Her condition is ot so good, it was reported today and she is premitted to see only immeidate members of her family.

Obituary: The Daily Courier, Connellsville, PA

4 Apr 1950

MRS. AMANDA HAMPSHIRE

Mrs. Amanda Alice Hampshire, 73, died at 10:40 o'clock Monday morning April 3, at her home at 1203 Vine Street after a lingering illness. She was born January 31, 1877 at Listonburg, a duaghter of the late Henry C. and Elizabeth Christner Diehl. She was a member of the First United Presbyterian Church. She was a widow of the late C. H. Hampshire.

Surviving are three sons, Frank D. of Republic, Harry D. of Cleveland OH and Clarence (Johnny) at home; five daughters, Mrs. James R. Crawford of republic, Mrs. Carl Shallenberger of Vanderbilt, Mrs. Fred Robbins of Poplar Grove and Mrs. Eloise Harvey and Mrs. Ray Gore of Connellsville; 22 grandchildren; nine great-grandchildren; four sisters, Mrs. Laura Hawkins of Dearth, Mrs. Mary Johnson of Normalville, Mrs. Andrew Taylor of Orient and Mrs. Emma Hennessey of Republic and two brothers, Samuel Diehl of Jerome and George of Greensburg.

The funeral service will be held at the home at 2 o'clock Wednesady afternoon with her pastor, Re. John E. Caughey, officiating. Internment will be in Green Ridge Memorial Park at Pennsville.

Residence: 1918 According To Henry C. Diehl's Obit She Lived In Connellsville, Fayette Co., PA

Residence: 1935 According To Wm. H. Diehl's Obit She Lived In Connellsville, Fayette Co., PA

Marriage license granted during the week ending Aug. 21, 1897 to Charles H. Hampshire of Connellsville, and Amanda Diehl of Broad Ford. The Courier, Connellsville, Aug. 27, 1897, p. 3.

Cause of death Carcinoma of rectum

More About AMANDA ALICE DIEHL:
Burial: 05 Apr 1950, Green Ridge Memorial Park Cemetery, Pennsville, Fayette Co., PA
Cause of death (Facts Pg): 03 Apr 1950, Carcinoma of Rectum
Census: 1910, PA, Fayette Co., Connellsville Twp.,: Series: T624 Roll: 1344   Page: 194
Death Certificate: File # 32095; Registered # 78; Fayette Co., PA
Occupation: Housewife
Residence: Bet. 1944 - 1950, 1203 Vine St., Connellsville, Fayette Co., PA

More About Amanda Alice Diehl:
Burial: 05 Apr 1950, Green Ridge Memorial Park Cemetery, Pennsville, Fayette Co., PA[2756,2757,2757,2758,2759,2760]
Cause of death (Facts Pg): 03 Apr 1950, Carcinoma of Rectum
Census: 1910, PA, Fayette Co., Connellsville Twp., : Series: T624 Roll: 1344   Page: 194
Death Certificate: File # 32095; Registered # 78; Fayette Co., PA
Occupation: Housewife/
Residence: 1930, Connellsville, Fayette Co., PA[2761]

Notes for Charles Henry Hampshire:
Marriage application #7722 - Married in New Haven, Broadford, Fayette Co,, PA by Justice of the Peace

Cause of death pnemonia.

Obituary: The Daily Courier
Connellsville, PA
4 Nov 1943 - 2 Nov. 1943

Charles H. Hampshire aged 69 of 1203 Vine Street, Connellsville, died at 10:15 o'clock Tuesday night, November 2, 1943, in Mercy Hospital, Pittsburgh of pnemonia after a brief illness. He was born in Casparis and was the last surviving member of his family. He had been employed by the Baltimore and OH railroad for the past 49 years and for several years had been a yard conductor. He was a member of Local no. 218, Brotherhood of Railroad Trainmen.

Surviving are his widow, Mrs. Amanda Diehl Hampshire, and the following children, Mrs. James R. Crawford and Frank Diehl of Republic; Mrs. Eloise Harden of Uniontown; Harry of Cleveland; Mrs. Carl F. Shallenberger, of Vanderbilt; Mrs. Fred Robbins and Mrs. Ray Gore of Connellsville; Clarence, at home. 18 grandchildren and four great grandchildren.

The funeral service will be held at 2 o'clock Saturday afternoon, at the home. In charge will be Rev. Joseph I. Krohn, pastor of the First United Presbyterian Church of Connellsville, officiating. Burial will follow in Green Ridge Memorial Park under the direction of the Charles A. McCormick Funeral Home, Connellsville.

Obituary: Morning Herald, 4 Nov 1943, p.8, col.7
Hampshire, Charles H. aged 69 of 1203 Vine Street, Connellsville, died of pnemonia Tuesday evening, November 2, 1943, in Mercy Hospital, Pittsburgh following a brief illness. He was born in Casparis and was the last surviving member of his family. He was a yard conductor in the B & O railroad's Connellsville yards for several years and was a member of Local no. 218, Brotherhood of Railroad Trainmen. Surviving are his widow, Mrs. Amanda Diehl Hampshire, and the following children, Mrs. James R. Crawford and Frank Diehl of Republic; Mrs. Eloise Harden of Uniontown; Harry of Cleveland; Mrs. Carl F. Shallenberger, of Vanderbilt; Mrs. Fred Robbins and Mrs. Ray Gore of Connellsville; Clarence, at home. 18 grandchildren and four great grandchildren. Funeral services will be held from the late home Saturday, November 6, at 2pm the Rev. J. I. Krohn, pastor of the First United Presbyterian Church of Connellsville, officiating. Burial will follow in Green Ridge Memorial Park under the direction of the Charles A. McCormick Funeral Home, Connellsville.

Charles registered for the Draft for WWI at the local draft board in Fayette Co., PA/

He was 44 years old when he registered and signed his draft card on Sep. 12, 1918. he worked for the B & O. Railroad. His home address was 1203 Vine St., Connellsville, Fayette Co., PA.

His description was medium build with blue eyes and brown hair.

More About Charles Henry Hampshire:
Burial: Green Ridge Memorial Park Cemetery, Pennsville, Fayette Co., PA
Census: 1910, PA, FAYETTE, CONNELLSVILLE TWP; Series: T624 Roll: 1344 Page: 194
Residence: 1920, Connellsville Ward 5, Fayette, PA[2762]

Children of Amanda Diehl and Charles Hampshire are:

	1611	i.	Frank[8] Hampshire.
+	1612	ii.	Margaret E. Hampshire, born 12 Mar 1898 in Connellsville, Fayette Co., PA; died 21 Jun 1989 in Connellsville, Fayette Co., PA.
+	1613	iii.	Eloise Hampshire, born 23 Jul 1899 in Connellsville, Fayette Co., PA; died Jan 1978 in Uniontown, Fayette Co., PA.
	1614	iv.	John Henry Hampshire, born Jul 1901 in Connellsville, Fayette Co., PA; died 07 Sep 1901 in Connellsville, Fayette Co., PA.
	1615	v.	Charles H. Hampshire[2763,2764], born Jul 1903 in Connellsville, Fayette Co., PA[2765,2766,2767]; died 20 Aug 1903 in Connellsville, Fayette Co., PA[2767,2768,2769].

Notes for Charles H. Hampshire:
The Daily Courier - 31 Oct 1937 - Connellsville, PA
The Daily Courier - 20 Aug 1903 - Connellsville, PA

More About Charles H. Hampshire:
Burial: 22 Aug 1903, Hill Grove Cemetery, Connellsville, Fayette Co., PA[2769]

	1616	vi.	Clara G. Hampshire[2770,2771], born 1905 in Connellsville, Fayette Co., PA[2772,2773,2774,2775]; died 02 Feb 1922 in Connellsville, Fayette Co., PA[2775,2775]. She married John Lakotish[2776] 14 Dec 1921 in Connellsville, Fayette Co., PA[2777].

Notes for Clara G. Hampshire:
Obituary: The Daily Courier, Connellsville, PA
3 Feb 1922

MRS. JOHN LAKOTICH

Mrs. Clara Hampshire Lakotich bride of seven woods, died Thursday morning at 11:35 o'clock at the home of her parents, Mr. and Mrs. C. H. Hampshire, 1203 Vine Street, from an abessed gland. She was married December 14, 1921 to John Lakotich of Elm Grove and had resided at Elm Grove ever since her marriage. Her brother-in-law Fred Harden who was store manager for the W. J. Rainey interests at Elm Grove dropped dead January 3, 1922. Her husband, parents and the following brothers and sisters survive: Mrs. James R. Crawford, Republic; Mrs. Eloise Harden, Elm Grove; Harry, Myrtle, Mary, Mildred Mae and Clarence, all at home. A step-brother Frank Diehl of Republic also survive.

The funeral service will be held Sunday afternoon at 3:30 o'clcok at the Hampshire home, with Rev. Francis J. Scott of the United Presbyterian Church of which the deceased was a member, officiating. The internment will be made in Hill Grove Cemetery.

The Daily Courier Connellsville, PA - 31 Oct 1937

More About Clara G. Hampshire:
Burial: 05 Feb 1922, Hill Grove Cemetery, Connellsville, Fayette Co., PA[2778]
Census: 1920, U.S. Census > 1920 United States Federal Census - PA - Fayette - Connellsville Ward 5 - District 14
Residence: 1920, Connellsville Ward 5, Fayette, PA[2779,2780]

+ 1617 vii. Harry O. Hampshire, born 01 Sep 1906 in Connellsville, Fayette Co., PA; died Jun 1983 in Connellsville, Fayette Co., PA.

+ 1618 viii. Myrtle R. Hampshire, born 16 Jan 1908 in Connellsville, Fayette Co., PA; died 13 Mar 2009 in Connellsville, Fayette Co., PA.

  1619 ix. Tressa Hampshire[2781,2782], born Aug 1909 in Connellsville, Fayette Co., PA[2783].

       More About Tressa Hampshire:
       Residence: 1950, Poplar Grove, Fayette Co., PA[2783]

+ 1620 x. Mildred Mae Hampshire, born 19 Aug 1912 in Connellsville, Fayette Co., PA; died 06 Apr 1985 in Connellsville, Fayette Co., PA.

  1621 xi. Clarence "Johnnie" R. Hampshire[2783,2784,2785], born 25 Apr 1914 in Connellsville, Fayette Co., PA[2785,2786,2787]; died 29 May 1994 in Connellsville, Fayette Co., PA[2787,2788,2789]. He married Dolores Trump; born 20 Apr 1929 in Connellsville, Fayette Co., PA; died 03 Oct 2007 in Mt. Pleasant, Westmoreland Co., PA.

       Notes for Clarence "Johnnie" R. Hampshire:
       SSDI:
       CLARENCE HAMPSHIRE
       Residence: 15425 Connellsville, Fayette, PA
       Born 25 Apr 1914 Last Benefit:
       Died 29 May 1994 Issued: PA (Before 1951)
       Nickname: Johnnie
       Social Security Number: 176-03-0939

       More About Clarence "Johnnie" R. Hampshire:
       Nickname: Johnnie
       Residence: 1920, Connellsville Ward 5, Fayette, PA[2790]
       Social Security Number: 176-03-0939/

+ 1622 xii. Mary H. Hampshire, born 1916 in Connellsville, Fayette Co., PA.

+ 1623 xiii. Esther L. Hampshire, born 04 Sep 1917; died 06 Jul 1979 in Connellsville, Fayette Co., PA.

500. Samuel[7] Diehl (Elizabeth[6] Christner, Jacob C.[5], John J.[4], Johannes John Hans[3], Christian[2], Christen[1])[2791,2792,2793,2794] was born 27 Sep 1878 in Connellsville, Fayette Co., PA[2795], and died 31 Dec 1948. He married **Carrie**[2795]. She was born 18 Jun 1882 in Connellsville, Fayette Co., PA[2795,2796], and died 15 Jul 1970 in

Allentown, Lehigh Co., PA[2796].

Notes for Samuel Diehl:
Birth: Sep. 27, 1878
Death: Dec. 31, 1948

Burial: Zionhill Evangelical Lutheran Church Cemetery, Zionhill, Bucks Co., PA

More About Samuel Diehl:
Residence: 1880, Hatfield, Montgomery Co., PA[2797]

Notes for Carrie:
Birth: Jun. 18, 1882
Death: Jul. 20, 1970

Burial: Zionhill Evangelical Lutheran Church Cemetery, Zionhill, Bucks Co., PA

More About Carrie:
Residence: 1910, East Buffalo, Union, PA[2798]
Social Security Number: 180-40-8574/[2799]
SSN issued: Connellsville, Fayette Co., PA[2799]

Children of Samuel Diehl and Carrie are:
+   1624   i.   Ella[8] Diehl, born 1918 in Connellsville, Fayette Co., PA.
     1625   ii. Marion Diehl[2800], born 1926 in Connellsville, Fayette Co., PA[2800,2801].

              More About Marion Diehl:
              Arrival: [2802]
              Residence: 1930, Salisbury, Lehigh, PA[2802]

501. Edna[7] Diehl (Elizabeth[6] Christner, Jacob C.[5], John J.[4], Johannes John Hans[3], Christian[2], Christen[1])[2803]
was born Oct 1879 in Somerset Co., PA[2803], and died 03 Oct 1960 in Republic, Fayette Co., PA[2803]. She married
Andrew A. Taylor 1898. He was born 17 Nov 1877 in Connellsville, Fayette Co., PA, and died 24 Oct 1964 in
Miami, Dade Co., FL.

Notes for Edna Diehl:
1920 Federal Census, Fayette Co., PA, Redstone Twp., 3rd prec., enum. dist. 78

Residence: 1918 According To Henry C. Diehl's Obit She Lived In Thompson Number 1, PA

Residence: 1935 According To Wm. h. Diehl's Obit She Lived In Republic, Fayette Co., PA

Obituary: The Daily Courier, Connellsville, PA - 5 Oct 1960

MRS. ANDREW TAYLOR

Mrs. Edna Diehl Taylor, 80 of Republic, died Monday.
She leaves her husband, Andrew; four sons, incuding Henry of Nemacolin and James of Tower Hill No. 2 and
Mrs. charles (Clara) Heaton of Merrittstown; 15 grandchildren; 27 great-grandchildren; two brothers and a sister.
The body will be in the Flack Marucci funeral home, Republic until 11:45 am, Thursday and in the First Christian
Church of Republic from noon to 1 pm the hour of the funeral service. Internment will be in the Park Place
Cemetery, Uniontown.

More About Edna Diehl:
Burial: 06 Oct 1960, Park Place Cemetery, Uniontown, Fayette Co., PA[2803]

Notes for Andrew A. Taylor:

Obituary: The Daily Courier, Connellsville, PA, 27 - Oct 1964
Andrew Taylor

More About Andrew A. Taylor:
Burial: Park Place Cemetery, Uniontown, Fayette Co., PA

Children of Edna Diehl and Andrew Taylor are:
    1626   i.   Henry[8] Taylor, born 1900.
    1627   ii. Earl A. Taylor, born 1901.

504. Samuel Cleveland[7] Diehl (Elizabeth[6] Christner, Jacob C.[5], John J.[4], Johannes John Hans[3], Christian[2], Christen[1]) was born 06 Mar 1885 in Listonburg, Addison Twp., Somerset Co., PA, and died 06 Aug 1975 in Johnstown, Cambria Co., PA[2804,2805,2805,2805,2806]. He married **Bertha I. Dean**[2807]. She was born 10 Apr 1889 in Pittsburgh, Allegheny Co., PA[2808,2809], and died 22 Oct 1953 in Jerome, Somerset Co., PA[2810,2811].

Notes for Samuel Cleveland Diehl:
Name: Samuel C. DIEHL
Sex: M
Birth: 6 MAR 1885 in Listonburg, Addison Twp., Somerset Co., PA
Death: 6 AUG 1975 in Johnstown, Cambria Co., PA
Census: 1910 lived with parents in Republic, Fayette Co., PA
Residence: 1918 According to Henry C. Diehl's obit he lived in West Salisbury, Somerset Co., PA
Burial: 10 AUG 1975 Park Place Cemetery, Uniontown, Fayette Co., PA

Title: Information provided by Jocelyn Seitzer, granddaughter of Samuel C. Diehl

Census 1910 - Fayette Co., PA
Henry C. Diehl
Age: 68 State: PA
Color: W Enumeration District: 8064
Birth Place: MD Visit: 0271
Co.: Fayette
Relation: Head of Household
Other Residents: Wife Elizabeth 65, Pennsylvania
Son Samuel 24, Pennsylvania
Son George 21, Pennsylvania
Granddaughter Lizzie 16, Pennsylvania
Grandson Frank 14, Pennsylvania
Grandson William Fulmer 20, Pennsylvania

SSDI:
SAMUEL DIEHL 06 Mar 1885 Aug 1975 15905 (Johnstown, Cambria Co., PA) 172-18-2459 Pennsylvania

OBITUARY:

Samuel C., 90, Johnstown, formerly of Jerome, died Aug. 6, 1975, at Memorial Hospital, Johnstown. Born Mar. 6, 1885, in Listonburg, son of Henry C. and Elizabeth (Christner) Diehl. Preceded in death by parents; wife, former Bertha Dean, who died Oct. 22, 1953; two infant sons; seven sisters; and three brothers. Survived by these children: Grace, wife of Roy Emerick, Jerome; Elizabeth, wife of William Jacobs, Warwick, R.I.; Thelma, wife of Purney Acker, Lexington, Mass.; Harry, married to the former Marion Kurtz; Fay, husband of Marie Steinkirchner; and Frank, married to the former Agnes Molchany, all of Johnstown; also 18 grandchildren and 14 great grandchildren. Was a charter member of Jerome Church of the Nazarene. Resident of Jerome for over 50 years. Interment Park Place Cemetery, Uniontown.

Obituary: Somerset American, August 8, 1975

DIEHL

Samuel C. Diehl, 90, of 847 E. Avenue, Johnstown, formerly of Jerome, died Aug. 6, 1975 at Memorial Hospital. Born March 6, 1885, in Listonburg, a son of Henry C. and Elizabeth (Christner) Diehl. Preceded in death by parents, wife, the former Bertha Dean who died Oct. 22, 1953, two infant sons, seven sisters and three brothers. Survived by these children: Grace, wife of Roy Emerick of Jerome; Elizabeth, wife of William Jacobs, Warwick, R.I.; Thelma, wife of Purney Acker, Lexington, Mass.; Harry, married to the former Marion Kurtz, Fay, wife of Marie Steinkirchner, Frank, married to the former Agnes Molchany, all of Johnstown; 18 grandchildren and 15 great-grandchildren. Charter member of Jerome Church of the Nazarene. Resident of Jerome for more than 50 years. Friends received from 7 to 9 p.m. Friday (today), 10 a.m. to 9 p.m. Saturday and until noon on Sunday at Joseph G. Hoffman Funeral Home, 409 Main St., Boswell, when the body will be removed to the Jerome Church of the Nazarene to lie in state until time of service at 2 p.m. with the Rev. Elwood R. Zandiver officiating. Interment, Park Place Cemetery, Uniontown. There will be no viewing at the Church. In lieu of flowers, family requests contributions be made to the Jerome Church of the Nazarene.

More About Samuel Cleveland Diehl:
Burial: 10 Aug 1975, Park Place Cemetery, Uniontown, Fayette Co., PA
Religion: Jerome Church of the Nazarene/
Residence: 1880, Hatfield, Montgomery Co., PA[2812]
Social Security Number: 172-18-2459/

More About Bertha I. Dean:
Burial: Park Place Cemetery, Uniontown, Fayette Co., PA
Residence: 1920, Elk Lick, Somerset Co., PA[2812]

Children of Samuel Diehl and Bertha Dean are:

1628   i.   Elizabeth[8] Diehl. She married William Jacobs.
1629   ii.   Grace A. Diehl, born 14 Apr 1911 in Pittsburgh, Allegheny Co., PA[2812]; died 07 Jun 2000 in Santa Maria, Santa Barbara Co., CA[2812]. She married Roy Emerick[2812,2813]; born 09 Jan 1908 in Pittsburgh, Allegheny Co., PA[2814,2815]; died 18 Apr 1994 in Santa Maria, Santa Barbara Co., CA[2816].

     Notes for Grace A. Diehl:
     U.S., Social Security Death Index, 1935-Current

     Name: Grace Emerick
     SSN: 193-24-7396
     Last Residence: 93458 Santa Maria, Santa Barbara Co., CA
     Born: 14 Apr 1911
     Died: 7 Jun 2000
     State (Year) SSN issued: PA (Before 1951)

     More About Grace A. Diehl:
     Residence: 1930, Conemaugh, Somerset Co., PA[2816]

     More About Roy Emerick:
     Residence: 1930, Conemaugh, Somerset Co., PA[2816]
     Social Security Number: 208-10-0705/[2817]

1630   iii.   Thelma C. Diehl[2818], born 11 Feb 1914 in PA[2818]; died 2001[2818]. She married Purney Acker.

     More About Thelma C. Diehl:
     Residence: 1930, Conemaugh, Somerset, PA[2818]

1631   iv.   Harry Diehl[2819], born 02 Jan 1917[2819]; died 12 Jul 1991[2819]. He married Marion Kutrz.

     More About Harry Diehl:
     Residence: 1975, Johnstown, Cambria Co., PA[2819]

1632   v.   Fay Emerson Diehl, born 18 Mar 1918 in Pittsburgh, Allegheny Co., PA[2820]; died 02 Jun 1994 in

Johnstown, Cambria Co., PA[2820]. He married Marie Steinkirchner.

More About Fay Emerson Diehl:
Residence: 1930, Conemaugh, Somerset Co., PA[2820]

1633 vi. Frank E. Diehl[2821], born 28 Aug 1920 in Pennsylvania, USA[2821]; died 26 Aug 2008 in Ebensburg, Cambria, Pennsylvania, USA[2821]. He married Agnes Molchany.

More About Frank E. Diehl:
Residence: 1992, Johnstown, Cambria Co., PA[2821]

505. George Oscar[7] Diehl (Elizabeth[6] Christner, Jacob C.[5], John J.[4], Johannes John Hans[3], Christian[2], Christen[1])[2822,2822,2823,2824] was born 14 Aug 1888 in Somerset, Somerset Co., PA[2825,2825,2825,2826,2827], and died 22 Mar 1970 in Cleveland, Cuyahoga Co., OH[2828,2828,2828,2829]. He married **Margaret Theresa Monaghan**[2829] 18 Aug 1915 in Republic, Fayette Co., PA[2829,2830]. She was born 02 Dec 1897[2831,2832], and died 01 Jan 1990 in Turbotville, Northumberland Co., PA.

Notes for George Oscar Diehl:
Name: George Oscar DIEHL
Sex: M
Birth: ABT. 1889 in Pennsylvania
Census: 1910 living with parents in Republic, Fayette Co., PA
Occupation: 1910 Moler (?), cleaner /Miner
Residence: 1918 According to Henry C. Diehl's obit he lived in Republic, Fayette Co., PA

Census 1910 - Fayette Co., PA
Henry C. Diehl
Age: 68 State: PA
Color: W Enumeration District: 8064
Birth Place: MD Visit: 0271
Co.: Fayette
Relation: Head of Household
Other Residents: Wife Elizabeth 65, Pennsylvania
Son Samuel 24, Pennsylvania
Son George 21, Pennsylvania
Granddaughter Lizzie 16, Pennsylvania
Grandson Frank 14, Pennsylvania
Grandson William Fulmer 20, Pennsylvania

SSDI:
GEORGE DIEHL 06 Nov 1889 Oct 1973 15132 (Mc Keesport, Allegheny, PA) (none specified) 194-05-9997 Pennsylvania

Census: 1910 Lived With Parents In Republic, Fayette Co., PA

Residence: 1918 According To Henry C. Diehl's Obit He Lived In Republic, Fayette Co., PA

Residence: 1935 According To Wm. h. Diehl's Obit He Lived In Republic, Fayette Co., PA

Title: WWI registration card

Title: Social Security Death Index

occupation: Coal Miner

Buried: Mt. Moriah Baptist Cemetery, Smithfield, Fayette Co., PA

More About George Oscar Diehl:
Census: 1910, Living With Parents In Republic, Fayette Co., PA[2833]
Residence: 1910, Redstone, Fayette Co., PA[2834]
Social Security Number: PA/
SSN issued: PA[2835]

Notes for Margaret Theresa Monaghan:
SSDI:
MARGARET T DIEHL 02 Dec 1897 01 Jan 1990 17772 (Turbotville, Northumberland, PA) (none specified)
176-16-3220 PA

More About Margaret Theresa Monaghan:
Residence: 1930, Redstone, Fayette, PA[2836]
Social Security Number: 176-16-3220/[2837]
SSN issued: PA[2837]

Children of George Diehl and Margaret Monaghan are:
  1634   i.   George E.[8] Diehl Jr., born 1920 in Connellsville, Fayette Co., PA; died 1968 in Greensburg,
                  Westmoreland Co. PA.
  1635   ii.   Mary Elizabeth Diehl[2838], born 09 Nov 1924 in Uniontown, Fayette Co., PA[2838]; died 27 Oct 2005 in
                  Mentor, Lake Co., OH[2838].

                  More About Mary Elizabeth Diehl:
                  Residence: 1960, Cleveland, OH[2838]

  1636   iii. Margaret Ellen Diehl[2838], born 18 Jan 1928 in Republic, Fayette, PA[2838]; died 23 Dec 1983 in Cleveland,
                  Cuyahoga Co., OH[2838].

                  More About Margaret Ellen Diehl:
                  Residence: Willowick, Lake, Ohio, United States[2838]

508. Elizabeth[7] Christner (Jacob (Lumix Jake)[6], Jacob C.[5], John J.[4], Johannes John Hans[3], Christian[2],
Christen[1])[2839] was born Mar 1868 in PA[2839], and died Nov 1947 in Meyersdale, Somerset Co., PA[2839]. She
married **Martin Foy** 22 Mar 1888 in Garrett, Somerset Co., PA. He was born Feb 1866 in Frostburg, Allegany
Co., MD[2839], and died 1934.

Notes for Martin Foy:

Children of Elizabeth Christner and Martin Foy are:
+ 1637   i.   Annie[8] Foy, born 19 Sep 1888 in Meyersdale, Somerset Co., PA; died 30 Oct 1966 in Lonaconing,
                  Allegany Co., MD.
   1638   ii.   Ida Foy[2839,2840], born Aug 1889 in PA[2841]. She married Norman T Kline[2842].
   1639   iii. Edith Foy[2843], born Mar 1893 in PA[2843].
   1640   iv.   Harrison Foy[2843], born 28 Jul 1898 in Someret Co., PA[2843].
   1641   v.   Ruth N. Foy[2843], born Abt. 1908 in PA[2843].

515. George Harrison[7] Gray (Mary Elizabeth[6] Christner, Jacob C.[5], John J.[4], Johannes John Hans[3],
Christian[2], Christen[1])[2844] was born 03 May 1890 in Meyersdale, Somerset Co., PA, and died 13 Dec 1969 in
Garrett, Somerset, PA[2844,2845]. He married **Mary E Heining**[2845] 06 Jul 1924. She was born 19 Apr 1899 in
Garrett, Somerset Co., PA[2845], and died 18 Aug 1979 in Garrett, Somerset Co., PA[2845].

More About George Harrison Gray:
Residence: 1930, Summit, Somerset Co., PA[2846,2847]

Children of George Gray and Mary Heining are:

1642   i.   Nora[8] Gray[2847], born 25 Apr 1921[2847]; died 26 Jan 1982 in Somerset Co., PA[2847].

1643   ii.   Margaret Gray[2847], born 05 Aug 1924 in Garrett, Somerset Co., PA[2847]; died 03 Mar 2005 in Garrett, Somerset Co., PA[2847].

519. Nora[7] Christner (Samuel[6], Jacob C.[5], John J.[4], Johannes John Hans[3], Christian[2], Christen[1])[2848,2849] was born Mar 1887 in Summit Twp., Somerset Co., PA. She married **Bernard William Cox**. He was born 17 Feb 1888 in Meyersdale, Somerset Co., PA[2850,2851], and died 09 Nov 1968 in Meyersdale, Somerset Co., PA[2852,2853].

More About Nora Christner:
Residence: 1920, Meyersdale, Somerset Co., PA[2854]

More About Bernard William Cox:
Residence: 1910, Johnstown Ward 8, Cambria Co., PA[2854]

Child of Nora Christner and Bernard Cox is:

+   1644   i.   Harry Robert[8] Christner, born 05 Nov 1903 in Connellsville, Fayette Co., PA; died 06 Dec 1962.

520. Susan[7] Christner (Samuel[6], Jacob C.[5], John J.[4], Johannes John Hans[3], Christian[2], Christen[1])[2855] was born 29 Jul 1889 in Summit Twp., Somerset Co., PA[2855], and died 10 Jan 1972. She married **Joseph Calvin Boden**[2856]. He was born 31 Jul 1891 in Connellsville, Fayette Co., PA[2857,2858], and died 15 Feb 1973 in Meyersdale, Somerset Co., PA.

Notes for Susan Christner:
Birth: Jul. 29, 1889
Death: Jan. 10, 1972

Mrs. Susan Ann Boden, 82, Meyersdale, died Jan. 10, 1972. Born July 29, 1889 in Somerset County, she was a daughter of the late Samuel and Lydia (Deal) Christner. Surviving are her husband, Calvin J. Boden; a son, Marne of McKeesport; two daughters, Mrs. Sadie Piechuta of Connecticut and Mrs. Lee Mimmie, Meyersdale; four grandchildren and two sisters, Mrs. Lloyd Clubaugh, Somerset; and Mrs. Sadie Gray, Jerome. Funeral service was held Jan. 13 in Konhaus Funeral Home, Meyersdale with Rev. Robert Robertson officiating. Interment in Highland Cemetery, Garrett.
Meyersdale Republican, January 20, 1972

Spouse: Joseph Calvin Boden (1891 - 1973)

Burial: Highland Cemetery, Garrett, Somerset Co., PA

More About Susan Christner:
Residence: 1920, Garrett, Somerset Co., PA[2859]

Notes for Joseph Calvin Boden:
Birth: Jul. 31, 1891
Death: Feb. 15, 1973

Joseph Calvin Boden, 81, of Garrett, died Feb. 15, 1973 in Meyersdale. Born July 31, 1891 in Somerset County, he was the son of the late Joseph and Martha (Smith) Boden. Surviving are a son, Marne of McKeesport; two daughters: Mrs. Joseph Piechuta, Southington, Conn.; and Mrs. Lee Mimna, Meyersdale; five grandchildren, six great-grandchildren and a sister, Mrs. Lillie Lohr, Garrett. Funeral service was held Sunday afternoon in Konhaus Funeral Home, Meyersdale, with Rev. William Phennicie officiating. Interment in Highland Cemetery, Garrett.
Meyersdale Republican, February 22, 1973

Spouse: Susan Ann Christner Boden (1889 - 1972)

Burial: Highland Cemetery, Garrett, Somerset Co., PA
Find A Grave Memorial# 76905640

More About Joseph Calvin Boden:
Residence: 1920, Garrett, Somerset Co., PA[2859]
Social Security Number: 172-18-9664/[2860]

Children of Susan Christner and Joseph Boden are:

1645   i.   Sadie M.[8] Boden[2861], born 1912 in Connellsville, Fayette Co., PA[2861].

        More About Sadie M. Boden:
        Residence: 1920, Garrett, Somerset Co., PA[2861]

1646   ii.   William J. Boden[2861], born 1915 in Connellsville, Fayette Co., PA[2861].

        More About William J. Boden:
        Residence: 1920, Garrett, Somerset Co., PA[2861]

1647   iii. Elenora B. Boden[2861], born 1917 in Connellsville, Fayette Co., PA[2861].

        More About Elenora B. Boden:
        Residence: 1920, Garrett, Somerset Co., PA[2861]

1648   iv.   Marne C. Boden[2861], born 1920 in Connellsville, Fayette Co., PA[2861].

        More About Marne C. Boden:
        Residence: 1920, Garrett, Somerset Co., PA[2861]

525. George[7] Kendall (Caroline (Carrie)[6] Christner, Jacob C.[5], John J.[4], Johannes John Hans[3], Christian[2], Christen[1]) died Oct 1964. He married **Ida**. She died May 1966.

Notes for George Kendall:
He owned a farm in Hyndman, PA his real mother was Tenia Logsdon she died 1960. This was Carrie's Sister. Carrie and Tenia or Tena's father was Jacob C. Christner and mother was Julian Rumiser.

Child of George Kendall and Ida is:

1649   i.   Ezra[8] Kendall, died Jun 1977. He married Geraldine 1939.

527. Mason Franklin[7] Christner (Franklin Grant[6], Jacob C.[5], John J.[4], Johannes John Hans[3], Christian[2], Christen[1])[2862,2863] was born 24 Apr 1891 in Bullskin Twp., Fayette Co., PA[2864], and died 04 Mar 1958 in Connellsville, Fayette Co., PA[2865]. He married **Cora Mae Stillwagon** 04 Aug 1910 in Moyer, Fayette Co., PA. She was born Feb 1890 in BullskinTwp., Fayette Co., PA[2866,2867], and died 1933 in Greensburg, Westmoreland Co., PA[2868].

Notes for Mason Franklin Christner:
He was good at and liked to play stringed instruments He was a Barber. He had a guardian (Jacob W. Grims) when he got married. 1910 soundex PA has him living at Jacobs home. 1920 census has him living at Westmoreland County, Greensburg, 310 ½ Alexander Street, Pennslvania with wife, Cora & Children, Charles, & Frank.

More About Mason Franklin Christner:
Occupation: Miner when married/

More About Cora Mae Stillwagon:
Residence: 1920, Age: 26; Marital Status: Married; Relation to Head of House: Wife/Greensburg Ward 5, Westmoreland, PA[2868]

Children of Mason Christner and Cora Stillwagon are:

+   1650   i.   Charles Edward[8] Christner, born 21 Feb 1910; died Aug 1974 in Greensburg, Westmoreland Co., PA.

+ 1651 ii. Frank Henry Christner, born 20 Mar 1917 in Brownsville, Fayette Co., PA; died Jun 1979 in Chicago, Cook Co., IL.
  1652 iii. Alice Mae Christner, born 1922; died 1985.
  1653 iv. Mason Franklin Christner Jr., born 1923; died 1933.
  1654 v. Jacob Russell Eugene Christner, born 1924; died 1926.

532. George West[7] Christner (Franklin Grant[6], Jacob C.[5], John J.[4], Johannes John Hans[3], Christian[2], Christen[1])[2869,2870] was born 22 Feb 1900 in Brownsville, Fayette Co., PA[2871,2872,2873,2874], and died Jun 1971 in Dover, York Co., PA[2875,2876]. He married **(1) Grace E. Coleman**[2877]. She was born 04 Sep 1901 in Connellsville, Fayette Co., PA[2878,2879,2880], and died 07 Feb 1989[2881]. He married **(2) Mabel Shirley Hayter Fenton**. She was born 1911, and died 1973.

Notes for George West Christner:
George Dropped The name Christner & used West around 1920 to 1928. 1920 census he used Christner not West. 1920 he lived at Fayette County, National Pike road.

More About George West Christner:
Namesake: 1920, George Dropped The name Christner & used West/
Residence: 1920, Brownsville, Fayette, PA[2882,2883,2884]

More About Grace E. Coleman:
Residence: 1920, Brownsville, Fayette, PA[2885,2886]
Social Security Number: 169-07-6986/[2887]
SSN issued: Connellsville, Fayette Co., PA[2887]

Children of George Christner and Grace Coleman are:
  1655 i. William E.[8] Christner[2888], born 07 Sep 1919[2888]; died 07 Nov 1988 in Hampton, Hampton Co., VA[2888].

   More About William E. Christner:
   Social Security Number: 161-18-8689/[2888]
   SSN issued: Connellsville, Fayette Co., PA[2888]

+ 1656 ii. Frances Lucille Christner, born 15 Aug 1920 in Pittsburgh, Allegheny Co., PA; died 02 Jun 2010 in Grove City Hospital, Mercer Co., PA.
  1657 iii. George William Christner[2889], born 1923[2889].

   More About George William Christner:
   Residence: 1930, Brownsville, Fayette, PA[2889]

Children of George Christner and Mabel Fenton are:
  1658 i. George Daniel[8] West, born 1929.
  1659 ii. Harry Allen West, born 1931; died 1934.
  1660 iii. Louise Shirley West, born 1934. She married Marling Allen Pletcher; born 1924.
  1661 iv. William Vincent West, born 1936; died 1938.
  1662 v. Hillard Fenton West, born 1939; died 1977.
  1663 vi. Dennis Elmer West, born 1941. He married Connie.
  1664 vii. Henry Karla West, born 1943; died 1991.
  1665 viii. Douglas Bradley West, born 1944.
  1666 ix. Leland Burnell West, born 1947.
  1667 x. Sidney Bruce West, born 1949. He married Donna.
  1668 xi. James Leonard West, born 1951.

533. James Allen[7] Christner (Franklin Grant[6], Jacob C.[5], John J.[4], Johannes John Hans[3], Christian[2], Christen[1])[2890,2891,2892,2893] was born 30 Aug 1902 in Connellsville, Fayette Co., PA[2894,2895,2896], and died 24 Apr 1998 in Anchorage, Anchorage Co., Alaska. He married **Melvina**. She was born Abt. 1910 in Pittsburgh, Allegheny Co., PA[2897,2898].

More About James Allen Christner:
Race: White/[2899]
Residence: 1910, South Union, Fayette Co., PA[2900,2901]

More About Melvina:
Race: White/[2902]
Residence: 1930, Luzerne, Fayette Co., PA[2903]

Child of James Christner and Melvina is:
    1669   i.   Edith M.[8] Christner[2903], born 1928[2903].

                More About Edith M. Christner:
                Race: White/[2904]
                Residence: 1930, Luzerne, Fayette Co., PA[2905]

536. Sadie Marie[7] Christner (Frank[6], Jacob C.[5], John J.[4], Johannes John Hans[3], Christian[2], Christen[1])[2906] was born 24 Mar 1911 in Pine Hill, Somerset Co., PA[2907], and died 05 Jun 2007 in Meyersdale, Somerset Co., PA. She married **Peter Franklin Housel Sr.**. He was born 02 May 1907 in Meyersdale, Somerset Co., PA, and died 15 Mar 1977 in Meyersdale, Somerset Co., PA.

Notes for Sadie Marie Christner:
Sadie talked about her brother James, who didn't even live a month. She was 18 years old at the time, and she felt guilty, her mom had died while giving birth to James and she didn't know what to food the baby, and he died. She talked about how mean and cruel her father was, he made her do all the work and take care of the kids, and he was really mad when Peter Housel asked her to marry him and she said yes because now he wouldn't have to do all the work.

Birth: Mar. 24, 1911
Pine Hill, Somerset Co., PA
Death: Jun. 5, 2007
Meyersdale, Somerset Co., PA

Sadie Marie Housel, 96, Meyersdale, devoted and loving wife, mother and grandmother, went to be with the Lord on June 5, 2007, at her North Street residence. Born March 24, 1911, in Goodtown (Pine Hill). A daughter of the late Frank and Margaret (Pletcher) Christner. Also preceded in death by her husband, Peter F. Housel Sr.; daughter, Betty Gnagey; sons-in-law, William Fogel, Donald Cober and Norton Mathers; great-grandson, Timmy; and these sisters and brothers, Margaret Albright, Dorothy Ohler, Emma Housel, Clyde, George, John and Albert Christner. Survived by these children, Eleanor Cober, Berlin; Marie Mathers, Meyersdale; Doris, wife of Gerald Oester, Meyersdale; Peter F. Housel Jr., and his wife Gloria Ann, Meyersdale; Verna, wife of Joseph Niedermeyer, Bethel Park; Anna, wife of Lloyd Hamilton, Rex, Ga.; Clyde Housel, and his wife Terry, Lovettsville, Va.; and son-in-law Max Gnagey, Meyersdale. Also 32 grandchildren, 45 great-grandchildren, and five great-great-grandchildren. She was a faithful member of the Main Street Brethren Church where she held many offices, was a deaconess, worked for many fundraisers, and was the janitor for many years. She worked cleaning houses for many families in the community and worked as a cleaning lady for the Meyersdale Community Hospital. She is best known to the community for her homemade bread and rolls, which she sold weekly. She was very competitive at board games, her favorite being checkers and Chinese checkers, and she rarely lost a game! Friends will be received 2 to 4 and 7 to 9 p.m. Friday at the Price Funeral Home, Meyersdale. A funeral service will be conducted 11 a.m. Saturday at the Main Street Brethren Church. The Rev. Robert Stahl officiating. Interment Pine Hill Cemetery. Memorials may be made to the Main Street Brethren Church in her memory. Arrangements by the William Rowe Price Funeral Home Inc., Meyersdale
Dailyamerican.com, June 5, 2007

Parents:
Frank Christner (1875 - 1946)
Margaret Mae Pletcher Christner (1890 - 1931)

Spouse: Peter F Housel (1907 - 1977)

Children: Betty I. Housel Gnagey (1935 - 1989)

Burial: Pine Hill Cemetery, Berlin, Somerset Co., PA

More About Sadie Marie Christner:
Residence: 1930, Brothersvalley, Somerset Co., PA[2908]
SSN issued: PA[2909]

Notes for Peter Franklin Housel Sr.:
Birth: May 2, 1907 - Meyersdale, Somerset Co., PA
Death: Mar. 15, 1977 - Meyersdale, Somerset Co., PA

Obituary: Meyersdale Republic, March 17, 1977

Peter F. Housel, 69, of Meyersdale, died March 15 at Meyersdale Community Hospital. Born May 2, 1907, in Meyersdale he was the son of the late John and Margaret (Ohler) Housel. He is survived by his wife, the former Sadie Marie Christner, two sons, Peter Jr., Meyersdale RD 1, and Clyde, Sterling Park, Va.; six daughters, Mrs. Eleanor Fogle, Garrett; Mrs. Marie Mathers, Millvale, N.J.; Mrs. Betty Gnagey, Meyersdale RD 3; Mrs. Verna Mae Neidermeyer, Pittsburgh; Mrs. Doris Oester, Meyersdale RD 4; and Mrs. Anna Hamilton, Stone Mountain, Georgia; also 26 grandchildren and one great-grandchild. Also surviving him are two brothers, Eugene, Hampton, Va., and George, Meyersdale RD 4; four sisters, Mrs. Catherine Ohler, Garrett RD 1; Mrs. Emma Christner, Mrs. Tillie Shuck, and Mrs. Alverta Sanner, all of Meyersdale. He was a member of the Main Street Brethren Church where he was a deacon and Sunday school teacher. Friends will be received from 2 to 4 p.m. and 7 to 9 p.m. Wednesday and Thursday at the Price Funeral Home, Meyersdale. Funeral services will be conducted at 11 a.m. Friday with Rev. Joseph Hanna officiating. Interment, Pine Hill Cemetery. The family suggests that expressions of sympathy take the form of contributions to the Main Street Brethren Church.

Spouse: Sadie Marie Christner Housel (1911 - 2007)

Children: Betty I. Housel Gnagey (1935 - 1989)

Burial: Pine Hill Cemetery, Berlin, Somerset Co., PA

More About Peter Franklin Housel Sr.:
Burial: Pine Hill Cemetery Somerset Co., PA
Funeral Service: 18 Mar 1977, 11:00 am Friday William Rowe Price Funeral Home Rev. Joseph Hanna

Children of Sadie Christner and Peter Housel are:
+	1670	i.	Eleanor Louise[8] Housel, born 02 Apr 1933 in Meyersdale, Somerset Co., PA.
	1671	ii.	Agnes Marie Housel, born 15 Apr 1934 in Meyersdale, Somerset Co., PA. She married Norton Mathers.
+	1672	iii.	Betty Irene Housel, born 27 Sep 1935 in Meyersdale, Somerset Co., PA; died 28 Feb 1989 in Cumberland, Allegany Co., MD.
+	1673	iv.	Verna Mae Housel, born 06 Sep 1937 in Meyersdale, Somerset Co., PA.
+	1674	v.	Doris Lavern Housel, born 14 Mar 1939 in Meyersdale, Somerset Co., PA.
+	1675	vi.	Peter Franklin Housel Jr, born 17 Oct 1941 in Meyersdale, Somerset Co., PA.
+	1676	vii.	Anna Catherine Housel, born 08 Mar 1944 in Meyersdale, Somerset Co., PA.
+	1677	viii.	Clyde Franklin Housel, born 08 Mar 1947 in Meyersdale, Somerset Co., PA.

537. Margaret M.[7] Christner (Frank[6], Jacob C.[5], John J.[4], Johannes John Hans[3], Christian[2], Christen[1]) was born 25 Nov 1912 in Berlin, Somerset Co., PA, and died 1994 in Trenton, Mercer Co., NJ. She married **Melvin C. Albright**. He was born in Berlin, Somerset Co., PA.

Notes for Margaret M. Christner:
BRISTOL TWP., PA - Funeral services for Margaret M. Albright, 82 of Bristol Twp. who died Wednesday at her daughter's home in Levittown, PA will be held Monday at 11a.m. at the First Baptist Church of Levittown-

Fairless Hills, 6131 Emilie Road, Levittown. Burial will be in Greenwood Cemetery, Trenton.

Calling hours will be Sunday from 7 to 9 p.m. at Beck-O'Neill-Strouse Funeral Directors, 7400 New Falls Road, Levittown.

Born in Berlin, PA Mrs. Albright resided in Trenton for many years before moving to Bristol Twp. seven years ago. She was a member of VFW Post 3525, Trenton, Terchon VFW Post, Levittown, and the Bristol Twp. Senior Citizens.

Widow of Melvin C. Albright, she is survived by two daughters, Margaret Custer of Levittown and Patricia Hollender of Camp Hill, PA; three sons, William of Swansea, NC, Robert of Hamilton and Donald of Trenton; three sisters, Marie and Emma Housel, both of Meyersdale, PA and Dorothy Ohler of Dunlo, PA; 10 grandchildren, 12 great grandchildren, and many nieces and nephews.

Memorial donations may be made to the Chandler Hall Hospice/Home Health Agency, Buck Road at Barclay Street, Newtown, PA 18940.

More About Margaret M. Christner:
Burial: Greenwood Cemetery, Trenton, PA

Children of Margaret Christner and Melvin Albright are:
1678	i.	Donald[8] Albright.
1679	ii.	Margaret Albright. She married Custer.
1680	iii.	Patricia Albright. She married Hollender.
1681	iv.	Robert Albright.
1682	v.	William Albright.

538. Clyde Franklin[7] Christner (Frank[6], Jacob C.[5], John J.[4], Johannes John Hans[3], Christian[2], Christen[1]) was born 15 Mar 1915 in Brothersvalley Twp., Somerset Co., PA, and died 01 Oct 1988 in Trenton, Mercer Co., NJ[2910]. He married **Emma Irene Housel**. She was born 03 Sep 1912 in Larimer Twp., Somerset Co., PA, and died 30 Sep 1980 in Meyersdale, Summit Twp., Somerset Co., PA[2910].

Notes for Clyde Franklin Christner:
Obituary: Clyde F. CHRISTNER, 1988, formerly of Meyersdale, Somerset County, PA - Daily American, October 3, 1988
Clyde F. Christner, 73, of Morrisville, PA formerly of Meyersdale, died
Oct. 1 in Trenton, N.J. Born March 15, 1915, Brothersvalley Twp., son of
the late Frank and Margaret (Pletcher) Christner. Preceded in death by his wife, the former Emma Housel. Also preceded by a son, Clyde E.; and two daughters, Ruth, and Margaret Butler. Survived by these children: Robert C., Kenneth F. and Betty Brocht, all of Meyersdale; 21 Grandchildren, 18 great-grandchildren. A brother of: Margaret Albight, Trenton, N.J.; Dorothy Ohler of Dunlo; Marie Housel and Emma Housel, both of Meyersdale; also a daughter-in-law, Mary Ann Christner of Morrisville. Member of V.F.W. Post 3504. Friends will be received 2-4 and 7-9 p.m. Tuesday at the Price Funeral Home, Meyersdale, where services will be conducted at 11 a.m. Wednesday with Pastor Oscar Ohler officiating. Interment, Union Cemetery.

More About Clyde Franklin Christner:
Burial: Union Cemetery
Residence: 1930, Brothersvalley, Somerset Co., PA[2910]

More About Emma Irene Housel:
Residence: 1920, Summit, Somerset Co., PA[2910]

Children of Clyde Christner and Emma Housel are:
	1683	i.	Kenneth F.[8] Christner.
	1684	ii.	Ruth Christner.
+	1685	iii.	Margaret Alverda Christner, born 26 Nov 1933 in Summit Twp., Somerset Co., PA; died 12 Jun 1983 in Meyersdale, Somerset Co., PA.

1686	iv.	Betty Marie Christner, born 23 Oct 1935. She married Ron Brocht.
1687	v.	Clyde Eugene Christner, born 05 Apr 1937[2910]; died 27 Aug 1982 in Trenton, Mercer Co., NJ[2910].
+ 1688	vi.	Robert C. Christner, born 29 Aug 1940; died 29 Mar 2001 in Meyersdale, Somerset Co., PA.

539. George L.[7] Christner (Frank[6], Jacob C.[5], John J.[4], Johannes John Hans[3], Christian[2], Christen[1])[2911] was born 07 Jul 1917, and died 02 Mar 1948 in Baltimore, Baltimore Co., MD. He married **Catherine Ohler**.

Notes for George L. Christner:
Birth: Jul. 7, 1917
Death: Mar. 2, 1948

Burial: Dunmyer Cemetery, Salix, Cambria Co., PA
Plot: Sec. 3

Obituary: George L. Christner, 1948, Somerset County - Meyersdale Republican, March 11, 1948

George L. Christner died on March 2, at the age of 30 years, in Baltimore, MD, where he was employed. He was the sonof Mr. and Mrs. Frank Christner, both deceased.

His body was taken to Dunlo, PA for interment in the Dunmire Cemetery, Saturday, March 6, at 2:30 p.m.

He is survived by his wife, Mrs. Catherine (Ohler) Christner; two children, Shirley, 7,and Eugene, 9, and by the following named brothers and sisters: Mrs. Pete Housel, Clyde Christner and Mrs. George Housel, Meyersdale; Mrs. Melvin Albright and Mrs. George Ohler, Jr., Dunlo and John Christner of OH.

More About George L. Christner:
Burial: 06 Mar 1948, Sat. 2:30 pm at Dunmire Cemetery, Dunlo, PA[2912]

Children of George Christner and Catherine Ohler are:
| 1689 | i. | Eugene[8] Christner, born 1939. |
| 1690 | ii. | Shirley Christner, born 1941. |

540. John W.[7] Christner (Frank[6], Jacob C.[5], John J.[4], Johannes John Hans[3], Christian[2], Christen[1])[2913] was born 07 May 1920 in Berlin, Somerset Co., PA, and died 03 Oct 1987 in Laurel Crest Manor, Somerset Co., PA. He married **Eva**.

Notes for John W. Christner:
Obituary: John W. CHRISTNER, 1987 of interest in Somerset Co., PA - The Republic, October 8, 1987

John W. Christner, 67 Laurel Crest Manor, formerly of Dunlo, died Oct 3, 1987 at the manor. He was born May 7, 1920, in Berlin son of Frank and Maggie (Pletcher) Christner. He was preceded in death by parents; wife, Eva; and brother, George. He is survived by sons, Russell and Steven, both of Roanoke Rapids, NC and granddaughter, Tiffany. He was a brother of Sadie Marie Housel, Meyersdale; Margaret Albright, Silver Spring, MD; Clyde, Morrisville; Emma Housel, Meyersdale; and Dorothy Ohler, Dunlo. He was a veteran of World War II; member of VFW.
Arrangements were by George Funeral Home, Salix. Funeral and burial arrangements at convenience of family.

More About John W. Christner:
Burial: Cremated[2913]
Military service: WW II/
Oganization: VFW
Residence: Dunlo ???

Children of John Christner and Eva are:
| 1691 | i. | Russell[8] Christner. |

More About Russell Christner:
Residence: Roanoke Rapids NC

1692 ii. Steven Christner.

More About Steven Christner:
Residence: Roanoke Rapids NC

541. Emma Catherine[7] Christner (Frank[6], Jacob C.[5], John J.[4], Johannes John Hans[3], Christian[2], Christen[1])[2914] was born 06 Jul 1923 in Somerset, Somerset Co., PA[2914], and died 30 Sep 1980. She married **George Clayton Housel**[2914] 1945 in Pittsburgh, Allegheny Co., PA[2914]. He was born 24 May 1919 in Meyersdale, Somerset Co., PA, and died 24 Apr 1990 in Meyersdale, Somerset Co., PA.

More About Emma Catherine Christner:
Residence: 1930, Brothersvalley, Somerset Co., PA[2914]

More About George Clayton Housel:
Burial: Union Cemetery
Residence: 1930, Larimer, Somerset, PA[2914]

Children of Emma Christner and George Housel are:

    1693 i. Leonard[8] Housel.
    1694 ii. Matilda Mae Housel. She married Shuck.
    1695 iii. Roger Paul Housel.
+ 1696 iv. Rose Marie Housel.
+ 1697 v. George Martin Housel, born 08 Oct 1939.
    1698 vi. Donald Clayton Housel, born 09 Feb 1946; died 05 Mar 1946.
+ 1699 vii. James Eward Housel, born 04 Mar 1947.
+ 1700 viii. William Eugene Housel, born 04 Mar 1947 in Meyersdale, Somerset Co., PA; died 14 Sep 2001 in Somerset, Somerset Co., PA.
+ 1701 ix. Thomas Richard Housel, born 26 Sep 1951.
+ 1702 x. Nancy Jane Housel, born 16 Jan 1952.
+ 1703 xi. Robert Harold Housel, born 29 Oct 1954 in Meyersdale, Somerset Co., PA; died 06 Sep 1985 in Meyersdale, Somerset Co., PA.
    1704 xii. Catherine Irene Housel, born 03 Nov 1956.
    1705 xiii. Emma Arlene Housel, born 03 Nov 1956. She married Beal.

Notes for Emma Arlene Housel:
OBIT: Emma I. (HOUSEL) CHRISTNER, 1980, Meyersdale, Somerset County, PA - The Republic, October 9, 1980

Emma I. Christner, 68, of Meyersdale, died Sept. 30, 1980 at Meyersdale Community Hospital. She was born Sept. 3, 1912 in Larimer Twp., a daughter of the late John M. and Margaret (Ohler) Housel. She is survived by her husband, Clyde F. and these children: Mrs. Margaret Butler, Mrs. Betty Brocht, Robert, and Kenneth, all of Meyersdale; and Clyde E. of Morrisville; 20 grandchildren; 12 great-grandchildren. She was a sister of Mrs. Tillie Shuck and Alverta Sanner, both of Meyersdale; Mrs. Catherine Ohler, Garrett RD 1; and Clay Housel, Meyersdale RD 4.

Friends were received at the Price Funeral Home, Meyersdale, where services were conducted by the Rev. Robert Payne. Interment, Union Cemetery.

+ 1706 xiv. Patricia Ann Housel, born 25 Feb 1958.
+ 1707 xv. Thomas Patrick Housel, born 01 Jan 1959.
    1708 xvi. Kenneth Franklin Housel, born 11 Apr 1961 in Meyersdale, Somerset Co., PA; died 05 Jun 1982 in Meyersdale, Somerset Co., PA.

More About Kenneth Franklin Housel:
Burial: Union Cemetery

    1709 xvii. Brenda Housel, born 03 Mar 1963; died 07 Mar 1963.

542. Dorothy Caroline[7] Christner (Frank[6], Jacob C.[5], John J.[4], Johannes John Hans[3], Christian[2], Christen[1]) was born 08 Oct 1926 in Brothersvalley Twp., Somerset Co., PA, and died 16 Apr 1996 in Pittsburgh, Allegheny Co., PA. She married **George W. "Bud" Ohler**. He was born 09 Apr 1913 in Cassellman, and died 23 Mar 1986.

Notes for Dorothy Caroline Christner:
Dorothy C., 69, Coulter Street, Dunlo, died April 16, 1996, at Montefiore Medical Center, Pittsburgh. Born Oct. 8, 1926, in Brothersvalley Township, daughter of Frank and Margaret (Pletcher) Christner. Preceded in death by parents; husband, George W. "Bud"; sons, Robert and George; daughter, Mary Ann; grandson, Jason; brothers, George, Clyde, and John; and sister, Margaret Albright. Survived by these children: Barbara, wife of Glenn Crum, Sidman; Margaret, wife of Howard Hill, Browns Mills, N.J.; Nancy, wife of George Yatsky, Dunlo; Kenneth, at home, Carol, wife of Richard Walters, Elkhart, Ind; and Norman Gene, Columbus, Ohio; 12 grandchildren and 6 great grandchildren. Sister of Sadie Marie Housel; Emma Housel, both of Meyersdale.

Also survived by best friend, Evelyn Seese of Dunlo; and Kenneth's fiancee, Terry Eicher. Member of Dunlo Ladies Fire Auxiliary, Dunlo American Legion, Post 573, auxiliary; Beaverdale Senior Citizens; Dunlo Citizens Club Bowling League; SNPJ Lodge 274, Dunlo; and Dunlo United Methodist Church.

Family will receive friends 2 to 4 and 6 to 9p..m. Friday and from 10a.m. until time of service at 2p.m. Saturday at Homer J. George Funeral Home, Salix, the Rev. Richard Ralph Interment, Dunmyer Cemetery. Dunlo American Legion Ladies Auxiliary will hold a service at 8p.m. Friday.

More About Dorothy Caroline Christner:
Burial: Dunmyer Cemetery

More About George W. "Bud" Ohler:
Burial: Dunmyer Cemetery

Children of Dorothy Christner and George Ohler are:
1710	i.	Barbara[8] Ohler. She married Glenn Crum.
1711	ii.	Carol Ohler. She married Richard Walters.
1712	iii.	George Ohler.
1713	iv.	Kenneth Ohler. He married Terry Eicher.
1714	v.	Margaret Ohler. She married Howard Hill.
1715	vi.	Mary Ann Ohler.
1716	vii.	Nancy Ohler. She married George Yatsky.
1717	viii.	Norman Gene Ohler.
1718	ix.	Robert Ohler.

558. John R.[7] Berg (Deliah[6] Christner, John[5], Peter[4], Johannes John Hans[3], Christian[2], Christen[1]) He married **Priscilla Christner** 1861 in They raised 5 childeren. John served in the 168th PA. Infantry, Company B in the Civil War./, daughter of John Christner and Susannah Griffith. She was born Dec 1835 in Somerset, Somerset Co., PA[2915], and died 1918 in Connellsville, Fayette Co., PA.

More About Priscilla Christner:
Residence: 1910, Mount Pleasant, Westmoreland, PA[2915]

Children are listed above under (155) Priscilla Christner.

569. Ananias Sipe[7] Christner (Peter[6], John[5], Peter[4], Johannes John Hans[3], Christian[2], Christen[1])[2916,2917] was born 26 Jul 1850 in Saltlick Twp, Fayette Co PA[2918,2919], and died Jan 1930 in Lost Springs, Marion Co., KS[2920,2921]. He married **Inez Elizabeth Benschooter**[2921] 08 Sep 1878 in Uniontown, Fayette Co., PA, daughter of Alexander Benschooter and Harriet. She was born 27 May 1852 in Seneca City, OH[2922,2923], and died 13 Jan 1913 in Lost Springs, Marion Co., KS[2923].

Notes for Ananias Sipe Christner:
Birth: Jul 26, 1850
Death: Jan 10, 1931

Spouse: Inez E. Christner (1852 - 1911)

Burial: Lost Springs Cemetery, Lost Springs, Marion Co., KS
Plot: Lot 5, block 3

More About Ananias Sipe Christner:
Residence: 1910, Lost Springs, Marion Co., KS[2923,2924]

Notes for Inez Elizabeth Benschooter:
Inez died of lung fever.

Birth: 1852
Death: 1911

Spouse: Ananias Christner (1850 - 1931)

Burial: Lost Springs Cemetery, Lost Springs, Marion Co., KS
Plot: Lot 5, block 3

The 1900 census has her listed as Inez Shristner.

More About Inez Elizabeth Benschooter:
Burial: 15 Jan 1911, IOOF Cemetery, Lost Springs, Marion Co., KS
Cause of Death: lung fever
Residence: 1910, Lost Springs, Marion Co., KS[2925,2926]

Children of Ananias Christner and Inez Benschooter are:

+	1719	i.	Elmer[8] Christner, born 10 Jun 1874 in Edgar, Clay Co., NE; died 14 May 1946 in Hutchinson, Reno Co., KS.
+	1720	ii.	Mary Allen Christner, born 09 Oct 1876 in Edgar, Clay Co., NE; died 17 Jun 1962 in Ellsworth, KS.
+	1721	iii.	Arthur Christner, born 08 Nov 1879 in Edgar, Clay Co., NE; died 21 Nov 1928 in Lost Springs, Marion Co., KS.
+	1722	iv.	Jay Christner, born 23 Nov 1881 in Edgar, Clay Co., NE; died 26 May 1953 in Independance, Montgomery Co., KS.
+	1723	v.	Herman Christner, born 05 Dec 1885 in Arapahoe, Furnas Co., NE; died 05 Dec 1970 in Herington, Dickinson Co., KS.
+	1724	vi.	Sara Elizabeth Christner, born 12 Apr 1888 in Chardoce, KS; died 1971 in Hutchinson, Reno Co., KS.

574. Winfield Scott[7] Christner (Peter[6], John[5], Peter[4], Johannes John Hans[3], Christian[2], Christen[1])[2927] was born 23 Sep 1863 in Wabash Co., IN, and died 11 May 1947 in Silver Lake, Kosciusko Co., IN. He married **(1) Rosa Day Evans** 04 Sep 1886. She was born 1869 in Wayne Twp., IN, and died 26 Feb 1926 in South Bend, St. Joseph Co., IN. He married **(2) Sarah Belle Lightcap**[2927] 17 Jun 1904 in Marriage book: M:300 (http://www.ingenweb.org/inkosciusko/mar20q1L.htm)/Kosciusko Co., IN[2927]. She was born Jul 1867 in Kosciusko Co., IN[2927], and died 25 Sep 1920 in Silver Lake, Kosciusko Co., IN[2927].

Notes for Winfield Scott Christner:
Winfield Scott Christner 9/23/1863-5/11/1947
There is not a lot of information about Winfield Christner, but what we know is that he was a clean man, but he had a drinking problem. The is conflicting information about how old he was, but it appears he was 83.

His Obituary states:

Funeral services were conducted by Rev. Levi Hill Tuesday afternoon at the Summe Funeral Home for Winfield Christner who died at 8:00 Sunday morning at a nursing home near Warsaw. Burial was made at South Pleasant Cemetery, Wabash County. Mr. Christner was 85 years old. He was born south of Silver Lake in Wabash County 9/25/1863, son of Peter and Martha Chrisnter. His entire life was spent in this locality. He was first married to Rose Evans, and was later married to Sarah Belle Lightcap in 1907 by S. Kauffman, Min. Belle died 9/25/1920. Surviving relatives include one son Elmer, by his first marriage and a son Peter by the second marriage, a sister Mrs. Alice Miller of near North Manchester, several grandchildren and great grandchildren.

From the Kosciusko County Courthouse his death information says. Winfield died on 5/11/1947, that the place of death was Kosciusko Co., IN Rural. It states his age as 83 years, 7 months & 16 days. It states he was widowed and that his burial was at South Pleasant Cemetery on 5/13/1947. The Undertaker was E. E. Summe, and the coroner was T. S. Schuldt. The cause of death was Mitral Regurgitation.

The Cemetery book for South Pleasant lists his burial plot in Row 8, South to North, Marker 12. I have not been able to locate any marker.

Winfield and Rosa Evans were married on 9/4/1886. The had 2 children, one son Elmer Sherman Christner who was born 6/26/1887, who died 9/8/1972. They also had a daughter named Bessie Virginia Christner who was born 1/21/1889, who preceded Winfield in death on 2/3/1931.

The story is that Winfield routinely drank up all their money, and that Jesse Evans (the father of Rosa) had bought them a good horse and that one night while drinking, Winfield had run out of money and traded the horse for money and continued to drink that away. When Rosa found out what he had done, she left him.

At the age of 40 he married Sarah Belle Lightcap, known as Effie. They married on 6/17/1904, when she was 33. She was born in 1867 and she died 9/25/1920 at the age of 53. They had one son, Devone G. Christner, known as Pete. Pete was born 5/13/1909 and he died 10/31/1974.

The 1880 Pleasant Township, Wabash County Census lists Winfield having the occupation of farmer that is also what his father is listed as. Winfield continued to drink away his life. He used to borrow money from Elmer, but once Elmer told him he could not give Winfield any more money to drink on, as Elmer had 10 children to raise Winfield had nothing to do with Elmer after that. He lived in a small cottage down by Silver Lake.
Sheri Christner Krichbaum

Birth: 1863
Death: 1947

Burial: South Pleasant Methodist Church Cemetery, North Manchester, Wabash Co., IN

More About Winfield Scott Christner:
Burial: 1947, South Pleasant Methodist Church Cemetery/North Manchester, Wabash, Indiana, USA[2927]
Residence: 1910, Lake, Kosciusko, Indiana[2927]

Notes for Rosa Day Evans:
Rosa Day Evans Christner Walburn Kesling

Rosa Day Evans was born in 1869 in Wayne Township. Her parents were Jesse Evans, who was born in 1831 in Virginia. He married Vesta Jane Holstead 4/4/1858. Rosa married Winfield Scott Christner 9/4/1886. They had two children, a son Elmer Sherman Christner 6/26/1887 who died 9/8/1972, and a daughter Bessie Virginia Christner 1/21/1889. This marriage did not last long, due to Winfield being a heavy drinker. The story goes that Jesse Evans had bought Winfield and Rosa a good horse and on one night when Winfield ran out of money while drinking he traded the horse for money and continued to drink that money away also. She then left him.

On 1/10/1893 in Silver Lake, IN, Rosa married her 2nd husband, Joel W. Walburn. Joel is the son of Peter Walburn (1816-10/14/1897). The marriage record is #J268 in the book of Marriages of Kosciusko County 1892-1895, Page 13. The strange thing about this is the father listed for the bride is James Halstedge. Vesta Jane Holstead is the mother of Rosa, so maybe a Holstead family member stood up for her instead of her father Jesse.

Joel must have been married before as the Republican Indianian of Silver Lake of 9/18/1884 reports the death of a 3 month old child of Joel Walburn was buried at Germantown graveyard, 3 1/2 miles northwest of Silver Lake and the same paper of 3/18/1886 reports that a boy was born to the wife of Joel Walburn on Sunday 3/14/1886. In the 12/9/1875 issue it is reported that Harvey Walburn died on Saturday at the house of his brother Joel in Silver Lake. His funeral was preached on that day at what is called Germany, which was about 3 miles north by Rev. J.B. Alleman West. Also reported in the 11/6/1884 issue that at the residence of Joel Walburn at Silver Lake Edwin Walburn was married to Martha I. Hiatt, on 11/2/1884, with D. Kiwitt officiating.

On 11/4/1922 in Kosciusko County Rosa married Frank Kesling. Rosa died on 2/26/1926 in South Bend, St. Joseph County of Complies at the age of 57.

She is buried at Oakwood Cemetery, Warsaw, Indiana on 2/28/1926. She is buried on the North 1/2 of 13 in Block 28. I have found her marker and photographed it. The odd thing is that even though she was married to Frank Kesling, Joel Walburn is buried in the North 1/4 of Block #38. Joel died 8/21/1929 in Warsaw, Indiana of Parslysis. At the age of 89.

Chain of Events in the life of Rosa Day Evans: 1869 Rosa Day Evans born in Wayne Township, Kosciusko Co., IN to Jesse & Vesta Jane Holstead Evans.

9/4/1886Rosa Marries Winfield Scott Christner

6/26/1887Rosa gives birth to Elmer Sherman Christner

1/21/1889Rosa gives birth to Bessie Virginia Christner

Rosa and Winfield Christner Divorce

1/10/1893Rosa marries Joel Wallllburn Walburn

Rosa and Joel Walburn Divorce

11/4/1922Rosa marries Frank Kesling

2/26/1926Rosa dies in South Bend of Complies, at the age of 57

2/28/1926Rosa is buried at Oakwood Cemetery, Warsaw, Indiana near her 2nd husband Joel Walburn. She has a marker

Sheri Christner Krichbaum

More About Rosa Day Evans:
Burial: Oakwood Cemetery, Warsaw, IN

More About Sarah Belle Lightcap:
Residence: 1910, Lake, Kosciusko, Indiana[2927]

Children of Winfield Christner and Rosa Evans are:

+ 1725   i.   Elmer Sherman[8] Christner, born 26 Jun 1887 in Disko, Wabash Co., IN; died 08 Sep 1972 in Palestine, Kosciusko Co., IN.

    1726   ii.   Bessie Virginia Christner, born 21 Jan 1889; died 03 Feb 1931 in Argos, IN. She married (1) Martin. She married (2) Ward. She married (3) Artie Hall 24 Dec 1902. She married (4) Fred Stoner 26 Mar 1910 in Kosciusko Co., IN; born 25 Jul 1887. She married (5) Mason Freeman 02 Jul 1912 in Kosciusko Co., IN.

           More About Bessie Virginia Christner:
           Burial: Oakwood Cemetery, Warsaw, Indiana NO STONE Section 28

Cause of Death: During an operation at Argos Indiana

More About Fred Stoner:
Other-Begin: Kosciusko Co.[2928]
Residence: Kosciusko Co., IN[2928,2929]

Child of Winfield Christner and Sarah Lightcap is:
   1727   i.   Devon G. "Pete"[8] Christner, born 13 May 1909 in Silver Lake, Kosciusko Co., IN; died 01 Nov 1974 in Silver Lake, Kosciusko Co., IN. He married Lucille.

               Notes for Devon G. "Pete" Christner:
The towns people bought his headstone   "Devone G. Christner known as Pete
At the age of 40 Winfield S. Christner marries Sarah Belle Lightcap, known as Effie, age 33. She was born in 1867 and she died Sep. 25, 1920.

May 13, 1909 Effie gave birth to Devone G. Christner, known as Pete. Pete Christner is well remembered in Silver Lake for his eccentricities. He liked to drink and had bottles hidden in the town of Silver Lake. At one time Pete worked and lived in Chicago. He was married to a woman named Lucille and she is remembered as being a sharp dresser with beautiful red hair. At one time she was a cosmetic demonstrator.

Pete continued to drink and ended up alone, living in a shack that was no more than a shed in Silver Lake. They say Pete was good hearted and if he liked you he would do anything for you, but if he did not like you he had nothing to do with you.

In my research, I have spoken with several of the old-timers of Silver Lake. I spoke with Lowell Zile, Bill and Evelyn (Kline) Jagger, Louise Newhouse and Gene and Catherine (Grubb) Arnold.

Sadly, Pete is most remembered for the fact that he always wore bib overalls with no under clothing and he never bothered to button the sides. He gave everyone quite a view, as he seemed to like to scratch himself a lot also. He was not very clean, and always smelled like wine. He sat out front of the stores of Silver Lake and chewed tobacco. He was interesting to talk to and had beautiful penmanship. In 1917 the Silver Lake Record published, when Pete was in 2nd grade he had perfect spelling for the month. He was not an ignorant individual, he just treasured drinking more than achieving a successful life.

At one time he had a job at the North Manchester Foundry, and they knew he was drinking but could not find the bottle. They watched him and finally found that he was hiding the bottle in the toilet tank and he was fired. In 1967 he painted the roof of the hardware store in Silver Lake. He did odd jobs, and no job was too dirty for him. He did a lot of work with the sewers and they all missed him when he passed, because he knew where every water pipe and sewer was.

Pete would never be available to do a job the day you asked him. He could come the next day, but never the day you asked him. He spent a lot of time in the Silver Inn Saloon, at the time Maurry Reid owned the tavern.

Mrs. Evelyn (Kline) Jagger remembers as a girl, that their dog named Sandy, which was good tempered hated Pete. Pete on rare occasions would go to the pond behind their house and bathe. He would just strip off his overalls and wash. But he was smelly and not very clean.

Pete was arrested by State Police officer Henry Cripe for carrying a gun. Pete had several. In the past Pete had done some dirty job for the sheriff of Kosciusko County Frank Lucas and Frank let Pete go.

Oct. 31, 1974, at the age of 65, Pete was found dead behind his shed and all of his guns were missing. His death was questioned, but ruled natural causes. A rumor was that Hayden Newhouse shot him. He was found on a Thursday morning, but the coroner ruled he had been dead since sometime Monday

Pete had no money and was buried in a cheap box. He is buried at South Pleasant Cemetery, Wabash County. Several men of Silver Lake went together and took up a collection and purchased Pete a stone. I have found and photographed his marker.
Sheri Christner Krichbaum

Birth: 1909

Death: 1974

Burial: South Pleasant Methodist Church Cemetery, North Manchester, Wabash Co., IN
Find A Grave Memorial# 34230258

More About Devon G. "Pete" Christner:
Burial: South Pleasant Cemetery, Wabash Co., IN
Residence: 1910, Lake, Kosciusko, Indiana[2930]

575. Alice D.[7] Christner (Peter[6], John[5], Peter[4], Johannes John Hans[3], Christian[2], Christen[1])[2931] was born 13 Apr 1871 in Wabash, Wabash Co., IN[2931], and died 21 Nov 1961 in North Manchester, IN. She married **(1) Mason H. Grogg**[2931] 19 Jan 1890 in Wabash Co., IN by David Swihart[2931]. He was born 06 Oct 1866 in On a farm east of Gilead, Indiana./Miami Co., IN[2931], and died 17 Oct 1940 in At his home two and a half miles southwest of Akron, Indiana./Miami Co., IN[2931]. She married **(2) Jacob H. Miller** Feb 1946. He was born 04 Mar 1869 in North Manchester, IN[2932], and died 30 Aug 1962 in Warsaw, Kosciusko Co., IN.

Notes for Alice D. Christner:
Birth: 1871
Death: 1961

Burial: Akron IOOF Cemetery, Akron, Fulton Co., IN
Find A Grave Memorial# 64502205

More About Alice D. Christner:
Burial: 24 Nov 1961, Odd Fellows Cemetery, Akron, IN

Notes for Mason H. Grogg:
Birth: 1866
Death: 1940

Burial: Akron IOOF Cemetery, Akron, Fulton Co., IN
Find A Grave Memorial# 64502225

More About Mason H. Grogg:
Burial: Odd Fellows Cemetery, Akron, IN

Marriage Notes for Alice Christner and Mason Grogg:
By David Swihart

Notes for Jacob H. Miller:
Farmer

More About Jacob H. Miller:
Burial: Pleasant Hill Cemetery
Occupation: Farmer/
Social Security Number: 317-34-1198/[2932]
SSN issued: IN[2932]

Children of Alice Christner and Mason Grogg are:
	1728	i.	Theresa[8] Grogg[2933], born 18 Jun 1892 in Fulton Co., IN[2933]; died 12 Dec 1977 in IN[2933]. She married (1) Dowell Landis. She married (2) Harley Bucher.
+	1729	ii.	Theron Defoe Grogg, born 21 Oct 1900 in IN; died 02 Feb 1952 in Fort Wayne, Allen Co., IN.
+	1730	iii.	Forrest Ivan Grogg, born 11 Mar 1906 in Near Gilead./Miami Co., IN; died 24 May 1990 in Life Care Center./Fulton Co., IN.

576. Clarissa[7] Christner (Cain[6], John[5], Peter[4], Johannes John Hans[3], Christian[2], Christen[1])[2934] was born 12 Apr 1853 in Indian Head, Saltlick Twp., Fayette Co., PA, and died 20 May 1930 in Connellsville, Fayette Co.,

PA. She married **Soloman Shaffer** 12 Jan 1872 in Connellsville, Fayette Co., PA. He was born 28 Feb 1852 in Connellsville, Fayette Co., PA, and died 19 Jan 1916 in Connellsville, Fayette Co., PA.

Notes for Clarissa Christner:
Birth: 1853
Death: 1930

Spouse: Solomon B. Shaffer (1852 - 1916)

Burial: Shaffer Cemetery, Fayette Co., PA
Find A Grave Memorial# 99666817

More About Clarissa Christner:
Burial: Shaffer Cemetery

Notes for Soloman Shaffer:
Soloman is the son of Samuel and Margaret Brooks Shaffer.

Child of Clarissa Christner and Soloman Shaffer is:

1731	i.	Agnes[8] Shaffer, born 03 Nov 1887 in Connellsville, Fayette Co., PA. She married Charles Sisley Flack 03 Sep 1938.

577. Mary[7] Christner (Cain[6], John[5], Peter[4], Johannes John Hans[3], Christian[2], Christen[1])[2934,2935] was born 29 Jul 1855 in Saltlick Twp., Fayette Co., PA[2935], and died 08 Apr 1933 in Glendo, Platte Co., WY. She married **Jacob S. Weimer** 28 Dec 1873 in Fayette Co., PA, Brides Parents, Home. He was born 08 Sep 1852 in Saltlick Twp., Fayette Co., PA[2935], and died 10 Oct 1918 in Glendo, Platte Co., WY.

More About Mary Christner:
Burial: Glendo Cem, Wyoming
Residence: 1920, Election District 13, Platte Co., Wyoming, USA[2935]

Notes for Jacob S. Weimer:
Jacob is the son of Joseph and Susan Shaffer Weimer. In 1900 Jacob and Mary moved to Russell Co, KS. In 1913 they homesteaded land in Glendo, WY.

More About Jacob S. Weimer:
Burial: Glendo Cem, Wyoming
Residence: 1915, Luray, Russell Co., Kansas, USA[2935]

Children of Mary Christner and Jacob Weimer are:

+	1732	i.	Harry Christner[8] Weimer, born 30 Nov 1874 in Connellsville, Fayette Co., PA; died 10 Sep 1938 in On a street corner while returning from work (walking)./Youngwood, Westmoreland Co., PA.
	1733	ii.	Samuel Weimer[2935], born 30 Nov 1874 in Connellsville, Fayette Co., PA; died 30 Nov 1874 in Connellsville, Fayette Co., PA.
+	1734	iii.	Cain C. Weimer, born 10 Nov 1876 in Connellsville, Fayette Co., PA; died 07 Sep 1945 in Lutheran Hospital/Fort Wayne, Allen Co., IN.
	1735	iv.	Edwin C. Weimer, born 13 Mar 1878 in Connellsville, Fayette Co., PA; died 29 Sep 1947 in Glendo, Platte Co., WY.

> More About Edwin C. Weimer:
> Burial: Glendo Cemetery
> Residence: 1910, Luray, Russell, Kansas[2935]

	1736	v.	David Weimer[2935], born 15 Sep 1879 in Connellsville, Fayette Co., PA; died 13 Aug 1882 in Connellsville, Fayette Co., PA.

> More About David Weimer:
> Residence: 1880, Springfield, Fayette Co., PA[2935]

1737	vi.	Simon Weimer[2935], born 18 Jun 1883 in Connellsville, Fayette Co., PA; died 11 Aug 1883 in Connellsville, Fayette Co., PA.
+ 1738	vii.	Susannah Pearl Weimer, born 14 May 1884 in Connellsville, Fayette Co., PA; died 20 Sep 1956 in Cheyenne, Laramie Co., WY.
1739	viii.	Joseph C. Weimer, born 20 Apr 1887 in Connellsville, Fayette Co., PA; died 18 Jan 1974 in Glendo, Platte Co., WY. He married Lydia A. Keatley.

More About Joseph C. Weimer:
Burial: Glendo Cemetery
Residence: 1900, Fairview Township (West Portion), Russell Co., KS[2935]

1740	ix.	James Russel Weimer[2935], born 24 Nov 1889 in Connellsville, Fayette Co., PA; died 04 Jan 1890 in Connellsville, Fayette Co., PA.
1741	x.	William Weimer[2935], born 16 Jul 1891 in Connellsville, Fayette Co., PA; died 09 Aug 1891 in Connellsville, Fayette Co., PA.
1742	xi.	John Lorenza Weimer, born 24 Jul 1892 in Connellsville, Fayette Co., PA; died 06 Oct 1960 in Glendo, Platte Co., WY. He married Deloris Mowrey Judy 26 Jul 1919; born 25 Apr 1904 in Montgomery Co., IL.

More About John Lorenza Weimer:
Burial: Glendo Cemetery
Residence: 1930, Glendo, Platte, Wyoming[2935]

1743	xii.	George Morris Weimer[2935], born 31 Mar 1895 in Connellsville, Fayette Co., PA; died 26 Apr 1895 in Connellsville, Fayette Co., PA.
1744	xiii.	Etta Prissilla Weimer[2935], born 02 Sep 1896 in Connellsville, Fayette Co., PA; died 08 Nov 1896 in Connellsville, Fayette Co., PA.

578. Susana Susannah[7] Christner (Cain[6], John[5], Peter[4], Johannes John Hans[3], Christian[2], Christen[1])[2936] was born 02 May 1857 in Connellsville, Fayette Co., PA, and died 12 Dec 1945 in Connellsville, Fayette Co., PA[2936]. She married **George F. Miller** 01 Aug 1875. He was born 05 Apr 1851, and died 16 Mar 1925.

More About Susana Susannah Christner:
Burial: Indian Head, Fayette Co., PA

Children of Susana Christner and George Miller are:

1745	i.	Mary Ann[8] Miller.
1746	ii.	Rebecca Miller, born 12 Feb 1876; died 08 Jan 1917. She married William Knopsnider.

Notes for Rebecca Miller:
Rebecca married William Knopsnider

1747	iii.	Elizabeth Miller, born 08 May 1877; died 25 Jan 1933. She married John Firestone.

Notes for Elizabeth Miller:
Elizabeth married John Firestone

1748	iv.	Quincy Miller, born 05 Mar 1879; died 13 Feb 1951. He married Lisa Weimer.

Notes for Quincy Miller:
Quincy married Lisa Weimer

1749	v.	David C. Miller, born 05 Dec 1880. He married Ida Myers.

Notes for David C. Miller:
David married Ida Myers

1750   vi.   Sarah Miller, born 15 Jun 1884; died 14 Dec 1954. She married William Nedrow.

        Notes for Sarah Miller:
        Sarah married William Nedrow

1751   vii.   Mary Ann Miller, born 05 Dec 1885; died 11 Mar 1958.
1752   viii. Tura Miller, born 20 Dec 1887; died 10 Jul 1909.
1753   ix.   Amos Christner Miller, born 12 Jun 1896; died 15 Sep 1964. He married Bessie Miller in Cumberland, Alleganey Co., MD.

        Notes for Amos Christner Miller:
        Amos married Bessie Miller

        The Daily Courier - 10 Jan 1920
        Connellsville, Fayette Co., PA

        Licensed to Wed

        Amos Christner Miller and Bessie Miller both of Indian Head were licensed to wed in Cumberland.

579. Priscilla[7] Christner (Cain[6], John[5], Peter[4], Johannes John Hans[3], Christian[2], Christen[1])[2936] was born 17 Mar 1863 in Saltlick Twp., Fayette Co., PA[2936], and died 18 May 1916 in Disco, Wabash Co., IN. She married **John Ohm** 05 Sep 1888.

Notes for Priscilla Christner:
This info came from Bob Weimer of Cockeysville, MD.   As a girl Priscilla went to live with her uncle Peter Christner near Silver Lake, IN.

More About Priscilla Christner:
Burial: RoanI.O.O.F., Wabash Co, IN
Residence: 1880, Saltlick Twp., Fayette Co., PA[2936]

Notes for John Ohm:
John lived on a farm 2 miles from Disco, Wabash City, IN.

Children of Priscilla Christner and John Ohm are:
1754   i.   Ruth V.[8] Ohm, born 12 Oct 1889 in Disco, Wabash Co., IN; died 1977 in Akron, Wabash Co, IN. She married Frank Dershern.

        Notes for Ruth V. Ohm:
        Ruth married Frank Dershem

1755   ii.   Tressa E. Ohm, born 18 Jul 1891 in Disco, Wabash Co., IN; died Dec 1966. She married P. M. Kinder.

        Notes for Tressa E. Ohm:

        More About Tressa E. Ohm:
        Burial: AkronI.O.O.F., Cem

1756   iii. Ruel R. Ohm, born 05 Sep 1892 in Disco, Wabash Co., IN.

        Notes for Ruel R. Ohm:
        Ruel was a vetern of WWI.

1757   iv.   Etta J. Ohm, born 14 Oct 1893 in Disco, Wabash Co., IN; died Jan 1965. She married Homer Luallin.

More About Etta J. Ohm:
Burial: LaHabia

1758   v.   Rebecca Irene Ohm, born 11 Apr 1895 in Disco, Wabash Co., IN; died Dec 1965. She married Merl McGlennen.

Notes for Rebecca Irene Ohm:

1759   vi.   Dewey Ohm, born 18 Aug 1898 in Disco, Wabash Co., IN. He married Nelda.

581. Winfield Scott[7] Christner (Samuel[6], John[5], Peter[4], Johannes John Hans[3], Christian[2], Christen[1])[2937] was born 18 Sep 1854 in Bullskin Twp., Fayette Co., PA, and died 07 Nov 1934 in Pittsfield, Washtenaw Co., MI[2937]. He married **(1) Sarah White**. She was born 09 Jan 1859, and died 07 Mar 1879. He married **(2) Emma C. Weimer**[2937] 1890. She was born Feb 1864 in Henry Co., IL[2937].

Notes for Winfield Scott Christner:
Headstone at Saltlick, Fayette Co., PA. Sarah w/o Winfield Christner 3/7/1879 20y 1m 29d this would make her born on January 6, 1859.

More About Winfield Scott Christner:
Residence: 1930, Pittsfield, Washtenaw, Michigan[2937]

Notes for Sarah White:
Buried in Keslar Cemetery, Fayette Co., PA.

More About Emma C. Weimer:
Residence: 1930, Pittsfield, Washtenaw, Michigan[2937]

Child of Winfield Christner and Sarah White is:
+   1760   i.   Reuel Stanley[8] Christner, born 31 Aug 1878 in Bullskin Twp., Fayette Co., PA; died 26 Jan 1971 in Uniontown, Fayette Co., PA.

Children of Winfield Christner and Emma Weimer are:
+   1761   i.   Earl Weimer[8] Christner, born 04 Feb 1885 in Fayette Co., PA; died 07 Dec 1962 in OH.
+   1762   ii.   Edith Arlene Christner, born 10 Mar 1890 in Connellsville, Fayette Co., PA; died 08 May 1984 in Geneseo, Henry Co., IL.
+   1763   iii.   Elwyn Christner, born 14 Feb 1892 in Mt. Olive Cemetery, Bullskin Twp., Fayette Co., PA; died 12 Mar 1993 in Geneseo, Henry Co., IL.
    1764   iv.   Esther A. Christner, born Jun 1898 in Connellsville, Fayette Co., PA[2938].

Notes for Esther A. Christner:
The info I have says this childs name is Either. I just cant beleive that so the child is listed as just E

583. Warren[7] Christner (Samuel[6], John[5], Peter[4], Johannes John Hans[3], Christian[2], Christen[1])[2939,2940,2941,2942] was born 26 Apr 1861 in Bullskin Twp., Fayette Co., PA, and died 07 Jul 1934 in Bullskin Twp., Fayette Co., PA[2943]. He married **(1) Amanda Raymond**. She was born Nov 1861 in Saltlick Twp., Fayette Co., PA, and died 15 Sep 1927. He married **(2) Sadie Sara E. Lyons** 22 Jun 1886 in Westmorland Co. PA. She was born 25 Jun 1863 in Saltlick Twp., Fayette Co., PA[2943], and died 04 Nov 1896 in Bullskin Twp., Fayette Co., PA[2943].

More About Warren Christner:
Burial: 1934, Mt. Joy Church Cemetery/Fayette Co, PA[2943]

Occupation: Teacher/
Residence: 1880, Saltlick Twp., Fayette Co., PA[2943]

Notes for Amanda Raymond:
OBITUARY: The Daily Courier - Connellsville, PA
15 Sep 1927

MRS. WARREN CHRISTNER, Mount Pleasant, Sept 15

Mrs. Amanda Christner, 65 years and 10 months old, wife of Warren Christner, died at her home near Paraside Church, Bullskin Township yesterday afternoon. She had not been in the best of health for some time but the fatal illness manifested itself only about two weeks ago.

Mrs. Christner was born in Saltlick Township, her maiden name being Raymond. Her first husband was Henry Ellenberger, who died many years ago. One daughter to this marriage survives. She is Mrs. Effie Dibler of Elizabethville, near Harrisburg. Mrs. Christner was a member of Fairview United Brethern Church.

The funeral service will be Saturday morning at 10 o'clock at the home. Burial will be in Mount Olive Cemetery.

More About Amanda Raymond:
Residence: 1900, Bullskin Twp., Fayette Co., PA[2944]

More About Sadie Sara E. Lyons:
Burial: Snyder Cemetery/Fayette Co, PA[2945]
Residence: 1880, Saltlick Twp., Fayette Co., PA[2945]

Children of Warren Christner and Amanda Raymond are:
    1765   i.   Effie[8] Ellenberger[2946], born Oct 1884 in Pittsburgh, Allegheny Co., PA[2946].

                 More About Effie Ellenberger:
                 Residence: 1900, Bullskin Twp., Fayette Co., PA[2946]

    1766   ii.   Jerusha Christner[2946,2947], born Mar 1892 in Pittsburgh, Allegheny Co., PA[2948,2949].

                 More About Jerusha Christner:
                 Residence: 1900, Bullskin Twp., Fayette Co., PA[2950]

Child of Warren Christner and Sadie Lyons is:
    1767   i.   Jerusha[8] Christner, born Mar 1892 in Connellsville, Fayette Co., PA[2951].

592. Sophia[7] Christner (Uriah[6], John[5], Peter[4], Johannes John Hans[3], Christian[2], Christen[1])[2952,2953,2954,2955] was born 06 Mar 1860 in Bullskin Twp., Fayette Co., PA, and died 22 Aug 1930 in Connellsville, Fayette Co., PA. She married **(2) John Sanner**. He was born 25 Dec 1855 in Saltlick Twp., Fayette Co., PA, and died 19 Dec 1931 in Connellsville, Fayette Co., PA.

More About Sophia Christner:
Burial: 25 Aug 1930, Hill Grove Cemetery, Connellsville, Fayette Co., PA

More About John Sanner:
Burial: Hill Grove Cemetery Connellville, Fayette Co. PA

Children of Sophia Christner and John Sanner are:
    1768   i.   Joseph[8] Sanner.
    1769   ii.   Celia Sanner, born 13 Oct 1880 in Connellsville, Fayette Co., PA; died 23 Oct 1955 in Connellsville, Fayette Co., PA.
    1770   iii.   Samuel H. Sanner, born 26 Jan 1884 in Connellsville, Fayette Co., PA; died 29 Aug 1953 in

Connellsville, Fayette Co., PA.

1771   iv. George E. Sanner, born 13 Jul 1886 in Normalville, Fayette Co., PA; died 1970 in Canada.

More About George E. Sanner:
Burial: Hill Grove Cemetery Connellville, Fayette Co. PA

1772   v. John Skelie Sanner, born 13 Jan 1889 in Connellsville, Fayette Co., PA; died 02 May 1937 in IN.

1773   vi. David C. Sanner, born 15 Apr 1891 in Connellsville, Fayette Co., PA; died 17 Apr 1935 in Uniontown, Fayette Co., PA. He married Mary A. McManus; born Oct 1872; died 26 Nov 1936.

Notes for David C. Sanner:
Birth: Jul. 18, 1870
Death: Nov. 28, 1940

Parents:
Jacob Sanner (1830 - 1899)
Flora Snyder Sanner (1836 - 1912)

Spouse: Mary A. McManus Sanner (1872 - 1936)

Burial: Dan Snyder Cemetery, Fayette Co., PA

Notes for Mary A. McManus:
Birth: Oct., 1872
Death: Nov. 26, 1936

Spouse: David C. Sanner (1870 - 1940)

Burial: Dan Snyder Cemetery, Fayette Co., PA

1774   vii. Joseph Sanner, born 23 Jun 1893; died in IA.

1775   viii. Deborah Lou Sanner, born 24 May 1895 in Connellsville, Fayette Co., PA; died 05 Jun 1895 in Connellsville, Fayette Co., PA.

More About Deborah Lou Sanner:
Burial: Dan Snyder Cemetery Fayette Co. PA

1776   ix. Michael McKinley Sanner, born 13 Jun 1896 in Connellsville, Fayette Co., PA; died 08 Aug 1945 in Searights, Fayette Co., PA.

Notes for Michael McKinley Sanner:
Micheal died August 8 1945Married Mary Emily Phillips b. 8/25/1898-d.8/26/1943. They had a child Gladys Marie Sanner b. April 10 1926 d. August 19, 1974. She married John Joseph Yank Sr. b. March 30 1923 d. November 19, 1991. They had a son John Joseph Yank, Jr. b. March 11, 1954 info from John J. Yank, Jr.

1777   x. Ralph C. Sanner, born 07 Aug 1899 in Connellsville, Fayette Co., PA; died 10 Sep 1975 in Connellsville, Fayette Co., PA.

1778   xi. Emma Lou Sanner, born 04 Aug 1903 in Connellsville, Fayette Co., PA; died 17 Nov 1964 in Connellsville, Fayette Co., PA.

596. Levi[7] Christner (Uriah[6], John[5], Peter[4], Johannes John Hans[3], Christian[2], Christen[1])[2956,2957,2958,2959,2960,2961] was born 13 Jul 1869 in Bullskin Twp., Fayette Co., PA[2961], and died 03 Aug 1947[2962,2963]. He married **Elizabeth Bond/Bend** 18 Dec 1904 in Bullskin Twp., Fayette Co., PA. She was born Abt. 1885 in Connellsville, Fayette Co., PA.

More About Levi Christner:
Occupation: Farmer[2963]
Residence: 1910, Saltlick Twp., Fayette Co., PA[2964]

More About Elizabeth Bond/Bend:

Nickname: Lizzie

Children of Levi Christner and Elizabeth Bond/Bend are:

1779   i.   Walter[8] Christner[2965], born 1909[2965].

1780   ii.   Lena Christner, born 25 Apr 1910 in PA[2966]; died 13 Sep 1994 in Markleysburg, Fayette Co., PA[2966]. She married (1) Tillman Henry Sanner[2966]; born 19 Mar 1910 in Fayette Co., PA[2966]; died 01 Jul 1984 in Fayette Co., PA[2966]. She married (2) Kirby King[2966]; born 1905[2966]; died 1983[2966].

More About Tillman Henry Sanner:
Residence: 1956, Scottdale, Westmoreland Co., Pa.[2966]

1781   iii. Wilmer Christner[2967,2968,2969], born 1913[2970,2971,2972].

601. Susannah[7] Bungard (Mahala A.[6] Christner, John[5], Peter[4], Johannes John Hans[3], Christian[2], Christen[1])[2973] was born 03 Mar 1838 in Fayette Co., PA[2974], and died 10 Feb 1916 in Fayette Co., PA[2974]. She married **Uriah Christner**[2974,2975,2976,2977] 07 Aug 1856 in Fayette Co., PA[2978,2979,2980,2981], son of John Christner and Susannah Griffith. He was born 01 Mar 1831 in Somerset, Somerset Co., PA[2982], and died 03 Oct 1902 in Indian Head, Saltlick Twp., Fayette Co., PA[2983,2984].

More About Susannah Bungard:
Baptised: 15 Jun 1838, Good Hope Lutheran Church, Saltlick Twp., Fayette Co., PA
Burial: Feb 1916, Daniel Snyder Cemetery, White, Fayette Co., PA
Residence: 1910, Fayette, PA[2985]

Notes for Uriah Christner:
Birth: Mar. 1, 1831
Death: Oct. 3, 1902

Uriah Christner
Enlisted on 9/30/1864 as a Private.
On 9/30/1864 he was drafted into "G" Co. PA 199th Infantry
He was transferred out on 2/13/1865
On 2/13/1865 he transferred into "A" Co. PA 97th Infantry (date and method of discharge not given)

b. 1 Mar 1831
d. 3 Oct 1902

Burial: Dan Snyder Cemetery, Fayette Co., PA

U.S. Civil War Soldiers, 1861-1865
Name: Uriah Christner
Side: Union
Regiment State/Origin: Pennsylvania
Regiment Name: 97 Pennsylvania Inf.
Regiment Name Expanded: 97th Regiment, Pennsylvania Infantry
Company: A
Rank In: Private
Rank In Expanded: Private
Rank Out: Private
Rank Out Expanded: Private
Alternate Name: Uriah/Christian
Film Number: M554 roll 19

More About Uriah Christner:
Burial: Oct 1902, Dan Snyder Cemetery, Fayette Co., PA[2986]
Military service: Served during Civil War-Co. A 97th Bat.[2986]

Residence: 1900, Saltlick Twp., Fayette Co., PA[2987]

Children are listed above under (153) Uriah Christner.

604. Josiah C.[7] Bungard (Mahala A.[6] Christner, John[5], Peter[4], Johannes John Hans[3], Christian[2], Christen[1]) was born 12 Mar 1856 in Saltlick Twp., Fayette Co., PA, and died 28 Mar 1944 in White, Fayette Co., PA. He married **(1) Sadie**. He married **(2) Susanna B. Wissinger** 24 Apr 1889 in Bullskin Twp., Fayette Co., PA. She was born 14 May 1863 in Stalstown, Westmoreland Co., PA, and died 02 Dec 1947 in Scottdale, Westmoreland Co., PA.

Notes for Josiah C. Bungard:
Notes for JOSIAH C. BUNGARD:
Fayette Co., PA. newspaper clipping

JOSIAH C. BUNGARD

Josiah C. Bungard, 88 years old, died at 2 o'clock Tuesday afternoon at his home at White Postoffice after a brief illness of complications.

Mr. Bungard was born in Saltlick township, near Indian Head, March 12, 1856, the son of the late Jacob and Mahala Christner Bungard, and had resided all of his life in that locality. He operated the FLour and feed mill of the late Lemuel Matthews of Davistown for 15 years. Retiring from that, he moved to a farm near White Post office in 1902 and followed farming until five years ago.

Surviving are his widow, Mrs. Susana Wissinger Bungard, and the following children: Mrs. Marie Keefer of Scottdale, Mrs. Sadie Keslar of Acme, Mrs. Alverta McGinnis of Jeannette R.D. 2, and Mrs. Blanche Flack of White with whom he had made his home. There are 26 grandchildren, six grandsons being in the armed forces, and six great-grandchildren. He was a brother of Mrs. Sarah Trump of Uniontown, Mrs. Malinda Kalp of Indian Head, Mrs. Sophia Trump of Connellsville, and Mrs. Alice Underwood of Mount Pleasant, R. D.

The funeral will be held Saturday afternoon. There will be a brief service at 2 o'clock at the home with full rites at 2:30 o'clock at the Buchanan Church of God in charge of Rev. John L. Woods, pastor. Burial will be made in the family plot in Eutsey cemetery.

FAYETTE Co., PA DEED BOOK 195; page 24:
JOSIAH BUNBGARD and wife Susannah to Lucinda Jane WELLING of Saltlick Twp., April 24, 1901.

Occupation: Flour & Feed Mill Operator, Farmer

Burial: Eutsey Cemetery, White, Saltlick Twp., Fayette Co., PA

More About Josiah C. Bungard:
Burial: 1944, Eutsey Cemetery, White, Saltlick Twp., Fayette Co., PA

More About Susanna B. Wissinger:
Burial: Dec 1947, Eutsey Cemetery, White, Saltlick Twp., Fayette Co., PA

Children of Josiah Bungard and Susanna Wissinger are:
+   1782   i.   Mary Marie[8] Bungard, born 14 Jan 1886 in Bullskin Twp., Fayette Co., PA; died 25 Feb 1965 in Scottdale, Westmoreland Co., PA.
+   1783   ii. Sadie Grace Bungard, born 08 Mar 1890 in Davistown, Fayette Co., PA; died 12 Jan 1960 in Donegal, Westmoreland Co., PA.
+   1784   iii. Lula Blanche Bungard, born 25 Sep 1891 in Bullskin Twp., Fayette Co., PA; died 22 Dec 1969.
+   1785   iv. Alverda M. Bungard, born 18 Jan 1893 in Bullskin Twp., Fayette Co., PA; died Dec 1981 in Greensburg, Westmoreland Co., PA.

608. Malinda[7] Bungard (Mahala A.[6] Christner, John[5], Peter[4], Johannes John Hans[3], Christian[2], Christen[1]) was born 11 Apr 1863 in Connellsville, Fayette Co., PA, and died 15 May 1944 in Davistown, Fayette Co., PA. She married **Davis C. Kalp**. He was born 02 Apr 1860 in Fayette Co., PA, and died 08 Jul 1919 in Fayette Co., PA.

Notes for Malinda Bungard:
Notes for MALINDA BUNGARD:
Fayette Co., Pa. newspaper clipping....

MRS. MALINDA KALP

Mrs. Malinda Kalp, 81 years old, widow of Davis C. Kalp, died at 3:50 o'clock this morning at her home near Davistown after a short illness.

Mrs. Kalp was born near Indian Head April 11, 1863, the daughter of the late Jacob and Mahala Christner Bungard, and had spent all of her life in that community. Her husband preceded her in death 25 years ago. Surviving children are Mrs. Hattie Strohm, Harry, Mrs. Annie Miller and Clyde Kalp, all of Mount Pleasant, Samuel R. Kalp of New York City, and Lloyd Kalp at home. There are 22 grandchildren, 16 great-grandchildren, and three sisters, Mrs. Sarah Trump of Uniontown, Mrs. Sophia Trump of Connellsville and Mrs. Alice Underwood of Mount Pleasant, R.D. A brother, Josiah Bungard, of near White Postoffice, died about two months ago.

The funeral will be held Thursday afternoon with a brief service at the home at 2 o'clock and full rites at the Davistown Evangelical Church, of which she was a member for 63 years, at 2:30 o'clock in charge of Rev. William Beal, pastor. Burial will be made in the family plot in Mount Calvary Cemetery.

Burial: Mount Calvary Cemetery

More About Malinda Bungard:
Burial: Mt. Calvary Cemetery
Fact 1: See Note Page

Children of Malinda Bungard and Davis Kalp are:

1786	i.	Charles R.[8] Kalp.
1787	ii.	Hattie Kalp, born Feb 1883 in Bullskin Twp., Fayette Co., PA; died 10 Nov 1969 in Mt. Pleasant Twp., Westmoreland Co., PA. She married (1) Bert Strom; born 1879; died 1960 in Mt. Pleasant Twp., Westmoreland Co., PA.
1788	iii.	Harry E. Kalp, born Feb 1886 in Bullskin Twp., Fayette Co., PA; died 1968 in Mt. Pleasant Twp., Westmoreland Co., PA. He married Ida B. Pletcher; born 18 Aug 1893 in Middle Creek Twp., Somerset Co., PA; died 20 Feb 1973.

More About Harry E. Kalp:
Burial: Mt. Pleasant Cemetery, Mt. Pleasant, Westmoreland Co., PA

More About Ida B. Pletcher:
Burial: Mt. Pleasant Cemetery, Mt. Pleasant, Westmoreland Co., PA

1789	iv.	Anna "Annie" Kalp, born Jul 1888 in Bullskin Twp., Fayette Co., PA; died Bet. 1902 - 1982. She married Thomas Wade Miller[2988] Bet. 1902 - 1935; born 23 Apr 1889 in given as 15 Apr 1889 in Wade's notes/Saltlick Twp., Fayette Co., PA[2988]; died 29 Aug 1971 in Normalville, Fayette, PA, USA[2988].

More About Thomas Wade Miller:
Burial: 31 Aug 1971, fr Wade's notes/Mt Joy Cemetery[2988]
Residence: 1930, Mt. Pleasant, Westmoreland Co., PA[2988]

1790	v.	Lloyd J. Kalp, born 11 Sep 1890 in Bullskin Twp., Fayette Co., PA; died 05 Mar 1962 in Davistown, PA.
+ 1791	vi.	Clyde B. Kalp, born May 1896 in Bullskin Twp., Fayette Co., PA; died 1970 in Mt. Pleasant Twp., Washington Co., PA.

1792	vii.	Gertrude "Gertie" Kalp, born 1898 in Bullskin Twp., Fayette Co., PA; died 1924. She married Elmer H. Schaffer Bet. 1914 - 1923; born 1899; died 1966.
1793	viii.	Samuel R. Kalp, born 1901 in Bullskin Twp., Fayette Co., PA; died 1951. He married Dorothy Shurburn.
1794	ix.	Daisy H. Kalp, born 1903 in Bullskin Twp., Fayette Co., PA; died 1928.

609. Isaiah[7] Bungard (Mahala A.[6] Christner, John[5], Peter[4], Johannes John Hans[3], Christian[2], Christen[1]) was born 23 Aug 1864 in Bullskin Twp., Fayette Co., PA, and died 1944 in Westmoreland Co., PA. He married **Mary Elizabeth Harman** Bet. 1885 - 1915. She was born 13 Apr 1872, and died 1957 in Westmoreland Co., PA.

Notes for Isaiah Bungard:
Notes for ISAIAH BUNGARD:

Fayette Co., PA Deed Book 121 pp.458-459 Dated 14 Feb 1893 (abstract)

FRANKLIN P. PEGG to *ISAAC BUNGARD (should be ISAIAH BUNGARD)

This indenture between Franklin O. PEGG, Amy Ann Pegg his wife of the Borough of Uniontown, Fayette Co., PA, parties of the first part and Isaac Bungard of the Borough, Co. and state aforesaid, party of the second part.... In consideration of the sum of $385, hereby acknowledged, have granted, bargained, sold, aliened.... to the second part.... all of a certain piece or parcel of ground situate and being in North Union township in Fayette Co., Penna. and more particularyly described by virture and bounds as follows, ..

Burial: St. Luke Cemetery, Pleasant Unity

More About Isaiah Bungard:
Burial: St. Luke Cemetery, Pleasant Unity
Fact 1: See Note Page

Notes for Mary Elizabeth Harman:
Burial: St. Luke Cemetery, Pleasant Unity

More About Mary Elizabeth Harman:
Burial: St. Luke Cemetery, Pleasant Unity
Fact 1: See Note Page

Children of Isaiah Bungard and Mary Harman are:

1795	i.	Kenneth[8] Bungard, born Jul 1891; died Bet. 1892 - 1981.
1796	ii.	Earl Bungard, born May 1892. He married Laura Barker; born 09 Sep 1894; died 18 Feb 1989.
1797	iii.	William Bungard, born 1894.
1798	iv.	Mary Bungard, born Abt. 1897.
1799	v.	Irene Bungard Bungard, born 03 Mar 1898.
1800	vi.	Edna Bungard, born Abt. 1900.

611. Sophia[7] Bungard (Mahala A.[6] Christner, John[5], Peter[4], Johannes John Hans[3], Christian[2], Christen[1]) was born 28 Jun 1868 in Indian Head, Saltlick Twp., Fayette Co., PA, and died 1953 in Bullskin Twp., Fayette Co., PA. She married **(1) Trump**.   She married **(2) Harry Trump** 15 Oct 1882 in Bullskin Twp., Fayette Co., PA. He was born Apr 1870 in Connellsville, Fayette Co., PA, and died Aft. 1953 in Connellsville, Fayette Co., PA.

Notes for Sophia Bungard:
Notes for SOPHIA BUNGARD:
Obituary clipping from Fayette Co.,PA Newspapers..
MRS. HARRY TRUMP
Mrs. Sophia B. Trump, 87, of 216 Gibson Terrace, died at her home at 2.50 o'clock this morning.

Born at Indian Head June 28, 1868, she was a daughter of the late Jacob and Mahalla Christner Bungard. She had lived in this city for 30 years and was member of the Church of the Brethren.

Surviving are her husband, Harry Trump; four daughters, Mrs. Mary Fritz of Elizabeth, Mrs. Cora Lee of Connellsville R. D. 1, and Mrs. Helen Collins and Mrs. Hazel Guard of Connellsville; seven sons, Earl, Samuel, Charles and Elmer of South Connellsville, Carl of Connellsville, Ralph of Akron, Ohio, and Arthur of Jeannette; a sister, Mrs. Alice Underwood of Mount Pleasant; 34 grandchildren; 45 great-grandchildren and two great-great-grandchildren. A son, Clarence G. died Oct. 21, 1955.

The funeral service will be held at the Brooks funeral home in East Green St. at 2:30 P.M. Thursday with the Rev. E. M. Hertzler officiating. Interment will be made in Mount Olive Cemetery.

Facts about this person:

Religion
Church of the Brethren

Burial
Mt. Ollive cemetery, Bullskin Twp., Fayette Co., PA

More About Sophia Bungard:
Burial: Mt. Ollive cemetery, Bullskin Twp., Fayette Co., PA, Fayette Co., PA
Fact 1: See Note Page

Notes for Harry Trump:

More About Harry Trump:
Fact 1: See Note Page

Children of Sophia Bungard and Harry Trump are:

1801	i.	Cora[8] Trump.
1802	ii.	Helen Trump.
1803	iii.	Samuel Trump.
1804	iv.	Charles Trump.
1805	v.	Elmer Trump.
1806	vi.	Clarence G. Trump.
1807	vii.	Carl Trump.
1808	viii.	Earl B. Trump, born 1884 in Bullskin Twp., Fayette Co., PA; died 1926 in Connellsville, Fayette Co., PA.
+ 1809	ix.	Mary Trump, born 25 Nov 1887 in Bullskin Twp., Fayette Co., PA; died 11 Dec 1986 in North Huntingdon, PA.
+ 1810	x.	Ralph V. Trump, born Abt. 1906 in S. Connellsville, Fayette Co., PA; died 06 Dec 1986 in Portage Lakes, OH.
1811	xi.	Hazel M. Trump, born 1911; died 1975. She married Thomas H. Guard.

614. Alice[7] Bungard (Mahala A.[6] Christner, John[5], Peter[4], Johannes John Hans[3], Christian[2], Christen[1]) was born 20 Aug 1875 in Saltlick Twp., Fayette Co., PA, and died 1956 in Mt. Pleasant, Westmoreland Co., PA. She married **(1) Underwood**.   She married **(2) James Sylvester Underwood** 21 Sep 1938 in Mt. Pleasant, Westmoreland, PA. He was born 1870 in Bullskin Twp., Fayette Co., PA, and died 1938 in Mt. Pleasant, Westmoreland Co., PA.

Notes for Alice Bungard:
Fayette Co., Pa. newspaper clipping

MRS. ALICE UNDERWOOD

Mrs. Alice Underwood, 81, of Mount Pleasant, R.D. 3, died at 1:20 o'clock this morning at her home after a lingering illness.

She was born in Saltlick township Aug. 20, 1875, a daughter of the late Jacob and Mahalia Christner Bungard, and had lived at her present address for the past 47 years. She was a member of the Mount Joy Church of the Brethren.

Surviving are three sons, Jesse and Charles at home and James of Mount Pleasant R.D. 3; three daughters, Mrs. Edna Cramer of Latrobe R.D. 1, Mrs. Grace Bungard of Mount Pleasant and Mrs. Elsie Shogan of Swissvale; 27 grandchildren and 30 great-grandchildren. She was preceded in death by her husband James Underwood in 1938.

The body will be at the deceased's home after 6 o'clock this evening and the funeral service will be held there at 2 o'clock Thursday afternoon with the Rev. John Geary officiating. Interment will be int he Mount Joy cemetery in charge of Brooks funeral service.

Burial: Mt. Joy Cemetery, Mount Joy Church of the Brethren

More About Alice Bungard:
Burial: Mt. Joy Cemetery
Cause of Death: Illness
Fact 1: See Note Page

Children of Alice Bungard and James Underwood are:
1812	i.	Jesse[8] Underwood.
1813	ii.	Edna Underwood.
1814	iii.	Elsie Underwood.
1815	iv.	Charles Underwood.
1816	v.	Emerson Underwood, born 22 Mar 1896 in Westmoreland Co. , PA; died Bet. 1897 - 1986.

Notes for Emerson Underwood:
EMERSON UNDERWOOD:
Delayed Birth Records, Fayette Co., PA
Birth Register, Fayette Co. Book I

#13. EMERSON UNDERWOOD, son of Sylvesta UNDERWOOD and Alice UNDERWOOD of Hammondville was born 22 Mar 1896 in   Westmoreland Co., PA (page 263).

+	1817	vi.	Grace Underwood, born 14 Apr 1909 in Mt. Pleasant Twp., Westmoreland Co., PA; died 23 Feb 1988 in Mt. Pleasant Twp., Westmoreland Co., PA.
	1818	vii.	James Underwood, born 1910 in Westmoreland Co., PA. He married Ortha Bungard; born 1910 in Westmoreland Co. , PA.

621. Richard E.[7] Christner (Cyrus John[6], John[5], Peter[4], Johannes John Hans[3], Christian[2], Christen[1])[2989] was born Nov 1867 in Connellsville, Fayette Co., PA[2989], and died 1948[2990,2991]. He married **Annie Bell Secrest** 14 Oct 1896 in Fayette Co., PA[2991]. She was born 01 Nov 1876 in Lower Tyrone Twp., Fayette Co., PA[2992], and died 16 Jun 1958 in Scottdale, Westmoreland Co., PA[2993].

Notes for Richard E. Christner:
Richard lived with M.L. Baint. This info may be a male or female. 1920 census he is living at Westmoreland Co., Coal Bank Hollow Rd.

More About Richard E. Christner:
Census: 16 Jun 1880, Bullskin Twp., Fayette Co., PA[2994]
Residence: 1930, East Huntingdon Tqp., Westmoreland Co., PA[2995]

Notes for Annie Bell Secrest:
Burial: Green Ridge Memorial Park, Connellsville, Fayette Co., PA

More About Annie Bell Secrest:
Burial: 19 Jun 1958, Greenridge Memorial Park, Connellsville, Fayette Co., PA[2996]
DeathCause: Congestive Heart Failure due to Diabetes Mellitus/[2996]
Residence: 1880, Upper Tyrone, Fayette Co., PA[2997]

Children of Richard Christner and Annie Secrest are:

1819   i.   Ebbert Clinton[8] Christner[2998], born 03 Aug 1897 in Connellsville, Fayette Co., PA[2999,3000]; died 06 May 1971 in Steubenville, Jefferson Co., OH[3001]. He married Ruth P. King[3001]; born 06 Jun 1902[3001]; died 18 Apr 1977 in Steubenville, Jefferson Co., OH[3001].

More About Ebbert Clinton Christner:
Residence: 01 Apr 1940, Steubenville, Jefferson, Ohio, United States[3002]
Social Security Number: 232-03-5606/[3003]
SSN issued: North Carolina or West Virginia[3003]

1820   ii. Roy E. Christner[3004,3005], born 1902 in Connellsville, Fayette Co., PA[3006]; died 1937[3006,3007]. He married Anna Orabetz[3008]; born 1907[3008].

More About Roy E. Christner:
Residence: 1920, East Huntingdon, Westmoreland Co., PA[3009]

1821   iii. Rachel Pearl Christner[3009], born 21 Aug 1903 in Lower Tyrone Township, Fayette Co., PA[3010]; died 14 Jul 2002 in At her home/RD#1, Scottdale, Westmoreland Co., PA[3010]. She married George E. Cotton[3010]; born 28 Apr 1898 in Charleroi, Fayette Co., PA[3010]; died 03 Dec 1976[3010].

More About Rachel Pearl Christner:
Arrival: 26 Nov 1923, New York, NY[3011]
Burial: Green Ridge Memorial Park/Mt. Olive Cemetery, Bullskin Twp., Fayette Co., PA[3012]
Member: Lifetime and oldest mmber of the Tyrone Presbyterian Church/[3012]
Occupation: Before retiring in 1973, she was employed for 18 years by Kelly and Cook Insurance in Scottdale, and for 12 years between Woolworth Company and McCrory's 5&10 Store./[3012]
Residence: 01 Apr 1940, East Huntingdon, Westmoreland Co., PA[3013]

1822   iv. Viola M. Christner, born 29 Jul 1905 in Upper Tyrone Twp, Fayette, PA[3013]; died 09 Jan 2001 in Scottdale, Westmoreland, PA[3013].

More About Viola M. Christner:
Residence: 01 Apr 1940, East Huntingdon, Westmoreland Co., PA[3013]

623. Samuel E.[7] Christner (Cyrus John[6], John[5], Peter[4], Johannes John Hans[3], Christian[2], Christen[1])[3014,3015,3016,3017,3018] was born 12 Sep 1872 in Pennsville, Bullskin Twp., Fayette Co., PA[3019,3020,3021,3022,3023,3024], and died 11 Jul 1937 in Connellsville, Fayette Co., PA[3025,3026,3027]. He married **Rachael Copeland Akins**[3028,3029,3030,3031] 02 Jun 1903, daughter of Robert Akins and Mary Steele. She was born 11 Aug 1875 in Westmoreland Co., PA[3032], and died 21 Mar 1958 in At her home, 14 Pearl St., Scottdale, Westmoreland Co., PA[3033,3034,3035].

Notes for Samuel E. Christner:
Samuel left home and came to Westmoreland Co, where he worked for 4 years for the Scottdale Sheet and Tin Plate Co. Then he went to work for his uncle Jacob Christner as an apprentice carpenter. He stayed 6 years and started to work for H.C. Frick & Company as aforman in the coke region.He then went to work for J.W. Ruth as a carpenter. One year later 1905 he started his own business in Scottdale, PA. Samuel is credited as building many of the businesses, churches and better homes of Scottdale. Samuel was a member of the Independent Order of Odd Fellows,a staunch Republican. He had an ability for music and was a member of the Grand Army Band of Scottville.

More About Samuel E. Christner:
Burial: Scottdale Cemetery/Scottdale, Westmoreland Co., PA[3035]
Census: 16 Jun 1880, Bullskin Twp., Fayette Co., PA[3036,3037,3038]
Member: First Presbyterian Church in Scottdale, Pa./[3039]

Occupation: General Building Contractor[3039]
Residence: 1910, Scottdale Ward 1, Westmoreland Co, PA[3040]

Notes for Rachael Copeland Akins:
Rachael is the daughter of Robert Akins and Mary Jane Steele Akins

More About Rachael Copeland Akins:
Burial: Scottdale Cemetery[3041]
Member: First Presbyterian Church in Scottdale, Pa.[3041]
Resided at: Scottdale for 56 years[3041]
Residence: 1910, Scottdale Ward 1, Westmoreland Co, PA[3042]

Children of Samuel Christner and Rachael Akins are:
+   1823   i.   Cyrus John[8] Christner, born 23 Feb 1904 in Fayette Co., PA; died 05 Sep 1980 in Scottdale, Westmoreland Co., PA.
+   1824   ii.   Samuel J. Christner, born 23 Feb 1904; died 05 Sep 1980 in Scottdale, Westmoreland Co., PA.
    1825   iii.   Walter Akins Christner[3042,3043,3044], born 16 Feb 1906 in Scottdale, Westmoreland Co., PA[3045,3046,3047,3048,3049]; died 13 Jun 1961 in Scottdale, Westmoreland Co., PA[3050,3051].

          More About Walter Akins Christner:
          Burial: Scottdale Cemetery, Scottdale, Westmoreland Co., PA[3052]
          Member: Brookman - Hernley Post VFW, Thomas Lewellyn Post Amer Legion[3052]
          Occupation: Carpenter and building inspector for dept of labor and industry[3052]
          Residence: 1910, Scottdale Ward 1, Westmoreland Co, PA[3053]
          Served: WWI - European Theater[3054]

    1826   iv.   Edith May Christner[3055,3056,3057,3058,3059], born 23 May 1907 in Scottdale, Westmoreland Co., PA[3060,3061,3062,3063,3064]; died 03 Oct 1996 in Mt. Pleasant, Westmoreland Co., PA[3064,3064]. She married Dalton Albert Foss[3064]; born 05 Jul 1905 in Connellsville, Fayette Co., PA[3064]; died May 1974 in Boardman, Mahoning, OH[3064].

          Notes for Edith May Christner:
          Birth: 1907
          Death: 1996

          Burial: Scottdale Cemetery, Scottdale, Westmoreland Co., PA
          Find A Grave Memorial# 86772831

          More About Edith May Christner:
          Residence: 1910, Scottdale Ward 1, Westmoreland Co, PA[3065]

    1827   v.   Mildred R. Christner[3066,3067], born 1911 in Connellsville, Fayette Co., PA[3068,3069].

          More About Mildred R. Christner:
          Residence: 1920, Scottdale Ward 2, Westmoreland Co., PA[3070]

    1828   vi.   Earl Robert Christner[3071,3072,3073,3074,3075,3076], born 08 Jun 1913[3076,3077,3078,3079,3080,3081]; died 20 Dec 1971 in Scottdale, Westmoreland Co., PA[3082]. He married Thelma Ruth Synder.

          More About Earl Robert Christner:
          Burial: Scottdale, Westmoreland[3083]
          Military service: 25 May 1943, Greensburg, Westmoreland Co., PA[3084]
          Residence: 1920, Scottdale Ward 2, Westmoreland Co., PA[3085,3086]
          Social Security Number: 210-01-7698/[3087]
          SSN issued: Connellsville, Fayette Co., PA[3087]

    1829   vii.   Samuel J. Christner[3088], born 1916 in Connellsville, Fayette Co., PA[3088]. He married Thelma D. Dickey.

          More About Samuel J. Christner:
          Residence: 1920, Scottdale Ward 2, Westmoreland Co., PA[3088]

1830   viii.   James S. Christner[3089], born 1916[3089]; died 15 Oct 1990 in Scottdale, Westmoreland Co., PA[3090]. He married Thelma Dickey.

More About James S. Christner:
Residence: 1930, Scottdale, Westmoreland Co., PA[3091]

1831   ix.   Harry R. Christner[3092,3093,3094], born 08 Jan 1918[3094]; died 05 Mar 1995 in Scottdale, Westmoreland Co., PA[3095,3096,3097]. He married Living Belle[3098].

More About Harry R. Christner:
Military service: 30 Apr 1942, Pittsburgh, Alleghaney Co., PA[3099]
Residence: 1920, Scottdale Ward 2, Westmoreland Co., PA[3100]
Social Security Number: 191-07-6048[3101]
SSN issued: PA[3101]

626. Amos D.[7] Christner (Jacob G.[6], John[5], Peter[4], Johannes John Hans[3], Christian[2], Christen[1])[3102,3103] was born Apr 1866 in Davistown, Fayette Co., PA[3104,3105], and died 1941. He married **Anna Elizabeth Garwichon**[3106,3107] 16 Oct 1887 in Connellsville, Fayette Co., PA. She was born Sep 1865 in Frostburg, Allegany Co., MD[3108], and died 1948.

Notes for Amos D. Christner:
Amos is the son of Jacob G. Christner and Sarah Davis

More About Amos D. Christner:
Burial: Mt.Joy
Residence: 1910, Westmoreland Co., PA[3109,3110]

More About Anna Elizabeth Garwichon:
Burial: Mt.Joy
Residence: 1930[3111,3112]

Children of Amos Christner and Anna Garwichon are:
+   1832   i.   Clayton Otis[8] Christner, born 13 Dec 1889 in Fayette, PA; died 1942.
+   1833   ii.   Curtis H. Christner, born 29 Dec 1891 in Connellsville, Fayette Co., PA.
     1834   iii.   May Oma Namomie-Naoma Christner[3113,3114], born Aug 1897 in Connellsville, Fayette Co., PA[3114,3115]; died 1943[3115].

Notes for May Oma Namomie-Naoma Christner:
This name is spelled several different ways. She never married..

More About May Oma Namomie-Naoma Christner:
Burial: Mt.Joy[3115]
Residence: 1910, Mt. Pleasant, Westmoreland Co., PA[3116]

     1835   iv.   May Anna Christner[3116], born Aug 1897 in Connellsville, Fayette Co., PA[3116]; died 1943.

More About May Anna Christner:
Residence: 1900, Mount Pleasant Ward 3, Westmoreland Co., PA[3116]

     1836   v.   Irene Christner[3116], born 1907 in Westmoreland Co., PA[3116].

More About Irene Christner:
Residence: 1910, Mt. Pleasant, Westmoreland Co., PA[3116]

     1837   vi.   Ivin C. Christner, born 1910 in Westmoreland Co., PA[3116].

More About Ivin C. Christner:
Residence: 1910, Mt. Pleasant, Westmoreland Co., PA[3116]

627. Anna Elizabeth[7] Hoffmeyer (Jacob G.[6] Christner, John[5], Peter[4], Johannes John Hans[3], Christian[2], Christen[1])[3117,3118,3119,3120] was born Jun 1868 in Connellsville, Fayette Co., PA[3121,3122,3123,3124,3125,3126], and died 1955 in Pittsburgh, Allegheny Co., PA[3126,3127,3127,3128]. She married **(1) Norman D. Christner**[3129]. He was born Oct 1867 in Connellsville, Fayette Co., PA[3130], and died 1943[3130,3131,3132]. She married **(2) Norman B. Christner**[3133,3134,3135,3136,3137] 03 Oct 1887 in Salisbury PA., son of Samuel Christner and Mary Shoemaker. He was born 13 Oct 1867 in Addison, Somerset Co., PA[3138], and died 02 Nov 1943 in Meyersdale, Somerset Co., PA[3138,3139].

More About Anna Elizabeth Hoffmeyer:
Burial: Meyersdale Cemetery, Meyersdale, Somerset Co., PA
Residence: 01 Apr 1940, Quemahoning, Somerset, PA, United States[3140]

More About Norman D. Christner:
Residence: 1910, Summit, Somerset Co., PA[3141]

Notes for Norman B. Christner:
Obituary: Norman B. CHRISTNER, 1943, Meyersdale, Somerset County, PA - Meyersdale Republican, November 4, 1943
Norman B. Christner, retired farmer living in Meyersdale, died Tuesday, Nov. 2, 1943 in the Windber Hospital, at the age of 76 years, 20 days. He was born Oct. 13, 1867, in Addison Township.

He is survived by his wife, Annie Hoffmeyer Christner, and the following children: Mrs. Grace Lint, Mrs. Henry Younkin and Mrs. Ernest Boden, Meyersdale; Ed Christner, Boynton; Mrs. Dan C. Specht and Mrs. D. W. Weaver, Stoystown, and Mrs. Sherman Gindlesperger, Boswell; also by 16 grandchildren and 8 great-grandchildren.

Mr. Christner began his career as a tenant farmer in Elk Lick Township at which he prospered until he bought a fine dairy farm near Stoystown which he successfully operated until failing health impelled him to dispose of his farm and retire from hard work. Their children all being grown up and established in homes of their own by that time, Mr. and Mrs. Christner bought a home in Meyersdale into which they moved several years ago to spend the sunset of their lives. Seeking relief from serious illness, he entered the Windber Hospital where he succumbed after a short stay.

Norman B. Christner was a sterling citizen, a good neighbor and kind husband and father. Funeral services will be held Friday at 2:30 p.m., at his late home on Broadway, With Rev. N. L. Wilson, Berlin, and Rev. Nelson C. Brown, Meyersdale, officiating. Interment in Union Cemetery. Pallbearers will be Josiah Lint, John Smearman, Charles Bolden, John Clark, John Gauntz and D. H. Bauman. H. R. Konhaus has charge of funeral arrangements.

More About Norman B. Christner:
Burial: Meyersdale Cemetery, Meyersdale, Somerset Co., PA
Residence: 01 Apr 1940, Quemahoning, Somerset, PA, United States[3142]

Children of Anna Hoffmeyer and Norman Christner are:
+ 1838   i.   Grace Alverta[8] Christner, born Apr 1888 in Somerset Co., PA; died in Sand Patch, Larimer Twp., Somerset Co., PA.
   1839   ii.   Emma P Christner[3142], born Mar 1890 in Somerset, Somerset Co., PA[3142]; died 19 Jan 1971 in Meyersdale, Somerset Co., PA[3142].

         More About Emma P Christner:
         Residence: 1910, Summit, Somerset Co., PA[3142]

   1840   iii.   Emma P. Christner[3143,3144], born 03 Mar 1890 in Elk Lick, Somerset Co., PA[3145]; died 19 Jan 1971 in Meyersdale, Somerset Co., PA[3146,3147,3148]. She married Henry Clay Younkin[3149]; born 18 Nov 1888[3149]; died 09 Feb 1982[3149].

         More About Emma P. Christner:
         Burial: Union Cemetery, Meyersdale, Somerset Co., PA[3149]
         Residence: 1920, Meyersdale, Somerset Co., PA[3150]

More About Henry Clay Younkin:
Burial: Union Cemetery, Meyersdale, PA[3151]

+ 1841   iv.   Ada O. Christner, born 08 Mar 1892 in Somerset Co., PA; died 23 Mar 1958.
   1842   v.   Edward Twain Christner[3152], born 06 Jul 1895 in Elklick Twp., Somerset Co., PA[3152].

     Notes for Edward Twain Christner:
     Maybe Edward I instead of T. Birthdate maybe July 1896.

     More About Edward Twain Christner:
     Residence: 1910, Summit, Somerset Co., PA[3152]

   1843   vi.   Edward T Christner[3153], born 06 Jul 1895 in Somerset, PA[3153].

     More About Edward T Christner:
     Residence: Somerset, PA[3153]

   1844   vii.   Samuel H. Christner, born 30 Nov 1896 in Somerset Co., PA; died 15 Jan 1897.

     Notes for Samuel H. Christner:
     Death: Jan. 15, 1897

     Inscription: s/o N.B.

     Burial: Maple Glen Church of the Brethren Cemetery, Somerset Co., PA

     More About Samuel H. Christner:
     Burial: Maple Glen Church of the Brethren Cemetery, Somerset Co., PA

   1845   viii.   Mary M. Christner[3154,3155], born 23 Feb 1898 in Elklick Township, Somerset Co., PA[3155,3156]; died 02 Dec 1988 in Jennerstown, PA[3157].

     More About Mary M. Christner:
     _UPD: 30 JUL 2010 09:19:05 GMT-5/[3157]
     Burial: Odd Fellows Cemetery, Stoystown, PA[3157]
     Residence: 1900, Greenville Twp., Somerset Co., PA[3158]

   1846   ix.   Mary M. Christner[3159], born 23 Feb 1898 in Elklick Township, Somerset Co., PA[3159,3160]; died 02 Dec 1988 in Jennerstown, PA[3161].

     More About Mary M. Christner:
     _UPD: 30 JUL 2010 09:19:05 GMT-5/[3161]
     Burial: Odd Fellows Cemetery, Stoystown, PA[3161]
     Residence: 1910, Summit, Somerset Co., PA[3162]

+ 1847   x.   Sadie Margaret Christner, born Mar 1900 in Somerset Co., PA.
   1848   xi.   Sadie M. Christner[3162,3163], born 18 Apr 1900 in Greenville Township, Somerset Co, PA[3163,3164]; died 12 Feb 1993 in White Star, PA[3165].

     More About Sadie M. Christner:
     Residence: 1910, Summit, Somerset Co., PA[3166]

   1849   xii.   Olive R. Christner[3166,3167], born Abt. 1902 in Connellsville, Fayette Co., PA[3167,3168].

     More About Olive R. Christner:
     Residence: 1910, Summit Twp., Somerset Co., PA[3169]

+ 1850   xiii.   Ruth Olive Christner, born 03 Nov 1902 in Greenville Twp, PA; died 07 Mar 1963.

628. Nelson D.[7] **Christner** (Jacob G.[6], John[5], Peter[4], Johannes John Hans[3], Christian[2], Christen[1]) was born 1871 in Connellsville, Fayette Co., PA, and died 1959. He married **Sallie Nellie Washabaugh** 27 Aug 1893.

She was born Nov 1877 in Connellsville, Fayette Co., PA, and died 1957.

Notes for Nelson D. Christner:
1900 Census has Nelson living on East Smithfield Street, Mt. Pleasant, Westmoreland Co., PA

Birth: 1871
Death: 1959

Burial: Mount Pleasant Cemetery, Mount Pleasant, Westmoreland Co., PA

More About Nelson D. Christner:
Residence: 1880, Saltlick Twp., Fayette Co., PA[3170]

Notes for Sallie Nellie Washabaugh:
She had her mother (Sarah) living with her in the 1910 soundex PA. Sarah was 74 in 1910 soundex PA.

Burial: Mount Pleasant Cemetery, Mount Pleasant, Westmoreland Co., PA

Children of Nelson Christner and Sallie Washabaugh are:

1851	i.	Stella M.[8] Christner, born Nov 1894 in Mt. Pleasant, Westmoreland Co., PA.
1852	ii.	Ruth Marie Christner, born Aug 1896 in Mt. Pleasant, Westmoreland Co., PA.
1853	iii.	Florence Christner, born 1909 in Connellsville, Fayette Co., PA.

631. Keturah May[7] Christner (Joseph[6], John[5], Peter[4], Johannes John Hans[3], Christian[2], Christen[1]) was born 26 Aug 1871 in Pittsburgh, Allegheny Co., PA[3171], and died 24 Jun 1957 in Poplar Grove, Connellsville, Fayette Co., PA[3171]. She married **John Elmer Bowser**[3172,3173]. He was born 12 Mar 1863 in Pittsburgh, Allegheny Co., PA[3174], and died 21 Mar 1935 in Mt. Vernon Park, Wooddale. PA[3174].

More About Keturah May Christner:
Residence: 1900, Donegal Township, Indian Creek District, Westmoreland Co., PA[3174]

More About John Elmer Bowser:
Burial: Mt Joy Cemetery near Mt Pleasant, Pa.[3175]
Medical Information: [3175]
Occupation: 1930, Farmer[3175]
Residence: 1900, Donegal Township, Indian Creek District, Westmoreland Co., PA[3176]

Children of Keturah Christner and John Bowser are:

1854	i.	Wade[8] Bowser[3176], died Oct 1934 in Pittsburgh, Allegheny Co., PA[3176].
1855	ii.	Mae Bowser[3176], died in RD, Scottdale, Westmoreland Co., PA[3176].
1856	iii.	Laura Bowser[3176], died in Wooddale, Bullskin Twp., Fayette Co., PA[3176].
+ 1857	iv.	Abbie Mae Bowser, born 10 Jul 1894 in Pittsburgh, Allegheny Co., PA; died 03 Mar 1972 in Mt Pleasant, Westmoreland Co., PA.
+ 1858	v.	Hazel V. Bowser, born 16 May 1896 in Pittsburgh, Allegheny Co., PA; died Mar 1978 in Connellsville, Fayette Co., PA.
1859	vi.	Jesse Ray Bowser[3177], born 04 Jul 1898 in Pittsburgh, Allegheny Co., PA[3177]; died 18 Oct 1934 in Bullskin Twp., Fayette Co., PA[3178,3179].

     Notes for Jesse Ray Bowser:
     Died in a truck accident near Ridgeview Schoolhouse in Bullskin Twp., Fayette Co., PA.

     More About Jesse Ray Bowser:
     Medical Information: [3179]
     Occupation: Worked in road construction[3179]
     Residence: 1900, Donegal Township, Indian Creek District, Westmoreland Co., PA[3180]

632. Frank Homer[7] Christner (Joseph[6], John[5], Peter[4], Johannes John Hans[3], Christian[2], Christen[1]) was born 07 Jun 1873 in Wilkinsburg, Allegheny Co., PA[3181], and died 30 Mar 1951[3181,3182]. He married **Mary Mabel Rodgers** 26 Apr 1899 in Greensburg, Westmoreland Co., PA. She was born Dec 1876 in Connellsville, Fayette Co., PA, and died 21 Oct 1931[3183,3184].

Notes for Frank Homer Christner:
Homer Franklin Christner unofficially changed his name to Frank H. Christner.

Children of Frank Christner and Mary Rodgers are:
    1860   i.   Gertrude Francina[8] Christner[3185], born 1901[3185]; died 1901[3185].
+   1861   ii.   Mildred Ruth Christner, born 20 Feb 1907 in Wilkinsburg, Allegheny Co., PA; died 04 Jul 1991 in Dade City, Pasco Co., FL.
    1862   iii. Mary Kathryn Christner[3185], born 21 Oct 1911 in Wilkinsburg, Allegheny Co., PA[3185].

642. Marguerite[7] Kooser (Clarissa[6] Christner, Levi[5], Peter[4], Johannes John Hans[3], Christian[2], Christen[1])[3186,3187] was born 1875 in Millrun, Fayette Co., PA[3188], and died in Pittsburgh, Allegheny Co., PA[3188]. She married **Walker F. Herwick**[3189]. He was born 13 Dec 1870 in Bullskin Co., PA[3189], and died 17 Dec 1937 in Millrun, Fayette Co., PA[3189].

More About Marguerite Kooser:
Residence: 1900, Connellsville, Fayette Co., PA[3190]

More About Walker F. Herwick:
Residence: 1880, Springfield, Fayette, PA, United States[3191]

Children of Marguerite Kooser and Walker Herwick are:
    1863   i.   Margaret Blance[8] Herwick[3191], born 10 Oct 1895 in Youngstown, Mahoning Co., OH; died 2007.
    1864   ii.   Clara Herwick[3191], born Abt. 1896 in Pittsburgh, Allegheny Co., PA[3191].

                More About Clara Herwick:
                Residence: 1930, Connellsville, Fayette Co., PA[3191]

    1865   iii. Ella Herwick[3191], born Abt. 1902 in Pittsburgh, Allegheny Co., PA[3191].

                More About Ella Herwick:
                Residence: 1920, Connellsville Ward 4, Fayette, PA[3191]

    1866   iv. Mildred Herwick[3191], born Abt. 1904 in Pittsburgh, Allegheny Co., PA[3191].

                More About Mildred Herwick:
                Residence: 1920, Connellsville Ward 4, Fayette, PA[3191]

    1867   v.   Margaret Belle Herwick[3191], born 1907 in Pittsburgh, Allegheny Co., PA[3191].

                More About Margaret Belle Herwick:
                Residence: 1930, Connellsville, Fayette Co., PA[3191]

    1868   vi. Walker Herwick[3191], born Abt. 1913 in Pittsburgh, Allegheny Co., PA[3191]; died 1965[3191].

                More About Walker Herwick:
                Residence: 1930, Connellsville, Fayette Co., PA[3191]

643. Bertha May[7] Christner (Elias[6], Levi[5], Peter[4], Johannes John Hans[3], Christian[2], Christen[1])[3192,3193,3194] was born 25 Feb 1870 in Bullskin Twp., Fayette Co., PA[3195,3196,3197], and died 02 Apr 1932 in BullskinTwp., Fayette Co., PA[3198,3199]. She married **James L. Newell**[3200] 27 Dec 1887 in Connellsville, Fayette Co., PA[3200]. He was born 23 Oct 1864 in Mt. Pleasant, Westmoreland Co., PA[3200], and died 22 Dec 1936 in BullskinTwp., Fayette Co., PA[3200].

Notes for Bertha May Christner:

Bertha May Christner (Elias-1) was born on February 25, 1870 in Fayette Co., PA. She appeared on the census on June 4, 1870 in Pennsville, Bullskin Twp., Fayette Co., PA. She appeared on the census in 1880 in Bullskin Twp., Fayette Co., PA. She appeared on the census on June 21, 1900 in Bullskin Twp., Fayette Co., PA. She appeared on the census on April 20, 1910 in Bullskin Twp., Fayette Co., PA. She resided in 1913 in Moyer, Fayette Co., PA. She appeared on the census on January 21, 1920 in Bullskin Twp., Fayette Co., PA. She appeared on the census in 1930 in Bullskin Twp., Fayette Co., PA. She died on April 2, 1932. She was buried on April 5, 1932 in Mt. Olive Cemetery, Connellsville, Fayette Co., PA

She was married to James L. NEWELL (son of Weston G. Newill and Ellen Porch) on December 27, 1887 in Connellsville, Fayette Co., PA. James L. Newell was born on October 23, 1864 in Mt. Pleasant, Westmoreland Co., PA. He was a Day Laborer on farm in June 1880. He appeared on the census on June 4, 1880 in Mt Pleasant Twp., Westmoreland Co., PA. He was a Laborer in a brickyard in June 1900 in Fayette Co., PA. He appeared on the census on June 21, 1900 in Bullskin Twp., Fayette Co., PA. He was a Superintendent in a Brick Yard in April 1910. He appeared on the census on April 20, 1910 in Bullskin Twp, Fayette, PA. He was a Coal Digger in 1913 in PA. He resided in 1913 in Moyer, Fayette Co, PA. He was a Public Works - Coal Mine in January 1920. He appeared on the census on January 21, 1920 in Bullskin Twp., Fayette Co., PA. He was a Miner - Coal Mine in 1930. He appeared on the census in 1930 in North Union, Fayette Co., PA. He died on December 22, 1936 in Connellsville, Fayette Co., PA. He was buried on December 26, 1936 in Mt. Olive Cemetery, Connellsville, Fayette Co., PA.

Birth: Feb. 25, 1870 - Fayette Co., PA
Death: Apr. 2, 1932 - Fayette Co., PA

Daughter of Elias Christner and Phoebe (Nicholson) Christner.
Married James L. Newell on 27 Dec 1887

Parents:
Elias Christner (1844 - 1923)
Phoebe Nicholson Christner (1835 - 1921)

Spouse: James L. Newell (1864 - 1936)

Burial: Mount Olive Cemetery, Connellsville, Fayette Co., PA
Find A Grave Memorial# 114025723

Christner, Bertha L.; Fayette Co.; Fayette Co.; 17; W; Dec 27, 1887; James L. Newill; Laborer; Fayette Co.; Westmd Co.; 23; W; Fayette Co. - Fayette County Genealogy Project
Marriages 1885-1889 Fayette County
(From Pennsylvania State Archives, Series #14.25)

More About Bertha May Christner:
Burial: 05 Apr 1932, Mt. Olive Cemetery, Connellsville, Fayette Co., PA[3200,3201]
Census: 1930, Bullskin Twp., Fayette Co., PA[3202,3203]
Marrcert: 27 Dec 1887[3204,3205]
Obi: 02 Apr 1932, The Daily Courier - Connellsville, Fayette Co., PA/[3206,3207]
Residence: 03 May 1915, Moyer, Fayette Co, PA[3208]

Notes for James L. Newell:
Info from Chris Newell, R.R.9 Box 910A. Pensacola, FL.

Birth: Oct. 23, 1864 - Mount Pleasant, Westmoreland Co., PA
Death: Dec. 22, 1936 - Fayette Co., PA

Son of Weston G. Newell and Ellen Porch.
Married Berth May Christner on 27 Dec 1887.

Spouse: Bertha May Christner Newell (1870 - 1932)

Burial: Mount Olive Cemetery, Connellsville, Fayette Co., PA
Find A Grave Memorial# 114025302

More About James L. Newell:
Burial: 26 Dec 1936, Mt.Olive Cemetery Connellsville, Fayette Co., PA[3208]
Census: 1930, North Union, Fayette, PA[3208]
Marrcert: 27 Dec 1887[3208]
Obi: 22 Dec 1936, The Daily Courier, Connellsville, Fayette Co., PA/[3208]
Occupation: 1930, Miner - Coal Mine/[3208]
Residence: 20 Apr 1910, Bullskin Twp., Fayette Co., PA[3208]

Children of Bertha Christner and James Newell are:

+ 1869   i.   Albert Moore[8] Newell, born 15 Sep 1888 in Moyer, Fayette Co, PA; died 23 May 1941 in Connellsville, Fayette Co., PA.

+ 1870   ii.   Olive Pearl Newell, born 12 Jun 1890 in Moyer, Fayette Co., PA; died 08 Nov 1914 in Pennsville, Bullskin Twp., Fayette Co., PA.

    1871   iii.   Lillian Newell[3208], born 18 Sep 1892 in Connellsville, Fayette Co., PA[3208]; died 04 Jul 1938[3208].

        More About Lillian Newell:
        Census: 20 Apr 1910, Bullskin Twp., Fayette Co., PA[3208]
        Occupation: 20 Apr 1910, laborer in a cigar factory/[3208]
        Residence: 1930, Redstone, Fayette, PA[3208]

    1872   iv.   Thomas H. Newell[3208], born 23 Feb 1896 in Connellsville, Fayette Co., PA[3208]; died 11 Aug 1954[3208]. He married Rose; born 1895 in Mid sea on the Atlantic Ocean.

        Notes for Thomas H. Newell:
        Thomas H. Newell (Bertha May CHRISTNER-2, Elias-1) was born on February 23, 1896 in Fayette Co., PA. He appeared on the census on June 21, 1900 in Bullskin Twp, Fayette, PA. He appeared on the census on April 20, 1910 in Bullskin Twp, Fayette, PA. He appeared on the census on January 21, 1920 in Bullskin Twp, Fayette, PA. He died on August 11, 1954.

        He was married to Rose before 1920. Rose was born about 1895 in Mid Sea on the Atlantic Ocean. She appeared on the census on January 21, 1920 in Bullskin Twp, Fayette, PA.

        More About Thomas H. Newell:
        Census: 21 Jan 1920, Bullskin Twp., Fayette Co., PA[3208]
        Marrcert: 27 Dec 1917[3208]
        News: 28 Dec 1917, Daily Courier - Connellsville, Fayette, PA[3208]
        Occupation: 17 Dec 1917, soldier/[3208]
        Residence: 1920, Bullskin Twp., Fayette Co., PA[3208]

    1873   v.   Bertha Newell[3208], born 17 Nov 1898 in Moyer, Fayette Co., PA[3208]; died 27 Nov 1986 in Odenton, Anne Arundel, MD[3208]. She married Ellis Colbert; born 13 Jan 1899 in Connellsville, Fayette Co., PA; died Jan 1975 in Connellsville, Fayette Co., PA.

        Notes for Bertha Newell:
        Bertha NEWELL (Bertha May CHRISTNER-2, Elias-1) was born on November 17, 1899 in Fayette Co., PA. She appeared on the census on June 21, 1900 in Bullskin Twp, Fayette, PA. She appeared on the census on April 20, 1910 in Bullskin Twp, Fayette, PA. She appeared on the census in 1920 in Dawson, Fayette, PA. She appeared on the census in 1930 in Bullskin Twp, Fayette, PA. She resided in 1986 in Odenton, Anne Arundel, MD. She died on November 27, 1986. She was named after after her mother.

        She was married to Ellis Colbert. Ellis Colbert was born on January 13, 1899 in PA. He appeared on the census in 1920 in Dawson, Fayette, PA. He died in January 1975 in PA.

        More About Bertha Newell:
        Census: 1930, Bullskin Twp., Fayette Co., PA[3208]

Marrcert: 28 Jun 1919[3208]
Namesake: after her mother/[3208]
Residence: 1986, Odenton, Anne Arundel, MD[3208]

1874   vi.   Fern Newell[3208], born 13 Apr 1901 in Bullskin Twp., Fayette Co., PA[3208]; died 18 Nov 1983[3208]. She
               married Moon.

               Notes for Fern Newell:
               Fern NEWELL (Bertha May CHRISTNER-2, Elias-1) was born on April 13, 1901 in Fayette Co., PA.
               She appeared on the census on April 20, 1910 in Bullskin Twp, Fayette, PA. She appeared on the census
               on January 21, 1920 in Bullskin Twp, Fayette, PA. She resided in 1983 in Mather, Greene Co, PA. She
               died on November 18, 1983. She was married to MOON.

               More About Fern Newell:
               Census: 21 Jan 1920, Bullskin Twp., Fayette Co., PA[3208]
               Marrcert: 21 Feb 1940[3208]
               News: 03 Feb 1932, Connellsville, Fayette Co., PA[3208]
               Residence: 1983, Mather, Greene Co, PA[3208]
               Social Security Number: 172-16-7213/[3208]

+   1875   vii.   Ethel Newell, born 15 Dec 1904 in Connellsville, Fayette Co., PA; died Mar 1986 in Mather, Greene
               Co., PA.
+   1876   viii. Florence Gladys Newell, born 04 Aug 1908 in Connellsville, Fayette Co., PA; died 21 Feb 1988 in
               Mather, Greene Co., PA.

644. Braden Hurst[7] Christner (Elias[6], Levi[5], Peter[4], Johannes John Hans[3], Christian[2],
Christen[1])[3209,3210,3211,3212,3213,3214,3215,3216] was born 01 Jun 1873 in Connellsville, Fayette Co., PA[3217,3218,3219],
and died Dec 1936[3220]. He married **Ella Mefford Smith**[3220,3221,3222] 1902[3223]. She was born 06 Oct 1881 in
Widnoon, Armstrong Co., PA[3223,3224,3225], and died 04 May 1939[3226].

Notes for Braden Hurst Christner:
Obituary:
Braden H. Christner (Elias-1) was born about 1873 in PA. He appeared on the census in 1880 in Bullskin Twp,
Fayette, PA. He was a General Auditor on January 8, 1920. He appeared on the census on January 8, 1920 in
Connellsville, Fayette Co, PA. He appeared on the census in 1930 in Connellsville, Fayette Co, PA.

He was married to Ella about 1902. Ella was born about 1882 in PA. She appeared on the census on January 8,
1920 in Connellsville, Fayette Co, PA. She appeared on the census in 1930 in Connellsville, Fayette Co, PA.

Buried: Hill Grove Cemetery, Connellsville, Fayette Co., PA

More About Braden Hurst Christner:
Census: 1930, Connellsville, Fayette Co., PA[3226]
Occupation: 08 Jan 1920, General Auditor/[3226,3227]
Residence: 18 Jun 1880, Bullskin Twp., Fayette Co., PA[3228,3229,3230,3231]

More About Ella Mefford Smith:
Census: 1930, Connellsville, Fayette Co., PA[3232]
Residence: 1920, Connellsville Ward 4, Fayette, PA[3233]

Children of Braden Christner and Ella Smith are:
+   1877   i.   Phoebe[8] Christner, born 16 Mar 1903 in Connellsville, Fayette Co., PA; died Jan 1978 in Connellsville,
               Fayette Co., PA.
    1878   ii.   Ora Louisa Christner[3234,3235,3236], born 16 Dec 1913 in Connellsville, Fayette Co., PA[3237,3238,3239]; died 26
               Feb 1969 in IA[3240]. She married Edward Sims Rishebarger[3241] 25 Sep 1937 in Connellsville, Fayette
               Co., PA[3241].

               Notes for Ora Louisa Christner:
               She appeared on the census on January 8, 1920 in Connellsville, Fayette Co, PA. She also appeared on

the census in 1930 in Connellsville, Fayette Co, PA.

More About Ora Louisa Christner:
Burial: Rock Island National Cemetery, Rock Island, IL[3242]
Census: 1930, Connellsville, Fayette Co., PA[3242]
Residence: 1969, Davenport IA[3242]

646. Martha (Mattie)[7] Christner (Charles[6], Levi[5], Peter[4], Johannes John Hans[3], Christian[2], Christen[1])[3243] was born 01 Nov 1869 in Prittstown, Fayette Co., PA[3244,3244], and died 30 Jun 1952 in Prittstown, Fayette Co., PA[3245,3246,3246]. She married **Thomas Mardis**[3247,3247] 1890[3247]. He was born 22 Apr 1869 in Liberty, Bedford Co., PA[3247], and died 28 Jun 1933 in Prittstown, Westmoreland Co., PA[3247].

More About Martha (Mattie) Christner:
Burial: Fayette Co, PA[3247]
Residence: 1880, Upper Tyrone, Fayette Co., PA[3248,3248]

Notes for Thomas Mardis:
Birth: 1868
Death: 1933

"Father" "In Loving Memory" (same stone as Martha)

Burial: Greenlick Cemetery, Fayette Co., PA
Find A Grave Memorial# 83045581

More About Thomas Mardis:
Burial: Fayette Co, PA[3249]
Residence: 1900, Bullskin, Fayette Co., PA[3249]

Children of Martha Christner and Thomas Mardis are:
1879   i. Samuel Adelma[8] Mardis[3249], born 14 Feb 1891 in Prittstown, Fayette Co., PA[3249]; died 14 Jun 1940 in Age: 49/Wooddale, Bullskin Twp., Fayette Co., PA[3249]. He married Grace L; born Abt. 1894 in Pittsburgh, Allegheny Co., PA[3250].

Notes for Samuel Adelma Mardis:
Cause fo death - heart attack.

More About Samuel Adelma Mardis:
Burial: Connellsville, Fayette Co., PA[3251]
Residence: 1930, Bullskin, Fayette Co., PA[3251]

More About Grace L:
Race: White/[3252]
Residence: 1920, Age: 26; Marital Status: Married; Relation to Head of House: Wife/Bullskin, Fayette Co., PA[3252]

1880   ii. Charles William Mardis[3253], born 08 Nov 1893 in Prittstown, Fayette, PA[3253]; died 29 Apr 1951 in Baltimore, Baltimore Co., MD[3253,3253].

More About Charles William Mardis:
Residence: 1942, Age: 49/Baltimore, Maryland[3253]

1881   iii. Lew V. Mardis[3253], born 05 Jul 1896 in Connellsville, Fayette Co., PA[3253]; died Oct 1971 in MS[3253].

More About Lew V. Mardis:
Residence: 1900, Age: 2; Marital Status: Single; Relation to Head of House: Son/Bullskin, Fayette Co., PA[3253]

1882   iv. Lavernon Mardis[3253], born 01 Jun 1897 in Pittsburgh, Allegheny Co., PA[3253,3253]; died 25 Nov 1964 in Age: 67/Connellsville, PA[3253,3253].

More About Lavernon Mardis:
Burial: Connellsville, Fayette County, PA, USA[3253]
Civil: Pittsburgh, Allegheny Co., PA[3253]
Residence: 1930, Age: 31; Marital Status: Married; Relation to Head of House: Head/Upper Tyrone, Fayette Co., PA[3253]

1883   v.   Grace Beatrice Mardis[3253], born 14 May 1902 in Prittstown, Fayette, PA[3253]; died 17 Sep 1976 in Woodale, Fayette, Pa[3253].

1884   vi. Theophilus Glenn Mardis[3253,3253], born Abt. 1910 in Pittsburgh, Allegheny Co., PA[3253,3253]; died Unknown[3253].

More About Theophilus Glenn Mardis:
Residence: 01 Apr 1940, Age: 30; Marital Status: Married; Relation to Head of House: Head/Upper Tyrone, Fayette Co., PA[3253]

1885   vii. Ruth T. Mardis[3253], born Abt. 1914 in Pittsburgh, Allegheny Co., PA[3253].

More About Ruth T. Mardis:
Residence: 1920, Age: 6; Marital Status: Single; Relation to Head of House: Daughter/Upper Tyrone, Fayette Co., PA[3253]

647.   Corriabell "Cora B"[7] Christner (Charles[6], Levi[5], Peter[4], Johannes John Hans[3], Christian[2], Christen[1])[3254] was born Nov 1872 in Connellsville, Fayette Co., PA[3255,3255], and died Bet. 1930 - 1940[3256]. She married **John McClure McGoogan**[3256] 1890[3257,3258]. He was born 20 Aug 1861 in Pittsburgh, Allegheny Co., PA[3258], and died 1920 in Pittsburgh, Allegheny Co., PA[3258].

Notes for Corriabell "Cora B" Christner:
1920 Census has Cora B living with her parents at 47 years old.

More About Corriabell "Cora B" Christner:
Residence: 1910, MT Pleasant Boro Ward 3, Westmoreland Co., PA[3259]

More About John McClure McGoogan:
Residence: 1910, Mt. Pleasant Boro Ward 3, Westmoreland Co., PA[3260]

Children of Corriabell Christner and John McGoogan are:
1886   i.   Harry H.[8] McGoogan[3260], born Jan 1891 in PA[3260]; died Bef. 1910 in 1910 census only 3 of 4 children of parents living/Pittsburgh, Allegheny Co., PA[3261].

More About Harry H. McGoogan:
Residence: 1900, Mt. Pleasant Ward 3, Westmoreland Co., PA[3262]

1887   ii. Charles Oral McGoogan[3263], born 01 Mar 1893 in Pittsburgh, Allegheny Co., PA[3263]; died Dec 1967 in Verona, Allegheny Co., PA[3263].

More About Charles Oral McGoogan:
Residence: 1910, Mt. Pleasant Boro Ward 3, Westmoreland Co., PA[3264]

1888   iii. Jessie B. McGoogan[3264], born Feb 1896 in PA[3264].

More About Jessie B. McGoogan:
Residence: 1910, Mt. Pleasant Boro Ward 3, Westmoreland Co., PA[3264]

1889   iv. Edgar McGoogan[3264], born 15 Apr 1899 in Pittsburgh, Allegheny Co., PA[3265].

More About Edgar McGoogan:
Residence: 1910, Mt. Pleasant Boro Ward 3, Westmoreland Co., PA[3266]
Unspecified: Westmoreland County[3267]

648. Elizabeth[7] **Christner** (Charles[6], Levi[5], Peter[4], Johannes John Hans[3], Christian[2], Christen[1])[3268,3268,3269] was born Jan 1876 in Fayette Co., PA[3270,3270]. She married **James Campbell Hager**[3271,3272,3273] 1892[3274,3275]. He was born 23 Jul 1873 in Connellsville, Fayette Co., PA[3276,3277], and died Dec 1966 in Cleveland, Cuyahoga Co., OH[3277].

More About Elizabeth Christner:
Residence: 1930, East Cleveland, Cuyahoga Co., OH[3278]

More About James Campbell Hager:
Residence: 1900, Duquesne Borough, Allegheny Co., PA[3279]
Social Security Number: 300-14-3096/[3280]
SSN issued: OH[3280]

Children of Elizabeth Christner and James Hager are:
 1890 i. Ruby V.[8] Hager[3281], born Jul 1893 in PA[3281].

      More About Ruby V. Hager:
      Residence: 1900, Duquesne Borough, Allegheny Co., PA[3281]

 1891 ii. Harold C. Hager[3281], born 07 Mar 1895 in Dickerson Run, Fayette Co., PA[3282,3283]; died Nov 1977 in Brookpark, Cuyahoga Co., PA[3283].

      More About Harold C. Hager:
      Other-Begin: Berea, Cuyahoga, Ohio, United States of America[3283]
      Residence: 1920, East Cleveland Ward 3, Cuyahoga Co., OH[3284]
      Social Security Number: 273-01-1245/[3285]
      SSN issued: Union Co., OH[3285]

652. Gertrude[7] **Christner** (Charles[6], Levi[5], Peter[4], Johannes John Hans[3], Christian[2], Christen[1])[3286,3286,3287,3288] was born Aug 1882 in Saltlick Twp., Fayette Co., PA[3289,3290,3290], and died Jun 1934 in Ligonier, Westmoreland Co., PA[3290]. She married **Harry E. Rhodes**[3291]. He was born 04 Apr 1872 in PA[3292,3293].

More About Gertrude Christner:
Residence: 1920, Ligonier, Westmoreland Co., PA[3293]

More About Harry E. Rhodes:
Residence: 1910, Ligonier, Westmoreland Co., PA[3293]

Children of Gertrude Christner and Harry Rhodes are:
 1892 i. Glen F.[8] Rhodes[3293,3293,3294], born 1903 in Ligonier, Westmoreland Co., PA[3294].

      More About Glen F. Rhodes:
      Residence: 1920, Ligonier, Westmoreland, PA[3294]

 1893 ii. Carl S. Rhodes[3295,3296,3297], born 12 Mar 1906 in Bitner, Fayette Co., PA[3298]; died 25 Mar 1968 in Died Washington Hosp./Washington Co., PA[3298]. He married Genevieve Mccoy[3298]; born 30 Jul 1912 in Swissvale, Allegheny Co., PA[3298]; died 14 Nov 1986 in Died in Brownsville General Hosp./Brownsville, Fayette Co., PA[3298].

      More About Carl S. Rhodes:
      Burial: Buried in Howe Cemetery/Coal Center, Washington Co., Pa.[3298]
      Residence: 1920, Ligonier, Westmoreland, PA[3299]

      More About Genevieve Mccoy:
      Residence: Bet. 1935 - 1993, Brownsville, Fayette Co., PA[3300]

653. Walter Joseph[7] **Christner** (Charles[6], Levi[5], Peter[4], Johannes John Hans[3], Christian[2],

Christen[1])[3301,3302,3303,3304,3305,3306,3306,3307,3308] was born 21 Jun 1885 in Prittstown, Fayette Co., PA[3309,3310,3311,3312,3313,3314,3314,3315,3316], and died 01 Apr 1934 in Mt Pleasant, Westmoreland Co., PA[3317,3318,3319,3320,3321]. He married **Elizabeth Ramsey**[3322,3323,3324,3325,3326] Abt. 1908[3327,3328]. She was born 18 Aug 1886 in Irwin, Westmoreland Co., PA[3329,3330,3331,3332,3333,3334,3335,3336], and died 15 Nov 1968 in Smithton, Westmoreland Co., PA[3337,3338,3339,3340,3341,3342].

Notes for Walter Joseph Christner:
Walter was a coal miner.

More About Walter Joseph Christner:
Residence: 1910, Mt. Pleasant, Westmoreland Co., PA[3343,3344,3345]

More About Elizabeth Ramsey:
Residence: 1910, Mt. Pleasant, Westmoreland Co., PA[3346]
Social Security Number: 176-40-7117/[3347]
SSN issued: Connellsville, Fayette Co., PA[3347]

Children of Walter Christner and Elizabeth Ramsey are:

+ 1894   i.   Richard[8] Christner Sr., born 14 Jun 1910 in Connellsville, Fayette Co., PA; died Jan 1978 in Kansas City, Jackson Co., MO.
+ 1895   ii.   Glenn R. Christner, born 11 Jul 1912 in Connellsville, Fayette Co., PA; died Feb 1984 in Smithton, Westmoreland Co., PA.
   1896   iii.   Leona Arlene Christner[3348,3349,3350,3351], born 31 Oct 1914 in Connellsville, Fayette Co., PA[3352,3353,3354,3355]; died 01 Jan 1993 in Dunbar Twp., Fayette Co., PA[3356,3357]. She married (1) Gilbert S. Sheard[3358]; born 07 Aug 1913 in Connellsville, Fayette Co., PA[3358,3359]; died Sep 1985 in Dunbar, FayetteCo., PA[3360]. She married (2) Charles Elbert Gregg[3361] 1930 in Brooke, WV[3361,3362].

More About Leona Arlene Christner:
Residence: 1930, South Huntingdon, Westmoreland Co., PA[3363]

More About Gilbert S. Sheard:
Residence: 1920, Dunbar, Fayette, PA[3364]
Social Security Number: 162-14-6998/[3365]

   1897   iv.   Arnold Christner[3366,3367,3368,3369,3370,3371], born 27 Sep 1916 in Connellsville, Fayette Co., PA[3372,3373,3374,3375]; died Dec 1983 in New Stanton, Westmoreland Co., PA[3376,3377].

More About Arnold Christner:
Residence: 1930, South Huntingdon, Westmoreland Co., PA[3377,3378,3379]
Social Security Number: 193-01-1329/[3380]
SSN issued: PA[3380]

+ 1898   v.   Charles Melvin "Chick" Christner Sr., born 07 Jan 1918 in Marguerite, Westmoreland Co., PA; died 07 Mar 2000 in Mt Pleasant, Westmoreland Co., PA.
+ 1899   vi.   Sarah Christner, born 12 Apr 1920 in Connellsville, Fayette Co., PA; died 06 May 1993 in Smithton, Westmoreland Co., PA.
   1900   vii.   Ernest Emerson Christner[3381,3382,3383,3384,3385], born 12 Sep 1923 in Searight, Fayette Co., PA[3386,3387,3388]; died 02 Oct 2006 in Jamestown, Chautauqua Co., NY[3389,3390,3391]. He married Mary Armita Wallace[3392,3393] 16 Oct 1943 in Westmoreland Co., PA[3394]; born 30 Sep 1927 in Greensburg, Westmoreland Co., PA[3395]; died 05 Sep 1964 in Dunkirk, Chautauqua Co., NY[3396].

More About Ernest Emerson Christner:
Residence: 1986, Jamestown, NY[3397]

+ 1901   viii.   Dorothy Christner, born 06 Nov 1925 in Smithton, Westmoreland Co., PA; died 07 Sep 2009 in Excela Health Westmoreland Hospital Greensburg.

654. George Washington[7] Christner (Charles[6], Levi[5], Peter[4], Johannes John Hans[3], Christian[2], Christen[1])[3398,3398] was born 28 Jan 1887 in Prittstown, Fayette Co., PA[3398,3398], and died 15 Dec 1948 in Hammondville, PA[3399]. He married **Anna Long** 15 Jan 1909 in Connellsville, Fayette Co., PA. She was born 02

Jan 1883 in Connellsville, Fayette Co., PA, and died 15 Jul 1969 in Connellsville, Fayette Co., PA[3400].

Notes for George Washington Christner:
Birth: Jan., 1887 - PA
Death: 1948

George was probably the son of George and Sarah Christner found in the 1900 census of Salt Lick Township, Fayette Co., PA. He married about 1909 to Anna Long. They lived in East Huntington Twp., Westmoreland Co., PA at the time of the 1910 census. They lived in Bullskin Twp., Fayette Co., PA in 1920, and in Connellsville, Fayette Co., PA in 1930. He was a coal miner.

Children of George and Anna:
Hazel M. Christner (ca.1913-unk)
Georgiane Christner (ca.1917-unk)

Spouse: Anna Long Christner (1883 - 1969)

Burial: Greenlick Cemetery, Fayette Co., PA

More About George Washington Christner:
Occupation: Teamster/
Residence: 1920, Bullskin Twp., Fayette Co., PA[3401]

Notes for Anna Long:
Birth: Jan 1883 - PA
Death: 1969

Anna was the daughter of William H. Long and Elizabeth Brothers.
She married about 1909 to George W. Christner.

They lived in East Huntington Township, Westmoreland Co., PA at the time of the 1910 census. They lived in Bullskin Township, Fayette Co., PA in 1920, and in Connellsville, Fayette Co., PA in 1930.

Children of George and Anna:
Hazel M. Christner (ca.1913-unk)
Georgiane Christner (ca.1917-unk)

Parents:
William H. Long (1861 - 1937)
Elizabeth Brothers Long (1866 - 1931)

Spouse: George W. Christner (1887 - 1948)

Burial: Greenlick Cemetery, Fayette Co., PA

More About Anna Long:
Residence: 1920, Bullskin Twp., Fayette Co., PA[3401]
Social Security Number: 183-40-5517/[3402]
SSN issued: Connellsville, Fayette Co., PA[3402]

Children of George Christner and Anna Long are:
+   1902   i.   Hazel Marie[8] Christner, born 23 Feb 1912 in Hammondsville, Jefferson Co., OH; died 16 Jun 1957 in Connellsville, Fayette Co., PA.
     1903   ii.   Georgeanna Christner, born 1916 in Connellsville, Fayette Co., PA.

658. William S.[7] Christner (Rufus[6], Levi[5], Peter[4], Johannes John Hans[3], Christian[2], Christen[1])[3403] was born 1873[3403], and died 1973[3403]. He married **Ida Alberta Odessa Wingrove**[3404]. She was born 31 Oct 1877 in

Hulltown, Lower Tyrone, Fayette, PA[3405], and died 24 Nov 1946 in Lower Tyrone Twp., Fayette Co., PA[3406,3407,3408].

Notes for William S. Christner:
He was a Justice of the peace in the Indian Head, Champion, Fayette Co., PA area.

More About William S. Christner:
Census: 1880, Bullskin Twp., Fayette Co., PA[3409]

Notes for Ida Alberta Odessa Wingrove:
She had 13 children with William Harvey Rimel. I'm not sure she was ever really married to William Christner, but we know she did have a child (John Ray Christner) by him.

More About Ida Alberta Odessa Wingrove:
Burial: 28 Nov 1946, buried next to her husband/Cochran Cemetery, Lower Tyrone Twp., Fayette Co., PA[3410]
Residence: 1900, Lower Tyrone, Fayette Co., PA[3411]

Child of William Christner and Ida Wingrove is:
+   1904   i.   John Ray[8] Christner, born 20 Oct 1895 in Connellsville, Fayette Co., PA; died 07 Dec 1978 in Dawson, Fayette Co., PA.

663.   Charles F. Russell[7] Christner (Rufus[6], Levi[5], Peter[4], Johannes John Hans[3], Christian[2], Christen[1])[3412] was born 08 Sep 1887 in Pittsburgh, Allegheny Co., PA[3412,3413], and died Dec 1918. He married **Lydia Lohr** 1915 in Uniontown, PA, USA[3414]. She was born 04 Jan 1889 in Melcroft, Fayette Co., PA[3414], and died 24 Aug 1981 in Champion, Fayette Co., PA[3414].

Notes for Charles F. Russell Christner:
Birth: 1887
Death: 1918

Burial: Mount Nebo Cemetery, Indian Head, Fayette Co., PA
Find A Grave Memorial# 94150185

Obituary - The Daily Courier - Connellsville, PA - 14 Dec 1918
Following an illness of influenza, Russell Christner, 30 years old, died Thursday at his home at Davistown. Funeral services will be held tomorrow morning at 9:30 o'clock from the house, followed by internment in Mount Nebo Cemetery. Mr. Christner is survived by his widow, two children, his parents, Mr. and Mrs. Rufus Christner of Davistown and several brothers and sisters, including Solomon Christner of Indian Head, Mrs. Edith Brown of Mount Pleasnt, Mrs. Lucy Howard of Indian Head and Hattie Christner at home.

More About Charles F. Russell Christner:
Other-Begin: Connellsville, Fayette Co., PA[3415]
Residence: 1900, Saltlick Twp., Fayette Co., PA[3416,3417]

Notes for Lydia Lohr:
Birth: 1889
Death: 1981

Burial: Mount Nebo Cemetery, Indian Head, Fayette Co., PA
Find A Grave Memorial# 94429157

Children of Charles Christner and Lydia Lohr are:
   1905   i.   Rex Everett[8] Christner[3418], died Aft. 1963 in New Castle, New Castle Co., PA[3418].
   1906   ii.   James Ruffus Christner[3418], born 1917 in Davistown, Fayette Co., PA[3418]; died 1972 in Augusta, Columbia Co., GA[3418].

       More About James Ruffus Christner:

Served: 1963, Master Sergeant in US Army at Fort Gordon, GA[3418]

668.   Elmer E.[7] Cramer (Elvina Belle[6] Christner, Levi[5], Peter[4], Johannes John Hans[3], Christian[2], Christen[1])[3419] was born 27 May 1893 in Rockwood, Somerset Co., PA[3420,3421], and died 09 Dec 1936 in Browntown, WV[3422,3423]. He married **Eunice E. Strickler**[3424] Abt. 1914[3424,3425]. She was born 18 Jul 1895 in Pittsburgh, Allegheny Co., PA[3425], and died Jun 1977 in Uniontown, Fayette Co., PA[3425].

Notes for Elmer E. Cramer:
The Daily Courier (Connellsville, PA), p. 6 December 10, 1936, Thursday Elmer E. Cramer-Killed In Mine Elemer E. Cramer, abt 42 years old, a former resident of Vanderbilt, was killed Wednesday (9 Dec 1936) morning in a coal mine at Browntown, West Virginia where he was employed as a coal cutting machine operator. It was said that he was demonstrating a new machine when he lost his life under a fall of slate. Besides his wife who was Miss Eunice STRICKLER, Mr. Cramer is survived by one son J.F. Cramer and three brothers and sisters; Mrs. Glenn GOE of Vanderbilt, Mrs. Samuel HAIR of Dickerson Run, Mrs. C.W. Lohr of Connellsville, Charles L. Cramer of Centerville, Edgar H. Cramer of Merrittstown, Mrs. James BIRD of Akron, Ohio, Mrs. I.N. CIPPERLEY and Mrs Clarence BAUMAN of Cleveland, Ohio, Mrs. A.D. NICOL of North Bloomfield, Ohio and Miss Olive Cramer of Chicago, Illinois. The body was removed by the undertaking firm of Ira Blair & sons of Perryopolis to the home of this mother, Mrs. Elvina Cramer at Vanderbilt where the funeral service will be conducted on Friday afternoon at 2:30 o'clock. Interment will be made in Dickerson Run Union Cemetery.

More About Elmer E. Cramer:
Burial: 1936, UNION CEMETERY/Dickerson Run, Fayette Co., PA[3426]
Occupation: COAL MINER/[3426]
Residence: 1900, New Centerville Borough, Somerset, PA[3427]

More About Eunice E. Strickler:
Residence: 01 Apr 1940, Franklin, Fayette, PA, United States[3428]

Child of Elmer Cramer and Eunice Strickler is:
      1907   i.   J. F.[8] Cramer.

680.   Minnie L.[7] Christner (Elijah H.[6], Levi[5], Peter[4], Johannes John Hans[3], Christian[2], Christen[1])[3429,3429] was born 01 May 1879 in Mt. Pleasant, Westmoreland Co., PA[3429,3429], and died 05 Dec 1961 in Charleroi, PA. She married **Harry F. Booth**.

Notes for Minnie L. Christner:
Obituary: The Valley Independent - Monessen, PA
5 Dec. 1961

Mrs. Minnie Christner Booth, 82 of 432 Center Ave., North Charleroi, died at her home yesterday at 6:40 pm. She was born in Mt. Pleasant, May 1, 1879.

Survivors are her husband, Harry F. Booth, three sons, Clarence O. Booth, Corning, NY, Alfred H. Booth, Detroit, MI and Kenneth D. Booth, Streator, IL, two daughters, Mrs. William (Helen) Schiffbauer, Nemacolin, Bernice E. Booth at home, one brother Hadd Christner, Mt. Pleasant, one sister, Mrs. Mabel Weight of Pittsburgh, six grandchildren and ten great granschildren.

Friends will be received at the Harol L. Schrock Funeral Home, 226 Fallowfield Ave., Charleroi during the hours of 2 to 5 and 7 to 10 pm.

More About Minnie L. Christner:
Residence: 1880, Bullskin, Fayette Co., PA[3429,3429]

Children of Minnie Christner and Harry Booth are:
      1908   i.   Clarence O.[8] Booth.

1909	ii.	Alfred H. Booth.
1910	iii.	Kenneth D. Booth.
1911	iv.	Helen Booth. She married William Schiffbauer.
1912	v.	Bernice E. Booth.

681. Mary Mae[7] Christner (Elijah H.[6], Levi[5], Peter[4], Johannes John Hans[3], Christian[2], Christen[1])[3429,3429] was born Mar 1882 in Pittsburgh, Allegheny Co., PA[3429,3429], and died 1962. She married **Braden Queer**. He was born 10 Jan 1881 in Buckeye, PA, and died 17 Jan 1962 in Hammondsville, Bullskin Twp., Fayette Co., PA.

More About Mary Mae Christner:
Residence: 1900, Bullskin Twp., Fayette Co., PA[3429,3429]

More About Braden Queer:
Burial: Green Lick Cemetery, Bullskin Twp., Fayette Co., PA
Residence: 1930, Bullskin Twp., Fayette Co., PA[3430]

Children of Mary Christner and Braden Queer are:

1913	i.	Stella[8] Queer.
1914	ii.	Irene Queer.
1915	iii.	Leroy Queer.

682. Harry Cramer[7] Christner (Elijah H.[6], Levi[5], Peter[4], Johannes John Hans[3], Christian[2], Christen[1])[3431,3431,3432] was born 04 Mar 1882[3432,3433], and died 19 Jul 1971 in Mt. Pleasant, Westmoreland Co., PA[3433]. He married **Mary Ann Nedrow**. She was born 12 Jan 1884 in Connellsville, Fayette Co., PA, and died 13 Sep 1936[3434].

Notes for Harry Cramer Christner:
Birth: 1882
Death: 1971

Spouse: Mary Ann Nedrow Christner (1884 - 1936)

Children:
Dorthea M. Christner Yothers (1908 - 1983)
Ralph H. Christner (1922 - 2003)
Dwight R. Christner (1925 - 1950)

Burial: Greenlick Cemetery, Fayette Co., PA

More About Harry Cramer Christner:
Residence: 1900, Bullskin, Fayette Co., PA[3435,3435]
Social Security Number: 172-18-7650/[3436]
SSN issued: PA[3436]

Notes for Mary Ann Nedrow:
Fergunson/Nedrow Cemetery and Nedrow Road are north of Donegal PA. off route 711.

1910 soundex PA has Catherine Lontz, Grandmother, 82, living with them, is this his or hers.

Birth: 1884
Death: 1936

Spouse: Harry C. Christner (1882 - 1971)

Children:
Dorthea M. Christner Yothers (1908 - 1983)

Ralph H. Christner (1922 - 2003)
Dwight R. Christner (1925 - 1950

Burial: Greenlick Cemetery, Fayette Co., PA

Children of Harry Christner and Mary Nedrow are:

	1916	i.	Unnamed[8] Christner, born 1904 in Connellsville, Fayette Co., PA.
+	1917	ii.	Elvy Elsworth Christner, born 22 Sep 1905 in Connellsville, Fayette Co., PA; died 02 Jun 2002 in Youngstown, Mahoning Co., OH.
	1918	iii.	Merle Christner, born 1907 in Connellsville, Fayette Co., PA; died 1907 in Connellsville, Fayette Co., PA.
	1919	iv.	Earl Christner[3437,3438], born 06 Jan 1907[3439]; died 22 Oct 1988 in Jeannette, Westmoreland Co., PA[3439]. He married Sarah Kepple; born 1910; died 1989.

More About Earl Christner:
Residence: 1910, Bullskin, Fayette, PA[3440]
Social Security Number: 169-03-7201/[3441]
SSN issued: Connellsville, Fayette Co., PA[3441]

+	1920	v.	Dorotha Minerva Christner, born 10 Nov 1908; died 06 Oct 1983 in Collier Co., FL.
	1921	vi.	Marie Louvenia Christner, born 1911 in Connellsville, Fayette Co., PA.
+	1922	vii.	Edna Mae Christner, born 15 Sep 1914; died 11 Aug 1999 in Mt. Pleasant, Westmoreland Co., PA.
	1923	viii.	Violet Christner, born 1916 in Connellsville, Fayette Co., PA; died 1918.
	1924	ix.	Olive Jean Christner, born 1918 in Connellsville, Fayette Co., PA.
	1925	x.	Raymond Alfred Christner, born 22 Jul 1920[3442]; died 22 Jul 1999 in Mt. Pleasant, Westmoreland Co., PA[3442]. He married Florence L. Sanders; born 16 Aug 1928; died 19 Mar 2005.

More About Raymond Alfred Christner:
Social Security Number: 172-18-7649/[3442]
SSN issued: PA[3442]

Notes for Florence L. Sanders:
Birth: Aug. 16, 1928
Death: Mar. 19, 2005

Spouse: Raymond A. Christner (1920 - 1999)

Burial: Greenlick Cemetery, Fayette Co., PA

	1926	xi.	Ralph Harry Christner, born 07 Jul 1922[3443,3444]; died 02 Jun 2003 in Connellsville, Fayette Co., PA[3445]. He married Shirley J; born 01 Jul 1944[3446].

Notes for Ralph Harry Christner:
Birth: Jul. 7, 1922
Death: Jun. 2, 2003

Parents:
Harry C. Christner (1882 - 1971)
Mary Ann Nedrow Christner (1884 - 1936)

Burial: Greenlick Cemetery, Fayette Co., PA

More About Ralph Harry Christner:
Military service: 08 Oct 1942, Pittsburgh, Alleghaney Co., PA[3447]
Residence: Westmoreland Co., PA[3447]
SSN issued: PA[3448]

Notes for Shirley J:
Greenlick Cemetery, Bullskin Twp., Fayette Co., PA.

More About Shirley J:
Residence: Mount Pleasant, PA[3449]

1927   xii.   Dwight R. Christner, born 1925; died 1950.

Notes for Dwight R. Christner:
Birth: 1925
Death: 1950

Parents:
Harry C. Christner (1882 - 1971)
Mary Ann Nedrow Christner (1884 - 1936)

Burial: Greenlick Cemetery, Fayette Co., PA

1928   xiii.   Nora Belle Christner, born 1928.

687. Jacob "Deets/Deitz" R.[7] Christner (George Deitz[6], Susan[5], David[4], Johannes John Hans[3], Christian[2], Christen[1]) was born 05 Oct 1863 in Trenton, Henry Co., IA[3450], and died 25 Sep 1933 in Henry Co., IA[3451]. He married **Fanny Rich**[3452,3453,3454,3455] 27 Aug 1885 in IA[3456,3457]. She was born 09 Feb 1868 in Henry Co., IA[3458], and died 11 May 1947 in Wayland, Henry Co., IA[3458,3459].

Notes for Jacob "Deets/Deitz" R. Christner:
Jacob is listed as the son of George and Mary Christner in the 1870 census.
George (a mulatto) is born George Deets or Deitz and why he has changed his name to Christner is unclear.

Birth: Aug 27, 1863 - IA
Death: Sep 25, 1933 - Henry Co., IA

Spouse: Fannie Rich Christner (1868 - 1947)

Children:
Bertha Christner Hill (1889 - 1977)
Nicholas Christner (1891 - 1977)

Burial: North Hill Cemetery, (Rural Wayland), Henry Co., IA

More About Jacob "Deets/Deitz" R. Christner:
Burial: Sep 1933, SE corner. From drive, row 4, grave 1./North Hill Cemetery, Wayland, Iowa, USA[3460,3461]
Residence: 1920, Jefferson, Henry Co., IA[3462]

Notes for Fanny Rich:
Birth: Feb 9, 1868 - Henry Co., IA
Death: May 11, 1947 - Henry Co., IA

Spouse: Jacob E. Christner (1863 - 1933)

Children:
Bertha Christner Hill (1889 - 1977)
Nicholas Christner (1891 - 1977)

Burial:North Hill Cemetery, (Rural Wayland), Henry Co., IA

Parents:
Nicholas Rich (1844 - 1920)
Anna Huser Rich (1843 - 1907)

Spouse: Jacob E. Christner (1863 - 1933)

Children:
David Christner (1885 - 1979)
Bertha Christner Hill (1889 - 1977)
Nicholas Christner (1891 - 1977)
Jakie Jacob Christner (1893 - 1974)
Barbara Christner Neff (1894 - 1963)
Anna Mae Christner Campbell (1897 - 1971)
Neoma Christner Schantz (1901 - 1981)
Lavina Christner Riley (1903 - 1997)
Clarence Rufus Christner (1909 - 1910)
Elmer Christner (1912 - 1999)

Burial: North Hill Cemetery, Rural Wayland, Henry Co., IA

More About Fanny Rich:
Burial: May 1947, SE corner. From drive, row 4, grave 1./North Hill Cemetery, Wayland, Iowa, USA[3463,3464]
Residence: 1930, Jefferson, Henry Co., IA[3465,3466,3467]

Children of Jacob Christner and Fanny Rich are:

1929   i.   David D.[8] Christner[3468,3469], born 31 Dec 1885 in Wayland, Henry Co., IA[3470,3471]; died 04 Nov 1979 in Wayland, Henry Co., IA[3472,3473]. He married Bertha Lorene Ackles[3474] 06 Jul 1946[3474]; born 24 Sep 1908 in IA[3474]; died 01 Nov 1968 in Wayland, Henry Co., IA[3474].

       Notes for David D. Christner:
       Birth: Dec 31, 1885 - Henry Co., IA
       Death: Nov 4, 1979 - IA

       Parents:
       Jacob E Christner (1863 - 1933)
       Fannie Rich Christner (1868 - 1947)

       Spouse: Bertha Lorene Ackles Christner (1908 - 1968)

       Burial: North Hill Cemetery (Rural Wayland), Henry Co., IA

       More About David D. Christner:
       Residence: 1930, Jefferson, Henry Co., IA[3475]
       Social Security Number: 485-60-6537/[3476]
       SSN issued: IA[3476]

       Notes for Bertha Lorene Ackles:
       Birth: Sep. 24, 1908 - IA
       Death: Nov. 1, 1968 - IA

       Spouse: David Christner (1885 - 1979)

       Burial: North Hill Cemetery, (Rural Wayland), Henry Co., IA

       More About Bertha Lorene Ackles:
       Residence: 1930, Trenton, Henry Co., IA[3477]

+   1930   ii.   Annie Mae Christner, born 08 Aug 1896 in Topeka, Lagrange Co., IN; died 13 Apr 1991 in Topeka, Lagrange Co., IN.

+   1931   iii.   Fannie Ada Christner, born 18 Feb 1899 in Washington Co., IA; died 02 Jun 1968 in Washington Hospital, Washington Co., IA.

    1932   iv.   Neoma Christner[3478,3479], born 15 Jun 1901 in Henry Co., IA[3480]; died 19 Sep 1981 in Wayland, Henry Co., IA[3480]. She married Edward R Schantz[3480] 16 Mar 1920[3480]; born 14 Apr 1899[3480]; died 27 Mar 1990[3480].

       More About Neoma Christner:

1933   v.   Veoma Christner[3482], born 15 Jun 1901 in Henry Co., IA[3482]; died 19 Sep 1981 in Henry Co., IA[3483,3484].

More About Veoma Christner:
Residence: 1915, Jefferson, Henry Co., IA[3484]

689. William Franklin Frank[7] Risher (Elizabeth[6] Christner, David[5], David[4], Johannes John Hans[3], Christian[2], Christen[1]) was born 13 Dec 1856 in Connellsville, Fayette Co., PA, and died 20 Dec 1943 in Johnstown, Cambria Co., PA. He married **Mary Katherine Beaner**[3485] 22 Feb 1881. She was born 25 Dec 1854 in Somerset Co., PA[3485], and died 09 Feb 1944 in Johnstown, Cambria Co., PA[3485].

Notes for William Franklin Frank Risher:
Gospel Herald Vol XXXVI No.41 pages 852 & 853 Jan. 6, 1944

Risher - Frank Risher, of near Thomas Dale, Somerset Co., PA was born Dec. 13, 1856; died Dec. 20, 1943, at the home of his son and daughter-in-law, Mr. and Mrs. L. L. Risher, Johnstown, PA; aged 87 y. 7 d. He had been in failing health for some time and was bedfast for about 6 months. He was married to Mrs. Mary Beaver Decker and together they shared the joys and sorrows of life for about 62 or 63 years. He is survived by his widow and the following children: Mrs. Elizabeth Doubt, Bedford, PA; George W., Pittsburgh, PA; Lemon L., Johnstown, PA; Harry A., Somerset Pike; also a stepdaughter (Mrs. Jennie Murphy, Ligonier, Pa.) and a number of grandchildren and greatgrandchildren. He was received into the Mennonite Church at Thomas Church, June 19, 1930. He took an active interest in the church and was a witness for the Lord. On Dec. 20, he peacefully fell asleep, answering the call for which he had been waiting. Services were conducted at the Thomas Church. Burial in the nearby cemetery.

More About William Franklin Frank Risher:
Burial: Thomas Mennonite Church Cemetery Somerset Co., , PA
Religion: Thomas Mennonite Church Somerset Co., PA/

More About Mary Katherine Beaner:
Burial: Thomas Mennonite Church Cem. Conemaugh TWP., Somerset Co., , PA

Children of William Risher and Mary Beaner are:
  1934   i.   Elizabeth[8] Risher, born 31 Aug 1881 in Somerset Co., PA. She married Jack Doubt.
  1935   ii.   George Webster Risher, born 13 Oct 1883 in Somerset Co., PA; died 25 Feb 1950 in Bedford, PA. He married Annie Edith Boyer 29 Jan 1905 in Johnstown, Cambria Co. PA.
  1936   iii. Lemon Lenhart Risher, born 22 Jun 1887.
  1937   iv.   Henry Albert Pete Risher, born 19 Jun 1894.

693. John[7] Christner (Samuel[6], David[5], David[4], Johannes John Hans[3], Christian[2], Christen[1])[3485,3486] was born 05 Apr 1868 in Jenner Twp., Somerset Co., PA[3487], and died 1932 in Conner, Jenner Twp., Somerset Co., , PA[3488]. He married **Harriet Hattie Decker**[3489] 12 Mar 1896 in Connor, Jenner Twp., Somerset Co., PA, daughter of Mary Katherine Beaner. She was born Jan 1876 in Somerset Co., PA[3489], and died 18 Jun 1943 in Somerset Co., PA[3489].

Notes for John Christner:
His parents and his wifes parents were both Mulatto. 1910 census living in Ferndale Cambria Co. PA worked at Stable Boss Coal Mine 1930 census he worked at a steel mill as a loader.

More About John Christner:
Residence: 1910, Ferndale, Cambria Co., PA[3489]

Notes for Harriet Hattie Decker:
Her Stepfather was Frank Risher. Color of her Parents was Mulatto as were his parents.

More About Harriet Hattie Decker:
Burial: Memorial Park Somerset Co., PA
Residence: 1920, Ferndale, Cambria Co., PA[3489]

Children of John Christner and Harriet Decker are:
1938   i.   Franklin Dewey[8] Christner, born 25 Mar 1899 in Jenner Twp., Somerset Co., PA[3489].

        More About Franklin Dewey Christner:
        Occupation: Moulder at a steel mill/
        Residence: 1910, Ferndale, Cambria Co., PA[3489]

1939   ii.   Mary Jeannette Christner, born 1901[3489]. She married Berkebile.

        Notes for Mary Jeannette Christner:
        She may have been married to a Berkebile & had a half brother Roy Heckman.

        More About Mary Jeannette Christner:
        Residence: 1910, Ferndale, Cambria Co., PA[3489]

1940   iii.   Edna Irene Christner, born 27 Dec 1903 in Jerome, Conemaugh Twp., Somerset Co., PA; died 05 Jul 1977 in Berlin, Somerset Co., PA. She married Ivan Oscar Ben Lambert 1935; born 24 Aug 1895 in Lambertsville, Somerset Co., PA; died 04 Feb 1984 in Stoystown, Somerset Co., PA.

        Notes for Edna Irene Christner:
        Edna was a stepmother to Josephine Lambert & Marjorie Lambert their natural mother was Ida Pearl Rankin she died Dec.26, 1935

        More About Edna Irene Christner:
        Burial: Memorial Park, Somerset Co., PA
        Religion: Trinity Lutheran Church/
        Residence: 1943 Reels Corner, Shade Twp., Somerset Co., , PA

        More About Ivan Oscar Ben Lambert:
        Burial: 1984, Somerset Memorial Park, Somerset Co., PA
        Education: Cambria Business College/
        Elected: Co. Commissioner/
        Military service: 110th Infantry, 28th Division, Coumpany C   Purple Heart/
        Occupation: Licensed Real Estate Salesman/
        Oganization: Somerset Lodge 358, F&AM
        Religion: Lutheran - St. Paul's Lutheran Church, Buckstown, PA/

1941   iv.   Edwin Christner[3489,3490], born 1904 in Connellsville, Fayette Co., PA[3491].

        More About Edwin Christner:
        Residence: 1910, Ferndale, Cambria Co., PA[3491]

1942   v.   Leo W. Christner[3491], born 23 Sep 1906[3491,3492]; died Apr 1985 in Johnstown, Cambria Co., PA[3492].

        More About Leo W. Christner:
        Other-Begin: Johnstown, Cambria Co., PA[3492]
        Residence: 1910, Ferndale, Cambria Co., PA[3493]
        Social Security Number: 196-07-8134/[3494]
        SSN issued: PA[3494]

1943   vi.   William Christner[3495], born 08 Sep 1911; died Aug 1980 in Baltimore, Baltimore Co., MD[3495].

        More About William Christner:
        Occupation: truck driver in the building construction industry/
        Social Security Number: 192-07-9314/[3495]
        SSN issued: PA[3495]

696. Jesse[7] Christner (Samuel[6], David[5], David[4], Johannes John Hans[3], Christian[2], Christen[1])[3496] was born

10 Jan 1872 in Jenner, Somerset Co., PA[3496], and died 25 Jun 1941 in Johnstown, Cambria Co., PA[3496]. He married **Catherine Katherine Dietz**[3496] 22 Nov 1894, daughter of David Dietz and Mary Thomas. She was born 17 Jul 1869 in Somerset Co., PA[3496], and died 20 May 1935 in Johnstown, Cambria Co., PA[3496].

Notes for Jesse Christner:
This info came from Robert Schaffer 119 Markley Ct. Johnstown, PA. Robert is the son of Mary Pauline, Jesses daughter.

More About Jesse Christner:
Burial: Grandview Cemetery, Johnstown, Cambria Co., PA
Residence: 1920, Johnstown Ward 8, Cambria Co., PA[3496]

Notes for Catherine Katherine Dietz:
Catherine is the daughter of David and Mary Thomas Dietz.

More About Catherine Katherine Dietz:
Residence: 1920, Johnstown Ward 8, Cambria Co., PA[3496]

Children of Jesse Christner and Catherine Dietz are:
> 1944   i.   Ora May[8] Christner[3497], born 10 Oct 1895 in Connellsville, Fayette Co., PA[3497]; died 14 May 1911.
>
> > More About Ora May Christner:
> > Residence: 1910, Johnstown Ward 8, Cambria Co., PA[3497]

+   1945   ii.   Naomi Ruth Christner, born 02 Aug 1899 in Johnstown, Cambria Co., PA; died 29 Apr 1976 in Johnstown, Cambria Co., PA.

+   1946   iii.   Harry Christner Sr., born 22 Feb 1902 in Johnstown, Cambria Co., PA; died 17 Dec 1982 in Glendale, Los Angeles Co., CA.

+   1947   iv.   Robert Christner Sr., born 25 Apr 1908 in Johnstown, Cambria Co., PA; died 13 Oct 1959 in Johnstown, Cambria Co., PA.

+   1948   v.   Mary Pauline Christner, born 21 Apr 1915 in Johnstown, Cambria Co., PA; died 08 May 1975 in Johnstown, Cambria Co., PA.

701. David[7] Christner (Samuel[6], David[5], David[4], Johannes John Hans[3], Christian[2], Christen[1])[3498,3499,3500] was born 30 Dec 1883 in Somerset Co., PA[3501,3502,3503,3504], and died 1945[3505]. He married **Nancy Berkey**[3506,3507] 1898[3507]. She was born Feb 1883 in Somerset Co., PA[3507,3508], and died 1930[3508,3509].

More About David Christner:
Residence: 1920, Jenner, Somerset Co., PA[3509,3510]

More About Nancy Berkey:
Residence: 1900, Jenner Township (East Part), Somerset Co., PA[3511,3512]

Children of David Christner and Nancy Berkey are:
> 1949   i.   Mabel[8] Christner[3513,3514], born 1904 in Somerset Co., PA[3514,3515].
>
> > More About Mabel Christner:
> > Residence: 1920, Jenner, Somerset Co., PA[3515,3516]
>
> 1950   ii.   Florence H. Christner[3517], born 1908 in Somerset Co., PA[3517].
>
> > More About Florence H. Christner:
> > Residence: 1920, Jenner, Somerset Co., PA[3517]
>
> 1951   iii.   Virgil Oscar Christner[3517], born 30 Oct 1911 in Bedford, Bedford Co., PA[3517]; died 27 Oct 1969 in York Co., PA[3517].
>
> > More About Virgil Oscar Christner:

Military service: 28 Oct 1942, Altoona, Blair Co., PA[3517]
Residence: 1920, Jenner, Somerset Co., PA[3517]
Social Security Number: 196-09-3228/[3517]
SSN issued: Connellsville, Fayette Co., PA[3517]

+ 1952   iv.   Ethel Frances Christner, born 08 Aug 1913 in Thomas Mills, Potter Co., PA; died 31 Oct 1980 in Johnstown, Cambria Co., PA.

1953   v.   Irene Christner, born 1917 in Connellsville, Fayette Co., PA.

702. Louisa Ellen[7] Lowry (Susanna Deitz[6] Christner, David[5], David[4], Johannes John Hans[3], Christian[2], Christen[1])[3518] was born 25 Dec 1860 in Somerset Co., PA, and died 11 Mar 1954 in Somerset Co., PA. She married **Jeremiah Pyle**[3518]. He was born 03 Apr 1829 in Middle Creek Twp., Somerset Co., PA, and died 01 Sep 1925 in Somerset Co., PA.

More About Louisa Ellen Lowry:
Residence: 1930, Somerset, Somerset Co., PA[3518]

More About Jeremiah Pyle:
Residence: 1920, Milford, Somerset Co., PA[3518]

Children of Louisa Lowry and Jeremiah Pyle are:
+ 1954   i.   Arthur Learoux[8] Pyle, born 08 Dec 1884; died 10 Jul 1955 in ,Ketchum, ID.
+ 1955   ii.   Susan E. Pyle, born 30 Apr 1894 in Middlecreek, Somerset Co., PA; died 12 Nov 1986 in Somerset Co., PA.

703. Albert W.[7] Lowry (Susanna Deitz[6] Christner, David[5], David[4], Johannes John Hans[3], Christian[2], Christen[1]) was born 03 Mar 1862 in Somerset Co., PA. He married **(1) Sadie Switzer**.   He married **(2) Daisy Wooley**.

Children of Albert Lowry and Sadie Switzer are:
1956   i.   Earl[8] Lowry.
1957   ii.   Lulu Lowry.

705. Amos Herbert[7] Lowry (Susanna Deitz[6] Christner, David[5], David[4], Johannes John Hans[3], Christian[2], Christen[1])[3519] was born 07 Nov 1866 in Middle Creek Twp., Somerset Co., PA, and died in PA[3519,3520]. He married **Annie Stayer**.

More About Amos Herbert Lowry:
Residence: 1930, McKeesport, Allegheny, PA[3521,3522]

Children of Amos Lowry and Annie Stayer are:
1958   i.   Clarence[8] Lowry.
1959   ii.   Mabel Lowry.
1960   iii.   Lester Lowry.

706. Cora Estelle[7] Lowry (Susanna Deitz[6] Christner, David[5], David[4], Johannes John Hans[3], Christian[2], Christen[1]) was born 31 Dec 1870 in Somerset Co., PA, and died 06 Sep 1937 in Aspenwall, PA.. She married **George Dempsey Pyle** 06 Jan 1891 in Somerset Co., PA. He was born 23 Sep 1863 in Middlecreek Twp. Somerset. Co. Pa., and died 01 Sep 1926 in Scottdale, Westmoreland Co., PA.

More About Cora Estelle Lowry:
Burial: Scottdale, Westmoreland Co., PA

More About George Dempsey Pyle:
Burial: Scottdale, Westmoreland Co., PA

Children of Cora Lowry and George Pyle are:

    1961   i.   Clyde[8] Pyle, born 28 Mar 1892 in Scottdale, Westmoreland Co., PA; died 14 Jul 1961 in Scottdale, Westmoreland Co., PA. He married Esther Andereson.

                   Notes for Clyde Pyle:
                   No Children

                   More About Clyde Pyle:
                   Burial: Scottdale, Westmoreland Co., PA

+   1962   ii. Edna Myrtle Pyle, born 07 Mar 1894 in Scottdale, Westmoreland Co., PA; died 05 Jul 1971 in Salt Lake CIty, UT.
+   1963   iii. Gladys Fay Pyle, born 08 Jun 1900 in Scottdale, Westmoreland Co., PA; died 19 Aug 1994 in Martinsburg PA.
+   1964   iv. Ida Mae Pyle, born 10 Apr 1905 in Scottdale, Westmoreland Co., PA; died 1997 in Salt Lake CIty, UT.

707. Ida Mae[7] Lowry (Susanna Deitz[6] Christner, David[5], David[4], Johannes John Hans[3], Christian[2], Christen[1]) was born 31 Dec 1870 in Somerset Co., PA, and died 1899 in Somerset Co., PA. She married **William Miller**.

Notes for Ida Mae Lowry:
All her children died of TB (turburculosis) brought into the home by the children of Rev. N. B. Christner who also married her.

Edna Pyle Tedrow offered to take care of (Ida's Daughter) Violet Miller's son but Edna's mother (Cora Estelle Lowry) said "NO, there's something wrong with that family, their all dying," so Violet's father kept the child. All of his sons died of TB also.

The whole gang of Millers are buried at Middle Church of the Brethern with Wasington and Susan (Christner) Lowry and 2 of their children.

Some say she born 5/22/1868 died 1906.

More About Ida Mae Lowry:
Burial: Middle Church of the Brethern

Children of Ida Lowry and William Miller are:

    1965   i.   Earl[8] Miller.
    1966   ii. Ernest Miller.
    1967   iii. Harry Miller.
+   1968   iv. Violet Miller.
    1969   v.   Ernest Miller.
    1970   vi. Harry Miller.

708. Anna B.[7] Lowry (Susanna Deitz[6] Christner, David[5], David[4], Johannes John Hans[3], Christian[2], Christen[1]) was born 15 Aug 1872 in Somerset Co., PA, and died 16 Mar 1950. She married **John Hyatt**.

Child of Anna Lowry and John Hyatt is:

    1971   i.   Hazel[8] Hyatt.

710. John E.[7] Lowry (Susanna Deitz[6] Christner, David[5], David[4], Johannes John Hans[3], Christian[2], Christen[1]) was born 06 Feb 1876 in Somerset Co., PA, and died 06 Feb 1961 in Milford Twp., Somerset Co., PA. He married **Hattie Uphouser**.

Children of John Lowry and Hattie Uphouser are:

    1972   i.   Mildred Bailey[8] Lowry.

1973   ii.   Stella McDevitt Lowry.

714. Cora Alice[7] Christner (John[6], Jessie[5], David[4], Johannes John Hans[3], Christian[2], Christen[1])[3523] was born 23 Sep 1873 in Goshen, Elkhart Co., IN[3523,3524], and died 18 Nov 1953 in Goshen, Elkhart Co., IN. She married **Alonzo Smith**[3525,3526] in Waterford, (Goshen), Elkhart Co., IN. He was born Apr 1866[3526], and died 21 Mar 1935.

More About Cora Alice Christner:
Residence: 1880, Elkhart, Elkhart Co., IN[3527]

More About Alonzo Smith:
Burial: Violett Cemetery, Goshen, Elkhart Co., IN
Residence: Waterford south of Goshen, IN

Children of Cora Christner and Alonzo Smith are:
1974   i.   Ray[8] Smith, born 29 May 1897 in Waterford Mills, Goshen, Elkhart Co., IN; died 24 Jul 1964.

Notes for Ray Smith:
He never married.

More About Ray Smith:
Burial: Violett Cemetery, Goshen, Elkhart Co., IN
Residence: 1900, Elkhart, Elkhart Co., IN[3528]

+ 1975   ii.   May Smith, born 17 Sep 1904 in Waterford Mills, Goshen, Elkhart Co., IN; died 25 Dec 1993 in Wakarusa Nursing Home Wakarusa, IN.
1976   iii.   Irvin Pete Smith, born 01 Oct 1905 in Waterford Mills, Goshen, Elkhart Co., IN; died 10 Dec 1954. He married Virginia Todd 06 Nov 1941 in Goshen, Elkhart Co., IN.

Notes for Irvin Pete Smith:
He was first married to Virginia (don't know her last name) second to Virginia Todd.

More About Irvin Pete Smith:
Burial: Violett Cemetery, Goshen, Elkhart Co., IN

1977   iv.   John Smith, born 17 May 1908 in Waterford Mills, Goshen, Elkhart Co., IN; died 16 May 1971 in MI. He married Virran.

Notes for Virran:
John was her second husband.

1978   v.   Minnie Smith, born 19 Nov 1909 in Waterford Mills, Goshen, Elkhart Co., IN; died 11 May 1959. She married Ray Cripe 24 Apr 1928 in Goshen, Elkhart Co., IN.

More About Minnie Smith:
Burial: Violett Cemetery, Goshen, Elkhart Co., IN
Residence: 1920, Elkhart, Elkhart Co., IN[3529]

1979   vi.   Nancy Smith, born 27 Aug 1911 in Waterford Mills, Goshen, Elkhart Co., IN; died 12 Dec 1973 in Goshen, Elkhart Co., IN. She married (1) Ben Lehman. She married (2) Robert Delcamp. She married (3) Martin Stewart 1951 in Goshen, Elkhart Co., IN.

More About Nancy Smith:
Burial: Violett Cemetery, Goshen, Elkhart Co., IN

715. Jesse Calvin[7] Christner (John[6], Jessie[5], David[4], Johannes John Hans[3], Christian[2], Christen[1])[3530] was born 02 Nov 1874 in Goshen, Elkhart Co., IN[3530]. He married **Jennie Lynn Webber** in Sugar Grove Church Cemetery, Goshen, Elkhart Co., IN.

More About Jesse Calvin Christner:

Residence: 1880, Elkhart, Elkhart Co., IN[3530]

Children of Jesse Christner and Jennie Webber are:

    1980   i.   Lois[8] Christner. She married Kauffman.

                    Notes for Lois Christner:
                    She lived at Bristol, IN.

+   1981   ii.   Myrtle Pauline Christner, died May 1962.
    1982   iii.   Esther E. Christner, born 03 Nov 1912.
    1983   iv.   Harold S. Christner[3531], born 05 Dec 1914 in Elkhart Co., IN; died 16 Aug 2000 in Goshen, Elkhart Co., IN. He married Betty E. Kitson 12 Apr 1946; born 04 May 1919 in Elkhart Co., IN[3532,3533]; died 23 Jun 1995 in Goshen, Elkhart Co., IN.

                    Notes for Harold S. Christner:
He died at Millers Merry Manor, Wakarusa. He was a farmer and his farm was at County Road 20 north of Goshen, Indiana. A member of Sugar Grove Church He lived at 313 Huron St Goshen,IN.

Birth: 1914
Death: 2000

Spouse: Betty E. Christner (1919 - 1995)

Burial: Sugar Grove Cemetery, Goshen, Elkhart Co., IN
Find A Grave Memorial# 93531387

More About Harold S. Christner:
Burial: Sugar Grove Church Cemetery, Goshen, Elkhart Co., IN
Education: Jefferson High School/
Occupation: Farmer/
Social Security Number: 312-01-2618/[3534]
SSN issued: IN[3534]

Notes for Betty E. Kitson:
She died at 5:50 P.M. in Greencroft Health Care in Goshen Indiana.where she had been for two weeks, she was only ill one month.

Birth: 1919
Death: 1995

Spouse: Harold S. Christner (1914 - 2000)

Burial: Sugar Grove Church Cemetery, Goshen, Elkhart Co., IN
Find A Grave Memorial# 93531377

More About Betty E. Kitson:
Burial: Sugar Grove Church Cemetery, Goshen, Elkhart Co., IN[3535]
Social Security Number: 309-05-5842/[3536]
SSN issued: IN[3536]

716. Harry[7] Christner (John[6], Jessie[5], David[4], Johannes John Hans[3], Christian[2], Christen[1])[3537,3538,3539] was born 13 Sep 1876 in Goshen, Elkhart Co., IN[3539], and died 09 Aug 1964 in Waterford Mills, Goshen, Elkhart Co., IN[3539]. He married **Elzina Miller** 20 Aug 1903. She was born 27 Feb 1884 in Goshen, Elkhart Co., IN, and died 27 Jan 1962 in Waterford Mills, Goshen, Elkhart Co., IN[3540].

Notes for Harry Christner:
He was a house Painter and spoke Pennsylvania Dutch.

SS# 308-05-4761

More About Harry Christner:

Residence: 1920, Elkhart, Elkhart Co., IN[3541]

Notes for Elzina Miller:
At age 12 she worked as a maid at the big white house south of Waterford bridge on Highway 15, South Goshen, IN.

Buried in Violet Cemetery, Goshen, IN

More About Elzina Miller:
Residence: 1910, Elkhart, Elkhart Co., IN[3541]

Child of Harry Christner and Elzina Miller is:
+   1984   i.   Wilma Irene[8] Christner, born 22 Sep 1905 in Waterford Mills, Goshen, Elkhar Co., IN; died 18 Sep 1982 in Waterford Mills, Goshen, Elkhar Co., IN.

719. Martha M.[7] Christner (John[6], Jessie[5], David[4], Johannes John Hans[3], Christian[2], Christen[1]) was born 16 Oct 1879 in Goshen, Elkhart Co., IN[3542]. She married **Jesse Close**.

More About Martha M. Christner:
Residence: 1880, Elkhart, Elkhart Co., IN[3542]

Children of Martha Christner and Jesse Close are:
    1985   i.   Kenneth J.[8] Close[3543], born 15 Aug 1904[3543]; died 20 May 1993 in Toledo, Lucas Co., OH[3543].

            More About Kenneth J. Close:
            Social Security Number: 292-07-8126/[3543]

    1986   ii.   ? Close, born 25 Oct 1905.
+   1987   iii.   Orval Clarence Close, born 25 Dec 1906 in OH; died 14 Nov 1978 in San Bernardino, San Bernardino Co., CA.

721. Matilda Garnetta[7] Christner (John[6], Jessie[5], David[4], Johannes John Hans[3], Christian[2], Christen[1])[3544] was born 18 Apr 1884 in Goshen, Elkhart Co., IN[3544]. She married **Charles Defreese**.

More About Matilda Garnetta Christner:
Residence: 1900, Elkhart Township (Excl. Goshen City), Elkhart, Indiana[3544]

Children of Matilda Christner and Charles Defreese are:
    1988   i.   ?[8] Defreese.
    1989   ii.   ? Defreese, born 30 Dec 1905.

723. Mable Persilla[7] Christner (John[6], Jessie[5], David[4], Johannes John Hans[3], Christian[2], Christen[1])[3544] was born 18 Nov 1888 in Goshen, Elkhart Co., IN[3544], and died 16 Nov 1918[3544]. She married **Albert Judy**.

More About Mable Persilla Christner:
Burial: Violet Cem Goshen. IN
Residence: 1900, Elkhart Township (Excl. Goshen City), Elkhart, Indiana[3544]

Children of Mable Christner and Albert Judy are:
    1990   i.   Leonard[8] Judy, born 27 Dec 1908.
    1991   ii.   Florence Judy, born 11 Nov 1909.
    1992   iii.   Irene Judy, born 1910.
    1993   iv.   Kenneth Judy, born 1913.
    1994   v.   Paul Judy, born 1915; died Aug 1918.
    1995   vi.   Robert Judy, born 1916.
    1996   vii.   Mable Judy, born 28 Jun 1918.

726. Ellen Mary (Lesh) Kolkhorst[7] Whetstone (Harriet "Hattie"[6] Christner, Jessie[5], David[4], Johannes John Hans[3], Christian[2], Christen[1])[3545] was born 06 Apr 1875 in IN[3545,3546], and died 06 Apr 1962 in Longmont, Boulder Co., CO[3547]. She married **(1) Fritz Hienrich Martin "Fred" Kolkhorst**[3548]. He was born Abt. 1883 in Germany[3548], and died 03 Feb 1962 in Denver, Colorado, United States[3548]. She married **(2) Ella Whetstone**[3549] 23 Nov 1893 in Elkhart[3549]. She married **(3) Otto L Lesh**[3550] 23 Nov 1893 in Elkhart Co., IN[3550]. He was born Mar 1863 in OH[3550].

More About Ellen Mary (Lesh) Kolkhorst Whetstone:
Residence: 1920, Lincoln Ward 5, Lancaster, NE[3551,3552]

More About Fritz Hienrich Martin "Fred" Kolkhorst:
Arrival: 1903[3552]
Departure: Hamburg[3552]
Residence: 1930, Lincoln, Lancaster, NE[3552]

More About Otto L Lesh:
Residence: 1870, Miami, Montgomery, Ohio, United States[3552]

Child of Ellen Whetstone and Fritz Kolkhorst is:
    1997   i.   John Jack[8] Kalkhorst[3552], born 02 Feb 1916 in NE[3552]; died 22 Oct 1995 in Arvada, Jefferson, Colorado, United States of America[3552].

                More About John Jack Kalkhorst:
                Residence: 1930, Lincoln, Lancaster, NE[3552]

745. Jonas Henry[7] Lowry (Tyrannus[6] Christner, Abraham D.[5], Joseph "Zep"[4], Johannes John Hans[3], Christian[2], Christen[1]) was born 1858, and died 1919. He married **Mary E. Kellerman**. She was born Jan 1856 in Meyersdale, Somerset Co., PA, and died 1902.

Notes for Jonas Henry Lowry:
These children never used the name of Eichner. He also did not use the name Henry so he called himself Jonas H. Lowry   He had 16 children many died before age 2

More About Jonas Henry Lowry:
Birth Name: Henry Jonas Maybe Eicher or Lowry

Children of Jonas Lowry and Mary Kellerman are:
    1998   i.   John[8] Lowry.
    1999   ii.   Robert Lowry.
+   2000   iii.   Minnie Opal Lowry, born Apr 1887 in Somerset Co., PA; died 1917.
    2001   iv.   Dorothy Cubanna Lowry, born 1898; died 1964 in Ross Co., OH. She married Dyer Mitchell.

                Notes for Dorothy Cubanna Lowry:
                Married a Dyer Mitchell or Mitchell Dyer

749. Mary "Pollie"[7] Lowry (Tyrannus[6] Christner, Abraham D.[5], Joseph "Zep"[4], Johannes John Hans[3], Christian[2], Christen[1]) was born 1860 in Somerset Co., PA, and died 1931. She married **William Henry Baer** 06 Dec 1885. He was born 18 Sep 1863 in Meyersdale, Somerset Co., PA, and died 1947.

More About William Henry Baer:
Burial: Union Cemetery Meyersdale PA.

Child of Mary Lowry and William Baer is:
+   2002   i.   William Joseph[8] Baer, born 21 Mar 1884 in Meyersdale, Somerset Co., PA; died 13 Dec 1947 in Windber, Somerset Co., PA.

758. Mahlon[7] Christner (Herman[6], Abraham D.[5], Joseph "Zep"[4], Johannes John Hans[3], Christian[2], Christen[1])[3553,3554,3555,3556,3557,3558] was born 15 Sep 1865 in Summit Twp., Somerset Co., PA[3559,3560,3561,3562], and died 24 Apr 1932 in Summit Garret Somerset Co., PA[3563]. He married **Mary Matilda Pritts**[3564,3565,3566,3567] 25 Mar 1890 in Garrett, Somerset Co., PA. She was born 14 Sep 1861 in Connellsville, Fayette Co., PA[3568,3569,3570,3571,3572], and died 02 Feb 1939.

Notes for Mahlon Christner:
Birth: Sep 15, 1865
Death: Apr 24, 1932

Burial: Highland Cemetery, Garrett, Somerset Co., PA

Mahlon was a railroad brakeman. Mahlon was shot and killed by his nephew Walter (son of Lewis) over the raise in rent on a house. Like most railroad men he had a part time occupation, his being a saw miller and a lumber dealer. Laurel Messinger,Nov 1966 Garrett was the first town in the county to have brick paved streets. Mayor W.A. Merrill,Councilmen J.Juday,W.Hoover,Simon Britz, U.Sober, Mahlon Christner year 1906. Mahlon built and owned the first dam at Bigby Run to supply the town of Garrett PA. with water. He later sold the dam to his half brother Lewis Christner.

1920 Census has Harry 27, Edward 24, Jacob 21, & Catherine,13 living at home with the parents.

More About Mahlon Christner:
Burial: Highland Cemetery, Garrett, Somerset Co., PA
Cause of Death: Shot by nephew
Residence: 1930, Garrett, Somerset Co., PA[3573,3574]

Notes for Mary Matilda Pritts:
Birth: Sep. 14, 1862
Death: 1939

w/o Mahlon

Burial: Highland Cemetery, Garrett, Somerset Co., PA
Find A Grave Memorial# 78171524

More About Mary Matilda Pritts:
Burial: Highland Cemetery, Garrett, Somerset Co., PA
Residence: 1930, Garrett, Somerset Co., PA[3575,3576]

Children of Mahlon Christner and Mary Pritts are:
+   2003   i.   George Curtis[8] Christner, born 20 Jul 1885 in Garrett, Summit Twp., Somerset Co., PA; died 08 Feb 1973 in Meyersdale, Summit Twp., Somerset Co., PA.
+   2004   ii.   Edna Bell Christner, born 30 Sep 1890 in Garrett, Summit Twp., Somerset Co., PA; died 09 Oct 1959 in Meyersdale, Somerset Co., PA.
+   2005   iii.   Harry Albert Christner, born 01 Jan 1893 in Cumberland, Allegany Co., MD; died 24 Mar 1974 in Martinsburg, Berkeley Co., WV.
     2006   iv.   Ida Christner[3577,3577], born 01 Mar 1893[3577]; died 03 Jun 1893 in Summit Twp., Somerset Co., PA.

          More About Ida Christner:
          Burial: Garrett Union, PA

+   2007   v.   Edward Carl Christner, born 09 Mar 1895 in Garrett, Summit Twp., Somerset Co., PA; died 09 May 1988 in Meyersdale, Somerset Co., PA.
     2008   vi.   Washington Christner[3578,3579], born May 1896 in Garrett, Summit Twp., Somerset Co., PA[3580]; died 30 Mar 1916 in Garrett, Somerset Co., PA[3581].

          Notes for Washington Christner:

Never Married   Was Electrocuted.

Birth: May 1896
Death: 30 Mar 1916

Meyersdale Commercial, Mar. 30, 1916

Young man electrocuted - Son of Mahlon Christner at Garrett Meets Terrible Death at His Home Tuesday Evening. Washington the nineteen year old son of Mr. and Mrs. Mahlon Christner of Garrett met death by accidently being electrocuted at his father's farm at about 5:30 o'clock on Tuesday evening. The young man was adjusting a broken electrical wire leading from the street to the barn. He climbed up along the side of the barn about ten feet and had taken hold of the electrical and a lightening rod on barn. Mr. Silas Deal noticed smoke escaping from the boy's glove and pulled him down. Death was almost instantaneous. The funeral services will be conducted by Rev. W. B. Carney of the Lutheran Church Friday afternoon. He is survived by his parents and the following brothers and sisters: George, Jacob, Harry, and Mrs. Edna Duecker, Katharine, and Edward all of Garrett. Washington was of excellent character and most dutiful to his parents. The funeral was in charge of Undertaker Tressler of Meyersdale. Sincere sympathy is extended to the family in their bereavement.

Meyersdale Commercial, Apr. 6, 1916
MAN SHOCKED TO DEATH - Attempts to Remove Tangle of Electrical Wires; Grasps Lightning Rod - Washington Christner, aged nineteen, of Garrett, near Rockwood, Pa., was killed by electricity at his home. Young Christner climbed unto the barn to untangle two electric wires which had crossed above the barn door. Grasping the lightning rod with one hand, he endeavored to untangle the wires with the other and was shocked to death.

Burial: Ridgeview Cemetery, Garrett, Somerset Co., PA

More About Washington Christner:
Burial: Garrett Highland Cemetery, Summit Twp., Somerset Co., PA
Residence: 1900, Summit, Somerset Co., PA[3582]

+   2009   vii.   Jacob Henry Christner, born 13 Sep 1899 in Garrett, Summit Twp., Somerset Co., PA; died 17 Feb 1952.
+   2010   viii.   Catharine M. Christner, born 29 Jun 1906 in Garrett, Summit Twp., Somerset Co., PA; died 22 Feb 1998 in Meyersdale, Somerset Co., PA.

759. Amanda[7] **Christner** (Herman[6], Abraham D.[5], Joseph "Zep"[4], Johannes John Hans[3], Christian[2], Christen[1])[3583,3584,3585] was born 13 Oct 1867 in Garrett, Summit Twp., Somerset Co., PA[3586,3587,3588], and died 28 Mar 1932 in Somerset, Somerset Co., PA[3589]. She married **(1) Samuel W. Husband**[3589,3590] 27 Feb 1880 in Connellsville, Fayette Co., PA. He was born 19 Jun 1846 in Tarr's Station, Westmoreland Co., PA[3591,3592], and died 23 Mar 1915[3593,3594]. She married **(2) Harry Griffith** 1916. He was born 04 Aug 1869 in Jenner Township PA, and died 20 Jan 1954.

Notes for Amanda Christner:
She owned a house in Garrett, Somerset Co., PA.

More About Amanda Christner:
Residence: 1900, Mount Pleasant Ward 3, Westmoreland Co., PA[3595]

Notes for Samuel W. Husband:
He worked as a clerk in Garrett, Somerset Co., PA.

More About Samuel W. Husband:
Residence: 1900, Telegraph operator/Mount Pleasant Ward 3, Westmoreland Co., PA[3595,3596]

Notes for Harry Griffith:
He was Pennsylvania Railroad engineer.

More About Harry Griffith:
Burial: Jennerstown Luthern Cemetery

Children of Amanda Christner and Samuel Husband are:

+   2011   i.   Benjamin Harrison[8] Husband, born 15 Nov 1888 in Mt. Pleasant, Westmoreland Co., PA; died 06 Dec 1959.
+   2012   ii.   Grace Lucille Husband, born 19 Aug 1893; died 06 Jan 1973 in Somerset Co., PA.

760. Albert Paul.[7] Christner Sr. (Herman[6], Abraham D.[5], Joseph "Zep"[4], Johannes John Hans[3], Christian[2], Christen[1])[3597,3598,3599] was born 20 Jan 1870 in Summit Twp. Somerset PA[3600,3601], and died Jul 1952 in Garrett, Somerset Co., PA[3602]. He married **Margaret Gretella Gardiner**[3602,3603] 1908 in Garrett, Somerset Co., PA[3604]. She was born 18 Feb 1890 in Glasgow, Scotland[3605,3606], and died 31 Jan 1977 in Meyersdale, Somerset Co., PA[3606,3607].

Notes for Albert Paul. Christner Sr.:
This info came from Cary Christner of Meyersdale, PA. Albert is the son of Harmon Christner and Susan Ringer. Some of this info came from Robert C. who is the son of Francis a brother of Albert. Robert says Albert was born in Feb 1870.

More About Albert Paul. Christner Sr.:
Burial: Highland Cemetery, Garrett, Somerset Co., PA
Christened: Garrett, Somerset Co., PA
Residence: 1930, Garrett, Somerset Co., PA[3608]

Notes for Margaret Gretella Gardiner:
Maggie Gardner Christner was the daughter of Daniel Gardner and Mary McCallister.

Obituary: Margaret (Gardiner) CHRISTNER, 1977, of Garrett, Somerset County, PA - Meyersdale Republican, February 3, 1977

Mrs. Margaret G. Christner, 86 died Jan 31 in Meyersdale Community Hospital. Born February 18, 1890, in Glasgow, Scotland, she was a daughter of the late Mr. and Mrs. Daniel Gardner. Her husband, Albert Christner, preceded her in death.

She is survived by two sons, Fred "Peg" Christner and Clyde Christner, both of Garrett; 13 grandchildren and 28 great-grandchildren.

The body is at the Price Funeral Home, Meyersdale, where friends will be received. Services will be held at the funeral home on Thursday at 2 p.m. by Rev. A. J. Shearer. Interment will be in Highland Cemetery.

Birth: Feb. 18, 1890, Scotland
Death: Jan. 31, 1977

Burial: Highland Cemetery, Garrett, Somerset Co., PA

More About Margaret Gretella Gardiner:
Burial: Feb 1977, Highland Cemetery, Garrett, Somerset Co., PA
Residence: 1930, Garrett, Somerset Co., PA[3609]

Children of Albert Christner and Margaret Gardiner are:

+   2013   i.   Glenn H.[8] Christner, born 04 Sep 1909 in Garrett, Somerset Co., PA; died 22 Jul 1974 in Meyersdale, Somerset Co., PA.
+   2014   ii.   Frederick H. Christner, born 17 Oct 1911 in Somerset Co., PA; died 21 Sep 1982 in Cumberland, Allegeny Co., MD.
+   2015   iii.   Clyde W. Christner, born 27 Jul 1913 in Garrett, Somerset Co., PA; died 22 Dec 1982 in Cumberland, Allegany Co., MD.
+   2016   iv.   Ethel M. Christner, born 02 Aug 1916 in Somerset Co., PA; died Dec 1952.
+   2017   v.   Albert Paul Christner Jr., born 23 Feb 1919 in Garrett, Somerset Co., PA; died 05 Jan 1977 in Dover, Kent Co., DE.

761. William H.[7] **Christner** (Herman[6], Abraham D.[5], Joseph "Zep"[4], Johannes John Hans[3], Christian[2], Christen[1])[3610,3611] was born 21 Jun 1874 in Summit Twp., Somerset Co., PA[3612,3613,3614,3615], and died 31 Mar 1930 in Flint, Genesee Co., MI[3616]. He married **Elizabeth Lane**. She was born Sep 1877 in Connellsville, Fayette Co., PA[3617,3618,3619], and died in Flint, MI.

More About William H. Christner:
Residence: 1880, Summit Twp., Somerset Co., PA[3620]

More About Elizabeth Lane:
Residence: 1900, Northampton, Somerset Co., PA[3621]

Children of William Christner and Elizabeth Lane are:

2018   i.   Carl Osborne[8] Christner, born 17 Dec 1897; died Dec 1975.

       Notes for Carl Osborne Christner:
       There is no sex listed for this child as i can't beleive the name is spelled
       right. Could this be Sharon?

       More About Carl Osborne Christner:
       Residence: 1900, Northampton, Somerset Co., PA[3621]

2019   ii.   Nellie M. Christner[3621,3622], born May 1898 in Connellsville, Fayette Co., PA[3623,3624].

       More About Nellie M. Christner:
       Residence: 1900, Northampton, Somerset Co., PA[3625]

+ 2020   iii.   Francis Guy Christner, born 18 Jul 1899 in Connellsville, Fayette Co., PA; died 1949 in Genesee Co., MI.

2021   iv.   Marie M. Christner[3626], born 1903 in Connellsville, Fayette Co., PA[3626].

       More About Marie M. Christner:
       Residence: 1910, Bacon, Charlotte Co., VA[3626]

2022   v.   Emma L. Christner[3626,3627], born 21 Feb 1903[3627]; died Dec 1975 in Prescott, Ogemaw Co., MI[3627].

       More About Emma L. Christner:
       Residence: 1910, Bacon, Charlotte Co., VA[3628]
       Social Security Number: 365-07-1245/[3629]

+ 2023   vi.   Mildred Ruth Christner, born 14 Jan 1908 in Auburn, King Co., WA; died 08 Oct 1977 in Flint, Genesee Co., MI.

762. Sadie[7] **Christner** (Herman[6], Abraham D.[5], Joseph "Zep"[4], Johannes John Hans[3], Christian[2], Christen[1])[3630] was born 16 Apr 1876 in Summit Twp., Somerset Co., PA[3630], and died 06 May 1955 in Cumberland, Allegany Co., MD. She married **(1) Frank**. She married **(2) George Bittner**. She married **(3) Harry Nickle**.

More About Sadie Christner:
Burial: Cumberland, Allegany Co., MD
Residence: 1880, Summit Twp., Somerset Co., PA[3630]

Children of Sadie Christner and George Bittner are:
2024   i.   Ann Lucille[8] Bittner.
2025   ii.   Eugene Bittner.

763. Francis A. "Wash"[7] **Christner** (Herman[6], Abraham D.[5], Joseph "Zep"[4], Johannes John Hans[3], Christian[2], Christen[1])[3631,3632] was born 24 Jan 1878 in Summit Twp., Somerset Co., PA[3633,3634], and died 13 Jun

1928[3635]. He married **Clara Rachel Hughes**[3636] 1902. She was born Jan 1882 in Palo Alto, PA, and died 14 Dec 1963 in Garrett, Somerset Co., PA.

Notes for Francis A. "Wash" Christner:
Birth: Jan 24, 1878
Death: Jun 13, 1928 - Somerset Co., PA

Inscription: Spanish American War Vet Org Co M 46 Reg Inf. U. S., Vol - Pvt

Burial: Highland Cemetery, Garrett, Somerset Co., PA
Find A Grave Memorial# 78645612

More About Francis A. "Wash" Christner:
Burial: Highland Cemetery, Garrett, Somerset Co., PA[3637]
Military service: 31 May 1901, San Francisco, San Francisco Co., CA[3638]

Notes for Clara Rachel Hughes:
Clara is the daughter of William Hughes and Lana Martz.

Birth: 1882
Death: 1963

Burial: Highland Cemetery, Garrett, Somerset Co., PA
Find A Grave Memorial# 100713799

More About Clara Rachel Hughes:
Burial: Highland Cemetery, Garrett, Somerset Co., PA

Children of Francis Christner and Clara Hughes are:

2026   i.   Alice V.[8] Christner[3639,3640,3641], born 25 Jun 1902 in Garrett, Somerset Co., PA[3642,3643,3644]; died Jan 1983 in Somerset, Somerset Co., PA[3644,3645]. She married Herman Miller[3645,3646] 1918; born 12 Feb 1899 in PA[3646]; died 27 Jan 1964[3647].

        More About Alice V. Christner:
        Residence: 1910, Summit, Somerset Co., PA[3648]
        Social Security Number: 160-50-0701/[3649]
        SSN issued: Connellsville, Fayette Co., PA[3649]

        Notes for Herman Miller:
        Birth: Feb. 12, 1899
        Death: Jan. 27, 1964

        Burial: Green Lawn Cemetery, Columbus, Franklin Co., OH
        Find A Grave Memorial# 71648034

        More About Herman Miller:
        Residence: 1930, Somerset, Somerset Co., PA[3650]

2027   ii.   Robert C. "Amos" Christner[3651], born 28 Sep 1903 in Garrett, Somerset Co., PA[3652]; died 09 Feb 1986 in Meyersdale, Somerset Co., PA.

        Notes for Robert C. "Amos" Christner:
        He went by Amos and was a PFC US Army World War II, 714th RY OPN BN Alaska Asiatic Pacific Theater. He worked for B & O Railroad and was a member of the American Legion & VFW.

        Obituary: Robert C. "Amos" Christner 1986, Garrett, Somerset County, PA - Daily American, February 10, 1986

        Robert C. (Amos) Christner, 82, Garrett, died Feb. 9, 1986, in Meyersdale Community Hospital. Born Sept. 28, 1903 in Garrett, son of late Francis and Clara (Hughes) Christner. Survived by two brothers,

Clarence, Garrett; and Millard, Portland, OR; and a number of nieces and nephews. Retired employee of B & O Railroad. Veteran of World War II. Member of Meyersdale American Legion and VFW. Friends will be received after 7 p.m. Monday at Leckemby Funeral Home, where service will be held at 2 p.m. Wednesday, the Rev. William Phennicie. Interment, Highland Cemetery, Garrett. Military graveside service will be conducted at cemetery.

More About Robert C. "Amos" Christner:
Burial: Highland Cemetery, Garrett, Somerset Co., PA
Social Security Number: 208-10-5025/[3653]
SSN issued: PA[3653]

+	2028	iii.	Grace Lucille Christner, born 25 Mar 1906 in Garrett, Somerset Co., PA; died 29 Nov 1969.
+	2029	iv.	Clarence H. Christner, born 29 Mar 1910 in Garrett, Somerset Co., PA; died 04 Dec 1993 in Grantsville, Garrett Co., MD.
+	2030	v.	Lawerence William Christner, born 29 Mar 1910 in Garrett, Somerset Co., PA; died 29 Nov 1969 in Somerset Co., PA.
+	2031	vi.	Millard Francis Christner, born 24 Jul 1919 in Garrett, Somerset Co., PA; died 07 Jul 2002 in Portland, Multnomah Co., OR.
	2032	vii.	Guy E. Christner, born May 1921; died Nov 1937.

Notes for Guy E. Christner:
Birth: 1921
Death: 1937

Burial: Highland Cemetery, Garrett, Somerset Co., PA

More About Guy E. Christner:
Burial: Highland Cemetery, Garrett, Somerset Co., PA

764. Lewis[7] Christner (Herman[6], Abraham D.[5], Joseph "Zep"[4], Johannes John Hans[3], Christian[2], Christen[1])[3654,3655,3656,3657,3658,3659] was born 20 Aug 1860 in Elk Lick Twp., Somerset Co., PA[3660,3661,3662], and died 14 Dec 1941 in Garrett, Somerset Co., PA[3663,3664,3665]. He married **Eliza Missouri Walters**[3666,3667,3668,3669,3670] 22 Jun 1887. She was born 24 Mar 1867 in Summit, Somerset Co., PA[3671,3672,3673], and died 09 Apr 1944 in Garrett, Somerset Co., PA[3674,3675,3676].

Notes for Lewis Christner:
Lewis's mother was Sadie White but there is no other info on Sadie. Lewis had one unnamed child who died at birth. Lewis's father Herman had 2 woman with child at the same time he raised both children. Lewis built an elegant brick mansion in Garrett, PA near the Western MD railroad track. Lewis Christner planned the house as a resort hotel for guests from Pittsburgh, but it didn't happen. When he applied for a liquor license, Judge Rupple, his political rival, denied the request. Instead Lewis ran a speakeasy, without the benefit of a license, Until the effects of prohibition and the depression bankrupted him in 1937.(Ref.Register of Wills index 1040. Vol.315, Pg., 152.) The property was sold to a man named Lenhart. Lenhart was killed by a Peter Myers, who was then hanged by the Somerset sheriff.

Mahlon Christner built and owned the first dam at Bigby Run to supply the town of Garrett PA with water. He later sold the dam to Lewis Christner. Lewis formed a company, sold stock in the dam. 1920 census has Charles 27, Stella 21, Bula D. 19, & Walter H.17, all living at home with the parents.

More About Lewis Christner:
Residence: 1870, Summit, Somerset Co., PA[3677]

Notes for Eliza Missouri Walters:
Eliza was the daughter of Sam Walters b.1827-d.1905 and Rose Ann Judy b.1832-d.1922 No S on tombstone. This is the time period the Walters became the Walter by dropping the (s).

OBIT: Eliza (WALTERS) CHRISTNER, 1944, Garrett, Somerset County, PA - ELIZA CHRISTNER

Mrs. Eliza Christner, 77, widow of Lewis Christner, died Thursday afternoon at her home in Garrett. She was a daughter of Samuel and Rose Ann (Judy) Walters. Surviving are eight children - Sylvester, Garrett; Mrs. William Murray, New Kensington; Edgar and Mrs. Estella Buckman, both of Somerset; Mrs. Charles Martin, Pittsburgh; Mrs. Stover Meyer, Somerset; Albert of Garrett and William, Dayton, O. She was a sister of Austin Walters, Garrett R.D. Funeral services were conducted at 2 o'clock Sunday afternoon at the home by Rev. Ellwood Stahl, pastor of the Garrett Lutheran Church. Interment was made in the Berlin I.O.O.F. Cemetery.

More About Eliza Missouri Walters:
Residence: 1930, Garrett, Somerset Co., PA[3678]

Children of Lewis Christner and Eliza Walters are:

+ 2033   i.   Sylvester[8] Christner, born 08 Apr 1887 in Garrett, Somerset Co., PA; died 06 Sep 1952 in Somerset Co., PA.

+ 2034   ii.   Eva Christner, born 18 Dec 1888 in Connellsville, Fayette Co., PA; died Nov 1964.

   2035   iii.   Robert Christner, born 27 Oct 1890; died 1890 in Died as an infant.

Notes for Robert Christner:
Died as an infant.

   2036   iv.   Charles H. Christner, born 05 May 1892 in Somerset Co., PA[3679]; died 04 Jan 1975 in Berlin, Somerset Co., PA.

Notes for Charles H. Christner:
Obituary: Somerset American, January 5, 1975
Charles H. Christner, 83, of Garrett, died Jan. 4, 1976 in Berlin. Born May 5, 1892, in Somerset County, a son of Lewis and Eliza (Walters) Christner. Survived by these brothers and sisters: Estella Buckman; Beulah, wife of Charles W. Martin; and Mary, wife of Stover C. Meyer, all of Somerset; Albert, of Garrett and William of Pittsburgh. Deceased brothers and sisters are Sylvester, Edgar, Eva Martin, and Pearl Murray.

He was a member of Trinity Lutheran Church and a retired coal miner.

Friends received after 7 p.m. Monday in Robert H. Halverson Funeral Home where service will be conducted Tuesday 1 p.m. Rev. H. James Meyers officiating. Interment I.O.O.F. Cemetery, Berlin.

Charles never married.

More About Charles H. Christner:
Residence: 1930, Garrett, Summit Twp., Somerset Co., PA[3680]
Social Security Number: 172-18-8470/[3681]
SSN issued: PA[3681]

+ 2037   v.   Elsie Pearl Christner, born 09 Jun 1894 in Connellsville, Fayette Co., PA; died 13 Oct 1956 in Connellsville, Fayette Co., PA.

+ 2038   vi.   Edgar James Christner, born 13 Jul 1896 in Connellsville, Fayette Co., PA; died Sep 1967 in Somerset, Somerset Co., PA.

+ 2039   vii.   Estella B. Christner, born 12 Mar 1898 in Garrett, Somerset Co., PA; died 06 Dec 1983.

+ 2040   viii.   Beulah D. Christner, born 20 Mar 1900 in Garrett, Somerset Co., PA; died 08 Oct 1990 in Somerset Co., PA.

+ 2041   ix.   Walter H. Christner, born 13 May 1902; died 24 Apr 1932.

+ 2042   x.   Mary B. Christner, born 20 Apr 1905; died 20 Jun 1992.

+ 2043   xi.   Albert Raymond Christner, born 05 Apr 1907 in Garrett, Somerset Co., PA; died 17 Aug 1978 in Pittsburgh, Allegheny Co., PA.

   2044   xii.   William Christner, born 30 May 1909; died 29 Sep 1992 in Connellsville, Fayette Co., PA. He married Pauline Vigliotti; born 22 Jun 1910 in New Eagle, Washington Co., PA; died 18 Apr 2012.

Notes for William Christner:
SS#169-07-0902 ISS PA   last address 16046 Pittsburgh PA

More About William Christner:
Burial: 02 Oct 1992

Notes for Pauline Vigliotti:
Pauline and William may have a child that died at birth.

765. William[7] Christner (Freeman L.[6], Abraham D.[5], Joseph "Zep"[4], Johannes John Hans[3], Christian[2], Christen[1]) was born Feb 1869 in Somerset Co., PA[3682]. He married **(1) Berttia Shultz.** He married **(2) Harriet Gastigen.** She was born Nov 1869 in Connellsville, Fayette Co., PA[3682].

More About William Christner:
Residence: 1900, Somerset, Somerset, PA[3682]

More About Harriet Gastigen:
Residence: 1900, Somerset, Somerset, PA[3682]

Children of William Christner and Harriet Gastigen are:

2045   i.   Herbert[8] Christner.

        Notes for Herbert Christner:
        Herbert never married.

2046   ii.   Margaret Christner. She married Lows.
2047   iii.   Jay William Christner Jr., born 20 Mar 1899 in Connellsville, Fayette Co., PA[3683,3684]; died Aug 1967 in Connellsville, Fayette Co., PA.

        Notes for Jay William Christner Jr.:
        SS#201-20-9308 ISS PA   last address 15212 Pittsburgh PA

        More About Jay William Christner Jr.:
        Residence: 1900, Somerset, Somerset, PA[3684]

+   2048   iv.   Ruth Blanche Christner, born 23 Jun 1903 in Somerset, Somerset Co., PA; died 27 Dec 1984 in Cadillac, Wexford Co., MI.

766. Hiram P. "Hiry"[7] Christner (Freeman L.[6], Abraham D.[5], Joseph "Zep"[4], Johannes John Hans[3], Christian[2], Christen[1])[3685] was born May 1870 in Connellsville, Fayette Co., PA[3685,3686]. He married **Elizabeth Berkey** 1895[3687]. She was born Nov 1878 in PA[3688], and died in Y/[3688].

Notes for Hiram P. "Hiry" Christner:
Harry P. had a son born April 1900 this son had 5 children
Dean--Edna--Jack--Helen--Ralph

More About Hiram P. "Hiry" Christner:
Race: White/[3689]
Residence: 1900, Derry, Westmoreland Co., PA[3690]

More About Elizabeth Berkey:
Race: White/[3691]
Residence: 1900, Derry, Westmoreland Co., PA[3692]

Children of Hiram Christner and Elizabeth Berkey are:
2049   i.   Edna[8] Christner.
2050   ii.   Wilbert D. Christner[3693], born Aug 1896 in Westmoreland Co., PA[3693].

        More About Wilbert D. Christner:
        Residence: 1900, Derry, Westmoreland Co., PA[3694]

2051   iii.   Willard Dean Christner[3695], born Aug 1896 in Westmoreland Co., PA[3695].

                 More About Willard Dean Christner:
                 Race: White/[3696]
                 Residence: 1900, Derry, Westmoreland Co., PA[3696]

+   2052   iv.   Christner, born Apr 1900 in Westmoreland Co., PA.
     2053   v.   Helen Christner[3697], born 01 Apr 1908 in Ligonier, Westmoreland Co., PA[3697]; died 17 Oct 2001 in Ligonier, Westmoreland Co., PA[3697].

767. Margaret[7] Christner (Henry A.[6], Abraham D.[5], Joseph "Zep"[4], Johannes John Hans[3], Christian[2], Christen[1])[3698] was born Jul 1864 in Pittsburgh, Allegheny Co., PA[3699]. She married **Jesse Holliday**[3700,3701,3702] 1885[3703]. He was born Jun 1866 in Pittsburgh, Allegheny Co., PA[3704].

More About Margaret Christner:
Residence: 1930, Elk Lick, Somerset Co., PA[3705]

More About Jesse Holliday:
Residence: 1880, Addison Twp., Somerset Co., PA[3706,3706]

Children of Margaret Christner and Jesse Holliday are:
     2054   i.   Howard[8] Holliday.
     2055   ii.   Arthur Earl Holliday, born 1887.
+   2056   iii.   Calvin Holliday, born Mar 1890 in Connellsville, Fayette Co., PA.
     2057   iv.   George Lester Holliday[3707,3708], born 22 Jun 1893 in Elklick Twp., Somerset Co., PA[3709]; died 24 Jan 1962[3709].

                 Notes for George Lester Holliday:
                 Coal Miner

                 More About George Lester Holliday:
                 Burial: [3709]
                 Other-Begin: [3710]
                 Residence: 1930, Benner, Centre, PA[3711]

     2058   v.   Florence A. Holliday, born 04 Oct 1896 in Elklick Twp., Somerset Co., PA.

                 More About Florence A. Holliday:
                 Residence: 1910, Addison, Somerset Co., PA[3711]

     2059   vi.   Elsie M. Holliday, born 1907; died in Young before 1920 censes.

                 More About Elsie M. Holliday:
                 Residence: 1910, Addison, Somerset Co., PA[3712]

770. Wilson Milton[7] Shumaker (Elizabeth[6] Christner, Abraham D.[5], Joseph "Zep"[4], Johannes John Hans[3], Christian[2], Christen[1])[3713] was born 02 Sep 1878 in Rairhope, Southampton Township, Somerset Co., PA[3713], and died 30 Oct 1956 in 28 Virginia Ave.[3713]. He married **Carrie Latta**.

Notes for Wilson Milton Shumaker:
Conductor for the B. & O. Railroad and St. Johns Lutheran Church. He also lived at Cumberland, MD.

More About Wilson Milton Shumaker:
Census: 08 Jun 1900, Fairhope Township, Somerset Co., PA[3713]

Children of Wilson Shumaker and Carrie Latta are:
     2060   i.   Elizabeth[8] Shumaker. She married Bartik.
     2061   ii.   William Shumaker.

+ 2062   iii.   Merle W. Shumaker, born 1909 in Berlin, Somerset Co., PA; died 16 Apr 1978 in 26 Virginia Ave..

772. Martha MO⁷ Christner (Elias⁶, Abraham D.⁵, Joseph "Zep"⁴, Johannes John Hans³, Christian², Christen¹) was born 1870. She married **William Henry Traup** 21 Nov 1891. He was born 1867.

Children of Martha Christner and William Traup are:
2063   i.   Arthur⁸ Traup, died 1959. He married Ethel Woy.

        Notes for Arthur Traup:
        He owned the Blacksmith shop in Rockwood, PA by the Casselman River.

+ 2064   ii. Martha Traup, born in Somerset Co., PA; died 18 Apr 1980 in Somerset Co., PA.

773. Louise⁷ Christner (Elias⁶, Abraham D.⁵, Joseph "Zep"⁴, Johannes John Hans³, Christian², Christen¹) was born 25 Nov 1874 in Garrett, Somerset Co., PA. She married **Eli H. Baker** 19 Oct 1893 in At stepfathers house Joseph Ringer. He was born 1848, and died 1925.

More About Louise Christner:
Burial: Casebeer Cemetery by the Lutheran Church

More About Eli H. Baker:
Residence: Lincoln Twp. PA

Marriage Notes for Louise Christner and Eli Baker:
He was 45 and she was 18

Child of Louise Christner and Eli Baker is:
+ 2065   i.   Lena Alverta⁸ Baker, born 13 Mar 1894 in Lincoln TWP.; died 15 Mar 1983 in Somerset Co., PA.

775. Francis M.⁷ Smith (Joanna⁶ Christner, Abraham D.⁵, Joseph "Zep"⁴, Johannes John Hans³, Christian², Christen¹) was born 07 Jun 1879 in Glencoe Somerset Co., PA, and died 1940 in 938 Lemon St. Dale. He married **Lucinda Bittner**.

More About Francis M. Smith:
Burial: Richland Cemetery

Children of Francis Smith and Lucinda Bittner are:
+ 2066   i.   Charles F.⁸ Smith.
  2067   ii. Mildred Smith.
+ 2068   iii. Howard E. Smith, born 11 Dec 1926 in Johnstown, Cambria Co., PA; died 20 Jun 1982.

776. William Harrison⁷ Smith (Joanna⁶ Christner, Abraham D.⁵, Joseph "Zep"⁴, Johannes John Hans³, Christian², Christen¹) was born 26 Aug 1888 in Northampton TWP., and died 21 Apr 1965 in Somerset Co., PA. He married **Virginia Mae Huff**.

More About William Harrison Smith:
Burial: Mt. Lebanon Cemetery Glencoe

Children of William Smith and Virginia Huff are:
2069   i.   Delores O.⁸ Smith.
2070   ii. Dorothy I. Smith.
2071   iii. Grace F. Smith.
2072   iv. William Harrison Smith Jr..

780. Mary A.[7] Shoemaker (Sally Sarah[6] Christner, Abraham D.[5], Joseph "Zep"[4], Johannes John Hans[3], Christian[2], Christen[1])[3714] was born 24 Nov 1852 in Addison Twp., Somerset Co., PA[3714], and died 25 Jan 1918[3714]. She married **Samuel J. "Matlick Sam" Christner**, son of Joseph Christner and Mary Keim. He was born 19 Apr 1847 in Elk Lick, Somerset Co., PA[3715], and died 01 Feb 1937 in Meyersdale, Somerset Co., PA.

Notes for Samuel J. "Matlick Sam" Christner:
Information from Mrs. Roy Linderman Meyersdale, PA is the daughter of Matlick Sam.

Birth: Apr 19, 1847 - PA
Death: Feb 1, 1937 - Meyersdale, Somerset Co., PA

The son of Joseph Christner, Jr. and Mary Salome Keim.

He married Ada Florence Wagner in 1878.

Parents:
Joseph Christner (1814 - 1897)
Mary Keim Christner (1818 - 1882)

Spouse: Ada Florence Wagner Christner (1850 - 1944)

Burial: St. Paul's Wilhelm Cemetery, Meyersdale, Somerset Co., PA
Find A Grave Memorial# 114109997

More About Samuel J. "Matlick Sam" Christner:
Residence: 1930, Clarksburg, Harrison Co., WV[3716]

Child is listed above under (246) Samuel J. "Matlick Sam" Christner.

789. Rudolph[7] Christner (John C.[6], Christian[5], Joseph "Zep"[4], Johannes John Hans[3], Christian[2], Christen[1]) was born Nov 1864 in Somerset Co., PA[3717], and died 1939. He married **(1) Amanda Newan** 18 Apr 1889. She was born 1867, and died 16 Jul 1894. He married **(2) Nettie Frickey** 28 Nov 1895 in Meyersdale, Somerset Co., PA. She was born Apr 1867 in PA 1910 soundex PA has 1876, and died 1928.

Notes for Rudolph Christner:
This info from Tom Christner Garrett, PA. micro film 558,970
They lived across the road from the (Abraham Christner up on the hill cemetery) N39° 51.400 by W79° 4.700.
He was a farmer west of Garrett, PA.

Birth: 1864
Death: 1939

Burial: Highland Cemetery, Garrett, Somerset Co., PA

More About Rudolph Christner:
Burial: Highland Cemetery, Garrett, Somerset Co., PA
Occupation: Farmer/
Residence: 1880, Garrett, Somerset Co., PA[3718]

More About Amanda Newan:
Burial: Highland Cemetery, Garrett, Somerset Co., PA

Notes for Nettie Frickey:
Birth: 1867
Death: 1928

Burial: Highland Cemetery, Garrett, Somerset Co., PA

More About Nettie Frickey:
Residence: 1910, Summit, Somerset Co., PA*3718*

Children of Rudolph Christner and Amanda Newan are:
2073   i.   Eurma Emma[8] Christner, born Jan 1890 in Garrett, Somerset Co., PA. She married Edward R. Sechler 18 May 1911 in Connellsville, Fayette Co., PA; born 1890 in Somerset Co., PA.

More About Eurma Emma Christner:
Residence: 1900, Summit, Somerset Co., PA*3718*

More About Edward R. Sechler:
Occupation: Railroader/

+ 2074   ii. Herbert Earl Christner, born 29 Feb 1892 in Garrett, Somerset Co., PA; died 22 Apr 1976 in Meyersdale, Somerset Co., PA.

Child of Rudolph Christner and Nettie Frickey is:
2075   i.   Sourie Grace[8] Christner, born 06 Feb 1897 in Garrett, Somerset Co., PA.

Notes for Sourie Grace Christner:
Birth: Feb. 6, 1897
Death: Sep. 14, 1897

Burial: Ridgeview Cemetery, Garrett, Somerset Co., PA

793. Sevilla[7] Christner (John C.[6], Christian[5], Joseph "Zep"[4], Johannes John Hans[3], Christian[2], Christen[1])*3719* was born Nov 1870 in Somerset Co., PA*3719*, and died in Somerset Co., PA*3719*. She married **Harvey W. Burkholder***3719* 11 Feb 1894 in Somerset Co. PA*3720*. He was born Aug 1866 in Somerset Co., PA*3721*, and died 23 Jan 1929 in Somerset Co., PA*3721*.

More About Sevilla Christner:
Residence: 1930, Summit, Somerset Co., PA*3722*

More About Harvey W. Burkholder:
Residence: 1900, Summit, Somerset Co., PA*3723*

Children of Sevilla Christner and Harvey Burkholder are:
2076   i.   Charles[8] Burkholder, born Aug 1894; died 1961 in Somerset Co. PA*3724*.
2077   ii. James Burkholder, born Oct 1897 in Summit Twp, Somerset, PA*3724*; died 08 Nov 1897 in Summit Twp, Somerset, PA*3724*.
2078   iii. Irvin Burkholder, born Jan 1899.

More About Irvin Burkholder:
Residence: 1930, Summit, Somerset Co., PA*3724*

2079   iv. Laura Burkholder, born Abt. 1902*3724*.
+ 2080   v.   Nellie Mae Burkholder, born 24 Oct 1902 in Somerset Co., PA; died 15 Nov 1988 in Meyersdale, Somerset Co., PA.
2081   vi. Leonard Burkholder, born 18 Mar 1906 in Garrett, Somerset Co., PA*3724*; died 17 Dec 1971 in Garrett, Somerset Co., PA*3724*.

More About Leonard Burkholder:
Residence: 1920, Summit, Somerset Co., PA*3724*

817. Aaron[7] Hostetter (Gabriel[6] Hostetler, Elizabeth[5] Christner, Joseph "Zep"[4], Johannes John Hans[3], Christian[2], Christen[1])*3725,3726* was born 16 Nov 1867 in Canaan, Wayne Co., OH*3727,3728*, and died 24 Jun 1938 in Canton, Stark Co., OH*3729,3730*. He married **Mary Ella Waggoner***3730* 1889 in OH*3730*. She was born 27 Feb

1868 in Waynesburg, Stark Co., OH[3730], and died 04 Mar 1952 in Canton, Stark Co., OH[3730].

More About Aaron Hostetter:
Burial: 27 Jun 1938, West Lawn Cemetery/Canton, Stark, Ohio[3730]
Residence: 1930, Canton, Stark, Ohio[3730]

More About Mary Ella Waggoner:
Burial: 08 Mar 1952, West Lawn Cemetery/Canton, Stark Co., OH[3730]
Residence: 1930, Canton, Stark, Ohio[3730]

Children of Aaron Hostetter and Mary Waggoner are:
    2082   i.   George E.[8] Hostetter[3730], born 13 Mar 1890 in Canton, Stark Co., OH[3730]; died 26 Jan 1970 in OH[3730].

                    More About George E. Hostetter:
                    Residence: Canton, Stark, Ohio[3730]

    2083   ii.   Vernel A. Hostetter[3730], born 12 Dec 1893 in Canton, Stark Co., OH[3730]; died 23 Dec 1968[3730].

                    More About Vernel A. Hostetter:
                    Residence: Canton, Stark, Ohio[3730]

829. Austin George[7] Christner (Zachariah[6], Christian[5], Joseph "Zep"[4], Johannes John Hans[3], Christian[2], Christen[1])[3731,3732,3733] was born 01 Oct 1863 in Somerset, Somerset Co., PA[3733], and died 1933 in Summit Twp., Somerset Co., PA. He married **(1) Sarah**[3734]. She was born 1877 in Frostburg, Allegany Co., MD. He married **(2) Lydia Burkholder**[3735,3736] 05 Feb 1888 in Garrett, Somerset Co., PA. She was born Dec 1866 in Somerset Co., PA[3737,3738], and died 14 May 1913 in Summit Twp., Somerset Co., PA.

Notes for Austin George Christner:
Birth: 1863
Death: 1933

Burial: Center Lutheran Church Cemetery, Summit Twp., Somerset Co., PA

More About Austin George Christner:
Burial: Center Church, Luthern, Union, Pa. or Pleasant Hill, Cem, Somerset Co, PA
Residence: 1930, Summit, Somerset Co, PA[3739]

Notes for Lydia Burkholder:
Lydia is the daughter of Noah and Caroline_____Burkholder.

Birth: 1866
Death: 1913

Burial: Center Lutheran Church Cemetery, Summit Twp., Somerset Co., PA

More About Lydia Burkholder:
Burial: Center Church, Luthern, Union, Pa. or Pleasant Hill, Cem, Somerset Co, PA
Residence: 1900, Summit, Somerset Co., PA[3740]

Children of Austin Christner and Lydia Burkholder are:
+   2084   i.   Carrie Agnes[8] Christner, born 21 Jan 1890 in Garrett, Somerset Co., PA; died 19 Oct 1975 in Frostburg, Allegeny Co., MD.
    2085   ii.   Roy Milton Christner[3740,3741], born 17 May 1892 in Garrett, Somerset Co., PA[3742].

                    More About Roy Milton Christner:
                    Residence: 1900, Summit, Somerset Co., PA[3743]

    2086   iii.   Maggie Ellen Christner[3743,3744], born 02 May 1896 in Garrett, Somerset Co., PA[3745,3746,3747]. She married

Seibert.

Notes for Maggie Ellen Christner:
Maggie either married a George Carter or a Seibert. This info on sister
Carrie's file because Carrie could of been married to either one of these men.

More About Maggie Ellen Christner:
Residence: 1900, Summit, Somerset Co., PA[3748]

+ 2087 iv. Melvin A. Christner, born 1904 in Garrett, Somerset Co., PA; died 23 Sep 1953 in Somerset, Somerset Co., PA.
  2088 v. Musin Christner[3749], born 1905 in Connellsville, Fayette Co., PA[3749].

More About Musin Christner:
Residence: 1910, Summit, Somerset Co., PA[3749]

831. MO[7] Christner (Zachariah[6], Christian[5], Joseph "Zep"[4], Johannes John Hans[3], Christian[2], Christen[1]) was born 1868. She married **George Judy** 12 Sep 1889.

Notes for George Judy:
George and Clara had 7 children only 3 lived.

Children of MO Christner and George Judy are:
  2089 i. Ralph Rudolph[8] Judy, born Apr 1890.
  2090 ii. Scott Judy, born May 1895.
  2091 iii. Ofelia M Judy, born Sep 1898.

832. Washington[7] Christner (Zachariah[6], Christian[5], Joseph "Zep"[4], Johannes John Hans[3], Christian[2], Christen[1]) was born Aug 1871 in Connellsville, Fayette Co., PA. He married **Emma Rector** 26 Jan 1892 in Somerset Co. PA maybe 1891. She was born 1873.

Notes for Washington Christner:
Worked for the railroad as a conductor on the Baltimore and Ohio Railway and lived in Garrett, PA.
Court cases for Washington 11/19/1889 VS Ida M. Lohr Dec. 1889 Fornication & Bastardy Somerset Co., PA.
Zacharia & Jacob both forfeited bonds due to non-appearance for court dates for Washington's.

Children of Washington Christner and Emma Rector are:
+ 2092 i. Velma G.[8] Christner, born Aug 1892 in Connellsville, Fayette Co., PA; died Apr 1984 in Somerset, Somerset Co., PA.
  2093 ii. Ruth L. Christner, born Feb 1894 in Connellsville, Fayette Co., PA.
  2094 iii. Equilla Christner[3750,3751], born 03 Nov 1895 in Connellsville, Fayette Co., PA; died Jan 1975 in Wayne Co., MI[3752]. She married Gill[3752].
  2095 iv. Madaline Christner, born Jun 1898 in Connellsville, Fayette Co., PA.
  2096 v. Howard Christner, born 1901 in Connellsville, Fayette Co., PA.
  2097 vi. Paul Christner, born 1907 in Connellsville, Fayette Co., PA.
  2098 vii. Wodrow Christner, born 1913 in Connellsville, Fayette Co., PA.
  2099 viii. Donald Edgar Christner[3753], born 26 Jun 1915 in Fayette Co., PA[3753,3754]; died 25 Dec 1985 in La Habra, Orange Co., CA[3755].

More About Donald Edgar Christner:
Social Security Number: 186-07-9497/[3756]
SSN issued: Pittsburgh, Allegheny Co., PA[3756]

833. George Washington[7] Christner (Zachariah[6], Christian[5], Joseph "Zep"[4], Johannes John Hans[3], Christian[2], Christen[1]) was born Aug 1871[3757], and died 1941. He married **Emma**[3757] Bef. 1892[3757]. She was born Jul 1873[3757].

Notes for George Washington Christner:
Obituary: George Washington Christner, 1941, Somerset, Somerset County, PA - Meyersdale Republican, April 17, 1941

George Washington Christner, 69, one of Somerset's well-known Baltimore and Ohio conductors, died at 1 o'clock Sunday morning at the home of his daughter, Mrs. Frank Walter of West Patriot Street, after an illness of several months.

Mr. Christner retired from active service as a conductor on the Baltimore and Ohio in 1938 and has since led a retired life.

He was a son of Zachariah and Magdalene (Hoover) Christner, both deceased. His wife, Emma (Rector) Christner, preceded him in death last December.

Surviving are the following children: Mrs. Frank Walter, Mrs. Charles Brick, Howard Christner, Melvin Christner, all of Somerset; Mrs. Ruth Weighley, Woodrow Christner and Donald Christner, all of Los Angeles, California.

Woodrow Christner left California by trans-continental plane late Sunday night and arrived in Pittsburgh shortly after noon Monday.

Mr. Christner was a brother of Theodore Christner of Hyndman, Wilson Christner of Pittsburgh and Mrs. Nathan Burkett of Tyrone.

Funeral services were conducted at 3 Tuesday afternoon at the late home on rear South Edgewood Avenue by the Rev. Dr. George L. Roth, pastor of the St. Paul's Evangelical and Reformed Church. Interment was in the Somerset County Memorial Park under the direction of Charles R. Hauger, Somerset mortician.

Children of George Christner and Emma are:
   2100   i.   Ruth[8] Christner[3757], born Feb 1894 in PA[3758,3759].

              More About Ruth Christner:
              Residence: 1900, Summit, Somerset Co., PA[3760]

   2101   ii. Magdalena Christner[3761], born Jun 1898[3761].

   834. Wilson William[7] Christner (Zachariah[6], Christian[5], Joseph "Zep"[4], Johannes John Hans[3], Christian[2], Christen[1]) was born 29 Sep 1873 in PA. He married **Elizabeth Lizzie Walter** 05 Oct 1891 in Summitt Twp., Somerset Co., PA. She was born Mar 1875 in Connellsville, Fayette Co., PA, and died 20 Oct 1928.

Notes for Wilson William Christner:
Info from Connie Yokum:

Children are Clinton born Nov 1891 Blanche born Jan 1893 Lelon/Lebosi/Leonoa born Nov 22 1895 The child Lelon may be a boy and Leonoa another child info from Dora Gilliliam children are Zachariah John Susan Caroline. Wilson worked for the Baltimore & Ohio railroad as a brakeman, in 4 years he has a freight conductor than 8 years later he became a passenger conductor on the Buffalo Valley Railroad. They lived in Berlin, PA. Berlin Luthern Church. A Democrat of the most stalwart type. He was affiliated with various fraternal and benefical orders. He was a great admirer of athletics.   He was manager of the Berlin baseball team who were the champions of the Somerset County League in 1905. He was a lover of good horses and delighted in speed contests between well trained and high bred animals. He loved to travel and visited every part of the United States, and journeyed to Mexico. In the fall of 1905, he made a tour of Europe, spending time in France and Germany, and also visited England, Scotland, and Ireland.

History of Bedford and Somerset Counties, Pennsylvania; Bedford County by E. Howard Blackburn; Somerset County by William H. Welfley; v.3, Pub. The Lewis Publishing Company, New York/Chicago 1906, ppg. 278-280

WILSON CHRISTNER

Wilson Christner, the popular and efficient conductor on the "Berlin Branch," was born near Garrett, Somerset Co., PA, September 29, 1873. His parents were Zachariah and Magdalene (Hoover) Christner. His grandfather Christopher Christner, was a native of Germany, who on emigrating to the United States settled in Somerset Co., PA, where both he and his wife died at advanced ages. He was a farmer by occupation. He was a consistent member of the Lutheran church, and in politics was a Democrat. His children were:

Zachariah, John, Caroline (Mrs. Christner), and Susan (Mrs. Hoover). Zachariah Christner, eldest child of Christopher Christner, was for many years a farmer in Summit township, Somerset Co., PA, and is now living a retired life in Canton, OH. He and his wife are both members of the Lutheran church. He was a Democrat in politics, and earnest in the maintenance of his views. He married Magdelena Hoover, and to them were born the following children: Austin, resides on the homestead farm; Washington, a conductor on the Baltimore & Ohio railway, resides in Garrett; Theodore, a conductor on the same road, and lives in Cumberland, Maryland; Carrie, lives with her parents in Canton, Ohio; MO (Mrs. George Judy), of Pennsylvania Furnace, Cambria county; Jennie (Mrs. Nathan Burkett), of Cumberland, Maryland; Wilson. Wilson Christner of the family last named, was five years old when his parents removed to Mount Pleasant, PA and he received his education in the common schools of that town. He gave himself to a life of industry from his very youth, and worked in and about the mines and factories until he was eighteen years old, when he entered the employ of the Baltimore and Ohio Railroad Company in the capacity of brakeman. He so proved his efficiency and fidelity that after four years' service he was advanced to the position of freight train conductor. He rendered efficient service as such for a period of eight years, when he was promoted to the place which he has uninterruptedly held to the present time, that of passenger conductor on the Buffalo Valley Railroad, a part of the Balitmore & Ohio system, enjoying the entire confidence of his superiors, and the esteem of the traveling public. He adheres to the religious faith of his ancestors, and is a member of the Berlin Lutheran church. In politics he is a Democrat of the most stalwart type. He is affiliated with various fraternal and beneficail orders: Connellsville Lodge, No. 503, Benevolent and Protective Order of Elks; Berlin Lodge, No. 503, Knights of Pythias; Connellsville Lodge, Order of Railway Conductors; and Berlin Lodge, Modern Woodmen. He is a great admirer of athletics, and his tastes cover the entire range of athletic sports. He is manager of the Berlin Base Ball team who were the champions of the Somerset County League in 1905. He is a lover of a good horse, and delights in speed contests between well trained and high bred animals. He is ardently fond of travel, and has visited every part of the United States, and journeyed into Mexico. In the autumn of 1905 he made a tour of Europe, spending some time in France and Germany, als also visiting England, Scotland and Ireland. While greatly enjoying the scenery of these distant lands, and deeply interested in the manners and customs of their peoples, he returned with a higher respect and love for his own country.

Mr. Christner married Elizabeth Walter, a daughter of Samuel and Rosanna (Judy) Walter, of Garrett, PA. Of this marriage were born four children: Clinton, Blanche, Lelon and Leona. The family residence is in Berlin.

Notes for Elizabeth Lizzie Walter:
1920 census has her living in Pittsburg (Ahlsrs Way) PA. & living with her are daughter Blanch (23), son Lelon (23), & Grandson Wilson born 1914 in Maryland.

Birth: 1874
Death: Oct. 20, 1928 - Somerset Co., PA

Inscription: 53y 6m 22d

Burial: Center Lutheran Church Cemetery, Summit Twp., Somerset Co., PA

Children of Wilson Christner and Elizabeth Walter are:
+   2102   i.   Clinton[8] Christner, born 17 Nov 1891 in Garrett, Somerset Co., PA; died May 1970 in Shanksville, Somerset Co., PA.
      2103   ii. Blanche P. Christner[3762], born Jan 1893 in Somerset Co., PA[3762].

            Notes for Blanche P. Christner:
            1920 census has these children as the same age. Blanch (23) 1897, son Lelon (23), 1897

More About Blanche P. Christner:
Residence: 1900, Summit, Somerset Co., PA[3762]

2104   iii. Lelon Christner, born Nov 1895 in Somerset Co., PA; died 10 Apr 1963[3763].

Notes for Lelon Christner:
1920 census has these children as the same age. Blanch (23) 1897, son Lelon (23), 1897

Pennsylvania, Veterans Burial Cards, 1777-1999
about Lellon Christner
Name: Lellon Christner
Birth Date: 22 Nov 1895
Death Date: 10 Apr 1963
Age: 67
Military Branch: Army
Cemetery Name: Mount Lebanon Cemetery
Cemetery Location: MT Lebanon, Allegheny County, Pennsylvania

More About Lelon Christner:
Burial: Allegheny Co.[3763]

+   2105   iv. Leona O. Christner, born 1901 in Somerset Co., PA; died 01 May 1964 in Pittsburgh, Allegheny Co., PA.

835. Theodore "Dorrie"[7] Christner (Zachariah[6], Christian[5], Joseph "Zep"[4], Johannes John Hans[3], Christian[2], Christen[1])[3764,3765,3766,3767] was born 18 Mar 1875 in Summit Twp., Somerset Co., PA[3768,3769,3770,3771,3772], and died 1947 in Hyndman, Bedford Co., PA[3773,3774,3775,3776,3777]. He married **Generva Minerva "MO" Beachley**[3778,3779] 09 Apr 1893 in Garrett, Somerset Co., PA. She was born 30 Sep 1872 in Brothersvalley Twp., Somerset Co., PA[3780,3781,3782,3783,3784], and died 18 Feb 1949 in Hyndman, Bedford Co., PA.

Notes for Theodore "Dorrie" Christner:
Info from Robert Christner, Connie Yokum and microfilm 558,970. He worked for the Baltimore & Ohio railroad. He was listed as a coal miner in 1893. He lived in the Cumberland/Hymdman/Garrett, PA area. From various sources, we learned that it was Carrie (With help from Sister Jennie) that promoted the idea that her father Theadore wanted to be buried between his father Zachariah and his mother Magdalena. Theadore was originally buried per that request, but Generva was greatly bothered by the fact that Theadore would not be buried with his own immediate family in the large plot purchased by Generva for the family. He was later reinterred (dug up & replanted) in the Madly Cemetery next to Generva. From oral family tradition, we know that Theadore did not take his wedding vows seriously. Theadore did not take his religion seriously either. Dorrie was a short, stocky man who loved to hunt and fish. This is the way Theadore spelled his name.

Birth: Mar. 18, 1875 - Summit Twp., Somerset Co., PA
Death: 1947 - Hyndman, Bedford Co., PA

Parents:
Zachariah Christner (1837 - 1918)
Magdalena M. Hoover Christner (1840 - 1917)

Spouse: Generva Minerva MO Beachley Christner (1872 - 1949)

Children:
Lloyd E. Christner (1901 - 1965)
Clyde S. Christner (1903 - 1968)
Thomas W. Christner (1910 - 1984)

Burial: Lybarger Cemetery, Madley, Bedford Co., PA

More About Theodore "Dorrie" Christner:
Burial: 1st Time Hyndman Cemetery   2nd Time Madly-Lybarger Cemetery[3784]
Census: 1920, Londonderry Twp., Bedford Co., PA[3785]
Occupation: Railroad Conductor/[3785,3786]
Residence: 1900, Summit Twp., Somerset Co., PA[3787]

Notes for Generva Minerva "MO" Beachley:
From various sources, we learned that it was Carrie (With help from Sister Jennie) that promoted the idea that her father Theodore wanted to be buried between his father Zachariah and his mother Magdalena. Theodore was originally buried per that request, but Generva was greatly bothered by the fact that Theodore would not be buried with his own immediate family in the large plot purchased by Generva for the family. He was later reinterred in the Madly Cemetery next to Generva. Theodore and Generva lived a number of years in Cumberland, MD. From oral family tradition, we know that Theodore did not take his wedding vows seriously. Generva's mother was from the Hauger family. Generva's grandfather was Will Hauger from the Berlin, PA area. Will was a devout member of the German Reformed Church. The Hauger home had a family altar and prayers were said each evening. Generva lived many years with her grandparents because her stepfather(Huffman) did not treat her kindly. Genera's strong faith took root in the home of her grandparents and had a great impact upon her children. The house had no porch when they moved there, but a neighbor (Mr. Bruck) built one. Irene and her mother Generva made an awning to decorate the porch. They were very proud of this dwelling, the scene of many family gatherings. There was a pond next to the house that provided fishing for the boys and ice skating for the town in winter. The pond was filled in and the house torn down in a road widening project and nothing remains of the site today. Generva then moved into town into a home Meyers bought for her and Theodore, just across from the Reformed church where she taught in the Sunday School, sang in the choir and where almost every activity saw her in attendance. Irene also sang in the choir, taught Sunday School and was active there until her move to Ohio. I did wonder where Generva came upon her spiritual roots. you will note that Generva's mother was a Hauger. The Haugers were German speaking people who were of the German Reformed faith. They lived in the vicinity of Berlin, PA which originally was a German settlement. In doing some genealogy work, Jimmy Madden (Irene's son), learned of Will Hauger who was Generva's grandfather. Jimmy tells us that "the Hauger home had a family altar and evening prayer took place there daily. It was in this household that Generva got her firm grounding in the Christian faith. Generva went to live with her Hauger grandparents because her stepfather was not kind to her and the grandparents said she could come live with them. Generva's parents were Frank or Ralph Beachley and _____ Hauger. They were never married. _____ Hauger eventually married a Huffman Generva's stepfather. She also went by the name Minerva. These events have caused some confusion with her name. Generva had two brothers Clayton (married Myrtle) and Ezra (Married Lizzie). Generva had a sister named Annie. In the winter of 1948-49, Generva went to live with Maudie and Earl Murray in Akron Ohio. Generva had a stroke while at Maudie's and died..

Birth: Sep. 30, 1872 - Brothersvalley Twp., Somerset Co., PA
Death: 1949 - Hyndman, Bedford Co., PA

Parents: Rebecca E. Hauger Hoffman (1856 - 1894)

Spouse: Theodore Christner (1875 - 1947)

Children:
Lloyd E. Christner (1901 - 1965)
Clyde S. Christner (1903 - 1968)
Thomas W. Christner (1910 - 1984)

Burial: Lybarger Cemetery,Madley, Bedford Co., PA

More About Generva Minerva "MO" Beachley:
Burial: Lybarger Lutheran Cemetery, Madley, Londonderry Twp., Bedford Co., PA[3788]
Residence: 1920, Londonderry, Bedford, PA[3789,3790,3791,3792]

Children of Theodore Christner and Generva Beachley are:
+   2106   i.   Orpha Maude[8] Christner, born 22 Oct 1893 in Summit Twp., Somerset Co., PA; died 28 Jun 1969 in

<table>
<tr><td></td><td></td><td>Canton, Stark Co., OH.</td></tr>
</table>

+ 2107   ii.   Myers Wilson "K.O." Christner, born 28 Dec 1894 in Garrett, Somerset Co., PA; died 15 Oct 1979 in Cuyahoga Falls, Summit Co., OH.

    2108   iii.   Robert Christner, born 1897 in Twin with Scott; died 05 Feb 1897.

    2109   iv.   Scott Christner, born 1897 in Twin with Robert; died 19 Feb 1897.

+ 2110   v.   Charles Theodore Christner, born 11 Dec 1899 in OH; died Apr 1974 in Akron, Summit Co., OH.

+ 2111   vi.   Lloyd E. Christner, born 01 Oct 1901; died 03 Nov 1965 in Hyndman, Bedford Co., PA.

+ 2112   vii.   Clyde S. Christner, born 1903 in Garrett, Somerset Co., PA; died 01 Jun 1968 in Pittsburgh, Allegheny Co., PA.

+ 2113   viii.   Gertrude Christner, born 04 Jun 1905 in Garrett, Somerset Co., PA; died 18 Apr 1986 in Hyndman, Bedford Co., PA.

+ 2114   ix.   Leota Irene Christner, born 25 Sep 1907; died 23 Mar 2002 in Hyndman, Bedford Co., PA.

+ 2115   x.   Thomas W. Christner, born 16 Dec 1910 in Hollsopple, Conemaugh Twp., Somerset Co., PA; died Mar 1984 in Hyndman, Bedford Co., PA.

842. Tena[7] Hoover (Susanna Lucy Anne[6] Christner, Christian[5], Joseph "Zep"[4], Johannes John Hans[3], Christian[2], Christen[1])[3793] was born 07 Oct 1867[3793], and died 20 Dec 1950 in Garrett, Someret Co., PA[3793]. She married **Jeremiah B. Phillippi**[3793]. He was born 28 Apr 1864[3793], and died 19 Nov 1939[3793].

Notes for Tena Hoover:
Birth: Oct. 7, 1867
Death: Dec. 20, 1950

Parents: John Hoover (1833 - 1896)

Spouse: Jeremiah B. Phillippi (1864 - 1939)

Children:
Elizabeth May Phillippi Dunbar (1888 - 1952)
Martin V Phillippi (1891 - 1934)
Fannie Viola Phillippi Pritts (1902 - 1979)
Jennie Marie Phillippi Rugg (1902 - ____)
Sylvester Phillippi (1908 - 1971)
James Irwin Phillippi (1910 - 1911)

Burial: Laurel Church Cemetery, Somerset Co., PA

Notes for Jeremiah B. Phillippi:
Birth: 1864
Death: 1939

Parents:
Noah Phillippi (1835 - 1915)
Isabelle Tressler Phillippi (1835 - 1924)

Spouse: Tena Hoover Phillippi (1867 - 1950)

Children:
Elizabeth May Phillippi Dunbar (1888 - 1952)
Martin V. Phillippi (1891 - 1934)
Jennie Marie Phillippi Rugg (1902 - ____)
Fannie Viola Phillippi Pritts (1902 - 1979)
Sylvester Phillippi (1908 - 1971)
James Irwin Phillippi (1910 - 1911)

Burial: Laurel Church Cemetery, Somerset Co., PA

More About Jeremiah B. Phillippi:

Burial: Laurel Cem.*3793*

Children of Tena Hoover and Jeremiah Phillippi are:

+ 2116   i.   Elizabeth May[8] Phillippi, born 14 Sep 1888 in Somerset Co., PA; died 27 Sep 1952 in Summit Township, Somerset Co., PA.

     2117   ii.   Martin V. Phillippi*3793*, born 20 Feb 1891 in Connellsville, Fayette Co., PA*3794,3795*; died 24 May 1934*3795,3796*.

         More About Martin V. Phillippi:
         Burial: Westmoreland Co., PA*3796*
         Other-Begin: Somerset Co.*3797*
         Residence: Somerset Co., PA*3797*

     2118   iii.   Charles Earl Phillippi*3798*, born 26 Dec 1892*3798*; died 01 Sep 1955*3798*.
     2119   iv.   Zachariah Henry Phillippi*3798*, born 15 Feb 1895*3798*; died 10 Oct 1918 in France (WW1)*3798*.
     2120   v.   Bertha Alice Phillippi*3798*, born 12 Oct 1897*3798*.
     2121   vi.   Calvin B. Phillippi*3798*, born 31 Jan 1900*3798*.
+ 2122   vii.   Jennie Marie Phillippi, born 20 Feb 1902.
+ 2123   viii.   Fannie Viola Phillippi, born 20 Feb 1902; died 02 Jan 1979.
     2124   ix.   Ralph Raymond Phillippi*3798*, born 07 Oct 1904*3798*; died 10 Dec 1947*3798*.
     2125   x.   Etta Louella Phillippi*3798*, born 29 Aug 1906*3798*.
     2126   xi.   Sylvester (Jim) Phillippi*3798*, born 24 Jun 1908*3798*; died 1971. He married Alverta; born 26 Oct 1921*3799*; died 05 Jan 2007 in Rockwood, Somerset Co., PA*3799*.

         Notes for Sylvester (Jim) Phillippi:
         Birth: 1908
         Death: 1971

         Son of Jeremiah B. and Tena Hoover Phillippi

         Parents:
         Jeremiah B. Phillippi (1864 - 1939)
         Tena Hoover Phillippi (1867 - 1950)

         Spouse: Alverta Phillippi (1921 - 2007)

         Burial: Laurel Church Cemetery, Somerset Co., PA

         Notes for Alverta:
         Birth: 1921
         Death: 2007

         Spouse: Sylvester Phillippi (1908 - 1971)

         Burial: Laurel Church Cemetery, Somerset Co., PA

         More About Alverta:
         SSN issued: Connellsville, Fayette Co., PA*3799*

     2127   xii.   James Irwin Phillippi, born 23 Jun 1910; died 01 Apr 1911.

         Notes for James Irwin Phillippi:
         Birth: Jun 23, 1910
         Death: Apr 1, 1911

         Parents:
         Jeremiah B. Phillippi (1864 - 1939)
         Tena Hoover Phillippi (1867 - 1950)

         Burial: Laurel Church Cemetery, Somerset Co., PA

850. Emma D.[7] **Christner** (Amos Dickey[6], Gabriel[5], Joseph "Zep"[4], Johannes John Hans[3], Christian[2],

Christen[1])[3800] was born 11 Jan 1877. She married **Lawerence M. Phillips**.

Notes for Emma D. Christner:
Emma D. or Emma M. married a Lawerence M. Phillips or a _____ Trimbath.
We have no last names on the children. Could be either name. The 1900 Census has her listed as a servant of Lawrence M. Phillips in Somerset, PA.

More About Emma D. Christner:
Residence: 1900, Age: 23; Marital Status: Single; Relation to Head of House: Servant/Somerset, Somerset Co., PA[3800]

Children of Emma Christner and Lawerence Phillips are:
2128	i.	Blair[8] Phillips.
2129	ii.	Dorothy Phillips.
2130	iii.	Louise Phillips.
2131	iv.	Marion Phillips.

851. Laura Ellen[7] Christner (Amos Dickey[6], Gabriel[5], Joseph "Zep"[4], Johannes John Hans[3], Christian[2], Christen[1])[3800] was born 30 Aug 1877 in Somerset Co., PA[3801], and died 20 Sep 1973 in Age: 95 Years/Danbury, Fairfield Co., CT[3802]. She married **Ross Oliver Bruner** 06 Mar 1895 in Luthern Parsonage Glades, PA or 1899.

Notes for Laura Ellen Christner:

More About Laura Ellen Christner:
Residence: 1880, Age: 9m; Marital Status: Single; Relation to Head of House: Daughter/Mt. Pleasant, Westmoreland Co., PA[3802]

Notes for Ross Oliver Bruner:
Sawmill Operator resides at Medford, PA.

More About Ross Oliver Bruner:
Occupation: Sawmill worker/
Residence: Milford PA

Children of Laura Christner and Ross Bruner are:
2132	i.	Unnamed[8] Bruner.
2133	ii.	Elwood Bruner, born 1899; died 1900.
2134	iii.	Dwight L. Bruner, born 1900; died 1908.
2135	iv.	Theodisia Bruner, born 1901.
2136	v.	Elwin C. Bruner, born 1908. He married Virginia Miller[3803]; born Abt. 1908 in PA[3803].

> Notes for Elwin C. Bruner:
> Elwin (Ed) & Virginia have 2 stores named Bruner's. They sell Antiques, Clocks, Guns, Coins & they also have a Hydroponic Nursery. Summer time sales are in Somerset, PA. Winter sales are at Alamo,TX.
>
> Notes for Virginia Miller:
> Virginia paternal ancestor was Jost Miller & her Maternal ancestor was Captain Michael Holderman She is an active member in the Daughters of the American Revolution in Somerset, PA.
>
> More About Virginia Miller:
> Education: Studied nursing at Jefferson Medical College and became an assistant to doctors in Philadelphia and New York/[3803]
> Residence: 1920, Somerset, Somerset, Pennsylvania[3803]

2137	vi.	Jaunita Bruner, born 1918. She married Goldstrohn.

852. Clarence Herbert[7] Christner (Amos Dickey[6], Gabriel[5], Joseph "Zep"[4], Johannes John Hans[3], Christian[2], Christen[1])[3804] was born 05 Jul 1881 in Westmoreland Co., PA[3805], and died in Pittsburgh, Allegheny Co., PA[3805]. He married **(1) Anna**[3805]. He married **(2) Ina Lee Williams**[3805]. She was born 27 Mar 1884 in Uniontown, Fayette Co., PA[3805], and died Sep 1965 in New Brighton, Beaver Co., PA[3805].

More About Clarence Herbert Christner:
Residence: 1910, Charleroi, Washington Co., PA[3805]

More About Ina Lee Williams:
Residence: 1930, New Brighton, Beaver Co., PA[3805]

Child of Clarence Christner and Ina Williams is:

2138   i.   Dorothy Jean[8] Christner[3805], born 18 Jun 1915 in Pittsburgh, Allegheny Co., PA[3805]; died 13 Jan 1995 in Saint Augustine, Saint Johns Co., FL[3805].

         More About Dorothy Jean Christner:
         Residence: 1930, New Brighton, Beaver Co., PA[3805]

854. Isa Olive[7] Christner (Amos Dickey[6], Gabriel[5], Joseph "Zep"[4], Johannes John Hans[3], Christian[2], Christen[1])[3806] was born 19 Mar 1889 in Milford, Somerset Co., PA[3807,3808], and died Aug 1978 in Scottdale, Westmoreland Co., PA[3809,3810]. She married **Cyrus Luther Rumbaugh**[3811] 22 Jul 1928 in Mt. Pleasant Twp., Westmoreland Co., PA[3811]. He was born 01 Jul 1877 in Mt. Pleasant Twp., Westmoreland Co., PA[3811], and died 07 May 1958 in Age at Death: 81/Mt. Pleasant Twp., Westmoreland Co., PA[3811].

Notes for Isa Olive Christner:
Isa married a Cyrus Rumbaugh. She owned and operated a store on West Main Street in Mount Pleasant, PA. 1920 Census she was living with her parents at Westmoreland County, Mt Pleasant Boro, West Main Street.

Birth: 1889
Death: 1978

Note: Same stone as Cyrus L. Rumbaugh

Burial: Saint Johns Union Cemetery, Mount Pleasant, Westmoreland Co., PA
Find A Grave Memorial# 30769652

More About Isa Olive Christner:
Burial: Mount Pleasant, Westmoreland County, PA, USA[3812,3813]
Residence: 1930, Mt. Pleasant, Westmoreland Co., PA[3814]
Social Security Number: 188-32-0313/[3815]
SSN issued: PA[3815]

More About Cyrus Luther Rumbaugh:
Burial: Mount Pleasant, Westmoreland County, PA, USA[3816]
Residence: 1880, Age: 2; Marital Status: Single; Relation to Head of House: Son/Mt. Pleasant, Westmoreland Co., PA[3816]

Child of Isa Christner and Cyrus Rumbaugh is:

2139   i.   Betty Jane[8] Rumbaugh. She married Fassold/Fasshold.

         Notes for Betty Jane Rumbaugh:
         Betty married _____Fassold/Fasshold

855. Barton Roy[7] Christner (Amos Dickey[6], Gabriel[5], Joseph "Zep"[4], Johannes John Hans[3], Christian[2], Christen[1])[3817] was born 04 Apr 1892 in Connellsville, Fayette Co., PA[3817], and died 18 Jul

1963[3818,3819,3820,3821,3822]. He married **Harriet M. "Hattie" McCulley**[3822]. She was born 06 May 1895 in WV[3822,3822,3822], and died 02 Mar 1961 in New Brighton, Beaver Co., PA[3822].

Notes for Barton Roy Christner:
SS#174-01-9205 ISS PA

1920 census has him living at Allegheny Co., PA.

More About Barton Roy Christner:
Residence: 1920, Duquesne Ward 1, Allegheny Co., PA[3822]
Social Security Number: 174-01-9205/[3823]
SSN issued: Connellsville, Fayette Co., PA[3823]

More About Harriet M. "Hattie" McCulley:
Residence: 1920, Duquesne Ward 1, Allegheny Co., PA[3824]

Children of Barton Christner and Harriet McCulley are:

+ 2140 i. Thayer H.[8] Christner, born 03 Apr 1913 in Pittsburgh, Allegheny Co., PA; died 07 Jan 2004 in Pittsburgh, Alleghaney Co., PA.

  2141 ii. Olive Mae Christner[3825], born 14 Dec 1914[3826]; died in Vero Beach, FL[3827]. She married Thompson.

  More About Olive Mae Christner:
  Race: White/[3828]
  Residence: 1920, Age: 5; Marital Status: Single; Relation to Head of House: Daughter/Duquesne Ward 1, Allegheny, Pennsylvania, USA[3828]

  2142 iii. Robert Christner, born 1917 in Connellsville, Fayette Co., PA.

+ 2143 iv. Roberta Samatha Christner, born 1923 in Pittsburgh, Allegheny Co., PA; died 25 Jul 2013 in New Brighton, Beaver Co., PA.

  2144 v. Harriet Jean Christner[3829], born 26 Jun 1924 in Connellsville, Fayette Co., PA[3829]; died 27 Jul 2006 in St. Petersburg, Pinellas Co., FL[3829].

  More About Harriet Jean Christner:
  Residence: 1983, Clearwater, FL[3829]

+ 2145 vi. Elizabeth Christner, born 28 Oct 1925 in Rochester, Beaver Co., PA; died 15 Oct 2005 in Donegal.

860. Gabriel Dickey "Milton"[7] Christner (Nelson Brown[6], Gabriel[5], Joseph "Zep"[4], Johannes John Hans[3], Christian[2], Christen[1])[3830,3831,3832] was born 18 Aug 1876 in Donegal, Westmoreland Co., PA[3833,3834,3835,3836], and died 17 Jul 1962 in McKeesport, Allegheny Co., PA[3837,3838,3839]. He married **Mary Ann Knight**[3840,3841] 23 Apr 1900[3842]. She was born 17 Mar 1882 in Williamsport, Lycoming Co., PA[3843,3844], and died 07 May 1970 in Mercer, Mercer Co., PA[3845,3846].

Notes for Gabriel Dickey "Milton" Christner:
Gabriel was named for his grandfather Gabriel and his grandmother Magdalena Dickey on his fathers side.

SS#;186-28-7772 Issued in PA.

His death maybe Sept. 30 1958. Franklin Ave.. McKeesport, Alleghany Co. PA.
1920 census his name was spelled Cristner

Birth: unknown
Death: Jul. 17, 1962

Burial: McKeesport and Versailles Cemetery, McKeesport, Allegheny Co., PA
Plot: Section O, Lot 82
Find A Grave Memorial# 33629780

More About Gabriel Dickey "Milton" Christner:
Burial: Versailles Cemetery, McKeesport, Allegheny Co., PA
Residence: 1930, McKeesport, Allegheny Co., PA, United States[3846,3847,3848]
Social Security Number: 186-28-7772/[3849]
SSN issued: Connellsville, Fayette Co., PA[3849]

More About Mary Ann Knight:
Residence: 1900, McKeesport City (East Side), Allegheny, PA[3850]

Children of Gabriel Christner and Mary Knight are:
+ 2146   i.   LaReine Mary[8] Christner, born 21 Jul 1901.
+ 2147   ii.   Alan Shirley Christner, born 11 Jun 1906 in McKeesport, Allegheny Co., PA; died 04 Aug 1994 in Holmes Beach, Manatee Co., FL.
+ 2148   iii. Lois Frances Christner, born 28 Sep 1912.

873. Amanda[7] Miller (Elizabeth[6] Christner, Joseph[5], Joseph "Zep"[4], Johannes John Hans[3], Christian[2], Christen[1]) was born 27 Aug 1864, and died 1903 in Lincoln, Lancaster Co., NE[3851]. She married **George Raffensparger**.

More About Amanda Miller:
Residence: 1920, Bryant, Fillmore Co., NE[3851]

Child of Amanda Miller and George Raffensparger is:
+ 2149   i.   Goldie Fern[8] Raffensparger, born 28 Dec 1883 in Spencer, IA; died 28 Sep 1973 in Orange Co., CA.

877. Savilla[7] Beal (Katherine[6] Christner, Joseph[5], Joseph "Zep"[4], Johannes John Hans[3], Christian[2], Christen[1])[3852] was born 10 Aug 1866[3852], and died 15 Dec 1896 in Enid, Garfield Co., OK[3852]. She married **Casper Habig**[3852] 18 Oct 1884 in Hanover, Washington Co., KS[3852]. He was born 1860[3852], and died 29 Jun 1895 in Hanover, Washington Co., KS[3852].

Child of Savilla Beal and Casper Habig is:
  2150   i.   Fern Edith[8] Habig[3852], born 04 Sep 1885 in Hanover, Washington Co., KS[3852]; died 1946 in Houston, Harris Co., TX[3852].

                More About Fern Edith Habig:
                Residence: 01 Mar 1895, Hanover, Washington, Kansas[3852]

880. Norman B.[7] Christner (Samuel J. "Matlick Sam"[6], Joseph[5], Joseph "Zep"[4], Johannes John Hans[3], Christian[2], Christen[1])[3853,3854,3855,3856,3857] was born 13 Oct 1867 in Addison, Somerset Co., PA[3858], and died 02 Nov 1943 in Meyersdale, Somerset Co., PA[3858,3859]. He married **Anna Elizabeth Hoffmeyer**[3860,3861,3862,3863] 03 Oct 1887 in Salisbury PA., daughter of Jacob Christner and Sarah Davis. She was born Jun 1868 in Connellsville, Fayette Co., PA[3864,3865,3866,3867,3868,3869], and died 1955 in Pittsburgh, Allegheny Co., PA[3869,3870,3870,3871].

Notes for Norman B. Christner:
Obituary: Norman B. CHRISTNER, 1943, Meyersdale, Somerset County, PA - Meyersdale Republican, November 4, 1943
Norman B. Christner, retired farmer living in Meyersdale, died Tuesday, Nov. 2, 1943 in the Windber Hospital, at the age of 76 years, 20 days. He was born Oct. 13, 1867, in Addison Township.

He is survived by his wife, Annie Hoffmeyer Christner, and the following children: Mrs. Grace Lint, Mrs. Henry Younkin and Mrs. Ernest Boden, Meyersdale; Ed Christner, Boynton; Mrs. Dan C. Specht and Mrs. D. W. Weaver, Stoystown, and Mrs. Sherman Gindlesperger, Boswell; also by 16 grandchildren and 8 great-grandchildren.

Mr. Christner began his career as a tenant farmer in Elk Lick Township at which he prospered until he bought a fine dairy farm near Stoystown which he successfully operated until failing health impelled him to dispose of his farm and retire from hard work. Their children all being grown up and established in homes of their own by that time, Mr. and Mrs. Christner bought a home in Meyersdale into which they moved several years ago to spend the sunset of their lives. Seeking relief from serious illness, he entered the Windber Hospital where he succumbed after a short stay.

Norman B. Christner was a sterling citizen, a good neighbor and kind husband and father. Funeral services will be held Friday at 2:30 p.m., at his late home on Broadway, With Rev. N. L. Wilson, Berlin, and Rev. Nelson C. Brown, Meyersdale, officiating. Interment in Union Cemetery. Pallbearers will be Josiah Lint, John Smearman, Charles Bolden, John Clark, John Gauntz and D. H. Bauman. H. R. Konhaus has charge of funeral arrangements.

More About Norman B. Christner:
Burial: Meyersdale Cemetery, Meyersdale, Somerset Co., PA
Residence: 01 Apr 1940, Quemahoning, Somerset, PA, United States[3872]

More About Anna Elizabeth Hoffmeyer:
Burial: Meyersdale Cemetery, Meyersdale, Somerset Co., PA
Residence: 01 Apr 1940, Quemahoning, Somerset, PA, United States[3872]

Children are listed above under (627) Anna Elizabeth Hoffmeyer.

882. George Calvin[7] Christner (Samuel J. "Matlick Sam"[6], Joseph[5], Joseph "Zep"[4], Johannes John Hans[3], Christian[2], Christen[1]) was born 24 Aug 1878 in Elk Lick, Somerset Co., PA[3873], and died 12 Jan 1965 in Brevard Co., FL[3873]. He married **(1) Bessie Hoover**. He married **(2) Nora McCavitt**[3873]. She died 1918[3873]. He married **(3) Bessie Mae Pickard**[3873]. She was born 26 Aug 1894 in IA[3873,3874,3875], and died 28 Dec 1980 in Brevard Co., FL[3876,3877].

Notes for George Calvin Christner:
He was married twice. The first one died when the 2 boys were young.

More About George Calvin Christner:
Residence: 1880, Elk Lick, Somerset Co., PA[3878]

Notes for Bessie Hoover:
---13369--B. Hochstedler-C. Stutzman book

More About Bessie Mae Pickard:
Other-Begin: Merritt Island, Brevard, Florida, United States of America[3879]
Residence: 1930, Leoni, Jackson Co., MI[3880]
Social Security Number: 365-20-6068/[3881]
SSN issued: MI[3881]

Child of George Christner and Bessie Hoover is:
    2151   i.   George[8] Christner Jr..

Children of George Christner and Nora McCavitt are:
    2152   i.   Samuel J.[8] Christner[3882], born 14 Sep 1906[3882,3883]; died 07 Aug 1971 in Jackson, Jackson Co., MI[3884].

                  More About Samuel J. Christner:
                  Social Security Number: 373-10-2509/[3885]
                  SSN issued: MI[3885]

    2153   ii.   Charles Christner[3886], born 20 Dec 1907 in PA[3886,3887]; died 15 May 1998 in Jackson, Jackson Co., MI[3888]. He married Esther; born 24 Mar 1910[3889]; died 16 Nov 1999 in Jackson, Jackson Co., MI[3889].

                  Notes for Charles Christner:

Birth: Dec. 20, 1907
Death: May 15, 1998

Son of George C. Christner and Nora McCavitt

Spouse: Esther Christner (1910 - 1999)

Burial: Hillcrest Memorial Park, Jackson, Jackson Co., MI
Plot: Section F
Find A Grave Memorial# 66659716

More About Charles Christner:
Residence: 1910, Somerset Co., PA[3890]
Social Security Number: 386-10-0551/[3891]
SSN issued: MI[3891]

Notes for Esther:
Birth: 1910
Death: 1999

Spouse: Charles Christner (1907 - 1998)

Burial: Hillcrest Memorial Park, Jackson, Jackson Co., MI
Plot: Section F
Find A Grave Memorial# 66659655

More About Esther:
Social Security Number: 381-28-1321/[3892]
SSN issued: MI[3892]

2154 iii. George I. Christner[3893], born 21 Aug 1910 in Defiance, Bedford Co., PA[3893,3894,3895]; died 20 Jul 1983 in Ann Arbor, Washtenaw Co., MI[3896].

More About George I. Christner:
Residence: Tompkins, Jackson Co., MI[3896,3897]
Social Security Number: 367-07-0198/[3898]
SSN issued: MI[3898]

Child of George Christner and Bessie Pickard is:
2155 i. Opal Arlene[8] Christner[3899], born 07 Mar 1927 in MI[3899]; died 07 Mar 1995 in Fort Mill, York Co., SC[3899].

More About Opal Arlene Christner:
Residence: 1930, Leoni, Jackson Co., MI[3899]

883. Hattie[7] Christner (Samuel J. "Matlick Sam"[6], Joseph[5], Joseph "Zep"[4], Johannes John Hans[3], Christian[2], Christen[1])[3900] was born Nov 1880 in Spring City, Berks, PA[3900]. She married **Lewis William Corley** 01 Aug 1906. He was born 16 Aug 1882 in New Buena Vistia, PA[3901].

Notes for Hattie Christner:
Hattie may of gotten married on Aug 1, 1906.

More About Hattie Christner:
Residence: 1920, Elk Lick, Somerset Co., PA[3901]

Notes for Lewis William Corley:
His parents John M.Corely & Maria E. Lowery.

More About Lewis William Corley:
Christened: Reformed
Residence: 1920, Elk Lick, Somerset Co., PA[3901]

Children of Hattie Christner and Lewis Corley are:
2156   i.   Evelyn[8] Corely.
2157   ii.   Guy Corely, born Abt. 1908 in PA[3901].

> More About Guy Corely:
> Residence: 1920, Elk Lick, Somerset Co., PA[3901]

2158   iii.   Ada Corely, born Abt. 1910 in PA[3901].

> More About Ada Corely:
> Residence: 1920, Elk Lick, Somerset Co., PA[3901]

2159   iv.   Clyde Corely, born 05 Apr 1912 in Connellsville, Fayette Co., PA[3901]; died 15 Jun 1993 in Baldwin, Lake Co., PA[3901].

> More About Clyde Corely:
> Residence: 1920, Elk Lick, Somerset Co., PA[3901]

2160   v.   Blair Corely, born 27 Oct 1917.

884. Irvin F.[7] Christner (Samuel J. "Matlick Sam"[6], Joseph[5], Joseph "Zep"[4], Johannes John Hans[3], Christian[2], Christen[1])[3902] was born 08 May 1883 in Connellsville, Fayette Co., PA[3903]. He married **Ada Pearl Chamberlin**. She was born 1890 in Connellsville, Fayette Co., PA.

More About Irvin F. Christner:
Residence: 1900, Elk Lick, Somerset Co., PA[3903]

Notes for Ada Pearl Chamberlin:
1920 census has her brother (Harry age 31) living with her & Irwin.

More About Ada Pearl Chamberlin:
Residence: 1930, Clarksburg, Harrison Co., WV[3903]

Child of Irvin Christner and Ada Chamberlin is:
2161   i.   Jack[8] Christner, born 08 Jun 1918 in Huntington, Huntington Co., IN[3904]; died 05 Oct 1973 in Valparaiso, Porter Co., IN[3904]. He married Elizabeth Rusbason[3904]; born 25 Sep 1923 in Perryapolis, Fayette Co., PA[3904,3905]; died 27 Sep 2001 in Valparaiso, Porter Co., IN[3905,3906].

> More About Jack Christner:
> Burial: 08 Oct 1973, St. Paul's Cemetery, Valparaiso, IN[3907]

> More About Elizabeth Rusbason:
> Social Security Number: 185-16-1362[3908]
> SSN issued: PA[3908]

885. Cornelia Mae[7] Christner (Samuel J. "Matlick Sam"[6], Joseph[5], Joseph "Zep"[4], Johannes John Hans[3], Christian[2], Christen[1])[3909,3910] was born 28 May 1885 in Elklick Twp., Bedford (now Somerset) Co., PA, and died 07 Nov 1964 in Waterloo, Black Hawk Co., IA[3911]. She married **Frank Johnson Peck** 21 Sep 1911 in Waterloo, Black Hawk Co., IA. He was born 12 Jan 1883 in Waterloo, Black Hawk Co, IA[3912], and died 08 Apr 1943.

Notes for Cornelia Mae Christner:
Birth: May 28, 1885
Somerset Co., PA
Death: Nov. 7, 1964

Waterloo, Black Hawk Co., IA

Spouse: Frank Johnson Peck (1883 - 1943)

Children: Evelyn I. Peck (1912 - 1987)

Burial: Orange Twp., Cemetery, Black Hawk Co., IA
Find A Grave Memorial# 42860192

More About Cornelia Mae Christner:
Burial: Nov 1964, Orange Center Cemetery, Orange Twp, Black Hawk Co, IA[3912]
Residence: 1900, Elk Lick Township (West Part), Somerset Co., PA[3913]

Notes for Frank Johnson Peck:
Frank is the son of Jeramia J. and Elizabeth Lichty Peck.

13372 Hochstedler/Stutzman.

Birth: Jan 12, 1883 - Black Hawk Co., IA
Death: Apr 8, 1943 - Waterloo, Black Hawk Co., IA

Spouse: Cornelia Mae Christner Peck (1885 - 1964)

Children: Evelyn I. Peck (1912 - 1987)

Burial: Orange Twp., Cemetery, Black Hawk Co., IA
Find A Grave Memorial# 42860121

More About Frank Johnson Peck:
Burial: 1943, Orange Center Cemetery, Orange Twp, Black Hawk Co, IA[3914]
Christened: Brethern

Child of Cornelia Christner and Frank Peck is:
 2162 i. Evelyn Irene[8] Peck[3914], born 12 Oct 1912 in IA[3914]; died 10 Feb 1987[3914].

     Notes for Evelyn Irene Peck:
     Birth: 1912
     Death: 1987

     Parents:
     Frank Johnson Peck (1883 - 1943)
     Cornelia Mae Christner Peck (1885 - 1964)

     Burial: Orange Township Cemetery, Black Hawk Co., IA
     Find A Grave Memorial# 95189455

886. Florence B.[7] Christner (Samuel J. "Matlick Sam"[6], Joseph[5], Joseph "Zep"[4], Johannes John Hans[3], Christian[2], Christen[1])[3915] was born Dec 1889 in Somerset, Somerset Co., PA[3915], and died 1963 in Meyersdale, Somerset Co., PA[3916]. She married **Roy Lindeman**. He was born 30 Oct 1884 in PA[3916], and died 1965 in Meyersdale, Somerset Co., PA[3916].

More About Florence B. Christner:
Residence: 1910, Elk Lick, Somerset, PA[3917]

Notes for Roy Lindeman:
13373 Hochstedler/Stutzman

More About Roy Lindeman:
Residence: *3918*

Children of Florence Christner and Roy Lindeman are:

2163   i.   Glenn E.[8] Lindeman*3918*, born 12 May 1911 in PA*3918*; died Sep 1969 in Meyersdale, Somerset Co., PA*3918*.

        More About Glenn E. Lindeman:
        Residence: 1930, Summit, Somerset Co., PA*3918*

2164   ii.   Thomas E. Lindeman*3918*, born Abt. 1912 in PA*3918*.

        More About Thomas E. Lindeman:
        Residence: 1920, Summit, Somerset Co., PA*3918*

2165   iii.   Viola A. Lindeman*3918*, born Abt. 1918 in PA*3918*; died in Somerset, Somerset Co., PA*3918*.

        More About Viola A. Lindeman:
        Residence: 1930, Pittsburgh, Allegheny, PA*3918*

2166   iv.   Floyd E. Lindeman*3918*, born 10 Feb 1919 in PA*3918*; died Oct 1984 in Meyersdale, Somerset Co., PA*3918*.

        More About Floyd E. Lindeman:
        Residence: 1930, Summit, Somerset Co., PA*3918*

2167   v.   Mary Ann Elizabeth Lindeman*3918*, born 03 Sep 1927 in PA*3918*; died 15 Jul 1988 in Pittsburgh, Alleghaney Co., PA*3918*.

887. Clyde Evans[7] Christner (Samuel J. "Matlick Sam"[6], Joseph[5], Joseph "Zep"[4], Johannes John Hans[3], Christian[2], Christen[1])*3919,3920,3921* was born 06 Aug 1894 in Meyersdale, Somerset Co., PA*3922,3923,3924*, and died Apr 1963 in OH*3924*. He married **Cora Edna Geisbert**pt_*3925,3926* 23 Dec 1917 in Meyersdale, Somerset Co., PA. She was born 08 Dec 1899 in Meyersdale, Somerset Co., PA*3926*.

Notes for Clyde Evans Christner:
13374 B.Hochstedler -- Stutzman Book-------Laborer SS# 192-01-4008 Iss.PA

More About Clyde Evans Christner:
Christened: Reformed
Residence: 1930, Johnstown, Cambria, PA*3926*
Social Security Number: 192-01-4008/*3927*
SSN issued: Connellsville, Fayette Co., PA*3927*

More About Cora Edna Geisbert:
Residence: 1900, Summit Township (South Part), Somerset Co., PA*3928*

Children of Clyde Christner and Cora Geisbert are:

2168   i.   Leo Irvin[8] Christner, died 24 Apr 1922.

2169   ii.   Bernice Mae Christner, born 24 Oct 1918 in Connellsville, Fayette Co., PA; died 1957*3929*. She married Donald Emerson Brown*3929*; born 04 Mar 1917 in Connellsville, Fayette Co., PA*3929,3930*; died 12 Nov 2001 in New Paris, Bedford Co., PA*3931*.

        More About Donald Emerson Brown:
        Social Security Number: 190-05-6078/*3932*
        SSN issued: PA*3932*

+   2170   iii.   Sylvester Francis Christner, born 25 Dec 1920 in Connellsville, Fayette Co., PA; died 25 May 1995 in Lorain, Lorain Co., OH.

2171   iv.   Tom Evans Christner*3933*, born 19 Aug 1929 in PA*3934,3935*; died 15 Oct 2002 in Canton, Stark Co., OH*3935*.

More About Tom Evans Christner:
Social Security Number: 181-24-8589/[3936]
SSN issued: Connellsville, Fayette Co., PA[3936]

892. Florence Ruth[7] Christner (Henry J.[6], Joseph[5], Joseph "Zep"[4], Johannes John Hans[3], Christian[2], Christen[1]) was born 10 Mar 1883 in Salisbury, Elk Lick Twp., Somerset C., PA[3937], and died 06 Jul 1975 in Jackson Co., MI. She married **(1) Wallace**.   She married **(2) Frank G. Argenbright** 18 Dec 1902 in Keim, PA, son of Samuel Argenbright and Margret Snellings. He was born 25 Dec 1881 in Staunton, Augusta Co., VA, and died 07 Nov 1947 in Huntingdon, Huntingdon Co., PA[3937].

Notes for Florence Ruth Christner:
Florence Ruth went by her middle name Ruth. She must have remarried as the 1920 census she is with Frank G. Argenbright & by 1934 she is listed as Mrs. Ruth Wallace. 1920 census she is with Frank G. Argenbright & her brother Hubert (age 27) is living with them.

More About Florence Ruth Christner:
Burial: Sylvania Hills Cemetery NB. PA.
Residence: 1930, Huntingdon, Huntingdon, PA[3937]

Notes for Frank G. Argenbright:
13378 Hochstedler/Stutzman

More About Frank G. Argenbright:
Burial: Tipton Indiana   Arcadia Cemetery
Residence: [3937]

Children of Florence Christner and Frank Argenbright are:
+   2172   i.   Flowella[8] Argenbright, born 20 Aug 1903 in W.Salisbury, PA; died 16 Nov 1983 in Oxnard CA..
+   2173   ii.   Mary Gertrude Argenbright, born 30 Apr 1905 in W.Salisbury, PA; died 09 Aug 1999 in York Co., PA.
+   2174   iii.   Annabelle Argenbright, born 20 Dec 1908 in W.Salisbury, PA; died Jun 1999 in Huntingdon Co. PA..
+   2175   iv.   Esther Mildred Argenbright, born 24 Mar 1910 in W.Salisbury, PA; died Nov 1999 in Jackson Co., MI.
     2176   v.   George O. Argenbright, born 16 Dec 1921 in W.Salisbury, PA; died 08 Apr 1922.

              Notes for George O. Argenbright:
              The headstone in the cemetery has the wrong death date, his mother was very old when she bought the stone.

              More About George O. Argenbright:
              Burial: I.O.O.F Cemetery in West Salisbury PA

+   2177   vi.   Joe Franklin Argenbright, born 25 May 1923 in Boyton PA or W.Salisbury, PA.

893. Harry Buford[7] Christner (Henry J.[6], Joseph[5], Joseph "Zep"[4], Johannes John Hans[3], Christian[2], Christen[1])[3938] was born 23 Dec 1889 in West Salisbury, Somerset Co., PA[3938], and died 29 Jul 1953 in Detroit, Wayne Co., MI[3938]. He married **(1) Mayme Alina Juntunen**[3938]. She was born 27 Jul 1907 in Nisula, Houghton Co., MI[3938], and died 06 Dec 1969 in Detroit, Wayne Co., MI[3938]. He married **(2) Florence Bassett**[3938] 03 Feb 1910 in Cumberland, Allegany Co., MD. She was born 05 Sep 1890 in South Fork, Cambria Co., PA[3938].

Notes for Harry Buford Christner:
Methodist---13383 B. Hochstetler C. Stutzman Book

Maybe born Dec.29 1892. 1910 soundex PA has them living in South Fork, Cambia County, PA.

Birth: Dec 23, 1889
Death: Jul 29, 1953

Inscription: MICHIGAN PVT BTRY A 104 FIELD ARTY WORLD WAR I

Burial: Grand Lawn Cemetery, Detroit, Wayne Co., MI
Plot: Section R

More About Harry Buford Christner:
Residence: 1920, Detroit Ward 9, Wayne Co., MI[3938]

More About Florence Bassett:
Residence: 1910, South Fork, Cambria Co., PA[3938]

Children of Harry Christner and Florence Bassett are:

2178   i.   Robert Lee[8] Christner[3939,3940], born 13 Sep 1910[3941,3942]; died 27 Nov 1985 in Farmington Hills, Oakland Co., MI[3943,3944].

        Notes for Robert Lee Christner:
        SS#372-07-2723 ISS MI   Last address Dearborn MI 48126

        Birth: 1910
        Death: 1985

        Burial: Mount Ever-Rest Memorial Park South, Kalamazoo, Kalamazoo Co., MI
        Plot: Four Seasons

        More About Robert Lee Christner:
        Residence: Dearborn, Wayne Co., MI[3945]
        Social Security Number: 372-07-2723/[3946]
        SSN issued: MI[3946]

2179   ii.   William Clayton Christner[3947,3948,3949], born 14 Apr 1912 in South Fork, Cambria Co., PA[3950,3951,3952]; died 14 Jun 1973 in Detroit, Wayne Co., MI[3953,3954,3955].

        Notes for William Clayton Christner:
        SS#362-01-2710 ISS MI   Last address 48215 Detroit MI

        More About William Clayton Christner:
        Social Security Number: 362-01-2710/[3955]
        SSN issued: MI[3955]

894. Hubert Eugene[7] Christner (Henry J.[6], Joseph[5], Joseph "Zep"[4], Johannes John Hans[3], Christian[2], Christen[1])[3956] was born 02 Mar 1892 in West Salisbury, Somerset Co., PA[3956], and died 15 Mar 1971 in Meyersdale, Somerset Co., PA[3956]. He married **Florence Lucinda Brown**[3956,3957] 10 Dec 1919 in Cumberland, Allegany Co., MD. She was born 02 Dec 1899 in Meyersdale, Summitt Twp., Somerset Co., PA[3958,3959], and died 16 May 1998 in Salisbury, Somerset Co., PA[3960].

Notes for Hubert Eugene Christner:
SS#;170-18-2245 Iss PA

He was a life time coal miner with black lung also a member of UMWA a united mine workers ass. union When he gave his word it was as good as gold. If he told you he would sell you his watch for $10.00 dollars and find out it was worth $100.00 later he would still sell it to you for what he said without being upset with you. He was very particular about everything he did and his appearance. His daughter Janet got this from him then she married a man just like her father which in this case was a good choice.

More About Hubert Eugene Christner:
Burial: old I.O.O.F Cemetery in Salisbury PA
Residence: 1900, Elk Lick, Somerset Co., PA[3961]
Social Security Number: 170-18-2245/[3962]

SSN issued: Connellsville, Fayette Co., PA[3962]

Notes for Florence Lucinda Brown:
Florence is the daughter of John P. Brown and Amanda Murray. At age 15 her father died and as she was an older child she was called upon to work out of the home for others, she worked on neighboring farms. When she was older she became a telephone operator. She loved to crochet in her free time becoming so good she could lok at a doily and make a another without instructions. She was in the care of her daughter from 1987 until her death, Janet expressed her joy in having her mother close with her. Her mother was very active until the last 10 months. She was a good Christian and caring person.

Obituary: Florence L. (Brown) Christner, 1998, Salisbury, Somerset County, PA - Daily American, May 18, 1998
Florence L. Christner, 98, 120 Mineral St., Salisbury, formerly of Boynton, died May 16, 1998, at her residence. Born Dec. 2, 1899, in Summit Township, she was a daughter of the late John and Amanda (Murray) Brown. Also preceded in death by husband, Hubert E. Christner, March 15, 1971; 3 sons, Paul, Earl and Everett; 3 grandchildren; 1 great- grandchild; 4 brothers, Maurice, Frank, Lloyd and Will Brown; and 3 sisters, Martha Miller, Ella Winters and Annie Marteney. Surviving are 3 daughters: Kathleen Gutowski and husband, William, Moscow, PA; Irene Ludy and husband, Harry, Glencoe; Janet Wahl and husband, Ray, Jr. "Tex", Salisbury, with whom she resided; 2 daughters-in-law, Emogen Christner and Kathleen Christner, both of Salisbury; a brother, Clarence Brown and a sister, Elizabeth Blocher, both of Salisbury; 11 grandchildren, 22 great-grandchildren and 15 great-great-grandchildren. Mrs. Christner was a charter member of Cornerstone Assembly of God, Boynton and was a homemaker. Friends received 2-4 and 7-9 p.m., Monday at the Newman Funeral Home Inc., Salisbury, where services will be conducted at 11 a.m., Tuesday, with the Rev. Gary L. Kipe officiating. Interment, Salisbury Cemetery.

Birth: Dec. 2, 1899
PA
Death: May 16, 1998
Summit Twp., Somerset Co., PA

SALISBURY, PENNSYLVANIA - Florence L. Christner, 98, of 120 Mineral St., Salisbury, formerly of Boynton, died Saturday, May 16, 1998, at her residence.

Born Dec. 2, 1899, in Summit Township, she was a daughter of the late John and Amanda (Murray) Brown. She also was preceded in death by her husband, Hubert E. Christner, on March 15, 1971; three sons, Paul, Earl and Everett; three grandchildren; one great-grandchild; four brothers, Maurice, Frank, Lloyd and Will Brown; and three sisters, Martha Miller Wheeling, Ella Winters and Annie Marteney.

Mrs. Christner was a charter member of the Cornerstone Assembly of God, Boynton, and was a homemaker. Surviving are three daughter, Kathleen Gutowski and husband William, Moscow, Pa., Irene Ludy and husband Harry, Glencoe, Pa., and Janet Wahl and husband Ray, Jr., "Tex," Salisbury, with whom she resided; two daughters-in-law, Emogen Christner and Kathleen Christner, both of Salisbury; a brother, Clarence Brown; and a sister, Elizabeth Blocher, both of Salisbury; 11 grandchildren; 22 great-grandchildren; and 15 great-great-grandchildren.
Friends will be received at the Newman Funeral Home, Salisbury, Monday from 2 to 4 and 7 to 9 p.m.
Services will be conducted at the funeral home Tuesday at 11 a.m. with the Rev. Garry L. Kipe officiating.
Interment will be in the Salisbury Cemetery.

Publication Date:Sunday, May 17, 1998
Cumberland Times-News, Cumberland, MD

Burial: IOOF Cemetery, Salisbury, Somerset Co., PA

More About Florence Lucinda Brown:
Burial: old I.O.O.F Cemetery in Salisbury PA
Other-Begin: 16 May 1998, United States[3963]
Residence: 1910, Elk Lick, Somerset Co., PA[3964]

Social Security Number: 188-40-5355/*3965*
SSN issued: PA*3965*

Children of Hubert Christner and Florence Brown are:

+ 2180   i.   Paul Jay⁸ Christner, born 30 Jun 1920 in Elk Lick Twp., Somerset Co., PA; died 09 Jul 1967 in Meyersdale, Somerset Co., PA.
+ 2181   ii. Earl Ray Christner, born 18 May 1922 in Boynton, Somerset Co., PA; died 06 Apr 1985 in Cumberland, Allegany Co., MD.
+ 2182   iii. Kathleen May Christner, born 27 May 1923 in Boynton, Somerset Co., PA; died 04 Aug 2009 in Moscow, Lackawanna Co., PA.
+ 2183   iv. Everett Fay Christner, born 08 Jun 1924 in Boynton, Somerset Co., PA; died 16 Feb 1973 in Meyersdale, Somerset Co., PA.
+ 2184   v.   Anna Irene Christner, born 26 May 1928 in Boynton, Somerset Co., PA.
   2185   vi. Janet Marie Christner, born 25 May 1938 in Boynton, Somerset Co., PA. She married Ray Wahl Jr. 07 Mar 1959 in Morgantown, Monongalia Co., WV; born 20 Mar 1934 in Elk Lick Twp. Somerset C. PA.

Notes for Janet Marie Christner:
Lives at First red brick ranch above the cemetery. She was a good mate for Tex as she was very particular about everything she did just as he was. She married a man just like her father which in this case was a good choice. She retired after 31 years from a shirt Mfg. Co. as a utility person which is a person the company can call upon to do most any job in the plant. As a utility person one would think she would sew, but the company reserved her for more important job such as ordering lining or correcting mistakes but never sewing. She took care of her mother from 1987 until her death, Janet expressed her joy in having her mother close with her. Her mother was very active until the last 10 months.

Notes for Ray Wahl Jr.:
He is also known as Tex. He was a Army veteran. His lifetime vocation was an automobile mechanic with a speciality for repairing General Motors automobiles like Cadillac, Buick, Oldsmobile, and Pontiac. He had an attraction to John Deere lawn tractors. He was very good at his work as he was a perfectionist, this even carried over to things like his lawn. He was very particular about everything he did. His free time was spent hunting and fishing.

898.   Earl Nevin⁷ Newman (Sevilla⁶ Christner, Joseph⁵, Joseph "Zep"⁴, Johannes John Hans³, Christian², Christen¹)*3966,3967* was born 06 Jun 1886 in St.Paul, PA, and died 17 Oct 1959 in Wenatchee, Chelan Co., WA*3968*. He married **Alta Thompson** 24 Sep 1911 in St Paul, PA*3969*. She was born 28 Aug 1890 in Caney, Montgomery Co., KS*3969*, and died 03 Sep 1976 in Wenatchee, Chelan Co., WA*3970*.

Notes for Earl Nevin Newman:
Birth: 1886
Death: Oct. 17, 1959

Burial: Wenatchee City Cemetery, Wenatchee, Chelan Co., WA
Plot: Section F

More About Earl Nevin Newman:
Residence: 1900, Eagle & Lincoln Townships, Black Hawk Co., IA*3970,3971*

More About Alta Thompson:
Residence: 1933, Wenatchee, Co., WA*3972*
Social Security Number: 539-16-7777/*3973*
SSN issued: Washington*3973*

Child of Earl Newman and Alta Thompson is:
   2186   i.   Gerald "Jerry" D⁸ Newman*3974*, born 22 May 1918 in Parkdale, Hood River Co., OR*3974*; died 25 Sep 1962 in Wenatchee, Chelan Co., WA*3974*.

More About Gerald "Jerry" D Newman:
Residence: 1930, Lincoln, Chelan Co., WA*3974*

901. Arthur Grover[7] Christner (Harvey[6], Joseph[5], Joseph "Zep"[4], Johannes John Hans[3], Christian[2], Christen[1]) was born 29 Nov 1884 in Salisburg, Elklick Twp., Somerset Co., PA. He married **Diantha Merle Glines**.

Notes for Arthur Grover Christner:
Adopted out to relatives with the last name Bender? His name was changed.

Child of Arthur Christner and Diantha Glines is:
+ 2187 i. Clair Glines[8] Bender, died 1987.

904. Ora[7] Christner (Urias Jonas[6], Jonas Yone[5], Joseph "Zep"[4], Johannes John Hans[3], Christian[2], Christen[1])[3975] was born 15 Jan 1898 in Connellsville, Fayette Co., PA, and died 15 Nov 1927 in Meyersdale, Somerset Co., PA. She married **Brown**.

Notes for Ora Christner:
Ora died at age 27 from injurys she received when her husband knocked her down a stairway.

More About Ora Christner:
Residence: 1920, Summit, Somerset Co., PA[3975]

Children of Ora Christner and Brown are:
   2188 i. Dorothy[8] Brown.
   2189 ii. George Brown.
   2190 iii. Helen Brown.
   2191 iv. Kathern Brown.

906. Karl J.[7] Christner (Urias Jonas[6], Jonas Yone[5], Joseph "Zep"[4], Johannes John Hans[3], Christian[2], Christen[1])[3976] was born 14 Jul 1899 in Meyersdale, Somerset Co., PA[3976,3977], and died 04 Sep 1967 in Meyersdale, Somerset Co., PA. He married **(1) Sallie Emma Gnagey**[3978] 24 Dec 1920 in Meyersdale, PA by Rev.T.R.Coffman, daughter of Daniel Gnagey and Civilla Saylor. She was born 06 Feb 1899 in Sipesville, Somerset, PA[3979,3980], and died 11 Jun 1980 in Berlin, Somerset, PA[3981]. He married **(2) Gladys M. Miller Hillegas** 11 Dec 1955 in Cumberland, Allegany Co., MD.

Notes for Karl J. Christner:
SS#;209-10-3807 Iss PA   Last address 15552 Meyersdale PA.

Obituary: Karl J. CHRISTNER, 1967, Meyersdale, Somerset County, PA - Meyersdale Republican, September 7, 1967

Karl J. Christner, 68, Meyersdale RD 1, died September 4 in his home.
Born July 14, 1899, in Meyersdale, he was a son of the late Urias and Sevilla (Coleman) Christner. He is survived by his wife, the former Gladys Miller, and three daughters: Mrs. Hilda Fink and Mrs. Anna Bertha Adams, both of Somerset: and Mrs. Bette Firl, Meyersdale RD 2; also 16 grandchildren. Four stepchildren also survive: Mrs. Ella Herak, Prospect Heights, Ill.; Zelma, wife of Francis Bittner Jr., Meyersdale RD 2; Mrs. Joanne Jrocano, Cleveland; and Clyde W. Hillegas, Edmons, WA. He was a brother of Orlan Christner and Mrs. Ula Kapphan, both of Pittsburgh; Steward A., MacMurray (Pa.); Urie of Coraopolis; Paul J., Meyersdale RD 3; Mrs. Freda Forrest, Meyersdale; and Mrs. Lucy C. Wright, Frostburg RD 2. Funeral service was held at Price Funeral Home, Meyersdale, on Wednesday morning, with Rev. William Snell officiating. Interment was made in Greenville Lutheran Cemetery.

More About Karl J. Christner:

Burial: Greenville Luthern Cemetery Salisbury PA
Christened: Brethern
Residence: 1930, Summit, Somerset Co., PA[3982]
Social Security Number: 209-10-3807/[3983]
SSN issued: PA[3983]

Notes for Sallie Emma Gnagey:

More About Sallie Emma Gnagey:
Residence: 1930, Summit, Somerset Co., PA[3984]
Social Security Number: 194-40-8816/[3985]
SSN issued: Connellsville, Fayette Co., PA[3985]

More About Gladys M. Miller Hillegas:
Burial: Greenville Luthern Cemetery Salisbury PA

Children of Karl Christner and Sallie Gnagey are:
+   2192   i.   Hilda Marie[8] Christner, born 24 Nov 1922 in Summit Twp.Somerset Co., PA; died Jul 2009 in Johnstown, Cambria Co., PA.
+   2193   ii.   Bette Lucile Christner, born 25 Oct 1926 in Meyersdale, Somerset Co., PA.
+   2194   iii.   Anna Bertha Christner, born 20 Jul 1936 in Meyerdale, Somerset Co., PA.

907.   **Stewart A.**[7] **Christner** (Urias Jonas[6], Jonas Yone[5], Joseph "Zep"[4], Johannes John Hans[3], Christian[2], Christen[1])[3986] was born 21 Feb 1901 in Connellsville, Fayette Co., PA[3986,3987], and died 13 Sep 1969 in Connellsville, Fayette Co., PA. He married **Francis Margaret Barnum**. She was born 02 Feb 1904[3988,3989], and died 11 Jan 1981 in Ballston Spa, Saratoga Co., NY[3990].

Notes for Stewart A. Christner:
This info came from Stewarts brother Paul. Stewart had 2 children but we only have a name of one child. Some records show him as Steward he had his name changed.

SS#193-10-0868 ISS PA

More About Stewart A. Christner:
Burial: Oak Springs Cem, Canonsburg, PA
Residence: 1930, Brentwood, Allegheny, PA[3991]
Social Security Number: 193-10-0868/[3992,3993]
SSN issued: PA[3994]

More About Francis Margaret Barnum:
Burial: Oak Springs Cem, Canonsburg, PA
Residence: 1930, Brentwood, Allegheny, PA[3995]
Social Security Number: 186-30-1142/[3996]
SSN issued: Connellsville, Fayette Co., PA[3996]

Children of Stewart Christner and Francis Barnum are:
+   2195   i.   Stewart Norman[8] Christner, born 27 Dec 1930 in McMurray, PA; died 04 Oct 2012 in SC.
     2196   ii.   Penny Christner, born 04 Jun 1942 in Canonsburg, PA; died 05 Jun 1942.

908.   **Freda**[7] **Christner** (Urias Jonas[6], Jonas Yone[5], Joseph "Zep"[4], Johannes John Hans[3], Christian[2], Christen[1]) was born 19 Nov 1902 in Meyersdale, Summit Twp., Somerset Co., PA[3997,3998], and died 03 Jun 1978 in Meyersdale, Somerset Co., PA. She married **Lloyd Forrest**. He was born 04 Jun 1898 in Meyersdale, Summit Twp., Somerset Co., PA[3998], and died 06 Nov 1968 in Meyersdale, Summit Twp., Somerset Co., PA[3998].

More About Freda Christner:
Burial: Union Cemetery, Meyersdale, Somerset Co., PA
Residence: 1930, Meyersdale, Somerset Co., PA[3998]
Social Security Number: 211-44-7242/[3999]
SSN issued: PA[3999]

More About Lloyd Forrest:
Residence: 1900, Summit, Somerset Co., PA[4000]

Children of Freda Christner and Lloyd Forrest are:
   2197   i.   Donald[8] Forrest.
   2198   ii.   Mary Louise Forrest.
   2199   iii. Ruth Elizabeth Forrest[4001], born 08 Mar 1922[4002,4003]; died 19 Nov 2005 in Meyersdale, Somerset Co.,
                 PA[4004].

                 More About Ruth Elizabeth Forrest:
                 Residence: 1930, Meyersdale, Somerset Co., PA[4004]

910. Ula[7] Christner (Urias Jonas[6], Jonas Yone[5], Joseph "Zep"[4], Johannes John Hans[3], Christian[2],
Christen[1])[4005,4006] was born 19 Aug 1906 in PA[4007,4008], and died 11 Nov 1980 in Pittsburgh, Allegheny Co.,
PA[4009]. She married **Albert Thomas Kapphan**. He was born 30 Jan 1908 in Pittsburgh, Allegheny Co., PA[4010],
and died 30 Dec 1960 in Pittsburg, Allegheny Co., PA[4010].

More About Ula Christner:
Burial: Allegheny, Memorial, Pittsburg, PA
Residence: 1920, Summit, Somerset Co., PA[4011]
Social Security Number: 187-26-5052/[4012]
SSN issued: Connellsville, Fayette Co., PA[4012]

More About Albert Thomas Kapphan:
Residence: 1920, Pittsburgh, Allegheny Co., PA[4013]

Child of Ula Christner and Albert Kapphan is:
   2200   i.   Carol[8] Kapphan.

913. Lucy Catherine[7] Christner (Urias Jonas[6], Jonas Yone[5], Joseph "Zep"[4], Johannes John Hans[3],
Christian[2], Christen[1]) was born 26 Mar 1912 in Meyersdale, Somerset Co., PA, and died 20 Oct 2001. She
married **Samuel Wright**[4014] 31 Dec 1931 in Cumberland, Allegany Co., MD. He was born 06 Aug 1902 in
Johnsons, Allegany Co., MD[4014], and died 12 Feb 1966[4014].

Notes for Samuel Wright:
Samuel is the son of John C. Wright and Eliza Meese Wright. He was a carpenter and a farmer.

More About Samuel Wright:
Burial: Greenville Cemetery, Meyersdale, Somerset Co., PA
Christened: Luthern

Children of Lucy Christner and Samuel Wright are:
   2201   i.   Joan C.[8] Wright, born 07 Sep 1932 in Garrett Co., MD.
   2202   ii.   John E. Wright, born 26 Dec 1933 in Garrett Co., MD.
   2203   iii. Karaha Jean Wright, born 18 Jan 1939 in Garrett Co., MD.
   2204   iv.   Gary A. Wright, born 04 Sep 1941 in Garrett Co., MD.
   2205   v.   David S. Wright, born 21 May 1944 in Garrett Co., MD.

914. Urias Bud[7] Christner (Urias Jonas[6], Jonas Yone[5], Joseph "Zep"[4], Johannes John Hans[3], Christian[2],

Christen[1])[4015] was born 20 Jul 1914 in Meyersdale, Somerset Co., PA, and died 12 Jan 1974 in Sewickley Valley Hospital. He married **Fern Swartzwelder**. She died Oct 1994.

Notes for Urias Bud Christner:
SS#211-05-7884 ISS PA   SS has death date of Jan.1974

OBIT: Urie "Bud" CHRISTNER, 1974, native of Meyersdale, Somerset County, PA - Meyersdale Republican, January 17, 1974

Urie (Bud) Christner, 59, of Moon Township RD 3, died Jan. 12, 1974, in Sewickley Valley Hospital. Born July 20, 1914, in Meyersdale, he was a son of Urias and Sebilla (Coleman) Christner.

Surviving are his wife, the former M. Fern Swartzwelder; two sons, James A. of South Heights and Robert G, of Aliquippa; four grandchildren; three sisters, Mrs. Freda Forrest, Meyersdale; Mrs. Ula Kapphan, Pittsburgh; and Mrs. Lucy Wright, Frostburg; and two brothers, Paul Christner, Salisbury; and Orlin of Deltona, FL.

He was a member of Aliquippa United Methodist Church; and F & AM 674 of Coraopolis. Funeral service was held Tuesday at Copeland Funeral Home, Coraopolis, with Rev. Richard Sanford officiating. Interment in Sylvania Hills, Rochester, PA.

More About Urias Bud Christner:
Burial: Coraopolis, PA
Residence: 1920, Summit, Somerset Co., PA[4015]
Social Security Number: 211-05-7884/[4015]
SSN issued: Connellsville, Fayette Co., PA[4015]

Children of Urias Christner and Fern Swartzwelder are:
    2206   i.   James[8] Christner.
    2207   ii.   Robert G. Christner.

915. Paul Jacob[7] Christner (Urias Jonas[6], Jonas Yone[5], Joseph "Zep"[4], Johannes John Hans[3], Christian[2], Christen[1]) was born 22 Jul 1916 in Meyersdale, Somerset Co., PA, and died 24 Mar 1988 in Salisbury, Somerset Co., PA. He married **Anna Bertha Gnagey** 05 Jun 1937 in Accident, Garrett Co., MD. She was born 17 Oct 1915 in Meyersdale, Somerset Co., PA, and died 02 Apr 2003 in Hartford City, CT.

Notes for Paul Jacob Christner:
Paul gave me this info himself. He sold coal in Summit Mills. PA. Being very industrious he also had his own roofing,spouting,and painting business. The last business he had was a contract earth moving for General Telephone Co. with his own Backhoes. He also owned a farm in Summit Mills where he enjoyed raising Beef Cattle.

Paul served in the U.S. Army 83rd infantry in Europe during WWII participating in the 3rd wave of the invasion of France, also in the battle of central France, Luxemborg, Hurgan Forest. He was involved in the invasion of Germany and the battle of the bulge. Paul was wounded four times, three times by artillery,and the last time by machine gun fire, receiving ten bullet wounds.
Paul received these awards: Purple Heart, 3 oak leaves, Bronze Star for gallantry in battle, Combat infantry medal.
SS#206-03-8288 ISS PA

He authored an article in a book called "Mongst The Hills Of Somerset". He worked with light steel products & lead plus tin which they called Tinner's. He lived in the Meyersdale PA. area.

OBIT: Paul J. CHRISTNER, 1988, Salisbury, Somerset Co., PA - Daily American, March 25, 1988

Paul J. Christner, 71, Salisbury, died March 24, 1988, at Veterans Hospital, Oakland. Born July 20, 1916, in

Summit Township, a son of the late Urias J. and Sevilla (Coleman) Christner. Survived by his wife, the former Anna Bertha Gnagey; daughter, Mrs. Trudy Hetrick, Bridgeport, W.Va.; and two grandsons. Brother of Mrs. Lucy Wright, Frostburg, MD. He was a veteran of the U.S. Army, WWII a member of the American Legion and the VFW. Friends will be received 7-9 p.m. Friday at Price Funeral Home, Meyersdale. Memorial service will be conducted noon Saturday at Meyersdale Church of the Brethren, with Pastor Richard Hanley officiating. Interment in Union Cemetery. In lieu of flowers, contributions may be made to the American Heart Association.

More About Paul Jacob Christner:
Burial: Union Cemetery, Meyersdale, Somerset Co., PA
Social Security Number: 206-03-8288/[4016]
SSN issued: PA[4016]

Notes for Anna Bertha Gnagey:
Anna is the daughter of Quinter Jonas Gnagey and Catherine Grace Miller Gnagey

Obituary: CHRISTNER - Daily American, April 4, 2003

Anna Bertha "Bercy" Christner, 87, of Hartford City, IN formerly of Salisbury, died April 2, 2003 in Hartford City. Born Oct. 17, 1915 in Meyersdale. A daughter of the late Quinter and Kate Grace (Miller) Gnagey. Also preceded in death by her husband Paul J. Christner, March 24,
1988 and a brother Robert Gnagey. Survived by daughter, Trudy K. wife of Marvin K. Hetrick, Hartford City, Ind.; two grandchildren, David P. Hetrick and Ronald L. Hetrick and his wife Kim; three great-grandchildren, Alex P. Hetrick, Jake A. Hetrick and Elizabeth G. Hetrick. A sister of Arlene wife of Richard Beal, Ashtabula, Ohio. A member of the Meyersdale Church of the Brethren. Bercy lived in Salisbury from 1969 to August 2000 at which time she moved to Hartford City so that she could be near her daughter Trudy and her family. Friends will be received 2 to 4 and 7 to 9 p.m. Friday at the Price Funeral Home, Meyersdale. A memorial service will be conducted 11 a.m. Saturday at the Meyersdale Church of the Brethren with the Rev. Michael Swick and the Rev. Randy Haulk officiating. Interment Union Cemetery, Meyersdale. Memorials may be made to Meyersdale Church of the Brethren Memorial Fund, Beachley St., Meyersdale, PA 15552.

Child of Paul Christner and Anna Gnagey is:
+   2208   i.   Trudy Kay[8] Christner, born 03 Jul 1943 in Meyersdale, Somerset Co., PA.

919. Leta M.[7] Christner (Charles[6], Jonas Yone[5], Joseph "Zep"[4], Johannes John Hans[3], Christian[2], Christen[1]) was born 18 Oct 1906 in Monroe, NE. She married **Elmer J. Martin** 25 Jan 1928 in Torrington, WY. He was born 17 Jul 1909 in Harrison, NE.

Notes for Leta M. Christner:
1930 censes shows Leta M. and her daughter Bonnie Jeanne Martin living with Charles,Goldie,Airial,Dale, and Fern at Spoon Buttes, Goshen WY.

Notes for Elmer J. Martin:
Elmer is the son of Joe and Sena Northnea Martin.
13357 Hochstedler/Stutzman
Elmer is a union mechanic.

Children of Leta Christner and Elmer Martin are:
    2209   i.   Bonnie Jeanne[8] Martin, born 27 Dec 1928.
    2210   ii.   Evadna JoAnne Martin, born 07 Mar 1931.

921. Dale Wilber[7] Christner (Charles[6], Jonas Yone[5], Joseph "Zep"[4], Johannes John Hans[3], Christian[2], Christen[1]) was born 07 Nov 1909 in Monroe, NE[4017], and died 30 Sep 1992 in Hi Desert Medical Center, Joshua Tree, CA. He married **Ruth Hope Lockhart**[4018] 22 Jun 1937. She was born 19 Jun 1921 in Troy, NY[4018,4019], and died 15 Apr 1981 in Los Angeles Co., CA[4020].

Notes for Dale Wilber Christner:
His son Ron thinks his name was Wilber Dale not Dale Wilber, but death Certificate states Dale Wilber.

Birth: Nov. 7, 1909
Death: Sep. 30, 1992

Spouse: Ruth Hope Lockhart Christner (1921 - 1981)

Inscription: BELOVED - HUSBAND-FATHER-GRANDFATHER

Burial: Twentynine Palms Cemetery, Twentynine Palms, San Bernardino Co., CA
Plot: Row 14A, lot 19, site 1
Find A Grave Memorial# 94569198

More About Dale Wilber Christner:
Burial: 29 Palms Cemetery, 29 Palms, San Bernardino Co., CA
Residence: 1991, 57460 Irway ct./Yucca Valley, San Bernardino, California, USA[4021]
Social Security Number: 508-07-7655/[4022]
SSN issued: NE[4022]

Notes for Ruth Hope Lockhart:
Birth: Jun. 19, 1921
Death: Apr. 15, 1981

Spouse: Dale Wilbur Christner (1909 - 1992)

Inscription: BELOVED WIFE-MOTHER-GRANDMOTHER
THE LORD IS MY SHEPHERD

Burial: Twentynine Palms Cemetery, Twentynine Palms, San Bernardino Co., PA
Plot: Row 14A, lot 19, site 2
Find A Grave Memorial# 94569245

More About Ruth Hope Lockhart:
Burial: 29 Palms Cemetery, 29 Palms, San Bernardino Co., CA
Other-Begin: Yucca Valley, San Bernardino Co., CA[4023]
Social Security Number: 507-18-5601/[4023]
SSN issued: NE[4023]

Children of Dale Christner and Ruth Lockhart are:
+   2211   i.   Ronald Dale[8] Christner, born 18 Apr 1938 in Lincoln, Lancaster Co., NE.
     2212   ii. Lorna Sue Christner[4024], born 05 Aug 1947; died 30 Jul 2005 in Las Vegas, Clark Co., NV[4024]. She
                      married (1) Jan Stacey. She married (2) Ken Crain. She married (3) Bill Kibridge. She married (4) Jan
                      H Kapustka[4025] 28 Mar 1964 in San Bernardino Co., CA[4025]; born 1943[4025].

                      More About Lorna Sue Christner:
                      Residence: 1981, Yucca Valley, San Bernardino, California, USA[4026]

     922. Linda[7] **Christner** (Calvin M.[6], Jonas Yone[5], Joseph "Zep"[4], Johannes John Hans[3], Christian[2],
Christen[1]) was born Dec 1888 in Somerset Co., PA[4027]. She married **Eli W. Weirner**. He was born 21 Sep
1880, and died 20 Apr 1975 in Meyerdale, Somerset Co., , PA.

More About Linda Christner:
Residence: 1900, Summit, Somerset Co., PA[4027]

More About Eli W. Weirner:
Burial: White Oak Cemetery, Somerset Co., , PA

Children of Linda Christner and Eli Weirner are:
  2213   i.   Archie[8] Weirner.
  2214   ii.   Betty Weirner.
  2215   iii. Howard Weirner.
  2216   iv.   Shirley Weirner.

923. Mary Etta[7] Christner (Calvin M.[6], Jonas Yone[5], Joseph "Zep"[4], Johannes John Hans[3], Christian[2], Christen[1])[4027] was born Mar 1894 in Connellsville, Fayette Co., PA[4027], and died 20 Apr 1972 in Summit Twp., Somerset Co., PA[4027]. She married **Millen Shuck**.

More About Mary Etta Christner:
Residence: 1910, Larimer, Somerset, PA[4027]

Children of Mary Christner and Millen Shuck are:
  2217   i.   Ada[8] Shuck.
  2218   ii.   Carl Shuck.
  2219   iii. Jaunita Shuck.
  2220   iv.   Pauline Shuck.

924. Clarence Cadalso[7] Christner (Calvin M.[6], Jonas Yone[5], Joseph "Zep"[4], Johannes John Hans[3], Christian[2], Christen[1])[4028,4029,4030] was born 09 Oct 1895 in Summit, Somerset Co., PA[4031,4032], and died 1971. He married **Mary Leona Knepp**[4033]. She was born 09 Nov 1899 in Deal, Somerset Co., PA[4033], and died 29 Jan 1994 in Berlin, Brothersvalley Township, Somerset Co., PA[4033].

Notes for Clarence Cadalso Christner:
Birth: 1891
Death: 1971

Children:
Lewis Calvin Christner (1918 - 1967)
Clarence Eugene Christner (1924 - 1988)
Ruth Arlene Christner Stone (1930 - 2005)

Burial: White Oak Cemetery, Wittenberg, Somerset Co., PA

More About Clarence Cadalso Christner:
Burial: White Oak Cem, PA
Residence: 1910, Larimer, Somerset, PA[4034,4035]

Notes for Mary Leona Knepp:
Birth: Nov. 9, 1899
Somerset Co., PA

Death: Jan. 29, 1994
Berlin, Somerset Co., PA

Children:
Lewis Calvin Christner (1918 - 1967)
Clarence Eugene Christner (1924 - 1988)
Ruth Arlene Christner Stone (1930 - 2005)

Burial: White Oak Cemetery, Wittenberg, Somerset Co., PA

Obituary: Mary Leona (KNEPP) CHRISTNER, 1994, Salisbury, Somerset Co., PA - Daily American, January 31, 1994

Mary Leona Christner, 94 of Salisbury died Jan. 29, 1994, at Maple
Mountain Manor Nursing Home, Berlin. Born Nov. 9, 1899, at Deal, PA she was a daughter of the late Lewis
and Agnes (Suder) Knepp. Preceded in death by her husband, Clarence C. Christner, and 3 sons - Lewis, Lester
and Eugene Christner. She was the last surviving member of a family of 11 children. She was a homemaker and
member of St. John's United Church of Christ, Salisbury. Survivors include a daughter, Ruth A. Stone, Salisbury;
9 grandchildren and 9 great-grandchildren. Friends will be received from 2 to 9 p.m. Monday at Newman Funeral
Home Inc., Salisbury. Interment will be at a later date in White Oak Cemetery, Meyersdale.

More About Mary Leona Knepp:
Burial: White Oak Cemetery, Somerset Co., PA
Residence: 1900, Saudpatch Village, Somerset, PA[4036]

Children of Clarence Christner and Mary Knepp are:
    2221   i.   Lester L.[8] Christner.

                    Notes for Lester L. Christner:
                    Frostburg RD 2 PA.

+   2222   ii.   Lewis Calvin Christner, born 26 Aug 1918 in Meyersdale, Somerset Co., PA; died 05 May 1967 in
                    Morgantown, Monongalia Co., WV.
    2223   iii.   Clarence Eugene Christner, born 07 Jul 1924 in Sand Patch, Somerset Co., PA; died 18 Aug 1988 in
                    Salisbury, Somerset Co., PA. He married Joann Bitner; born 20 Nov 1926 in Meyerdale, Somerset Co.,
                    PA; died 04 Mar 2002 in Johnstown, Cambria Co., PA.

                    Notes for Clarence Eugene Christner:
                    Obituary: Clarence Eugene "Gene" CHRISTNER, 1988, Salisbury, Somerset Co., PA - Daily American,
                    August 20, 1988
                    Clarence Eugene "Gene" Christner, 64, of Salisbury, died Aug. 18, 1988, at home. Born July 7, 1924,
                    in Sand Patch, son of Mary L. (Knepp) Christner of Berlin and the late Clarence C. Christner. Also
                    preceded in death by a brother, Lewis Christner. Besides his mother, also survived by his wife, the
                    former Joan Bittner; and two sons, Terry and Gary Christner, both of Salisbury; a granddaughter, Kelly
                    Jo Christner; one sister, Mrs. Ruth Stone, Salisbury; and one brother, Lester, Finzel, Md. He was the
                    owner and operator of Chris' Tavern of Salisbury and a former superintendent for the Manley Sand
                    Company of Cumberland, Md., for 23 years. He was a member of the Mt. Carmel Lutheran Church. He
                    was a veteran of World War II.

                    Member of Salisbury American Legion, D.A.V. of Meyersdale and the Meyersdale Elks, No. 1951.
                    Friends will be received Saturday, 2-4 and 7-9 p.m., at the Thomas Funeral Home, Salisbury, where
                    funeral service will be held Sunday at 4 p.m. with the Rev. David E. Fetter officiating. Internment,
                    White Oak Cemetery.

                    Birth: Jul. 7, 1924
                    Sand Patch, Somerset Co., PA
                    Death: Aug. 18, 1988
                    Salisbury, Somerset Co., PA

                    Parents:
                    Clarence C. Christner (1891 - 1971)
                    Mary Leona Knepp Christner (1899 - 1994)

                    Spouse: Joann Bittner Christner (1926 - 2002)

                    Burial: White Oak Cemetery, Wittenberg, Somerset Co., PA
                    Find A Grave Memorial# 73088496

                    Notes for Joann Bitner:
                    Birth: Oct. 20, 1926
                    Meyersdale, Somerset Co., PA
                    Death: May 4, 2002
                    Johnstown, Cambria Co., PA

Spouse: Clarence Eugene Christner (1924 - 1988)

Burial: White Oak Cemetery, Wittenberg Somerset Co., PA

2224   iv.   Ruth Arlene Christner, born 03 May 1930 in Meyersdale, Somerset Co., PA[4037]; died 17 Mar 2005 in Meyersdale, Somerset Co., PA. She married Wayne F. Stone[4038]; born 04 Jan 1926 in sand Patch, Somerset Co., PA[4038]; died 02 May 1995 in Meyersdale, Somerset Co., PA.

Notes for Ruth Arlene Christner:
Meyersdale PA We thought her name was Annebell born 1924 but this info maybe was for her brother Lewis's wife.

Birth: May 3, 1930
Meyersdale, Somerset Co., PA
Death: Mar. 17, 2005
Meyersdale, Somerset Co., PA

Parents:
Clarence C. Christner (1891 - 1971)
Mary Leona Knepp Christner (1899 - 1994)

Spouse: Wayne F. Stone (1926 - 1995)

Burial: White Oak Cemetery, Wittenberg, Somerset Co., PA

More About Ruth Arlene Christner:
Burial: White Oak Cemetery, Somerset Co., PA
SSN issued: PA[4039]

Notes for Wayne F. Stone:
Birth: Jan. 4, 1926 - Sand Patch, Somerset Co., PA
Death: May 2, 1995 - Meyersdale, Somerset Co., PA

Served in World War II

Spouse: Ruth Arlene Christner Stone (1930 - 2005)

Burial: White Oak Cemetery, Wittenberg, Somerset Co., PA

More About Wayne F. Stone:
Social Security Number: 205-16-0202/[4040]
SSN issued: PA[4040]

925. Walter C.[7] Christner (Calvin M.[6], Jonas Yone[5], Joseph "Zep"[4], Johannes John Hans[3], Christian[2], Christen[1])[4041] was born 14 Jan 1899 in Meyersdale, Somerset Co., PA[4041], and died 27 Dec 1975 in Meyersdale, Somerset Co., PA. He married **Lydia Smith**. She was born 18 Mar 1904 in PA, and died 1990.

Notes for Walter C. Christner:
Birth: 1904
PA
Death: 1990

Spouse: Walter C. Christner (1899 - 1975)

Burial: White Oak Cemetery, Wittenberg, Somerset Co., PA

More About Walter C. Christner:
Residence: 1910, Larimer, Somerset, PA[4041]

Notes for Lydia Smith:

Birth: 1904
PA
Death: 1990

Spouse: Walter C. Christner (1899 - 1975)

Burial: White Oak Cemetery, Wittenberg, Somerset Co., PA

Children of Walter Christner and Lydia Smith are:
+   2225   i.   Norma Alberta[8] Christner, born 29 Mar 1924 in Wittenberg, Somerset Co., PA; died 18 Feb 1983 in Cumberland, Allegany Co., MD.
+   2226   ii.   JoAnn Christner, born 06 May 1931 in Wittenburg, PA.

927. Sadie Sarah[7] Christner (Calvin M.[6], Jonas Yone[5], Joseph "Zep"[4], Johannes John Hans[3], Christian[2], Christen[1])[4041] was born 31 Oct 1903 in Larimer Twp., Somerset Co., PA[4041], and died 1951 in Hollsopple, Conemaugh Twp., Somerset Co., PA[4041]. She married **Joseph Jesse Lint**[4042] 1924 in Somerset Co., PA[4042]. He was born 15 Apr 1904 in Greenville Twp., Somerset Co., PA[4042], and died 06 Nov 1985 in Beaver Co., PA[4042].

More About Sadie Sarah Christner:
Buried at: Union Cemetery, Meyersdale, Somerset Co., PA/[4043]
Married: once[4044]
Occupation: housewife/[4045]
Point of Contact: Gary Lint[4046]
Residence: 1930, Conemaugh, Somerset Co., PA[4047]

More About Joseph Jesse Lint:
Buried at: Union Cemetery, Meyersdale, Somerset Co., PA[4048]
Children: six (6)[4048]
Last entry date: 18 Mar1998 by GBL[4048]
Married: once[4048]
Point of Contact: Greg Lint[4048]
Religion: German Baptist Church[4048]

Child of Sadie Christner and Joseph Lint is:
  2227   i.   Joseph Jay[8] Lint[4048], born 24 Sep 1930 in Brøderbund Family Archive #110, Vol. 1, Ed. 3, Social Security Records: U.S., SS Death Benefit Records, Surnames Beginning with L, Date of Import: 8 Apr 1996, Internal Ref. #1.111.3.127742.114/Conemaugh Twp., Somerset Co., PA[4048]; died 22 Apr 1978 in Brøderbund Family Archive #110, Vol. 1, Ed. 3, Social Security Records: U.S., SS Death Benefit Records, Surnames Beginning with L, Date of Import: 8 Apr 1996, Internal Ref. #1.111.3.127742.114/Cleveland, Cuyahoga co., Ohio[4048].

        More About Joseph Jay Lint:
        Buried at: Twinsburg, Ohio (?)[4048]
        Children: uncertain[4048]
        Coded sources: 9 (Gary & Greg Lint), 5, 29 (PRL), 3[4048]
        Last entry date: 20 Dec 1997 by GBL[4048]
        Married: at least once[4048]
        Military service: unknown[4048]
        Occupation: unknown[4048]
        Point of Contact: Greg Lint[4048]
        Religion: unknown[4048]
        Social Security: 200-24-4372[4048]
        Tombstone: unknown[4048]

929. Miles E[7] Christner (Calvin M.[6], Jonas Yone[5], Joseph "Zep"[4], Johannes John Hans[3], Christian[2], Christen[1])[4049] was born 1908 in Connellsville, Fayette Co., PA[4049]. He married **Twila**.

More About Miles E Christner:
Residence: 1910, Larimer, Somerset, PA*4049*

Child of Miles Christner and Twila is:
  2228   i. Richard[8] Christner.

932. Ralph[7] Christner (Rufus J.[6], Jonas Yone[5], Joseph "Zep"[4], Johannes John Hans[3], Christian[2], Christen[1])[4050,4051,4052,4053,4054] was born 27 Feb 1897 in Coal Run, Somerset Co., PA[4055], and died 16 Mar 1985 in Akron, Summit Co., OH[4056]. He married **Sadie Alma Yoder**[4057,4058] 17 Jul 1928 in Cumberland, Allegany Co., MD. She was born 18 Apr 1910 in Salisbury, Somerset Co., PA[4059,4060], and died 01 Dec 1972 in Meyersdale, Somerset Co., PA[4061,4062].

Notes for Ralph Christner:
Obituary: Ralph Christner 1985, formerly of Meyersdale, Somerset County, PA - Daily American, March 18, 1985

Ralph Christner, 88 Akron, OH formerly of Meyersdale RD 1, died March 16, 1985, in Cuyahoga Falls, OH General Hospital. Born Feb. 27, 1897 in Rockwood, son of late Rufus and Susan (Marker) Christner. Preceded in death by wife, former Sadie A. Yoder, and daughter, Betty. Survived by three sons: Ray S., Jack A. and James C., all of Akron, OH; two daughters: Mrs. Eva M. Hotchkiss, Mogadore, OH and Mrs. Janet R. Gilpin, Akron, OH; sister, Mrs. Vila Silvrants, Denver, CO; also 18 grandchildren and 14 great-grandchildren. Retired coal miner. Veteran of World War I. Friends will be received from 2-4 and 7-9 p.m. Monday (today) at Thomas Funeral Home, Salisbury, where service will be held at 2 p.m. Tuesday, the Rev. Elam C. Bender officiating. Interment, St. Paul Cemetery.

More About Ralph Christner:
Burial: St. Paul Cemetery, Elk Lick, Somerset Co., PA*4063*
Residence: 1900, Summit Township (South Part), Somerset Co., PA*4064*
Social Security Number: 163-14-2491/*4065*
SSN issued: PA*4065*

Notes for Sadie Alma Yoder:
Sadie Alma is the daughter of Abraham J. and Nellie Hawn Yoder

OBIT: Sadie Yoder CHRISTNER, 1972, Meyersdale, Somerset County, PA - Meyersdale Republican, December 7, 1972

MRS. RALPH CHRISTNER

Mrs. Sadie Christner, 62, of Meyersdale RD 1, died Dec. 1, 1972 in Memorial Hospital, Cumberland.

Born in Somerset County, April 17, 1910 she was a daughter of the late Abraham and Nellie (Hahn) Yoder. Surviving are her husband, Ralph Christner; sons, Ray, Jack and James, all of Akron, Ohio; daughters, Mrs. Leroy Christner, Meyersdale RD 1; Mrs. David Hotchkiss, Mogadore, Ohio; Mrs. Grady Gilpin, Akron, Ohio; 18 grandchildren, one great-grandchild; four brothers, Arthur and Charles Yoder, Baltimore, Md.; Melvin Yoder, Friedens; and Albert Yoder, Salisbury; and a sister, Mrs. James Blubaugh, Akron, OH.

Funeral service was conducted Monday afternoon in Konhaus Funeral Home, Meyersdale, with Rev. Lloyd Sechriest officiating. Interment in St. Paul's Cemetery.

More About Sadie Alma Yoder:
Residence: 1920, Fairhaven, Huron Co., MI*4066*
Social Security Number: 190-30-2730/*4067*
SSN issued: Connellsville, Fayette Co., PA*4067*

Children of Ralph Christner and Sadie Yoder are:

+ 2229   i.   Ray Sandow[8] Christner Sr., born 20 Jan 1929 in Somerset Co., PA; died 11 Oct 2004 in Akron, Summit Co., OH.
+ 2230   ii.   Betty Dean Christner, born 02 Jun 1930 in Summitt Twp., Somerset Co., PA; died 30 Oct 1975 in Cumberland, Cumberland Co., MD.
+ 2231   iii.   Jack Allen Christner, born 28 Jul 1934 in Meyersdale, Somerset Co., PA.
+ 2232   iv.   Eva Marie Christner, born 14 Jun 1936 in Meyersdale, Somerset Co., PA; died 22 Apr 2003 in Grand Rapids, Kent Co., MI.
+ 2233   v.   Janet Ruth Christner, born 17 Apr 1943 in Meyersdale, Somerset Co., PA.
+ 2234   vi.   James Cornett Christner, born 29 Aug 1945 in Meyersdale, Somerset Co., PA.

941. Harrison Simon[7] Pritts (Mary Ann[6] Christner, Moses C.[5], Joseph "Zep"[4], Johannes John Hans[3], Christian[2], Christen[1])[4068,4069,4070,4071,4072] was born 13 Oct 1859 in Black Twp., PA[4073], and died 11 Mar 1948 in Rockwood (Wilson Creek), Somerset, PA[4074,4075,4076]. He married **(1) Barbara Ellen Romesburg**[4077] 1880 in Somerset Co., PA. She was born 17 Feb 1865 in Somerset Co., PA[4077], and died 12 Mar 1902 in Black Twp., Somerset, PA[4077,4078]. He married **(2) Emma Mathilda Rector**[4079] 1910[4080], daughter of Jacob Rector and Sarah Cunningham. She was born 1857 in Somerset Co., PA[4081], and died 1938 in Age at Death: 80/Black, Somerset Co., PA[4082].

Notes for Harrison Simon Pritts:
They had at least one son Charles born Aug 10 1884 in Black Twp., PA. His middle or first name maybe Simon.

Birth: 1860
Death: 1848

Inscription: "At Rest"

Burial: Hauger Church Cemetery, Blackfield, Somerset Co., PA

More About Harrison Simon Pritts:
Burial: Sanner Church, Rockwood, PA
Residence: 1870, closest post office./Somerset, Somerset, Pennsylvania[4082]

Notes for Barbara Ellen Romesburg:
Inscription: "At Rest"

Burial: Hauger Church Cemetery, Blackfield, Somerset Co., PA

More About Barbara Ellen Romesburg:
Burial: Hauger Cemetery, Somerset, Somerset Co., PA[4083,4084]
Residence: 1900, Casselman borough, Somerset, PA[4084]

More About Emma Mathilda Rector:
Burial: Rockwood IOOF Cemetery; Find A Grave Memorial# 96451147; headstone photo posted to memorial page./Somerset Co., PA[4085]
Residence: 1930, Age: 71; Marital Status: Married; Relation to Head of House: Wife/Black, Somerset, Pennsylvania[4085]

Children of Harrison Pritts and Barbara Romesburg are:

+ 2235   i.   Charles A. "Cappy"[8] Pritts, born 10 Aug 1884 in Black Twp., Somerset Co., PA; died 26 Aug 1966 in Meyersdale Community Hospital, Somerset Co., PA.
   2236   ii.   George Pritts[4086,4087], born 13 Jan 1886 in Somerset Co., PA[4088,4089]; died 25 Aug 1968 in Rockwood, Somerset Co., PA[4089]. He married Annie G; born 1888; died 1961.

         Notes for George Pritts:
         Birth: 1886
         Death: 1968

Spouse: Annie G. Pritts (1888 - 1961)

Burial: Rockwood IOOF Cemetery, Rockwood, Somerset Co., PA
Find A Grave Memorial# 96705226

More About George Pritts:
Burial: Rockwood IOOF Cemetery, Somerset Co., PA[4090]
Social Security Number: 206-01-6857/[4091]
SSN issued: Pittsburgh, Allegheny Co., PA[4091]

Notes for Annie G:
Birth: 1888
Death: 1961

Spouse: George B. Pritts (1886 - 1968)

Burial: Rockwood IOOF Cemetery, Rockwood, Somerset Co., PA
Find A Grave Memorial# 96705245

2237	iii.	James Clarence Pritts[4092], born 06 Sep 1887 in Black Twp., Somerset Co., PA[4092]; died 22 Jan 1968 in Franklin, Gloucester Co., NJ[4092].
+ 2238	iv.	Irene "Grace" Pritts, born 19 Mar 1889 in Black Twp., Somerset Co., PA; died 13 Mar 1986 in Rockwood, Somerset Co., PA.
2239	v.	Joseph Pritts[4092], born 27 Dec 1890 in Somerset Co., PA[4092]; died 15 Apr 1905 in Black Twp., Somerset Co., PA[4092].

Notes for Joseph Pritts:
Birth: Dec. 28, 1890
Death: Apr. 15, 1905

Inscription: "Son of H & E Pritts"

Burial: Hauger Church Cemetery, Blackfield, Somerset Co., PA

More About Joseph Pritts:
Burial: Hauger Cemetery, Rockwood, Somerset Co., PA[4092]

2240	vi.	Irvin Milton Pritts[4092], born 17 Feb 1893 in Rockwood, (Wilson Creek), Somerset Co., PA[4092]; died 07 Aug 1933 in Rockwood, (Wilson Creek), Somerset Co., PA[4092].

More About Irvin Milton Pritts:
Burial: Rockwood IOOF Cemetery, Somerset Co., PA[4092]

+ 2241	vii.	Elmer Isreal Pritts, born 02 Oct 1894 in Black Twp., Somerset Co., PA; died 22 Nov 1983 in Somerset, Somerset Co, PA.
2242	viii.	Mary Pearl Pritts[4092], born 18 Nov 1896 in Somerset Co., PA[4092]; died 06 Sep 1965[4092].

More About Mary Pearl Pritts:
Burial: Somerset Memorial Park, Somerset, Somerset, PA[4092]

2243	ix.	Nellie Mae Pritts[4092], born 31 Mar 1899 in Black Twp., Somerset Co., PA[4092]; died 09 Nov 1986 in Somerset, Somerset, PA[4092].

More About Nellie Mae Pritts:
Burial: Somereset Co. Memorial Park, Somerset, PA[4092]

2244	x.	Alice May Pritts[4092], born 30 Mar 1900[4092]; died 31 Oct 1900[4092].
2245	xi.	Infant Pritts[4092], born 1902[4092]; died 1902[4092].

942. Catherine Amanda[7] Pritts (Mary Ann[6] Christner, Moses C.[5], Joseph "Zep"[4], Johannes John Hans[3],

Christian[2], Christen[1])[4093] was born 24 Feb 1862 in Summit, Somerset Co., PA[4094], and died 21 May 1926 in Connellsville, Fayette Co., PA[4095]. She married (1) Crutchfield. She married (2) William Richard Miller[4096] 03 May 1891. He was born 15 Nov 1864 in PA[4096,4097], and died 22 Dec 1937[4098,4099].

More About Catherine Amanda Pritts:
Residence: 1900, Casselman borough, Somerset, PA[4100]

Notes for William Richard Miller:
Birth: 1864
Death: 1937

Spouse: Mae A Miller (1888 - 1967)

Burial: Sanner's Lutheran Church Cemetery, Somerset Co., PA
Find A Grave Memorial# 93018028

More About William Richard Miller:
Residence: 1930, Black Twp., Somerset Co., PA[4100]

Child of Catherine Pritts and Crutchfield is:
    2246   i.   Mary Ellen[8] Crutchfield. She married Harry Baker.

Children of Catherine Pritts and William Miller are:
    2247   i.   Nellie[8] Miller.
    2248   ii.   George Miller.
    2249   iii.   William Richard Miller Jr.[4100], born 1888[4100]; died 1972[4100].

943. Jacob Lewis[7] Pritts (Mary Ann[6] Christner, Moses C.[5], Joseph "Zep"[4], Johannes John Hans[3], Christian[2], Christen[1]) was born 09 May 1865 in Somerset Co., PA[4101], and died 30 Mar 1894 in Somerset Co., PA[4102]. He married **Emma Grace Romesberg**[4103]. She was born 19 May 1869 in Somerset Co., PA[4104], and died 27 Oct 1908 in Wilsoncreek, Somerset Co., PA[4104].

More About Jacob Lewis Pritts:
Burial: Hauger Cemetery, Rockwood, Somerset Co., PA[4104]
Residence: 1870, Summit, Somerset Co, PA[4104]

More About Emma Grace Romesberg:
Burial: Hauger Cemetery, Rockwood, Somerset Co., PA[4104]
Residence: 1900, Casselman borough, Somerset, PA[4104]

Children of Jacob Pritts and Emma Romesberg are:
    2250   i.   Frank[8] Pritts[4105,4106], born Abt. 1889[4107,4108]; died 23 Apr 1901 in Somerset Co., PA[4109].

                More About Frank Pritts:
                Burial: Hauger Cemetery, Rockwood, Somerset Co., PA[4110]
                Occupation: Killed In Coal Mine At Age 11 Yrs, 10m, 14d's/[4110]

    2251   ii.   William Pritts[4111,4112], born 05 Jun 1890 in Somerset Co., PA[4113,4114]; died 21 Nov 1975 in Garrett, Somerset Co., PA[4114].

                More About William Pritts:
                Burial: 24 Nov 1975, Highland Cemetery, Garrett, Somerset Co., PA[4114]
                Residence: 1920, Brothersvalley, Somerset Co., PA[4115,4116]

    2252   iii.   Ephraim Pritts[4117], born 25 Nov 1892[4117]; died Mar 1986 in Clearfield, PA[4117].
    2253   iv.   Fannie Pritts[4117], born 18 Sep 1894 in Somerset Co., PA[4117]; died Aft. 1922[4117].

944. Irene Milissa[7] Pritts (Mary Ann[6] Christner, Moses C.[5], Joseph "Zep"[4], Johannes John Hans[3], Christian[2], Christen[1])[4118] was born 22 May 1869 in Somerset, Somerset Co., PA[4118], and died 04 Dec 1953 in Rockwood, Somerset Co., PA[4118]. She married **William F. Kincaid**[4119] 1902[4119]. He was born 12 Mar 1867 in Somerset, Somerset Co., PA[4119], and died 24 Dec 1938 in Black Twp, Somerset, PA[4120].

Notes for Irene Milissa Pritts:
Her name may be spelled Ruenna Malisa. She is buried in Sanner's Lutheran Church Cemetery.

More About Irene Milissa Pritts:
Residence: 1900, Black Twp., Somerset Co., PA[4121]

Notes for William F. Kincaid:
Buried in Sanner's Lutheran Church Cemetery.

More About William F. Kincaid:
Residence: 1880, Age: 14; Marital Status: Single; Relation to Head of House: Son/Union, Bedford, PA, United States[4122,4123]

Children of Irene Pritts and William Kincaid are:

2254   i.   George Garman[8] Kincaid[4123,4124], born 20 May 1903 in Brothersvalley, Somerset Co., PA[4125]; died 13 Jun 1984 in Somerset, Somerset Co., PA[4125].

              More About George Garman Kincaid:
              Residence: 1910, Age in 1910: 6; Marital Status: Single; Relation to Head of House: Son/Black Twp., Somerset Co., PA[4126,4127]

2255   ii.   William L. Kincaid[4127], born 1909 in Brothersvalley, Somerset Co., PA[4127,4128]; died 1919 in Somerset, Somerset Co., PA[4129].

              Notes for William L. Kincaid:
              Birth: 1909
              Death: 1919

              Parents:
              William F Kincaid (1867 - 1938)
              Irene Kincaid (1869 - 1953)

              Burial: Sanner's Lutheran Church Cemetery, Somerset Co., PA
              Find A Grave Memorial# 93019062

              More About William L. Kincaid:
              Residence: 1910, Age in 1910: 1; Marital Status: Single; Relation to Head of House: Son/Black Twp., Somerset Co., PA[4130,4131]

945. Irvin Franklin[7] Pritts (Mary Ann[6] Christner, Moses C.[5], Joseph "Zep"[4], Johannes John Hans[3], Christian[2], Christen[1])[4132] was born 05 Oct 1871 in Somerset, Somerset Co., PA[4132], and died 23 Jun 1950 in Somerset, Somerset Co., PA[4132]. He married **Elizabeth Shaffer**[4133] 31 Jul 1897. She was born Abt. 1878 in Pittsburgh, Allegheny Co., PA[4134], and died 1976.

Notes for Irvin Franklin Pritts:
Birth: Oct. 5, 1871
Death: Jun. 23, 1950

Parents:
Israel Pritts (1837 - 1904)
Mary Pritts (1841 - 1909)

Spouse: Eliza Shaffer Pritts (1878 - 1936)

Children: Israel Harmon Pritts (1898 - 1971)

Burial: Rockwood IOOF Cemetery, Rockwood, Somerset Co., PA
Find A Grave Memorial# 83307125

More About Irvin Franklin Pritts:
Residence: 1930, Black Twp., Somerset Co., PA[4134]

Notes for Elizabeth Shaffer:
Birth: 1878
Death: 1936

Parents:
Herman Shaffer (1846 - 1914)
Adaline Shaffer (1845 - 1920)

Spouse: Irvin Franklin Pritts (1871 - 1950)

Children: Israel Harmon Pritts (1898 - 1971)

Burial: Rockwood IOOF Cemetery, Rockwood, Somerset Co., PA
Find A Grave Memorial# 83307199

More About Elizabeth Shaffer:
Residence: 1920, Black Twp., Somerset Co., PA[4134]

Children of Irvin Pritts and Elizabeth Shaffer are:
+   2256   i.   Israel Harmon "Jumbo"[8] Pritts, born 26 Apr 1898; died 30 May 1971 in Rockwood, Somerset Co., PA.
     2257   ii. Harrison Jacob Pritts, born 17 Dec 1899[4135]; died Mar 1964[4135].

                    Notes for Harrison Jacob Pritts:
                    Birth: 1899
                    Death: 1964

                    Burial: Hauger Cemetery, Blackfield, Somerset Co., PA
                    Find A Grave Memorial# 98004775

                    More About Harrison Jacob Pritts:
                    Social Security Number: 209-07-5938/[4135]
                    SSN issued: Pittsburgh, Allegheny Co., PA[4135]

     2258   iii. Mary Ellen Pritts, born 1901.
     2259   iv. Catherine Pritts, born 1903.
     2260   v.   Martha Pritts, born 01 May 1905 in Black Twp., Somerset Co., PA[4136]; died 31 May 1975 in Rockwood,
                    Somerset Co., PA[4136].
     2261   vi. George Pritts, born 1906; died 1906.
     2262   vii. Iva Pritts, born 1906; died 1906.
     2263   viii. Nelson Pritts[4137], born 1909; died 1967.

                    More About Nelson Pritts:
                    Residence: 1920, Black Twp., Somerset Co., PA[4137]

     2264   ix. Lucy J. Pritts, born 1912; died 1912.
     2265   x.   Clinton T. Pritts[4138], born 29 Jan 1912[4138]; died 04 Dec 1912[4138].
     2266   xi. Luther F. Pritts[4139], born 17 May 1913[4139]; died 15 Jan 2002 in Kent, Portage Co., OH[4139].

                    More About Luther F. Pritts:
                    Social Security Number: 209-09-7738/[4139]

SSN issued: Pittsburgh, Allegheny Co., PA[4139]

946. Caroline "Carrie" Earl[7] Pritts (Mary Ann[6] Christner, Moses C.[5], Joseph "Zep"[4], Johannes John Hans[3], Christian[2], Christen[1]) was born 30 Apr 1874 in Somerset, Somerset Co., PA[4140], and died 16 Jul 1930 in Connellsville, Fayette Co., PA[4140]. She married **John Bittner**.

Children of Caroline Pritts and John Bittner are:

2267	i.	Harry[8] Bittner.
2268	ii.	Ralph Bittner.
2269	iii.	Joseph Bittner.
2270	iv.	Mary Bittner.

948. Ida Masouri[7] Pritts (Mary Ann[6] Christner, Moses C.[5], Joseph "Zep"[4], Johannes John Hans[3], Christian[2], Christen[1])[4140] was born 17 Oct 1876 in Somerset, Somerset Co., PA[4140], and died 03 Dec 1903 in Somerset, Somerset Co., PA[4140]. She married **Emery Pressler**[4141] 25 Jan 1902.

Notes for Ida Masouri Pritts:
Birth: Oct. 17, 1876
Death: Jan. 18, 1904

Inscription: "Wife of Emry Pressler"

Burial: Hauger Cemetery, Blackfield, Somerset Co., PA
Find A Grave Memorial# 29593517

More About Ida Masouri Pritts:
Residence: 1900, Black Twp., Somerset Co., PA[4142]

Children of Ida Pritts and Emery Pressler are:

2271   i.   Carrie Irene[8] Presler, born 1903 in PA[4143]; died 18 Oct 1976 in Somerset Co., PA[4143].

2272   ii.   Mary Elizabeth Presler, born 26 Nov 1903; died 02 May 1966[4144]. She married Myron R. Coughenour[4145,4146]; born 08 Mar 1901 in Pittsburgh, Allegheny Co., PA[4147]; died Jan 1972 in Charleston, Kanawha Co., WV[4147].

        Notes for Mary Elizabeth Presler:
        Died May 2 1966

        More About Mary Elizabeth Presler:
        Residence: 1930, Fairmont, Marion Co., WV[4147]

        More About Myron R. Coughenour:
        Residence: 1930, Fairmont, Marion Co., WV[4147]

950. Laura Virginia[7] Christner (Jacob M.[6], Moses C.[5], Joseph "Zep"[4], Johannes John Hans[3], Christian[2], Christen[1]) was born 29 Dec 1869, and died 27 Apr 1942. She married **Fred W. Gilland Gilliland**. He was born 02 Jun 1874 in Nauvoo, Hancock IL, and died 20 Aug 1940.

Notes for Laura Virginia Christner:
Some have her married to Freds Brother George (Dec.3 1894 at Hebron) She said her first marriage was to a man named Prophet but everyone thought it was a cover for being pregnant with Boyd. Boyd was to use the Christner name not Prophet or Gilliland.

Birth: Dec 29, 1869
Death: Mar 27, 1942

Spouse: George Winfred Gilliland (1874 - 1940)

Burial: Prairie Lawn Cemetery, Willard, Logan Co., CO
Find A Grave Memorial# 39261516

More About Laura Virginia Christner:
Burial: Willard, Colo.

More About Fred W. Gilland Gilliland:
Burial: Willard, Colorado

Child of Laura Christner and Fred Gilliland is:
+   2273   i.   Boyd[8] Christner, born 31 Aug 1890 in NE; died 1914.

951. Geneive Rebecca[7] Christner (Jacob M.[6], Moses C.[5], Joseph "Zep"[4], Johannes John Hans[3], Christian[2], Christen[1]) was born 01 Oct 1871 in Garrett, Somerset Co., PA, and died 01 Jun 1943 in Boulder, Boulder Co., CO. She married **Obedia Stark Muckel** 25 Oct 1888 in Davenport, Thayer Co., NE. He was born 17 Feb 1863 in Ephrata, Lancaster Co., PA, and died 25 Jun 1953 in Franklin Co., NE.

More About Geneive Rebecca Christner:
Burial: Riverton, Franklin Co., NE

Notes for Obedia Stark Muckel:
His marrage licence has his name as Muckle. He lived at Riverton, Franklin Co., NE.

More About Obedia Stark Muckel:
Occupation: Clerk/
Religion: Presbyterian/

Children of Geneive Christner and Obedia Muckel are:
     2274   i.   Lena May[8] Muckel, born 19 Jul 1889 in NE; died 25 Jul 1973 in Riverton, Franklin Co., NE. She married Jack Ziegler; born 1889; died 1956.

               More About Lena May Muckel:
               Burial: Riverton, Franklin Co., NE

     2275   ii.   Harry W. Muckel, born 1891; died 1946. He married Julia H; born 1895; died 1932.
     2276   iii. Harold Warren Muckel, born 05 Aug 1891; died 1946 in Franklin Co., NE. He married Julia Schegg; born 1895; died 1932.

               More About Harold Warren Muckel:
               Burial: Bloomington, Franklin, Neb.

+   2277   iv.   Arthur Benjamin Muckel, born 11 Jun 1893 in Hebron, Thayer Co., NE; died 05 Apr 1976 in Bloomington, Franklin Co., NE.
     2278   v.   Florence M. Muckel, born 18 Feb 1897[4148]; died 11 Apr 1989 in Bloomington, Franklin Co., NE[4148].

               More About Florence M. Muckel:
               Social Security Number: 505-60-3841/[4148]

     2279   vi.   Hazel Marguerite Muckel, born 09 Nov 1899 in Pilger, Stanton Co., NE; died 1973 in Riverton, Franklin Co., NE. She married Harlan H. Harrington 02 Jul 1922.
     2280   vii. Don Cecil Muckel, born 22 Aug 1903; died 21 May 1986. He married Claire Vitaline.

               More About Don Cecil Muckel:
               Burial: Bayside Cemetery, Laconia, NH

     2281   viii. Dean Christner Muckel, born 17 Jun 1907 in Riverton, Franklin Co., NE[4149]. He married Helen Lucille Waste 28 May 1939 in Los Angeles Co., CA; born 17 Jun 1907 in MO[4149].

Notes for Dean Christner Muckel:

More About Dean Christner Muckel:
Census: 1940, 32 yrs old/San Jose, Los Angeles Co., CA[4149]
Occupation: civil engineer/[4149]
Residence: 1945, US City directory/Pomona, Los Angeles, California, USA[4149]

More About Helen Lucille Waste:
Census: 1940, San Jose, Los Angeles Co., CA[4149]

952. Hannah Bell[7] Christner (Jacob M.[6], Moses C.[5], Joseph "Zep"[4], Johannes John Hans[3], Christian[2], Christen[1])[4150] was born 02 Oct 1873 in Garrett, Somerset Co., PA[4150], and died 09 Jun 1952 in Denver, Denver Co., CO[4150]. She married **Milton A. Lantz** 05 Nov 1891 in Hebron, Thayer Co., NE. He was born 29 Jan 1868 in Williams, Northhampton Co., PA[4150], and died 06 Aug 1950 in Yuma, Yuma Co., CO[4150].

Notes for Hannah Bell Christner:
People that knew her said she was a GOOD GOOD woman but because of her husband's problem. (He suffered from alcoholism). She had to move when ever the rent got behind and had no worldly goods. She had hip surgery and while in recovery a blood clot took her life.

Notes for Milton A. Lantz:
He suffered from alcoholism.

Children of Hannah Christner and Milton Lantz are:

2282   i.   Clifford W.[8] Lantz, born 20 Aug 1893 in Hebron, Thayer Co., NE[4150]; died 28 Nov 1985 in Yuma, Yuma Co., CO[4150]. He married Rachel Florence Clark[4151]; born 16 May 1900 in Council Bluffs, IA[4151]; died 17 Apr 1973 in Yuma, Yuma Co., CO[4151].

Notes for Clifford W. Lantz:
The Descendants of John J. Christner, privately published February 1961, p. 100.

Notes for Rachel Florence Clark:
The Descendants of John J. Christner, privately published February 1961, p. 100.

2283   ii.   Leo J. Lantz, born 28 Aug 1894; died 18 Oct 1970 in Denver, Arapahoe Co., CO. He married Georgia Anita Bowman[4152]; born 18 Sep 1905 in East St. Louis, Illinois[4152]; died 09 Mar 1977 in Aurora, Arapahoe Co., Colorado[4152].

2284   iii.   Ruby M. Lantz, born 19 Jul 1901 in Louisburg, Miami Co., KS[4153]; died 1970[4153]. She married R. Rankin Archer.

953. Warren Jacob (Grant)[7] Christner (Jacob M.[6], Moses C.[5], Joseph "Zep"[4], Johannes John Hans[3], Christian[2], Christen[1]) was born 29 Aug 1875 in Garrett, Somerset Co., PA, and died 17 May 1940 in Willard, Logan Co., CO. He married **Flora Flo Peck** 06 May 1906 in Kansas City, Jackson Co., MO. She was born in Kansas City, MO, and died Sep 1960 in Greeley, Weld Co., CO.

Notes for Warren Jacob (Grant) Christner:
Warren was born 6 months after his fathers death. One name for his father and the other two for army generals. Warren served in the Spanish American War (Dorington Scouts) which disillusioned him greatly. Family story is he TRAMPED around the world. He was in England for coronation of King Edward (Victoria's son) and on the ship back to states - he and a friend using imagination and whatever was available on board ship - invented a carnival ride (remember the "bucket seats on chains that swing out on centrifugal force) and sold the "idea" to a Kansas City Amusement park for $200.00 - where WJG worked for some time and met his wife there. He was living in Kansas City when his mother died.

More About Flora Flo Peck:
Burial: Sunset Memorial, Greeley, Weld Co., CO

Children of Warren Christner and Flora Peck are:

2285   i.   Charlotta⁸ Christner, born 21 Sep 1911 in Kansas City, MO. She married (1) Arthur Corbin. She married (2) George Hunter.

              Notes for Charlotta Christner:
              She was married to Arthur twice, number 1 and 3. She was divorced for 35 years from Arthur Corbin and remarried him after being widowed from George Hunter.

+ 2286   ii.   Jack Christner, born 11 Apr 1918 in Willard, Logan Co., CO; died 14 Sep 2003 in Carson City, Carson Co., NV.

2287   iii.   Beatrice Christner, born 25 Jun 1922 in Willard, Logan Co., CO⁴¹⁵⁴; died 28 Mar 1985 in Greeley, Weld Co., CO. She married George Hoecher 29 Aug 1946.

              More About Beatrice Christner:
              Social Security Number: 522-28-9406/⁴¹⁵⁴
              SSN issued: CO⁴¹⁵⁴

954. John Joseph⁷ Lenhart (Adeline Polly⁶ Christner, Moses C.⁵, Joseph "Zep"⁴, Johannes John Hans³, Christian², Christen¹)⁴¹⁵⁵,⁴¹⁵⁶,⁴¹⁵⁷ was born 16 Mar 1871 in Somerset Co., PA⁴¹⁵⁸,⁴¹⁵⁹, and died 1948 in Guthrie, Logan Co., OK⁴¹⁵⁹. He married **Lurenia Isabella "Rea" Smith**⁴¹⁵⁹ 1899 in OK⁴¹⁵⁹. She was born 28 Jun 1872 in IL⁴¹⁵⁹, and died 1937 in OK⁴¹⁵⁹.

Notes for John Joseph Lenhart:
John married Lurenia Isabelle Smith (Rea) in 1899.
Johns grandson John Lawerence (he is known by both names) was killed in a car accident. John Lawerence's parents Carl and Maggie were visited and taken care of by the other boys involved in the accident that killed John Lawerence out of their great friendship for him.

John named Lockridge Oklahoma because it was the corner of Logan,Oklahoma, Canadian and Kingfisher counties(where they met) and was on a ridge L-O-C-K ridge.The town is actually in Logan Co and the cemetary is in Oklahoma Co. The town of Lockridge was started by John and his father when they built a store near the railroad. This was a general store. Then came a blacksmith
shop,grocery and hotel. At its peak Lockridge had 5 general stores, drugstore,and 2 saloons. A post office was added on Nov 7 1903. There were 2 elevators, cotton gin,lumber yard,cream store and finally a bank. John actually was the first "banker" as he extended credit and made small loans to the area people. John bulit The Farmers Guarantee Bank. The railroad left for good around 1924/25 and the post office stopped service Nov 30, 1928. John was the last resident to leave the town.

More About John Joseph Lenhart:
Burial: Christner Cemetery, , Oklahoma, Oklahoma⁴¹⁵⁹
Residence: 1880, Sherman, Furnas Co., NE⁴¹⁶⁰,⁴¹⁶¹

More About Lurenia Isabella "Rea" Smith:
Burial: Christner Cemetery, , Oklahoma, Oklahoma⁴¹⁶¹
Residence: 1910, Spring Creek, Logan Co., OK⁴¹⁶¹

Children of John Lenhart and Lurenia Smith are:

2288   i.   Carl Edward⁸ Lenhart⁴¹⁶¹, born 09 Jul 1903 in Lockridge, Logan, Oklahoma Territory USA⁴¹⁶¹; died Nov 1979 in Edmond, Oklahoma Co., OK⁴¹⁶¹.

              More About Carl Edward Lenhart:
              Residence: 1930, Deer Creek, Oklahoma Co., OK⁴¹⁶¹

2289   ii.   Vergel Lucille Lenhart⁴¹⁶¹, born 07 Aug 1907 in Lockridge, Logan Co., OK⁴¹⁶¹; died 12 Feb 1998 in

Hutchinson, Reno Co., KS[4161].

More About Vergel Lucille Lenhart:
Burial: Christner Cemetery/Edmond, Oklahoma Co., OK[4161]
Residence: 1910, Spring Creek, Logan Co., OK[4161]

955. Charles Wallace[7] Lenhart (Adeline Polly[6] Christner, Moses C.[5], Joseph "Zep"[4], Johannes John Hans[3], Christian[2], Christen[1])[4162,4163,4164] was born 23 Jan 1872 in Somerset Co., PA[4165,4166], and died 1940 in OK[4167]. He married **Emma Rosalie Logsdon**[4168] 1901 in PA[4168], daughter of George Logsdon and Harriet Logsdon. She was born 07 Jul 1884 in Somerset Co., PA[4168], and died 1962 in Cooke Mills, PA[4168].

Notes for Charles Wallace Lenhart:

More About Charles Wallace Lenhart:
Residence: 1920, Spring Creek, Logan Co., OK[4169]

More About Emma Rosalie Logsdon:
Residence: 1920, Spring Creek, Logan Co., OK[4170]

Children of Charles Lenhart and Emma Logsdon are:
   2290   i.   Elva Mae[8] Lenhart[4170], born 22 Jun 1902 in Oklahoma[4170]; died in Okahoma City, Oklahoma, Oklahoma[4170].

            More About Elva Mae Lenhart:
            Residence: 1920, Spring Creek, Logan Co., OK[4170]

   2291   ii. Hattie Lucelle Lenhart[4170], born 10 May 1906[4170]; died 1908 in Cooke Mills, PA[4170].
   2292   iii. Eugene George Lenhart[4170], born 27 Aug 1909 in Oklahoma[4170]; died 13 Nov 1957 in Oklahoma City, OKlahoma, Oklahoma[4170].

            More About Eugene George Lenhart:
            Residence: 1930, Albany, Berks, Pennsylvania[4170]

959. Emma Elizabeth[7] Lenhart (Adeline Polly[6] Christner, Moses C.[5], Joseph "Zep"[4], Johannes John Hans[3], Christian[2], Christen[1])[4171,4172,4173] was born 25 Mar 1881 in Wilsonville, Furnas Co., NE[4174,4175], and died 24 Feb 1975 in Guthrie, Logan Co., OK[4176]. She married **Benjamin Franklin Hatfield**[4177] 20 Dec 1900 in Logan Co., OK[4177], son of Francis Hatfield and Rebecca Marshall. He was born 12 Jul 1879 in Ozark, Franklin Co., AR[4177], and died 02 Apr 1958 in Oklahoma City, Oklahoma Co., OK[4177].

Notes for Emma Elizabeth Lenhart:
Benjamin born July 12 1879 Ozark Ark. son of Francis Marion and Rebecca Marshall Hatfield. Benjamin died April 2 1958.

More About Emma Elizabeth Lenhart:
Burial: Nazarene Church, Cashion, Oklahoma
Residence: 01 Apr 1940, Spring Creek, Logan, Oklahoma, United States[4177]

More About Benjamin Franklin Hatfield:
Residence: 01 Apr 1940, Spring Creek, Logan, Oklahoma, United States[4177]

Children of Emma Lenhart and Benjamin Hatfield are:
   2293   i.   Mabel Irene[8] Hatfield[4177], born 04 Jul 1901 in Marshall, Logan, Oklahoma, United States[4177]; died 24 Jul 1971 in Guthrie, Logan, Oklahoma, United States[4177].

            More About Mabel Irene Hatfield:

Residence: 01 Apr 1940, Crescent, Logan, Oklahoma, United States[4177]

2294 ii. Cora Mae Hatfield[4177], born 17 May 1906 in Cashion, Kingfisher, Oklahoma, United States[4177]; died 03 May 1999 in Kingfisher, Kingfisher Co., OK[4177].

More About Cora Mae Hatfield:
Residence: Bet. 1935 - 1993, Kingfisher, OK[4177]

2295 iii. Clifford Ananias Hatfield[4177], born 04 Nov 1907 in Mangum, Greer, Oklahoma, United States[4177]; died 06 Feb 1989 in Guthrie, Logan Co., OK[4177].

More About Clifford Ananias Hatfield:
Residence: 1910, Madge, Harmon, Oklahoma[4177]

2296 iv. Rebecca Madge Hatfield[4177], born 03 Apr 1914 in Lockridge, Logan, Oklahoma, United States[4177]; died 10 Nov 2009 in Guthrie, Logan, Oklahoma, United States[4177].

More About Rebecca Madge Hatfield:
Residence: 1920, Spring Creek, Logan, Oklahoma[4177]

2297 v. Juanita Elaine Hatfield[4177], born 13 Apr 1922 in Lockridge, Logan, Oklahoma, United States[4177]; died 07 Feb 1987 in Oklahoma City, Oklahoma Co., OK[4177].

More About Juanita Elaine Hatfield:
Residence: 01 Apr 1940, Spring Creek, Logan, Oklahoma, United States[4177]

961. James Blaine[7] Lenhart (Adeline Polly[6] Christner, Moses C.[5], Joseph "Zep"[4], Johannes John Hans[3], Christian[2], Christen[1])[4178,4179,4180] was born 02 Nov 1885 in Humbolt, Richardson Co., NE[4181,4182], and died 06 Apr 1961 in Hawthorne, Los Angeles Co., CA[4183]. He married **Ida Mae Jones**[4184] 1908 in OK[4184]. She was born 08 Oct 1888 in MO[4184], and died 13 Nov 1973 in Hawthorne, Orange Co., CA[4184].

Notes for James Blaine Lenhart:
James children were very musical inclined and on his farm S. of Lockridge he had a wooden platform erected and held dances on Sat night. The band consisted of James's children, Pete Blem and a couple others. In the early 1930's (aprox 1930) James and family moved to California where son Billy played Bass Fidle in "Our Gang Comedies".Other members of the band played with the Sons of
the Pioneers and Jim played bit parts in the movies. Son Ike stayed in Oklahoma to run the family farm and was killed in an accident. Son Billy now has a night club in California.

More About James Blaine Lenhart:
Residence: 01 Apr 1940, Age: 55; Marital Status: Married; Relation to Head of House: Head/Los Angeles, Los Angeles Co., CA[4184]

More About Ida Mae Jones:
Residence: 01 Apr 1940, Age: 51; Marital Status: Married; Relation to Head of House: Wife/Los Angeles, Los Angeles Co., CA[4184]

Children of James Lenhart and Ida Jones are:
2298 i. Everett Casimir[8] Lenhart[4184], born 12 Sep 1909 in OK[4184]; died 05 Apr 1983 in Pecos, Reeves Co., TX[4184].

More About Everett Casimir Lenhart:
Residence: 1935, Edmond, Oklahoma Co., OK[4184]

2299 ii. Lottie Marie Lenhart[4184], born 08 Nov 1911 in Logan Co., OK[4184]; died 27 Apr 1913 in Logan Co., OK[4184].

More About Lottie Marie Lenhart:
Burial: 1913, Cashion Cemetery, Cashion, Kingfisher Co., OK[4184]

2300 iii. James Warren "Ike" Lenhart[4184], born 20 Apr 1914 in OK[4184]; died 23 Jul 1938 in OK[4184].

    More About James Warren "Ike" Lenhart:
    Residence: 1920, Deer Creek, Oklahoma Co., OK[4184]

2301 iv. Lola Mae Lenhart[4184], born 27 Sep 1918 in OK[4184]; died 24 Mar 1919 in OK[4184].

    More About Lola Mae Lenhart:
    Burial: 1919, Cashion Cemetery/Cashion Cemetery, Cashion, Kingfisher Co., OK[4184]

2302 v. Ray Andrew Lenhart[4184], born 23 Jul 1920 in OK[4184]; died 05 Nov 1998 in Magalia, Butte Co., CA[4184].

    More About Ray Andrew Lenhart:
    Residence: 1930, Spring Creek, Oklahoma Co., OK[4184]

2303 vi. Norma Lucy Lenhart[4184], born 26 Mar 1924 in OK[4184]; died 30 May 2001 in Laguna Niguel, Orange Co., CA[4184].

    More About Norma Lucy Lenhart:
    Residence: 1935, Edmond, Oklahoma Co., OK[4184]

2304 vii. Adaline Lenhart[4184], born 22 Mar 1929 in OK[4184]; died 25 Mar 1929 in OK[4184].

    More About Adaline Lenhart:
    Burial: 1929, Cashion Cemetery, Cashion, Kingfisher Co., OK[4184]

2305 viii. Billy Joe Lenhart[4184], born 14 Dec 1930 in OK[4184]; died 19 Feb 2013 in CA[4184].

    More About Billy Joe Lenhart:
    Residence: 1935, Edmond, Oklahoma Co., OK[4184]

962. Ida Victoria[7] Hoover (Rena[6] Christner, Moses C.[5], Joseph "Zep"[4], Johannes John Hans[3], Christian[2], Christen[1])[4185] was born 07 Dec 1869 in Brothersvalley Twp., Somerset Co., PA[4185], and died 19 Dec 1944 in Garrett, Somerset Co., PA[4185]. She married **William Lewis Brant** in Garrett, Somerset Co., PA. He was born 10 Oct 1869, and died 1916.

Notes for Ida Victoria Hoover:
info from Dora
Ida married William Lewis Brant born Oct 10 1869 died 1916. William is also buried at Highland Cemetery, Garrett, PA.

They had 9 children. Verda who married Mike Herboldheimer had an old Christner bible.

More About Ida Victoria Hoover:
Burial: Highland Cemetery, Garrett, Somerset Co., PA
Residence: 1880, Garrett, Somerset Co., PA[4185]

More About William Lewis Brant:
Burial: Highland Cemetery Garrett PA

Child of Ida Hoover and William Brant is:
2306 i. Verda[8] Brant. She married Mike Herboldheimer.

    Notes for Verda Brant:
    Verda who married Mike Herboldheimer had an old (Froschauer) Christner bible.

    The 1548 Froschauer Bible that is in the Goshen College Historical Library. It was donated in 1971 by
    Levi D. Christner. Levi born 1897 & died 1984. There is another story, the bible was thrown into a fire

and a little girl saved it from the fire. We don't know how it got to an auction in Lagrange Co., IN.

967. Mary[7] Christner (Joseph M.[6], Moses C.[5], Joseph "Zep"[4], Johannes John Hans[3], Christian[2], Christen[1])[4186] was born 27 Mar 1887 in Marysville, Marshall Co., KS[4186,4186], and died 27 Feb 1973 in Longmont, Boulder Co., CO. She married **Jesse Gilbert Wright**[4186] 1908[4186]. He was born 10 Sep 1884 in Neligh, Antelope Co., NE[4186], and died 29 May 1962 in Longmont, Boulder Co., CO[4186].

Notes for Mary Christner:
Mary traveled in a covered wagon as a small child to Edmond, Oklahoma in 1889.

My grandmother told us that her mother had been working at a general store and while she was sweeping the walk way in front of the store a handsome man with beautiful red hair came riding up on a white horse and that was the beginning of Mary Christner and Jesse Wrights legacy.

More About Mary Christner:
Burial: Mountain View Cemetery, Longmont, Boulder Co., CO
Residence: 01 Apr 1940, Age: 53; Marital Status: Married; Relation to Head of House: Wife/Frederick, Weld Co., CO[4186]

Notes for Jesse Gilbert Wright:
Jesse worked in the area coal mines.

More About Jesse Gilbert Wright:
Burial: Longmont, Boulder Co., CO
Residence: 01 Apr 1940, Frederick, Weld Co., CO[4186]

Children of Mary Christner and Jesse Wright are:

2307   i.   Edgar Joseph[8] Wright[4186], born 13 Dec 1909 in Longmont, Boulder Co., CO[4186,4186]; died 18 Jan 1953 in Longmont, Boulder Co., CO. He married Regina Romans[4187]; born 02 Mar 1915[4187]; died 27 Mar 1990 in Longmont, Boulder Co., CO[4187].

         Notes for Edgar Joseph Wright:

         More About Edgar Joseph Wright:
         Burial: Longmont, Boulder Co., CO[4188]
         Residence: 1930, Frederick, Weld Co., CO[4188]

+ 2308   ii.   Ruby Alice Wright, born 05 Aug 1912 in Billings, Yellowstone Co., MT; died 24 Feb 1992 in Fayetteville, AR.

2309   iii.   Ella Mae Wright[4189,4190], born 16 Oct 1914 in Miles City, Custer Co., MT[4190]; died 05 Apr 1990 in Montrose, Montrose Co., CO[4190]. She married (1) Eugene Pulver[4191]; born 29 Jun 1906[4191]; died 30 Jun 1970 in Denver, Adams, CO[4191]. She married (2) Clyde R. Duncam. She married (3) Edward V. Hanna.

         Notes for Ella Mae Wright:
         Ella married Clyde R. Duncan. They divorced and then she married 2nd Edward V. Hanna; They diroved; then married 3rd Eugene E. Pulver.

         More About Ella Mae Wright:
         Residence: 01 Apr 1940, Frederick, Weld Co., CO[4191,4192]
         Social Security Number: 524-30-4594/[4193]
         SSN issued: CO[4193]

+ 2310   iv.   Ethel Marie Wright, born 16 Oct 1914 in Miles City, Custer Co., MT; died 03 Sep 2004 in Montrose, Montrose Co., CO.

2311   v.   Elmer Harold Wright, born 14 Mar 1916; died 20 Jun 1916 in MT.

2312   vi.   Jesse Willard Wright[4194], born 21 Apr 1917 in OK[4194]; died 07 Mar 2003 in Longmont, Boulder Co., CO[4194]. He married Margorie Hutcherson.

Notes for Jesse Willard Wright:

More About Jesse Willard Wright:
Residence: 1992, Longmont, Boulder Co., CO[4194]

2313   vii.   Mary Belle Wright, born 20 Jul 1919. She married Ivan Clair[4195]; born 18 Aug 1916[4195]; died 21 Jun 2001 in Colorado Springs, El Paso Co., CO[4195].

Notes for Mary Belle Wright:
Mary married Ivan Clair

Notes for Ivan Clair:
Birth: Aug. 18, 1916
Tuttle, Grady Co., OK
Death: Jun. 21, 2001
Colorado Springs, El Paso Co., CO

Ivan Everette Clair, 84, of Colorado Springs, a superintendent, died June 21. Graveside services were June 25 in Highland Cemetery.

Clair was born Aug. 18, 1916, in Tuttle, OK. In August 1936, he married Mary Belle Wright.

He was superintendent of the Thornton water and sewer department. His interests included travel, camping and fishing.

He is survived by his wife; a daughter, Linda Albrandt, Colorado Springs; six grandchildren; 14 great-grandchildren; and one great-great-grandson.

Source: Published in the Denver Post in Denver, CO on July 19, 2001.

Inscription:
TOGETHER FOREVER

Burial:
Olinger Highland Mortuary and Cemetery, Thornton,
Adams Co., CO

+   2314   viii.   Laura Jane Wright, born 25 Apr 1921 in CO; died 28 May 1995 in Lakewood, Jefferson Co., CO.
2315   ix.   Melvin Dewey Wright, born 30 Jul 1926. He married Rita Gabel; born 23 Feb 1930.

Notes for Melvin Dewey Wright:
Melvin married Rita Gabel born Feb 23 1930

969. Jacob J.[7] Christner (Joseph M.[6], Moses C.[5], Joseph "Zep"[4], Johannes John Hans[3], Christian[2], Christen[1])[4196] was born 11 Aug 1888 in Marysville, Marshal Co., KS[4196], and died 07 Feb 1960 in Bellevue, Sarpy Co., NE[4196]. He married **Adeline M. Meers**[4196,4197] 14 Jun 1911 in NE[4198]. She was born 30 Mar 1895 in Davenport, Nuckolls, NE[4198,4199], and died 15 Sep 1988 in Bellevue, Sarpy Co., NE[4200].

Notes for Jacob J. Christner:
This info came from Dora Lue Gilliam.

More About Jacob J. Christner:
Burial: BElleview, Neb.

Occupation: worked in round house for Union Pacific Railroad/[4200]
Residence: 1910, Deer Creek, Oklahoma Co., OK[4200]

More About Adeline M. Meers:
Residence: 1910, Davenport, Thayer Co., NE[4201]

Child of Jacob Christner and Adeline Meers is:

+ 2316   i.   Violet Lauretta[8] Christner, born 03 Jan 1913 in Davenport, Nuckolls, NE; died 26 Dec 1977 in Bellevue, Sarpy Co., NE.

    970. Kate[7] Christner (Joseph M.[6], Moses C.[5], Joseph "Zep"[4], Johannes John Hans[3], Christian[2], Christen[1])[4202] was born 27 Jan 1890 in Guthrie, Logan Co., OK[4202], and died 18 Feb 1974 in Ponca, Kay Co., OK[4202]. She married **Clyde Charles Burright**[4203,4204] 1912 in Guthrie, Logan Co., OK[4204]. He was born 04 Jun 1879 in Salem, Dent Co., MO[4205], and died 1951 in Kildare, Kay Co., OK[4205].

More About Kate Christner:
Burial: Christner Cemetery, Oklahoma Co., OK
Residence: 1900, Deer Creek Township, Oklahoma Co., OK[4206]

Notes for Clyde Charles Burright:
Birth: Jun. 4, 1879
Salem, Dent Co., MO
Death: 1951
Kildare, Kay Co., OK

Parents:
Charles Colby Burright (1855 - 1934)
Lilly Ella Hotchkiss Burright (1862 - 1914)

Spouse: Kate Christner Burright (1890 - 1974)

Children:
Irene Mildred Burright (1914 - 1990)
Wesley Edward Burright (1919 - 1994)

Burial: Christner Cemetery, Oklahoma Co., OK

Clyde is the son of Charles C. Burright and Lily E. Charles born Aug 23 1855 died June 1, 1934. Lily born April l4 1862 died April 9, 1914.

More About Clyde Charles Burright:
Burial: Christner Cemetery, Oklahoma Co., OK
Residence: 1920, Miller, Kay Co., OK[4207]

Children of Kate Christner and Clyde Burright are:

     2317   i.   James Orville[8] Burright[4208], born 21 Mar 1913 in Guthrie, Logan Co., OK[4208]; died 21 Mar 1913 in Guthrie, Logan Co., OK[4208].

             Notes for James Orville Burright:
             Birth: 21 Mar., 1913
             Death: 21 Mar., 1913

             Inscription: Burright-double stone.

             Note: Double stone with his infant sister Verlin Glyde Burright, below.

             Burial: Summit View Cemetery, Guthrie, Logan Co., OK
             Plot: Blk 01 - Lot 21

Find A Grave Memorial# 50029820

More About James Orville Burright:
Burial: Guthrie, Logan Co., OK

2318   ii.   Irene M. Burright, born 15 Feb 1914 in Guthrie, Logan Co., OK[4208]; died 17 Sep 1990 in Anadarko, Caddo Co., OK[4208].

Notes for Irene M. Burright:
Birth: Feb. 15, 1914 - Guthrie, Logan Co., OK
Death: Sep. 17, 1990 - Anadarko, Caddo Co., OK

Parents:
Clyde Charles Burright (1879 - 1951)
Kate Christner Burright (1890 - 1974)

Burial: Christner Cemetery, Oklahoma Co., OK

More About Irene M. Burright:
Burial: Christner Cemetery, Oklahoma Co., OK
Residence: 1930, Kildare, Kay Co., OK[4208]

2319   iii.   Verlin Clyde Burright, born 26 May 1916 in Guthrie, Logan Co., OK[4208]; died Jun 1918 in Guthrie, Logan Co., OK[4208].

More About Verlin Clyde Burright:
Burial: Guthrie, Logan Co., OK

+   2320   iv.   Wesley Edward Burright, born 02 Mar 1919 in Guthrie, Logan Co., OK; died 29 Jan 1994 in Ponca, Kay Co., OK.

2321   v.   Donald Gene Burright, born 26 Jul 1931.

971. Archie B.[7] **Christner** (Joseph M.[6], Moses C.[5], Joseph "Zep"[4], Johannes John Hans[3], Christian[2], Christen[1])[4209,4210] was born 22 Sep 1892 in Lockridge, Logan Co., OK[4211], and died 08 Nov 1962 in Los Angeles, Los Angeles Co., CA[4211]. He married **Marvie Ruth Waugh**[4211] 1914[4211]. She was born 05 Mar 1895[4211], and died 26 Dec 1981 in Whittier, Los Angeles Co., CA[4211].

Notes for Archie B. Christner:
Birth: Mar 4, 1913
Death: Nov 21, 2003

Spouse: Marie V. Christner (1915 - 2002)

Burial: White Oak Cemetery, Trenton, Henry Co., IA

More About Archie B. Christner:
Residence: 1930, Montebello, Los Angeles Co., CA[4211]

Notes for Marvie Ruth Waugh:
Birth: Nov. 19, 1915
Death: Jul. 29, 2002

Spouse: Archie M. Christner (1913 - 2003)

Burial: White Oak Cemetery, Trenton, Henry Co., IA

Children of Archie Christner and Marvie Waugh are:
2322   i.   Kenneth McCoy[8] Christner[4211], born 06 Jul 1915[4211]; died 17 Apr 1981 in Whittier, Los Angeles Co., CA[4211].

2323   ii.   Wilma G. Christner[4211], born 05 Mar 1918[4211]; died Nov 1936 in Whittier, Los Angeles Co., CA[4211].

+ 2324   iii. William Eugene Christner, born 16 Jul 1928 in CA; died Jan 1982 in Sunset Beach, Orange Co., CA.

972. Sampson Samuel[7] Christner (Joseph M.[6], Moses C.[5], Joseph "Zep"[4], Johannes John Hans[3], Christian[2], Christen[1])[4212] was born 16 Aug 1893 in Downs, Kingfisher Co., OK[4212,4213], and died 04 Mar 1919 in Oklahoma City, Oklahoma Co., OK[4213,4214]. He married **Edna Olive Burright**[4215,4216,4217] 23 Nov 1912 in Guthrie, Logan Co., OK. She was born 23 Aug 1893 in OK[4218], and died 25 Feb 1958 in Edmond, Oklahoma Co., OK[4219,4220,4220].

Notes for Sampson Samuel Christner:
Birth: Aug. 16, 1893
Death: Mar. 4, 1919

Burial: Christner Cemetery, Oklahoma Co., OK

More About Sampson Samuel Christner:
Burial: Christner Cemetery, Oklahoma Co., OK
Residence: 1910, Deer Creek, Oklahoma Co., OK[4221]

Notes for Edna Olive Burright:
Birth: Aug. 23, 1893 - OK
Death: Feb. 28, 1958 - Edmond, Oklahoma Co., OK

Parents:
Charles Colby Burright (1855 - 1934)
Lilly Ella Hotchkiss Burright (1862 - 1914)

Spouses:
John Marshall (1895 - 1989)
Sampson S. Christner (1893 - 1919)

Children:
Thelma G. Christner Cravens (1913 - 1997)
Chester Joseph Christner (1916 - 1933)
Margaret Faye Marshall Darr (1928 - 2003)

Burial: Christner Cemetery, Oklahoma Co., OK
Find A Grave Memorial# 89045057

More About Edna Olive Burright:
Burial: Christner Cemetery, Oklahoma Co., OK
Residence: 27 Apr 1910, Spring Creek, Logan Co., OK[4222,4223,4223]

Children of Sampson Christner and Edna Burright are:
2325   i.   Thelma G.[8] Marshal, born 02 Sep 1913 in Lockridge, Logan Co., OK[4224]; died 08 Aug 1997 in Guthrie, Logan Co., OK[4224]. She married Charles A. Cravens; born 21 Jul 1912[4225]; died 04 Jul 1980[4225].

       Notes for Thelma G. Marshal:
       Birth: Sep. 2, 1913 - Logan Co., OK
       Death: Aug. 8, 1997 - Guthrie, Logan Co., OK

       Parents:
       Sampson S. Christner (1893 - 1919)
       Edna Olive Burright Christner (1893 - 1958)

       Spouse: Charles A. Cravens (1912 - 1980)

       Burial: Christner Cemetery, Oklahoma Co., OK

Find A Grave Memorial# 89155630

More About Thelma G. Marshal:
Burial: Christner Cemetery, Oklahoma Co., OK
Social Security Number: 442-10-2924/[4226]
SSN issued: [4226]

Notes for Charles A. Cravens:
Birth: Jul. 21, 1912 - OK
Death: Jul. 4, 1980 - Guthrie, Logan Co., OK

Spouse: Thelma G. Christner Cravens (1913 - 1997)

Burial: Christner Cemetery, Oklahoma Co., OK
Find A Grave Memorial# 89045315

More About Charles A. Cravens:
Burial: Christner Cem, Oklahoma
Other-Begin: Guthrie, Logan Co., OK[4227]
Social Security Number: 441-10-5810/[4227]
SSN issued: OK[4227]

2326   ii.   Chester Joseph Christner, born 20 Jul 1916 in OK; died 1933 in OK.

Notes for Chester Joseph Christner:
Chester is buried in Christner Cemetery and there is no last name on the grave.

He is in row 13 and it says Chester "Bucky" Chesters daughter Thelma and her husband Charles Cravens is also burried there.

Birth: Jul. 20, 1916 - OK
Death: 1933 - OK

Parents:
Sampson S. Christner (1893 - 1919)
Edna Olive Burright Christner (1893 - 1958)

Burial: Christner Cemetery, Oklahoma Co., OK
Find A Grave Memorial# 89157255

More About Chester Joseph Christner:
Burial: Christner Cemetery, Oklahoma Co., OK

973. Lauretta[7] Christner (Joseph M.[6], Moses C.[5], Joseph "Zep"[4], Johannes John Hans[3], Christian[2], Christen[1])[4228] was born 17 Apr 1895 in Oklahoma City, Oklahoma, Oklahoma, United States[4229,4230], and died 03 Feb 1946 in Denver, Denver, CO[4230,4231]. She married **James Miller Moore**[4232]. He was born 08 Sep 1895 in NE[4232,4233], and died 1977 in Denver, Arapahoe Co., CO.

More About Lauretta Christner:
Residence: 01 Apr 1940, Denver, Denver, Colorado, United States[4233]

More About James Miller Moore:
Residence: 01 Apr 1940, Denver, Denver, Colorado, United States[4233]

Children of Lauretta Christner and James Moore are:
    2327   i.   Harold Celland[8] Moore, born 03 Mar 1918; died 1977 in Denver, Arapahoe Co., CO.
    2328   ii.   Clarence Miller Moore, born 12 Sep 1919.
    2329   iii.   Dorothy Fern Moore, born 12 May 1921. She married Charles E. Adams Jr.; born 22 Sep 1919.
    2330   iv.   Thomas James Moore[4233], born 13 Jul 1923 in Denver, Denver County, Colorado[4233]; died 18 Oct 1982 in Wiscosin[4233]. He married (1) June Ryan. He married (2) Joan.

More About Thomas James Moore:
Residence: 01 Apr 1940, Denver, Denver, Colorado, United States[4233]

2331 v. Vivian Richard Moore, born 13 Mar 1926. He married Nettie Pacettie; born 22 Dec 1924.

Notes for Vivian Richard Moore:

+ 2332 vi. Robert Eugene Moore, born 24 Aug 1927 in Denver, Denver, CO; died 17 Feb 2004 in Denver, Denver, CO.

2333 vii. Vernon Leroy Moore, born 16 Feb 1929. He married Elberta White; born 30 Sep 1930.

2334 viii. Marvin Kenneth Moore, born 18 Sep 1930.

2335 ix. Betty Jean Moore, born 27 Jul 1932.

2336 x. Donald Edward Moore, born 08 May 1937.

975. Nannie[7] Christner (Joseph M.[6], Moses C.[5], Joseph "Zep"[4], Johannes John Hans[3], Christian[2], Christen[1]) was born 15 Aug 1899 in Lockridge, Logan, OK[4234], and died 30 Dec 1979 in Brea, Los Angeles Co., CA[4234]. She married **Charles L. Smothers**[4234] 1917 in Guthrie, Logan Co., OK[4234]. He was born 30 May 1896 in Macomb, MO[4234], and died 27 Dec 1979 in Brea, Los Angeles Co., CA[4234].

Notes for Nannie Christner:
Nannie is a twin to annie.

More About Nannie Christner:
Burial: Brea CA[4234]
Residence: 1910, Deer Creek, Oklahoma Co., OK[4234,4234]

More About Charles L. Smothers:
Residence: 1930, San Gabriel, Los Angeles Co., CA[4234]

Child of Nannie Christner and Charles Smothers is:
2337 i. Charles Louis[8] Smothers[4234,4234], born 03 Apr 1918 in Guthrie, Logan Co., OK[4234,4235]; died 21 Oct 1967 in Los Angeles Co., CA[4236,4237].

More About Charles Louis Smothers:
Military service: 13 Apr 1944, Fort Macarthur San Pedro, California[4238]
Residence: Alameda, California[4238]

976. Annie[7] Christner (Joseph M.[6], Moses C.[5], Joseph "Zep"[4], Johannes John Hans[3], Christian[2], Christen[1])[4239] was born 15 Aug 1899 in OK[4239], and died 15 Jun 1976 in Hawthorne, CA[4239]. She married **Emmett George Surber** 1920[4239]. He was born 25 Dec 1897 in CO[4239], and died 16 May 1954 in Hawthorne, Los Angeles Co., CA[4239].

Notes for Annie Christner:
Annie is a twin to Nannie.

More About Annie Christner:
Burial: Hawthorne CA[4239]
Residence: 1900, Deer Creek, Oklahoma Co., OK[4239]

More About Emmett George Surber:
Residence: 1930, Montebello, Los Angeles Co., CA[4239]

Children of Annie Christner and Emmett Surber are:

+ 2338   i.   George B.[8] Surber, born 29 Jul 1921 in Guthrie, Logan Co., OK.
    2339   ii.   Robert Calvin Surber, born 02 Jan 1925 in Los Angeles, Los Angeles Co., CA[4239]; died 17 Feb 1993 in Los Angeles Co., CA[4239]. He married Esther; born 30 May 1924.

> Notes for Robert Calvin Surber:
> Birth: Jan 2, 1925
> Death: Feb 17, 1993
>
> Burial: Green Hills Memorial Park, Rancho Palos Verdes, Los Angeles Co., CA
> Plot: Holly, 166, E
> Find A Grave Memorial# 72148471

    2340   iii.   Emmert Joseph Surber, born 31 May 1939. He married (1) Julia A. Junge[4240] 04 Feb 1961 in Los Angeles Co., CA[4240]; born 23 Feb 1940[4240]. He married (2) Carolyne F. Dahlberg[4240] 25 Feb 1984 in Orange Co., CA[4240]; born 27 Oct 1945[4241]. He married (3) Carolyne F. Erickson[4242] 25 Feb 1984 in Orange Co., CA[4242]; born 13 Sep 1947[4243].

> More About Carolyne F. Dahlberg:
> Residence: 1993, Age: 48/Huntington Beach, CA[4244]
>
> More About Carolyne F. Erickson:
> Residence: 1982, Age: 35/Melbourne, FL[4245]

978. Pearl[7] Christner (Joseph M.[6], Moses C.[5], Joseph "Zep"[4], Johannes John Hans[3], Christian[2], Christen[1])[4246] was born 22 Dec 1903 in OK[4246,4247], and died 28 Nov 1989 in Norwalk, Los Angeles, California, USA[4248]. She married **(1) Leonard Howell**[4248]. He was born 12 Aug 1895 in Colorado USA[4248], and died in Los Angeles Co., CA. She married **(2) Henry Harry Robinson** 1924[4248]. He was born 1903 in KS[4248].

Notes for Pearl Christner:
Pearl is a twin to Charles.

Birth: Dec. 22, 1903
Death: Nov. 28, 1989

Burial: Little Lake Cemetery, Santa Fe Springs, Los Angeles Co., CA
Find A Grave Memorial# 10613794

More About Pearl Christner:
Residence: 01 Apr 1940, San Antonio, Los Angeles, California, United States[4248]
Social Security Number: 561-22-6338/[4249]

More About Leonard Howell:
Residence: 01 Apr 1940, San Antonio, Los Angeles, California, United States[4250]

More About Henry Harry Robinson:
Residence: 1930, Covina, Los Angeles Co., CA[4250]

Children of Pearl Christner and Henry Robinson are:
    2341   i.   Henry[8] Robinson Jr., born 1925; died 05 Jan 1974 in CA[4250].
    2342   ii.   Oscar Eldridge ROBINSON[4250], born 10 Jan 1927 in Los Angeles, California USA[4250]; died 02 Jul 1983 in San Bernardino Co., CA[4250].

> More About Oscar Eldridge ROBINSON:
> Residence: 1930, Covina, Los Angeles Co., CA[4250]

    2343   iii.   Wayne Robinson, born 1931.

980. Daisy Victoria[7] Christner (Joseph M.[6], Moses C.[5], Joseph "Zep"[4], Johannes John Hans[3], Christian[2],

Christen[1])[4251,4252] was born 16 Apr 1905 in OK[4253,4254], and died 16 Jan 1992 in Arkansas City, Cowley Co., KS[4255,4256]. She married **(1) Jewel Derington**[4256] 1922[4256]. He was born 05 Mar 1900 in OK[4256], and died 21 Feb 1948 in Kansas City, Wyandotte, Kansas, USA[4256]. She married **(2) Nobel B. Lowry**[4256] 21 May 1949 in Wellington, Sumner Co., KS[4256]. He was born 26 Jun 1911 in Oxford, Sumner Co., KS[4256,4257], and died 16 Apr 1995 in Arkansas City, Cowley Co., KS[4258].

Notes for Daisy Victoria Christner:
Birth: Apr. 16, 1905
Death: Jan. 16, 1992

Wife of Noble B. Lowry - Married May 21, 1949

Obituary: The Wichita Eagle (KS) - January 18, 1992

Daisy V. Lowry, 86, retired Rodeo Meats employee, died Thursday, Jan. 16, 1992. Service 10:30 a.m. Monday, Riverview Cemetery. Survivors: husband, Noble; sons, Charles H. Derington of Commerce City, Colo., Robert L. Derington of Arkansas City; sister Elviria Stonum of El Monte, Calif.; seven grandchildren; 16 great-grandchildren; six great-great- grandchildren. Memorial has been established with Hospice Inc. Rindt-Erdman Funeral Home.

Spouse: Noble Ben Lowry (1911 - 1995)

Burial: Riverview Cemetery, Arkansas City, Cowley Co., KS
Find A Grave Memorial# 46715240

More About Daisy Victoria Christner:
Residence: 1920, Oklahoma, Oklahoma Co., OK[4258]

More About Jewel Derington:
Burial: KS
Residence: 1930, Kansas City, Wyandotte Co., KS[4258]

Notes for Nobel B. Lowry:
Birth: Jun. 26, 1911
Death: Apr. 16, 1995

Obituary: The Wichita Eagle (KS) - April 20, 1995

Lowry, Noble Ben, 83, General Electric retired press operator, died Sunday, April 16, 1995. Service 10 a.m. Friday, Riverview Cemetery. Survivors: stepson, Charles Derington of Commerce City, Colo.; six step grandchildren; 16 step-great-grandchildren; seven step-great-great- grandchildren. Memorial has been established with Hospice, Inc. Rendt-Erdman Funeral Home.

Spouse: Daisy V. Lowry (1905 - 1992)

Burial: Riverview Cemetery, Arkansas City, Cowley Co., KS
Find A Grave Memorial# 46715275

More About Nobel B. Lowry:
Social Security Number: 515-03-3091/[4259]
SSN issued: KS[4259]

Children of Daisy Christner and Jewel Derington are:
    2344   i.   Jewel Monroe[8] Derington[4260], born 12 Oct 1923[4260]; died 03 Aug 1990[4260]. He married Nadine Cook; born 27 Aug 1923.
    2345   ii.   Charles Hugh Derington[4260], born 15 Dec 1925; died May 1978[4260]. He married Judith Elaine Ramsey; born 14 Jun 1945.
    2346   iii.   Robert Lavern Derington[4260], born 03 Feb 1928[4260]; died 10 Mar 1994 in Arkansas City, Cowley Co.,

KS[4260]. He married Ina Mae Winegarner; born 17 Nov 1927; died 29 Sep 1993.

Notes for Robert Lavern Derington:
Robert married Ina Mae Winegarner born Nov 17, 1927.

Notes for Ina Mae Winegarner:
Birth: Nov. 17, 1927
Death: Sep. 29, 1993

Wife of Robert L. Derington
Married Sept 17, 1945

Spouse: Robert L. Derington (1928 - 1994)

Children:
Charlene Jean Derington Day (1945 - 2010)
Ronald Lee Derington (1947 - 1947)
Cynthia Jo Derington (1957 - 1963)

Burial: Riverview Cemetery, Arkansas City, Cowley Co., KS
Find A Grave Memorial# 41561651

2347   iv. Eugenia Mae Derington[4260], born 04 May 1932[4260]; died 17 Nov 1989 in OK[4260]. She married Donald P. Cook; born 31 Dec 1926.

Notes for Donald P. Cook:
U.S. Veterans Gravesites, ca.1775-2006

Name: Donald E Cook
Service Info.: SGT US ARMY KOREA, VIETNAM
Birth Date: 31 Dec 1926
Death Date: 8 Jun 1966
Interment Date: 16 Jun 1966
Cemetery: Golden Gate National Cemetery, 1300 Sneath Lane, San Bruno, CA 94066
Buried At: Section B Site 77-A

984. Sidney Lewis[7] **Christner** (Nelson "Nels"[6], Moses C.[5], Joseph "Zep"[4], Johannes John Hans[3], Christian[2], Christen[1])[4261,4262] was born 30 Aug 1890 in Lockridge, Logan Co., OK[4263,4264,4265], and died 12 Jan 1970 in Oklahoma City, Oklahoma Co., OK[4266,4267,4268]. He married **Lydia Ruth Burright**[4269,4270,4271] 23 Nov 1912 in Guthrie, Logan Co., OK. She was born 16 Oct 1896 in Lockridge, Logan Co., OK[4272,4273], and died 07 Mar 1986 in Oklahoma City, Oklahoma Co., OK[4274,4275].

Notes for Sidney Lewis Christner:
Birth: Aug. 30, 1890
Logan Co., OK
Death: Jan. 12, 1970
Oklahoma City, Oklahoma Co., OK

Spouse:
Lydia Ruth Burright Christner (1896 - 1986)

Children:
Bessie Marie Christner Kordis (1916 - 1999)
Beryl Mable Christner Deaton (1920 - 1973)

Burial: Christner Cemetery, Oklahoma Co., OK
Find A Grave Memorial# 89060945

Sidney was born in a sod house. He was a farmer all his life.

SS#446-24-8700 ISS OK

More About Sidney Lewis Christner:
Burial: Christner Cemetery, Oklahoma Co., OK
Residence: 1920, Spring Creek, Logan Co., OK[4276]
Social Security Number: 446-24-8700/[4277]
SSN issued: OK[4277]

Notes for Lydia Ruth Burright:
Lydia was a housewife all her life and a very active member of Draper Park Christian Church.

Birth: Oct. 13, 1896 - Logan Co., OK
Death: Mar. 7, 1986 - Oklahoma City, Oklahoma Co., OK

Parents:
Charles Colby Burright (1855 - 1934)
Lilly Ella Hotchkiss Burright (1862 - 1914)

Spouse: Sidney Lewis Christner (1890 - 1970)

Children:
Bessie Marie Christner Kordis (1916 - 1999)
Beryl Mable Christner Deaton (1920 - 1973)

Burial: Christner Cemetery, Oklahoma Co., OK
Find A Grave Memorial# 89061443

More About Lydia Ruth Burright:
Burial: 10 Mar 1986, Christner Cemetery, Oklahoma Co., OK
Residence: 1910, Spring Creek, Logan Co., OK[4278]

Children of Sidney Christner and Lydia Burright are:
+   2348   i.   Bessie Marie[8] Christner, born 21 Oct 1916 in OK; died 29 Jan 1999 in Kingfisher, Kingfisher Co., OK.
+   2349   ii.   Beryl Mabel Christner, born 15 Aug 1920 in Lockridge, Logan Co., OK; died 1973 in Oklahoma City, Oklahoma Co., OK.
+   2350   iii.   Betty Ruth Christner, born 07 Jul 1926 in Edmond, OK; died 23 Jan 2003 in Le Claire, Scott Co., IA.

985. Earl Harrison[7] Christner (Nelson "Nels"[6], Moses C.[5], Joseph "Zep"[4], Johannes John Hans[3], Christian[2], Christen[1])[4279] was born 16 Sep 1892 in Lockridge, Logan Co., OK[4279], and died 13 Aug 1958 in North Platte, Lincoln Co., NE[4280]. He married **Blanch Emily Vanek**[4281,4282] 03 May 1925[4283,4284]. She was born 23 Feb 1902 in WI[4284], and died 19 Oct 1994 in North Platte, Lincoln Co., NE[4285].

Notes for Earl Harrison Christner:
Earl was a Army Veteran of WWI.

Birth: Sep. 16, 1892
Death: Aug. 13, 1958

Pvt. US ARMY

Burial: Fort McPherson National Cemetery, Maxwell, Lincoln Co., NE
Plot: Q, 0, 141
Imported from: US Veteran's Affairs
Find A Grave Memorial# 490322

More About Earl Harrison Christner:

Burial: Fort McPherson National Cemetery, Maxwell, Lincoln Co., NE
Occupation: worked for Union Pacific RR with Jake Christener/[4285]
Residence: 1900, Cedar & Spring Creek Townships, Logan Co., OK[4286,4287]
Social Security Number: 712-05-9444/[4288]
SSN issued: Railroad Board (Issued Through)[4288]

Children of Earl Christner and Blanch Vanek are:

	2351	i.	Donald[8] Christner.
+	2352	ii.	Gladys Opal Christner, born 25 Nov 1925 in NE; died 24 May 2007 in Orange, Orange Co., CA.
+	2353	iii.	Roy Marvin Christner, born 25 Jan 1928 in NE; died 03 Aug 1994.
+	2354	iv.	Theodore Eugene Christner, born 08 Jul 1932 in North Platte, Lincoln Co., NE; died 19 Apr 2007 in Sacramento, Sacramento Co., CA.
+	2355	v.	Richard Christner, born 16 Jan 1937; died 20 Feb 2003 in North Platt, Lincoln Co., NE.
+	2356	vi.	Conrad Christner, born 23 Apr 1939.

986. Musetta[7] Christner (Nelson "Nels"[6], Moses C.[5], Joseph "Zep"[4], Johannes John Hans[3], Christian[2], Christen[1])[4289,4290] was born 20 Oct 1894 in Lockridge, Logan Co., OK, and died 06 Aug 1928 in Cashion, Kingfisher Co., OK[4290,4291]. She married **Otto Karns Collins**[4292] 1917[4293]. He was born 18 Sep 1891 in Havensville, Pottawatomie Co., KS[4294], and died 28 Feb 1973 in Guthrie, Logan Co., OK[4294].

Notes for Musetta Christner:
Birth   20 October 1895
Death   6 August 1928
Cemetery Cashion Cemetery, Cashion, OK

More About Musetta Christner:
Burial: Aug 1928, Cashion Cemetery, Cashion, Kingfisher Co., OK
Residence: 1920, Cedar, Logan, Oklahoma USA[4295]

More About Otto Karns Collins:
Residence: 01 Apr 1940, Age: 47; Marital Status: Married; Relation to Head of House: Head/Lawrie, Logan, Oklahoma, United States[4296]

Child of Musetta Christner and Otto Collins is:

	2357	i.	Vera Luella[8] Collins[4296], born 12 Jan 1918 in her Mother died/born West of Guthrie[4296]; died 31 May 2009 in Guthrie, Logan, Oklahoma[4296].

More About Vera Luella Collins:
Residence: 1920, Cedar, Logan Co., OK[4296]

987. Dewey Guy[7] Christner (Nelson "Nels"[6], Moses C.[5], Joseph "Zep"[4], Johannes John Hans[3], Christian[2], Christen[1])[4297,4298] was born 25 Jan 1897 in Lockridge, Logan Co., OK[4299], and died 01 Dec 1971 in Guthrie, Logan Co., OK[4300]. He married **Iclee Derington**[4300]. She was born 14 Apr 1904[4300], and died 15 Apr 1967 in Guthrie, Logan Co., OK[4300].

Notes for Dewey Guy Christner:
Dewey was a veteran of WWI and served in France. He lived in Guthrie, Ok most of his life. He worked in Guthrie, OK making cheese and ice cream.

SS# 440-05-3304 Iss. OK   Last zip 73044

Birth: Jun. 25, 1897
Death: Dec. 1, 1971

Inscription: Christner (west) - Willford (east)-double family stone. Service Stone: Oklahoma Private, Infantry - WWI

Burial: Summit View Cemetery, Guthrie, Logan Co., OK
Plot: Blk 40 - Lot 95
Find A Grave Memorial# 50711703

More About Dewey Guy Christner:
Burial: Guthrie Cemetery, Logan Co., OK
Residence: 1930, Guthrie, Logan Co., OK[4301]
Social Security Number: 440-05-3304/[4302]
SSN issued: OK[4302]

Notes for Iclee Derington:
Birth: Apr. 14, 1914
Death: Apr. 15, 1967

Inscription: Willford-Christner - double family stone. w/ Dewey G. Christner.

Burial: Summit View Cemetery, Guthrie, Logan Co., OK
Plot: Blk 40 - Lot 95
Find A Grave Memorial# 50711771

More About Iclee Derington:
Burial: Guthrie Ok.

Child of Dewey Christner and Iclee Derington is:
   2358   i.   Almede Iclee[8] Christner[4303], born 25 Feb 1923[4303]; died in Pueblo, Pueblo Co., CO[4304]. She married Lionel DeLoy Willford[4304]; born 30 Oct 1921[4304]; died 04 Dec 1991 in Pueblo, CO[4304].

         More About Almede Iclee Christner:
         Residence: 1993, Pueblo, CO[4305]

         Notes for Lionel DeLoy Willford:
         Lionel was a member of the American Legion, Pueblo Fraternal Order of the Eagles, Rio Grande Veterans Club. He was a terminal manager of the Rio Grande Motorway for 33 years. He served in WWII from June 25 1942 to Dec 29, 1945.

         More About Lionel DeLoy Willford:
         Burial: Summit View Cemetery Pueblo Co., CO

988. Jeanette "Nettie"[7] Christner (Nelson "Nels"[6], Moses C.[5], Joseph "Zep"[4], Johannes John Hans[3], Christian[2], Christen[1]) was born 25 Oct 1898 in Lockridge, Logan Co., OK, and died 16 Jan 1963 in Fort Collins, Laramie Co., CO[4306]. She married **Frank D. Souders** 05 Jul 1920[4307]. He was born 30 Mar 1891 in Lamar, Chase Co., NE[4307], and died 26 Jan 1965 in Fort Collins, Larimer Co., CO[4307].

Notes for Jeanette "Nettie" Christner:
Nettie worked in a pickle factory and was a worker for the Salvation Army.

More About Jeanette "Nettie" Christner:
Burial: Ft. Collins, Colorado
Residence: 1910, Spring Creek, Logan Co., OK[4308,4309]

Children of Jeanette Christner and Frank Souders are:
+   2359   i.   Lloyd Nelson[8] Souders, born 21 Sep 1921; died 19 Sep 2008 in Sterling, Logan Co., CO.
+   2360   ii.   Cecil Ermit Souders, born 25 Apr 1923; died 09 Jan 2008 in Sterling, Logan Co., CO.
+   2361 iii.   Marvin L Souders Sr., born 29 Apr 1925; died 25 Apr 1994 in Fort Collins, Larimer Co., CO.
+   2362 iv.   Raymond Souders, born 26 Feb 1927.
+   2363   v.   Dorothy Souders, born 16 Mar 1930.

+	2364	vi.	Wayne Souders, born 28 Dec 1931 in Sterling, Logan Co., CO; died 03 Jun 1996 in Ft Collins, Larimer Co., CO.
+	2365	vii.	Dale Souders, born 01 Jan 1935.
	2366	viii.	Catherine Souders[4309], born 11 May 1940[4309]; died in In infancy.

989. Ermit Theodore "Erm"[7] Christner (Nelson "Nels"[6], Moses C.[5], Joseph "Zep"[4], Johannes John Hans[3], Christian[2], Christen[1])[4310,4311,4312] was born 06 Nov 1900 in Lockridge, Logan Co., OK[4313,4314], and died 14 Dec 1979 in Minco, Grady Co., OK[4314]. He married **Nora Pauline Burright**[4315,4316,4317,4318,4319]. She was born 02 Dec 1904 in Guthrie, Logan Co., OK[4320], and died 05 Dec 1985 in Chickasha, Grady Co., OK.

Notes for Ermit Theodore "Erm" Christner:
Ermit was a auctioneer and a farmer. He also operated a grocery store and a cream station at one time. He was known by Colonel E. J. when he did his auctioneering.

SS# 441-28-8315 Iss. OK Last zip 73059

Birth: Nov 6, 1900 - Logan Co., OK
Death: Dec 14, 1979 - Chickasha, Grady Co., OK

Spouse: Nora Pauline Burright Christner (1904 - 1985)

Burial: Evergreen Cemetery, Minco, Grady Co., OK

More About Ermit Theodore "Erm" Christner:
Residence: 1930, Spring Creek, Logan Co., OK[4320]
Social Security Number: 441-28-8315/[4321]
SSN issued: OK[4321]

Notes for Nora Pauline Burright:
Birth: Dec 2, 1904 - Guthrie, Logan Co., OK
Death: Dec 5, 1985 - Chickasha, Grady Co., OK

Parents:
Charles Colby Burright (1855 - 1934)
Lilly Ella Hotchkiss Burright (1862 - 1914)

Spouse: Ermit Theodore Christner (1900 - 1979)

Burial: Evergreen Cemetery, Minco, Grady Co., OK

More About Nora Pauline Burright:
Residence: 01 Apr 1940, Minco, Grady Co., OK[4322,4323]

Children of Ermit Christner and Nora Burright are:

| + | 2367 | i. | Imogine Pauline[8] Christner, born 23 Apr 1925 in Lockridge, Logan Co., OK; died 09 Sep 2012 in Everett, Snohomish Co., WA. |
| | 2368 | ii. | Orville Ermit Christner, born 08 Jul 1934 in Minco, Grady Co., OK; died 05 Jun 1951. |

Notes for Orville Ermit Christner:
Birth: Jul. 8, 1934
Minco, Grady Co., OK
Death: Jun. 5, 1951
Minco, Grady Co., OK

Burial: Evergreen Cemetery, Minco, Grady Co., OK

More About Orville Ermit Christner:
Burial: Evergreen Cemetery, Minco, Grady Co., OK

990. Elva O.[7] **Christner** (Nelson "Nels"[6], Moses C.[5], Joseph "Zep"[4], Johannes John Hans[3], Christian[2], Christen[1])[4324] was born 06 Dec 1902 in Lockridge, Logan Co., OK[4325], and died 30 Aug 1993 in Oklahoma City, Oklahoma Co., OK[4326,4327]. She married **Frank Dewitt Thompson**[4328] 09 Jan 1927. He was born 07 Nov 1899 in TX[4329], and died Dec 1964[4330].

Notes for Elva O. Christner:
Elva is a school teacher and a secretary.

Birth: Dec. 9, 1902
Death: Aug. 30, 1993

Elva O., a resident of St. Ann's Home, died Monday, August 30, 1993. Elva was born in Logan County, Oklahoma, December 9, 1902 to Sarah and Nelson Christner. After graduating from Hills Business College of OKC, Elva worked in Grandfield, Okla. where she met her future husband. In 1927, she married Frank D. Thompson who preceded her in death in 1964. While raising her 3 children, Elva assisted her husband after he founded Capitol Stage Equipment Co. of OKC. Elva was an active member of Eighth Street Methodist Church until its dissolution. She then joined Wesley United Methodist Church. She enjoyed traveling. Elva is survived by 3 children: daughter, Dixie Galloway and son-in-law, Tom of OKC; son, Don F. Thompson, Texas; son, Larry B. Thompson and daughter-in-law, Shirley of OKC; also survived by 7 grandchildren, Brian Roth, Bob Thompson, Sharon Shawn, Barry Roth, Susan Rupe, all of OKC, and Michelle and Jacob Thompson, Texas; also 4 great grandchildren; a sister, Verdell Perry of Edmond; and many nieces and nephews.

Spouse: Frank D. Thompson (1899 - 1964)

Burial: Memorial Park Cemetery, Oklahoma City, Oklahoma Co., OK
Plot: Section#18
Find A Grave Memorial# 62875805

More About Elva O. Christner:
Race: White/[4331]
Residence: 1920, Spring Creek, Logan Co., OK[4332]
Social Security Number: 440-48-7804/[4333]
SSN issued: OK[4333]

Notes for Frank Dewitt Thompson:
Birth: Nov. 7, 1899
Death: Dec., 1964

Spouse: Elva O. Christner Thompson (1902 - 1993)

Burial:Memorial Park Cemetery, Oklahoma City, Oklahoma Co., OK
Plot: Section#18
Find A Grave Memorial# 62875786

More About Frank Dewitt Thompson:
Burial: Memorial Park Cemetery, Oklahoma City, Oklahoma Co., OK
Residence: 1910, Age: 10; Marital Status: Single; Relation to Head of House: Son/Alfalfa, Tillman, Oklahoma[4334]

Children of Elva Christner and Frank Thompson are:
> 2369　　i.　Dixie Irene[8] Thompson[4335], born 04 Dec 1929 in Potter Co., TX[4335]. She married George Roth III.
>
>> More About Dixie Irene Thompson:
>> Residence: 1930, Amarillo, Potter Co., TX[4336]
>
> 2370 .　　ii.　Larry Benton Thompson, born 07 Dec 1930 in Bastrop, TX[4337]; died 2011 in San Diego, San Diego Co., CA[4337]. He married Shirley Ann Haddock.

More About Larry Benton Thompson:
Residence: 1993, Age: 63/Julian, CA[4337]

2371   iii.   Don Francis Thompson[4338,4339], born 13 Apr 1931 in Gray, TX[4339].

Notes for Don Francis Thompson:
Don taught puclic school and worked with the blind. He lives in San Antonio, TX.

More About Don Francis Thompson:
Race: White/[4340]
Residence: 01 Apr 1940, Age: 8; Marital Status: Single; Relation to Head of House: Son/Oklahoma City, Oklahoma, Co., OK[4340]

991. Alma[7] Christner (Nelson "Nels"[6], Moses C.[5], Joseph "Zep"[4], Johannes John Hans[3], Christian[2], Christen[1])[4341,4342] was born 28 Dec 1905 in Lockridge, Logan Co., OK[4343,4344], and died 09 Aug 1991 in Guthrie, Logan Co., OK[4345,4346]. She married **Macy Virgil Perry**[4346] 30 Jul 1924 in Guthrie, Logan Co., OK[4346], son of William Perry and Saline Brinkley. He was born 01 Oct 1898 in Norwood, Wright Co., MO, and died 02 Jan 1987 in Guthrie, Logan Co., OK[4346].

Notes for Alma Christner:
Alma was a housewife all her life and lived in Logan Co., OK.

Birth: Dec. 28, 1905
Death: Aug. 9, 1991

Spouse: Macy Perry (1898 - 1987)

Burial: Christner Cemetery, Oklahoma Co., OK
Find A Grave Memorial# 37027476

More About Alma Christner:
Burial: 13 Aug 1991, Christner Cemetery, Oklahoma Co., OK
Residence: 1930, Spring Creek, Logan Co., OK[4347]
Social Security Number: 442-48-2733/[4348]
SSN issued: OK[4348]

Notes for Macy Virgil Perry:
Macy is the son of William and Saline Binkley Perry.

Birth: Oct. 1, 1898
Death: Jan. 2, 1987

Spouse: Alma Perry (1905 - 1991)

Burial: Christner Cemetery, Oklahoma Co., OK
Find A Grave Memorial# 37027493

More About Macy Virgil Perry:
Burial: Christer Cemetery, Deer Creek, OK[4349]

Children of Alma Christner and Macy Perry are:
+   2372   i.   Valda Elaine[8] Perry, born 26 Dec 1924 in Cashion, Logan Co., OK.
+   2373   ii.   Floyd Wayne "Moe" Perry, born 22 Mar 1927 in Seward, Logan Co., OK; died 12 May 1985.
+   2374   iii. Eunice Irene Perry, born 03 Apr 1929 in Seward, Logan Co., OK; died 30 Apr 2001 in Guthrie, Logan Co., OK.
    2375   iv.   Leola Evelyn Perry, born 02 Jul 1932 in Seward, Logan Co., OK; died 10 Jul 1984 in Oklahoma City, Oklahoma Co., OK. She married Kenneth Leslie Harris[4350] 02 Jul 1949 in Guthrie, Logan Co., OK; died

Abt. 1990[4350].

Notes for Leola Evelyn Perry:
Leola worked as adminstrative secretary for the Langston Coop Extension, she was also very active in 4-H. She was a member of the First Baptist church of Coyle and the Perkins Eastern Star Leola married Kenneth Harris July 2, 1949 Guthrie, OK.

More About Leola Evelyn Perry:
Burial: 13 Jul 1984, Summit View Cem

+   2376   v.   Delbert Jerald Perry, born 12 Nov 1939 in Seward, Logan Co., OK.

992. Verdell[7] Christner (Nelson "Nels"[6], Moses C.[5], Joseph "Zep"[4], Johannes John Hans[3], Christian[2], Christen[1])[4351,4352] was born 04 Apr 1908 in Lockridge, Logan Co., OK[4353], and died 29 Oct 1994 in Edmond, Logan Co., OK. She married **George Elmer Perry**[4354]. He was born 27 Mar 1902 in OK[4354,4355], and died 08 Jun 1983 in Edmond, Logan Co., OK[4356].

Notes for Verdell Christner:
Verdell was a homemaker and worked at Britton Laundry and Dry Cleaners.

Birth: Jan. 4, 1908
Death: Oct. 29, 1994

Spouse: George Elmer Perry (1902 - 1983)

Burial: Christner Cemetery, Oklahoma Co., OK

More About Verdell Christner:
Residence: 1930, Choctaw, Oklahoma Co., OK[4357,4358,4359]

Notes for George Elmer Perry:
Elmer was born in a tent in what is now Oklahoma City, OK. He was a wheat farmer. In earlier years, Elmer enjoyed playing the fiddle with his brother at barn dances.

Birth: Mar. 27, 1902
Death: Jun. 8, 1983

Spouse: Verdell Christner Perry (1908 - 1994)

Burial: Christner Cemetery, Oklahoma Co., OK

More About George Elmer Perry:
Residence: 1910, Spring Creek, Oklahoma Co., OK[4359]

Children of Verdell Christner and George Perry are:
2377   i.   Eileen[8] Perry, born 10 Feb 927[4360]; died 12 Apr 2006. She married J. O. Baker.

             More About Eileen Perry:
             Race: White/[4360]
             Residence: 01 Apr 1940, Age: 13; Marital Status: Single; Relation to Head of House: Daughter/Edmond, Oklahoma Co., OK[4360]

+   2378   ii. Leon George Perry, born 12 Jan 1925 in OK; died 26 Feb 1987 in Edmond, Logan Co., OK.

993. Gladys Irene[7] Christner (Nelson "Nels"[6], Moses C.[5], Joseph "Zep"[4], Johannes John Hans[3], Christian[2], Christen[1])[4361] was born 12 Jan 1910 in OK[4361], and died 24 Oct 1981 in Mangum, Greer Co., OK[4361]. She married **Leroy James "Jake" Davis**[4361,4362] 20 Jan 1938 in Oklahoma City, Oklahoma Co., OK, son of Benjamin

Davis and Frances Casey. He was born 29 Sep 1906 in Logan Co., OK[4362], and died 22 Aug 1976 in Guthrie, Logan Co., OK.

Notes for Gladys Irene Christner:
Gladys was the 13th of 14th children. She walked to Spring Creek School. When she was 15, her father, Nelson,"Nels" passed away, and her oldest brother Arthur returned to Oklahoma to help his mother run the farm. Gladys graduated from Deer Creek High School, attended Central State Teachers College in Edmond, OK Co., OK, and was on the swim team. She married Leroy James Davis in Oklahoma City. Early on she became a single parent and raised her children on the Christner homestead. She was a home maker and helped brother Arthur run the homestead. After Arthur's death, Gladys was employed at Rockwell International, Bethany, OK Division, in aircraft manufacturing. After retiring, she purchased a home and moved to Mangum, Oklahoma, to be near her daughter and grandchildren. Gladys loved fishing, hunting rabbits, sewing, gardening, teaching children, making crafts, and playing cards. She was a life-long teacher and learner.

Birth: Jan 12, 1910
Death: Oct 24, 1981

Burial: Christner Cemetery, Oklahoma Co., OK
Find A Grave Memorial# 37051030

More About Gladys Irene Christner:
Burial: Christer Cemetery, Deer Creek, Oklahoma Co., OK[4363]
Residence: 01 Apr 1940, Esculapia, Benton Co., AR[4363]

More About Leroy James "Jake" Davis:
Residence: 1935, Rural, Benton, Arkansas[4363]
Social Security Number: 444-14-0724/[4364]
SSN issued: OK[4364]

Children of Gladys Christner and Leroy Davis are:
   2379   i.   Darrel Wayne[8] Davis[4365], born 03 Sep 1934[4365]; died 13 Mar 2006 in Mangum, Greer Co., OK[4365].

                  Notes for Darrel Wayne Davis:
                  From his sister - Roberta

                  Darrel grew up on the family homestead in Logan Co, OK. When he was almost ten years old, his younger sister, Frances, died from an accident involving a gas storage tank. He graduated from Cashion High School, was active in Future Farmers of America and enjoyed exhibiting his show pigs and cattle. He continued living on the farm and enjoyed helping his mother and sisters. He loved all animals and could easily train dogs to do tricks. Darrel loved music and enjoyed playing his many records for others. He worked as a farm hand, in furniture manufacturing, in airplane fabrication at Rockwell International, Bethany Division, and was a small engine mechanic.

                  He moved to Mangum, OK, and was church custodian, cleaned businesses and repaired lawnmowers and bicycles. He was well known for his memory for numbers, for telling jokes and stories, and making others laugh.

                  Birth: Sep. 3, 1934
                  Death: Mar. 13, 2006

                  Darrel Wayne Davis peacefully passed from this life to be with his Lord and Savior on March 13, 2006. He was born in the Lockridge Community near Cashion, OK to Gladys Christner Davis on September 3, 1934.

                  He grew up on the Christner family farm south of Cashion with his mother, sisters and Uncle Arthur Christner. He attended Cashion schools twelve years, graduating with the Class of 1953.

                  FFA was Darrel's passion, and he continued to win ribbons at State Fairs after graduation. He loved the outdoors, animals and people. He was known for teaching dogs unusual tricks, his vast musical collection, his sense of humor and love of life.

He entertained everyone with his many original jokes, limericks and euphemisms. His capacity to remember numbers, especially dates and phone numbers was phenomenal. He enjoyed games, from shooting pool to throwing darts.

Darrel lived in Cashion until moving to Mangum in 1980. He was a member of Mangum First United Methodist Church.

He was employed as a farm laborer and custom harvester. He worked for the Cashion Farmer's Coop, Oklahoma Furniture Manufacturing Company, Aero Commander/Rockwell International and was a certified small engine repairman.

He was preceded in death by sister Francis Catherine Davis and mother Gladys Irene Davis and a host of aunts and uncles, cousins and friends.

He is survived by: sisters Roberta Williams and Iris Deurmyer of Mangum and brother-in-law Richard Williams (who Darrel considered his real brother); nieces and nephews Shari and Brian Kloos, Erin, Logan and Casen Kloos all of Amarillo; Dr. Brian Williams of Tulsa, OK; Chris and Alice Deurmyer of Oswego, KS;
Jeremy Deurmyer of Texarkana, TX; and many beloved cousins and friends.

Visitation services will be at Greer Funeral Home in Mangum on Friday, March 17, 2006 from 6:00 PM to 8:00 PM. Funeral services will be at Baggerly Funeral Home in Edmond, Oklahoma on Saturday, March 18, 2006, with visitation services at 1:00 PM followed by funeral service at 2:00 PM. Interment will be at the Christner Family Cemetery west of Edmond.

Burial: Christner Cemetery, Oklahoma Co., OK
Find A Grave Memorial# 15077907

2380 ii. Frances Catherine Davis[4366], born 16 Jun 1937 in OK[4366]; died 12 Aug 1945 in Logan Co., OK[4366].

Notes for Frances Catherine Davis:
Birth 16 June 1937
Death 12 August 1945

Buried: Christner Cemetery, Edmond, OK
Inscription: Our Darling

More About Frances Catherine Davis:
Burial: Christer Cemetery, Deer Creek, Oklahoma Co., OK[4366]

+ 2381 iii. Roberta Sue Davis, born 27 Dec 1943 in Edmond, Oklahoma Co., OK.
+ 2382 iv. Iris Davis, born 13 Apr 1948 in Edmond, Oklahoma Co., OK.

994. Roy M.[7] Christner (Nelson "Nels"[6], Moses C.[5], Joseph "Zep"[4], Johannes John Hans[3], Christian[2], Christen[1])[4367] was born 19 Sep 1913 in Lockridge, Logan Co., OK[4368,4369], and died 15 Apr 1993 in Oklahoma City, Oklahoma Co., OK[4370]. He married **Donna Lois Mallony**[4370]. She was born 01 Jul 1915[4370], and died 06 Apr 1971 in OK[4370].

Notes for Roy M. Christner:
Roy was in the Navy and he married late in life. He lived in OK. Roy was a farmer for over 20 years and also worked for Mustang Fuel.

SS#556-03-6016 ISS CA Last address Oklahoma 73122

Birth: Sep. 19, 1913
Death: Apr. 15, 1993

Burial: Christner Cemetery, Oklahoma Co., OK

More About Roy M. Christner:

Residence: 1930, Spring Creek, Logan Co., OK[4370]
Social Security Number: 556-03-6016/[4371]
SSN issued: CA[4371]

Notes for Donna Lois Mallony:
Birth: Jul. 1, 1915
Death: Apr. 6, 1971

Burial: Christner Cemetery, Oklahoma Co., OK

More About Donna Lois Mallony:
Burial: Christner Cemetery, Oklahoma Co., OK

Child of Roy Christner and Donna Mallony is:
+   2383   i. Carol Ann[8] Christner.

995. Josephine[7] Christner (Alexander[6], Moses C.[5], Joseph "Zep"[4], Johannes John Hans[3], Christian[2], Christen[1])[4372,4373,4374,4375] was born 06 Jun 1881 in Stella, Richardson Co., NE[4375], and died 21 Nov 1925 in Guthrie, Logan Co., OK[4376,4377]. She married **Penilton Taylor Stewart** 04 Oct 1898 in Hennessey, Kingfisher Co., OK[4377]. He was born 18 Sep 1878[4378], and died 31 Jul 1974 in Hobart, Kiowa Co., OK[4379,4380].

Notes for Josephine Christner:
Nellie died of a ruptured appendix January 30, 1914 in hospital in Longmont, CO. While she was living in Lyons, Colorado. This information from her death certificate. Her daughter in law Mina Boren-Christner had this certificate in her possession. Now it is in my hands I am her granddaughter Donna Christner-Reese.

More About Josephine Christner:
Burial: 21 Nov 1925, Bridgeport, Caddo Co., OK[4381]
Census: 14 Jan 1920, Waconda, Caddo Co., OK[4381]
Residence: 1910, Estes Park, Larimer Co., CO[4382]

Notes for Penilton Taylor Stewart:
Birth: 1878
Death: 1974

Burial: Lone Wolf Cemetery, Lone Wolf, Kiowa Co., OK
Find A Grave Memorial# 24512552

More About Penilton Taylor Stewart:
Burial: Lone Wolf, OK
Residence: 01 Apr 1940, Age: 64; Marital Status: Widowed; Relation to Head of House: Head/Waconda, Caddo, Oklahoma, United States[4383]
Social Security Number: 444-09-9826/[4384]
SSN issued: OK[4384]

Children of Josephine Christner and Penilton Stewart are:
    2384   i. Arvel B[8] Stewart[4385], born 25 Feb 1897 in Oklahoma, United States[4385]; died 13 Apr 1956 in Little, Seminole, Oklahoma, United States[4385].
    2385   ii. Earl Edwin Stewart[4386,4387], born 06 Jul 1899 in Bridgeport, Caddo Co., CA[4388]; died 24 Oct 1943 in Bakerfield, CA. He married Alice Clara Trell; born 10 Sep 1908.

                    Notes for Earl Edwin Stewart:
                    Earl married Alice Clara Trell. In 1992 Alice was living in Greenwood Ark. Alice born Sept 10, 1908.

                    Birth: 1899

Death: 1943

Burial: Geary Cemetery, Geary,Blaine Co., OK.
Find A Grave Memorial# 27719057

More About Earl Edwin Stewart:
Burial: Geary, OK
Residence: 1910, Age in 1910: 10; Marital Status: Single; Relation to Head of House: Son/Fort Morgan, Morgan, Colorado[4389]

2386   iii.   Bessie Stewart[4390], born 1900[4390]; died 1900.

        Notes for Bessie Stewart:
        She was stillborn.

+   2387   iv.   Florence Louise Stewart, born 06 Jun 1901 in Hennessey, Kingfisher Co., OK; died 11 Mar 1996 in Woodland Yolo, CA.
     2388   v.   Chester Leroy Stewart[4391], born 26 Mar 1905 in OK[4391]; died 15 Aug 1906 in Hydro, Blaine Co., OK[4391].
     2389   vi.   Mildred Marie "Midge" Stewart[4391,4392], born 21 Oct 1906 in Hydro, Caddo Co., OK[4393]; died 07 Jul 1972 in Oroville, Butte Co., CA[4393]. She married Leo Vinson McDonnell.

        More About Mildred Marie "Midge" Stewart:
        Residence: 1910, Age in 1910: 3; Marital Status: Single; Relation to Head of House: Daughter/Estes Park, Larimer Co., CO[4394,4395]

2390   vii.   John Leslie Stewart[4395,4396], born 14 Aug 1909 in Estes Park, CO[4397,4398]; died 30 Apr 1996 in Compton, Los Angeles Co, CA[4399]. He married Louise Thelma Clary; born 18 Jan 1915.

        More About John Leslie Stewart:
        Residence: 1910, Age in 1910: 0; Age in 1910: 8/12; Marital Status: Single; Relation to Head of House: Son/Estes Park, Larimer Co., CO[4400,4401]
        Social Security Number: 710-01-8456/[4402]
        SSN issued: Railroad Board (Issued Through)[4402]

2391   viii.   Vera Ione Stewart[4403], born 01 Jan 1912 in Lyons, Boulder Co., CO[4403]; died 08 Feb 1932 in Geary, OK.

        Notes for Vera Ione Stewart:
        Vera married Charlie Baker. she died from complications from childbirth.

        Birth: 1912
        Death: 1932

        Burial: Geary Cemetery, Geary, Blaine Co., OK
        Find A Grave Memorial# 27719087

        More About Vera Ione Stewart:
        Residence: 1920, Waconda, Caddo Co., OK[4403]

2392   ix.   Fred Lewis Stewart[4404], born 03 Oct 1915 in Hydro, Caddo Co., OK; died 08 Jan 2002 in Bangor, Butte Co., CA[4404]. He married Marie Edna Shirey in Los Angeles Co., CA; born 17 Oct 1920; died 08 May 1976.
2393   x.   Penilton Taylor "Penny" Stewart[4404], born 02 Mar 1918 in Bridgeport, OK[4404,4405]; died 12 Apr 1998 in Sacramento, CA[4406]. He married Mabel Tucker.

        Notes for Penilton Taylor "Penny" Stewart:
        Penery married Mabel Tucker and 2nd to Frances _____.
        In 1992 Pen lives is Sacremento California

        More About Penilton Taylor "Penny" Stewart:
        Social Security Number: 441-12-2085/[4407]
        SSN issued: OK[4407]

2394   xi.   Leonard Leroy Stewart, born 29 Jan 1920 in Bridgeport, OK; died 12 Apr 2012 in Age at Death:

92/Springfield, Lane, Oregon, USA[4408]. He married (1) Berit Marianne Paulson; born 29 Nov 1932 in Sweden. He married (2) Vella Vernice Watson; born 05 Feb 1922; died 11 Aug 1984.

Notes for Leonard Leroy Stewart:
Leonard maybe born Jan. 20.

More About Leonard Leroy Stewart:
Residence: 1993, Springfield, OR[4408]

2395   xii.   Elton Neal Stewart[4409,4410], born 10 Aug 1922 in Bridgeport, Caddo Co., CA[4411]; died 27 Feb 1988 in Lone Wolf, OK.

Notes for Elton Neal Stewart:
Elton married Betty Jean Hill born Sept 10 1922 Carnegie Oklahoma

More About Elton Neal Stewart:
Residence: 01 Apr 1940, Age: 17; Marital Status: Single; Relation to Head of House: Son/Waconda, Caddo, Oklahoma, United States[4412]

2396   xiii.   Elma Elva Stewart, born 14 Feb 1924[4413]; died 07 Jul 2007 in Sacramento, Sacramento Co., CA[4413]. She married Garland Sellers; born 01 Jul 1923.

More About Elma Elva Stewart:
SSN issued: CA[4413]

997. Philo Leroy (Roy P)[7] Christner (Alexander[6], Moses C.[5], Joseph "Zep"[4], Johannes John Hans[3], Christian[2], Christen[1])[4414,4415] was born 11 Jan 1886 in Oxford, Crowley Co., KS[4416], and died 21 Feb 1954 in Denver, Arapahoe Co., CO. He married **Mina Ethel Boren**[4417,4418] 23 Dec 1911 in Boulder, Boulder Co., CO. She was born 03 Jan 1893 in Bartlesville, OK, and died 21 May 1993 in Kiowa, CO[4419].

Notes for Philo Leroy (Roy P) Christner:
His name is maybe Philo Lee Ray Christner.

Birth: Jan. 11, 1886
Death: Feb. 21, 1954

Burial: Mount View Cemetery, Bennett, Adams Co., CO
Find A Grave Memorial# 35274619

More About Philo Leroy (Roy P) Christner:
Burial: 26 Feb 1954, Montview Cemetery Bennett, Colorado[4420,4421]
Fact 1: only went to the 8th grade in school[4422]
Fact 2: he was a whiz in math[4422]
Fact 3: he had a jolly personality loved life[4422]
Fact 4: 23 Dec 1911, married Mina E. Boren[4422]
Fact 5: he was a hard worker loved to garden[4422]
Fact 6: loved to plant and care for his Roses kept a beautiful yard.[4422]
Fact 7: 21 Feb 1954, died of carcinoma 1 kidney cancer and uremia[4422]
Fact 8: drove a stage from Lyons to Estes Park[4422]
Fact 9: helped transport the Elk into Roosevelt national park[4422]
Fact 10: proved up on his homestead 7 mi. no. of Strasburg, Co.[4422]
Fact 11: worked on building the Stanley Hotel in Estes Park, Co.[4422]
Fact 12: worked on the Fall River road crewbuilding the road[4422]
Residence: Adams Co., CO[4423]

Notes for Mina Ethel Boren:
Birth: Jan. 3, 1893
Death: May 21, 1993

Burial: Mount View Cemetery, Bennett, Adams Co., CO
Find A Grave Memorial# 35274652

More About Mina Ethel Boren:
Burial: 26 May 1993, Bennett Cemetery, Bennett, CO
Fact 1: Attended school in Lyons Colorado[4424,4425]
Fact 2: 1898, homesteaded once with father Robert P Boren[4426,4427]
Fact 3: 1911, homesteaded with her husband Roy Christner[4428,4429]
Fact 4: Mina was always a lady[4430,4431]
Fact 5: played the piano & pump organ[4432,4433]
Fact 6: 23 Dec 1911, Mina married Roy in Boulder , Colorado[4434,4435]
Fact 7: Mina sang in the church choir in Strasburg, Co.[4436,4437]
Fact 8: She was a practical nurse or nurse's aid[4438,4439]
Fact 9: she gave blood worked for the war II effort[4440,4441]
Fact 10: member of the presbyterian church[4442,4443]
Fact 11: She loved to & got to travel a lot in her later yrs.[4444,4445]
Fact 12: she was a loving disapplinarian[4446,4447]
Residence: 1900, Estes Park, Larimer Co., CO[4448]

Children of Philo Christner and Mina Boren are:

+   2397   i.   Gilbert Leroy[8] Christner, born 31 Jul 1912 in Estes Park, Larimer Co., CO; died 13 Dec 1981 in Aurora, Arapahoe Co., CO.

+   2398   ii.   Eva Lucile Christner, born 22 Dec 1914 in Estes Park, CO; died 12 Dec 1994 in Denver, Arapahoe Co., CO.

    2399   iii.   Muriel Edna Christner, born 10 Aug 1918 in Strasburg Co., CO; died 07 Sep 1918 in Strasburg Co., CO.

           More About Muriel Edna Christner:
           Burial: Montview Cemetery, Bennett, Adams Co., CO

+   2400   iv.   Richard Robert Christner, born 29 Sep 1923 in North of Strasburg, CO; died 26 Mar 2002 in Afton, Ottawa Co., OK.

+   2401   v.   Donna Lee Christner, born 10 May 1932 in Strasburg, Arapaho Co., CO.

+   2402   vi.   Neil Wesley Christner, born 07 Aug 1934 in Strasburg Co., CO.

998. Eva Geneva Idella[7] Ackerman (Leah[6] Christner, Moses C.[5], Joseph "Zep"[4], Johannes John Hans[3], Christian[2], Christen[1])[4449,4450] was born 1880 in Northampton, Somerset Co., PA[4451,4452], and died 1920. She married **James A. Bittner**[4453]. He was born 09 Mar 1878 in Glencoe, PA, USA[4453], and died 21 Apr 1933 in Glencoe, PA, USA[4453].

More About Eva Geneva Idella Ackerman:
Residence: 1920, Northampton, Somerset Co., PA[4454,4455]

More About James A. Bittner:
Residence: 1920, Northampton, Somerset Co., PA[4455]

Children of Eva Ackerman and James Bittner are:

    2403   i.   Geneva Elizabeth[8] Bittner[4455], born 21 Sep 1901 in Glencoe, PA[4455]; died 21 Apr 1991 in Glencoe, PA[4455].

           More About Geneva Elizabeth Bittner:
           Residence: 1930, Northampton, Somerset Co., PA[4455]

    2404   ii.   Cyrus Paul Bittner[4455], born 19 Apr 1904 in Northampton, Somerset Co., PA[4455].

           More About Cyrus Paul Bittner:
           Residence: 1910, Northampton, Somerset Co., PA[4455]

    2405   iii.   William Austin Bittner[4455], born 10 May 1907 in Northampton Township, Somerset, PA[4455]; died Oct

1909 in Northampton Township, Somerset, PA[4455].

2406   iv.   Henry Philip Bittner[4455], born 13 Jul 1909 in Connellsville, Fayette Co., PA[4455]; died 24 Jun 1966 in Berlin, Somerset Co., PA[4455].

More About Henry Philip Bittner:
Residence: 1910, Northampton, Somerset Co., PA[4455]

2407   v.   James Albert Bittner[4455], born 06 Oct 1919 in Northampton, Somerset Co., PA[4455]; died 25 Feb 1976 in McKeesport, Allegheny Co., PA[4455].

More About James Albert Bittner:
Residence: 1920, Northampton, Somerset Co., PA[4455]

1007. Irvin Gibert[7] Christner (George Washington[6], Moses C.[5], Joseph "Zep"[4], Johannes John Hans[3], Christian[2], Christen[1]) was born 24 Aug 1889 in OK[4456], and died 27 Mar 1961 in Sterling, Logan Co., CO. He married **Fannie Emma Lenhart**[4457,4458] 04 Apr 1915. She was born 21 Sep 1895 in Garrett, Somerset Co., PA[4459], and died 28 Nov 1968 in Sterling, Logan Co., CO[4459].

Notes for Irvin Gibert Christner:
Birth: Aug 24, 1889
Death: Mar 27, 1961

Spouse: Fannie Emma Lenhart Christner (1895 - 1968)

Children:
Irvin Gilbert Christner (1917 - 1995)
George N Christner (1919 - 1981)
Marie A Christner Petteys (1927 - 2006)

Burial: Sunset Memorial Gardens, Sterling, Logan Co., CO

More About Irvin Gibert Christner:
Burial: Sterling, Logan Co., CO[4460]
Residence: 1930, Age in 1930: 38; Marital Status: Married; Relation to Head of House: Head/Willard, Logan Co., CO[4460,4461]

More About Fannie Emma Lenhart:
Census: 21 Jun 1900, Summit Twp, Somerset, PA, USA[4462]
Residence: 1930, Willard, Logan Co., CO[4463]

Children of Irvin Christner and Fannie Lenhart are:
+   2408   i.   Virginia Wynona[8] Christner, born 25 Dec 1915; died 17 Aug 1976 in Sterling, Logan Co., CO.
+   2409   ii.   Irvin Christner Jr., born 12 Jun 1917 in Garrett, Somerset Co., PA; died 15 Apr 1995 in Sterling, Logan Co., CO.
+   2410   iii.   George N. Christner, born 15 May 1919; died Aug 1981 in Sterling, Logan Co., CO.
+   2411   iv.   Marie Arlene Christner, born 21 Aug 1927; died 14 Feb 2006.
+   2412   v.   Allen B. Christner Sr., born 03 Feb 1935 in CO.

1009. Bessie Vera[7] Christner (George Washington[6], Moses C.[5], Joseph "Zep"[4], Johannes John Hans[3], Christian[2], Christen[1])[4464,4465,4466] was born 16 Feb 1898 in OK[4467,4468,4469,4470], and died 23 Jul 1979 in Cashion, Kingfisher Co., OK[4471,4472]. She married **William F. Cobb**[4473] Abt. 1915[4474]. He was born 06 Jul 1891[4475], and died Dec 1965 in Cashion, Kingfisher Co., OK[4476,4477,4478].

Notes for Bessie Vera Christner:
Dora writes that Bessie's mother was May Crumb Christner and that she was the mother of all 3 children. Bessie was raised in an Masonic orphanage near ElReno., OK and that Bill Cobb was a teacher there and that is how they met. Could be that Mable Jones is the second wife of George. I don't have any dates so it is very hard to check

this out.

More About Bessie Vera Christner:
Burial: Cashion, Kingfisher Co., OK[4479]
Residence: 1920, Downs, Kingfisher Co., OK[4480]
Social Security Number: 441-52-4616/[4481,4482]
SSN issued: OK[4483]

More About William F. Cobb:
Burial: Cashion, Kingfisher Co., OK
Residence: 1930, Downs, Kingfisher Co., OK[4484,4485]
Social Security Number: 443-38-5657/[4486]
SSN issued: OK[4486]

Children of Bessie Christner and William Cobb are:

2413   i.   Clois Cornelius[8] Cobb, born 29 Aug 1916 in OK[4487]; died 07 Oct 2000 in Oklahoma City, Oklahoma Co., OK[4488]. He married Ola Thorpe.

> More About Clois Cornelius Cobb:
> Residence: 1993, Oklahoma City, OK[4488,4489]
> Social Security Number: 444-30-4768/[4489]
> SSN issued: OK[4489]

+   2414   ii.   Elizabeth Vera Cobb, born 13 Feb 1920; died 23 Mar 2002.

2415   iii. Jaunita Oleta Cobb, born 10 Oct 1922; died 1935.

1014. Mabel[7] Christner (Richard W.[6], Moses C.[5], Joseph "Zep"[4], Johannes John Hans[3], Christian[2], Christen[1])[4490] was born 09 May 1907 in Connellsville, Fayette Co., PA[4490,4491,4492], and died 19 May 1985 in Lima, Allen Co., OH[4493]. She married **John W Rittenour**[4494]. He was born 1910 in PA[4495].

More About Mabel Christner:
Residence: 1930, Garrett, Somerset, PA[4496]
Social Security Number: 292-20-5391/[4497]
SSN issued: OH[4497]

More About John W Rittenour:
Residence: 1930, Garrett, Somerset Co., PA[4498]

Children of Mabel Christner and John Rittenour are:

2416   i.   William Donald[8] Rittenour[4499], born 24 Oct 1927 in Somerset Co., PA[4499,4500,4501]; died 26 Sep 1992 in Akron, Summit Co., OH[4502].

> More About William Donald Rittenour:
> Residence: 1930, Garrett, Somerset Co., PA[4502]
> Social Security Number: 300-22-5856/[4503]
> SSN issued: OH[4503]

2417   ii.   James Rittnour, born 1930.

1016. Blanche Beloye[7] Christner (Richard W.[6], Moses C.[5], Joseph "Zep"[4], Johannes John Hans[3], Christian[2], Christen[1]) was born 10 Mar 1910 in Garrett, Somerset Co., PA[4504], and died 01 Oct 1980 in Berlin, Somerset Co., PA. She married **Eugene Arthur Walters Sr.**.

Notes for Blanche Beloye Christner:
Birth: Mar. 10, 1910 - Garrett, Somerset Co., PA
Death: Oct. 1, 1980 - Berlin, Somerset Co., PA

Burial: Somerset County Memorial Park, Somerset, Somerset Co.,
Find A Grave Memorial# 55338570

More About Blanche Beloye Christner:
Burial: Somerset County, Memorial Park, Somerset, Somerset Co., PA[4505]
Christened: United Church, Christ
Residence: 1920, Summit, Somerset Co., PA[4506]
Social Security Number: 186-32-3550/[4507]
SSN issued: PA[4507]

Child of Blanche Christner and Eugene Walters is:

2418   i.   Eugene Arthur[8] Walters Jr., born 05 Sep 1930 in Garrett, Somerset Co., PA; died 13 Nov 2001 in Somerset, Somerset Co., PA. He married Evelyn; born 1933.

Notes for Eugene Arthur Walters Jr.:
Birth: Sep 5, 1930 - Garrett, Somerset Co., PA
Death: Nov 13, 2001 - Somerset, Somerset Co., PA

Parents: Blanch Beloye Christner Walters (1910 - 1980)

Burial: Somerset County Memorial Park, Somerset, Somerset Co., PA
Find A Grave Memorial# 55338472

1020. Bertha Idella "Della"[7] Judy (Cornelius[6], Eve[5] Christner, Joseph "Zep"[4], Johannes John Hans[3], Christian[2], Christen[1])[4508] was born 12 Feb 1880 in Pittsburgh, Allegheny Co., PA[4508], and died 12 Nov 1980 in Somerset, Co., PA[4508]. She married **John Ray**.

More About Bertha Idella "Della" Judy:
Residence: 1900, Age: 20; Marital Status: Single; Relation to Head of House: Daughter/Brothersvalley, Somerset, PA[4508]

Child of Bertha Judy and John Ray is:
+   2419   i.   Harry[8] Ray.

1021. Elias F.[7] Judy (Cornelius[6], Eve[5] Christner, Joseph "Zep"[4], Johannes John Hans[3], Christian[2], Christen[1])[4508] was born 27 Mar 1884 in Pittsburgh, Allegheny Co., PA[4508], and died 11 Mar 1973 in Garrett, Somerset Co., PA[4508]. He married **Mary Ellen Mullen**[4509] 26 Dec 1911 in Somerset Co., PA[4509]. She was born 24 Jan 1884 in Minerville, Bedford Co., PA[4509], and died 04 Jul 1964 in Age at Death: 80/Brothersvalley, Somerset Co., PA[4509].

More About Elias F. Judy:
Burial: Somerset Co., PA[4509]
Residence: 1900, Age: 16; Marital Status: Single; Relation to Head of House: Son/Brothersvalley, Somerset, PA[4510]

More About Mary Ellen Mullen:
Burial: Somerset Co., PA[4511]
Residence: 1935, Brothers Valley, Somerset, Pennsylvania[4511]

Children of Elias Judy and Mary Mullen are:

2420   i.   Paul Eugene[8] Judy[4511], born 05 Nov 1911 in PA[4511]; died 02 May 1978 in Berlin, Somerset, Pennsylvania, United States of America[4511].

More About Paul Eugene Judy:
Burial: Somerset Co., PA[4511]
Residence: 1930, Age: 18; Marital Status: Single; Relation to Head of House: Son/Brothersvalley,

Somerset, Pennsylvania[4511]

2421   ii.   Pauline Naomi Judy[4511], born 05 Nov 1911 in Fogletown, Brothersvalley Twp, Somerset Co., PA[4511]; died 06 Aug 2012 in Titusville, Brevard Co., Florida[4511].

More About Pauline Naomi Judy:
Residence: 1935, Reading, Berks, Pennsylvania[4511]

1031. Albert Barton[7] Judy (Jerome Henry[6], Eve[5] Christner, Joseph "Zep"[4], Johannes John Hans[3], Christian[2], Christen[1])[4512,4513,4514] was born 02 Mar 1888 in Garrett, Somerset Co., PA[4515,4516], and died 1960 in Garrett, Somerset Co., PA[4517,4518]. He married **Margaret Mae Romesberg**[4519,4520] 28 Apr 1910[4521,4522]. She was born 27 Dec 1891 in Garrett, Somerset Co., PA[4523,4524], and died 1960 in Garrett, Somerset, PA[4524].

More About Albert Barton Judy:
Residence: 1930, Age: 42; Marital Status: Married; Relation to Head of House: Head/Garrett, Somerset, Pennsylvania[4524]

More About Margaret Mae Romesberg:
Residence: 1930, Age: 38; Marital Status: Married; Relation to Head of House: Wife/Garrett, Somerset, Pennsylvania[4524]

Children of Albert Judy and Margaret Romesberg are:
2422   i.   Charlotte Margaret[8] Judy[4524], born 25 Jan 1911 in Garrett, Somerset, PA[4524]; died 1953 in Age at Death: 42/Garrett, Somerset, Pennsylvania, USA[4524].

More About Charlotte Margaret Judy:
Burial: Garrett, Somerset County, Pennsylvania, USA[4524]
Residence: 1920, Age: 8; Marital Status: Single; Relation to Head of House: Daughter/Garrett, Somerset, Pennsylvania[4524]

2423   ii.   Emaline R Judy[4524], born 14 Mar 1916 in Garrett, Somerset, PA[4524]; died 05 Nov 1973 in Garrett, Somerset, PA[4524].

More About Emaline R Judy:
Residence: 1920, Age: 3; Age: 3 9/12; Marital Status: Single; Relation to Head of House: Daughter/Garrett, Somerset, Pennsylvania[4524]

2424   iii.   Regina B Judy[4524], born 05 Jul 1918 in PA[4524]; died 29 Mar 2006 in Garrett, Somerset, Pennsylvania[4524].

More About Regina B Judy:
Residence: 1920, Age: 1; Age: 1 6/12; Marital Status: Single; Relation to Head of House: Daughter/Garrett, Somerset, Pennsylvania[4524]

2425   iv.   Ivadene Louise Judy[4524], born 15 Nov 1920 in Garrett, Somerset, PA[4524]; died 08 Apr 1983 in Garrett, Somerset, PA[4524].

More About Ivadene Louise Judy:
Residence: 1930, Age: 9; Marital Status: Single; Relation to Head of House: Daughter/Garrett, Somerset, Pennsylvania[4524]

2426   v.   Albert Devon Judy[4524], born 19 Jul 1927 in Garrett, Somerset, PA[4524]; died 12 Apr 2006[4524].

More About Albert Devon Judy:
Residence: 1930, Age: 2; Age: 2 9/12; Marital Status: Single; Relation to Head of House: Son/Garrett, Somerset, Pennsylvania[4524]

1042. Elizabeth Amelia[7] Christner (William Henry[6], Solomon McKenzie[5], Benjamin[4], Johannes John Hans[3], Christian[2], Christen[1])[4525] was born 29 Aug 1869 in Grey, York, Ontario, Canada[4525], and died 10 Oct 1940 in Lincoln, Lancaster Co., NE[4525]. She married **Alexander Beam** Dec 1889. He was born 19 Jan 1861 in Fort Wayne, Allen Co., IN, and died 23 Apr 1938 in Lincoln, Lancaster Co., NE.

More About Elizabeth Amelia Christner:
Residence: 1880, Painesville, Lake Co., OH[4525]

Children of Elizabeth Christner and Alexander Beam are:
2427   i.   Edith[8] Beam.
2428   ii. Herbert Rollin Beam, born 13 Feb 1891; died 08 Aug 1891.
2429   iii. Ethyl May Beam, born 23 Jun 1892 in Denton, NE. She married Lawrence Moses 09 Mar 1923 in
            Marysville, Marshal Co., KS.
2430   iv. Grace Beam, born 12 Oct 1893. She married George Wilson 12 Jun 1919 in Denton NE.
2431   v.   Victoria Marie Beam, born 23 May 1895; died 30 May 1895.
2432   vi. William Beam[4526], born 1900 in NE[4526].

            More About William Beam:
            Residence: 1910, Denton, Lancaster, NE[4526]

1046. Sarah Etta[7] Christner (William Henry[6], Solomon McKenzie[5], Benjamin[4], Johannes John Hans[3], Christian[2], Christen[1])[4527] was born 30 May 1874 in Canada[4527], and died 17 Jan 1939[4527]. She married **Mason J. Wagey** 23 Dec 1890. He was born 04 Jul.

More About Sarah Etta Christner:
Residence: 1880, Painesville, Lake Co., OH[4527]

Children of Sarah Christner and Mason Wagey are:
2433   i.   Clara[8] Wagey. She married (1) Bill Schiller. She married (2) Jimmy Cameron.
2434   ii. Evelyn Ruth Wagey. She married Sherwood Turner.
2435   iii. Harold Christner Wagey, born 15 Jul 1899; died in New Lexington, PA. He married Eva Perry 1920.

1047. Frederick Walter[7] Christner (William Henry[6], Solomon McKenzie[5], Benjamin[4], Johannes John Hans[3], Christian[2], Christen[1])[4527,4528,4529,4530] was born 14 Aug 1876 in Canada[4531,4532,4533], and died 10 Jan 1945 in San Luis Obispo, CA[4534,4535,4536]. He married **Lola May King** 22 Dec 1903. She was born 01 Jun 1886 in MO[4537,4538], and died 16 Jun 1968 in San Luis Obispo, CA[4539].

More About Frederick Walter Christner:
Arrival: 1887[4540]
Residence: 1880, Painesville, Lake Co., OH[4541]

More About Lola May King:
Residence: 1910, Clay, Douglas, MO[4542]
Social Security Number: 559-03-6657/[4543]
SSN issued: CA[4543]

Children of Frederick Christner and Lola King are:
2436   i.   Cleda[8] Christner[4544,4545], born Bet. 1905 - 1906 in MO[4546].

            More About Cleda Christner:
            Residence: 1910, Clay, Douglas, MO[4546]

2437   ii. Della D. Christner[4546,4547], born 25 Oct 1906 in MO[4548]; died 21 Jun 1940 in Kern, CA[4548].

            More About Della D. Christner:
            Residence: 1910, Clay, Douglas, MO[4549]

2438   iii. Walter Christner[4549], born 1910 in MO[4549,4550].

            More About Walter Christner:
            Residence: 1910, Clay, Douglas, MO[4551]

1048. Rosa Mae⁷ Christner (William Henry⁶, Solomon McKenzie⁵, Benjamin⁴, Johannes John Hans³, Christian², Christen¹)*⁴⁵⁵²,⁴⁵⁵³,⁴⁵⁵³* was born 27 Jul 1878 in Painesville, Lake Co., OH*⁴⁵⁵⁴,⁴⁵⁵⁵*, and died Apr 1974 in Lincoln, Lancaster Co., NE*⁴⁵⁵⁵*. She married **John William Fuhrer***⁴⁵⁵⁶* 30 Apr 1902. He was born 1880 in IL*⁴⁵⁵⁶*.

More About Rosa Mae Christner:
Residence: 1880, Painesville, Lake Co., OH*⁴⁵⁵⁷*
Social Security Number: 326-20-5202/*⁴⁵⁵⁸*
SSN issued: IL*⁴⁵⁵⁸*

More About John William Fuhrer:
Residence: 1910, Pittsburg Ward 2, Crawford, Kansas*⁴⁵⁵⁹*

Children of Rosa Christner and John Fuhrer are:
+ 2439　　i.　　Mary A.⁸ Fuhrer*⁴⁵⁵⁹*, born 1903 in NE*⁴⁵⁵⁹*.

　　　　　　　More About Mary A. Fuhrer:
　　　　　　　Residence: 1910, Pittsburg Ward 2, Crawford, Kansas*⁴⁵⁵⁹*

+ 2440　　ii.　　Lorema C. Fuhrer*⁴⁵⁵⁹*, born 1906 in NE*⁴⁵⁵⁹*.

　　　　　　　More About Lorema C. Fuhrer:
　　　　　　　Residence: 1910, Pittsburg Ward 2, Crawford, Kansas*⁴⁵⁵⁹*

1050. Lena Belle⁷ Christner (William Henry⁶, Solomon McKenzie⁵, Benjamin⁴, Johannes John Hans³, Christian², Christen¹)*⁴⁵⁶⁰,⁴⁵⁶¹* was born 28 Jun 1882 in Painesville, Lake Co., OH*⁴⁵⁶²*, and died 31 Aug 1954 in Lindsay, Tulare Co., CA*⁴⁵⁶²*. She married **Soloman Leonard Pugh** 14 Sep 1902 in Olathe, Douglas Co., MO. He was born 25 Jul 1879 in Romney, Hampshire Co., WV*⁴⁵⁶³*, and died 13 Feb 1957 in Lindsay, Tulare Co., CA*⁴⁵⁶³*.

More About Lena Belle Christner:
Residence: 1930, Long Beach, Los Angeles, California*⁴⁵⁶³*

More About Soloman Leonard Pugh:
Residence: 1930, Long Beach, Los Angeles, California*⁴⁵⁶³*

Children of Lena Christner and Soloman Pugh are:
+ 2441　　i.　　Thelma Marie⁸ Pugh*⁴⁵⁶³*, born 10 Dec 1903 in Olathe, Douglas Co., MO*⁴⁵⁶³*; died 13 Sep 1994 in Lindsay, Tulare Co., CA*⁴⁵⁶³*.

　　　　　　　More About Thelma Marie Pugh:
　　　　　　　Residence: 1930, Long Beach, Los Angeles, California*⁴⁵⁶³*

+ 2442　　ii.　　Everett Fowler Pugh*⁴⁵⁶³*, born 19 May 1905 in Olathe, Douglas Co., MO*⁴⁵⁶³*; died 26 Oct 1926 in Long Beach, Los Angeles Co., CA*⁴⁵⁶³*.

　　　　　　　More About Everett Fowler Pugh:
　　　　　　　Residence: 1910, Clay, Douglas, MO*⁴⁵⁶³*

+ 2443　　iii.　　Mary Lillian Pugh*⁴⁵⁶³*, born 03 Feb 1907 in Olathe, Douglas Co., MO*⁴⁵⁶³*; died 19 Oct 1909 in Olathe, Douglas Co., MO*⁴⁵⁶³*.

1053. Grace Estelle⁷ Christner (William Henry⁶, Solomon McKenzie⁵, Benjamin⁴, Johannes John Hans³, Christian², Christen¹)*⁴⁵⁶⁴* was born 07 Oct 1884 in Painesville, Lake Co., OH*⁴⁵⁶⁴,⁴⁵⁶⁵*, and died 13 Jun 1967 in Lindsay, Tulare Co., CA. She married **Lawrence Dennis Pugh** 30 Mar 1902 in Olathe, Douglas Co., MO. He was born 02 Oct 1881 in Pleasant Dale, Hampshire Co., WV*⁴⁵⁶⁶*, and died 14 Dec 1959 in Modesto St.Hosp., Modesto, Stanislaus, CA*⁴⁵⁶⁶*.

More About Grace Estelle Christner:
Burial: 16 Jun 1967, Olive Cemetery, Lindsay, Tulare, CA[4566]
Social Security Number: 573-30-8179/[4567]
SSN issued: CA[4567]

More About Lawrence Dennis Pugh:
Burial: Olive Cemetery, Lindsay, Tulare, CA[4568]

Children of Grace Christner and Lawrence Pugh are:

2444	i.	Living[8] Pugh[4568].
2445	ii.	Buelah Belle Pugh[4568], born 01 Nov 1902 in Olathe, Douglas Co., MO[4568]; died 13 May 1984 in Victorville, San Bernardino Co., CA[4568].
2446	iii.	Florence Agnes Pugh[4568], born 21 May 1904 in Olathe, Douglas Co., MO[4568].
2447	iv.	Elmer Jesse Pugh[4568], born 17 Jan 1906 in Olathe, Douglas Co., MO[4568]; died 18 Jul 1914 in Olathe, Douglas Co., MO[4568].

> More About Elmer Jesse Pugh:
> Burial: Fairview Cemet, Olathe, Douglas, Mo[4568]

2448	v.	Earl William Pugh[4568], born 27 Oct 1908 in Olathe, Douglas Co., MO[4568]; died 17 Sep 1970 in Anaheim, Orange Co., CA[4568].

> More About Earl William Pugh:
> Burial: Loma Vista, Fullerton, Orange, CA[4568]

2449	vi.	Bert Leonard Pugh[4568], born 13 Oct 1910 in Olathe, Douglas Co., MO[4568]; died 10 May 1975 in Lindsay Hosp., Lindsay, Tulare Co., CA[4568].

> More About Bert Leonard Pugh:
> Burial: 13 May 1975, Olive Cemetery, Lindsay, Tulare, CA[4568]

1059. Bertha Ida[7] Christner (William Henry[6], Solomon McKenzie[5], Benjamin[4], Johannes John Hans[3], Christian[2], Christen[1])[4569,4570,4571] was born 02 Dec 1896 in Olathe, Douglas Co., MO[4572,4573,4574,4575], and died Dec 1986 in Pittsburg, Crawford Co., KS[4575,4576]. She married **John William Lemon**[4577] 23 Feb 1918 in Pittsburg, Salina Co., KS. He was born 1897 in KS[4577].

More About Bertha Ida Christner:
Residence: 1910, Clay, Douglas, MO[4578]
Social Security Number: 510-68-4809/[4579]
SSN issued: KS[4579]

More About John William Lemon:
Residence: 1930, Pittsburg, Crawford, Kansas[4580]

Children of Bertha Christner and John Lemon are:

2450	i.	Billy[8] Lemon[4580], born 1919[4580].

> More About Billy Lemon:
> Residence: 1930, Pittsburg, Crawford, Kansas[4580]

2451	ii.	Jinnie Lemon[4580], born 1921[4580].

> More About Jinnie Lemon:
> Residence: 1930, Pittsburg, Crawford, Kansas[4580]

2452	iii.	Jack Lemon[4580], born 1924[4580].

> More About Jack Lemon:
> Residence: 1930, Pittsburg, Crawford, Kansas[4580]

1060. William John[7] Merrill (Jane Elizabeth[6] Christner, Solomon McKenzie[5], Benjamin[4], Johannes John Hans[3], Christian[2], Christen[1]) was born 02 Mar 1860, and died 01 Jun 1927 in Southeastern NE.

More About William John Merrill:
Burial: Crete, NE

Child of William John Merrill is:
+ 2453   i.   Charles LeRoy[8] Merrill, born 1887.

1061. Benjamin Christner[7] Merrill (Mary Ann[6] Christner, Solomon McKenzie[5], Benjamin[4], Johannes John Hans[3], Christian[2], Christen[1])[4581] was born 07 Jun 1864 in Ontario, Canada[4581], and died 08 Jul 1941 in Hayes Co., NE[4581]. He married **(1) Edith E. Fox**[4581] Nov 1892[4581]. She was born Oct 1864 in MO[4581], and died 1912 in Hayes Co., NE[4581]. He married **(2) Anna Robb**[4581] 03 Apr 1921[4581]. She was born Abt. 1863[4581].

Notes for Benjamin Christner Merrill:
Birth: Jun 7, 1864
Death: Jul 8, 1941

Parents:
William H. Merrill (1837 - 1917)
Mary Ann Christner Merrill (1841 - 1914)

Spouse: Edith E. Fox Merrill (1864 - 1912)

Burial: Elmer Cemetery, Hayes Co., NE
Find A Grave Memorial# 37222717

More About Benjamin Christner Merrill:
Arrival: 1878[4581]
Burial: Elmer Cemetery, Elmer, Hayes, Nebraska[4581]
Residence: 1930, Antelope, Hayes, Nebraska[4581]

Notes for Edith E. Fox:
Birth: Oct 1864
Death: 1912

Spouse: Benjamin Christner Merrill (1864 - 1941)

Burial: Elmer Cemetery, Hayes Co., NE
Find A Grave Memorial# 40723868

More About Edith E. Fox:
Burial: Elmer Cemetery, Elmer, Hayes, Nebraska[4581]
Residence: 1930, Antelope, Hayes, Nebraska[4581]

More About Anna Robb:
Residence: 1930, Antelope, Hayes, Nebraska[4581]

Children of Benjamin Merrill and Edith Fox are:
+ 2454   i.   Martha Marcella "Marcella"[8] Merrill, born 02 Feb 1894 in NE; died Jul 1981 in Elsie, Perkins Co., NE.
  2455   ii.   Harry Edward Merrill[4581], born 16 Oct 1896 in Stratton, Hitchcock, Nebraska[4581]; died 26 Jul 1940 in York, York, Nebraska[4581].

More About Harry Edward Merrill:

Burial: Riverside Cemetery, Wauneta, Chase, Nebraska[4581]
Residence: 1920, Yankee, Perkins, Nebraska[4581]

2456   iii.   Benjamin W Merrill[4581], born 06 Jul 1904 in Dundy Co., NE[4581]; died 11 Jun 1959 in Sutherland, Lincoln Co., NE[4581].

More About Benjamin W Merrill:
Burial: Riverside Cemetery, Wauneta, Chase, Nebraska[4581]
Residence: 1930, Antelope, Hayes, Nebraska[4581]

+   2457   iv.   John Theron Merrill, born 02 Jan 1908 in NE; died Aug 1978 in Wauneta, Chase Co., NE.

1062. William Henry[7] Merrill Jr. (Mary Ann[6] Christner, Solomon McKenzie[5], Benjamin[4], Johannes John Hans[3], Christian[2], Christen[1])[4582] was born 12 May 1869 in Ontario, Canada[4582], and died 15 Oct 1916 in railroad accident/Railroad, York Co., PA[4582]. He married **Clara B. Reed**[4582] 1898[4582]. She was born Dec 1870 in IL[4582].

Notes for William Henry Merrill Jr.:
Birth: May 12, 1869 - Canada
Death: Oct 15, 1916 - York, York Co., PA

Parents:
William H. Merrill (1837 - 1917)
Mary Ann Christner Merrill (1841 - 1914)

Burial: Riverside Cemetery, Wauneta, Chase Co., NE
Plot: 39-2-4
Find A Grave Memorial# 37222638

More About William Henry Merrill Jr.:
Arrival: 1876[4582]
Burial: Riverside Cemetery, Wauneta, Chase, Nebraska[4582]
Residence: 1910, Harrison, Hayes, Nebraska[4582]

More About Clara B. Reed:
Residence: 1920, Lincoln Ward 7, Lancaster, Nebraska[4582]

Child of William Merrill and Clara Reed is:
2458   i.   Herbert K.[8] Merrill[4582], born 04 Nov 1901 in NE[4582,4583]; died 25 Sep 1977 in Ceres, Stanislaus Co., CA[4584,4585].

More About Herbert K. Merrill:
Residence: 1920, Lincoln Ward 7, Lancaster, Nebraska[4586]
Social Security Number: 543-16-6005/[4587]

1065. Jessie Amanda[7] Merrill (Mary Ann[6] Christner, Solomon McKenzie[5], Benjamin[4], Johannes John Hans[3], Christian[2], Christen[1])[4588,4589,4590] was born 17 Oct 1885 in NE[4591,4592], and died 07 Mar 1951 in Riverside, Burt Co., NE[4592,4593]. She married **Elmer Henry Carpenter**[4593,4594,4595], son of Theron Carpenter and Caroline Olson. He was born 08 Sep 1882 in LaSalle County, Illinois[4596,4597,4598], and died 10 May 1968 in Stratton, Hitchcock, Nebraska[4599,4600,4601].

Notes for Jessie Amanda Merrill:
Birth: Sep 18, 1882
Death: Mar 7, 1951

Parents:
William H. Merrill (1837 - 1917)
Mary Ann Christner Merrill (1841 - 1914)

Spouse: Elmer Henry Carpenter (1882 - 1968)

Children:
Ellis E. Carpenter (1911 - 2003)
Ruth Alberta Carpenter (1916 - 1925)

Burial: Riverside Cemetery, Wauneta, Chase Co., NE
Find A Grave Memorial# 37237674

More About Jessie Amanda Merrill:
Burial: Riverside Cemetery, Wauneta, Chase, Nebraska[4602]
Residence: 1900, Precinct I, Seward, Nebraska[4602,4602]

Notes for Elmer Henry Carpenter:
Birth: Sep 8, 1882
Death: May 10, 1968

Parents:
Theron Virgil Bradford Carpenter (1856 - 1920)
Caroline Isabel Olson Carpenter (1856 - 1940)

Spouse: Jessie Amanda Merrill Carpenter (1882 - 1951)

Children:
Ellis E. Carpenter (1911 - 2003)
Ruth Alberta Carpenter (1916 - 1925)

Burial: Riverside Cemetery, Wauneta, Chase Co., NE
Find A Grave Memorial# 37237521

More About Elmer Henry Carpenter:
Burial: Riverside Cemetery, Wauneta, Chase, Nebraska[4602,4603]
Residence: 1920, Wauneta, Chase, Nebraska[4603,4604,4605,4606]

Children of Jessie Merrill and Elmer Carpenter are:
    2459   i.   Merril[8] Carpenter[4607], born 1910 in NE[4607]; died Jan 1974 in Mead, Weld, Colorado, United States of America[4607].

        More About Merril Carpenter:
        Residence: 01 Apr 1940, Stratton, Hitchcock, Nebraska, United States[4607]

    2460   ii.   Ellis E. Carpenter, born 04 Sep 1911 in Eden, Hitchcock Co., NE[4608]; died 02 Sep 2003 in North Platte, Lincoln Co., NE[4608]. He married Irene Della Egle[4608] 01 Aug 1936[4608]; born 15 Nov 1914 in NE[4608]; died 05 May 1986 in North Platte, Lincoln Co., NE[4608].

        Notes for Ellis E. Carpenter:
        Birth: Sep 4, 1911 - Wauneta, Chase Co., NE
        Death: Sep 2, 2003 - North Platte, Lincoln Co., NE

        NORTH PLATTE - Ellis E. Carpenter, 91, died Tuesday (Sept. 2, 2003) at Linden Court Nursing Home.

        He was born Sep 4, 1911, Elmer and Jessie Carpenter northwest of Wauneta. He grew up in the Eden community in Hitchcock County and graduated From Wauneta High School.

        On Aug 1, 1936 he married Irene D. Egle. The couple made their home in the Eden community and participating in farming there until 1983 where the couple retired and moved to North Platte.

He was a member of the Eden Missionary Church, a barber shop quartet, North Platte Senior Center and Intra Church Reserve.

He was preceded in death by his parents; his wife, Irene; one brother, Merrill; and one sister, Ruth.

Survivors include his sister, Glenda Schwenk of Mesa, Ariz.; two sisters-in-law, Bonnie and husband, Herman Bley of North Platte and Viola Miller of Lancaster, Pa.; and one brother-in-law, Donald and wife, Iola Egle of Bella Vista, Ark.

Services are Friday, 10:30 a.m. (MST), at Riverside Cemetery in Wauneta. Visitation is Friday, 9:30-10:15 a.m. (MST), at the Wauneta Methodist Church.
Memorials are suggested to the Salvation Army or the Alzheimer's Association.
Carpenter Funeral Home of North Platte is in charge of arrangements.

Parents:
Elmer Henry Carpenter (1882 - 1968)
Jessie Amanda Merrill Carpenter (1882 - 1951)

Spouse: Irene Della Egle Carpenter (1914 - 1986)

Burial:Riverside Cemetery, Wauneta, Chase Co., NE
Plot: 43-3-5
Find A Grave Memorial# 12848839

More About Ellis E. Carpenter:
Burial: Sep 2003, Wauneta, Chase County, Nebraska, USA[4608]
Religion: Eden Missionary Church/Eden, Hitchcock, Nebraska, United States[4608]
Residence: 01 Apr 1940, Age: 28; Marital Status: Married; Relation to Head of House: Head/Eden, Hitchcock, Nebraska, United States[4608]

Notes for Irene Della Egle:
Birth: Nov 15, 1914
Death: May 1986

Parents:
Dan Egle (1889 - 1950)
Martha Egle (1890 - 1965)

Spouse: Ellis E. Carpenter (1911 - 2003)

Burial: Riverside Cemetery, Wauneta, Chase Co., NE
Find A Grave Memorial# 37237891

More About Irene Della Egle:
Burial: May 1986, Riverside Cemetery/Wauneta, Chase County, Nebraska, USA[4608]
Residence: 01 Apr 1940, Age: 25; Marital Status: Married; Relation to Head of House: Wife/Eden, Hitchcock, Nebraska, United States[4608]

2461   iii.   Glenda J. Carpenter[4609], born 11 Jun 1913 in NE[4610,4611]; died 30 Aug 2004 in Mesa, Maricopa Co., AZ[4611,4612]. She married Alton Schwenk[4612]; born 28 Nov 1909 in NE[4612]; died Jun 1987 in Mesa, Maricopa Co., AZ[4612].

More About Glenda J. Carpenter:
Residence: 1995, Mesa, Maricopa Co., AZ[4612,4613]

2462   iv.   Ruth Alberta Carpenter[4614], born 03 Apr 1916 in Chase Co., NE[4614]; died 01 Jul 1925.

Notes for Ruth Alberta Carpenter:
Birth: Apr 3, 1916
Death: Jul 1, 1925

Parents:

Elmer Henry Carpenter (1882 - 1968)
Jessie Amanda Merrill Carpenter (1882 - 1951)

Burial: Riverside Cemetery, Wauneta, Chase Co., NE
Plot: 43-3-4
Find A Grave Memorial# 37237919

More About Ruth Alberta Carpenter:
Burial: Riverside Cemetery, Wauneta, Chase, Nebraska[4614]
Residence: 1920, Wauneta, Chase, Nebraska[4614]

1067. William Arthur[7] Christner (Moses Isaac[6], Solomon McKenzie[5], Benjamin[4], Johannes John Hans[3], Christian[2], Christen[1])[4615] was born 09 Sep 1879 in Painesville, Lake Co., OH[4615], and died 18 Sep 1946 in Golden Gate National Cemetery, Marin, CA[4616]. He married **Ethel E. Eastwood**[4616,4617] 04 Mar 1908 in M E Church/Tacoma, Pierce Co., WA[4618]. She was born 30 Jun 1888 in NE[4619,4620], and died 13 Aug 1982 in Seattle, King Co., WA[4620].

More About William Arthur Christner:
Burial: 21 Sep 1946, CA[4621]
Military service: 10 Jul 1899[4621]
Residence: 1920, Tacoma Ward 7, Pierce Co., WA[4622]

More About Ethel E. Eastwood:
Residence: 1930, Skagway, First Judicial District, Alaska Territory[4622]

Child of William Christner and Ethel Eastwood is:
    2463   i.   Robert L.[8] Christner[4623], born 12 Oct 1909 in Tacoma, Pierce Co., WA[4623,4624]; died Apr 1975 in Seattle, King Co., WA[4625,4626].

                   More About Robert L. Christner:
                   Residence: 1930, Skagway, First Judicial District, Alaska Territory[4626]

1070. Elizabeth[7] Peacock (Eliza[6] Irvine, Mary Jane[5] Christner, Benjamin[4], Johannes John Hans[3], Christian[2], Christen[1]) She married **William Root**.

Children of Elizabeth Peacock and William Root are:
    2464   i.   Fred[8] Root.
    2465   ii.   Goldie Root.
    2466   iii.   Irvine Root.

1079. Frank O.[7] Irvine (James[6], Mary Jane[5] Christner, Benjamin[4], Johannes John Hans[3], Christian[2], Christen[1]) was born 1889, and died 1960 in IL. He married **Genevieve Sedlack**.

Children of Frank Irvine and Genevieve Sedlack are:
    2467   i.   James Weston[8] Irvine.
    2468   ii.   Patricia J. Irvine.
    2469   iii.   Dorothy M. Irvine.

1080. May Adelaide[7] Irvine (James[6], Mary Jane[5] Christner, Benjamin[4], Johannes John Hans[3], Christian[2], Christen[1]) was born 05 Nov 1894 in Weston, York Co., Canada, and died 24 Mar 1984. She married **John Bernard Knapp** 30 Nov 1929 in St. Philips Ang. Church, York Co., Toronto, Canada. He was born 20 Sep 1894 in Toronto, Canada, and died 24 Mar 1984 in Toronto, Canada.

More About May Adelaide Irvine:
Burial: Riverside Cemetery by Lawrence Ave. & Royal York Road Toronto CA.

More About John Bernard Knapp:
Burial: Riverside Cemetery by Lawrence Ave. & Royal York Road Toronto CA.

Children of May Irvine and John Knapp are:
+   2470   i.   Mary Jane[8] Knapp, born 06 Nov 1933.
     2471   ii.   Marjorie Knapp, born 21 Jun 1939. She married Ronald F. Mossman 01 Jul 1961.

1081. Harry Foreman[7] Irvine (James[6], Mary Jane[5] Christner, Benjamin[4], Johannes John Hans[3], Christian[2], Christen[1]) was born 08 Aug 1897 in Weston, York Co., Canada, and died 27 Dec 1953. He married **Doris Bourke** 01 Oct 1937 in Toronto, Canada.

More About Harry Foreman Irvine:
Burial: Riverside Cemetery by Lawrence Ave. & Royal York Road Toronto CA.

Child of Harry Irvine and Doris Bourke is:
     2472   i.   John[8] Irvine.

1120. John[7] Christner (Peter C.[6], Christian[5], Peter[4], Christian[3], Christian[2], Christen[1])[4627] was born 06 Nov 1870 in Miami Co., IN, and died 13 Apr 1941 in Age at Death: 72/Wawpecong, Miami County, Indiana - Buried - Kokomo Memorial Park Cemetery, Kokomo, Howard County, Indiana[4627]. He married **Amanda Carrie Schrock**[4628] 06 May 1893, daughter of John Schrock and Elizabeth Christner. She was born 18 Nov 1870 in Licking Co., OH[4629], and died 11 Jun 1948 in Wawpecong, Miami County, Indiana - Buried - Memorial Park Cemetery, Kokomo, Howard County, Indiana[4629].

Notes for John Christner:
Amish

More About John Christner:
Religion: Amish/
Residence: 1900, Clay Township, Miami Co., IN[4630]

Notes for Amanda Carrie Schrock:
Birth: 1870
Death: Jun. 11, 1948

Burial: Kokomo Memorial Park Cemetery, Kokomo, Howard Co., IN
Plot: Sec: Memorial

More About Amanda Carrie Schrock:
Residence: 1910, Clay Township, Miami Co., IN[4631]

Children are listed above under (428) Amanda Carrie Schrock.

1121. Christian C "Chris"[7] Christner (Peter C.[6], Christian[5], Peter[4], Christian[3], Christian[2], Christen[1])[4632] was born 02 Aug 1849 in Elkhart, Elkhart Co., IN[4632], and died 19 Oct 1926 in Wayland, Henry Co., IA[4632]. He married **Barbara S "Barbry" "Barbra" Van Gunden**[4632] 21 Jan 1872. She was born 05 Sep 1849 in Butler Co., OH[4632], and died 20 Jan 1929 in Wayland City, Henry Co., IA[4633].

Notes for Christian C "Chris" Christner:
Christner - Christian C. Christner was born in Elkhart Co., IN, Aug. 2, 1849; died at his home in Wayland, IA Oct 19, 1926; aged 77 y. 2 m. 17 d. He came to Iowa with his parents when a boy, residing on a farm near Rome. On Jan. 21, 1872 he was married to Barbara Gunden. They opened their home to a foster daughter and later two children were born to this union. In his youth he accepted Christ as his Savior, uniting with the Amish Mennonite Church and remained a faithful member until called by death. He leaves his bereaved wife, the foster daughter (Mrs. Oscar Martin), one son (John) and one daughter (Mrs. John Wenger); a half-sister (Mrs. Ephraim Miller), six grandchildren, four foster grandchildren, and a host of friends and neighbors to mourn their loss. The funeral

was held at the Sugar Creek Church conducted by the home ministers (Daniel Graber and Simon Gingerich) assisted by Bro. H. J. Schrag of Wayland. Texts, Job 5: 26; I Pet. 1: 23-25. Interment in the cemetery nearby.

Birth: Aug. 2, 1849 - Elkhart Co., IN
Death: Oct. 19, 1926 - Wayland, Henry Co., IA

Christner - Christian C. Christner was born in Elkhart Co., IN Aug. 2, 1849; died at his home in Wayland, IA Oct 19, 1926. He came to IA with his parents when a boy, residing on a farm near Rome.

On Jan 21, 1872, he was married to Barbara Gunden. They opened their home to a foster daughter and later two children were born to this union.

In his youth he accepted Christ as his Savior, uniting with the Amish Mennonite Church and remained a faithful member until called by death.

He leaves his bereaved wife, the foster daughter (Mrs. Oscar Martin), one son (John) and one daughter (Mrs. John Wenger); a half-sister (Mrs. Ephraim Miller), six grandchildren, four foster grandchildren, and a host of friends and neighbors to mourn their loss.

Spouse: Barbara S. Gunden Christner (1848 - 1929)

Children: Katie Ann Christner Wenger (1882 - 1980)

Burial: Sugar Creek Cemetery, Wayland, Henry Co., IA

More About Christian C "Chris" Christner:
Burial: Sugar Creek Cemetery, Wayland, Henry Co., IA
Residence: 01 Jan 1925[4634]

Notes for Barbara S "Barbry" "Barbra" Van Gunden:
Barbara is the daughter of John V. and Catherine Schmidt Gunden.

Christner - Barbara (Gunden) Christner was born in Butler Co., Ohio, Sept. 5, 1848. She came to Lee Co., Iowa, with her parents when she was eight years old. A few years later they moved to Henry Co., Iowa, near the country town of Trenton. Here she grew to womanhood. She accepted Christ as her Savior and united with the Amish Mennonite Church and remained faithful until death. On Jan 21, 1872, she was united in marriage to Christian C. Christner who preceded her in death Oct 19, 1926. They opened their home to a foster daughter and 1 daughter and 1 son were born to this union. She was a kind and affectionate mother. She was sick only a week, passing away very suddenly at the home of her daughter Sunday evening, Jan 20, 1929 at the age of 80 y. 4 m. 15 d. She leaves her daughter, Mrs. John R. Wenger, her son, John, both of Wayland, Iowa, her foster daughter, Mrs. Oscar Martin, Noble, Iowa; 3 brothers, John and Joe Gunden, Pigeon, Mich., and Jacob Gunden, Wellman, Iowa; 1 sister, Mrs. Tena Swartzendruber, Noble, Iowa; 6 grandchildren and a large number of acquaintances and friends to mourn her loss. The funeral was held at the Sugar Creek Church, Jan 23, conducted by the home ministers. Text, II Tim. 4:6-8; Jno. 17:24. Interment in the cemetery near by.

Birth: Sep. 5, 1848
Butler Co., OH
Death: Feb. 7, 1929
Henry Co., IA

Spouse: Christian C. Christner (1849 - 1926)

Children: Katie Ann Christner Wenger (1882 - 1980)

Burial: Sugar Creek Cemetery, Wayland, Henry Co., IA

More About Barbara S "Barbry" "Barbra" Van Gunden:

Burial: Sugar Creek Cemetery, Wayland, Henry Co., IA
Residence: 1920[4634,4635,4636]

Children of Christian Christner and Barbara Gunden are:

2473   i.   May[8] Christner[4637], born Abt. 1880 in Jefferson Twp., Henry Co., IA[4637].

        More About May Christner:
        Residence: 1885, Jefferson Twp., Henry Co., IA[4637]

+   2474   ii.   Katherine "Katie" Ann Christner, born 14 Dec 1882 in Wayland, Henry Co., IA; died 25 Sep 1980 in Parkview Home Wayland, Henry Co., IA.

+   2475   iii. John G. Christner, born 03 Jan 1885 in Jefferson Twp., Henry Co., IA; died 24 Nov 1962 in Mount Pleasant, Henry Co., IA.

1122. Lydia[7] Christner (Peter C.[6], Christian[5], Peter[4], Christian[3], Christian[2], Christen[1])[4638] was born 29 Jun 1851 in Elkhart, Elkhart Co., IN[4638], and died 19 Aug 1882 in Miami, Miami Co., IN[4638]. She married **Jonas Stineman**. He was born 13 Mar 1846 in Shanesville, Holmes Co., OH[4638], and died 29 Sep 1919 in Clay, Miami Co., IN[4638].

Notes for Jonas Stineman:
Jonas is the son of Peter and Veronica Hochstetler Stineman.

Child of Lydia Christner and Jonas Stineman is:

2476   i.   Fannie[8] Stineman[4638], born 07 Jan 1872 in Miami, IN[4638]; died 21 Jan 1922 in Home, Miami, IN/[4638].

1133. Susanna[7] Christner (Jacob[6], Christian[5], Peter[4], Christian[3], Christian[2], Christen[1])[4639] was born 10 Jun 1852 in Elkhart, Elkhart Co., IN[4639], and died 23 Nov 1881 in Clinton, Elkhart Co., IN[4640]. She married **Christian J. Troyer** 04 Jan 1870 in Goshen, Elkhart Co., IN[4640]. He was born 15 Apr 1847 in New Bedford, Holmes Co., OH, and died 08 Jun 1917 in Elkhart Co., IN.

Notes for Susanna Christner:
Amish and Amish Mennonite Genealogies; CHC52, p. 61

Buried Nisley Cemetery, Goshen, Elkhart Co., IN.

More About Susanna Christner:
Residence: 1880, Clinton, Elkhart Co., IN[4640]

Notes for Christian J. Troyer:
Christian is the son of Jeptha and Elizabeth Yoder Troyer. Christian married the 2nd time to Elizabeth Schlabach. Deacon in the Amish church ordained May 8, 1884.

More About Christian J. Troyer:
Residence: 1910, Clinton, Elkhart Co., IN[4640]

Children of Susanna Christner and Christian Troyer are:

+   2477   i.   Jacob C.[8] Troyer, born 23 Apr 1871 in Goshen, Elkhart Co., IN; died 26 Feb 1929 in Goshen, Elkhart Co., IN.

+   2478   ii.   Elizabeth Troyer, born 09 Dec 1872; died 18 Mar 1935 in Bremen, Marshall Co., IN.

+   2479   iii. Magdalena Mattie Troyer, born 31 Mar 1874 in Goshen, Elkhart Co., IN; died 24 Nov 1947 in Goshen, Elkhart Co., IN.

2480   iv.   Veronica Fannie Troyer[4640], born 19 Aug 1875 in Goshen, Elkhart Co., IN[4640]; died 27 Feb 1951. She married Noah S. Miller.

        More About Veronica Fannie Troyer:

Residence: 1930, English River, Washington Co., Iowa[4640]

Notes for Noah S. Miller:
He is an Amish deacon.

+ 2481   v.   Jeptha Troyer, born 17 Jul 1878; died 03 Nov 1956 in Lagrange Co., IN.
   2482   vi.   Mary Troyer, born 01 Sep 1880 in Goshen, Elkhart Co., IN[4640]; died 26 Aug 1906 in Nappanee, Elkhart Co., Indiana[4640].

More About Mary Troyer:
Residence: 1900, Clinton, Elkhart Co., IN[4640]

1134. Elizabeth[7] Christner (Jacob[6], Christian[5], Peter[4], Christian[3], Christian[2], Christen[1])[4641,4642] was born 19 Jul 1853 in Elkhart Co., IN[4643,4644], and died 03 Nov 1917 in Haven, Reno Co., KS[4644]. She married **Jeremiah D. Yoder**[4644] 26 Mar 1875. He was born 10 Mar 1852 in Somerset Co., PA[4644], and died 29 Nov 1933 in Haven, Reno Co., KS[4644].

Notes for Elizabeth Christner:
Amish and Amish Mennonite Genealogies; CHC53, p. 61

More About Elizabeth Christner:
Residence: 1915, Yoder, Reno Co., KS[4644]

Notes for Jeremiah D. Yoder:
Amish and Amish Mennonite Genealogies; CHC53, p. 61

Jeremiah is the son of David C. and Susanna Miller Yoder? was David married twice? Some say David is the son of Christian who is the son of Christian?

More About Jeremiah D. Yoder:
Residence: 1930, Yoder, Reno Co., KS[4644]

Children of Elizabeth Christner and Jeremiah Yoder are:
+ 2483   i.   Fannie E.[8] Yoder, born 03 Dec 1875 in Elkhart Co., IN; died 30 Apr 1964 in Yoder, KS.
+ 2484   ii.   Jacob E. Yoder, born 23 Aug 1877 in Middlebury, Elkhart Co., IN; died 20 Apr 1954 in Age at Death: 76/.
+ 2485   iii.   David J. Yoder, born 26 Feb 1880 in Middlebury, Elkhart Co., IN; died 28 Jul 1970 in Hutchinson, Reno Co., KS.
   2486   iv.   Mary Yoder, born 20 Apr 1882; died 06 Feb 1888.
   2487   v.   Andrew Yoder, born 01 Apr 1885; died 18 Jul 1901.
+ 2488   vi.   Susan Yoder, born 01 May 1887 in Middlebury, Elkhart Co., IN; died 29 Jul 1981 in Schowalter Villa, Hesston Co., KS.
   2489   vii.   Anna Yoder, born 25 Feb 1889; died 15 Aug 1889.

1135. Samuel[7] Christner (Jacob[6], Christian[5], Peter[4], Christian[3], Christian[2], Christen[1])[4645,4646,4647,4648,4649,4650] was born 12 Nov 1854 in Elkhart Co., IN[4651,4652,4653,4654], and died 20 Oct 1937 in Nursing home at Eureka, IL. He married **Elizabeth Mast**[4655] 1875. She was born 04 Aug 1859 in Pigeon, Huron Co., MI[4656], and died 19 Nov 1916 in Oliver, Huron Co., MI[4657].

Notes for Samuel Christner:
Amish and Amish Mennonite Genealogies; CHC54, p. 61

Sometimes you have a child you can't do anything with, that was Jacob's son Samuel.

Coming from a family and father that was very neat and organized, straight rows, square corners, no weeds, take responsability for your own actions. Where did Samuel get his ways? He let his wife in 1912, no one knew where he was for 15 years when he showed up at his sister's (Barbara) home when she was living with her son Oba

Miller in 1930 to 1933. From there he went to live in a nursing home until he died Aug. 20,1937.His headstone is marked wrong, Birth date is marked 1863, so be 1854.

More About Samuel Christner:
Arrival: 08 Sep 1928, Emerson, Manitoba[4657]
Burial: Peter Miller Cemetery, Riverside, IA near Kalona, IA
Residence: 1860, Clinton, Elkhart Co., IN[4658]

Notes for Elizabeth Mast:
Amish and Amish Mennonite Genealogies; CHC54, p. 61

Elizabeth lived with her son John after her husband left her.

More About Elizabeth Mast:
Burial: Nov 1916, Pigeon River Mennonite Church Cemetery, Pigeon, Huron Co., MI
Residence: 1880, Clinton, Elkhart Co., IN[4659]

Children of Samuel Christner and Elizabeth Mast are:

+	2490	i.	Daniel J.[8] Christner, born 06 Mar 1879 in Elkhart Co., IN; died 03 Apr 1943 in Buried Pigeon River Mennonite Church Cemetery, Pigeon, Huron Co., Michigan/Huron Co., MI.
+	2491	ii.	John Adam Christner, born 05 Sep 1880 in Middlebury, Elkhart Co., IN; died 09 Sep 1920 in Pigeon, Huron Co., MI.
+	2492	iii.	Barbara Christner, born 14 Sep 1882 in IN; died 22 Mar 1915 in Hubbard, Marion Co., OR.
+	2493	iv.	Jacob Christner, born 11 Jun 1884 in Goshen, Elkhart Co., IN; died 06 Dec 1960 in Pigeon, Huron Co., MI.

1136. Frances Frany[7] Christner (Jacob[6], Christian[5], Peter[4], Christian[3], Christian[2], Christen[1])[4660] was born 23 Apr 1856 in Goshen, Elkhart Co., IN[4661,4662], and died 24 May 1934 in Goshen, Elkhart Co., IN[4663,4664]. She married **Simon D. Schlabach**[4664] 15 Jun 1887 in Elkhart Co., IN[4664], son of David Schlabach and Catherine Miller. He was born 25 Jan 1851 in Charm, Holmes Co., OH[4664], and died 13 Oct 1932[4664].

Notes for Frances Frany Christner:
Amish and Amish Mennonite Genealogies; CHC55, p. 61

Schlabach - Frances Christner was born Apr. 23, 1856; died at the home of her daughter (Mrs. Noah Miller) near Goshen, Ind., May 24, 1934; aged 78 y. 1 m. 1 d. In her young years she united with the Amish Mennonite Church and continued in this faith to the end. On June 15, 1881, she was united in marriage with Simeon Schlabach. To this union were born 2 sons and 3 daughters. One son preceded her in death. She leaves 1 son, 3 daughters, 3 brothers, 10 grandchildren, 4 great-grandchildren, and a host of relatives and friends-not to mourn her departure but to rejoice that her suffering is ended and believe that her soul is at rest. Funeral services at the home by Samuel Hostetler and Nathaniel Miller in German and D. J. Johns in English.
Birth: Apr. 23, 1856
Death: May 25, 1934

Spouse: Simeon D. Schlabach (1851 - 1932)

Children:
Elizabeth Schlabach Miller (1883 - 1973)
Osa Schlabach (1887 - 1977)

Note: Dau of Jacob and Elizabeth (Walter) Christner

Burial: Nisley Cemetery, Goshen, Elkhart Co., IN
Plot: Row 8 #38
Find A Grave Memorial# 55232878

More About Frances Frany Christner:

Burial: Nisley Cemetery, Goshen, Elkhart Co., IN
Residence: 1930, Clinton, Elkhart Co., IN[4664]

Notes for Simon D. Schlabach:
Amish and Amish Mennonite Genealogies; CHC55, p. 61

Simon is a farmer. He was O. O. Amish and the son of David J. and Catherine Miller Schlabaugh.

More About Simon D. Schlabach:
Burial: Nisley Cemetery, Goshen, Elkhart Co., IN
Residence: 1920, Clinton, Elkhart Co., IN[4664]

Children of Frances Christner and Simon Schlabach are:

+   2494   i.   Elizabeth Lizzie[8] Schlabaugh, born 18 Oct 1883 in Goshen, Elkhart Co., IN; died 05 Jul 1973 in Goshen, Elkhart Co., IN.

     2495   ii.   Catherine Katie Schlabaugh, born 18 Jul 1885 in Goshen, Elkhart Co., IN; died 09 Aug 1958 in Kalona, Washington Co., IA. She married William Schrock 18 Feb 1919; born 24 Feb 1885; died 19 Jul 1966.

         Notes for Catherine Katie Schlabaugh:
         Katie married William Schrock on Feb 18, 1919. William born Feb 24 1885 died July 19, 1966. William son of Noah and Elizabeth Kinsinger Schrock. He was a Conservative Mennonite.

         More About Catherine Katie Schlabaugh:
         Religion: conservative Mennonite/

+   2496   iii.   Osa Schlabaugh, born 16 Dec 1887 in Goshen, Elkhart Co., IN; died 09 Apr 1977 in Goshen, Elkhart Co., IN.

     2497   iv.   Dora Schlabaugh, born 04 Mar 1889 in Goshen, Elkhart Co., IN; died 21 Feb 1978. She married Moses N. Weaver 13 Feb 1912; born 11 Feb 1893; died 14 Aug 1949.

         Notes for Moses N. Weaver:
         Moses son of Noah I. Weaver. He was Old Order Amish and a farmer.

         More About Moses N. Weaver:
         Occupation: Farmer/
         Religion: Old Order Amish/

1137. Mary[7] Christner (Jacob[6], Christian[5], Peter[4], Christian[3], Christian[2], Christen[1])[4665,4666] was born 06 Apr 1858 in Elkhart Co., IN[4667,4668], and died 22 Mar 1923 in Elkhart Co., IN[4669]. She married **John J. L. Miller** 25 Dec 1877. He was born 15 Mar 1855 in Holmes Co., OH, and died 03 Oct 1938.

Notes for Mary Christner:
Amish and Amish Mennonite Genealogies; CHC56, p. 61

Miller - Mary (Christner) Miller, wife of Pre. John J. Miller, died at her home near Goshen, Ind., March 22, 1923, of dropsy, at the age of 64 y. 11 m. 16 d. She had been in failing health for 3 years, in which time she was only able to attend church a few times. She bore her sufferings patiently. She leaves her husband, 6 sons (David, Jacob, Levi, and John, of Goshen, Ind., Harvey and Oby of Howard Co., Ind.), 3 daughters (Mrs. Samuel Kauffman of Shipshewana, Ind., Mrs. Andy Yoder and Mrs. Menno Kuhns of Nappanee, Ind.), 51 grandchildren, 3 brothers (Jacob of Iowa, Samuel of Kansas, David of N. Y.), 1 sister (Mrs. Simon Schlabach of Goshen, Ind.). She was a member of the Old Order Amish Church. Funeral was held at Solomon Schrock's Mar. 25, by Nathaniel Miller and Emanuel Hershberger in German, and Dan Johns in English. Texts, II Cor. 5 and I Cor. 15, beginning at verse 39.

More About Mary Christner:
Burial: Clinton Union Cemetery, Elkhart Co., IN N41°34.072'xW85°44.270'
Cause of Death: Dropsy

Notes for John J. L. Miller:
Amish and Amish Mennonite Genealogies; CHC56, p. 61

He was Old Order Amish, farmer/minister. John is the son of John L. and Anna Hochstetler Miller.

Buried: Clinton Union Cemetery, Elkhart Co., IN N41°34.072'xW85°44.270'; Row 10, Plot 16

More About John J. L. Miller:
Burial: Clinton Union Cemetery, Elkhart Co., IN N41°34.072'xW85°44.270'

Children of Mary Christner and John Miller are:

2498	i.	Lizzie J.[8] Miller.
+ 2499	ii.	David J.C. Miller, born 04 Dec 1878 in Goshen, Elkhart Co., IN; died 15 Oct 1945 in Goshen, Elkhart Co., IN.
+ 2500	iii.	Levi J. Miller, born 25 Sep 1881 in Elkhart Co., IN; died 04 Jan 1959.
2501	iv.	John J. C. Miller, born 12 Jul 1883 in Elkhart Co., IN; died 1964 in Row 10 Plot 18. He married Mary E. Hostetler 22 Jul 1909; born 20 Feb 1894 in Newton Co., IN.

Notes for John J. C. Miller:
Mary is the daughter of Eli E. and Emma Lehman Hostetler. He was a Mennonite farmer.

More About John J. C. Miller:
Burial: Clinton Union Cemetery Co Rd. 34 Elkhart Co Indiana

+ 2502	v.	Jacob J. C. Miller, born 01 Nov 1885 in Elkhart Co., IN; died 07 Nov 1959.
2503	vi.	Harvey J. Miller, born 21 Oct 1887 in Elkhart Co., IN. He married Fanny Helmuth 27 Oct 1907; born 14 Jan 1887 in Lagrange Co., IN.

Notes for Harvey J. Miller:
Harvey married Fanny Helmuth on Oct 27, 1907. Fanny is the daughter of Abraham and Mattie Yoder Helmuth.

Fanny born Jan 14, 1887 Lagrange Co., IN. he was Old Order Amish.

+ 2504	vii.	Mary J. Miller, born 30 Jun 1889 in Goshen, Elkhart Co., IN; died 13 Mar 1926 in Lagrange Co., IN.
2505	viii.	Oba J. Miller, born 06 Mar 1891. He married Elmina C. Miller 19 Dec 1910; born 10 Jul 1891.
+ 2506	ix.	Mattie J. Miller, born 01 Jan 1896 in Reno Co., KS; died 17 Jul 1985 in Goshen, Elkhart Co., IN.
2507	x.	Fannie J. Miller, born 06 May 1898. She married Menno M. Kuhns.

Notes for Fannie J. Miller:
Fannie married Menno M.Kuhns

1138. Barbara[7] Christner (Jacob[6], Christian[5], Peter[4], Christian[3], Christian[2], Christen[1])[4669] was born 06 Apr 1860 in Elkhart Co., IN[4669], and died 25 Apr 1921 in Elkhart Co., IN[4669]. She married **Joas S. Miller** 23 Apr 1879, son of Lloyd Miller. He was born 04 Dec 1857 in Lagrange Co., IN, and died 04 Sep 1890.

Notes for Barbara Christner:
Amish and Amish Mennonite Genealogies; CHC57, p. 61

More About Barbara Christner:
Burial: Nisley Cemetery, Goshen, Elkhart Co., IN

Notes for Joas S. Miller:
Joas is the son of Simon and Lydia Miller. He is Old Order Amish and a farmer.

More About Joas S. Miller:

Burial: Nisley Cemetery, Goshen, Elkhart Co., IN

Children of Barbara Christner and Joas Miller are:

2508   i.   Oba J.[8] Miller, born 06 Feb 1880 in Elkhart Co., IN; died 14 May 1957. He married (1) Mary Miller 1901; born 26 Apr 1879 in Holmes Co., OH. He married (2) Mary Miller 1901.

       Notes for Oba J. Miller:
       He is Old Order Amish and a farmer.

       More About Oba J. Miller:
       Burial: Peter Miller Cemetery (864) North of Kalona/Johnson, Iowa, USA[4670]
       DBH Book: 6912/[4670]
       Religion: Old Order Amish Mennonite/[4670]

2509   ii.   Samuel J. Miller, born 22 Oct 1881 in Elkhart Co., IN; died 13 Aug 1968.

       Notes for Samuel J. Miller:
       Samuel was a farmer and Mennonite. Samuel married Jan 24, 1907 to Mary Yoder daughter of Jacob J. and Elizabeth Bontrager Yoder. Mary born Oct 31, 1885 Elkhart Co., IN died May 24, 1990.

       More About Samuel J. Miller:
       Burial: St Johnstown Cemetery, Greenwood, DE

2510   iii.   Henry Miller, born 12 Jan 1884; died 23 Aug 1884.
2511   iv.   Miller, born 25 Dec 1885; died 25 Dec 1885.
2512   v.   Mahlon Miller, born 04 Feb 1886; died 09 May 1886.
2513   vi.   Ezra J. Miller, born 23 Jun 1888 in Elkhart Co., IN; died 13 Aug 1956. He married Susan Weaver 13 Dec 1908; born 18 Feb 1890; died 06 Dec 1978.

       Notes for Ezra J. Miller:
       Ezra was Old Order Amish and a farmer. Ezra died as a result of an accident, he was thrown against a tree while moving a cabin. This caused a head injury. After 4 different operations he lapst in unconsciousness and lived only 3 more days. The accident happened June 25, 1956.

       Notes for Susan Weaver:
       Susan daughter of Noah I and Mattie Coblentz Weaver.

2514   vii.   Liddie Miller, born 12 Jun 1890; died Sep 1892.

1140. Jacob J.[7] Christner (Jacob[6], Christian[5], Peter[4], Christian[3], Christian[2], Christen[1])[4671,4672,4673,4674] was born 23 Sep 1862 in Middlebury, Elkhart Co., IN[4675,4676,4677,4678], and died 06 Feb 1939 in Johnson Co., IA[4678]. He married **Veronica A. Yoder**[4679,4680] 20 Jan 1889. She was born 21 Jun 1861 in Shanksville, Somerset Co., PA[4681,4682,4683], and died 05 Jan 1929 in Iowa City, Johnson Co., IA[4683,4684].

Notes for Jacob J. Christner:
Amish and Amish Mennonite Genealogies; CHC58, p. 61

Birth: Sep 23, 1862
Death: Feb 6, 1939

Obituary: Iowa City Press-Citizen - 7 Feb 1939, p.14-Tuesday

Headline: JACOB CHRISTNER OF SHARON CENTER DIES
Mr. Jacob Christner died suddenly at his home, north of Sharon Center, Monday. Death was the result of a heart attack. 9 Feb 1939, p.10

Headline: FUNERAL SERVICES FOR JACOB CHRISTNER ARE HELD AT SHARON
Funeral services for Mr. Jacob Christner, aged resident of Sharon Township, were held at the home of his son Anan Christner Wednesday at 1 p.m. Of his immediate family, 6 sons are living: Abner, Anan and Elim of Sharon, Jesse of South Bend, Ind., Simon of Michigan and Gideon who recently moved to Mississippi and was

unable to attend the funeral.

Parents: Jacob Christner (1828 - 1893)

Spouse: Fannie A. Yoder Christner (1861 - 1929)

Children:
Abner O. Christner (1890 - 1977)
Anan U. Christner (1893 - 1969)
Jesse M. Christner (1896 - 1958)

Burial: Eash Cemetery, Johnson Co., IA

More About Jacob J. Christner:
Burial: Eash Cemetery, Sharon Center, Johnson Co., IA

Notes for Veronica A. Yoder:
Birth: Jun. 21, 1861
Death: Jan. 5, 1929

Obituary - Gospel Herald, January 24, 1929

Fannie Christner, daughter of Abner and Veronica (Schrock) Yoder, was born June 21, 1861, in Somerset Co.,
PA; died in Iowa City Hospital Jan. 5, 1929; aged 67 y. 6 m. 14 d. At the age of 16 she accepted Christ as her
Savior and united with the Amish Mennonite Church of which she remained a faithful member till death. She had
been in failing health for a number of years but remained cheerful till the end. She had no fear of the future and
was ready and willing to depart because she had confidence in Him in whom she believed.
On Jan. 20, 1889 she was united in marriage to Jacob J. Christner. To this union were born 7 children (Abner,
Elam, Ammon, and Gideon, of the immediate community; Jess and Simon of South Bend, IN). One daughter
(Mrs. Reuben Mast) preceded her in death March 19, 1926. She leaves her husband, 6 sons, 3 brothers, 2 sisters,
10 grandchildren, besides many other relatives and friends.
Funeral services were held at the home Jan. 8, 1929, conducted by Isaac Helmuth and S. J. Kemp. Burial in Eash
cemetery near Sharon Center.

Parents:
Abner Yoder (1814 - 1883)
Veronica Schrock Yoder (1819 - 1886)

Spouse: Jacob Christner (1862 - 1939)

Children:
Abner O. Christner (1890 - 1977)
Anan U. Christner (1893 - 1969)
Jesse M. Christner (1896 - 1958)

Burial: Eash Cemetery, Johnson Co., IA

More About Veronica A. Yoder:
Burial: 08 Jan 1929, Eash Cemetery, Sharon Center, Johnson Co., IA
Religion: Amish/

Children of Jacob Christner and Veronica Yoder are:
+   2515   i.   Abner Ozias[8] Christner, born 09 May 1890 in Kalona, Washington Co., IA; died 11 Dec 1977 in Kalona,
                     Washington Co., IA.
+   2516   ii.   Elam Josiah Christner, born 16 Jan 1892 in Near Middlebury, Elkhart Co., IN; died 06 Sep 1969 in
                     Kalona, Washington Co., IA.
     2517   iii. Anan Uriah Christner, born 25 Nov 1893 in Iowa City, Wright Co., IA[4685]; died 29 Jul 1969 in Kalona,
                     Washington Co., IA. She married Rachel Hostetler 02 Jan 1916; born 24 May 1889; died 1952.

Notes for Anan Uriah Christner:
Anan and his wife Rachel adopted his sister Mary Elizabeth's daughter after her death and change the child's last name to Christner.

Fannie Edith Mast/Fannie Edith Christner #3306   SS# 482-42-8709 Iss.IA Last zip 52247

Birth: Nov. 12, 1893
Death: Jul. 29, 1969

Parents:
Jacob Christner (1862 - 1939)
Fannie A. Yoder Christner (1861 - 1929)

Spouse: Rachel Christner (1884 - 1952)

Burial: Eash Cemetery, Johnson Co., IA

More About Anan Uriah Christner:
Burial: Eash Cemetery, Sharon Center, Johnson Co., IA
Social Security Number: 482-42-8709/[4685]
SSN issued: Kalona, Washington Co., IA[4685]

Notes for Rachel Hostetler:
Rachel is the daughter of Jonathan D and Fanny Stutzman Hostetler.

Birth: May 24, 1884
Death: Dec. 28, 1952

Spouse: Anan U. Christner (1893 - 1969)

Burial: Eash Cemetery, Johnson Co., IA

More About Rachel Hostetler:
Burial: Eash Cemetery, Sharon Center, Johnson Co., IA

2518   iv.   Jesse Matthias Christner, born 05 Apr 1896 in Iowa Co., IA; died 11 Oct 1958 in Greencastle, Putnam Co., IN.

Notes for Jesse Matthias Christner:
Christner, Jesse M., son of Jacob J. and Fannie (Yoder) Christner; born April 15, 1896, in Iowa Co., Iowa; died Oct. 11, 1958, at Greencastle, IN; aged 62 y. 5 m. 26 d. His parents, one sister and one brother preceded him in death. Survivors are 4 brothers (Abner, Iowa City; Elam and Anan, Kalona, and Gideon, Wellman). Employed for many years by the Studebacker Co., South Bend, IN. Member of the Miami Brethren Church, after locating in Indiana. Funeral services at East Union, Kalona Co., IA in charge of Elmer G. Swartzendruber and D. J. Fisher; interment in the Eash Cemetery.

More About Jesse Matthias Christner:
Burial: Eash Cemetery, Sharon Center, Johnson Co., IA

+   2519   v.   Gideon Andrew Christner, born 25 Nov 1897 in Parnell, Iowa Co., IA; died 26 Jul 1978 in Wellman, Washington Co., IA.
+   2520   vi.   Simon Peter Christner, born 25 Mar 1900 in Wellman, IA; died 15 Jun 1943.
+   2521   vii. Mary Elizabeth Christner, born 17 Aug 1902 in Iowa City, Wright Co., IA; died 19 Mar 1926.

1141. David J.[7] **Christner** (Jacob[6], Christian[5], Peter[4], Christian[3], Christian[2], Christen[1])[4686,4687,4688] was born 10 Mar 1865 in Elkhart, Elkhart Co., IN[4689,4690,4691,4692], and died 10 Apr 1941 in Shelbyville, Bedford Co., OH[4693,4694,4695]. He married **Lovina D. Raber**[4696,4697] 11 Nov 1886 in Farmerstown, Holmes Co., OH[4698]. She was born 25 Jul 1868 in Farmerstown, Holmes Co., OH[4699,4700,4701], and died 26 May 1938 in Shelbyville, Shelby Co., IL[4702,4703].

Notes for David J. Christner:
Lived across from the Clinton Center School Co Rd 34 about 5 miles east of Goshen In . N41°34.835' by W85°43.263'

For a complete history of David and his family read H. Walter Christner's book Our Immigrants. Christian and Elizabeth Christner's Family at Goshen College, Goshen, IN.

More About David J. Christner:
Burial: Mt. Hermon A.M. Church Cemetery, Clarksburg RD. off Route 66 near Shelbyville, IL.
Residence: 1910, Clinton, Elkhart Co., IN[4703,4704,4705]

Notes for Lovina D. Raber:
Christner - Lovina, wife of David J. Christner and daughter of Daniel and Anna Raber, was born in Holmes Co., Ohio, July 25, 1868; died in her home near Shelbyville, Ill., May 26, 1938; aged 69 y. 10 m. 1 d. To this union were born 5 sons and 4 daughters. She leaves her husband, 6 children (Lovina Yoder of Gevena, Ind.; Daniel of Akron, N.Y.; Anna Brenneman of Kalona, Iowa; Lulu Guengerich of Low Point, N.Y.; Joe of Shelbyville; David of Corfu, N.Y.); 41 grandchildren, and 2 great-grandchildren. Three children (Jerry, Fannie Kauffman, and Elmer) preceded her in death. She united with the Amish church in her youth, and remained faithful until death. The day before her death she said, "I see the glory of God. Oh, it is so beautiful. Get your families ready for that place, for we don't want to miss it."

More About Lovina D. Raber:
Burial: Mt. Hermon A.M. Church Cemetery, Clarksburg RD. off Route 66 near Shelbyville, IL.
Religion: Amish/
Residence: 1930, Pembroke, Genesee Co., NY[4706,4707]

Children of David Christner and Lovina Raber are:

2522   i.   Jeremiah[8] Christner, born 31 Oct 1889; died 09 May 1920 in Shelbyville, IN.

    More About Jeremiah Christner:
    Burial: Mt. Hermon A.M. Church Cemetery, Clarksville RD. off Route 66 near Shelbyville IL.

+   2523   ii.   Fanny Mae Christner, born 12 Feb 1891 in Goshen, Elkhart Co., IN; died 15 Jan 1921 in Age: 29/Shelbyville, Shelby Co., IL.

+   2524   iii.   Daniel D. Christner, born 11 Jul 1892 in Goshen, Elkhart Co., IN; died 04 Feb 1979 in Alden, NY or Batavia, NY.

+   2525   iv.   Anna Faye Christner, born 08 Jun 1894 in Goshen, Elkhart Co., IN; died 12 Jun 1983 in Kolona, Washington Co., IA.

+   2526   v.   Joseph Davis Christner, born 08 Dec 1895 in Goshen, Elkhart Co., IN; died 01 Apr 1972 in Shelbyville, Shelby Co., IL.

+   2527   vi.   David J. Christner Jr., born 22 Jan 1899 in Goshen, Elkhart Co., IN; died 23 Jul 1956 in Goshen, Elkhart Co., IN.

+   2528   vii.   Lovina Lulu Christner, born 10 Feb 1903 in Goshen, Elkhart Co., IN; died 28 Aug 1995 in Greenwood, DE.

2529   viii.   Elmer Christner[4708,4709], born 23 Jun 1909[4710,4711]; died 25 May 1930 in 5 friends Killed in a Auto/Train Accident all buried in one grave.

    Notes for Elmer Christner:
    The Descendants of John J. Christner, privately published February, 1961, p. 67.

    More About Elmer Christner:
    Burial: Co. Line Union Cemetery, Alden., NY
    Residence: 1930, Pembroke, Genesee Co., NY[4712,4713]

1142. Joseph[7] Christner (Jacob[6], Christian[5], Peter[4], Christian[3], Christian[2], Christen[1]) was born 10 Mar 1865 in Elkhart, Elkhart Co., IN[4714], and died 10 Apr 1941 in Shelbyville, Bedford Co., OH[4714]. He married **Lovina D. Raber**[4714,4715] 11 Nov 1886 in Farmerstown, Holmes Co., OH[4716]. She was born 25 Jul 1868 in Farmerstown, Holmes Co., OH[4717,4718,4719], and died 26 May 1938 in Shelbyville, Shelby Co., IL[4720,4721].

More About Joseph Christner:
Residence: 1930, Pembroke, Genesee Co., NY[4722]

Notes for Lovina D. Raber:
Christner - Lovina, wife of David J. Christner and daughter of Daniel and Anna Raber, was born in Holmes Co., Ohio, July 25, 1868; died in her home near Shelbyville, Ill., May 26, 1938; aged 69 y. 10 m. 1 d. To this union were born 5 sons and 4 daughters. She leaves her husband, 6 children (Lovina Yoder of Gevena, Ind.; Daniel of Akron, N.Y.; Anna Brenneman of Kalona, Iowa; Lulu Guengerich of Low Point, N.Y.; Joe of Shelbyville; David of Corfu, N.Y.); 41 grandchildren, and 2 great-grandchildren. Three children (Jerry, Fannie Kauffman, and Elmer) preceded her in death. She united with the Amish church in her youth, and remained faithful until death. The day before her death she said, "I see the glory of God. Oh, it is so beautiful. Get your families ready for that place, for we don't want to miss it."

More About Lovina D. Raber:
Burial: Mt. Hermon A.M. Church Cemetery, Clarksburg RD. off Route 66 near Shelbyville, IL.
Religion: Amish/
Residence: 1930, Pembroke, Genesee Co., NY[4723,4724]

Child of Joseph Christner and Lovina Raber is:
+   2530   i.   Laura D.[8] Christner, born 22 Sep 1887 in Goshen, Elkhart Co., IN; died 21 Apr 1961 in Sturgis, St. Joseph Co., MI.

1146. Elizabeth[7] Christner (Daniel S.[6], Christian[5], Peter[4], Christian[3], Christian[2], Christen[1])[4725] was born 11 Sep 1856 in Pulaski, Davis Co., IA, and died 08 Aug 1898 in Altmota, Whitman Co., WA. She married **Jacob Stevig**[4726] 1877 in IA[4727]. He was born Nov 1848 in Alsace-Lorraine[4728].

More About Elizabeth Christner:
Residence: 1885, Roscoe, Davis Co., IA[4728]

More About Jacob Stevig:
Arrival: 1880[4728]
Residence: 1900, Almota, Whitman, Washington[4728]

Children of Elizabeth Christner and Jacob Stevig are:
   2531   i.   John[8] Stevick[4729], born 31 Oct 1878 in Davis Co., IA[4730,4731]; died 10 Nov 1959 in Spokane, Spokane Co., WA[4732].

              More About John Stevick:
              Residence: 1930, Spokane, Spokane, Washington[4732]

   2532   ii.   Nancy Stevig[4732], born Oct 1880 in Roscoe, Davis Co., IA[4732]; died 23 Jun 1941 in Colfax, Whitman Co., WA[4732].

              More About Nancy Stevig:
              Residence: 1930, Colfax, Whitman, Washington[4732]

   2533   iii.   Eka E Wilson[4732], born 1889 in NE[4732].
   2534   iv.   Roy A Stevig[4732], born Apr 1889 in NE[4732].
   2535   v.   Effie G Stevig[4732], born Mar 1890[4732].
   2536   vi.   Eunice Stevig[4732], born Mar 1892 in NE[4732].
   2537   vii.   Culver G Stevig[4732], born 1899 in Roscoe, Davis Co., IA[4732].

1148. John Hubert[7] Christner (Daniel S.[6], Christian[5], Peter[4], Christian[3], Christian[2], Christen[1]) was born 12 Jan 1860 in Pulaski, Davis Co., IA, and died 30 Mar 1941 in Hidalgo, TX[4733]. He married **Augusta Louise "Gussie" DeGarmo**. She was born 1864, and died 15 Jun 1959.

Notes for John Hubert Christner:

Birth: Jan 12, 1860 - Pulaski, Davis Co., IA
Death: Mar 30, 1941 - Weslaco, Hidalgo Co., TX

My paternal Great Grandfather. The son of Daniel S Christner and Magdalena Miller. By 1910 he had moved to NE and by 1920 he had moved to Hildago Co. in Texas where lived until his death. Married Augusta "Gussie" DeGarmo.

Children: James Blaine Christner (1892 - 1976)

Spouse: Augusta Louise DeGarmo Christner (1864 - 1959)

Burial: Weslaco Cemetery, Weslaco, Hidalgo Co., TX

More About John Hubert Christner:
Residence: 1930, Precinct 7, Hidalgo, Texas[4733]

Notes for Augusta Louise "Gussie" DeGarmo:
Birth: 1864
Death: Jun. 15, 1959

Parents:
McGregor DeGarmo (1832 - 1915)
Jane Louisa Wiswell DeGarmo (1838 - 1903)

Spouse: John Hubert Christner (1860 - 1941)

Burial: Weslaco Cemetery, Weslaco, Hidalgo Co., TX

More About Augusta Louise "Gussie" DeGarmo:
Residence: 1930, Precinct 7, Hidalgo, Texas[4733]

Child of John Christner and Augusta DeGarmo is:
+ 2538   i.   James Blaine[8] Christner, born 13 Dec 1892 in NE; died 11 Sep 1976 in Shamrock, Wheeler Co., TX.

1149. Michael M.[7] Christner (Daniel S.[6], Christian[5], Peter[4], Christian[3], Christian[2], Christen[1])[4734] was born 02 Jan 1862 in Pulaski, Davis Co., IA[4734], and died 26 Mar 1946 in Pulaski, Davis Co., IA[4735]. He married **(1) Paula G. "Polly" Boehm**[4736,4737] 1890[4738]. She was born 23 Feb 1869 in Germany[4739,4740,4741,4742], and died 19 Nov 1943 in Hayes Center, Hayes Co., NE[4743]. He married **(2) Nannie E.**[4744] 1910 in Antelope, Hayes Co., NE[4744]. She was born 1873 in MO[4744].

More About Michael M. Christner:
Residence: 1880, Bloomfield, Davis Co., IA[4745]

More About Paula G. "Polly" Boehm:
Residence: 1910, Government, Hayes Co., NE[4745]

More About Nannie E.:
Residence: 1910, Wauneta, Chase Co., NE[4746]

Children of Michael Christner and Paula Boehm are:
   2539   i.   Mary[8] Christner.
+ 2540   ii.   Arthur George Christner, born 19 Feb 1891 in NE; died 28 Dec 1976 in Wauneta, Chase Co., NE.
   2541   iii.   Oscar Beno Christner[4746,4747], born 10 Jun 1894 in NE[4748,4749]; died 21 Jul 1967 in Hayes Center, Hayes Co., NE[4750]. He married Evalyn Hahn[4751] 27 Dec 1932[4751]; born 27 Dec 1911 in NE[4751,4752]; died 28 Jun 1982 in Wauneta, Chase Co., NE[4753].

     More About Oscar Beno Christner:

Burial: Meadowlawn Cemetery, Hamlet, Hayes Co., NE[4754]
Residence: 1917, Hayes Co., NE[4755]
Social Security Number: 507-52-9970/[4756]
SSN issued: NE[4756]

More About Evalyn Hahn:
Residence: 1930, Hamlet, Hayes Co., NE[4757]
Social Security Number: 505-68-3558/[4758]

2542   iv.   Annie Christner[4759], born 1897 in NE[4759].

                More About Annie Christner:
                Residence: 1900, Fairfield, Government & High Ridge Precincts, Hayes Co., NE[4759]

2543   v.   Mary Christner[4759], born 1899 in NE[4759].

                More About Mary Christner:
                Residence: 1900, Fairfield, Government & High Ridge Precincts, Hayes Co., NE[4759]

2544   vi.   Roosevelt T. Christner[4760], born 17 May 1906 in Hayes Center, Hayes Co., NE[4760]; died 31 Oct 1937 in Estille Cemetery, Hayes Center, Hayes Co., NE[4760].

                Notes for Roosevelt T. Christner:
                Birth: May 17, 1906
                Death: Oct. 31, 1937

                Burial: Hayes Center Cemetery, Hayes Center, Hayes Co., NE
                Find A Grave Memorial# 67995525

                More About Roosevelt T. Christner:
                Residence: 1920, Antelope, Hayes Co., NE[4760]

1150. Daniel Lincoln[7] Christner (Daniel S.[6], Christian[5], Peter[4], Christian[3], Christian[2], Christen[1])[4761,4762,4763,4764,4765,4766,4767,4768,4769,4770,4771,4772,4773] was born 15 May 1863 in Pulaski, Davis Co., IA[4774,4775,4776,4777], and died 13 Jul 1954 in Orland, Glenn Co., CA[4778,4779,4780]. He married **Harriet "Hattie" (Christner) Denton**[4780,4781,4782,4783,4784,4785] 22 Dec 1895 in Lancaster Co., NE[4786]. She was born Mar 1877 in Lancaster Co., NE[4787,4788], and died 18 Aug 1937 in Palisade, Hitchcock Co., NE[4789,4790].

Notes for Daniel Lincoln Christner:
He was a Mennonite and a livestock farmer.
His ashes buried in Grandmother Mattie's grave in Grandview Cemetery.

More About Daniel Lincoln Christner:
Burial: Meadowlawn Cemetery, Hamlet, Hayes Co., NE[4791]
Residence: 1930, Age in 1930: 66; Marital Status: Married; Relation to Head of House: Head/Hamlet, Hayes, Nebraska[4792,4793,4794,4795]

More About Harriet "Hattie" (Christner) Denton:
Burial: Meadowlawn Cemetery, Hamlet, Hayes Co., NE[4796]
Residence: 1930, Age in 1930: 54; Marital Status: Married; Relation to Head of House: Wife/Hamlet, Hayes, Nebraska[4797,4797]

Children of Daniel Christner and Harriet Denton are:
2545   i.   Emery L.[8] Christner, born 29 Dec 1895 in NE[4798]; died Apr 1918 in Hayes Co., NE[4798].

                Notes for Emery L. Christner:
                Birth: 1895
                Death: 1918

Burial: Hayes Center Cemetery, Hayes Center, Hayes Co., NE
Find A Grave Memorial# 59863056

More About Emery L. Christner:
Residence: 05 Jun 1917, Hayes Co., NE[4798]

2546   ii.   John Elmer Christner[4799], born 07 Feb 1897 in NE[4799]; died 04 Feb 1911 in Hayes Co., NE[4799].

Notes for John Elmer Christner:
Birth: Feb 7, 1897 - Hayes Co., NE
Death: Feb 4, 1911 - Hayes Co., NE

John Elmer Christner

John Elmer Christner, son of Mr. and Mrs. Daniel Christner was born in Hayes County on February 7, 1897, died at his home west of town on February 4, 1911, aged 13 years, 11 months, 27 days, after a short illness. His condition was not thought at all serious until the day before his death when a physician was called, but it was too late, and the little fellow was called higher up the next morning. Funeral services were held at the farm last Thursday and burial took place in the Hayes Center Cemetery, which was attended by a large number of friends and relatives. Only the memory of the lovely boy is left yet how sweet, how uplifting its influence. For after all, death is but the slipping off of the outer body. "When death strikes down the innocent and young, for every fragile form which he lets the panting spirit free, a hundred virtues rise, in shapes of mercy, charity, and love to walk the world and bless it. Of every tear that sorrowing mortals shed on such green graves, some born good is born, some gentle nature comes". The bereaved family have the heartfelt sympathy in their sad hours of all.

CARD OF THANKS
To those who have been with us in our bereavement and by kind words and kindly acts have tried to lessen our sorrow, we extend our sincere thanks.
Mr. and Mrs. Daniel Christner
Jan 12, 1911

Burial: Hayes Center Cemetery, Hayes Center, Hayes Co., NE
Find A Grave Memorial# 59863049

More About John Elmer Christner:
Burial: Hayes Center, Hayes County, Nebraska, USA[4799]
Residence: 1900, Age: 3; Marital Status: Single; Relation to Head of House: Son/Hayes Center, Hayes, Nebraska, USA[4799]

+   2547   iii. Jason Oliver Christner, born 24 Feb 1898; died 22 May 1990 in Hayes Co., NE.
+   2548   iv.   Clarence Herbert Christner, born 30 Jan 1900 in NE; died 27 Jun 1977 in Wauneta, Chase Co., NE.
    2549   v.   Willis Earnest Christner[4800], born 04 May 1901 in NE[4800,4801]; died 29 Jan 1964 in WI[4802].

More About Willis Earnest Christner:
Residence: 1910, Government, Hayes Co., NE[4803]
Social Security Number: 391-22-8049/[4804]

+   2550   vi.   Richard Earl Christner, born 29 Sep 1902; died 15 Apr 1985 in McCook, Red Willow Co., NE.
    2551   vii. Elba May "Eggy" Christner, born 15 Nov 1903 in NE[4805]; died 29 Jun 1971 in Contra Costa Co., CA[4806]. She married Perry Alan Eagy[4807,4808]; born 20 Oct 1900[4809]; died 22 Dec 1977 in Concord, Contra Costa Co., CA[4810,4811].

More About Elba May "Eggy" Christner:
Residence: 1910, Government, Hayes Co., NE[4812]

More About Perry Alan Eagy:
Other-Begin: El Sobrante, Contra Costa, CA[4813]
Residence: 1930, Palisade, Hitchcock, NE[4814]
Social Security Number: 507-01-1194/[4815]
SSN issued: NE[4815]

    2552   viii. Florence Christner, born 1905; died 05 Jul 1965 in Never married/Alameda, Alameda Co., CA[4816].

More About Florence Christner:
Residence: 1910, Government, Hayes Co., NE[4816]

2553　ix.　Dorthy Elaine Christner, born 1907 in NE[4817].

More About Dorthy Elaine Christner:
Residence: 1920, Swan Lake, Hayes Co., NE[4817]

2554　x.　Hazel Hughes Christner, born 30 Mar 1910 in IN[4818]; died 07 Oct 2002 in Fort Collins, Larimer Co., CO[4819].

More About Hazel Hughes Christner:
CauseOfDeath: Ashes buried in grandmother Mattie's grave in Grandview cemetery/[4820]
Residence: 1910, Government, Hayes Co., NE[4820]

2555　xi.　Daniel Leroy "Roy" Christner, born 11 Jul 1912 in Hayes Co., NE[4821]; died May 1974 in CA[4822,4823,4824].

More About Daniel Leroy "Roy" Christner:
Residence: 1920, Swan Lake, Hayes Co., NE[4824]
Social Security Number: 553-03-2278/[4825]
SSN issued: CA[4825]

2556　xii.　Joseph Denton Christner[4826], born 22 Sep 1913 in NE[4827,4828,4829]; died 21 Oct 1979 in El Sobrante, Contra Costa Co., CA[4829,4830].

More About Joseph Denton Christner:
Arrival: 02 May 1944, Sailed from Alexandria, Egypt on US Liberty ship, Ferdinand Westfald/Baltimore, Maryland[4831]
Departure: 24 Apr, Alexandria, Egypt On Liberty Ship, Ferdinand Westdahl[4831]
Residence: 1930, Hamlet, Hayes Co., NE[4831,4832]
Social Security Number: 553-03-3010/[4833]

2557　xiii.　Martha Christner[4834], born 06 Jun 1915 in NE[4834]; died 10 Jan 1982 in Marin Co., CA[4834].

1152. Pheobe Or Philipine[7] Christner (Daniel S.[6], Christian[5], Peter[4], Christian[3], Christian[2], Christen[1]) was born 17 Apr 1865 in Pulaski, Davis Co., IA, and died 04 May 1932 in Holdridge, Phelps Co., NE[4835]. She married **William Culver Wilson**[4835] 1887 in Culbertson. NE[4835]. He was born 26 Apr 1860 in Greene Co., PA[4835], and died 06 Feb 1934 in Hayes Center, Hayes Co., NE[4835].

More About Pheobe Or Philipine Christner:
Residence: 1930, High Ridge, Hayes Co., NE[4835]

More About William Culver Wilson:
Residence: 1930, High Ridge, Hayes Co., NE[4835]

Children of Pheobe Christner and William Wilson are:
2558　i.　Eska E[8] Wilson[4835], born 27 Oct 1887 in Hayes Center, Hayes Co., NE[4835]; died 12 Oct 1972 in Costa Mesa, Orange, California[4835].

More About Eska E Wilson:
Residence: 1920, Los Angeles Assembly, District 66, Los Angeles, Co., CA[4835]

2559　ii.　Roy A Wilson[4835], born 02 Jan 1889 in Hayes Center, Hayes Co., NE[4835]; died 09 May 1972 in Bell, Los Angeles, California[4835].

More About Roy A Wilson:
Residence: 1930, Alameda, Alameda, California[4835]

2560　iii.　Effie Grace Wilson[4835], born 30 Mar 1890 in Rain, , NE[4835]; died 1938[4835].

More About Effie Grace Wilson:

Residence: 1910, High Ridge, Hayes Co., NE[4835]

2561   iv. Eunice M Wilson[4835], born 16 Mar 1892 in Hayes Center, Hayes Co., NE[4835]; died 1972 in NE[4835].

More About Eunice M Wilson:
Residence: 1900, High Ridge, Hayes Co., NE[4835]

2562   v. Culver Glenn Wilson[4835], born 15 Apr 1899 in Hayes Center, Hayes Co., NE[4835]; died 04 Sep 1966 in , Los Angeles, California[4835].

More About Culver Glenn Wilson:
Residence: 1920, Los Angeles Assembly, District 66, Los Angeles, Co., CA[4835]

2563   vi. Richard R. Wilson[4835], born 31 Jan 1903 in Hayes Center, Hayes Co., NE[4835]; died 08 Feb 1903[4835].
2564   vii. Ruby R Wilson[4835], born Abt. 1906 in NE[4835]; died in of California[4835].

More About Ruby R Wilson:
Residence: 1930, High Ridge, Hayes Co., NE[4835]

1153. Joseph J.[7] Christner (Daniel S.[6], Christian[5], Peter[4], Christian[3], Christian[2], Christen[1])[4836] was born 25 Jan 1868 in or Sept. 1868 Quincy, Hickory Co., MO[4836], and died 10 Jan 1959[4837,4838]. He married **Minnie Miranda Heater**[4839,4840,4841] 1893[4842], daughter of Isaac Heater and Mary Stoutsenbarger. She was born 09 Oct 1875 in Stuart, Guthrie Co., IA[4843,4844], and died 24 Sep 1966 in Imperial, Chase Co., NE[4845,4846].

Notes for Joseph J. Christner:
Birth: Jan 25, 1868
Death: Jan 10, 1959

His father was Daniel L. Christner and the mother's was Mattie.

In 1886, an 18 year old Joseph and his family moved from Iowa to Hayes County, Nebraska.

After Joe and Minnie's marriage in 1892, the young couple homesteaded their property while living in a sod house.

In 1900 Joseph was a farmer and started to preach as a local preacher in the school houses in neighboring communities, He was 32 years old.

In 1905 at 37, he sold his equipment and livestock and moved to Fort Wayne, Indiana to attend the Bible Training School for two years. After returning to Nebraska, he held tent meetings as an evangelist.

By the 1910 Census he was a minister of the gospel in Wauneta, Chase, Nebraska.
When William Phillip Pegg died in 1915 he was the minister officiating at the funeral.

He served the Methodist Church in Nebraska at Stockville, Grant, Farnham, Wauneta, Gretna, Palisade, Crab Orchard, Hopewell, Courtland, and Mt Zion. He retired from the ministry in 1934 and they moved to live in Wauneta, Nebraska.

Spouse: Minnie Miranda Heater Christner (1875 - 1966)

Children:
Joseph Dewey Christner (1898 - 1918)
Mattie Rosella Christner (1902 - 1909)
Elizabeth Grace Christner (1912 - 1916)

Burial:Riverside Cemetery, Wauneta, Chase Co., NE
Find A Grave Memorial# 37414914

More About Joseph J. Christner:
Burial: Riverside Cemetery, Wauneta, Chase Co., NE[4847]
Residence: 1930, Sterling, Johnson, Nebraska[4848,4849]

Notes for Minnie Miranda Heater:
Birth: Oct 9, 1875
Death: Sep 24, 1966

As a child of 8 in 1884, she moved to Nebraska in a covered wagon where her father was preparing to homestead (for the third time) in Hayes County.

She married Joseph J. Christner, 23 October 1892, when she was 17 and he 24.
They had 8 daughters and 2 sons.

Eva May Christner Born: 29 September 1893
Mary Blanche Christner Born: 12 March 1897
Joseph Dewey Christner Born: 21 September 1898
Benjamin H Christner Born: 04 June 1901
Mattie Rosella Christner Born: 17 September 1902
Orpha Rachel Christner Born 20 October 1904
Ruth Adeline. Christner Born 1908 in Nebraska
Margaret M Christner Born 1910 in Nebraska
Elizabeth Christner Born: 11 February 1912
Ernesta B. Christner Born 1915 in Nebraska

They began farming around Hayes County and lived in a sod house. In 1900 Joseph began lay preaching at school houses and in local communities. In 1905, at age 37, he attended the Bible Training Institute in Fort Wayne, Indiana, for 2 years. The Christners then returned to Nebraska and they moved to several communities in Eastern Nebraska in pursuing their ministry. Joseph retired from an active ministry in 1934 but continued to preach at several churches after retirement.

Parents:
Isaac Heater (1833 - 1920)
Mary Stoutsenbarger Heater (1836 - 1879)

Spouse: Joseph J. Christner (1868 - 1959)

Children:
Joseph Dewey Christner (1898 - 1918)
Mattie Rosella Christner (1902 - 1909)
Elizabeth Grace Christner (1912 - 1916)

Burial: Riverside Cemetery, Wauneta, Chase Co., NE
Find A Grave Memorial# 37414951

More About Minnie Miranda Heater:
Residence: 1910[4850,4851,4852,4853]

Children of Joseph Christner and Minnie Heater are:
+   2565   i.   Ava[8] Christner, born 29 Sep 1893 in NE; died 11 Oct 1935 in North Platte, Lincoln Co., NE.
     2566   ii.   Mary Blanche Christner, born 12 Mar 1897 in NE.
     2567   iii.   Joseph Dewey Christner[4854], born 21 Sep 1898 in NE[4854]; died 07 Dec 1918[4854].

        Notes for Joseph Dewey Christner:
        Birth: Sep 21, 1898
        Death: Dec 7, 1918

Dewey registered for the draft on 12 September 1918. He described himself as medium height, medium build, grey eyes and brown hair. He was a farmer working for his father Joseph J. Christner.

Dewey, as everyone called him, was active in the young men's Christian group, the M. E. (Methodist) church, and the Epworth League. He was attending the agriculture school at University of Nebraska in Lincoln.

His obituary wasn't very specific as to cause of death, but it very likely could have been the influenza that struck down so many young people at this time.

Parents:
Joseph J. Christner (1868 - 1959)
Minnie Miranda Heater Christner (1875 - 1966)

Burial:Riverside Cemetery, Wauneta, Chase Co., NE
Find A Grave Memorial# 37414866

More About Joseph Dewey Christner:
Residence: 1900, Fairfield, Government & High Ridge Precincts, Hayes Co., NE[4854]

2568   iv.   Mattie Rosella Christner, born 17 Sep 1902; died 31 Dec 1909.

Notes for Mattie Rosella Christner:
Birth: Sep 17, 1902
Death: Dec 31, 1909

Obituary: WAUNETA BREEZE MATTIE CHRISTNER'S DEATH - 6 Jan 1910

Mattie, the seven year old child of Rev. and Mrs. J. J. Christner was terribly burned yesterday afternoon, (last Wed.) and may lose her life as a result. Just how the accident occurred is not definitely known but it seems that she was standing near the stove possibly stirring the fire when the gas in the stove exploded and the girl's clothing caught fire, She ran out of-doors-and away- from an older. sister, who attempted to throw her in the snow. She was finally caught and the flames-smothered in rugs. She fainted as. soon as. the fire was extinguished and it was thought when she was taken to the house that she was dead but she soon revived. Dr. Case who is in attendance states that there is but little hope for her recovery, although there has been little change during the past twenty-four hours. Her breast, head and neck were severely burned. She is unconscious a great deal of the time.

Mr. and Mrs. Christner were away at the time of the accident the former being out in the Zion Hill neighborhood and the latter visiting with her parents in Hayes county. Mattie died Friday morning (Dec 31) at 2 o'clock. Her mother arrived Thursday evening at 6 o'clock.

Parents:
Joseph J. Christner (1868 - 1959)
Minnie Miranda Heater Christner (1875 - 1966)

Burial: Riverside Cemetery, Wauneta, Chase Co., NE
Find A Grave Memorial# 37414942

2569   v.   Elizabeth Grace Christner, born 11 Feb 1912; died 03 Apr 1916.

Notes for Elizabeth Grace Christner:
Birth: Feb 11, 1912
Death: Apr 3, 1916

As her obituary said: "She was sick only a few hours and her sudden death was a shock to all."

She died of the croup.

Parents:
Joseph J. Christner (1868 - 1959)
Minnie Miranda Heater Christner (1875 - 1966)

Burial: Riverside Cemetery, Wauneta, Chase Co., NE

Find A Grave Memorial# 37414893

1156. Leah[7] Christner (Daniel S.[6], Christian[5], Peter[4], Christian[3], Christian[2], Christen[1])[4855] was born 14 Apr 1874 in Quincy, Hickory Co., MO[4855], and died 23 Mar 1932 in Hamlet, Hayes Co., NE[4855]. She married **(1) Filmore Potter**[4855]. He was born Apr 1870 in PA[4855]. She married **(2) Valmore Poitras**[4855]. He was born 14 Aug 1905 in MA[4855], and died Oct 1979[4855].

More About Leah Christner:
Residence: 1920, High Ridge, Hayes, Nebraska[4855]

More About Filmore Potter:
Residence: 1920, High Ridge, Hayes, Nebraska[4855]

Children of Leah Christner and Filmore Potter are:
    2570   i.   Mattie E[8] Potter[4855], born 1897 in NE[4855].

                More About Mattie E Potter:
                Residence: 1910, High Ridge, Hayes, Nebraska[4855]

    2571   ii.   Edna L Potter[4855], born 1898 in NE[4855].

                More About Edna L Potter:
                Residence: 1920, High Ridge, Hayes, Nebraska[4855]

    2572   iii.   Joseph H Potter[4855], born 1900 in NE[4855].

                More About Joseph H Potter:
                Residence: 1920, High Ridge, Hayes, Nebraska[4855]

    2573   iv.   Faith B Potter[4855], born 1902 in NE[4855].

                More About Faith B Potter:
                Residence: 1920, High Ridge, Hayes, Nebraska[4855]

    2574   v.   Hubert G Potter[4855], born Abt. 1905 in NE[4855].

                More About Hubert G Potter:
                Residence: 1920, High Ridge, Hayes, Nebraska[4855]

    2575   vi.   Filmore Jr. Potter[4855], born 1907 in NE[4855].

                More About Filmore Jr. Potter:
                Residence: 1920, High Ridge, Hayes, Nebraska[4855]

    2576   vii.   Leola M Potter[4855], born 1909 in Nebrask[4855].

                More About Leola M Potter:
                Residence: 1920, High Ridge, Hayes, Nebraska[4855]

Child of Leah Christner and Valmore Poitras is:
    2577   i.   Victor Joy[8] Potter[4855], born 01 Apr 1920[4855]; died 10 Jul 1998 in Omaha, Douglas, Nebraska, USA[4855].

1157. Mary C.[7] Christner (Daniel S.[6], Christian[5], Peter[4], Christian[3], Christian[2], Christen[1]) was born 30 Sep 1876 in Pulaski, Davis Co., IA, and died 05 May 1968 in Springfield, MO. She married **Henry Ensign Moore** 17 Apr 1901 in Hayes Co.. He was born 11 Dec 1875 in Albert Lea, MN, and died 05 Jan 1963 in Ozark, MO.

Children of Mary Christner and Henry Moore are:
    2578   i.   Gladys[8] Moore.

2579	ii.	Raymond Victor Moore, born 09 Jul 1902.
2580	iii.	Hazel Faye Moore, born 24 Oct 1903.
2581	iv.	Wesley Andrew Moore, born 18 Dec 1904.
2582	v.	Helen Marie Moore, born 15 Dec 1915.

1158. Joseph B. "Just"[7] Christner (John B.[6], Peter[5], Peter[4], Christian[3], Christian[2], Christen[1])[4856] was born 06 May 1857 in Henry Co., IN[4856], and died 17 May 1937 in Kent Co., DE[4856]. He married **Susanna B. Weirich**[4856,4857,4858] 29 Dec 1878. She was born 10 Sep 1860 in Lagrange, Lagrange Co., IN[4859,4860,4861], and died 26 Mar 1928 in Dover, DE[4862,4863,4864,4865].

Notes for Joseph B. "Just" Christner:
Joseph was Old Order Amish. Joseph has the nickname of Just.

Amish and Amish Mennonite Families; CHB11; p. 60

More About Joseph B. "Just" Christner:
Residence: 1920, Precinct 29, Yamhill Co., OR[4866,4866]

Notes for Susanna B. Weirich:
Susanna is the daughter of Bendict and Mary Plank Weirich.

Christner - Susanna (Weirich) Christner, wife of Joseph B. Christner was born Sep 10, 1860; died at the home of her daughter Elizabeth Miller, Dover, DE on March 26, 1928; aged 67 y. 6 m. 16 d. She was the mother of 12 children. One child died in infancy. Surviving are her husband, and these children; Elizabeth, wife of David Miller; Mary, wife of A. M. Beachy, Somerset Co., PA; Rachel, wife of Joseph Schrock, Curtiss, WI; Samuel S. of Orrville, OH; Benedict J. of Beach City, Ohio; Malinda, wife of Andy Yoder, Amity, OR; Susanna and Ada Christner, Lancaster Co., PA; Fannie, widow of Menno C. Beachy, Lancaster Co., PA; Ollie, wife of Rudy Miller, Bird-in-hand, PA; Elva, wife of Aaron Kauffman, Bird-in-hand, PA. 1 brother, 4 sisters, 41 grandchildren, and 12 great-grandchildren also survive, as well as many other relatives and friends. With her husband she left McMinnville, OR to be with their children in the east. She was failing in health about a year, but was very patient in her sickness, which at last turned to Bright's Disease. She took her bed on Thursday afternoon and died the next Monday. The funeral sermon was preached by Will Byler and Iddo Yoder. Text, Rev. 7; Psalm 19.

More About Susanna B. Weirich:
Cause of Death: Bright's Disease
Residence: 1920, Precinct 29, Yamhill Co., OR[4866,4866]

Children of Joseph Christner and Susanna Weirich are:

| 2583 | i. | Edna[8] Christner. |
| 2584 | ii. | Susanna Christner. |

Notes for Susanna Christner:
Christner. - Susanna, daughter of Joseph and Susanna (Weirich) Christner was born near Hubbard, Ore., July 13, 1892; died Sept. 6, 1931; aged 39 y. 1 m. 24 d. She leaves to mourn, father, and brothers and sisters; Mrs. David Miller of Hartley, Del.; Mrs. Alvin Beachy of Plain City, O.; Mrs. Joseph Schrock of Curtiss, Wis.; Samuel Christner of Orrville, O.; Benedict Christner of Wilmot. O.; Mrs. Andrew Yoder of Kalona, Ia.; Mrs. Fannie Beachy of Bareville, PA; Mrs. Rudy Miller, Miss Ada Christner, and Mrs. Aaron Kauffman of Witmer, PA; and many other relatives and friends. She united with the Amish Mennonite Church in her younger years. In the fall of 1927, she, with her father and mother, moved from McMinnville, Ore., to Lancaster Co., PA. In the spring of 1928 her mother preceded her in death; also a sister at the age of 18 months. In January she became ill and had been in the care of doctors but it seemed nothing could be done. About two months before her death her ailment was pronounced cancer of the bowels. She was very patient with her suffering. Funeral services where held at the Amish Mennonite church at Morgantown, Pa., by David Yoder and John S. Mast. Burial in adjoining cemetery.

	2585	iii.	William Christner, died in Lagrange Co., IN.
+	2586	iv.	Elizabeth J. Christner, born 01 Oct 1879 in Elkhart Co., IN; died 05 Mar 1937 in Kent Co., DE.
+	2587	v.	Mary Christner, born 02 Dec 1880 in IN; died 11 Aug 1956.
+	2588	vi.	Rachel J. Christner, born 14 Dec 1882 in Goshen, Elkhart Co., IN; died 05 Aug 1971 in Blair Co., WI.

+ 2589   vii.   Samuel S. Christner, born 02 Apr 1884 in Lagrange Co., IN; died 09 Mar 1951 in Orrville, OH.

2590   viii.   Edna Christner[4867], born 13 Dec 1885 in Goshen, Elkhart Co., IN[4867]; died 29 Aug 1887 in Goshen, Elkhart Co., IN[4867].

+ 2591   ix.   Benedict J. Christner, born 29 Feb 1888 in Reno, Reno Co., KS; died 13 Jun 1957.

+ 2592   x.   Malinda Christner, born 14 Mar 1891.

2593   xi.   Susanna Christner, born 13 Jul 1892 in Hubbard, Marion Co., OR; died 06 Sep 1931.

     Notes for Susanna Christner:
     Birth: Jul. 13, 1892
     Death: Sep. 6, 1931

     Christner. - Susanna, daughter of Joseph and Susanna (Weirich) Christner was born near Hubbard, Ore., July 13, 1892; died Sept. 6, 1931; aged 39 y. 1 m. 24 d. She leaves to mourn, father, and brothers and sisters; Mrs. David Miller of Hartley, DE; Mrs. Alvin Beachy of Plain City, OH; Mrs. Joseph Schrock of Curtiss, Wis.; Samuel Christner of Orrville, OH; Benedict Christner of Wilmot. O.; Mrs. Andrew Yoder of Kalona, IA; Mrs. Fannie Beachy of Bareville, PA; Mrs. Rudy Miller, Miss Ada Christner, and Mrs. Aaron Kauffman of Witmer, PA and many other relatives and friends. She united with the Amish Mennonite Church in her younger years. In the fall of 1927, she, with her father and mother, moved from McMinnville, OR to Lancaster Co., PA. In the spring of 1928 her mother preceded her in death; also a sister at the age of 18 months. In January she became ill and had been in the care of doctors but it seemed nothing could be done. About two months before her death her ailment was pronounced cancer of the bowels. She was very patient with her suffering. Funeral services where held at the Amish Mennonite church at Morgantown, PA by David Yoder and John S. Mast. Burial in adjoining cemetery.

     Burial: Conestoga Mennonite Church Cemetery, Lancaster Co., PA

     More About Susanna Christner:
     Burial: Amish Mennonite Church Cemetery at Morgantown PA.
     Cause of Death: Cancer of the bowels

+ 2594   xii.   Ollie Christner, born 11 Mar 1897 in Hubbard, Marion Co., OR; died 26 Apr 1988 in Lancaster Co., PA.

+ 2595   xiii.   Ada A. Christner, born 03 Aug 1900 in Yamhill Co., OR; died 17 Mar 1988 in Lancaster, Lancaster Co., PA.

1160. John E.[7] **Christner** (John B.[6], Peter[5], Peter[4], Christian[3], Christian[2], Christen[1])[4868,4869] was born 01 May 1861 in Henry Co., IN[4870,4871], and died 22 Feb 1939 in Newbury, Lagrange Co., IN[4872,4873,4874,4875]. He married **(1) Emma J. Christner**[4876,4877] 1883 in by David Kauffman Lagrange Co, IN, daughter of John Christner and Susanna Mast. She was born 22 Sep 1865 in Topeka, Lagrange Co., IN[4878], and died 15 Mar 1901 in Topeka, Lagrange Co., IN[4879,4880,4881]. He married **(2) Elizabeth "Lizzie" M. Miller** 09 Jan 1896. She was born 02 Nov 1876 in Newbury, Lagrange Co., IN[4882], and died 15 Dec 1965.

Notes for John E. Christner:
Amish and Amish Mennonite Families; CHB13; p. 60

The Descendants of John J. Christner, privately published February 1961, p. 46.

He was Old Order Amish.

John E. is the son of John B.(Hans) Christner and Rachel Miller. John B. was born in Alsace-Lorraine France June 9, 1829. Rachel was born in Somerset Co., PA on Nov 21, 1837. John B and Rachel were married in 1855.

Birth: May 1, 1861
Death: Feb. 22, 1939

Burial: Forks Yoder Cemetery, Lagrange Co., IN

More About John E. Christner:
Amish and Amish Mennonite: CHB13/[4883]
Burial: Yoder Cemetery, Forks, Lagrange Co., IN
Occupation: Farmer/

Religion: Old Order Amish/
Residence: 1930, Newbury, Lagrange Co., IN[4884]

Notes for Emma J. Christner:
Amish and Amish Mennonite Families; CH2121b, CHB1; p. 60

The Descendants of John J. Christner, privately published 1961, pp. 4, 46.

Birth: Sep. 24, 1865
Death: Mar. 15, 1901

Inscription: Wife of John E. Christner, aged 35 Y 5 M 21 D

Burial: Christner Cemetery, Honeyville, Lagrange Co., IN
Row 5 plot 18

More About Emma J. Christner:
Burial: Christner Cemetery, Honeyville, Lagrange Co., IN
DBH Book: 11086/[4885,4886]
Religion: Old Order Amish/
Residence: 1900, Eden, Lagrange Co., IN[4887]

Notes for Elizabeth "Lizzie" M. Miller:
Title: Amish and Amish Mennonite Families
Author: Hugh F. Gingerich and Rachel W. Kreider, 1986; ML232b46, CHB1; p. 60

Elizabeth is the daughter of Manasses M. and Anna Miller. She was married to 1st to Samuel C. Miller, 2nd to Jacob M. Troyer, 3rd to John E. Christner.

Birth: Nov. 2, 1876
Death: Dec. 15, 1965

Burial: Forks Yoder Cemetery, Lagrange Co., IN
Plot: wife of John Christner

More About Elizabeth "Lizzie" M. Miller:
Burial: N41°38.827xW85°38.184/Yoder Cemetery, Forks, Lagrange Co., IN

Children are listed above under (399) Emma J. Christner.

Children of John Christner and Elizabeth Miller are:

2596	i.	Levi[8] Christner.
2597	ii.	Sylvia Christner.
+ 2598	iii.	Anna S. Miller, born 26 Jan 1899 in Lagrange Co., IN; died 21 Jun 1973.
+ 2599	iv.	Emma J. Christner, born 02 Mar 1901 in Topeka, Lagrange Co., IN; died 09 Jul 1969.
+ 2600	v.	Cletus S. Christner, born 18 Oct 1911 in Topeka, Lagrange Co., IN; died 08 Nov 1990 in Geneva, Adams Co., IN.
+ 2601	vi.	Alvin S. Christner, born 15 Jul 1914 in Topeka, Lagrange Co., IN; died 20 Jan 2012 in Berne, Adams Co., IN.
+ 2602	vii.	Elmina J. Christner, born 13 Jun 1919; died 17 Jan 1970.
+ 2603	viii.	Edna Christner, born 21 Jul 1922.
2604	ix.	Ida Christner, born 21 Jul 1933.

1161. Margaret[7] Christner (John B.[6], Peter[5], Peter[4], Christian[3], Christian[2], Christen[1])[4888] was born 25 Oct 1865 in or 1863 Trenton, Henry Co., IN[4888], and died 15 Oct 1929 in Goshen, Elkhart Co., IN. She married **Harry C. Schrock**[4888] 20 Dec 1885 in IN. He was born 07 Dec 1866 in Lagrange Co., IN[4888], and died 21 Nov 1962 in Lagrange Co., IN[4888].

Notes for Margaret Christner:
Schrock, Maggie Christner, wife of Harry C. Schrock, was born at Trenton, IA Oct. 25, 1865; died at her home near Goshen, IN Oct. 15, 1929; aged 63 y. 11 m. 20 d. In 1865 she was married to Harry Schrock, to which union were born 2 sons (John and Cornelius), and 3 daughters (Lizzie, Edna, and Lena), all of whom with her husband, survive. Besides these she leaves 20 grandchildren, 5 brothers, (Joseph, John, Samuel, Peter, and Edward), and one sister (Sadie), who, together with a host of friends, mourn her death. Early in life she united with the Mennonite Church and remained devoted to her faith until death. During the seven years of her suffering from the ailment which caused her death, she was always patient, hopeful, and ready to do the will of God. Funeral services were conducted at the home near Goshen, IN by Bros. A. L. Buzzard and S. C. Yoder and at the Shore church near Shipshewana, Ind., by Bros. S. C. Yoder and Oscar Hostetler, after which the remains were laid away in the cemetery adjoining the church.

Amish and Amish Mennonite Families; CHB14; p. 60

More About Margaret Christner:
Burial: Shore Church Shipshewana IN.

Notes for Harry C. Schrock:
Harry is the son of Cornelius and Magdalena Bontrager Schrock. Margaret died and Harry married Elvina Miller. Elvina died and Harry married Savilla Esch born Mar 15, 1880.

Title: Amish and Amish Mennonite Families
Author: Hugh F. Gingerich and Rachel W. Kreider, 1986; SK32149, CHB1; p. 60

Children of Margaret Christner and Harry Schrock are:

2605   i.   Lizzie[8] Schrock, born 29 Mar 1886. She married Lee L. Yoder.

Notes for Lizzie Schrock:
Lizzie married Lee L. Yoder

+ 2606   ii.   John Foster Schrock, born 03 Oct 1887 in Lagrange Co., IN; died 10 Jan 1940 in Huntington, IN.

2607   iii.   Cornelius M. Schrock, born 27 Jan 1890; died 18 Jan 1965. He married Emma Slouter; born Abt. 1890 in Iowa[4889].

Notes for Cornelius M. Schrock:
Birth: Jan. 7, 1890
Death: Jan. 18, 1965

Spouse: Emma Schrock (1890 - 1974)

Burial: Shore Cemetery, Shipshewana, Lagrange Co., IN
Find A Grave Memorial# 51051076

More About Emma Slouter:
Race: White[4889]
Residence: 1930, Age: 40; Marital Status: Married; Relation to Head of House: Wife/Concord, Elkhart, Indiana[4889]

+ 2608   iv.   Edna Sarah Schrock, born 06 May 1892 in Lagrange Co., IN; died 16 Jan 1974 in Sarasota, Manatee Co., FL.

2609   v.   Lena Schrock, born 16 May 1896. She married Archie Rice.

Notes for Lena Schrock:
Lena married Archie Rice or Leana She divorced him and left him with the 5 boys/sons She lives in Chicago Il.

1162. Peter J.[7] Christner (John B.[6], Peter[5], Peter[4], Christian[3], Christian[2], Christen[1]) was born 18 Mar 1867 in Lagrange Co., IN, and died 31 Jan 1948 in Three Rivers, St Joseph Co., MI[4890,4891]. He married **Elizabeth Beachy**[4891] 07 Mar 1897 in Lagrange Co., IN[4891]. She was born Abt. 1870 in Henry Co., IA[4891].

Notes for Peter J. Christner:
Amish and Amish Mennonite Families; CHB15; p. 60

More About Peter J. Christner:
Burial: 03 Feb 1948, Three Rivers, St Joseph Co., MI[4892]
Residence: 1930, Three Rivers, St Joseph Co., MI[4893]

Notes for Elizabeth Beachy:
Title: Amish and Amish Mennonite Families
Author: Hugh F. Gingerich and Rachel W. Kreider, 1986; BC1b4b, CHB1; p. 60

More About Elizabeth Beachy:
Residence: 1930, Three Rivers, St Joseph Co., MI[4893]

Children of Peter Christner and Elizabeth Beachy are:

2610   i.   Hewlitt[8] Christner[4893], born 15 Jan 1898 in Lagrange Co., IN[4893]; died 01 Aug 1989 in Three Rivers, St Joseph Co., MI[4893].

     More About Hewlitt Christner:
     Residence: 1910, Van Buren, Lagrange Co., IN[4893]

2611   ii.   Leona Christner[4893], born Abt. 1900 in Lagrange Co., IN[4893].

     More About Leona Christner:
     Residence: 1910, Van Buren, Lagrange Co., IN[4893]

2612   iii.   Howard Christner[4893], born 05 Dec 1902 in Lagrange Co., IN[4893]; died 17 Mar 1995 in Kalamazoo, Kalamazoo Co., MI[4893].

     More About Howard Christner:
     Residence: 1930, Three Rivers, St Joseph Co., MI[4893]

2613   iv.   Lucile Christner[4893], born Abt. 1906 in Lagrange Co., IN[4893].

     More About Lucile Christner:
     Residence: 1910, Van Buren, Lagrange Co., IN[4893]

2614   v.   Fannie Christner[4893], born Abt. 1908 in St Joseph Co., MI[4893].

     More About Fannie Christner:
     Residence: 1910, Van Buren, Lagrange Co., IN[4893]

2615   vi.   Lena Christner[4893], born Abt. 1910 in Lagrange Co., IN[4893].

     More About Lena Christner:
     Residence: 1910, Van Buren, Lagrange Co., IN[4893]

2616   vii.   Freeland Christner[4893], born 18 May 1910 in Lagrange Co., IN[4893]; died 01 Aug 1973 in Ann Arbor, Washtenaw Co., MI[4893].

     More About Freeland Christner:
     Residence: Lockport, St. Joseph Co., MI[4893]

1165. Sarah[7] Christner (John B.[6], Peter[5], Peter[4], Christian[3], Christian[2], Christen[1]) was born 07 Aug 1873 in Lagrange Co., IN, and died 05 Mar 1964 in Elkhart Co., IN[4894]. She married **(1) Milton Williams**[4894]. She married **(2) Amos J. Lambright**[4894,4895]. He was born 20 Nov 1872 in Lagrange, Lagrange Co., IN[4895], and died 18 Apr 1961 in Topeka, Lagrange Co., IN[4895]. She married **(3) William G. S. Smith** 02 Apr 1902. He was born

Abt. 1873 in IN[4896].

Notes for Sarah Christner:
Amish and Amish Mennonite Families; CHB18; p. 60

More About Sarah Christner:
Residence: 1930, Middlebury, Elkhart Co., IN[4896]

More About Amos J. Lambright:
Burial: Hawpatch Cemetery/Topeka, Lagrange Co., IN[4897]

More About William G. S. Smith:
Residence: 1930, Middlebury, Elkhart Co., IN[4898]

Child of Sarah Christner and Amos Lambright is:
    2617   i.   Fannie Alzoa[8] Lambright[4898], born 31 May 1891 in Lagrange Co., IN[4898]; died 04 Jun 1925 in Elyria, Lorain, Ohio[4898].

                More About Fannie Alzoa Lambright:
                Residence: 1900, Elkhart, Elkhart Co., IN[4898]

Child of Sarah Christner and William Smith is:
    2618   i.   Harry J W[8] Smith[4898], born Abt. 1907 in Elkhart Co., IN[4898].

                More About Harry J W Smith:
                Residence: 1910, Jefferson, Elkhart, Indiana[4898]

1166. Samuel J.[7] Christner (John B.[6], Peter[5], Peter[4], Christian[3], Christian[2], Christen[1]) was born 17 Dec 1875 in Lagrange Co., IN, and died 05 Nov 1971 in Shipshewana Lagrange Co., IN[4899]. He married **Veronica Fannie Miller**. She was born 1875, and died 27 Apr 1946[4899].

Notes for Samuel J. Christner:
Amish and Amish Mennonite Families; CHB19; p. 60

More About Samuel J. Christner:
Burial: Bontreger North Cemetery, Lagrange Co., IN
Residence: 1930, Newbury, Lagrange Co., IN[4899]

Notes for Veronica Fannie Miller:
Amish and Amish Mennonite Families; ML223744, CHB1; p. 60

More About Veronica Fannie Miller:
Burial: Bontrager North Cemetery, Lagrange Co., IN
Residence: 1910, Newbury, Lagrange Co., IN[4899]

Children of Samuel Christner and Veronica Miller are:
    2619   i.   Nora[8] Christner, born 02 May 1899; died 05 Dec 1916 in Lagrange Co., IN.

                More About Nora Christner:
                Burial: N41°40.560xW85°37.884/Bontreger North Cemetery, Lagrange Co., IN

+   2620   ii.   Sarah Ann Christner, born 16 Jan 1902 in Shipshewana Lagrange Co., IN; died 06 Feb 1994.
+   2621   iii.   John S. Christner, born 03 Sep 1905 in Shipshewana, Elkhart Co., IN; died 07 Mar 1983 in Shipshewana, Elkhart Co., IN.
+   2622   iv.   Olen S. Christner, born 23 Sep 1909 in Lagrange Co., IN; died 02 May 1992 in Lagrange Co., IN.
+   2623   v.   Ida Christner, born 16 May 1912 in Shipshewana, Elkhart Co., IN; died 19 Dec 1996 in Shipshewana, Lagrange Co., IN.

1168. Edward J.[7] Christner (John B.[6], Peter[5], Peter[4], Christian[3], Christian[2], Christen[1]) was born 28 Oct 1883 in Lagrange Co., IN[4900], and died 12 Nov 1960 in Huntington Park, Los Angeles Co., CA[4900,4901]. He married **Lydia Eash**[4902] 22 Dec 1907 in Lagrange Co., IN[4902], daughter of Christian Eash and Amanda. She was born 14 Nov 1888 in Lagrange Co., IN[4902], and died 29 Nov 1980 in Gainesville, Hall Co., GA[4903].

Notes for Edward J. Christner:
Amish and Amish Mennonite Families; CHB1b; p. 60

More About Edward J. Christner:
Burial: Bontrager South Cemetery, Lagrange Co., IN
Residence: 1930, Goshen, Elkhart Co., IN[4904]

Notes for Lydia Eash:
Amish and Amish Mennonite Families; EFR280, CHB1; p. 60

Birth: 1888
Death: 1980

Burial: Bontrager South Cemetery, Lagrange Co., IN
Find A Grave Memorial# 82428782

More About Lydia Eash:
Burial: Bontrager South Cemetery, Lagrange Co., IN
Residence: 1930, Goshen, Elkhart Co., IN[4904]

Children of Edward Christner and Lydia Eash are:

2624　　i.　Mary Winifred[8] Christner, born 11 Nov 1908 in Middlebury, Elkhart Co., IN[4904]; died 21 Nov 1908 in W85°37.533 x N41°37.512/Bontrager South Cemetery, Lagrange Co., IN.

More About Mary Winifred Christner:
Burial: Beside Parents

2625　　ii.　Marlen Christner[4904], born 1909 in Middlebury, Elkhart Co., IN[4904]. He married Rose.

More About Marlen Christner:
Residence: 1930, Goshen, Elkhart Co., IN[4904]

2626　　iii.　Kenneth La Mar Christner[4904], born 29 Jul 1913 in Middlebury, Elkhart Co., IN[4904]; died 04 Jun 1918 in Middlebury, Elkhart Co., IN[4904].

Notes for Kenneth La Mar Christner:
Christner - Kenneth La Mar Christner was born July 29. 1913; died June 4, 1918; aged 4 y. 10 m. 6 d.
He leaves a father, mother two brothers (Marlen and Wayne), four grandparents and a host of friends and relatives.
"Dear Kenneth, how we miss you
Your kind and smiling face,
But God did call you home.
To give you a better resting place."
Funeral services by S. S. Yoder and D. D. Miller at Forks Church near Middlebury, IN.

More About Kenneth La Mar Christner:
Burial: Bontrager South Cemetery, Lagrange Co., IN

2627　　iv.　Wayne B. Christner, born 09 May 1916; died 08 Jan 2009 in Nappanee, Elkhart Co., IN[4905].

More About Wayne B. Christner:
Residence: 1930, Goshen, Elkhart Co., IN[4905]

2628　　v.　Dallas Christner, born 22 Nov 1921.

1169. Veronica Fannie[7] Christner (Peter[6], Peter[5], Peter[4], Christian[3], Christian[2], Christen[1]) was born 04 Mar 1859 in Wayland, Henry Co., IA[4906], and died 18 Jan 1894 in Peach Orchard, Clay Co., AR[4906]. She married **Moses P. Miller** 20 Feb 1877 in IN[4906]. He was born 31 Aug 1851 in Holmes Co., OH, and died 29 Jul 1932 in OR.

Notes for Veronica Fannie Christner:
Family History of Christian Schmucker and Catherine Christner, p. 9

They lived in Howard Co., IN and later in AR.

Veronica was a popular name with the early Christner family. Veronica was the woman who gave Jesus a cloth to wipe his face while he carried the cross. This name comes from the fourteen Stations of the Cross, including the extra-biblical character, Veronica, who wipes Jesus' bloody face with her veil which retains the image of his face imprinted upon it, left as a gift for her and for Christians to contemplate forever. This is a medieval Roman Catholic Holdover from their early religion.

Fannie Frannie Freny Frany Freni are all nicknames for Veronica as the german pronunciation uses an F sound instead of a V as in Furronica. (roll the R's) so like many languages if you add a Y sound to the end of a name you have a nickname. Example Johnny, Dickie or Dicky, Bobby, Maggie, Lizzie.

Last names had the same problem, Schantz became Johns as you can play with the word in german it will sound like (chaunts) the a is ah.

Notes for Moses P. Miller:
Family History of Christian Schmucker and Catherine Christner, p. 9.

Moses was married to Susanna Keim before he married Veronica.
Moses is the son of Peter J. and Veronica Miller Miller.

More About Moses P. Miller:
Residence: 1930, Liberal, Clackamas, Oregon[4906]

Children of Veronica Christner and Moses Miller are:

2629	i.	Fannie Jane[8] Miller[4906], born 06 May 1879 in Kokomo, Howard Co., IN[4906]; died 01 Apr 1967 in Marion Co., OR[4906].
2630	ii.	Ezra M. Miller[4906], born 25 Jan 1883 in Needy, Clackamas Co., OR[4906]; died 03 Dec 1968 in Orrville, Wayne., Wayne Co., OH[4906].
2631	iii.	Amelia Miller[4906], born 23 Apr 1885 in Kokomo, Howard Co., IN[4906]; died 09 Feb 1975 in Albany, Linn Co., OR[4906].
2632	iv.	Peter M. Miller[4906], born 22 Feb 1890 in Daviess Co., IN[4906]; died in Sugarcreek, Tuscarawas Co., OH[4906].

1170. Catherine[7] Christner (Peter[6], Peter[5], Peter[4], Christian[3], Christian[2], Christen[1])[4907,4908,4909] was born 09 Mar 1860 in Henry Co., IA[4910,4911,4912], and died 26 Nov 1933 in Nappanee, Elkhart Co., IN[4913,4914,4915]. She married **(1) Christian C. Schmucker**[4915,4916,4917] 1877 in Howard Co., IN[4917,4918], son of John Schmucker and Elizabeth Nisley. He was born 18 Apr 1856 in Kokomo, Howard Co., IN[4919,4920,4921], and died 17 Mar 1909 in Liberty Township, Howard, Indiana, United States[4921,4922,4923]. She married **(2) Jacob J. Kauffman**[4924] 1913 in Howard Co. IN., son of Jacob Kauffman and Elizabeth Miller. He was born 1845 in Elkhart Co., IN[4924], and died 25 Oct 1925 in Elkhart, Elkhart Co., IN[4924]. She married **(3) John J. Miller** 10 Jul 1927 in Nappanee, IN. He was born 02 Feb 1856 in Holmes Co., OH, and died 04 Jan 1947.

Notes for Catherine Christner:
Family History of Christian Schmucker and Catherine Christner, p. 9.

Catherine was married 3 times She and her sister (Fannie) stayed in Indiana when the rest of the family moved to Eugene, Oregon in 1881. She went to visit her father in April 1910 in Oregon after not seeing him for 29 years.

Her youngest son, Noah, went with her. After her second marriage she went for another visit and later her father took sick so she went again and was able to be with him when he died. Old Order Amish   She died of cancer of the stomach she underwent an operation and had much pain.

Catherine had a foster child Ada Hershberger b.Dec. 4 1894 died of Pneumonia on Nov.3 1910.

Katie Christner Miller, daughter of Peter and barbara Christner was born March 9, 1860 in Missouri and died at her home near nappanee, IN., Nov. 26, 1933 at the age of 73 years, 8 mo., 17bdays.

She was married to Christian C. Schmucker in the year 1877 and lived in the Holy Bonds of Matrimony 32 years. To this union were born 6 children, namely: Marbara, wife of Emanuel C. Hochstedler, John C. Schmucker and Mattie, wife of John C. Hochstedler of Howard Co., IN, Joseph C. Schmucker of Midland, MI, Jacob C. Schmucker of Topeka, IN and Noah C. Schmucker of Millersburg, IN.

Twenty - six grandchildren, 40 great-grandchildren, 4 brothers living in Oregon, a breaved husband and a host of friends to mourn her departures. We do not mourn as though we have no hope.

More About Catherine Christner:
Cause of Death: cancer of the stomach
Residence: 1900, Howard Township, Howard, Indiana[4925]

Notes for Christian C. Schmucker:
When his health left him unable to farm he made furniture until his rheumatism slowed him down.

Family History of Christian Schmucker and Catherine Christner, Edited by Mrs. George E. Hoover, Rt. 3, Box 100, Goshen, IN, 1957, pp. 4, 13, 14

Christian Schmucker son of John and elizabeth Nisley Schmucker was born in Howard Co., IN, April 18, 1856 where he grew to manhood. Some time in the year 1877 he was married to Catherine Christner, daughter of Peter and Barnara Hass/Haas Christner. They made their home and raised a family of six children - four sons and two daughters, also giving a home to a foster daughter.

On March 17, 1909 Christian died after suffering for at least 20 years with rheumatism. After he was not able to do his farming he made some furniture and tried to keep busy as long as he was able.

In April of 1910 Catherine decided to go see her Father in Oregon, whom she had not seen for 29 years. So the family decided that her youngest son, Noah should go with her. her Mother had passed away 12 years before, so she never got to see her Mother after they moved to Oregon.

In 1913 she was married the second time to Jacob Kauffman, Hea was born feb. 9, 1845 and died Oct 25, 1925, age 80 years 8 mo. 16 days.

Some time in the marriage they together made a trip to Oregon to visit her father. Then later on, when she heard her Father was not well, she made another trip to see him. He died while she was there.

Catherine was married the third time on July 10, 1927 to John J. Miller. His home was at the east edge of Nappanee, IN. She moved there with him and kept house for him until she took sick with cancer and died Nov. 26, 1933, age 73 years, 8 mo., 17 days.

Obituary: Katie (Christner) Miller
The death angel has again been in our midst and called away our beloved Mother.

More About Christian C. Schmucker:
Occupation: Farmer/
Residence: 1900, Howard Township, Howard, Indiana[4925]

More About Jacob J. Kauffman:
Residence: 1910, Clay, Miami, Indiana[4926]

Notes for John J. Miller:
John was 1st married to Susanna Frey, 2nd marriage 5 Nov 1905 to Lydia Gingerich. John is the son of John F and Magdalena Miller Miller.

Children of Catherine Christner and Christian Schmucker are:

+ 2633 i.   Barbara[8] Schmucker, born 13 Jul 1878 in Greentown, Howard Co., IN; died 01 Apr 1940 in Greentown, Howard, Indiana, United States.
+ 2634 ii. John C. Schmucker, born 08 Dec 1879 in Greentown, Howard Co., IN; died 28 Dec 1950.
+ 2635 iii. Joseph P. Schmucker, born 18 Apr 1881 in Greentown, Howard Co., IN; died 04 May 1948.
+ 2636 iv. Jacob Schmucker, born 07 Jan 1883 in Greentown, Howard Co., IN.
   2637 v.   Magdalena C Schmucker[1927,1928,1929], born 26 Aug 1884 in Kokomo, Howard Co., IN[4930,4931]; died 10 Jul 1982 in Kokomo, Howard Co., IN[4932].

            More About Magdalena C Schmucker:
            Residence: 1900, Howard Township, Howard, Indiana[4932]

+ 2638 vi. Noah C. Schmucker, born 17 Mar 1891 in Greentown, Howard Co., IN; died 05 Jun 1975 in Middlebury, Elkhart Co., IN.

1171. Jacob[7] Christner (Peter[6], Peter[5], Peter[4], Christian[3], Christian[2], Christen[1]) was born 30 Mar 1861 in Henry Co., IA, and died 1933. He married **Veronica Frany Miller**. She was born 19 May 1865 in Lagrange Co., IN, and died 13 Feb 1886 in Hubbard, Marion Co., OR.

Notes for Jacob Christner:
Family History of Christian Schmucker and Catherine Christner, p. 9

Christner, Young son - On the 20th of February, in Hubbard, Oregon, a son of Jacob and Veronica Christner, aged 2 months and 18 days. The funeral services were held by John Miller and Jacob Schwartzentruber. Text, Mark 10:13.

Notes for Veronica Frany Miller:
Family History of Christian Schmucker and Catherine Christner, p. 9

Veronica is the daughter of Daniel D. and Anna Kauffman Miller

CHRISTNER- On the 12th of Feb., near Hubbard, OR of fourteen months suffering with consumption, Fanny, wife of Jacob Christner, aged 20 years, 8 months and 24 days. She was a faithful member of the Amish Mennonite church. She was patient unto the end. Ten days before her death she and her husband were conveyed to the home of Bro. P. Mishler, where she died. In her last days she often desired singing, praying and reading, which was always done at her request. She was buried on Sunday, the 14th of Feb., at the Miller graveyard. Services were held by P. Mishler and W. H. Palmer from Luke 13:23- 29. She leaves a sorrowing husband and one child.

More About Veronica Frany Miller:
Burial: Miller Graveyard, OR

Child of Jacob Christner and Veronica Miller is:
+ 2639 i.   Levi[8] Christner, born 12 Dec 1884 in Hubbard, Marion Co., OR; died 15 May 1953 in Clackamas Co., OR.

1172. Magdalena "Mattie"[7] Christner (Peter[6], Peter[5], Peter[4], Christian[3], Christian[2], Christen[1]) was born 21 Jul 1862 in Trenton, Henry Co., IA, and died 28 Mar 1929 in Hubbard, Marion Co., OR. She married

Solomon L. Miller Jun 1880. He was born 30 Sep 1857 in Lagrange Co., IN, and died 31 Jan 1941 in OR.

Notes for Magdalena "Mattie" Christner:
Family History of Christian Schmucker and Catherine Christner, p. 9.

Miller - Mattie (Christner) Miller daughter of Peter and Barbara Christner was born July 21, 1862, near Trenton, Henry, Co., IA died near Hubbard, OR March 28, 1929; aged 66 y. 8 m. 7 d. In youth she with her parents moved to Hickory Co., MO and a few years later to Howard Co., IN. In June, 1880 she was united in marriage to Solomon L. Miller. In the fall of the same year they moved to Hubbard, OR where she lived until death, except ten years when she lived in Lane Co., OR. She is survived by her husband, four daughters and one son: Mrs. Delilah Kauffman, Warrenton, OR; Mrs. Polly Kropf, Woodburn, OR; Samuel S., Mrs. Mary Kropf, and Mrs. Tilly Jones of Hubbard, OR. She is also survived by 33 grandchildren, 4 great-grandchildren, 5 brothers, and 1 sister. Two brothers and one sister preceded her in death. In her youth she gave her life to her Master, united with the Mennonite Church, and remained faithful to the end. For six months she suffered, which kept her at home, where loving hands administered to her wants. During her last six days she was cared for in the Hubbard Sanitarium, where her loving Father called her home. Funeral services were conducted by A. P. Troyer and E. Z. Yoder. Text, Jno. 14:2. The remains were laid to rest in the cemetery near by.

Birth: Jul. 21, 1862
Death: Mar. 28, 1929

Children: Samuel Serious Miller (1883 - 1967)

Burial: Zion Mennonite Cemetery, Clackamas Co., OR
Plot: row 5 plot 2 sec 1 s

Notes for Solomon L. Miller:
Family History of Christian Schmucker and Catherine Christner, p. 9

Birth: Sep. 30, 1857
Death: Jan. 31, 1941

Gospel Herald - Vol. XXXIII, No 47 - February 20, 1941 - pp. 1006, 1007

Miller,- Solomon L., son of Daniel and Anna Miller was born Sept. 30, 1857 at Elkhart, IN; died Jan. 31, 1941 at the home of his daughter, Mrs. Harvey Kropf, near Hubbard, Oregon; aged 83 y. 4 m. 1 d. When a young man he, with his parents moved to Oregon. Later he returned to Indiana where he was united in marriage to Mattie Christner. Returning to Oregon he made his home in Lane County for about ten years, moving then to the vicinity of Hubbard, where he has since resided. He was the father of 1 son and 4 daughters: Mrs. C. I. Kropf of Woodburn, Samuel S., Mrs. Harvey Kropf, and Mrs. A. E. Jones of Hubbard. His wife and daughter Mary preceded him in death. Two brothers, 33 grandchildren, 31 great-grandchildren, and many other relatives and friends also survive him. In his youth he united with the Amish Church, later affiliating with the Mennonite Church in which faith he lived and died. Funeral services at the Zion Church were conducted by N. A. Lind, assisted by Nick Birky and E. Z. Yoder. Text, Acts 7:55, 56.

Spouse: Mattie Christner Miller (1862 - 1929)

Children:
Barbara Delila Miller Kauffman Krofpt (1881 - 1982)
Samuel Serious Miller (1883 - 1967)
Polly Miller Kropf (1885 - 1952)
Mary Ann Miller Kropf (1887 - 1936)
Katie Matilda Miller Jones (1890 - 1972)

Solomon is the son of Daniel D. and Anna Kauffman Miller. Solomon and Veronica are brother and sister. They married brother and sister.

Birth: Sep. 30, 1857
Death: Jan. 31, 1941

Children: Samuel Serious Miller (1883 - 1967)

Burial: Zion Mennonite Cemetery, Clackamas Co., OR
Plot: row 5 plot 1 sec 1 s

Children of Magdalena Christner and Solomon Miller are:

	2640	i.	Tilly[8] Miller. She married Jones.
	2641	ii.	Mary Miller. She married Kropf.
+	2642	iii.	Barbara Delilah "Lila" Miller, born 02 Apr 1881 in Woodburn, Marion Co., OR; died 03 Apr 1982 in Woodburn, Marion Co., OR.
+	2643	iv.	Samuel Serious Miller, born 04 Apr 1883 in Hubbard, Marion Co., OR; died 22 Jul 1967 in Salem, Marion Co., OR.
+	2644	v.	Polly Miller, born 20 Mar 1885 in Brooks, Marion Co., OR; died 14 Sep 1952 in Silverton, Marion Co., OR.

1176. Christian S.[7] Christner (Peter[6], Peter[5], Peter[4], Christian[3], Christian[2], Christen[1])[4933,4934,4935] was born 13 Feb 1871 in Wheatland, Hickory Co., MO, and died 09 Jan 1945 in Molalla, Clackamas Co., OR[4935,4936,4937]. He married **Adeline Roth**[4937,4938,4939] 14 Apr 1898 in Clackamas Co., OR[4940]. She was born 05 Feb 1875 in Wheatland, Hickory Co., MO[4941,4941], and died 13 Jan 1943 in Molalla, Clackamas Co., OR[4941,4942,4943].

Notes for Christian S. Christner:
Family History of Christian Schmucker and Catherine Christner, p. 9

Gospel Herald - Vol. XXXVII, No . 47 - February 23, 1945 - page 958

Christner, Chris, son of Peter and Barbara Christner was born near Wheatland, MO Feb. 13, 1872; passed away Jan. 9, 1945; aged 72 y. 10 m. 27 d. He came to Lane Co., OR with his parents, when nine years old. On April 14, 1898, he was married to Ada Roth, who preceded him in death Jan. 13, 1943. In 1900 they moved to the Molalla, OR community where he resided since. He is survived by one daughter and 4 sons (Inez Lantz, Clinton C., Loren, Harley S., of Molalla, and Earl J., of Portland), one brother (Noah, of Portland), one granddaughter, 5 grandsons, and many nieces, nephews, and friends. In his younger years he became discouraged in the Christian life, but on Oct. 31, 1920, he renewed his covenant with the Lord and the Mennonite Church. Soon after this he was afflicted through sickness and never fully recovered. Funeral services were conducted by F. J. Gingerich and J. W. Hess.

Parents:
Peter Christner (1833 - 1912)
Barbara Haus Christner (1828 - 1898)

Spouse: Adaline Roth Christner (1875 - 1943)

Children:
Clinton C. Christner (1901 - 1987)
Barbara May Christner (1907 - 1907)

Burial: Zion Mennonite Cemetery, Ninety-one, Cackamas Co., OR
Plot: 10N-1

More About Christian S. Christner:
Burial: Zion Mennonite Cemetery, Hubbard, Oregon[4944,4945]
Residence: 01 Apr 1940, Age: 68; Marital Status: Married; Relation to Head of House: Head/Needy, Clackamas Co., OR[4946]

Notes for Adeline Roth:
Christner - Ada Roth was born Feb. 5, 1875, near Wheatland, Hickory Co., Mo.; emigrated with her parents by

wagon and tram (in August, 1862) to Arkansas, and in 1892 by train to Hubbard, Oreg. April 14, 1898, she was married to Chris Christner. They made their home in Lane County for awhile and since then near Molalla, OR. She accepted Christ as her Savior in her youth and united with the Mennonite Church, passing out of this life in faith as a communicant member of said church. The last few years she was afflicted with heart trouble, which caused her much suffering, death relieving her Jan. 13, 1943; aged 67 y. 11m. 8 d. She leaves her husband, daughter (Mrs. Iness Lantz), 4 sons (Clifton and Harley of Molalla; Lorn of Oregon City, Earl of Portland)and five grandchildren, also 5 sisters (Lizzie Nofzinger of Molalla, Lena Nofziger, Katie Yoder of Canby, Rose Strubbar of Woodburn, Emma Headings of Hubbard), 3 brothers (Will of Coquille, Oreg., Joe of Birmingham, AL, Simon of Molalla), besides many cousins, relatives, and friends. Funeral services at the Zion Church and graveyard. Text, Psa. 107: 8, 14, 21, 31.

Birth: Feb. 5, 1875
Death: Jan. 13, 1943

Burial: Zion Mennonite Cemetery, Clackamas Co., OR
Plot: row 10 plot 2 sec 1 n

More About Adeline Roth:
Burial: Zion Mennonite Cemetery, row 10 plot 2 sec 1 n/Estacada, Clackamas, Oregon, USA
Residence: 1920, Needy, Clackamas Co., OR[4947,4947,4948]

Children of Christian Christner and Adeline Roth are:
+ 2645   i.   Inez Katherine[8] Christner, born 01 Jun 1899 in Lane Co., OR; died 24 Sep 1979 in Molalla, Clackamas Co., OR.

+ 2646   ii.   Clinton Chris Christner, born 29 Jan 1901 in Needy, Clackamas Co., OR; died 22 Dec 1987 in Molalla, Clackamas Co., OR.

2647   iii.   Loren P. Christner, born 31 Dec 1903 in Molalla, Clackamas Co., OR[4949]; died 20 Jul 1982 in Molalla, Clackamas Co., OR[4949]. He married Lena D. Babcock[4949]; born 19 Dec 1905 in Hoxie, KS[4949]; died 19 Jan 1949[4949].

     More About Loren P. Christner:
     Residence: 1930, Needy, Clackamas Co., OR[4949]
     Social Security Number: 541-03-3673/[4950]

     More About Lena D. Babcock:
     Residence: 1930, Needy, Clackamas Co., OR[4951]

2648   iv.   Earl Joseph Christner[4952,4952,4953,4954], born 24 Sep 1905 in Needy, Clackamas Co., OR[4955,4955,4956]; died 27 May 1983 in Lake Oswego, Clackamas Co., OR[4957,4957,4958]. He married Evelyn Christner[4959,4960] 1926 in OR[4961]; born 09 May 1908[4961]; died 08 Nov 1971 in Lake Oswego, Clackamas Co., OR[4961].

     More About Earl Joseph Christner:
     Residence: 1920, Needy, Clackamas Co., OR[4961,4961]
     Social Security Number: 541-12-7850/[4962]
     SSN issued: OR[4962]

     More About Evelyn Christner:
     Social Security Number: 544-09-9763/[4963]
     SSN issued: OR[4963]

2649   v.   Barbara May Christner[4964], born 10 Nov 1907 in Clackamas Co., OR[4964]; died 11 Nov 1907 in Clackamas Co., OR[4964].

     Notes for Barbara May Christner:
     Birth: Nov. 10, 1907
     Death: Nov. 11, 1907

     Parents:
     Christian C. Christner (1871 - 1945)
     Adaline Roth Christner (1875 - 1943)

Burial: Zion Mennonite Cemetery, Ninety-one, Clackamas Co., OR
Plot: 10N-8

+   2650   vi.   Harley Simon Christner, born 02 Feb 1914 in Molalla, Clackamas Co., OR; died 17 May 1984 in
                    Estacada, Clackamas Co., OR.

1178. Magdalena "Lena"[7] Christner (Jacob[6], Peter[5], Peter[4], Christian[3], Christian[2], Christen[1]) was born 08 Jun 1861 in Henry Co., IA[4965], and died 19 Apr 1943 in IA[4965]. She married **Jacob Hirschy**[4965]. He was born 29 Feb 1864 in Alsace, France[4965], and died 20 Feb 1946 in Wayland IA[4965].

Notes for Magdalena "Lena" Christner:
Birth: 1861
Death: 1943

Parents:
Jacob Christner (1836 - 1904)
Barbara Egli Christner (1835 - 1915)

Spouse: Jacob Hirschy (1864 - 1946)

Children:
Infant Daughter 3 Hirschy (_____ - 1900)
Infant Son 1 Hirschy
Infant Daughter 1 Hirschy
Infant Daughter 2 Hirschy
David Hirschy (1891 - 1891)
Ida Hirschy (1893 - 1899)

Burial: Sugar Creek Cemetery, Wayland, Henry Co., IA
Plot: Row 16

Children of Magdalena Christner and Jacob Hirschy are:
    2651   i.   Joseph Christner[8] Hirschy[4965], born 23 Nov 1889 in Wayland IA[4965]; died 30 Mar 1976 in Wayland
                  IA[4965].
    2652   ii.   David Hirschy[4965], born 14 Apr 1891 in Wayland, Henry Co., IA[4965]; died 19 Apr 1891 in Wayland,
                  Henry Co., IA[4965].

                  Notes for David Hirschy:
                  Birth: Apr 14, 1891
                  Death: Apr 19, 1891

                  Parents:
                  Jacob Hirschy (1864 - 1946)
                  Magdalena Christner Hirschy (1861 - 1943)

                  Burial: Sugar Creek Cemetery, Wayland, Henry Co., IA
                  Plot: Row 16

    2653   iii. Ida Hirschy[4965], born 18 Jun 1893 in Wayland, Henry Co., IA[4965]; died 15 Jun 1899 in Wayland, Henry
                  Co., IA[4965].

                  Notes for Ida Hirschy:
                  Birth: Jun 18, 1893
                  Death: Jun 15, 1899

                  Daughter of Jacob and Lena

                  Parents:
                  Jacob Hirschy (1864 - 1946)
                  Magdalena Christner Hirschy (1861 - 1943)

Burial: Sugar Creek Cemetery, Wayland, Henry Co., IA
Plot: Row 16

2654   iv.   Ada Marie Hirschy[4965], born 22 Aug 1896 in IA[4965]; died 21 Sep 1982 in Wayland, Henry Co., IA[4965].
2655   v.   Ellen Hirschy[4965], born 24 Aug 1901 in Wayland, Henry Co., IA[4965]; died 02 Nov 1935 in IA[4965].
2656   vi.   Edwin J. Hirschy[4965], born 18 Mar 1905 in IA[4965]; died 04 Nov 1919 in Wayland, Henry Co., IA[4965].

1179. Jacob E.[7] Christner (Jacob[6], Peter[5], Peter[4], Christian[3], Christian[2], Christen[1])[4966] was born 27 Aug 1863 in Henry Co., IA[4967], and died 25 Sep 1933 in Henry Co., IA[4968]. He married **Fanny Rich**[4969,4970,4971,4972] 27 Aug 1885 in IA[4973]. She was born 09 Feb 1868 in Henry Co., IA[4974], and died 11 May 1947 in Wayland, Henry Co., IA[4974,4975].

Notes for Jacob E. Christner:
Birth: Aug 27, 1863 - IA
Death: Sep 25, 1933 - Henry Co., IA

Parents:
Jacob Christner (1836 - 1904)
Barbara Egli Christner (1835 - 1915)

Spouse: Fannie Rich Christner (1868 - 1947)

Children:
David Christner (1885 - 1979)
Bertha Christner Hill (1889 - 1977)
Nicholas Christner (1891 - 1977)
Jakie Jacob Christner (1893 - 1974)
Barbara Christner Neff (1894 - 1963)
Anna Mae Christner Campbell (1897 - 1971)
Neoma Christner Schantz (1901 - 1981)
Lavina Christner Riley (1903 - 1997)
Clarence Rufus Christner (1909 - 1910)
Elmer Christner (1912 - 1999)

Burial: North Hill Cemetery, Henry Co., IA

More About Jacob E. Christner:
Burial: Iowa Gravestone Photo Project/North Hill Cemetery, Wayland, IA[4976]
Residence: 1910, Jefferson, Henry Co., IA[4976]

Notes for Fanny Rich:
Birth: Feb 9, 1868 - Henry Co., IA
Death: May 11, 1947 - Henry Co., IA

Spouse: Jacob E. Christner (1863 - 1933)

Children:
Bertha Christner Hill (1889 - 1977)
Nicholas Christner (1891 - 1977)

Burial:North Hill Cemetery, (Rural Wayland), Henry Co., IA

Parents:
Nicholas Rich (1844 - 1920)
Anna Huser Rich (1843 - 1907)

Spouse: Jacob E. Christner (1863 - 1933)

Children:
David Christner (1885 - 1979)
Bertha Christner Hill (1889 - 1977)
Nicholas Christner (1891 - 1977)
Jakie Jacob Christner (1893 - 1974)
Barbara Christner Neff (1894 - 1963)
Anna Mae Christner Campbell (1897 - 1971)
Neoma Christner Schantz (1901 - 1981)
Lavina Christner Riley (1903 - 1997)
Clarence Rufus Christner (1909 - 1910)
Elmer Christner (1912 - 1999)

Burial: North Hill Cemetery, Rural Wayland, Henry Co., IA

More About Fanny Rich:
Burial: May 1947, SE corner. From drive, row 4, grave 1./North Hill Cemetery, Wayland, Iowa, USA[4977,4978]
Residence: 1930, Jefferson, Henry Co., IA[4979,4980,4981]

Children of Jacob Christner and Fanny Rich are:

+ 2657   i.   Bertha[8] Christner, born 23 Jan 1889 in Wayland, Henry Co., IA; died 12 Dec 1977 in Mt. Pleasant, Henry Co., IA.

+ 2658   ii.   Nicholas Christner, born 13 Jan 1891 in Washington Co., IA; died 05 May 1977 in Mt. Pleasant, Henry Co., IA.

+ 2659   iii.   Jacob Christner, born 04 Jan 1893 in Henry Cty., IA; died 28 Apr 1974 in Buried: North Hill Cemetery/.

     2660   iv.   Barbara Christner[4982,4983,4984,4985], born 16 Dec 1894 in Wayland, Henry Co., IA[4985,4986,4987]; died 22 Mar 1963 in Mount Pleasant, Henry, IA[4988]. She married Benjamin Harrison Neff[4988] 08 Feb 1913 in Wayland, Henry Co., IA[4988]; born 15 Jun 1889 in Coppack, Henry Co. IA[4988]; died 05 Oct 1969 in Mt. Pleasant, Henry Co., IA[4988].

         Notes for Barbara Christner:
         Buried: North Hill Cemetery

         More About Barbara Christner:
         Residence: 01 Apr 1940, Jefferson, Henry Co., IA[4988]

         More About Benjamin Harrison Neff:
         Residence: 01 Apr 1940, Jefferson, Henry Co., IA[4988]

     2661   v.   Anna Mae Christner[4989], born 21 Feb 1897 in IA[4989]; died 20 Mar 1971 in Wayland, Henry Co., IA[4989].

         Notes for Anna Mae Christner:
         Buried: North Hill Cemetery, Wayland, Henry Co., IA

         More About Anna Mae Christner:
         Residence: 1905, Walnut, Jefferson Co., IA[4989]

     2662   vi.   Ada Fanny Christner[4989,4990], born 18 Feb 1899 in Washington Co., IA[4990,4991]; died 02 Jun 1968 in Washington Hospital, Washington Co., IA[4992,4993].

         More About Ada Fanny Christner:
         Residence: 01 Jan 1925, Marion, Washington Co., IA[4994]

     2663   vii.   Lavina Christner[4995,4996], born 19 Sep 1903 in Jefferson Co., IA[4996,4997]; died 25 Dec 1997 in Washington, Washington Co., IA[4998].

         More About Lavina Christner:
         Residence: 1920, Jefferson, Henry Co., IA[4999]

     2664   viii.   Ezra Christner[4999,5000,5001,5002], born 03 Mar 1906 in IA[5003,5004,5005]; died 18 Jan 1991 in Washington,

Washington Co., IA[5006,5007,5008].

More About Ezra Christner:
Residence: 1920, Jefferson, Henry Co., IA[5009]
Social Security Number: 330-09-4955/[5010]
SSN issued: IL[5010]

2665   ix.   Clarence Rufas Christner[5011], born 07 Jun 1909 in Henry Co., IA[5012,5013]; died 21 Aug 1910 in Henry Co., IA[5014].

More About Clarence Rufas Christner:
Residence: 1910, Jefferson, Henry Co., IA[5015]

1180. Christian E.[7] Christner (Jacob[6], Peter[5], Peter[4], Christian[3], Christian[2], Christen[1])[5016,5017] was born 20 Jan 1868 in Trenton, Henry Co., IA[5018], and died 02 Dec 1951 in Wayland, Henr Co., PA[5018]. He married **Emma Estalena Conrad**[5018,5019,5020] 08 Feb 1899 in Wayland, Henry Co., IA[5021]. She was born 05 Mar 1876 in Henry Co.. IA[5022], and died 04 Jan 1965 in Henry Co.. IA[5022].

Notes for Christian E. Christner:
Gospel Herald - Volume XLIV , Number 52 - December 25, 1951 - page 1242

Christner, Christian E., son of Jacob and Barbara (Egli) Christner was born near Trenton in Henry Co., Jan. 20, 1868; departed this life after a short illness, aged 83 y. 10 m. 12 d. When he was ten years old his parents moved to a farm near Olds, Iowa, where he grew to manhood. As a young man he accepted Christ as his Saviour and united with the Sugar Creek Mennonite Church, remaining a faithful member until death. On Feb. 8, 1899, he was married to Emma Conrad. This union was blessed with 6 children: Irvin and Ralph, at home; Nina-Mrs. Joseph Unterahrer, Florence-Mrs. Herman Lleichty, Erna-Mrs. Jesse Roth and Verda-Mrs. Glen Reschly, all of the home community, Wayland, Iowa. He leaves his companion, 6 children, 18 grandchildren, 2 great-grandchildren, one sister (Mrs. Mary Gisser), and 2 brothers (Enos, Wayland, Iowa; Amos, Blakesburg, Iowa). He was a loving husband and a considerate father and grandfather who will be missed in the family circle. The funeral was held at the Sugar Creek Church Dec 4 conducted by the home ministers. Interment was made in the cemetery near by.

More About Christian E. Christner:
Burial: Sugar Creek Church, Wayland, Henry Co., IA[5022]
Residence: 1930, Wayne, Henry Co., IA[5022]

Notes for Emma Estalena Conrad:
Gospel Herald - Volume LVIII, Number 4 - January 26, 1965 - pages 86, 87

Christner, Emma Estalena, daughter of Martin and Anna (Klopfinstein) Conrad, was born in Henry Co., Iowa, March 5, 1876; died at her home in Henry Co., Jan. 4, 1965; aged 88 y. 9 m. 30 d. On Feb. 8, 1899, she was married to Christian E. Christner, who died Dec. 2, 1951. Surviving are 2 sons (Irvin and Ralph), 4 daughters (Nina - Mrs. Joseph Unternahrer, Florence - Mrs. Herman Leichty, Erna - Mrs. Jesse Roth, and Verda - Mrs. Glen Reschly), 19 grandchildren, 35 great-grandchildren, and one sister. One sister, one brother, and 2 great-grandchildren also preceded her in death. She was a member of the Sugar Creek Church, where funeral services were held Jan. 6, in charge of Simon Gingerich, Robert Hartzler, and Vernon S. Gerig.

More About Emma Estalena Conrad:
Burial: Sugar Creek Church, Wayland, Henry Co., IA[5022]
Residence: 1930, Wayne, Henry Co., IA[5022]

Children of Christian Christner and Emma Conrad are:
2666   i.   Irvin Lloyd[8] Christner[5023], born 05 Feb 1900 in Wayland, Henry Co., IA; died 11 Apr 1976 in Wapello, Louisa Co., IA[5023].

Notes for Irvin Lloyd Christner:
Christner, Irvin Lloyd, son of Christian and Emma E. (Conrad) Christner was born near Wayland, Iowa,

Feb. 5, 1900; died at the Wapello Nursing Home, Apr. 11, 1976; aged 76 y. Surviving are one brother (Ralph) and 3 sisters (Florence, - Mrs. Herman Leichty, Erna Mrs. Jesse Roth, and Verda Mrs. Glen Reschley). He was preceded in death by one sister (Nina Mrs. Joseph Unternahrer). He was a member of Sugar Creek Mennonite Church, where funeral services were held on Apr. 13, in charge of Orie L. Roth and Willard Leichty; interment in the church cemetery.

More About Irvin Lloyd Christner:
Burial: Sugar Creek Church, Wayland, Henry Co., IA
Residence: 1930, Wayne, Henry Co., IA[5024,5025]

2667   ii.   Nina Marie Christner[5025], born 02 Apr 1903 in Noble Co., IA; died 28 Nov 1968 in Auto Accident. She married Joseph Unterahrer 17 Aug 1947; born 31 Jul 1896 in Baden, Germany; died 21 Jul 1980 in Wayland, Henry Co., IA.

Notes for Nina Marie Christner:
UNTERNAHRER, NINA MARIE, daughter of C. E. and Emma (Conrad) CHRISTNER, was born near Noble, Iowa, Apr. 2, 1903; died instantly in an automobile accident the afternoon of Thanksgiving Day, Nov. 28, 1968; aged 65 y. 7 m. 26 d. On Aug. 17, 1947, she was married to Joseph Unternahrer, who survives. Also surviving are 2 brothers (Irvin and Ralph) and 3 sisters (Florence--Mrs. Herman Leichty, Erna--Mrs. Jesse Roth, and Verda--Mrs. Glen Reschly). She was a member of the Sugar Creek Church, where funeral services were held Nov. 30, with Vernon S. Gerig and Robert Hartzler officiating.

More About Nina Marie Christner:
Burial: Sugar Creek Church
Residence: 01 Apr 1940, Wayne, Henry Co., IA[5025]

More About Joseph Unterahrer:
Burial: 24 Jul 1980, Sugar Grove Church Cemetery Wayland, Iowa
Religion: Sugar Grove Church Wayland, Iowa/

+ 2668   iii.   Florence Anna Christner, born 28 Jan 1905 in Henry Co., IA; died 05 May 1994 in Wayland, Henry Co., IA.
+ 2669   iv.   Erna Barbara Christner, born 19 May 1908 in Henry Co., IA; died 18 Jan 2001 in Wayland, Henry Co., IA.
2670   v.   Ralph Peter Christner[5025], born 11 Nov 1910 in Henry Co.. IA; died 15 Mar 1928 in Wayland, Henry Co., IA.

Notes for Ralph Peter Christner:
Christner, Ralph P., son of Chris and Emma (Conrad) Christner, was born at Henry Co., Iowa, Nov. 11, 1910; died at Wayland, Iowa, Mar. 15, 1928; aged 71 y. He was a member of Sugar Creek Mennonite Church, where funeral services were held, in charge of Ed Miller, Oliver Yutzy, and Arnold C. Roth.

More About Ralph Peter Christner:
Burial: Sugar Creek Church Cemetery Henry Co., Wayland Co., IA
Residence: 01 Apr 1940, Wayne, Henry Co., IA[5025]

+ 2671   vi.   Verda Emma Christner, born 21 Nov 1915 in Henry Co., IA; died 04 Aug 1999 in Wayland, Henry Co., IA.

1181. Benjamin E.[7] Christner (Jacob[6], Peter[5], Peter[4], Christian[3], Christian[2], Christen[1]) was born 04 Feb 1877 in Trenton, Henry Co., IA, and died 06 Jan 1919 in Trenton, Henry Co., IA. He married **Della May Messer**[5026], daughter of Samuel Messer and Cylinda Parker. She was born 19 Sep 1883 in Trenton, Henry Co., IA[5027,5028], and died 15 Jul 1966 in Washington, Washington Co., IA[5028].

Notes for Benjamin E. Christner:
Birth: Feb. 4, 1877
Trenton, Henry Co., IA
Death: Jan. 6, 1919
Trenton, Henry Co., IA

Parents:

Jacob & Barbara (Egli) Christner
Children to Benjamin E Christner were as follows........
Ida Leona, died in infancy, Luther Hansel, Basil Iliff, Samuel Jacob,John Thomas, Joseph Harold, Welcome Gertrude, Leola Lucille, and Freda May.

Children: John Thomas Christner (1907 - 1956)

Burial: Green Mound Cemetery, Henry Co., IA

More About Della May Messer:
Burial: 1968, Green Mound Cemetery, Trenton, Henry County, Iowa[5028]
Residence: 01 Jan 1925, Trenton, Henry, Iowa, USA[5028]

Child of Benjamin Christner and Della Messer is:
+   2672   i.   John Thomas[8] Christner, born 31 Dec 1907 in Wayne, Henry Co., IA; died 27 May 1956 in Iowa City, Johnson Co., IA.

1183. Amos[7] Christner (Jacob[6], Peter[5], Peter[4], Christian[3], Christian[2], Christen[1])[5029,5030] was born 27 Mar 1883 in Henry Co., IA[5031], and died Aug 1968 in Washington, Washington Co., IA[5031]. He married **Mollie Vera Farmer**[5031] 24 Mar 1909 in Olds, Henry Co., IA[5031]. She was born 19 Mar 1891 in Wayland, Henry Co., IA[5031], and died 02 Jan 1966 in Henry Co., IA[5031].

Notes for Amos Christner:
Birth: Mar. 27, 1883
Henry Co., IA
Death: Aug. 12, 1968
IA

Parents:
Jacob Christner (1836 - 1904)
Barbara Egli Christner (1835 - 1915)

Spouse: Mollie Vera Farmer Christner (1891 - 1966)

Burial: Wayland Methodist Church Cemetery, Henry Co., IA
Plot: Row 11

More About Amos Christner:
Burial: Wayland Cemetery[5031]
Residence: 1920, Trenton, Henry Co., IA[5032]
Social Security Number: 479-60-8508/[5033]
SSN issued: Kalona, Washington Co., IA[5033]

Notes for Mollie Vera Farmer:
Birth: Mar. 19, 1891
IA
Death: Jan. 2, 1966
IA

Spouse: Amos Christner (1883 - 1968)

Burial: Wayland Methodist Church Cemetery, Henry Co., IA
Plot: Row 11

More About Mollie Vera Farmer:
Burial: Wayland Cemetery[5033]

Residence: 1915, Walnut, Jefferson Co., IA[5034]

Child of Amos Christner and Mollie Farmer is:

2673   i.   Hazel Arlene[8] Christner[5035], born 25 Jan 1910 in Trenton, Henry Co., IA[5035]; died 03 Dec 1933 in Trenton, Henry Co., IA[5035]. She married Eldon Hall.

More About Hazel Arlene Christner:
Residence: 1930, Center, Henry Co., IA[5035]

1184. Christian[7] Christner (Josef[6], Josef[5], Peter[4], Christian[3], Christian[2], Christen[1]) was born 1876, and died 1960. He married **Leni Springer**. She was born 1880, and died 1967.

Child of Christian Christner and Leni Springer is:

2674   i.   Josef[8] Christner, born 1905; died 1987. He married Babette Weber; born 1925.

1185. Jacob[7] Good (Christian[6] Guth, Barbara[5] Christner, John Johann[4], Christian[3], Christian[2], Christen[1]) was born 28 Mar 1870, and died 25 May 1937 in Kokomo, Howard Co., IN. He married **Emma Mary Garber**. She was born 06 Feb 1871 in Woodford Co., IL, and died 20 Oct 1939 in Kokomo, Howard Co., IN.

Notes for Jacob Good:
Jacob changed the name to Good from Guth from Gut all of them mean good as the opposite of bad. In german it would be ///das ih guut/// this is good in english.

Child of Jacob Good and Emma Garber is:

+   2675   i.   Emery Levi[8] Good, born 18 May 1892 in Hopedale, IL; died 15 Nov 1961 in Hopedale, IL.

1188. Ida[7] Christner (Daniel[6], Christian[5], John Johann[4], Christian[3], Christian[2], Christen[1]) was born 29 Jun 1880 in Wilmot Twp, Waterloo Co, Ontario, Canada.[5036] She married **George Wesley Battler**[5037] 21 Dec 1904 in Wilmot Twp, Waterloo Co., Ontario Province, Canada[5037]. He was born 25 May 1874 in Wilmot Twp, Waterloo Co., Ontario Province, Canada[5037].

More About Ida Christner:
Residence: 1911, Waterloo South, Ontario, Canada[5037]

More About George Wesley Battler:
Residence: 1911, Waterloo South, Ontario, Canada[5037]

Children of Ida Christner and George Battler are:

2676   i.   Christina[8] Battler[5037], born Mar 1906 in Ontario, Canada[5037].

More About Christina Battler:
Residence: 1911, Waterloo South, Ontario, Canada[5037]

2677   ii.   Christian Thomas Battler[5037], born 05 Mar 1906 in Wilmot Twp, Waterloo Co., Ontario Province, Canada[5037]; died Dec 1979 in Elkhart, Elkhart Co., IN[5037].

More About Christian Thomas Battler:
Residence: 1911, Waterloo South, Ontario, Canada[5037]

2678   iii.   Clarence Arthur Battler[5037], born 23 May 1908 in Wilmot Twp, Waterloo Co., Ontario Province, Canada[5037]; died 1946[5037].

More About Clarence Arthur Battler:
Residence: 1911, Waterloo South, Ontario, Canada[5037]

2679   iv.   Howard David Battler[5037], born 25 Feb 1911 in Wilmot Twp, Waterloo Co., Ontario Province, Canada[5037]; died 17 Jul 1987 in Breslau, Woolwich Twp, Waterloo Co., Ontario Province, Canada[5037].

More About Howard David Battler:
Residence: 1911, Waterloo South, Ontario, Canada[5037]

1200. Charles Albert[7] **Christner** (Enos H.[6], Christian[5], John Johann[4], Christian[3], Christian[2], Christen[1]) was born 12 Jul 1894, and died 1982. He married **Violet Otto**[5038,5039]. She was born 12 Feb 1898 in Waterloo Co., Ontario, Canada[5040], and died 1971.

Notes for Charles Albert Christner:
Birth: Jul. 12, 1894
Death: 1982

Parents:
Enos Christner (1850 - 1936)
Hannah "Adeline" Feick Christner (1866 - 1924)

Spouse: Violet Otto Christner (1898 - 1971)

Children:
Raymond John Christner (1928 - 1990)
Bob Christner (1932 - 2011)

Burial: Riverside Cemetery, Waterloo Co., Ontario, Canada

Notes for Violet Otto:
Birth: Feb 12, 1898
Death: 1971

Parents:
John T. Otto (1859 - 1921)
Elizabeth Ratz Otto (1858 - 1942)

Spouse: Charles Albert Christner (1894 - 1982)

Children:
Raymond John Christner (1928 - 1990)
Bob Christner (1932 - 2011)

Burial: Riverside Cemetery, Waterloo Co., Ontario, Canada
Find A Grave Memorial# 51266620

More About Violet Otto:
Residence: 1911, Waterloo South, Ontario, Canada[5041,5042]

Children of Charles Christner and Violet Otto are:
    2680   i.   Raymond John[8] Christner[5043], born 1928[5043]; died 1990[5043].

                Notes for Raymond John Christner:
                Birth: 1928
                Death: 1990

                Parents:
                Charles Albert Christner (1894 - 1982)
                Violet Otto Christner (1898 - 1971)

                Burial: Riverside Cemetery, Waterloo Co., Ontario, Canada
                Find A Grave Memorial# 51266733

More About Raymond John Christner:
Burial: New Hambug, Ontario, Canada[5043]

2681   ii.   Robert Christner, born 1932; died 26 Aug 2011.

Notes for Robert Christner:
Birth: 1932
Death: Aug. 26, 2011

CHRISTNER, Bob Passed away on Friday, August 26, 2011 at St. Mary's General Hospital, Kitchener. Bob was born 79 years ago in Kitchener and was the son of the late Charles and Violet (Otto) Christner. Beloved husband of Dianne (Naumann) Christner who were married for 51 years. Dear father of Tom Christner and friend Terry Shaw and Dave and wife Sherry Christner all of New Hamburg. Loving grandpa of Callan and Cohen. Missed by his brother Burt and wife Helen Christner of New Hamburg, mother-in-law Viola Naumann of Baden, brother-in-law Larry and wife Donna Naumann of Baden, sisters-in-law Shirley Christner of Aurora and Gloria (nee Naumann). Bob was predeceased by brothers Bill Christner, Ray Christner and brother-in-law Ken Naumann and father-in-law Sylvester Naumann. Also remembered by a number of nieces and nephews. Bob was employed at Electrohome in Kitchener for over thirty years. Bob enjoyed hunting and fishing in his younger years and loved watching his sons and grandsons play hockey and ball. Cremation has taken place. A memorial service to celebrate Bob's life will take place on Sunday, September 11, 2011 at 1:00 p.m. at the Mark Jutzi Funeral Home, 291 Huron Street, New Hamburg. A reception will follow at the Royal Canadian Legion, Branch 532, New Hamburg. As expressions of sympathy, donations may be made to the Grand River Regional Cancer Centre. On-line condolences and donation information available at:

Parents:
Charles Albert Christner (1894 - 1982)
Violet Otto Christner (1898 - 1971)

Burial: Cremated

1219. Milton[7] Otto (Elizabeth[6] Christner, Peter L.[5], John Johann[4], Christian[3], Christian[2], Christen[1])[5044] was born 27 Aug 1889 in Ontario, Canada[5044], and died 24 May 1956. He married **Beatrice Rohr**[5044] 14 Apr 1921 in Wilmot Township[5044]. She was born 07 Nov 1889 in Wilmot Township[5044], and died 11 Sep 1977.

Notes for Milton Otto:
Birth: Aug. 27, 1889
Death: May 24, 1956

Son of Elizabeth (Christner) and Christian Otto, husband to Beatrice Rohr.

Parents:
Christian Otto (1846 - 1911)
Elizabeth Christner Otto (1853 - 1928)

Spouse: Beatrice Rohr Otto (1889 - 1977)

Children: Arthur Harry Otto (1923 - 2009)

Burial: Riverside Cemetery, Waterloo Co., Ontario, Canada

More About Milton Otto:
Residence: 1911, Waterloo South, Ontario, Canada[5044]

Notes for Beatrice Rohr:
Birth: Nov. 7, 1889
Death: Sep. 11, 1977

Daughter of Josephine (Golbeck) and Henry Rohr, wife of Milton Otto.

Spouse: Milton Otto (1889 - 1956)

Children: Arthur Harry Otto (1923 - 2009)

Burial: Riverside Cemetery, Waterloo Co., Ontario, Canada

More About Beatrice Rohr:
Residence: 1911, Waterloo South, Ontario, Canada[5044]

Child of Milton Otto and Beatrice Rohr is:
    2682   i.   Arthur Harry[8] Otto, born 12 Jun 1923; died 05 Dec 2009. He married Joan Dinger.

> Notes for Arthur Harry Otto:
> Birth: Jun. 12, 1923
> Death: Dec. 5, 2009
>
> OTTO, Arthur Harry Passed away in his sleep on Saturday, December 5, 2009 at his home in New Hamburg at the age of 86 years. Arthur was born June 12, 1923 in Wilmot Township to the late Milton and Beatrice (Rohr) Otto. Art is survived by Joan (Dinger) Otto, his wife of 56 years. Loving father and grandfather of son Howard and his children Janessa, Jennifer and her fiancé Greg Rabus, Janet and her fiancé Joe Sales; daughter Margaret Swoboda and her husband Frank and their children Jonathan and his wife Swati, Dwayne, Jeremy, Andrew and Bethany; son James and his wife Mary and their children Michael, Andrea, Christine, Kathryn, Matthew and Daniel; son David and his wife Lorraine and their children Joshua, Stephanie, Graham and Serena. Also survived by sister-in-law Hazel Zehr and her husband Ray and brother-in-law Don Zarnke and wife Gwen. Predeceased by his parents, his beloved sister June Zarnke and his wife's parents Victor and Elma (Sararas) Dinger. Art lived on the family farm (Haysville) until 1982, when he and Joan moved to New Hamburg. Art was employed as a Road Foreman for the Region of Waterloo for many years until his retirement in 1988. He was a faithful member of New Dundee Baptist Church. Art enjoyed helping on the farm, where he gardened for the whole family each summer and also enjoyed traveling. Family and friends are invited to share their memories with the family at the Mark Jutzi Funeral Home , 291 Huron Street, New Hamburg on Tuesday December 8, 2009 from 2-4 and 7-9 p.m. The funeral service will be held on Wednesday December 9, 2009 at 11:00 a.m. at New Dundee Baptist Church, 1173 Queen Street, New Dundee with Rev. Paul Kowtecky officiating. Interment in Riverside Cemetery, New Hamburg. In Art's memory donations may be made to New Dundee Baptist Church or the Cardiac Care Unit of St. Mary's Hospital, Kitchener. On line condolences and donation information available at www.markjutzifuneralhomes.ca
>
> Parents:
> Milton Otto (1889 - 1956)
> Beatrice Rohr Otto (1889 - 1977)
>
> Burial: Riverside Cemetery, Waterloo Co., Ontario, Canada

1224. George Samuel[7] Zimmerman (Lucinda[6] Christner, Peter L.[5], John Johann[4], Christian[3], Christian[2], Christen[1])[5045] was born 26 Feb 1885 in Yamhill Co., OR[5045], and died 25 Sep 1976 in Age: 91/[5045]. He married **Oka Swingle**. She was born 31 Aug 1890 in Lorella, Klamath Co., OR[5045], and died 25 Oct 1980 in Age: 90/OR[5045].

Notes for George Samuel Zimmerman:
Birth: Feb. 26, 1885 - Yamhill Co., OR
Death: Sep. 25, 1976

GEORGE ZIMMERMAN DIES AT AGE 91
Pioneer Yamhill County farmer and businessman George Samuel Zimmerman 91, Yamhill, died Saturday, Sept. 25. - News-Register, McMinnville, Oregon, Monday, September 27, 1976

He served as county commissioner from 1920 to 1924, where his special interest was easier access to, and realignment of, county roads. The first state market road, between Yamhill and Newberg, was built under his leadership.

He was one of the early advocates of the Nestucca Road across the coast range to Highway 101 and for years promoted Highway 47 between McMinnville and Vernonia as a scenic road.

Zimmerman built and operated the first prune dryer in the area that used electric forced air drying.

In 1913 he became the first commercial livestock buyer in this region and in 1916 he built a commercial grain elevator. It was incorporated as the George S. Zimmerman Grain Co. in 1952 and he was active in its management for over 60 years.

He also helped establish the Yamhill County Health Association and the first Union High School District in the state. He acted as member and clerk of several farmer-owned cooperatives, was an adult sponsor of the Future Farmers of America, and with his brother rejuvenated the Yamhill-Carlton Pioneer Cemetery, serving as its president for many years.

Zimmerman was listed as a "distinguished citizen" in "Who's Who for Oregon".

At the time of his death he was the oldest alumnus of Yamhill-Carlton Union High School and be was the last living charter member of the Oregon Feed, Seed and Suppliers Association. He was a charter member of the Withycombe Club organization.

Services will be Wednesday, Sept. 29, at 1:30 p.m. at the Yamhill United Methodist Church.

Services for Yamhill County Pioneer George Samuel Zimmerman, 91, Yamhill, will be Wednesday, Sept. 29, 1976, at 1:30 p.m. at the United Methodist Church in Yamhill with interment in Yamhill-Carlton Pioneer Cemetery.

He died Sept. 25. Son of Christian and Louise Nolte Zimmerman, he was born Feb. 26, 1885, in Yamhill County.

He attended local schools and graduated from Oregon Agricultural College (now Oregon State University) with a degree in agriculture in 1910.

On Jan. 1, 1911, he married Oka Swingle of Klamath Falls.

He was a member of the United Methodist Church, Yamhill Grange and Yamhill County Farm Bureau.

Survivors include his wife, Oka, Newberg; daughters, Celia Dromgoole, McMinnville, and Lenola Walter, San Pedro, Calif.; son, Gordon N., San Francisco; brother, Ed, Yamhill; grandsons, Gordon, Yamhill, and Paul Dromgoole, Seattle; and two great-grandchildren.

Memorial Contributions may be made to Yamhill-Carlton Pioneer Cemetery.

Parents:
Christian Zimmerman (1848 - 1934)
Louise Nolte Zimmerman (1857 - 1938)

Spouse: Oka Swingle Zimmerman (1890 - 1980)

Children:
Celia Ruth Zimmerman Dromgoole (1915 - 2006)
Lenola (Nona) Zimmerman Riggs (1921 - 2003)
Lenola O Zimmerman Walter (1922 - 2003)

Burial: Yamhill-Carlton Cemetery, Yamhill, Yamhill Co., OR
Find A Grave Memorial# 11911283

More About George Samuel Zimmerman:

Burial: Yamhill, Yamhill County, Oregon, USA*5045*

Notes for Oka Swingle:
Birth: Aug 31, 1890 - Lorella, Klamath Co., OR
Death: Oct 25, 1980

Services for Oka Zimmerman, 90 member of a pioneer Yamhill County family and a longtime Yamhill resident who had lived the past 13 years in Newberg, will be held at 2 p.m. Thursday in the Chapel of Macy & Son Funeral Directors. Mrs. Zimmerman died Oct. 25, 1980, in a Newberg care center.

The Rev. Bob Kuykendall will officiate and interment will be in the Yamhill-Carlton Pioneer Cemetery.

Born Aug. 31, 1890, in Lorella, OR daughter of Charles J. and Orpha Fryer Swingle, she was raised and educated in Klamath Falls, graduating from high school there. Her grandparents, the Joseph Swingles of Jackson County and the Alexander Fryers of Yamhill County came to the Oregon Territory in 1852 and 1854, respectively. Her great-grandfather, Peter Smith, took up a donation land claim where the town of Carlton in situated.

She and George W. Zimmerman, who preceded her in death in 1976, were married Jan. 1, 1911, in Klamath Falls. After her marriage, she attended Pacific University in Forest Grove as a music student. She was a former member of the Yamhill County Extension unit in Yamhill, of the Cove Orchard Grange and the Yamhill Chamber of Commerce. A 50 year member of the Yamhill Methodist Church, she was a member of the Newberg Nazarene Church at the time of her death. She also was a charter member of the Yamhill County and the Oregon Historical societies. She was well known in Yamhill for the beautiful flowers she raised and shared with the community.

Survivors include two daughters, Celia Dromgoole of McMinnville and Lenola Walter, of California; a son, Gordon Zimmerman of California; two grandchildren and two great-grandchildren.

Memorial contributions may be made to the Yamhill County Historical Society.

Parents:
Charles Jackson Swingle (1866 - 1947)
Orpha Fryer Swingle (1868 - 1945)

Spouse: George Samuel Zimmerman (1885 - 1976)

Children:
Celia Ruth Zimmerman Dromgoole (1915 - 2006)
Lenola (Nona) Zimmerman Riggs (1921 - 2003)
Lenola O Zimmerman Walter (1922 - 2003)

Burial: Yamhill-Carlton Cemetery, Yamhill, Yamhill Co., OR
Find A Grave Memorial# 11911431

More About Oka Swingle:
Burial: Yamhill, Yamhill County, Oregon, USA*5045*

Children of George Zimmerman and Oka Swingle are:
    2683   i. Celia Ruth[8] Zimmerman, born 13 Sep 1915; died 17 May 2006.

                Notes for Celia Ruth Zimmerman:
                Birth: Sep. 13, 1915
                Death: May 17, 2006

                News-Register, McMinnville, Oregon, May 20, 2006

                Former Yamhill and McMinnville resident Celia Ruth Zimmerman Dromgoole of Milwaukie died in her home in Rose Villa Assisted Living Center on Wednesday, May 17, 2006. Memorial services will be held at 1:30 p.m. at First Baptist Church in McMinnville. The Rev. Kent Harrop will officiate. Private family interment will take place in the Yamhill-Carlton Pioneer Cemetery. Contributions may be made to the Yamhill County Mental Health Department, care of Macy & Son Funeral Directors, 135 N.E. Evans St., McMinnville, OR 97128.

She is survived by two sons, Gordon of Yamhill and Paul of Seattle; a brother, George Zimmerman of San Francisco; two grandsons and one great-grandson.

The following obituary was published as a paid notice on May 20, 2006:

In Loving Memory
Celia Ruth Zimmerman Dromgoole
1915-2006

Celia Ruth Zimmerman Dromgoole died at her home in Rose Villa, Milwaukie OR on May 17, 2006. Daughter of George and Oka Zimmerman of Yamhill, Mrs. Dromgoolewas born September 1915 in Yamhill, Oregon. She attended Yamhill schools and Linfield College (1934-1935) graduating from the University of Washington with degrees in Sociology and Business Administration.

Mrs. Dromgoole worked as an employment counselor at the Mullins Agency in Seattle during her college and post college years. She and Emmett Dromgoole were married in 1943 moving to the Yamhill family farm in 1948. She was the bookkeeper for Zimmerman Grain Co., of Yamhill for a number of years.

In 1967 Celia and Emmett relocated to McMinnville. In 1975 they retired and moved to Lincoln City. They enjoyed living at the beach for several years before moving to Rose Villa in Milwaukie in 1990.

Even though Mrs. Dromgoole had a lifetime physical handicap she was a high-energy lady who was very involved in her community. She and Emmett were members of First Baptist Church, McMinnville while living in Yamhill and McMinnville. They were members of Lincoln City Baptist in their retirement years at the coast. Mrs. Dromgoole was one of the first members of the Yamhill County Mental Health Committee and was interested in helping adults and children with mental and physical disabilities.

Celia loved to travel and was always on the go. Her keen interests in her family's history lead her to involvement in the Yamhill and Oregon State Historical Societies. The material she collected on family and local history was very useful to her brother, Gordon Zimmerman when writing his book "The Song of Yamhill".

She was preceded in death by her husband, Emmett Dromgoole and her sister, Nona Zimmerman. Her brother Gordon Zimmerman of San Francisco, 2 sons Gordon of Yamhill and Paul of Seattle, 2 grandsons, Kevin of McMinnville and Darren of Lake Oswego and one great grandson survive her.

Memorial Services will be held on Saturday, May 27, 2006 at 1:30 PM at the First Baptist Church in McMinnville with Pastor Kent Harrop presiding. Private family committal services were held at Yamhill Carlton Pioneer Cemetery. Memorial contributions can be made to Yamhill County Mental Health c/o Macy & Son.

Parents:
George Samuel Zimmerman (1885 - 1976)
Oka Swingle Zimmerman (1890 - 1980)

Note: Husband Emmett.

Burial: Yamhill-Carlton Cemetery, Yamhill, Yamhill Co., OR
Find A Grave Memorial# 17359706

2684   ii.   Lenola Zimmerman, born 1921; died 2003. She married Oliver Riggs; died 1968.

Notes for Lenola Zimmerman:
Birth: Oct. 13, 1921
Death: Oct. 15, 2003

News-Register, McMinnville, Oregon, October 18, 2003

A private family graveside service for Lenola O. Walter, also known as Nona Zimmerman Riggs of Downey, CA will be held in Yamhill-Carlton Pioneer Cemetery, Yamhill.

Ms. Walter died Oct. 15, 2003, in Downey Care Center. She was 81.

She was born Oct. 13, 1922, in Yamhill, the daughter of George S. and Oka Swingle Zimmerman. She was raised and educated in Yamhill. She graduated from Oregon State College in 1943 with the highest grade point average to have been achieved in the college at the time. She belonged to Phi Beta Kappa scholastic honor society and many other campus groups. She was chosen as the graduating senior who had contributed most to performing music in her college career.

She studied voice at the University of Washington and performed as an alto soloist with many groups in the Seattle area, including the Seattle Symphony. In the early 1950s, she moved to Santa Barbara, Calif., and studied with opera star Lotte Lehman in the Music Academy of the West. In the late 1950s, Ms. Walter was a teacher at the University of California at Santa Monica. She had been under the care of her family for the last 30 years.

Survivors include a brother, Gordon Zimmerman of Yamhill, and a sister, Celia Dromgoole of Milwaukie.

She was preceded in death by her husband, Oliver Riggs, in 1968.

Memorial contributions may be made to the National Alliance for the Mentally Ill in care of Macy & Son Funeral Directors, 135 N.E. Evans St., McMinnville, OR 97128.

Parents:
George Samuel Zimmerman (1885 - 1976)
Oka Swingle Zimmerman (1890 - 1980)

Note: Daughter to George S. & Oka Zimmerman

Burial: Yamhill-Carlton Cemetery, Yamhill, Yamhill Co., OR
Find A Grave Memorial# 17359665

1231. Kathryn "Katie" Ann[7] Christner (Christopher N.[6], Peter L.[5], John Johann[4], Christian[3], Christian[2], Christen[1]) was born 26 Jul 1899 in Wilmot Twp., Waterloo Co., Ontario Canada[5046], and died 30 Jan 1993 in New Hamburg, Waterloo Co., Ontario Canada[5046]. She married **Joseph Howard Lederman** 10 Jul 1926 in Wilmot Twp., Waterloo Co., Ontario Canada[5046]. He was born Oct 1898 in New Hamburg, Waterloo Co., Ontario Canada[5046], and died 29 Aug 1973 in Ontario Canada[5046].

Notes for Kathryn "Katie" Ann Christner:
Birth: Jul. 26, 1899
Death: 1993

Parents:
Chris N Christner (1862 - 1917)
Ellen Clyde Brash Christner (1873 - 1932)

Spouse: Joseph Howard Lederman (1898 - 1973)

Children: Joseph Karl Lederman (1936 - 2010)

Burial: Wilmot Mennonite Cemetery, Waterloo Co., Ontario, Canada
Find A Grave Memorial# 51276858

Notes for Joseph Howard Lederman:
Birth: Oct. 16, 1898
Death: 1973

Parents:

Charles B Lederman (1870 - 1937)
Annie Roth Lederman (1869 - 1932)

Spouse: Katie Ann Christner Lederman (1899 - 1993)

Children: Joseph Karl Lederman (1936 - 2010)

Burial: Wilmot Mennonite Cemetery, Waterloo Co., Ontario, Canada

Children of Kathryn Christner and Joseph Lederman are:
    2685   i.   Kathryn[8] Lederman. She married Joseph Hallas.
    2686   ii.   Joseph Karl Lederman[5047], born 04 Feb 1936 in Plattsville, Ontario, Canada; died 10 Jul 2010 in
                      Kitchener, Ontario, Canada[5047]. He married Barbara Aiken.

                Notes for Joseph Karl Lederman:
                Birth: Feb. 4, 1936
                Death: Jul. 10, 2010

                LEDERMAN, Joseph Karl It is with the deepest sorrow that the family of Joseph Karl Lederman announce his passing on Saturday, July 10, 2010. He was surrounded in the loving arms of his family after a long and courageous battle with cancer. Joseph was born in 1936, in Plattsville, Ontario and was the dear son of the late Joseph and Katie Lederman. Beloved husband of Barbara (nee Aitken) for 54 years. He was the proud father of seven children; Joseph David Lederman and Christina (London), James Lederman and Glenna (Cambridge), LuAnn Lederman (Kitchener), Katie and Rick Plant (Kitchener), Barb and Jason Schmidt (New Hamburg), Tim Lederman and Steph (Guelph), Kris Lederman and Nikki (Kitchener), 13 grandchildren; Joey, Janice, Jaime, Jesse, Trevor, Tyler, Kaitlyn, Justin, Jordan, Matthew, Cassandra, Coleson, Alyssa and three great-grandchildren Brayden, Avery and Dylan. Joseph served in the Canadian Armed Forces from 1957 until 1960, when he joined the Waterloo Police Force. He spent several years as head of the Juvenile Department, and in the Cambridge, Kitchener and New Hamburg detachments. In 1977, Joseph formed the Emergency Response Unit, a tactical team that protected the community from the highest level of threats. Joseph and his wife Barbara formed the Kitchener-Waterloo Cadet Organization Police School in 1970 to help troubled youth in the community. This organization is still in operation today. Joseph and Barbara were foster parents from 1970 until 2005 to over 60 children at risk. He was the president of the Waterloo Regional Police Association from 1984 until he retired with the rank of Staff Sergeant in 1988. Following his retirement, Joseph formed the Waterloo Police Retirees as well as, the Ontario Police Retirees.

                He wrote and published two books illustrating the life he lived as a police officer and serving the community for over 50 years. Joseph was a strong believer in God and his faith as a member of the Cambridge Community Church. We wish to thank the doctors and nurses at the Grand River Hospital and Dr. Boutill and staff at the Grand River Cancer Centre. For all of their compassion and care, we wish to thank the entire staff at Lisaard House. A special thanks to Pastor and family friend, Rob Heintz for his comfort and support throughout Joe's difficult journey. We will forever miss our hero. Visitation will be held at the Ratz-Bechtel Funeral Home, 621 King St. W. on Monday and Tuesday evenings from 6-9 p.m. The funeral service will be held in the Chapel on Wednesday, July 14, 2010 at 2 p.m. A private family interment at Chesterfield United Church Cemetery will take place. Memorial donations to the Grand River Cancer Centre or Lisaard House would be appreciated.

                Joe Lederman: Tough cop, top-notch dad

                July 12, 2010

                By Cherri Greeno and Frances Barrick, Record staff
                PLATTSVILLE --Joseph Lederman, a man described as an old-school police officer who was both revered and feared, has died. He was 74.
                "He was a man who helped so many," said Staff Sgt. Ray Massicotte, president of the Waterloo Regional Police Association, a group that Lederman himself headed for many years. "He was an outstanding all around guy. He was a good man who did a lot for this community."

                Lederman died Saturday from cancer. He became a police officer in 1960. His tactics were sometimes questioned, leading him to be at the centre of an Ontario Police Commission inquiry into allegations of police brutality. The allegations related to an infamous 1978 police raid on the Henchmen biker clubhouse.

At the time, Lederman headed the newly-formed tactical squad, which was criticized during the inquiry. In the end, Lederman was demoted. The police chief at the time, Syd Brown, was fired. Brown fought the firing and was re-instated in name only. Waterloo Region ended up with two police chiefs: Harold Basse was the other.

Years later, Lederman chronicled those controversial years in an autobiographical novel, Tainted Blue, which he described as the cop's story that was never told.

In the book, Lederman blamed the force's top brass for his demotion and accused senior officers of incompetence and a lack of professionalism.
He also charged that there was a conspiracy to get rid of Brown because senior officers did not like his style.

"There were so many people who wanted him to quit," said Barbara Lederman, his wife of 54 years. "I really, really admired him for that. He was honest and stuck to his principals and he never gave in."
She described her husband as a "big bear."
"We were the best of friends," she said.
Lederman was perhaps best known as a devoted husband and father who committed his life to bettering the lives of children.

He and Barbara founded the K-W C.O.P.S. army cadet corps, to help troubled youth. Along with having seven children of their own, the couple fostered more than 60 kids.

Lederman also co-founded the Waterloo Regional Police Retirees Association and the Police Retirees of Ontario, Inc. He was also president of the Waterloo Regional Police Association.

Most recently he helped form CARO - Children At Risk - Ontario. He tried to convince politicians to increase funding for child-protection agencies and school boards so that educators could reinstate family studies and life skills programs.

When he fell ill, he had to set aside CARO.

"He was a role model to me," said daughter LuAnn Lederman. "He was a great dad."

LuAnn and her sister, Katie Plant, fondly remember their father trying to scare off their dates by pretending to clean his gun when they walked through the door.

"He'd say, 'So, where are you taking my daughter? And, 'What time are you going to be home,'" recalled Plant with a laugh.
"Some were brave and stuck around."
Plant said her father was very "soft-hearted," despite his "tough guy" persona, "He was so loving and caring, not just about his family but for everyone," she said.

Her husband Rick said Lederman believed in everyone he met.

"He didn't judge you on what you did but on what you'd do to correct it, and how you were going to move forward," he said.

His children fondly remember dinners where their father would share his stories about policing. Sometimes, the dinner table would be so full of kids that some had to go eat in another room.
The fact that Lederman took in so many troubled youth taught his own children about a different kind of life - one in which kids didn't have it so good. It taught them to appreciate the love they had.

"He was always there and always helped me out in any way he could," said son James Lederman. "He was always a good Dad."

After Tainted Blue, Lederman wrote When Good Men Do Nothing. The book chronicles the lives of people Lederman knew and incidents he saw during his police career.

Waterloo Regional Police Supt. Steve Beckett said the service is "deeply saddened by (Lederman's) passing."

"He made tremendous personal and professional contributions to our service and will be sincerely missed."

The funeral will be held Wednesday, 2 p.m., at the Ratz-Bechtel Funeral Home in Kitchener. Visitation will take place Tuesday, 6-9 p.m.

Parents:
Joseph Howard Lederman (1898 - 1973)
Katie Ann Christner Lederman (1899 - 1993)

Burial: Chesterfield United Cemetery, Oxford Co., Ontario, Canada

More About Joseph Karl Lederman:
Residence: 2002, Plattsville, Ontario, Canada[5047]

1233. John Melvin[7] Christner (Aaron[6], Peter L.[5], John Johann[4], Christian[3], Christian[2], Christen[1])[5048,5049,5050] was born 10 Mar 1875 in Elkhart Co., IN[5051,5052,5053], and died 15 Feb 1944 in Elkhart, Elkhart Co., IN[5054]. He married **Marie "Minnie" Smith**[5054] 04 Sep 1897[5054]. She was born 16 Jan 1881[5054], and died 29 Apr 1962 in Elkhart, Elkhart Co., IN[5054].

More About John Melvin Christner:
Residence: 1880, Harrison, Elkhart Co., IN[5055,5056]

Children of John Christner and Marie Smith are:
	2687	i.	Hazel[8] Christner.
	2688	ii.	Virgil Christner.
+	2689	iii.	Howard Franklin Christner, born 14 Aug 1897 in Elkhart Co., IN; died 19 Nov 1986 in St Petersburg, Pinellas Co., FL.

1235. Charles Franklin[7] Christner (Aaron[6], Peter L.[5], John Johann[4], Christian[3], Christian[2], Christen[1])[5057] was born 11 Sep 1877 in Elkhart Co., IN[5057], and died 10 Sep 1965 in Goshen, Elkhart Co., IN[5058]. He married **(1) Nora E. Michaels** 15 Oct 1901 in Elkhart Co., IN. She was born 1881, and died 31 Aug 1909. He married **(2) Mabel A. Michaels** 18 Jan 1913 in Elkhart Co., IN. She was born 26 May 1888, and died 14 Aug 1962.

Notes for Charles Franklin Christner:
Birth: 1877
Death: 1965

Charles F. Christner, son of Aaron Christner & his wife Elizabeth aka Anna Elizabetha Pletcher Christner

1st married Nora E. Michael Christner, daughter of John P. Michael.

2nd married 1913 Mabel

Parents:
Aaron Christner (1843 - 1902)
Elizabeth A. Pletcher Christner (_____ - 1933)

Spouses:
Nora E. Michael Christner (1881 - 1909)
Mabel A. Christner (1888 - 1962)

Children:
Elizabeth Christner (1909 - 1909)
Pauline Elizabeth Christner (1913 - 1914)

Burial: Yellow Creek Brick Cemetery, Southwest, Elkhart Co., IN

More About Charles Franklin Christner:
Burial: Yellow Creek Cemetery, Elkhart Co., IN
Residence: 1880, Harrison, Elkhart Co., IN[5059]
Social Security Number: 307-26-8416/[5060]
SSN issued: IN[5060]

Notes for Nora E. Michaels:
Birth: 1881
Death: 1909

Mrs Chas. Christner, aged about 30 years, died of consumption at 11 o'clock on August 31, at her home 5 miles east of Wakarusa. Besides her husband she leaves her father, John P Michael and one son, Paul. The funeral was held last Friday morning at 10 o'clock at Yellow Creek church. Rev Wm. Moore of this place officiating. Burial in the Yellow Creek cemetery.

Wakarusa Tribune
9 September 1909

Family links:
Spouse:
Charles F. Christner (1877 - 1965)

Children:
Elizabeth Christner (1909 - 1909)

Inscription:
Wife

Burial:
Yellow Creek Brick Cemetery, Southwest, Elkhart Co., IN

More About Nora E. Michaels:
Burial: Yellow Creek Cemetery, Elkhart Co., IN

Notes for Mabel A. Michaels:
Obituary: Wakarusa Tribune - 22 August 1962
Mrs Mabel A Christner, 74, of Foraker, died at 10 am Aug. 14 in the Goshen Hospital. Death was the result of a heart attack. She had been ill for a day. She was born Nov. 26, 1888, in Goshen and lived in that vicinity all her life. On Jan. 18, 1913, she married Charles F. Christner, who survives. Also surviving are a son, Paul, of Goshen; two daughters, Mrs Howard Schrock and Mrs. Noble Detweiler, both of Goshen; nine grandchildren; 11 great-grandchildren; and three brothers, Leonard, Ralph, and Kenneth Michael of Goshen.

Services were held in the Southwest Ebenezer Church. The Rev Cecil Clien, pastor, officiated. Burial was in Yellow Creek cemetery.

Birth: 1888
Death: 1962

Spouse: Charles F. Christner (1877 - 1965)

Children: Pauline Elizabeth Christner (1913 - 1914)

Burial: Yellow Creek Brick Cemetery, Southwest, Elkhart Co., IN

More About Mabel A. Michaels:

Burial: Yellow Creek Cemetery, Elkhart Co., IN

Children of Charles Christner and Nora Michaels are:

+ 2690   i.   Paul G.[8] Christner, born 05 Feb 1902 in Elkhart Co., IN; died 13 Apr 1996 in Goshen, Elkhart Co., IN.
   2691   ii.   Elizabeth Christner, born 1909; died 1909.

> Notes for Elizabeth Christner:
> Birth: 1909
> Death: 1909
>
> Parents:
> Charles F. Christner (1877 - 1965)
> Nora E. Michael Christner (1881 - 1909)
>
> Inscription: Daughter
>
> Burial: Yellow Creek Brick Cemetery, Southwest, Elkhart Co., IN
>
> More About Elizabeth Christner:
> Burial: N41°33.086xW85°56.717/Yellow Creek Cemetery, Elkhart Co., IN

Child of Charles Christner and Mabel Michaels is:

   2692   i.   Pauline Elizabeth[8] Christner, born 03 Nov 1913 in Harrison Twp., Elkhart Co., IN; died 06 Nov 1914.

> Notes for Pauline Elizabeth Christner:
> Birth: 1913
> Death: 1914
>
> Pauline Elizabeth Christner, daughter of Charles and Mabel Christner, was born in Harrison township, Elkhart county, Ind, Nov 3, 1913 and died Nov 6, 1914, aged 1 year and 3 days. She leaves a father, mother, one brother, 3 grandparents, uncles and aunts. Funeral services were held on Sabbath afternoon Nov 8th, at the Yellow Creek church. Services were conducted by A. B. Yoder.
>
> Mr. and Mrs. Christner have the sympathies of all good people with this, their loss.
>
> Wakarusa Tribune
> 12 Nov 1914
>
> Parents:
> Charles F Christner (1877 - 1965)
> Mabel A Christner (1888 - 1962)
>
> Burial: Yellow Creek Brick Cemetery, Southwest, Elkhart Co., IN

1236. Henry Edward[7] Christner (Aaron[6], Peter L.[5], John Johann[4], Christian[3], Christian[2], Christen[1])[5061,5062,5063,5064] was born 31 Dec 1878 in Elkhart Co., IN[5065,5066], and died 24 Mar 1956 in Union, Cass Co., MI[5067]. He married **Lucy Ann Wise**[5067,5068] 17 Mar 1898 in Elkhart Co., IN. She was born 12 Aug 1883 in Wakarusa, Elkhart Co., IN[5069,5070], and died 27 Mar 1967 in MI[5071].

More About Henry Edward Christner:
Residence: 01 Apr 1940, Mason, Cass Co., MI[5072]

More About Lucy Ann Wise:
Residence: 01 Apr 1940, Mason, Cass Co., MI[5072]

Children of Henry Christner and Lucy Wise are:

+ 2693   i.   Ralph O.[8] Christner, born Aug 1897 in IN; died 1947.
+ 2694   ii.   Ora A. Christner, born 27 Jan 1900 in Wakarusa, Elkhart Co., IN; died 01 Feb 1973 in Edwardsburg, MI.
+ 2695   iii.   Beulah Christner, born 29 Jul 1903; died 20 Oct 1991 in Jefferson, Cass Co., MI.

2696   iv.   Bernice Christner[5073], born Abt. 1911 in MI[5073]. She married Francis Edward Garman[5073]; born 15 Aug 1897 in Ottwoo Twp., Cass Co., MI[5073]; died 23 Nov 1949 in Mason, Cass Co., MI[5073].

More About Bernice Christner:
Residence: 01 Apr 1940, Age: 29; Marital Status: Married; Relation to Head of House: Wife/Mason, Cass, Michigan, United States[5073]

More About Francis Edward Garman:
Burial: 27 Nov 1949, Cass Co.[5073]
Residence: Cass, Michigan[5073]

+   2697   v.   Charles E. Christner, born 19 Jul 1914 in MI; died 02 Feb 1980 in Union, Cass Co., MI.

1239. Sarah Mandella[7] Christner (Aaron[6], Peter L.[5], John Johann[4], Christian[3], Christian[2], Christen[1])[5074] was born 12 Jul 1884 in Elkhart Co., IN[5075,5076], and died 13 Jan 1921 in Goshen, Elkhart Co., IN[5077,5078]. She married **(1) Billings**. She married **(2) Schrock**. She married **(3) John M. Loucks** 08 Apr 1904 in Elkhart Co., IN. She married **(6) David C. Rathburn** 11 Apr 1914 in Elkhart Co., IN. He was born 16 Mar 1873[5079], and died 31 Jan 1956 in Columbia City, Dubois, IN[5079].

Child of Sarah Christner and Billings is:
2698   i.   Treva[8] Billings.

Child of Sarah Christner and Schrock is:
2699   i.   Frances[8] Schrock.

Child of Sarah Mandella Christner is:
+   2700   i.   Jaunita Fern[8] Christner, born 08 Mar 1911 in Elkhart Co., IN; died 18 Mar 2003 in Age: 92/Miller's Merry Manor, Wakarusa, Elkhart Co., IN.

1241. Orange Vandever Eugene[7] Christner (Aaron[6], Peter L.[5], John Johann[4], Christian[3], Christian[2], Christen[1]) was born 06 Mar 1889 in Elkhart Co., IN, and died 15 Sep 1966 in Elkhart, Elkhart Co., IN. He married **Leona Wagner** 30 Jan 1915 in Elkhart Co., IN. She was born 24 Jul 1888 in Nappanee, Elkhart Co., IN, and died 11 Sep 1966 in Bremen, IN.

Notes for Orange Vandever Eugene Christner:
Birth: 1889
Death: 1966

Burial: Union Center East Cemetery, Nappanee, Elkhart Co., IN

More About Orange Vandever Eugene Christner:
Burial: N41°28.337XW85°56.703/Union Center Cemetery, Elkhart Co., IN

Notes for Leona Wagner:
Birth: 1888
Death: 1966

Burial: Union Center East Cemetery, Nappanee, Elkhart Co., IN

More About Leona Wagner:
Burial: Union Center Cemetery, Elkhart Co., IN

Children of Orange Christner and Leona Wagner are:
+   2701   i.   William Dale[8] Christner, born 11 Dec 1916 in Elkhart Co., IN; died 08 Jan 2009 in Nappanee, Elkhart Co., IN.
+   2702   ii.   Elizabeth Evelyn Christner, born 09 Nov 1918 in Union Twp. Elkhart Co., IN; died 31 Mar 2006 in

Hubbard Hill Retirement Home Elkhart, IN.

1243. Iva Madgerene[7] Christner (Aaron[6], Peter L.[5], John Johann[4], Christian[3], Christian[2], Christen[1]) was born 03 Dec 1892, and died 18 Sep 1982 in Kalamazoo, MI. She married **Macy Grippen Scott** 07 Oct 1911 in Elkhart Co. IN.

Notes for Macy Grippen Scott:
Macy was born a Grippen but changed his last name to Scott when he went into the military.

Child of Iva Christner and Macy Scott is:
 2703 i. Phyles[8] Scott.

1245. Allan[7] Bechtel (Menno[6], Veronica Luckenbill[5] Christner, John Johann[4], Christian[3], Christian[2], Christen[1]) was born 08 Mar 1870 in Waterloo Co., Ontario, Canada[5080], and died 26 Jul 1942. He married **Julia Kaufman**. She was born 20 Dec 1869, and died 1949.

Notes for Allan Bechtel:
Birth: Mar. 8, 1870
Death: Jul. 26, 1942

Son of Menno & Isabella (Shirk) Bechtel. Husband of Julia Kaufman.

Parents:
Menno Bechtel (1842 - 1902)
Isabella Shirk Bechtel (1847 - 1919)

Spouse: Julia Kaufman Bechtel (1869 - 1949)

Children: John Wilfred Bechtel (1904 - 1986)

Burial: Saint Peters Lutheran Cemetery, Kitchener, Ontario, Canada
Find A Grave Memorial# 47272432

Notes for Julia Kaufman:
Birth: Dec. 20, 1869
Death: 1949

Daughter of Henry & Elizabeth (Henkel) Kaufman. Wife of Allan Bechtel.

Spouse: Allan Bechtel (1870 - 1942)

Children: John Wilfred Bechtel (1904 - 1986)

Burial: Saint Peters Lutheran Cemetery, Kitchener, Ontario, Canada
Find A Grave Memorial# 47272507

Child of Allan Bechtel and Julia Kaufman is:
 2704 i. John Wilfred[8] Bechtel, born 21 Oct 1904 in Waterloo Co., Ontario, Canada; died 1986.

       Notes for John Wilfred Bechtel:
       Birth: Oct. 21, 1904
       Death: 1986

       Parents:
       Allan Bechtel (1870 - 1942)
       Julia Kaufman Bechtel (1869 - 1949)

Generation No. 8

1260. Milo[8] Hamsher (Andrew[7], Elizabeth "Betsy"[6] Sipe, Elizabeth[5] Christner, Christian J.[4], Johannes John Hans[3], Christian[2], Christen[1])[5081,5082,5083,5084,5085,5086] was born 27 Jul 1893 in Trail, Holmes Co., OH[5087,5088], and died 22 May 1974 in Dover, Tuscarawas Co., OH[5089]. He married **Ollie Miller**[5090] 27 Oct 1917 in Tuscarawas, Tuscarawas Co., OH[5090]. She was born 22 Sep 1897 in Walnut Creek, Holmes Co., OH[5090], and died 05 Jan 1996 in Sugarcreek, Tuscarawas Co., OH[5090].

More About Milo Hamsher:
Religion: -/[5090]
Residence: 1920, Walnut Creek, Holmes Co., OH[5090]
Social Security Number: 282-09-1244/[5091]
SSN issued: OH[5091]

More About Ollie Miller:
Religion: -/[5092]
Residence: 1920, Walnut Creek, Holmes Co., OH[5092]

Children of Milo Hamsher and Ollie Miller are:

2705   i.   Dallas Eugene[9] Hamsher[5092], born 17 Apr 1918 in Walnut Creek, Holmes, Ohio, United States[5092]; died 31 Aug 1992 in Orrville, Wayne., Wayne Co., OH[5092].

More About Dallas Eugene Hamsher:
Residence: 1920, Walnut Creek, Holmes Co., OH[5092]

2706   ii.   John Henry Hamsher[5092], born 18 Mar 1920 in Walnut Creek, Holmes Co., OH[5092]; died 29 Jan 2002 in Dover, Tuscarawas Co., OH[5092].

More About John Henry Hamsher:
Residence: 01 Apr 1940, Shanesville, Tuscarawas, Ohio, United States[5093]

2707   iii.   Daniel M Hamsher[5093], born 1922 in OH[5093].

More About Daniel M Hamsher:
Residence: 01 Apr 1940, Shanesville, Tuscarawas, Ohio, United States[5093]

2708   iv.   Reuben Andrew Hamsher[5094], born 03 Jul 1923 in Walnut Creek, Holmes Co., OH[5094]; died 04 Sep 2009 in Walnut Creek, Holmes Co., OH[5094].

More About Reuben Andrew Hamsher:
Residence: 01 Apr 1940, Shanesville, Tuscarawas, Ohio, United States[5095]

2709   v.   Thomas Franklin Hamsher[5096], born 08 Jun 1925 in Walnut Creek, Holmes Co., OH[5096]; died 23 Mar 2002 in Sugarcreek, Tuscarawas Co., OH[5096].

More About Thomas Franklin Hamsher:
Religion: -/[5096]
Residence: Bet. 1935 - 1993, Sugarcreek, Tuscarawas Co., OH[5096]

2710   vi.   Mary E Hamsher[5097], born 1928 in OH[5097].

More About Mary E Hamsher:
Residence: 01 Apr 1940, Shanesville, Tuscarawas, Ohio, United States[5097]

2711   vii.   Edward D Hamsher[5098,5099], born 25 Jul 1929 in Walnut Creek, Holmes Co., OH[5100]; died 20 Nov 2004 in Dover, Tuscarawas Co., OH[5100].

More About Edward D Hamsher:
Residence: 01 Apr 1940, Shanesville, Tuscarawas, Ohio, United States[5101]

2712   viii.   Betty J Hamsher[5101], born 1932 in OH[5101].

More About Betty J Hamsher:
Residence: 01 Apr 1940, Shanesville, Tuscarawas, Ohio, United States[5101]

2713   ix.   Robert D Hamsher[5101], born 1937 in OH[5101].

More About Robert D Hamsher:
Residence: 01 Apr 1940, Shanesville, Tuscarawas, Ohio, United States[5101]

2714   x.   James A Hamsher[5101], born 1940 in OH[5101].

More About James A Hamsher:
Residence: 01 Apr 1940, Shanesville, Tuscarawas, Ohio, United States[5101]

1267. Malinda[8] Mishler (Andrew S.[7], Sarah[6] Sipe, Elizabeth[5] Christner, Christian J.[4], Johannes John Hans[3], Christian[2], Christen[1])[5102] was born 15 Jan 1887 in Lagrange Co., IN[5102], and died Aft. 1952 in Millersburg, Elkhart Co., IN[5102]. She married **William Hershberger**[5102] 30 Oct 1910[5102]. He was born 07 Nov 1882 in Trail, Holmes Co., Ohio[5102], and died 04 Dec 1955 in Millersburg, Elkhart Co., IN[5102].

More About William Hershberger:
Religion: Conservative/[5102]
Residence: Goshen, Elkhart Co., IN[5102]

Child of Malinda Mishler and William Hershberger is:
+   2715   i.   Edna Mae[9] Hershberger, born 15 Aug 1911 in Near Honeyville, Lagrange Co., IN; died 01 May 2001 in Topeka, Lagrange Co., IN.

1268. Amanda[8] Christner (Joseph J.[7], John J.[6], Joseph C.[5], Christian J.[4], Johannes John Hans[3], Christian[2], Christen[1])[5103,5104,5105,5106] was born 24 Oct 1861 in Holmes Co., OH[5107,5108], and died 10 Mar 1947 in Chappell, Deuel Co., NE[5109,5110]. She married **Adam Stutzman**[5110,5111,5112] 13 Aug 1882[5112,5112]. He was born 27 Feb 1861 in Holmes Co., OH[5112], and died 17 Dec 1921 in Chappell, Deuel Co., NE[5112].

Notes for Amanda Christner:
Stutzman - Amanda daughter of Joseph and Sarah Christner, was born in Holmes Co., Ohio on Oct. 24, 1861; died at her home in Chappell, NE March 10, 1947; aged 85 y. 4 m. 14 d. As a young girl she moved to Milford, NE and on Aug. 13, 1882 she was united in marriage to Adam Stutzman. In 1886, they moved to Chappell, Nebr., where they were the first Mennonite settlers. Her husband preceded her in death on Dec. 17, 1921. Surviving are 3 sons and 3 daughters (Wesley and Frank of Chappell; Belva-Mrs. Joe F. Yoder, Wellman, Iowa; Clara, at home; Minerva-Mrs. Ezra J. Yoder, Oshkosh, Nebr.; and Joe, of Chappell), one foster son (Joe Christenham, Moorpark, Calif.), 18 grandchildren, 13 great-grandchildren, one sister (Mrs. Katie Ann Gerber, of Ohio), 4 brothers (John, William, Henry, and Harvey, all of Ohio), and other relatives. In her youth she united with the Mennonite Church. Funeral services were held at the Chappell Mennonite Church, in charge of W. R. Eicher and Fred Gingerich. Interment was made in the nearby cemetery.

More About Amanda Christner:
Baptism: Holmes Co., OH[5113]
Burial: Chappell Mennonite Church Cemetery, Chappell, Deuel Co., NE
Residence: 1880, Precinct O, Seward Co., NE[5114]

Notes for Adam Stutzman:
Birth: Feb. 27, 1861
Death: Dec. 17, 1921

Stutzman. - Adam Stutzman was born in Holmes Co., OH Feb. 27, 1861. Dec. 14, 1918, he had a paralytic stroke from which he died Dec. 17, 1921, at his home near Chappel, NE; aged 60 y. 9 m. 20 d. He accepted Christ as His Savior in his youth and remained faithful until death. He left OH at the age of 12, moving to Milford, NE, where he remained until 1886, at which time he moved to Chappel, NE, where he has since made his home. On Aug. 13, 1882, he was married to Amanda Christner. To this union were born 3 sons and 3 daughters, who with his life companion, 14 grandchildren, 2 brothers, 2 sisters, and many relatives and friends remain to mourn his departure. Funeral services at the A. M. Church near Chapple, Neb., conducted by N. M. Birky. Interment in cemetery adjoining.

Spouse: Amanda Christner Stutzman (1861 - 1947)

Children:
Wesley C. Stutzman (1883 - 1948)
Frank Stutzman (1885 - 1972)
Clara Stutzman (1889 - 1960)
Joe Stutzman (1895 - 1948)

Burial: Mennonite Cemetery, Chappell, Deuel Co., NE
Find A Grave Memorial# 20842784

More About Adam Stutzman:
Burial: Chappell Mennonite Church Cemetery/Chappell, Deuel Co., NE[5115]
DBH Book: 10818/[5115]
Residence: 1920, Swan, Deuel Co., NE[5116]

Children of Amanda Christner and Adam Stutzman are:

+ 2716   i.   Wesley C.[9] Stutzman, born 31 May 1882 in Milford, Seward Co., NE; died 26 Oct 1948 in Chappell, Deuel Co., NE.

+ 2717   ii.   Frank Stutzman, born 31 Jan 1885 in Milford, Seward Co., NE; died 15 Jan 1972 in Chappell, Deuel Co., NE.

+ 2718   iii.   Belva Stutzman, born 07 Apr 1888 in Chappell, Deuel Co., NE; died 23 Jul 1963 in Goshen, Elkhart Co., IN.

   2719   iv.   Clara Stutzman[5117], born Dec 1889 in NE[5117]; died 1960 in Chappell, Deuel Co., NE[5117,5118].

         Notes for Clara Stutzman:
         Birth: Dec 1889 - NE
         Death: 1960 - Deuel Co., NE

         Daughter of Adam & Amanda (Christner) Stutzman.

         Parents:
         Adam Stutzman (1861 - 1921)
         Amanda Christner Stutzman (1861 - 1947)

         Burial: Mennonite Cemetery, Chappell, Deuel Co., NE
         Find A Grave Memorial# 74539175

   2720   v.   Minerva Stutzman[5119], born 16 Jan 1892 in Chappell, Deuel Co., NE[5119]; died in Chappell, Deuel Co., NE[5119]. She married Ezra J. Yoder.

   2721   vi.   Elizabeth Bessy Stutzman, born 31 Jan 1892.

+ 2722   vii.   Joseph Stutzman, born 24 Oct 1895 in Chappell, Deuel Co., NE; died 07 Sep 1948.

1269. John D.[8] Christner (Joseph J.[7], John J.[6], Joseph C.[5], Christian J.[4], Johannes John Hans[3], Christian[2], Christen[1])[5120,5121,5122] was born 28 Oct 1875 in Honeyville, Lagrange Co., IN[5122], and died 29 May 1942 in Shipshewana, Lagrange Co., IN[5123]. He married **Lucretia Renner**[5124,5125] 25 Nov 1900 in IN[5126]. She was born 04 Sep 1881 in IN[5127], and died 27 Jun 1948[5128,5129].

Notes for John D. Christner:
OBITUARY - Gospel Herald - Vol. XXXV, No . 12 - June 18, 1942 - pp. 254, 255

Christner - John D. son of Joseph and Amanda (Folk) Christner was born near Topeka, IN Oct. 28, 1875; died at his home in Shipshewana May 29, 1942, after an illness of nearly 2 1/2 years; aged 66 y. 7 m. 1 d. He was united in marriage to Lucretia Renner Nov. 25, 1900. To this union were born 5 children (Oscar of Shipshewana, Beulah Mochler of Middlebury, Venona Barnell of Scott, Dana of Lagrange and Luella Troyer of near Lagrange). He leaves his wife, 2 sons, 3 daughters, 17 grandchildren, 4 sisters (Anna Miller, Lydia Eash, Mary Christner, and Bessie Hershberger), 5 brothers (Abraham, Joseph, Ira, and Eli, all of Lagrange Co., and Noah of Plain City, OH), with other relatives and a host of friends who were a source of greatest enjoyment to him. Preceding him in death were his father and mother, 1 sister, and 1 grandson. He had been a member of the Forks Mennonite Church for the past forty years. His wife has lost an affectionate husband, the children a kind father, and the community a friend and neighbor of sterling worth. Funeral services were held at the Forks Mennonite Church by Bishop D. D. Miller. Text, Job 19:25. Burial in the Forest Grove Cemetery.

John was a Mennonite. He was a farmer and a live stock broker. The farm was North of Shipshewana Indiana on State Rd. 120. John was bedfast for the last 2 1/2 years of his life.

The Descendants of John J. Christner, privately published 1961, February 1961, p. 4.

More About John D. Christner:
Burial: Forest Grove Cemetery
Religion: Forks Mennonite Church/

Notes for Lucretia Renner:
Lucretia was the daughter of Jacob Renner and Catherine Farmwald.

The Descendants of John J. Christner, privately published February1961, p. 4.

More About Lucretia Renner:
Burial: Forest Grove Cemetery, Elkhart Co., IN

Children of John Christner and Lucretia Renner are:

+ 2723   i.   Oscar Ira⁹ Christner, born 08 Mar 1901 in Eden, Lagrange Co., IN; died 15 Nov 1970 in Lagrange, Lagrange Co., IN.
+ 2724   ii.   Beulah V. Christner, born 16 Mar 1905 in Middlebury, Elkhart Co., IN; died 24 Sep 1996 in Goshen, Elkhart Co., IN.
+ 2725   iii.   Venona L. Christner, born 06 May 1907 in White Pigeon, St. Joseph Co., MI; died 27 Dec 2002 in Sturgis, St Joseph Co., MI.
+ 2726   iv.   Dana R. Christner, born 11 Jul 1909 in Topeka, Lagrange Co., IN; died 14 Jan 2000 in Mesa, Maricopa Co., AZ.
+ 2727   v.   Luella Mae Christner, born 31 May 1917 in Van Buren, Lagrange Co., IN; died 09 Oct 2008 in Shipshewana, Lagrange Co., IN.

1271. Annie J.⁸ Christner (Joseph J.⁷, John J.⁶, Joseph C.⁵, Christian J.⁴, Johannes John Hans³, Christian², Christen¹)⁵¹³⁰ was born 29 Aug 1879 in Holmes Co., OH⁵¹³⁰, and died 18 Sep 1957⁵¹³⁰. She married **Ezra J. Miller** 19 Nov 1896 in Honeyville, Lagrange Co., IN. He was born 13 Nov 1876 in Lagrange Co., IN, and died 25 Jan 1933.

Notes for Annie J. Christner:
Eash book says Anna was born in Lagrange Co. Aug 29, 1877. Last address Shipshewana, IN.

The Descendants of John J. Christner, privately published February 1961, pp. 4, 6.

More About Annie J. Christner:
Burial: Yoder Corner Cemetery, Lagrange Co., IN
Religion: Amish/⁵¹³¹

Notes for Ezra J. Miller:

In 1906 Ezra bought 80 acre farm, 2 1/2 miles south of Shipshewana on the west side of State Road 5. All his children were born and raised here. This farm was known as the Klondyke and also the Arbagast. Ezra did carpenter work and he built the Honeyville Store In LaGrange Co., IN. He was Old Order Amish.

Ezra is the son of Johathan J. and Veronica V. Yoder Miller. Ezra did carpenter work and he built the Honeyville Store In LaGrange Co., IN.

Birth: Nov. 13, 1876
Death: Jan. 25, 1933

Burial: Yoder Cemetery, Shipshewana, Lagrange Co., IN

The Descendants of John J. Christner, privately published February 1961, p. 6.

Children of Annie Christner and Ezra Miller are:
- + 2728 i. Edna Mae[9] Miller, born 11 Sep 1897 in Shipshewana, Lagrange Co., IN; died 23 Jun 1976.
- + 2729 ii. Willis E. Miller, born 29 Jan 1899 in Shipshewana, Lagrange Co., IN; died 14 Sep 1980 in Shipshewana, Lagrange Co., IN.
- + 2730 iii. Mary E. Miller, born 01 Oct 1900 in Honeyville, Eden Twp., Lagrange Co., IN; died 29 Dec 1998 in Goshen, Elkhart Co., IN.
- + 2731 iv. Enos E. Miller, born 12 Mar 1903 in Shipshewana, Lagrange Co., IN; died 15 Feb 1988 in IN.
- + 2732 v. Ada E. Miller, born 31 Jul 1906 in Lagrange Co., IN; died 06 Jul 1994 in Lagrange Co., IN.
- + 2733 vi. Sylvia E. Miller, born 10 May 1909 in Lagrange Co., IN; died 30 Dec 2002 in Lagrange Co., IN.
- + 2734 vii. Emma E. Miller, born 08 Sep 1911 in Shipshewana, Lagrange Co., IN; died 12 Jan 2004 in 0330 South Indiana State Road 5 at 12:30 AM.
- + 2735 viii. Alma E. Miller, born 12 Dec 1912 in Middlebury, Elkhart Co., IN; died 06 Jun 1942.
- + 2736 ix. Amos E. Miller, born 12 Dec 1912 in Lagrange Co., IN; died 22 Aug 1969 in Home, Middlebury, IN.

1273. Lydia J.[8] Christner (Joseph J.[7], John J.[6], Joseph C.[5], Christian J.[4], Johannes John Hans[3], Christian[2], Christen[1])[5132,5133] was born 08 Dec 1884 in Honeyville, Lagrange Co., IN[5133], and died 24 Nov 1943 in Rome City, Noble Co., IN[5133]. She married **(1) Daniel J. Eash**. He was born 17 Apr 1881, and died 24 Nov 1962 in Row3 Plot 10. She married **(2) Daniel J. Eash** 12 Sep 1903[5134]. He was born 17 Apr 1881, and died 24 Nov 1962 in Row3 Plot 10.

Notes for Lydia J. Christner:
OBIT: Gospel Herald - Vol. XXXVI, No. 42 - January 13, 1944, page 895

Eash - Lydia (Christner), daughter of Joseph J. and Amanda (Folk) Christner, was born in Lagrange Co., IN, Dec. 8, 1884; passed from this life Nov. 24, 1943, at the Kniepp Springs Sanitarium, Rome City, IN where she was taken just a week before death; aged 58 y. 11 m. 16 d. On Sept. 12, 1903, she was united in marriage to Daniel J. Eash. She confessed and accepted Christ in her youth and remained a faithful servant until death. She leaves to mourn her departure, her loving companion, 5 children (Alma, wife of Christ L. Miller, Topeka; Alva in Sicily; Levi and Wilma, wife of Ernest Miller, both of Topeka; and Irma, wife of Tobias Bontrager, Middlebury, Ind.), 11 grandchildren, 4 brothers (Noah, Abraham, Eli, and Ira), and 3 sisters (Anna, Mary, and Bessie). Two children and one grandchild preceded her in death. She was a devoted wife and a loving mother. She suffered much but bore it very patiently and complained little. In May, 1939, she had a severe heart attack and was bedfast 5 weeks. Since that she had a number of attacks and never regained her usual health. This past summer she grew weaker but at the Sanitarium she was feeling much better until the morning of her death when she had an attack and in a short time peacefully passed away. In her long illness she attended church services whenever her health permitted. Funeral services were held at the Townline Church, Nov. 27, conducted by Bros. John J. S. Yoder and Noah Zehr, and also in the church basement by Bros. Manasses R. Miller and Jonas D. Miller.

The call was sudden, the shock severe.
We little thought the end so near;
And only those who lost can tell
The loss of a loved one without farewell.

Birth: Dec. 8, 1884
Death: Nov. 24, 1943

Parents:
Joseph J. Christner (1851 - 1925)
Amanda Folk Christner (1857 - 1920)

Spouse: Daniel J. Eash (1881 - 1962)

Burial: Christner Cemetery, Honeyville, Lagrange Co., IN

The Descendants of John J. Christner, privately published February 1961, p. 4, 12.

More About Lydia J. Christner:
Burial: Christner Cemetery, Honeyville, IN - Row3 Plot 11 - N 41°34.500-W 85°35.900

Notes for Daniel J. Eash:
The Descendants of John J. Christner, privately published February 1961, p. 12.

He was called : Daniel J. "Thrasher Dan" Eash

Thrasher Dan is the son of Josiah and Sarah Hershberger Eash Dan owned 4 rigs at one time for thrashing. Lydia died, Dan married Barbara Yoder Graber.

Birth: Apr. 17, 1881
Death: Nov. 24, 1962

18 Dec 1962 -- Eash, Daniel J., son of Josiah and Sarah (Herschberger) Eash, was born in Lagrange Co., Ind., April 17, 1881; died at the Westview Convalescent Home, Elkhart, Ind., Nov. 24, 1962; aged 81 y. 7 m. 7 d. On Sept. 12, 1903, he was married to Lydia Christner, who died Nov. 24, 1943. On Aug. 20, 1944, he was married to Barbara Gerber, who survives. He was ordained as deacon of the Townline C.M. Church, Shipshewana, Ind., in May, 1932. Surviving are 4 children (Alma-Mrs. Chris Miller, Alva, Erma-Mrs. Tobias Bontrager, and Wilma-Mrs. Ernest Miller), 18 grandchildren, 21 great-grandchildren, one stepson, 4 stepdaughters, one sister, Mrs. Samuel T. Eash), and one brother (John). Three children preceded him in death. He was a member of the Townline Church, where funeral services were held Nov. 26, in charge of John J. S. Yoder and Eli D. Miller. ~Gospel Herald - Volume LV, Number 49 - page 1095.

Spouses:
Lydia Eash (1884 - 1943)
Barbara Yoder Gerber/Eash (1886 - 1978)

Burial:Christner Cemetery, Honeyville, Lagrange Co., IN

More About Daniel J. Eash:
Burial: Christner Cemetery, Honeyville, Lagrange Co., IN

Notes for Daniel J. Eash:
The Descendants of John J. Christner, privately published February 1961, p. 12.

He was called : Daniel J. "Thrasher Dan" Eash

Thrasher Dan is the son of Josiah and Sarah Hershberger Eash Dan owned 4 rigs at one time for thrashing. Lydia died, Dan married Barbara Yoder Graber.

Birth: Apr. 17, 1881
Death: Nov. 24, 1962

18 Dec 1962 -- Eash, Daniel J., son of Josiah and Sarah (Herschberger) Eash, was born in Lagrange Co., Ind., April 17, 1881; died at the Westview Convalescent Home, Elkhart, Ind., Nov. 24, 1962; aged 81 y. 7 m. 7 d. On Sept. 12, 1903, he was married to Lydia Christner, who died Nov. 24, 1943. On Aug. 20, 1944, he was married to Barbara Gerber, who survives. He was ordained as deacon of the Townline C.M. Church, Shipshewana, Ind., in May, 1932. Surviving are 4 children (Alma-Mrs. Chris Miller, Alva, Erma-Mrs. Tobias Bontrager, and Wilma-Mrs. Ernest Miller), 18 grandchildren, 21 great-grandchildren, one stepson, 4 stepdaughters, one sister, Mrs. Samuel T. Eash), and one brother (John). Three children preceded him in death. He was a member of the Townline Church, where funeral services were held Nov. 26, in charge of John J. S. Yoder and Eli D. Miller. ~Gospel Herald - Volume LV, Number 49 - page 1095.

Spouses:
Lydia Eash (1884 - 1943)
Barbara Yoder Gerber/Eash (1886 - 1978)

Burial:Christner Cemetery, Honeyville, Lagrange Co., IN

More About Daniel J. Eash:
Burial: Christner Cemetery, Honeyville, Lagrange Co., IN

Children of Lydia Christner and Daniel Eash are:
+   2737   i.   Alma D.⁹ Eash, born 10 Mar 1904 in Topeka, Lagrange Co., IN; died 22 Aug 1994 in Topeka, Lagrange Co., IN.
+   2738   ii.   Levi D. Eash, born 14 Dec 1913 in Topeka, Lagrange Co., IN; died 31 Mar 1954.
+   2739   iii.   Erma Eash, born 29 Jul 1915 in Topeka, Lagrange Co., IN.
     2740   iv.   Enos Eash, born 04 Dec 1920 in Topeka, Lagrange Co., IN; died 04 Dec 1920.
+   2741   v.   Wilma Eash, born 27 Jun 1922 in Topeka, Lagrange Co., IN.
     2742   vi.   Edna Eash, born 23 Jul 1924 in Topeka, Lagrange Co., IN; died 06 Aug 1924.

Child of Lydia Christner and Daniel Eash is:
+   2743   i.   Elva⁹ Eash, born 13 Dec 1909 in Topeka, Lagrange Co., IN.

1274. Noah J.⁸ Christner (Joseph J.⁷, John J.⁶, Joseph C.⁵, Christian J.⁴, Johannes John Hans³, Christian², Christen¹)[5134,5135,5136,5137,5138] was born 12 Apr 1887 in Honeyville, Lagrange Co., IN[5139,5140,5141], and died 12 Mar 1947[5142,5143,5144,5145]. He married **(1) Magdalena Yoder**[5146,5147]. She was born 22 Mar 1884 in IL[5148,5149,5150], and died 30 Aug 1964[5151,5152]. He married **(2) Magdalena Yoder**[5153,5154]. She was born 22 Mar 1884 in IL[5155,5156,5157], and died 30 Aug 1964[5158,5159]. He married **(3) Magdalena Yoder**[5160,5161] 20 Jul 1907. She was born 22 Mar 1884 in IL[5162,5163,5164], and died 30 Aug 1964[5165,5166].

Notes for Noah J. Christner:
Amish farmer from Plain City, OH.

The Descendants of John J. Christner, privately published 1961, February 1961, pp. 4, 13.

More About Noah J. Christner:
Burial: Plain City, Madison Co., OH
Christened: O.O.Amish
Other-Begin: Madison Co.[5167,5168]
Residence: Madison, OH[5169,5170,5171]

Notes for Magdalena Yoder:
The Descendants of John J. Christner, privately published February 1961, p. 13.

Magdalena is the daughter of Mahlon S. and Rebecca Kauffman Yoder.

More About Magdalena Yoder:
Burial: Plain City, Madison Co., OH
Residence: 1930, Canaan, Madison, OH[5172]

Notes for Magdalena Yoder:
The Descendants of John J. Christner, privately published February 1961, p. 13.

Magdalena is the daughter of Mahlon S. and Rebecca Kauffman Yoder.

More About Magdalena Yoder:
Burial: Plain City, Madison Co., OH
Residence: 1930, Canaan, Madison, OH[5172]

Notes for Magdalena Yoder:
The Descendants of John J. Christner, privately published February 1961, p. 13.

Magdalena is the daughter of Mahlon S. and Rebecca Kauffman Yoder.

More About Magdalena Yoder:
Burial: Plain City, Madison Co., OH
Residence: 1930, Canaan, Madison, OH[5172]

Children of Noah Christner and Magdalena Yoder are:

    2744   i.   Clara[9] Christner, born 22 Oct 1907 in Topeka, Lagrange Co., IN; died 22 Oct 1907 in Topeka, Lagrange Co., IN.

                  Notes for Clara Christner:
                  The Descendants of John J. Christner, privately published February 1961, p. 13.

                  Clara and Carrie were twins. Clara lived less then one day.

                  Birth: Oct. 22, 1907
                  Death: Oct. 22, 1907

                  Inscription: Infant Dau of N.J. & M. Christner

                  Note: Twin sister of Carrie Christner Stutzman. "The Descendants of John J. Christner", Feb 1961.

                  Burial: Christner Cemetery, Honeyville, Lagrange Co., IN
                  Row4 plot 29
                  Find A Grave Memorial# 24708563

                  More About Clara Christner:
                  Burial: Christner Cemetery, Honeyville, Lagrange Co., IN

+   2745   ii.   Joseph Mahlon Christner, born 22 Dec 1909 in Plain City, Madison Co., OH; died 07 Jan 1989 in Columbus., OH.

+   2746   iii.   Ollie N. Christner, born 08 Feb 1912 in Honeyville, Lagrange Co., IN; died 13 Apr 1987 in Plain City, Madison Co., OH.

+   2747   iv.   Edna Mae Christner, born 24 Mar 1913 in Honeyville, Lagrange Co., IN; died 13 Aug 1992 in Plain City, Madison Co., OH.

+   2748   v.   Eli N. Christner, born 30 Mar 1915 in Plain City, Madison Co., OH; died 08 Jan 1982 in New Philadelphia, Tuscarawas Co., OH.

+   2749   vi.   Lula Hellen Christner, born 13 Jan 1918 in Plain City, Madison Co., OH; died 20 Jan 1993 in Plain City, Madison Co., OH.

+   2750   vii.   Mary Janet Christner, born 27 Mar 1921 in Plain City, Madison Co., OH; died 09 Dec 2002 in Cantpn, Stark Co., OH.

+   2751   viii.   Willis N. Christner, born 24 Dec 1922 in Plain City, Madison Co., OH; died 07 Sep 2006 in Glendale, Maricopa Co., AZ.

    2752   ix.   Glen N. Christner, born 08 Apr 1925 in Plain City, Madison Co., OH; died 20 May 1987 in Medway, Clark Co., OH[5173]. He married Edna E. Troyer 10 Nov 1946; born 12 Jul 1927.

Notes for Glen N. Christner:
The Descendants of John J. Christner, privately published February 1961, pp. 13, 15.

More About Glen N. Christner:
Residence: Clark, Holmes Co., OH[5173,5173]
Social Security Number: 289-30-4121/[5173]
SSN issued: OH[5173,5173]

Notes for Edna E. Troyer:
The Descendants of John J. Christner, privately published February 1961, p. 13.

Edna is the daughter of Eli M. and Malinda Farmwald Troyer.

+ 2753   x.   Paul N. Christner, born 07 Oct 1930 in Plain City, Madison Co., OH; died 20 May 1987 in Dayton, OH.

Child of Noah Christner and Magdalena Yoder is:
+ 2754   i.   Carrie[9] Christner, born 22 Oct 1907 in Topeka, Lagrange Co., IN; died 29 Oct 1984 in Plain City, Madison Co., OH.

1275. Abraham A.[8] Christner (Joseph J.[7], John J.[6], Joseph C.[5], Christian J.[4], Johannes John Hans[3], Christian[2], Christen[1])[5174,5175,5176] was born 19 Mar 1889 in Honeyville, Lagrange Co., IN[5177], and died 12 May 1959 in Lagrange, Lagrange Co., IN. He married **Mary D. Yoder** 31 Dec 1914 in Topeka, Lagrange Co., IN[5178]. She was born 05 Feb 1897 in Lagrange Co., IN[5178], and died 01 Sep 1979 in Goshen, Elkhart Co., IN[5178].

Notes for Abraham A. Christner:
The Descendants of John J. Christner, privately published February 1961, pp. 4, 16.

Abe and his brother Joe owned the Honeyville Store. Fishing was his favorite pastime. Abe owned a parrot for 45 years. Abe raised silver fox (bought by his brother Ira J.). The offsprings were to be divided for Abe keeping them. Ira never got any of the offsprings so he traded the foxes for some new implements. Abe had a heart problem for 10 years prior to his death. This problem let to other complications which caused his death.

Christner Brothers., Joe and Abe, bought Seagly Bros. in Topeka. Seagly Bros. was a hardware store plus farm implements,coal, fence, and fertilizer. That was in 1929,by 1930 they had a fire and they took what they could salvage to Honeyville Store. The building was sold to Greenawalt Bros. after rebuilding it they moved in their furniture and undertaking businesses in until 1953. The Greenawalts sold this business to another Christner Bros., LeRoy and Verlo in 1953.

Burial: Christner Cemetery, Honeyville, Lagrange Co., IN

Obituary: Gospel Herald - June 2, 1959 - page 526

Christner, Abraham A., son of Joseph and Amanda (Foulk) Christner; born March 19, 1889, at Topeka, Ind.; died May 12, 1959, at the Lagrange Co. Hospital, Lagrange, Ind., from a heart condition; aged 70 y. 1 m. 13 d. He was married on Dec. 31, 1914, at Topeka, Ind., to Mary Yoder, who survives. Two children preceded him in death. Also surviving are 2 brothers (Eli, Millersburg, Ind.; and Ira, Topeka, Ind.), and 2 sisters (Mary, Topeka; and Bessie-Mrs. Joseph Hershberger, Goshen, Elkhart Co., INd.). He was a member of the Townline C. M. Church, where funeral services were held May 16, in charge of Calvin Borntrager and Eli D. Miller; interment in Christner Cemetery.

Amish and Amish Mennonite Genealogies;

More About Abraham A. Christner:
Burial: Christner Cemetery., Honeyville, Lagrange Co., IN - Row 4, plot 24
Cause of Death: Heart Attack

Christened: Conservative
Obituary: Gospel Herald - Volume LII, Number 22 - June 2, 1959-page 526[5179]

Notes for Mary D. Yoder:
The Descendants of John J. Christner, privately published February 1961, p. 16.

Birth: Feb. 5, 1897
Death: 1979

Spouse: Abraham A Christner (1889 - 1959)

Burial: Christner Cemetery, Honeyville, Lagrange Co., IN
Died at the Fountainview Nursing home.

More About Mary D. Yoder:
Burial: Christner Cemetery/Honeyville, Lagrange Co., IN[5180]
Social Security Number: 307-48-3655/[5180]
SSN issued: IN[5180]

Children of Abraham Christner and Mary Yoder are:
    2755   i. Infant[9] Christner[5180], died 29 Oct 1916 in Lagrange Co., IN.

                  Notes for Infant Christner:
                  The Descendants of John J. Christner, privately published February 1961, p. 16.

                  Birth: Oct 30, 1916 - Lagrange Co., IN
                  Death: Oct 30, 1916 - Lagrange Co., IN

                  Christner, Abraham A, Mary Yoder, M, W, Oct 30 1916 H10 84 Index to Birth Records Lagrange Co.,
                  Indiana 1882 - 1920 Volume 1 A-L; Compiled by Indiana Works Progress Administration 1939.
                  Lagrange County Public Library.

                  Christner, M, W, -- Oct 30 1916 Eden Twp H-16 71
                  Index to Death Records, Lagrange County Indiana 1882 - 1924 Volume 1 A-Z Inclusive; Compiled by
                  Indiana Works Progress Administration 1939. Lagrange County Public Library.

                  Inscription:Infant son of A.A. & M.D. Christner

                  Burial: Christner Cemetery, Honeyville, Lagrange Co., IN
                  Row 4, plot 28

                  More About Infant Christner:
                  Burial: N 41°34.500-W 85°35.900/Christner Cemetery, Honeyville, Lagrange Co., IN

    2756   ii. Alta Bernice Christner[5180,5181,5182], born 19 Aug 1915 in Topeka, Lagrange Co., IN[5182,5183,5184]; died 01
                  Sep 1926 in Topeka, Lagrange Co., IN[5185,5186].

                  Notes for Alta Bernice Christner:
                  The Descendants of John J. Christner, privately published February 1961, p. 16.

                  Birth: Aug. 19, 1915
                  Death: Sep. 1, 1926

                  Inscription: Dau of A. A. & M. Christner 1915 - 1926

                  Burial: Christner Cemetery, Honeyville, Lagrange Co., IN

                  More About Alta Bernice Christner:
                  Burial: Christner Cemetery, Honeyville, Lagrange Co., IN[5186]
                  Residence: 1920, Eden, Lagrange Co., IN[5187]

1277. Eli J.[8] Christner (Joseph J.[7], John J.[6], Joseph C.[5], Christian J.[4], Johannes John Hans[3], Christian[2], Christen[1])[5188,5189,5190] was born 19 Aug 1894 in Millersburg, Elkhart Co., IN[5191,5192], and died 31 May 1972 in Topeka, Lagrange Co., IN[5193]. He married **Polly D. Yoder**[5194] 20 Feb 1919[5195]. She was born 07 Mar 1895 in Lagrange Co., IN[5196], and died 16 Oct 1979.

Notes for Eli J. Christner:
Eli was a farmer in Honeyville, IN and was bed redden the last 7 years of his life.

SS# 316-34-2875 Iss. IN

Birth: 1894
Death: 1972

Spouse: Polly D. Christner (1895 - 1979)

Children: Freeman E. Christner (1924 - 2012)

Burial: Town Line Cemetery,Topeka, Lagrange Co., IN

The Descendants of John J. Christner, privately published 1961, February 1961, pp. 4, 16.

More About Eli J. Christner:
Burial: Townline Cemetery, Lagrange Co., IN
Residence: 1910, Eden, Lagrange Co., IN[5197]
Social Security Number: 316-34-2875 issued IN/

Notes for Polly D. Yoder:
The Descendants of John J. Christner, privately published February 1961, p. 16.

Birth: 1895
Death: 1979

Spouse: Eli I. Christner (1894 - 1972)

Children: Freeman E, Christner (1924 - 2012)

Burial: Town Line Cemetery, Topeka, Lagrange Co., IN

More About Polly D. Yoder:
Burial: Town Line Cemetery, Topeka, Lagrange Co., IN
Residence: 1930, Eden, Lagrange Co., IN[5198]

Children of Eli Christner and Polly Yoder are:
+   2757   i.   Wilbur E.[9] Christner, born 02 Dec 1919 in Topeka, Lagrange Co., IN; died 12 Jun 1987 in Goshen, Elkhart Co., IN.
+   2758   ii.   Freeman E. Christner, born 28 Jan 1924 in Topeka, Lagrange Co., IN; died 04 Aug 2012 in IN.
+   2759   iii. Vernon E. Shorty Christner, born 01 Apr 1929 in Topeka, Lagrange Co., IN.

1279. Ira J.[8] Christner (Joseph J.[7], John J.[6], Joseph C.[5], Christian J.[4], Johannes John Hans[3], Christian[2], Christen[1])[5199] was born 27 May 1897 in Honeyville, Lagrange Co., IN[5200], and died 21 Aug 1982 in Carl Christner Home, Lagrange Co., IN[5200,5201]. He married **Sylvia Swartzentruber**[5201] 28 Feb 1918[5202]. She was born 22 Jun 1893 in Topeka, Lagrange Co., IN[5203], and died 26 Jun 1981 in Ft. Wayne, Allen Co., IN[5204].

Notes for Ira J. Christner:

Ira was a farmer and a cattle dealer most of his life. When he first started dealing in cattle he drove them from sale to sale on foot. In 1932/33 the fall of 1932 he contracted to buy peppermint oil from other farmers. That winter there was very little snow and it was extremely windy. It blew the roots of the mint out of the ground. Since his contracts called for all their mint he got what there was. The price of peppermint kept going up and Ira dug a hole in the Floor of the tool shed and burried the mint oil.He covered the hole with boards and his implements so it was not able to be stolen. A few weeks later he sold the oil at the top of the market ($28.00 a pound) and became a very wealthy man. A few weeks later the bottom dropped out of the mint market.
He lost his right eye as a very small child. He was playing with a 22 bullet cap and hit it on an anvil, it exploded and he lost his eye. He died from a heart attack at his son Carl's home in Honeyville. Ira was a farmer and a cattle dealer most of his life. When he first started dealing in cattle he drove them from sale to sale on foot. In 1932/33 the fall of 1932 he contracted to buy peppermint oil from other farmers. That winter there was very little snow and it was extremely windy. It blew the roots of the mint out of the ground. Since his contracts called for all their mint he got what there was. The price of peppermint kept going up and Ira dug a hole in the floor of the tool shed and burried the mint oil.He covered the hole with boards and his implements so it was not able to be stolen. A few weeks later he sold the oil at the top of the market ($28.00 a pound) and became a very wealthy man. A few weeks later the bottom dropped out of the mint market.
SS#;308-40-0641 Iss IN.

Ira had a water drainage clay tile the length of his many fields. These at times can plug up for several reasons then filling with water and not draining that part of the field. The fix for this problem was to get a peach branch in the shape of a Y, then give it to his Grandson (Steven Carl Christner) and have him walk across the field, when the stick bends down that where to dig. It worked every time although I don't know how.

His farm was at Honeyville IN.N41°34.841xW85°36.322, it was also owned by his father and Grandfather.

Ira was a farmer and a cattle dealer most of his life. When he first started dealing in cattle he drove them from sale to sale on foot. He was a very good judge of a cow's weight, buying them at farm auctions where they have no scales and selling them at large auctions where they have a scales and many more buyers. He was also very good at letting in pardners on individual deals such as the Auctioneers at the next auction he is taking the cows to sell.

Birth: May 27, 1897
Death: Aug. 25, 1982

Burial: Town Line Cemetery,Topeka, Lagrange Co., IN

The Descendants of John J. Christner, privately published 1961, February 1961, pp. 4, 16.

More About Ira J. Christner:
Burial: Townline Cemetery, Lagrange Co., IN
Funeral Service: Pall Bearers Freeman, Ollie, Wilbur, Willis & Vernon Christner & Lloyd Hershberger
Religion: Conservative Division of Amish/Mennonite
Social Security Number: 308-40-0641/[5204]
SSN issued: IN[5204]

Notes for Sylvia Swartzentruber:
The Descendants of John J. Christner, privately published February 1961, p. 16.

Sylvia is the daughter of John Swartzentruber and Sarah Weirich. Sylvia SS# 316-54-9632 ISS IN

Birth: 1893
Death: 1981

Burial: Town Line Cemetery, Topeka, Lagrange Co., IN

More About Sylvia Swartzentruber:

Burial: 29 Jun 1981, Townline Cemetery, Lagrange Co., IN
Social Security Number: 316-54-9632/[5204,5205]
SSN issued: IN[5205]

Children of Ira Christner and Sylvia Swartzentruber are:
+ 2760   i.   Carl I.⁹ Christner, born 24 Mar 1921 in Honeyville, Lagrange Co., IN; died 09 Apr 2005 in Goshen, Elkhart Co., IN.
+ 2761   ii.   Freda Christner, born 03 Jul 1927 in Goshen, Elkhart Co., IN; died 16 Jul 1997 in Sarasota, Sarasota Co., FL.

1280. Bessie Amanda⁸ Christner (Joseph J.⁷, John J.⁶, Joseph C.⁵, Christian J.⁴, Johannes John Hans³, Christian², Christen¹)[5206,5207,5208] was born 09 Dec 1899 in Goshen, Elkhart Co., IN, and died 01 Oct 1966[5209,5210,5211]. She married **Joseph Eli Harshberger**[5212,5213] 16 Mar 1926 in IN[5214,5215]. He was born 26 Dec 1900 in Middlebury, Elkhart Co., IN[5216,5217,5218,5219], and died 25 Jan 1975 in Home[5220].

Notes for Bessie Amanda Christner:
The Descendants of John J. Christner, privately published 1961, February 1961, pp. 4, 16.

More About Bessie Amanda Christner:
Burial: Thomas Cemetery, Goshen, Elkhart Co., IN - N41°36.182 by W85°43.380
Religion: Old Order Amish/

Notes for Joseph Eli Harshberger:
The Descendants of John J. Christner, privately published February 1961, p. 16.

In some books they are named Hershberger however they chose Harshberger for all of there tombstone's except Ida, she made sure hers read Hershberger. I drove to their house and asked them, they said Oh it's the same thing!

He was Old Order Amish and a farmer.

More About Joseph Eli Harshberger:
Burial: Thomas Cemetery, Goshen, Elkhart Co., IN - N41°36.182 by W85°43.380
Occupation: Farmer in Clinton Twp. Elkhart Co. East of Goshen, Indiana/
Religion: Old Order Amish/

Children of Bessie Christner and Joseph Harshberger are:
+ 2762   i.   Lloyd J.⁹ Harshberger, born 21 Mar 1927 in Goshen, Elkhart Co., IN; died 14 Aug 1992 in Elkhart Co., IN.
   2763   ii.   Alvin Harshberger[5220,5221], born 15 Apr 1928 in Goshen, Elkhart Co., IN[5221]; died 30 Apr 1935 in Goshen, Elkhart Co., IN[5222,5223].

       Notes for Alvin Harshberger:
       The Descendants of John J. Christner, privately published February 1961, p. 17.

       More About Alvin Harshberger:
       Burial: Thomas Cemetery, Goshen, Elkhart Co., IN - N41°36.182 by W85°43.380

+ 2764   iii.   Eli J. Harshberger, born 18 Aug 1929 in Goshen, Elkhart Co., IN; died 10 Oct 1970 in St Joe River, Berrien Springs, MI.
   2765   iv.   Infant Son Harshberger[5224], born 06 Nov 1930 in Goshen, Elkhart Co., IN; died 06 Nov 1930 in Goshen, Elkhart Co., IN[5224].

       Notes for Infant Son Harshberger:
       The Descendants of John J. Christner, privately published February 1961, p 17.

       More About Infant Son Harshberger:
       Burial: Thomas Cem, ELKHART CO, GOSHEN, IN. N41°36.182byW85°43.380

2766 v. Ida J. Harshberger[5224,5225], born 07 May 1932 in Elkhart Co., IN[5226,5227,5228]; died 01 Mar 2002 in Goshen General Hospital, Elkhart Co., IN[5229,5230,5231].

Notes for Ida J. Harshberger:
The Descendants of John J. Christner, privately published February 1961, p 17.

Ida never married. She was a seamstress and Old Order Amish. Her tombstone has her last name mispelled, Hershberger on her stone, her parents buried nearby have Harshberger for them and three of their children. More on the tombstone!!!

In some books they are named Hershberger however they chose Harshberger for all of there tombstone's except Ida, she made sure hers read Hershberger. I drove to their house and ask them, they said Oh it's the same thing?!?!?

More About Ida J. Harshberger:
Burial: Thomas Cemetery, Goshen, Elkhart Co., IN - N41°36.182 by W85°43.380
Occupation: Seamstress/
Religion: Old Order Amish/
Social Security Number: 312-54-9484/[5231]
SSN issued: IN[5231]

2767 vi. Infant Son Harshberger, born 02 Oct 1934; died 02 Oct 1934.

Notes for Infant Son Harshberger:
The Descendants of John J. Christner, privately published February 1961, p 17.

More About Infant Son Harshberger:
Burial: Thomas Cem, ELKHART CO, GOSHEN, IN. N41°36.182byW85°43.380

2768 vii. Alma Harshberger, born 02 Jun 1936.

Notes for Alma Harshberger:
The Descendants of John J. Christner, privately published February 1961, p. 17.

Alma never married.

2769 viii. Infant Son Harshberger, born 07 Jun 1940; died 07 Jun 1940.

Notes for Infant Son Harshberger:
The Descendants of John J. Christner, privately published February 1961, p. 17.

More About Infant Son Harshberger:
Burial: Thomas Cem, ELKHART CO, GOSHEN, IN. N41°36.182byW85°43.380

+ 2770 ix. Ray J. Harshberger, born 16 Nov 1941.
   2771 x. Infant Dau. Harshberger, born 23 Jul 1945; died 23 Jul 1945.

Notes for Infant Dau. Harshberger:
The Descendants of John J. Christner, privately published February 1961, p 17.

More About Infant Dau. Harshberger:
Burial: Thomas Cem, ELKHART CO, GOSHEN, IN. N41°36.182byW85°43.380

1281. Cornelius D.[8] Christner (David J.[7], John J.[6], Joseph C.[5], Christian J.[4], Johannes John Hans[3], Christian[2], Christen[1])[5232] was born 22 Jan 1883 in Topeka, Lagrange Co., IN[5232,5233,5234,5235], and died 15 Sep 1954 in IN[5236,5237,5237,5238]. He married **Susannna V. Yoder** 18 Dec 1902 in IN[5239,5240]. She was born 04 Sep 1884 in IN[5241,5242,5243], and died 22 Apr 1962.

Notes for Cornelius D. Christner:
The Descendants of John J. Christner, privately published Februaury 1961, p. 17.

He was ordained to the ministry May 5, 1905 and a Bishop, May 12, 1918. He was Old Order Amish.

Birth: Jan 22, 1883
Death: Sep 15, 1954

Burial: Miller Amish Cemetery, Lagrange, Lagrange Co., IN
Plot: Row 1, lot 4

More About Cornelius D. Christner:
Burial: Miller Cemetery, Lagrange Co., IN
Occupation: 05 May 1905, Ordained Minister and Bishop/
Residence: 1942, Lagrange Co., IN[5244]

Notes for Susannna V. Yoder:
Birth: Sep 4, 1884
Death: Apr 22, 1962

Burial: Miller Amish Cemetery, Lagrange, Lagrange Co., IN
Plot: Row 1, lot 5
Find A Grave Memorial# 66591538

More About Susannna V. Yoder:
Burial: Miller Cemetery, Lagrange Co., IN
Residence: 1930, Clearspring, Lagrange Co., IN[5244]

Child of Cornelius Christner and Susannna Yoder is:
+   2772   i.   Annie C.[9] Christner, born 01 Oct 1903 in Lagrange Co., IN; died 08 Oct 1982.

1283. Eddranis D.[8] Christner (David J.[7], John J.[6], Joseph C.[5], Christian J.[4], Johannes John Hans[3], Christian[2], Christen[1]) was born 10 May 1886 in Topeka, Lagrange Co., IN[5245], and died 27 Aug 1963 in IN[5245]. He married **(1) Harriet Elizabeth Renner** 18 Oct 1908. She was born 26 Feb 1889 in New Bedford, OH, and died 02 Mar 1950 in Near Topeka, IN. He married **(2) Deilia Cordelia Yoder** 10 May 1955. She was born 03 Oct 1882 in Elkhart Co., IN, and died 27 Dec 1969 in Goshen, Elkhart Co., IN.

Notes for Eddranis D. Christner:
The Descendants of John J. Christner, privately published 1961, p. 19.

Maybe spelled Eddranis. SS# 308-40-2395   Iss. IN Farmer.

Birth: 1886
Death: 1963

Spouse: Harriet E. Renner Christner (1889 - 1950)

Children:
LeRoy Christner (1911 - 1985)
Verlo E. Christner (1916 - 1971)
Ida E. Christner (1920 - 2010)

Burial: Maple Grove Cemetery, Topeka, Lagrange Co., IN

More About Eddranis D. Christner:
Burial: Maple Grove Topeka Indiana
Residence: 1930, Eden, Lagrange Co., IN[5246,5247]
Social Security Number: 308-40-2395/[5248]

SSN issued: IN[5248]

Notes for Harriet Elizabeth Renner:
The Descendants of John J. Christner, privately published February 1961, p. 18.

Christner, Harriet Elizabeth, daughter of George and Barbara Renner, was born Feb. 26, 1889, in New Bedford, Ohio; died at her late home near Topeka, Ind., March 2, 1950; aged 61 y. 5 d. She was united in marriage to Eddranis D. Christner on Oct. 18, 1908. To this union were born 4 sons (Glen, Goshen, Ind.; LeRoy, at home; George, Elkhart, Ind.; Verla, of Topeka) and 2 daughters (Ida, at home; and Irene, who preceded her mother in death). Besides her husband and children she leave 6 grandchildren, 2 sisters (Mrs. Otis Mehl, Shipshewana, Ind.; and Mrs. Ida Paulus, Ligonier, Ind.), and 2 brothers (Milo and Nolen Renner, both of Ligonier). She accepted Christ and became a member of the Maple Grove Mennonite Church at an early age and remained a faithful member until death. Funeral services were held March 4 at the Maple Grove Mennonite Church, Topeka, Ind., conducted by Amos Hostetler and Edwin J. Yoder. Burial was made in the Maple Grove Cemetery.

Birth: 1889
Death: 1950

Spouse: Eddranis D Christner (1886 - 1963)

Children:
LeRoy Christner (1911 - 1985)
Verlo E. Christner (1916 - 1971)
Ida E. Christner (1920 - 2010)

Burial: Maple Grove Cemetery, Topeka, Lagrange Co., IN

More About Harriet Elizabeth Renner:
Burial: Maple Grove Cemetery Topeka IN

Notes for Deilia Cordelia Yoder:
Delia lived at the Andersen Nursing home in Goshen, IN from April 1969 till her death. She lived in Topeka and Goshen all her life.

Children of Eddranis Christner and Harriet Renner are:

2773	i.	Irene[9] Christner, died 1931.
2774	ii.	Irene Christner.
+ 2775	iii.	Glen E. Christner, born 23 Sep 1909 in Topeka, Lagrange Co., IN; died 11 Jun 1980 in Goshen, Elkhart Co., IN.
2776	iv.	Leroy E. Roy Christner[5249], born 26 Mar 1911 in Topeka, Lagrange Co., IN[5249]; died 28 May 1985 in Ft. Wayne, Allen Co., IN[5249].

Notes for Leroy E. Roy Christner:
The Descendants of John J. Christner, privately published 1961, p. 18.

Roy owned Christner Furniture, Main Street Topeka, Lagrange Co., IN for many years. (1953 to 1973) He was helped in the business by his brother Verlo.

Roy never married. World War II Army Veteran.
SS#303-16-2584 ISS.IN

Birth: Mar. 26, 1911
Death: May 29, 1985

Parents:
Eddranis D Christner (1886 - 1963)
Harriet E Renner Christner (1889 - 1950)

Burial: Maple Grove Cemetery, Topeka, Lagrange Co., IN

More About Leroy E. Roy Christner:
Burial: Maple Grove Cem, Lagrange Co, IN
Military: 04 Jun 1942, Toledo, OH[5249]
Social Security Number: 303-16-2584/[5249]
SSN issued: IN[5249]

+ 2777   v.   George E. Christner, born 25 Apr 1914 in Topeka, Lagrange Co., IN; died 27 Apr 1985 in Elkhart Co., IN.

+ 2778   vi.   Verlo Christner, born 29 Jun 1916 in Topeka, Lagrange Co., IN; died 04 Jul 1971 in Topeka, Lagrange Co., IN.

  2779   vii.   Ida Christner, born 01 Jan 1920 in Topeka, Lagrange Co., IN; died 11 Mar 2010 in Goshen, Elkhart Co., IN[5250].

Notes for Ida Christner:
Ida never married.

Birth: Jan 1, 1920 - Topeka, Lagrange Co., IN
Death: Mar 11, 2010 - Goshen, Elkhart Co., IN

Obituary:

Ida E. Christner, 90, of Goshen, died at her home on Thursday, March 11, 2010.

She was born in Topeka, Indiana, on January 1, 1920, the late Eddranis and Harriet (Renner) Christner. She moved to Goshen in 2007 from Topeka where she had lived her whole life.

A member of Maple Grove Church, Topeka, Miss Christner worked in sales for her brother, LeRoy at Christner Furniture Store in Topeka.

She is survived by nieces and nephews.

She was preceded in death by an infant sister, Irene and four brothers, Glen, LeRoy, George and Verlo Christner.

Friends may call 1 to 5 p.m., Sunday, March 14, at the funeral home.

A 10:00 a.m., Monday, March 15, 2010, funeral service will be conducted at Yoder-Culp Funeral Home. Burial will follow in Maple Grove Cemetery, Topeka, IN.

Memorial contributions may be made to United Cancer Services of Elkhart County.

Parents:
Eddranis D. Christner (1886 - 1963)
Harriet E. Renner Christner (1889 - 1950)

Burial: Maple Grove Cemetery, Topeka, Lagrange Co., IN

More About Ida Christner:
Residence: 1930, Eden, Lagrange Co., IN[5250]

1284. Mary Ann[8] Christner (David J.[7], John J.[6], Joseph C.[5], Christian J.[4], Johannes John Hans[3], Christian[2], Christen[1])[5251,5252] was born 12 Jan 1888 in Honeyville, Lagrange Co., IN, and died 20 Jan 1958 in IN[5252]. She married **Harvey S. Frye** 13 Jan 1910 in IN[5252,5252]. He was born 28 Jan 1889 in Emma, Lagrange Co., IN, and died 23 Oct 1991 in Greencroft, Nursing Home, Goshen, Elkhart Co., IN.

Notes for Mary Ann Christner:
The Descendants of John J. Christner, privately published 1961, pp. 17, 19.

Elkhart Prairie Cemetery, Goshen, IN. N41°33'xW85°48' is at Kercher Road(Co.Rd.38) and Dierdorff Road (Co.Rd.27). center for east/west & south side.
Some sources have her death as 1958 this is in error, it's 1954. Frye, Mary Ann, daughter of David and Elizabeth

Christner, was born near Honeyville, Ind., Jan. 12, 1888; died Jan. 20, 1954; aged 70 y. 9 d. She had been in failing health for the past few years but died very suddenly as the result of a heart ailment. At an early age she accepted Christ as her Saviour and continued in that faith throughout life. She held membership in the North-Goshen Mennonite Church. On Jan. 13, 1910, she was married to Harvey S. Frye and had resided in New Paris, IN for twenty years. Surviving in addition to her husband are 6 sons (E. Jay, Goshen, IN; Samuel, Chicago, IL; Ernest, South Bend, IN; Edward and LeRoy, Long Beach, Calif.; and Freeman, Edwardsburg, MI), one daughter (Mrs. Dorothy Roe, Wawaka, Ind.), 2 brothers (Edd and Levi, both of Topeka, IN), one sister (Mrs. Katie J. Miller, Topeka, IN), and 3 grandchildren. Funeral services were held at the North Goshen Church, Jan. 22, in charge of Paul Mininger and Russell Krabill. Interment in the Elkhart Prairie Cemetery.

More About Mary Ann Christner:
Burial: Elkhart Prairie Cem. Goshen, IN.N41°33'xW85°48'
Cause of Death: Heart Ailment
Religion: Mennonite/
Residence: 1910, Clearspring, Lagrange Co., IN[5252]

Notes for Harvey S. Frye:
The Descendants of John J. Christner, privately published February 1961, p. 19.

Harvey wrote several articles and had them published. He had a very distinct style of writing. He used punctuation no one else used. He was a typesetter for Farmers Exchange Newspaper in Elkhart County. He also developed a numbering system for county roads. It started at the center of the county, for example five miles south of the county seat was 500S. S for South and nine and one half miles west of the county seat was 950W. W for west. This is still in use in 2002. I (Steven Carl Christner) was born 1/8 mile north of 500S.& 950W.Harvey was an independent thinker with no tolerance for other peoples ideas. He was a member of Sunny side Mennonite Church in Dunlap Near Elkhart, IN.

More About Harvey S. Frye:
Burial: Elkhart Prairie Cem. Goshen, IN.N41°33'xW85°48'
Other-Begin: Lagrange County[5252]
Residence: 1942, employed by 1XL Furniture Company/New Paris, Indiana[5252]
Social Security Number: 304-09-3764/[5252]
SSN issued: IN[5252]

Children of Mary Christner and Harvey Frye are:

2780   i.   Elizabeth Mae[9] Frye, born 27 Nov 1912 in Topeka, Lagrange Co., IN[5252]; died 19 Oct 1972 in Elkhart Co., IN[5252].

Notes for Elizabeth Mae Frye:
The Descendants of John J. Christner, privately published February 1961, p. 19.

Cause of death - polycythemia.

More About Elizabeth Mae Frye:
Burial: Belliville PA

+ 2781   ii.   Elias Jay Frye, born 27 Oct 1914 in Topeka, Lagrange Co., IN; died 08 Oct 1998 in Wakarusa, Elkhart Co., IN.

2782   iii.   Samuel H. Frye, born 27 Jul 1917 in Lagrange Co., IN; died 1964.

Notes for Samuel H. Frye:
The Descendants of John J. Christner, privately published February 1961, p. 19.

Birth: 1917
Death: 1964

Burial: Elkhart Prairie Cemetery, Goshen, Elkhart Co., IN
Find A Grave Memorial# 89672238

More About Samuel H. Frye:
Burial: Elkhart Prairie Cem. Goshen, IN.N41°33'xW85°48'

+ 2783   iv.   Ernest R. Frye, born 18 Jul 1919 in South Bend, St. Joseph Co., IN; died 03 Oct 1996 in South Bend, St Joseph Co., IN.

2784   v.   Edward Frye[5252], born 06 Apr 1921; died 11 Jun 1998 in Bristol, Elkhart Co., IN[5252,5252].

Notes for Edward Frye:
The Descendants of John J. Christner, privately published February 1961, p. 19.

More About Edward Frye:
Social Security Number: 309-14-0409/[5252]
SSN issued: IN[5252]

2785   vi.   Freeman H. Frye, born 02 Feb 1924 in Topeka, Lagrange Co., IN[5252]; died 04 Jan 2002 in Goshen, Elkhart Co., IN. He married Louise Wise 19 Aug 1969 in Goshen, Elkhart Co., IN; born 07 May 1918; died 12 Jan 1992.

Notes for Freeman H. Frye:
The Descendants of John J. Christner, privately published February 1961, p.19.

Yellow Creek Mennonite Church   He worked at Concord Schools as a custodian. Mary was married before she married Freeman.

More About Freeman H. Frye:
Burial: Yellow Creek Mennonite Cemetery Elkhart, Co. IN.
Military: 24 Mar 1944, Fort Benjamin Harrison, Indiana[5252]
Residence: Elkhart Co., IN[5252]
Social Security Number: 306-20-8741/[5252]
SSN issued: IN[5252]

2786   vii.   Ira Frank Frye[5252], born 10 Jan 1926; died 22 Nov 1953[5252].

Notes for Ira Frank Frye:
The Descendants of John J. Christner, privately published February 1961, p. 19.

More About Ira Frank Frye:
Burial: Elkhart Prairie Cem. Goshen, IN.N41°33'xW85°48'

+ 2787   viii.   Dorothy June Frye, born 03 Jun 1928; died 23 Oct 2010 in Tonawanda, Erie Co., NY.
2788   ix.   Leroy Frye, born 09 Mar 1931.

Notes for Leroy Frye:
The Descendants of John J. Christner, privately published February 1961, p. 19.

1285. David D.[8] **Christner** (David J.[7], John J.[6], Joseph C.[5], Christian J.[4], Johannes John Hans[3], Christian[2], Christen[1])[5253,5254,5255,5256,5257,5258] was born 08 Jun 1889 in Topeka, Lagrange Co., IN[5259,5260,5261,5262], and died 25 Nov 1948 in Lagrange Co., IN[5262]. He married **(1) Lydia Ann T. Yoder**[5263] 10 Feb 1910 in IN. She was born 18 Jan 1892 in Eden, Lagrange Co., IN[5264], and died 07 May 1923 in Clear Spring, Lagrange Co., IN[5264]. He married **(2) Catherine M. "Katie" Hershberger**[5265] 15 Apr 1926 in Elkhart, Elkhart Co., IN[5265]. She was born 13 May 1883 in OH[5265], and died 04 Aug 1935 in Elkhart, Elkhart Co., IN[5265]. He married **(3) Katie Chupp Miller** 28 Oct 1941 in Locke Twp., Elkhart Co., IN. She was born 16 Sep 1901, and died 30 Nov 1976.

Notes for David D. Christner:
The Descendants of John J. Christner, privately published February 1961, pp. 17, 19.

He was a farmer and made an ordained minister on May 31, 1916. David was Old Order Amish. He was 1st married to Lydia Ann T. Yoder 10 Feb 1910. He then married Catherine M. "Katie" Hershberger 15 Apr 1926. His 3rd marriage was to Katie Chupp Miller on Oct. 28, 1941. She was born Sept. 16 1901.

He had 1 son by his 2nd wife Milo William born July 4, 1928 in Elkhart, IN. Milo married Betty Joe Davis on Sept 8, 1956. David D. died in St. Joseph Hospital, Lancaster, PA from a fisula of the esophagus & removal of part of his lung. He & his wife left Oct. 3 1948 for Lancaster was xrayed & operated on for a growth in his throat & had his tonsils burned out with electricity. Left for home Oct. 26.

1948 to stay 4 weeks rest he seamed a little better the first few days but got worse with coughing--Eating & drinking with difficulty & got weaker with pain in his back. Left home again on Penicillin & also given shots.

David seemed pretty strong & well before his operation but lived only around 24 hours after.

Story of his broken leg.
He was herding cows in to the barn and stepped on a corn cob and fell down. Well I think it was more up and then down. He didn't want to see a doctor (they charge money you know) so he had his brother Levi (who owned a tin shop) make a brace for his broken leg out of light steel.

Birth: Jun. 8, 1889
Death: Nov. 25, 1948

Spouses:
Katie M. Christner (1888 - 1935)
Lydia A. Christner (1892 - 1923)
Katie Ann Miller Christner (1901 - 1976)

Children:
Levi Christner (____ - 1923)
Infant Boy Christner (____ - 1920)
Eli Christner (____ - 1923)
Lilly Mae Christner (1912 - 1912)
Harley D. Christner (1914 - 1914)
Tobias D. Christner (1917 - 1918)
John D. Christner (1922 - 1923)

Burial: Miller Amish Cemetery, Lagrange, Lagrange Co., IN
Plot: Row 8, lot 19

More About David D. Christner:
Burial: N41°35.348'xW85°28.937'Row8plot19/Miller Amish Cemetery, Lagrange, Lagrange Co., IN
Military Draft: World War I and World War II/[5265]
Religion: 31 May 1916, Ordained Minister Old Order Amish/
Residence: 1920, Clearspring, Lagrange Co., IN[5266]

Notes for Lydia Ann T. Yoder:
The Descendants of John J. Christner, privately published February 1961, p. 19.

Birth: 1892
Death: 1923

Spouse: David D. Christner (1889 - 1948)

Children:
Infant Boy Christner (____ - 1920)
Eli Christner (____ - 1923)
Levi Christner (____ - 1923)
Lilly Mae Christner (1912 - 1912)
Harley D. Christner (1914 - 1914)
Tobias D. Christner (1917 - 1918)

John D. Christner (1922 - 1923)

Burial: Miller Amish Cemetery, Lagrange, Lagrange Co., IN
Plot: Row 8, lot 20

More About Lydia Ann T. Yoder:
Burial: N41°35.348'xW85°28.937' Row 8 plot 20/Miller Amish Cemetery, Lagrange, Lagrange Co., IN
N41°35.348'xW85°28.937'Row8plot20
Residence: 1910, Clearspring, Lagrange Co., IN[5266]

Notes for Catherine M. "Katie" Hershberger:
Catherine was the child of Mannasses Hershberger and Katie J. MIller. Catherine 1st marriage was to Joseph B. Mullet.

Birth: Sep. 16, 1901
Death: Nov. 20, 1976

Wife of David D. Christner

Spouse: David D. Christner (1889 - 1948)

Burial: Miller Amish Cemetery, Lagrange, Lagrange Co., IN
Plot: Row 8, lot 17

More About Catherine M. "Katie" Hershberger:
Burial: Miller Cemetery, Lagrange Co., IN
Cause of Death: Sarcoma Cancer

Notes for Katie Chupp Miller:
Birth: Sep. 16, 1901
Death: Nov. 20, 1976

Katie married Eli E Miller on Jan 18, 1923. Their children:
Elmer Ray born Jan 1, 1924
Matilta born and died Apr 12, 1926
Mary Ellen born Jan 17, 1928
Amanda E born Oct 3, 1929
Sylvia E born Jul 1, 1931
Emma E born Dec 8, 1932
Clara Jane born Apr 3, 1934
Eli died May 16, 1935 at Plymouth, Marshall County, IN
Katie married David D Christner Oct 21, 1941 at Locke Twp., Elkhart County, IN.

Parents:
Daniel E Miller (1878 - 1925)
Emma M Hochstetler Miller (1880 - 1971)

Spouses:
David D. Christner (1889 - 1948)
Eli E Miller (1900 - 1935)

Inscription: 75 YR 2 MO 14 DA

Burial: Miller Amish Cemetery, Lagrange, Lagrange Co., IN
Plot: Row 8, lot 17

Children of David Christner and Lydia Yoder are:

+ 2789   i.   Soloma[9] Christner, born 10 Dec 1910 in Lagrange Co., IN; died 07 Nov 1997 in 11322 Co.Rd.34 Goshen, Elkhart Co., IN.

   2790   ii.   Lilly Mae Christner, born 19 Feb 1912 in Lagrange Co., IN; died 19 Feb 1912 in Lagrange Co., IN.

Notes for Lilly Mae Christner:
The Descendants of John J. Christner, privately published February 1961, p. 19.

Birth: Feb. 19, 1912
Death: Feb. 19, 1912

Parents:
David D. Christner (1889 - 1948)
Lydia A. Christner (1892 - 1923)

Burial: Miller Amish Cemetery, Lagrange, Lagrange Co., IN

More About Lilly Mae Christner:
Burial: Miller Cem, Lagrange Co, IN. N41°35.348'xW85°28.937'Row8plot25

+ 2791   iii.   Wilma L. Christner, born 25 May 1913 in Lagrange Co., IN; died 15 Apr 1977 in Lagrange Co., IN.

   2792   iv.   Harley D. Christner, born 09 Jul 1914 in Lagrange Co., IN; died 09 Jul 1914 in Lagrange Co., IN.

Notes for Harley D. Christner:
The Descendants of John J. Christner, privately published February 1961, p. 19.

Birth: Jul 9, 1914
Death: Jul 9, 1914

Parents:
David D. Christner (1889 - 1948)
Lydia A. Christner (1892 - 1923)

Burial: Miller Amish Cemetery, Lagrange, Lagrange Co., IN

More About Harley D. Christner:
Burial: N41°35.348'xW85°28.937' Row8 plot24/Miller Amish Cemetery, Lagrange, Lagrange Co., IN

+ 2793   v.   Uriah D. Christner, born 16 Sep 1915 in Clearspring Twp., Lagrange Co., IN; died 31 Oct 2003 in Lagrange Hospital Lived at 5615 W--500 S//N41°34.128xW85°31.962.

   2794   vi.   Tobias D. Christner, born 20 Apr 1917 in Lagrange Co., IN; died 17 Oct 1918 in Lagrange Co., IN[5267].

Notes for Tobias D. Christner:
The Descendants of John J. Christner, privately published February 1961, p. 19.

Birth: Apr. 20, 1917
Death: Oct. 17, 1918

Parents:
David D. Christner (1889 - 1948)
Lydia A. Christner (1892 - 1923)

Burial: Miller Amish Cemetery, Lagrange, Lagrange Co., IN
Plot: Row 8, lot 22

More About Tobias D. Christner:
Burial: Oct 1918, N41°35.348'xW85°28.937'Row8plot22/Miller Cemetery. Lagrange Co., IN

+ 2795   vii.   Mattie L. Christner, born 09 Oct 1918 in Topeka, Lagrange Co., IN; died 26 Feb 1999 in Lagrange Co., IN.

   2796   viii.   Not Named Christner, born 22 May 1920 in Lagrange Co., IN; died 22 May 1920 in Lagrange Co., IN.

Notes for Not Named Christner:
The Descendants of John J. Christner, privately published February 1961, p.19.

Birth: 22 May 1920
Death: 22 May 1920

Parents:
David D. Christner (1889 - 1948)
Lydia A. Christner (1892 - 1923)

Burial: Miller Amish Cemetery, Lagrange, Lagrange Co., IN
Plot: Row 8, lot 23

More About Not Named Christner:
Burial: Miller Cemetery, Lagrange Co., IN

2797   ix.   John D. Christner, born 09 Jan 1922 in Lagrange Co., IN; died 04 Jan 1923 in Lagrange Co., IN[5268].

Notes for John D. Christner:
The Descendants of John J. Christner, privately published February 1961, p., 19.

Birth: Jul. 9, 1914
Death: Jul. 9, 1914

Parents:
David D. Christner (1889 - 1948)
Lydia A. Christner (1892 - 1923)

Burial: Miller Amish Cemetery, Lagrange, Lagrange Co., IN

More About John D. Christner:
Burial: Miller Cem, Lagrange Co, IN. N41°35.348'xW85°28.937'Row8plot21

2798   x.   Eli Christner[5269], born 06 May 1923 in Lagrange Co., IN; died 15 May 1923 in Lagrange Co., IN[5269].

Notes for Eli Christner:
The Descendants of John J. Christner, privately published February 1961, p. 19.

Birth: 06 May 1923
Death: 15 May 1923

Infant, twin to Levi

Parents:
David D. Christner (1889 - 1948)
Lydia A. Christner (1892 - 1923)

Burial: Miller Amish Cemetery, Lagrange, Lagrange Co., IN

More About Eli Christner:
Burial: N41°35.348'xW85°28.937'/Miller Cemetery, Lagrange Co., IN

2799   xi.   Levi Christner, born 06 May 1923 in Lagrange Co., IN; died 13 May 1923 in Lagrange Co., IN.

Notes for Levi Christner:
The Descendants of John J. Christner, privately published February 1961, p. 19.

Birth: 06 May 1923
Death: 13 May 1923

Infant, twin to Eli

Parents:

David D. Christner (1889 - 1948)
Lydia A. Christner (1892 - 1923)

Burial: Miller Amish Cemetery, Lagrange, Lagrange Co., IN
Plot: Row 8, lot 27

More About Levi Christner:
Burial: Miller Cemetery, Lagrange Co., IN

Child of David Christner and Catherine Hershberger is:

+ 2800   i.   Milo William[9] Christner, born 04 Jul 1928 in Elkhart, Elkhart Co., IN; died 27 Jun 1965 in Elkhart, Elkhart Co., IN.

Children of David Christner and Katie Miller are:

2801   i.   Elmer Ray[9] Christner, born 01 Jan 1924.
2802   ii.   Matilta Christner, born 12 Apr 1926.
2803   iii.   Mary Ellen Christner, born 17 Jan 1928.
2804   iv.   Amanda E. Christner, born 03 Oct 1929.
2805   v.   Sylvia E. Christner, born 01 Jul 1931.
2806   vi.   Emma E. Christner, born 08 Dec 1932.
2807   vii.   Clara Jane Christner, born 03 Apr 1934.
2808   viii.   Eli Christner, born 16 May 1935 in Plymouth, Marshall Co., IN.

1286. Katie D.[8] Christner (David J.[7], John J.[6], Joseph C.[5], Christian J.[4], Johannes John Hans[3], Christian[2], Christen[1])[5270] was born 22 Feb 1891 in Topeka, Lagrange Co., IN[5270], and died 28 Mar 1959 in Lagrange, Lagrange Co., IN[5271]. She married **Jacob J. M. Miller**[5272] 01 Apr 1909. He was born 06 May 1890 in Lagrange Co., IN[5272], and died 03 Jul 1963 in Lagrange Co., IN[5272].

Notes for Katie D. Christner:
The Descendants of John J. Christner, privately published 1961, pp., 17, 21.

More About Katie D. Christner:
Religion: Old Order Amish/[5273]

Notes for Jacob J. M. Miller:
The Descendants of John J. Christner, privately published February 1961, p. 22.

Jacob is Old Order Amish. He was known as Jake Jake and his children were known as Jake Jake's Susie or Jake Jake's Alice. One son was known as triple Jake.

Children of Katie Christner and Jacob Miller are:

+ 2809   i.   Susan J.[9] Miller, born 17 Mar; died 10 Oct 1968 in Lagrange Co., IN.
+ 2810   ii.   Mary Ann Miller, born 26 Jul 1909 in Topeka, Lagrange Co., IN; died 24 Jul 1930.
+ 2811   iii.   Alice J. Miller, born 10 May 1911 in Topeka, Lagrange Co., IN; died 17 Jul 2001 in Middlebury, Elkhart Co., IN.
+ 2812   iv.   Tobias J. Miller, born 02 Feb 1913 in Topeka, Lagrange Co., IN.
+ 2813   v.   Amos J. Miller, born 19 Oct 1915 in Lagrange Co., IN; died 04 Apr 1987 in Sarasota, Sarasota Co., FL.
+ 2814   vi.   Eli J. Miller, born 02 Apr 1919 in Shipshewana, Lagrange Co., IN; died 26 Nov 2004 in Montezuma, GA.
   2815   vii.   Edd J. Miller, born 14 Sep 1921 in Columbus, Franklin Co., OH. He married Myrtice Surrency 16 Aug 1947; born 23 Dec 1916.

         Notes for Edd J. Miller:
         The Descendants of John J. Christner, privately published February 1961, pp. 21, 22.

         Edd married Myrtice Surrency Aug 16, 1947 in Sarasota, Florida. They owned a auto drive in restaurant, they bring the food to your automobile.

Notes for Myrtice Surrency:
The Descendants of John J. Christner, privately published February 1961, p. 22.

+	2816	viii.	Jacob Willis Miller, born 28 Dec 1923 in Topeka, Lagrange Co., IN; died in This is triple Jake as his dad was called Jake Jake.
+	2817	ix.	Amzie J. Miller, born 22 Sep 1926 in Goshen, Elkhart Co., IN.
+	2818	x.	Obie J. Miller, born 03 Jul 1928 in Topeka, Lagrange Co., IN.
+	2819	xi.	Wanetia Katie Miller, born 09 Mar 1931 in Shipshewana, Lagrange Co., IN.
+	2820	xii.	Edna Ellen Miller, born 08 Mar 1935 in Topeka, Lagrange Co., IN.

1287. Emma D.[8] Christner (David J.[7], John J.[6], Joseph C.[5], Christian J.[4], Johannes John Hans[3], Christian[2], Christen[1]) was born 18 Apr 1893 in Topeka, Lagrange Co., IN, and died 15 Apr 1928 in IN[5274,5275]. She married **Menno J. S. Yoder**[5276] 14 Apr 1911. He was born 04 Jul 1892 in Lagrange Co., IN[5277], and died 11 Jul 1967[5278,5279,5280].

Notes for Emma D. Christner:
The Descendants of John J. Christner, privately published February 1961, p. 23.

More About Emma D. Christner:
Burial: Miller Cem, Lagrange Co, IN. N41°35.348'xW85°28.937'
Residence: 1910, Clearspring, Lagrange Co., IN[5281]

Notes for Menno J. S. Yoder:
The Descendants of John J. Christner, privately published February 1961, p., 23.

Menno was 1st married to Emma D. Christner. Emma died April 15, 1928 and then he married Susie J. Christner Bontrager.

More About Menno J. S. Yoder:
Alt. Birth: 03 Jul 1892[5282]
Burial: Miller Cem, Lagrange Co, IN. N41°35.361'xW85°28.925' row 7 Plot 56
Religion: Amish (Deacon)[5283,5284]

Children of Emma Christner and Menno Yoder are:

+	2821	i.	Leo M.[9] Yoder, born 13 Oct 1911 in Topeka, Lagrange Co., IN; died 19 Apr 1997 in at his home Lagrange Co, IN N41°37.750' by W85°28.375'.
+	2822	ii.	Susanna M. Yoder, born 18 Feb 1913 in Lagrange, Lagrange Co., IN.
+	2823	iii.	Edna M. Yoder, born 06 Aug 1914 in Lagrange, Lagrange Co., IN; died 30 Aug 1982 in Lagrange Co., IN.
+	2824	iv.	John M. Yoder, born 21 Jun 1917 in Lagrange, Lagrange Co., IN; died 12 Dec 1993 in Lagrange Co., IN.
+	2825	v.	Levi M. Yoder, born 06 Apr 1920 in Topeka, Lagrange Co., IN.
+	2826	vi.	Cornelius M. Yoder, born 29 Dec 1922 in Topeka, Lagrange Co., IN; died 03 Oct 2000 in Topeka, Lagrange Co, IN.
	2827	vii.	Daniel M. Yoder[5285], born 20 Apr 1925 in Topeka, Lagrange Co., IN; died 28 Sep 1997 in Shipshewana, Elkhart Co., IN. He married Lydia Mae Hochstetler 02 Mar 1952 in Lagrange Co., IN[5285]; born 19 Sep 1931 in Howard Co., IN[5285]; died in IN[5285].

Notes for Daniel M. Yoder:
The Descendants of John J. Christner, privately published February 1961, pp. 23, 25.

Retired farmer Old Order Amish. Lived at 4185 North & 675 West in LaGrange Co., IN.

More About Daniel M. Yoder:
Burial: East Barren Cemetery, Shipshewana, Lagrange Co., IN
Occupation: Farmer/
Religion: Old Order Amish/
Residence: 01 Apr 1940, Age: 14; Marital Status: Single; Relation to Head of House: Son/Clearspring, Lagrange Co., IN[5285]

Notes for Lydia Mae Hochstetler:
The Descendants of John J. Christner, privately published February 1961, p. 25.

More About Lydia Mae Hochstetler:
Residence: 01 Apr 1940, Age: 8; Marital Status: Single; Relation to Head of House: Daughter/Howard, Howard, Indiana, United States[5285]

1289. Levi D.[8] Christner (David J.[7], John J.[6], Joseph C.[5], Christian J.[4], Johannes John Hans[3], Christian[2], Christen[1])[5286,5287,5288,5289,5290,5290] was born 20 Aug 1897 in Topeka, Lagrange Co., IN[5291,5292,5293,5294,5295,5295], and died 08 Nov 1985 in Elklick Twp., Bedford (now Somerset) Co., PA[5296,5297,5298,5299]. He married **(1) Goldie O'Neil Eash**[5300,5301,5302,5303,5304,5304] 15 Jul 1916 in Lagrange Co., IN[5304,5304]. She was born 12 Dec 1896 in Elkhart Co., IN[5305,5306,5307,5308,5309,5309], and died 08 Jan 1966 in Lagrange Co., IN[5310,5311,5312,5313]. He married **(2) Edna Schlabuagh Miller**[5313] Feb 1967[5313], daughter of David Miller and Elizabeth Christner. She was born 30 Sep 1901 in McMinnville, Yamhill Co., OR[5313,5313], and died 25 Mar 1987 in Elklick Twp., Somerset Co., PA[5313].

Notes for Levi D. Christner:
The Descendants of John J. Christner, privately published February 1961, p. 25.

Levi and Goldie moved to Willington, Delaware from IN Dec 1928 and returned home about 1 year later. They went by train along with all the livestock and the farm implements. He was very affluent in reading and writing high German. He built 11 grandfather clocks. He owned and operated a Farm and sheet metal shop north of Topeka, IN. (N41°34.800 x W85°31.250) for many years. He got too successful in the sheet metal venture so the Bishop's forced him to curtail the sales. They upset him to the point of selling all the equipment to Christian Hochstetler who started Honeyville Metal, Inc. which became a large enterprise. He also had a peppermint distillery on his land. He spent over 20 years of his life working on the Christner genealogy. If it were not for his small scraps of paper with notes, the work that has been accomplished would of been nearly impossible. He had so many little tid bits of info that it took several years just to connect them all, but it was well worth the time.

He bought a farm along the west side of Messick Lake and Mud Lake in Lagrange Co., IN when he retired. His hobbies were fishing and reading. He moved to Elklick Twp., Somerset Co., PA with his second wife Edna Christner Schlabaugh in 1977. The farm on Messick lake was the entire west side from river to dam. He was a very organized man and planned more to do in a day than most men could accomplish, but he could get it done. He had a very bright personality and an extra ordinary drive for knowledge. He had a buggy horse "NELLIE" that he kept for many many years and Nellie knew which Sunday was church Sunday and would have herself backed into the buggy when he got to the barn. Hans Christner wife Frany Johns brought the 1548 Froschauer Bible with her. The bible is at Goshen College Goshen, Indiana. The Bible was given to the College by Levi D. Christner (born 8/20/1897) this is Frany's 3rd. great grandson. Levi got the Bible at an auction in Lagrange Co. Indiana about 1960 to 1965. Monroe Yoder ask him if he (Levi) wanted to buy a bible for $20.00 as it has Christner family infomation in it. Levi said NO as he knew he knew Monroe didn't pay that much for it and he (Levi) didn't want him to make a profit on selling this bible. Later he (Monroe Yoder) came to him and ask him (Levi) if he can pay him just what he paid for it and Levi agreed to pay him the $17.00. This was the 1548 Froschauer Bible.

When Jonathon Miller died Levi bought his suit.

Obituary: Levi D. CHRISTNER, 1984, Salisbury, Somerset County, PA - The Republic, November 22, 1984

Levi D. Christner, 87, of Salisbury RD 1, died November 8, 1984 at Meyersdale Community Hospital.

He was born August 20, 1897, at Lagrange, IN. He was the son of David and Elizabeth (Burlingcourt) Christner. Besides his parents, he was preceded in death by his first wife, Goldie O'Neal.

He is survived by his wife Edna (Miller) Christner and sons: Menno of Wawaka, IN David, of Lagrange, Indiana; Christian, of Shipshewana, IN Amos of Huntsville, AL; Samuel of Nappanee, Indiana; John of Stockton, California; Levi, of Goshen, IN; Arthur, of Topeko, IN, Also daughters: Mrs. Lizzie Ann Miller of Goshen, IN; Mrs. Sue Christner of Millersburg, IN; Mrs. Mary Ann Fereva, of Manteca, CA; Mrs. Edith Lyons of Lagrange,

IN. Stepsons: Joseph Slabaugh, Grantsville RD 1, Maryland; Ruffs Slabaugh, Trenton, KY.

Stepdaughters: Mrs. Anna Zook, Meyersdale RD 1; Mrs. Lizzie. Yoder, Salisbury RD 1: Mrs. Ida Bender, Catlett, VA; also 37 grandchildren, 51 great-grandchildren and one great-great grandson.

He was a member of the Old Order Amish Church of Summit Mills. Services were held November 9, at the Summit Mills Amish Church with the Rev. Noah J. Yoder officiating and on November 11, at Lagrange, IN. Interment, Clear Spring Amish Cemetery, Lagrange Co., IN.

More About Levi D. Christner:
Burial: Miller Cem, Lagrange Co, IN. N41°35.339'xW85°28.937'Row 12 Plot 19--21
Cause of Death: Stroke
Christened: Amish
Residence: 1910, Clearspring, Lagrange Co., IN[5313,5314,5315]

Notes for Goldie O'Neil Eash:
The Descendants of John J. Christner, privately published February 1961, p., 25.

Goldie was the birth daughter of Peter O'Neil and Florence Bowen Pennington. Florence was born Jan 26 1874 in Lagrange Co., IN and died March 12, 1924. Peter deserted his family in east Goshen, Indiana when Goldie was very young and she was taken to Mishawaka IN. to an orphanage. The Northern Indiana Orphans Home up on a hill across from the Saint Joe river on one of the first national highways the old Lincoln highway .

In 2003 the name of the home was Family & Children's Center at 1411 Lincoln Way West Mishawaka IN. 46544 ----- N41°39.47' by W86°11.85'

She was placed at the orphanage July 22, 1902. On Nov 1902 Benjamin Troyer from South Bend, IN. They returned her on April 16, 1903. On March 24, 1904 She was adopted by Samuel S. Eash and Susan J.(Miller) Eash from Topeka, IN. The Samuel S. Eash home farm was located at _____ ¼ west of State Road 5, on Cr 500S in Lagrange Co., IN Southeast of Honeyville. It was ½ west of where Levi Christner (her husband) grew up.

To learn more about this Eash Family read DESCENDANTS OF SAMUEL S. EASH & SUSAN J. MILLER COMPILED BY Ora E. Eash 627 W. 6th St. McMinnville,OR. 97128. She was about 7 years old at this time. She was raised Amish. She did in later life make a connection with her natural Mother who lived in east Goshen, IN and brothers Charles and Arthur O'Neil from South Bend, IN.

Charles O'Neil was an electrician and died from electrocution. Arthur O'Neil Managed Channel 22 CBS Television Broadcasting Station in South Bend, IN.

Burial at Miller Cemetery, LaGrange Co., IN. N41°35.339'xW85°28.937' Row 7 Plot 38, Short row north of the south entrance, between rows 7 & 8. This cemetery is located at County Roads 300S and 300W -- 3 miles south & 3 miles west of the Lagrange County Court House.

Birth: Dec. 12, 1896
Death: Jan. 8, 1966

Wife of LD

Children: Goldie L. Christner (1933 - 1950)

Burial: Miller Amish Cemetery, Lagrange, Lagrange Co., IN
Plot: Row 12, lot 19

More About Goldie O'Neil Eash:
Adoption: 1910, Adopted by Samuel & Susanna Eash[5316]
Burial: Miller Cem, Lagrange Co, IN. N41°35.339'xW85°28.937'row 12 plot 19-21

Residence: 1930, Clearspring, Lagrange Co., IN[5317,5318]

Notes for Edna Schlabuagh Miller:
Edna was married to Amos Schlabaugh. She was the daughter of David Y. Miller and Elizabeth Christner Miller.
Edna's grandfather was Joseph Christner and her Great Grandfather was John B. Christner.

Joseph's nickname was Just Christner.

OBIT: Edna (MILLER) CHRISTNER, 1987 of interest in Somerset Coo., PA - The Republic, April 2, 1987

EDNA CHRISTNER

Edna Christner, 85, died March 26, 1987 at her home in Elk Lick Township. She was born Sept. 30, 1901 at McMinnville, Oregon a daughter of the late David Y. and Elizabeth (Christner) Miller. Also preceded in death by husbands Amos Slabaugh and Levi Christner.

She is survived by sons, Rufus Slabaugh of Guthrie, KY; Joseph Slabaugh of Grantsville, MD; daughters Mrs. Ida (Joseph) Beer of
Cattlet, VA; Mrs. Annie (Amos) Zook of Meyersdale; Mrs. Elizabeth (Wilmer) Yoder of Salisbury. She was the sister of Jacob Miller of Stuarts Draft, VA; Enos Miller of Mifflinburg; Mrs. Susannah Yoder of Meyersdale. Also survived by 32 grandchildren, 54 great-grandchildren and ten stepchildren.

She was a member of the Old Order Amish Church, of Summit Mills. Services were held Friday at 10 a.m. at the Old Order Amish Church with Noah J. Yoder officiating. Interment, Summit Mills Amish Cemetery.

More About Edna Schlabuagh Miller:
Residence: 1930, District 4, Kent, Delaware[5319]

Children of Levi Christner and Goldie Eash are:

+ 2828   i.   Menno L.[9] Christner, born 15 Feb 1917 in Topeka, Lagrange Co., IN; died 11 Feb 1995 in Moulton, Lawrence Co., AL.
+ 2829   ii.   Lizzie Ann Christner, born 17 Jul 1918 in Topeka, Lagrange Co., IN; died 22 Dec 1999 in Goshen, Elkhart Co., IN.
+ 2830   iii. Susanna L. Christner, born 05 Aug 1919 in Topeka, Lagrange Co., IN; died 12 Nov 2010 in Topeka, Lagrange Co., IN.
+ 2831   iv.   David L. Christner, born 29 Mar 1921 in Lagrange Co., IN; died 10 Nov 2010 in Wolcottville, Lagrange Co., IN.
+ 2832   v.   Christian L. Christner, born 10 Jun 1922 in Topeka, Lagrange Co., IN; died 01 Sep 1994 in Shipshewana, Lagrange Co., IN.
+ 2833   vi.   Emma L. Christner, born 06 Dec 1923 in Topeka, Lagrange Co., IN; died 20 Oct 1955 in Dhamtari, Chhattisgarh, India.
  2834   vii. Amos R. Christner[5320], born 10 Mar 1925 in Lagrange Co., IN[5320]; died 05 Dec 1985 in Huntsville, Madison Co., AL[5321,5322]. He married Dovie Lorraine Hughes[5323] 11 Nov 1950 in Huntsville, Madison Co., AL[5323]; born 17 Apr 1911[5323]; died 13 Aug 1992 in Huntsville, Madison Co., AL.

Notes for Amos R. Christner:
The Descendants of John J. Christner, privately published February 1961, p. 26.

Amos has the middle initial of L. but during his military service he went by the name of Rocky, this is why you find him listed as Amos R. He later worked for the government at the Redstone Arsenal in Huntsville, AL. He was a missile inspector for the missile plant. He worked with the first Missile's to put a satellite into space, the first man into space, the first man on the moon, the first space shuttle. He had collected a lot of space memorabilia that was signed by many different astronauts. Amos is buried in Huntsville Ala. Many of the family members traveled to the funeral in a commercial bus. The sight of this bus in the funeral precessional was a sight to see. Amos was a member of the Werhner VonBraun rocket development team. He died of cancer. He retired from NASA.

SS# 309-20-6672 Iss.IN .

More About Amos R. Christner:
Military: 20 May 1943, Toledo, OH[5323]
Residence: 1930, Clearspring, Lagrange Co., IN[5324]
Social Security Number: 309-20-6672[5325]
SSN issued: IN[5325]

Notes for Dovie Lorraine Hughes:
The Descendants of John J. Christner, privately published February 1961, p., 26.

Dovie is the daughter of Thea E. Isebell Huges or Hughes and Lula Pidmore. Amos and Dovie never had any children. When Amos died Dovie cut the ties with the Christner Family that day.

+   2835   viii.   Mary Ann Christner, born 31 Dec 1926 in Topeka, Lagrange Co., IN.
    2836   ix.   Samuel L. Christner, born 11 Mar 1928 in Topeka, Lagrange Co., IN. He married (1) Pauline "Polly" Schrock 18 Jan 1953 in Reno, NV; born 07 Nov 1930 in Holmes Co., OH. He married (2) Dorothy Mae Holderman 20 Jan 1979 in Nappanee, Elkhart Co., IN; born 17 Apr 1908 in Nappanee, Elkhart Co., IN; died 22 Jul 1994 in Nappanee, Elkhart Co., IN.

Notes for Samuel L. Christner:
The Descendants of John J. Christner, privately published February 1961, p. 26.

Sam served in the military and saw a lot of action. He is one of the children of Levi that has a grandfather clock. His father, Levi Made the clock. Sam enlisted on June 11, 1952,discharged Mar 24 1954. He made corporal on July 12, 1953. Honors earned Korean Service Ribbon 2 bronze service stars United Nations Service Medal National defense service medal merit unit citation combat medical badge. He drove an Ambulance in the Korean War. He told me about having a flat tire (shot out) & getting out to put a good tire on gut the enemy shot at the dirt close to him so he let go of the tire & ran for cover and the tire rolled down the hill. After a while he went after the tire all the way down the hill & rolled it back up the hill. When he got within a few feet of the Ambulance the enemy shot the dirt by him again so he left go of the tire and dove for cover and the tire rolled down the hill again. After the third trip the enemy let him have his tire. Even in War boys will be boys. His uncle (Cornelias Neal Christner) taught him how to shoe a horse. He later divorced Pauline.
Sam served in the military and saw a lot of action. He is one of the children of Levi that has a grandfather clock. His father, Levi Made the clock. Sam enlisted on June 11 1952,discharged Mar 24 1954. He made corporal on July 12 1953 Honors earned Korean Service Ribbon 2 bronze service stars United Nations Service Medal National defence service medal merit unit citation combat medical badge. He drove an Ambulance in the Korean War. He told me about having a flat tire (shot out) & getting out to put a good tire on gut the enemy shot at the dirt close to him so he let go of the tire & ran for cover and the tire rolled down the hill. After a while he went after the tire all the way down the hill & rolled it back up the hill. When he got within a few feet of the Ambulance the enemy shot the dirt by him again so he left go of the tire and dove for cover and the tire rolled down the hill again. After the third trip the enemy let him have his tire. Even in War boys will be boys. His uncle (Cornelias Neal Christner) taught him how to shoe a horse.

Notes for Pauline "Polly" Schrock:
Polly was the daughter of Noah J. Schrock and Emma Miller
Sam and Polly never had any children.

Polly's father Noah J. Schrock from R.D.2 Dundee Ohio was the author of many genology books.

DECENDANTS OF PETER C SCHROCK AND MAGDALENA J. JOHNS
Polly is #12 in this book. Magdalena is the grandaughter of Joseph J. Johns.
Joseph is the brother of Frany Johns who married John Hans Christner.
Polly was a lot of fun to be around as she enjoyed life and made every one around her have a good time.

Notes for Dorothy Mae Holderman:
They are buried at Union Center Cemetery, Nappanee, IN. Sam and Dorothy never had any children.

+   2837   x.   John Levi Christner, born 09 Dec 1929 in Topeka, Lagrange Co., IN; died 31 May 1990 in Stockton, San Joaquin Co., CA.
+   2838   xi.   Levi Lee Christner, born 12 Sep 1931 in Topeka, Lagrange Co., IN; died 22 Jul 2001 in Goshen, Elkhart Co., IN.

2839   xii.   Goldie L. Christner[5326,5326], born 19 Jun 1933 in Topeka, Lagrange Co., IN[5326,5326]; died 29 May 1950 in heart disease, probably congenital[5326,5327].

Notes for Goldie L. Christner:
Christner, Goldie L. daughter of Levi and Goldie (O'Neil) Christner, was born northeast of Topeka, Ind., June 19, 1933; died May 29, 1950; aged 16 y. 11 m. 10 d. She had been suffering from heart trouble for five years; death followed six days after a severe attack. She was received in to the Old Order Amish Church by baptism May 25, 1950. Surviving are her parents, 8 brothers and 5 sisters (Menno, Rawleigh, IN; Lizzie Ann, Milford, IN; David, Bellevue, Ohio; Suzanna, Millersburg, IN; Christian, Wolcottville, IN; Emma, Topeka, IN; Amos, Huntsville, Ala.; Mary, Stockton, CA; John, Placerville, CA; Samuel, Levi, Edith, and Arthur, at home), 4 nieces, 9 nephews, 7 uncles, 2 aunts, and a large number of other relatives and friends. Funeral services were held at the home May 31 by David Nissley and John S. Miller. Her body was laid to rest in the Miller Cemetery. Burial at Miller Cemetery, LaGrange Co, IN. N41°35.339'xW85°28.937' Row 7 Plot 38, Short row north of the south entrance, between rows 7 & 8. This cemetery is located at County Roads 300S and 300W -- 3 miles south & 3 miles west of the Lagrange Co. Court House.

Birth: Jun 19, 1933
Death: May 29, 1950

Daughter of Levi D. & Goldie

Parents: Goldie Christner (1896 - 1966)

Burial: Miller Amish Cemetery, Lagrange, Lagrange Co., IN
Plot: Row 12, lot 20

More About Goldie L. Christner:
Baptism: 25 May 1950, Old Order Amish Church[5328]
Burial: Miller Cem, Lagrange Co, IN. N41°35.339'xW85°28.937' row 12 Plot 19-21

+   2840   xiii.   Edith L. Christner, born 23 Jun 1935 in Topeka, Lagrange Co., IN; died 18 Mar 1987 in Howe, Lagrange Co., IN.

+   2841   xiv.   Arthur L. Christner, born 13 Jun 1939 in Topeka, Lagrange Co., IN; died 07 Oct 2000 in Topeka, Lagrange Co., IN.

1290. Katherine[8] Christner (John J.[7], John J.[6], Joseph C.[5], Christian J.[4], Johannes John Hans[3], Christian[2], Christen[1]) was born 17 Mar 1879 in Millersburg, Elkhart Co., IN, and died 01 Oct 1962 in Row 2 plot 7. She married **John D. "Buck Johnny" Miller** 22 Feb 1906 in By Eli Bontrager, son of Freeman Miller and Mary Miller. He was born 10 Jul 1885 in Elkhart Co., IN, and died 01 Jun 1960 in Row 2 plot 6.

Notes for Katherine Christner:
The Descendants of John J. Christner, privately published February 1961, p. 26.

More About Katherine Christner:
Burial: Christner Cemetery, Honeyville, Lagrange Co., IN

Notes for John D. "Buck Johnny" Miller:
The Descendants of John J. Christner, privately published February 1961, p. 26.

Buck Johnny had a feed grinding business on his farm. His wife's (Katherine Christner) father gave her the farm at N41°33.900 x W85°36.400 Honeyville, Indiana. He was a jovial man with a big belly. His horse and buggy always leaned to the right side because of his big belly.

John was the son of David and Fannie Miller. O. O. Amish.

More About John D. "Buck Johnny" Miller:
Burial: Christner Cemetery, Honeyville, Lagrange Co., IN
Nickname: Buck

Religion: Old Order Amish/

Child of Katherine Christner and John Miller is:

+ 2842   i.   Adopted Mary F.[9] Yoder, born 26 Sep 1914 in Millersburg, Elkhart Co., IN; died 02 May 2005 in at 4:45 PM   Row 2 plot 4.

1293. Lydia M.[8] Christner (John J.[7], John J.[6], Joseph C.[5], Christian J.[4], Johannes John Hans[3], Christian[2], Christen[1])[5329] was born 04 Nov 1888 in Honeyville, Lagrange Co., IN, and died 15 Jan 1990 in Honeyville, Lagrange Co., IN. She married **David R. Bontrager**[5329] 21 Jan 1909 in IN[5330]. He was born 26 Jun 1888 in Middlebury, Lagrange Co., IN, and died 19 Mar 1967 in Millersburg, Elkhart Co., IN[5330].

Notes for Lydia M. Christner:
The Descendants of John J. Christner, privately published February 1961, pp. 26, 27.

Lydia and her sisters Annie and Mary wrote the first Christner history book printed in 1961. They lived in Honeyville, IN.

Buried in the Christner Cemetery, Honeyville, LaGrange Co, IN row 7 plot 15.

Birth: Nov. 4, 1888
Death: Jan. 15, 1990

Note: Lydia M. Christner wife of D.R. Bontrager Ag 101 YR 2 MO 11 DAYS

Burial: Christner Cemetery, Honeyville, Lagrange Co., IN

More About Lydia M. Christner:
Burial: N 41°34.500-W 85°35.900/Christner Cemetery, Honeyville, Lagrange Co., IN

Notes for David R. Bontrager:
The Descendants of John J. Christner, privately published February 1961, p. 27.

His parents Reuben Bontrager and Elizabeth Yoder Bontrager. David was a farmer. David and his brother Levi R. married sisters. He was Old Order Amish and a farmer.

Buried in the Christner Cemetery, Honeyville, LaGrange Co, IN row 7 plot 15

More About David R. Bontrager:
Burial: Christner Cemetery, Honeyville, Lagrange Co., IN
Christened: Amish

Children of Lydia Christner and David Bontrager are:

+ 2843   i.   Amanda Mae[9] Bontrager, born 25 Nov 1909 in Millersburg, Elkhart Co., IN; died 05 Mar 1936 in Elkhart, Elkhart Co., IN.
+ 2844   ii.   Levi D. Bontrager, born 01 Jan 1914 in Millersburg, Elkhart Co., IN; died 20 Nov 2004 in Honeyville, Lagrange Co., IN.
+ 2845   iii.   Amos D. Bontrager, born 04 Jul 1916 in Millersburg, Elkhart Co., IN; died 04 Oct 2003 in Millersburg, Elkhart Co., IN.
+ 2846   iv.   Elizabeth D. Bontrager, born 30 Nov 1918 in Honeyville, Lagrange Co., IN; died 17 Jul 2006 in Lagrange Co., IN/.
+ 2847   v.   Katie Mae Bontrager, born 18 Jun 1920 in Kenton, OH.
+ 2848   vi.   Mary Bontrager, born 13 Jun 1922 in Ligonier, Bureau Co., IN; died 04 May 2011 in Ligonier, Noble Co., IN.

1295. Mary M.[8] Christner (John J.[7], John J.[6], Joseph C.[5], Christian J.[4], Johannes John Hans[3], Christian[2], Christen[1])[5331] was born 15 Aug 1901 in Lagrange Co., IN, and died 28 Dec 1999 in Honeyville, Lagrange Co., IN[5331]. She married **Manelius C. Hochstetler**[5331] 04 Dec 1919 in Lagrange Co., IN[5331]. He was born 21 Jan

1899 in Lagrange Co., IN[5331], and died 24 Jul 1995 in Honeyville, Lagrange Co., IN[5331].

Notes for Mary M. Christner:
The Descendants of John J. Christner, privately published February 1961, p. 29.

Lydia and her sisters Annie and Mary wrote the first Christner history book printed in 1961. They lived in Honeyville IN. Manas and Mary were the oldest living married Amish couple in the United States.

A quote from the H/H/H/Family Newsletter states, They moved to Mary's home farm just northwest of the Historic Honeyville store (owned by her cousin's Joe and Abe Christner) in Lagrange Co. Indiana in 1919 when they got married, and they have lived there ever since. The young couple then bought the farm from Mary's parents in 1927. In 1958 they moved into the adjoining "Daudy Haus"when they turned the farm over to a son-in-law who has also now retired, and a grandson continues the farming. The Hochstetlers have raised five children. In there retirment years Manas developed a saw filing business, while Mary pieced "dozens" of quilts. Her quilts and wall hangings are still in demand and have been distributed widely. A 1937 70"x87" Pot of Flowers quilt made by Mary is part of the David Pottinger collection of Indiana Amish Quilts which has been displayed from coast to coast, from the Smithsonian in Washington, DC to Switzerland!

More About Mary M. Christner:
Burial: Row 2 Plot11/Christner Cemetery, Honeyville, Lagrange Co., IN
Religion: Old Order Amish/
Residence: 1910, Eden, Lagrange Co., IN[5331]

Notes for Manelius C. Hochstetler:
The Descendants of John J. Christner, privately published February 1961, p. 29.

Manas is the son of Christian D. and Katie M. (Bontrager) Hochstetler. Manas lived in Honeyville, Lagrange Co., IN was a farmer and Old Order Amish.

Manas had two brothers still living at the time of his death, Harry Lived at Wolcottville and Joni lived at Middlebury, 5 sisters and 5 brothers proceded him in death. Burial in Christner Cemetery at Honeyville, IN. His last address was 9775 West 400 South LaGrange IN. Manas and Mary were the oldest living married Amish couple in the United States. Manas is the son of Christian D. and Katie M. (Bontrager) Hochstetler.

More About Manelius C. Hochstetler:
Burial: Christner Cemetery, Honeyville, Lagrange Co., IN
Occupation: Farmer/
Religion: Old Order Amish/
Residence: 1910, Clearspring, Lagrange Co., IN[5331]

Children of Mary Christner and Manelius Hochstetler are:
+   2849   i.   Ada[9] Hochstetler, born 25 Feb 1922 in Topeka, Lagrange Co., IN; died 13 Feb 1990.
+   2850   ii.   Katie M. Hochstetler, born 25 Feb 1922 in Topeka, Lagrange Co., IN; died 11 Aug 2002 in Topeka, Lagrange Co., IN   N 41° 35.451' x W 85° 31'.
+   2851   iii. Lydia Mae Hochstetler, born 24 Apr 1929 in Lagrange Co., IN.
+   2852   iv.   Edna Hochstetler, born 09 Sep 1932 in Millersburg, IN.
      2853   v.   Rosa Hochstetler, born 29 Jul 1940. She married William A. Hochstetler 08 Oct 1964; born 24 Feb 1946.

                      Notes for Rosa Hochstetler:
                      William is a farmer and factory employee.

1299. Nathan[8] Christner (Abraham J.[7], John J.[6], Joseph C.[5], Christian J.[4], Johannes John Hans[3], Christian[2], Christen[1])[5332,5333] was born 26 Nov 1887 in Millersburg, Elkhart Co., IN, and died 05 Nov 1964 in Aurora, NE[5333]. He married **Sarah Schrock**[5333] 22 Jul 1909[5334,5335]. She was born 04 May 1892 in Topeka, Lagrange Co., IN[5335,5336], and died 02 Jun 1972 in Goshen, Elkhart Co., IN[5337].

Notes for Nathan Christner:
The Descendants of John J. Christner, privately published February 1961, p. 30.

Nathan and Sarah were members North Goshen Mennonite Church.

OBITUARY - GOSPEL HERALD - Volume LVII, Number 48 - December 15, 1964 - pp 1078, 1079

Christner, Nathan, son of Abraham and Mattie (Miller) Christner, was born near Topeka, Ind., Nov. 26, 1887; died at Goshen, Elkhart Co., INd., Nov. 5, 1964; aged 76 y. 11 m. 10 d. On July 22, 1909, he was married to Sarah Schrock, who survives. On son lost his life in a plane crash about 10 years ago. Surviving are 5 children (Mrs. Delilah Sark, Salina-Mrs. Carl Dintaman, Rufus, Ernest, and Truman), 21 grandchildren, 10 great-grandchildren, 2 brothers (Dan and John), and 4 sisters (Mattie-Mrs. Tobias Yoder, Elizabeth, Mary-Mrs. Noah Glick, and Mrs. Saloma Erb). He was a member of the North Goshen Church, where funeral services were held Nov. 7, in charge of Russell Krabill; burial in Violett Cemetery.

Nathan and Sarah were members North Goshen Mennonite Church. He was a farmer.

Nathen's roaming home
David J. Christner Farm and house at Raymond Eash (N41°34.026'xW85°36.335') old home. was first at Ezra Yoder's N41°34.444 x W85°36.000 till they build the big house. Then moved the little old house north of our place between the mint still N41°34.320'xW85°36.502' and Ray Miller's building. Joe (Preacher) Yoder lived there. Uncle John owned the land but sold the house to Uncle Abe for his son Nathan Christner. The small barn (built 1880) at Ezra Yoder's was Grandpa David J. Christner's barn before he got the big barn built in 1908. In 1908 moved to N41°34.727'x W85°31.325' Clearspring Township, Lagrange Co., Indiana. 1909 the coal fired steam dredge put the ditch in on Arthur Christner's Property which he got from his father Levi and Levi got from his father David J. this ditch is at N41°34.969'xW85°31.325'. Grandpa David J. gave $50 to Noah.

More About Nathan Christner:
Burial: Violet Cemetery, Goshen, Elkhart Co., IN
Cause of death (Facts Pg): Train/Car accident
Residence: Elkhart Co., IN[5338]

Notes for Sarah Schrock:
The Descendants of John J. Christner, privately published February 1961, p. 30.

Sarah is the daughter of John Schrock and Delilah Werich Schrock.

Obit no date says Sarah was a patient since May 18 (1972) in Goshen General Hospital.

More About Sarah Schrock:
Burial: Jun 1972, Violet Cemetery, Goshen, Elkhart Co., IN
Social Security Number: 315-22-9464/[5339,5340]
SSN issued: IN[5340,5341]

Children of Nathan Christner and Sarah Schrock are:

+ 2854   i.   Harley[9] Christner, born 06 Nov 1910 in Near Topeka, IN; died 03 Jul 1954.
+ 2855   ii.   Delilah Mae Christner, born 25 Jul 1912 in Honeyville, Lagrange Co., IN; died 27 Apr 2001 in Goshen, Elkhart Co., IN.
+ 2856   iii.   Salina Christner, born 16 Aug 1914 in Lagrange Co., IN; died 20 Oct 1973 in Lagrange Co., IN.
+ 2857   iv.   Rufus Christner, born 25 Sep 1916 in Topeka, Lagrange Co., IN; died 07 Jun 1993 in Goshen, Elkhart Co., IN.
+ 2858   v.   Ernest Christner, born 19 Jul 1919; died 09 Sep 2009 in Saline, Washtenaw Co., MI.
+ 2859   vi.   Truman Christner, born 29 Jul 1921 in Honeyville, Lagrange Co., IN; died 17 Sep 1977 in Iowa City, Johnson Co., IA.

1300. Daniel A.[8] Christner (Abraham J.[7], John J.[6], Joseph C.[5], Christian J.[4], Johannes John Hans[3], Christian[2], Christen[1])[5342,5343,5344,5345] was born 04 Aug 1889 in Lagrange Co., IN[5346,5347], and died 29 Sep 1976 in Shipshewana, Lagrange Co., IN[5347,5348]. He married **(1) Amelia Schrock**[5348] 18 Feb 1909[5349]. She was born 15 Sep 1888 in Newbury, Lagrange Co., IN[5350], and died 19 Oct 1918 in Lagrange Co., IN[5350]. He married **(2) Mary Ann Hershberger** 09 Oct 1919. She was born 16 Jul 1893 in Lagrange Co., IN, and died 23 Dec 1965 in Lagrange Co., IN.

Notes for Daniel A. Christner:
The Descendants of John J. Christner, privately published February 1961, pp. 30, 31.

Daniel's 2nd Wife was Mary ann Hershberger Born July 16, 1893. Daughter of Emanuel Hersbergerand Amanda Hochstetler they were married on Oct 9, 1919.

SS# 315-22-8619 Iss.IN Last zip 46565,

Birth: 1889
Death: 1975

Spouse: Amelia Christner (1888 - 1918)

Burial: Yoder Cemetery, Shipshewana, Lagrange Co., IN

More About Daniel A. Christner:
Burial: Yoder Cem. South of Shipshewana IN.
Military Draft: World War I and World War II[5351]
Social Security Number: 315-22-8619[5352]
SSN issued: IN[5352]

Notes for Amelia Schrock:
The Descendants of John J. Christner, privately published February 1961, p. 31.

Birth: 1888
Death: 1918

Spouse: Daniel A. Christner (1889 - 1975)

Burial: Yoder Cemetery, Shipshewana, Lagrange Co., IN

More About Amelia Schrock:
Burial: Yoder Cemetery, South of Shipshewana IN

Notes for Mary Ann Hershberger:
Christner, Mary Ann, daughter of Emanuel and Amanda (Hochstetler) Hershberger, was born in Lagrange Co., Ind., July 16, 1893; died at the Lagrange County Hospital, Dec. 23, 1965; aged 72 y. 5 m. 7 d. She had been ill for five years. On Oct. 2, 1919, she was married to Daniel A. Christner, who survives. Also surviving are 4 sons (Menno, Wayne, Jonas, and Earl), one daughter (Elizabeth Ann), 3 stepchildren (Monroe, Barbara Blough, and Clara), 12 grandchildren, 7 stepgrandchildren, 8 stepgreat-grandchildren, one brother (Edward), one half brother (Emanuel), and one half sister (Sylvia). Two sons preceded her in death. She was a member of the Marion Church, where funeral services were conducted Dec. 27, in charge of Paul Lauver and Aldine Haarer.

More About Mary Ann Hershberger:
Burial: .N41°37.552xW85°35.240/Yoder Cemetery, South of Shipshewana IN

Children of Daniel Christner and Amelia Schrock are:
+   2860   i.   Monroe D.[9] Christner, born 21 Oct 1911 in Newbury, Lagrange Co., IN; died 29 Jan 1986 in Topeka, Lagrange Co., IN.
+   2861   ii. Barbara Ann Christner, born 18 Aug 1913 in Newbury, Lagrange Co., IN; died Feb 1992 in Goshen,

Elkhart Co., IN.

2862   iii.   Clara Christner, born 28 Jul 1916 in Lagrange Co., IN; died 08 Jul 1997 in Lagrange Co., IN.

Notes for Clara Christner:
The Descendants of John J. Christner, privately published February 1961, p. 31.
Clara never married & was a lifetime resident of Topeka, Lagrange Co., IN & Maple Grove Mennonite Church. She retired from Starcraft Boat Company. Her aunt Ida never married and lived with her.

More About Clara Christner:
Burial: Yoder Corner Cemetery/Lagrange Co IN Yoder Cem. South of Shipshewana IN

Children of Daniel Christner and Mary Hershberger are:

+   2863   i.   Menno[9] Christner, born 04 Mar 1920; died in Shore Mennonite Church.
+   2864   ii.   Jonas Christner, born 08 Jul 1921 in Sturgis, St. Joseph Co., MI.
     2865   iii.   Betty Lizzie Ann Christner, born 03 Feb 1923.

Notes for Betty Lizzie Ann Christner:
The Descendants of John J. Christner, privately published February 1961, p. 31.

     2866   iv.   Edward Christner, born 30 Mar 1927 in York, Elkhart Co., IN[5353]; died 30 Mar 1927 in York, Elkhart Co., IN[5353].
     2867   v.   Cleteus Christner, born 09 Feb 1928; died 20 Feb 1928.
+   2868   vi.   Earl Christner, born 22 Apr 1930; died 15 May 2008 in Vicksburg, Kalamazoo Co., MI.
+   2869   vii.   Wayne Christner, born 30 Dec 1935.

1301. Mattie A.[8] Christner (Abraham J.[7], John J.[6], Joseph C.[5], Christian J.[4], Johannes John Hans[3], Christian[2], Christen[1]) was born 19 Sep 1891 in Honeyville, Lagrange Co., IN, and died 20 Oct 1975 in Goshen, Elkhart Co., IN[5354]. She married **Tobias E. Yoder** 14 Dec 1916 in Honeyville, Lagrange Co., IN. He was born 08 Dec 1894 in Newton Co., IN, and died 31 Mar 1968 in Elkhart Co., IN Nursing Home row 5 plot 26.

Notes for Mattie A. Christner:
The Descendants of John J. Christner, privately published February 1961, pp. 30, 32.

Mattie married Tobias E. Yoder December 14 1916.

Birth: 1891
Death: 1975

Children: Jemima M Yoder Miller (1912 - 1999)

Burial: Christner Cemetery, Honeyville, Lagrange Co., IN
Find A Grave Memorial# 24708637

More About Mattie A. Christner:
Burial: Christner Cemetery, Honeyville, Lagrange Co., IN
Christened: O.O.Amish
Residence: 1930, Eden, Lagrange Co., IN[5354]

Notes for Tobias E. Yoder:
The Descendants of John J. Christner, privately published February 1961, p. 32.

Tobias is the son of Enos and Sarah Yoder. Burial at Christner Cemetery in Honeyville, IN. He was Old Order Amish. This man had the nickname (POOR TOBY) however he left this earth RICH in friends and few enemys if any. Toby was a kind and gentle man who had time to hear your problems and comfort your soul.

Birth: 1894
Death: 1968

Children: Jemima M Yoder Miller (1912 - 1999)

Burial: Christner Cemetery, Honeyville, Lagrange Co., IN
row 5 plot 26
Find A Grave Memorial# 24708640

More About Tobias E. Yoder:
Burial: Christner Cemetery, Honeyville, Lagrange Co., IN
Christened: O.O.Amish

Children of Mattie Christner and Tobias Yoder are:

+   2870   i.   Jemima Mae[9] Yoder, born 10 Sep 1912 in Honeyville, Lagrange Co., IN; died 14 Jul 1999 in 10877 C.R. 46 Millersburg, Elkhart Co., IN.

     2871   ii.   Abraham T. Yoder, born 08 Apr 1919 in Wolcottville, Lagrange Co., IN; died 26 Feb 1920 in Row5 plot 22.

       Notes for Abraham T. Yoder:
       The Descendants of John J. Christner, privately published February 1961, p. 32.

       More About Abraham T. Yoder:
       Burial: Christner Cemetery, Honeyville, Lagrange Co., IN

     2872   iii.   Ina Mae Yoder, born 28 Feb 1921 in Wolcottville, Lagrange Co., IN; died 27 Aug 1921.

       Notes for Ina Mae Yoder:
       The Descendants of John J. Christner, privately published February 1961, p. 32.

       Buried in row 4 plot 20.

       More About Ina Mae Yoder:
       Burial: Christner Cemetery, Honeyville, Lagrange Co., IN

+   2873   iv.   Alvin Jay Yoder, born 14 Jul 1922 in Wolcottville, Lagrange Co., IN; died 31 Aug 1999 in Goshen, Elkhart Co., IN.
+   2874   v.   Mary Jane Yoder, born 08 Aug 1924 in Honeyville, Indiana N41°34.0575byW85°36.9472; died 09 Jan 2006 in Greencroft, Goshen, IN.
+   2875   vi.   Mable Marie Yoder, born 18 Dec 1927.
     2876   vii.   Edith Yoder, born 14 Jun 1929; died 14 Jun 1929 in Still born   Row 3 Plot 6.

       Notes for Edith Yoder:
       The Descendants of John J. Christner, privately published February 1961, p. 32.

       More About Edith Yoder:
       Burial: Christner Cemetery, Honeyville, Lagrange Co., IN

+   2877   viii.   Edna Ellen Yoder, born 14 Mar 1931; died 15 Nov 1975.

1302. John A.[8] Christner (Abraham J.[7], John J.[6], Joseph C.[5], Christian J.[4], Johannes John Hans[3], Christian[2], Christen[1]) was born 16 Jan 1895 in Millersburg, Elkhart Co., IN[5355], and died 02 Apr 1965 in IN[5356,5357]. He married **Martha Glick**[5358] 17 Apr 1923[5358]. She was born 29 Jul 1903 in Lagrange Co., IN, and died 04 Jan 1983 in Goshen, Elkhart Co., IN.

Notes for John A. Christner:
The Descendants of John J. Christner, privately published February 1961, pp. 30, 33.

John worked on the railroad as a section hand at Millersburg, IN. He was also a farmer for many years. SS# 317-18-1107 Iss IN.

Birth: Jan. 16, 1895

Death: Apr. 2, 1965

Inscription: Son of A & M Christner. 70 Yrs 3 Mos 17 Days

Burial: Christner Cemetery, Honeyville, Lagrange Co., IN

More About John A. Christner:
Burial: N 41°34.500-W 85°35.900/Christner Cemetery, Honeyville, Lagrange Co., IN
Residence: Elkhart Co., IN[5359]
Social Security Number: 317-18-1107/[5360]
SSN issued: IN[5360]

Notes for Martha Glick:
The Descendants of John J. Christner, privately published February 1961, p. 33.

More About Martha Glick:
Burial: Christner Cemetery, Honeyville, Lagrange Co., IN
Cause of Death: Cancer
Religion: Fairhaven Amish-Mennonite Church/

Children of John Christner and Martha Glick are:
+   2878   i.   Raymond[9] Christner, born 13 Jun 1924 in Lagrange Co., IN.
     2879   ii. Freeman Christner, born 25 Oct 1925 in Lagrange Co., IN; died 02 Jan 1926.

                    Notes for Freeman Christner:
                    The Descendants of John J. Christner, privately published February 1961, p. 33.

     2880   iii. Mary Ellen Christner, born 08 Mar 1927 in Lagrange Co., IN; died 27 Oct 1937.

                    Notes for Mary Ellen Christner:
                    The Descendants of John J. Christner, privately published February 1961, p. 33.

                    Birth: Mar. 8, 1927
                    Death: Oct. 27, 1937

                    Inscription: Dau of John A & M Christner

                    Burial: Christner Cemetery, Honeyville, Lagrange Co., IN

                    More About Mary Ellen Christner:
                    Burial: Christner Cemetery, Honeyville, Lagrange Co., IN

+   2881   iv. Noah J. Christner, born 06 Mar 1928 in Lagrange Co., IN; died 31 Aug 2010 in Spokane, Spokane Co.,
                    WA.
+   2882   v.   Clara Christner, born 19 Aug 1931 in Lagrange Co., IN.
+   2883   vi. Lizzie Mae Christner, born 08 Feb 1936 in Lagrange Co., IN; died 26 Jul 2010 in Elkhart, Elkhart Co.,
                    IN.
+   2884   vii. Floyd Christner, born 29 Jun 1939 in Lagrange Co., IN; died 11 Oct 2007 in Marlow, OK.

1303. Elizabeth A.[8] Christner (Abraham J.[7], John J.[6], Joseph C.[5], Christian J.[4], Johannes John Hans[3], Christian[2], Christen[1]) was born 18 Sep 1897 in Lagrange Co., IN, and died 30 Dec 1992 in Goshen. Elkhart Co., IN.

Notes for Elizabeth A. Christner:
The Descendants of John J. Christner, privately published February 1961, p. 30.

She was a homemaker and was employed at Miles Laboratories for 17 years in the packaging dept. Elizabeth was a member of Hively Ave Mennonite Church, Elkhart, IN. Burial at Christner Cemetery, Honeyville, IN. She never married. She had a Daughter named Malinda Goldie, Malinda was for her great grand mother and Goldie was for Goldie O'Neil/Eash. She lived 3 years 8 months 8 days.

Birth: Sep. 18, 1897
Death: Dec. 30, 1992

Burial: Christner Cemetery, Honeyville, Lagrange Co., IN

More About Elizabeth A. Christner:
Burial: Christner Cemetery, Honeyville, Lagrange Co., IN

Child of Elizabeth A. Christner is:
    2885   i.   Malinda Goldie[9] Christner, born 28 Feb 1915; died 28 Nov 1918 in Row4 plot 19.

                Notes for Malinda Goldie Christner:
                Birth: Feb 28, 1915
                Death: Nov 28, 1918

                Inscription: Malinda (_____) Dau of E Christner Aged 3 Y 8 M 8 D

                Burial: Christner Cemetery, Honeyville, Lagrange Co., IN

                More About Malinda Goldie Christner:
                Burial: Christner Cemetery, Honeyville, Lagrange Co., IN

1305. Mary Nan[8] Christner (Abraham J.[7], John J.[6], Joseph C.[5], Christian J.[4], Johannes John Hans[3], Christian[2], Christen[1])[5361,5362,5362] was born 28 Sep 1903 in Millersburg, Elkhart Co., IN[5362], and died 20 Jan 1975 in Goshen, Elkhart Co., IN. She married **Noah N. Glick**[5362] 07 Jan 1925 in Lagrange Co., IN[5362,5363]. He was born 28 Jun 1905 in Topeka, Lagrange Co., IN[5364], and died 20 Feb 1984 in Goshen, Elkhart Co., IN[5364].

Notes for Mary Nan Christner:
The Descendants of John J. Christner, privately published February 1961, pp. 30, 34.

Mary Nan married Noah N. Glick on January 7, 1925.

Glick, Mary Nan, daughter of Abraham and Magdalena (Miller) Christner, was born at Millersburg, IN Sep 28, 1903; died of a heart ailment at Goshen General Hospital, Goshen, IN Jan 20, 1975; aged 71 y. On Jan 7, 1925, she was married to Noah N. Glick, who survives. Also surviving are 4 sons (Harvey C., Stanley N., Gerald, and Walter N.), 3 daughters (Maggie, Ruby - Mrs. Nathan Nussbaum, and Viola - Mrs. Oliver Farmwald), 17 grandchildren, 3 stepgrandchildren, one brother (Daniel), and 3 sisters (Mattie - Mrs. Tobias Yoder, Elizabeth Christner, and Saloma - Mrs. David Erb). One son (Virgil) preceded her in death, Dec. 13, 1945. She was a member of Emma Mennonite Church, where funeral services were held on Jan. 22, in charge of Ivan M. Miller, Amos O. Hostetler, and Ken Bontreger; interment in Millers Cemetery.
Mary Nan married Noah N. Glick on January 7, 1925.

More About Mary Nan Christner:
Burial: Miller Cemetery, 7 Mile Curve, Lagrange Co., IN
Social Security Number: 310-48-7856/[5364]
SSN issued: IN[5364]

Notes for Noah N. Glick:
The Descendants of John J. Christner, privately published February 1961, p. 34.

Noah is the son of Noah and Cora Ream Glick. Emma Mennonite Church Emma, IN. Retired from the Lagrange Co., IN Highway Department. He was a farmer and farm supply salesman.

More About Noah N. Glick:
Burial: N41°35.316'xW85°28.937 row 13 plot 3/Miller Cemetery, Lagrange Co., IN.

Children of Mary Christner and Noah Glick are:

2886   i.   Maggie Irene[9] Glick, born 22 Jun 1926.

Notes for Maggie Irene Glick:
The Descendants of John J. Christner, privately published February 1961, p. 34.

Maggie in her normal state of reverent modesty admits to being only the editor of Abraham J. Christner & Magdalena Miller book. It is a work well done. Some think about doing while Maggie just does it. Maggie has made a good example of a life by giving to others.

+   2887   ii.   Harvey C. Glick, born 27 Jul 1927.

2888   iii.   Virgil N. Glick[5364], born 26 Oct 1929[5364]; died 13 Dec 1945[5364].

Notes for Virgil N. Glick:
The Descendants of John J. Christner, privately published February 1961, p. 34.

+   2889   iv.   Alice Ruby Glick, born 23 Apr 1931.
+   2890   v.   Stanley N. Glick, born 12 Jul 1932 in Lagrange Co., IN; died 20 Nov 2001 in Lagrange Co., IN.
+   2891   vi.   Viola Elizabeth Glick, born 15 Jul 1933.
+   2892   vii.   Gerald N. Glick, born 28 Feb 1941.
+   2893   viii.   Walter N. Glick, born 17 Sep 1944.

1306. Soloma[8] Christner (Abraham J.[7], John J.[6], Joseph C.[5], Christian J.[4], Johannes John Hans[3], Christian[2], Christen[1]) was born 31 May 1905 in Millersburg, Elkhart Co., IN[5365], and died 18 Feb 1998 in Orrville, Wayne Co., OH[5365]. She married **David S. Erb** 12 Jun 1930 in Lagrange Co., IN, son of Seth Erb and Magdalena Hershberger. He was born 23 Apr 1903 in German Holmes Co., OH[5366], and died 18 Apr 1956[5366].

Notes for Soloma Christner:
The Descendants of John J. Christner, privately published February 1961, pp. 30, 35.

Soloma married David Erb on June 12 1930.

Erb - Saloma Christner, 93 Orrville, OH died Feb. 18. Survivors: children Violet Northern, Marie MacKnight, Clyde; six grandchildren; four great-grandchildren; two step-grandchildren; six step-great-grandchildren. Burial: Kidron, OH by Terry Shue and Herman Myers.

More About Soloma Christner:
Burial: Kidron OH
Religion: Conservative Mennonite/
Social Security Number: 277-38-8498/[5367]
SSN issued: OH[5367]

Notes for David S. Erb:
The Descendants of John J. Christner, privately published February 1961, p. 35.

Children of Soloma Christner and David Erb are:

2894   i.   Mildred[9] Erb, born 17 Feb 1931 in Lagrange Co., IN.

Notes for Mildred Erb:
The Descendants of John J. Christner, privately published February 1961, p. 35.

2895   ii.   Violet Elizabeth Erb, born 07 Sep 1932. She married Northern.

Notes for Violet Elizabeth Erb:
The Descendants of John J. Christner, privately published February 1961, p. 35.

2896   iii.   Omer Erb, born 09 Jan 1936.

        Notes for Omer Erb:
        The Descendants of John J. Christner, privately published February 1961, p. 35.

2897   iv.   Marie Erb[5368], born 30 Mar 1938[5368]. She married Ian W. MacKnight 16 Oct 1976 in Wayne Co.,
        OH[5368]; born Abt. 1930[5368].

        Notes for Marie Erb:
        The Descendants of John J. Christner, privately published February 1961, p. 35.

        More About Marie Erb:
        Residence: OH[5368]

        Notes for Ian W. MacKnight:
        Ohio Marriage Index, 1970, 1972-2007

        Name: Iain W. MacKnight
        Age: 46
        Birth Year: abt 1930
        Residence County: Out of State
        Spouse's Name: Marie Erb
        Spouse's Age: 38
        Spouse's Birth Year: abt 1938
        Spouse's Residence County: Wayne
        Marriage Date: 16 Oct 1976
        Marriage License County: Wayne
        Cerificate Number: 78754
        Volume Number: 8783

        More About Ian W. MacKnight:
        Residence: OH[5368]

2898   v.   Clyde Erb, born 12 Aug 1944.

        Notes for Clyde Erb:
        The Descendants of John J. Christner, privately published February 1961, p. 35.

1308. Bertha[8] Kemp (Mary[7] Christner, John J.[6], Joseph C.[5], Christian J.[4], Johannes John Hans[3], Christian[2], Christen[1]) was born 10 Jul 1894 in Shipshewana, Lagrange Co., IN, and died 07 Dec 1936. She married **Jacob Jones**. He was born 10 Apr 1894, and died 1976.

Notes for Bertha Kemp:
The Descendants of John J. Christner, privately published February 1961, p. 35.

Bertha married Jacob Jones She was adopted by Tobias & Mary Christner Kemp.

Birth: 1892
Death: 1936

Burial: Yoder Cemetery, Shipshewana, Lagrange Co., IN

More About Bertha Kemp:
Adoption: Adopted
Christened: Adopted

Notes for Jacob Jones:
The Descendants of John J. Christner, privately published February 1961, p. 35.

Birth: 1892
Death: 1976

Burial: Yoder Cemetery, Shipshewana, Lagrange Co., IN

Children of Bertha Kemp and Jacob Jones are:

+ 2899   i.   Fred[9] Jones, born 11 Sep 1913.
   2900   ii.   Toby Jones, born 10 Jan 1915; died 26 Feb 1915.

> Notes for Toby Jones:
> The Descendants of John J. Christner, privately published February 1961, p. 35.
>
> Birth: Jan. 10, 1915
> Death: Feb. 26, 1915
>
> Son of JF & BM
>
> Burial: Yoder Cemetery, Shipshewana Lagrange Co., IN

   2901   iii.   Nellie Jones, born 15 Dec 1915. She married Albert Schlabach.

> Notes for Nellie Jones:
> The Descendants of John J. Christner, privately published February 1961, p. 35.
>
> Birth: unknown
> Death: Mar. 26, 1926
>
> Burial: Yoder Cemetery, Shipshewana, Lagrange Co., IN
>
> Notes for Albert Schlabach:
> The Descendants of John J. Christner, privately published February 1961, p. 35.

   2902   iv.   Elizabeth Jones, born 24 Oct 1917; died 08 Feb 1921.

> Notes for Elizabeth Jones:
> The Descendants of John J. Christner, privately published February 1961, p. 35.
>
> Birth: unknown
> Death: Feb. 8, 1921
>
> Burial: Yoder Cemetery, Shipshewana, Lagrange Co., IN

   2903   v.   Neal Jones, born 30 Dec 1919; died 26 Mar 1926.

> Notes for Neal Jones:
> The Descendants of John J. Christner, privately published February 1961, p. 35.
>
> Birth: unknown
> Death: Mar. 26, 1926
>
> Burial: Yoder Cemetery, Shipshewana, Lagrange Co., IN

+ 2904   vi.   Nathaniel J. Jones, born 14 Jan 1922.
+ 2905   vii.   Levi Jones, born 04 Mar 1924 in Topeka, Lagrange Co., IN.
+ 2906   viii.   Jacob Jones Jr., born 23 Apr 1925.
+ 2907   ix.   Amelia Jones, born 12 Jul 1926.
   2908   x.   Abe Jones, born 01 Oct 1927.

> Notes for Abe Jones:
> The Descendants of John J. Christner, privately published February 1961, p. 35.

+ 2909   xi.   Perry J. Jones, born 01 Mar 1930.
+ 2910   xii.   Mary Anna Jones, born 11 Jul 1931 in Oregon City, OR.

+ 2911   xiii.   David J. Jones, born 03 May 1933.

1309. Eli I.[8] Schrock (Anna[7] Christner, John J.[6], Joseph C.[5], Christian J.[4], Johannes John Hans[3], Christian[2], Christen[1]) was born 11 Sep 1885 in Topeka, Lagrange Co., IN. He married **Iva Viola Dunithan** 16 Dec 1906. She was born 13 Oct 1885, and died 23 Jul 1952 in Dodge City, KS.

Notes for Eli I. Schrock:
The Descendants of John J. Christner, privately published February 1961, p. 37.

Notes for Iva Viola Dunithan:
The Descendants of John J. Christner, privately published February 1961, p. 37.

More About Iva Viola Dunithan:
Burial: Maple Grove Cemetery Dodge City Kansas

Children of Eli Schrock and Iva Dunithan are:
+ 2912   i.   Ruth Annie[9] Schrock, born 29 Mar 1908.
+ 2913   ii.   Dorothy Marie Schrock, born 01 Jul 1910.
+ 2914   iii.   Bessie Viola Schrock, born 09 Aug 1912.
    2915   iv.   Mildred Irene Schrock, born 16 Sep 1914; died 06 Aug 1918 in Dodge City, KS.

                 Notes for Mildred Irene Schrock:
                 The Descendants of John J. Christner, privately published February 1961, p. 37.

+ 2916   v.   Oma Evelyn Schrock, born 24 Oct 1920 in Dodge City, KS.

1310. Amos I.[8] Schrock (Anna[7] Christner, John J.[6], Joseph C.[5], Christian J.[4], Johannes John Hans[3], Christian[2], Christen[1]) was born 13 Feb 1887 in Topeka, Eden Twp., Lagrange Co., IN[5369], and died 02 Nov 1944 in of accute Nephritis. He married **Beulah Cleora Hershberger** 07 Jan 1912 in Middlebury, Elkhart Co., IN[5369]. She was born 12 Mar 1891 in Middlebury Township, Elkhart Co., IN[5369], and died 09 Mar 1939 in Goshen, Elkhart Co., IN[5369].

Notes for Amos I. Schrock:
The Descendants of John J. Christner, privately published February 1961, p. 38.

Amos married Beulah C. Hershberger Jan 7, 1912. Cause of death of accute Nephritis.

More About Amos I. Schrock:
Burial: Rock Run Cemetery Southeast of Goshen IN
Residence: 27 Apr 1942, Lagrange Co., IN[5369]

Notes for Beulah Cleora Hershberger:
The Descendants of John J. Christner, privately published February 1961, p. 39.

She died of cancer.

More About Beulah Cleora Hershberger:
Burial: Rock Run Cemetery Southeast of Goshen IN
Residence: 14 Apr 1930, Edentwp., Lagrange Co., IN[5369]

Children of Amos Schrock and Beulah Hershberger are:
+ 2917   i.   Ethel Fern[9] Schrock, born 01 May 1913 in Lagrange, Lagrange Co., IN; died 09 Apr 1974 in Sarasota, Sarasota Co., FL.
+ 2918   ii.   Ernest Isaac Schrock, born 17 Sep 1917 in Topeka, Lagrange Co., IN.
+ 2919   iii.   Virgil Kenneth Schrock, born 08 Apr 1923 in Topeka, Lagrange Co., IN.

1311. Cornelius I.[8] Schrock (Anna[7] Christner, John J.[6], Joseph C.[5], Christian J.[4], Johannes John Hans[3], Christian[2], Christen[1])[5370] was born 01 Dec 1888 in Topeka, Lagrange Co., IN[5370], and died Jul 1969 in Phoenix, Maricopa Co., AZ[5370]. He married **(1) Pearl Edith Weaver**[5371,5372] 22 Apr 1906 in Elkhart Co., IN[5372]. She was born 24 Jul 1886 in Middlebury, Elkhart Co., IN[5372,5373], and died Jul 1991 in Goshen, Elkhart Co., IN[5373,5374]. He married **(2) Delzie Bontrager** 1949.

Notes for Cornelius I. Schrock:
The Descendants of John J. Christner, privately published February 1961, p. 37.

Lived in Richards, MO.

More About Cornelius I. Schrock:
Residence: 27 Apr 1942, Goshen, Clinton Township, Elkhart Co., IN[5374]

Notes for Pearl Edith Weaver:
The Descendants of John J. Christner, privately published February 1961, p. 36.

divorced 1948

Birth: Jul. 24, 1886
Death: Jul., 1991

Social Securty Records:
Date of Birth: Saturday July 24, 1886
Date of Death: July 1991
Est. Age at Death: 104 years, 11 months

Children: Irma C. Schrock (1913 - 1913)

Burial: Forest Grove Cemetery, Middlebury, Elkhart Co., IN
Plot: Section 5-Row 6-Site 2
Find A Grave Memorial# 87221918

More About Pearl Edith Weaver:
Residence: 30 Apr 1930, Clinton Township, Elkhart Co., IN[5374]
Social Security Number: 306-44-4780/[5375]
SSN issued: IN[5375]

Notes for Delzie Bontrager:
The Descendants of John J. Christner, privately published February 1961, p. 36.

Children of Cornelius Schrock and Pearl Weaver are:
+   2920   i.   Goldie Bernice[9] Schrock, born 11 Dec 1907 in IN; died 21 Oct 2006 in Leadville, Lake Co., CO.
       2921   ii.   Irma Gladys Schrock, born 14 Jun 1913[5376]; died 30 Jul 1991[5376]. She married (1) Elmer Witmer. She married (2) Rosco Loy.

                      Notes for Irma Gladys Schrock:
                      Birth: 1913
                      Death: 1913

                      Parents: Pearl E Schrock (1886 - 1991)

                      Burial: Forest Grove Cemetery, Middlebury, Elkhart Co., IN
                      Plot: Section 5-Row 6-Site 2
                      Find A Grave Memorial# 87222022

                      More About Irma Gladys Schrock:
                      Social Security Number: 316-07-1848/[5376]

SSN issued: IN[5376]

Notes for Elmer Witmer:
The Descendants of John J. Christner, privately published February 1961, p. 37.

Notes for Rosco Loy:
The Descendants of John J. Christner, privately published February 1961, p. 37.

+ 2922   iii.   Pauline Annie Schrock, born 17 Sep 1917.
2923   iv.   Maxine Mae Schrock, born 28 May 1924. She married Ernest D. Sailor 14 May 1950.

Notes for Maxine Mae Schrock:
The Descendants of John J. Christner, privately published February 1961, p. 37.

Notes for Ernest D. Sailor:
The Descendants of John J. Christner, privately published February 1961, p. 37.

Child of Cornelius Schrock and Delzie Bontrager is:
2924   i.   Sheryl Gail[9] Schrock, born 16 Sep 1955.

Notes for Sheryl Gail Schrock:
The Descendants of John J. Christner, privately published February 1961, p. 36.

1312. Susanna I.[8] Schrock (Anna[7] Christner, John J.[6], Joseph C.[5], Christian J.[4], Johannes John Hans[3], Christian[2], Christen[1])[5377] was born 13 Dec 1888 in Topeka, Lagrange Co., IN[5377,5378], and died 26 Nov 1983 in Wolcottville, Lagrange Co., IN[5378,5379]. She married **(1) Henry L. Miller**[5379]. He was born 23 Jul 1885 in Elkhart, IN[5379], and died 28 Dec 1935 in Goshen, IN[5379]. She married **(2) Henry L. Miller** 06 Feb 1908. He was born 23 Jul 1885 in Goshen, Elkhart Co., IN[5380], and died 28 Dec 1935 in Topeka, Lagrange Co., IN[5380].

Notes for Susanna I. Schrock:
The Descendants of John J. Christner, privately published February 1961, p. 39.

A son was born May 28 1909 died May 30 1909 age 2 days. She died at her daughter's home.
A son was born may 28 1909 died May 30 1909 age 2 days

More About Susanna I. Schrock:
Burial: Christner Cemetery, Honeyville, Lagrange Co., IN[5380,5380]

Notes for Henry L. Miller:
The Descendants of John J. Christner, privately published February 1961, p. 39.

Died 4 days after Appendictes operation. He was Old Order Amish.

More About Henry L. Miller:
Burial: Christner Cemetery/Honeyville, Lagrange, IN[5380,5380]
Occupation: Farmer/
Religion: Old Order Amish/

Child of Susanna Schrock and Henry Miller is:
+ 2925   i.   Ervin H[9] Miller, born 10 Aug 1920; died May 1969.

Children of Susanna Schrock and Henry Miller are:
2926   i.   Infant[9] Miller, born 28 May 1909 in Topeka, Lagrange Co., IN; died 30 May 1909 in Lagrange Co., IN.

Notes for Infant Miller:
The Descendants of John J. Christner, privately published February 1961, p. 39.

2927   ii.   Annie Viola Miller, born 04 Oct 1911.

Notes for Annie Viola Miller:
The Descendants of John J. Christner, privately published February 1961, p. 39.

+   2928   iii.   Lydia Mae Miller, born 08 Oct 1913 in Lagrange Co., IN; died 10 Aug 1950 in IN.
+   2929   iv.   Verna Elizabeth Miller, born 04 Sep 1915 in Lagrange Co., IN; died 22 Dec 1968 in Lagrange Co., IN.
+   2930   v.   Ammon H. Miller, born 17 Apr 1917 in Topeka, Lagrange Co., IN; died 14 May 1979.
+   2931   vi.   Beulah Moda Miller, born 07 Sep 1919 in Topeka, Lagrange Co., IN.
    2932   vii.   Ervin H. Miller, born 10 Aug 1921.

Notes for Ervin H. Miller:
The Descendants of John J. Christner, privately published February 1961, p. 39.

+   2933   viii.   Wilma Mabel Miller, born 22 Jan 1924.
+   2934   ix.   Verlo H. Miller, born 27 Jan 1927.

1313. Levi I.[8] Schrock (Anna[7] Christner, John J.[6], Joseph C.[5], Christian J.[4], Johannes John Hans[3], Christian[2], Christen[1]) was born 22 Oct 1891 in Topeka, Lagrange Co., IN, and died 21 Aug 1971 in Row 6 plot 16. He married **Mary C. Schlabach** 21 Dec 1916. She was born 22 Jul 1892 in Holmes Co., OH, and died 11 Sep 1935 in Near Topeka, Lagrange Co., IN[5381].

Notes for Levi I. Schrock:
The Descendants of John J. Christner, privately published February 1961, p. 40.

Levi died from a stroke. He was Old Order Amish and a farmer.

More About Levi I. Schrock:
Burial: Christner Cemetery, Honeyville, Lagrange Co., IN
Occupation: Farmer/
Religion: Old Order Amish/

Notes for Mary C. Schlabach:
The Descendants of John J. Christner, privately published February 1961, p. 41.

Dies of of Organic Heart Lessions.

Buried in row 6 plot 17

More About Mary C. Schlabach:
Burial: Christner Cemetery, Honeyville, Lagrange Co., IN
Residence: 1930, Eden, Lagrange, Indiana[5381]

Children of Levi Schrock and Mary Schlabach are:
+   2935   i.   Ella Pauline[9] Schrock, born 12 Jun 1918 in Lagrange Co., IN.
+   2936   ii.   Annie L. Schrock, born 19 Jan 1920.
+   2937   iii.   Truman L. Schrock, born 19 Jan 1921 in Shipshewana, Elkhart Co., IN; died 26 Apr 2007.
+   2938   iv.   Lydia L. Schrock, born 07 Sep 1922 in Topeka, Lagrange Co., IN; died 26 Oct 1994 in Lagrange, Lagrange Co., IN.
    2939   v.   Viola Schrock, born 09 Aug 1924; died 16 Jul 1946 in Elkhart Co., IN.

Notes for Viola Schrock:
Died of General Hospital of Spinal Meningitus
Buried in row 6 plot 18

More About Viola Schrock:
Burial: Christner Cemetery, Honeyville, Lagrange Co., IN
Cause of Death: Spinal Meningitus

+   2940   vi.   Fannie Mae Schrock, born 11 Jun 1927 in Topeka, Lagrange Co., IN.
       2941   vii.   Freeman Schrock, born 08 Sep 1928 in Lagrange Co., IN; died 07 Aug 1955 in Oakland, Alameda Co., CA.

               Notes for Freeman Schrock:
               He lived with Edna Kuhns from Plain City., OH. He died in a Motel at Oakland, CA.

               Birth: Sep. 8, 1928
               Death: Aug. 7, 1955

               Inscription: Freeman L. Son of Levi and Mary Schrock Age 26 YR 11 MO

               Burial: Christner Cemetery, Honeyville, Lagrange Co., IN
               Buried in row 6 plot 19.
               Find A Grave Memorial# 24605172

               More About Freeman Schrock:
               Burial: 11 Aug 1955, Beside his sister Viola Christner Cemetery Honeyville IN N 41°34.500-W 85°35.900
               Cause of Death: Rheumatic Heart

+   2942   viii.   Ammon L. Schrock, born 11 Mar 1930.
+   2943   ix.   Raymond L. Schrock, born 21 Jul 1935 in Shipshewana, Elkhart Co., IN; died in Died 7 weeks old.

1314. Mary I.[8] Schrock (Anna[7] Christner, John J.[6], Joseph C.[5], Christian J.[4], Johannes John Hans[3], Christian[2], Christen[1]) was born 28 Mar 1894 in Topeka, Lagrange Co., IN, and died 29 Mar 1946 in Lagrange, Lagrange Co., IN. She married **Frederick A. Mishler**[5382] 08 Jul 1911 in Lagrange, Lagrange Co., IN[5382]. He was born 19 Aug 1894 in Lagrange, Lagrange Co., IN[5382], and died 16 Oct 1936 in Lagrange, Lagrange Co., IN[5382].

Notes for Mary I. Schrock:
The Descendants of John J. Christner, privately published February 1961, p., 41

Mary's birhtday may be Mar 28, 1894. She died of a stroke and cerebral hemorrhage.

More About Mary I. Schrock:
Burial: Miller Cemetery, Lagrange Co., IN
Cause of Death: Cerebral Hemorage
Religion: Old Order Amish/
Residence: 28 Apr 1930, Clearspring Township, Lagrange Co., IN[5382]

Notes for Frederick A. Mishler:
The Descendants of John J. Christner, privately published February 1961, p. 41.

He was ordained Oct 22, 1933 and Bishop in May 21, 1936 of intestinal ulcers or cancer. He was Old Order Amish.

More About Frederick A. Mishler:
Burial: Miller Cemetery, Lagrange Co., IN
Cause of Death: intestinal ulcers (cancer)
Religion: Old Order Amish/
Residence: 1930, Clearspring, Lagrange Co., IN[5382]

Children of Mary Schrock and Frederick Mishler are:
       2944   i.   Lydia Ann[9] Mishler[5382], born 31 Jan 1912; died 28 Oct 1991[5382]. She married Abner B. Miller 22 Jan 1953; born 31 Dec 1901 in Lagrange Co., IN.

Notes for Lydia Ann Mishler:
The Descendants of John J. Christner, privately published February 1961, p. 42.

More About Lydia Ann Mishler:
Burial: Miller Cemetery, Lagrange Co., IN
Religion: Old Order Amish/
Residence: 29 Apr 1930, Clearspring Township, Lagrange Co., IN[5382]

Notes for Abner B. Miller:
Source:
The Descendants of John J. Christner, privately published February 1961, p. 42.

He was Old Order Amish.

More About Abner B. Miller:
Religion: Old Order Amish/

+   2945   ii.   Goldie Berniece Mishler, born 27 Jan 1914 in Lagrange Co., IN; died 14 May 1959 in Paoli, Orange
                   Co., Indiana from Heart Dropsey.
+   2946   iii. Amos F. Mishler, born 20 Sep 1917 in Lagrange, Lagrange Co., IN; died 09 May 1982 in Home.
+   2947   iv.   Harry F. Mishler, born 21 Apr 1920 in Lagrange Co., IN; died 24 Mar 1965 in Lagrange Co., IN.
     2948   v.   Annie Mishler, born 20 Oct 1924; died 17 May 1926.

                   Notes for Annie Mishler:
                   The Descendants of John J. Christner, privately published February 1961, p. 42.

                   More About Annie Mishler:
                   Burial: Miller Cemetery, Lagrange Co., IN

+   2949   vi.   Ervin F. Mishler, born 20 Mar 1927.
     2950   vii. Noah Mishler, born 23 Mar 1929; died 23 Mar 1929.

                   Notes for Noah Mishler:
                   The Descendants of John J. Christner, privately published February 1961, p. 42.

                   More About Noah Mishler:
                   Burial: Miller Cemetery, Lagrange Co., IN

+   2951   viii. John F. Mishler, born 01 Feb 1931.

1315. John I.[8] Schrock (Anna[7] Christner, John J.[6], Joseph C.[5], Christian J.[4], Johannes John Hans[3], Christian[2], Christen[1]) was born 26 May 1896 in Topeka, Lagrange Co., IN, and died 31 Aug 1952 in Lagrange Co. IN of Cancer. He married **Elizabeth Wingard** 01 Jan 1920. She was born 26 Mar 1900.

Notes for John I. Schrock:
The Descendants of John J. Christner, privately published February 1961, p. 42.

He was Old Order Amish.

More About John I. Schrock:
Cause of Death: Cancer
Occupation: farmer/
Religion: Old Order Amish/

Notes for Elizabeth Wingard:
The Descendants of John J. Christner, privately published February 1961, p. 42.

Children of John Schrock and Elizabeth Wingard are:
+   2952   i.   Cletus J.[9] Schrock, born 27 Mar 1921.
+   2953   ii.   Beulah Elizabeth Schrock, born 22 Sep 1922 in Miami, Dade Co., FL.
+   2954   iii. Ida Mae Schrock, born 01 Dec 1925 in Drayton Plains, MI.

+ 2955   iv.   Anna Pauline Schrock, born 16 Jun 1927.
+ 2956   v.   Mary Ellen Schrock, born 26 Feb 1930 in Millersburg, Lagrange Co., IN; died 11 Oct 2006 in 4770 S - 1125W Lagrange Co., IN.
+ 2957   vi.   Edna Irene Schrock, born 22 Dec 1931.
   2958   vii.   Alice Schrock, born 04 Jan 1934.

       Notes for Alice Schrock:
       The Descendants of John J. Christner, privately published February 1961, p. 42.

   2959   viii.   Lucille Schrock, born 28 Dec 1935. She married Rudy C. Miller 29 Nov 1956; born 13 Jan 1935.

       Notes for Lucille Schrock:
       The Descendants of John J. Christner, privately published February 1961, p. 42.

       More About Lucille Schrock:
       Religion: Old Order Amish/

       Notes for Rudy C. Miller:
       The Descendants of John J. Christner, privately published February 1961, p. 43.

       He was Old Order Amish.

       More About Rudy C. Miller:
       Religion: Old Order Amish/

   2960   ix.   Elmer Jay Schrock, born 21 Mar 1938.

       Notes for Elmer Jay Schrock:
       The Descendants of John J. Christner, privately published February 1961, p. 42.

+ 2961   x.   Katie Mae Schrock, born 06 Sep 1939 in Middlebury, Elkhart Co., IN.
   2962   xi.   Wilma Elizabeth Schrock, born 18 Aug 1942.

       Notes for Wilma Elizabeth Schrock:
       The Descendants of John J. Christner, privately published February 1961, p. 42.

   2963   xii.   Menno Schrock, born 12 Feb 1944.

       Notes for Menno Schrock:
       The Descendants of John J. Christner, privately published February 1961, p. 42.

1316. Andrew I.[8] Schrock (Anna[7] Christner, John J.[6], Joseph C.[5], Christian J.[4], Johannes John Hans[3], Christian[2], Christen[1]) was born 07 May 1898 in Lagrange Co., IN. He married **Lilly J. Schrock** 23 Apr 1918. She was born 09 Mar 1901.

Notes for Andrew I. Schrock:
The Descendants of John J. Christner, privately published February 1961, p. 43.

Children of Andrew Schrock and Lilly Schrock are:
   2964   i.   Orla[9] Schrock, born 14 Sep 1918; died 14 Sep 1918.

       Notes for Orla Schrock:
       The Descendants of John J. Christner, privately published February 1961, p. 43.

+ 2965   ii.   Harley Schrock, born 02 Dec 1919; died 17 Jan 1952.
+ 2966   iii.   Freeman A. Schrock, born 24 May 1922 in MI; died 10 Mar 2005 in Lagrange, Lagrange Co., IN.
+ 2967   iv.   Nedra Lucille Schrock, born 14 Oct 1925 in MI; died 22 Aug 1968 in Centreville, St. Joseph Co., MI.
+ 2968   v.   Rollin Schrock, born 17 Apr 1931.
+ 2969   vi.   Frank Schrock, born 12 Apr 1934.
+ 2970   vii.   Fred Schrock, born 12 Apr 1934.
   2971   viii.   Marion Schrock, born 11 Sep 1935; died 28 Oct 1936 in Pneumonia.

Notes for Marion Schrock:
The Descendants of John J. Christner, privately published February 1961, p. 43.

1317. Lydia I.[8] Schrock (Anna[7] Christner, John J.[6], Joseph C.[5], Christian J.[4], Johannes John Hans[3], Christian[2], Christen[1]) was born 01 Nov 1900 in Topeka, Lagrange Co., IN. She married **Daniel H. Mast** 20 Dec 1922. He was born 22 Jan 1901 in Arthur, IL.

Notes for Lydia I. Schrock:
The Descendants of John J. Christner, privately published February 1961, pp. 44, 64.

More About Lydia I. Schrock:
Religion: Old Order Amish/

Notes for Daniel H. Mast:
The Descendants of John J. Christner, privately published February 1961, pp. 44, 64.

He was Old Order Amish and a farmer.

More About Daniel H. Mast:
Occupation: Farmer/
Religion: Old Order Amish/

Children of Lydia Schrock and Daniel Mast are:

| | 2972 | i. | Viola[9] Mast, born 14 Nov 1923. |

Notes for Viola Mast:
The Descendants of John J. Christner, privately published February 1961, p. 44.

+	2973	ii.	Harley Mast, born 27 Sep 1925.
+	2974	iii.	Henry Elvin Mast, born 24 Mar 1928.
+	2975	iv.	Jerry Mast, born 08 May 1930 in Kokomo, IN.
	2976	v.	Annie Mast, born 26 Mar 1932.

Notes for Annie Mast:
The Descendants of John J. Christner, privately published February 1961, p. 44.

| | 2977 | vi. | Mary Beulah Mast, born 14 Nov 1933. |

Notes for Mary Beulah Mast:
The Descendants of John J. Christner, privately published February 1961, p. 44.

| + | 2978 | vii. | Freeman Mast, born 09 Mar 1935. |
| | 2979 | viii. | Edna Mast, born 28 Jul 1937. |

Notes for Edna Mast:
The Descendants of John J. Christner, privately published February 1961, p. 44.

| | 2980 | ix. | Elva Mast, born 07 Mar 1939. |

Notes for Elva Mast:
The Descendants of John J. Christner, privately published February 1961, p. 44.

| | 2981 | x. | Wilma Mast, born 14 Sep 1941. |

Notes for Wilma Mast:
The Descendants of John J. Christner, privately published February 1961, p. 44.

2982   xi.   Elma Mast, born 28 Jun 1943.

          Notes for Elma Mast:
          The Descendants of John J. Christner, privately published February 1961, p. 44.

2983   xii.   Fanny Mae Mast, born 30 Apr 1946.

          Notes for Fanny Mae Mast:
          The Descendants of John J. Christner, privately published February 1961, p. 44.

1318. Amanda I.[8] Schrock (Anna[7] Christner, John J.[6], Joseph C.[5], Christian J.[4], Johannes John Hans[3], Christian[2], Christen[1])[5383] was born 18 Nov 1902 in Topeka, Lagrange Co., IN, and died 15 Feb 1929 in Scarlet Fever. She married **William A. Beechy**[5383] 20 May 1921 in 0/Lagrange Co., IN[5383]. He was born 10 Apr 1903 in Lagrange Co., IN[5383], and died 30 Oct 1980 in Topeka, Lagrange Co., IN[5383].

Notes for Amanda I. Schrock:
The Descendants of John J. Christner, privately published February 1961, pp. 44, 45.

Amanda married William A. Beachy May 20/21, 1921. She died of Scarlet Fever 9 days after Amanda was born.

More About Amanda I. Schrock:
Cause of Death: Scarlet Fever
Fact 4: Old Order Amish/[5383]
Fact 10: DBH11085/[5383]
Fact 11: Descendants of Daniel J. Hochstetler & Barbara C. Miller 1842-1990 by Dan A. Hoc/[5383]
Fact 12: Family Record of Daniel J. Hochstetler, 1842-1968, by Alvin & Susie Bontrager/[5383]
Fact 13: The Descendants of John J. Christner by Mr. & Mrs. David R. Bontrager... 1961/[5383]
Marriage Fact: 0/Married by Rev. Thomas A. Estell[5383]
Religion: Old Order Amish/

Notes for William A. Beechy:
Source:
The Descendants of John J. Christner, privately published February 1961, p., 44

Birth: Apr. 10, 1903
Death: Oct. 30, 1980

Burial:
Hawpatch Cemetery
Topeka
Lagrange County
IN

He was Old Order Amish.

More About William A. Beechy:
Fact 1: Farmer, saw filing & lawn mower shop/[5383]
Fact 4: Old Order Amish/[5383]
Fact 5: last known residence 46571 zip code/[5383]
Fact 6: S.S. # 310-36-7936, U.S. Social Security Records/[5383]
Fact 10: DJHochstetler 427/[5383]
Fact 11: Descendants of Daniel J. Hochstetler & Barbara C. Miller 1842-1990 by Dan A. Hoc/[5383]
Fact 12: Descendants of Jacob Raber, 1794-1977/[5383]
Fact 13: The Descendants of John J. Christner by Mr. & Mrs. David R. Bontrager... 1961/[5383]
Marriage Fact: 0/married by Bishop Joseph Yoder[5383]

Religion: Old Order Amish/

Children of Amanda Schrock and William Beechy are:
+ 2984   i.   Ammon W.[9] Beechy, born 26 Jul 1921 in Shipshewana, Elkhart Co., IN.
+ 2985   ii.   Elva Beachy, born 27 Feb 1923.
+ 2986   iii.   Vernon W. Beachy, born 20 May 1924; died 25 Feb 1977.
+ 2987   iv.   Mary Elizabeth Beachy, born 06 Oct 1925.
+ 2988   v.   Anna Mae Beechy, born 15 Nov 1927 in Topeka, Lagrange Co., IN; died 18 Aug 2005 in Goshen, Elkhart Co., IN.
+ 2989   vi.   Amanda W. Beachy, born 07 Feb 1929 in Topeka, Lagrange Co., IN.

1319. Ammon I.[8] Schrock (Anna[7] Christner, John J.[6], Joseph C.[5], Christian J.[4], Johannes John Hans[3], Christian[2], Christen[1])[5384] was born 20 Dec 1904 in Topeka, Lagrange Co., IN[5384], and died 20 Apr 1994 in Manatee Co., FL[5384]. He married **Mabel Kauffman**[5384] 14 Feb 1933[5384]. She was born 13 Apr 1907[5384], and died 21 Dec 1989 in IN[5384].

Notes for Ammon I. Schrock:
The Descendants of John J. Christner, privately published February 1961, p. 45.

Notes for Mabel Kauffman:
The Descendants of John J. Christner, privately published February 1961, p. 45.

Child of Ammon Schrock and Mabel Kauffman is:
   2990   i.   Nedra Irene[9] Schrock, born 03 Aug 1945.

       Notes for Nedra Irene Schrock:
       The Descendants of John J. Christner, privately published February 1961, p. 45.

1320. Fanny I.[8] Schrock (Anna[7] Christner, John J.[6], Joseph C.[5], Christian J.[4], Johannes John Hans[3], Christian[2], Christen[1]) was born 03 Sep 1907 in Topeka, Lagrange Co., IN, and died 09 Aug 1953. She married **Samuel J. Bontrager** 09 Feb 1928. He was born 02 Aug 1902 in Near Middlebury, Lagrange Co., IN, and died 06 Dec 1961[5385].

Notes for Fanny I. Schrock:
The Descendants of John J. Christner, privately published February 1961, p. 45.

Fanny married Samuel J. Bontrager Feb 9 1928.

Birth: Sep. 3, 1907
Death: Aug. 9, 1953

Spouse: Samuel J. Bontrager (1902 - 1961)

Children: Viola S. Bontrager (1945 - 1961)

Burial: Hawpatch Cemetery, Topeka, Lagrange Co., IN -650S. x 700W. N41°32.800' x W85°33.500'
Find A Grave Memorial# 81322178

More About Fanny I. Schrock:
Burial: Hawpatch Cemetery West of Topeka IN. N41° 32.8190' W85°33.5060'
Cause of Death: Cirrhosis of the liver

Notes for Samuel J. Bontrager:
The Descendants of John J. Christner, privately published February 1961, p. 45.

The evening of December 6, 1961 Sam and his five youngest daughters went to the German Spelling. On the way home, coming from the south on SR 5, as he was about to turn in the lane, a fast moving car came over a knoll from the north and hit the double buggy broadside, just as they were turning. Leonard Spann, the driver was a buyer at Shipshewana Auction.

Sam was instantly killed. The girls were scattered on the road and beside the road. Erma who was hurt the least, ran in the lane to tell brother Daniel and sister Edna, who were at home.

Elma had a skull fracture and numerous other injuries. Irene had very swollen knees and other injuries. Elma was taken to Parkview Hospital in Ft. Wayne, IN. J. D. Hochstetler came upon the accident and took Viola and Ruby to Lagrange Hospital by car. Ruby had a broken right leg above the knee and was in the hospital six weeks in traction. Viola had a concussion and other injuries. She died 24 hrs later on December 7, 1961. Her age was 15 yrs., 11 mo., 23 days. Age one week less than 16 years. She left two brothers, ten sisters, seven nephews, and eight nieces.

Double funeral services were held for Dad and Viola on December 9, 1961 at the Orla Troyer residence, with burial at Hawpatch Cemetary beside Mother.

AUTO-BUGGY CRASH TAKES LIVES OF
SAMUEL J. BONTRAGER, DAUGHTER

A 59-year-old Topeka area man, Samuel J. Bontrager, was killed at 11:10 o' clock last Wednesday night when the buggy in which he and five of his daughters were riding was hit by an auto four miles southwest of Topeka on SR 5.

One of the daughters, Viola S., 15, died at 9:30 PM. last Thursday at the Lagrange Co. Hospital, about 22 hours after suffering head injuries and knee lacerations in the crash.

The accident occurred at the entrance of the lane leading to the Bontrager residence. Sheriff Myron A. Welker, one of the investigating officers, said that the marks on the pavement, showing the point of impact, revealed that the horse and buggy and begun its turn into the driveway and was hit nearly broadside.

Sheriff Welker reported that one of Bontrager's daughters told him that the driver of the buggy felt there was still time to complete the turn before the auto approached the driveway area.

Bontrager and his daughters were thrown from the demolished buggy. Bontrager was killed instantly when he was dragged under the auto for 108 feet.

The girls and the driver of the auto, Jesse L. Spann Jr., 45, of North Manchester route 2, were taken to the Lagrange Co. Hospital by private ambulance and auto.

Elma S. Bontrager,12 was rushed to Parkview Hospital in Fort Wayne for treatment of a head injury. Her twin sister, Erma, who suffered body bruises was treated at the county hospital and released.

Ruby S., 10, suffered a broken right leg and Fannie Irene, 14 received minor lacerations to her body. Both were hospitalized. Viola S. who succumbed to her injuries last Thursday, was first listed as "fair" but her condition became worse during the evening.

Spann was released from the county hospital after receiving treatment for body bruises and multiple lacerations to his face. He told the investigating officers that he was driving south on the state highway, en-route to his home after attending a sale.

The Bontragers were headed north. Their horse was killed and the buggy was smashed to splinters. Spann's 1962 auto was nearly demolished.

Bontrager's body was wedged beneath the auto when the investigating officers arrived and an auto wrecker was called to free it. Lagrange Co. Coroner Marlin K. Shoup said Bontrager died of a broken back, a severe skull fracture and multiple leg fractures.

Sheriff Welker and State Troopers Tom Jack and Sidney Fish said that Spann's auto skidded 129 feet before hitting the buggy. The auto skidded another 108 feet after the impact. The tire skid marks on the highway confirmed Spann's statement that he was traveling at a speed of 65 miles per hour.

Spann was not held following the investigation.

Birth: Aug. 2, 1902
Death: Dec. 6, 1961

Spouse: Fanny Bontrager (1907 - 1953)

Children: Viola S. Bontrager (1945 - 1961)

Burial: Hawpatch Cemetery, Topeka, Lagrange Co., IN
Find A Grave Memorial# 81322137

More About Samuel J. Bontrager:
Burial: 09 Dec 1961, Hawpatch Cemetery West of Topeka IN. N41° 32.8190' W85°33.5060'
Cause of Death: Automobile and Horse & Buggy Crash
Occupation: Farmer/
Religion: Old Order Amish/
Residence: 1930, Edentwp., Lagrange Co., IN[5385]

Children of Fanny Schrock and Samuel Bontrager are:

+ 2991   i.   Wilma[9] Bontrager, born 06 Dec 1928.
+ 2992   ii.   Anna S. Bontrager, born 06 Feb 1930.
+ 2993   iii. Nettie Bontrager, born 18 Aug 1932 in Topeka, Lagrange Co., IN; died 19 Nov 2010 in IN.
   2994   iv.   Mary S. Bontrager, born 29 Oct 1934.

           Notes for Mary S. Bontrager:
           The Descendants of John J. Christner, privately published February 1961, p. 45.

   2995   v.   Daniel S. Bontrager, born 10 Nov 1937.

           Notes for Daniel S. Bontrager:
           The Descendants of John J. Christner, privately published February 1961, p. 45.

   2996   vi.   Elmer S. Bontrager, born 10 Jul 1939; died 31 Jan 1969.

           Notes for Elmer S. Bontrager:
           The Descendants of John J. Christner, privately published February 1961, p. 45.

   2997   vii. Ida Mae Bontrager, born 10 Jun 1941.

           Notes for Ida Mae Bontrager:
           The Descendants of John J. Christner, privately published February 1961, p. 45.

   2998   viii. Edna Bontrager, born 08 Jan 1943.

           Notes for Edna Bontrager:
           The Descendants of John J. Christner, privately published February 1961, p., 45.

   2999   ix.   Viola Bontrager, born 14 Dec 1945; died 07 Dec 1961 in Auto/Buggy Crash.

           Notes for Viola Bontrager:
           The Descendants of John J. Christner, privately published February 1961, p. 45.

           AUTO-BUGGY CRASH TAKES LIVES OF
           SAMUEL J. BONTRAGER, DAUGHTER

A 59-year-old Topeka area man, Samuel J. Bontrager, was killed at 11:10 o' clock last Wednesday night when the buggy in which he and five of his daughters were riding was hit by an auto four miles southwest of Topeka on SR 5.

One of the daughters, Viola S., 15, died at 9:30 P.M. last Thursday at the Lagrange Co. Hospital, about 22 hours after suffering head injuries and knee lacerations in the crash.

The accident occurred at the entrance of the lane leading to the Bontrager residence. Sheriff Myron A. Welker, one of the investigating officers, said that the marks on the pavement, showing the point of impact, revealed that the horse and buggy and begun its turn into the driveway and was hit nearly broadside.

Sheriff Welker reported that one of Bontrager's daughters told him that the driver of the buggy felt there was still time to complete the turn before the auto approached the driveway area.

Bontrager and his daughters were thrown from the demolished buggy. Bontrager was killed instantly when he was dragged under the auto for 108 feet.

The girls and the driver of the auto, Jesse L. Spann Jr., 45 of North Manchester route 2, were taken to the Lagrange Co. Hospital by private ambulance and auto.

Elma S. Bontrager,12 was rushed to Parkview Hospital in Fort Wayne for treatment of a head injury. Her twin sister, Erma, who suffered body bruises , was treated at the county hospital and released.

Ruby S., 10, suffered a broken right leg and Fannie Irene, 14 received minor lacerations to her body. Both were hospitalized. Viola S., who succumbed to her injuries last Thursday, was first listed as "fair" but her condition became worse during the evening.

Spann was released from the county hospital after receiving treatment for body bruises and multiple lacerations to his face. He told the investigating officers that he was driving south on the state highway, en-route to his home after attending a sale.

The Bontragers were headed north. Their horse was killed and the buggy was smashed to splinters. Spann's 1962 auto was nearly demolished.

Bontrager's body was wedged beneath the auto when the investigating officers arrived and an auto wrecker was called to free it. Lagrange Co. Coroner Marlin K. Shoup said Bontrager died of a broken back, a severe skull fracture and multiple leg fractures.

Sheriff Welker and State Troopers Tom Jack and Sidney Fish said that Spann's auto skidded 129 feet before hitting the buggy. The auto skidded another 108 feet after the impact. The tire skid marks on the highway confirmed Spann's statement that he was traveling at a speed of 65 miles per hour.

Spann was not held following the investigation.

The evening of December 6, 1961, Sam and his five youngest daughters went to the German Spelling. On the way home, coming from the south on SR 5, as he was about to turn in the lane, a fast moving car came over a knoll from the north and hit the double buggy broadside, just as they were turning. Leonard Spann, the driver, was a buyer at Shipshewana Auction.

Sam was instantly killed. The girls were scattered on the road and beside the road. Erma who was hurt the least, ran in the lane to tell brother Daniel and sister Edna, who were at home.

Elma had a skull fracture and numerous other injuries. Irene had very swollen knees and other injuries. Elma was taken to Parkview Hospital in Ft. Wayne, IN. J. D. Hochstetler came upon the accident and took Viola and Ruby to Lagrange Hospital by car. Ruby had a broken right leg above the knee and was in the hospital six weeks in traction. Viola had a concussion and other injuries. She died 24 hrs. later on December 7, 1961. Her age was 15 yrs., 11 mo., 23 days. Age one week less than 16 years. She left two brothers, ten sisters, seven nephews, and eight nieces.

Double funeral services were held for Dad and Viola on December 9, 1961, at the Orla Troyer residence, with burial at Hawpatch Cemetary beside Mother.

Hawpatch Cemetery West of Topeka, Lagrange Co., IN 650S.x700W. N41°32.800' x W85°33.500'

Birth: Dec. 14, 1945
Death: Dec. 7, 1961

Parents:
Samuel J. Bontrager (1902 - 1961)
Fanny Bontrager (1907 - 1953)

Hawpatch Cemetery,Topeka, Lagrange Co., IN
Find A Grave Memorial# 81322242

More About Viola Bontrager:
Burial: Hawpatch Cemetery West of Topeka IN. N41° 32.8190' W85°33.5060'

3000 x. Fanny Irene Bontrager, born 18 Oct 1947.

Notes for Fanny Irene Bontrager:
The Descendants of John J. Christner, privately published February 1961, p. 45.

3001 xi. Elma Bontrager, born 11 Feb 1949.

Notes for Elma Bontrager:
The Descendants of John J. Christner, privately published February 1961, p. 45.

3002 xii. Erma Bontrager, born 11 Feb 1949.

Notes for Erma Bontrager:
The Descendants of John J. Christner, privately published February 1961, p. 45.

3003 xiii. Ruby S. Bontrager, born 15 Jan 1951.

Notes for Ruby S. Bontrager:
The Descendants of John J. Christner, privately published February 1961, p. 45.

1321. Elmer J.[8] Christner (John E.[7], John B.[6], Peter[5], Peter[4], Christian[3], Christian[2], Christen[1])[5386] was born 12 Oct 1886 in Topeka, Lagrange Co., IN[5386], and died 26 Nov 1917 in Goshen, Elkhart Co., IN[5386]. He married **Madgelina "Mattie" S. Miller**[5386] 27 May 1906 in White Cloud, Newaygo Co., MI. She was born 31 Jul 1887 in Goshen, Elkhart Co., IN[5386], and died 12 Jul 1959 in IN[5386].

Notes for Elmer J. Christner:
The Descendants of John J. Christner, privately published February 1961, p. 46.

Amish---11087-B. Hochstedler--C. Stutzman-book. Elmer stopped at his sister Amanda Wingard's in the morning carrying a gun to hunt for rabbits, crossed the road, crawled over the fence and tried to pull the gun through the fence. He was shot and died the same day.

Birth: Oct. 12, 1886
Death: Nov. 26, 1917

Burial: Christner Cemetery, Honeyville, Lagrange Co., IN

More About Elmer J. Christner:
Burial: Row 5 plot 19/Christner Cemetery, Honeyville, Lagrange Co., IN
Cause of Death: Accidentally shot himself
Religion: Old Order Amish/
Residence: 1910, Eden, Lagrange Co., IN[5387]

Notes for Madgelina "Mattie" S. Miller:
The Descendants of John J. Christner, privately published February 1961, p., 46.

Second husband - Emanuel E. Bontrager, Married March 20, 1927 Emanuel born November 11, 1878 Lagrange Co., IN.

Birth: Jul. 8, 1865
Death: Jun. 6, 1926

Spouse: Abraham J Christner (1856 - 1931)

Children: Amelia Christner (1900 - 1901)

Inscription: Wife of A. J. Christner

Burial: Christner Cemetery, Honeyville, Lagrange Co., IN
Row 5 plot 17

More About Madgelina "Mattie" S. Miller:
Burial: Christner Cemetery, Honeyville, Lagrange Co., IN
Religion: Old Order Amish/
Residence: 1910, Eden, Lagrange Co., IN[5387]

Children of Elmer Christner and Madgelina Miller are:

+   3004   i.   Melvin E.[9] Christner, born 26 Nov 1906 in Topeka, Lagrange Co., IN; died 02 Feb 1996 in Goshen, Elkhart Co., IN.
+   3005   ii.   Ida E. Christner, born 24 Nov 1908 in Topeka, Lagrange Co., IN; died 22 Oct 2001 in Greenville, Greenville Co., SC.
+   3006   iii. Leland E. Christner, born 19 Oct 1913 in Cochranton, Crawford Co., PA; died 13 Jul 1987 in Crawford Co., PA.
     3007   iv.   Alphus Christner[5388,5389,5390], born 02 Feb 1916 in Shipshewana, Lagrange Co., IN[5390,5390,5391]; died 16 May 2003 in Apache Junction, Pinal Co., AZ[5392,5392].

                   Notes for Alphus Christner:
                   The Descendants of John J. Christner, privately published February 1961, p. 46.

                   More About Alphus Christner:
                   Residence: 1930, Middlebury, Elkhart Co., IN[5393]
                   Social Security Number: 309-05-5877/[5394,5394]
                   SSN issued: IN[5394,5394]

+   3008   v.   Erma Christner, born 10 May 1917 in Shipshewana, Lagrange Co., IN; died 09 May 1989 in Elkhart Co., IN.

1322. Samuel J.[8] Christner (John E.[7], John B.[6], Peter[5], Peter[4], Christian[3], Christian[2], Christen[1])[5395,5396,5397] was born 27 Mar 1888 in Topeka, Lagrange Co., IN[5398,5399], and died 14 Dec 1980 in Scott, Kosciusko Co., IN[5400]. He married **Elizabeth Ann Miller**[5400,5401,5402] 12 Oct 1907, daughter of Simon Miller and Magdalena Lantz. She was born 17 Jun 1887 in Lagrange Co., IN[5403,5404,5405], and died 05 Feb 1985[5406].

Notes for Samuel J. Christner:
The Descendants of John J. Christner, privately published February 1961, pp. 46, 47.

More About Samuel J. Christner:
Residence: 1920, Scott, Kosciusko Co., IN[5406,5407]

Notes for Elizabeth Ann Miller:
The Descendants of John J. Christner, privately published February 1961, pp. 47, 102.

More About Elizabeth Ann Miller:
Residence: 1920, Scott, Kosciusko Co., IN[5408,5409]

Children are listed above under (440) Elizabeth Ann Miller.

1323. Susie J.[8] **Christner** (John E.[7], John B.[6], Peter[5], Peter[4], Christian[3], Christian[2], Christen[1]) was born 04 Mar 1890 in Topeka, Lagrange Co., IN[5410], and died 11 Aug 1981. She married **(1) Abraham R. Bontrager**[5411] 02 Mar 1911 in Lagrange Co., IN, son of Reuben Bontrager and Elizabeth Yoder. He was born 12 Sep 1890 in Lagrange Co., IN, and died 22 Oct 1918 in Lagrange Co, IN. She married **(2) Menno J. S. Yoder**[5412] 12 Dec 1929 in IN[5413]. He was born 04 Jul 1892 in Lagrange Co., IN[5413], and died 11 Jul 1967[5414,5415,5416].

Notes for Susie J. Christner:
The Descendants of John J. Christner, privately published February 1961, p., 48

Susie later (11 years 21 days later) married Deacon Menno J. S. Yoder. Dec. 12, 1929.

More About Susie J. Christner:
Alt. Birth: 04 Mar 1890[5417]
Burial: Miller Cem, Lagrange Co, IN. N41°35.361'xW85°28.925' row 7 Plot 56
DBH Book: 14543/[5418]
Religion: Old Order Amish/

Notes for Abraham R. Bontrager:
The Descendants of John J. Christner, privately published February 1961, p. 48.

He is Old Order Amish and farmer near Topeka, IN. He died of Influenza.

More About Abraham R. Bontrager:
Cause of Death: Influenza
Occupation: Farmer/
Religion: Old Order Amish/

Notes for Menno J. S. Yoder:
The Descendants of John J. Christner, privately published February 1961, p., 23.

Menno was 1st married to Emma D. Christner. Emma died April 15, 1928 and then he married Susie J. Christner Bontrager.

More About Menno J. S. Yoder:
Alt. Birth: 03 Jul 1892[5419]
Burial: Miller Cem, Lagrange Co, IN. N41°35.361'xW85°28.925' row 7 Plot 56
Religion: Amish (Deacon)/[5420,5421]

Children of Susie Christner and Abraham Bontrager are:
    3009   i.   Amelia A.[9] Bontrager, born 12 Sep 1911 in Lagrange Co., IN.

                Notes for Amelia A. Bontrager:
                The Descendants of John J. Christner, privately published February 1961, p. 48.

+   3010   ii.   Amos A. Bontrager, born 28 Sep 1913 in Lagrange Co., IN; died 08 Jun 1982 in Lagrange Co., IN.
    3011   iii. Harley A. Bontrager, born 09 May 1915 in Lagrange Co., IN; died 05 Feb 2001[5422]. He married Mary D. Miller 16 Feb 1939 in By Cornelius Christner; born 13 Aug 1911 in Holmes Co., OH; died 23 Aug 1992.

                Notes for Harley A. Bontrager:
                The Descendants of John J. Christner, privately published February 1961, p. 48.

                He was Old Order Amish and is buried at Miller Cemetery, Lagrange, IN.

                More About Harley A. Bontrager:

Occupation: Farmer/[5422]
Religion: Amish/[5422]

Notes for Mary D. Miller:
The Descendants of John J. Christner, privately published February 1961, p. 48.

+   3012   iv.   Abraham A. Bontrager, born 22 Jan 1919 in Lagrange Co., IN.

Child of Susie Christner and Menno Yoder is:
   3013   i.   Daniel M[9] Yoder[5422], born 20 Apr 1925 in Topeka, Lagrange Co., IN[5422]; died 28 Sep 1997 in Shipshewana, Lagrange Co., IN[5422]. He married Lydia Mae Hochstedler; born 19 Sep 1931.

More About Daniel M Yoder:
Occupation: Farmer & factory worker/[5422]
Religion: Amish/[5422]

1324. Mary J.[8] Christner (John E.[7], John B.[6], Peter[5], Peter[4], Christian[3], Christian[2], Christen[1]) was born 05 Dec 1892 in Topeka, Lagrange Co., IN, and died 14 Jan 1979 in Shipshewana, Lagrange Co., IN. She married **Jacob E. Hochstetler** 24 Jan 1918. He was born 03 Apr 1894 in Lagrange Co., IN, and died 29 Nov 1978.

Notes for Mary J. Christner:
The Descendants of John J. Christner, privately published February 1961, p., 49.

More About Mary J. Christner:
Burial: Naylor Cemetery, Lagrange Co., IN
Religion: Old Order Amish/

Notes for Jacob E. Hochstetler:
The Descendants of John J. Christner, privately published February 1961, p. 49.

Jacob is the son of Gideon J. and Elizabeth Schrock Hochstetler. He was Old Order Amish.

More About Jacob E. Hochstetler:
Burial: Naylor Cemetery, Lagrange Co., IN
Religion: OLd Order Amish/

Children of Mary Christner and Jacob Hochstetler are:
+   3014   i.   Celesta J.[9] Hochstetler, born 13 Jan 1921; died 08 Sep 2006 in her home at 10740W--500South Lagrange Co. IN.
+   3015   ii.   Harley J. Hochstetler, born 07 Jul 1922 in Lagrange Co., IN; died 21 Oct 1996 in Lagrange Co., IN.
+   3016   iii.   Susie J. Hochstetler, born 23 Apr 1928.
+   3017   iv.   Eli J. Hochstetler, born 23 Jul 1929.
+   3018   v.   Gideon J. Hochstetler, born 09 Apr 1933; died 10 Nov 1959.

1325. Amanda J.[8] Christner (John E.[7], John B.[6], Peter[5], Peter[4], Christian[3], Christian[2], Christen[1])[5423,5424] was born 01 Jun 1895 in Topeka, Lagrange Co., IN[5425,5426,5427], and died 18 Oct 1981 in Shipshewana, Lagrange Co., IN[5428]. She married **Levi J. Wingard**[5429] 31 Jan 1915 in Shipshewana, Lagrange Co., IN[5429]. He was born 31 Oct 1894 in Lagrange Co., IN[5429], and died 16 Apr 1970 in Lagrange Co., IN[5429].

Notes for Amanda J. Christner:
The Descendants of John J. Christner, privately published February 1961, p. 49.

More About Amanda J. Christner:
Burial: N41°40.560 x W85°37.884/Bontrager North Cemetery, Lagrange Co., IN
Religion: Old Order Amish/
Residence: 1910, Eden, Lagrange Co., IN[5430]

Social Security Number: 306-70-7217/[5431]
SSN issued: IN[5431]

Notes for Levi J. Wingard:
The Descendants of John J. Christner, privately published February 1961, pp. 49, 50.

Levi is the son of Jacob P and Elizabeth Yoder Wingard. Levi was Old Order Amish and a farmer.

More About Levi J. Wingard:
Burial: N41°40.560 x W85°37.884/Bontrager North Cemetery, Lagrange Co., IN
Religion: Old Order Amish/

Children of Amanda Christner and Levi Wingard are:

+	3019	i.	Alta Marie[9] Wingard, born 16 Jun 1915 in Lagrange Co., IN; died 17 Apr 1991 in Goshen General, Hospital, Goshen, Elkhart Co., IN.
+	3020	ii.	Elizabeth L. Wingard, born 05 Nov 1918 in Lagrange Co., IN; died 11 Feb 1966 in Lagrange Co., IN.
+	3021	iii.	Wilma A. Wingard, born 26 Oct 1922 in Lagrange Co., IN; died 03 Mar 1994 in Honeyville, Lagrange Co., IN.
	3022	iv.	Edna A. Wingard[5432], born 23 Sep 1925[5432]; died 25 Oct 1925[5432].

Notes for Edna A. Wingard:
The Descendants of John J. Christner, privately published February 1961, p. 49.

+	3023	v.	Anna A. Wingard, born 16 Jun 1927.
+	3024	vi.	Freeman L. Wingard, born 25 Jul 1928 in Lagrange Co., IN; died 21 Nov 1995 in Goshen, Elkhart Co., IN.

1326. Levi J.[8] Christner (John E.[7], John B.[6], Peter[5], Peter[4], Christian[3], Christian[2], Christen[1]) was born 10 Jun 1897 in Topeka, Lagrange Co., IN, and died 06 Aug 1984 in Lagrange, Lagrange Co., IN[5433]. He married **Susie Schrock** 27 Jul 1924 in Canton, Stark Co., OH[5433], daughter of Joseph Schrock and Rachel Christner. She was born 02 Jul 1903 in Middlefield, OH, and died 07 Jan 1987 in Rome City, Noble Co., IN[5433].

Notes for Levi J. Christner:
The Descendants of John J. Christner, privately published February 1961, pp. 48, 50.
He was Old Order Amish.

More About Levi J. Christner:
Burial: Miller Cem.Lagrange Co. IN. N41°35.361xW85°28.925 Row 8 Plot 56
Occupation: worked at a Paper Mill and a farmer/White Pigeon, Michigan, USA[5434]
Religion: Old Order Amish/
Residence: Not Stated, Lagrange, Indiana[5435,5436]

Notes for Susie Schrock:
The Descendants of John J. Christner, privately published February 1961, p. 50.

More About Susie Schrock:
Burial: Miller Cem.Lagrange Co. IN. N41°35.361xW85°28.925 Row 8 Plot 56
Religion: Old Order Amish/
Residence: 1920, Precinct 15, Yamhill Co., OR[5436]

Children of Levi Christner and Susie Schrock are:

+	3025	i.	Jaunita[9] Christner, born 07 Jan 1925.
+	3026	ii.	Kenneth Christner, born 09 Oct 1927.
+	3027	iii.	Merle Christner, born 20 Sep 1931 in Lagrange Co., IN.
+	3028	iv.	Mervin Roy Christner, born 13 May 1936 in Lagrange Co., IN; died 01 Apr 2007 in Sturgis, Saint Joseph Co., MI.
+	3029	v.	Freida Christner, born 12 May 1939 in White Pigeon, St. Joseph Co., MI; died 15 Feb 2011 in Avilla, Noble Co., IN.

3030   vi.   Freeman Christner, born 12 May 1939 in White Pigeon, St. Joseph Co., MI.

Notes for Freeman Christner:
The Descendants of John J. Christner, privately published February 1961, p. 50.
Freeman is a twin to Freida.

+   3031   vii.   Anna Marie Christner, born 02 Mar 1948 in Lagrange Co., IN.

1327. Amos J.[8] Christner (John E.[7], John B.[6], Peter[5], Peter[4], Christian[3], Christian[2], Christen[1]) was born 06 Apr 1899 in Wolcottville, Lagrange Co., IN, and died 06 Oct 1963[5437]. He married **Elizabeth D. Bontrager** 14 Dec 1926 in Lagrange Co., IN[5437]. She was born 12 Jun 1905 in Lagrange Co., IN, and died 25 Jul 1983 in Goshen, Elkhart Co., IN.

Notes for Amos J. Christner:
The Descendants of John J. Christner, privately published February 1961, p. 50.

He was Old Order Amish and a farmer. He buried two infants at Forks/Yoder Cemetery 1925 & 1930.

Birth: Apr. 6, 1899
Death: Oct. 6, 1963

Burial: Forks Yoder Cemetery, Lagrange Co., IN

More About Amos J. Christner:
Burial: Yoder Cemetery, Forks, Lagrange Co., IN
Religion: Old Order Amish/
Residence: 1930, Middlebury, Elkhart Co., IN[5437]

Notes for Elizabeth D. Bontrager:
The Descendants of John J. Christner, privately published February 1961, p. 50.

Birth: 1905
Death: 1983

Burial: Forks Yoder Cemetery, Lagrange Co., IN

Elizabeth is the daughter of Dan R. Bontrager and Amelia Wingard Elizabeth married the 2nd time to Willis E. Miller son of Eza and Annie Christner Miller.

More About Elizabeth D. Bontrager:
Burial: Yoder Cemetery, Lagrange Co., IN
Religion: Old Order Amish/
Residence: 1930, Middlebury, Elkhart Co., IN[5437]

Children of Amos Christner and Elizabeth Bontrager are:
    3032   i.   Infant[9] Christner, born 1925; died 1925.

                Notes for Infant Christner:
                Birth: 1925
                Death: 1925

                Child of Amos & Lizzie

                Burial: Forks Yoder Cemetery, Lagrange Co., IN

    3033   ii.   Ervin C. Christner, born 07 Mar 1928 in Lagrange Co., IN; died 07 Mar 1928 in Lagrange Co., IN.

                Notes for Ervin C. Christner:

He was born stillborn.

	3034	iii.	Wilma Christner, born 1929; died 1929.
+	3035	iv.	Ida Christner, born 12 Apr 1929 in Lagrange Co., IN; died 12 Oct 1994 in Kokomo, Miami Co., IN.
	3036	v.	Infant Christner, born 1930; died 1930.

Notes for Infant Christner:
Birth: 1930
Death: 1930

Child of Amos & Lizzie

Burial: Forks Yoder Cemetery, Lagrange Co., IN

+	3037	vi.	Gertie Christner, born 11 Sep 1931 in Wollcotville, Lagrange Co., IN; died 18 Feb 2009 in IN.
+	3038	vii.	Elmer A. Christner, born 22 Nov 1934 in Lagrange Co., IN.
+	3039	viii.	Samuel A. Christner, born 26 Feb 1937 in Wollcotville, Lagrange Co., IN.
	3040	ix.	Ivan Christner, born 11 Oct 1938 in Homer, Calhoun Co., MI; died 14 Oct 1938.

More About Ivan Christner:
Burial: Yoder Cemetery

1328. Elizabeth Lizzie[8] Schlabach (Mary D.[7] Frey, Elizabeth J.[6] Christner, Joseph C.[5], Christian J.[4], Johannes John Hans[3], Christian[2], Christen[1])[5438] was born 20 Oct 1872 in Topeka, Lagrange Co., IN, and died 07 May 1927[5438]. She married **Maneleus D. Hochstetler** 06 Apr 1893 in Married by Bishop Emanuel L. Miller. He was born 21 Aug 1870 in Lagrange, Lagrange Co., IN[5439], and died 15 Nov 1960[5440].

Notes for Elizabeth Lizzie Schlabach:
The Descendants of John J. Christner, privately published February 1961, p. 52.

Birth: Oct. 20, 1872
Death: May 7, 1927

Spouse: M. D. Hochstetler (1870 - 1960)

Children: Amos Hochstetler (1912 - 1926)

Burial: Miller Amish Cemetery, Lagrange, Lagrange Co., IN

More About Elizabeth Lizzie Schlabach:
Religion: Old Order Amish/

Notes for Maneleus D. Hochstetler:
The Descendants of John J. Christner, privately published February 1961, p. 52.

He was Old Order Amish.

Birth: Aug. 21, 1870
Death: Nov. 15, 1960

Spouse: Elizabeth Hochstetler (1872 - 1927)

Children: Amos Hochstetler (1912 - 1926)

Burial: Miller Amish Cemetery, Lagrange, Lagrange Co., IN

More About Maneleus D. Hochstetler:
DJH Book: 6158/[5440]

Occupation: Farmer & undertaker/[5440]
Religion: Old Order Amish/

Children of Elizabeth Schlabach and Maneleus Hochstetler are:

	3041	i.	Infant[9] Hochstetler.
+	3042	ii.	Albert M. Hochstetler, born 31 Jan 1894 in Topeka, Lagrange Co., IN; died 18 May 1972 in Lagrange Co., IN.
	3043	iii.	Infant Hochstetler, born 13 Oct 1896; died 19 Oct 1896.

Notes for Infant Hochstetler:
The Descendants of John J. Christner, privately publishedFebruary 1961, p. 52.

+	3044	iv.	Tobias M. Hochstetler, born 13 Jun 1898 in Lagrange Co., IN; died 08 Nov 1970 in Lagrange Co., IN.
+	3045	v.	Daniel M. Hochstetler, born 15 May 1900; died 16 Aug 1973.
+	3046	vi.	Urias M. Hochstetler, born 29 Mar 1901 in Topeka, Lagrange Co., IN; died 11 Jun 1987 in Hardin Memorial Hospital/Kenton, Hardin Co., OH.
+	3047	vii.	Christian M. Hochstetler, born 05 Aug 1906.
+	3048	viii.	Anna M. Hochstetler, born 28 May 1910.
	3049	ix.	Amos M. Hochstetler, born 19 Mar 1913; died 30 Aug 1926.

Notes for Amos M. Hochstetler:
The Descendants of John J. Christner, privately published February 1961, p. 52.

Birth: Mar. 19, 1912
Death: Aug. 30, 1926

Parents:
M. D. Hochstetler (1870 - 1960)
Elizabeth Hochstetler (1872 - 1927)

Burial: Miller Amish Cemetery, Lagrange, Lagrange Co., IN

1329. Joseph J.[8] Schlabach (Mary D.[7] Frey, Elizabeth J.[6] Christner, Joseph C.[5], Christian J.[4], Johannes John Hans[3], Christian[2], Christen[1])[5441] was born 23 Dec 1874 in Lagrange Co., IN[5442,5443], and died 30 May 1951 in Anderson, Indiana[5444]. He married **(1) Clara V. Yoder** 28 Nov 1895. She was born 16 Nov 1878, and died 03 Mar 1903. He married **(2) Hallie May Miles Rice**[5444] 17 Jul 1907 in Lafayette, Indiana[5444]. She was born 16 Jan 1885 in Danville, Indiana[5444,5445], and died Feb 1977[5445].

Notes for Joseph J. Schlabach:
The Descendants of John J. Christner, privately published February 1961, pp. 52, 57.

Notes for Clara V. Yoder:
The Descendants of John J. Christner, privately published February 1961, p. 57.

Notes for Hallie May Miles Rice:
The Descendants of John J. Christner, privately published February 1961, p. 57.

More About Hallie May Miles Rice:
Other-Begin: Anderson, Madison Co., IN[5445]
Social Security Number: 313-26-9889/[5445]
SSN issued: IN[5445]

Children of Joseph Schlabach and Clara Yoder are:

+	3050	i.	Amos Clifford[9] Schlabach, born 27 Nov 1896 in Anderson, Madison Co., IN; died 18 Dec 1990 in Anderson, Madison Co., IN.
+	3051	ii.	Albert J. Schlabach, born 28 Jun 1899; died Jan 1974 in Anderson, Madison, Indiana, United States of America.

Children of Joseph Schlabach and Hallie Rice are:

3052   i.   Mable Grace[9] Schlabach, born 09 Oct 1910; died 18 Oct 1910.

3053   ii.   Joyce Marie Schlabach, born 09 Jul 1913.

Notes for Joyce Marie Schlabach:
The Descendants of John J. Christner, privately published February 1961, p. 57.

3054   iii.   William Ernest Schlabach, born 29 Jan 1916.

Notes for William Ernest Schlabach:
The Descendants of John J. Christner, privately published February 1961, p. 57.

1330. Jacob J.[8] Schlabach (Mary D.[7] Frey, Elizabeth J.[6] Christner, Joseph C.[5], Christian J.[4], Johannes John Hans[3], Christian[2], Christen[1])[5446] was born 13 Mar 1877 in Topeka, Lagrange Co., IN[5447,5448,5449,5449]. He married **Lydiann D. Yoder**[5450] 20 Dec 1898. She was born 20 Nov 1874 in Nappanee, Elkhart Co., IN[5451,5452,5453].

Notes for Jacob J. Schlabach:
The Descendants of John J. Christner, privately published February 1961, pp. 52, 58.

More About Jacob J. Schlabach:
Description: 12 Sep 1918, medium height/build, blue eyes, brown hair/Goshen, Elkhart Co., IN[5453]
Occupation: 12 Sep 1918, baggageman, NY Central Railroad/Goshen, Elkhart Co., IN[5453]
Other-Begin: Elkhart County[5453]
Residence: 1930, Union City Twp, Elkhart, IN[5453]

Notes for Lydiann D. Yoder:
The Descendants of John J. Christner, privately published February 1961, p. 58.

More About Lydiann D. Yoder:
Residence: 1930, Union City Twp, Elkhart, IN[5453]

Children of Jacob Schlabach and Lydiann Yoder are:
3055   i.   Simon J.[9] Schlabach[5454], born 04 Nov 1899[5454,5455,5456,5456]; died Jun 1982 in Elkhart Co., IN[5457]. He married Helen V. Booker[5458] 15 Jul 1924; born 09 Jun 1907[5458]; died Jul 1996 in Elkhart, Elkhart Co., IN[5458].

Notes for Simon J. Schlabach:
The Descendants of John J. Christner, privately published February 1961, p. 58.

More About Simon J. Schlabach:
Residence: 01 Apr 1940, Elkhart, Elkhart Co., IN[5459]
Social Security Number: 308-05-4536/[5460,5461]
SSN issued: IN[5462,5463]

Notes for Helen V. Booker:
The Descendants of John J. Christner, privately published February 1961, p. 58.

More About Helen V. Booker:
Residence: 1930, Jackson, Elkhart Co., IN[5463]
Social Security Number: 308-05-6229/[5464]
SSN issued: IN[5464]

3056   ii.   Beulah J. Schlabach, born 05 May 1901; died 12 Nov 1906.

Notes for Beulah J. Schlabach:
The Descendants of John J. Christner, privately published February 1961, p. 58.

3057   iii.   Lula J Schlabach, born 17 May 1902; died 26 Nov 1906.

Notes for Lula J Schlabach:

The Descendants of John J. Christner, privately published February 1961, p. 58.

3058   iv.   Ira Leonard Schlabach, born 06 Sep 1903; died 28 Jul 1905.

Notes for Ira Leonard Schlabach:
The Descendants of John J. Christner, privately published February 1961, p. 58.

3059   v.   Lawrence J. Schlabach, born 21 Oct 1904.

Notes for Lawrence J. Schlabach:
The Descendants of John J. Christner, privately published February 1961, p. 58.

3060   vi.   Infant Son Schlabach, born 04 Nov 1907; died 04 Nov 1907.

Notes for Infant Son Schlabach:
The Descendants of John J. Christner, privately published February 1961, p. 58.

1331. Daniel J.[8] Schlabach (Mary D.[7] Frey, Elizabeth J.[6] Christner, Joseph C.[5], Christian J.[4], Johannes John Hans[3], Christian[2], Christen[1])[5465] was born 17 Apr 1879 in IN[5466,5467,5468,5469]. He married **Katherine Yoder** 12 Nov 1904 in Lagrange Co., IN[5470,5471]. She was born 03 Nov 1882 in Lagrange Co., IN[5472], and died 09 Sep 1970[5472].

Notes for Daniel J. Schlabach:
The Descendants of John J. Christner, privately published February 1961, pp. 52, 58.

More About Daniel J. Schlabach:
Other-Begin: Elkhart County[5473]
Residence: 1920, Goshen Ward 4, Elkhart, Indiana[5474,5475,5476]

Notes for Katherine Yoder:
The Descendants of John J. Christner, privately published February 1961, p. 58.

More About Katherine Yoder:
Residence: 1910, Clearspring, Lagrange Co., IN[5476]

Children of Daniel Schlabach and Katherine Yoder are:
    3061   i.   Glen[9] Schlabach, born 30 May 1906 in IN[5476]; died 10 Dec 1906 in IN[5476].

Notes for Glen Schlabach:
The Descendants of John J. Christner, privately published February 1961, p. 58.

    3062   ii.   Opal Fern Schlabach[5476], born 20 Jan 1908; died 21 Sep 1926[5476].

Notes for Opal Fern Schlabach:
The Descendants of John J. Christner, privately published February 1961, p. 58.

More About Opal Fern Schlabach:
Residence: 1920, Goshen Ward 4, Elkhart, Indiana[5476]

1332. Barbara J.[8] Schlabach (Mary D.[7] Frey, Elizabeth J.[6] Christner, Joseph C.[5], Christian J.[4], Johannes John Hans[3], Christian[2], Christen[1]) was born 31 Dec 1881 in Emma, Lagrange Co., IN[5477], and died Mar 1975 in Elkhart, Elkhart Co., IN[5477,5478]. She married **Dalton S. Miller** 02 Aug 1902 in Home of Bride by Rev Menno S Yoder/Emma, Lagrange Co., IN[5478]. He was born 01 Oct 1879 in Lagrange, Lagrange Co., IN[5478], and died 18 Aug 1913 in Topeka, Lagrange Co., IN[5478].

Notes for Barbara J. Schlabach:
The Descendants of John J. Christner, privately published February 1961, pp. 52, 58.

More About Barbara J. Schlabach:
Residence: 1930, Age: 48; Marital Status: Widowed; Relation to Head of House: Head/Elkhart, Elkhart Co., IN[5478]
Social Security Number: 309-38-7565/[5479]
SSN issued: IN[5479]

Notes for Dalton S. Miller:
The Descendants of John J. Christner, privately published February 1961, p. 58.

More About Dalton S. Miller:
Residence: 1910, Age in 1910: 30; Marital Status: Married; Relation to Head of House: Head/Newbury, Lagrange Co., IN[5480]

Children of Barbara Schlabach and Dalton Miller are:

+ 3063   i.   Paul E.[9] Miller, born 27 Apr 1903 in Topeka, Lagrange Co., IN; died Mar 1987 in Grover Beach, San Luis Obispo Co., CA.

   3064   ii.   Joe Miller[5480], born 12 Jul 1905 in Emma, Lagrange Co., IN[5480]; died 03 May 1906 in Emma, Lagrange Co., IN[5480].

      Notes for Joe Miller:
      The Descendants of John J. Christner, privately published February 1961, p. 58.

+ 3065   iii.   Silas Miller, born 30 Oct 1906 in Emma, Lagrange Co., IN; died 06 Nov 1990 in Oxford, Benton Co., IN.

   3066   iv.   Mary Ellen Miller, born 26 Mar 1909 in Goshen, Elkhart Co., IN[5480]; died 17 Dec 2010 in Goshen, Elkhart Co., IN[5480].

      Notes for Mary Ellen Miller:
      The Descendants of John J. Christner, privately published February 1961, p. 58.

      More About Mary Ellen Miller:
      Residence: 1930, Age: 19; Marital Status: Single; Relation to Head of House: Daughter/Elkhart, Elkhart Co., IN[5480]

   3067   v.   Martha M Miller[5480], born Abt. 1910 in IN[5480]; died 17 Feb 1998 in Goshen, Elkhart Co., IN[5480].

      Notes for Martha M Miller:
      The Descendants of John J. Christner, privately published February 1961, p. 58.

      More About Martha M Miller:
      Residence: 1920, Age: 10; Marital Status: Single; Relation to Head of House: Daughter/Newbury, Lagrange Co., IN[5480]

   3068   vi.   Frank Russell Miller[5480], born 12 Feb 1914 in Emma, Lagrange Co., IN[5480]; died Sep 1917 in Emma, Lagrange Co., IN[5480].

      Notes for Frank Russell Miller:
      The Descendants of John J. Christner, privately published February 1961, p. 58.

1333. Anna J.[8] Schlabach (Mary D.[7] Frey, Elizabeth J.[6] Christner, Joseph C.[5], Christian J.[4], Johannes John Hans[3], Christian[2], Christen[1])[5481] was born 19 Apr 1884 in Lagrange Co., IN. She married **(1) Urias V. Yoder** 19 Apr 1900. He was born 29 Nov 1881[5482].

Notes for Anna J. Schlabach:
The Descendants of John J. Christner, privately published February 1961, pp. 52, 59 .

Birth: Apr. 19, 1884
Death: Nov. 23, 1968

Spouse: Urias V. Yoder (1881 - 1967)

527

Burial: Miller Amish Cemetery, Lagrange, Lagrange Co., IN
Find A Grave Memorial# 66591728

Notes for Urias V. Yoder:
The Descendants of John J. Christner, privately published February 1961, p. 59.

Birth: Nov. 29, 1881
Death: Sep. 28, 1967

Spouse: Anna Yoder (1884 - 1968)

Burial: Miller Amish Cemetery, Lagrange, Lagrange Co., IN
Find A Grave Memorial# 66591686

More About Urias V. Yoder:
Residence: Lagrange, Lagrange Co., IN[5482]

Children of Anna Schlabach and Urias Yoder are:
    3069   i.   Elenora[9] Yoder, born 19 Sep 1900; died 09 Jul 1901 in High Chair Accident.

        Notes for Elenora Yoder:
        The Descendants of John J. Christner, privately published February 1961, p. 59.

        More About Elenora Yoder:
        Burial: KS

+   3070   ii.   Elizabeth U. Yoder, born 17 May 1902 in Lagrange Co., IN; died 23 Feb 1981 in Lagrange Co., IN.
+   3071   iii. Amos N. Yoder, born 08 Apr 1914 in Lagrange Co., IN; died Bef. 1989.

1334. Ezra J.[8] Schlabach (Mary D.[7] Frey, Elizabeth J.[6] Christner, Joseph C.[5], Christian J.[4], Johannes John Hans[3], Christian[2], Christen[1]) was born 20 Mar 1887 in Topeka, Lagrange Co., IN[5483,5484], and died Oct 1975 in Topeka, Lagrange Co., IN[5484]. He married **Jemima Hostetler** 18 Jun 1910 in IN[5485]. She was born 27 Feb 1893 in Emma, Lagrange Co., IN[5485,5485], and died 15 Apr 1946[5485].

Notes for Ezra J. Schlabach:
The Descendants of John J. Christner, privately published February, 1961, p. 60.

More About Ezra J. Schlabach:
Other-Begin: Lagrange County[5485]
Residence: Lagrange Co., IN[5485]
Social Security Number: 315-22-7975[5486,5487]
SSN issued: IN[5488,5489]

Notes for Jemima Hostetler:
The Descendants of John J. Christner, privately published February 1961, p. 60.

Children of Ezra Schlabach and Jemima Hostetler are:
+   3072   i.   Gerald[9] Schlabach, born 10 Jan 1911 in Topeka, Lagrange Co., IN; died Dec 1976 in Topeka, Lagrange Co., IN.
+   3073   ii.   Neva Schlabach, born 21 Oct 1912 in Topeka, Lagrange Co., IN; died 13 Dec 1998 in Lagrange Co., IN.
+   3074   iii. Gretshen Schlabach, born 21 May 1919.

1335. Eleanora[8] Schlabach (Mary D.[7] Frey, Elizabeth J.[6] Christner, Joseph C.[5], Christian J.[4], Johannes John Hans[3], Christian[2], Christen[1]) was born 04 Mar 1892. She married **Samuel Edward Dooty** 01 Dec 1923. He was born 01 Apr 1889.

Notes for Eleanora Schlabach:
The Descendants of John J. Christner, privately published February 1961, p. 60.

Notes for Samuel Edward Dooty:
They have been engaged in Church work for over 40 years in Kansas, Iowa, California, Michigan, & Indiana. They later lived at 107 Spring Street, Three Rivers, Michigan.

The Descendants of John J. Christner, privately published February, 1961, p. 60.

Children of Eleanora Schlabach and Samuel Dooty are:
+   3075   i.   Samuella Fern[9] Dooty, born 22 Aug 1924 in Cedar Rapids, IA.
     3076   ii.   Vera Mae Dooty, born 22 Aug 1924; died 22 Aug 1924.

> Notes for Vera Mae Dooty:
> The Descendants of John J. Christner, privately published February, 1961, p. 60.

1337. Daniel B.[8] Miller (Barbara D.[7] Frey, Elizabeth J.[6] Christner, Joseph C.[5], Christian J.[4], Johannes John Hans[3], Christian[2], Christen[1])[5490,5490] was born 24 Apr 1878 in Lagrange, Lagrange Co., IN[5490,5490], and died 14 Mar 1944[5490,5490]. He married **Mattie C. Miller** 23 Nov 1899. She was born 09 Oct 1879, and died 02 Sep 1943.

Notes for Daniel B. Miller:
The Descendants of John J. Christner, privately published February 1961, p. 61.

More About Daniel B. Miller:
Religion: Old Order Amish/
Residence: 1930, Clinton, Elkhart Co., IN[5490,5490]

Notes for Mattie C. Miller:
The Descendants of John J. Christner, privately published February 1961, pp. 61, 62.

Children of Daniel Miller and Mattie Miller are:
     3077   i.   Elmina[9] Miller, born 09 Feb 1901; died 18 Dec 1901.

> Notes for Elmina Miller:
> The Descendants of John J. Christner, privately published February 1961, p. 61.

+   3078   ii.   Saloma D. Miller, born 30 Apr 1904 in Lagrange Co., IN; died 29 Jan 1977 in Elkhart Co., IN.
     3079   iii.   Mary Ann Miller, born 16 Oct 1906; died 15 Jan 1907.
     3080   iv.   Infant Miller, born 09 Feb 1908; died 09 Feb 1908.

> Notes for Infant Miller:
> The Descendants of John J. Christner, privately published February 1961, p. 62.

     3081   v.   Infant Miller, born 17 Mar 1909; died 17 Mar 1909.

> Notes for Infant Miller:
> The Descendants of John J. Christner, privately published February, 1961, p. 62.

+   3082   vi.   Ada D. Miller, born 15 Jun 1912.
     3083   vii.   Barbara D. Miller, born 25 Nov 1914 in Goshen, Elkhart Co., IN. She married David A. Yoder 14 Feb 1946 in By Perry Nisley; born 19 Aug 1914.

> Notes for Barbara D. Miller:
> The Descendants of John J. Christner, privately published February 1961, p. 62.

> Notes for David A. Yoder:
> The Descendants of John J. Christner, published February 1961, p. 62.

> More About David A. Yoder:

Religion: Old Order Amish/

3084   viii.   Joseph Miller, born 01 Aug 1917; died 12 May 1920.

Notes for Joseph Miller:
The Descendants of John J. Christner, privately published February 1961, p. 62.

+   3085   ix.   Erma D. Miller, born 10 Feb 1923 in Colon, MI.

1338. Joseph B.[8] Miller (Barbara D.[7] Frey, Elizabeth J.[6] Christner, Joseph C.[5], Christian J.[4], Johannes John Hans[3], Christian[2], Christen[1])[5491,5492] was born 01 Aug 1880 in Lagrange Co., IN[5493,5494], and died 23 Mar 1936 in Lagrange Co., IN[5495,5496]. He married **Sarah E. Troyer**[5497] 12 Feb 1903 in Lagrange Co., IN[5497]. She was born 07 Jun 1884 in Lagrange Co., IN[5497], and died 25 May 1931 in Lagrange Co., IN[5497].

Notes for Joseph B. Miller:
The Descendants of John J. Christner, privately published February 1961, p. 62.

He was Old Order Amish.

More About Joseph B. Miller:
Religion: Old Order Amish/

Notes for Sarah E. Troyer:
The Descendants of John J. Christner, privately published February 1961, p. 62.

Children of Joseph Miller and Sarah Troyer are:
+   3086   i.   Samuel J.[9] Miller, born 07 Dec 1903 in Topeka, Lagrange Co., IN; died 07 Jan 1960.
+   3087   ii.   William J. Miller, born 16 Mar 1905 in Topeka, Lagrange Co., IN; died 01 Aug 1969 in IN.
+   3088   iii.   Jacob Miller, born 16 Mar 1905.
    3089   iv.   Lydia J. Miller[5497], born 05 May 1907 in Topeka, Lagrange Co., IN[5497].

Notes for Lydia J. Miller:
The Descendants of John J. Christner, privately published February 1961, p. 62.

+   3090   v.   Daniel S. Miller, born 22 Sep 1908 in Topeka, Lagrange Co., IN; died 17 Jul 1985 in Lagrange Co., IN.
+   3091   vi.   Joseph J. Miller, born 28 Dec 1911 in Lagrange Co., IN; died Apr 1986 in Luzerne, PA.
    3092   vii.   Lizzie Miller[5497], born 09 Aug 1914 in Topeka, Lagrange Co., IN[5497]; died 21 Feb 1916 in Topeka, Lagrange Co., IN[5497].

Notes for Lizzie Miller:
The Descendants of John J. Christner, privately published February 1961, p. 62.

+   3093   viii.   Amos J. Miller, born 12 May 1917 in Shipshewana, Elkhart Co., IN; died 27 Oct 2006 in Shipshewana, Lagrange Co., IN.

1339. Elizabeth B.[8] Miller (Barbara D.[7] Frey, Elizabeth J.[6] Christner, Joseph C.[5], Christian J.[4], Johannes John Hans[3], Christian[2], Christen[1])[5498,5498] was born 31 Jan 1885 in Lagrange Co., IN[5498,5498]. She married **Benjamin M. Bontrager** 02 Feb 1904. He was born 12 Nov 1877, and died 02 May 1959.

Notes for Elizabeth B. Miller:
The Descendants of John J. Christner, privately published February 1961, p. 64.

Notes for Benjamin M. Bontrager:
The Descendants of John J. Christner, privately published February 1961, p. 64.

More About Benjamin M. Bontrager:
Religion: Old Order Amish/

Children of Elizabeth Miller and Benjamin Bontrager are:

+ 3094   i.   Joseph[9] Bontrager.
+ 3095   ii.   Manas B. Bontrager, born 21 Feb 1905 in Topeka, Lagrange Co., IN.
+ 3096   iii.   Noah B. Bontrager, born 27 Aug 1907; died 03 Oct 1969.
+ 3097   iv.   Joseph B. Bontrager, born 05 Jan 1910; died 17 Nov 1984 in Lagrange, Lagrange Co., IN.
    3098   v.   Saloma Bontrager, born 15 Dec 1912.

> Notes for Saloma Bontrager:
> The Descendants of John J. Christner, privately published February 1961, p. 64.

+ 3099   vi.   Barbara Bontrager, born 05 Feb 1917; died 21 Jul 2011 in Topeka, Lagrange Co., IN.
+ 3100   vii.   Lydia Bontrager, born 01 Jun 1921.

1340. Noah B.[8] Miller (Barbara D.[7] Frey, Elizabeth J.[6] Christner, Joseph C.[5], Christian J.[4], Johannes John Hans[3], Christian[2], Christen[1])[5498,5498] was born 25 Feb 1891 in South Bend, St Joseph, IN[5498,5498]. He married **Edna G. Streeter** 20 May 1915. She was born 05 Oct 1896.

Notes for Noah B. Miller:
The Descendants of John J. Christner, privately published February 1961, p. 65.

More About Noah B. Miller:
Other-Begin: Lagrange Co.[5498]
Residence: Not Stated, Lagrange, Indiana[5498]

Notes for Edna G. Streeter:
The Descendants of John J. Christner, privately published February 1961, p. 65.

Child of Noah Miller and Edna Streeter is:
    3101   i.   Robert Frank[9] Miller, born 03 Feb 1925.

> Notes for Robert Frank Miller:
> The Descendants of John J. Christner, privately published February 1961, p. 65.

1342. Simon J.[8] Frey (John D.[7], Elizabeth J.[6] Christner, Joseph C.[5], Christian J.[4], Johannes John Hans[3], Christian[2], Christen[1]) was born 18 Dec 1882 in Holmes Co., OH, and died 1956 in Goshen, Elkhart Co., IN[5499]. He married **Fannie S Miller** 25 Dec 1906 in in Newaygo Co. Michigan by Valentine Hostetler[5499]. She was born 23 Aug 1884, and died 1970 in Goshen, Elkhart Co., IN[5499].

Notes for Simon J. Frey:
The Descendants of John J. Christner, privately published February 1961, p. 82.

Notes for Fannie S Miller:
The Descendants of John J. Christner, privately published February 1961, p. 82.

Children of Simon Frey and Fannie Miller are:

+ 3102   i.   Edward S[9] Frey, born 24 Apr 1908 in Bristol, Elkhart Co., IN; died 26 Nov 2000 in Isleton, Sacramento Co., CA.
+ 3103   ii.   Irvin S. Frey, born 07 Sep 1909 in Bristol, Elkhart Co., IN; died Jun 1985 in Goshen, Elkhart Co., IN.
+ 3104   iii.   Susannah S. Frey, born 07 Jul 1911; died 31 May 2010 in Elkhart, Elkhart Co., IN.
+ 3105   iv.   Walter Harley Frey, born 25 Mar 1914 in Bristol, Elkhart Co., IN; died Aug 1986 in Elkhart, Elkhart Co., IN.
+ 3106   v.   Mayme Maude Frey, born 08 Jan 1918 in Bristol, Elkhart Co., IN; died Jul 1989 in Elkhart Co., IN.
+ 3107   vi.   William Owen Frey, born 01 Dec 1920.
+ 3108   vii.   Vernon Jay Frey, born 06 May 1923.
+ 3109   viii.   Frances Darlene Frey, born 23 Apr 1925.

1345. Elmer J.[8] Frey (John D.[7], Elizabeth J.[6] Christner, Joseph C.[5], Christian J.[4], Johannes John Hans[3], Christian[2], Christen[1]) was born 26 Oct 1888. He married **Lydia L. Kaser** 22 Jan 1910. She was born 26 Mar 1888.

Notes for Elmer J. Frey:
The Descendants of John J. Christner, privately published February 1961, pp. 82, 83.

Notes for Lydia L. Kaser:
The Descendants of John J. Christner, privately published February 1961, p. 83.

Children of Elmer Frey and Lydia Kaser are:

3110   i.   John E.[9] Frey, born 09 Aug 1910.

         Notes for John E. Frey:
         The Descendants of John J. Christner, privately published February 1961, p. 83.

3111   ii.   Emanuel E Frey, born 22 Dec 1911.

         Notes for Emanuel E Frey:
         The Descendants of John J. Christner, privately published February 1961, p. 83.

3112   iii.   Lizzie E. Frey, born 19 Feb 1913.

         Notes for Lizzie E. Frey:
         The Descendants of John J. Christner, privately published February 1961, p. 83.

3113   iv.   Rosemary E. Frey, born 29 Feb 1916; died 18 May 1924.

         Notes for Rosemary E. Frey:
         The Descendants of John J. Christner, privately published February 1961, p. 83.

3114   v.   Wesley E. Frey, born 24 Nov 1918.

         Notes for Wesley E. Frey:
         The Descendants of John J. Christner, privately published February 1961, p. 83.

3115   vi.   Joseph E. Frey, born 12 Jan 1920.

         Notes for Joseph E. Frey:
         The Descendants of John J. Christner, privately published February 1961, p. 83.

1346. Sarah J.[8] Frey (John D.[7], Elizabeth J.[6] Christner, Joseph C.[5], Christian J.[4], Johannes John Hans[3], Christian[2], Christen[1]) was born 22 Oct 1891. She married **Eli Chupp**. He was born 16 Jul 1882.

Notes for Sarah J. Frey:
The Descendants of John J. Christner, privately published February 1961, pp. 82, 83.

Notes for Eli Chupp:
The Descendants of John J. Christner, privately published February 1961, p. 83.

Children of Sarah Frey and Eli Chupp are:

+   3116   i.   Edna[9] Chupp, born 02 Oct 1909 in White Cloud, Newago Co., MI.
     3117   ii.   Jonas Chupp, born 24 Nov 1910; died 21 May 1918.

         Notes for Jonas Chupp:
         The Descendants of John J. Christner, privately published February 1961, p. 84.

3118   iii.   Amos Chupp, born 17 Jul 1912.

Notes for Amos Chupp:
The Descendants of John J. Christner, privately published February 1961, p. 84.

3119   iv.   Nathaniel Chupp, born 05 Sep 1914; died 05 Sep 1914.

Notes for Nathaniel Chupp:
The Descendants of John J. Christner, privately published February 1961, p. 84.

3120   v.   Wilis Chupp, born 17 May 1916.

Notes for Wilis Chupp:
The Descendants of John J. Christner, privately published February 1961, p. 84.

3121   vi.   Adaline Chupp, born 03 Feb 1919.

Notes for Adaline Chupp:
The Descendants of John J. Christner, privately published February 1961, p. 84.

3122   vii.   Infant Chupp, born 17 Mar 1921.

Notes for Infant Chupp:
The Descendants of John J. Christner, privately published February 1961, p. 84.

1350. Andrew J.[8] **Frey** (John D.[7], Elizabeth J.[6] Christner, Joseph C.[5], Christian J.[4], Johannes John Hans[3], Christian[2], Christen[1]) was born 10 Jun 1897 in Muskegon, MI. He married **Ida J. Chupp** 27 Dec 1916. She was born 14 Sep 1898 in Goshen, Elkhart Co., IN.

Notes for Andrew J. Frey:
The Descendants of John J. Christner, privately published February 1961, p. 82.

More About Andrew J. Frey:
Occupation: Auto Garage Mechanic/

Notes for Ida J. Chupp:
The Descendants of John J. Christner, privately published February 1961, p. 83.

Children of Andrew Frey and Ida Chupp are:
3123   i.   Eli Jesse[9] Frey, born 01 Nov 1917.

Notes for Eli Jesse Frey:
The Descendants of John J. Christner, privately published February 1961, p. 83.

3124   ii.   Annie Frances Frey, born 24 Nov 1919.

Notes for Annie Frances Frey:
The Descendants of John J. Christner, privately published February 1961, p. 83.

3125   iii.   Albert Clarence Frey, born 24 Mar 1921.

Notes for Albert Clarence Frey:
The Descendants of John J. Christner, privately published February 1961, p. 83.

3126   iv.   William Frey, born 24 Jan 1923; died 24 Jan 1923.

Notes for William Frey:
The Descendants of John J. Christner, privately published February 1961, p. 83.

1352. Daniel J.[8] **Frey** (John D.[7], Elizabeth J.[6] Christner, Joseph C.[5], Christian J.[4], Johannes John Hans[3], Christian[2], Christen[1]) was born 19 Aug 1915. He married **Lydia G. Helmuth** 21 Oct 1937. She was born 11

Dec 1918.

Notes for Daniel J. Frey:
The Descendants of John J. Christner, privately published February 1961, p. 84.

Notes for Lydia G. Helmuth:
The Descendants of John J. Christner, privately published February 1961, p. 84.

Children of Daniel Frey and Lydia Helmuth are:

 3127 i. Elizabeth Mae[9] Frey, born 23 Aug 1938; died 24 Aug 1938.

      Notes for Elizabeth Mae Frey:
      The Descendants of John J. Christner, privately published February 1961, p. 84.

 3128 ii. John Olen Frey, born 13 Jun 1939.

      Notes for John Olen Frey:
      The Descendants of John J. Christner, privately published February 1961, p. 84.

 3129 iii. Henry Frey, born 24 Nov 1940; died 26 Nov 1940.

      Notes for Henry Frey:
      The Descendants of John J. Christner, privately published February 1961, p. 84.

 3130 iv. Jacob Frey, born 08 Sep 1942.

      Notes for Jacob Frey:
      The Descendants of John J. Christner, privately published February 1961, p. 84.

 3131 v. Christie Frey, born 29 Aug 1943.

      Notes for Christie Frey:
      The Descendants of John J. Christner, privately published February 1961, p. 84.

 3132 vi. Joseph Frey, born 16 Mar 1945.

      Notes for Joseph Frey:
      The Descendants of John J. Christner, privately published February 1961, p. 84.

 3133 vii. Daniel Frey Jr., born 11 Dec 1946.

      Notes for Daniel Frey Jr.:
      The Descendants of John J. Christner, privately published February 1961, p. 84.

 3134 viii. Susie Frey, born 06 Dec 1947; died 06 Dec 1947.

      Notes for Susie Frey:
      The Descendants of John J. Christner, privately published February 1961, p. 84.

 3135 ix. Mary Ellen Frey, born 07 Aug 1949.

      Notes for Mary Ellen Frey:
      The Descendants of John J. Christner, privately published February 1961, p. 84.

 3136 x. Clarence Jay Frey, born 23 Oct 1952.

      Notes for Clarence Jay Frey:
      The Descendants of John J. Christner, privately published February 1961, p. 84.

 3137 xi. Samuel Frey, born 31 Dec 1953; died 01 Jan 1954.

      Notes for Samuel Frey:
      The Descendants of John J. Christner, privately published February 1961, p. 84.

1353. Willard J.[8] **Frey** (John D.[7], Elizabeth J.[6] Christner, Joseph C.[5], Christian J.[4], Johannes John Hans[3], Christian[2], Christen[1]) was born 03 Feb 1918. He married **Hartense W. Parker** 17 Dec 1942. She was born 09 Oct 1921.

Notes for Willard J. Frey:
The Descendants of John J. Christner, privately published February 1961, p. 84.

Notes for Hartense W. Parker:
The Descendants of John J. Christner, privately published February 1961, p. 84.

Children of Willard Frey and Hartense Parker are:

    3138   i.   Judith Kay[9] Frey, born 16 Feb 1943.

                  Notes for Judith Kay Frey:
                  The Descendants of John J. Christner, privately published February 1961, p. 84.

    3139   ii.   James D. Frey, born 30 Mar 1946.

                  Notes for James D. Frey:
                  The Descendants of John J. Christner, privately published February 1961, p. 84.

    3140   iii.   Jeffery Lynn Frey, born 13 Sep 1957.

                  Notes for Jeffery Lynn Frey:
                  The Descendants of John J. Christner, privately published February 1961, p. 84.

    3141   iv.   Jane Sue Frey, born 01 Oct 1958.

                  Notes for Jane Sue Frey:
                  The Descendants of John J. Christner, privately published February 1961, p. 84.

1354. Samuel J.[8] **Frey** (John D.[7], Elizabeth J.[6] Christner, Joseph C.[5], Christian J.[4], Johannes John Hans[3], Christian[2], Christen[1])[5500] was born 13 Jan 1920 in Lagrange Co., IN[5500], and died 27 Oct 1999 in Auburn, Dekalb Co., IN[5500]. He married **(1) Bracey Alice Parker**[5500] 14 Mar 1942[5500]. She was born 28 Jan 1923 in Elkhart, Elkhart Co., IN[5500], and died 26 Jul 1953 in Lagrange, Lagrange Co., IN[5500]. He married **(2) Rosa Marie Whysong** 16 Oct 1954. She was born 21 Jun 1932.

Notes for Samuel J. Frey:
The Descendants of John J. Christner, privately published February 1961, p. 84.

Notes for Bracey Alice Parker:
The Descendants of John J. Christner, privately published February 1961, p. 84.

Notes for Rosa Marie Whysong:
The Descendants of John J. Christner, privately published February 1961, p. 84.

Children of Samuel Frey and Bracey Parker are:

    3142   i.   Jerry Lee[9] Frey, born 26 Feb 1943.

                  Notes for Jerry Lee Frey:
                  The Descendants of John J. Christner, privately published February 1961, p. 84.

    3143   ii.   Jack S. Frey, born 03 Mar 1946.

                  Notes for Jack S. Frey:
                  The Descendants of John J. Christner, privately published February 1961, p. 84.

1355. Elizabeth J.[8] Fry (Joseph D.[7] Frey, Elizabeth J.[6] Christner, Joseph C.[5], Christian J.[4], Johannes John Hans[3], Christian[2], Christen[1]) was born 24 Jan 1879 in Emma, Lagrange Co., IN[5501], and died 23 Aug 1933 in Yoder, KS. She married **Daniel N. Miller**[5502] 09 Dec 1897. He was born 04 Feb 1872, and died 17 Aug 1961 in Hutchinson, Reno Co., KS[5502].

Notes for Elizabeth J. Fry:
The Descendants of John J. Christner, privately published February 1961, p. 66.

Notes for Daniel N. Miller:
The Descendants of John J. Christner, privately published February 1961, p. 66.

Children of Elizabeth Fry and Daniel Miller are:

    3144   i.   Barbara D.[9] Miller, born 15 Oct 1898; died 31 Jan 1899.

                      Notes for Barbara D. Miller:
                      The Descendants of John J. Christner, privately published February 1961, p. 67.

    3145   ii.   Roy D. Miller, born 02 Jan 1900; died 07 Jan 1900.

                      Notes for Roy D. Miller:
                      The Descendants of John J. Christner, privately published February 1961, p. 67.

+   3146   iii.   Katie Miller, born 12 Feb 1901 in Hutchinson, Reno Co., KS; died 09 Jun 1934 in Hutchinson, Reno Co., KS.
+   3147   iv.   Mary Miller, born 10 Aug 1903.
+   3148   v.   Alvin Miller, born 14 Dec 1905 in Corfu, NY.
+   3149   vi.   Joe Alvin Miller, born 14 Dec 1905 in Corfu, NY; died 02 Mar 2001 in Rockingham, VA.
    3150   vii.   Mamie Miller, born 13 May 1908; died 25 May 1930 in 5 friends Killed in a Auto/Train Accident all buried in one grave.

                      Notes for Mamie Miller:
                      The Descendants of John J. Christner, privately published February 1961, p. 67.

+   3151   viii.   Joe Miller, born 21 Feb 1911.
+   3152   ix.   Ray Miller, born 02 Mar 1913.
    3153   x.   Alice D. Miller, born 30 Dec 1915.

                      Notes for Alice D. Miller:
                      The Descendants of John J. Christner, privately published February 1961, p. 67.

                      More About Alice D. Miller:
                      Occupation: School Teacher at Tonawanda, New York/

+   3154   xi.   Cora Miller, born 01 Nov 1919.
+   3155   xii.   Nora Miller, born 19 Jun 1922.

1356. Mary J.[8] Fry (Joseph D.[7] Frey, Elizabeth J.[6] Christner, Joseph C.[5], Christian J.[4], Johannes John Hans[3], Christian[2], Christen[1])[5503] was born 24 Aug 1880 in Kalona, Washington Co., IA[5503], and died 13 Oct 1964[5503]. She married **Harvey C. Miller** 06 May 1901[5503]. He was born 06 Feb 1881 in IN[5503], and died 07 Dec 1949[5503].

Notes for Mary J. Fry:
The Descendants of John J. Christner, privately published February 1961, pp. 66, 68.

More About Mary J. Fry:
Burial: South Gingerich Cemetery (110) Northwest of Kalona/Washington County, Iowa, USA[5503]

More About Harvey C. Miller:
Burial: South Gingerich Cemetery (111) Northwest of Kalona/Washington County, Iowa, USA[5503]

Children of Mary Fry and Harvey Miller are:

+ 3156   i.   Barbara[9] Miller, born 08 Feb 1902 in Haven, Reno Co., KS; died 09 May 1974 in Grantsville, Garrett Co., MD.
+ 3157   ii.   Clemens Miller, born 12 Dec 1903 in Haven, Reno Co., KS; died 15 Jul 1934 in Drowning/.
   3158   iii.   Infant Son Miller, born 06 May 1905; died 13 May 1905.
+ 3159   iv.   Amos H. Miller, born 11 Oct 1906 in KS; died 23 Jun 1942.
+ 3160   v.   Clarence M. Miller, born 08 Sep 1907 in Kalona, Washington Co., IA; died 29 Jul 2001 in Kalona, Washington Co., IA.
+ 3161   vi.   Samuel H. Miller, born 08 Oct 1908 in Haven, Reno Co., KS; died 20 Aug 1998.
   3162   vii.   Ezra Miller[5503], born 05 May 1911[5503]; died 22 Feb 1920[5503].
+ 3163   viii.   Lydian Miller, born 07 Jul 1912; died 29 Jul 1947.
+ 3164   ix.   Susan H. Miller, born 23 Jan 1914; died 09 May 1988 in Holmes Co., OH.
   3165   x.   Enos H. Miller, born 09 Mar 1915 in KS[5503]; died 29 Dec 2001[5503]. He married Ada Glick 22 Dec 1936; born 03 Mar 1915.

       Notes for Enos H. Miller:
       The Descendants of John J. Christner, privately published February 1961, p. 72.

       Obituary:

       MILLER, Enos H; 86; Yoder, KS>Sarasota FL; Sarasota H-T; 2001-12-30; sarcher

       Notes for Ada Glick:
       The Descendants of John J. Christner, privately published February 1961, p. 72.

+ 3166   xi.   Magdalena H Miller, born 17 Oct 1916 in Haven, Reno Co., KS; died 17 Nov 2003 in Kalona, Washington Co., IA.
+ 3167   xii.   Mary H. Miller, born 12 Jun 1918 in Yoder, Reno Co., KS; died 05 Feb 2009.
+ 3168   xiii.   Edna M. Miller, born 30 Aug 1919.
+ 3169   xiv.   Harvey H. Miller, born 29 Jul 1921 in Conway Springs, Sumner Co., KS; died 02 Sep 2012 in Mercy Hospital/Iowa City, Johnson Co., IA.
+ 3170   xv.   Henry M. Miller, born 29 Jul 1921 in Kalona, Washington Co., IA; died 16 Mar 1997.

1357. John J.[8] Fry (Joseph D.[7] Frey, Elizabeth J.[6] Christner, Joseph C.[5], Christian J.[4], Johannes John Hans[3], Christian[2], Christen[1])[5504] was born 02 Jul 1882 in Lagrange Co., IN[5504,5505], and died 13 Dec 1966 in Shipshewana, Lagrange Co., IN[5505]. He married **(1) Mahala Miller** 08 Dec 1903. She was born 12 Apr 1884 in Ford Co., KS[5506], and died 08 Dec 1939[5506]. He married **(2) Anna Bontrager Yoder** 19 Jan 1941. She was born 18 Aug 1895.

Notes for John J. Fry:
The Descendants of John J. Christner, privately published February 1961, pp. 66, 72.

More About John J. Fry:
Social Security Number: 363-24-2999/[5507]
SSN issued: MI[5507]

Notes for Mahala Miller:
The Descendants of John J. Christner, privately published February 1961, p. 72.

Notes for Anna Bontrager Yoder:
The Descendants of John J. Christner, privately published February 1961, p. 74.

I think her maiden name was Bontrager.

Children of John Fry and Mahala Miller are:

+ 3171   i.   Elizabeth[9] Fry, born 12 Jun 1905 in Haven, Reno Co., KS; died 21 May 1995 in Catlett, Fauquier Co., VA.
+ 3172   ii.   Freddie Fry, born 28 May 1911 in Middlebury, Elkhart Co., IN.

+   3173   iii.   Sadie J. Fry, born 07 Aug 1916 in Nappanee, Elkhart Co., IN; died 16 Mar 2000.

1358. Daniel J.[8] Fry (Joseph D.[7] Frey, Elizabeth J.[6] Christner, Joseph C.[5], Christian J.[4], Johannes John Hans[3], Christian[2], Christen[1])[5508] was born 24 Jan 1884 in Lagrange Co., IN[5508], and died 24 Nov 1911 in Haven, Reno Co., KS[5508]. He married **Anna V. Yoder** 14 Dec 1905. She was born 06 Feb 1885[5508], and died 01 Jan 1962[5508].

Notes for Daniel J. Fry:
The Descendants of John J. Christner, privately published February, 1961, p. 66

More About Daniel J. Fry:
Alt. Birth: 24 Jan 1884[5508]

Notes for Anna V. Yoder:
The Descendants of John J. Christner, privately published February 1961, p. 74.

Children of Daniel Fry and Anna Yoder are:
+   3174   i.   David D.[9] Fry, born 28 Sep 1906 in Reno Co., KS; died 19 Feb 1991 in Lagrange Co., IN.
+   3175   ii.   Harvey D. Fry, born 13 Sep 1908 in Topeka, Lagrange Co., IN.
+   3176   iii.   Willie D. Fry, born 05 May 1910 in Yoder, Reno Co., KS; died 24 Aug 1991 in Lagrange Co., IN.
     3177   iv.   Daniel Fry, born 15 Jun 1912 in Shipshewana Lagrange Co., IN[5509]; died 24 Aug 1994[5509]. He married Fannie Gingerich[5510,5510] 22 Dec 1936; born 17 Jun 1912 in Wild Horse, Cheyenne Co., CO[5510,5511]; died 08 Jul 2004 in Shipshewana, Lagrange Co., IN[5511,5512].

Notes for Daniel Fry:
The Descendants of John J. Christner, privately published February 1961, pp. 74, 75.

More About Daniel Fry:
Burial: Shipshewana, Lagrange County, Indiana, USA[5513]

Notes for Fannie Gingerich:
The Descendants of John J. Christner, privately published February 1961, pp. 74, 75.

More About Fannie Gingerich:
Residence: 1930, Newbury, Lagrange Co., IN[5514]
Social Security Number: 315-42-8381/[5515]
SSN issued: IN[5515]

1359. Amos J.[8] Fry (Joseph D.[7] Frey, Elizabeth J.[6] Christner, Joseph C.[5], Christian J.[4], Johannes John Hans[3], Christian[2], Christen[1])[5516,5517] was born 20 Nov 1885 in Lagrange Co., IN[5518], and died 29 Nov 1967 in Reno Co., KS[5518]. He married **Sarah Ann Yoder**[5518,5519,5520] 21 Jan 1909 in Reno Co., KS[5521]. She was born 19 May 1890 in Haven, Reno Co., KS[5521,5522], and died 24 Dec 1972 in Reno Co., KS[5522].

Notes for Amos J. Fry:
The Descendants of John J. Christner, privately published February 1961, p. 66.

More About Amos J. Fry:
Social Security Number: 510-42-5855/[5523,5524]
SSN issued: KS[5525,5526]

Notes for Sarah Ann Yoder:
The Descendants of John J. Christner, privately published February 1961, p. 75.

Children of Amos Fry and Sarah Yoder are:
+   3178   i.   Christian A.[9] Fry, born 09 Oct 1909 in Hutchinson, Reno Co., KS; died 29 Apr 1990 in Mesa, Maricopa Co., AZ.
     3179   ii.   Barbara A. Fry, born 02 Nov 1911. She married Louie Knetich 04 Feb 1952; born 31 Aug 1927.

Notes for Barbara A. Fry:
The Descendants of John J. Christner, privately published February 1961, p. 76.

Notes for Louie Knetich:
The Descendants of John J. Christner, privately published February 1961, p. 76.

+   3180   iii.   Mattie A. Fry, born 30 Aug 1913 in Reno Co., KS; died 30 Jun 1997 in Wichita, Sedgwick Co., KS.
+   3181   iv.   Joseph A. Fry, born 17 Mar 1916 in Reno Co., KS; died 26 Dec 1999 in Middlebury, Elkhart Co., IN.
+   3182   v.   Enos A Fry, born 16 Mar 1918.
+   3183   vi.   Alvin LeRoy Fry, born 26 Apr 1924; died 17 Nov 2000 in Los Angeles, Los Angeles Co., CA.
+   3184   vii.   Ora Floyd Fry, born 02 May 1928 in Haven, Reno Co., KS; died 06 Jan 2002 in Haven, Reno Co., KS.

1360. Fannie J.[8] Fry (Joseph D.[7] Frey, Elizabeth J.[6] Christner, Joseph C.[5], Christian J.[4], Johannes John Hans[3], Christian[2], Christen[1]) was born 21 Mar 1887 in Lagrange Co., IN[5527], and died 07 Sep 1934[5527]. She married **Clarence F. Bontrager**[5527] 17 Dec 1908. He was born 19 Jun 1887 in Middlebury, Elkhart Co., IN[5527], and died 29 Jul 1965 in Lagrange, Lagrange Co., IN[5527].

Notes for Fannie J. Fry:
The Descendants of John J. Christner, privately published February 1961, p. 66.

Notes for Clarence F. Bontrager:
The Descendants of John J. Christner, privately published February 1961, p. 77.

More About Clarence F. Bontrager:
Residence: 1915, Lincoln, Reno, Kansas[5527]

Child of Fannie Fry and Clarence Bontrager is:
+   3185   i.   Amos C. F.[9] Bontrager, born 21 Apr 1919 in Deer Park, Custer Co., OK; died Jul 1969.

1362. Enos J.[8] Fry (Joseph D.[7] Frey, Elizabeth J.[6] Christner, Joseph C.[5], Christian J.[4], Johannes John Hans[3], Christian[2], Christen[1])[5528] was born 14 Apr 1890 in Lagrange Co., IN[5528], and died 29 May 1966 in Lagrange Co., IN[5528]. He married **Mattie D. Yoder**[5528] 26 Jan 1911 in Reno Co., KS[5528]. She was born 13 Mar 1892 in Reno Co., KS[5528].

Notes for Enos J. Fry:
The Descendants of John J. Christner, privately published February 1961, pp. 66, 78.

More About Enos J. Fry:
Ordination: 21 Apr 1926, Old Order Amish Preacher in Somner Co. Kansas
Residence: 04 Mar 1941, Moved from Kanas to Topeka Indiana

Notes for Mattie D. Yoder:
The Descendants of John J. Christner, privately published February 1961, pp. 78, 96.

More About Mattie D. Yoder:
Alt. Birth: 13 Mar 1892[5528]

Children of Enos Fry and Mattie Yoder are:
  3186   i.   Susan[9] Fry[5528], born 08 Apr 1912 in Reno Co., KS[5528]; died 08 Apr 1912 in Reno Co., KS[5528].

      Notes for Susan Fry:
      The Descendants of John J. Christner, privately published February 1961, p. 78.

+   3187   ii.   Katie Fry, born 12 Feb 1916 in Haven, Reno Co., KS; died 21 Feb 1982 in Lagrange Co., IN.
+   3188   iii.   Amos E. Fry, born 20 Mar 1918.
+   3189   iv.   Elizabeth Fry, born 08 Nov 1920.

+ 3190　　v.　Levi E. Fry, born 27 Jul 1922 in KS; died 06 Jun 1983 in Lagrange Co., IN.
+ 3191　　vi.　Joseph E. Fry, born 23 Mar 1924 in Lagrange Co., IN; died 08 Oct 1969 in Lagrange Co., IN.
+ 3192　　vii.　Mary Fry, born 30 Apr 1926.
　 3193　　viii.　David Fry, born 19 Dec 1928; died 19 Dec 1928.

　　　　　　　Notes for David Fry:
　　　　　　　The Descendants of John J. Christner, privately published February 1961, p. 78.

　 3194　　ix.　Felty Fry, born 03 May 1930; died 03 May 1930.

　　　　　　　Notes for Felty Fry:
　　　　　　　The Descendants of John J. Christner, privately published February 1961, p. 78.

　 3195　　x.　Ada Fry, born 27 Jul 1932; died 05 Feb 1933.

　　　　　　　Notes for Ada Fry:
　　　　　　　The Descendants of John J. Christner, privately published February 1961, p. 78.

　 3196　　xi.　Barbara Fry, born 19 Jun 1934; died 19 Jun 1934.

　　　　　　　Notes for Barbara Fry:
　　　　　　　The Descendants of John J. Christner, privately published February 1961, p. 78.

1363. Manileus J.[8] Fry (Joseph D.[7] Frey, Elizabeth J.[6] Christner, Joseph C.[5], Christian J.[4], Johannes John Hans[3], Christian[2], Christen[1]) was born 13 Nov 1891, and died 10 Jan 1919. He married **Clara R. Bontrager** 19 Aug 1915. She was born 21 Oct 1896.

Notes for Manileus J. Fry:
The Descendants of John J. Christner, privately published February 1961, pp. 66, 79.

More About Manileus J. Fry:
Residence: Yoder, KS

Notes for Clara R. Bontrager:
The Descendants of John J. Christner, privately published February, 1961, p. 79.

Children of Manileus Fry and Clara Bontrager are:
+ 3197　　i.　Elizabeth[9] Fry, born 17 Apr 1916; died 06 Apr 1946.
　 3198　　ii.　Sylvia Fry, born 06 Jun 1918; died 20 Mar 1919.

　　　　　　　Notes for Sylvia Fry:
　　　　　　　The Descendants of John J. Christner, privately published February 1961, p. 79.

1364. Barbara Ann[8] Fry (Joseph D.[7] Frey, Elizabeth J.[6] Christner, Joseph C.[5], Christian J.[4], Johannes John Hans[3], Christian[2], Christen[1])[5529,5530] was born 03 May 1893 in Haven, Reno Co., KS[5531,5532], and died 06 Sep 1975 in ID[5533,5534]. She married **Joseph Levi Garver**[5535,5536] 29 May 1913. He was born 23 Jul 1892 in Hutchinson, Reno Co., KS[5537,5537,5538], and died 28 Jan 1970 in Council, Adams Co., ID[5539,5540].

Notes for Barbara Ann Fry:
The Descendants of John J. Christner, privately published February 1961, pp. 66, 79.

Birth: 1893
Death: 1975

Burial: Odd Fellows Cemetery, Council, Adams Co., ID
Plot: 4533

More About Barbara Ann Fry:

Residence: 01 Apr 1940, Lincoln, Grant, Kansas, United States[5541,5542]

Notes for Joseph Levi Garver:
The Descendants of John J. Christner, privately published February 1961, p. 79.

Birth: 1892
Death: 1970

Burial: Odd Fellows Cemetery, Council, Adams Co., ID
Plot: 4533

More About Joseph Levi Garver:
Residence: 01 Apr 1940, Lincoln, Grant, Kansas, United States[5543,5544]

Children of Barbara Fry and Joseph Garver are:
+ 3199   i.   Gertrude[9] Garver, born 24 Jan 1914 in KS; died 11 Jun 2010 in Weiser, Washington Co., ID.
+ 3200   ii.   Lloyd Garver, born 07 Feb 1915 in KS; died 07 Jan 1949 in Ada.
   3201   iii.   Stephen Garver, born 13 Sep 1916 in Anchorage, Alaska. He married Alta Calvin Dec 1946; born 30 Jan.

       Notes for Stephen Garver:
       The Descendants of John J. Christner, privately published February 1961, p. 80.

       Notes for Alta Calvin:
       The Descendants of John J. Christner, privately published February 1961, p. 80.

   3202   iv.   Roy Garver, born 15 May 1919; died 13 Apr 1924.

       Notes for Roy Garver:
       The Descendants of John J. Christner, privately published February 1961, p. 79.

+ 3203   v.   Edith Garver, born 02 Feb 1921 in Ulysses, Grant Co., KS; died 25 Jun 2005 in Ulysses, Grant Co., KS.
+ 3204   vi.   Mary Ellen Garver, born 29 Dec 1926.
+ 3205   vii.   Edward Garver, born 25 Aug 1929.

1365. Noah J.[8] Fry (Joseph D.[7] Frey, Elizabeth J.[6] Christner, Joseph C.[5], Christian J.[4], Johannes John Hans[3], Christian[2], Christen[1])[5545] was born 03 Nov 1894 in Haven, Reno Co., KS, and died 22 Aug 1977 in Lagrange Co., IN[5545]. He married **Mary J. Bontrager** 03 Jun 1917. She was born 09 Jun 1897 in Haven, Reno Co., KS, and died 09 Jun 1990 in Macon, Noxubee Co., MS[5545].

Notes for Noah J. Fry:
The Descendants of John J. Christner, privately published February 1961, pp. 66, 80.

More About Noah J. Fry:
Religion: Old Order Amish/
Residence: near Topeka, Indiana

Notes for Mary J. Bontrager:
The Descendants of John J. Christner, privately published February 1961, p. 80.

Children of Noah Fry and Mary Bontrager are:
+ 3206   i.   Joseph N.[9] Fry, born 21 Sep 1921 in Topeka, Lagrange Co., IN; died 19 Jul 2001 in Lagrange Co., IN.
+ 3207   ii.   Sara N. Fry, born 12 Oct 1924.
+ 3208   iii.   Ezra N. Fry, born 10 Oct 1926 in Topeka, Lagrange Co., IN.
+ 3209   iv.   Jacob N. Fry, born 30 Dec 1929 in Topeka, Lagrange Co., IN.

1366. Mattie[8] Fry (Joseph D.[7] Frey, Elizabeth J.[6] Christner, Joseph C.[5], Christian J.[4], Johannes John Hans[3],

Christian[2], Christen[1]) was born 11 Mar 1896 in Hutchinson, Reno Co., KS. She married **Eli J. Gingerich** 12 Nov 1914. He was born 16 Dec 1892.

Notes for Mattie Fry:
The Descendants of John J. Christner, privately published February 1961, pp. 66, 81.

Notes for Eli J. Gingerich:
The Descendants of John J. Christner, privately published February 1961, p. 81.

Children of Mattie Fry and Eli Gingerich are:
+   3210   i.   Joseph E.[9] Gingerich, born 18 Oct 1915 in Hutchinson, Reno Co., KS.
+   3211   ii.   John M. Gingerich, born 08 Oct 1917 in Kendall, KS.
+   3212   iii. Fred E. Gingerich, born 12 Nov 1919 in Hutchinson, Reno Co., KS.
+   3213   iv.   Merl M. Gingerich, born 01 Jan 1922 in Hutchinson, Reno Co., KS.
+   3214   v.   Velma M. Gingerich, born 04 Feb 1925 in Hutchinson, Reno Co., KS.
+   3215   vi.   Mary Lou Gingerich, born 11 Jul 1927 in Hutchinson, Reno Co., KS.
+   3216   vii. Lovelle Fanny Gingerich, born 30 Jul 1929.

1368. Noah S.[8] Frye (Samuel D.[7] Frey, Elizabeth J.[6] Christner, Joseph C.[5], Christian J.[4], Johannes John Hans[3], Christian[2], Christen[1]) was born 23 Jul 1891 in Wolcottville, Lagrange Co., IN. He married **Elizabeth Glick** 24 Dec 1917. She was born 18 Apr 1899.

Notes for Noah S. Frye:
The Descendants of John J. Christner, privately published February 1961, p. 84.

More About Noah S. Frye:
Religion: Old Order Amish/

Notes for Elizabeth Glick:
The Descendants of John J. Christner, privately published February 1961, p. 84.

Children of Noah Frye and Elizabeth Glick are:
+   3217   i.   Daniel N.[9] Frye, born 14 Apr 1919.
+   3218   ii.   Ada Mae Frye, born 01 Dec 1920; died 20 Nov 1998 in Hillsdale, MI.
+   3219   iii. Martha N. Frye, born 23 Jan 1923.
+   3220   iv.   Harley N. Frye, born 30 Mar 1925.

1370. Henry S.[8] Frye (Samuel D.[7] Frey, Elizabeth J.[6] Christner, Joseph C.[5], Christian J.[4], Johannes John Hans[3], Christian[2], Christen[1]) was born 26 Jul 1896 in Topeka, Lagrange Co., IN[5546], and died 05 Oct 1947 in Lagrange Co., IN[5546]. He married **Lydia Ann Troyer**[5546] 09 Jan 1919 in IN[5546]. She was born 08 Apr 1897 in Topeka, Lagrange Co., IN[5546], and died 22 Mar 1966 in Lagrange Co., IN[5546].

Notes for Henry S. Frye:
The Descendants of John J. Christner, privately published February 1961, pp. 84, 85.

More About Henry S. Frye:
Religion: Old Order Amish/
Residence: Topeka, Lagrange Co., IN

Notes for Lydia Ann Troyer:
The Descendants of John J. Christner, privately published February 1961, p. 85.

Children of Henry Frye and Lydia Troyer are:
+   3221   i.   Joas H.[9] Frye, born 21 Dec 1919 in Topeka, Lagrange Co., IN; died 27 Aug 1998 in Middlebury, Elkhart Co., IN.
+   3222   ii.   Susan Frye, born 02 Nov 1921.

+	3223	iii.	Katie H. Frye, born 09 Sep 1923 in Topeka, Lagrange Co., IN; died 11 Oct 2010 in Topeka, Lagrange Co., IN.
+	3224	iv.	Elvie H. Frye, born 23 Sep 1925 in Topeka, Lagrange Co., IN; died 18 Nov 2001 in Shipshewana, Lagrange Co., IN.
+	3225	v.	Noah H. Frye, born 22 Nov 1927.
	3226	vi.	Lovina Frye[5546], born 24 Jul 1930 in Topeka, Lagrange Co., IN[5546]; died 25 Jan 1933 in Topeka, Lagrange Co., IN[5546].
+	3227	vii.	Edna Frye, born 03 Dec 1932.
+	3228	viii.	Ella Frye, born 26 Oct 1935 in IN.
	3229	ix.	Samuel Frye, born 06 Mar 1937.
	3230	x.	Calvin Frye, born 27 May 1938.

1371. Cassie S.[8] Fry (Samuel D.[7] Frey, Elizabeth J.[6] Christner, Joseph C.[5], Christian J.[4], Johannes John Hans[3], Christian[2], Christen[1]) was born 02 Aug 1899 in Topeka, Lagrange Co., IN. She married **Eli J Miller** 18 Dec 1917. He was born 13 Oct 1898.

Notes for Cassie S. Fry:
The Descendants of John J. Christner, privately published February 1961, p. 84.

More About Cassie S. Fry:
Religion: Mennonite/

Children of Cassie Fry and Eli Miller are:
| + | 3231 | i. | Harry[9] Miller, born 06 May 1920. |
| + | 3232 | ii. | Susie Marion Miller, born 12 Mar 1922. |

1376. Elizabeth D.[8] Frey (Daniel D.[7], Elizabeth J.[6] Christner, Joseph C.[5], Christian J.[4], Johannes John Hans[3], Christian[2], Christen[1]) was born 22 Jan 1891 in Lagrange Co., IN. She married **Noah J. Miller** 03 Dec 1914 in By Emanuel I. Miller. He was born 19 Mar 1883.

Notes for Elizabeth D. Frey:
The Descendants of John J. Christner, privately published February 1961, p. 87.

Notes for Noah J. Miller:
The Descendants of John J. Christner, privately published February 1961, p. 87.

More About Noah J. Miller:
Religion: Old Order Amish/

Children of Elizabeth Frey and Noah Miller are:
| + | 3233 | i. | Mahlon[9] Frey, born 20 Jul 1912 in Wellman, Washington Co., IA; died Oct 1964. |
| | 3234 | ii. | Susann Miller, born 05 Apr 1915; died 06 Apr 1915. |

Notes for Susann Miller:
The Descendants of John J. Christner, privately published February 1961, p. 87.

	3235	iii.	Sarahann Miller, born 05 Apr 1915; died 06 Apr 1915.
+	3236	iv.	Mary Ann Miller, born 01 May 1916 in Lagrange Co., IN.
	3237	v.	John N. Miller, born 19 Aug 1917; died 27 Oct 1918.

Notes for John N. Miller:
The Descendants of John J. Christner, privately published February 1961, p. 87.

1377. Catherine D.[8] Frey (Daniel D.[7], Elizabeth J.[6] Christner, Joseph C.[5], Christian J.[4], Johannes John Hans[3], Christian[2], Christen[1]) was born 08 Jul 1892 in Monroe, IN. She married **Daniel J. Schwartz** 01 Sep 1912. He was born 22 Jan 1889.

Notes for Catherine D. Frey:
The Descendants of John J. Christner, privately published February 1961, p. 87.

Notes for Daniel J. Schwartz:
The Descendants of John J. Christner, privately published February 1961, p. 87.

More About Daniel J. Schwartz:
Ordination: 24 Apr 1927, Deacon Old Order Amish
Religion: Old Order Amish/

Children of Catherine Frey and Daniel Schwartz are:
+   3238   i.   Menno D.[9] Schwartz, born 25 Dec 1912 in Geneva, IN.
     3239   ii.   Mary Ann Schwartz, born 27 Apr 1914; died 30 Dec 1918.

                   Notes for Mary Ann Schwartz:
                   The Descendants of John J. Christner, privately published February 1961, p. 87.

     3240   iii. Anna D. Schwartz, born 22 Jan 1916. She married Andrew D. Mast Mar 1954; born 13 Jun 1909.

                   Notes for Anna D. Schwartz:
                   The Descendants of John J. Christner, privately published February 1961, p. 88.

                   Notes for Andrew D. Mast:
                   The Descendants of John J. Christner, privately published February 1961, p. 88.

+   3241   iv.   Daniel D. Schwartz, born 22 Jan 1916 in Camden, MI.
+   3242   v.   Jacob D. Schwartz, born 09 Apr 1917.

   1379. Daniel D. M.[8] Frey (Daniel D.[7], Elizabeth J.[6] Christner, Joseph C.[5], Christian J.[4], Johannes John Hans[3], Christian[2], Christen[1]) was born 13 Sep 1895 in Emma, Lagrange Co., IN[5547], and died 21 Oct 1972[5547]. He married **Elizabeth J. Miller** 06 Sep 1914 in By Emanuel I. Miller. She was born 22 Aug 1895 in Lagrange Co., IN[5547], and died 13 Aug 1958[5547].

Notes for Daniel D. M. Frey:
The Descendants of John J. Christner, privately published February 1961, pp. 48, 88.

More About Daniel D. M. Frey:
Burial: 24 Oct 1972, Miller Cemetery/Lagrange Co., IN[5547]
Religion: Old Order Amish/

Notes for Elizabeth J. Miller:
The Descendants of John J. Christner, privately published February 1961, pp. 48, 88.

More About Elizabeth J. Miller:
Burial: Miller Cemetery/Lagrange Co., IN[5547]

Children of Daniel Frey and Elizabeth Miller are:
+   3243   i.   Tobias D.[9] Frey, born 29 Jan 1915.
+   3244   ii.   Joseph E. Frey, born 12 Jul 1916; died 24 Nov 1991.
+   3245   iii.   Anna D. Frey, born 02 Apr 1918; died 23 Mar 2006 in Ligonier, Noble Co., IN.
+   3246   iv.   Mary Ellen Frey, born 31 Jan 1920.
+   3247   v.   Barbara D. Frey, born 30 Aug 1920 in Topeka, Lagrange Co., IN.
+   3248   vi.   John William Frey, born 30 Mar 1923.
+   3249   vii.   Daniel E. Frey, born 06 Nov 1924.
+   3250   viii. Elizabeth Frey, born 24 Dec 1927.
     3251   ix.   Edna Mae Frey[5547], born 06 May 1935 in Topeka, Lagrange Co., IN; died 04 Mar 1959[5547]. She married Tobias M. Hochstetler[5548] 07 Nov 1957[5549]; born 29 Jan 1935[5549,5550]; died 01 Jul 2009 in Parkview Lagrange Hospital/Lagrange, Lagrange Co., IN[5551].

Notes for Edna Mae Frey:
The Descendants of John J. Christner, privately published February 1961, pp. 88, 89.

Birth: May 6, 1935
Death: Mar. 4, 1959

Wife of TM

Burial: Miller Amish Cemetery, Lagrange, Lagrange Co., IN
Plot: Row 9, lot 5
Find A Grave Memorial# 66641753

Notes for Tobias M. Hochstetler:
The Descendants of John J. Christner, privately published February 1961, p. 89.

Birth: Jan. 29, 1935 - Marshall Co., IN
Death: Jul. 1, 2009 - Lagrange, Lagrange Co., IN

Tobias M. Hochstetler, 74 of 14448 CR 34, son of Mannasses D. and Amella (Borkholder) Hochstetler. On Nov. 7, 1967, he married Fannie Mae Nisley. She survives in additions to one daughter, Barbara (Walter) Helmuth of Nappanee; three sons, Wilber and Arlen R Hochstetler, both of Goshen, and Earl J (Rebecca) Hochstetler of Curtiss, WI; nine grandchildren; three sisters, Anna Gingerich of Jamesport, MO, and Judith (Allen) Kauffman and Clara Hochstetler, both of Middlebury; four brothers, Ezra (Patricia) Hochstetler of Goshen, John H (Mary Ellen) Hichstetler of Middlebury, Ura (Miriam) Hochstetler of Nappanee and Wilbur (Susie) Hochstetler of Charlotte, MI.

One brother, Clarence Hochstetler, preceeded him in death.
Mr Hochstetler was a farmer and member of the Old Order Amish Church.

The funeral service was held at 9:30 am Saterday, July 4 at the Simon Schmucker home, 14592 CR 34, Goshen. Bishop Siomom Schmucker and the home ministers wil officiate. Buriel in Nisley Cemetery, Goshen. Miller-Stewart Funeral Home, 1003 S Main St., Middlebury, assisted with the arrangements.

Burial: Nisley Cemetery, Goshen, Elkhart Co., IN
Find A Grave Memorial# 39153869

More About Tobias M. Hochstetler:
Occupation: Farmer[5551]
Religion: Amish[5551]
Social Security Number: 304-40-4282[5551]
SSN issued: IN[5551,5552]

1380. Anna D.[8] Frey (Daniel D.[7], Elizabeth J.[6] Christner, Joseph C.[5], Christian J.[4], Johannes John Hans[3], Christian[2], Christen[1])[5553] was born 12 Apr 1899 in Topeka, Lagrange Co., IN, and died 05 Oct 1982 in Lagrange Co., IN[5553]. She married **John A. Beechy** 13 Nov 1919 in By Cornelius Christner. He was born 21 Mar 1901 in Lagrange Co., IN[5553], and died 27 Oct 1984 in Lagrange Co., IN[5553].

Notes for Anna D. Frey:
The Descendants of John J. Christner, privately published February 1961, pp. 87, 90.

More About Anna D. Frey:
Residence: 01 Apr 1940, Clearspring, Lagrange Co., IN[5553]

Notes for John A. Beechy:
The Descendants of John J. Christner, privately published February 1961, p. 90.

More About John A. Beechy:
Religion: Old Order Amish/

Residence: 01 Apr 1940, Clearspring, Lagrange Co., IN[5553]

Children of Anna Frey and John Beechy are:

+ 3252   i.   Mary Ann[9] Beechy, born 18 Apr 1920 in Topeka, Lagrange Co., IN.
+ 3253   ii.   Barbara J. Beechy, born 15 Oct 1921 in Lagrange Co., IN; died 06 Aug 1961 in Lagrange Co., IN.
+ 3254   iii.   Katie J. Beechy, born 05 May 1923 in Topeka, Lagrange Co., IN.
+ 3255   iv.   Elizabeth J. Beechy, born 31 May 1924 in Lagrange Co., IN; died 21 Sep 2005 in Lagrange Co., IN.
   3256   v.   Infant Son, born 28 May 1925.

> Notes for Infant Son:
> The Descendants of John J. Christner, privately published February 1961, p. 90.

+ 3257   vi.   Daniel J. Beechy, born 22 Apr 1926.
+ 3258   vii.   Joseph J. Beechy, born 01 Oct 1927.
+ 3259   viii.   John W. Beechy, born 17 Nov 1929.
+ 3260   ix.   Lydia J. Beechy, born 26 Feb 1931.
+ 3261   x.   Alvin Jay Beechy, born 17 Mar 1933.
+ 3262   xi.   Ora J. Beechy, born 22 Sep 1934.
+ 3263   xii.   Anna Mae Beechy, born 08 Sep 1936.
   3264   xiii.   Viola Beechy, born 29 Apr 1938.

> Notes for Viola Beechy:
> Source:
>
> The Descendants of John J. Christner, privately published 1961, February 1961, p. 90

+ 3265   xiv.   Aaron Leroy Beechy, born 13 Sep 1940.

1381. Barbara D.[8] Frey (Daniel D.[7], Elizabeth J.[6] Christner, Joseph C.[5], Christian J.[4], Johannes John Hans[3], Christian[2], Christen[1])[5554] was born 30 Mar 1902[5554]. She married **Levi M. Miller**[5554] 02 Mar 1922. He was born 07 Feb 1902[5554], and died 06 Sep 1955.

Notes for Barbara D. Frey:
The Descendants of John J. Christner, privately published February 1961, p. 87.

Notes for Levi M. Miller:
The Descendants of John J. Christner, privately published February 1961, p. 87, 92.

More About Levi M. Miller:
Religion: Old Order Amish/

Children of Barbara Frey and Levi Miller are:
   3266   i.   Anna L.[9] Miller, born 28 Jan 1924; died 26 Jan 1934.

> Notes for Anna L. Miller:
> The Descendants of John J. Christner, privately published February 1961, p. 92.

+ 3267   ii.   Daniel L. Miller, born 21 Mar 1925 in Topeka, Lagrange Co., IN; died 22 May 1971.
+ 3268   iii.   Amos L. Miller, born 17 Aug 1926 in Arthur, IL.
   3269   iv.   Elizabeth Miller, born 28 Jul 1928; died 03 Apr 1929.

> Notes for Elizabeth Miller:
> The Descendants of John J. Christner, privately published February 1961, p. 92.

+ 3270   v.   Mary Ellen Miller, born 30 Apr 1930.
   3271   vi.   Ray L. Miller, born 10 Mar 1932.

> Notes for Ray L. Miller:
> The Descendants of John J. Christner, privately published February 1961, p. 92.

3272   vii.   John L. Miller, born 12 Nov 1933.

           Notes for John L. Miller:
           The Descendants of John J. Christner, privately published February 1961, p. 92.

3273   viii.   Susanna L. Miller, born 21 Sep 1938.

           Notes for Susanna L. Miller:
           The Descendants of John J. Christner, privately published February 1961, p. 92.

3274   ix.   Fannie Mae Miller, born 01 Jan 1940.

           Notes for Fannie Mae Miller:
           The Descendants of John J. Christner, privately published February 1961, p. 92.

3275   x.   LeRoy L. Miller, born 01 Jun 1942.

           Notes for LeRoy L. Miller:
           The Descendants of John J. Christner, privately published February 1961, p. 92.

1382. John D.[8] Frey (Daniel D.[7], Elizabeth J.[6] Christner, Joseph C.[5], Christian J.[4], Johannes John Hans[3], Christian[2], Christen[1]) was born 24 Jun 1903. He married **Lydia L. Raber** 03 Dec 1929. She was born 12 May 1909.

Notes for John D. Frey:
The Descendants of John J. Christner, privately published February 1961, p. 87.

More About John D. Frey:
Ordination: 30 Oct 1930, Old Order Amish Minister

More About Lydia L. Raber:
Religion: Old Order Amish/

Children of John Frey and Lydia Raber are:
+   3276   i.   Katie D.[9] Fry, born 23 Nov 1932.
    3277   ii.   Fannie D. Fry, born 19 May 1937.
    3278   iii.   Mary D. Fry, born 30 Sep 1938.
    3279   iv.   Paul D. Fry, born 01 Oct 1942.

1383. Joseph D. M.[8] Frey (Daniel D.[7], Elizabeth J.[6] Christner, Joseph C.[5], Christian J.[4], Johannes John Hans[3], Christian[2], Christen[1]) was born 04 May 1905. He married **Katie T. Yoder** 06 Feb 1936. She was born 10 Jul 1908.

Notes for Joseph D. M. Frey:
The Descendants of John J. Christner, privately published February 1961, pp. 87, 92.

More About Joseph D. M. Frey:
Religion: Old Order Amish/

Children of Joseph Frey and Katie Yoder are:
+   3280   i.   Erma J.[9] Frey, born 27 Jul 1938.
    3281   ii.   Irene Fry, born 16 Dec 1941.

1385. Daniel R.[8] Borntrager (Elizabeth D.[7] Frey, Elizabeth J.[6] Christner, Joseph C.[5], Christian J.[4], Johannes John Hans[3], Christian[2], Christen[1]) was born 18 Nov 1890 in Ligonier, Noble Co., IN[5555]. He married **Katie S. Miller** 18 Nov 1915 in By Bishop Jonas D. Borntrager in Reno Co., KS. She was born 05 Mar 1894 in Hubbard, Marion Co., OR.

Notes for Daniel R. Borntrager:
The Descendants of John J. Christner, privately published February 1961, p. 93.

More About Daniel R. Borntrager:
Other-Begin: Reno Co.[5555]
Religion: Old Order Amish/
Residence: Noble, Indiana[5555]

Notes for Katie S. Miller:
The Descendants of John J. Christner, privately published February 1961, p. 93.

More About Katie S. Miller:
Religion: Old Order Amish/

Children of Daniel Borntrager and Katie Miller are:
+ 3282   i.   Elizabeth D.[9] Borntrager, born 20 Oct 1916 in Reno Co., KS.
+ 3283   ii.   Lydia D. Borntrager, born 29 Dec 1918 in Reno Co., KS.
+ 3284   iii.   Rudolph D. Borntrager, born 13 Sep 1920 in Reno Co., KS.
+ 3285   iv.   Samuel D. Borntrager, born 22 Dec 1922 in Reno Co., KS.
+ 3286   v.   Edna D. Borntrager, born 09 Dec 1924 in Butler Co., MO.
   3287   vi.   Andrew Borntrager, born 22 May 1927 in Belle City, MO; died 23 May 1927 in Belle City, MO.

     Notes for Andrew Borntrager:
     The Descendants of John J. Christner, privately published February 1961, p. 93.

+ 3288   vii.   Mary D. Borntrager, born 13 Jun 1928 in Tanner, MO.
+ 3289   viii.   Ida Mae Borntrager, born 30 Apr 1932 in Tanner, MO.

1386. Susan R.[8] Borntrager (Elizabeth D.[7] Frey, Elizabeth J.[6] Christner, Joseph C.[5], Christian J.[4], Johannes John Hans[3], Christian[2], Christen[1]) was born 25 Oct 1892 in Haven, Reno Co., KS[5555], and died 15 Jan 1919[5555]. She married **Andrew I. Chupp** 29 Apr 1909 in By Bishop Eli Beachy in Anderson, Co. Kansas. He was born 22 Feb 1888, and died 26 Nov 1941 in Sturgi, MI.

Notes for Susan R. Borntrager:
The Descendants of John J. Christner, privately published February 1961, pp. 93, 94.

Notes for Andrew I. Chupp:
The Descendants of John J. Christner, privately published February 1961, p. 94.

Children of Susan Borntrager and Andrew Chupp are:
   3290   i.   Rudolph[9] Chupp, born 26 Oct 1909; died 07 Mar 1911.

     Notes for Rudolph Chupp:
     The Descendants of John J. Christner, privately published February 1961, p. 94.

+ 3291   ii.   Levi A. Chupp, born 01 Mar 1911 in Middlebury, Elkhart Co., IN.
+ 3292   iii.   Lizzie A. Chupp, born 12 Feb 1912 in Goshen, Elkhart Co., IN.
   3293   iv.   Infant Chupp, born 09 Apr 1916; died 09 Apr 1916.

     Notes for Infant Chupp:
     The Descendants of John J. Christner, privately published February 1961, p. 94.

+ 3294   v.   Mattie A. Chupp, born 30 Oct 1916 in IN; died 11 Aug 2010 in South Bend, St. Joseph Co., IN.

1387. Henry R.[8] Borntrager (Elizabeth D.[7] Frey, Elizabeth J.[6] Christner, Joseph C.[5], Christian J.[4], Johannes John Hans[3], Christian[2], Christen[1]) was born 07 Nov 1893 in Goshen, Elkhart Co., IN[5556], and died 16 Apr 1957 in Goshen, Elkhart Co., IN[5556]. He married **Clara Schrock** 08 Nov 1917 in By Bishop Jonas D Borntrager. She was born 14 Apr 1896 in Haven, Reno Co., KS[5557,5558], and died 06 Dec 1986[5558].

Notes for Henry R. Borntrager:
The Descendants of John J. Christner, privately published February 1961, pp. 93, 95.

Died of cancer.

More About Henry R. Borntrager:
Other-Begin: Reno Co.[5559]
Religion: Mennonite/
Residence: Not Stated, Reno, Kansas[5559]

Notes for Clara Schrock:
The Descendants of John J. Christner, privately published February 1961, p. 95.

Children of Henry Borntrager and Clara Schrock are:
+ 3295   i.   Susan[9] Borntrager, born 02 Sep 1918 in Millersburg, Elkhart Co., IN; died 18 Jan 2000 in Elkhart Co., IN.
+ 3296   ii.   Albert C. Borntrager, born 09 Sep 1919 in Nappanee, IN.
   3297   iii.   Elizabeth Borntrager, born 22 Nov 1923.

       Notes for Elizabeth Borntrager:
       The Descendants of John J. Christner, privately published February 1961, p. 95.

   3298   iv.   Rudolph Borntrager, born 23 Apr 1925.

       Notes for Rudolph Borntrager:
       The Descendants of John J. Christner, privately published February 1961, p. 95.

+ 3299   v.   Harvey C. Borntrager, born 14 Dec 1926 in Goshen, Elkhart Co., IN.
   3300   vi.   Jonas Borntrager, born 07 Dec 1927 in Yoder, Reno Co., KS[5560]; died 31 Aug 2001 in Baltimore, Baltimore, MD[5560].

       Notes for Jonas Borntrager:
       The Descendants of John J. Christner, privately published February 1961, p. 95.

       More About Jonas Borntrager:
       Social Security Number: 310-28-6303/[5560]
       SSN issued: IN[5560]

   3301   vii.   Barbara Borntrager, born 02 Jan 1929.

       Notes for Barbara Borntrager:
       The Descendants of John J. Christner, privately published February 1961, p. 95.

   3302   viii.   Esther Borntrager[5561], born Jul 1932; died Bef. 2008[5561].

       Notes for Esther Borntrager:
       The Descendants of John J. Christner, privately published February 1961, p. 95.

+ 3303   ix.   Lloyd Borntrager, born 10 Oct 1933.

1388. Samuel R.[8] Borntrager (Elizabeth D.[7] Frey, Elizabeth J.[6] Christner, Joseph C.[5], Christian J.[4], Johannes John Hans[3], Christian[2], Christen[1])[5562] was born 28 Nov 1896 in Curryville, Pike Co., MO[5562,5563]. He married **Lizzie Yoder**[5564] 29 May 1919. She was born 21 Aug 1900.

Notes for Samuel R. Borntrager:
The Descendants of John J. Christner, privately published February 1961, pp. 93, 96.

More About Samuel R. Borntrager:
Other-Begin: Reno Co.[5564,5565]
Religion: OLd Order Amish/
Residence: Not Stated, Reno, Kansas[5565]

Notes for Lizzie Yoder:
The Descendants of John J. Christner, privately published February 1961, p. 96.

More About Lizzie Yoder:
Religion: Old Order Amish/
Residence: 01 Mar 1905, Haven, Reno Co., KS[5566]

Children of Samuel Borntrager and Lizzie Yoder are:

+	3304	i.	Mary S.[9] Borntrager, born 20 Jul 1920 in Clark Co., MO.
	3305	ii.	Edna Borntrager[5566], born 10 Oct 1921 in Reno, KS[5566]; died 22 Apr 1922 in Poplar Bluff, MO[5566].
+	3306	iii.	Katie S. Borntrager, born 09 Feb 1923 in Butler Co., MO; died Aug 1992 in Reno, KS.
+	3307	iv.	David S. Borntrager, born 17 Jan 1925.
+	3308	v.	Alma S. Borntrager, born 03 Feb 1927 in Hazleton, IA.
+	3309	vi.	Fanny S. Borntrager, born 30 Jan 1929 in Clarence, MO.
+	3310	vii.	Levi S. Borntrager, born 02 Jul 1930 in Anabel, MO.
	3311	viii.	Sarah Borntrager[5566], born 17 Jul 1932[5566]; died 06 Feb 1934[5566].
+	3312	ix.	Willard S. Borntrager, born 12 Nov 1934 in Curryville, Pike Co., MO.
+	3313	x.	Rudy S. Borntrager, born 14 Feb 1936 in Bowling Green, MO.
	3314	xi.	Laura Borntrager, born 22 Sep 1938 in Curryville, Pike Co., MO. She married Amos Eicher 02 Apr 1959; born 06 Feb 1939.

> Notes for Laura Borntrager:
> The Descendants of John J. Christner, privately published February 1961, p. 97.
>
> Notes for Amos Eicher:
> The Descendants of John J. Christner, privately published February 1961, p. 97.

	3315	xii.	Elnora Borntrager, born 22 Sep 1938 in Curryville, Pike Co., MO. She married August P. Girod 02 Apr 1959; born 10 Sep 1937.

> Notes for Elnora Borntrager:
> The Descendants of John J. Christner, privately published February 1961, p. 97.
>
> Notes for August P. Girod:
> The Descendants of John J. Christner, privately published February 1961, p. 97.
>
> More About August P. Girod:
> Religion: Old Order Amish/

	3316	xiii.	Borntrager, born 11 Sep 1942; died 11 Sep 1942.

1389. Mary[8] **Borntrager** (Elizabeth D.[7] Frey, Elizabeth J.[6] Christner, Joseph C.[5], Christian J.[4], Johannes John Hans[3], Christian[2], Christen[1])[5567] was born 28 Sep 1899 in Haven, Reno Co., KS[5567,5568], and died 26 Nov 1983[5568]. She married **Daniel N. Glick**[5569,5570] 04 Mar 1920 in Reno Co., KS by Bishop Jonas D Borntraber. He was born 31 Oct 1895 in Elkhart Co., IN[5571], and died 13 Jan 1970 in Lagrange Co., IN[5572].

Notes for Mary Borntrager:
The Descendants of John J. Christner, privately published February 1961, pp. 93, 98.

Notes for Daniel N. Glick:

The Descendants of John J. Christner, privately published February 1961, p. 98.

More About Daniel N. Glick:
Religion: Mennonite/
Residence: Lagrange, Lagrange Co., IN[5573,5574]

Child of Mary Borntrager and Daniel Glick is:
+   3317   i.   Elizabeth Mae[9] Glick, born 16 Apr 1924 in Lagrange Co., IN; died 23 Dec 1960.

1390. Harvey R.[8] Borntrager (Elizabeth D.[7] Frey, Elizabeth J.[6] Christner, Joseph C.[5], Christian J.[4], Johannes John Hans[3], Christian[2], Christen[1]) was born 15 Jun 1901 in Haven, Reno Co., KS, and died 02 Dec 1991 in Haven, Reno Co., KS[5575]. He married **Lena Keim** 21 Nov 1918 in By Jonas D Borntrager. She was born 13 Sep 1898.

Notes for Harvey R. Borntrager:
The Descendants of John J. Christner, privately published February 1961, pp. 93, 98.

More About Harvey R. Borntrager:
Religion: Old Order Amish/

Notes for Lena Keim:
The Descendants of John J. Christner, privately published February 1961, p. 98.

Children of Harvey Borntrager and Lena Keim are:
+   3318   i.   Emma[9] Borntrager, born 23 Feb 1919 in Weatherford, OK.
    3319   ii.   Laura Borntrager, born 05 Aug 1920 in Hutchinson, Reno Co., KS. She married William A. Bontrager May 1958; born 10 Oct 1898.

                  Notes for Laura Borntrager:
                  The Descendants of John J. Christner, privately published February 1961, pp. 98, 99.

                  Notes for William A. Bontrager:
                  The Descendants of John J. Christner, privately published February 1961, pp. 98, 99.

                  More About William A. Bontrager:
                  Religion: Yoder Mennonite Church/

    3320   iii.   Rudy Borntrager, born 20 Dec 1921; died 01 Jan 1922.

                  Notes for Rudy Borntrager:
                  The Descendants of John J. Christner, privately published February 1961, p. 98.

+   3321   iv.   Mattie Borntrager, born 29 Dec 1922 in Clark Co., MO.
+   3322   v.   Elizabeth Borntrager, born 22 Feb 1925 in Hutchinson, Reno Co., KS.
+   3323   vi.   Leander H. Borntrager, born 23 Dec 1927 in Dumas Texas Trailer City.
    3324   vii.   Edwin Borntrager, born 08 Feb 1932.

                  Notes for Edwin Borntrager:
                  The Descendants of John J. Christner, privately published February 1961, p. 98.

+   3325   viii.   Ada Borntrager, born 05 Aug 1935 in Haven, Reno Co., KS.

1394. Clemens R.[8] Borntrager (Elizabeth D.[7] Frey, Elizabeth J.[6] Christner, Joseph C.[5], Christian J.[4], Johannes John Hans[3], Christian[2], Christen[1]) was born 23 Nov 1909 in Medford, WI. He married **Polly Schrock** 08 Nov 1928 in By Bishop M.E. Borntrager at Sikeston, MO. She was born 07 Sep 1903.

Notes for Clemens R. Borntrager:

The Descendants of John J. Christner, privately published February 1961, pp. 93, 99.

More About Clemens R. Borntrager:
Ordination: 06 Apr 1942, Deacon Old Order Amish at Fairbank, Iowa
Religion: Old Order Amish/

Notes for Polly Schrock:
The Descendants of John J. Christner, privately published February 1961, p. 99.

Children of Clemens Borntrager and Polly Schrock are:
+ 3326 i. Lydia Lorene[9] Borntrager, born 28 Aug 1930 in Curtiss, WI.
+ 3327 ii. Elizabeth Borntrager, born 24 Feb 1933 in Medford, WI.
  3328 iii. Lovina Borntrager, born 24 Feb 1933; died 24 Feb 1933.

    Notes for Lovina Borntrager:
    The Descendants of John J. Christner, privately published February 1961, p. 99.

+ 3329 iv. Mary Borntrager, born 26 Nov 1935 in Medford, WI.
  3330 v. Susie Borntrager, born 09 Nov 1938.

    Notes for Susie Borntrager:
    The Descendants of John J. Christner, privately published February 1961, p. 99.

  3331 vi. Harvey Borntrager, born 18 Aug 1941.

    Notes for Harvey Borntrager:
    The Descendants of John J. Christner, privately published February 1961, p. 99.

  3332 vii. Infant Dau. Borntrager, born 23 Oct 1943; died 23 Oct 1943.

    Notes for Infant Dau. Borntrager:
    The Descendants of John J. Christner, privately published February 1961, p. 99.

  3333 viii. Ella Borntrager, born 13 Dec 1946.

    Notes for Ella Borntrager:
    The Descendants of John J. Christner, privately published February 1961, p. 99.

1395. Ura R.[8] Miller (Martha[7], Barbara[6] Christner, John J.[5], Christian J.[4], Johannes John Hans[3], Christian[2], Christen[1]) He married **Mae Hostetler**.

Child of Ura Miller and Mae Hostetler is:
  3334 i. J. Virgil[9] Miller. He married Susan.

    Notes for J. Virgil Miller:
    J. Virgil Miller and Levi Christner worked on the Christner history.

1426. Harry[8] Gerber (Catherine Ann[7] Christner, Joseph J.[6], John J.[5], Christian J.[4], Johannes John Hans[3], Christian[2], Christen[1]) was born 04 May 1900 in Bars Mills, OH, and died 19 Oct 1990 in Baltic, Tuscarawas Co., OH. He married **Kate Hershberger** 07 Feb 1925.

Notes for Harry Gerber:
He was Mennonite.

More About Harry Gerber:
Burial: 22 Oct 1990, Walnut Creek Church Cemetery OH

Children of Harry Gerber and Kate Hershberger are:

3335	i.	Alice[9] Gerber.
3336	ii.	June Gerber.
3337	iii.	Stanley Gerber.
3338	iv.	Wayne Gerber.
3339	v.	Harry Gerber Jr..

1428. Niva[8] Christner (William J.[7], Joseph J.[6], John J.[5], Christian J.[4], Johannes John Hans[3], Christian[2], Christen[1])[5576] was born 20 Dec 1896 in Tuscarawas Co., OH[5576], and died 13 Apr 1947[5576]. She married **John G. Miller** 11 Jan 1918 in Portage Co., OH[5576]. He was born 16 Oct 1891 in Shanesville, Tuscarawas Co., OH[5576], and died 18 Sep 1958[5576].

Children of Niva Christner and John Miller are:

	3340	i.	Arland[9] Miller.
	3341	ii.	Hazel Miller.
	3342	iii.	David Miller.
	3343	iv.	George Miller.
	3344	v.	John Miller.
	3345	vi.	Paul Miller.
+	3346	vii.	Grace Miller, born 15 May 1922 in Aurora, Portage Co., OH; died 28 Dec 2001 in Apple Creek, Wayne Co., OH.
	3347	viii.	Mary Louise Miller, born 11 Aug 1925 in Aurora, Portage Co., OH; died 07 Jan 1988 in Goshen, Elkhart Co., IN.

Notes for Mary Louise Miller:
She was a mennonite and is buried in the Church Cemetery in Aurora, Portage Co., OH.

More About Mary Louise Miller:
Burial: 09 Jan 1988, Aurora, Portage Co., OH

3348	ix.	James Ray Miller[5576], born 30 Jan 1929 in Aurora, Portage Co., OH[5576]; died 05 Feb 1930 in Aurora, Portage Co., OH[5576].

1429. Velma[8] Christner (William J.[7], Joseph J.[6], John J.[5], Christian J.[4], Johannes John Hans[3], Christian[2], Christen[1]) was born 26 Apr 1898 in Baltic, Tuscarawas Co., OH, and died 25 Mar 1987 in Achbold, OH. She married **Daniel Stuckey** 14 Jan 1920. He died 04 Feb 1971.

Notes for Velma Christner:
Stuckey, Velma Christner, daughter of William and Mary (Hershberger) Christner, was born near Baltic, Ohio, Apr. 26, 1898; died at Fairlawn Haven, Archbold, Ohio, Mar. 25, 1987; aged 88 y. On Jan. 14, 1920, she was married to Daniel Stuckey, who died on Feb. 4, 1971. Surviving are 3 children (LaMar, Fern Wyse, and Arlene Milliman), 6 grandchildren, 12 great-grandchildren, one brother (Rollie Christner), and 3 sisters (Beulah Schrock, Elvesta Grieser, and Lorene Johnson). She was a member of Lockport Mennonite Church, where funeral services were held in charge of Merle Wyse and James Groeneweg; interment in Lockport Cemetery.

More About Velma Christner:
Burial: Lockport Mennonite Church Cemetery

Children of Velma Christner and Daniel Stuckey are:

3349	i.	Arlene[9] Stuckey. She married Milliman.
3350	ii.	Fern Stuckey. She married Wyse.
3351	iii.	LaMar Stuckey.

1430. Malinda Leona[8] Christner (William J.[7], Joseph J.[6], John J.[5], Christian J.[4], Johannes John Hans[3], Christian[2], Christen[1]) was born 20 Dec 1899 in Baltic, Tuscarawas Co., OH, and died 19 Oct 1962 in Streetsboro, Portage Co., OH. She married **Ernie R. Bontrager** 03 Nov 1921. He died 17 Nov 1960.

Notes for Malinda Leona Christner:
Bontrager, Malinda Leona, daughter of William J. and Mary (Hershberger) Christner, was born near Baltic, Ohio, Dec. 20, 1899; died of a heart attack at her home in Streetsboro, Ohio, Oct. 19, 1962; aged 62 y. 9 m. 29 d. On Nov. 3, 1921, she was married to Ernie R. Bontrager, who died Nov. 17, 1960. Surviving are 3 daughters and one son (Bertha-Mrs. Walter Steiner, Mildred-Mrs. Edward Roth, Norma-Mrs. Robert Miller, and Gerald), her mother (Mrs. Mary Christner), 4 sisters (Velma-Mrs. Dan Stucky, Beulah-Mrs. Noah Schrock, Lorene-Mrs. Frank Johnson, and Elvesta-Mrs. Lloyd Grieser), and 3 brothers (Wade, Floyd, and Rollie). One sister, one brother, and one grandchild preceded her in death. She was a member of the Plainview Church, where funeral services were held Oct. 22, in charge of David Miller, Eugene Yoder, and Elmer Stoltzfus.

More About Malinda Leona Christner:
Burial: 22 Oct 1962

Children of Malinda Christner and Ernie Bontrager are:
    3352   i.   Gerald[9] Bontrager.
    3353   ii. Mildred Bontrager. She married Edward Roth.
    3354   iii. Norma Bontrager. She married Robert Miller.
+   3355   iv. Bertha Bontrager, born 1925; died 04 May 2006 in Dalton, OH.

1431. Beulah Fern[8] Christner (William J.[7], Joseph J.[6], John J.[5], Christian J.[4], Johannes John Hans[3], Christian[2], Christen[1])[5577,5578] was born 06 Feb 1901 in Tuscarawas Co., OH[5579], and died 10 Mar 1999 in Stryker, OH, USA[5579]. She married **Noah M Schrock**[5579] 1926 in OH[5579]. He was born 29 Aug 1892 in Woodford Ct, Illinois[5579], and died 06 Apr 1976 in Burlington, Iowa[5579].

Notes for Beulah Fern Christner:
Schrock, Beulah Christner, 98, Stryker, Ohio, died March 10. Spouse: Noah Schrock (deceased). Survivors: children Berneda Wyse, Shirley, Janice Prowant; 13 grandchildren; 30 great-grandchildren; three great-great-grandchildren. Funeral: March 12 at Pine Grove Mennonite Church, Stryker.

More About Beulah Fern Christner:
Burial: Pine Grove Mennonite Church Stryker OH
Publication: 18 Mar 1999[5579]
Residence: Williams, OH, United States[5579]
Social Security Number: 273-62-5039/[5579]
SSN issued: OH[5579]

Children of Beulah Christner and Noah Schrock are:
    3356   i.   Shirley[9] Schrock.
    3357   ii. Berneda Schrock.
    3358   iii. Janice Schrock.

1437. William J.[8] Christner (Harvey C.[7], Joseph J.[6], John J.[5], Christian J.[4], Johannes John Hans[3], Christian[2], Christen[1])[5580,5580,5581] was born 01 Nov 1904 in Coshocton, Coshocton Co., OH[5582,5583], and died 25 Aug 1966 in Dover, Tuscarawas Co., OH[5584,5584,5585]. He married **Hazel Neletta Lint**[5585,5586,5587] 02 Jun 1923 in Tuscarawas Co., OH[5588]. She was born 05 Oct 1901 in Baltic, Buck Twp., Tuscarawas Co., OH[5588,5589,5590], and died 30 Jun 1976 in Dover, Tuscarawas Co., OH[5591,5592,5593].

Notes for William J. Christner:
Birth: Nov. 1, 1903
Coshocton Co., OH
Death: Aug. 25, 1966

Spouse: Hazel N. Lint Christner (1901 - 1976)

Burial: West Lawn Cemetery
Baltic, Tuscarawas Co., OH

Obituary:

William J. Christner 62, died this morning in his home following a long illness. Born in Coshocton Co., he was the son of the late Harvey and Amanda Lower Christner.

Surving are his widow, the former Hazel Lint, a daughter Mrs. Myron (Norma Jean) Ott of Dover; a son George of Stone Creek; a sister Mrs. Hugo Miller of a Shanesville and 4 grandchildren. One grandchild preceeded him in death.

Services are pending at Lingler-Geckler Funeral home.

More About William J. Christner:
Residence: 1930, Baltic, Tuscarawas Co., OH[5594,5595,5595]

Notes for Hazel Neletta Lint:
Birth: Sep. 5, 1901 - Tuscarawas Co., OH
Death: Jun. 30, 1976 - Dover, Tuscarawas Co., OH

Spouse: William J Christner (1903 - 1966)

Burial: West Lawn Cemetery, Baltic, Tuscarawas Co., OH

More About Hazel Neletta Lint:
Residence: 1930, Baltic, Tuscarawas Co., OH[5596,5597]
Social Security Number: 268-50-9048/[5598]
SSN issued: OH[5598]

Child of William Christner and Hazel Lint is:
    3359   i.   Norma Jean[9] Christner[5599], born 23 Aug 1927 in Baltic, Tuscarawas Co., OH[5599]; died 09 Mar 1998 in Dover, Tuscarawas Co., OH[5599]. She married Myron Ott.

            More About Norma Jean Christner:
            Residence: 1930, Baltic, Tuscarawas Co., OH[5599]

1439. Bertha[8] Christner (John[7], Peter C.[6], Christian[5], Peter[4], Christian[3], Christian[2], Christen[1]) was born 18 Dec 1892, and died Apr 1977 in Kokomo, Howard Co., IN[5600]. She married **Milton E. Stepler** 20 Feb 1909. He was born 07 Dec 1887, and died 1925 in North Grove, Miami Co., IN[5601].

More About Bertha Christner:
Other-Begin: Greentown, Howard Co., IN[5602]
Social Security Number: 316-05-4121/[5602]
SSN issued: IN[5602]

Notes for Milton E. Stepler:
Descendants of Jacob Hochstetler book Copyright 1977

More About Milton E. Stepler:
Other-Begin: Miami Co.[5603]
Residence: Miami Co., IN[5603]

Children of Bertha Christner and Milton Stepler are:
    3360   i.   Lowell Paul[9] Stepler, born 02 Jan 1910.
    3361   ii.   Charles Stepler[5604], born 04 Nov 1911 in North Grove, Miami Co., IN[5604]; died Jan 1978 in Greentown, Howard Co., IN[5604].

More About Charles Stepler:
Social Security Number: 316-10-0760/[5604]
SSN issued: IN[5604]

3362   iii.   Russell H. Stepler[5604], born 11 May 1918 in North Grove, Miami Co., IN[5604]; died 06 Jun 1992 in Kokomo, Howard Co., IN[5604].

More About Russell H. Stepler:
Military: 31 Jan 1945, Indianapolis, Indiana[5604]
Residence: Indiana, U.S. At Large[5604]
Social Security Number: 311-03-3821/[5604]
SSN issued: IN[5604]

1440. Harry Irvin[8] Christner (John[7], Peter C.[6], Christian[5], Peter[4], Christian[3], Christian[2], Christen[1]) was born 18 Aug 1894, and died 22 Feb 1971. He married **Grace E. Shively** 13 Mar 1917 in Miami Co., IN. She was born 22 Feb 1898 in Miami Co., IN[5605], and died Nov 1984 in Peru, Miami Co., IN[5605].

Notes for Harry Irvin Christner:
Birth: Aug. 18, 1894
Death: Feb. 22, 1971

Spouse: Grace E. Shively Christner (1898 - 1984)

Children: Weldon W. Christner (1825 - 1979)

Burial: Park Lawn Cemetery, Amboy, Miami Co., IN

More About Harry Irvin Christner:
Residence: 1930, North Grove, Miami, Indiana[5605]
Social Security Number: 313-18-8896/[5606]
SSN issued: IN[5606]

Notes for Grace E. Shively:
Birth: Feb. 22, 1898
Death: Nov., 1984

Parents:
William H Shively (1872 - 1955)
Alice L. Jenkins Shively (1874 - 1919)

Spouse: Harry I. Christner (1894 - 1971)

Children: Weldon W. Christner (1825 - 1979)

Burial: Park Lawn Cemetery, Amboy, Miami Co., IN

Child of Harry Christner and Grace Shively is:
    3363   i.   Weldon W.[9] Christner, born 09 Dec 1925[5607]; died Aug 1979[5607].

Notes for Weldon W. Christner:
Birth: Dec. 9, 1925
Death: Aug., 1979

Parents:
Harry I. Christner (1894 - 1971)
Grace E. Shively Christner (1898 - 1984)

Burial: Park Lawn Cemetery, Amboy, Miami Co., IN

More About Weldon W. Christner:
Social Security Number: 317-16-8694/[5607]
SSN issued: IN[5607]

1445. Raymond Russell "Friz"[8] Christner (John[7], Peter C.[6], Christian[5], Peter[4], Christian[3], Christian[2], Christen[1]) was born 11 Dec 1905 in Waupecong, IN[5608], and died Apr 1976 in Bradford, Miami Co., OH[5609]. He married **Clara Catherine Rody**[5610]. She was born 29 May 1910 in Plevna, IN[5610], and died 12 Nov 1993 in Buried - Miami Memorial Park Cemetery in Newberry Township, Miami County, Ohio/Athens, OH[5610].

More About Raymond Russell "Friz" Christner:
Residence: 1946, Employee at Turner Field/41 Wm. Binns Homes, Albany, GA[5610]
Social Security Number: 308-09-2078/[5611]
SSN issued: IN[5611]

Notes for Clara Catherine Rody:
Buried - Miami Memorial Park Cemetery in Newberry Twp., Miami Co., OH

More About Clara Catherine Rody:
Residence: 1946, 41 Wm. Binns Homes, Albany, GA[5612]

Children of Raymond Christner and Clara Rody are:

3364   i.   Phyllis Geraldine[9] Christner[5612], born 01 Aug 1931 in Howard Co., IN[5612]; died 03 Dec 2006 in Tallapoosa, Haralson Co., GA[5612]. She married Moore.

        Notes for Phyllis Geraldine Christner:
        Buried - Glen Haven Memorial Gardens, New Carlisle, Clark Co., OH

        More About Phyllis Geraldine Christner:
        Residence: 01 Apr 1940, Center Township, Howard County, Indiana[5612]

3365   ii. Gerald Max Christner[5612], born 20 Sep 1942 in Columbus, Loundes Co., MS[5612]; died 29 Nov 2007 in Thomson, GA[5612].

        Notes for Gerald Max Christner:
        Buried - Savannah Valley Memorial Gardens, Thomson, McDuffie Co., GA

        More About Gerald Max Christner:
        Residence: 1995, 622 Southwinds Ct, Rock Hill, South Carolina[5612]

1447. Treva[8] Lantz (Edward[7], Philip[6], Veronica Fannie[5] Christner, Christian J.[4], Johannes John Hans[3], Christian[2], Christen[1]) was born 15 Jul 1922 in Goshen, Elkhart Co., IN[5613], and died 22 Sep 2009 in Indianapolis, Marion Co., IN[5613]. She married **David J. Miller**[5614] 07 Feb 1946. He was born 26 Feb 1920[5614], and died 14 Feb 2003 in Goshen, Elkhart Co., IN[5614,5615].

Notes for Treva Lantz:
The Descendants of John J. Christner, privately published February 1961, p. 100.

More About Treva Lantz:
SSN issued: IN[5616]

Notes for David J. Miller:
The Descendants of John J. Christner, privately published February 1961, p. 199.

More About David J. Miller:
Residence: 1930, Van Buren, Lagrange Co., IN[5617]
Social Security Number: 310-18-9601/[5618]
SSN issued: IN[5618]

Children of Treva Lantz and David Miller are:

3366   i.   Barbara Eilene[9] Miller, born 10 Dec 1948.

     Notes for Barbara Eilene Miller:
     The Descendants of John J. Christner, privately published February 1961, p. 100.

3367   ii.   Lorris David Miller, born 30 Jan 1951.

     Notes for Lorris David Miller:
     The Descendants of John J. Christner, privately published February 1961, p. 100.

3368   iii.   Denis Ann Miller, born 06 Jun 1953.

     Notes for Denis Ann Miller:
     The Descendants of John J. Christner, privately published February 1961, p. 100.

3369   iv.   John Edward Miller, born 12 Mar 1956.

     Notes for John Edward Miller:
     The Descendants of John J. Christner, privately published February 1961, p. 100.

3370   v.   Elizabeth Miller, born 06 Oct 1965.

     Notes for Elizabeth Miller:
     The Descendants of John J. Christner, privately published February 1961, p. 100.

1448. Delbert[8] Lantz (Edward[7], Philip[6], Veronica Fannie[5] Christner, Christian J.[4], Johannes John Hans[3], Christian[2], Christen[1]) was born 01 May 1924. He married **June Ettline** 29 Mar 1947. She was born 25 Aug 1929.

Notes for Delbert Lantz:
The Descendants of John J. Christner, privately published February 1961, p.100.

Notes for June Ettline:
The Descendants of John J. Christner, privately published February 1961, p. 100.

Children of Delbert Lantz and June Ettline are:

3371   i.   Stephen Kent[9] Lantz, born 24 Nov 1947.

     Notes for Stephen Kent Lantz:
     The Descendants of John J. Christner, privately published February 1961, p. 100.

3372   ii.   Delbert Edward Lantz, born 27 Dec 1949.

     Notes for Delbert Edward Lantz:
     The Descendants of John J. Christner, privately published February 1961, p. 100.

3373   iii.   Allen Dwight Lantz, born 07 Jun 1951.

     Notes for Allen Dwight Lantz:
     The Descendants of John J. Christner, privately published February 1961, p. 100.

1449. Virgil[8] Lantz (Edward[7], Philip[6], Veronica Fannie[5] Christner, Christian J.[4], Johannes John Hans[3], Christian[2], Christen[1]) was born 25 Mar 1926, and died 29 Sep 1958. He married **Mary Alice Blough** 30 Jun 1951. She was born 04 May 1932, and died 31 Oct 1957.

Notes for Virgil Lantz:
The Descendants of John J. Christner, privately published February 1961, p.100.

Notes for Mary Alice Blough:
The Descendants of John J. Christner, privately published 1961, February 1961, p.100.

Child of Virgil Lantz and Mary Blough is:
3374 i. Sharon Diane[9] Lantz, born 23 Jun 1952.

     Notes for Sharon Diane Lantz:
     The Descendants of John J. Christner, privately published February 1961, p. 100.

1450. Floyd[8] Lantz (Edward[7], Philip[6], Veronica Fannie[5] Christner, Christian J.[4], Johannes John Hans[3], Christian[2], Christen[1]) was born 04 Dec 1927. He married **(1) Mildred Bailey**.   He married **(2) Hellen Frey**. She was born 07 Mar 1934.

Notes for Floyd Lantz:
The Descendants of John J. Christner, privately published February 1961, p. 99.

Notes for Mildred Bailey:
The Descendants of John J. Christner, privately published February 1961, p. 100.

Notes for Hellen Frey:
The Descendants of John J. Christner, privately published February 1961, p.100.

Children of Floyd Lantz and Mildred Bailey are:
3375 i. Roger[9] Lantz, born 12 Aug 1946.

     Notes for Roger Lantz:
     The Descendants of John J. Christner, privately published February 1961, p. 100.

3376 ii. Danny Lantz, born 16 Jan 1949.

Children of Floyd Lantz and Hellen Frey are:
3377 i. Diane Lynn[9] Lantz, born 29 Aug 1955.
3378 ii. Charles Dewayne Lantz, born 13 Dec 1956.

1451. Barbara Ellen[8] Lantz (Edward[7], Philip[6], Veronica Fannie[5] Christner, Christian J.[4], Johannes John Hans[3], Christian[2], Christen[1]) was born 12 Mar 1930 in Topeka, Lagrange Co., IN. She married **Jacob Stoltzfus** 15 Jul.

Notes for Barbara Ellen Lantz:
The Descendants of John J. Christner, privately published February 1961, pp. 99, 100.

Notes for Jacob Stoltzfus:
The Descendants of John J. Christner, privately published February 1961, p. 100.

More About Jacob Stoltzfus:
Residence: 1410 Kune Ave., Dunlap, Elkhart, Indiana

Child of Barbara Lantz and Jacob Stoltzfus is:
3379 i. Harlen Keith[9] Stoltzfus, born 26 Aug 1958.

     Notes for Harlen Keith Stoltzfus:
     The Descendants of John J. Christner, privately published February 1961, p. 100.

1453. Omar[8] **Lantz** (Edward[7], Philip[6], Veronica Fannie[5] Christner, Christian J.[4], Johannes John Hans[3], Christian[2], Christen[1]) was born 11 Apr 1936. He married **Katherine Miller** 28 Feb 1958. She was born 30 Sep 1940.

Notes for Omar Lantz:
The Descendants of John J. Christner, privately published February 1961, pp. 99, 100.

Notes for Katherine Miller:
The Descendants of John J. Christner, privately published February 1961, p. 100.

Child of Omar Lantz and Katherine Miller is:
 3380 i. Sheryl Ann[9] Miller, born 28 Sep 1959.

      Notes for Sheryl Ann Miller:
      The Descendants of John J. Christner, privately published February 1961, p. 100.

1454. Truman Lavoid[8] **Lantz** (Ezra[7], Philip[6], Veronica Fannie[5] Christner, Christian J.[4], Johannes John Hans[3], Christian[2], Christen[1]) was born 11 Jan 1921[5619], and died 16 Jul 1999 in Lagrange Co., IN[5619]. He married **Lois Jane Mason** 08 Jun 1945. She was born 02 Aug 1928.

Notes for Truman Lavoid Lantz:
The Descendants of John J. Christner, privately published February 1961, p. 101.

Children of Truman Lantz and Lois Mason are:
 3381 i. Jerry Lee[9] Lantz[5620,5621,5622], born 13 Sep 1947[5623,5624,5625]. He married (1) Joyce E. Rogers[5626,5627] 25 Jun 1977[5627,5628]; born Abt. 1952[5628,5629]. He married (2) Patricia A. Newman[5630] 22 May 1985 in Harris Co., TX[5630]; born Abt. 1959[5630].

      More About Joyce E. Rogers:
      Residence: Stark, Ohio, United States[5631]

 3382 ii. Kathryn Jane Lantz, born 28 Jan 1949; died 20 Jan 1956.
 3383 iii. Lina Elain Lantz, born 19 Mar 1952.
 3384 iv. Rebecca Jo Lantz, born 09 Aug 1957.

1455. Gladys Barbra[8] **Lantz** (Ezra[7], Philip[6], Veronica Fannie[5] Christner, Christian J.[4], Johannes John Hans[3], Christian[2], Christen[1]) was born 27 Dec 1923. She married **Amos E. Yoder**[5632] 18 Feb 1940. He was born 21 Nov 1918 in Middlebury, Elkhart Co., IN[5632], and died 08 Apr 1982[5632].

Notes for Gladys Barbra Lantz:
The Descendants of John J. Christner, privately published February 1961, p. 101.

Children of Gladys Lantz and Amos Yoder are:
 3385 i. Dean Roger[9] Yoder[5632], born 16 Jan 1942 in Middlebury, Elkhart Co., IN[5632]; died 24 Jul 1994 in River Ridge, Jefferson, Louisiana, USA[5632].
 3386 ii. Frances Joan Yoder, born 01 Jun 1947.

1456. Irma Arlene[8] **Lantz** (Ezra[7], Philip[6], Veronica Fannie[5] Christner, Christian J.[4], Johannes John Hans[3], Christian[2], Christen[1]) was born 23 Mar 1925. She married **Aldine C. Haarer** 26 Jul 1942. He was born 06 Sep 1912.

Notes for Irma Arlene Lantz:
The Descendants of John J. Christner, privately published February 1961, p. 101.

Notes for Aldine C. Haarer:

The Descendants of John J. Christner, privately published February 1961, p. 101.

Children of Irma Lantz and Aldine Haarer are:
 3387   i.   Richard Lavern[9] Haarer, born 16 May 1946.

         Notes for Richard Lavern Haarer:
         The Descendants of John J. Christner, privately published February 1961, p. 101.

 3388   ii.   Dennis Lynn Haarer, born 05 May 1953.

         Notes for Dennis Lynn Haarer:
         The Descendants of John J. Christner, privately published February 1961, p. 101.

1458. Glendon Ezra[8] Lantz (Ezra[7], Philip[6], Veronica Fannie[5] Christner, Christian J.[4], Johannes John Hans[3], Christian[2], Christen[1]) was born 02 Nov 1934. He married **Esther Kuhns** 29 Jun 1958. She was born 19 Dec 1939.

Notes for Glendon Ezra Lantz:
The Descendants of John J. Christner, privately published February 1961, p. 101.

Notes for Esther Kuhns:
The Descendants of John J. Christner, privately published February 1961, p. 101.

Child of Glendon Lantz and Esther Kuhns is:
 3389   i.   Rodney Wayne[9] Lantz, born 05 Sep 1959.

         Notes for Rodney Wayne Lantz:
         The Descendants of John J. Christner, privately published February 1961, p. 101.

1459. Harold[8] Lantz (Earl[7], Philip[6], Veronica Fannie[5] Christner, Christian J.[4], Johannes John Hans[3], Christian[2], Christen[1]) was born 03 Mar 1923. He married **Cleo Mae Hershberger** 15 Feb 1948. She was born 25 Mar 1926, and died 18 Jun 1958 in Auto Accident at US 30 & IN 19.

Notes for Harold Lantz:
The Descendants of John J. Christner, privately published February 1961, p. 101

He had a millwright buisiness with Joseph J. Byler. They build & repair feed mills. anything that moves food products like corn or wheat from storage bin to anywhere else.   Steven Carl Christner owned 5 % of this Corp. in the 1970s.

More About Harold Lantz:
Religion: Conservative Amish/

Notes for Cleo Mae Hershberger:
The Descendants of John J. Christner, privately published February 1961, p. 101.

Children of Harold Lantz and Cleo Hershberger are:
 3390   i.   David Michael[9] Lantz, born 21 Nov 1951.

         Notes for David Michael Lantz:
         The Descendants of John J. Christner, privately published February 1961, p. 101.

 3391   ii.   Linda Irene Lantz, born 15 Feb 1953.

         Notes for Linda Irene Lantz:
         The Descendants of John J. Christner, privately published February 1961, p. 101.

 3392   iii. Steven Dwayne Lantz, born 04 Jan 1955.

Notes for Steven Dwayne Lantz:
The Descendants of John J. Christner, privately published February 1961, p. 101.

3393   iv. Cynthia Lou Lantz, born 26 Mar 1956.

Notes for Cynthia Lou Lantz:
The Descendants of John J. Christner, privately published February 1961, p. 101.

3394   v. Johnny Joe Lantz, born 29 Apr 1958.

Notes for Johnny Joe Lantz:
The Descendants of John J. Christner, privately published February 1961, p. 101.

1460. Dorothy Ellen⁸ Lantz (Earl⁷, Philip⁶, Veronica Fannie⁵ Christner, Christian J.⁴, Johannes John Hans³, Christian², Christen¹) was born 24 Dec 1927. She married **Edwin H. Bontrager** 18 Jul 1948. He was born 22 Oct 1923.

Notes for Dorothy Ellen Lantz:
The Descendants of John J. Christner, privately published February 1961, p. 101.

Notes for Edwin H. Bontrager:
The Descendants of John J. Christner, privately published February 1961, p. 101.

Children of Dorothy Lantz and Edwin Bontrager are:
3395   i. Mary Katherine⁹ Bontrager, born 10 Mar 1949.

Notes for Mary Katherine Bontrager:
The Descendants of John J. Christner, privately published February 1961, p.101.

3396   ii. Glenda Fern Bontrager, born 09 Oct 1950.

Notes for Glenda Fern Bontrager:
The Descendants of John J. Christner, privately published February 1961, p. 101.

3397   iii. Larry Eugene Bontrager, born 17 Mar 1953.

Notes for Larry Eugene Bontrager:
The Descendants of John J. Christner, privately published February 1961, p. 101.

He has a very successful painting Buisiness in Topeka, IN. For many years him and his faithful wife & Business partner painted auto vans & motor homes.

1461. Kenneth⁸ Lantz (Earl⁷, Philip⁶, Veronica Fannie⁵ Christner, Christian J.⁴, Johannes John Hans³, Christian², Christen¹) was born 22 May 1930. He married **Esther Miller** 30 Apr 1949, daughter of Amos Miller and Polly Miller. She was born 25 May 1930.

Notes for Kenneth Lantz:
The Descendants of John J. Christner, privately published February 1961, pp. 70, 101.

Notes for Esther Miller:
The Descendants of John J. Christner, privately published February 1961, p. 69.

Children of Kenneth Lantz and Esther Miller are:
3398   i. Marvin Eugene⁹ Lantz, born 16 Nov 1950.

Notes for Marvin Eugene Lantz:
The Descendants of John J. Christner, privately published February 1961, p. 70.

3399   ii.   Kenneth Wayne Lantz, born 03 Feb 1953.

        Notes for Kenneth Wayne Lantz:
        The Descendants of John J. Christner, privately published February 1961, p. 70.

3400   iii. Gerry Lee Lantz, born 05 Mar 1955.

        Notes for Gerry Lee Lantz:
        The Descendants of John J. Christner, privately published February 1961, p. 70.

3401   iv.   Roy Dean Lantz, born 20 May 1957.

        Notes for Roy Dean Lantz:
        The Descendants of John J. Christner, privately published February 1961, p. 70.

1467. Emma Marie[8] Miller (Phineas S.[7], Magdalena Mattie[6] Lantz, Veronica Fannie[5] Christner, Christian J.[4], Johannes John Hans[3], Christian[2], Christen[1]) was born 07 May 1907, and died 19 Feb 1994. She married **Perry Bontrager** 12 Sep 1927. He was born 15 Feb 1907, and died 03 Jun 1971.

Notes for Emma Marie Miller:
The Descendants of John J. Christner, privately published February 1961, p. 102.

Birth: May 7, 1907
Death: Feb. 19, 1994

Burial: Christner Cemetery, Wawpecong, Miami Co., IN
Find A Grave Memorial# 35379874

Notes for Perry Bontrager:
The Descendants of John J. Christner, privately published February 1961, p.102.

Birth: Feb. 15, 1907
Death: Jun. 3, 1971

Burial: Christner Cemetery, Wawpecong, Miami Co., IN
Find A Grave Memorial# 35379973

Children of Emma Miller and Perry Bontrager are:
+   3402   i.   Marilyn Louise[9] Bontrager, born 23 Feb 1932.
+   3403   ii.   Lonita Eveylin Bontrager, born 22 Jun 1935 in Kokomo, Howard Co., IN.
     3404   iii. Richard Dwaine Bontrager, born 23 Mar 1938 in Kokomo, Howard Co., IN[5633]; died 30 Jun 2008 in Seattle, King Co., WA[5633]. He married Mary Alice Struwing 29 Nov 1959; born 24 Oct 1939.

              Notes for Richard Dwaine Bontrager:
              The Descendants of John J. Christner, privately published February 1961, p.102.

              Obituary: Kokomo Tribune - (Aug/4/2008)
              Richard Dwaine Bontrager

              Richard Dwaine Bontrager, passed away peacefully on Monday, June 30, 2008, at home into the arms of God, after a long battle with cancer.

              More About Richard Dwaine Bontrager:
              SSN issued: IN[5633]

              Notes for Mary Alice Struwing:
              The Descendants of John J. Christner, privately published February 1961, p.102.

3405 iv. Judith Ann Bontrager, born 02 Aug 1941.

    Notes for Judith Ann Bontrager:
    The Descendants of John J. Christner, privately published February 1961, p. 102.

3406 v. Larry Eugene Bontrager, born 01 Dec 1946.

    Notes for Larry Eugene Bontrager:
    The Descendants of John J. Christner, privately published February 1961, p.102.

1468. Ammon Leo[8] Miller (Phineas S.[7], Magdalena Mattie[6] Lantz, Veronica Fannie[5] Christner, Christian J.[4], Johannes John Hans[3], Christian[2], Christen[1]) was born 07 Oct 1909, and died 16 Nov 1960. He married **Barbara Rozyehic** 09 Oct 1948. She was born 21 Jun 1917 in IL.

Notes for Ammon Leo Miller:
The Descendants of John J. Christner, privately published February 1961, p. 102.

Notes for Barbara Rozyehic:
The Descendants of John J. Christner, privately published February 1961, p. 102.

Child of Ammon Miller and Barbara Rozyehic is:
 3407 i. Sandra Lee[9] Miller, born 19 Nov 1949.

    Notes for Sandra Lee Miller:
    The Descendants of John J. Christner, privately published February 1961, p. 102.

1469. Alvin Elias[8] Miller (Phineas S.[7], Magdalena Mattie[6] Lantz, Veronica Fannie[5] Christner, Christian J.[4], Johannes John Hans[3], Christian[2], Christen[1]) was born 22 Jan 1913. He married **Esther Hertzler** 30 Aug 1941 in Morgantown, PA by John S Mast. She was born 20 Jan 1920.

Notes for Alvin Elias Miller:
The Descendants of John J. Christner, privately published February 1961, p. 102.

Notes for Esther Hertzler:
The Descendants of John J. Christner, privately published February 1961, p. 102.

Children of Alvin Miller and Esther Hertzler are:
 3408 i. Clair Elvin[9] Miller, born 15 Jul 1946.

    Notes for Clair Elvin Miller:
    The Descendants of John J. Christner, privately published February 1961, p. 102.

 3409 ii. Gene Carlyle Miller, born 10 Nov 1949.

    Notes for Gene Carlyle Miller:
    The Descendants of John J. Christner, privately published February 1961, p. 102.

 3410 iii. Marianne Elizabeth Miller, born 09 Mar 1957.

    Notes for Marianne Elizabeth Miller:
    The Descendants of John J. Christner, privately published February 1961, p. 102.

1470. Magdalena Opal[8] Miller (Phineas S.[7], Magdalena Mattie[6] Lantz, Veronica Fannie[5] Christner,

Christian J.[4], Johannes John Hans[3], Christian[2], Christen[1]) was born 03 Apr 1915[5634], and died 23 Sep 1997 in Maricopa Co., AZ[5634]. She married **Obadiah J. Bontrager**[5634,5634] 05 Aug 1933[5634]. He was born 05 Oct 1908 in Lagrange Co., IN[5634,5634], and died 24 May 2000 in Maricopa Co., AZ[5634].

Notes for Magdalena Opal Miller:
The Descendants of John J. Christner, privately published February 1961, p. 102.

Notes for Obadiah J. Bontrager:
The Descendants of John J. Christner, privately published February 1961, p. 103.

Children of Magdalena Miller and Obadiah Bontrager are:
+ 3411   i.   Douglas LaMar[9] Bontrager, born 01 Nov 1933.
+ 3412   ii.   Betty Kathryn Bontrager, born 13 Jun 1935.
+ 3413   iii.   Helen Jean Bontrager, born 02 Aug 1937.
   3414   iv.   Robert Dale Bontrager, born 10 Nov 1940.

     Notes for Robert Dale Bontrager:
     The Descendants of John J. Christner, privately published February 1961, p.103.

   3415   v.   Velva Lee Bontrager, born 04 Aug 1943.

     Notes for Velva Lee Bontrager:
     The Descendants of John J. Christner, privately published February 1961, pp. 102, 103.

1472. Harold Marvin[8] Miller (Phineas S.[7], Magdalena Mattie[6] Lantz, Veronica Fannie[5] Christner, Christian J.[4], Johannes John Hans[3], Christian[2], Christen[1]) was born 06 Jul 1921 in Nappanee, Elkhart Co., IN. He married **Joy Belle Sechrist** 13 May 1951. She was born 31 Mar 1927.

Notes for Harold Marvin Miller:
The Descendants of John J. Christner, privately published February 1961, p. 102.

Notes for Joy Belle Sechrist:
The Descendants of John J. Christner, privately published February 1961, p.103.

Children of Harold Miller and Joy Sechrist are:
   3416   i.   Diana Elaine[9] Miller, born 31 Aug 1949.

     Notes for Diana Elaine Miller:
     The Descendants of John J. Christner, privately published February 1961, p. 103.

   3417   ii.   Patricia Jo Miller, born 11 Dec 1952.

     Notes for Patricia Jo Miller:
     The Descendants of John J. Christner, privately published February 1961, p. 103.

   3418   iii.   Harold Marvin Miller, born 08 Dec 1957.

     Notes for Harold Marvin Miller:
     The Descendants of John J. Christner, privately published February 1961, p. 103.

   3419   iv.   Kathryn Mae Miller, born 31 Aug 1960.

     Notes for Kathryn Mae Miller:
     The Descendants of John J. Christner, privately published February 1961, p. 103.

1473. Ruby Elizabeth[8] Miller (Phineas S.[7], Magdalena Mattie[6] Lantz, Veronica Fannie[5] Christner, Christian J.[4], Johannes John Hans[3], Christian[2], Christen[1]) was born 20 Jul 1924. She married **Dewey Samples** 08 Aug 1948. He was born 02 Apr 1924.

Notes for Ruby Elizabeth Miller:
The Descendants of John J. Christner, privately published February 1961, pp. 102, 103.

Notes for Dewey Samples:
The Descendants of John J. Christner, privately published February 1961, p. 103.

Children of Ruby Miller and Dewey Samples are:
    3420   i.   David Nolan[9] Samples, born 01 Dec 1949.

                Notes for David Nolan Samples:
                The Descendants of John J. Christner, privately published February 1961, p. 103.

    3421   ii.   Donna Elizabeth Samples, born 08 Apr 1951.

                Notes for Donna Elizabeth Samples:
                The Descendants of John J. Christner, privately published February 1961, p. 103.

    3422   iii.   Brian Scott Samples, born 13 Dec 1953; died 19 Mar 1954.

                Notes for Brian Scott Samples:
                The Descendants of John J. Christner, privately published February 1961, p. 103.

    3423   iv.   Dennis Patrick Samples, born 21 Sep 1955.

                Notes for Dennis Patrick Samples:
                The Descendants of John J. Christner, privately published February 1961, p. 103.

    3424   v.   James Jeffrey Samples, born 09 Nov 1957.

                Notes for James Jeffrey Samples:
                The Descendants of John J. Christner, privately published February 1961, p. 103.

1475. Mahlon M. S.[8] Miller (Milo S.[7], Magdalena Mattie[6] Lantz, Veronica Fannie[5] Christner, Christian J.[4], Johannes John Hans[3], Christian[2], Christen[1]) was born 13 Aug 1915 in Middlefield, OH, and died 03 Feb 2002 in Geauga Co., OH[5635]. He married **Katie Yoder**[5635] 14 Dec 1949. She was born 14 Feb 1912 in Geauga Co., OH[5635], and died 13 Apr 1999 in Geauga Co., OH[5635].

Notes for Mahlon M. S. Miller:
The Descendants of John J. Christner, privately published February 1961, pp. 103, 104.

More About Mahlon M. S. Miller:
Residence: Geauga Co., OH[5635]

Notes for Katie Yoder:
The Descendants of John J. Christner, privately published February 1961, pp. 103, 104.

More About Katie Yoder:
Residence: 1930, Burton, Geauga, Ohio[5635]

Children of Mahlon Miller and Katie Yoder are:
    3425   i.   Owen M.[9] Miller, born 15 Sep 1940 in Geauga Co., OH[5635]; died 04 Feb 2000 in Cleveland, Cuyahoga, Ohio[5635].

                Notes for Owen M. Miller:
                The Descendants of John J. Christner, privately published February 1961, p. 103.

                More About Owen M. Miller:
                Residence: Cleveland, Cuyahoga, Ohio, United States[5635]

3426   ii.   William Henry Miller, born 06 Feb 1943.

Notes for William Henry Miller:
The Descendants of John J. Christner, privately published February 1961, p. 104.

3427   iii.   Marvin Miller[5635], born 23 Jun 1947[5635]; died 23 Jun 1947[5635].

Notes for Marvin Miller:
The Descendants of John J. Christner, privately published February 1961, p. 104.

3428   iv.   Mark Miller[5635], born 23 Jun 1947[5635]; died 23 Jun 1947[5635].

Notes for Mark Miller:
The Descendants of John J. Christner, privately published February 1961, p. 104.

3429   v.   Freeman M. Miller, born 03 Sep 1949.

Notes for Freeman M. Miller:
The Descendants of John J. Christner, privately published February 1961, p. 104.

3430   vi.   Mary Ann Miller, born 07 Sep 1952.

Notes for Mary Ann Miller:
The Descendants of John J. Christner, privately published February 1961, p. 104.

1476. Henry M.[8] Miller (Milo S.[7], Magdalena Mattie[6] Lantz, Veronica Fannie[5] Christner, Christian J.[4], Johannes John Hans[3], Christian[2], Christen[1]) was born 20 Sep 1922 in Nappanee, Elkhart Co., IN[5636], and died 18 Jul 2000 in Riceville, Howard Co., IA[5636]. He married **Katie Troyer** 22 Apr 1943. She was born 01 May 1914.

Notes for Henry M. Miller:
The Descendants of John J. Christner, privately published February 1961, pp. 103, 104.

More About Henry M. Miller:
Occupation: Farmer/[5636]
Religion: Amish (Bishop)/[5636]

Notes for Katie Troyer:
The Descendants of John J. Christner, privately published February 1961, p. 104.

Children of Henry Miller and Katie Troyer are:
3431   i.   Emma H.[9] Miller, born 05 May 1947.

Notes for Emma H. Miller:
The Descendants of John J. Christner, privately published February 1961, p. 104.

3432   ii.   Eli H. Miller, born 11 Apr 1949.

Notes for Eli H. Miller:
The Descendants of John J. Christner, privately published February 1961, p. 104.

3433   iii.   Levi H. Miller, born 04 Oct 1951.

Notes for Levi H. Miller:
The Descendants of John J. Christner, privately published February 1961, p. 104.

3434   iv.   Daniel H. Miller, born 16 Sep 1952.

Notes for Daniel H. Miller:
The Descendants of John J. Christner, privately published February 1961, p. 104.

3435   v.   Susan H. Miller, born 07 May 1954.

Notes for Susan H. Miller:
The Descendants of John J. Christner, privately published February 1961, p. 104.

1477. Levi M.[8] Miller (Milo S.[7], Magdalena Mattie[6] Lantz, Veronica Fannie[5] Christner, Christian J.[4], Johannes John Hans[3], Christian[2], Christen[1]) was born 26 Jun 1925 in Stoneboro, PA. He married **Fannie Byler** 23 Oct 1947. She was born 28 Dec 1926.

Notes for Levi M. Miller:
The Descendants of John J. Christner, privately published February 1961, pp. 103, 104.

Children of Levi Miller and Fannie Byler are:
3436   i.   Mahlon L.[9] Miller, born 12 Oct 1950.

Notes for Mahlon L. Miller:
The Descendants of John J. Christner, privately published February 1961, p. 104.

3437   ii.   Clara L. Miller, born 14 Mar 1952.

Notes for Clara L. Miller:
The Descendants of John J. Christner, privately published February 1961, p. 104.

3438   iii. Owen L. Miller, born 17 Apr 1953.

Notes for Owen L. Miller:
The Descendants of John J. Christner, privately published February 1961, p. 104.

3439   iv.   Benjamin L. Miller, born 26 May 1954.

Notes for Benjamin L. Miller:
The Descendants of John J. Christner, privately published February 1961, p. 104.

3440   v.   Sarah L. Miller, born 21 Sep 1955.

Notes for Sarah L. Miller:
The Descendants of John J. Christner, privately published February 1961, p. 104.

3441   vi.   Milo L. Miller, born 27 Jun 1957.

Notes for Milo L. Miller:
The Descendants of John J. Christner, privately published February 1961, p. 104.

3442   vii. Emma L. Miller, born 17 Aug 1958.

Notes for Emma L. Miller:
The Descendants of John J. Christner, privately published February 1961, p. 104.

1478. Ida M.[8] Miller (Milo S.[7], Magdalena Mattie[6] Lantz, Veronica Fannie[5] Christner, Christian J.[4], Johannes John Hans[3], Christian[2], Christen[1]) was born 19 Jun 1931 in Mercer, PA. She married **Daniel N. Yoder** 25 Apr 1950. He was born 29 Sep 1924.

Notes for Ida M. Miller:
The Descendants of John J. Christner, privately published February 1961, pp.103, 104.

Notes for Daniel N. Yoder:
The Descendants of John J. Christner, privately published February 1961, p. 104.

Children of Ida Miller and Daniel Yoder are:

3443 i. Sally Ann[9] Yoder, born 18 Oct 1951.

> Notes for Sally Ann Yoder:
> The Descendants of John J. Christner, privately published February 1961, p. 104.

3444 ii. Emma D. Yoder, born 10 Apr 1953.

> Notes for Emma D. Yoder:
> The Descendants of John J. Christner, privately published February 1961, p. 104.

3445 iii. Aaron D. Yoder, born 07 Sep 1954.

> Notes for Aaron D. Yoder:
> The Descendants of John J. Christner, privately published February 1961, p. 104.

3446 iv. Alvin D. Yoder, born 07 Sep 1954.

> Notes for Alvin D. Yoder:
> The Descendants of John J. Christner, privately published February 1961, p. 104.

3447 v. Levi D. Yoder, born 20 Oct 1955.

> Notes for Levi D. Yoder:
> The Descendants of John J. Christner, privately published February 1961, p. 104.

3448 vi. Cora D. Yoder, born 30 May 1957.

> Notes for Cora D. Yoder:
> The Descendants of John J. Christner, privately published February 1961, p. 104.

3449 vii. Samuel D. Yoder, born 16 Oct 1958.

> Notes for Samuel D. Yoder:
> The Descendants of John J. Christner, privately published February 1961, p. 104.

1479. Owen M.[8] Miller (Milo S.[7], Magdalena Mattie[6] Lantz, Veronica Fannie[5] Christner, Christian J.[4], Johannes John Hans[3], Christian[2], Christen[1]) was born 19 Jun 1931 in Mercer, PA. He married **Mary Detweiler** 27 Mar 1952. She was born 18 Jan 1930.

Notes for Owen M. Miller:
The Descendants of John J. Christner, privately published February 1961, p. 103.

Notes for Mary Detweiler:
The Descendants of John J. Christner, privately published February 1961, p. 104.

Children of Owen Miller and Mary Detweiler are:

3450 i. Raymond[9] Miller, born 04 Feb 1953; died 08 Jun 1959.

> Notes for Raymond Miller:
> The Descendants of John J. Christner, privately published February 1961, p. 104.

3451 ii. Rebecca O. Miller, born 06 Apr 1954.

> Notes for Rebecca O. Miller:
> The Descendants of John J. Christner, privately published February 1961, p. 104.

3452 iii. Sarah O. Miller, born 08 Aug 1955.

> Notes for Sarah O. Miller:
> The Descendants of John J. Christner, privately published February 1961, p. 104.

3453   iv.   Henry O. Miller, born 01 Aug 1957.

Notes for Henry O. Miller:
The Descendants of John J. Christner, privately published February 1961, p. 104.

3454   v.   Ida O. Miller, born 30 Oct 1958.

Notes for Ida O. Miller:
The Descendants of John J. Christner, privately published February 1961, p. 104.

1481. Emma S.[8] Christner (Samuel J.[8], John E.[7], John B.[6], Peter[5], Peter[4], Christian[3], Christian[2], Christen[1]) was born 12 Aug 1916 in Topeka, Lagrange Co., IN. She married **John S. Girod** 18 Jan 1940. He was born 29 Sep 1917 in Berne, Adams Co., IN.

Notes for Emma S. Christner:
The Descendants of John J. Christner, privately published February 1961, p. 48.

Notes for John S. Girod:
The Descendants of John J. Christner, privately published February 1961, p. 48.

Children of Emma Christner and John Girod are:
    3455   i.   Elizabeth[9] Girod, born 31 Mar 1942.

Notes for Elizabeth Girod:
The Descendants of John J. Christner, privately published February 1961, p. 48.

    3456   ii.   Josephine Girod, born 30 Jul 1943.

Notes for Josephine Girod:
The Descendants of John J. Christner, privately published February 1961, p. 48.

    3457   iii.   Miriam Girod, born 07 Oct 1947.

Notes for Miriam Girod:
The Descendants of John J. Christner, privately published February 1961, p. 48.

    3458   iv.   Samuel Girod, born 23 Oct 1948.

Notes for Samuel Girod:
The Descendants of John J. Christner, privately published February 1961, p. 48.

    3459   v.   Levi Girod, born 18 Feb 1950.

Notes for Levi Girod:
The Descendants of John J. Christner, privately published February 1961, p. 48.

+   3460   vi.   Lovina Girod, born 18 Feb 1952.
    3461   vii.   Reuben Girod, born 21 Oct 1954.

Notes for Reuben Girod:
The Descendants of John J. Christner, privately published February 1961, p. 48.

    3462   viii.   Mark Girod, born 17 Mar 1957.

Notes for Mark Girod:
The Descendants of John J. Christner, privately published February 1961, p. 48.

1482. Levi S.[8] Christner (Samuel J.[8], John E.[7], John B.[6], Peter[5], Peter[4], Christian[3], Christian[2], Christen[1]) was born 06 Jul 1920 in Topeka, Lagrange Co., IN, and died 10 Feb 2011 in Decatur, Adams Co., IN. He married **Josephine M. Schwartz** 28 Mar 1946. She was born 21 Apr 1919.

Notes for Levi S. Christner:
The Descendants of John J. Christner, privately published February 1961, p. 48.

Birth: Jul. 6, 1920
Nappanee, Elkhart Co., IN
Death: Feb. 10, 2011
Decatur, Adams Co., IN

Source: Bluffton News-Banner
Date: 02-12-2011

The father of a Bluffton resident, Levi S. Christner, 90, of Geneva, died at 3:59 a.m. Thursday, Feb. 10, 2011, at Adams Memorial Hospital in Decatur.

He was born in Nappanee on July 6, 1920, to Sam J. and Elizabeth (Miller) Christner.

Surviving relatives include his wife, Josephine M. Christner of Geneva; three sons, Samuel J. (Emma) Christner of Monroe, Jacob J. (Mary) Christner of Berne and Levi J. (Martha) Christner of Geneva; five daughters, Margaret (Tobe) Wickey of Geneva, Lizzie (Martin) Schwartz of Geneva, Fannie (Menno N.) Schwartz of Monroe, Rebecca (Jacob L.) Wickey of Decatur and Barbara (Amos E.) Wickey of Bluffton; one brother, Alvin S. Christner of Berne; four sisters, Edna Schwartz of Hamilton, Emma Girod of Berne, Sylvia Eicher of Geneva and Ida Lengacher of Harlan; and 76 grandchildren and 253 great grandchildren.

Mr. Christner was preceded in death by one daughter, Josephine Christner, and one brother, Cletus S. Christner.

Calling hours will be from noon to 8 p.m. Friday, Feb. 11, and from 9 a.m. to 8 p.m. Saturday, Feb. 12, at the Christner residence. Funeral services will be at 9 a.m. Sunday, Feb. 13, at the Christner residence. Burial will be at Bunker Hill Cemetery in Geneva.

Downing and Glancy Funeral Homes in Geneva are in charge of arrangements.

Burial:
Bunker Hill Cemetery, Geneva, Adams Co., IN

Notes for Josephine M. Schwartz:
The Descendants of John J. Christner, privately published February 1961, p. 48.

Children of Levi Christner and Josephine Schwartz are:
+   3463   i.   Margaret J.[9] Christner, born 27 Feb 1947 in Geneva, Adams Co., IN.
+   3464   ii. Samuel J. Christner, born 31 Aug 1948 in Geneva, Adams Co., IN.
+   3465   iii. Jacob J. Christner, born 07 Aug 1949 in Geneva, Adams Co., IN.
    3466   iv. Elizabeth J. Christner, born 21 May 1953 in Geneva, Adams Co., IN. She married Martin K. Schwartz 09 Sep 1982 in Adams Co., IN; born 08 Jul 1949 in Berne, Adams Co., IN.

        Notes for Elizabeth J. Christner:
        The Descendants of John J. Christner, privately published February 1961, p. 48.

+   3467   v.   Fannie J. Christner, born 21 Jun 1954 in Geneva, Adams Co., IN.
+   3468   vi. Levi J. Christner, born 26 Jun 1955 in Geneva, Adams Co., IN.
    3469   vii. Josephine Christner, born 10 Oct 1956; died 17 Jan 1957 in Adams Co., IN.

        Notes for Josephine Christner:
        The Descendants of John J. Christner, privately published February 1961, p. 48.

+   3470   viii. Rebecca J. Christner, born 04 Jan 1958 in Geneva, Adams Co., IN.
+   3471   ix. Barbara J. Christner, born 27 Jan 1960 in Geneva, Adams Co., IN.

1483. Edna S.[8] **Christner** (Samuel J.[8], John E.[7], John B.[6], Peter[5], Peter[4], Christian[3], Christian[2], Christen[1])[5637] was born 06 Jan 1925 in Nappanee, Elkhart Co., IN. She married **Amos M. Schwartz** 18 Mar 1948. He was born 06 Feb 1929 in Monroe, Adams Co., IN.

Notes for Edna S. Christner:
The Descendants of John J. Christner, privately published February 1961, p. 48.

More About Edna S. Christner:
Residence: 1930, Scott, Kosciusko Co., IN[5637]

Notes for Amos M. Schwartz:
The Descendants of John J. Christner, privately published February 1961, p. 48.

Children of Edna Christner and Amos Schwartz are:

    3472   i.   Elizabeth A.[9] Schwartz, born 08 Jan 1949.

                        Notes for Elizabeth A. Schwartz:
                        The Descendants of John J. Christner, privately published February 1961, p.,48.

    3473   ii.   Mary A. Schwartz, born 15 Apr 1950.

                        Notes for Mary A. Schwartz:
                        The Descendants of John J. Christner, privately published February 1961, p. 48.

    3474   iii.   Jacob A. Schwartz, born 20 Feb 1952.

                        Notes for Jacob A. Schwartz:
                        The Descendants of John J. Christner, privately published February 1961, p. 48.

    3475   iv.   Syliva A. Schwartz, born 05 Jul 1954.

                        Notes for Syliva A. Schwartz:
                        The Descendants of John J. Christner, privately published February 1961, p. 48.

    3476   v.   Edna A. Schwartz, born 06 Jan 1958.

                        Notes for Edna A. Schwartz:

                        The Descendants of John J. Christner, privately published February 1961, p. 48.

    3477   vi.   Martha A. Schwartz, born 19 Sep 1959.

                        Notes for Martha A. Schwartz:
                        The Descendants of John J. Christner, privately published February 1961, p. 48.

    3478   vii.   Fannie A. Schwartz, born 17 Jan 1962.
    3479   viii.   Rebecca A. Schwartz, born 11 Jul 1964.

1484. Sylvia S.[8] **Christner** (Samuel J.[8], John E.[7], John B.[6], Peter[5], Peter[4], Christian[3], Christian[2], Christen[1]) was born 20 Oct 1927 in Nappanee, Elkhart Co., IN. She married **Joseph J. Eicher** 31 Oct 1957. He was born 20 Mar 1936 in Berne, Adams Co., IN.

Notes for Sylvia S. Christner:
The Descendants of John J. Christner, privately published February 1961, p. 48.

Notes for Joseph J. Eicher:

The Descendants of John J. Christner, privately published February 1961, p. 48.

Children of Sylvia Christner and Joseph Eicher are:

3480   i.   Benjamin S.[9] Eicher, born 07 Sep 1958.

                Notes for Benjamin S. Eicher:
                The Descendants of John J. Christner, privately published February 1961, p. 48.

3481   ii.   Elizabeth S. Eicher, born 26 Nov 1960.
3482   iii. Marie S. Eicher, born 12 Jul 1963 in Adams Co., IN; died 31 Aug 1963.
3483   iv. Edna S. Eicher, born 27 Oct 1965.
3484   v.   John S. Eicher, born 25 Dec 1967 in Adams Co., IN.
3485   vi. Jerry S. Eicher, born 15 Jul 1969.

1485. Ida S.[8] Christner (Samuel J.[8], John E.[7], John B.[6], Peter[5], Peter[4], Christian[3], Christian[2], Christen[1]) was born 21 Jul 1933 in Berne, Adams Co., IN. She married **John A. Lengacher** 23 Feb 1969. He was born 26 Nov 1930 in Grabill, Allen Co., IN, and died 27 Sep 1978 in Grabill, Allen Co., IN.

Children of Ida Christner and John Lengacher are:

3486   i.   David[9] Lengacher, born 23 Dec 1969.
3487   ii.   Joseph Lengacher, born 13 Mar 1971 in Allen Co. IN.
3488   iii. Nathan Lengacher, born 05 Sep 1972 in Allen Co. IN.
3489   iv. Elizabeth Lengacher, born 04 Nov 1974 in Allen Co. IN.
3490   v.   Paul Lengacher, born 28 Jun 1976 in Allen Co. IN.

1486. Ervin N.[8] Gingerich (Sarah[7] Hershberger, Magdalena Mattie[6] Lantz, Veronica Fannie[5] Christner, Christian J.[4], Johannes John Hans[3], Christian[2], Christen[1]) was born 06 Jan 1916 in Millerburg, Holmes Co., OH. He married **Esther Burkholder**[5638]. She was born 14 Jun 1918 in Nappanee, Elkhart County, Indiana, US[5638], and died 07 May 2001 in Holmes Co., OH, US[5638].

Notes for Esther Burkholder:
The Descendants of John J. Christner, privately published February 1961, p. 104.

More About Esther Burkholder:
Burial: 10 May 2001, Coblentz Cemetery, Berlin Township, Holmes Co., OH, US[5638]

Children of Ervin Gingerich and Esther Burkholder are:

3491   i.   Merle[9] Gingerich, born 08 Nov 1941.

                Notes for Merle Gingerich:
                The Descendants of John J. Christner, privately published February 1961, p. 104.

3492   ii.   Allen Gingerich, born 04 Mar 1943.

                Notes for Allen Gingerich:
                The Descendants of John J. Christner, privately published February 1961, p. 104.

3493   iii. Edna Gingerich, born 10 Dec 1945.

                Notes for Edna Gingerich:
                The Descendants of John J. Christner, privately published February 1961, p. 104.

3494   iv. Betty Gingerich, born 14 Feb 1949.

                Notes for Betty Gingerich:
                Descendants of John J. Christner, privately published February 1961, p. 104.

3495   v.   Raymond Gingerich, born 25 Mar 1950.

Notes for Raymond Gingerich:
The Descendants of John J. Christner, privately published February 1961, p. 104.

3496   vi.   David Gingerich, born 15 Apr 1951.

Notes for David Gingerich:
The Descendants of John J. Christner, privately published February 1961, p. 104.

3497   vii.   Barbara Gingerich, born 22 Nov 1952.

Notes for Barbara Gingerich:
The Descendants of John J. Christner, privately published February 1961, p. 104.

3498   viii.   Martha Gingerich, born 04 Sep 1955.

Notes for Martha Gingerich:
The Descendants of John J. Christner, privately published February 1961, p.104.

1487. Alvin N.[8] Gingerich (Sarah[7] Hershberger, Magdalena Mattie[6] Lantz, Veronica Fannie[5] Christner, Christian J.[4], Johannes John Hans[3], Christian[2], Christen[1]) was born 17 Mar 1918 in Millerburg, Holmes Co., OH. He married **Mae Miller** 10 Feb 1944.

Notes for Alvin N. Gingerich:
The Descendants of John J. Christner, privately published February 1961, p. 105.

Notes for Mae Miller:
The Descendants of John J. Christner, privately published February 1961, p. 105.

Children of Alvin Gingerich and Mae Miller are:
3499   i.   Ruth[9] Gingerich, born 06 Oct 1945.

Notes for Ruth Gingerich:
The Descendants of John J. Christner, privately published February 1961, p. 105.

3500   ii.   Naomi Gingerich, born 26 Jun 1947.

Notes for Naomi Gingerich:
The Descendants of John J. Christner, privately published February 1961, p. 105.

3501   iii.   Mahlon Gingerich, born 08 May 1949.

Notes for Mahlon Gingerich:
The Descendants of John J. Christner, privately published February 1961, p.105.

3502   iv.   Ada Gingerich, born 23 Jan 1952.

Notes for Ada Gingerich:
The Descendants of John J. Christner, privately published February 1961, p. 105.

3503   v.   Mary Gingerich, born 17 Dec 1953.

Notes for Mary Gingerich:
The Descendants of John J. Christner, privately published February 1961, p. 105.

3504   vi.   Daniel Gingerich, born 26 Sep 1957.

Notes for Daniel Gingerich:

The Descendants of John J. Christner, privately published February 1961, p. 105.

1488. Edna^8 Gingerich (Sarah^7 Hershberger, Magdalena Mattie^6 Lantz, Veronica Fannie^5 Christner, Christian J.^{4}, Johannes John Hans^3, Christian^2, Christen^1) was born 20 Apr 1920 in Millerburg, Holmes Co., OH. She married **Mel Beachy**.

Notes for Edna Gingerich:
The Descendants of John J. Christner, privately published February 1961, p. 105.

Notes for Mel Beachy:
The Descendants of John J. Christner, privately published February 1961, p. 105.

Children of Edna Gingerich and Mel Beachy are:
  3505   i.   Marianna^9 Beachy, born 17 Jan 1957.

              Notes for Marianna Beachy:
              The Descendants of John J. Christner, privately published February 1961, p. 105.

  3506   ii.   Galen Beachy, born 26 Sep 1959.

              Notes for Galen Beachy:
              The Descendants of John J. Christner, privately published February 1961, p. 105.

1489. Mary^8 Gingerich (Sarah^7 Hershberger, Magdalena Mattie^6 Lantz, Veronica Fannie^5 Christner, Christian J.^{4}, Johannes John Hans^3, Christian^2, Christen^1) was born 11 Jul 1922 in Millerburg, Holmes Co., OH. She married **Samuel Yoder**.

Children of Mary Gingerich and Samuel Yoder are:
  3507   i.   Elsie^9 Yoder, born 12 Jan 1946.
  3508   ii.   Ellen Yoder, born 22 Oct 1948.

1490. Ernest N.^{8} Miller (Sarah^7 Hershberger, Magdalena Mattie^6 Lantz, Veronica Fannie^5 Christner, Christian J.^{4}, Johannes John Hans^3, Christian^2, Christen^1) was born 29 Nov 1923. He married **Elizabeth A. Hochstetler** 29 Nov 1945 in by David D. Nisley, daughter of Albert Hochstetler and Anna Miller. She was born 01 Sep 1927 in Topeka, Lagrange Co., IN.

Notes for Ernest N. Miller:
The Descendants of John J. Christner, privately published February 1961, p. 53.

More About Ernest N. Miller:
Occupation: Cattle Feed Mill Operator & Farmer/
Religion: Old Order Amish/

Notes for Elizabeth A. Hochstetler:
The Descendants of John J. Christner, privately published February 1961, p. 53.

He was Old Order Amish, farmer and feed mill operator.

More About Elizabeth A. Hochstetler:
Religion: Old Order Amish/

Children of Ernest Miller and Elizabeth Hochstetler are:
  3509   i.   Anna Marie^9 Miller, born 03 Jul 1948.

Notes for Anna Marie Miller:
The Descendants of John J. Christner, privately published February 1961, p. 53.

3510   ii.   Freeman E. Miller, born 06 Sep 1950.

Notes for Freeman E. Miller:
The Descendants of John J. Christner, privately published February 1961, p. 53.

3511   iii.   Orpha E Miller, born 19 Oct 1952.

Notes for Orpha E Miller:
The Descendants of John J. Christner, privately published February 1961, p. 53 .

3512   iv.   Orva E Miller, born 19 Oct 1952.

Notes for Orva E Miller:
The Descendants of John J. Christner, privately published February 1961, p. 53.

3513   v.   Alvin Jay Miller, born 23 Oct 1953.

Notes for Alvin Jay Miller:
The Descendants of John J. Christner, privately published February 1961, p. 53.

3514   vi.   Freeda Miller, born 28 Jun 1956.

Notes for Freeda Miller:
The Descendants of John J. Christner, privately published February 1961, p. 53.

1491. Fannie[8] Gingerich (Sarah[7] Hershberger, Magdalena Mattie[6] Lantz, Veronica Fannie[5] Christner, Christian J.[4], Johannes John Hans[3], Christian[2], Christen[1]) was born 28 Apr 1924 in Millerburg, Holmes Co., OH, and died 14 Feb 1975 in Holmes Co., OH[5639]. She married **Yost Miller** 20 Feb 1947.

Children of Fannie Gingerich and Yost Miller are:
3515   i.   Nelson[9] Miller, born 22 Apr 1947.
3516   ii.   Clarence Miller, born 30 Jul 1950.
3517   iii.   Esther Miller, born 17 Feb 1954.
3518   iv.   Ellis Miller, born 04 Feb 1955.
3519   v.   Phillip Miller, born 20 Jul 1959.

1492. Emma[8] Gingerich (Sarah[7] Hershberger, Magdalena Mattie[6] Lantz, Veronica Fannie[5] Christner, Christian J.[4], Johannes John Hans[3], Christian[2], Christen[1]) was born 27 Dec 1926 in Sugarcreek, Tuscarawas Co., OH. She married **Ervin D. Miller**.

Notes for Emma Gingerich:
The Descendants of John J. Christner, privately published February 1961, p. 105.

Notes for Ervin D. Miller:
The Descendants of John J. Christner, privately published February 1961, p. 105.

Children of Emma Gingerich and Ervin Miller are:
3520   i.   Christian[9] Miller, born 12 Sep 1953.

Notes for Christian Miller:
The Descendants of John J. Christner, privately published February 1961, p. 105.

3521   ii.   Jerry Miller, born 12 Nov 1955.

Notes for Jerry Miller:

The Descendants of John J. Christner, privately published February 1961, p. 105.

3522 iii. Rosetta Miller, born 12 Nov 1959.

   Notes for Rosetta Miller:
   The Descendants of John J. Christner, privately published February 1961, p. 105.

1493. Mahlon[8] Gingerich (Sarah[7] Hershberger, Magdalena Mattie[6] Lantz, Veronica Fannie[5] Christner, Christian J.[4], Johannes John Hans[3], Christian[2], Christen[1]) was born 12 Mar 1929 in Millerburg, Holmes Co., OH. He married **Anna Mae Troyer**.

Notes for Mahlon Gingerich:
The Descendants of John J. Christner, privately published February 1961, p. 105.

Notes for Anna Mae Troyer:
The Descendants of John J. Christner, privately published February 1961, p.105.

Children of Mahlon Gingerich and Anna Troyer are:
 3523 i. Wilma[9] Gingerich, born 28 Dec 1952.
 3524 ii. Orpha Gingerich, born 26 May 1954.
 3525 iii. Ruby Gingerich, born 03 Jun 1956.
 3526 iv. Myron Gingerich, born 14 Jan 1958.

1497. Cletus[8] Miller (Amos S.[7], Magdalena Mattie[6] Lantz, Veronica Fannie[5] Christner, Christian J.[4], Johannes John Hans[3], Christian[2], Christen[1]) was born 01 Feb 1924 in Topeka, Lagrange Co., IN. He married **Esther Troyer** 17 Mar 1947. She was born 07 Aug 1926 in Holmes Co., OH.

Notes for Cletus Miller:
The Descendants of John J. Christner, privately published February 1961, p. 105.

Notes for Esther Troyer:
The Descendants of John J. Christner, privately published February 1961, p. 105.

Children of Cletus Miller and Esther Troyer are:
 3527 i. Joanna[9] Miller, born 09 Sep 1951.

   Notes for Joanna Miller:
   The Descendants of John J. Christner, privately published February 1961, p. 105.

 3528 ii. Ruthann Miller, born 18 Jun 1953.

   Notes for Ruthann Miller:
   The Descendants of John J. Christner, privately published February 1961, p. 105.

 3529 iii. Infant Miller, born 25 Jan 1958; died 25 Jan 1958.

   Notes for Infant Miller:
   The Descendants of John J. Christner, privately published February 1961, p. 105.

1498. Anna[8] Miller (Amos S.[7], Magdalena Mattie[6] Lantz, Veronica Fannie[5] Christner, Christian J.[4], Johannes John Hans[3], Christian[2], Christen[1]) was born 08 Feb 1927 in Topeka, Lagrange Co., IN. She married **Elmer C. Miller** 16 Jun 1950. He was born 28 Jul 1925[5640], and died 21 Jul 1999[5640].

Notes for Anna Miller:

The Descendants of John J. Christner, privately published February 1961, p. 105.

Notes for Elmer C. Miller:
The Descendants of John J. Christner, privately published February 1961, p. 105.

More About Elmer C. Miller:
DBH Book: 8059/[5640]

Children of Anna Miller and Elmer Miller are:

    3530   i.   Roger Allen[9] Miller, born 13 Dec 1950.

                 Notes for Roger Allen Miller:
                 The Descendants of John J. Christner, privately published February 1961, p. 106.

    3531   ii.   Phyllis Ann Miller, born 01 Jul 1952.

                 Notes for Phyllis Ann Miller:
                 The Descendants of John J. Christner, privately published February 1961, p. 106.

    3532   iii.   Karen Louise Miller, born 13 Jan 1958.

                 Notes for Karen Louise Miller:
                 The Descendants of John J. Christner, privately published February 1961, p. 106.

1499. Ellis L.[8] Miller (Levi S.[7], Magdalena Mattie[6] Lantz, Veronica Fannie[5] Christner, Christian J.[4], Johannes John Hans[3], Christian[2], Christen[1])[5641] was born 27 May 1923 in Lagrange Co., IN[5642,5643], and died 09 May 2000 in Fort Wayne, Allen Co., IN[5643,5644]. He married **Phyllis Kitchen**.

Notes for Ellis L. Miller:
The Descendants of John J. Christner, privately published February 1961, p. 106.

More About Ellis L. Miller:
Social Security Number: 317-26-1124/[5645,5646]
SSN issued: IN[5647,5648]

Notes for Phyllis Kitchen:
Source:

The Descendants of John J. Christner, privately published 1961, February 1961, p. 106

Children of Ellis Miller and Phyllis Kitchen are:

    3533   i.   Richard Edward[9] Miller, born 12 Sep 1955.

                 Notes for Richard Edward Miller:
                 The Descendants of John J. Christner, privately published February 1961, p. 106.

    3534   ii.   Peggy Joan Miller, born 09 Jun 1957.

                 Notes for Peggy Joan Miller:
                 The Descendants of John J. Christner, privately published February 1961, p. 106.

1501. Edna Lucy[8] Miller (Levi S.[7], Magdalena Mattie[6] Lantz, Veronica Fannie[5] Christner, Christian J.[4], Johannes John Hans[3], Christian[2], Christen[1])[5649] was born 29 Dec 1926 in Lagrange Co., IN[5649], and died 11 Sep 1999 in Clark, Randolph Co., MO[5649]. She married **Ezra J. Miller** 18 Apr 1946. He was born 10 Jan 1925.

Notes for Edna Lucy Miller:
The Descendants of John J. Christner, privately published February 1961, p. 106.

Notes for Ezra J. Miller:
The Descendants of John J. Christner, privately published February 1961, p. 106.

Children of Edna Miller and Ezra Miller are:

3535   i.   Anna[9] Miller, born 28 Dec 1947.

        Notes for Anna Miller:
        The Descendants of John J. Christner, privately published February 1961, p. 106.

3536   ii.   Susie Miller, born 25 Nov 1948.

        Notes for Susie Miller:
        The Descendants of John J. Christner, privately published February 1961, p. 106.

3537   iii.   John Henry Miller, born 31 Dec 1949.

        Notes for John Henry Miller:
        The Descendants of John J. Christner, privately published February 1961, p. 106.

3538   iv.   Clara Miller, born 26 Mar 1951.

        Notes for Clara Miller:
        The Descendants of John J. Christner, privately published February 1961, p. 106.

3539   v.   Clarence Miller, born 25 May 1955.

        Notes for Clarence Miller:
        The Descendants of John J. Christner, privately published February 1961, p. 106.

3540   vi.   Mary Miller, born 25 Feb 1956.

        Notes for Mary Miller:
        The Descendants of John J. Christner, privately published February 1961, p. 106.

3541   vii.   Ezra Miller, born 03 Jun 1957.

        Notes for Ezra Miller:
        The Descendants of John J. Christner, privately published February 1961, p. 106.

3542   viii.   Mahlon Miller, born 15 Sep 1958.

        Notes for Mahlon Miller:
        The Descendants of John J. Christner, privately published February 1961, p. 106.

1504. Fannie L.[8] Miller (Levi S.[7], Magdalena Mattie[6] Lantz, Veronica Fannie[5] Christner, Christian J.[4], Johannes John Hans[3], Christian[2], Christen[1]) was born 01 Jul 1934. She married **Adin G. Yutzy** 13 Oct 1953. He was born 19 May 1934.

Notes for Fannie L. Miller:
The Descendants of John J. Christner, privately published February 1961, p. 106.

Notes for Adin G. Yutzy:
The Descendants of John J. Christner, privately published February 1961, p. 106.

More About Adin G. Yutzy:
Residence: Vilonia, Arkansas

Children of Fannie Miller and Adin Yutzy are:
    3543   i.   Vernon[9] Yutzy, born 13 Mar 1954.

                   Notes for Vernon Yutzy:
                   The Descendants of John J. Christner, privately published February 1961, p. 106.

    3544   ii. Mary Arlene Yutzy, born 22 Jun 1956.

                   Notes for Mary Arlene Yutzy:
                   The Descendants of John J. Christner, privately published February 1961, p. 106.

    3545   iii. Paul Yutzy, born 23 Jul 1959.

                   Notes for Paul Yutzy:
                   The Descendants of John J. Christner, privately published February 1961, p. 106.

1508. Alma L.[8] Miller (Levi S.[7], Magdalena Mattie[6] Lantz, Veronica Fannie[5] Christner, Christian J.[4], Johannes John Hans[3], Christian[2], Christen[1]) was born 03 Sep 1957. She married **Monroe A. Mast**. He was born 11 Dec 1935.

Notes for Alma L. Miller:
The Descendants of John J. Christner, privately published February 1961, pp. 99, 106.

Notes for Monroe A. Mast:
The Descendants of John J. Christner, privately published February 1961, p. 106.

Children of Alma Miller and Monroe Mast are:
    3546   i.   Edna[9] Mast, born 18 Apr 1956.

                   Notes for Edna Mast:
                   The Descendants of John J. Christner, privately published February 1961, p. 106.

    3547   ii. Ella Mast, born 26 Mar 1959.

                   Notes for Ella Mast:
                   The Descendants of John J. Christner, privately published February 1961, pp. 99, 106.

1509. Orva Eldon[8] Miller (Fannie Elmina[7], Magdalena Mattie[6] Lantz, Veronica Fannie[5] Christner, Christian J.[4], Johannes John Hans[3], Christian[2], Christen[1])[5650] was born 29 Jan 1922[5650,5651], and died Feb 1971[5652,5653]. He married **Mayzel Evelyn Kline** 22 Feb 1952. She was born 24 Sep 1921[5654], and died 31 Oct 2009 in North Webster, Kosciusko Co., IN[5654].

Notes for Orva Eldon Miller:
The Descendants of John J. Christner, privately published February 1961, p. 8.

Birth: 1922 - IN
Death: Feb. 22, 1971

Orva was the son of Willis & Fannie Elmina Miller. He had four brothers and a sister: Arlene, Orla Vernon, Glen, Raymond and Floyd.

Orva married Gladys May Cook, daughter of Earl & Pearl, in Goshen on November 22nd of 1948.

Spouse: Mayzel E. Miller (1921 - 2009)

Burial: Mock Cemetery, North Webster, Kosciusko Co., IN
Plot: Section 1 row 2
Find A Grave Memorial# 69555074

More About Orva Eldon Miller:
Social Security Number: 306-20-7928/[5655]
SSN issued: IN[5655]

Notes for Mayzel Evelyn Kline:
Source:
The Descendants of John J. Christner, privately published 1961, p. 8.

Birth: Sep. 24, 1921
Death: Oct. 31, 2009

Family links:
Spouse:
Orva Eldon Miller (1922 - 1971)

Burial:
Mock Cemetery, North Webster, Kosciusko Co., IN
Plot: Section 1 row 2
Find A Grave Memorial# 69555718

More About Mayzel Evelyn Kline:
SSN issued: IN[5656]

Children of Orva Miller and Mayzel Kline are:
    3548   i.   Richard Dean[9] Miller, born 20 Aug 1951.

                      Notes for Richard Dean Miller:
                      The Descendants of John J. Christner, privately published February 1961, p. 8.

    3549   ii.   Sally Jo Miller, born 30 Jan 1953.

                      Notes for Sally Jo Miller:
                      The Descendants of John J. Christner, privately published February 1961, p. 8.

1511. Orla Vernon[8] Miller (Fannie Elmina[7], Magdalena Mattie[6] Lantz, Veronica Fannie[5] Christner, Christian J.[4], Johannes John Hans[3], Christian[2], Christen[1]) was born 01 Apr 1925 in Lagrange Co., IN[5657], and died 07 Jan 1993 in Fort Wayne, Allen Co., IN. He married **Ada Eash** 22 Nov 1945 in Lagrange Co., IN. She was born 07 Jun 1925 in Shipshewana, Elkhart Co., IN.

Notes for Orla Vernon Miller:
The Descendants of John J. Christner, privately published February 1961, p. 8.

More About Orla Vernon Miller:
Burial: Yoder Cemetery Shipshewana IN
Religion: Old Order Amish/

Notes for Ada Eash:
The Descendants of John J. Christner, privately published February 1961, p. 8.

Children of Orla Miller and Ada Eash are:
    3550   i.   Calvin A.[9] Miller, born 12 Jan 1947 in Middlebury, Elkhart Co., IN.

Notes for Calvin A. Miller:
The Descendants of John J. Christner, privately published February 1961, p. 8.

3551   ii.   Infant Son Miller, born 05 May 1948 in Sturgis, St. Joseph Co., MI; died 05 May 1948.

Notes for Infant Son Miller:
The Descendants of John J. Christner, privately published February 1961, p. 8.

3552   iii. David V. Miller, born 17 Aug 1949 in Sturgis, St. Joseph Co., MI.

Notes for David V. Miller:
The Descendants of John J. Christner, privately published February 1961, p. 8.

+   3553   iv.   Esther Miller, born 28 Oct 1951 in Sturgis, St. Joseph Co., MI.
    3554   v.   LeRoy Miller, born 01 Apr 1955 in Sturgis, St. Joseph Co., MI.

Notes for LeRoy Miller:
The Descendants of John J. Christner, privately published February 1961, p. 8.

3555   vi.   Elsie Miller, born 08 Mar 1958 in Sturgis, St. Joseph Co., MI.

Notes for Elsie Miller:
The Descendants of John J. Christner, privately published February 1961, p. 8.

3556   vii. Eileen Miller, born 01 Mar 1962 in Sturgis, St. Joseph Co., MI.

Notes for Eileen Miller:
The Descendants of John J. Christner, privately published February 1961, p. 8.

3557   viii. Ernest V. Miller, born 05 Feb 1966 in Sturgis, St. Joseph Co., MI.

Notes for Ernest V. Miller:
The Descendants of John J. Christner, privately published February 1961, p. 8.

1513. Ruby Ellen[8] Miller (Fannie Elmina[7], Magdalena Mattie[6] Lantz, Veronica Fannie[5] Christner, Christian J.[4], Johannes John Hans[3], Christian[2], Christen[1])[5657] was born 07 Jul 1927 in Lagrange Co., IN, and died 07 Apr 2006 in Shipshewana, Elkhart Co., IN. She married **Levi W. Bontrager** 20 Jan 1948. He was born 12 Nov 1926.

Notes for Ruby Ellen Miller:
The Descendants of John J. Christner, privately published February 1961, p 8.

More About Ruby Ellen Miller:
Burial: Yoder Cemetery Shipshewana Indiana N41°37.536xW85°35.241
Religion: Old Order Amish/

Notes for Levi W. Bontrager:
The Descendants of John J. Christner, privately published February 1961, p. 8.

Children of Ruby Miller and Levi Bontrager are:
    3558   i.   Perry[9] Bontrager, born 18 Oct 1948.

Notes for Perry Bontrager:
The Descendants of John J. Christner, privately published February1961, p. 8.

3559   ii.   Fannie Bontrager, born 02 Jan 1950.

Notes for Fannie Bontrager:
The Descendants of John J. Christner, privately published February 1961, p. 8.

3560   iii. William Bontrager, born 17 Jul 1951.

Notes for William Bontrager:
The Descendants of John J. Christner, privately published February 1961, p. 8.

3561   iv.   Amos Bontrager, born Sep 1953.

Notes for Amos Bontrager:
The Descendants of John J. Christner, privately published February 1961, p. 8.

3562   v.   Levi Bontrager Jr., born 19 Feb 1955.

Notes for Levi Bontrager Jr.:
The Descendants of John J. Christner, privately published February 1961, p. 8.

3563   vi.   Abie Bontrager, born 16 Jul 1956.

Notes for Abie Bontrager:
The Descendants of John J. Christner, privately published February 1961, p. 8.

3564   vii.   Edna Bontrager, born 17 Jan 1959.

Notes for Edna Bontrager:
The Descendants of John J. Christner, privately published 1961, p. 8.

1517.   Mary Magdalene[8] **Miller** (Fannie Elmina[7], Magdalena Mattie[6] Lantz, Veronica Fannie[5] Christner, Christian J.[4], Johannes John Hans[3], Christian[2], Christen[1])[5658] was born 03 Feb 1936 in Shipshewanna, Lagrange Co., IN[5658], and died 09 Jun 1998 in Goshen, Elkhart Co., IN[5658]. She married **(1) Daniel Helmuth**.   She married **(2) Orley Lamar Swoveland**[5658]. He was born 29 Nov 1934 in Goshen, Elkhart Co., IN[5658], and died 12 Mar 1999 in Ft. Wayne, Allen, IN[5658]. She married **(3) Orla Swovaland** Jun 1959.

Notes for Mary Magdalene Miller:
The Descendants of John J. Christner, privately published February 1961, p. 8.

Notes for Daniel Helmuth:
The Descendants of John J. Christner, privately published February 1961, p. 8.

Children of Mary Miller and Daniel Helmuth are:
3565   i.   Norman Ray[9] Helmuth, born 18 Oct 1955.

Notes for Norman Ray Helmuth:

The Descendants of John J. Christner, privately published February 1961, p. 8.

3566   ii.   Cheryl Anna Helmuth, born 10 Feb 1957.

Notes for Cheryl Anna Helmuth:
The Descendants of John J. Christner, privately published February 1961, p. 8.

1519.   Wilma[8] **Miller** (Edna Mae[7], Magdalena Mattie[6] Lantz, Veronica Fannie[5] Christner, Christian J.[4], Johannes John Hans[3], Christian[2], Christen[1]) was born 13 Sep 1926. She married **David M. Hostetler** 07 Mar 1946. He was born 04 Jan 1926 in Shipshewana, Indiana, USA[5659], and died 20 Nov 2001 in Middlebury, Elkhart, Indiana, United States of America[5659].

Notes for Wilma Miller:
The Descendants of John J. Christner, privately published February 1961, p. 107.

Notes for David M. Hostetler:
The Descendants of John J. Christner, privately published February 1961, p. 107.

More About David M. Hostetler:
Residence: Hayward, WI[5659]

Children of Wilma Miller and David Hostetler are:

| 3567 | i. | Ernest Eugene[9] Hostetler, born 29 Jan 1947. |

Notes for Ernest Eugene Hostetler:
The Descendants of John J. Christner, privately published February 1961, p. 107.

| 3568 | ii. | Loretta Mae Hostetler, born 23 Aug 1948. |

Notes for Loretta Mae Hostetler:
The Descendants of John J. Christner, privately published February 1961, p. 107.

| 3569 | iii. | Richard Lee Hostetler, born 30 Jan 1951. |

Notes for Richard Lee Hostetler:
Source:

The Descendants of John J. Christner, privately published 1961, February 1961, p. 107

| 3570 | iv. | Shirley Ann Hostetler, born 07 May 1954. |

Notes for Shirley Ann Hostetler:
The Descendants of John J. Christner, privately published February 1961, p.107.

1520. Ada Marie[8] Miller (Edna Mae[7], Magdalena Mattie[6] Lantz, Veronica Fannie[5] Christner, Christian J.[4], Johannes John Hans[3], Christian[2], Christen[1]) was born 28 Apr 1931. She married **Richard Lambright**. He was born 07 Oct 1925.

Notes for Ada Marie Miller:
The Descendants of John J. Christner, privately published February 1961, p. 107.

Notes for Richard Lambright:
The Descendants of John J. Christner, privately published February 1961, p. 107.

Children of Ada Miller and Richard Lambright are:

| 3571 | i. | Betty Fern[9] Lambright, born 21 Jan 1952. |

Notes for Betty Fern Lambright:
The Descendants of John J. Christner, privately published February 1961, p. 107.

| 3572 | ii. | Diana Kay Lambright, born 10 May 1953; died 13 May 1953. |

Notes for Diana Kay Lambright:
The Descendants of John J. Christner, privately published February 1961, p. 107.

| 3573 | iii. | Eugene Ray Lambright, born 25 Dec 1955. |

Notes for Eugene Ray Lambright:
The Descendants of John J. Christner, privately published February 1961, p. 107.

| 3574 | iv. | Gerald Dean Lambright, born 11 Mar 1957. |

Notes for Gerald Dean Lambright:
The Descendants of John J. Christner, privately published February 1961, p. 107,

| 3575 | v. | Devon Jay Lambright, born 14 Mar 1958. |

Notes for Devon Jay Lambright:
The Descendants of John J. Christner, privately published February 1961, p. 107.

3576   vi.   Gary Lee Lambright, born 20 Feb 1960.

Notes for Gary Lee Lambright:
The Descendants of John J. Christner, privately published February 1961, p. 107.

1537. Charles[8] **Christner** (John Riley[7], Jacob[6], John[5], John J.[4], Johannes John Hans[3], Christian[2], Christen[1]) was born 01 Mar 1895 in Monoghelia, Marion Co., WV, and died 10 Dec 1970 in Pearce Hospital, Salina, IL. He married **Gertrude Nolen** 01 Jul 1923 in Shawneetown, IL. She was born 31 Oct 1902, and died 23 Aug 1982.

Notes for Charles Christner:
Birth: Mar. 1, 1895
Death: Dec. 10, 1970

Spouse: Gertie Christner (1902 - 1982)

Inscription: ILLINOIS
PFC US ARMY WWI

Burial: Big Ridge Cemetery, Harrisburg, Saline Co., IL
Find A Grave Memorial# 97796900

More About Charles Christner:
Burial: 12 Dec 1970, Big Ridge Cemetary Rt#4 Harrisburg IL
Cause of Death: Extreme Arteriiosclerosis
Military service: Discharged on Nov.21 1918 U.S.Army at Camp Meade MD/
Occupation: Coal Miner/
Social Security Number: 342-10-3703/

More About Gertrude Nolen:
Burial: Big Ridge Cemetary Rt#4 Harrisburg IL
Social Security Number: 350-50-0875/

Child of Charles Christner and Gertrude Nolen is:
+   3577   i.   Charles Ray[9] Christner, born 19 Apr 1924 in Muddy, IL; died 21 Apr 2005 in Harrisburg, Saline Co., IL.

1538. Pearl Ada[8] **Christner** (John Riley[7], Jacob[6], John[5], John J.[4], Johannes John Hans[3], Christian[2], Christen[1]) was born 12 Apr 1897 in Monoghelia, Marion Co., WV[5660], and died 20 Aug 1981 in Milton Cabell Co. WV. She married **Asa Nicholas Payne** 04 Sep 1920 in Oakland, Garrett Co., MD. He was born 01 Oct 1894 in Dola, Harrison Co., WV, and died 15 Sep 1971 in Charleston, Kanawha Co., WV.

More About Pearl Ada Christner:
Burial: Koontz Cemetary, Clendenin, WV
Social Security Number: 233-96-8030/[5660]
SSN issued: WV[5660]

More About Asa Nicholas Payne:
Burial: Koontz Cemetary, Clendenin, WV

Children of Pearl Christner and Asa Payne are:
+   3578   i.   Madeline Lucille[9] Payne, born 07 Jul 1921 in Rachel Marion Co WV; died 07 Mar 1973 in Charleston, Kanawha Co., WV.
+   3579   ii.   Kenneth Charles Payne, born 03 May 1923 in Rachel Marion Co WV; died 04 Nov 1990 in Charleston,

Kanawha Co., WV.

+ 3580   iii.   Billie Payne, born 05 Apr 1927 in Rachel Marion Co WV; died 21 Mar 1978 in Charleston, Kanawha Co., WV.

+ 3581   iv.   Noreita Ann Payne, born 02 Jan 1935 in Corton Kanawha Co. WV.

1539. Carl[8] Danley (Nora Delia[7] Christner, Jacob[6], John[5], John J.[4], Johannes John Hans[3], Christian[2], Christen[1]) was born 14 Aug 1895 in Clarksburg, Harrison Co., WV, and died 17 Apr 1967 in Clarksburg, Harrison Co., WV. He married **Clara Viola Feather** 04 Sep 1920 in Oakland, Garrett Co., MD. She was born 25 Aug 1899, and died 01 Jan 1946.

More About Carl Danley:
Burial: 19 Apr 1967, Greenlawn Cemetary Clarksburg Harrison Co. WV

Child of Carl Danley and Clara Feather is:

+ 3582   i.   Frances[9] Danley, born 12 Jun 1921 in CA; died Oct 1993 in Clarksburg, Harrison Co., WV.

1544. Ruby[8] Christner (Alfred[7], Jacob[6], John[5], John J.[4], Johannes John Hans[3], Christian[2], Christen[1]) was born 15 Jul 1913[5661], and died 20 Feb 1994 in Fairmont, Marion Co., WV[5661]. She married **Sherman Bragg**.

More About Ruby Christner:
Social Security Number: 232-36-9999/[5661]

Child of Ruby Christner and Sherman Bragg is:

+ 3583   i.   Mary Ann[9] Bragg, born 18 Oct 1948.

1545. Horace Alfred[8] Christner (Alfred[7], Jacob[6], John[5], John J.[4], Johannes John Hans[3], Christian[2], Christen[1])[5662] was born 15 Jan 1916 in Clarksburg, Harrison Co., WV[5663], and died 02 Jan 1994 in Capistrano, Orange Co., CA[5664,5665]. He married **Lucille Eloise Jack** in Marion Co., WV. She was born 24 Jul 1919 in Fairmont, Marion Co., WV, and died 04 Jul 1991 in Capistrano, Orange Co., CA.

More About Horace Alfred Christner:
Residence: 1930, Eagle, Harrison Co., WV[5666]
Social Security Number: 236-03-9937/[5667]
SSN issued: WV[5667]

Children of Horace Christner and Lucille Jack are:

   3584   i.   Judy[9] Christner, born 14 Feb 1940.
   3585   ii.   Susan Christner, born 14 Feb 1940.
   3586   iii.   Thomas G. Christner, born 1942.

1548. Nora[8] Christner (James Hoy[7], Jacob[6], John[5], John J.[4], Johannes John Hans[3], Christian[2], Christen[1]) was born 13 Oct 1919[5668], and died 16 Apr 1990 in Republic, Ferry Co., WA[5668]. She married **(1) Matt Oversby**. He was born 05 Dec 1905 in Republic, Ferry Co., WA, and died 28 Mar 1994 in Republic, Ferry Co., WA. She married **(2) Robert E. Pipkin** in Marion Co., WV.

More About Nora Christner:
Burial: Republic, Ferry Co., WA
Social Security Number: 532-28-5034/[5668]
SSN issued: Washington[5668]

More About Matt Oversby:
Burial: Republic, Ferry Co., WA

Children of Nora Christner and Robert Pipkin are:

   3587   i.   Ann[9] Pipkin.

3588   ii.   Judy Pipkin.

1549. Lee Edward[8] Christner (James Hoy[7], Jacob[6], John[5], John J.[4], Johannes John Hans[3], Christian[2], Christen[1]) was born 01 Jul 1921 in Harlan, KY, and died 24 Mar 1984 in Fairmont, Marion Co., WV. He married **Margaret Ann Levelle** 10 Apr 1946 in Marion Co., WV. She was born 10 Jan 1925 in Mannington, Marion Co., WV.

Notes for Lee Edward Christner:
Birth: Jul. 1, 1921
Death: Mar. 24, 1984

Burial: Mannington Memorial Park Cemetery, Mannington, Marion Co., WV

More About Lee Edward Christner:
Burial: Mar 1984, Mannington Cemetery, Marion Co., WV

Child of Lee Christner and Margaret Levelle is:
3589   i.   Regina[9] Christner, born 1946.

1552. Alfred Hoy[8] Christner (James Hoy[7], Jacob[6], John[5], John J.[4], Johannes John Hans[3], Christian[2], Christen[1])[5669,5670,5671,5672,5673] was born 28 Aug 1927 in Dakota, Marion Co., WV[5674,5675], and died 12 Jul 1992 in Fairmont, Marion Co., WV[5676]. He married **Martha Lee Michael**[5676] 04 Oct 1946 in Hundred, Wetzel Co., WV. She was born 23 Apr 1927 in Mannington, Marion Co., WV[5676,5677], and died 15 Aug 2000 in Morgantown, Monongalia Co., WV[5678].

Notes for Alfred Hoy Christner:
Alfred worked most of his life in No., 9 mine, Farmington, WV. He missed two explosions during his tenure at the mine. The first explosion in "55", was missed because he went deer hunting and the second explosion which occured in 1968, exploded just as he was getting ready to enter the mine. No., 9 mine has a reputation of being one of the gaseous mines in the state.

There were niney-nine miners in the mine when the explosion occurred, seventy-eight of whom died as a result of the explosion. Alfred was on the rescue team at No., 9. I can remember watching the various mining teams compete at Hough Park, Mannington, WV when I was small. Each mine had a unique uniform, shirt, pants and shoes.

Birth: Aug. 28, 1927
Dakota, Marion Co., WV
Death: Jul. 12, 1992

Son of Hoy and Eva Christner
WWII Veteran
Married Martha Lee Michael, daughter of Francis and Stella Michael, October 4, 1946 in Hundred, Marion Co., WV

Parents:
James Hoy Christner (1886 - 1950)
Eva Blanche Christner (1900 - 1952)

Spouse: Martha Lee Michael Christner (1927 - 2000)

Children: Gary Lee Christner (1947 - 1947)

Burial: Grandview Memorial Gardens, Fairmont, Marion Co., WV
Find A Grave Memorial# 97047388

CHRISTNER, ALFRED HOY
S 2/c. U. S. Navy. Born Aug. 28,, 1927. Entered service Sep. 17, 1944, Great Lakes, Ill.; Cuba; Pacific; Okinawa; Yokohama, Japan. Awarded two Battle Stars. Attended Manington H. S. Methodise. Son of Mr. and Mrs. H. J. Christner, 139 high St., Mannington, WV.

More About Alfred Hoy Christner:
Burial: 14 Jul 1992, Grandview Memorial Cemetery, East Grafton Rd., WV
Cause of Death: Sclerderma
Military service: 17 Sep 1944[5679]
Occupation: Coal Miner/
Oganization: VFW post 826 & American Legion Post #0068
Residence: 1930, Fairmont, Marion Co., WV[5680,5681]
Retirement: From Consolidated Coal Co.#9 Mine
Social Security Number: 235-34-6456/[5682]
SSN issued: WV[5682]

Notes for Martha Lee Michael:
Birth: Apr. 23, 1927
Mannington, Marion Co., WV
Death: Aug. 15, 2000

Daughter of Francis and Stella Michael
Married Alfred Hoy Christner October 4, 1946 in Hundred, Marion Co., WV

Parents:
Francis A. Michael (1893 - 1979)
Stella M. Michael (1899 - 1950)

Spouse: Alfred Hoy Christner (1927 - 1992)
Children: Gary Lee Christner (1947 - 1947)

Burial: Mannington Memorial Park Cemetery, Mannington, Marion Co., WV
Find A Grave Memorial# 93248162

More About Martha Lee Michael:
Residence: 1930, Mannington, Marion Co., WV[5683]
Social Security Number: 235-40-4068/[5684]
SSN issued: WV[5684]

Children of Alfred Christner and Martha Michael are:
    3590   i.   Sharon Sue[9] Christner, born 10 May 1948.
    3591   ii. Larry Kevin Christner, born 25 Sep 1950.

1553. Mary Jo[8] Christner (James Hoy[7], Jacob[6], John[5], John J.[4], Johannes John Hans[3], Christian[2], Christen[1]) was born 18 Oct 1930 in Barracksville, Marion Co., WV, and died Mar 1957 in Fairmont, Marion Co., WV. She married **Arden Shock** in Marion Co., WV. He was born 30 Nov 1924 in Huntington WV, and died 12 Oct 1989 in Monoghelia, Marion Co., WV.

Notes for Mary Jo Christner:
Mary Jo was my favorite Aunt. Life at her house was always interesting and full of activity. Mary Jo never let anything bother her, if she was in the middle of painting and the paint bucket fell off the ladder and spilled over her brand new encyclopedias, so be it. She would just pack the kids in the car and away they would go.

More About Mary Jo Christner:
Burial: Mannington Cemetery, Marion Co., WV
Cause of Death: Encephalitis

Religion: Primary Sunday School Teacher/

More About Arden Shock:
Burial: 14 Oct 1989, Pricetown Cemetary

Children of Mary Christner and Arden Shock are:
    3592   i.   Mark Edward[9] Shock, born 1952.
    3593   ii.   Richard Lee Shock, born 1953.

1554. Dorothy[8] McKenzie (Mary Olive[7], Sarah Ellen "Helena"[6] Christner, John[5], John J.[4], Johannes John Hans[3], Christian[2], Christen[1])[5685,5686] was born in MD[5686], and died in MD[5686]. She married **Godfrey D. (Tapper) Stott** 21 Mar 1928 in Hagerstown, Washington Co., MD. He was born 1905 in Frostburg, Allegany Co., MD[5687], and died 26 Feb 1967 in Frostburg, Allegany Co., MD[5687].

Children of Dorothy McKenzie and Godfrey Stott are:
    3594   i.   Homer[9] Stott.
+   3595   ii.   Martha Stott, born 29 Nov in MD; died in MD.
    3596   iii.   Delores E. Stott[5687], born 16 Feb 1937 in Frostburg, Allegany Co., MD; died 30 Jul 2006 in Frostburg, Allegany Co., MD[5687].

> Notes for Delores E. Stott:
> Delores E. Cessna, 69, of McCulloh Street, Frostburg, died Sunday, July 30, 2006, at her residence. Born Feb. 16, 1937, in Frostburg, she was the daughter of the late Godfrey "Tapper" Stott and Dorothy (McKenzie) Stott. In addition to her parents, she was preceded in death by one daughter, Diane K. (Cessna) Mamich; two brothers, Homer Stott and Larry Stott; and one sister, Martha (Stott) Cobb. Delores was retired from Hills Department Store, Cumberland and formerly worked at Prichards Hardware Store, Frostburg. She was a devoted wife, mother, and grandmother, and she cherished her family. Surviving are her husband of 49 years, Herbert "Buzz" Cessna; one daughter, Vickie Mazer and husband Barry, Frostburg; two granddaughters, Andrea Mamich and Jordin Mazer; one son-in-law, Thomas Mamich, Cleveland, Ohio. Delores also loved her special nieces and nephews Rick Cobb, Debbie (Cobb) Hook, Wanda (Cobb) Wickensheimer and Michelle Morris (Cobb) Wickensheimer. She was especially close to her sisters-in-law, Mary Heinrich and husband Gus, Oldtown and Sue Holt and husband Allen, Baltimore. A memorial service will be held at the Durst Funeral Home P.A., 57 Frost Ave., Frostburg on Thursday, Aug. 3, 2006, at 1:15 p.m. She will be cremated in accordance with her wishes following the service.   Cumberland Times-News

    3597   iv.   Larry Stott[5687], born 1941; died 13 Dec 1948 in Frostburg, Allegany Co., MD.

> Notes for Larry Stott:
> Seven-year-old Larry Stott, Frostburg, died this morning at 11:30 to Miners' Hospital, Frostburg, from injuries suffered when he was struck by a car near his home late yesterday afternoon. A second grade student at Hill Street School, the child was enroute home from an errand when hit by an auto driven by Lowry Newton Moser, 48, of 56 Green Street, Frostburg. The child was a son of Mr. and Mrs. Godfrey Stott, 204 McCulloch Street. Hospital attendants said he suffered a fractured skull, concussion of the brain and fractured right leg. State Trooper George Coddington said Moser, a carpenter at the Celanese plant, reported he was enroute home from work at 4:30 and driving south on Grant Street when the boy ran in front of his machine. The boy was returning home from a Grant Street grocery store at the time of the accident. A passing motorist took him to the hospital. Trooper Coddington said a passenger in Moser's car, Robert Delaney, corroborated Moser's account of the mishap. Trooper Coddington indicated no charges will be preferred pending completion of the investigation. The child is survived by his parents; a brother, Homer Stott, and two sisters, Martha and Dolores Stott, all at home. He was a member of St. Michael's Catholic Church and was to have appeared in the Christmas operetta at Hill Street School tomorrow in a scene "The Living Christmas Tree." The Cumberland Evening Times, December 14, 1948

1555. Edward Joseph[8] McKenzie (Mary Olive[7], Sarah Ellen "Helena"[6] Christner, John[5], John J.[4], Johannes John Hans[3], Christian[2], Christen[1])[5688] was born 02 Aug 1887 in MD[5688], and died 29 Aug 1957 in Frostburg, Allegany Co., MD[5688]. He married **Mary E. Freal**[5689] 01 Sep 1909. She was born Abt. 1889 in Frostburg, Allegany Co., MD[5689], and died 23 Mar 1971 in Frostburg, Allegany Co., MD[5689].

Notes for Edward Joseph McKenzie:
FROSTBURG - Mrs. Mary E. McKenzie, 82, of 201 McCulloch Street, died yesterday. She had been in failing health for five years. A native of Frostburg, she was a daughter of the late Patrick and Anna (McGregor) Freal and was the widow of Edward J. McKenzie. She was a member of Jehovah's Witnesses. Surviving are two daughters, Mrs. Catherine Canning, Chicago, Illinois; Mrs. Anna J. Filer, Carlos; two sons, Robert E. and William A. McKenzie, Frostburg; three sisters, Mrs. Gertrude Eisentrout, Mrs. Margaret Arnold, here; Mrs. Helen Blank, Eckhart, and 11 grandchildren. The body is at the Durst Funeral Home where friends will be received from 7 until 9 p.m. today and tomorrow from 2 until 4 and 7 until 9 p.m. Services will be conducted Friday at 1:30 p.m. in the funeral home by Mr. James Pryor. Interment will be in Frostburg Memorial Park. Pallbearers will be Lafe L. McKenzie, Eugene McKenzie, Francis McKenzie, Reges McKenzie, William Wright and David Freal. The Cumberland Evening Times, March 24, 1971. She was buried on 26 Mar 1971 in Frostburg Memorial Park, Frostburg, Allegany Co., MD.

More About Edward Joseph McKenzie:
Residence: 1920, Cumberland Ward 1, Allegany, MD[5690]

More About Mary E. Freal:
Residence: 1920, Cumberland Ward 1, Allegany, MD[5691]

Children of Edward McKenzie and Mary Freal are:
3598	i.	Anna Jane[9] McKenzie.
3599	ii.	Catherine McKenzie.
3600	iii.	Irvin E. (Lindy) McKenzie.
3601	iv.	William A. McKenzie.

1557. Rose Blanche[8] McKenzie (Mary Olive[7], Sarah Ellen "Helena"[6] Christner, John[5], John J.[4], Johannes John Hans[3], Christian[2], Christen[1])[5692,5693] was born 17 Jan 1891 in Union District, Grant Co., WV[5694], and died 30 Dec 1969 in Akron, Summit Co., OH[5694]. She married **Thomas Wright Ravenscroft**[5695]. He was born 24 Jun 1882 in Frostburg, Allegany Co., MD[5695], and died 29 Mar 1960 in Akron, Summit Co., OH[5695].

Notes for Rose Blanche McKenzie:
Obituary: The Cumberland Evening Times, January 5, 1970

FROSTBURG - Mrs. Rose B. Ravenscroft, 78 of 460 Killiea Road, Akron, Ohio, died December 30, in St. Thomas Hospital, there, following a long illness. Born in Frostburg, she was the daughter of the late Louis and Mary (McKenzie) McKenzie. She had resided in the Akron area 25 years. Surviving are one daughter, Mrs. Edith Starkey, Akron; four brothers, John McKenzie, Akron; James McKenzie, Staunton, VA and Leonard McKenzie and Thomas McKenzie, both of Frostburg; two sisters, Mrs. Ruth Pursley, Akron, and Mrs. Dorothy Stott, Frostburg; one granddaughter and five great-grandchildren. Mass and interment were held in Akron, Saturday. She was buried on 3 Jan 1970 in Akron, Summit Co., OH.

More About Rose Blanche McKenzie:
Residence: Summit Co., OH[5695]

Notes for Thomas Wright Ravenscroft:
Obituary: The Cumberland Evening Times, March 29, 1960

Thomas W. Ravenscroft, 77, a native of Frostburg, died this morning at his home in Akron. He was a son of the late Thomas and Maria (Murphy) Ravenscroft. Survivors include his widow, Mrs. Rose (McKenzie) Ravenscroft; Mrs. Edith Starkey, a daughter, at home; a brother, Merlon L. Ravenscroft, RD 2, Frostburg; two sisters, Mrs. Stella Wiland, Frostburg, and Mrs. Vincent Minnick, Akron; a granddaughter and a great-grandchild. The body is at the Hummel Funeral Home, Exchange Street, Akron. Services will be conducted on Thursday at 9:30 a. m. in St. Francis Xavier Church. Interment will be in the Holy Cross Cemetery there.

More About Thomas Wright Ravenscroft:
Residence: Garrett, MD[5695]

Child of Rose McKenzie and Thomas Ravenscroft is:

3602   i.   Edith L[9] Ravenscroft[5695], born Abt. 1909 in MD[5695].

More About Edith L Ravenscroft:
Residence: 1920, Akron Ward 5, Summit, Ohio[5695]

1558. Leonard Clarence[8] McKenzie (Mary Olive[7], Sarah Ellen "Helena"[6] Christner, John[5], John J.[4], Johannes John Hans[3], Christian[2], Christen[1])[5696] was born 27 Jan 1893 in Eckhart, Allegany Co., MD[5696], and died 25 Jan 2011 in Cumberland, Allegany Co., MD. He married **Edna Elizabeth Smith**. She was born 15 Dec 1898, and died 22 Jan 1983.

Notes for Leonard Clarence McKenzie:
Obituary: Meyersdale Republican, May 8, 1972

Leonard C. McKenzie, 79, of Finzel, Md., died May 12, 1972, at his home. Born in Garrett County, Md., he was a son of the late Louis and Mary (McKenzie) McKenzie. He was a member of St. Michael's Catholic Church and a retired construction worker. Surviving are his wife, the former Edna Smith; four sons, Francis A. McKenzie, Finzel; Henry L. McKenzie, Hagerstown; Joseph E. McKenzie, Millersville, Md.; and Ervin W. McKenzie, Mt. Savage, Md.; seven daughters, Mrs. Genevieve Lapp and Mrs. Mary McKenzie, both of Cresaptown, Md.; Mrs. Edna McCurry, College Park, Md.; Mrs. Anna Brode, Frostburg; Mrs. Alice Albright, Finzel; Mrs. Mildred Middleton, St. Clair Shores, Mich.; and Mrs. Helen Baker, Cumberland; 34 grandchildren, 38 great-grandchildren; three brothers, James McKenzie, Sykesville, Md.; John McKenzie, Akron, Ohio; and Thomas McKenzie, Frostburg Star Route; and two sisters, Mrs. Ruth Pursley, Akron, Ohio; and Mrs. Dorothy Stott, Frostburg. A Mass of the Resurrection was celebrated Monday morning in St. Michael's Catholic Church. Interment in Finzel Cemetery, Finzel, Garrett Co., MD.

Children of Leonard McKenzie and Edna Smith are:

3603   i.   Alice G.[9] McKenzie, born 10 Jul 1931.

Notes for Alice G. McKenzie:
Obituary: Cumberland Times-News, January 26, 2011

FROSTBURG - Alice G. Albright, 79 of Frostburg died Tuesday, Jan 25, 2011, at the Western Maryland Regional Medical Center. Born July 10, 1931, in Eckhart, she was the daughter of the late Leonard C. McKenzie and Edna (Smith) McKenzie. She was also preceded in death by five brothers and four sisters. Surviving are her husband of 59 years, Carl E. Albright Sr.; two daughters, Delores Williams and husband Danny, of Mount Savage and Barbara Bolden and husband Donald, of Gallipolis, Ohio; one son, Carl E. Albright Jr. and wife Elyse, of Frostburg; five grandchildren, Stacey Frank-enberry and husband Joe, Dr. Donna Bolden-Clinger and husband Todd, Chris Bolden, Scott Williams, and Natalie Long and husband Justin; twelve great-grandchildren and 2 great great-grandchildren. Also surviving are two sisters, Mary McKenzie and Mildred Middleton and numerous nieces and nephews. Mrs. Albright was a member of Emmanuel United Methodist Church in Finzel, and enjoyed spending time with her friends at Frostburg Heights apartment complex. Friends will be received at the Durst Funeral Home P.A., 57 Frost Ave., Frostburg, on Thursday, Jan. 27, 2011, from 2 to 4 and 7 to 9 p.m. Funeral services will be conducted in the Emmanuel United Methodist Church, Route 40, West of Finzel, on Friday, Jan 28, 2011, at 11 a.m. with the Rev. Dan Agnew officiating. Friends may be received at the church one hour prior to service. Interment will be in the Finzel Cemetery. In lieu of flowers, donations can be made to Emmanuel United Methodist Church, 29 Pocahontas Road, Frostburg, MD 21532 or the American Cancer Society, 182 North Mechanic St., Cumberland, MD 21502. Condolences may be sent to the family at durstfuneralhome.com

3604   ii.   Helen Delores McKenzie[5697], born 21 Jan 1935[5697]; died 18 Oct 1981 in Cumberland, Allegany Co., MD[5697]. She married (1) Baker. She married (2) Canton.

1563. Thomas Patrick[8] McKenzie (Mary Olive[7], Sarah Ellen "Helena"[6] Christner, John[5], John J.[4], Johannes John Hans[3], Christian[2], Christen[1])[5698,5699] was born 25 Jan 1906 in MD[5699,5700], and died 17 Nov 1991 in Cumberland, Allegany Co., MD[5700]. He married **Nellie Leona Garlitz**[5701]. She was born 25 Sep 1909 in

GarrettCo., MD[5701,5702], and died Aug 1988 in Frostburg, Allegany Co., MD[5702,5703].

Notes for Thomas Patrick McKenzie:
Birth: Jan. 25, 1905
Death: Nov. 17, 1991

Children:
Joseph Alfred McKenzie (1931 - 2000)
Roger Michael McKenzie (1950 - 2012)

Burial: Saint Anns Cemetery, Avilton, Garrett Co., MD
Find A Grave Memorial# 74571216

More About Thomas Patrick McKenzie:
Occupation: 24 Apr 1930, Farmer Laborer for Lewis McKenzie/[5703]
Residence: Nov 1991, Cumberland, Allegany Co., MD[5703]
Soc Sec #: Bef. 1951, 214-16-2593/MD[5703]

Notes for Nellie Leona Garlitz:
Birth: Sep. 25, 1909
Death: Aug. 10, 1988

Children:
Joseph Alfred McKenzie (1931 - 2000)
Roger Michael McKenzie (1950 - 2012)

Burial: Saint Anns Cemetery, Avilton, Garrett Co., MD
Find A Grave Memorial# 74571236

More About Nellie Leona Garlitz:
Residence: 02 Apr 1920, Johnsons, Garrett Co., MD[5703]
Soc Sec #: 1963, 218-48-9538/MD[5703]

Children of Thomas McKenzie and Nellie Garlitz are:

	3605	i.	Ralph[9] McKenzie.
+	3606	ii.	Joseph Alfred McKenzie, born 07 Jul 1931 in GarrettCo., MD; died 27 Apr 2000 in Cumberland, Allegany Co., MD.
	3607	iii.	Patrick McKenzie, born 08 Jun 1941[5704,5705]; died 05 Jun 1997 in Grantsville, Garrett Co., MD[5705,5706].

> More About Patrick McKenzie:
> Residence: 05 Jun 1997, Grantsville, Garrett, Maryland[5706]
> Soc Sec #: 1959, 220-40-0934/MD[5706]
> Social Security Number: 220-40-0934/[5707]
> SSN issued: MD[5707]
> Zip: 05 Jun 1997, 21536/[5708]

+	3608	iv.	Roger Michael McKenzie, born 20 Mar 1950 in Frostburg, Allegany Co., MD; died 05 Mar 2012 in Frostburg, Allegany Co., MD.

1565. Verna Virginia[8] McKenzie (George Thomas[7], Sarah Ellen "Helena"[6] Christner, John[5], John J.[4], Johannes John Hans[3], Christian[2], Christen[1])[5709,5709] was born 11 Jun 1909 in WV[5709,5709], and died 12 Jan 1999 in Upper Glade, Webster Co., WV[5709,5709]. She married **Leo David McClure**[5709] 11 Apr 1927 in Pocahontas, Somerset Co., PA[5709]. He was born 19 Mar 1907 in Pocahontas, Somerset Co., PA[5709,5710], and died 28 Dec 1955 in Pocahontas, Somerset Co., PA[5711,5712].

Notes for Verna Virginia McKenzie:
Charleston Gazette, December 5, 2003 - Verna V. McClure

MANASSAS, VA - Verna V. McClure, 89, of Manassas, formerly of Upper Glade, WV died Jan. 12, 1999, in Annaburg Manor Nursing Home after a long illness.She was former operator of the McClure Grocery Store, Upper Glade, and a Methodist. Surviving: daughter, Kathleen Luchsinger of O'Fallon, Ill.; sons, Troy of Winlock, WA Douglas of London, KY, Merlin "Thomas" of Marshall; sisters, Ruby Cottrill of Upper Glade, Myrtle Woodring of Cowen, WV Rhoda Kilpatrick of Sun City Center, FL, Georgia Hildreth of Alexandria; 18 grandchildren; 24 great-grandchildren.Service will be 11 a.m. Saturday at Morris Funeral Home, Cowen, with the Rev. Okey Wayne officiating. Burial will be in Handschumacher Cemetery, Upper Glade. Friends may call from 6 to 8 p.m. today at the funeral home.

More About Leo David McClure:
Social Security Number: 235-03-9154/*5712*
SSN issued: WV*5712*

Children of Verna McKenzie and Leo McClure are:

- 3609 i. Kathleen V.[9] McClure. She married Luchsinger.
- 3610 ii. Merlin Thomas McClure.
- + 3611 iii. Asa Albert McClure, born 24 Apr 1928 in Upper Glade, Webster Co., WV; died 19 Jul 1972 in Webster Co., WV.
- 3612 iv. Troy Lee McClure*5713*, born 15 Aug 1932.
- 3613 v. Douglas McClure*5714*, born 09 Nov 1934 in WV*5714*; died 03 Mar 2004 in London, Laurel Co., KY*5714*.

1595. Henry C.[8] Diehl (William Henry[7], Elizabeth[6] Christner, Jacob C.[5], John J.[4], Johannes John Hans[3], Christian[2], Christen[1])*5715,5716* was born 08 Mar 1891 in Connellsville, Fayette Co., PA*5717,5718*, and died 17 Nov 1968 in Meyersdale, Somerset Co., PA*5719*. He married **Eva Cochran** in Somerset Co., PA. She was born 18 Oct 1892 in Salisbury, Somerset Co., PA, and died 09 Dec 1973 in Grantsville, Garrett Co., MD.

Notes for Henry C. Diehl:
Delayed Birth Records - PA

He was on page 424 - The number in the far right hand column was 34-1953

Henry C. DIEHL b. Mar 8, 1891 in Connellsville to William H. DIEHL and Fredericka GEORCKE

Obituary: Meyersdale Republican, November 23, 1967

HENRY C. DIEHL

Henry C. Diehl, 76, West Salisbury, died Nov. 17 at Meyersdale. Born March 8, 1891, in Elk Lick Twp., he was a son of William H. and Fredericka (Gurke) Diehl. He is survived by his wife, the former Eva C. Cochrane; three sons: William J., Kampsville, Ill.; Roy E., Atlantic City, N.J.; and George E., El Paso, Texas; five daughters: Miss Kathryn Diehl, Meyersdale; Mrs. Isabelle Rodamer, Flagtown, N.J.; Mrs. Ethel Zabawa, Manville, N.J.; Mrs. Ruth Ansell, Cumberland; and Mrs. Jean Rembold, Springs. Three brothers: William J., Salisbury; George E., Somerville, N.J.; and Earl, Somerset; three sisters: Mrs. Edna Glotfelty, Pittsburgh; Mrs. Edith Bowman, Boynton and Mrs. Marguerite Brown, Salisbury; 26 grandchildren and six great-grandchildren. Mr. Diehl was a member of Salisbury Methodist Church, Salisbury IOOF and an honorary life member of Salisbury Volunteer Fire Department. Service was held Monday afternoon at Thomas Funeral Home with the Rev. William A. Cassidy officiating. Interment followed in Salisbury IOOF Cemetery.

Birth: 1891
Death: 1967

Burial: Salisbury IOOF Cemetery, Salisbury, Somerset Co., PA

More About Henry C. Diehl:
Burial: IOOF Cemetery, Salisbury, Somerset Co., PA
Other-Begin: *5720*

Residence: 1910, Elk Lick, Somerset Co., PA[5721]
Social Security: 163-14-2485 issued PA
Social Security Number: 163-14-2485/[5722]
SSN issued: PA[5722]

Notes for Eva Cochran:
Obituary: Meyersdale Republican, December 13, 1973

MRS. HENRY C. DIEHL

Eva C. Diehl, 81, Salisbury, died Dec. 9, 1973, in Goodwill Mennonite Home, Grantsville. She was born Oct. 18, 1892, in Salisbury, a daughter of the late William and Ida (Fogle) Cochrane. She was also preceded in death by her husband, Henry C. Diehl. Surviving are these children: William Diehl, Kampsville, Ill.; Roy Diehl, Atlantic City, N.J.; George Diehl, El Paso, Texas; Miss Kathryn Diehl, Meyersdale; Mrs. Isabelle Rodamer and Mrs. Ethel Zabawa, both of Manville, N.J.; Mrs. Ruth nsel, Cumberland, Md.; and Mrs. Jean Rembold of Springs; also 25 grandchildren and a number of great-grandchildren. She was a sister of Mrs. Emma Younkin and Mrs. LaVerne Carter, both of Akron, OH; eorge Cochrane, Baden, Pa.; and Allen Cochrane, Fairmount City, Pa. She was a member of the United Methodist Church. Funeral service was held Wednesday afternoon in Thomas Funeral Home, Salisbury, with Rev. John H. Kraybill officiating. Interment in Salisbury Cemetery.

Birth: 1891
Death: 1973

Burial: Salisbury IOOF Cemetery, Salisbury, Somerset Co., PA

More About Eva Cochran:
Burial: Salisbury IOOF Cemetery, Salisbury, Somerset Co., PA
Social Security Number: 193-24-7205/[5723]
SSN issued: Connellsville, Fayette Co., PA[5723]

Children of Henry Diehl and Eva Cochran are:
   3614   i.   Joseph[9] Diehl.
   3615   ii. Isabel Diehl, born in W. Salisbury, Somerset Co., PA; died 1985 in Flagtown, Somerset Co., NJ. She married James Rodamer[5724]; born in W. Salisbury, Somerset Co., PA; died 1974 in Somerville, NJ.

             More About Isabel Diehl:
             Other-Begin: Somerville, Somerset, New Jersey, United States of America[5725]
             Social Security Number: 160-12-3649/[5725]
             SSN issued: Connellsville, Fayette Co., PA[5725]

   3616   iii. Jean Diehl.
   3617   iv. Ruth Diehl.
   3618   v.   William J. Diehl.
   3619   vi. Kathryn Diehl, born 11 Sep 1912 in W. Salisbury, Somerset Co., PA; died 30 May 1987 in Meyersdale, Somerset Co., PA.

             Notes for Kathryn Diehl:
             Obituary: Daily American, June 1, 1987

             DIEHL

             Kathryn R. (Sis) Diehl, 74, of Meyersdale, died May 30, 1987, in Middlecreek Township. Born Sept. 11, 1912, in Salisbury, a daughter of the late Henry C. and Eva C. (Cochran) Diehl. Also preceded in death by a sister, Isabelle Rodamer. She is survived by three brothers: William of Kampsville, Ill.; Roy E., Atlantic City, N.J.; and George of El Paso, Tex.; three sisters: Mrs. Ethel Zabawa of Manville, N.J.; Mrs. Ruth Ansel, Cumberland, Md.; and Mrs. Jean Rembold of Springs; also a number of nieces and nephews. She was a retired LPN with 30 years of service at Meyersdale Community Hospital. Member of the Sts. Philip and James Catholic Church, Meyersdale, the hospital auxiliary and the Ladies of the Elks. Friends will be received from 7-9 p.m. Monday and 2-4, 7-9 p.m. Tuesday at the Price Funeral Home, Meyersdale, where services will be conducted Wednesday at 2 p.m. with the Rev. James Bunn.

Interment, Salisbury Cemetery.

Birth: 1913
Death: 1987

Burial: Salisbury IOOF Cemetery, Salisbury, Somerset Co., PA

More About Kathryn Diehl:
Burial: Salisbury IOOF Cemetery, Salisbury, Somerset Co., PA

+ 3620 vii. Ethel Diehl, born 11 Apr 1917 in West Salisbury, Somerset Co., PA; died 23 Apr 1988 in Manville, Somerset Co., N.J..

3621 viii. George E. Diehl[5726,5727], born 12 Feb 1918 in West Salisbury, Somerset Co., PA[5728,5729]; died Jan 1968[5730,5731,5732]. He married Iva Mae Shaneyfelt[5732]; born 1916[5732]; died 1988 in Greensburg, Westmoreland Co., PA[5732].

More About George E. Diehl:
Social Security Number: 200-05-0201/[5733]
SSN issued: Connellsville, Fayette Co., PA[5733]

3622 ix. Roy Edward Diehl, born 05 Aug 1924 in W. Salisbury, Somerset Co., PA; died 19 Sep 1997 in Cumberland, Allegany Co., MD.

Notes for Roy Edward Diehl:
Obituary: Published Sep 20,1997 - Cumberland Times-News, Cumberland,Maryland

Birth: Aug. 5, 1924 - West Salisbury, Somerset Co., PA
Death: Sep. 19, 1997 - Atlantic City, Atlantic Co., NJ

ATLANTIC CITY, N.J. - Roy Edward Diehl, 73, of 1801 Atlantic Avenue, Atlantic City, died Friday, Sept. 19, 1997, at Memorial Hospital, Cumberland, MD

Born Aug. 5, 1924, in West Salisbury, Pa., he was a son of the late Henry C. and Eva C. (Cochrane) Diehl.

Mr. Diehl was a graduate of Johns Hopkins Hospital, School of X-ray Technicians. He was an X-ray therapist and manager of the Emergency Room X-ray Department at Atlantic City Medical Center. A U.S. Navy veteran of World War II, he was a member of the American Legion Post 1000, Trenton. He was a Methodist by faith.

Surviving are a brother, George E. Diehl, El Paso, Texas; two sisters, Ruth Ansel, Cumberland, and Jean Rembold, Springs, Pa.; a sister-in-law, Eris Diehl, Kampsville, Ill.; an uncle, George "Joe" Diehl, Salisbury, Pa.; and numerous nieces and nephews.

Friends will be received at the Newman Funeral Home, Salisbury, on Tuesday from 10 to 11 a.m.

Services will be conducted at the funeral home on Tuesday at 11 a.m. with the Rev. Steven Heatwole officiating. Interment will be in Salisbury Cemetery. Expressions of sympathy may be directed to Memorial Hospital Hospice or to the charity of choice.

Obituary: New Republic, September 25, 1997

ROY E. DIEHL

Roy E. Diehl, 73, of Atlantic City, NJ died Friday, Sept. 19, 1997, at Memorial Hospital, Cumberland, MD. Born Aug. 5, 1924, at West Salisbury, he was a son of the late Henry C. and Eva C. (Cochrane) Diehl. Mr. Diehl was a graduate of Johns Hopkins Hospital School of X-Ray Technicians, was an X-ray therapist and manager of the emergency room X-ray department at Atlantic City Medical Center. A U.S. Navy veteran of World War II, he was a member of the American Legion Post 1000, Trenton, NJ. He was a Methodist by faith. Mr. Diehl is survived by a brother, George E. Diehl of El Paso, TX; two sisters: Ruth Ansel, Cumberland, MD; and Jean Rembold of Springs; a sister-in-law, Eris Diehl of Kampsville, IL; an uncle, George "Joe" Diehl of Salisbury; and numerous nieces and nephews. Friends were received at Newman Funeral Home, Inc., Salisbury, on Sept. 23. Services were conducted at the funeral home the same day, with the Rev. Steven Heatwold officating. Interment, Salisbury Cemetery. Expressions of sympathy may be directed to Memorial Hospital Hospice or the charity of the donor's choice.

Birth: Aug. 5, 1924 - West Salisbury, Somerset Co., PA
Death: Sep. 19, 1997 - Atlantic City, Atlantic Co., NJ
Burial: Salisbury IOOF Cemetery, Salisbury, Somerset Co., PA

More About Roy Edward Diehl:
Burial: Salisbury Cemetery, Salisbury, Somerset Co., PA

1596. Elizabeth Wilhelmina[8] Diehl (William Henry[7], Elizabeth[6] Christner, Jacob C.[5], John J.[4], Johannes John Hans[3], Christian[2], Christen[1]) was born 28 Jul 1893 in Connellsville, Fayette Co., PA[5734], and died 29 Mar 1955 in Meyersdale, Somerset Co., PA. She married **Holler** in Somerset Co., PA.

More About Elizabeth Wilhelmina Diehl:
Burial: IOOF Cemetery, Salisbury, Somerset Co., PA
Nickname: Minnie
Residence: 1910, Elk Lick, Somerset Co., PA[5734]

Children of Elizabeth Diehl and Holler are:
3623	i.	Doris May[9] Holler, born in Connellsville, Fayette Co., PA; died 2001 in Ocala, Marion Co., FL. She married Lowrey.
3624	ii.	William A. Holler, born 27 Nov 1920.
3625	iii.	Selene Jane Holler, born 04 Feb 1923.
+ 3626	iv.	James Robert Holler, born 28 Dec 1924 in Connellsville, Fayette Co., PA.

1598. William James[8] Diehl (William Henry[7], Elizabeth[6] Christner, Jacob C.[5], John J.[4], Johannes John Hans[3], Christian[2], Christen[1])[5734,5735,5736] was born 28 Jan 1896 in Connellsville, Fayette Co., PA[5737,5738], and died 13 Apr 1974 in Cumberland, Allegany Co., MD. He married **Daisy Kate James** in Salisbury, Somerset Co., PA. She was born 02 Jan 1897 in Cornwall, England, and died 30 Jul 1986 in Meyersdale, Somerset Co., PA.

Notes for William James Diehl:
SSDI:
WILLIAM DIEHL
SSN 170-18-3042 Residence: 15558 Salisbury, Somerset, PA
Born 28 Jan 1896 Last Benefit:
Died Apr 1974 Issued: PA (Before 1951)

Obituary: Somerset Bulletin, April 15, 1974
DIEHL

William J. Diehl, 78, of Salisbury, died Saturday, at Cumberland, Md. Born Jan. 28, 1896, in West Salisbury, son of the late William H. Diehl and Fredericka Gerke Diehl. Survived by his wife, Daisy K. James; one son, James, Bedford, OH; two brothers, Joe, of Somerville, N.J., and Earl, Somerset; three sisters, Mrs. Edna Glotfelty, Monroeville, Mrs. Edith Bowman, Boynton, and Mrs. Joan Brown, Salisbury; and five grandchildren. Was a member of the Salisbury Methodist Church, and Meyersdale Lodge 554, F & AM. Friends are being received at the Thomas Funeral Home, where services will be held Tuesday at 2 p.m., Rev. Ernest N. Rumbaugh officiating. Interment Salisbury Cemetery.

More About William James Diehl:
Burial: IOOF Cemetery, Salisbury, Somerset Co., PA
Residence: 1910, Elk Lick, Somerset Co., PA[5739]
Social Security Number: 170-18-3042/

Notes for Daisy Kate James:
Obituary: Daily American - July 31, 1986

Daisy K. Diehl, 90 of Salisbury, died July 30, 1986, in Meyersdale Community Hospital. Born Jan. 2, 1896, in Cornwall, England, daughter of the late George P. and Elizabeth (Prynn) James. Preceded in death by her husband, William J. Diehl; a brother, Luke P. James; and two sisters, Myrtle Conner and Violet Jones. Survived by a son, James R. of Salisbury; five grandchildren and one great-grandson. Member of the Methodist Church of Salisbury. She owned and operated Diehl's Variety Store in Salisbury for 37 years. Friends will be received Friday 2-4 and 7-9 p.m. in the Thomas Funeral Home, where funeral services will be held Saturday 2 p.m. with the Rev. David E. Fetter officiating. Interment, Salisbury Cemetery.

More About Daisy Kate James:
Burial: IOOF Cemetery, Salisbury, Somerset Co., PA

Child of William Diehl and Daisy James is:
    3627   i.   James R.[9] Diehl, born 13 Sep 1926 in Salisbury, Somerset Co., PA; died 19 Jul 1988 in Cumberland, Allegany Co., MD.

                  Notes for James R. Diehl:
                  Obituary: Daily American, July 21, 1988
                  DIEHL

                  James R. Diehl, 61, of Salisbury, died July 19, 1988, in Sacred Heart Hospital in Cumberland, Md. Born Sept. 13, 1926, in Salisbury, son of the late William and Daisy (James) Diehl. Survived by his wife, the former Alice Hall, and these children: Charles, Cleveland, OH; Mrs. Rhonda Minick, Salisbury; Beverly, Loretta and Doretta, all at home; also three grandchildren. He was a retired employee of Seaway Foods of Bedford Heights, OH; a veteran of W.W. II and a member of Salisbury V.F.W. Friends will be received at the Thomas Funeral Home in Salisbury today (Thursday) from noon to 4 p.m., at which time the funeral services will be held with the Rev. David E. Fetter officiating. Interment, Salisbury Cemetery.

                  More About James R. Diehl:
                  Burial: Salisbury IOOF Cemetery, Salisbury, Somerset Co., PA

1599. Edna May[8] Diehl (William Henry[7], Elizabeth[6] Christner, Jacob C.[5], John J.[4], Johannes John Hans[3], Christian[2], Christen[1])[5739,5740,5741] was born 25 Aug 1898 in Connellsville, Fayette Co., PA[5742,5743], and died 26 Mar 1991 in Monroeville, Allegheny Co., PA. She married **Miles Lee Glotfelty**. He was born 20 Jul 1899 in Connellsville, Fayette Co., PA, and died 26 Feb 1966 in Monroeville, Allegheny Co., PA.

Notes for Edna May Diehl:
SSDI:
EDNA GLOTFELTY
SSN 208-18-3341 Residence:
Born 25 Aug 1898 Last Benefit:
Died 26 Mar 1991 Issued: PA (Before 1951)

More About Edna May Diehl:
Residence: 1910, Elk Lick, Somerset Co., PA[5744]

Children of Edna Diehl and Miles Glotfelty are:
    3628   i.   Glenn Lee[9] Glotfelty, born 08 Aug 1927 in Connellsville, Fayette Co., PA; died Sep 1974 in Connellsville, Fayette Co., PA.
    3629   ii.   Elaine Glotfelty, born 29 Aug 1930 in Connellsville, Fayette Co., PA.

                  More About Elaine Glotfelty:
                  Adoption: Unknown

    3630   iii.   Dale Edward Glotfelty, born 28 Aug 1933 in Connellsville, Fayette Co., PA; died 2004.

1600. Edith Mary[8] **Diehl** (William Henry[7], Elizabeth[6] Christner, Jacob C.[5], John J.[4], Johannes John Hans[3], Christian[2], Christen[1])[5744,5745,5746] was born 24 Dec 1904 in W. Salisbury, Somerset Co., PA[5747,5748], and died 19 Dec 1985 in Boynton, Somerset Co., PA. She married **Paul E. Bowman**. He was born 16 Jan 1909[5749], and died 20 Mar 1958 in Meyersdale, Somerset Co., PA.

Notes for Edith Mary Diehl:
Obituary:

Edith M. Bowman, 80 Boynton, died Dec. 19, 1985 at home. Born Dec. 24, 1904, in West Salisbury, daughter of the late William H. and Fredericka (Gerke) Diehl. Preceded in death by her husband, Paul E. Bowman. Survived by one son, Paul Daniel Bowman, Boynton: one brother, George E. Diehl, Salisbury; and two sisters: Mrs. Edna Glotfelty, Monroeville; and Mrs. Joan Brown, Salisbury. She was a member of the Salisbury Methodist Church. Friends will be received Friday from 2-4 and 7-9 pm at the Thomas Funeral Home, Salisbury, where funeral services will be held Saturday at 2 pm, with the Rev. Charles F. Harper officiating. Interment, Salisbury Cemetery.

More About Edith Mary Diehl:
Burial: 21 Dec 1985, I. O. O. F. Cemetery, Salisbury, Somerset Co., PA
Residence: 1910, Elk Lick, Somerset Co., PA[5750]

Notes for Paul E. Bowman:
SSDI:
PAUL BOWMAN
SSN 163-14-2276 Residence:
Born 16 Jan 1909 Last Benefit:
Died Mar 1958 Issued: PA (Before 1951)

More About Paul E. Bowman:
Burial: Mar 1958, I. O. O. F. Cemetery, Salisbury, Somerset Co., PA
Social Security Number: 163-14-2276[5751]
SSN issued: Connellsville, Fayette Co., PA[5751]

Child of Edith Diehl and Paul Bowman is:
> 3631   i.   Paul Daniel[9] Bowman, born 30 Jul 1942 in Morgantown, Monongalia Co., WV; died 29 Aug 1995 in W. Salisbury, Somerset Co., PA.
>
>   Notes for Paul Daniel Bowman:
>   Obituary: Daily American, August 30, 1995
>
>   Paul Daniel Bowman, 53, of Boynton, died Aug. 29, 1995, in Salisbury. Born July 30, 1942, at Frostburg, Md., he was the son of the late Paul Eugene and Edith Mary (Diehl) Bowman. He is survived by an aunt, June Shoemaker, Salisbury; 2 uncles, Grant Bowman and George "Joe" Diehl, both of Salisbury, and a number of nieces, nephews and cousins. Member of Salisbury American Legion Home Aid Association, Meyersdale Moose and Methodist Church. Graveside services will be conducted at 11 a.m. Friday at the Salisbury Cemetery, with the Rev. David E. Fetter officiating. Interment will follow. Newman Funeral Home, Salisbury, has charge of arrangements.
>
>   More About Paul Daniel Bowman:
>   Burial: Salisbury Cemetery, Salisbury, Somerset Co., PA

1601. Marguerite Christianna Gerke[8] **Diehl** (William Henry[7], Elizabeth[6] Christner, Jacob C.[5], John J.[4], Johannes John Hans[3], Christian[2], Christen[1])[5752,5753] was born 16 Oct 1908 in W. Salisbury, Somerset Co., PA[5754,5755], and died 11 Oct 1994 in W. Salisbury, Somerset Co., PA. She married **Leon Ira Brown** 23 Feb 1923 in Somerset Co., PA. He was born 03 Sep 1906 in Somerset Co., PA, and died 19 May 1990 in W. Salisbury, Somerset Co., PA.

Notes for Marguerite Christianna Gerke Diehl:
SSN 160-12-3650 Salisbury, Somerset, PA
Born 16 Oct 1908
Died 11 Oct 1994 Issued: PA (Before 1951)

Obituary: Daily American, October 14, 1994

Marguerite C. "Joan" Brown, 85 Salisbury, died Oct. 11, 1994 at Conemaugh Hospital, Johnstown. Born Oct. 16, 1908 at West Salisbury. Daughter of the late William and Fredericka (Gerke) Diehl. Preceded in death by her husband, Leon I. "Peanut" Brown, on May 19, 1990. Survivors include a son, Donald "Peanut" S. Brown, Salisbury; a daughter, Kathy Layman, Somerset; a brother, George "Joe' Diehl, Salisbury; 7 grandchildren; 7 great grandchildren. Member of Salisbury Church of the Brethren. Friends were received Thursday evening and will be received from 9 a.m. to time of service at 1 p.m. today (Friday) at Newman Funeral Home, Inc., Salisbury, with the Rev. Daniel Whitacre officiating. Interment, Salisbury Cemetery. Expressions of sympathy may be directed to Salisbury Church of the Brethren.

More About Marguerite Christianna Gerke Diehl:
Burial: IOOF Cemetery, Salisbury, Somerset Co., PA
Residence: 1920, Elk Lick, Somerset, PA[5756]
Social Security Number: 160-12-2650/

Notes for Leon Ira Brown:
SSN 191-07-8563
Born 3 Sep 1906 Last Benefit:
Died 19 May 1990 Issued: PA (Before 1951)

Obituary: Daily American, May 21, 1990

Leon I. (Peanut) Brown, 83 of Route 1, Salisbury, PA passed away at his home Saturday, May 19, 1990. Born Sept. 3, 1906 in Salisbury. He was a son of the late Samuel and Sarah (Baker) Brown. Preceded in death by one grandchild. He is survived by his wife, Marguerite (Diehl) Brown; one son, Donald Brown of Salisbury and one daughter, Kathy Layman, Somerset; also seven grandchildren and six greatgrandchildren. He was a self-employed carpenter and member of the Salisbury Church of the Brethren. Friends will be received at the Newman Funeral Home, Salisbury, formerly the Thomas Funeral Home, from 2 to 4 and 7 to 9 p.m. Monday. The service will be at 2 p.m. Tuesday from the funeral home with Rev. Daniel Whitacre. Interment, Salisbury Cemetery. In lieu of flowers, an expression of sympathy may be made to Salisbury Church of the Brethren.

More About Leon Ira Brown:
Burial: IOOF Cemetery, Salisbury, Somerset Co., PA
Nickname: Peanut
Social Security Number: 191-07-8563/

Child of Marguerite Diehl and Leon Brown is:
+   3632   i.   Donald Samuel[9] Brown, born 12 May 1931 in Salisbury, Somerset Co., PA; died 25 May 2002 in Salisbury, Somerset Co., PA.

1602. George Edward[8] Diehl (William Henry[7], Elizabeth[6] Christner, Jacob C.[5], John J.[4], Johannes John Hans[3], Christian[2], Christen[1])[5757,5758,5759] was born 31 Mar 1911 in W. Salisbury, Somerset Co., PA[5760,5761], and died 09 Oct 2002 in Meyersdale, Somerset Co., PA. He married **Mary Margaret Lowry**[5762] 07 Dec 1945 in New York City, New York Co., NY. She was born 08 Mar 1910 in Pittsburg, Allegheny Co., PA[5763], and died 10 Apr 1975 in Somerville, Somerset Co., NJ[5763].

Notes for George Edward Diehl:
Obituary: Daily American, October 10, 2002

George Edward "Joe" Diehl 91 of Floral City, FL and formerly of Salisbury, died Oct. 9, 2002 at Meyersdale Medical Center, Meyersdale. Born March 31, 1911 in West Salisbury, he was the son of the late William H. and Fredericka (Gerke) Diehl. He was proceeded in death by his wife, Mary (Lowry) Diehl and one granddaughter, Mary Cathryn Bartlett. Survivors include one daughter, Shirley A. Bartlett, Smyra, GA and one grandson Robert T. Bartlett. Mr. Diehl was a member of the Meyersdale United Methodist Church, U. S. Navy veteran of the World War II, Salisbury American Legion and VFW and was a retired house painter. Friends will be received 2 to 4 pm Thursday at Newman Funeral Home, Inc. 9168 Mason-Dixon Hwy, Salisbury. Graveside serives and internment will be held Saturday in Piscataway, NJ.

More About George Edward Diehl:
Burial: Lake Nelson Memorial Park, Piscatawy, Somerset Co., NJ
Nickname: Joe
Residence: 1920, Elk Lick, Somerset Co., PA[5764]

Notes for Mary Margaret Lowry:
Obituary: Meyersdale Republic, April 24, 1975

MRS. GEORGE E. DIEHL

Mrs. Mary Lowry Diehl, 65, of Somerville, N.J., formerly of Cumberland and Grantsville, Md., died April 10, 1975 in Somerset Hospital. Born in Pittsburgh, she was a daughter of the late Lewis D. and Gladys (Cochran) Lowry. Surviving are her husband, George E. Diehl; a daughter, Mrs. Shirley Barlett, Issaquah, Wash.; a brother, Roy Lowry, Elton, Pa.; and three sisters, Mrs. Flora Clark, Hunker, Pa.; Mrs. Vernie Carnahan, Shelocta; and Mrs. Frances Shehee, Cumberland. Funeral service was held April 14, in New Jersey, with interment in Lake Nelson Memorial Park there.

More About Mary Margaret Lowry:
Burial: 10 Apr 1975, Lake Nelson Memorial Park, Somerset, Somerset Co., NJ
Social Security Number: 217-18-4223/[5765]
SSN issued: MD[5765]

Children of George Diehl and Mary Lowry are:
+ 3633   i.   Shirley Ann[9] Diehl, born 17 Apr 1947 in Somerville, Somerset Co., NJ.
  3634   ii.   David Delone Diehl, born Aug 1957 in Somerville, Somerset Co., NJ; died Aug 1957 in Somerville, Somerset Co., NJ.

1603. Earl Robert[8] Diehl (William Henry[7], Elizabeth[6] Christner, Jacob C.[5], John J.[4], Johannes John Hans[3], Christian[2], Christen[1])[5766,5767,5768] was born 16 Aug 1914 in W. Salisbury, Somerset Co., PA[5769,5770], and died 18 Sep 1977 in Salisbury, Somerset Co., PA. He married **Grace Baer**. She was born 03 Dec 1921.

Notes for Earl Robert Diehl:
SSDI:
EARL DIEHL
SSN 201-01-7075 Residence: 15558 Salisbury, Somerset, PA
Born 16 Aug 1914 Last Benefit: 15558 Salisbury, Somerset, PA
Died Sep 1977 Issued: PA (Before 1951)

Obituary: The Republic, September 22, 1977

EARL R. DIEHL

Earl R. Diehl, 63, Salisbury, died September 18, 1977, at Somerset Community Hospital. He was born August 16, 1914, in West Salisbury, a son of the late William and Fredricka (Gerke) Diehl. He is survived by one son, Ronald, of Meyersdale, and three daughters: Mrs. Glenda Geiger, Meyersdale; Mrs. Connie Kinsinger and Mrs. Patty Bittinger, both of Grantsville, Md. He is also survived by three sisters: Mrs. Edna Glofelty, Monroeville;

Mrs. Edith Bowman, Boynton; and Mrs. Joan Brown, Salisbury; one brother, Joseph, Summervill [sic], N.J. and nine grandchildren. He was a member of the F.O.E. area No. 1801. Services were held Wednesday at the Thomas Funeral Home with Rev. John H. Kraybill officiating. Interment, Salisbury Cemetery.

More About Earl Robert Diehl:
Burial: Sep 1977, I. O. O. F. Cemetery, Salisbury, Somerset Co., PA
Residence: 1920, Elk Lick, Somerset Co., PA[5771]
Social Security Number: 201-01-7075/

Children of Earl Diehl and Grace Baer are:

3635	i.	Glenda[9] Diehl.
3636	ii.	Ronald Diehl.
3637	iii.	Connie Diehl.
3638	iv.	Patricia Diehl.

1604. Clara Elizabeth[8] Hawkins (Laura Catherine[7] Diehl, Elizabeth[6] Christner, Jacob C.[5], John J.[4], Johannes John Hans[3], Christian[2], Christen[1]) was born 15 Apr 1885 in Mountain Lake Park, Garrett Co., MD, and died 02 Dec 1967 in Indiana, Indiana Co., PA. She married **Charles Henry Donavan**[5772]. He was born 18 Mar 1887 in Tarrs, Westmoreland Co., PA, and died 27 Nov 1947 in Uniontown, Fayette Co., PA.

Notes for Clara Elizabeth Hawkins:
Birth: Apr. 15, 1885 - Mountain Lake Park, Garrett Co., MD
Death: Dec. 2, 1967 - Indiana, Indiana Co., PA

Obituary:

Mrs. Clara Donovan, 82 of 1302 Water St., Indiana, died Saturday, Dec 2, 1967 in the Indiana Hospital. Born April 15, 1885, in Mountain Lake Park, MD, she had lived at her present address for the past four years. She was a daughter of George and Laura Diehl.

Surviving her is a son, Charles E. of Indiana; four daughters: Mrs. J.F. (Laura) Anderson of Indiana; Mrs. Edward (Jean) Laird, Detroit, Michigan, Mrs. John (Rebecca) Blackstone of Nigeria, Africa; and Mrs. Edwin (Virginia) Randolph of Uniontown; 12 grandchildren and 10 great-grandchildren.

Friends will be received at Robinson - Lytle's in Indiana from 2 to 4 and 7 to 9 p.m. today where Pastor Roy S. Shultz will conduct services Tuesday at 3 p.m. Interment will be made in Oakland Cemetery, IN.

Parents: Laura C. Diehl Hawkins (1865 - 1959)

Spouse: Charles Henry Donavan (1887 - 1947)

Children:
Rebecca Lois Donavan Blackstone (1918 - 2000)
Virginia F. Donavan (1920 - 1995)

Note: No headstone

Burial: Oakland Cemetery and Mausoleum, Indiana, Indiana Co., PA
Plot: T-131

More About Clara Elizabeth Hawkins:
Residence: 1930, Everett, Bedford Co., PA[5773]

Notes for Charles Henry Donavan:
Birth: Mar. 18, 1887 - Tarrs, Westmoreland Co., PA
Death: Nov. 27, 1947 - Uniontown, Fayette Co., PA

Spouse: Clara Elizabeth Donavan (1885 - 1967)

Children:
Rebecca Lois Donavan Blackstone (1918 - 2000)
Virginia F. Donavan (1920 - 1995)

Note: No headstone

Burial: Sylvan Heights Memorial Gardens, Uniontown, Fayette Co., PA
Plot: East Extension section, row G

More About Charles Henry Donavan:
Residence: 1920, Indiana, Allegheny Co., PA[5773]

Children of Clara Hawkins and Charles Donavan are:

    3639   i.   Laura May Elizabeth[9] Donavan[5774], born 22 May 1909 in Brownsville, Fayette Co., PA[5774]; died 08 Feb 1978 in Indiana, Indiana Co., PA[5774]. She married (1) Joseph Alexander Steele[5774] 16 Nov 1928 in New Castle, Lawrence, Pennsylvania, United States[5774]; born 19 Feb 1906[5774]; died 18 Sep 1983 in Fort Myers, Lee, Florida, United States[5774]. She married (2) James Franklin Anderson[5774] 28 Sep 1948 in Winchester, Frederick Co., VA[5774]; born 30 Mar 1913 in Pittsburgh, Allegheny Co., PA[5774]; died 12 Oct 1988 in Virginia Beach, Princess Anne Co., VA[5774].

        More About Laura May Elizabeth Donavan:
        Residence: 1920, Indiana, Allegheny, Pennsylvania[5774]

        More About Joseph Alexander Steele:
        Residence: Bet. 1935 - 1993, Fort Myers, FL[5774]

+   3640   ii.   Rebecca Lois "Becky" Donavan, born 12 Jan 1918 in Donora, Washington Co., PA; died 10 Mar 2000 in De Land Highlands, Volusia Co., FL.

    3641   iii.   Virginia F. Donavan, born 07 Apr 1920 in Pittsburgh, Allegheny Co., PA; died 18 Jan 1995 in Redstone, Fayette Co., PA. She married Edwin N. Randolph; born 31 Jan 1914 in Redstone Twp., Fayette Co., PA; died 27 Oct 1972 in Redstone, Fayette Co., PA.

        Notes for Virginia F. Donavan:
        Birth: Apr. 7, 1920 - Pittsburgh, Allegheny Co., PA
        Death: Jan. 18, 1995 - Redstone, Fayette Co., PA

        Obituary: The Herald Standard, Uniontown, PA, 19 Jan 1995

        Virginia F. Randolph, 74, of New Salem, R.D. 1, passed away suddenly Wednesday, Jan. 18, 1995, at her residence. She was born April 7, 1920 in Pittsburg, PA, a daughter of the late Charles and Clara Diehl Donavan. In addition to her parents she was predeceased by her husband, Edwin in 1972.

        She was a member of the Pleasant View Presbyterian Church, the Franklin Grange 1169, and the Pamona and State Grange. Surviving are two sons, Richards of Val Pariso (sic), IN and Robert, at home; four grandchildren, Heath, Chris, Kara and Karly; two sisters, Jean Laird of Birmingham, MI and Rebecca Blackstone of Paisley, FL.

        Friends will be received in the Dearth Funeral Home, New Salem, today after 7 p.m., Friday from 2 to 4 and 7 to 9 p.m., and Saturday until 11 a.m., the hour of service, with her pastor, the Rev. Keith Conover officiating. Interment will follow in Lafayette Memorial Park.

        Parents:
        Charles Henry Donavan (1887 - 1947)
        Clara Elizabeth Donavan (1885 - 1967)

        Spouse: Edwin N. Randolph (1914 - 1972)

        Burial: LaFayette Memorial Park, Brier Hill, Fayette Co., PA
        Plot: St. Matthew section, 187-1

Notes for Edwin N. Randolph:
Birth: Jan 31, 1914 - Redstone, Fayette Co., PA
Death: Oct 27, 1972 - Redstone, Fayette Co., PA

Spouse: Virginia F. Donavan (1920 - 1995)

Burial: LaFayette Memorial Park, Brier Hill, Fayette Co., PA
Plot: St. Matthew section, 187-1

1612. Margaret E.[8] Hampshire (Amanda Alice[7] Diehl, Elizabeth[6] Christner, Jacob C.[5], John J.[4], Johannes John Hans[3], Christian[2], Christen[1])[5775,5776,5777,5778,5779] was born 12 Mar 1898 in Connellsville, Fayette Co., PA[5780,5781,5782,5783,5784,5785,5786,5787], and died 21 Jun 1989 in Connellsville, Fayette Co., PA[5788,5789,5790]. She married **James Ray Crawford**[5791,5792]. He was born 09 Oct 1892 in Dunbar Twp., Fayette Co., PA[5793], and died 24 Oct 1971 in Connellsville, Fayette Co., PA[5793,5794].

More About Margaret E. Hampshire:
Residence: 01 Apr 1940, Redstone, Fayette Co., PA[5795]
Social Security Number: 161-30-8710/[5796]
SSN issued: PA[5796]

Notes for James Ray Crawford:
Birth: Oct. 9, 1892 - Fayette Co., PA
Death: Oct. 24, 1971 - Connellsville, Fayette Co., PA

JAMES R. CRAWFORD

James R. Crawford, 79, of 6-A Greenwood Heights, formerly of Republic, was dead on arrival at 7:30 a.m. Sunday at Connellsville State General Hospital.

He was born Oct. 9, 1892, in Dunbar, the son of the late Frank and Lydia Dean Crawford, and had lived in Connellsville for three years, having resided in Republic prior to that.

A retired coal miner with Republic Steel, he was a member of the UMWA 668, Clyde Local of Fredericktown, the Juniors, Dunlap Council 48 of Merrittstown; the Youghiogheny Lodge 340, United Transportation Union, the Greenwood United Methodist Church and formerly was a member of the Christian Church at Tower Hill 1.

Surviving are his wife, Mrs. Margaret E. Hampshire Crawford; three sons, James R. Crawford, Jr., of SC, Robert E. Crawford of Lanham, Md., and Tech Sgt. William L. Crawford of the Forbes Air Force Base, Topeka, Kan, one daughter, Mrs. Ivan (Betty Louise) Gore of South Connellsville; eight grandchildren, one great-grandchild, and two sisters, Mrs. Paul (Rhea) Roby and Mrs. Matthew (Luea) Lowden, both of Uniontown.

He was predeceased by a daughter, June, in 1919, a brother, Frank Crawford, Jr. and two sisters, Mrs. Edna Gough and Mrs. Lillian Lowden.

FUNERAL NOTICES

CRAWFORD-Friends of James R. Crawford, of 6-A Greenwood Heights, who died Sunday, Oct 24, 1971, may call after 7 p.m. today at the Samuel C. Brooks Funeral Home, 111 East Green St., where the funeral service will be conducted at 1:30 p.m. Wednesday with the Rev. Roland M. O'Brian and the Rev. Robert Critchlow in charge. Interment in LaFayette Memorial Park.

Monday, October 25, 1971,
page 15, column 8
The Daily Courier (Connellsville, Pennsylvania)

Parents:
Franklin McDonald Crawford (1863 - 1929)

Eliza Jane Dean Crawford (1870 - 1936)

Burial: LaFayette Memorial Park, Brier Hill, Fayette Co., PA
Find A Grave Memorial# 65908997

More About James Ray Crawford:
Residence: 1910, Redstone, Fayette Co., PA[5797]
Social Security Number: 190-10-7571/[5798]
SSN issued: PA[5798]

Children of Margaret Hampshire and James Crawford are:

3642   i.   June[9] Crawford, died 1919.

3643   ii.   James R. Crawford Jr., born 1917 in Pittsburgh, Allegheny Co., PA[5799].

    More About James R. Crawford Jr.:
    Residence: 1920, Redstone, Fayette Co., PA[5799]

3644   iii. Betty Louise. Crawford[5800], born 1922 in Pittsburgh, Allegheny Co., PA[5800]. She married Ivan Gore.

    More About Betty Louise. Crawford:
    Residence: 01 Apr 1940, Redstone, Fayette Co., PA[5800]

3645   iv.   Robert Eugene Crawford Sr[5801,5802], born 25 Nov 1930 in Uniontown, Fayette Co., PA[5803]; died 07 Dec 1991 in Cumberland, Allegany Co., PA[5803].

    More About Robert Eugene Crawford Sr:
    Residence: 01 Apr 1940, Age: 9; Marital Status: Single; Relation to Head of House: Son/Redstone, Fayette Co., PA[5803]

3646   v.   William Lee Crawford[5804], born 1938 in Pittsburgh, Allegheny Co., PA[5804].

    More About William Lee Crawford:
    Residence: 01 Apr 1940, Redstone, Fayette Co., PA[5804]

1613. Eloise[8] Hampshire (Amanda Alice[7] Diehl, Elizabeth[6] Christner, Jacob C.[5], John J.[4], Johannes John Hans[3], Christian[2], Christen[1])[5805,5806,5807] was born 23 Jul 1899 in Connellsville, Fayette Co., PA[5808,5809,5810,5811,5812,5813,5814,5815,5816], and died Jan 1978 in Uniontown, Fayette Co., PA[5817,5818,5819,5820]. She married **(1) Fred Harden**[5821,5822] 22 Feb 1919 in Republic, Fayette Co., PA[5823]. He was born 15 Apr 1891 in Brownsville, Fayette Co., PA[5824], and died 03 Jan 1922 in Elm Grove, Fayette Co., PA[5825,5826,5827,5828]. She married **(2) Fred Harden**[5829,5830] 22 Feb 1919. He was born 15 Apr 1891 in Brownsville, Fayette Co., PA[5831], and died 03 Jan 1922 in Elm Grove, Fayette Co., PA[5832,5833,5834,5835]. She married **(3) Wiley Stevens Harvey** 25 May 1944 in Beckley, WV. He was born 27 Jun 1900[5836], and died 30 Apr 1947 in USVA Hospital, Aspinwall, Allegheny Co., PA[5836].

Notes for Eloise Hampshire:
The Daily Courier - Connellsville, PA
Saturday, February 22, 1919

Announcement has been made of the marriage of Miss Eloise Hampshire, daughter of Mr. And Mrs. C. H. Hampshire of Connellsville and Fred Hardin, son of Mr. and Mrs. Thomas Hardin of Republic, solemnized Tuesday evening in the home of the bridegrooms parents. Rev. J. S. Manley of Cardale officiated. Following the ceremony a wedding supper was served, covers being laid for 60 guests. Miss Hampshire previous to her marriage was employed at the Woolworth store and is widely and favorably known. The bridegroom is manager of the W. J. Rainey store at Elm Grove. Mr. and Mrs. hardin left yesterday for a wedding trip to Baltimore and other points of interest. Out of town guests at the wedding were Mrs. Fred Addis of Brownsville, Mr. and Mrs. James hardin, Mr. and Mrs. Thomas Hennessy and family of allison and Mrs. Smith Newcomer and daughter, Mrs. arthur Graham and son, Arthur Jr., of Connellsville.

The Daily Courier - Connellsville, PA
31 May 1944

Eloise H. Harden, Former Local Woman weds Uniontown Man

Announcement is made of the marriage of Eloise Hampshire Harden of Uniontown, formerly of Connellsville and
W. S. Harvey of Uniontown, the ceremony taking place Thursday, May 26, at Becklely, WV in the parsonage of
the First Christian Church there. Dr. Ware performed the ceremony.

The bride wore a navy blue ensemble with white accessories and a corsage of tallisman roses and baby breath.

Mr. and Mrs. G. M. Harvey, brother and sister-in-law of the bridegroom were the only attendants. As matron of
honor, Mrs. Harvey was attired in Navy blue and a chose a corsage of gardenias.

The ceremony was followed by a reception in the Harvey home. Twenty-five guests attended. A three-tiered
wedding cake, topped with a miniature sailor bride and groom and flanked by American flags, formed the
centerpiece.

Mr. Harvey recently received a medical discharge from the service. Prior to that time he served as a petty officer
2/c with the U. S. Navy and participated in te battles of Casablanca, North Africa and Italy. He is also a veteran
of World War I.

The Harvey's are residing at 45 Pittsburgh Street., Uniontown.

Title: The Daily Courier
Publication: 31 Oct 1937
Note: Connellsville, PA
Note: The Daily Courier,31 May 1944
wedding announcement
The Daily Courier
Connellsville, PA
31 May 1944
Eloise H. Harden, Former Local Woman weds Uniontown Man
Announcement is made of the marriage of Eloise Hampshire Harden of Uniontown, formerly of Connellsville and
W. S. Harvey of Uniontown, the ceremony taking place Thursday, May 26, at Becklely, WV in the parsonage of
the First Christian Church there. Dr. Ware performed the ceremony.
The bride wore a navy blue ensemble with white accessories and a corsage of tallisman roses and baby breath.
Mr. and Mrs. G. M. Harvey, brother and sister-in-law of the bridegroom were the only attendants. As matron of
honor, Mrs. Harvey was attired in Navy blue and a chose a corsage of gardenias.
The ceremony was followed by a reception in the Harvey home. Twenty-five guests attended. A three-tiered
wedding cake, topped with a miniature sailor bride and groom and flanked by American flags, formed the
centerpiece.
Mr. Harvey recently received a medical discharge from the service. Prior to that time he served as a petty officer
2/c with the U. S. Navy and participated in te battles of Casablanca, North Africa and Italy. He is also a veteran
of World War I.
The Harvey's are residing at 45 Pittsburgh Street., Uniontown.
Title: Social Security Death Index
Title: The Daily Courier
Publication: 31 Oct 1937
Note: Connellsville, PA
Note: The Daily Courier,31 May 1944
wedding announcement
More About ELOISE HAMPSHIRE:
Soc Sec #: 171-16-7238

The Daily Courier - Connellsville, PA
31 May 1944

Eloise H. Harden, Former Local Woman weds Uniontown Man
Announcement is made of the marriage of Eloise Hampshire Harden of Uniontown, formerly of Connellsville and
W. S. Harvey of Uniontown, the ceremony taking place Thursday, May 26, at Becklely, WV in the parsonage of
the First Christian Church there. Dr. Ware performed the ceremony.

The bride wore a navy blue ensemble with white accessories and a corsage of tallisman roses and baby breath.

Mr. and Mrs. G. M. Harvey, brother and sister-in-law of the bridegroom were the only attendants. As matron of
honor, Mrs. Harvey was attired in Navy blue and a chose a corsage of gardenias.
The ceremony was followed by a reception in the Harvey home. Twenty-five guests attended. A three-tiered
wedding cake, topped with a miniature sailor bride and groom and flanked by American flags, formed the
centerpiece.

Mr. Harvey recently received a medical discharge from the service. Prior to that time he served as a petty officer
2/c with the U. S. Navy and participated in te battles of Casablanca, North Africa and Italy. He is also a veteran
of World War I.

The Harvey's are residing at 45 Pittsburgh Street., Uniontown.

Title: The Daily Courier
Publication: 31 Oct 1937
Note: Connellsville, PA

Note: The Daily Courier,31 May 1944
wedding announcement
More About ELOISE HAMPSHIRE:
Soc Sec #: 171-16-7238 PA

Buried: Hill Grove Cemetery, Connellsville, Fayette Co., PA

More About Eloise Hampshire:
Residence: 1910, Connellsville, Fayette Co., PA[5837]
Social Security Number: 171-16-7238/[5838]
SSN issued: Connellsville, Fayette Co., PA[5838]

Notes for Fred Harden:
Note: The Daily Courier, 18 Feb 1919
marriage license announcement.
Title: The Daily Courier
Publication: 31 Oct 1937

Buried: Hill Grove Cemetery, Connellsville, Fayette Co., PA

More About Fred Harden:
Residence: 1920, Franklin, Fayette Co., PA[5839]

Notes for Fred Harden:
Note: The Daily Courier, 18 Feb 1919
marriage license announcement.
Title: The Daily Courier
Publication: 31 Oct 1937

Buried: Hill Grove Cemetery, Connellsville, Fayette Co., PA

More About Fred Harden:
Residence: 1920, Franklin, Fayette Co., PA[5839]

Notes for Wiley Stevens Harvey:
Obituary: The Daily Courier, Connellsville, PA
1 May 1947

WILEY S. HARVEY

Wiley S. Harvey, 46 of 45 Pittsburg St., Uniontown died early Wednesday morning in the U. S. Veterans Hospital at Aspinwall after a lingering illness.

A veteran of World Wars I & II, he was a member of the Veterans of Foreign Wars, Junior Order of United American Mechanics; Loyal Order of Moose and Fraternal Order of the Eagles.

Survving are his widow, Mrs. Eloise Harden Harvey; two step-daughters, Mrs. Esther Hampshire of South Connellsville and Mrs. Eloise Liddle of Jackson, OH; one stepson, Charles Harden of Uniontown; one sister, Mrs. Earl Hair of Lynchburg, VA; two brothers, Clyde Harvey, also of Lynchburg and George M. Harvey of Beckley, WV and two half-brothers Alex and Audrey Woodridge of Lynchburg.

Title: The Daily Courier
Publication: 31 Oct 1937
Note: Connellsville, PA
Note: The Daily Courier, 1 May 1947
Obituary
Title: The Daily Courier
Publication: 31 Oct 1937
Repository:
Note: Connellsville, PA
Note: The Daily Courier, 31 May 1944
wedding announcement
Title: The Daily Courier
Publication: 31 Oct 1937
Repository:
Note: Connellsville, PA
Note: The Daily Courier,31 May 1944
wedding announcement
More About WILEY S. HARVEY:
Military: WWI & WWII, US Navy - Petty Officer2/c, medical discharge, 1944

Title: The Daily Courier
Publication: 31 Oct 1937
Repository:
Note: Connellsville, PA
Note: The Daily Courier, 1 May 1947
Obituary
Title: The Daily Courier
Publication: 31 Oct 1937
Repository:
Note: Connellsville, PA
Note: The Daily Courier, 31 May 1944
wedding announcement

Title: The Daily Courier
Publication: 31 Oct 1937
Repository:
Note: Connellsville, PA
Note: The Daily Courier,31 May 1944
wedding announcement

More About WILEY S. HARVEY:
Military: WWI & WWII, US Navy - Petty Officer2/c, medical discharge, 1944

Buried: Hill Grove Cemetery, Connellsville, Fayette Co., PA

More About Wiley Stevens Harvey:
Burial: Connellsville, Fayette Co., PA[5840]

Children of Eloise Hampshire and Fred Harden are:
+   3647   i.   Charles Edward[9] Harden Sr., born 01 Feb 1920 in Connellsville, Fayette Co., PA; died 22 Nov 1988 in
                     Macomb, Macomb Co., MI.
     3648   ii.   Eloise T. Harden, born 16 Mar 1921 in Connellsville, Fayette Co., PA[5841]; died 07 Sep 1986 in Warren,
                     Trumbull Co., OH[5841]. She married Ralph E. Liddle[5841] 10 Nov 1939 in Uniontown, Fayette Co., PA;
                     born 27 Sep 1920 in Connellsville, Fayette Co., PA[5842]; died 19 Sep 1985 in Warren, Trumbull Co.,
                     OH[5843].

                     Notes for Eloise T. Harden:
                     The Daily Courier - Connellsville, PA
                     14 Nov 1939

                     ELOISE HARDEN BECOMES BRIDE OF RALPH LIDDIE

                     Announcement is made of the marriage of Miss Eloise Harden, daughter of Mrs. Eloise Harden and late
                     Fred Harden of Gallentin Avenue, Uniontown and Ralph Liddie. The wedding tok place Friday,
                     Novemeber 10, at the Manse of the Third Prysbeterian Church, Uniontown and was very quite, because
                     of the illnes of the beides grandmother, Mrs. C. H. Hampshire of this city. Rev. Clarence W. Kerr
                     officiated.

                     The bride wore a navy blue dress with black accessories and a corsage of Joanna Hill roses and lillies of
                     the valey. The couple will reside at Cannonsburg.

                     Birth: 1921
                     Death: 1986

                     Spouse: Ralph E Liddle (1920 - 1985)

                     Burial: Johnston Township Cemetery, Johnston, Trumbull Co., OH

                     More About Eloise T. Harden:
                     Residence: Trumbull Co., OH[5843]

                     Notes for Ralph E. Liddle:
                     Birth: 1920
                     Death: 1985

                     Spouse: Eloise T. Liddle (1921 - 1986)

                     Burial: Johnston Township Cemetery, Johnston, Trumbull Co., OH

                     More About Ralph E. Liddle:
                     Residence: Connellsville, Fayette Co., PA[5843]
                     Social Security Number: 184-14-4569/[5844]
                     SSN issued: Connellsville, Fayette Co., PA[5844]

   Child of Eloise Hampshire and Fred Harden is:
     3649   i.   Kenneth[9] Harden[5845], born 1914 in Connellsville, Fayette Co., PA[5845].

                     More About Kenneth Harden:
                     Residence: 1920, Franklin, Fayette Co., PA[5845]

Children of Eloise Hampshire and Wiley Harvey are:
>   3650   i.   Clyde[9] Harvey.
>   3651   ii. George M. Harvey.

1617. Harry O.[8] Hampshire (Amanda Alice[7] Diehl, Elizabeth[6] Christner, Jacob C.[5], John J.[4], Johannes John Hans[3], Christian[2], Christen[1])[5846,5847,5848,5848,5849] was born 01 Sep 1906 in Connellsville, Fayette Co., PA[5850,5851,5852,5853,5854,5855], and died Jun 1983 in Connellsville, Fayette Co., PA[5856,5857,5858,5859]. He married **Ruth Edenfield** 31 Oct 1937 in New Salem, Fayette Co., PA. She was born 1907 in Pittsburgh, Allegheny Co., PA[5860].

Notes for Harry O. Hampshire:
HARRY HAMPSHIRE
SSN 172-18-6188 Residence: 15425 Connellsville, Fayette, PA
Born 1 Sep 1906 Last Benefit:
Died Jun 1983 Issued: PA (Before 1951)

More About Harry O. Hampshire:
Census: 1920, U.S. Census > 1920 United States Federal Census - PA - Fayette - Connellsville Ward 5 - District 14
Residence: 01 Apr 1940, Uniontown, Fayette Co., PA[5860]
Social Security Number: 172-18-6188/[5861]
SSN issued: Pittsburgh, Allegheny Co., PA[5861]

More About Ruth Edenfield:
Residence: 01 Apr 1940, Uniontown, Fayette Co., PA[5862]

Children of Harry Hampshire and Ruth Edenfield are:
>   3652   i.   Dolores G.[9] Helleim[5862], born 1929 in Pittsburgh, Allegheny Co., PA[5862].
>
>   More About Dolores G. Helleim:
>   Residence: 01 Apr 1940, Uniontown, Fayette Co., PA[5862]
>
>   3653   ii. Jacguelyn Helleim[5862], born 1931 in Pittsburgh, Allegheny Co., PA[5862].
>
>   More About Jacguelyn Helleim:
>   Residence: 01 Apr 1940, Uniontown, Fayette Co., PA[5862]

1618. Myrtle R.[8] Hampshire (Amanda Alice[7] Diehl, Elizabeth[6] Christner, Jacob C.[5], John J.[4], Johannes John Hans[3], Christian[2], Christen[1])[5863,5864] was born 16 Jan 1908 in Connellsville, Fayette Co., PA[5865,5866,5867,5868], and died 13 Mar 2009 in Connellsville, Fayette Co., PA[5869]. She married **(1) Fred R. Robbins**. He was born 05 May 1905, and died 27 Nov 1955. She married **(2) Joseph Leroy Harshman**[5870,5871] 19 Jan 1965 in Connellsville, Fayette Co., PA[5872]. He was born 27 Dec 1903 in Connellsville, Fayette Co., PA[5873], and died 19 Feb 1991[5874,5875].

More About Myrtle R. Hampshire:
Census: 1920, U.S. Census - 1920 United States Federal Census - PA - Fayette - Connellsville Ward 5 - District 14
Residence: 1910, Connellsville, Fayette, PA[5876]
Social Security Number: 199-32-4226/[5877]
SSN issued: Connellsville, Fayette Co., PA[5877]

Notes for Fred R. Robbins:
Birth   5 May 1905
Death   27 November 1955

Buried: Green Ridge Memorial Park, Connellsville, Fayette Co., PA

Notes for Joseph Leroy Harshman:
Buried: Green Ridge Memorial Park, Connellsville, Fayette Co., PA

More About Joseph Leroy Harshman:
Military service: 27 Jun 1941[5878]
Residence: 1920, German, Fayette Co., PA[5879]
Social Security Number: 189-10-3426/[5880,5881]
SSN issued: Connellsville, Fayette Co., PA[5882]

Child of Myrtle Hampshire and Fred Robbins is:

3654　　i.　Fred R.[9] Robbins Jr., born 1926. He married Joanne B. "Joy"; born 1934; died 2008.

　　　　　Notes for Joanne B. "Joy":
　　　　　Birth: 1934
　　　　　Death: 2008

　　　　　Buried: Green Ridge Memorial Park, Connellsville, Fayette Co., PA

Child of Myrtle Hampshire and Joseph Harshman is:

3655　　i.　Esther L.[9] Harshman.

1620. Mildred Mae[8] Hampshire (Amanda Alice[7] Diehl, Elizabeth[6] Christner, Jacob C.[5], John J.[4], Johannes John Hans[3], Christian[2], Christen[1])[5883,5884,5885] was born 19 Aug 1912 in Connellsville, Fayette Co., PA[5886,5887,5888,5889,5890], and died 06 Apr 1985 in Connellsville, Fayette Co., PA[5890,5891,5892]. She married **(1) Arthur L. Beard**[5893,5894,5895,5896,5897,5898]. He was born 1903 in Pittsburgh, Allegheny Co., PA[5899], and died Oct 1982 in Connellsville, Fayette Co., PA[5900]. She married **(2) Carl Frederick Shallenberger**[5901,5902,5903] 14 Jan 1931 in Dickerson Run, Fayette Co., PA. He was born 13 Dec 1907 in Liberty, Dunbar Twp., Fayette Co., PA[5904,5905,5906,5907], and died 17 Jun 1950 in Magee Hospital, Pittsburgh, Allegheny Co., PA.

Notes for Mildred Mae Hampshire:
Obituary: Mildred M. Hampshire Shallenberger Beard - Connellsville Courier

Beard, Mildred M. (TOOTS) - aged 72 years of 318 E. Crawford Ave., Connellsville, died April 6, 1985 in Connellsville State General Hospital. She was born Aug 9, 1912 at Connellsville, a daughter of the late Charles H. and Amanda Alice Diehl Hampshire. She was a resident of Connellsville most of her life, but was a resident of Vanderbilt for 14 years. She was a member of the First Baptist Church of Connellsville, Ladies auxiliary of the Eagles and a former member of the Secret Pal Club. Surviving are three Sons, Charles and Earl Shallenberger, both of California, and T. C. Shallenberger of Connellsville, three daughters, Mrs. Steve (Patricia) Katona of South Connellsville, Mrs. Jerry (Mary) Johnson of Mira Loma, California and Mrs. Anthony (Verna) Moreira of Swansea, Mass., a stepson Robert a. Beard of Cocoa Beach, FL, two step daughters, Mrs. Doris Bell of Clearfeild, Utah, and Mrs. Anthony (Mary) Carbonara of South Connellsville, 25 grandchildren, eight great-grandchildren, eight step - great- grandchildren, five step great grandchildren, one brother Clarence (Johnny) Hampshire of Connellsville, three sisters, Mrs. Margaret Crawford and Mrs. Leroy (Myrtle) Harshman, both of Connellsville and Mrs. Ray (Mary) Gore of Bristol, PA. She was preceded in death by her first husband, Carl F. Shallenberger in 1950, her second husband, Arthur L. Beard in 1982, a daughter Mrs. Ruth C. Easter, two brothers, Frank Diehl and Harry Hampshire; two sisters, Mrs. Eliose Harvey and Mrs. Clara Lakotish; two infant brothers; one granddaughter, a step grandson and a step - great granddaughter. Friends will be received today from 10 am to 9 PM today at the Brooks Funeral Home, Inc. 111 E. Green St., Connellsville, where services will be held Wednesday at 11 am with Rev. William Shellhammer officiating. Internment will follow in green Ridge Memorial Park.

More About MILDRED MAE HAMPSHIRE:
Burial: 10 Apr 1985, Greenridge Memorial Park, Connellsville, Fayette Co., PA (Sec. B. 121 #4)
Cause of death (Facts Pg): Cardiac Arrest and Coronary Artery Disease, and Renal insufficiency

Death Certificate: 036408 - PA
Social Security Number: 199-24-3463

Brooks Funeral Home, Inc., 111 E. Green Street, Connellsville, PA 15425

More About Mildred Mae Hampshire:
Burial: 10 Apr 1985, Greenridge Memorial Park, Connellsville, Fayette Co., PA (Sec. B. 121 #4)
Cause of death (Facts Pg): Cardiac Arrest and Coronary Artery Disease, and Renal insufficiency
Death Certificate: 036408 - PA
Residence: 01 Apr 1940, Dunbar, Fayette Co., PA[5908]
Social Security Number: 199-24-3463/

Notes for Arthur L. Beard:
SSDI:
ARTHUR BEARD 04 Aug 1902 Oct 1982 15425 (Connellsville, Fayette, PA) (none specified) 178-07-1390 PA
More About ARTHUR L. BEARD:
Burial: Oct 1982, Greenridge Memorial Park, Connellsville, Fayette Co., PA (Sec. B. 139 #4)
Occupation: Prudential Insurance Co., Crawford & Pittsburg St., Connellsvile, Fayette Co., PA

Residence: 1936, 316 S. 9th St., Connellsville, Fayette Co., PA

More About Arthur L. Beard:
Burial: Oct 1982, Greenridge Memorial Park, Connellsville, Fayette Co., PA (Sec. B. 139 #4)
Occupation: Prudential Insurance Co., Crawford & Pittsburg St., Connellsvile, Fayette Co., PA/
Residence: 01 Apr 1940, Age: 37; Marital Status: Married; Relation to Head of House: Head/Connellsville,
Fayette Co., PA[5909]
Social Security Number: 178-07-1390/[5910]
SSN issued: Connellsville, Fayette Co., PA[5910]

Notes for Carl Frederick Shallenberger:

Buried in Dickerson Run Union Cemetery - Section 1, Lot 103
Death Certificate - PA file# 57045
Died from Intra Cranial Tumor - fell off the roof of his home nine years prior. He was a laborer for the railroad.
He died at 8:20 PM on 17 June 1950 at the Magee Hospital in Pittsburgh, Allegheny Co., PA.

Obituary:
Shallenberger, Carl F. - aged 42 of Vanderbilt died Saturday , June 17 1950 at 9:45 PM in the Magee Hospital in
Pittsburgh following a brief illness. Surviving are his wife Mildred Hampshire Shallenberger, seven children:
Patricia Ann, Ruth Carol, Charles Henry, Earl, Terrance, Mary Elizabeth and Verna Mae at home. His parents
Mr. and Mrs. O. H. Shallenberger of Vanderbilt, three brothers, Donald S. of Vanderbilt, Walter of Charleroi, ,
Jesse of Connellsville, and one sister Mrs. Mabel Blackstone of Connellsville. Friends are being received at the
Galley Funeral home, Dawson, where prayer service will be held Tuesday, June 20, 1950 at 2:30 PM followed by
additional rites in the Church of Christ, Vanderbilt, at 3 o'clock with Rev. Walter T. Merrick officiating.
Internment will be in Dickerson Run Union Cemetery.

Burial: 20 Jun 1950, Sec. 1, Lot 103, Dickerson Run Union Cemetery, Vanderbilt, Fayette Co., PA
Cause of death (Facts Pg): Intra cranial tumor
Death Certificate: 17 Jun 1950, PA - Certificate file # 57045
Social Security Number: PA - 200-05-1597

More About Carl Frederick Shallenberger:
Burial: 20 Jun 1950, Sec. 1, Lot 103, Dickerson Run Union Cemetery, Dunbar Twp., Fayette Co., PA
Cause of death (Facts Pg): Intra cranial tumor

Death Certificate: 17 Jun 1950, PA - Certificate file # 57045
Residence: 01 Apr 1940, Dunbar, Fayette Co., PA[5911]
Social Security Number: PA - 200-05-1597/

Children of Mildred Hampshire and Carl Shallenberger are:

+	3656	i.	Patricia Ann[9] Shallenberger, born 31 May 1932 in Connellsville, Fayette Co., PA; died 22 Sep 2013 in Mt Pleasant, Westmoreland Co., PA.
+	3657	ii.	Ruth Carol Shallenberger, born 31 Jan 1934 in Connellsville, Fayette Co., PA; died 09 Apr 1970 in Tampa, Hillsborough Co., FL.
+	3658	iii.	Charles Henry Shallenberger, born 03 Jul 1936 in Connellsville, Fayette Co., PA.
+	3659	iv.	Earl Shallenberger, born 05 Aug 1938 in Connellsville, Fayette Co., PA; died 10 Jan 2008 in Freedom, Santa Cruz Co., CA.
+	3660	v.	Mary Elizabeth Shallenberger, born 09 Feb 1940 in Connellsville, Fayette Co., PA.
+	3661	vi.	Terrance Carl Shallenberger, born 12 Feb 1942 in Connellsville, Fayette Co., PA.
+	3662	vii.	Verna Mae Shallenberger, born 29 Aug 1944 in Connellsville, Fayette Co., PA.

1622. Mary H.[8] Hampshire (Amanda Alice[7] Diehl, Elizabeth[6] Christner, Jacob C.[5], John J.[4], Johannes John Hans[3], Christian[2], Christen[1])[5912] was born 1916 in Connellsville, Fayette Co., PA[5912]. She married **Arthur Ray Gore**[5913,5914,5915,5916,5917,5918] 12 Aug 1937 in Connellsville, Fayette Co., PA. He was born 23 Apr 1914 in Connellsville, Fayette Co., PA[5918,5919,5920,5921,5922,5923], and died 03 Apr 2006 in Sharonvile, OH[5924,5925,5926].

More About Mary H. Hampshire:
Residence: 1920, Connellsville Ward 5, Fayette, PA[5927]

Notes for Arthur Ray Gore:
Obituary: The Connellsville Daily Courier - April 5, 2006

Arthur Ray Gore - Sharonville, Ohio

Formerly of Connellsville and Bristol, PA
Arthur Ray Gore, 92, of Sharonville, Ohio, formerly of Connellsville and Bristol, PA passed away on Monday, April 3, 2006. Arthur was a motorman/streetcar driver for over 20 years for West Penn Railways and retired after 20 years as security for Thiokol Chemical. He was preceded in death by his parents and seven brothers. Arthur is survived by his wife of 68 years, Mary H. (Hampshire) Gore of Sharonville; two sons, William (Nancy) Gore, of Cincinnati, Ohio, and Daniel (Anne) Gore, of Delaware; two grandchildren, Les, of Fairfield, Ohio, and Richard Gore, of Reading, Ohio; three stepgrandchildren, Robert, of New Jersey, and Christopher Marshall, of Liberty Township, Ohio, and Beverly Grubbs, of Canton, Ohio; and eight stepgreat-grandchildren. Services will be held at the convenience of the family. Memorial donations may be made in his memory to the Gideons International, P.O. Box 36325-0325, Cincinnati, OH 45236.

More About Arthur Ray Gore:
Other-Begin: 04 Apr 2006, United States[5928]
Residence: Sharonville, Hamilton, Ohio, United States[5929]
Social Security Number: 189-10-3577/[5930]
SSN issued: Connellsville, Fayette Co., PA[5930]

Children of Mary Hampshire and Arthur Gore are:

3663	i.	Daniel L.[9] Gore.
3664	ii.	William Ray Gore, born 15 Oct 1938 in Connellsville, Fayette Co., PA.

1623. Esther L.[8] Hampshire (Amanda Alice[7] Diehl, Elizabeth[6] Christner, Jacob C.[5], John J.[4], Johannes John Hans[3], Christian[2], Christen[1]) was born 04 Sep 1917[5931,5932], and died 06 Jul 1979 in Connellsville, Fayette Co., PA. She married **(1) William S. Showman**.   She married **(2) Harold Thomas Copeland**.

Notes for Esther L. Hampshire:
Birth: 1917

Death: 1979

Cemetery: - Mt. Olive Evangelical Cemetery, Bullskin Twp., Fayette Co., PA

More About Esther L. Hampshire:
Other-Begin: Connellsville, Fayette Co., PA[5933]
Residence: Connellsville, PA[5934]
Social Security Number: 159-14-8914/[5935]
SSN issued: Pittsburgh, Allegheny Co., PA[5935]

Notes for William S. Showman:
Mt. Olive Evangelical Cemetery, Bullskin Twp., Fayette Co., PA

Child of Esther Hampshire and William Showman is:
+   3665   i.   Rhoda Jean⁹ Hampshire, born 23 Oct 1936 in Connellsville, Fayette Co., PA; died 09 Oct 1980.

1624. Ella⁸ Diehl (Samuel⁷, Elizabeth⁶ Christner, Jacob C.⁵, John J.⁴, Johannes John Hans³, Christian², Christen¹)[5936,5937] was born 1918 in Connellsville, Fayette Co., PA[5938,5939,5940].

More About Ella Diehl:
Arrival: [5941]
Residence: 1930, Salisbury, Lehigh, PA[5941]

Child of Ella Diehl is:
     3666   i.   Gertrude⁹ Diehl[5942], born 1935 in Connellsville, Fayette Co., PA[5942].

                      More About Gertrude Diehl:
                      Residence: 01 Apr 1940, Allentown, Lehigh, PA[5942]

1637. Annie⁸ Foy (Elizabeth⁷ Christner, Jacob (Lumix Jake)⁶, Jacob C.⁵, John J.⁴, Johannes John Hans³, Christian², Christen¹)[5943,5944] was born 19 Sep 1888 in Meyersdale, Somerset Co., PA[5945], and died 30 Oct 1966 in Lonaconing, Allegany Co., MD[5945]. She married **William Clayton Platter Sr.**[5946] He was born 15 Jan 1888 in Summit Twp., Somerset Co., PA[5946], and died 1957[5946].

Notes for Annie Foy:
Birth: Sep. 19, 1888 - Meyersdale, Somerset Co., PA
Death: Oct. 30, 1966 - Lonaconing, Allegany Co., MD

Spouse: William Clayton Platter (1888 - 1957)

Burial: Union Cemetery, Meyersdale, Somerset Co., PA

More About Annie Foy:
Burial: Union Cemetery, Meyersdale, Somerset Co., PA[5947,5948]

Notes for William Clayton Platter Sr.:
Birth: Jan. 15, 1888 - Summit Township, Somerset Co., PA
Death: 1957

Spouse: Annie Foy Platter (1888 - 1966)

Burial: Union Cemetery, Meyersdale, Somerset Co., PA

More About William Clayton Platter Sr.:
Burial: Union Cemetery, Meyersdale, Somerset Co., PA[5948]

Children of Annie Foy and William Platter are:

3667   i.   William Clayton[9] Platter Jr.[5948], born 04 Nov 1915 in Meyersdale, Somerset Co., PA[5948]; died 18 Oct 1997 in Meyersdale, Somerset Co., PA[5948].

More About William Clayton Platter Jr.:
Burial: St. Paul Wilhelm United Church of Christ Cemetery, St. Paul, Elk Lick Twp., Somerset Co., PA[5948]
Military service: U.S Army Veteran of World War II/[5948]
Occupation: Baltimore & Ohio Railroad/[5948]

3668   ii.   Margaret Elizabeth Platter[5948], born 20 Aug 1918 in Meyersdale, Somerset Co., PA[5948]; died 07 May 1985 in Somerset, Somerset Co., PA[5948].

More About Margaret Elizabeth Platter:
Burial: Rockwood I.O.O.F Cemetery, Rockwood, Somerset Co., PA[5948]

3669   iii.   Anna Ruth Platter[5948], born 14 May 1921 in Meyersdale, Somerset Co., PA[5948]; died 28 Jan 2001 in Cumberland, Allegany Co., MD[5948].

More About Anna Ruth Platter:
Burial: Rocky Gap Veterans Cemetery, Flintstone, MD[5948]

3670   iv.   Nellie Mae Platter[5948], born 30 May 1923 in Meyersdale, Somerset Co., PA[5948]; died 08 Oct 1978 in Wellersburg, Somerset Co., PA[5948].

1644. Harry Robert[8] Christner (Nora[7], Samuel[6], Jacob C.[5], John J.[4], Johannes John Hans[3], Christian[2], Christen[1])[5949,5950,5951] was born 05 Nov 1903 in Connellsville, Fayette Co., PA[5951], and died 06 Dec 1962[5952,5953,5954,5955]. He married **Florence Margaret Kraushouer**[5956] 1926 in Meyersdale, Somerset Co., PA[5956]. She was born 18 Jun 1908 in Connellsville, Fayette Co., PA[5956], and died 14 Mar 1993 in Pottsville, Schuylkill Co., PA[5956].

More About Harry Robert Christner:
Residence: 1910, Johnstown Ward 8, Cambria Co., PA[5957]
Social Security Number: 210-03-5205/[5958]
SSN issued: Connellsville, Fayette Co., PA[5958]

More About Florence Margaret Kraushouer:
Residence: 1910, South Fork, Cambria, PA[5959]
Social Security Number: 187-24-3408/[5960]

Child of Harry Christner and Florence Kraushouer is:

3671   i.   Robert Henry[9] Christner[5961,5962], born 02 Jun 1927 in Pittsburgh, Allegheny Co., PA[5963]; died 04 Dec 2004 in Winchester, Frederick Co., VA[5963,5964].

More About Robert Henry Christner:
Residence: 1994, Berryville, VA[5965]

1650. Charles Edward[8] Christner (Mason Franklin[7], Franklin Grant[6], Jacob C.[5], John J.[4], Johannes John Hans[3], Christian[2], Christen[1])[5966] was born 21 Feb 1910[5966], and died Aug 1974 in Greensburg, Westmoreland Co., PA[5966]. He married **Anna Jane Trout** 25 Apr 1945. She was born 11 Nov 1920.

Notes for Charles Edward Christner:
Birth: Feb. 21, 1910
Death: Aug. 17, 1974

Burial: Hillview Cemetery, Greensburg, Westmoreland Co., PA

More About Charles Edward Christner:
Residence: 1920, Greensburg Ward 5, Westmoreland, PA[5967]
Social Security Number: 175-03-6624/[5968]
SSN issued: Connellsville, Fayette Co., PA[5968]

Children of Charles Christner and Anna Trout are:
    3672   i.   Charles[9] Christner.
    3673   ii. Linda Christner.

1651. Frank Henry[8] Christner (Mason Franklin[7], Franklin Grant[6], Jacob C.[5], John J.[4], Johannes John Hans[3], Christian[2], Christen[1])[5969] was born 20 Mar 1917 in Brownsville, Fayette Co., PA[5969], and died Jun 1979 in Chicago, Cook Co., IL[5970]. He married **Ruth Olive Heckman**. She was born 1917, and died 1974.

More About Frank Henry Christner:
Residence: 1920, Age: 2; Age: 2 10/12; Marital Status: Single; Relation to Head of House: Son/Greensburg Ward 5, Westmoreland, PA[5971]
Social Security Number: 169-09-8672/[5972]
SSN issued: Connellsville, Fayette Co., PA[5972]

Children of Frank Christner and Ruth Heckman are:
+   3674   i.   Mason Joseph[9] Christner, born 1937.
    3675   ii. James Lewis Christner, born 1938.

1656. Frances Lucille[8] Christner (George West[7], Franklin Grant[6], Jacob C.[5], John J.[4], Johannes John Hans[3], Christian[2], Christen[1])[5973] was born 15 Aug 1920 in Pittsburgh, Allegheny Co., PA[5974], and died 02 Jun 2010 in Grove City Hospital, Mercer Co., PA[5975]. She married **David Nicholas Hough**[5975,5976]. He was born 22 Jul 1914 in Connellsville, Fayette Co., PA[5977], and died 17 Aug 1988 in Jackson Center, Mercer Co., PA[5978].

Notes for Frances Lucille Christner:
Birth: Aug. 16, 1920
Death: Jun. 2, 2010

Burial: Belle Vernon Cemetery, Belle Vernon, Westmoreland Co., PA
Plot: CHAPEL D Lot Column 6 Grave 6
Find A Grave Memorial# 93673517

More About Frances Lucille Christner:
Residence: 1930, Brownsville, Fayette, PA[5979]
SSN issued: PA[5980]

Notes for David Nicholas Hough:
Birth: Jul. 22, 1914
Death: Aug. 17, 1988

Parents:
Kennedy Ewing Hough (1864 - 1937)
Blanche N. Hough (1878 - 1948)

Burial: Mount Auburn Cemetery, Fayette City, Fayette Co., PA
Find A Grave Memorial# 82448839

More About David Nicholas Hough:
Residence: 01 Apr 1940, Age: 25; Marital Status: Single; Relation to Head of House: Son/Fayette City, Fayette Co., PA[5981]
Social Security Number: 191-10-0225/[5982]
SSN issued: PA[5982]

Child of Frances Christner and David Hough is:

3676   i.   Dorothy Jean[9] Hough[5983], born 11 Apr 1945 in Chaleroi- Monesson Hospital, Fayette Co., PA[5983]; died 03 Apr 2008 in Route 58. Mercer Co., PA[5983].

1670. Eleanor Louise[8] Housel (Sadie Marie[7] Christner, Frank[6], Jacob C.[5], John J.[4], Johannes John Hans[3], Christian[2], Christen[1]) was born 02 Apr 1933 in Meyersdale, Somerset Co., PA. She married **(1) Donald Glenn Cober Sr.**. He was born 28 Nov 1927 in Berlin, Somerset Co., PA[5984,5985], and died 01 Dec 2006 in Berlin, Somerset Co., PA[5985,5986]. She married **(2) William R. Fogel** 06 Jun 1953. He was born 08 Dec 1926, and died 31 Jul 1992 in Garrett, Somerset Co., PA.

Notes for Eleanor Louise Housel:
Her second husband was her youngest childs husband. Donald Glann Cober Jr

Notes for Donald Glenn Cober Sr.:
Obituary: The Tribune-Democrat - Dec/4/2006

COBER - Donald G. Sr., 79, Berlin, died Dec. 1, 2006, at home. Family will receive friends from 2 to 4 and 7 to 9 p.m. Monday at Deaner Funeral Home, Berlin. Viewing from 10 a.m. until service at 11 a.m. Tuesday at Holy Trinity Lutheran Church, Berlin. In lieu of flowers, contributions may be given to In Touch Hospice, 223 S. Pleasant Ave., Somerset, Pa. 15501, or Holy Trinity Lutheran Church, Berlin, Pa. 15530.

More About William R. Fogel:
Burial: Beachdale Cemetery
Residence: Fogletown, PA

Children of Eleanor Housel and William Fogel are:

+   3677   i.   Donald William[9] Fogel, born 1955.
+   3678   ii.   Timothy Edward Fogel, born 1957.
+   3679 iii.   Esther Ellen Fogel, born 1960.
+   3680 iv.   Janet Marie Fogel, born 1962.

1672. Betty Irene[8] Housel (Sadie Marie[7] Christner, Frank[6], Jacob C.[5], John J.[4], Johannes John Hans[3], Christian[2], Christen[1]) was born 27 Sep 1935 in Meyersdale, Somerset Co., PA, and died 28 Feb 1989 in Cumberland, Allegany Co., MD[5987]. She married **Max E. Gnagey** 04 Jun 1958.

Notes for Betty Irene Housel:
Birth: Sep. 27, 1935 - Meyersdale, Somerset Co., PA
Death: Feb. 28, 1989 - Cumberland, Allegany Co., MD

GNAGEY - Daily American, March 2, 1989

Betty I. Gnagey, 53, Meyersdale RD 3, died Feb. 28, 1989, at Sacred Heart Hospital, Cumberland, Md. Born Sept. 27, 1935, in Meyersdale, daughter of Mrs. Sadie Marie (Christner) Housel, Meyersdale and the late Peter F. Housel. Survived by husband, Max E. Gnagey, and these children, Richard L. and Gary J., both of Elkridge, MD. A sister of Mrs. Eleanor Fogle, Garrett; Mrs. Marie Mathers, Millville, NJ; Mrs. Verna Mae Niedermeyer, Pittsburgh; Mrs. Doris Oester, Meyersdale RD 4; Peter, Meyersdale RD 1; Clyde, Clifton, VA; and Mrs. Anna Hamilton, Decatur, GA. Member of Main Street Brethren Church, Meyersdale. Friends will be received from 2-4 and 7-9 p.m. Thursday at Price Funeral Home, Meyersdale where services will be conducted at 11 a.m. Friday with Pastor Robert Stahl officiating. Interment, Pine Hill Cemetery.

Parents:
Peter F Housel (1907 - 1977)
Sadie Marie Christner Housel (1911 - 2007)

Burial: Pine Hill Cemetery, Berlin, Somerset Co., PA

More About Betty Irene Housel:
Cause of Death: Asthma

Children of Betty Housel and Max Gnagey are:
    3681   i.   Richard L.[9] Gnagey, born 07 Jan 1960.
    3682   ii.   Gary J. Gnagey, born 02 Feb 1963.

1673. Verna Mae[8] Housel (Sadie Marie[7] Christner, Frank[6], Jacob C.[5], John J.[4], Johannes John Hans[3], Christian[2], Christen[1]) was born 06 Sep 1937 in Meyersdale, Somerset Co., PA. She married **Joseph Paul Niedermeyer** 28 Jun 1958 in Pittsburgh, Allegheny Co., PA. He was born 22 Jun 1936 in Pittsburgh, Allegheny Co., PA.

Children of Verna Housel and Joseph Niedermeyer are:
+   3683   i.   Christina Marie[9] Niedermeyer, born 18 May 1959 in Pittsburgh, Allegheny Co., PA.
    3684   ii.   Karen Lynne Niedermeyer, born 05 Aug 1960 in Pittsburgh, Allegheny Co., PA.
+   3685   iii.   Joseph Paul II Niedermeyer, born 14 Feb 1963 in Pittsburgh, Allegheny Co., PA.
+   3686   iv.   Randall Peter Niedermeyer, born 25 Nov 1965.
+   3687   v.   Kevin Paul Niedermeyer, born 21 May 1967.
+   3688   vi.   Brian David Niedermeyer, born 18 Jul 1969.
+   3689   vii.   Rebecca Anna Niedermeyer, born 25 Oct 1973.

1674. Doris Lavern[8] Housel (Sadie Marie[7] Christner, Frank[6], Jacob C.[5], John J.[4], Johannes John Hans[3], Christian[2], Christen[1]) was born 14 Mar 1939 in Meyersdale, Somerset Co., PA. She married **Gerald Nicholson Oester** 02 Sep 1961 in Cove, MD. He was born 08 Jun 1924 in Wadsworth, OH.

Children of Doris Housel and Gerald Oester are:
+   3690   i.   Creed[9] Oester.
+   3691   ii.   Gerald Dana Oester.
    3692   iii.   Karl N. Oester.
+   3693   iv.   Thomas Paul Oester.
+   3694   v.   Caroline Oester.
+   3695   vi.   John Charles Oester, born 24 Oct 1962.
+   3696   vii.   Martha Jane Oester, born 03 Oct 1964.
+   3697   viii.   Maryann Oester, born 28 May 1967.

1675. Peter Franklin[8] Housel Jr (Sadie Marie[7] Christner, Frank[6], Jacob C.[5], John J.[4], Johannes John Hans[3], Christian[2], Christen[1]) was born 17 Oct 1941 in Meyersdale, Somerset Co., PA. He married **Gloria Ann Klink**. She was born 1948.

Child of Peter Housel and Gloria Klink is:
    3698   i.   Carl Eugene[9] Housel, born 1966.

1676. Anna Catherine[8] Housel (Sadie Marie[7] Christner, Frank[6], Jacob C.[5], John J.[4], Johannes John Hans[3], Christian[2], Christen[1]) was born 08 Mar 1944 in Meyersdale, Somerset Co., PA. She married **Lloyd Blakeley Hamilton**.

Children of Anna Housel and Lloyd Hamilton are:
+   3699   i.   Tammy Lee[9] Hamilton, born 04 Jan 1964.
+   3700   ii.   Victoria Marie Hamilton, born 14 Jan 1965.
+   3701   iii.   Sherry Ann Hamilton, born 01 Mar 1968.

1677. Clyde Franklin[8] Housel (Sadie Marie[7] Christner, Frank[6], Jacob C.[5], John J.[4], Johannes John Hans[3], Christian[2], Christen[1]) was born 08 Mar 1947 in Meyersdale, Somerset Co., PA. He married **(1) Linda Susan Shelton** 1970. She was born 08 Nov 1950. He married **(2) Terry Lynn Chason** Dec 1989. She was born 24

Apr 1957.

Children of Clyde Housel and Linda Shelton are:
+   3702   i.   Stephanie Lynn[9] Housel, born 30 Aug 1974.
+   3703   ii.   Stacie Dawn Housel, born 18 Jun 1978.

1685. Margaret Alverda[8] Christner (Clyde Franklin[7], Frank[6], Jacob C.[5], John J.[4], Johannes John Hans[3], Christian[2], Christen[1]) was born 26 Nov 1933 in Summit Twp., Somerset Co., PA, and died 12 Jun 1983 in Meyersdale, Somerset Co., PA. She married **John M. Butler.**

More About Margaret Alverda Christner:
Burial: Union Cemetery

Children of Margaret Christner and John Butler are:
     3704   i.   Claude[9] Butler.
     3705   ii.   Debbie Butler. She married Bittner.
     3706   iii.   John R. Butler.
     3707   iv.   Kathy Butler. She married Boden.
     3708   v.   Linda Sue Butler.
     3709   vi.   Mary Ann Butler.

1688. Robert C.[8] Christner (Clyde Franklin[7], Frank[6], Jacob C.[5], John J.[4], Johannes John Hans[3], Christian[2], Christen[1])[5988] was born 29 Aug 1940, and died 29 Mar 2001 in Meyersdale, Somerset Co., PA. He married **Clara Oester.**

Notes for Robert C. Christner:
Obituary: Robert C. "Brown Bottle" CHRISTNER, 2001, Meyersdale, Somerset County, PA - Daily American, March 31, 2001

Robert C. "Brown Bottle" Christner, 60, of Meyersdale died March 29, 2001, in Meyersdale. Born Aug. 29, 1940, a son of the late Clyde F. Christner and Emma Irene (Housel) Christner. He was preceded in death by a brother, Clyde Christner Jr. and a sister Margaret (Peggy) Butler. Surviving are his wife, Clara (Oester) Christner; a son, Jeffrey of Meyersdale; a sister, Betty Brocht of Meyersdale; a brother Kenneth Christner and wife Linda of Meyersdale, and many nieces and nephews. Friends will be received from 2 to 4 and 7 to 9 p.m. Sunday at the Leckemby Funeral Home where service will be held at 11 a.m. Monday with Pastor Albert Valentine officiating. Interment, Union Cemetery.

More About Robert C. Christner:
Social Security Number: 171-32-7897/[5988]
SSN issued: PA[5988]

Child of Robert Christner and Clara Oester is:
     3710   i.   Jeffrey[9] Christner.

1696. Rose Marie[8] Housel (Emma Catherine[7] Christner, Frank[6], Jacob C.[5], John J.[4], Johannes John Hans[3], Christian[2], Christen[1]) She married **(1) Kenneth Edward Wilt.** She married **(2) Richard Shrug.**

Children of Rose Housel and Richard Shrug are:
     3711   i.   Mike[9] Shrug.
     3712   ii.   Connie Shrug.
     3713   iii.   Julie Shrug.
     3714   iv.   Kenneth Shrug.

1697. George Martin[8] Housel (Emma Catherine[7] Christner, Frank[6], Jacob C.[5], John J.[4], Johannes John Hans[3], Christian[2], Christen[1]) was born 08 Oct 1939. He married **Lucille Trott.**

Children of George Housel and Lucille Trott are:
- 3715   i.   Lisa[9] Housel.
- 3716   ii.   Steve Housel.

1699. James Eward[8] Housel (Emma Catherine[7] Christner, Frank[6], Jacob C.[5], John J.[4], Johannes John Hans[3], Christian[2], Christen[1]) was born 04 Mar 1947. He married **Beatrice Bouser**.

Children of James Housel and Beatrice Bouser are:
- 3717   i.   James[9] Housel.
- 3718   ii.   Margie Housel.
- 3719   iii. Maryann Housel.
- 3720   iv.   Ricky Housel.
- 3721   v.   Theresa Housel.

1700. William Eugene[8] Housel (Emma Catherine[7] Christner, Frank[6], Jacob C.[5], John J.[4], Johannes John Hans[3], Christian[2], Christen[1])[5989] was born 04 Mar 1947 in Meyersdale, Somerset Co., PA[5989], and died 14 Sep 2001 in Somerset, Somerset Co., PA[5989]. He married **Joyce Knopsnyder**.

Children of William Housel and Joyce Knopsnyder are:
- 3722   i.   Karen[9] Housel.
- 3723   ii.   Susan Housel.
- 3724   iii. Tommy Housel.

1701. Thomas Richard[8] Housel (Emma Catherine[7] Christner, Frank[6], Jacob C.[5], John J.[4], Johannes John Hans[3], Christian[2], Christen[1]) was born 26 Sep 1951. He married **Glenna Peterman**.

Children of Thomas Housel and Glenna Peterman are:
- 3725   i.   Landra[9] Housel.
- 3726   ii.   Shelly Housel.
- 3727   iii. Tina Housel.

1702. Nancy Jane[8] Housel (Emma Catherine[7] Christner, Frank[6], Jacob C.[5], John J.[4], Johannes John Hans[3], Christian[2], Christen[1]) was born 16 Jan 1952. She married **Ronnie Roodman**.

Children of Nancy Housel and Ronnie Roodman are:
- 3728   i.   Joseph[9] Roodman.
- 3729   ii.   Scott Roodman.

1703. Robert Harold[8] Housel (Emma Catherine[7] Christner, Frank[6], Jacob C.[5], John J.[4], Johannes John Hans[3], Christian[2], Christen[1])[5989] was born 29 Oct 1954 in Meyersdale, Somerset Co., PA, and died 06 Sep 1985 in Meyersdale, Somerset Co., PA. He married **Cathy Fox**.

More About Robert Harold Housel:
Burial: St. Johns Cemetery

Children of Robert Housel and Cathy Fox are:
- 3730   i.   Sheila[9] Foy.
- 3731   ii.   Wendy Foy.

1706. Patricia Ann[8] Housel (Emma Catherine[7] Christner, Frank[6], Jacob C.[5], John J.[4], Johannes John Hans[3], Christian[2], Christen[1]) was born 25 Feb 1958. She married **Paul Miller**.

Child of Patricia Housel and Paul Miller is:

3732   i.   Melissa Ann[9] Miller.

1707. Thomas Patrick[8] Housel (Emma Catherine[7] Christner, Frank[6], Jacob C.[5], John J.[4], Johannes John Hans[3], Christian[2], Christen[1]) was born 01 Jan 1959. He married **Debra Hittie**.

Child of Thomas Housel and Debra Hittie is:
    3733   i.   Amy Sue[9] Housel.

1719. Elmer[8] Christner (Ananias Sipe[7], Peter[6], John[5], Peter[4], Johannes John Hans[3], Christian[2], Christen[1])[5990,5991] was born 10 Jun 1874 in Edgar, Clay Co., NE[5992], and died 14 May 1946 in Hutchinson, Reno Co., KS. He married **Elma Harrison**. She was born Abt. 1882 in KS[5993].

More About Elmer Christner:
Residence: 1900, Lost Springs, Marion Co., KS[5994]

More About Elma Harrison:
Residence: 1930, Hutchinson, Reno Co., KS[5995]

Children of Elmer Christner and Elma Harrison are:
    3734   i.   Living[9] Christner[5995].
+   3735   ii. Homer Eugene Christner, born 29 Apr 1909 in Hutchinson, Reno Co., KS; died 30 May 1983 in 93243 Lebec, Kern Co., CA.

1720. Mary Allen[8] Christner (Ananias Sipe[7], Peter[6], John[5], Peter[4], Johannes John Hans[3], Christian[2], Christen[1]) was born 09 Oct 1876 in Edgar, Clay Co., NE[5996], and died 17 Jun 1962 in Ellsworth, KS. She married **(1) H.V.Brown**. She married **(2) H. V. Brown**. She married **(3) Reader Jackson**.

More About Mary Allen Christner:
Residence: 1900, Lost Springs, Marion Co., KS[5996]

Children of Mary Christner and Reader Jackson are:
    3736   i.   Ivan[9] Jackson.
    3737   ii. Mina Jackson.

1721. Arthur[8] Christner (Ananias Sipe[7], Peter[6], John[5], Peter[4], Johannes John Hans[3], Christian[2], Christen[1])[5997,5998,5999] was born 08 Nov 1879 in Edgar, Clay Co., NE[6000,6001,6002], and died 21 Nov 1928 in Lost Springs, Marion Co., KS[6003,6004]. He married **Florence Catherine Terry**[6005,6006,6007] 25 Jun 1899, daughter of Alfred Terry and Nancy Coleman. She was born 16 Apr 1879 in Lost Springs, Marion Co., KS[6008,6009,6010,6011], and died 23 Apr 1934 in Burdick, Morris Co., KS[6012,6013].

Notes for Arthur Christner:
Birth: Nov. 8, 1879
Death: Nov. 21, 1928

Spouse: Florence Katherine Christner (1879 - 1934)

Burial: Lost Springs Cemetery, Lost Springs, Marion Co., KS
Plot: Lot 77, block 4

More About Arthur Christner:
Residence: 1920, Lost Springs, Marion Co., KS[6013,6014]

Notes for Florence Catherine Terry:
Birth: Apr. 16, 1879

Death: Apr. 23, 1934

Spouse: Arthur Christner (1879 - 1928)

Children: Simon "Pete" S Christner (1906 - 1976)

Burial: Lost Springs Cemetery, Lost Springs, Marion Co., KS
Plot: Lot 77, block 4

More About Florence Catherine Terry:
Burial: Lost Springs, Marion Co., KS
Residence: 1930, Lost Springs, Marion Co., KS[6015,6016,6017]

Children of Arthur Christner and Florence Terry are:

    3738   i.   Baby[9] Christner[6017,6018], born 24 Jul 1900[6019,6020]; died 24 Jul 1900[6021,6022].

+   3739   ii.   Alfred Arthur Christner, born 11 Aug 1901 in Lost Springs, Marion Co., KS; died 13 Apr 1968 in Macks Creek, Camden, MO.

+   3740   iii.   Melvin LeRoy Christner, born 17 Feb 1903 in Lost Springs, Marion Co., KS; died 18 Jan 2002 in Burdick, Morris Co., KS.

+   3741   iv.   Nancy Ann Christner, born 25 Jan 1905 in Lost Springs, Marion Co., KS; died 24 Mar 1970 in San Bernardino, San Bernardino Co., CA.

+   3742   v.   Simon Sipe (Pete) Christner, born 21 Aug 1906 in Lost Springs, Marion Co., KS; died 21 Nov 1976 in Herington, Herington Co., KS.

+   3743   vi.   Inez Elizabeth Christner, born 19 Oct 1909 in Lost Springs, Marion Co., KS; died Dec 1995 in Council Grove, Morris Co., KS.

+   3744   vii.   Frank Laverne Christner, born 05 Oct 1910 in Lost Springs, Marion Co., KS; died 18 Dec 1998 in Herington, Dickinson Co., KS.

+   3745   viii.   Walter Orville Christner, born 09 Nov 1912 in Lost Springs, Marion Co., KS; died 24 Feb 1971 in Pocatello, Bannock Co., ID.

    3746   ix.   Roy Dimple Christner[6022,6023], born 30 Sep 1914 in Lost Springs, Marion Co., KS[6024,6025,6026]; died Dec 1978[6027,6028].

                  Notes for Roy Dimple Christner:
                  Birth: 1914
                  Death: 1978

                  Burial: Lost Springs Cemetery, Lost Springs, Marion Co., KS
                  Plot: Lot 77, block 4
                  Find A Grave Memorial# 36848558

                  More About Roy Dimple Christner:
                  Residence: 1920, Lost Springs, Marion Co., KS[6029,6030]
                  Social Security Number: 513-32-6641[6031]

+   3747   x.   Donald Ray Christner, born 04 Oct 1917 in Lost Springs, Marion Co., KS; died 12 Oct 1998 in Phoenix, Maricopa Co., AZ.

+   3748   xi.   Sylvia Florence Christner, born 13 Jan 1920; died 20 Jul 2002 in Eugene, Lane Co., OR.

1722. Jay[8] Christner (Ananias Sipe[7], Peter[6], John[5], Peter[4], Johannes John Hans[3], Christian[2], Christen[1])[6032] was born 23 Nov 1881 in Edgar, Clay Co., NE[6033], and died 26 May 1953 in Independance, Montgomery Co., KS. He married **Matilda Albertina Blume**[6034,6035] 31 Dec 1902 in Woodbine, Dickinson Co., KS[6036]. She was born 17 Jun 1879 in Morris Co., KS[6036], and died 23 Dec 1958 in KS[6036,6037,6038].

More About Jay Christner:
Residence: 1900, Lost Springs, Marion Co., KS[6039]

More About Matilda Albertina Blume:
Residence: 1900, Liberty & Rhinehart Townships, Dickinson, Kansas[6040,6041]

Children of Jay Christner and Matilda Blume are:

3749	i.	Infant[9] Christner.
3750	ii.	Walter Christner[6042], born Oct 1903 in KS[6042]; died Nov 1903 in KS[6042].
3751	iii.	Floyd Harry Christner, born 25 Oct 1904 in KS[6042]; died 04 Jul 1925 in Barttesviulle, Washington Co., OK[6042].

> Notes for Floyd Harry Christner:
> He was at a picnic, ran to the river to swim, jumped in and hit his head on the bottom and drown.
>
> More About Floyd Harry Christner:
> Cause of Death: Drowning

3752	iv.	Comer Forrest Christner, born 30 Jul 1906 in KS[6042]; died 09 Jun 1935[6042].

> More About Comer Forrest Christner:
> Cause of Death: Brain Tumor

+	3753	v.	Erma Christner, born Oct 1918.

1723. Herman[8] Christner (Ananias Sipe[7], Peter[6], John[5], Peter[4], Johannes John Hans[3], Christian[2], Christen[1])[6043,6044] was born 05 Dec 1885 in Arapahoe, Furnas Co., NE[6045,6046,6047], and died 05 Dec 1970 in Herington, Dickinson Co., KS[6048]. He married **Stella Young**[6048]. She was born Abt. 1885 in KS[6048].

More About Herman Christner:
Residence: 1930, Lost Springs, Marion Co., KS[6048]
Social Security Number: 709-18-5774/[6049]
SSN issued: Railroad Board (Issued Through)[6049]

More About Stella Young:
Residence: 1930, Lost Springs, Marion Co., KS[6050]

Children of Herman Christner and Stella Young are:

3754	i.	Clarence[9] Christner.
3755	ii.	Helen Christner.
3756	iii.	Raymond Christner. He married Edna Beisel.
3757	iv.	Beulah Christner[6050], born 29 Jun 1919 in KS[6050,6051]; died Feb 1983 in La Porte, Harris Co., TX[6052]. She married Ralph Hugh McAninch[6052] 29 Jun 1940 in McPherson, McPherson, Kansas; born 16 Mar 1915 in Manhattan, KS[6052]; died 28 Jun 2003 in Pasadena, Harris Co., TX[6052].

> More About Beulah Christner:
> Residence: 1930, Lost Springs, Marion Co., KS[6052]
> Social Security Number: 514-07-6705/[6053]
> SSN issued: KS[6053]
>
> More About Ralph Hugh McAninch:
> Residence: La Porte, Texas[6054]

1724. Sara Elizabeth[8] Christner (Ananias Sipe[7], Peter[6], John[5], Peter[4], Johannes John Hans[3], Christian[2], Christen[1]) was born 12 Apr 1888 in Chardoce, KS, and died 1971 in Hutchinson, Reno Co., KS. She married **John Johannes**.

Notes for Sara Elizabeth Christner:
Also known as Bertha.

More About Sara Elizabeth Christner:
Residence: 1900, Lost Springs, Marion Co., KS[6055]

Children of Sara Christner and John Johannes are:

3758	i.	Inez Meta[9] Johannes, born 1907; died 1908.

+ 3759   ii.   Everett Johannes, born 1909.
+ 3760   iii.   Lowell Johannes, born 1911; died 1956.
   3761   iv.   Velber Johannes, born 1916; died 1944. She married Ollie.

1725. Elmer Sherman[8] Christner (Winfield Scott[7], Peter[6], John[5], Peter[4], Johannes John Hans[3], Christian[2], Christen[1])[6056,6057] was born 26 Jun 1887 in Disko, Wabash Co., IN[6058,6059], and died 08 Sep 1972 in Palestine, Kosciusko Co., IN[6060]. He married **Elva Marie Myers**[6061,6062] 10 Nov 1906. She was born 19 Feb 1890 in Wabash Co., IN[6063], and died 21 Aug 1977 in Warsaw, Kosciusko Co., IN.

Notes for Elmer Sherman Christner:
He was raised by his grandfather Peter Christner.

More About Elmer Sherman Christner:
Burial: Oakwood Cemetery, Warsaw, IN
Residence: 1930, Seward, Kosciusko Co., IN[6063]
Social Security Number: 311-24-9193/[6064]
SSN issued: IN[6064]

More About Elva Marie Myers:
Burial: Oakwood Cemetery, Warsaw, IN
Residence: 1930, Seward, Kosciusko Co., IN[6065]

Children of Elmer Christner and Elva Myers are:
+ 3762   i.   Cleo Fern[9] Christner, born 25 Jan 1907 in Wabash Co., IN; died 04 Dec 1995 in Warsaw, Kosciusko Co., IN.
   3763   ii.   Claude Devayne Christner[6066,6067], born 07 Jul 1908 in Wabash Co., IN[6068]; died 27 Sep 2001 in Millers Merry Manor, Warsaw, Kosciusko Co., IN. He married (1) Imogene McCurtain. He married (2) Dorothy Elizabeth Martz 30 Dec 1944; died 31 Mar 1996.

           Notes for Claude Devayne Christner:
           Birth: Jul. 7, 1908
           Death: Sep. 21, 2001

           Burial: Oakwood Cemetery, Warsaw, Kosciusko Co., IN

           More About Claude Devayne Christner:
           Burial: 01 Oct 2001, Oakwood Cemetery, Warsaw, IN
           Other-Begin: 28 Sep 2001, Allen Co., IN[6069]
           Social Security Number: 305-07-9423/[6070]
           SSN issued: IN[6070]

           More About Dorothy Elizabeth Martz:
           Burial: Oakwood Cemetery, Warsaw, IN

+ 3764   iii.   Mildred Ruth Christner, born 26 Feb 1910 in Wabash Co., IN; died Sep 1977 in Warsaw, Kosciusko Co., IN.
+ 3765   iv.   Roy Lemoine Christner, born 31 May 1912 in Wabash Co., IN.
+ 3766   v.   Wilbur Ray Christner, born 05 Dec 1914; died 03 Jul 1974.
+ 3767   vi.   Genieve Irene Christner, born 18 Dec 1918 in Silver Lake, Kosciusko Co., IN; died 27 Aug 1988 in Palestine, Kosciusko Co., IN.
+ 3768   vii.   John Robert Christner, born 13 Mar 1920 in Silver Lake, Kosciusko Co., IN; died 08 Jul 2003 in IN.
+ 3769   viii. Audrey Marciel Christner, born 26 Aug 1922 in Silver Lake, Kosciusko Co., IN.
+ 3770   ix.   Raymond Mack Christner, born 29 Oct 1925 in Silver Lake, Kosciusko Co., IN.
+ 3771   x.   Virginia Bessie Christner, born 29 Oct 1928 in Silver Lake, Kosciusko Co., IN; died 29 Sep 1975 in Carmel, Hamilton Co., IN.

1729. Theron Defoe[8] Grogg (Alice D.[7] Christner, Peter[6], John[5], Peter[4], Johannes John Hans[3], Christian[2], Christen[1])[6071] was born 21 Oct 1900 in IN[6071], and died 02 Feb 1952 in Fort Wayne, Allen Co., IN[6071]. He married **Beatrice Titus**.

Children of Theron Grogg and Beatrice Titus are:
    3772   i.   Catherine[9] Grogg.
    3773   ii.   Earl Grogg.
    3774   iii. Josephine Grogg.
    3775   iv.   Marylin Grogg.
    3776   v.   Viginia Grogg.

1730. Forrest Ivan[8] Grogg (Alice D.[7] Christner, Peter[6], John[5], Peter[4], Johannes John Hans[3], Christian[2], Christen[1])[6071] was born 11 Mar 1906 in Near Gilead./Miami Co., IN[6071], and died 24 May 1990 in Life Care Center./Fulton Co., IN[6071]. He married **Ruth Conrad**.

Children of Forrest Grogg and Ruth Conrad are:
    3777   i.   Un-Named[9] Grogg.
    3778   ii.   Malinda Grogg.

1732. Harry Christner[8] Weimer (Mary[7] Christner, Cain[6], John[5], Peter[4], Johannes John Hans[3], Christian[2], Christen[1])[6072] was born 30 Nov 1874 in Connellsville, Fayette Co., PA[6072], and died 10 Sep 1938 in On a street corner while returning from work (walking)./Youngwood, Westmoreland Co., PA[6072]. He married **Frances Elizabeth "Fannie" McArdle**[6072], daughter of Michael McArdle and Catherine. She was born May 1881 in Upper Tyrone Twp., Fayette Co., PA[6072], and died 28 Aug 1956 in Silver Spring, Montgomery Co., MD[6072].

Notes for Harry Christner Weimer:
Harry married Frances E. McArdle born 1879 died Aug 28 1956. Buried with Harry.

More About Harry Christner Weimer:
Burial: St.John Catholic Cemetery, Scottdale, Westmoreland Co., PA[6072]
Occupation: 1938, Conductor on Pennsylvania Railroad/[6072]
Residence: 1930, Youngwood, Westmoreland, PA[6073]

More About Frances Elizabeth "Fannie" McArdle:
Residence: 1947, Washington DC[6074]

Children of Harry Weimer and Frances McArdle are:
    3779   i.   Weimer96[6074], born in Youngwood, Westmoreland Co., PA[6074]; died Bef. 1910[6074].
    3780   ii.   Mary Catherine Weimer[6074], born 1910 in Youngwood, Westmoreland Co., PA[6074].

              More About Mary Catherine Weimer:
              Residence: 1938, Youngwood, Westmoreland Co., PA[6074]

1734. Cain C.[8] Weimer (Mary[7] Christner, Cain[6], John[5], Peter[4], Johannes John Hans[3], Christian[2], Christen[1]) was born 10 Nov 1876 in Connellsville, Fayette Co., PA, and died 07 Sep 1945 in Lutheran Hospital/Fort Wayne, Allen Co., IN[6075]. He married **Florence Adella Hill**[6075] 11 Jun 1903 in Pleasant Twp., Wabash Co., IN[6075]. She was born 06 Nov 1877 in IN[6075], and died 18 Jun 1960 in Wabash, Wabash Co., IN[6075].

Notes for Cain C. Weimer:
Cain married Florence Adella Hill June 11, 1903. Florence born Nov 6, 1877 died June 18, 1960 buried with Cain.

Robert Weimer found this letter. A letter written by Cain Christner in Fayette Co. PA. to his grandson Cain Weimer in Wabash Co. Indiana, Circa November 1 1905. The following are the last four pages. I don't know what happened to the first four pages.

Well you wish to know about that little anvil indeed Cain if I had it yet I would make present to you if you wish to have itbut it went with the rest of my things I had to sell and give em away I give somethings away and some that ware sold dident fetch much   our kitchen stove with eleven joints of stove pipe on it fetcht 75 cents   the heating stove in the room also eleven joints pipe on it fetcht 100 my Buggy fetcht 100 my two horse waggon with one wheel broke down fetcht a quarter dollar four waggon wheels that your pap filled them before he went to Kansas the first time he filld them for Sol Schaffer I got them of Sol he had got the howns and axels put in his other waggon then I got thee wheels of him I allowed him twelve dollars for the wheels well the fetcht 20 cents thats the way most of the things went except the cow and the mare the fetcht all the wer worth and hay fetcht 11 dollars a tun wheat 86 per bushel cow 40 dollars mare 42 corn 40 cents for single bushel them are all the articles that fetcht what the wer worth the other things all went nearly for nothing   a Beauro that i paid 12 doll fetcht 3 dol a Corner Cubbard that i paid 11 dol fetcht 5 doll I give some bedsteads away i give a coalstove without pipe for a quarter dol I have never been to a salr in my life that things went so low the blacksmith tools brought about twelve altogether i dident sell them all on a lump that is the way it goes sometimes well Cain tell uncle Peter Delila Berg is dead and buried she was buried last week   she was within a few weeks eighty one years old if Peter lives until next April he will be eighty if I live until next August i will be seventy nine brother Sam is about seventy six Well Cain as you belong into our family I will give you a short history of our family I was 25 and granmother was 21 when we got married we wer married just one year when we had the first baby well we lived together fifty three years   Raised four children the wer all over eighteen when the got married now we have thirty one granchildren living and four or five of em dead I am only counting the living ones and thirty geat granchildren counting your baby but yours is not the youngest one there is one Younger yet then yours no more at present but remain ever your granfather Cain

Cain married Florence Adella Hill June 11 1903

Florence born Nov 6 1877 died June 18 1960 buried with Cain

Obituary - 20 Sep 1945
The Daily Courier - Connellsville, Fayette Co., PA

CAIN C. Weimer

Wod has been received here of the death of Cain C. Weimer at North Manchester, Ind., on September 14.

He was the son of the late Jacob and Mary Christner Weimer former residents of Indian Head, where he was born. He is survived by his widow, three sons and one daughter.

Obituary says he died 14 Sep 1945.

Birth: 1876
Death: 1945

Children:
Ruth M. Weimer (1905 - 1907)
Mildred L. Weimer (1911 - 1916)
Ruby M. Weimer (1913 - 1915)

Burial: South Pleasant Methodist Church Cemetery, North Manchester, Wabash Co., IN
Find A Grave Memorial# 34451431

More About Cain C. Weimer:
Burial: South Pleasent, Cem
Occupation: Bet. 1898 - 1900, teacher, Lininger Public School, District No. 7/Clear Creek Twp., Huntington Co., IN[6075]
Residence: 01 Apr 1940, North Manchester, Wabash Co., IN[6075]

Notes for Florence Adella Hill:
Birth: 1877
Death: 1960

Children:
Ruth M. Weimer (1905 - 1907)

Mildred L. Weimer (1911 - 1916)
Ruby M. Weimer (1913 - 1915)

Burial: South Pleasant Methodist Church Cemetery, North Manchester, Wabash Co., IN
Find A Grave Memorial# 34451451

More About Florence Adella Hill:
Burial: 23 Jun 1960, South Pleasant Cemetery/Pleasant Twp., Wabash Co., IN[6075]
Residence: 01 Apr 1940, North Manchester, Wabash Co., IN[6075]

Children of Cain Weimer and Florence Hill are:

3781   i.   Meriam Ruth[9] Weimer[6075], born 28 Feb 1905 in Wabash Co., IN[6075]; died 16 Feb 1907 in Wabash Co., IN[6075].

         Notes for Meriam Ruth Weimer:
         Birth: Feb. 28, 1905
         Death: Sep. 16, 1907

         Parents:
         Cain C. Weimer (1876 - 1945)
         Florence Adella Hill Weimer (1877 - 1960)

         Burial: South Pleasant Methodist Church Cemetery, North Manchester, Wabash Co., IN
         Find A Grave Memorial# 34451625

         More About Meriam Ruth Weimer:
         Burial: 18 Sep 1907, South Pleasant Cemetery/Pleasant Twp., Wabash Co., IN[6075]

3782   ii.   Harry Raymond Weimer[6075], born 09 Dec 1906 in Pleasant Twp., Wabash Co., IN[6075]; died 15 Dec 1970 in Hallway of Chemistry Building, Manchester College/North Manchester, Wabash Co., IN[6075].

         More About Harry Raymond Weimer:
         Burial: 18 Dec 1970, South Pleasant Cemetery, Pleasant Twp., Wabash Co., IN[6075]
         Graduation: May 1933, Ph. D. degree (chemistry), Ohio State University/Columbus, Franklin Co., Ohio, USA[6075]
         Occupation: Bet. 1945 - 1970, Professor of Chemistry, Department Head, Chairman of Science Division, Manchester College/North Manchester, Wabash Co., IN[6075]
         Residence: 01 Apr 1940, North Manchester, Wabash Co., IN[6075]

3783   iii.   Albert John Weimer[6075], born 05 Oct 1908 in Pleasant Twp., Wabash Co., IN[6075]; died 11 Feb 1996 in Phoenix, Maricopa Co., AZ[6075].

         More About Albert John Weimer:
         Residence: 01 Apr 1940, North Manchester, Wabash Co., IN[6075]

3784   iv.   Mildred Lulu Weimer[6075], born 02 Aug 1911 in Wabash Co., IN[6075]; died 10 Aug 1916 in North Manchester, Wabash Co., IN[6075].

         Notes for Mildred Lulu Weimer:
         Birth: Aug. 2, 1911
         Death: Aug. 10, 1916

         Parents:
         Cain C. Weimer (1876 - 1945)
         Florence Adella Hill Weimer (1877 - 1960)

         Burial: South Pleasant Methodist Church Cemetery, North Manchester, Wabash Co., IN
         Find A Grave Memorial# 34451586

         More About Mildred Lulu Weimer:
         Burial: 11 Aug 1916, South Pleasant Cemetery/Pleasant Twp., Wabash County, IN[6075]

3785   v.   Ruby May Weimer[6075], born 06 Aug 1913 in Wabash Co., IN[6075]; died 06 Feb 1915 in North Manchester, Wabash Co., IN[6075].

More About Ruby May Weimer:
Burial: 08 Feb 1915, South Pleasant Cemetery/Pleasant Twp., Wabash Co., IN[6075]

3786   vi.   Mabel Lois Weimer[6075], born 08 Jun 1916 in North Manchester, Wabash Co., IN[6075]; died 27 May 2008 in Fort Wayne, Allen Co., IN[6075].

More About Mabel Lois Weimer:
Burial: 30 May 2008, Oak Lawn Cemetery/North Manchester, Wabash Co., IN[6075]
Graduation: May 1933, Central High School/North Manchester, Wabash Co., IN[6075]
Residence: 1930, North Manchester, Wabash, Indiana[6075]

1738. Susannah Pearl[8] Weimer (Mary[7] Christner, Cain[6], John[5], Peter[4], Johannes John Hans[3], Christian[2], Christen[1])[6076,6077] was born 14 May 1884 in Connellsville, Fayette Co., PA[6077], and died 20 Sep 1956 in Cheyenne, Laramie Co., WY. She married **Fred Augustus Homewood**[6077] 20 Aug 1902, son of William Homewood and Anna Thomas. He was born 28 Jul 1880 in Luray, KS[6077], and died 23 Mar 1948 in Holtville, Imperial Co., CA[6077].

Notes for Susannah Pearl Weimer:
Susannah married Fred Augustus Homewood Aug 20 1902 in Russel Co., KS
Fred born July 28 1880 died Mar 23, 1948. Fred buried with Susannah.

More About Susannah Pearl Weimer:
Burial: Sep 1956, Lakeview Cemetery, Cheyenne, Laramie Co., Kansas, USA[6078]
Residence: 01 Mar 1905, Lucas, Russell, Kansas[6079,6080]

More About Fred Augustus Homewood:
Residence: 01 Apr 1940, Imperial, California, United States[6081]

Children of Susannah Weimer and Fred Homewood are:
3787   i.   Charles F[9] Homewood[6081], born 1904 in KS[6081].

More About Charles F Homewood:
Residence: 1910, Waldo, Russell, Kansas[6081]

3788   ii.   Mary A Homewood[6081], born 1906 in KS[6081].

More About Mary A Homewood:
Residence: 1930, Age: 24; Marital Status: Married; Relation to Head of House: Wife/Four Jay, Platte, Wyoming[6081]

3789   iii.   Anna Fredonia Homewood[6081], born 08 Jan 1913 in Covert, Osborne, Kansas, United States[6081]; died 12 May 1990 in Tulsa, Tulsa, Oklahoma[6081].

More About Anna Fredonia Homewood:
Residence: 1930, Glendo, Platte, Wyoming[6081]

1760. Reuel Stanley[8] Christner (Winfield Scott[7], Samuel[6], John[5], Peter[4], Johannes John Hans[3], Christian[2], Christen[1])[6082,6082] was born 31 Aug 1878 in Bullskin Twp., Fayette Co., PA[6082], and died 26 Jan 1971 in Uniontown, Fayette Co., PA[6083,6084]. He married **Eliza Jane Kinneer**[6084,6084]. She was born 20 Jul 1880 in Salt Lick, Fayette, PA[6084], and died 29 Oct 1974 in Uniontown, Fayette Co., PA[6084].

Notes for Reuel Stanley Christner:
Some spell it Reuel.

Birth: Aug. 31, 1878
Death: Jan. 26, 1971

Spouse: Eliza J. Kinneer Christner (1880 - 1974)

Children:
Maybelle Marie Christner Wolfe (1907 - 1980)
Ruth M. Christner Blystone (1909 - 1983)

Burial: Greenlick Cemetery, Fayette Co., PA

More About Reuel Stanley Christner:
Member: Church of the Brethren[6085]
Occupation: 1930, Coal Miner[6085]
Residence: 1930, Bullskin Twp., Fayette Co., PA[6086]
Social Security Number: 190-01-2126/[6087]
SSN issued: Connellsville, Fayette Co., PA[6087]

Notes for Eliza Jane Kinneer:
Birth: Jul. 20, 1880
Death: Oct. 29, 1974

Spouse:
Reuel S. Christner (1878 - 1971)

Children:
Maybelle Marie Christner Wolfe (1907 - 1980)
Ruth M. Christner Blystone (1909 - 1983)

Burial: Greenlick Cemetery, Fayette Co., PA

More About Eliza Jane Kinneer:
Member: Uniontown Church of the Brethren[6088,6089]
Residence: 1930, Bullskin Twp., Fayette Co., PA[6090]

Children of Reuel Christner and Eliza Kinneer are:

3790   i.   Hazel Irene[9] Christner[6090,6091], born 1903 in Connellsville, Fayette Co., PA[6092,6093,6094]; died in Uniontown, Fayette Co., PA[6094]. She married Eugene Van Bremer; born Abt. 1894 in Pittsburgh, Allegheny Co., PA[6094].

       More About Hazel Irene Christner:
       Residence: 1974, Uniontown, Fayette Co., PA[6094]

       More About Eugene Van Bremer:
       Residence: 1930, Uniontown, Fayette Co., PA[6094]

3791   ii.   Maybelle Marie Christner, born 23 Jul 1907 in Connellsville, Fayette Co., PA[6095,6096]; died 09 Jun 1980 in Uniontown, Fayette Co., PA[6097]. She married Charles Wolfe; born 1906 in Henry Clay Township, Fayette Co., PA[6098]; died 29 Jul 1984 in Uniontown, Fayette Co., PA.

       More About Maybelle Marie Christner:
       Social Security Number: 189-22-6720/[6099]
       SSN issued: Connellsville, Fayette Co., PA[6099]

       More About Charles Wolfe:
       Burial: Greenlick Cemetery/[6100]
       Member: Church of the Brethren/[6100]
       Residence: 1964, 58 East Wine Street, Uniontown, Fayette Co., Pa.[6100]

3792   iii.   Ruth M. Christner, born 01 Jun 1909 in Connellsville, Fayette Co., PA[6101]; died 21 Feb 1983. She married Gilbert Blystone.

More About Ruth M. Christner:
Social Security Number: 162-16-6221/[6101]
SSN issued: PA[6101]

1761. Earl Weimer[8] Christner (Winfield Scott[7], Samuel[6], John[5], Peter[4], Johannes John Hans[3], Christian[2], Christen[1])[6102,6103,6104,6105] was born 04 Feb 1885 in Fayette Co., PA[6106,6107,6108], and died 07 Dec 1962 in OH[6109,6110]. He married **Ruby Christner**[6111]. She was born 1900[6111].

Notes for Earl Weimer Christner:
SS# 384-07-4111 Iss. MI

More About Earl Weimer Christner:
Residence: 1900, Bullskin Twp., Fayette Co., PA[6112,6113]
Social Security Number: 384-07-4111/[6114]
SSN issued: MI[6114]

More About Ruby Christner:
Residence: 1930, Pittsfield, Washtenaw Co., MI[6115]

Children of Earl Christner and Ruby Christner are:

> 3793   i.   Alice[9] Christner[6115], born 1915[6115].
>
> > More About Alice Christner:
> > Residence: 1930, Pittsfield, Washtenaw Co., MI[6115]
>
> 3794   ii.   Beth E. Christner[6115], born 1917[6115].
>
> > More About Beth E. Christner:
> > Residence: 1930, Pittsfield, Washtenaw Co., MI[6115]

1762. Edith Arlene[8] Christner (Winfield Scott[7], Samuel[6], John[5], Peter[4], Johannes John Hans[3], Christian[2], Christen[1])[6116,6116] was born 10 Mar 1890 in Connellsville, Fayette Co., PA[6116,6117], and died 08 May 1984 in Geneseo, Henry Co., IL[6118]. She married **Arvid Emmet Johnson**[6118] 21 Feb 1912 in Geneseo, Henry Co., IL[6118,6118]. He was born 14 Jul 1886 in Geneseo, Henry Co., IL[6118], and died 25 Sep 1966 in Geneseo, Henry Co., IL[6118,6118,6118].

More About Edith Arlene Christner:
Burial: Abt. 10 May 1984, Oakwood Cemetery, Geneseo, Henry Co., IL[6118]
Residence: 1930, Geneseo, Henry Co., IL[6118]
Social Security Number: 333-40-8430/[6119]
SSN issued: IL[6119]

More About Arvid Emmet Johnson:
Burial: Abt. 28 Aug 1966, Oakwood Cemetery, Geneseo, Henry Co., IL[6120]
Residence: 1942, WWII Draft Registration Card/Geneseo, Henry Co., IL[6120]

Children of Edith Christner and Arvid Johnson are:

> 3795   i.   Harlan[9] Johnson[6120], born 12 Oct 1912 in Geneseo, Henry Co., IL[6120]; died 23 Oct 1912 in Geneseo, Henry Co., IL[6120].
>
> 3796   ii.   Janet Edith Johnson[6120], born 07 Oct 1917 in Geneseo, Henry Co., IL[6120]; died 11 Jun 2011 in Genesis Medical Center, East Rusholme Street/[6120].
>
> > More About Janet Edith Johnson:
> > Residence: 1993, Bettendorf, Scott Co., Iowa, USA[6120]
>
> 3797   iii.   Cyril Arvid Johnson[6120], born 08 Jun 1919 in Geneseo, Henry Co., IL[6120]; died 10 Dec 2003 in Hillcrest

Home/Geneseo, Henry Co., IL[6120].

More About Cyril Arvid Johnson:
Burial: Abt. 13 Dec 2003, Oakwood Cemetery/Geneseo, Henry Co., IL[6120]
Residence: 1930, Geneseo, Henry Co., IL[6120]

1763. Elwyn[8] Christner (Winfield Scott[7], Samuel[6], John[5], Peter[4], Johannes John Hans[3], Christian[2], Christen[1])[6121,6122,6122] was born 14 Feb 1892 in Mt. Olive Cemetery, Bullskin Twp., Fayette Co., PA[6122,6123], and died 12 Mar 1993 in Geneseo, Henry Co., IL[6123]. She married **Carl Frederick Wetterhall**[6124]. He was born Abt. 1885 in IL[6124].

More About Elwyn Christner:
Residence: 1930, Muncie, Delaware Co., IN[6124]
Social Security Number: 385-54-8435/[6125]

More About Carl Frederick Wetterhall:
Residence: 1920, Geneseo, Henry Co., IL[6126]

Children of Elwyn Christner and Carl Wetterhall are:

3798 i. Ruth E.[9] Wetterhall[6126], born 14 Jan 1914 in Geneseo, Henry Co., IL[6126]; died 30 Aug 2008 in Hot Springs Village, Garland Co., AR[6126].

   More About Ruth E. Wetterhall:
   Residence: 1920, Geneseo, Henry Co., IL[6126]

3799 ii. Roy C. Wetterhall[6126], born 21 Feb 1922[6126,6127]; died Nov 1980 in SelfDeathAge: 58/[6127,6128].

   More About Roy C. Wetterhall:
   Residence: 1930, Muncie, Delaware Co., IN[6128]
   Social Security Number: 376-14-8301/[6129]

1782. Mary Marie[8] Bungard (Josiah C.[7], Mahala A.[6] Christner, John[5], Peter[4], Johannes John Hans[3], Christian[2], Christen[1]) was born 14 Jan 1886 in Bullskin Twp., Fayette Co., PA, and died 25 Feb 1965 in Scottdale, Westmoreland Co., PA. She married **Daniel M. Keffer** 18 Jan 1907 in Bullskin Twp., Fayette Co., PA. He was born 07 Feb 1880 in Connellsville, Fayette Co., PA, and died 18 Apr 1942 in Scottdale, Westmoreland Co., PA.

Notes for Mary Marie Bungard:
Memory Card.

Mary Marie KEEFER
Date of birth: January 14, 1886
Date of death: February 25, 1965
Services: Sunday, February 28, 1965
Clergy: Rev. Edwin Alderfer
Rev. James D. Mowrey
Interment: Green Ridge Memorial Park
W. George Barr Funeral Home

More About Mary Marie Bungard:
Burial: Green Ridge Memorial Park, Fayette Co., PA

Notes for Daniel M. Keffer:
Fayette Co., PA newspaper clipping...

DANIEL M. KEEFER, 62 years old, of Scottdale, Star Route, Walnut Hill, was the son of Abram and the late

Susanna Miller Keefer of White Post office.

Beside his father, he leaves his widow, Mrs. Mary Bungard Keefer and the following children: Wilmer, Emory, Meade, Willa, and Ruth, at home; Glenn, Ligonier; Daniel, White Post office, and Charles, St. Mary's. He was a brother of Benjamin, Somerset, R. D.; Jacob and Harry, Wooddale; Grant, Mount Pleasant; William, Masontown; Mrs. Samuel Coffman, Connellsville; Mrs. Harry Craig, Acme; Mrs. Minerva Mull and Mrs. John Grimm, Mount Pleasant, and Mrs. Omar Miller and Mrs. William Coffman, White Post office.

The funeral service will be held at 3 o'clock Wednesday afternoon at the Mennonite Church in charge of Rev. John Horst, pastor of the Mennonite Church, and Rev. W. S. Harr, pastor of the Evangelical Church. Interment will be made in Green Ridge Memorial Park.

More About Daniel M. Keffer:
Burial: Green Ridge Memoral Park, Fayette Co., PA

Children of Mary Bungard and Daniel Keffer are:

3800	i.	Willa[9] Keffer.
3801	ii.	Ligonier Keffer.
3802	iii.	Infant Keffer, born 1907; died 1907.
3803	iv.	Wilmer Keffer, born 04 Feb 1910.
3804	v.	Oscar Lloyd Keffer, born 15 Sep 1911; died 08 Oct 1913.
3805	vi.	Josiah Glenn Keffer, born 12 Oct 1912. He married Margaret Tosh; born 01 Aug 1916; died 13 Oct 1938.
3806	vii.	Daniel Lee Keffer, born 10 Sep 1916 in Kingview, PA; died 16 Jun 1984 in Mt. Pleasant, Westmoreland Co., PA. He married Delrosa Snyder Forrest 16 Aug 1955; born 06 Apr 1921.

More About Daniel Lee Keffer:
Burial: Scottdale Cemetery

3807	viii.	Charles Emerson Keffer, born 03 Mar 1918 in Connellsville, Fayette Co., PA. He married (1) Martha Niterite. He married (2) Lillian (Noch) Wilkins 10 Apr 1946.
3808	ix.	Emory Thaddeus Keffer, born 14 Mar 1920. He married Marjorie June Myers 10 Apr 1946; born 17 Aug 1923.
3809	x.	Meade Wayne Keffer, born 05 Feb 1922. He married Mary Theona Leonard 14 Jul 1950; born 07 Sep 1929.
3810	xi.	Ruth Marie Keffer, born 09 Mar 1928. She married John Ivan Stoner 28 Mar 1947.

1783. Sadie Grace[8] Bungard (Josiah C.[7], Mahala A.[6] Christner, John[5], Peter[4], Johannes John Hans[3], Christian[2], Christen[1]) was born 08 Mar 1890 in Davistown, Fayette Co., PA[6130], and died 12 Jan 1960 in Donegal, Westmoreland Co., PA. She married **Forrest Iven Keslar**[6131] 31 Mar 1909 in Bullskin Twp., Fayette Co., PA. He was born 12 Nov 1890 in Acme, Fayette Co., PA[6132], and died 29 Apr 1955 in Acme, Fayette Co., PA.[6133].

Notes for Sadie Grace Bungard:
Fayette Co., PA newspaper clipping....

MRS. SADIE KESLAR

Mrs. Sadie Grace Keslar, 69, of Donegal, died Tuesday morning in Somerset Community Hospital after a lingering illness. She was born March 8, 1890, at Davistown, a daughter of the late Josiah C. and Susanna B. Wissinger Bungard, and lived in Donegal for the past four years and prior to that in the Acme and White vicinity.

She is survived by nine sons, Carl of White, Morris of Kregaar, Meryl of Graterford, Gilbert of Acme, Ivan of Torrance, Claude and Shelby of Indian Head, Theodore of Standard Shaft and Arden of Donegal; two daughters, Mrs. Clyde (Luella) Anderson of Macungie and Mrs. Gay (Hazel) Chacken of Acme; 28 grandchildren; five great-grandchildren, and three sisters, Mrs. Marie Keefer and Mrs. Emery (Blanche) Flack of Scottdale, Star Route, and Mrs. Harry (Alverda) McGinnis of Greensburg, R. D. 6. Her husband, Forrest I. Keslar, preceded her in death August. 29, 1955 as did a son and a daughter.

The body will be at the Brooks funeral home at Indian Head after 7:30 P.M. today where the funeral will be held at 2 P.M. Saturday. The Rev. Wesly Myers will officiate. Interment will be in Brown Cemetery.

More About Sadie Grace Bungard:
Burial: Brown Cemetery, Saltlick Twp., Fayette Co., PA
Residence: 1930, Saltlick, Fayette, PA[6134]

Notes for Forrest Iven Keslar:
Occupation: Farmer

More About Forrest Iven Keslar:
Burial: Brown Cemetery, Acme, Fayette Co., PA
Residence: 1930, Saltlick, Fayette, PA[6134]

Marriage Notes for Sadie Bungard and Forrest Keslar:
[Geo. White.FTW]

_STATMARRIED

Children of Sadie Bungard and Forrest Keslar are:
  3811   i.   Infant[9] Keslar.
  3812   ii. Carl Welfred Keslar, born 22 Oct 1909 in Connellsville, Fayette Co., PA.
  3813   iii. Luella Irene Keslar[6135], born 02 Dec 1912[6136,6137]. She married Clyde Anderson.

            More About Luella Irene Keslar:
            Residence: 1930, Saltlick, Fayette, PA[6138]

  3814   iv. Morris Woodrow Keslar, born 20 Dec 1913; died 04 Jun 1989.
  3815   v.   Hazel Catherine Keslar, born 07 Feb 1914. She married Gay Chacken.
  3816   vi. Gilbert Edmond Keslar, born 28 Jul 1916 in Acme, Fayette Co., PA; died 19 Dec 1985 in Latrobe, Westmoreland Co., PA. He married Mary Kinneer; born 26 Oct 1923; died 19 Dec 1985 in Acme, Fayette Co., PA.

            Notes for Gilbert Edmond Keslar:
            Obituary: Fayette Co., PA newspaper clipping

            Gilbert E. Keslar, 69, of Star Route, Acme, died Thursday evening at Latrobe Hospital.

            He was born July 28, 1916 at Acme, a son of the late Forrest and Sadie Bungard Keslar.

            He was a resident of Acme all his life. He was a former employee of White Lumber Co., with more than 40 years service. He was also a member of Calvary United Methodist Church, Salt Lick township.

            Surviving are his wife, Mary K. Kinneer Keslar; a son, Blaine Keslar of Acme, R. D. 1; two daughters, Mrs. Jack (Claudia) Terhorst of Acme, R. D. 1, and Amy Keslar, at home; six grandchildren; six brothers, Carl Keslar of White, Morris Keslar of Stahlstown, Claude Keslar of Normalville, Arden Keslar of Donegal, Shelby Keslar of Indian Head and Theodore Keslar; and two sisters, Mrs. Clyde (Luella) Anderson of Emaus and Mrs. Gay (Hazel) Chakan of Acme.

            He was predeceased by an infant son; three brothers, Ivan, Josiah and Meryl Keslar, and an infant sister. (Note: burial was in Brown Cemetery... death date: Dec. 19, 1985)

            More About Gilbert Edmond Keslar:
            Burial: Brown Cemetery, Acme, Fayette Co., PA

  3817   vii. Ivan Harold Keslar, born 14 Feb 1919 in Acme, Fayette Co., PA; died 21 Oct 1963[6139].

            More About Ivan Harold Keslar:
            Burial: Brown Cemetery, Acme, Fayette Co., PA
            Record Change: 14 Jul 2002[6139]

| 3818 | viii. | Claude Laverne Keslar, born 03 May 1921. |
| 3819 | ix. | Josiah Bungard Keslar, born 26 Oct 1923 in Connellsville, Fayette Co., PA; died 18 Mar 1945 in Iwo Jima. |

> More About Josiah Bungard Keslar:
> Record Change: 14 Jul 2002[6139]

+	3820	x.	Shelby Otis Keslar, born 30 Nov 1925 in Indian Head, Fayette Co., PA; died 29 Nov 2010 in Indian Head, Saltlick Twp., Fayette Co., PA.
	3821	xi.	Vernon Theodore Keslar, born 10 Jun 1928.
	3822	xii.	Arden Fay Keslar, born 19 Sep 1929.

1784. Lula Blanche[8] Bungard (Josiah C.[7], Mahala A.[6] Christner, John[5], Peter[4], Johannes John Hans[3], Christian[2], Christen[1]) was born 25 Sep 1891 in Bullskin Twp., Fayette Co., PA, and died 22 Dec 1969. She married **Emery C. Flack** 24 Sep 1914 in Bullskin Twp., Fayette Co., PA. He was born 08 Dec 1892 in McKeesport, Allegheney Co., PA, PA, and died 09 Aug 1972 in Scottdale, Westmoreland Co., PA.

Notes for Lula Blanche Bungard:
Memory Card.

Blanche L. Flack
Date of birth: September 25, 1891
Date of death: December 22, 1969
Services: Wednesday, December 24, 1969
Clergy: Rev. John E. Wood
Interment: Eutsey Cemetery
Brooks Funeral Service

More About Lula Blanche Bungard:
Burial: Eutsey Cemetery, White, Saltlick Twp., Fayette Co., PA

Notes for Emery C. Flack:
Notes for EMERY C. Flack:

A Letter from Velma Cuppett in 1990:
"I'm sending a page of some of my interest of the Bungards. I am no relation as I know of to Bungards only by marriage to Blanche & Emory's nephew."
JACOB Flack b: 7/31/1860 d. 11/21/1919
m. Dorothea A. TEDROW b: 6/12/1860 d. 2/6/1936.
5 children:
l. Homer Flack   b. 8/5/1883 d. 1/21/1958
m. Elma ECHARD b. 6/16/1889 d. 5/16/1936.
Four sons:
a. Sherman Flack m. Susan Snyder
b. Eugene Flack b. 9/14/1910 d. 1/27/1967
m. VELMA White b. 8/16/1912, m.2nd Bruce CUPPETT, b. 10/31/1906.
c. Gerald Flack m. Grace Delgross
d. Jesse R. Flack m. Emma Lou Myers
2. Phillip Flack b. 4/4/1891 d. 7/13/1962
m. Luzetta Coffman
3. Stella Flack b. 9/12/1886 d. 1985 aged 99yrs
m. Jesse ECHARD b. 6/30/1883 d. 1930
4. Russell Flack b. 5/26/1889 d.____
m. Hattie White b. 7/18/1884 d. 11/11/1960
5. EMERY Flack b. 12/8/92 d. 8/9/1972
m. BLANCHE BUNGARD b. 8/25/1892 d. 12/22/1969

no issue.

More About Emery C. Flack:
Burial: Eutsey Cemetery, White, Saltlick Twp., Fayette Co., PA
Social Security: 198-18-1972 PA

Child of Lula Bungard and Emery Flack is:
    3823   i.   Infant[9] Flack, born 17 Jun 1919; died 17 Jun 1919.

                More About Infant Flack:
                Burial: Eutsey Cemetery, White, Saltlick Twp., Fayette Co., PA

1785. Alverda M.[8] Bungard (Josiah C.[7], Mahala A.[6] Christner, John[5], Peter[4], Johannes John Hans[3], Christian[2], Christen[1]) was born 18 Jan 1893 in Bullskin Twp., Fayette Co., PA, and died Dec 1981 in Greensburg, Westmoreland Co., PA. She married **Harry McGinnis**. He was born 11 Nov 1888, and died 15 Nov 1975 in Jeanette, Westmoreland Co., PA.

More About Alverda M. Bungard:
Social Security: 162-50-5743 PA

Children of Alverda Bungard and Harry McGinnis are:
    3824   i.   Dorothy Suzannah[9] McGinnis, born 02 Nov 1913. She married Albert Gettemy.
    3825   ii.   Gladys Catherine McGinnis, born 19 Oct 1915. She married Glen McClain.
    3826   iii.   Edwin Albert McGinnis, born 27 Apr 1918.
    3827   iv.   Blanche Elizabeth McGinnis, born 08 May 1920. She married Seybert.
    3828   v.   Eugene Alvin McGinnis, born 09 Dec 1927; died 15 Feb 1929.
    3829   vi.   Ross Franklin McGinnis, born 16 Dec 1932.
    3830   vii.   Cora Alsetta McGinnis, born 08 Apr 1933; died 27 Jun 1944.

1791. Clyde B.[8] Kalp (Malinda[7] Bungard, Mahala A.[6] Christner, John[5], Peter[4], Johannes John Hans[3], Christian[2], Christen[1]) was born May 1896 in Bullskin Twp., Fayette Co., PA, and died 1970 in Mt. Pleasant Twp., Washington Co., PA. He married **(1) Goldie M. Welsh**. She was born Abt. 1897. He married **(2) Ethen N. Miller**.

Child of Clyde Kalp and Goldie Welsh is:
    3831   i.   Robert[9] Kalp, born 1917.

1809. Mary[8] Trump (Sophia[7] Bungard, Mahala A.[6] Christner, John[5], Peter[4], Johannes John Hans[3], Christian[2], Christen[1]) was born 25 Nov 1887 in Bullskin Twp., Fayette Co., PA, and died 11 Dec 1986 in North Huntingdon, PA. She married **Wesley J. Fritz**.

Notes for Mary Trump:
Fayette Co., PA Newspaper Clippings....

MARY FRITZ

Mary Trump Fritz, 99, of North Huntingdon, died Thursday, Dec. 11, 1986. She was born Nov. 4, 1904 in Mill Run, a daughter of the late Harry and Sophia Bungard Trump.

She was preceded in death by her husband, Wesley J. Fritz; a daughter, Helen Whetsel; two grandchildren; seven brothers; and three sisters.

She is survived by a daughter, Alverta G. Coffman of North Huntingdon; a granddaughter, Jill Coffman with whom she resided and three other grandchildren; four great-grandchildren; one great-great grandchild; and a brother Ralph Trump of Oak Hill, FL.

A memorial service was held in the First Presbyterian Church of Irwin, with the Dr. Larry A. Dunster officiating. Burial followed in Glade Cemetery, Somerset Co.. Those wishing may contribute to the First Presbyterian Church of Irwin Memorial Fund, William Snyder Funeral Home, 521 Main St., Irwin, in charge of arrangements.

More About Mary Trump:
Burial: Glade Cemetery, Somerset Co., PA

Children of Mary Trump and Wesley Fritz are:
 3832 i. Alverta G.[9] Fritz. She married Coffman.
 3833 ii. Helen Fritz. She married Whetsel.

1810. Ralph V.[8] Trump (Sophia[7] Bungard, Mahala A.[6] Christner, John[5], Peter[4], Johannes John Hans[3], Christian[2], Christen[1]) was born Abt. 1906 in S. Connellsville, Fayette Co., PA, and died 06 Dec 1986 in Portage Lakes, OH. He married **(1) Adelia Soisson**. He married **(2) Alverda Shaffer**. He married **(3) Mary**.

Notes for Ralph V. Trump:
Obituary: Clippng from Fayette Co., PA Newspapers

RALPH V. TRUMP

Ralph Trump, 80 of Akron, OH formerly of South Connellsville, died Dec. 26 (1986). He was born in South Connellsville, a son of the late Henry and Sophia Bungard Trump.

Surviving are his wife, Mary; a daughter, Doris Tennant of Akron, OH; six grandchildren, and nine great-grandchildren.

He was the last surviving member of his immediate family, being predeceased by his first wife, Alverta Shaffer Trump; his second wife, Adelia Soisson Trump; a son, Gilbert; seven brothers, Clarence, Charles, Earl, Samuel, Elmer, Carl and Arthur Trump, and four sisters, Mary Fritz, Cora Lee, Hazel Guard and Helen Collins.

Burial was in Akron, Ohio. (Buried Greenlawn Cemetery, Akron, OH)

Ohio Newspaper clipping..
PORTAGE LAKES

Ralph V. Trump, 80, passed away Dec. 26. A resident of Portage Lakes for 50 years he worked at PPG Industries for over 40 years. He was an active member of the First Baptist Church.

Mr. Trump is survived by wife, Mary, daughter and son-in-law, Doris and Bob Tennant of Akron; daughter-in-law, Joanne Trump of FL; six grandchildren; and nine great-grandchildren.

Funeral services Tuesday, 11 A.M. at First Baptist Church, Rev. William Malanowski and Rev. Harold officiating. Burial Greenlawn Cemetery. Visitation Monday, 2 to 4 and 7 to 9 P.M., at the funeral home and one hour prior to services at the Church. (Campfield-Hickman, Barberton.)

More About Ralph V. Trump:
Burial: Greelawn Cemetery, Akron, OH
Fact 1: See Note Page

Children of Ralph Trump and Alverda Shaffer are:
 3834 i. Gilbert[9] Trump, died Bef. Dec 1986. He married Joanne.
 3835 ii. Doris Trump. She married Robert Tennant.

1817. Grace[8] Underwood (Alice[7] Bungard, Mahala A.[6] Christner, John[5], Peter[4], Johannes John Hans[3], Christian[2], Christen[1]) was born 14 Apr 1909 in Mt. Pleasant Twp., Westmoreland Co., PA, and died 23 Feb 1988 in Mt. Pleasant Twp., Westmoreland Co., PA. She married **William Earl Bungard** Bet. 1923 - 1946. He was born 09 Oct 1904 in Westmoreland Co. , PA, and died 25 Nov 1954 in Mt. Pleasant Twp., Westmoreland Co., PA.

Notes for Grace Underwood:
Fayette Co., PA Newspaper clippings

FUNERALS: BUNGARD - Mrs. Grace I. Bungard of Spring Garden Mobil Home Court, Mount Pleasant, died Tuesday, February. 23, 1988. Friends will be received at Eugene G. Saloom Funeral Home, Main St., Mount Pleasant, today from 7 to 9 P.M., where services will be held at 1 P.M. Friday with the Rev. Durward Hayes officiating. Interment will follow in Mount Pleasant Cemetery.

OBITUARIES - MRS. GRACE I. BUNGARD

Mrs. Grace I. Bungard, 78, of Spring Garden Mobile Home Court, Mount Pleasant, died Tuesday evening at her home. She was born April 14, 1909 in Mount Pleasant, daughter of the late James and Alice Bungard Underwood.

Surviving are five sons, Walter, Ray, and Richard Bungard all of Mount Pleasant, Norman Bungard of Southwest and William Bungard of Scottdale; four daughters, Mrs. Darrell (FLorence) Thomas, Mrs. William (Hazel) Tempest, both of Mount Pleasant, Mrs. Michael (Janet) Garchar of Scottdale and Doris Shrum of York, Pa.; 37 grandchildren; 28 great-grandchildren; one brother, James Underwood of Scottdale, and one sister, Mrs. Elsie Shogan of Swissvale.

She was predeceased by her husband, William Bungard; one son Robert Bungard; three daughters, Kathryn, Zella, and Nancy Bungard; two brothers, Jesse and Charles Underwood, and one sister, Mrs. Edna Cramer.

More About Grace Underwood:
Burial: Mt. Pleasant Cemetery, Mt. Pleasant, PA[6140]
Fact 1: See Note Page
Social Security Number: 163-24-4354/[6141]
SSN issued: Connellsville, Fayette Co., PA[6141]

More About William Earl Bungard:
Burial: Mt. Pleasant Cemetery, Mt. Pleasant Twp., Westmoreland Co., PA
Member: American Flint Glass Workers Union #597 and the Mount Joy Church of the Brethren/[6142]
Occupation: Employed at Bryce Brothers Glass/[6142]
Social Security Number: 168-22-0538/[6143]
SSN issued: Connellsville, Fayette Co., PA[6143]

Children of Grace Underwood and William Bungard are:
    3836   i.   Ray[9] Bungard. He married Arlene O. Harper; died 25 Nov 2003 in Allegheny General Hospital, Pittsburgh, Allegheny Co., PA.

                        Notes for Arlene O. Harper:
                        Obituary: Arlene O. HARPER - Herald Standard Newspaper- Sunday, 11/30/2003

                        Arlene O. HARPER Bungard, 74, of Mount Pleasant, PA died Tuesday, November 25, 2003 in Allegheny General Hospital, Pittsburgh, PA.

                        She is survived by her husband, Ray E. BUNGARD; children: Edward BUNGARD, of White Oak, Pa., Kenneth BUNGARD of Mount Pleasant, PA, Mrs. Orrin (Carol) Ritenour, of Mount Pleasant, PA, Mrs. William (Joyce) Gower of Scottdale, PA, Mrs. Jeffrey (Bonnie) Tucker of Bridgeton, NC and Mrs. Edward (Edith) Luckas of Greensburg, PA; five grandchildren and nine great-grandchildren.

                        Arrangements were under direction of the Eugene G. Saloom Funeral Home Inc., 730 West Main Street, Mount Pleasant, PA.

3837   ii.   Kathryn Bungard, born in Died young; died Bef. 1954[6144].

More About Kathryn Bungard:
Fact1: Died young.[6144]

3838   iii.   Zella Bungard, born in Died young; died Bef. 1954[6144].

More About Zella Bungard:
Fact1: Died young.[6144]

3839   iv.   Nancy Bungard, born in Died young.
3840   v.   Norman Bungard. He married Betty Sheets.
3841   vi.   William Bungard. He married Barbara Rhodes.
3842   vii.   Florence Bungard. She married Darrell Thomas.
3843   viii.   Hazel Bungard. She married William Tempest.
3844   ix.   Janet Bungard. She married Michael Garchar.
3845   x.   Doris Bungard. She married Larry Carlan.
3846   xi.   Robert Bungard Sr.[6144], born 09 Jun 1927; died 03 Jun 1982 in Stahlstown, PA. He married Nina Thomas; died Aft. 1982.

More About Robert Bungard Sr.:
Residence: 1954, Mt Pleasant, Westmoreland Co., PA[6144]

+ 3847   xii.   Walter Bungard, born 06 Jun 1931 in East Huntingdon Twp., Westmoreland Co., PA; died 12 Oct 1998 in Greensburg, Westmoreland Co., PA.
+ 3848   xiii.   Richard Bungard, born 11 May 1936 in Mt. Pleasant, Westmoreland Co., PA; died 22 Jan 1999 in Mt. Pleasant, Westmoreland Co., PA.

1823. Cyrus John[8] Christner (Samuel E.[7], Cyrus John[6], John[5], Peter[4], Johannes John Hans[3], Christian[2], Christen[1])[6145] was born 23 Feb 1904 in Fayette Co., PA[6145], and died 05 Sep 1980 in Scottdale, Westmoreland Co., PA[6145]. He married **Elizabeth Battenfield**[6145] 21 Aug 1929 in Reformed Church of Greensburg, Westmoreland Co., PA[6145]. She was born 1907 in Scottdale, Westmoreland Co., PA[6145], and died in Scottdale, Westmoreland Co., PA[6145].

Notes for Cyrus John Christner:
Birth: 1904
Death: 1980

Burial: Scottdale Cemetery, Scottdale, Westmoreland Co., PA
Find A Grave Memorial# 102435957

More About Cyrus John Christner:
Residence: 1910, Scottdale Ward 1, Westmoreland Co, PA[6146]
Social Security Number: 173-18-1894/[6147]
SSN issued: Connellsville, Fayette Co., PA[6147]

Notes for Elizabeth Battenfield:
Birth: 1907
Death: 1997

Burial: Scottdale Cemetery, Scottdale, Westmoreland Co., PA
Find A Grave Memorial# 102435992

Child of Cyrus Christner and Elizabeth Battenfield is:
3849   i.   Robert[9] Christner[6148], died in Connellsville, Fayette Co., PA[6148].

1824. Samuel J.[8] Christner (Samuel E.[7], Cyrus John[6], John[5], Peter[4], Johannes John Hans[3], Christian[2],

Christen[1]) was born 23 Feb 1904[6149,6150], and died 05 Sep 1980 in Scottdale, Westmoreland Co., PA[6151]. He married **Elizabeth Battenfield**[6152] in Reformed Church of Greensburg, Westmoreland Co., PA[6152]. She was born 1907 in Scottdale, Westmoreland Co., PA[6152], and died in Scottdale, Westmoreland Co., PA[6152].

More About Samuel J. Christner:
Residence: 1910, Scottdale Ward 1, Westmoreland Co, PA[6153]
Social Security Number: 173-18-1894/[6154]
SSN issued: PA[6154]

Notes for Elizabeth Battenfield:
Birth: 1907
Death: 1997

Burial: Scottdale Cemetery, Scottdale, Westmoreland Co., PA
Find A Grave Memorial# 102435992

Child of Samuel Christner and Elizabeth Battenfield is:
  3850   i.   John Samuel[9] Christner[6155], died in Mt Pleasant, Westmoreland Co., PA[6155].

            More About John Samuel Christner:
            Graduated: Indiana State Teachers College, and attended Wisconsin State College at Milwaukee, Wisconsin and the University of Pittsburgh[6155]
            Occupation: Teaches at Scottdale High School[6155]

1832. Clayton Otis[8] Christner (Amos D.[7], Jacob G.[6], John[5], Peter[4], Johannes John Hans[3], Christian[2], Christen[1])[6156] was born 13 Dec 1889 in Fayette, PA[6157,6158,6159,6160], and died 1942. He married **Myrtle E. Griffin**[6161]. She was born 1891 in PA[6161], and died 1965.

More About Clayton Otis Christner:
Burial: Mt.Joy
Residence: 1900, Mount Pleasant Ward 3, Westmoreland Co., PA[6162]

More About Myrtle E. Griffin:
Residence: 1930, Mt. Pleasant, Westmoreland Co., PA[6163]

Children of Clayton Christner and Myrtle Griffin are:
  3851   i.   Nevin Jacob[9] Christner[6163], born 13 Nov 1910 in PA[6163]; died 25 Sep 1966 in Winter Park, Orange Co., FL[6163].

            More About Nevin Jacob Christner:
            Residence: 1920, Mt. Pleasant, Westmoreland Co., PA[6163]

  3852   ii.   Dwane Christner[6163], born Abt. 1919 in PA[6163]; died Mar 1987 in Orlando, Orange Co., FL[6163].

            More About Dwane Christner:
            Residence: 1920, Mt. Pleasant, Westmoreland Co., PA[6163]

1833. Curtis H.[8] Christner (Amos D.[7], Jacob G.[6], John[5], Peter[4], Johannes John Hans[3], Christian[2], Christen[1])[6164,6165] was born 29 Dec 1891 in Connellsville, Fayette Co., PA[6166,6167,6168]. He married **Lizzie I. Pore**[6169,6170]. She was born 26 Mar 1888 in Connellsville, Fayette Co., PA[6171,6172,6173], and died Oct 1973 in Mt. Pleasant, Westmoreland Co., PA[6174,6175].

More About Curtis H. Christner:
Residence: 1900, Mount Pleasant Ward 3, Westmoreland Co., PA[6176]

Notes for Lizzie I. Pore:
Birth: 1888

Death: 1973

Note: Same stone as Curtis H. Christner

Burial: Saint Johns Union Cemetery, Mount Pleasant, Westmoreland Co., PA

More About Lizzie I. Pore:
Residence: 1930, Mt. Pleasant, Westmoreland Co., PA[6177]
Social Security Number: 159-42-5086/[6178]
SSN issued: PA[6178]

Children of Curtis Christner and Lizzie Pore are:
    3853   i.   Mildred[9] Christner[6179], born 04 Dec 1911 in Connellsville, Fayette Co., PA[6179]; died 18 Apr 2005 in Youngstown, Mahoning Co., OH[6179].

                 More About Mildred Christner:
                 Residence: 1930, Mt. Pleasant, Westmoreland Co., PA[6179,6180]

+   3854   ii. Melvin P. Christner, born 04 Dec 1911 in Connellsville, Fayette Co., PA; died Jan 1987 in Mt. Pleasant, Westmoreland Co., PA.
    3855   iii. Howard Jacob Christner[6181], born 24 Jan 1914 in Mt. Pleasant, Westmoreland Co., PA[6181]; died 12 Nov 1997 in Youngstown, Mahoning Co., OH[6181].

                 More About Howard Jacob Christner:
                 Residence: 1993, Austintown, OH[6181]

1838. Grace Alverta[8] Christner (Norman B.[7], Samuel J. "Matlick Sam"[6], Joseph[5], Joseph "Zep"[4], Johannes John Hans[3], Christian[2], Christen[1])[6182,6183] was born Apr 1888 in Somerset Co., PA[6184], and died in Sand Patch, Larimer Twp., Somerset Co., PA[6185]. She married **John Calvin Lint** 23 Dec 1906 in Cumberland, Allegany Co., MD[6185], son of Noah Lint and Sarah Glotfelty. He was born 22 Jun 1875 in Sand Patch, Larimer Twp., Somerset Co., PA[6185], and died 18 Oct 1941 in Sand Patch, Larimer Twp., Somerset Co., PA[6185].

More About Grace Alverta Christner:
Children: four (4)[6185]
Married: once[6185]
Occupation: housewife[6185]
Religion: German Reformed Church[6185]
Residence: 1930, Meyersdale, Somerset Co., PA[6186]

Notes for John Calvin Lint:

More About John Calvin Lint:
Children: four (4)[6187]
Religion: German Reformed Lutheran Church[6187]

Children of Grace Christner and John Lint are:
    3856   i.   Mary Leora[9] Lint, born 19 Jul 1907; died 24 Jan 1991 in Brøderbund Family Archive #110, Vol. 1, Ed. 3, Social Security Records: U.S., SS Death Benefit Records, Surnames Beginning with B, Date of Import: 27 Mar 1996, Internal Ref. #1.111.3.24422.88/Summit Twp., Somerset Co., PA[6187].

                 More About Mary Leora Lint:
                 Buried at: Meyersdale, PA (?)[6187]
                 Children: unknown[6187]
                 Coded sources: 45 (1037), 5, 26[6187]
                 Last entry date: 26 Mar 1996 by GBL[6187]
                 Married: at least once[6187]
                 Military service: female N/female N/A[6187]

Occupation: housewife[6187]
Point of Contact: Barbara Walukas[6187]
Religion: Lutheran[6187]
Social Security: 184-18-3742[6187]
Tombstone: unknown[6187]

3857   ii.   Paul W. Lint[6187], born 24 Apr 1913 in Brøderbund Family Archive #110, Vol. 1, Ed. 3, Social Security Records: U.S., SS Death Benefit Records, Surnames Beginning with L, Date of Import: 24 Mar 1996, Internal Ref. #1.111.3.127743.6/Sand Patch, Larimer Twp., Somerset Co., PA[6187]; died Jul 1959 in Brøderbund Family Archive #110, Vol. 1, Ed. 3, Social Security Records: U.S., SS Death Benefit Records, Surnames Beginning with L, Date of Import: 24 Mar 1996, Internal Ref. #1.111.3.127743.6/Cumberland, Allegany co., MD (?)[6187].

More About Paul W. Lint:
Children: two (2)[6187]
Coded sources: 1, 7 (J.N.Lint), 2 (EL), 5, 3, 11[6187]
Last entry date: 31 Dec 1997 by GBL[6187]
Married: at least once[6187]
Military service: unknown[6187]
Occupation: unknown[6187]
Religion: unknown[6187]
Social Security: 194-01-7845[6187]

3858   iii.   Kenneth E. Lint[6187], born 04 Aug 1918 in Brøderbund Family Archive #110, Vol. 1, Ed. 3, Social Security Records: U.S., SS Death Benefit Records, Surnames Beginning with L, Date of Import: 24 Mar 1996, Internal Ref. #1.111.3.127742.119/Sand Patch, Larimer Twp., Somerset Co., PA[6187]; died 17 Feb 1991 in Brøderbund Family Archive #110, Vol. 1, Ed. 3, Social Security Records: U.S., SS Death Benefit Records, Surnames Beginning with L, Date of Import: 24 Mar 1996, Internal Ref. #1.111.3.127742.119/Meyersdale Borough, Somerset co., PA (?)[6187].

More About Kenneth E. Lint:
Buried at: Meyersdale, Somerset co., PA (?)[6187]
Children: at least three (3)[6187]
Coded sources: 1, 7 (J.N.Lint), 2 (EL), 5, 3, 11[6187]
Last entry date: 31 Dec 1997 by GBL[6187]
Married: at least once[6187]
Military service: unknown[6187]
Occupation: unknown[6187]
Religion: unknown[6187]
Social Security: 209-03-4052[6187]
Tombstone: unknown[6187]

3859   iv.   Robert Lint[6187], born 1923 in Brøderbund Family Archive #110, Vol. 1, Ed. 3, Social Security Records: U.S., SS Death Benefit Records, Surnames Beginning with L, Date of Import: 24 Mar 1996, Internal Ref. #1.111.3.127743.34/Sand Patch, Larimer Twp., Somerset Co., PA[6187].

More About Robert Lint:
Coded sources: 1, 7 (John Noah Lint), 2 (Ellen Lint), 5[6187]
Last entry date: 20 Mar 1997 by GBL[6187]

1841. Ada O.[8] Christner (Norman B.[7], Samuel J. "Matlick Sam"[6], Joseph[5], Joseph "Zep"[4], Johannes John Hans[3], Christian[2], Christen[1])[6188,6189,6190] was born 08 Mar 1892 in Somerset Co., PA[6191,6192], and died 23 Mar 1958[6192,6193,6194,6195,6196]. She married **Ernest Bodes**[6197,6198] 1915 in Somerset, Somerset Co., PA[6198]. He was born 17 Oct 1888 in Elk Lick Twp, Somerset Co., PA[6199], and died 12 Mar 1959[6199,6200].

More About Ada O. Christner:
Residence: 1900, Greenville Township, Somerset Co., PA[6201,6202]

More About Ernest Bodes:
Residence: 1910, Elk Lick, Somerset Co., PA[6203]

Children of Ada Christner and Ernest Bodes are:

3860   i.   Helen Viola[9] Bodes[6203], born 14 Jul 1916 in St. Paul[6203]; died 28 Feb 2003 in bur 04 Mar 2003/Bedford, Bedford Co., PA[6203].

More About Helen Viola Bodes:
Residence: 1930, Elk Lick, Somerset Co., PA[6203]

3861   ii.   Donald Eugene Bodes[6203], born 21 Dec 1918 in Connellsville, Fayette Co., PA[6203]; died 12 Jun 1990 in Richland Co., OH[6203].

More About Donald Eugene Bodes:
Residence: 1920, Elk Lick, Somerset, PA[6204]

3862   iii.   Eleanor Mae Bodes[6204], born 23 Oct 1924 in Connellsville, Fayette Co., PA[6204]; died 13 Dec 1993 in High Point, Guilford Co., NC[6204].

More About Eleanor Mae Bodes:
Residence: 1930, Elk Lick, Somerset, PA[6204]

1847. Sadie Margaret[8] Christner (Norman B.[7], Samuel J. "Matlick Sam"[6], Joseph[5], Joseph "Zep"[4], Johannes John Hans[3], Christian[2], Christen[1])[6205] was born Mar 1900 in Somerset Co., PA[6205]. She married **Norman Edward Seibert**[6206]. He was born 21 Jan 1889 in PA[6206].

Notes for Sadie Margaret Christner:
Maybe Sadie H.

More About Sadie Margaret Christner:
Residence: 1920, Summit Twp., Somerset Co., PA[6207]

More About Norman Edward Seibert:
Residence: 1910, Summit, Somerset Co., PA[6208]

Child of Sadie Christner and Norman Seibert is:

3863   i.   Charles E[9] Seibert[6208], born 10 Jun 1924[6208]; died 30 Sep 2009 in Chandler, Maricopa, Arizona[6208].

More About Charles E Seibert:
Residence: PA[6208]

1850. Ruth Olive[8] Christner (Norman B.[7], Samuel J. "Matlick Sam"[6], Joseph[5], Joseph "Zep"[4], Johannes John Hans[3], Christian[2], Christen[1]) was born 03 Nov 1902 in Greenville Twp, PA, and died 07 Mar 1963. She married **Sherman G. Gindlesperger** 14 Jun 1924 in Oakland, Garrett Co., MD. He was born 28 May 1899 in Berlin, PA Somerset Co., and died Apr 1976.

Children of Ruth Christner and Sherman Gindlesperger are:

3864   i.   Deanna June[9] Gindlesperger.
3865   ii.   Dorthy Louise Gindlesperger, born 29 Nov 1925 in Stoyestown, PA.
3866   iii.   Sherman G. Gindlesperger Jr., born 29 Jul 1927 in Stoyestown, PA; died 28 May 1985.

1857. Abbie Mae[8] Bowser (Keturah May[7] Christner, Joseph[6], John[5], Peter[4], Johannes John Hans[3], Christian[2], Christen[1])[6209] was born 10 Jul 1894 in Pittsburgh, Allegheny Co., PA[6209], and died 03 Mar 1972 in Mt Pleasant, Westmoreland Co., PA[6210]. She married **Charles Roy Atkinson**[6210] 1911[6210]. He was born 01 Dec 1886[6210], and died 04 Sep 1963 in Mt Pleasant, Westmoreland Co., PA[6210].

More About Abbie Mae Bowser:
Residence: 1900, Donegal Township, Indian Creek District, Westmoreland Co., PA[6211]

Child of Abbie Bowser and Charles Atkinson is:

3867   i.   Glenn Roy[9] Atkinson[6212], born 02 Aug 1915[6212,6213,6214]; died 26 Jun 1973 in Mt Pleasant, Westmoreland Co., PA[6215].

           Notes for Glenn Roy Atkinson:
           Glenn was a veteran of WWII.

           More About Glenn Roy Atkinson:
           Burial: Mt. Joy cemetery, Mt.Pleasant, Westmoreland Co., PA[6216]
           Social Security Number: 189-14-7294/[6217]

1858. Hazel V.[8] Bowser (Keturah May[7] Christner, Joseph[6], John[5], Peter[4], Johannes John Hans[3], Christian[2], Christen[1])[6218] was born 16 May 1896 in Pittsburgh, Allegheny Co., PA[6218,6219], and died Mar 1978 in Connellsville, Fayette Co., PA[6220,6221]. She married **James Myrl Wilson**[6221]. He was born 21 Jun 1897 in Pittsburgh, Allegheny Co., PA[6221], and died 17 Sep 1988[6221].

More About Hazel V. Bowser:
Residence: 1930, Redstone, Fayette Co., PA[6222,6223]

More About James Myrl Wilson:
Residence: 1930, Redstone, Fayette Co., PA[6223]

Child of Hazel Bowser and James Wilson is:
+   3868   i.   Harold Ross "Barney"[9] Wilson, born 21 Jul 1920 in Wooddale, Bullskin Twp., Fayette Co., PA; died 18 Jul 2010 in Johnstown, Cambria Co., PA.

1861. Mildred Ruth[8] Christner (Frank Homer[7], Joseph[6], John[5], Peter[4], Johannes John Hans[3], Christian[2], Christen[1])[6224,6225] was born 20 Feb 1907 in Wilkinsburg, Allegheny Co., PA[6226], and died 04 Jul 1991 in Dade City, Pasco Co., FL[6226]. She married **Clarence Alexander Nolton**[6227] 27 Apr 1941[6227]. He was born 26 Jan 1895 in Kittanning, Armstrong Co., PA[6227], and died 14 Jul 1979 in Dade City, Pasco Co., FL[6227].

Child of Mildred Christner and Clarence Nolton is:
   3869   i.   Living[9] Nolton[6227].

1869. Albert Moore[8] Newell (Bertha May[7] Christner, Elias[6], Levi[5], Peter[4], Johannes John Hans[3], Christian[2], Christen[1])[6228] was born 15 Sep 1888 in Moyer, Fayette Co, PA[6228], and died 23 May 1941 in Connellsville, Fayette Co., PA[6228]. He married **Jessie Eugenia McCreary** 03 May 1915 in Uniontown, Fayette Co., PA.. She was born 06 May 1892 in Leetsdale, Allegheny Co, PA., and died 18 Dec 1970 in Pensacola FL..

Notes for Albert Moore Newell:
Albert Moore Newell (Bertha May CHRISTNER -2, Elias-1) was born on September 15, 1888 in Moyer, Fayette Co, PA. He appeared on the census on June 21, 1900 in Fayette Co., PA. He appeared on the census on April 10, 1910 in Bullskin Twp., Fayette, PA living with his grandfather Elias Christner. He appeared on the census in 1920 in Bullskin Twp., Fayette Co., PA. He was a Steel Worker in 1930. He appeared on the census in 1930 in Bullskin Twp., Fayette, PA. He was buried in May 1941 in Mt. Olive Cemetery, Fayette Co., PA.

More About Albert Moore Newell:
Burial: May 1941, Mt Olive Cemetery, Fayette, PA[6228]
Census: 1930, Bullskin Twp., Fayette Co., PA[6228]
Marrcert: 03 May 1915[6228]
Occupation: 1930, Steel Worker/[6228]
Residence: 03 May 1915, Moyer, Fayette Co, PA[6228]

Notes for Jessie Eugenia McCreary:
She appeared on the census in 1920 in Bullskin Twp, Fayette Co., PA. She appeared on the census in 1930 in Bullskin Twp., Fayette Co., PA.

Children of Albert Newell and Jessie McCreary are:

3870   i.   Dorothy[9] Newell, born 1916.

        Notes for Dorothy Newell:
        Dorothy Newell was born about 1916 in PA. She appeared on the census in 1920 in Bullskin Twp, Fayette, PA. She appeared on the census in 1930 in Bullskin Twp., Fayette Co., PA.

3871   ii.   Hellen Newell, born Dec 1917.

        Notes for Hellen Newell:
        Hellen Newell was born about December 1917 in PA. She appeared on the census in 1920 in Bullskin Twp., Fayette Co., PA. She appeared on the census in 1930 in Bullskin Twp., FayetteCo., PA.

3872   iii.   James Newell, born 1920.

        Notes for James Newell:
        James A. Newell was born about 1920 in PA. He appeared on the census in 1930 in Bullskin Twp., Fayette Co., PA.

3873   iv.   Frank Holland Newell, born Mar 1922 in Bridgeport Westmoreland PA; died 03 Dec 1943 in De Land Volusia Co. FL..

        Notes for Frank Holland Newell:
        Frank Holland Newell was born in March 1922 in Bridgeport, Westmoreland Co., PA. He appeared on the census in 1930 in Bullskin Twp., Fayette Co., PA. He died on December 3, 1943 in DeLand, Volusia Co., FL. He was buried in Mt. Olive Cemetery, Connellsville, Fayette Co., PA.

        More About Frank Holland Newell:
        Burial: Mt. Olive Cemetery Connellsville Fayette Co. PA.

3874   v.   Robert T. Newell, born 1924 in PA.

        Notes for Robert T. Newell:
        Robert T. Newell was born about 1924 in PA. He appeared on the census in 1930 in Bullskin Twp., Fayette Co., PA.

1870. Olive Pearl[8] Newell (Bertha May[7] Christner, Elias[6], Levi[5], Peter[4], Johannes John Hans[3], Christian[2], Christen[1])[6228,6229] was born 12 Jun 1890 in Moyer, Fayette Co., PA[6230,6231], and died 08 Nov 1914 in Pennsville, Bullskin Twp., Fayette Co., PA[6232]. She married **Frank Hagan Stouffer**[6233] 22 Sep 1913 in Uniontown, Fayette Co., PA. He was born 19 Apr 1891 in Pennsville, Bullskin Twp., Fayette Co., PA[6233], and died 23 Mar 1943 in McKeesport, Allegheny Co, PA[6233].

Notes for Olive Pearl Newell:
Olive Pearl NEWELL (Bertha May CHRISTNER-2, Elias-1) was born on June 12, 1890 in Moyer, Fayette Co., PA. She appeared on the census on June 21, 1900 in Bullskin Twp., Fayette, PA. She appeared on the census on April 20, 1910 in Bullskin Twp, Fayette, PA. She resided in 1913 in Moyer, Fayette Co, PA. She died on November 8, 1914 in Pennsville, Bullskin Township, Fayette, PA. She was buried on November 10, 1914 in Mt. Olive Cemetery, Connellsville, Fayette Co., PA. She was ill with Typhoid fever Oct 1913 - Nov 1914 in Pennsville, Bullskin Twp., Fayette Co., PA. She was a Housewife in Pennsville, Bullskin Twp., Fayette Co., PA. She resided in Pennsville, Bullskin Twp., Fayette Co., PA. She was named after Olive Newell - her aunt on her father's side.

More About Olive Pearl Newell:
Burial: 10 Nov 1914, Mt. Olive Cemetery Connellsville Fayette Co. PA.[6234,6235]
Census: 20 Apr 1910, Bullskin Twp., Fayette Co., PA[6236,6237]
DeathCert: 08 Nov 1914[6238,6239]
Illness: Bet. Oct 1913 - Nov 1914, Typhoid fever/Pennsville, Bullskin Twp., Fayette Co., PA[6240]
Namesake: Olive Newell - her aunt on her father's side/[6240,6241]
Occupation: 20 Apr 1910, servant in a private home/[6242,6243]
Residence: 1900, Bullskin Township, Precinct 1, Fayette, PA[6243,6244]

Notes for Frank Hagan Stouffer:
She was married to Frank Hagan STOUFFER (son of Charles Howard STOUFFER and Sarah Jane FLANIGAN) on September 22, 1913 in Uniontown, Fayette County, PA. Frank Hagan STOUFFER was born on April 19, 1891 in Pennsville, Bullskin Township, Fayette, PA. He appeared on the census on June 18, 1900 in Bullskin Twp, Fayette, PA. He appeared on the census on May 10, 1910 in Bullskin Twp, Fayette, PA. He was a Laborer on January 28, 1920. He appeared on the census on January 28, 1920 in Bullskin Twp, Fayette, PA. He died on March 23, 1943 in McKeesport, Allegheny Co, PA. He was buried on March 26, 1943 in Mt Olive Cemetery, Fayette, PA. He served in the military World War I.

More About Frank Hagan Stouffer:
Burial: 26 Mar 1943, Mt. Olive Cemetery Connellsville Fayette Co. PA.[6245]
Census: 18 Apr 1930, Bullskin Twp., Fayette Co., PA[6245]
Military: [6245]
Obi: 24 Mar 1943, The Daily Courier - Connellsville, Fayette, PA/[6245]
Occupation: 1942, employee of Duquesne Steel Company/Duquesne, Allegheny, PA[6245]
Religion: a member of Pennsville Evangelical Church/[6245]
Residence: Connellsville, Fayette Co., PA[6245]

Child of Olive Newell and Frank Stouffer is:
+   3875   i.   Ray Newell[9] Stouffer, born 05 Dec 1913 in Connellsville, Fayette Co., PA; died 31 Jul 1978 in McKeesport, Allegheny Co., PA.

1875. Ethel[8] Newell (Bertha May[7] Christner, Elias[6], Levi[5], Peter[4], Johannes John Hans[3], Christian[2], Christen[1])[6246] was born 15 Dec 1904 in Connellsville, Fayette Co., PA[6246], and died Mar 1986 in Mather, Greene Co., PA[6246]. She married **Roy E. Flesher** 1922. He was born 05 Jul 1902 in Connellsville, Fayette Co., PA, and died Apr 1966.

Notes for Ethel Newell:
Ethel NEWELL (Bertha May CHRISTNER-2, Elias-1) was born on December 15, 1904 in Fayette Co., PA. She appeared on the census on April 20, 1910 in Bullskin Twp, Fayette, PA. She appeared on the census on January 21, 1920 in Bullskin Twp, Fayette, PA. She resided in 1986 in Mather, Greene Co., PA. She died in March 1986.

She was married to Roy E. Flesher about 1922. Roy E. Flesher was born on July 5, 1902 in PA. He appeared on the census in 1930 in Luzerne Twp., Fayette, PA. He died in April 1966 in Mather, Greene Co, PA. He was a Coal Miner.

More About Ethel Newell:
Census: 21 Jan 1920, Bullskin Twp., Fayette Co., PA[6246]
Residence: 1986, Mather, Greene Co, PA[6246]

Children of Ethel Newell and Roy Flesher are:
     3876   i.   Betty L.[9] Flesher, born 1923.
     3877   ii.   Fern A. Flesher, born 1925.

1876. Florence Gladys[8] Newell (Bertha May[7] Christner, Elias[6], Levi[5], Peter[4], Johannes John Hans[3], Christian[2], Christen[1])[6246] was born 04 Aug 1908 in Connellsville, Fayette Co., PA[6246], and died 21 Feb 1988 in Mather, Greene Co., PA[6246]. She married **Joseph Harshman**. He was born 30 Aug 1903 in Connellsville, Fayette Co., PA, and died 26 Aug 1973 in McKeesport, Allegheny Co., PA.

Notes for Florence Gladys Newell:
Florence Gladys "Gladys" NEWELL (Bertha May CHRISTNER-2, Elias-1) was born on August 4, 1908 in Fayette Co., PA. She appeared on the census on April 20, 1910 in Bullskin Twp., Fayette Co., PA. She appeared on the census on January 21, 1920 in Bullskin Twp., Fayette Co., PA. She died on February 21, 1988 in Mather, Greene Co., PA.

More About Florence Gladys Newell:
Census: 21 Jan 1920, Bullskin Twp., Fayette Co., PA[6246]
Residence: 20 Apr 1910, Bullskin Twp., Fayette Co., PA[6246]
Social Security Number: 164-20-2713/[6246]

Notes for Joseph Harshman:
Florence Newell and Joseph Harshman (son of John Harshman and Frances Oaks) were married on April 22, 1924 in Cumberland, Allegany Co, MD.

Joseph Harshman was born on August 30, 1903 in Connellsville, Fayette Co, PA. He was a president/bus agent of Amalgamated Street Electric Railway and Motor Coach Employees of America, Loc between 1943 and 1956. He died on August 26, 1973 in McKeesport, Allegheny Co, PA. He was buried on August 28, 1973 in Hillgrove Cemetery. He was a Penn Transit driver in PA. He was Christianity - Baptist. He resided 339 Third Street, Mather, PA in Mather, Greene Co., PA. He resided Long Run Road, McKeesport, PA in McKeesport, Allegheny Co., PA.

More About Joseph Harshman:
Burial: 28 Aug 1973, Hillgrove Cemetery

Children of Florence Newell and Joseph Harshman are:
　　3878　　i.　John Lee[9] Harshman, born in Connellsville, Fayette Co., PA. He married (1) Joan Monohan Jul 1950 in NY. He married (2) Rita Jorzick 1965 in Frankfort, Germany.
　　3879　　ii.　Josephine Harshman. She married Robert W. Fawcett 05 Apr 1948 in McKeesport, Allegheny Co., PA.

　　1877. Phoebe[8] Christner (Braden Hurst[7], Elias[6], Levi[5], Peter[4], Johannes John Hans[3], Christian[2], Christen[1])[6247,6248,6249] was born 16 Mar 1903 in Connellsville, Fayette Co., PA[6250,6251,6252], and died Jan 1978 in Connellsville, Fayette Co., PA[6253]. She married **Strickler**.

Notes for Phoebe Christner:
Phoebe Christner (Braden H-2, Elias-1) was born about 1904 in PA. She appeared on the census on January 8, 1920 in Connellsville, Fayette Co, PA. She appeared on the census in 1930 in Connellsville, Fayette Co, PA.

She was married to Strickler between 1920 and 1930 in PA. She was divorced from Strickler between 1920 and 1930 in PA. Phoebe Christner and Strickler had the following children:

Lester Strickler was born about 1925 in PA. He appeared on the census in 1930 in Connellsville, Fayette Co., PA.

More About Phoebe Christner:
Census: 1930, Connellsville, Fayette Co., PA[6253]
Residence: 1930, Connellsville, Fayette, PA[6254]

Child of Phoebe Christner and Strickler is:
　　3880　　i.　Lester[9] Strickler, born 1925.

　　　　　　　Notes for Lester Strickler:
　　　　　　　Phoebe Christner (Braden H-2, Elias-1) was born about 1904 in PA. She appeared on the census on January 8, 1920 in Connellsville, Fayette Co, PA. She appeared on the census in 1930 in Connellsville, Fayette Co, PA.

　　　　　　　She was married to Strickler between 1920 and 1930 in PA. She was divorced from Strickler between 1920 and 1930 in PA. Phoebe Christner and Strickler had the following children:

　　　　　　　Lester STRICKLER was born about 1925 in PA. He appeared on the census in 1930 in Connellsville, Fayette Co, PA.

1894. Richard[8] Christner Sr. (Walter Joseph[7], Charles[6], Levi[5], Peter[4], Johannes John Hans[3], Christian[2], Christen[1])[6255,6256,6257,6258,6259,6260,6261] was born 14 Jun 1910 in Connellsville, Fayette Co., PA[6262,6263,6264,6265], and died Jan 1978 in Kansas City, Jackson Co., MO[6266,6267,6268]. He married **Mabel Marie Ashbaugh**[6268,6269] 05 Dec 1935 in Westmoreland Co., PA[6270]. She was born 31 Aug 1916 in Export, Westmoreland Co., PA[6270,6271], and died 08 Jan 1994 in Kansas City, Jackson Co., MO[6272].

More About Richard Christner Sr.:
Residence: 01 Apr 1940, South Huntingdon, Westmoreland Co., PA[6273]
Social Security Number: 193-01-1330/[6274]
SSN issued: PA[6274]

More About Mabel Marie Ashbaugh:
Race: White/[6275,6276]
Residence: 1920, Delmont, Westmoreland Co., PA[6277]
Social Security Number: 500-70-6009/[6278]
SSN issued: MO[6278]

Child of Richard Christner and Mabel Ashbaugh is:

3881 i. Shirley Irene[9] Christner[6279,6280], born 1937 in Smithton, Westmoreland Co., PA[6281]; died 1939 in Smithton, Westmoreland Co., PA[6281].

    Notes for Shirley Irene Christner:
    Birth: 1937
    Death: 1939

    Burial: Olive Branch Cemetery, Belle Vernon, Westmoreland Co., PA

1895. Glenn R.[8] Christner (Walter Joseph[7], Charles[6], Levi[5], Peter[4], Johannes John Hans[3], Christian[2], Christen[1])[6282,6283,6284,6285] was born 11 Jul 1912 in Connellsville, Fayette Co., PA[6286,6287,6288,6289,6290,6291], and died Feb 1984 in Smithton, Westmoreland Co., PA[6292,6293,6294]. He married **(1) Marjorie Ashbaugh**[6294,6295] 30 May 1942 in Westmoreland Co., PA, USA[6296]. She was born Abt. 1912 in Connellsville, Fayette Co., PA[6296], and died Bef. 1959 in Smithton, Westmoreland Co., PA[6296]. He married **(2) Mary J. Weyandt**[6296] 14 May 1960 in Westmoreland Co., PA, USA[6296]. She was born Abt. 1918 in Greensburg, Westmoreland Co., PA[6296], and died Bef. 1977 in Smithton, Westmoreland Co., PA[6296]. He married **(3) Julia Jubic**[6296] 30 Mar 1978 in Westmoreland Co., PA[6296]. She was born 20 Dec 1919 in Connellsville, Fayette Co., PA[6296], and died 20 Apr 2009 in Greensburg, Westmoreland Co., PA[6296].

Notes for Glenn R. Christner:
Birth: 1912
Death: 1984

Burial: Olive Branch Cemetery, Belle Vernon, Westmoreland Co., PA

More About Glenn R. Christner:
Residence: 01 Apr 1940, South Huntingdon, Westmoreland Co., PA[6297,6298]
Social Security Number: 193-01-1492/[6299]
SSN issued: Connellsville, Fayette Co., PA[6299]

More About Marjorie Ashbaugh:
Residence: 1920, Delmont, Westmoreland Co., PA[6300]

More About Mary J. Weyandt:
Residence: 1920, Salem, Westmoreland, PA[6301]

Notes for Julia Jubic:
Birth: 1919
Death: 2009

Burial: Olive Branch Cemetery, Belle Vernon, Westmoreland Co., PA

Children of Glenn Christner and Marjorie Ashbaugh are:

3882   i.   Elizabeth[9] Christner[6301,6302,6303], born 01 Sep 1935 in Smithton, Westmoreland Co., PA[6304,6305]; died 15 Jun 2007 in Mc Clellandtown, Fayette Co., PA[6306]. She married Robert Raymond Lemley[6307,6308] 01 Nov 1952 in PA[6309]; born 10 Aug 1932 in Van Meter, Westmoreland Co., PA[6309,6310]; died 13 Jan 1997 in Dunbar, Fayette Co., PA[6311].

        Notes for Elizabeth Christner:
        Birth: Sep. 1, 1935
        Death: Jun. 15, 2007

        Burial: Olive Branch Cemetery, Belle Vernon, Westmoreland Co., PA
        Find A Grave Memorial# 86462254

        More About Elizabeth Christner:
        Burial: Belle Vernon, Westmoreland County, PA, USA[6312]

        More About Robert Raymond Lemley:
        Burial: Belle Vernon, Westmoreland County, PA, USA[6312]
        Residence: 01 Apr 1940, Age: 7; Marital Status: Single; Relation to Head of House: Son/Rostraver, Westmoreland, PA, United States[6312]
        Social Security Number: 202-24-3920/[6313]

3883   ii.   Lorraine Christner[6314], born 25 Feb 1938 in Smithton, Westmoreland Co., PA[6314]; died 15 Aug 1996 in Smithton, Westmoreland Co., PA[6314].

3884   iii. Glenn L. Christner Sr[6314], born 24 Nov 1939 in Smithton, Westmoreland Co., PA[6314]; died 17 Dec 1993 in Smithton, Westmoreland Co., PA[6314].

        Notes for Glenn L. Christner Sr:
        Birth: 1939
        Death: 1993

        Burial: Olive Branch Cemetery, Belle Vernon, Westmoreland Co., PA

        More About Glenn L. Christner Sr:
        Social Security Number: 182-30-8170/[6315]
        SSN issued: Connellsville, Fayette Co., PA[6315]

3885   iv.   Charles Christner[6316], born 30 Aug 1944 in Smithton, Westmoreland Co., PA[6316,6317]; died 05 Oct 2000 in Smithton, Westmoreland Co., PA[6318].

        More About Charles Christner:
        Other-Begin: [6319]
        Social Security Number: 187-34-1197/[6319]
        SSN issued: PA[6319]

1898. Charles Melvin "Chick"[8] Christner Sr. (Walter Joseph[7], Charles[6], Levi[5], Peter[4], Johannes John Hans[3], Christian[2], Christen[1])[6320,6321,6322,6323,6324,6325,6326,6327] was born 07 Jan 1918 in Marguerite, Westmoreland Co., PA[6328,6329,6330,6331,6332,6333,6334,6335], and died 07 Mar 2000 in Mt Pleasant, Westmoreland Co., PA[6336,6337,6338,6339,6340]. He married **Anna Marie Johnston**[6341,6342] 16 May 1942 in Smithton, Westmoreland Co., PA[6343]. She was born 07 Jul 1925 in Smithton, Westmoreland Co., PA[6343,6344], and died 26 May 1994 in Lung Cancer/West Newton, Westmoreland Co., PA[6345,6346].

Notes for Charles Melvin "Chick" Christner Sr.:
Liberator of Dachau
1945 , Germany

Charles was a member of the 157th Infantry regiment of the 45th Infantry Division of the United States Army during World War II. Their trek started in North Africa, went through Sicily, Italy, France, and eventually into

Germany for the Battle of the Buldge. He was awarded 2 Bronze stars during his tour of duty. One for his actions at the Battle of Anzio. The other for his actions during the liberation of the notorious Nazi death camp Dachau. I knew my grandfather well. He was as tough as they come. The images that he saw those days at Dachau had a profound effect on him. His disdain for the men who ran that prison camp was still quite evident to me over 50 years later.

Charles was a highly decorated WWII veteran and was a retiree from US Steel.

More About Charles Melvin "Chick" Christner Sr.:
Military service: Bet. 1942 - 1945, Served in North Africa, Sicily, France, and Germany Attained rank of Staff SGT and was awarded 2 Bronze Stars/World War II Co H 157th Inf Reg 45th Inf Div[6347,6348,6349,6350]
Residence: 1930, South Huntingdon, Westmoreland Co., PA[6350,6351,6352,6353]
Social Security Number: 201-03-1851/[6354]
SSN issued: Connellsville, Fayette Co., PA[6354]

Notes for Anna Marie Johnston:
Birth: 1925
Death: 1994

Burial: Olive Branch Cemetery, Belle Vernon, Westmoreland Co., PA

Anna Marie was a wonderful Grandma and died of lung cancer.

More About Anna Marie Johnston:
Residence: 1930, South Huntingdon, Westmoreland Co., PA[6355,6356]

Children of Charles Christner and Anna Johnston are:
+ 3886   i.   Charles Melvin[9] Christner Jr., born 18 Jul 1947 in Pittsburgh, Allegheny Co., PA.
   3887   ii.   Kathy Ann Christner[6357,6358], born 20 Dec 1950 in Mt Pleasant, Westmoreland Co., PA[6359,6360]; died 15 Jul 1997 in Collinsburg, Westmoreland Co., PA[6361,6362]. She married (1) Living Steiner[6362]. She married (2) Living Risku[6362].

     Notes for Kathy Ann Christner:
     Cause of death - heart attack.

     More About Kathy Ann Christner:
     Residence: 1995, West Newton, PA[6363,6364]

1899. Sarah[8] Christner (Walter Joseph[7], Charles[6], Levi[5], Peter[4], Johannes John Hans[3], Christian[2], Christen[1])[6365,6366,6367] was born 12 Apr 1920 in Connellsville, Fayette Co., PA[6368,6369,6370,6371], and died 06 May 1993 in Smithton, Westmoreland Co., PA[6372,6373]. She married **Charles J. Ashbaugh**[6374]. He was born 02 Feb 1916 in PA[6374], and died Oct 1981[6374].

Notes for Sarah Christner:
Birth: 1920
Death: 1993

Burial: Olive Branch Cemetery, Belle Vernon, Westmoreland Co., PA
Find A Grave Memorial# 86329899

More About Sarah Christner:
Residence: 1930, South Huntingdon, Westmoreland Co., PA[6375,6376,6377]
Social Security Number: 202-14-7369/[6378]

More About Charles J. Ashbaugh:
Residence: 1942, Smithton, PA[6379]

Child of Sarah Christner and Charles Ashbaugh is:

    3888   i.   William[9] Ashbaugh[6379], born 08 Apr 1948 in Smithton, Westmoreland Co., PA[6379]; died Jul 1981[6379].

1901. Dorothy[8] Christner (Walter Joseph[7], Charles[6], Levi[5], Peter[4], Johannes John Hans[3], Christian[2], Christen[1])[6380,6381,6382,6383] was born 06 Nov 1925 in Smithton, Westmoreland Co., PA[6384,6385,6386], and died 07 Sep 2009 in Excela Health Westmoreland Hospital Greensburg[6387]. She married **Maurice O. Weyandt**[6387]. He was born 28 May 1922[6387], and died 23 Feb 1990 in Pittsburgh, Allegheny Co., PA[6387].

More About Dorothy Christner:
Residence: 1930, South Huntingdon, Westmoreland Co., PA[6388,6389,6390]

Children of Dorothy Christner and Maurice Weyandt are:

    3889   i.   Maurice A[9] Weyandt[6391], born 15 Jan 1944[6391]; died Sep 1991[6391].
    3890   ii.   Walter Weyandt[6391], born 13 May 1945[6391]; died 05 Nov 2004[6391].

1902. Hazel Marie[8] Christner (George Washington[7], Charles[6], Levi[5], Peter[4], Johannes John Hans[3], Christian[2], Christen[1])[6392] was born 23 Feb 1912 in Hammondsville, Jefferson Co., OH[6392], and died 16 Jun 1957 in Connellsville, Fayette Co., PA[6392]. She married **Charles H. Gilson**[6392]. He was born 04 Jun 1910 in Nacogdoches, TX[6392], and died 26 Jan 1976 in Marcellus, Cass Co., MI[6392].

More About Hazel Marie Christner:
Residence: 1930, Connellsville, Fayette Co., PA[6392]

More About Charles H. Gilson:
Residence: 1930, San Antonio, Bexar, Texas[6392]

Children of Hazel Christner and Charles Gilson are:

    3891   i.   Charles Larry[9] Gilson[6392], born Feb 1945 in Connellsville, Fayette Co., PA[6392].
    3892   ii.   John Edward Gilson[6392], born Abt. 1946 in Connellsville, Fayette Co., PA[6392].
    3893   iii. Sandra Lee Gilson[6392], born Abt. 1950 in Connellsville, Fayette Co., PA[6392].
    3894   iv. Dana Ann Gilson[6392], born Abt. 1951 in Connellsville, Fayette Co., PA[6392].

1904. John Ray[8] Christner (William S.[7], Rufus[6], Levi[5], Peter[4], Johannes John Hans[3], Christian[2], Christen[1])[6393] was born 20 Oct 1895 in Connellsville, Fayette Co., PA[6393], and died 07 Dec 1978 in Dawson, Fayette Co., PA[6393]. He married **Margaret Elizabeth Sullenberger**[6393] 29 Jan 1917 in Dawson, Lower Tyrone, Fayette Co., PA[6393]. She was born 24 Feb 1900 in Lower Tyrone Twp, Fayette, PA[6393], and died Jan 1985 in Dickerson Run, Fayette Co., PA[6393].

Notes for John Ray Christner:
JOHN Christner SSN 211-05-6334
Residence: 15428 Dawson, Fayette, PA
Coal Miner at the W. J. Rainy Coal & Coke Co. & The Fort Hill Mines. He had light brown eyes & hair.

More About John Ray Christner:
Burial: Greenridge Memorial Park, Connellsville, Fayette Co., PA[6393]
Occupation: Retired carpenter and was also self-employed as a gunsmith at his Dawson home/[6394]
Residence: 1930, Lower Tyrone Township, Fayette Co., Pa.[6394]
Social Security Number: 211-05-6334 - PA/

Notes for Margaret Elizabeth Sullenberger:
Margaret Christner SSN 197-50-8465
Residence: 15430 Dickerson Run, Fayette, PA

More About Margaret Elizabeth Sullenberger:
Burial: 23 Jan 1985, Greenridge Memorial Park, Connellsville, Fayette Co., PA[6395]
DeathCause: Cardiopulmonary arrest; Congestive Heart Failure/[6395]
Social Security: 197-50-8465 - PA

Children of John Christner and Margaret Sullenberger are:

3895   i.   Ralph Leroy[9] Christner, born in Lwr. Tyrone Twp., Fayette Co., PA; died 25 Jul 2007 in Dawson, Fayette, PA[6396]. He married Irma Laverne.

More About Ralph Leroy Christner:
Obituary: 26 Jul 2007, The Herald Standard Newspaper, Fayette Co., PA[6397]
SSN issued: PA[6398]

3896   ii. Carl Eugene Christner. He married Eunice.
3897   iii. George David Christner. He married Janice.
3898   iv. John William "Bill" Christner, born 25 Aug 1917 in Lower Tyrone Twp., Fayette Co., PA; died 29 Apr 2006 in Dawson, Fayette Co., PA. He married Margaret Blanche Keffer[6399,6400]; born 12 May 1922 in PA[6400,6401]; died 29 Mar 1996 in Dawson, Fayette Co., PA[6402,6403].

Notes for John William "Bill" Christner:
Birth: Aug. 25, 1917
Death: Apr. 29, 2006

John W. "Bill" Christner, age 88, of Dawson, PA died Saturday morning, April 29, 2006 in his home. He was born in Lower Tyrone Twp., Fayette Co., PA on August 25, 1917, the son of John Ray Christner and Margaret Sullenberger Christner."Bill" was a member of the Dawson Baptist Church where he was a Life Deacon.He served with the United States Army in the 38th Cyclone Division, 152nd Infantry in the South Pacific, Luzon Campaign in the Philippines.

During his military career he was awarded the Combat Infantry Badge, the Good Conduct Medal, the Asiatic-Pacific Theatre of Operations Medal, the Philippine Liberation Medal with one Bronze Star and the World War II Victory Medal.He was a member of the American Legion Post 301 and the Veterans of Foreign Wars Post No. 21 both in Connellsville, PA.
"Bill" had been employed as a Track Foreman and Equipment Operator by the B&O Railroad and retired in 1979 with 36 years service.

He was a Past Master of the James Cochran Lodge No. 614 F. & A. M., the Uniontown Lodge of Perfection and the Council Chapter Consistory of Pittsburgh, Pa., and was a member of the Dawson Council for four years.
He was preceded in death by his parents, his wife, Margaret Blanche Keffer Christner and a sister, Ora Catherine Christner Lape.

Surviving are a sister, Esther Belle Swank of Dawson, PA; five brothers: Duane Christner and his wife, Priscilla of Dawson, PA, Ellis Howard Christner and his wife, Mildred of Dawson, PA, Carl Eugene Christner and his wife, Eunice, of Brunswick, OH, Ralph Leroy Christner and his wife, Irma Laverne, of Dawson, PA and George David Christner and his wife, Janice of LaPlata, MD.

Friends will be received in the RALPH E. GALLEY FUNERAL HOME, Railroad and Laughlin streets, Dawson, PA on Monday, May 1, from 7 to 9 p.m., Tuesday from 2 to 4 and 7 to 9 p.m. and Wednesday, May 3, until 11 a.m., the hour of the Service. Officiating minister will be the Rev. Chip Norton.Interment will follow in Green Ridge Memorial Park, Pennsville, PA where Military Honors and Rites will be accorded.James Cochran Lodge No. 614 F. & A. M. will conduct a Service in the Funeral Home on Tuesday at 7:30 p.m.

Burial: Green Ridge Memorial Park, Connellsville, Fayette Co., PA

More About John William "Bill" Christner:
Burial: Green Ridge Memorial Park, Fayette Co., PA
Military service: WWII Army 38th Cyclone Div. 152nd Infantry S. Pacific, Luzon Campaign Philippines/
Religion: Dawson Baptist Church, Life Deacon/

More About Margaret Blanche Keffer:

Social Security Number: 163-22-9202/[6404]

	3899	v.	Duane "Hud" Christner, born 29 Dec 1918 in Lwr. Tyrone Twp., Fayette Co., PA; died 12 Mar 1987 in Orlando, Orange Co., FL. He married Priscilla.

More About Duane "Hud" Christner:
Social Security Number: 173-18-4346 - PA/

+	3900	vi.	Esther Bell Christner, born 14 Feb 1920 in Dawson, Fayette Co., PA; died 06 Mar 2011 in Connellsville, Fayette Co., PA.
	3901	vii.	Jesse C. Christner, born 1923 in Lwr. Tyrone Twp., Fayette Co., PA; died 1991.

More About Jesse C. Christner:
Burial: Greenridge Memorial Park, Connellsville, Fayette Co., PA

+	3902	viii.	Ora Catherine Christner, born 07 Mar 1923 in Lower Tyrone Twp., Fayette Co., PA; died Nov 1987 in Dickerson Run, Fayette Co., PA.

1917. Elvy Elsworth[8] Christner (Harry Cramer[7], Elijah H.[6], Levi[5], Peter[4], Johannes John Hans[3], Christian[2], Christen[1]) was born 22 Sep 1905 in Connellsville, Fayette Co., PA[6405], and died 02 Jun 2002 in Youngstown, Mahoning Co., OH[6405]. He married **Helen Susan Williams**. She was born 26 Aug 1904[6406], and died Feb 1995 in Mount Pleasant, Westmoreland Co., PA[6406].

Notes for Elvy Elsworth Christner:
1910 soundex PA he was living in Somerset Co. PA & they spelled his name E L I R E ????

More About Elvy Elsworth Christner:
Social Security Number: 208-07-9088/[6407]
SSN issued: PA[6407]

More About Helen Susan Williams:
Social Security Number: 193-32-8167/[6408]

Children of Elvy Christner and Helen Williams are:
+	3903	i.	E. Wayne[9] Christner, born 01 Aug 1928.
+	3904	ii.	Galen M. Christner, born 18 Feb 1931.

1920. Dorotha Minerva[8] Christner (Harry Cramer[7], Elijah H.[6], Levi[5], Peter[4], Johannes John Hans[3], Christian[2], Christen[1])[6409] was born 10 Nov 1908[6410,6411,6412], and died 06 Oct 1983 in Collier Co., FL[6413,6414]. She married **Chester Eugene Yothers**. He was born 1911, and died 1979.

Notes for Dorotha Minerva Christner:
Birth: Nov. 10, 1908
Death: Oct. 6, 1983

Parents:
Harry C. Christner (1882 - 1971)
Mary Ann Nedrow Christner (1884 - 1936)

Spouse: Chester E. Yothers (1911 - 1979)

Children: Melvin Ray Yothers (1944 - 1944)

Burial: Greenlick Cemetery, Fayette Co., PA

More About Dorotha Minerva Christner:
Residence: 1920, Bullskin Twp., Fayette Co., PA[6415]

Social Security Number: 176-36-4107/[6416]
SSN issued: Connellsville, Fayette Co., PA[6416]

Notes for Chester Eugene Yothers:
Birth: Apr. 18, 1911
Death: Aug. 24, 1979

Spouse: Dorthea M. Christner Yothers (1908 - 1983)

Children: Melvin Ray Yothers (1944 - 1944)

Burial: Greenlick Cemetery, Fayette Co., PA

Child of Dorotha Christner and Chester Yothers is:
    3905   i.   Melvin Ray[9] Yothers, born 1944; died 1944.

                Notes for Melvin Ray Yothers:
                Birth: 1944
                Death: 1944

                Parents:
                Chester E. Yothers (1911 - 1979)
                Dorthea M. Christner Yothers (1908 - 1983)

                Burial: Greenlick Cemetery, Fayette Co., PA

1922. Edna Mae[8] Christner (Harry Cramer[7], Elijah H.[6], Levi[5], Peter[4], Johannes John Hans[3], Christian[2], Christen[1]) was born 15 Sep 1914[6417], and died 11 Aug 1999 in Mt. Pleasant, Westmoreland Co., PA[6417]. She married **Grant Snyder**[6418]. He was born 1913, and died Aug 1969[6418].

More About Edna Mae Christner:
Burial: Green Lick Cemetery, Bullskin Twp., Fayette Co., PA
Social Security Number: 189-42-0062/[6419]
SSN issued: PA[6419]

More About Grant Snyder:
Burial: Green Lick Cemetery, Bullskin Twp., Fayette Co., PA
Social Security Number: 169-03-7294/[6420]
SSN issued: PA[6420]

Children of Edna Christner and Grant Snyder are:
    3906   i.   Marvin[9] Snyder.
    3907   ii.   Connie Snyder.
    3908   iii.   Mary Ane Snyder.

1930. Annie Mae[8] Christner (Jacob "Deets/Deitz" R.[7], George Deitz[6], Susan[5], David[4], Johannes John Hans[3], Christian[2], Christen[1])[6421,6422,6422] was born 08 Aug 1896 in Topeka, Lagrange Co., IN[6422,6422], and died 13 Apr 1991 in Topeka, Lagrange Co., IN[6422]. She married **Levi R. Bontrager**[6422,6422] 16 Sep 1917 in IN[6422,6422]. He was born 05 Dec 1893 in Lagrange Co., IN[6422], and died 18 Sep 1967 in Row 7 plot 16.

Notes for Annie Mae Christner:
The Descendants of John J. Christner, privately published February 1961, pp. 26, 27.

Burial at Christner Cemetery Honeyville IN. Old Order Amish Lydia and her sisters Annie and Mary wrote the first Christner history book printed in 1961. They lived in Honeyville IN. at N41°35.513 x W85° 36.380 Annie was a rug weaver. She would get old rags & old clothes, cut them in strips & weave them into rug runners.

Birth: Aug. 8, 1896
Death: Apr. 14, 1991

Note: Wife of Levi R. 94 Y 8 M. 5 D.

Burial: Christner Cemetery, Honeyville, Lagrange Co., IN

More About Annie Mae Christner:
Burial: Christner Cemetery, Honeyville, Lagrange Co., IN
Residence: 1920, Jefferson, Henry Co., IA[6423]

Notes for Levi R. Bontrager:
The Descendants of John J. Christner, privately published February 1961, p. 29.

Levi is the son of Rueben E Bontrager and Elizabeth Yoder Bontrager. Levi was a farmer. Levi and his brother David R. married sisters.

Birth: Dec. 5, 1893
Death: Sep. 18, 1967

Note: 73 Y. 9 M. 13 D.

Burial: Christner Cemetery, Honeyville, Lagrange Co., IN

More About Levi R. Bontrager:
Burial: Christner Cemetery, Honeyville, Lagrange Co., IN
Christened: Amish
Religion: Old Order Amish/

Children of Annie Christner and Levi Bontrager are:
+   3909   i.   Edna Mae[9] Bontrager, born 24 Jan 1918 in Topeka, Lagrange Co., IN; died 16 Jun 1986.
     3910   ii. Ida Bontrager[6424,6424], born Nov 1922 in Topeka, Lagrange Co., IN[6424,6424]; died Nov 1922 in Topeka, Lagrange Co., IN[6424,6424].

              More About Ida Bontrager:
              Burial: Christner Cemetery/Honeyville, Lagrange Co., IN[6424]

     3911   iii. David L. Bontrager, born 04 Feb 1924. He married Susie Miller 31 Jan 1946; born 27 Nov 1919.

              Notes for David L. Bontrager:
              The Descendants of John J. Christner, privately published February 1961, p. 29..

              More About David L. Bontrager:
              Religion: Old Order Amish/

              Notes for Susie Miller:
              The Descendants of John J. Christner, privately published February 1961, p. 29.

1931. Fannie Ada[8] Christner (Jacob "Deets/Deitz" R.[7], George Deitz[6], Susan[5], David[4], Johannes John Hans[3], Christian[2], Christen[1])[6425] was born 18 Feb 1899 in Washington Co., IA[6426,6427], and died 02 Jun 1968 in Washington Hospital, Washington Co., IA[6428]. She married **David R. Schantz**[6428] 21 Jan 1920 in Wayland, Henry Co., IA[6428]. He was born 18 Jun 1894 in Washington Co., IA[6428], and died 25 Mar 1989 in Washington Hospital, Washington Co., IA[6428].

More About Fannie Ada Christner:
Residence: 1915, Jefferson, Henry Co., IA[6428]

More About David R. Schantz:

Residence: 01 Jan 1925, Marion, Washington Co., IA[6428]

Children of Fannie Christner and David Schantz are:

    3912   i.   Viola May[9] Schantz[6428], born 16 Jun 1920 in IA[6428]; died 16 Jun 1920[6428].

    3913   ii.   Verda Maxine Schantz[6428], born 06 Jul 1921 in Washington, Washington Co., IA[6428]; died 02 Jul 1993 in Johnson Co., IA[6428].

    3914   iii.   Rex C Schantz[6428], born 21 Jan 1923 in IA[6428]; died 21 Jan 1923[6428].

1945. Naomi Ruth[8] Christner (Jesse[7], Samuel[6], David[5], David[4], Johannes John Hans[3], Christian[2], Christen[1]) was born 02 Aug 1899 in Johnstown, Cambria Co., PA, and died 29 Apr 1976 in Johnstown, Cambria Co., PA. She married **Hubert Wesley Chrislop** 30 Oct 1916 in Cumberland, Allegany Co., MD. He was born 25 Oct 1895 in Heaters, Braxton Co., WV[6429], and died 04 Apr 1953 in Johnstown, Cambria Co., PA.

More About Naomi Ruth Christner:
Burial: 03 May 1976, Grandview Cemetery, Johnstown, Cambria Co., PA
Christened: 09 Feb 1913, St. Paul, Evangelical, Brethern, Johnstown, Cambria Co., PA
Residence: 1930, Ferndale, Cambria Co., PA[6429]

Notes for Hubert Wesley Chrislop:
His parents James Crislip & Margret Hinkle.

More About Hubert Wesley Chrislop:
Burial: Stahl Mennonite, Church
Residence: 1942, WWII Draft Registration/Johnstown, Cambria, PA[6429]

Children of Naomi Christner and Hubert Chrislop are:

    3915   i.   Lewis Wesley[9] Chrislop, born 09 Nov 1919 in Johnstown, Cambria Co., PA; died 20 Mar 1959. He married (1) Helen Kelly. He married (2) Irene McDaniel.

                  Notes for Lewis Wesley Chrislop:
                  Lewis married Helen Kelly and then married Irene McDaniel.

                  More About Lewis Wesley Chrislop:
                  Residence: 1930, Ferndale, Cambria Co., PA[6429]

    3916   ii.   Leona Mae Chrislop, born 19 May 1925 in Johnstown, Cambria Co., PA.

                  Notes for Leona Mae Chrislop:
                  Leona married Ray Waterhouse April 20/21, 1947 in Gary, IN.

    3917   iii.   Dorthy Louise Chrislop, born 20 Jan 1929 in Johnstown, Cambria Co., PA.

                  Notes for Dorthy Louise Chrislop:
                  Dorthy married Dwight Earbaugh Jan 24, 1948 Johnstown, Cambria Co., PA.

    3918   iv.   Hubert Albert "Bud" Chrislop, born 24 Feb 1931 in Johnstown, Cambria Co., PA; died 17 May 1988 in Findlay, Hancock Co., OH[6429].

                  Notes for Hubert Albert "Bud" Chrislop:
                  Bud married Betty Geiser and then married Sally Baker

                  More About Hubert Albert "Bud" Chrislop:
                  Residence: 1988, Ohio Deaths, 1908-1932, 1938-1944, 1958-2002/Findlay, Hancock Co., OH[6429]

1946. Harry[8] Christner Sr. (Jesse[7], Samuel[6], David[5], David[4], Johannes John Hans[3], Christian[2], Christen[1])[6430,6431,6432,6432] was born 22 Feb 1902 in Johnstown, Cambria Co., PA[6433,6434], and died 17 Dec 1982 in Glendale, Los Angeles Co., CA[6435]. He married **Irene L. Cole**. She was born 21 Oct 1904 in Gramplan, PA[6436], and died 24 Jan 1973 in Glendale, Los Angeles Co., CA.

Notes for Harry Christner Sr.:

More About Harry Christner Sr.:
Residence: 1920, Johnstown Ward 8, Cambria Co., PA[6436]
Social Security Number: 196-09-4604/[6437]
SSN issued: Connellsville, Fayette Co., PA[6437]

More About Irene L. Cole:
Burial: 29 Jan 1973, Glendale, Los Angeles Co., CA
Residence: 1930, Ferndale, Cambria, PA[6438]

Children of Harry Christner and Irene Cole are:
    3919   i.   Harry[9] Christner Jr..
    3920   ii. James R. Christner, died 30 Jun 1958.

1947. Robert[8] Christner Sr. (Jesse[7], Samuel[6], David[5], David[4], Johannes John Hans[3], Christian[2], Christen[1])[6439] was born 25 Apr 1908 in Johnstown, Cambria Co., PA, and died 13 Oct 1959 in Johnstown, Cambria Co., PA. He married **Theresa Mildred Labick**. She was born 15 Feb 1909 in Pittsburgh, Alleghaney Co., PA, and died 12 Dec 1968 in Johnstown, Cambria Co., PA.

Notes for Robert Christner Sr.:
SS#196-09-3945 ISS PA

More About Robert Christner Sr.:
Burial: Grandview Cemetery, Johnstown, Cambria Co., PA
Social Security Number: 196-09-3945/[6439]
SSN issued: PA[6439]

Notes for Theresa Mildred Labick:
Theresa is the daughter of Andrew Labick.

More About Theresa Mildred Labick:
Burial: Grandview Cemetery, Johnstown, Cambria Co., PA

Children of Robert Christner and Theresa Labick are:
    3921   i.   Betty Delores[9] Christner. She married Louis Keyes.
    3922   ii. Charlotte Jean Christner. She married Eugene Parks.
    3923   iii. Lois Pauline Christner. She married Edward Bridges.
    3924   iv. Robert Christner Jr..
    3925   v. Kenneth Raymond Christner, born 30 May.
+ 3926   vi. Rita Mae Christner, born 11 Jul 1928; died 18 Aug 2008 in Johnstown, Cambria, PA.
+ 3927 vii. Audrey Ann Christner, born Jul 1944 in IL.
    3928 viii. Carol Louise Christner, born 07 Nov 1946. She married (1) Hockenberry. She married (2) Ross Camut.

1948. Mary Pauline[8] Christner (Jesse[7], Samuel[6], David[5], David[4], Johannes John Hans[3], Christian[2], Christen[1]) was born 21 Apr 1915 in Johnstown, Cambria Co., PA, and died 08 May 1975 in Johnstown, Cambria Co., PA. She married **James M. Shaffer** 27 Oct 1932 in Ferndale, Evangelical, Church, Johnstown Pa. He was born 11 Sep 1911 in Somerset Co., PA.

Notes for Mary Pauline Christner:
Marys son is Robert Shaffer.

More About Mary Pauline Christner:
Burial: 10 May 1975, Benshoff Hill, Cem, Johnstown, PA

Notes for James M. Shaffer:
Jame is the son of Henry and Lucy Hershberger Shaffer.

Children of Mary Christner and James Shaffer are:

3929　　i.　Anna Catherine[9] Shaffer, born 20 Oct 1933 in Johnstown, Cambria Co., PA. She married Lancelot A. Whyte 14 Feb 1953.

　　　　　　　Notes for Anna Catherine Shaffer:
　　　　　　　Anna married Lancelot A. Whyte Feb 14 1953

3930　　ii.　Helen Irene Shaffer, born 15 Jan 1936 in Johnstown, Cambria Co., PA. She married Robert O. Brownley 02 Jan 1959.

3931　　iii.　Barbara Jean Shaffer, born 23 Jul 1941 in Johnstown, Cambria Co., PA. She married Robert E. Ashcom 26 Jun 1960.

　　　　　　　Notes for Barbara Jean Shaffer:

3932　　iv.　James Donald Shaffer, born 17 Jun 1944 in Johnstown, Cambria Co., PA. He married Patricia A. Smith 19 Jun 1971.

　　　　　　　Notes for James Donald Shaffer:
　　　　　　　James married Patricia A. Smith June 19 1971

3933　　v.　Robert Wade Shaffer, born 18 Nov 1954 in Johnstown, Cambria Co., PA. He married Vicki L. Orris 13 Oct 1979; born 17 Jul 1957.

　　　　　　　Notes for Robert Wade Shaffer:

3934　　vi.　Lucy Louise Shaffer, born 18 Feb 1958 in Johnstown, Cambria Co., PA.

1952. Ethel Frances[8] Christner (David[7], Samuel[6], David[5], David[4], Johannes John Hans[3], Christian[2], Christen[1])[6440] was born 08 Aug 1913 in Thomas Mills, Potter Co., PA[6440], and died 31 Oct 1980 in Johnstown, Cambria Co., PA[6440]. She married **Good**.

Notes for Ethel Frances Christner:
Good, Ethel F. daughter of David and Nancy (Berkey) Christner was born in Thomas Mills, PA, Aug. 8, 1913; died at Memorial Hospital, Johnstown, PA, Oct. 31, 1980; aged 67 y. Surviving are 5 daughters (Emma Martin, Delores Cleman, Janet North, Nancy Vickroy, and Harriet Mirilovich), 3 sons (David, Michael, and Robert), 21 grandchildren, 2 great-grandchildren, 2 sisters, and one brother. She was a member of First Mennonite Church, where funeral services were held on Nov. 3, in charge of Phil King and Jim Thomas; interment in Maple Spring Cemetery.

More About Ethel Frances Christner:
Burial: Maple Springs, Cem, Johnstown, PA
Christened: Mennonite
Residence: 1920, Jenner, Somerset Co., PA[6440]
Social Security Number: 187-42-9734[6441]
SSN issued: PA[6441]

Children of Ethel Christner and Good are:

| 3935 | i. | David[9] Good. |
| 3936 | ii. | Delores Good. She married Cicman. |

Notes for Delores Good:
Delores married_____Cicman

| 3937 | iii. | Emma Good. She married Martin. |

Notes for Emma Good:
Emma married_____Martin

| 3938 | iv. | Harriet Good. She married Mirilovich. |

Notes for Harriet Good:
Harriet married_____Mirilovich

3939	v.	Michael Good.
3940	vi.	Robert Good.
3941	vii.	Janet Good. She married North.

Notes for Janet Good:
Janet married_____North

| 3942 | viii. | Nancy Good. She married Vickroy. |

Notes for Nancy Good:
Nancy married _____Vickroy

1954. Arthur Learoux[8] Pyle (Louisa Ellen[7] Lowry, Susanna Deitz[6] Christner, David[5], David[4], Johannes John Hans[3], Christian[2], Christen[1]) was born 08 Dec 1884, and died 10 Jul 1955 in ,Ketchum, ID. He married **Sara Blanche Randolph**.

Child of Arthur Pyle and Sara Randolph is:

+ 3943   i.   Arthur Randolph[9] Pyle, born 21 Aug 1917 in ,Ketchum, ID; died 14 Dec 1968 in ,Ketchum, ID.

1955. Susan E.[8] Pyle (Louisa Ellen[7] Lowry, Susanna Deitz[6] Christner, David[5], David[4], Johannes John Hans[3], Christian[2], Christen[1])[6442] was born 30 Apr 1894 in Middlecreek, Somerset Co., PA[6442,6443], and died 12 Nov 1986 in Somerset Co., PA. She married **James Albert Critchfield**[6444,6445] 16 Oct 1912 in Rockwood, Somerset, PA[6445]. He was born 17 Nov 1881 in Dixon, Edwards Co., IL[6446], and died 09 Aug 1949 in Somerset Co., PA[6447,6448].

Notes for Susan E. Pyle:
Obituary: Daily American, November 14, 1986

Sue E. Critchfield, 92, Somerset, died Nov. 12, 1986, at Siemon Lakeview Manor Estate. Born April 30, 1894, in Middlecreek Township, daughter of the late Jeremiah and Ellen (Lowry) Pyle. Preceded in death by husband, James A., and brother, Arthur H. Pyle. Survived by these children: Donald A., Attorney Robert W., Attorney James A. Jr., all of Somerset; these grandchildren: Jon A., R. Eric, Richard N., Elizabeth and Ann Critchfield and Sally (Critchfield) Urban; great-grandchildren: Allison and Angela Urban, Brian E. and Jon Stephen Critchfield. Member of the Somerset Church of the Brethren; Somerset Trinity Chapter #138, Order of Eastern Star; Somerset Garden Club. Friends received from 2 - 4 and 7-9 p.m. Friday at the Hauger-Zeigler Funeral Home, where private services will be held at 11 a.m. Saturday, with the Rev. Roger L. Forty officiating.

Interment, Somerset County Memorial Park. Family suggests contributions may be made to the Somerset Church of the Brethren.

More About Susan E. Pyle:
Residence: 1910, New Centerville, Somerset Co., PA[6449]
Social Security Number: 159-38-9705[6450]
SSN issued: Pittsburgh, Allegheny Co., PA[6450]

More About James Albert Critchfield:
Occupation: 1940, General Contractor[6451]
Residence: 01 Apr 1940, Somerset, Somerset Co., PA[6451,6452]

Children of Susan Pyle and James Critchfield are:
+   3944   i.   Donald[9] Critchfield, born 12 Apr 1916 in Somerset, Somerset Co., PA; died 19 Oct 2004 in Somerset, Somerset Co., PA.
      3945   ii.   Robert Critchfield, born 24 Jan 1920.
      3946   iii.   James Critchfield, born 23 Mar 1926.

1962. Edna Myrtle[8] Pyle (Cora Estelle[7] Lowry, Susanna Deitz[6] Christner, David[5], David[4], Johannes John Hans[3], Christian[2], Christen[1]) was born 07 Mar 1894 in Scottdale, Westmoreland Co., PA, and died 05 Jul 1971 in Salt Lake CIty, UT. She married **Reese Benjamin Tedrow** in Scottdale, Westmoreland Co., PA.

More About Edna Myrtle Pyle:
Burial: Scottdale, Westmoreland Co., PA

Child of Edna Pyle and Reese Tedrow is:
+   3947   i.   Dr. Jack Lowry[9] Tedrow, born 22 Mar 1919 in Scottdale, Westmoreland Co., PA.

1963. Gladys Fay[8] Pyle (Cora Estelle[7] Lowry, Susanna Deitz[6] Christner, David[5], David[4], Johannes John Hans[3], Christian[2], Christen[1]) was born 08 Jun 1900 in Scottdale, Westmoreland Co., PA, and died 19 Aug 1994 in Martinsburg PA. She married **James Elmer Otho Butts** 20 Aug 1925 in Scottdale, Westmoreland Co., PA. He was born 12 Oct 1891 in Altoona, PA., and died 02 Aug 1963 in Roaring Spring, PA.

More About Gladys Fay Pyle:
Burial: Martinsburg, PA.

More About James Elmer Otho Butts:
Burial: Martinsburg, PA.

Children of Gladys Pyle and James Butts are:
+   3948   i.   Joyce Edna[9] Butts, born 23 May 1932 in Roaring Spring PA.
+   3949   ii.   Jane Estelle Butts, born 07 Nov 1936 in Roaring Spring PA.

1964. Ida Mae[8] Pyle (Cora Estelle[7] Lowry, Susanna Deitz[6] Christner, David[5], David[4], Johannes John Hans[3], Christian[2], Christen[1])[6453] was born 10 Apr 1905 in Scottdale, Westmoreland Co., PA[6453], and died 1997 in Salt Lake CIty, UT. She married **Willard F. Fleming**[6453] 05 Oct 1927 in Scottdale, Westmoreland Co., PA. He was born 19 Mar 1900 in Connellsville, Fayette Co., PA[6453], and died 1992.

More About Ida Mae Pyle:
Burial: CO
Residence: 1930, Butler, Butler, PA[6453]

More About Willard F. Fleming:
Burial: CO
Residence: 1930, Butler, Butler, PA[6453]

Children of Ida Pyle and Willard Fleming are:
+   3950   i.   Joan⁹ Fleming, born 29 Aug 1928 in Butler PA.
+   3951   ii.   Joel Frederic Fleming, born 12 Nov 1931 in Butler PA.

1968. Violet⁸ Miller (Ida Mae⁷ Lowry, Susanna Deitz⁶ Christner, David⁵, David⁴, Johannes John Hans³, Christian², Christen¹) She married **Orlin Barron**.

Notes for Violet Miller:
She died of T.B. at age 22 when her son was 1 year old. Edna Pyle Tedrow offered to take care of Violet Miller's son but Edna's mother (Cora Estelle Lowry) said "NO, there's something wrong with that family, their all dying," so Violet's father kept the child. All of his sons died of TB also.

Child of Violet Miller and Orlin Barron is:
+   3952   i.   William Miller⁹ Barron, born 28 May 1921 in Somerset Co., PA; died 22 Jun 2006 in Derry, Westmoreland Co., PA.

1975. May⁸ Smith (Cora Alice⁷ Christner, John⁶, Jessie⁵, David⁴, Johannes John Hans³, Christian², Christen¹) was born 17 Sep 1904 in Waterford Mills, Goshen, Elkhart Co., IN, and died 25 Dec 1993 in Wakarusa Nursing Home Wakarusa, IN. She married **Chester B. Carpenter** 06 Jan 1923 in Goshen, Elkhart Co., IN. He was born 13 Dec 1903 in Wabash, IN, and died 17 Oct 1981 in Goshen, Elkhart Co., IN.

More About May Smith:
Burial: Violett Cemetery Goshen, IN
Religion: St. Marks United Methodist Church Goshen, IN/

More About Chester B. Carpenter:
Burial: Violett Cemetery, Goshen, Elkhart Co., IN

Children of May Smith and Chester Carpenter are:
     3953   i.   Vivian⁹ Carpenter, born 28 Aug 1924 in Goshen, Elkhart Co., IN. She married Harold Lee Goodman 06 Apr 1947 in Goshen, Elkhart Co., IN; born in Louisville, KY.
     3954   ii.   Chester B. "Bud" Carpenter Jr., born 11 Jun 1926 in Goshen, Elkhart Co., IN; died 06 May 1982 in Syracuse, Onondaga Co., NY. He married Shirley Ketring 07 Sep 1946 in Goshen, Elkhart Co., IN.

                     More About Chester B. "Bud" Carpenter Jr.:
                     Burial: Violett Cemetery, Goshen, Elkhart Co., IN

     3955   iii. Keith Carpenter, born 17 Mar 1928 in Goshen, Elkhart Co., IN; died 17 Oct 1940 in Goshen, Elkhart Co., IN.

                     More About Keith Carpenter:
                     Burial: Violett Cemetery, Goshen, Elkhart Co., IN

+   3956   iv.   LaWanda Carpenter, born 17 Mar 1928 in Goshen, Elkhart Co., IN.

1981. Myrtle Pauline⁸ Christner (Jesse Calvin⁷, John⁶, Jessie⁵, David⁴, Johannes John Hans³, Christian², Christen¹) died May 1962. She married **Robert C. Fields**[6454,6455,6456] 15 Feb 1941. He was born 07 Jun 1919 in Mount Hood, OR[6457,6458,6459], and died 21 Jun 2006 in Elkhart, Elkhart Co., IN[6460].

Notes for Robert C. Fields:
He lived in the area about sixty years. He was a Machinist at L & J Press from 1950 to 1981. He grew up in Woodruff, IN.

More About Robert C. Fields:
Burial: Sugar Grove Church   Elder & Teacher
Graduation: 1937, Wolcottville High School

Hobby: Farming
Military service: World War II Navy USS LSM (R) 196 radar man/
Oganization: Sexton of Sugar Grove Cemetery
Religion: Sugar Grove Church/
Residence: 1930, Johnson, Lagrange Co., IN[6461]
Social Security Number: 314-28-4472/[6462]
SSN issued: IN[6462]

Children of Myrtle Christner and Robert Fields are:

3957	i.	Carl R.[9] Fields.
3958	ii.	Joan Fields. She married Bill Brennan.
3959	iii.	Paul L. Fields.

1984. Wilma Irene[8] Christner (Harry[7], John[6], Jessie[5], David[4], Johannes John Hans[3], Christian[2], Christen[1])[6463] was born 22 Sep 1905 in Waterford Mills, Goshen, Elkhar Co., IN[6463], and died 18 Sep 1982 in Waterford Mills, Goshen, Elkhar Co., IN[6463]. She married **George Daniel Turnbow**[6463] 10 Dec 1925 in Goshen, Elkhart Co., IN[6463]. He was born 22 Sep 1901 in Bogue Chitto, Lincoln Co., MS[6463], and died 20 May 1961 in Goshen, Elkhart Co., IN[6463].

Notes for Wilma Irene Christner:
She worked at the hat store in Goshen, IN. It became Klines Store. at that time in history hats for woman were a big deal and that store was the place to be and be seen.

More About Wilma Irene Christner:
Residence: 1910, Elkhart, Elkhart Co., IN[6464]

Notes for George Daniel Turnbow:
He met his wife on a blind date. He always had a dog. He was very proud of his 1946 Ford auto. He was in the hospital for 13 days & died from a heart ailment.

More About George Daniel Turnbow:
Occupation: worked part time at Maple City Ice Cream/

Children of Wilma Christner and George Turnbow are:

	3960	i.	Helen Jean[9] Turnbow, born 31 Jul 1926 in Waterford south of Goshen, IN; died 23 Sep 1938 in Waterford south of Goshen, IN.
+	3961	ii.	George Daniel Turnbow Jr., born 10 Oct 1927 in Waterford south of Goshen, IN; died 11 Oct 1985 in LA.
	3962	iii.	Twins Turnbow, born 1929 in Waterford south of Goshen, IN; died 1929 in Waterford south of Goshen, IN.
+	3963	iv.	Alice Jane Turnbow, born 24 May 1937 in Waterford south of Goshen, IN.
+	3964	v.	Patricia Elaine Turnbow, born 28 Jan 1941 in Goshen, Elkhart Co., IN; died 27 May 1997 in Elkhart Co., IN.

1987. Orval Clarence[8] Close (Martha M.[7] Christner, John[6], Jessie[5], David[4], Johannes John Hans[3], Christian[2], Christen[1])[6465] was born 25 Dec 1906 in OH[6466], and died 14 Nov 1978 in San Bernardino, San Bernardino Co., CA[6466,6467]. He married **Alice**[6467]. She was born Abt. 1906 in OH[6467].

More About Orval Clarence Close:
Residence: 01 Apr 1940, Toledo, Lucas, Ohio, United States[6467]
Social Security Number: 283-01-8949/[6468]

More About Alice:
Residence: 01 Apr 1940, Toledo, Lucas, Ohio, United States[6469]

Child of Orval Close and Alice is:

3965	i.	Orval Ray[9] Close[6469], born 17 Feb 1939 in OH[6469]; died 03 Jan 1997 in Greer, Greenville Co., SC[6469].

More About Orval Ray Close:
Residence: Bet. 1935 - 1993, Greer, SC[6469]

2000. Minnie Opal[8] Lowry (Jonas Henry[7], Tyrannus[6] Christner, Abraham D.[5], Joseph "Zep"[4], Johannes John Hans[3], Christian[2], Christen[1]) was born Apr 1887 in Somerset Co., PA, and died 1917. She married **John Turvey Jr.** 1903 in Connellsville, Fayette Co., PA. He was born Nov 1882 in Hanging Rock, Lawrence Co., OH.

Notes for Minnie Opal Lowry:
She had 11 Children in 14 years. she died 2 weeks after giving birth to her son Ray Lee.

Children of Minnie Lowry and John Turvey are:

3966	i.	Dorothy Louise[9] Turvey.
3967	ii.	Elmer Williard Turvey.
3968	iii.	John Morgan Turvey.
3969	iv.	Opal Grace Turvey.
3970	v.	Ray Lee Turvey.
3971	vi.	Robert Carey Turvey.
3972	vii.	Walter Eugene Turvey.
3973	viii.	Edgar Maurice Turvey, born 1904 in Connellsville, Fayette Co., PA.
3974	ix.	Charles Oscar Turvey, born 1905 in OH.
3975	x.	Albert Henry Turvey, born 1906 in OH.

2002. William Joseph[8] Baer (Mary "Pollie"[7] Lowry, Tyrannus[6] Christner, Abraham D.[5], Joseph "Zep"[4], Johannes John Hans[3], Christian[2], Christen[1])[6470] was born 21 Mar 1884 in Meyersdale, Somerset Co., PA[6470], and died 13 Dec 1947 in Windber, Somerset Co., PA[6470]. He married **Anna R. Donohoe**. She was born 12 Oct 1886, and died 10 Dec 1971.

Notes for William Joseph Baer:
Undertaker in Windber

More About William Joseph Baer:
Burial: Union Cemetery Meyersdale PA.
Residence: 1910, Connellsville Ward 1, Fayette, PA[6470]

More About Anna R. Donohoe:
Burial: Union Cemetery Meyersdale PA.

Children of William Baer and Anna Donohoe are:

+	3976	i.	Pauline[9] Baer.
+	3977	ii.	Mary Baer, born 03 Feb 1919 in Connellsville, Fayette Co., PA; died 15 May 2003 in Windber, Somerset Co., PA.

2003. George Curtis[8] Christner (Mahlon[7], Herman[6], Abraham D.[5], Joseph "Zep"[4], Johannes John Hans[3], Christian[2], Christen[1])[6471,6472,6473,6474] was born 20 Jul 1885 in Garrett, Summit Twp., Somerset Co., PA[6475,6476,6477,6478,6479,6480], and died 08 Feb 1973 in Meyersdale, Summit Twp., Somerset Co., PA[6481]. He married **Pearl C. Herwig**[6481,6482,6483] Abt. 1906 in Cumberland, Allegheny Co., PA[6483]. She was born 04 Feb 1886 in Garrett, Somerset Co., PA[6484,6485,6486,6487], and died 01 Nov 1976 in Meyersdale, Summit Twp., Somerset Co., PA[6488].

Notes for George Curtis Christner:
OBIT: George C. CHRISTNER, 1973, Meyersdale, Somerset Co., PA - Meyersdale Republican, February 15, 1973

George C. Christner, 87, Meyersdale RD 3, died Feb. 8, 1973 in Meyersdale Community Hospital. Born July

20, 1885, in Garrett, he was a son of the late Mahlon and Matilda (Pritts) Christner.

Surviving are his wife, the former Pearl Herwig; a son, A. E. Christner, Overgard, Ariz.; a daughter, Mrs. Emma Werner, Meyersdale RD 3; four grandchildren seven great-grandchildren; two brothers, Edward Christner, Meyersdale, and Harry, Cumberland; and a sister, Mrs. Catherine Brant, of Garrett. Funeral service was held Sunday afternoon in Price Funeral Home, Meyersdale, with Rev. Harold Appel officiating. Interment in Sunset Memorial Park, Cumberland.

SS# 215-05-2115 Iss MD Last address Meyersdale, PA. 15552

More About George Curtis Christner:
Burial: Sunset Memorial Park , Cumberland, Allegheny Co., MD
Residence: 1900, Summit, Somerset Co., PA[6489]

Notes for Pearl C. Herwig:
OBIT: Pearl C. (HERWIG) CHRISTNER, 1976, Meyersdale RD, Somerset County, PA - Daily American, November 2, 1976

Mrs. Pearl C. Christner, 90, of Meyersdale RD 3, died Nov. 1, 1976 in
Meyersdale Community Hospital. Born Feb. 4, 1886 in Garrett, a daughter of the late John and Mary Haer Herwig. Preceded in death by her husband, George. Survived by these children: A. E. Christner of Scottsdale, AZ and Mrs. Carl (Emma) Werner of Meyersdale RD 3, four grandchildren and seven great-grandchildren. A sister of Mrs. Evelyn Grant of Fairchance.
Friends will be received from 2 to 4 and 7 to 9 p.m. Tuesday and Wednesday at the Price Funeral Home, Meyersdale, where services will be conducted at 1 p.m. Thursday with the Rev. David Fetter officiating. Interment, Sunset Memorial Park, Cumberland, MD.

MRS. GEORGE CHRISTNER - Meyersdale Republican, November 4, 1976
Mrs. Pearl C. Christner, 90, of Meyersdale RD 3, died Nov. 1 at Meyersdale Community Hospital. Born in Garrett, she was a daughter of the late John and Mary (Haer) Herwig, and was the widow of George Christner. Surviving are a son, A.E. Christner, Scottsdale, Ariz.; a daughter, Mrs. Emma Werner, Meyersdale RD 3; a sister, Mrs. Evelyn Grant, Fairchance; four grandchildren and seven great-grandchildren.
Funeral services will be conducted at Price Funeral Home Thursday at 1 p.m. with Rev. David Fetter officiating. Interment will follow in Sunset Memorial Park, Cumberland, MD.

More About Pearl C. Herwig:
Burial: Sunset Memorial Park, Cumberland, Allegheny Co., MD
Residence: 1920, Summit, Somerset Co., PA[6490]

Children of George Christner and Pearl Herwig are:
+ 3978   i.   Authur E.[9] Christner, born 11 Feb 1908 in Connellsville, Fayette Co., PA; died 04 Oct 1989 in Somerset Co., PA.
+ 3979   ii.   Emma Marie Christner, born 25 Dec 1909 in Garrett, Somerset Co., PA; died 28 Mar 1982 in Meyersdale, Summit Twp., Somerset Co., PA.

2004. Edna Bell[8] Christner (Mahlon[7], Herman[6], Abraham D.[5], Joseph "Zep"[4], Johannes John Hans[3], Christian[2], Christen[1])[6491] was born 30 Sep 1890 in Garrett, Summit Twp., Somerset Co., PA[6491], and died 09 Oct 1959 in Meyersdale, Somerset Co., PA. She married **William Forest Decker** 03 Jul 1909 in Connellsville, Fayette Co., PA, son of Willis Decker and Mary Burkholder. He was born 02 Oct 1884 in Garrett, Somerset Co., PA, and died 02 Mar 1968.

More About Edna Bell Christner:
Burial: Garrett Highland Cemetery, Summit Twp., Somerset Co., PA
Residence: 1900, Summit, Somerset Co., PA[6491]

More About William Forest Decker:

Burial: Highland Cemetery, Garrett, Somerset Co., PA
Christened: Lutheran, Garrett, Somerset Co., PA

Children of Edna Christner and William Decker are:

+ 3980   i.   Eugene Mahlon Jeff[9] Decker, born 23 Dec 1909 in Garrett, Somerset Co., PA; died 03 May 1953.
+ 3981   ii.   Robert Woodrow Decker, born 14 Nov 1915 in Garrett, Somerset Co., PA; died 10 Nov 1991.
   3982   iii.   Ethel Marie Decker, born 17 Dec 1917 in Garrett, Somerset Co., PA; died 07 Jun 1982 in Meyersdale PA.. She married Clyde Brown 1939; born 29 Apr 1916 in Meyersdale, Somerset Co., PA; died 29 Aug 1994.

> Notes for Ethel Marie Decker:
> She maybe born December 18, 1913. She was also a member Mt. Tabor Church, Garrett, PA. They had no children.

> More About Ethel Marie Decker:
> Burial: Union Cemetery, Meyersdale, Somerset Co., PA

> Notes for Clyde Brown:
> They had no children.

> More About Clyde Brown:
> Burial: Union Cemetery, Meyersdale, Somerset Co., PA

+ 3983   iv.   Millard Decker, born 28 Sep 1920 in Garrett, Somerset Co., PA; died 19 Nov 1999.
+ 3984   v.   William Walter Decker, born 19 Jan 1923 in Garrett, Somerset Co., PA; died 17 Aug 1973.
+ 3985   vi.   Preston Dean Decker, born 14 Apr 1925 in Garrett, Somerset Co., PA; died 02 Dec 1988 in Somerset Co., PA.
   3986   vii.   Richard L. Decker, born 12 May 1927 in Garrett, Somerset Co., PA; died 05 Apr 1932.

> More About Richard L. Decker:
> Burial: Highland Cemetery Garrett, PA

+ 3987   viii.   Ruth Lucille Decker, born 12 May 1930 in Garrett, Somerset Co., PA.

2005. Harry Albert[8] Christner (Mahlon[7], Herman[6], Abraham D.[5], Joseph "Zep"[4], Johannes John Hans[3], Christian[2], Christen[1])[6491,6492,6493] was born 01 Jan 1893 in Cumberland, Allegany Co., MD[6493], and died 24 Mar 1974 in Martinsburg, Berkeley Co., WV. He married **Edith L. Grew** 20 Dec 1920 in Cumberland, Allegany Co., MD. She was born 02 Mar 1903 in Meyersdale, Somerset Co., PA, and died 02 Apr 1990.

Notes for Harry Albert Christner:
Obituary: Harry Albert Christner 1974, native of Garrett, Somerset County, PA - Daily American, 26 March 1974

Harry Albert Christner, 81, of LaVale, MD died March 24 in Veterans' Hospital, Martinsburg, WV born Jan 1, 1893 in Garrett son of the late Mahlon and Matilda Pritts Christner. Survived by a son, Leroy, Meyersdale RD 1; daughters Mrs. Mike Dneaster of Garrett and Mrs. Harold Miller, Garrett RD 1; a brother, Edward of Meyersdale; a sister, Mrs. Catherine Brant of Garrett; six grandchildren, and four great-grandchildren. Funeral services Wednesday at 2 p.m. in the Konhaus Funeral Home, Rev. William Snyder officiating. Interment Rest Lawn Memorial Gardens, LaVale.

More About Harry Albert Christner:
Burial: Veterans Cemetery Cumberland, MD
Christened: Brethern
Other-Begin: Somerset County[6494]
Residence: 1900, Summit, Somerset Co., PA[6495]
Social Security Number: 210-01-8889/[6496]
SSN issued: PA[6496]

Notes for Edith L. Grew:

Birth: Mar. 2, 1903
Death: Apr. 2, 1990

Edith is the daughter of Adam and Sarah Miller Grew
Lutheran.

Obituary: Edith L. (GREW) CHRISTNER, 1990, Garrett, Somerset County, PA - Daily American, April 4, 1990

Edith L. Christner, 87, of Garrett, died Apr. 2, 1990, at Meyersdale Manor. Born Mar. 2, 1903, in Summit Mills, a daughter of the late Adam and Sadie (Miller) Grew. Also preceded in death by a son, Robert, and a brother, John Grew. Survived by these children: Leroy Christner, Meyersdale RD 1; Odette, wife of Michael Dneaster, Garrett, and June, wife of Harold Miller, Garrett RD 1. Grandchildren: Roger, Kim, Terry, Bonnie, Donna and Michael. Great-Grandchildren: Tammy, Teresa, Steve, Greg, Lisa, Mary Beth and Johnny. Great-great-grandchildren: Jonathon and Justin.

Life member of the Mt. Tabor Lutheran Church of Garrett and the Garrett Senior Citizens. Friends will be received from 2-4 and 7-9 p.m. Wednesday at the Price Funeral Home, Meyersdale, where service will be conducted at 2 p.m. Thursday, with Pastor Pamela Armstrong and Pastor Charles Lady officiating. Interment Highland Cemetery, Garrett.

Burial: Highland Cemetery, Garrett, Somerset Co., PA

More About Edith L. Grew:
Burial: Garrett Highland Cemetery, Summit Twp., Somerset Co., PA
Christened: Lutheran

Children of Harry Christner and Edith Grew are:

+   3988   i.   Leroy Emerson[9] Christner, born 07 Jun 1921 in Garrett, Somerset Co., PA; died 16 Jan 2005 in Meyersdale, Somerset Co., PA.

     3989   ii.   Robert Burns Christner, born 04 Mar 1923 in Garrett, Somerset Co., PA; died 10 Apr 1923.

                   More About Robert Burns Christner:
                   Burial: Highland Cemetery, Garrett, Somerset Co., PA

+   3990   iii. June Matilda Christner, born 09 May 1925 in Garrett, Somerset Co., PA.
+   3991   iv.   Odette Lucille Christner, born 27 Nov 1927 in Garrett, Somerset Co., PA; died 05 Jul 2010 in Garrett, Somerset Co., PA.

2007. Edward Carl[8] Christner (Mahlon[7], Herman[6], Abraham D.[5], Joseph "Zep"[4], Johannes John Hans[3], Christian[2], Christen[1])[6497,6498,6499,6500] was born 09 Mar 1895 in Garrett, Summit Twp., Somerset Co., PA[6501,6502,6503,6504,6505,6506], and died 09 May 1988 in Meyersdale, Somerset Co., PA[6507]. He married **(1) Gertrude E. Engle**[6508], daughter of John Engle and Amanda Swerner. She was born 1904 in Connellsville, Fayette Co., PA[6509]. He married **(2) Louella Donahue**[6509] 21 Nov 1969 in Mineral, WV[6510]. She was born 1904 in Garrett, Somerset Co., PA[6511], and died 18 Jun 1974 in Meyersdale, Garrett, Somerset Co., PA[6511].

Notes for Edward Carl Christner:
Birth: Mar. 9, 1885
Death: May 9, 1988

Spouse: Louella Donahue Christner (1904 - 1974)

Burial: Highland Cemetery, Garrett, Somerset Co., PA

SS# 191-07-4298 Iss. PA   Last zip 15552

Obituary: Edward C. Christner, 1988 Meyersdale, Somerset Co., PA
Edward C. Christner, 93, of Meyersdale. Friends will be received Wednesday, 2-4 and 7-9 p.m., at Leckemby

Funeral Home, Meyersdale, where services will be Thursday at 2 p.m. with the Rev. Charles Lady officiating. Interment, Highland Cemetery, Garrett.

Obituary: Daily American May 10, 1988

Edward C. Christner, 93 of Meyersdale was dead on arrival at the Meyersdale Community Hospital on May 9, 1988. Born Mar 9, 1885 in Garrett, a son of the late Mahlon and Matilda (Pritts) Christner. Also preceded in death by two wives, Gertrude Engle and Louella Donahue. Survived by a son, Carlson, of Hermosa Beach, CA. Also survived by a sister, Catherine Brant, of Meyersdale. He was a member of the Mt. Tabor Lutheran Church in Garrett, the Meyersdale American Legion and the Meyersdale V.F.W. Arrangements, in charge of the Leckemby Funeral Home in Meyersdale are incomplete.

More About Edward Carl Christner:
Burial: Garrett Highland Cemetery, Summit Twp., Somerset Co., PA
Christened: Lutheran, Garrett, Somerset Co., PA
Military service: Bet. 1918 - 1919[6512]
Residence: 01 Apr 1940, Meyersdale, Somerset Co., PA[6512]
Social Security Number: 191-07-4298/[6513]
SSN issued: PA[6513]

Notes for Gertrude E. Engle:
Gertie's father was John Engle and her mother was Amanda Swerner. Information by Tom Christner, RR# 1, Garrett, PA.

More About Gertrude E. Engle:
Residence: 01 Apr 1940, Canton, Stark Co., OH[6514]

Notes for Louella Donahue:
Birth: 1904
Death: Jun. 18, 1974 - PA

Spouse: Edward C. Christner (1885 - 1988)

Burial: Highland Cemetery, Garrett, Somerset Co., PA

More About Louella Donahue:
Burial: Garrett Highland Cemetery, Summit Twp., Somerset Co., PA
Residence: 1930, Summit, Somerset Co., PA[6515]

Child of Edward Christner and Gertrude Engle is:
    3992   i.   Carlson Drew[9] Christner[6516,6517], born 31 Aug 1921 in Pittsburgh, Allegheny Co., PA[6518,6519]; died 29 Jan 1990 in Hermosa Beach, Los Angeles Co., CA[6520,6521]. He married Clarice Marie Fega[6522] 24 Feb 1962 in NV[6523]; born 01 Sep 1920 in KS[6524]; died 30 Apr 1989 in Hermosa Beach, Los Angeles Co., CA[6524].

                Notes for Carlson Drew Christner:
                Information from Tom Christner RR#1 Garrett, PA.

                Burial: Green Hills Memorial Park, Rancho Palos Verdes, Los Angeles Co., CA
                Plot: Summit Lawn, 508, C
                Find A Grave Memorial# 71287359

                More About Carlson Drew Christner:
                Military service: 23 Mar 1944, Los Angeles Co., CA[6525]
                Residence: 1975, Hermosa Beach, CA[6526]
                Social Security Number: 284-14-0747/[6527]
                SSN issued: OH[6527]

                Notes for Clarice Marie Fega:

Burial: Green Hills Memorial Park, Rancho Palos Verdes, Los Angeles Co., CA
Plot: Summit Lawn, 508, C
Find A Grave Memorial# 71287360

More About Clarice Marie Fega:
Residence: 1930, Burr Oak, Jewell, Kansas[6528]

2009. Jacob Henry[8] Christner (Mahlon[7], Herman[6], Abraham D.[5], Joseph "Zep"[4], Johannes John Hans[3], Christian[2], Christen[1])[6529,6530,6531,6532,6533] was born 13 Sep 1899 in Garrett, Summit Twp., Somerset Co., PA[6534,6535,6536], and died 17 Feb 1952[6536]. He married **Edna Leora Haer**[6536,6537] 19 Jun 1920 in Cumberland, Alleganey Co., MD. She was born 20 Jun 1902 in Garrett, Somerset Co., PA, and died 27 Jun 2002 in Meyersdale, Summit Twp., Somerset Co., PA[6538].

Notes for Jacob Henry Christner:

More About Jacob Henry Christner:
Burial: Garrett Highland Cemetery, Summit Twp., Somerset Co., PA[6539]
Christened: Luthern, Garrett, Somerset Co., PA[6539]
Residence: 01 Apr 1940, Garrett, Somerset Co., PA[6540]

Notes for Edna Leora Haer:
Edna's Father was Noah Haer & mother was Viola Mae Grove. What a woman! "Little Edna" she was known to her friends and relatives. She was a small woman but mighty as she raised her ten children after the death of husband "Jake" who passed away fifty years ago. Edna's goal seemed to be to live to reach 100 yours old which she did on June 20, 2002. Her birthday was announced by Willard Scott on national TV and repeated on WJAC-TV. Her children gathered together on her birthday, except for Nancy Stoner because her mother-in-law died at the same time, to receive communion with her and celebrate her life. Saterday following her birthday she received family and friends at Meyersdale Church of the Brethern again. She was so happy to reach this milestone. The other childern not named were Thomas,Mack,Harold,Sprawls,Arlene Houston, and Hazel Hoover. Sprawls and Hazel are deceased. After the celebration ended, Little Edna slowly declined for one week until granddaughter Debbie Myers, a nurse found she had slept away to join her beloved husband Jake. On July 1, 2002, nearly 100 family and friends celebrated her life recalling many happy events from the past, sharing the love which emanated from her to all she met. Little Edna gave birth to 10 childern at her home in Garrett, PA. There she baked bread, washed,ironed,and kept house for her family. There she also had room for all the neighborhood children who gathered to play hide and seek, kick the can and tag around the light pole in front of the house. After she left Garrett, she made more friends as she lived with daughter Miriam Sembower Stephens in Rockwood and "Tootie" Mary Catherine Hanks in Friedens at the flower shop and greenhouse, continuing activities in "Over 55 Speeders Club" and tacking care of children. Later she went to live with her daughter Barbara Myers in Meyersdale PA. until the end. Truly this was a woman! What a woman! Written by Rev. Jay Lewis Christner from Albert Raymond From Lewis From Hermon From Joseph(Zep) From John (Hans) and Frany.

OBIT: Edna L. (HAER) CHRISTNER, 2002, Meyersdale, Somerset County, PA

CHRISTNER

Edna L. Christner, 100, of Meyersdale, formerly of Somerset, died June 27, 2002 at her daughter Barbara's residence. Born June 20, 1902 in Summit Township, she was the daughter of Noah C. and Viola (Grove) Haer. She was preceded in death by her parents, husband Jacob H. Christner (1952); children Hazel Hoover and Sprawls Christner; sister Audrey Schrock; and brothers Otto and Glenn Haer. She is survived by children, Harold married to the former Helen Haer, Garrett; Miriam Stephens, Somerset; Barbara, married to Glenn Meyers, Meyersdale; Thomas, married to the former Peggy Haer, Garrett; Arlene, married to Frank Houston, Chardon, OH; Mack, married to the former Bernice Suder, Meyersdale; Nancy, married to Donald Stoner, Murrysville; Mary, married to Barry Hanks, Somerset; 26 grandchildren; 48 great-grandchildren; 18 great-great-grandchildren; sisters, Dorothy, married to Oscar Steinly, Garrett; Betty, married to John Weigle, Somerset; and close friends, Dr. Thomas Strunk and family, Johnstown. Edna attended Mt. Tabor Lutheran Church, Garrett and was a member of the "Over 55 Speeders Club." Family will receive friends from 2 to 4 and 7 to 9 p.m. Monday at Deaner Funeral Home, Berlin, where services will be held 11 a.m. Tuesday with Rev. Jay Christner officiating.

Interment, Highland Cemetery, Garrett. Memorial contributions may be sent to Mt. Tabor Lutheran Church, Garrett, PA 15542.

Daily American, June 29, 2002

More About Edna Leora Haer:
Burial: Garrett Highland Cemetery, Summit Twp., Somerset Co., PA
Christened: Luthern, Garrett, Somerset Co., PA
Residence: 1930, Garrett, Somerset Co., PA[6541]

Children of Jacob Christner and Edna Haer are:

+ 3993   i.   Harold Dean (Kosh)[9] Christner, born 23 Jan 1921 in Garrett, Somerset Co., PA; died 22 Apr 2006 in Windber, Cambria Co., PA.

+ 3994   ii.   Hazel M. Christner, born 15 Apr 1922 in Garrett, Somerset Co., PA; died 23 Aug 1984 in Garrett, Somerset Co., PA.

+ 3995   iii.   Miriam Virginia Christner, born 21 Mar 1924 in Garrett, Somerset Co., PA.

+ 3996   iv.   Barbara Christner, born 06 Jun 1926 in Garrett, Somerset Co., PA; died 05 Apr 2013 in Meyersdale. Somerset Co., PA.

+ 3997   v.   Thomas Jacob Christner, born 18 Sep 1928 in Garrett, Somerset Co., PA; died 27 Sep 2010 in Garrett, Somerset Co., PA.

   3998   vi.   Sprawls Edward Christner, born 31 Aug 1930 in Garrett, Somerset Co., PA[6542,6543]; died 24 Jul 1978 in Little Rock, Pulaski Co., AR[6544]. He married Pauline Pritts.

> Notes for Sprawls Edward Christner:
> Birth: Aug. 31, 1930
> Death: Jul. 24, 1978
>
> SS#187-24-4193 ISS PA   Last address 72117 Little Rock, AR
>
> Obituary: Sprawls E. CHRISTNER, 1978 formerly of Garrett, Somerset Co., PA - The Republic, July 27, 1978
>
> Sprawls E. Christner, 47, of Little Rock, Arkansas, formerly of Garrett, died July 24, 1978 in Veteran's Hospital Little Rock. Born August 31, 1930 in Garrett, he was the son of the late Jacob Christner and Edna (Haer) Christner of Friedens. He is survived by widow, Paula Christner of Little Rock. He was a brother of Harold, Thomas and Mack, all of Garrett; Mrs. Cloyd (Hazel) Hoover, Markleton; Mrs. Howard (Miriam) Stephens, Somerset; Mrs. Glenn (Barbara) Meyers, Meyersdale; Mrs. Frank (Arlene) Houston, Chardon, Ohio; Mrs. Donald (Nancy) Stoner, Murraysville; Mrs. Barry (Mary) Hanks, Friedens. He was a career veteran of U.S. Air Force and a member of VFW and American Legion in Somerset. Family received friends at the Deaner Funeral Home, Stoystown. Remains were removed to Garrett Lutheran Church to lie in state until services at 2 p.m. Thursday, the Rev. Jason Stanton officiating. Interment, Garrett Cemetery.
>
> Burial: Highland Cemetery, Garrett, Somerset Co., PA
>
> More About Sprawls Edward Christner:
> Burial: 17 Jul 1978, Garrett Cem.PA.
> Social Security Number: 187-24-4193/[6545]
> SSN issued: Connellsville, Fayette Co., PA[6545]

+ 3999   vii.   Arlene Christner, born 28 Oct 1932 in Garrett, Somerset Co., PA.

+ 4000   viii.   Mack Eugene Christner, born 08 May 1935 in Garrett, Somerset Co., PA.

+ 4001   ix.   Nancy Christner, born 27 Apr 1937 in Garrett, Somerset Co., PA.

+ 4002   x.   Mary Catherine Christner, born 01 Feb 1939 in Garrett, Somerset Co., PA.

2010. Catharine M.[8] Christner (Mahlon[7], Herman[6], Abraham D.[5], Joseph "Zep"[4], Johannes John Hans[3], Christian[2], Christen[1])[6546] was born 29 Jun 1906 in Garrett, Summit Twp., Somerset Co., PA[6546,6547], and died 22

Feb 1998 in Meyersdale, Somerset Co., PA. She married **Walter J. Brant** 05 Jul 1923. He was born 10 Apr 1903[6548], and died May 1964[6548].

Notes for Catharine M. Christner:
Birth: Jun. 29, 1906
Death: Feb. 22, 1998

Obituary: Daily American, February 24, 1998

Catherine Brant, 91, of Garrett, died Feb. 22, 1998, at Meyersdale Medical Center. Born June 29, 1906, in Garrett. A daughter of the late Mahlon and Matilda (Pritts) Christner. Also preceded in death by her husband, Walter J. Brant, May 1964; a sister, Edna Decker, and five brothers: George, Edward, Harry, Jacob and Washington Christner. Survived by four children: Delores, wife of Robert Schrock, Meyersdale; James C., married to the former Doris Estnick, and Elisabeth, wife of Albert Judy, both of Garrett, and Mary Louise, wife of Charles Arnold, Seville, Ohio. Also 12 grandchildren,19 great-grandchildren, and 3 great-great-grandchildren. Member of the Mt. Tabor Lutheran Church, Garrett. Friends will be received from 2-4 and 7-9 p.m. Tuesday at the Price Funeral Home, Meyersdale, where service will be conducted at 1:30 p.m. Wednesday, with Pastor Randall Marburger officiating. Interment, Highland Cemetery, Garrett.

Burial: Highland Cemetery, Garrett, Somerset Co., PA
Find A Grave Memorial# 77198743

More About Catharine M. Christner:
Burial: Garrett Highland Cemetery, Summit Twp., Somerset Co., PA
Christened: Lutheran, Garrett, Somerset Co., PA
Residence: 1920, Summit, Somerset Co., PA[6549]
Social Security Number: 211-12-6927/[6550]
SSN issued: PA[6550]

Notes for Walter J. Brant:
His parents Bengiman Brant & Elizabeth Sheeler.

Birth: 1903
Death: 1964

Burial: Highland Cemetery, Garrett, Somerset Co., PA
Find A Grave Memorial# 78072797

More About Walter J. Brant:
Burial: Garrett, Highland, Cem. PA.
Christened: Lutheran, Garrett, Somerset Co., PA
Social Security Number: 210-03-6214/[6551]
SSN issued: Pittsburgh, Allegheny Co., PA[6551]

Children of Catharine Christner and Walter Brant are:
4003	i.	Louise[9] Brant, born 16 Aug 1925 in Garrett, Somerset Co., PA. She married Charles Arnold.
4004	ii.	James Brant, born 20 Aug 1927 in Garrett, Somerset Co., PA. He married Doris Estnick.
4005	iii.	Elizabeth Brant, born 14 Jan 1929 in Garrett, Somerset Co., PA. She married Albert Judy.
4006	iv.	Delores Brant, born 27 Aug 1930 in Garrett, Somerset Co., PA. She married Robert Schrock.

2011. Benjamin Harrison[8] Husband (Amanda[7] Christner, Herman[6], Abraham D.[5], Joseph "Zep"[4], Johannes John Hans[3], Christian[2], Christen[1])[6552,6553] was born 15 Nov 1888 in Mt. Pleasant, Westmoreland Co., PA[6554,6555], and died 06 Dec 1959. He married **Lucy P. Husband**[6556]. She was born Abt. 1882 in Pittsburgh, Allegheny Co., PA[6556].

More About Benjamin Harrison Husband:
Residence: 1930, Connellsville, Fayette, PA[6557]

More About Lucy P. Husband:
Residence: 1930, Connellsville, Fayette, PA[6558]

Children of Benjamin Husband and Lucy Husband are:
    4007   i.   William H.[9] Husband, died 23 May 1985. He married Bessie Mae.
    4008   ii.   Edna P. Husband, died 08 Jul 1968.

2012. Grace Lucille[8] Husband (Amanda[7] Christner, Herman[6], Abraham D.[5], Joseph "Zep"[4], Johannes John Hans[3], Christian[2], Christen[1])[6559] was born 19 Aug 1893[6559], and died 06 Jan 1973 in Somerset Co., PA[6559]. She married **Charles Harrison Brallier**. He was born 1888, and died 12 Dec 1942 in Somerset Co., PA.

Notes for Grace Lucille Husband:
She didn't use her first name Grace but used a middle initial of H. maybe for Husband.

More About Grace Lucille Husband:
Burial: Husband Cemetery
Residence: 1920, Somerset, Somerset, PA[6559]

Notes for Charles Harrison Brallier:
He was an electriction for the Pennsylvania Electric Co. and as an assistant to the mortician Walter S. Hoffman. He was a member of First Christian Church of Somerset PA. Somerset Lodge #353 F. & A.M. New Castle consistory, Jaffa Shrine, Modern Woodmen.

He died from Paralysis of the Throat and was confined to his bed for several months.

He bought 2 parcels of land (48 & 45 acres) from Herman Christners Children. The land was bought Feb. 13 1935. He had to buy 3/7 interest of Mahlon, Albert, and Clarissa Christner for back taxes. They got the land March 8, 1899 see deed book vol. 117 page 197 Somerset, PA and see deed book vol. 337 page 41 Somerset, PA.

Child of Grace Husband and Charles Brallier is:
+   4009   i.   Charles Husband[9] Brallier, born 03 Sep 1919 in Somerset Co., PA; died 22 Nov 1990 in Somerset, Somerset Co., PA.

2013. Glenn H.[8] Christner (Albert Paul.[7], Herman[6], Abraham D.[5], Joseph "Zep"[4], Johannes John Hans[3], Christian[2], Christen[1]) was born 04 Sep 1909 in Garrett, Somerset Co., PA, and died 22 Jul 1974 in Meyersdale, Somerset Co., PA. He married **Mary Agnes Aggie Smith**. She was born 16 Aug 1911 in Meyersdale, Somerset Co., PA, and died 08 Jul 1995 in Hagerstown, Washington Co., MD.

Notes for Glenn H. Christner:
OBIT: Glenn H. CHRISTNER, 1974, Meyersdale, Somerset County, PA - Meyersdale Republican, July 25, 1974

Glenn H. Christner, 64, of 317 Lincoln Avenue, Meyersdale, died at his home July 22, 1974. Born in Garrett, Sept. 4, 1909, he was a son of Margaret (Gardner) Christner and the late Albert Christner. He was a retired B & O Railroad conductor, with 30 years of service, and a member of the Loyal Order Of Moose, Meyersdale. Surviving are his wife, the former Mary Agnes Smith; three daughters, Mrs. Robert (Dolores) Mitchell, Hooversville; Mrs. Donald (Joan) Kline, Martinsburg, WV; and Mrs. Lynn (Bonnie) Durst, Damascus, Md.; six grandchildren, two great-grandchildren; his mother, of Meyersdale; and three brothers, Fred and Clyde Christner, Garrett; and Paul Christner of Dover, DE. Friends are being received at Price Funeral Home, Meyersdale, where funeral service will be.

Birth: Sep. 1, 1909
Death: Jul. 22, 1974

Burial: Highland Cemetery, Garrett, Somerset Co., PA

More About Glenn H. Christner:
Burial: 25 Jul 1974, Highland Cem., Garrett, Pa.
Residence: 01 Apr 1940, Garrett, Somerset Co., PA*6560*

Notes for Mary Agnes Aggie Smith:
OBIT: Mary Agnes (SMITH) CHRISTNER, 1995, formerly of Meyersdale, Somerset County, PA - Daily American, July 10, 1995

Mary Agnes Christner, 83, of Boonsboro, MD formerly of Meyersdale, died July 8, 1995, at Washington County Hospital, Hagerstown, MD. Born Aug 16, 1911 in Meyersdale. A daughter of the late William A. and Hanna M. (Kraushaur) Smith. Also preceded in death by her husband, Glenn Herbert Christner. Survived by three daughters: Dolores, wife of Robert Mitchell, Hooversville; Joan, wife of Donald Kline, Martinsburg, WV and Bonnie, wife of Rodney McKenzie, Frederick, MD. Also five grandchildren and 2 great-grandchildren. Friends received from 7 to 9 p.m. Tuesday at the Price Funeral Home, Meyersdale, where service will be conducted at 2 p.m. Wednesday, with Pastor Barry Weyant officiating. Interment in Highland Cemetery, Garrett, PA.

More About Mary Agnes Aggie Smith:
Burial: Highland Cemetery, Garrett, Somerset Co., PA
Residence: 01 Apr 1940, Garrett, Somerset Co., PA*6560*

Children of Glenn Christner and Mary Smith are:
    4010   i.   Bonnie⁹ Christner. She married Lynn Durst.
    4011   ii. Joan Christner. She married Donald Kline.
    4012   iii. Dolores Christner*6560*, born 1931 in Pittsburgh, Allegheny Co., PA*6560*. She married Robert Mitchell.

        More About Dolores Christner:
        Residence: 01 Apr 1940, Garrett, Somerset Co., PA*6560*

2014. Frederick H.⁸ Christner (Albert Paul.⁷, Herman⁶, Abraham D.⁵, Joseph "Zep"⁴, Johannes John Hans³, Christian², Christen¹)*6561* was born 17 Oct 1911 in Somerset Co., PA*6561*, and died 21 Sep 1982 in Cumberland, Allegeny Co., MD*6561*. He married **Pearl E. Klink** 26 Sep 1934 in Garrett, Somerset Co., PA. She was born 10 Dec 1918 in Summit Twp., Somerset Co., PA, and died 02 Jan 1984 in Meyersdale, Somerset Co., PA.

Notes for Frederick H. Christner:
OBIT: Frederick H. CHRISTNER, 1982, Somerset, Somerset Co., PA - The Republic, September 30, 1982

Frederick H. Christner, 70, of Garrett, died Sept. 21, 1982, at Sacred Heart Hospital, Cumberland, MD. He was born Oct. 17, 1911, in Garrett, a son of the late Albert and Margaret (Gardner) Christner. He is survived by his wife, the former Pearl Klink; and these children:Fred, of Bossier City, LA; and Mrs. Doris Burkhart, Hagerstown, MD.; also five grandchildren and a great-granddaughter. He was a brother of Clyde of Garrett.

He retired from the Western Maryland Railroad after 44 years of service. He was a member of Moose Lodge No. 76, B.P.O.E. Lodge Number 1951, American Legion Home Aid, Garrett Hunting Camp, Laurel Falls Association and the Garrett Volunteer Fire Department. Friends were received at the Price Funeral Home, Meyersdale, where services were conducted with the Rev. William Phennicie officiating. Interment, Highland Cemetery, Garrett.

Birth: Oct. 17, 1911
Death: Sep. 21, 1982

Burial: Highland Cemetery, Garrett, Somerset Co., PA

More About Frederick H. Christner:
Burial: Highland Cemetery, Garrett, Somerset Co., PA
Residence: 1920, Summit, Somerset Co., PA*6561*

Notes for Pearl E. Klink:

Pearl is the daughter of Daniel Klink and Alice Bocker. This info came from Cary Christner of Meyersdale, Somerset Co., PA.

Obituary: Pearl E. (KLINK) CHRISTNER, 1984, Garrett, Somerset Co., PA - Daily American, January 3, 1984
Pearl E. Christner, 65, Garrett RD 1, died Jan. 2, 1984, Meyersdale Community Hospital. Born Dec. 10, 1918, Summit Twp., daughter of the late Daniel and Alice (Bockes) Klink. Preceded in death by her husband, Frederick H. Survived by a son, Fred, Bossier City, LA; daughter, Mrs. Doris Burkhart, Hagerstown, Md.; five grandchildren; and a great-granddaughter. A sister of Eugene Klink, Garrett RD l; Mrs. Margaret Forrest, Meyersdale RD 1; Mrs. Miriam Burkholder, Garrett RD 1; and Mrs. Hazel Bluebaugh, Berlin RD. She retired from the Meyersdale Mfg. Co. after 30 years of service. Friends will be received from 7-9 p.m. Tuesday, 2 - 4 and 7-9 p.m. Wednesday at Price Funeral Home, Meyersdale, where services will be conducted at 1 p.m. Thursday, with the Rev. William Phennicie. Interment, Highland Cemetery, Garrett.

More About Pearl E. Klink:
Burial: Highland Cemetery, Garrett, Somerset Co., PA
Christened: Jun 1919, St.Paul Church, St.Paul, Pa.

Children of Frederick Christner and Pearl Klink are:
+   4013   i.   Fred[9] Christner Jr., born 24 Mar 1935 in Summit Twp., Somerset Co., PA.
+   4014   ii. Doris Christner, born 15 Aug 1940 in Garrett, Somerset Co., PA.

2015. Clyde W.[8] Christner (Albert Paul.[7], Herman[6], Abraham D.[5], Joseph "Zep"[4], Johannes John Hans[3], Christian[2], Christen[1])[6562,6563,6564] was born 27 Jul 1913 in Garrett, Somerset Co., PA[6565,6566,6567], and died 22 Dec 1982 in Cumberland, Allegany Co., MD[6568,6569]. He married **Belva R. Burkholder**[6570] 25 Apr 1936 in Morgantown, Monongalia Co., WV. She was born 13 Aug 1918 in Garrett, Somerset Co., PA[6570], and died 04 May 1996 in Johnstown, Cambria Co., PA[6570].

Notes for Clyde W. Christner:
Obituary: Clyde W. Christner, Sr., 1982, Garrett, Somerset County, PA - The Republic, December 30, 1982

Clyde W. Christner Sr., 69 of Garrett died Dec 22, 1982, in Sacred Heart Hospital, Cumberland, Md. He was born Jul 27, 1913, in Garrett, a son of the late Albert and Margaret (Gardner) Christner. He is survived by his widow, the former Belva Burkholder; two sons and one daughter: Clyde W. Jr., Garrett; Cary, Meyersdale RD 3; and Janie, wife of William Ohler, Sipesville; 11 grandchildren. He was a retired PennDOT Assistant Superintendent; President of the Laurel Falls Association; president of the Brooklyn Hunting Club; and a member of the Hack Club. Friends were received in the Lecekbmy Funeral Home, where services were held with the Rev. William Phennicie officiating. Interment, Garrett Cemetery.

Birth: Jul. 22, 1913
Death: Dec. 22, 1982

Burial: Highland Cemetery, Garrett, Somerset Co., PA
Find A Grave Memorial# 78080034
SS# 705-12-8902 Iss.RR last zip 15542

More About Clyde W. Christner:
Burial: Highland Cemetery, Garrett, Somerset Co., PA
Residence: 1920, Summit, Somerset Co., PA[6571]
Social Security Number: 705-12-8902/[6572]
SSN issued: Railroad Board (Issued Through)[6572]

Notes for Belva R. Burkholder:
Obituary: Daily American, May 6, 1996

Belva R. Christner, 77 of Garrett died May 4, 1996 at Memorial Medical Center, Johnstown. Born Aug. 13,

1918, in Garrett. Daughter of the late John J. and Belva (Weddle) Burkholder. Preceded in death by husband, Clyde W., in 1982, and these brothers and sisters: Carl W., Robert, Clyde, Ellen Jean Walters and Peggy Burkholder and grandson, Kriss Gumbert. Survived by two sons, Clyde W. Jr., Garrett, and Gary, Meyersdale and daughter, Janie, wife of William Ohler, Sipesville; also 11 grandchildren, 22 great-grandchildren. Sister of Libert, Garrett RD 1, and Jeanette Romesberg, Cuyahoga Falls, OH. Member of Mt. Tabor Lutheran Church. Charter member of Laurel Falls Association. Also member of Hack Club. Friends will be received from 2 to 4 and 7 to 9 p.m. Monday at the Leckemby Funeral home, where service will be held at 2 p.m. Tuesday. Interment, Highland Cemetery, Garrett.

Birth: Aug. 13, 1918
Death: May 4, 1996

Burial: Highland Cemetery, Garrett, Somerset Co., PA
Find A Grave Memorial# 29764812

More About Belva R. Burkholder:
Burial: Highland Cemetery, Garrett, Somerset Co., PA
Christened: 1932, Garrett, Somerset Co., PA

Children of Clyde Christner and Belva Burkholder are:

+ 4015   i.   Clyde W. "Mush"[9] Christner Jr., born 18 Jan 1937 in Garrett, Somerset Co., PA.
+ 4016   ii.   Cary A. Christner, born 13 Feb 1940 in Garrett, Somerset Co., PA; died 10 Oct 1999 in Meyersdale, Somerset Co., PA.
+ 4017   iii.   Janie Kay Christner, born 22 May 1947 in Garrett, Somerset Co., PA.

2016. Ethel M.[8] Christner (Albert Paul.[7], Herman[6], Abraham D.[5], Joseph "Zep"[4], Johannes John Hans[3], Christian[2], Christen[1]) was born 02 Aug 1916 in Somerset Co., PA, and died Dec 1952. She married **Jarvis Brant** 1936 in Cumberland, Allegany Co., MD. He died Aug 1974 in Meyersdale, Somerset Co., PA.

More About Jarvis Brant:
Burial: Cleveland, OH

Children of Ethel Christner and Jarvis Brant are:

4018   i.   Jim[9] Brant, born in OH.
4019   ii.   Donna Brant, born 10 Sep 1939 in Beachdale, Brothersvalley Twp., Somerset Co., PA. She married Phillip Bluhme.

            Notes for Donna Brant:

4020   iii.   Gay Anne Brant, born Sep 1951 in OH.

2017. Albert Paul[8] Christner Jr. (Albert Paul.[7], Herman[6], Abraham D.[5], Joseph "Zep"[4], Johannes John Hans[3], Christian[2], Christen[1])[6573,6574] was born 23 Feb 1919 in Garrett, Somerset Co., PA[6575,6576,6577,6578], and died 05 Jan 1977 in Dover, Kent Co., DE[6579]. He married **Ferne Elizabeth Custer**[6580] 24 Mar 1940 in Garrett, Somerset Co., PA[6580]. She was born 19 Jun 1921 in Berlin, Somerset Co., PA[6580], and died 15 Aug 2008 in Phoenix, Maricopa Co., AZ[6580].

Notes for Albert Paul Christner Jr.:
Obituary - Meyersdale Republican, January 13, 1977

Albert P. Christner, 57, of Dover, DE, formerly of Garrett, died Jan 5, 1977 in Dover. He was born Feb 23, 1919, in Garrett, the son of Albert and Margaret (Gardner) Christner. Preceded in death by his father and a brother, Glenn, he is survived by his wife, the former Ferne Custer, and these children: Mrs. Jean Dockel of Dover, DE; Mrs. Marylyn Robinson of Philadelphia; also by his mother, Margaret of Berlin and five grandchildren. He was a brother of Fred and Clyde, both of Garrett. Funeral services were held in the Johnson and Son Funeral Home,

Berlin, with the Rev. Wayne Trout officiating. Internment, Berlin IOOF Cemetery.

More About Albert Paul Christner Jr.:
Burial: Berlin, Somerset Co., PA
Residence: 1920, Summit, Somerset Co., PA[6581]
Social Security Number: 159-12-1327/[6582]
SSN issued: Connellsville, Fayette Co., PA[6582]

Notes for Ferne Elizabeth Custer:

Children of Albert Christner and Ferne Custer are:
    4021   i.   Jean[9] Christner, born 07 Jun 1942 in Somerset Co., PA.
    4022   ii.   Marilyn Christner, born Oct 1944 in Somerset Co., PA.

2020. Francis Guy[8] Christner (William H.[7], Herman[6], Abraham D.[5], Joseph "Zep"[4], Johannes John Hans[3], Christian[2], Christen[1])[6583,6584,6585,6586,6587] was born 18 Jul 1899 in Connellsville, Fayette Co., PA[6588,6589,6590,6591], and died 1949 in Genesee Co., MI. He married **Mary E.** She was born 1906, and died 1986 in Genesee Co., MI.

More About Francis Guy Christner:
Residence: 1920, Burton, Genesee Co., MI[6592,6593]

Notes for Mary E:
Birth: 1906
Death: 1986 - Genesee Co., MI

Spouse: Francis G Christner (1899 - 1949)

Children: Billy Christner (1936 - 1939)

Burial: Evergreen Cemetery, Grand Blanc, Genesee Co., MI

Child of Francis Christner and Mary E is:
    4023   i.   Billy[9] Christner, born 1936; died 1939 in Genesee Co., MI.

        Notes for Billy Christner:
        Birth: 1936
        Death: 1939 - Genesee Co., MI

        Parents:
        Francis G Christner (1899 - 1949)
        Mary E Christner (1906 - 1986)

        Burial: Evergreen Cemetery, Grand Blanc, Genesee Co., MI

2023. Mildred Ruth[8] Christner (William H.[7], Herman[6], Abraham D.[5], Joseph "Zep"[4], Johannes John Hans[3], Christian[2], Christen[1])[6594] was born 14 Jan 1908 in Auburn, King Co., WA[6594], and died 08 Oct 1977 in Flint, Genesee Co., MI[6594]. She married **Dahl Melvin Johnson**[6594] 24 Dec 1935[6594]. He was born 29 Jul 1907[6594], and died 04 Apr 1997 in Burton, Genesee Co., MI[6594].

More About Mildred Ruth Christner:
Residence: 1910, Bacon, Charlotte Co., VA[6595]

Notes for Dahl Melvin Johnson:
Social Security Death Index

Name:Dahl M. Johnson
SSN:385-07-3087
Last Residence:48529 Burton, Genesee, MI
Born:29 Jul 1907
Died: 4 Apr 1997
State (Year) SSN issued:Michigan (Before 1951)

More About Dahl Melvin Johnson:
Residence: 1930, Burton, Genesee Co., MI[6596]

Child of Mildred Christner and Dahl Johnson is:

4024　　i.　Lloyd Arthur[9] Johnson[6597], born 11 Dec 1932 in Flint, Genesee Co., MI[6597]; died 03 Sep 1996 in Burton, Genesee Co., MI[6597].

　　　　　More About Lloyd Arthur Johnson:
　　　　　Residence: Burton, Genesee Co., MI[6597]

2028.　Grace Lucille[8] Christner (Francis A. "Wash"[7], Herman[6], Abraham D.[5], Joseph "Zep"[4], Johannes John Hans[3], Christian[2], Christen[1]) was born 25 Mar 1906 in Garrett, Somerset Co., PA, and died 29 Nov 1969. She married **William T. Larkin** 24 Feb 1932 in Somerset Co., PA. He was born 12 Nov 1896 in Paw Paw Co., WV[6598,6599], and died 30 Mar 1960 in Martinsburg, Berkeley Co., WV[6599].

Notes for William T. Larkin:
William is the son of Thomas Joseph and Catherine Shives Larkin.

William T., Larkin
WWi - Pvt. 6th Co., 2nd Battalion, 155th Depot Brig. Tr. Center
Camp Lee, VA

Enlisted 15 Aug 1918
Discharged 7 Jan 1919
Buried in Camp Hill Cemetery, Paw Paw, WV
Service Number: 34 68 589
Pension/VA Claim Number - XC 21 349 875

More About William T. Larkin:
Burial: 02 Apr 1960, Paw Paw Co., WV

Child of Grace Christner and William Larkin is:

4025　　i.　Joseph Francis[9] Larkin, born 27 May 1933 in Cumberland, Allegany Co., MD; died 02 Nov 1963.

2029.　Clarence H.[8] Christner (Francis A. "Wash"[7], Herman[6], Abraham D.[5], Joseph "Zep"[4], Johannes John Hans[3], Christian[2], Christen[1]) was born 29 Mar 1910 in Garrett, Somerset Co., PA, and died 04 Dec 1993 in Grantsville, Garrett Co., MD. He married **Leona Haer** 1938. She was born 15 Apr 1912 in Pittsburgh, Allegheny Co., PA, and died 12 Aug 2002.

Notes for Clarence H. Christner:
Obituary: Clarence H. CHRISTNER, 1993, Garrett, Somerset Co., PA - Daily American, December 6, 1993

Clarence H. Christner, 83 Garrett, died Dec 4, 1993, in Goodwill Nursing Center, Grantsville. Born Mar 29, 1910, in Garrett, son of the late Francis and Clara (Hughes) Christner. Survived by widow, Leona (Haer) and these children: Millard Christner, Portland, OR; Eleve wife of the late Spurgeon Romesburg; Lynnie, wife of Kenneth O'Neal and Karen wife of Paul Meyers, all of Meyersdale, and Aletha wife of Elvin Sanner, Cleveland, OH; also these grandchildren: Kimberly Thompson, Steven and Timothy Meyers, Ryan and Roger O'Neal, and two great-grandchildren, Matthew and Jessica Thompson. Retired B&O Railroad trackman. Friends received from 2 to 9 p.m. Monday at Leckemby Funeral Home, where service will be at 11 a.m. Tuesday, Pastor Robert Stahl. Interment, Highland Cemetery, Garrett. Family suggests contributions be made to Alzheimer's Disease Fund.

CLARENCE CHRISTNER - New Republic, December 16, 1993
Clarence H. Christner, 83, of Garrett, died Dec. 4, 1993, in Goodwill Nursing Center, Grantsville, MD. He was born on March 29, 1910, in Garrett, a son of the late Francis and Clara (Hughes) Christner. He is survived by widow, Leona (Haer); these children; Eleve, wife of the late Spurgeon Romesburg; Lynnie, wife of Kenneth O'Neal, and Karen, wife of Paul Meyers, all of Meyersdale, and Aletha, wife of Elvin Sanner, Cleveland, OH; also these grandchildren: Kimberly Thompson, Steven and Timothy Meyers, Ryan and Roger O'Neal; two great grandchildren: Matthew and Jessica Thompson; and a brother, Millard Christner, Portland, OR. Mr. Christner was a retired B & O Railroad trackman. Friends were received Monday at Leckemby Funeral Home, where service was held Tuesday; Pastor Robert Stahl officiating. Interment, Highland Cemetery, Garrett.

Burial: Highland Cemetery, Garrett, Somerset Co., PA
Find A Grave Memorial# 76586162

She was very nasty woman and very mean.

More About Clarence H. Christner:
Burial: Highland Cemetery, Garrett, Somerset Co., PA
Residence: 01 Apr 1940, Garrett, Somerset Co., PA[6600]

Notes for Leona Haer:
Birth: Apr. 15, 1912
Death: Aug. 13, 2002

Obituary: Leona Pauline (HAER) CHRISTNER, 2002 formerly of Meyersdale, Somerset County, PA - Daily American, August 13, 2002

Leona Pauline Christner, 90, of Ridgeley, WV formerly of Meyersdale, died Aug. 12, 2002 at Sacred Heart Hospital, Cumberland, MD. Born April 15, 1912 in Garrett. A daughter of the late Howard and MO (Walters) Haer. She was preceded in death by her husband, Clarence H. Christner on Dec. 4, 1993. Surviving are four daughters: Eleve, wife of the late Spurgeon Romesburg, Karen, wife of Paul Meyers, both of Meyersdale, Lynnie, wife of Kenneth O'Neil, Ridgeley, WV and Aletha, wife of Elvin Sanner, Cleveland, OH; one brother, Merle Haer and wife Peggy, Sandusky, OH; one sister, Peggy, wife of Tom Christner, Garrett; five grandchildren: Kimberly Romesburg, Steven Meyers and wife Cathy, Timothy Meyers, Ryan O'Neil and wife Jacque and Roger O'Neil; and three great-grandchildren: Matthew and Jessica Thompson and Ashley Meyers. She was a member of the Meyersdale Main Street Brethren Church. At the request of the deceased, there will be no public viewing or visitation. Private funeral services will be held at 2 p.m. Tuesday at the M. Ray Leckemby Funeral Home with Rev. Robert Stahl officiating. Interment, Highland Cemetery, Garrett. In lieu of flowers, contributions may be made to the Meyersdale Main Street Brethren Church.

Burial: Highland Cemetery, Garrett, Somerset Co., PA

More About Leona Haer:
Burial: Highland Cemetery, Garrett, Somerset Co., PA
Residence: 01 Apr 1940, Garrett, Somerset Co., PA[6600]

Children of Clarence Christner and Leona Haer are:
+   4026   i.   Eleve[9] Christner, born 21 Oct 1935 in Pittsburgh, Allegheny Co., PA.
       4027   ii.   Aletha Christner, born 19 Feb 1939. She married Elvin Sanner 28 Jun 1958.
+   4028   iii. Lynnie Christner, born 27 Dec 1946.
+   4029   iv.   Karen Christner, born 02 Oct 1949.

2030. Lawerence William[8] Christner (Francis A. "Wash"[7], Herman[6], Abraham D.[5], Joseph "Zep"[4], Johannes John Hans[3], Christian[2], Christen[1]) was born 29 Mar 1910 in Garrett, Somerset Co., PA, and died 29

Nov 1969 in Somerset Co., PA. He married **Evelyn Rebecca Boden**[6601] 27 Jul 1936. She was born 27 Nov 1918 in Garrett, Somerset Co., PA, and died 03 Mar 2006 in Somerset, Somerset Co., PA[6601].

Notes for Lawerence William Christner:
Birth: Mar 29, 1910
Death: Nov 29, 1969

Burial: Highland Cemetery, Garrett, Somerset Co., PA

More About Lawerence William Christner:
Burial: Highland Cemetery, Garrett, Somerset Co., PA
Residence: 1910, Summit, Somerset Co, PA[6602]

Notes for Evelyn Rebecca Boden:
ROMESBERG - Evelyn. Rebecca (Boden) ,Christner Romesberg, 87 of :Somerset, formerly of Garrett, passed away on March. 3, 2006 at Somerset Hospital. Born Nov. 27, 1918 in Garrett, she is the daughter of' the late George W. and Laura (Hoover) Boden. She is preceded in death by her first husband, "Lawrence W. Christner "and second husband, Wilbur Romesberg, brothers Joseph and Nortan Boden, and sister, Gladys (Boden) Kadvekar. She is survived by'. her children, William Christner, Garrett; Gary Christner. and wife Barbara, Garrett; and Lana Lafferty, Somerset; grandchildren Donna Warnick and husband Donni; Casey Christner" and wife Deb Michelle Gilbert and husband, David; Amy Lafferty and Melissa Christner; and fiance. Ron; and great grandchildren; Bryan' Basinger, Shawn. Warnick, Mathew Christner, Kayla Lafferty, Jacob Gilbert; Leigha and Dakota Critchfield, and Keriann Beard. She is also survived by these brothers and sisters: George Boden, Meyersdale; Hazel Clark, Maple Heights, OH; Bruce Boden, Glade Springs, VA; Edna Grace Bethel, Durrant, OK; Gladys Shelson, MD and numerous nieces and nephews. She had been an employee of Meyersdale Manufacturing and Clapper Manufacturing. She loved working with flowers, gardening and Pittsburgh Pirates baseball. She also enjoyed spending time with her father family and grandchildren The family will receive friends from 2 to 5 p.m.Sunday at Miller Funeral Home, Somerset, where a service will be held at 1 p.m.,Monday, The. Rev. Ruth _____officiating. Interment at Highland Cemetery.

Birth: Nov. 27, 1918
Death: Mar. 3, 2006

Burial: Highland Cemetery, Garrett, Somerset Co., PA

More About Evelyn Rebecca Boden:
Burial: Highland Cemetery Garrett, PA
Residence: 1930, Garrett, Somerset Co., PA[6603]

Children of Lawerence Christner and Evelyn Boden are:
+   4030   i.   William Dale[9] Christner, born 15 Jun 1937 in Pittsburgh, Allegheny Co., PA; died 11 Aug 2009 in
                       Garrett, Summit Twp., Somerset Co., PA.
+   4031   ii.   Gary Christner, born 13 Jun 1939 in Pittsburgh, Allegheny Co., PA.
+   4032   iii.   Lana Sue Christner, born 13 Apr 1950.

2031. Millard Francis[8] Christner (Francis A. "Wash"[7], Herman[6], Abraham D.[5], Joseph "Zep"[4], Johannes John Hans[3], Christian[2], Christen[1])[6604] was born 24 Jul 1919 in Garrett, Somerset Co., PA[6605], and died 07 Jul 2002 in Portland, Multnomah Co., OR[6606]. He married **(1) Frances**[6607].   He married **(2) Maida Joan Conrad** 01 Nov 1952 in Seattle, King Co., WA. She was born 11 Jul 1925 in Harmattan, Mountain View, Alberta, Canada. He married **(3) Lorraine Kendall**[6608] 30 Nov 1963 in Multnomah Co., OR[6608].

Notes for Millard Francis Christner:
Maida and Millard divorced in 1961.

Obituary:
CHRISTNER, Millard F Sr; 82; Garrett PA>Portland OR; Oregonian; 2002-7-11;

More About Millard Francis Christner:
Residence: 1930, Garrett, Summit Twp., Somerset Co., PA[6609]
Social Security Number: 200-05-4229/[6610]
SSN issued: PA[6610]

Notes for Maida Joan Conrad:
Maida told me this story: Sep 2013

I had to chuckle to myself - our ancestry seems pretty German, Scotch and Irish - but my mother said there was a rumor of an American Indian in the wood pile somewhere - and I believe it is true because my maternal grandfather; two of my brothers, and a nephew certainly could 'pass' ! To me that would be so funny.

In the early 30's - an Indian tribe that was on a res about 30 miles sw of our farm came by w/teepees, horses, dogs, wives and children. They set up in a grove of threes across the road from our home area and worked for my father picking roots on a quarter section he was clearing for planting grain - and they worked for a beef (starving on the res). There was a young boy the same age as my bro. 6 yrs. older than me that played with my brothers. My mother gave him some of their clothes to wear. A girl was riding by our house on her way to some cousins and saw what she thought was my brother
standing in the yard; she spoke to him and he didn't answer - turns out it was the Indian boy who didn't speak English.

My brothers had a lot of fun that summer playing together - they learned to make a bow and arrows w/feathers and stone tips - how to throw knives, etc. What every 10 and 12 year old boy would love to do.

The boy's mother brought me a leather beaded indian purse and had tea with my Mom. I had it for years but guess it didn't make it though some of the later moves from the farm, etc. A few years later I got an Indian pony - buckskin w/black main and tail. She was so pretty and very fast. My means of transportation for years.

Childhood memories in the Canadian wilderness - which it is no longer.

Children of Millard Christner and Maida Conrad are:

+   4033   i.   Mary Teresa[9] Christner, born 09 Aug 1953 in C.B. Naval Base, Pt. Hueneme, Oxnard, Ventura Co., CA.
+   4034   ii.   Millard Francis. Christner Jr., born 11 Feb 1956 in Mitchel AFB, Hempstead, Nassau Co., NY.
     4035   iii.   Warren Joseph Christner, born 13 Jul 1957 in Mitchel AFB, Hempstead, Nassau Co., NY. He married Dana Deanne Wendt 14 Oct 2001 in Hillsboro, OR; born 23 Jan 1958.
     4036   iv.   Marilyn Ann Christner, born 22 Feb 1959 in Aurora, Arapahoe Co., CO. She married Bradley Hoffman 04 Aug 1979 in Ft. Collins, Larimer Co., CO; born 03 Sep 1957.
+   4037   v.   John Thomas Christner, born 21 Jun 1961 in Aurora, Arapahoe Co., CO.

2033. Sylvester[8] Christner (Lewis[7], Herman[6], Abraham D.[5], Joseph "Zep"[4], Johannes John Hans[3], Christian[2], Christen[1])[6611,6612,6613] was born 08 Apr 1887 in Garrett, Somerset Co., PA, and died 06 Sep 1952 in Somerset Co., PA. He married **Ruth Huston**. She was born 1889 in Somerset Co., PA, and died 01 Sep 1959 in Somerset Co., PA.

Notes for Sylvester Christner:
1910 soundex PA has Sylvester living at his (at the time) girlfriends parents house. He is listed as a son in law.

More About Sylvester Christner:
Residence: 01 Apr 1940, Somerset, Somerset Co., PA[6613]

More About Ruth Huston:
Residence: 01 Apr 1940, Somerset, Somerset Co., PA[6613]

Children of Sylvester Christner and Ruth Huston are:
     4038   i.   Paul Clayton "Pont"[9] Christner, born 15 Jul 1911 in Somerset Co., PA; died 22 Apr 1971. He married (1) Beth Flick. He married (2) Leona Pritts.

Notes for Paul Clayton "Pont" Christner:
Pont was paralyzed by a stroke at age 47 and spent the remaining years in a wheel chair.

SS#209-01-5380 ISS PA   -   Last address Rockwood near Somerset, PA

Notes for Leona Pritts:
Obituary: Leona Mae (Pritts) Christner 1984, Rockwood, Somerset County, PA - Daily American, September 19, 1984

Leona Mae Christner, 59 of Main Street, Rockwood died Sept. 18, 1984, in Somerset Community Hospital. Born Dec. 3, 1924, in Somerset, daughter of Isabelle (Yoder) Pritts, and the late Edmund Pritts. Preceded in death by her father; her husband, Paul; and one sister, Frances Gary. Survived by her mother, of Rockwood; one brother, Fred Pritts, Wilkensburg; two sisters, Mary Louise Faidley, and Shirley, wife of James Leasock, both of Rockwood; six nieces and 11 nephews. Friends will be received after 7 p.m. today (Wednesday) and 2 to 4 and 7 to 9 p.m. Thursday at Robert H. Halverson Funeral Home, where service will be conducted Friday at 11 a.m., the Rev. Steven Forsythe. Interment, Somerset County Memorial Park.

+ 4039   ii.   Samuel Lewis Christner, born 13 Aug 1913 in Somerset Co., PA; died Sep 1983 in Tucson, Pima, Co., AZ.
+ 4040   iii. Janet Winifred Christner, born 23 Nov 1914 in Somerset Co., PA; died 27 Aug 1965 in Somerset Co., PA.
+ 4041   iv.   Clyde Donald "Teet" Christner, born 28 Sep 1915 in Somerset Co., PA; died 28 Nov 1972.
+ 4042   v.   Dorothy Lucille Christner, born 08 Sep 1919 in Somerset Co., PA; died 17 Sep 1999 in Somerset, Somerset Co., PA.
+ 4043   vi.   John Frederick Christner, born 11 May 1921 in Somerset Co., PA; died 04 Nov 2005 in Conebaugh, Cambria Co., PA.
+ 4044   vii. Jack Winters Christner, born 30 Dec 1924 in Somerset, Somerset Co., PA; died 06 Oct 1966 in Somerset, Somerset Co., PA.

2034. Eva[8] Christner (Lewis[7], Herman[6], Abraham D.[5], Joseph "Zep"[4], Johannes John Hans[3], Christian[2], Christen[1]) was born 18 Dec 1888 in Connellsville, Fayette Co., PA[6614], and died Nov 1964[6614]. She married **John Martin**[6615]. He was born 1887 in Connellsville, Fayette Co., PA[6615].

More About Eva Christner:
Social Security Number: 159-12-8409[6616]
SSN issued: PA[6616]

Children of Eva Christner and John Martin are:
4045   i.   Eva Rose[9] Martin.
4046   ii.   Grace Martin.
4047   iii. Mary B. Martin.

2037. Elsie Pearl[8] Christner (Lewis[7], Herman[6], Abraham D.[5], Joseph "Zep"[4], Johannes John Hans[3], Christian[2], Christen[1])[6617] was born 09 Jun 1894 in Connellsville, Fayette Co., PA, and died 13 Oct 1956 in Connellsville, Fayette Co., PA[6617]. She married **William Jennings Murray**. He was born 05 Apr 1894 in Kecksburg, Westmoreland Co., PA[6617], and died 04 Jul 1970 in Norvelt, Westmoreland Co., PA[6617,6617].

More About Elsie Pearl Christner:
Residence: 1930, Springdale, Allegheny Co., PA[6617]

More About William Jennings Murray:
Residence: 1942, 345 Fourth Ave. Coal miner for Hillman Coal and Coke Co. at Berking, PA in Allegheny Co../New Kensington, Westmoreland Co., PA[6617]

Children of Elsie Christner and William Murray are:
+ 4048   i.   William Louis[9] Murray, born 22 Aug 1915; died 25 May 1991.

4049 ii. Beulah Mae Murray, born 21 Jan 1918; died 01 Mar 2003. She married Telford Leland Mostoller; born 05 Oct 1912; died 04 May 1985.

    More About Beulah Mae Murray:
    Residence: 1930, Springdale, Allegheny Co., PA[6617]

+ 4050 iii. Paul Murray, born 08 Apr 1921 in PA; died 14 Jul 1983.
+ 4051 iv. Jerry Murray, born 30 May 1923; died 14 Feb 2000.

2038. Edgar James[8] Christner (Lewis[7], Herman[6], Abraham D.[5], Joseph "Zep"[4], Johannes John Hans[3], Christian[2], Christen[1]) was born 13 Jul 1896 in Connellsville, Fayette Co., PA, and died Sep 1967 in Somerset, Somerset Co., PA[6618]. He married **Helen Mimna**. She was born 23 Aug 1904 in Somerset, Somerset Co., PA[6619], and died 12 Oct 1975 in Odenton, Anne Arundel Co., MD[6619].

Notes for Edgar James Christner:
This info came from Tom Christner R.R. 1 Garrett, PA.

More About Edgar James Christner:
Residence: 1900, Garrett Borough, Somerset, PA[6620,6621,6622]
Social Security Number: 170-18-1854/[6623]
SSN issued: PA[6623]

Notes for Helen Mimna:
OBIT: Helen L. (MIMNA) CHRISTNER, 1975, Somerset, Somerset Co., PA -Somerset American, October 13, 1975

Mrs. Helen L. Christner, 71, Somerset RD 5, (Oak Ridge), died Oct. 12, 1975 at the Arundel Convalescent Home, Glen Burnie, Md. She was born Aug. 23, 1904 in Somerset and was a daughter of the late Charles and Laura (Winters) Mimna. She was preceded in death by her husband, Edgar, and a daughter, Fern Zeigler. Survived by her son, Charles C. of Odenton, MD. She was a sister of Mrs. Freda Gill, Pittsburgh, Mrs. Gladys Saylor, Johnstown, Curtis of McLean, Va., Mrs. Mary Jane Toney, Victoria, Tex. Mrs. Katherine Walmsly, and Kenneth of Flagstaff, Ariz. She was a member of Grace United Methodist Church and was a retired employe of Howard Johnsons. Friends are received from 7-9 p.m. Monday and 2 4 and 7-9 p.m. Tuesday in the Richard E. Hauger Funeral Home where service will be conducted Wednesday at 10:30 a.m. Rev. Charles Rummel officiating. Interment Somerset County Memorial Park.

Birth: Aug. 23, 1904 - Somerset Co., PA
Death: Oct. 12, 1975 - Glen Burnie, Anne Arundel Co., MD

Parents:
Charles Mimna (1874 - 1941)
Laura Ellen Winter Mimna (1879 - 1920)

Burial: Somerset County Memorial Park, Somerset, Somerset Co., PA
Find A Grave Memorial# 100532640

More About Helen Mimna:
Social Security Number: 198-20-1125/[6624]
SSN issued: PA[6624]

Children of Edgar Christner and Helen Mimna are:
 4052 i. Fern[9] Christner[6625], born 15 May 1928; died 25 Feb 1967. She married Dean Zeigler; died in Spring Grove, York Co., PA[6625].

    More About Fern Christner:
    Residence: 1930, Somerset, Somerset Co., PA[6625]

Notes for Dean Zeigler:
Dean is from York Pa.?

+ 4053   ii.   Charles Cavell 'Bud' Christner, born 16 Nov 1931 in Somerset Co., PA; died 08 Feb 2012 in Frederick, MD.

2039. Estella B.[8] Christner (Lewis[7], Herman[6], Abraham D.[5], Joseph "Zep"[4], Johannes John Hans[3], Christian[2], Christen[1]) was born 12 Mar 1898 in Garrett, Somerset Co., PA, and died 06 Dec 1983. She married **Russell Emmett Buckman** 16 Aug 1922 in Somerset Co., PA.

Notes for Estella B. Christner:
Trinity Lutheran Church

More About Estella B. Christner:
Burial: I.O.O.F. Cemetery Berlin PA

Child of Estella Christner and Russell Buckman is:
    4054   i.   Kathleen[9] Buckman. She married Floyd.

2040. Beulah D.[8] Christner (Lewis[7], Herman[6], Abraham D.[5], Joseph "Zep"[4], Johannes John Hans[3], Christian[2], Christen[1]) was born 20 Mar 1900 in Garrett, Somerset Co., PA[6626,6627], and died 08 Oct 1990 in Somerset Co., PA. She married **(1) Alfred Brocht.** She married **(2) Charles Martin.** He was born 12 Sep 1910 in Loyalhanna, and died 30 Jul 1991 in East Church St. Somerset PA.

Notes for Beulah D. Christner:
Trinity Luthern Church Somerset PA. She was the former owner of the Sugar bowl.

More About Beulah D. Christner:
Burial: I.O.O.F. Cemetery Berlin PA.
Residence: 1910, Summit, Somerset Co., PA[6628]

More About Charles Martin:
Burial: I.O.O.F. Cemetery Berlin PA.

Children of Beulah Christner and Alfred Brocht are:
    4055   i.   Alfred[9] Brocht Jr..
    4056   ii.   Betty Brocht.
+ 4057   iii. Beatrice Ann Brocht, born 02 Apr 1921 in Garrett, Somerset Co., PA.

2041. Walter H.[8] Christner (Lewis[7], Herman[6], Abraham D.[5], Joseph "Zep"[4], Johannes John Hans[3], Christian[2], Christen[1]) was born 13 May 1902, and died 24 Apr 1932. He married **Helen Lohr Beattie**.

Notes for Walter H. Christner:
Walter shot his uncle Mahlon Christner (son of Lewis) and then shot himself. This death/suicide was over the increase in rent on a house.

Birth: Mar. 13, 1902
Death: Apr. 24, 1932

Burial: Highland Cemetery, Garrett, Somerset Co., PA

More About Walter H. Christner:
Burial: Highland Cemetery, Garrett, Somerset Co., PA
Residence: 1930, Garrett, Somerset Co., PA[6629]

Child of Walter Christner and Helen Beattie is:

4058   i.   Walter[9] Christner Jr., born 31 May 1931 in Garrett, Somerset Co., PA; died 28 Dec 2001 in New Brighton, Beaver Co., PA[6629]. He married Bessie Lenhart.

> Notes for Walter Christner Jr.:
> Obituary: The New Republic, February 7, 2002
>
> Budd Christner, 70, of New Brighton, formerly of Baden, died Dec. 28, 2001 in Kendred Hospital, formerly Vencor Hospital.
>
> Born May 31, 1931 in Garrett, he was a son of the late Walter and Helen Lohr Christner Beattie. In addition to his parents, he was preceded in death by a brother, Robert Beattiel, a sister, Martha (Annie) Mimna, and a grandson; Richard Belcher Jr.
>
> He is survived by his wife; Bessie (Lenhart) Christner; a son and daughter-in-law, David and Darlene Christner, Economy; a daughter and son-in-law, Julie Belcher Baskel and her husband Ronlad, Aliquippa; grandchildren: Lori and Richard Lockhart, David Christner Jr. and Joseph Christner, all of Economy; and Brian and Jennifer Belcher, Baldwin; two great-grandchildren, Joshua and Taylor Lockhart; two brothers and sisters-in-law, Samuel and Sonja, Beattie, Meyersdale; and Charles and Elaine Beattie, Berlin; and a loving companion, Judy Kuzma, New Brighton.
>
> There was no public viewing. A memorial service was held at the Paul E. Bohn Funeral Home, Ambridge, with the Rev. Cletus Fahrion, Zion Lutheran Church, officiating.
>
> More About Walter Christner Jr.:
> Burial: Highland Cemetery, Garrett, Somerset Co., PA

2042. Mary B.[8] Christner (Lewis[7], Herman[6], Abraham D.[5], Joseph "Zep"[4], Johannes John Hans[3], Christian[2], Christen[1]) was born 20 Apr 1905, and died 20 Jun 1992. She married **Stover C. Meyer**. He was born 25 Jul 1903 in Bellefonte PA, and died 28 Mar 1988.

Children of Mary Christner and Stover Meyer are:

4059   i.   Mary Jane[9] Meyer.
4060   ii.   John H. Meyer.

2043. Albert Raymond[8] Christner (Lewis[7], Herman[6], Abraham D.[5], Joseph "Zep"[4], Johannes John Hans[3], Christian[2], Christen[1])[6630,6631,6632] was born 05 Apr 1907 in Garrett, Somerset Co., PA[6633,6634,6635], and died 17 Aug 1978 in Pittsburgh, Allegheny Co., PA[6636,6637]. He married **Viola M. Krug**[6638] 26 Jun 1928 in Frostburg, Allegany Co., MD. She was born 01 Dec 1912 in Elk Lick, Somerset Co., PA[6638,6639], and died 07 Oct 2008.

Notes for Albert Raymond Christner:
Birth: Apr. 5, 1907
Death: Aug. 17, 1978

Albert is the son of Lewis Christner and Eliza Walters
SS# 162-16-7614 Iss.PA Last address zip-15542

Obituary: The Republic, August 24, 1978
Albert R. Christner, 71, of Garrett died August 17, 1978 at Shadyside Hospital, Pittsburgh. Born April 5, 1907, in Garrett, he was the son of the late Lewis and Eliza (Walter) Christner. He is survived by one son, Jay of Somerset and two daughters, Avalon Keefer of Somerset and Kay Carol McLaughlin, Corpus Christi, Texas; eight grandchildren; and seven great-grandchildren. He was a brother of Estella Buckman; Beulah Martin; Mary Blach Meyer, all of Somerset; and William Christner of Pittsburgh. He was a member of Trinity Lutheran Church of Somerset. Friends were received at the Robert H. Halverson Funeral Home where services were conducted at 1:30 p.m. Saturday, with the Rev. Robert Driesen officiating. Interment, Highland Cemetery, Garrett.

Burial: Highland Cemetery, Garrett, Somerset Co., PA

More About Albert Raymond Christner:
Burial: Highland Cemetery, Garrett, Somerset Co., PA[6640]
Residence: 1930, Garrett, Somerset, PA[6640,6641,6642]

More About Viola M. Krug:
Residence: 1930, Garrett, Somerset, PA[6642]

Children of Albert Christner and Viola Krug are:
+   4061   i.   Rev. Jay Lewis[9] Christner, born 29 Oct 1929 in Garrett, Somerset Co., PA.
+   4062   ii.   Avalon Mae Christner, born 25 Feb 1932; died 30 Jul 2008 in Somerset, Somerset Co., PA.
+   4063   iii.   Kay Carol Christner, born 23 Aug 1945 in Garrett, Somerset Co., PA.

2048. Ruth Blanche[8] Christner (William[7], Freeman L.[6], Abraham D.[5], Joseph "Zep"[4], Johannes John Hans[3], Christian[2], Christen[1])[6643] was born 23 Jun 1903 in Somerset, Somerset Co., PA[6644], and died 27 Dec 1984 in Cadillac, Wexford Co., MI. She married **Ross Emerson Boyer**[6645,6646]. He was born 12 Dec 1897 in Somerset Co., PA[6647,6648], and died 08 Jun 1966 in Cumberland, Allegany Co., MD[6649].

More About Ruth Blanche Christner:
Burial: Husband Cemetery
Residence: 1930, Somerset, Somerset, PA[6650]

More About Ross Emerson Boyer:
Residence: 1930, Somerset, Somerset, PA[6650]

Children of Ruth Christner and Ross Boyer are:
      4064   i.   Gene L.[9] Boyer.
+   4065   ii.   Donald L. Boyer, born 23 Sep 1920 in Berlin, Somerset Co., PA; died 12 Aug 1983 in Alpena Co., MI.
      4066   iii.   Ardith Justice Boyer, born 1923[6650].

                     More About Ardith Justice Boyer:
                     Residence: 1930, Somerset, Somerset, PA[6650]

      4067   iv.   Irene L Boyer[6650], born 1930[6650].

                     More About Irene L Boyer:
                     Residence: 1930, Somerset, Somerset, PA[6650]

2052. Christner[8] (Hiram P. "Hiry"[7], Freeman L.[6], Abraham D.[5], Joseph "Zep"[4], Johannes John Hans[3], Christian[2], Christen[1])[6651,6652,6653] was born Apr 1900 in Westmoreland Co., PA[6654].

More About Christner:
Residence: 1900, Derry, Westmoreland, PA[6654]

Children of Christner are:
      4068   i.   Edna[9] Christner.
      4069   ii.   Dean Christner.
      4070   iii.   Helen Christner.
      4071   iv.   Ralph Christner.

2056. Calvin[8] Holliday (Margaret[7] Christner, Henry A.[6], Abraham D.[5], Joseph "Zep"[4], Johannes John Hans[3], Christian[2], Christen[1]) was born Mar 1890 in Connellsville, Fayette Co., PA. He married **Clara Blanch**. She was born 1888.

Notes for Calvin Holliday:
Occupation - Coal Miner

More About Calvin Holliday:
Residence: 1930, Grantsville, Garrett, MD[6655]

Children of Calvin Holliday and Clara Blanch are:
    4072   i.   Margaret L^9 Holiday[6656,6657], born 1917.

                  More About Margaret L Holiday:
                  Residence: 1920, Salisbury, Somerset, PA[6657]

    4073   ii. Anna Holliday, born 1920.

2062. Merle W.^{8} Shumaker (Wilson Milton^7, Elizabeth^6 Christner, Abraham D.^{5}, Joseph "Zep"^{4}, Johannes John Hans^3, Christian^2, Christen^1) was born 1909 in Berlin, Somerset Co., PA, and died 16 Apr 1978 in 26 Virginia Ave.. He married **Laura L. Lacy**.

Notes for Merle W. Shumaker:
Avid hunter and fisherman He died while fishing at Glades Run near Hyndman PA. Worked at B. & O. Railroad.

More About Merle W. Shumaker:
Burial: Hillcrest Burial Park

Children of Merle Shumaker and Laura Lacy are:
    4074   i.   Leon M.^{9} Shumaker.
    4075   ii. Vincent M. Shumaker.

2064. Martha^8 Traup (Martha MO^7 Christner, Elias^6, Abraham D.^{5}, Joseph "Zep"^{4}, Johannes John Hans^3, Christian^2, Christen^1) was born in Somerset Co., PA, and died 18 Apr 1980 in Somerset Co., PA. She married **McCaffrey**.

More About Martha Traup:
Burial: Weller Cemetery

Child of Martha Traup and McCaffrey is:
    4076   i.   William^9 McCaffrey.

2065. Lena Alverta^8 Baker (Louise^7 Christner, Elias^6, Abraham D.^{5}, Joseph "Zep"^{4}, Johannes John Hans^3, Christian^2, Christen^1) was born 13 Mar 1894 in Lincoln TWP., and died 15 Mar 1983 in Somerset Co., PA. She married **Harry B. Nair**.

More About Lena Alverta Baker:
Burial: Casebeer Cemetery by the Lutheran Church

Children of Lena Baker and Harry Nair are:
    4077   i.   Fred^9 Nair.
    4078   ii.   Joe Nair.
    4079   iii. Louise Nair.

2066. Charles F.^{8} Smith (Francis M.^{7}, Joanna^6 Christner, Abraham D.^{5}, Joseph "Zep"^{4}, Johannes John Hans^3, Christian^2, Christen^1) He married **Mary Louise**. She died 09 Aug 1981 in Lakeland Florida.

Children of Charles Smith and Mary Louise are:
    4080   i.   Bonnelle Louise^9 Smith.
    4081   ii.   Charlene F. Smith.
+ 4082   iii. Lucinda Smith.

2068. Howard E.[8] **Smith** (Francis M.[7], Joanna[6] Christner, Abraham D.[5], Joseph "Zep"[4], Johannes John Hans[3], Christian[2], Christen[1]) was born 11 Dec 1926 in Johnstown, Cambria Co., PA, and died 20 Jun 1982. He married **Lois Clark**.

Notes for Howard E. Smith:
He owned Smittys Parking Lot for 38 years. Automobile pay for parking area.

More About Howard E. Smith:
Burial: Richland Cemetery

Children of Howard Smith and Lois Clark are:

4083	i.	Deborah[9] Smith.
4084	ii.	James Smith.
4085	iii.	Linda Smith.
4086	iv.	Sharon Smith.
4087	v.	Terry Smith.
4088	vi.	Harry Smith.

2074. Herbert Earl[8] **Christner** (Rudolph[7], John C.[6], Christian[5], Joseph "Zep"[4], Johannes John Hans[3], Christian[2], Christen[1]) was born 29 Feb 1892 in Garrett, Somerset Co., PA[6658], and died 22 Apr 1976 in Meyersdale, Somerset Co., PA[6658]. He married **Lelia Lucille Baughman**[6658,6659]. She was born 07 Sep 1899 in Brothers Valley Twp., Somerset Co., PA[6660,6661], and died 14 May 1979 in Meyersdale, Somerset Co., PA[6662].

Notes for Herbert Earl Christner:
Birth: Feb 29, 1892
Death: Apr 22, 1976

This is the Earl that lived on what is referred as the Earl Christner Farm. Earl's great-grand father Joseph Zep Christner married to Barbara Burkholder had a land grant on the farm in1840. He (Zep) died after the 1850 census. Christner Cemetery. at Garrett PA. on Johnson Road and Phillippi Road. Part of the cemetery is under the road.on the farm of Earl Christner Southwest of the buildings about 50 rods on the hill above a spring along road leading from Garrett to Cross Roads Church is a cemetery There is a stone marked Franklin Christner born Jan.8 1878 Aged 6 MO (Son of Rufus) ???
Also Christian Christner died   10, 1888 aged 77y-3m--17d

Abraham Christner died March 4, 1879 71y--5m--4d ////// On April 28 1832 Christian Burkholder sold 200 acres in Elk Lick for $100.00 to Abraham Christner. The land is on Phillippi Road just south of the Center Luthern Church Near Garrett PA. This farm was first owned by Christian Burkholder's father John.

Jonas Christner died Jan. 26, 1881 67y--4m---12d

OBIT: H. Earl CHRISTNER, 1976, Garrett, Somerset County, PA - Meyersdale Republican, April 29, 1976

H. Earl Christner, 84, of Garrett RD 1, died April 22 in Meyersdale Community Hospital.   He was born Feb. 29, 1892, in Garrett, a son of the late Rudolph and   Amanda (Newman) Christner. Surviving are his wife, the former Leila Baughman and these children: Orville of Frostburg RD 2; Alfred of Berlin; Mrs. Ernest (Margaret) White of Meyersdale RD 3 and Mrs. Clyde (Betty) Clay of Rockwood RD; also eight grandchildren and seven great grandchildren.

He was a veteran of World War I and a member of the Meyersdale VFW.   Services were conducted at the Price Funeral Home April 25 with the Rev. David Fetter officiating. Interment, the Highland Cemetery in Garrett.

He (Earl) served in the Wagoner Supply Co. 320th INF 80th DIV. WW1
Herbert is his real FIRST name but he did not like to use it.

Burial: Highland Cemetery, Garrett, Somerset Co., PA

More About Herbert Earl Christner:
Burial: Highland Cem, Garrett, Somerset, PA[6662]
Christened: Lutheran
Residence: 01 Apr 1940, Summit, Somerset Co, PA[6663]

Notes for Lelia Lucille Baughman:
Birth: Sep 7, 1899
Death: May 15, 1979

OBIT: Leila L. (BAUGHMAN) CHRISTNER, 1979, Meyersdale, Somerset County, PA - The Republic, May 17, 1979

Mrs. Leila L. Christner, 79, of Meyersdale RD 3, formerly of Garrett RD 1, died May 14, 1979, at the Meyersdale Community Hospital. Born Sept. 7, 1899, in Brothersvalley Township she was a daughter of the late Harvey and Minerva (Pritz) Baughman. She was preceded in death by husband, H. Earl. She is survived by these children: Orville of Frostburg, Md. RD 2; Alfred of Monaca; Mrs. Margaret White of Meyersdale RD 3; Mrs. Betty Clay of Rockwood RD 1; also eight grandchildren and eight great-grandchildren. She was a sister of Harold of Jerome, Mrs. Leora Samuel of Boswell, Mrs. Mariam Wilkenson of Tire Hill and Mrs. Ruth Frye of Somerset RD. She was a member of the Mt. Tabor Lutheran Church. Friends will be received 2-4 p.m. and 7-9 p.m. Wednesday at the Price Funeral Home, Meyersdale, where services will be conducted at 2 p.m. Thursday with the Rev. David Fetter. Interment, Highland Cemetery, Garrett.

Burial: Highland Cemetery, Garrett, Somerset Co., PA

Leila (Lee la) was the great-grand daughter of the Baughmans rocks story at Mt. Davis, west of Garrett, PA.

More About Lelia Lucille Baughman:
Burial: Highland Cem, Garrett, Somerset, PA[6664]
Christened: Lutheran
Residence: 1930, Summit, Somerset Co., PA[6665]

Children of Herbert Christner and Lelia Baughman are:
+   4089   i.   Margaret[9] Christner.
+   4090   ii.   Orville R. "Speedy" Christner, born 1921 in Pittsburgh, Allegheny Co., PA.
+   4091   iii.   Betty Louise Christner, born 01 Jun 1923 in Summit Twp., Garrett, Somerset Co., PA; died 20 Oct 1996 in Somerset Co., PA.
+   4092   iv.   Alfred R. "Boots" Christner, born 1925.

2080. Nellie Mae[8] Burkholder (Sevilla[7] Christner, John C.[6], Christian[5], Joseph "Zep"[4], Johannes John Hans[3], Christian[2], Christen[1])[6666] was born 24 Oct 1902 in Somerset Co., PA[6666], and died 15 Nov 1988 in Meyersdale, Somerset Co., PA[6666]. She married **Roy Ackerman**[6666,6667]. He was born 17 Apr 1903 in Somerset Co., PA[6668,6669], and died 18 Jul 1972 in Somerset Co., PA[6670,6671].

More About Nellie Mae Burkholder:
Residence: 1910, Summit, Somerset Co., PA[6672]

More About Roy Ackerman:
Social Security Number: 211-12-7794/[6673]
SSN issued: Connellsville, Fayette Co., PA[6673]

Children of Nellie Burkholder and Roy Ackerman are:
   4093   i.   Zelda[9] Baker[6674], born 06 Jun 1924 in Summit Twp., Somerset Co., PA[6674]; died 04 Jun 1999 in Somerset, Somerset Co., PA[6674].
   4094   ii.   Elwood Burkholder[6674], born 15 Oct 1927 in Somerset Co., PA[6674]; died 15 Sep 1998 in Confluence, Somerset Co., PA[6674].

2084. Carrie Agnes⁸ Christner (Austin George⁷, Zachariah⁶, Christian⁵, Joseph "Zep"⁴, Johannes John Hans³, Christian², Christen¹)⁶⁶⁷⁵ was born 21 Jan 1890 in Garrett, Somerset Co., PA⁶⁶⁷⁶,⁶⁶⁷⁷, and died 19 Oct 1975 in Frostburg, Allegeny Co., MD. She married **George Carter**⁶⁶⁷⁸,⁶⁶⁷⁹. He was born 1884 in Pittsburgh, Allegheny Co., PA⁶⁶⁸⁰, and died 1955.

Notes for Carrie Agnes Christner:
Lived in Garrett PA.   She was the organist at Mt. Tabor Lutheran Church in Garrett, PA.

Birth: Jan. 21, 1890
Death: Oct. 19, 1975

Mrs. Carrie A. Carter, 85 of Garrett, died Oct 19, 1975, in Frostburg Community Hospital. Born Jan 21, 1890, in Garrett, she was a daughter of the late Austin and Lydia (Burkholder) Christner and was the widow of George Carter. She was a member of Mt. Tabor Lutheran Church, where she had been Sunday School teacher and choir director, and was a charter member of Garrett American Legion Auxiliary and a member of the Ladies Auxiliary to the Garrett Volunteer Fire Department. Surviving are two sons, William and George Carter, of Beaver Falls; two daughters, Mrs. Charlotte Zeller, Frostburg; and Mrs. Ruth Hall of Horsham, Pa.; nine grandchildren and eight great-grandchildren. Funeral service was held Wednesday afternoon in Mt. Tabor Lutheran Church with Rev. J. David Menchhofer officiating. Interment in Highland Cemetery, Garrett under the direction of Price Funeral Home, Meyersdale.
Meyersdale Republican, October 23, 1975

Burial: Highland Cemetery, Garrett, Somerset Co., PA
Find A Grave Memorial# 76911524

More About Carrie Agnes Christner:
Residence: 1900, Summit, Somerset Co., PA⁶⁶⁸¹

Notes for George Carter:
Birth: 1889
Death: 1955

Burial: Highland Cemetery, Garrett, Somerset Co., PA
Find A Grave Memorial# 78087982

More About George Carter:
Residence: 1930, Emmaus, Lehigh Co., PA⁶⁶⁸²

Children of Carrie Christner and George Carter are:
    4095   i.   Beulah⁹ Carter.
    4096   ii.   Leona Carter.
    4097   iii.   William Carter⁶⁶⁸³, born 1914 in Garrett, Somerset Co., PA⁶⁶⁸³.

                More About William Carter:
                Residence: 01 Apr 1940, Garrett, Somerset Co., PA⁶⁶⁸³

    4098   iv.   Isabel Carter⁶⁶⁸⁴, born 1916 in Pittsburgh, Allegheny Co., PA⁶⁶⁸⁴.

                More About Isabel Carter:
                Arrival: ⁶⁶⁸⁴
                Residence: 1930, Emmaus, Lehigh Co., PA⁶⁶⁸⁴

    4099   v.   Charlotte Carter⁶⁶⁸⁵, born 22 Jan 1916 in Garrett, Somerset Co., PA⁶⁶⁸⁵; died 15 Sep 2007 in Frostburg, Allegany Co., MD⁶⁶⁸⁵. She married Darrell Gustav Zeller⁶⁶⁸⁵ 13 Jun 1940⁶⁶⁸⁵; born 20 Nov 1912 in Frostburg, Allegany Co., MD⁶⁶⁸⁵; died 03 Dec 1990 in Frostburg, Allegany Co., MD⁶⁶⁸⁵.

                Notes for Charlotte Carter:

Died young was retarded

4100   vi.   George Carter Jr.[6686], born 1918 in Pittsburgh, Allegheny Co., PA[6686].

        More About George Carter Jr.:
        Residence: 01 Apr 1940, Garrett, Somerset Co., PA[6686]

4101   vii. Ruth Carter[6686], born 1921 in Pittsburgh, Allegheny Co., PA[6686].

        More About Ruth Carter:
        Residence: 01 Apr 1940, Garrett, Somerset Co., PA[6686]

4102   viii. Jessatine Carter[6687], born 1922 in Pittsburgh, Allegheny Co., PA[6687].

        More About Jessatine Carter:
        Arrival: [6687]
        Residence: 1930, Emmaus, Lehigh Co., PA[6687]

4103   ix.   Walter Carter[6688], born 1926 in Pittsburgh, Allegheny Co., PA[6688].

        Notes for Walter Carter:
        had 4 children

        More About Walter Carter:
        Residence: 01 Apr 1940, Garrett, Somerset Co., PA[6688]

2087. Melvin A.[8] Christner (Austin George[7], Zachariah[6], Christian[5], Joseph "Zep"[4], Johannes John Hans[3], Christian[2], Christen[1])[6689] was born 1904 in Garrett, Somerset Co., PA[6689], and died 23 Sep 1953 in Somerset, Somerset Co., PA. He married **Winifred J. Bird**[6689] 02 Jun 1923 in Somerset Co., PA[6689]. She was born 03 Feb 1903 in Rockwood, Somerset Co., PA[6690], and died 09 May 1980 in Somerset, Somerset Co., PA[6690].

Notes for Melvin A. Christner:
Birth: 1904
Garrett, Somerset Co., PA
Death: Sep. 23, 1953
Somerset, Somerset Co., PA

Spouse: Winifred J. Bird Christner (1903 - 1980)

Burial: Somerset County Memorial Park, Somerset, Somerset Co., PA
Find A Grave Memorial# 72445346

More About Melvin A. Christner:
Residence: 01 Apr 1940, 315 Court Alley, same in '35/telephone lineman/Somersetboro, Somerset, PA, United States[6691]

Notes for Winifred J. Bird:
Birth: Feb. 3, 1903
Rockwood, Somerset Co., PA
Death: May 9, 1980
Somerset, Somerset Co., PA

Grave Marker under husband

Parents:
Frank Ross Bird (1877 - 1953)
Harriet Florence Koontz Bird (1879 - 1943)

Spouse: Melvin A. Christner (1904 - 1953)

More About Winifred J. Bird:
Residence: 01 Apr 1940, 315 Court Alley, same in '35/Somersetboro, Somerset, PA, United States[6691]
Social Security Number: 194-50-1794/[6692]
SSN issued: Pittsburgh, Allegheny Co., PA[6692]

Child of Melvin Christner and Winifred Bird is:

    4104   i.   David M.[9] Christner[6693], born 08 Nov 1943 in Somerset Co., PA[6693]; died 09 May 2004 in Arroyo Grande, San Luis Obispo Co., CA[6693].

                  Notes for David M. Christner:
                  SS card issued Penn. 1960/61

                  More About David M. Christner:
                  Cremation: 14 May 2004, Grover Beach, San Luis Obispo Co., CA[6693]
                  Residence: 1993, 620 Bennett Ave/ 307 Sweet Springs Ln./ both shown in same year/Arroyo Grande, CA[6693]

2092. Velma G.[8] Christner (Washington[7], Zachariah[6], Christian[5], Joseph "Zep"[4], Johannes John Hans[3], Christian[2], Christen[1]) was born Aug 1892 in Connellsville, Fayette Co., PA, and died Apr 1984 in Somerset, Somerset Co., PA[6694]. She married **Frank Albert Walter**[6695]. He was born 03 Mar 1890[6695,6696], and died 21 Feb 1968[6696].

More About Velma G. Christner:
Residence: United States[6697]
Social Security Number: 453-98-4184/[6698]
SSN issued: TX[6698]

Notes for Frank Albert Walter:
Pennsylvania Veterans Burial Cards, 1777-1999

Name: Frank A Walter
Birth Date: 3 Mar 1890
Death Date: 21 Feb 1968
Age: 77
Military Branch: Army
Veteran of Which War: WWI
Cemetery Name: Somerset County Memorial Park
Cemetery Location: Somerset; Somerset Co., PA

More About Frank Albert Walter:
Burial: Somerset, Somerset Co.[6699]

Child of Velma Christner and Frank Walter is:

    4105   i.   Blaine Foster[9] Walter[6700], born 10 Nov 1910 in Rockwood, Somerset Co., PA[6700,6701,6702]; died 28 Jul 1990[6703].

                  More About Blaine Foster Walter:
                  Military service: 29 Nov 1943, Altoona, PA[6704]
                  Residence: [6704]
                  Social Security Number: 169-05-9576/[6705]
                  SSN issued: Connellsville, Fayette Co., PA[6705]

2102. Clinton[8] Christner (Wilson William[7], Zachariah[6], Christian[5], Joseph "Zep"[4], Johannes John Hans[3], Christian[2], Christen[1])[6706,6707,6708] was born 17 Nov 1891 in Garrett, Somerset Co., PA[6709,6710,6711], and died May 1970 in Shanksville, Somerset Co., PA[6711]. He married **Ruth Baldwin**. She was born 21 Jan 1892 in Berlin, Somerset Co., PA[6712], and died 17 Jan 1972 in Berlin, Somerset Co., PA.

Notes for Clinton Christner:
This info is not set in stone. All except his name came from the 1920 Census He was living at Somerset County, Berlin, PA on Meadow Street.

More About Clinton Christner:
Residence: 1930, Stonycreek, Somerset, PA[6712,6713]
Social Security Number: 172-18-9202/[6714]
SSN issued: Connellsville, Fayette Co., PA[6714]

Notes for Ruth Baldwin:
OBIT: Ruth (BALDWIN) CHRISTNER, 1972, Shanksville, Somerset County, PA - Meyersdale Republican, January 20, 1972

Mrs. Ruth Christner, 79, Shanksville, died Jan. 17, 1972, in Berlin. Born Jan. 21, 1892, in Berlin, she was a daughter of Edwin and Cora (Walker) Baldwin. She was preceded in death by her parents; her husband, Clinton C. Christner; a daughter, Mrs. Mary Wambaugh; an infant son and two brothers. Surviving are these children: Edwin and Gene, both of Shanksville; Mrs. William (Evelyn) Hillegass and Mrs. Fred (Betty) Knupp, both of Somerset; and Mrs. Dwight (Marjorie) Maust. Berlin; also 12 grandchildren, 15 great-grandchildren; and three sisters, Mrs. Myrtle Albright and Mrs. Vera Davis, both of Somerset; and Mrs. Catherine Adams, Johnstown. She was a member of St. Mark's Lutheran Church, Shanksville. Funeral service will be held this (Thursday) afternoon in Charles R. Deaner Funeral Home, Stoystown, with Rev. Herbert G. Hohman officiating. Interment in Walker Cemetery, Shanksville.

More About Ruth Baldwin:
Residence: 1930, Stonycreek, Somerset, PA[6715]

Children of Clinton Christner and Ruth Baldwin are:
4106   i.   Edwin B.[9] Christner, born 15 Jul 1913 in Pittsburgh, Alleghaney Co., PA[6715,6716]; died 28 Nov 1983 in Johnstown, Cambria Co., PA. He married Pauline Nicola Addleman; born 17 Sep 1910 in Conemaugh Twp., Somerset Co., PA[6717]; died 01 Jun 1999 in Berlin, Somerset Co., PA[6717].

Notes for Edwin B. Christner:
Obituary: Edwin B. CHRISTNER, 1983, Shanksville, Somerset Co., PA -
Daily American, November 30, 1983

Edwin B. Christner, 70, Shanksville, died Nov. 28, 1983, at Lee Hospital, Johnstown. Born July 15, 1913, in Pittsburgh, son of Clinton and Ruth (Baldwin) Christner. Preceded in death by parents; sister, Mary Wambaugh, and an infant brother, Billy. Survived by wife, the former Pauline Nicola Addleman; and children: Bruce Addleman, married to Sarah Jane Fox, Shanksville, and Donna Hamilton, Johnstown. Also six grandchildren and three great-grandchildren. Brother of: Mrs. William (Evelyn) Hillegass and Mrs. James (Betty Lou) Conrad, both of Somerset; Mrs. Dwight (Marjorie) Maust, Berlin; and Eugene, married to Winifred Gindlesperger, Shanksville.

Retired truck driver for Letty Lane Candy Co. and former janitor at Shanksville-Stonycreek schools. Member of St. Mark Lutheran Church, Shanksville, and Forbes Area Senior Citizens. Presently a Shanksville borough councilman. Played guitar with various Country and Western groups. Family received friends Tuesday evening and will receive friends from 2-4 and 7-9 p.m. Wednesday at Deaner Funeral Home, Stoystown, where service will be held 2 p.m. Thursday with the Rev. Patricia Harrington officiating. Interment, Walker Cemetery, Shanksville.

More About Edwin B. Christner:
Residence: 1930, Stonycreek, Somerset, PA[6718]
Social Security Number: 710-09-5215/[6719]
SSN issued: Railroad Board (Issued Through)[6719]

Notes for Pauline Nicola Addleman:
Obituary: Pauline C. (NICOLA) ADDLEMAN CHRISTNER, 1999, Berlin, Somerset Co., PA - Daily American June 2, 1999

ADDLEMAN-CHRISTNER

Pauline C. Addleman Christner, 88, of Berlin, formerly of Shanksville, died June 1, 1999, at Windber Medical Center. Born Sept 17, 1910, in Confluence. Daughter of Calvin and Al Della (Morrison) Nicola. Preceded in death by parents; first husband, Miles B. Addleman; second husband, Edwin B. Christner; two brothers and a sister. Survived by these children: M. Bruce Addleman, married to the former Sarah Jane Fox, and Donna, marrried to Leonard Reighard, both of Shanksville: grandchildren: Douglas, Steven, and Ronald Addleman, Janalee Zimmerman, Lori Newpher and Terri Jones; 17 great-grandchildren, Member of St. Mark Lutheran Chruch, Shanksville. Family will receive friends from 3-5 and 7-9 pm Thursday at Deaner Funeral Home. Stoystown, where service will be held at 11 am Friday. Rev. Richard T. Carter officiating. Interment, Walker Cemetery, Shanksville.

More About Pauline Nicola Addleman:
Social Security Number: 174-16-2201/[6720]
SSN issued: PA[6720]

4107	ii.	Evelyn Christner, born 1916 in Connellsville, Fayette Co., PA.
4108	iii.	Marjory Christner, born 1918 in Connellsville, Fayette Co., PA.
4109	iv.	Mary Christner, born 1919 in Connellsville, Fayette Co., PA.
4110	v.	Wilbur Christner, born 1920 in Connellsville, Fayette Co., PA.

2105. Leona O.[8] Christner (Wilson William[7], Zachariah[6], Christian[5], Joseph "Zep"[4], Johannes John Hans[3], Christian[2], Christen[1]) was born 1901 in Somerset Co., PA, and died 01 May 1964 in Pittsburgh, Allegheny Co., PA[6721]. She married **Arthur Streng**[6721,6722]. He was born 12 Apr 1896[6722], and died Jul 1976 in Pittsburgh, Allegheny Co., PA[6722].

More About Arthur Streng:
Social Security Number: 206-01-0077/[6722]
SSN issued: PA[6722]

Child of Leona Christner and Arthur Streng is:
4111	i.	Berniece[9] Streng[6723], born 20 Sep 1921 in Meyersdale, Somerset Co., PA[6723]; died 06 Jan 1994 in New Brunswick, Canada[6723].

2106. Orpha Maude[8] Christner (Theodore "Dorrie"[7], Zachariah[6], Christian[5], Joseph "Zep"[4], Johannes John Hans[3], Christian[2], Christen[1])[6724] was born 22 Oct 1893 in Summit Twp., Somerset Co., PA, and died 28 Jun 1969 in Canton, Stark Co., OH[6725]. She married **Earl Murray**[6726,6727]. He was born 04 Apr 1892 in Boynton, Somerset Co., PA[6728,6728], and died 24 Aug 1965 in Massillon, Stark Co., OH[6728,6728].

Notes for Orpha Maude Christner:
Moved to Akron, hio to work in the new RUBBER industry with several of her brothers. The following is from the David Christner notes. Early on Earl lived in Cumberland and knew KO Meyers. I believe that Cumberland is where Maudie met Earl. Earl and Maudie married very young. Both Earl and KO Meyers later migrated to the Akron area because of the booming rubber industry and the availability of jobs. Earl worked for the Goodyear tire and rubber company from which he retired.Earl and Maudie lived in the Akron and Massillon, Ohio area. They had a farm near Rootstown. Earl loved the farm. Earl liked to take a "nip" every now and then and hide private stashes around the farm from his wife. Earl and Maudie later moved to Akron and lived near the Goodyear Company on East Market Street. Later still they retired to a country home on US 241 south of Green and north of Massillon.

More About Orpha Maude Christner:
Burial: Hillside Cemetery in Akron OH Section 9[6728]
Residence: Stark Co., OH[6729]

More About Earl Murray:
Burial: Hillside Cemetery in Akron OH Section 9[6730]
Other-Begin: Akron City[6730]
Residence: Stark, Ohio, United States[6730]
Social Security Number: 291-03-7602/[6730]

SSN issued: OH[6730]

Children of Orpha Christner and Earl Murray are:

4112   i.   Clarence[9] Murray, died in died as infant.

            Notes for Clarence Murray:
            Died in Infancy

+   4113   ii.   Orpha Murray.

4114   iii.   Charles Clifford Murray[6731,6732], born 21 May 1914 in OH[6733,6734,6735]; died 08 Aug 1993 in Lakeland, Polk Co., FL[6736]. He married Yvonne Reynolds[6736]; born 12 Jun 1915 in McCaysville, Fannin Co., GA[6736]; died 11 Jan 2010 in Canton, Stark Co., OH[6736].

Notes for Charles Clifford Murray:
The Reynolds farm was adjacent to the Murray's farm in Rootstown,OH. They both graduated from Rootstown High School where they started dating. Clifford was driving a famr truck on the highway when he was involved in an accident. The truck went off the road, glass broke, and the blood was spurting from an artery. Clifford prayed and promised God that he would serve him if God saved his life. After the accident, Clifford went to Bible college in Minn. Yvonne was Pentecostal and Clifford joined her church.They lived for a long time in the Canton area. Clifford became an Apostolic pastor and founded the Lighthouse Apostolic Church on Tuscarawas Avenue between Canton and Massillon Ohio. Later he estaglished a Bible College in the church and Bob Jeffers was trained there. Betty and Bob Force became involved with Cliffords church. I have some memories of uor visits and Maudie's prayer practices. Clifford and his wife did not have any children. Clifford trained an assistant pastor and eventually gave the church to him, when he retired. Clifford and Yvonne retired to Florida where Clifford passed away. Clifford is buried in Florida and Yvonne is still living there. these notes were written by Rev. David Christner.

More About Charles Clifford Murray:
Residence: 1993, Lakeland, FL[6736]
Social Security Number: 274-05-8408/[6737]
SSN issued: OH[6737]

Notes for Yvonne Reynolds:
She had a sister Sarah married to a Letvin.

Obituary: YVONNE REYNOLDS MURRAY, 94
Professional Interior Designer - Ledger on January 12, 2010

LAKELAND - Yvonne Reynolds Murray, 94, died of natural causes Monday (Jan. 11, 2010). She was born June 12, 1915 in McCaysville, GA. In 1934, Yvonne married the love of her life, Rev. Charles C. Murray. Their journey together deeply touched the lives of relative and friends. Yvonne and her husband eventually made their home in the Canton, OH area until retiring to Florida 25 years ago.

Yvonne was a professional interior designer operating her business for many years in the Canton area. Throughout her life, Yvonne's passion for music was enjoyed by all who knew her. She shared her talent by playing the piano and organ for churches she attended for the past 82 years. Most recently she played for chapel at Victory Church in Lakeland, FL. Yvonne filled each day with Christian purpose. Her humble style and grace will be missed by her relatives and countless dear friends.

Preceded in death by parents Daniel and Maude Reynolds, husband Rev. Charles C. Murray, brothers Howard and Earl Reynolds and sister, Esther Moore.

Survived by sister, Sarah (Pauline) Letvin; nieces, Carol Young and Marie Walters; nephews, Duane and David Brown, Eugene Reynolds, Jim Letvin, Tom Dustman and many great nieces and nephews. Visitation will be held from 10 to 11 am on Thursday, January 14, 2010 at Victory Church Chapel. Funeral services will follow at 11 am.
Gentry Morrison Funeral Home, Northside.

More About Yvonne Reynolds:
Residence: 1993, Lakeland, FL[6738]

+ 4115   iv.   Claude E. Murray, born 11 Apr 1920; died 1985 in Washington, DC.

2107. Myers Wilson "K.O."[8] Christner (Theodore "Dorrie"[7], Zachariah[6], Christian[5], Joseph "Zep"[4], Johannes John Hans[3], Christian[2], Christen[1]) was born 28 Dec 1894 in Garrett, Somerset Co., PA[6739], and died 15 Oct 1979 in Cuyahoga Falls, Summit Co., OH[6740]. He married **Elizabeth Josephine Hiaduk** 06 Nov 1917 in San Antonio, TX. She was born 04 Nov 1893 in TX[6740], and died 07 Jun 1986 in Akron, Summit Co., OH[6740].

Notes for Myers Wilson "K.O." Christner:
Obituary:
Myers K.O. Christner 84 of Cuyahoga Falls, Ohio a native of Garrett died Monday at his home. Christner move to the Akron area after W.W. 1 service with the 37th Infantry Div. in which he was a 1st sergeant in Co. K. He had also served with the unit during the Mexican border war against Pancho Villa in 1916. Christner had nearly 250 pro fights during a boxing career that spanned the 1926 to1933, including 45 matches in one year. He fought such boxing greats as Max Bear and Jack Dempsey, Johnny Risko, Primo Canera, Arther DeKuh and Maloney. His most famous fight came Dec 4, 1928 when he knocked out THE FIGHTING DANE Knute Hansen in the 8th round of the Christmas Fund feature in Cleveland Public Hall.

He had been Babe Ruth's catcher when they were 12 year old members of the 3rd Dormitory team at St. Mary's Industrial School in Baltimore, where he had been sent because of chronic absenteeism from the public school in Garrett.

After his retirement from the ring he opened a bowling alley(Capital Bowling Alley) in Cumberland, Md. and he operated it until he retired in 1967. He then returned to Akron Ohio. SS#295-18-5848 ISS OH He first moved to Akron Ohio to work in a new industry called rubber for automobile tires. As a boy KO Meyers would jump a train out of Hyndman to visit relatives in Somerset for days. His parents had no control of him so they sent him to St. Marys Industrial School in Baltimore. Al Jolsen was also a classmate. He met his wife while stationed in Texas. He was a contender for the heavyweight Crown in 1929 the same year he had 3 matches in New York City in the Madison Square Garden and Yankee Stadium.   Court case Somerset Co., PA Dec. 1905 for Burglary.

OBIT: Meyers "K.O." CHRISTNER, 1979, native of Garrett, Somerset County, PA - The Republic, November 1, 1979

Meyers "K.O." Christner, 84, of Cuyahoga Falls, OH a native of Garrett, died Monday at his home. Christner moved to the Akron, OH area after World War I service with the 37th Infantry Division in which he was a first sergeant in Company K. He had also served with the unit during the Mexican border war against Pancho Villa in 1916.

Christner had nearly 250 pro fights during a boxing career that spanned the 1920's and 1930's, including 45 matches in one year. He fought such boxing greats as Max Baer and Jack Dempsey, and his most famous fight came on Dec. 4, 1928, when he knocked out "the fighting Dane," Knute Hansen in the eighth round of the Christmas Fund feature in Cleveland Public Hall.

He had been Babe Ruth's catcher when they were 12 year-old members of the Third Dormitory team at St. Mary's Industrial School in Baltimore, where he had been sent because of chronic absenteeism from the public school in Garrett.

After his retirement from the ring, he opened a bowling alley in Cumberland, MD and he operated it until he retired in 1967. He then returned to the Akron, Ohio area.

He leaves his wife of 62 years, Elizabeth; son, Milton of Cuyahoga Falls, Ohio; daughter, Betty Force, of Tallmadge, Ohio; brother, Tom of Hyndman; sisters, Gertrude Ritchey, of Hyndman and Irene Waggle of Akron, Ohio, four grandchildren and eight great-grandchildren.

Services were held at the Redmon Funeral Home in Stow, OH.

More About Myers Wilson "K.O." Christner:

Burial: Northlawn Cemetery
Residence: 1930, Akron, Summit Co., OH[6740]
Social Security Number: 295-18-5848/[6741]
SSN issued: OH[6741]

Notes for Elizabeth Josephine Hiaduk:
She was nicknamed Buddy by husband KO they are buried at Northlawn Cemetery on old route 8, North of Cuyahoga Falls. Section 4 lot 201. Her family lived on a cattle ranch near Las Gallinas, TX which is just south of San Antonio, TX.

More About Elizabeth Josephine Hiaduk:
Burial: Northlawn Cemetery
Residence: 1930, Akron, Summit Co., OH[6742]

Children of Myers Christner and Elizabeth Hiaduk are:
+ 4116   i.   Milton Earl[9] Christner, born 24 Jun 1920 in Akron, Sumitt Co., OH.
+ 4117   ii.   Betty Delores Christner, born 22 Sep 1922; died Apr 2001.

2110. Charles Theodore[8] Christner (Theodore "Dorrie"[7], Zachariah[6], Christian[5], Joseph "Zep"[4], Johannes John Hans[3], Christian[2], Christen[1]) was born 11 Dec 1899 in OH[6743], and died Apr 1974 in Akron, Summit Co., OH[6743]. He married **Mary Kobb**. She was born 1897 in Overton, OH, and died 1996.

Notes for Charles Theodore Christner:
Moved to Akron Ohio to work in the new RUBBER industry with his brother and sister. Nickname is Chic. 1919 to1942 he worked for Goodyear Aircraft Co. as an expditer and surplus salesman. He retired from Goodyear in 1964. Around 1930 - 1932 he tried his hand at boxing. He became the Featherweight Champion of Goodyear. He was a Sunday School Superintendant for many years at the East Market Reformed Church in Akron Ohio. He was also the president of Consistory.

More About Charles Theodore Christner:
Burial: Rose Hill Cemeter, Akron, OH
Social Security Number: 274-03-7048/[6743]
SSN issued: OH[6743]

Notes for Mary Kobb:
Mary met Charles while working at the General Tire Co. with her sister Sadie Repp. Charles lived with his sister Maudie Murry, across on Bauer Blvd. in Akron Ohio. Mary worked Goodyear Aircraft as a riveter from 1943 to 1945. As a child she had worked in the muck farms near Lodi Ohio. She enjoyed gardening cooking and keeping a nice home. Mary had a brother named Lucian who had both legs removed and moved around on a cart. They liked to watch boxing matces on television.

More About Mary Kobb:
Burial: Rose Hill Cemeter, Akron, OH

Children of Charles Christner and Mary Kobb are:
+ 4118   i.   Harold Maynard[9] Christner, born 30 Aug 1922 in Akron, Sumitt Co., OH; died 30 Apr 2006 in Akron, Sumitt Co., OH.
+ 4119   ii.   Doris Loiuse Christner, born 1926 in Akron, Sumitt Co., OH.

2111. Lloyd E.[8] Christner (Theodore "Dorrie"[7], Zachariah[6], Christian[5], Joseph "Zep"[4], Johannes John Hans[3], Christian[2], Christen[1]) was born 01 Oct 1901[6744], and died 03 Nov 1965 in Hyndman, Bedford Co., PA. He married **Nancy Belle Horner** 27 Jun 1927. She was born 13 Apr 1905 in Ellerslie, Allegany Co., MD, and died 20 Jul 1997 in Hyndman, Bedford Co., PA.

Notes for Lloyd E. Christner:
Lloyd began his 43 years at Kelly Springfield Rubber Co. in 1917. When he retired in 1965 he Division A

Superintendent. He was the mayer of Hyndman Ohio for many years. As a youth, Lloyd was a super baseball player. He was active in the Masonic organization.

Birth: Oct. 1, 1901
Meyersdale, Somerset Co., PA
Death: Nov. 3, 1965
Hyndman. Bedford Co., PA

Parents:
Theodore Christner (1875 - 1947)
Generva Minerva MO Beachley Christner (1872 - 1949)

Spouse: Nancy Belle Horner Christner (1905 - 1997)

Burial: Lybarger Cemetery, Madley, Bedford Co., PA

More About Lloyd E. Christner:
Burial: Madly-Lybarger Cemetery 8 miles Norh of Hyndman, PA on Rt.96
Social Security Number: 214-05-9885/*6744*
SSN issued: MD*6744*

Notes for Nancy Belle Horner:
Birth: Apr. 13, 1905
Ellerslie, Allegany Co., MD
Death: Jul. 20, 1997
Hyndman, Bedford Co., PA

Spouse: Lloyd E. Christner (1901 - 1965)

Burial: Lybarger Cemetery, Madley, Bedford Co., PA

More About Nancy Belle Horner:
Burial: Madly-Lybarger Cemetery 8 miles Norh of Hyndman, PA on Rt.96

Children of Lloyd Christner and Nancy Horner are:
4120   i.   Clara Jeanne[9] Christner, born 11 Jun 1924 in Hyndman, Bedford Co., PA; died 26 Mar 2007 in Pirrafield, MA. She married Roy E. Himeswere 30 Jun 1946.

               Notes for Clara Jeanne Christner:
               Pittsfield, MA. Clara Jeanne Himes 82 of 247 Eleanor Road, died Monday Mar 26, 2007 at home.

               Born in Hyndman, PA on June 11,1924 daughter of Lloyd and Nancy Horner Christner, she was valedictorian of the 1942 class at Hyndman High School. Mrs Himes worked in Akron, OH on the airplane assembly line to support the war effort while her husband served in the navy during world war 2. She was also office manager at Randall Trophies which is owned by her son Randall A. Himes. She retired in 1992. Mrs.Himes was a member of First United Methodist Church was a Sunday School teacher for many years. She enjoyed reading politics and sports. She and her husband Roy E. Himes were married Jun 30, 1946. Besides her husband and son of Pittsfield, she leaves two brothers, Lloyd Christner of Hyndman and William Christner of Crossville, TN a sister Sara Ann Cambell of Hyndman and a grandson.

               Memorial services will conducted Monday April 2 by Rev. Robert Rennie at the Wellington Funeral Home Calling hours from 5 PM until time of service.In lieu of flowers donations may be made in Mrs. Himes memory to the Jimmy fund in care of the funeral home.

               She also leaves a daughter in law Deborah Himes of Pittsfield and a grandson Christopher Munson of Troy, NY. Burial in Pittsfield, MA.

+   4121   ii.   Lloyd Elwood Christner Jr., born 13 Aug 1932 in Hyndman, Bedford Co., PA.
+   4122   iii.   Sara Ann Christner, born 07 Sep 1938 in Hyndman, Bedford Co., PA.

+ 4123   iv. William Lee Christner, born 08 Nov 1940 in Hyndman, Bedford Co., PA.

2112. Clyde S.⁸ Christner (Theodore "Dorrie"⁷, Zachariah⁶, Christian⁵, Joseph "Zep"⁴, Johannes John Hans³, Christian², Christen¹)⁶⁷⁴⁵ was born 1903 in Garrett, Somerset Co., PA⁶⁷⁴⁵, and died 01 Jun 1968 in Pittsburgh, Allegheny Co., PA⁶⁷⁴⁵. He married **Lillian Iva Dean Burkett**. She was born 1906 in Hyndman, Bedford Co., PA, and died 1988 in Connellsville, Fayette Co., PA.

Notes for Clyde S. Christner:
They lived for a long time in the Pittsburgh PA. area and worked for Baltimore and Ohio Railroad as a brakeman and conductor.

Birth: 1903 - Garrett, Somerset Co., PA
Death: Jun. 1, 1968 - Pittsburgh, Allegheny Co., PA

Parents:
Theodore Christner (1875 - 1947)
Generva Minerva MO Beachley Christner (1872 - 1949)

Spouse: Lillian Ivadeen Burkett Christner (1906 - 1988)

Burial: Hyndman Cemetery, Hyndman, Bedford Co., PA

More About Clyde S. Christner:
Burial: Madly-Lybarger Cemetery
Residence: 1910, Benson, Somerset, PA⁶⁷⁴⁵

Notes for Lillian Iva Dean Burkett:
One child died in infancy

Birth: 1906 - Hyndman, Bedford Co., PA
Death: 1988 - PA

Spouse: Clyde S. Christner (1903 - 1968)

Burial: Hyndman Cemetery, Hyndman, Bedford Co., PA

More About Lillian Iva Dean Burkett:
Burial: Madly-Lybarger Cemetery

Children of Clyde Christner and Lillian Burkett are:
+ 4124   i. Clyde S.⁹ Christner Jr..
+ 4125   ii. Betty Christner.

2113. Gertrude⁸ Christner (Theodore "Dorrie"⁷, Zachariah⁶, Christian⁵, Joseph "Zep"⁴, Johannes John Hans³, Christian², Christen¹)⁶⁷⁴⁶ was born 04 Jun 1905 in Garrett, Somerset Co., PA⁶⁷⁴⁶, and died 18 Apr 1986 in Hyndman, Bedford Co., PA⁶⁷⁴⁶. She married **Harry Clay Richey** 30 Jan 1923 in Cumberland, Alleganey Co., MD. He was born 1891, and died 1971.

Notes for Gertrude Christner:
Grertrude was always close to KO Meyers and very sympathetic toward him. She had Alzeheimers.

More About Gertrude Christner:
Burial: Madly-Lybarger Cemetery 8 miles Norh of Hyndman, PA on Rt.96

Notes for Harry Clay Richey:
The bridge first built on Wills Creek was adjacent to the property now owned by cousin Grace Pollock. This was

the home of Harry C. Ritchey's parents earlier. Gertrude and Harry had retired back to Hyndman after many years in mining towns. The core of the house is the original log cabin. Harry was a coal miner primarily in Central City, PA.

More About Harry Clay Richey:
Burial: Madly-Lybarger Cemetery 8 miles Norh of Hyndman, PA on Rt.96

Children of Gertrude Christner and Harry Richey are:

4126	i.	Earl Irvin[9] Richey, born 29 Nov 1923 in Hyndman, Bedford Co., PA.

Notes for Earl Irvin Richey:
Coal miner in Central City PA.   Married, Divorced Remarried.

+	4127	ii.	Minerva Grace Richey, born 14 Dec 1925.
+	4128	iii.	Annelee Margaret Richey, born 31 Oct 1928.

2114. Leota Irene[8] Christner (Theodore "Dorrie"[7], Zachariah[6], Christian[5], Joseph "Zep"[4], Johannes John Hans[3], Christian[2], Christen[1]) was born 25 Sep 1907, and died 23 Mar 2002 in Hyndman, Bedford Co., PA. She married **(1) Vernon Madden**. He was born 1901, and died 1950. She married **(2) Charles Waggle** 1957. He was born 1915, and died 1990.

More About Leota Irene Christner:
Burial: Madly-Lybarger Cemetery

Notes for Vernon Madden:
He was fascinated by new automobiles was schooled as an auto mechanic. He also learned the finer art of Painting, Lettering, and Lining Auto's. They lived in the Hyndman PA area.

More About Vernon Madden:
Burial: Madly-Lybarger Cemetery 8 miles Norh of Hyndman, PA on Rt.96

Notes for Charles Waggle:
He worked a long time for Goodyear Tire and Rubber in Akron, Ohio.

Child of Leota Christner and Vernon Madden is:

4129	i.	James V.[9] Madden, born 12 Mar 1939 in Cumberland, Alleganey Co., MD.

Notes for James V. Madden:
James grew up and lived in Hyndman, PA until 1957 when Irene and Jim moved to OH. After a brief stay at Maudie's home, Irene remained in Akron, obtained an apartment, and began working at the Sumner Home (a retirement residence). Jim moved to Orrville to begin a 42 yr. career with the Schantz Organ Company. While in Akron, Irene met Charles Waggle. Charles was a long time employee of the Goodyear Tire and Rubber Company. Charles and Irene waited until Jim returned from Army duty in Japan so he could play the organ for their wedding. They were married by Rev. Clifford Murray (Maudie's son). They lived on the East side of Akron before retiring to Columbus, OH.

James always enjoyed and exhibited a talented gift with the keyboard. In OH, James became involved with pipe organs and worked for the Schantz Organ Company of Orrville, Oh. He was for years District Manager for a three state territory. He designed organs for schools, colleges, and churches. He also served as organist-choirmaster in a number of churches. Later, James moved to Columbus, OH.

Chuck and Irene eventually retired to Columbus, OH and lived in Cardinal Village. After Chuck's death, Irene moved to Bristol Village in Waverly, OH. Where Jim had retired too. Jim bought a home and the two lived together until her failing health (arthritus) forced her to move into a nursing home. Irene died in March of 2002. James retired in 1999-2000, but still keeps his hands in music by playing the keyboard in local churches.

2115. Thomas W.[8] Christner (Theodore "Dorrie"[7], Zachariah[6], Christian[5], Joseph "Zep"[4], Johannes John

Hans[3], Christian[2], Christen[1])[6747,6748] was born 16 Dec 1910 in Hollsopple, Conemaugh Twp., Somerset Co., PA[6749], and died Mar 1984 in Hyndman, Bedford Co., PA[6749]. He married **Marian May**. She was born 20 Dec 1913 in Elersia, MD.

Notes for Thomas W. Christner:
He worked at the Cellanese Textile Plant in Cumberland PA. Died of Cancer.

Birth: Dec. 16, 1910
Benson, Somerset Co., PA
Death: Mar., 1984
Hyndman, Bedford Co., PA

Parents:
Theodore Christner (1875 - 1947)
Generva Minerva MO Beachley Christner (1872 - 1949)

Burial: Lybarger Cemetery, Madley, Bedford Co., PA
There is no tombstone, just a marker from the Ziegler funeral home.

More About Thomas W. Christner:
Burial: Madly-Lybarger Cemetery 8 miles Norh of Hyndman, PA on Rt.96
Residence: 1920, Londonderry, Bedford Co., PA[6749]
Social Security Number: 214-07-0152/[6750]
SSN issued: MD[6750]

Notes for Marian May:
Lived with her son Lynwood.

Child of Thomas Christner and Marian May is:
+   4130   i.   Lynwood[9] Christner, born 14 Jun 1945 in Cumberland, Allegany Co., MD.

2116. Elizabeth May[8] Phillippi (Tena[7] Hoover, Susanna Lucy Anne[6] Christner, Christian[5], Joseph "Zep"[4], Johannes John Hans[3], Christian[2], Christen[1])[6751] was born 14 Sep 1888 in Somerset Co., PA[6751], and died 27 Sep 1952 in Summit Township, Somerset Co., PA[6751]. She married **Campbell W. Dunbar**. He was born 1887, and died 1962.

Notes for Elizabeth May Phillippi:
Birth: Sep. 14, 1888 - Somerset Co., PA
Death: Sep. 27, 1952 - Summit Twp., Somerset Co., PA

Parents:
Jeremiah B. Phillippi (1864 - 1939)
Tena Hoover Phillippi (1867 - 1950)

Spouse: Campbell W. Dunbar (1887 - 1962)

Children: Kenneth E. Dunbar (1914 - 1984)

Burial: Center Lutheran Church Cemetery, Summit Twp., Somerset Co., PA

Notes for Campbell W. Dunbar:
Birth: 1887
Death: 1962

Spouse: Elizabeth May Phillippi Dunbar (1888 - 1952)

Children: Kenneth E Dunbar (1914 - 1984)

Burial: Center Lutheran Church Cemetery, Summit Township., Somerset Co., PA

Child of Elizabeth Phillippi and Campbell Dunbar is:

4131   i.   Kenneth E.[9] Dunbar, born 12 Jan 1914; died 12 Aug 1984.

> Notes for Kenneth E. Dunbar:
> Birth: Jan. 12, 1914
> Death: Aug. 12, 1984
>
> Parents:
> Campbell W Dunbar (1887 - 1962)
> Elizabeth May Phillippi Dunbar (1888 - 1952)
>
> Burial: Center Lutheran Church Cemetery, Summit Twp., Somerset Co., PA

2122. Jennie Marie[8] Phillippi (Tena[7] Hoover, Susanna Lucy Anne[6] Christner, Christian[5], Joseph "Zep"[4], Johannes John Hans[3], Christian[2], Christen[1])[6751] was born 20 Feb 1902[6751]. She married **Peter Rugg**. He was born 18 Sep 1890, and died 1948.

Notes for Jennie Marie Phillippi:
Birth: Feb. 20, 1902
Death: unknown

Parents:
Jeremiah B. Phillippi (1864 - 1939)
Tena Hoover Phillippi (1867 - 1950)

Children: Ada Viola Rugg (1922 - 2000)

Burial: MT. Zion United Brethern Cemetery, Upper Turkeyfoot, Somerset Co., PA

Child of Jennie Phillippi and Peter Rugg is:

4132   i.   Ada Viola[9] Rugg, born 18 Oct 1922; died 04 Jul 2000.

> Notes for Ada Viola Rugg:
> Birth: Oct. 18, 1922
> Death: Jul. 4, 2000
>
> Obituary: Daily American, July 5, 2000
>
> Ada V. Rugg, 77, of Somerset, formerly of Rockwood, passed away July 4, 2000, at Siemon Lakeview Manor Estate. Born Oct. 18, 1922, in Somerset, daughter of Peter and Jennie (Phillippi) Rugg. Preceded in death by parents and sister, Esther Rugg. Survived by daughter, Marian Martin (and Lloyd), Stoystown; and son, Barry, married to Phyllis Rugg, Stoystown. Sister of Louise Scarlet of Connellsville; Opal, married to Oscar Harbaugh of Somerset; Nellie, married to Peter Faix of McKeesport; Dolly Limley of McKeesport; Shirley, married to Ray Brubaker, Hollsopple; and Robert, married to Debbie Rugg of Denver, Colo. Also survived by seven grandchildren and 19 great-grandchildren. Retired employee of Specht Plastic and a cook for Siemon's Nursing Home and the former L&N Restaurant. Attended the Rockwood Christian and Missionary Alliance Church. Friends will be received from 12 to 4 p.m. Thursday at Miller Funeral Home, Rockwood, where a service will be held at 11 a.m. Friday, with Pastor James Vandervort officiating. Interment, Mount Zion Cemetery, Markleton. In lieu of flowers, contributions may be sent to the Alzheimer's Association, 1011 Old Salem Road, Greeensburg, PA 15601.
>
> Parents: Jennie Marie Phillippi Rugg (1902 - ____)

Burial: MT. Zion United Brethern Cemetery, Upper Turkeyfoot
Somerset Co., PA

2123. Fannie Viola[8] **Phillippi** (Tena[7] Hoover, Susanna Lucy Anne[6] Christner, Christian[5], Joseph "Zep"[4], Johannes John Hans[3], Christian[2], Christen[1])[6751] was born 20 Feb 1902[6751], and died 02 Jan 1979. She married **Israel Harmon "Jumbo" Pritts**, son of Irvin Pritts and Elizabeth Shaffer. He was born 26 Apr 1898[6752,6753], and died 30 May 1971 in Rockwood, Somerset Co., PA[6754].

Notes for Fannie Viola Phillippi:
Birth: Feb. 20, 1902
Death: Jan. 2, 1979

Obituary: The Republic, January 11, 1979
Fannie (Phillippi) Pritts, 76, of Rockwood RD 1, died Jan 2, 1979 in the Somerset Community Hospital. She was born Feb 20, 1902 in Rockwood, a daughter of Jermiah and Tina (Hoover) Phillippi. She is survived by four sons: Earl, Norval, and Richard, all of Rockwood RD 1, and James of Somerset; also by four daughters: Mrs. Mary Metz of Somerset; Mrs. Elloise Barndt of Rockwood RD 1; Mrs. Ethel Murray, with whom she resided at Rockwood RD 1; and Mrs. Audrey Kubis of Alliquippa; one sister, Mrs. Etta Handwork of Osterburg; 19 grandchildren and 11 great-grandchildren. She was preceded in death by husband, Israel "Jumbo" Pritts, May 30, 1971. She was a member of the Christian Gospel Tabernacle of Rockwood and senior citizens' group. Friends were received in the William J. Wood Funeral Home, Rockwood, where services were conducted with the Rev. Arnold Ansell officiating; Interment, Rockwood I.O.O.F. Cemetery.

Parents:
Jeremiah B. Phillippi (1864 - 1939)
Tena Hoover Phillippi (1867 - 1950)

Spouse: Israel Harmon Pritts (1898 - 1971)

Children: Mary Elizabeth Pritts Metz (1928 - 1996)

Burial: Rockwood IOOF Cemetery, Rockwood, Somerset Co., PA

Notes for Israel Harmon "Jumbo" Pritts:
Birth: Apr. 26, 1898 - Wilson Creek, Somerset Co., PA
Death: May 30, 1971 - Black Twp., Somerset Co., PA

Obituary: Daily American, June 3, 1971

Israel "Jumbo" Pritts, 73, RD 1, Rockwood, died May 30, 1971, in the Somerset Community Hospital. He was born April 26, 1898 in Rockwood, a son of Irvin and Eliza (Shaffer) Pritts. He is survived by his wife Fannie (Phillippi) Pritts, RD 1, Rockwood. Four sons, Earl, Norval (Gene), Richard, all of RD 1, Rockwood, also James, Ohio. Four daughters, Mrs. Mary Metz, Rockwood; Mrs. Ellouise Barndt, RD 1, Rockwood; Mrs. Ethel Murray, RD 1, Rockwood, and Mrs. Audrey Kubis, Aliquippa, Pa. One brother, Luther, Kent, Ohio. One sister, Mrs. Martha Kendall, RD 1, Rockwood. Sixteen grandchildren and four great grandchildren. He was preceded in death by five brothers and three sisters. He was a retired United Mine Worker.

Parents:
Irvin Franklin Pritts (1871 - 1950)
Eliza Shaffer Pritts (1878 - 1936)

Spouse: Fannie Viola Phillippi Pritts (1902 - 1979)

Children: Mary Elizabeth Pritts Metz (1928 - 1996)

Burial: Rockwood IOOF Cemetery, Rockwood, Somerset Co., PA

More About Israel Harmon "Jumbo" Pritts:
Social Security Number: 209-09-7736/[6754]
SSN issued: Connellsville, Fayette Co., PA[6754]

Child of Fannie Phillippi and Israel Pritts is:

4133   i.   Mary Elizabeth[9] Pritts, born 26 Apr 1928; died 24 Mar 1996.

Notes for Mary Elizabeth Pritts:
Birth: Apr. 26, 1928 - Wilbur, Somerset Co., PA
Death: Mar. 24, 1996 - Rockwood, Somerset Co., PA

Obituary: Somerset Daily American, March 25, 1996

Mary E. (Pritts) Metz, 67, of Rockwood died March 24, 1996, at home. Born April 26, 1928, in Black Township, daughter of the late Israel and Fannie (Phillippi) Pritts. Survived by sons: Lawrence, Rockwood; Vernon, Berlin, and Jerome, Somerset. Also survived by grandchildren: Mark, Joel, Jeremy, Kerri, Jason and Erin Metz, and great-granddaughter, Jeannette Metz. Friends will be received from 2 to 4 and 7 to 9 p.m. Tuesday at the Wilbur D. Miller Funeral Home, Rockwood, where funeral service will be conducted at 1 p.m. Wednesday, Rev. Wayne Sautter officiating. Interment, Rockwood IOOF Cemetery.

Parents:
Israel Harmon Pritts (1898 - 1971)
Fannie Viola Phillippi Pritts (1902 - 1979)

Burial: Rockwood IOOF Cemetery, Rockwood, Somerset Co., PA

2140. Thayer H.[8] Christner (Barton Roy[7], Amos Dickey[6], Gabriel[5], Joseph "Zep"[4], Johannes John Hans[3], Christian[2], Christen[1])[6755,6755] was born 03 Apr 1913 in Pittsburgh, Allegheny Co., PA[6755,6755], and died 07 Jan 2004 in Pittsburgh, Alleghaney Co., PA[6756]. He married **Nan H**. She was born Abt. 1913 in MS[6757].

More About Thayer H. Christner:
Residence: 01 Apr 1940, Pittsburgh, Allegheny, PA, United States[6758]
SSN issued: PA[6759]

More About Nan H:
Race: White/[6760]
Residence: 01 Apr 1940, Age: 27; Marital Status: Married; Relation to Head of House: Wife/Pittsburgh, Allegheny, PA, United States[6760]

Children of Thayer Christner and Nan H are:

4134   i.   James[9] Christner.
4135   ii.   Edward Christner, born Abt. 1935 in Pittsburgh, Allegheny Co., PA[6760].

More About Edward Christner:
Race: White/[6760]
Residence: 01 Apr 1940, Age: 5; Marital Status: Single; Relation to Head of House: Son/Pittsburgh, Allegheny, PA, United States[6760]

2143. Roberta Samatha[8] Christner (Barton Roy[7], Amos Dickey[6], Gabriel[5], Joseph "Zep"[4], Johannes John Hans[3], Christian[2], Christen[1])[6761] was born 1923 in Pittsburgh, Allegheny Co., PA[6761], and died 25 Jul 2013 in New Brighton, Beaver Co., PA. She married **Melvin R. Miller**[6762,6763]. He was born 06 Sep 1918 in New Brighton, Beaver Co., PA[6764], and died 13 Nov 2006 in New Brighton, Beaver Co., PA[6765].

Notes for Roberta Samatha Christner:
Obituary: Beaver Times Newspaper - 30 Jul 2013

Roberta Samantha Christner Miller, 91, passed away on July 25, 2013 at Good Samaritan Hospice of Heritage Valley Beaver. She was surrounded by loving family members and friends during her brief stay at the medical center.

More About Roberta Samatha Christner:
Residence: 1930, Rochester, Beaver Co., PA[6766]

Notes for Melvin R. Miller:
Obituary: Beaver County Times
Melvin R. Miller
11/17/2006

NEW BRIGHTON - Melvin R. Miller, Ph.D. of New Brighton, PA, died Nov 13, 2006 at the Worthington at Adams Nursing Home in Mars, PA.

He passed away quietly surrounded by many loving family members.

Dr. Melvin Miller was born Sept. 6, 1918, in New Brighton, PA. He attended New Brighton Public Elementary and High Schools. In high school, in addition to being an honor roll student, he was an athletic star in both basketball and football. As a young man, he was known for his enthusiasm and leadership at school, in sports and throughout the community. He attended Westminster College in New Wilmington, PA where his stellar athletic and academic careers continued. Mel helped both the Westminster basketball and football teams to winning seasons all four of his years there and was a charter member of the Sigma Phi Epsilon social fraternity.

After graduation, he returned to his beloved New Brighton to take teaching and coaching positions at his alma mater.

He soon married his loving wife, Roberta Christner. They had five children: Janice McCrea, New Brighton; Melvin E. (Loren) Miller, Montpelier, Vt.; Marilyn (Duane) Maietta, Ellwood City; Thomas (Diane) Miller, Pearland, Texas, and Nancy Miller, New Brighton. Mel and Roberta have 15 grandchildren: Natalie (Stephen) Semonik, Dianna (William) Kompa, Jennifer West, Melissa and Aaron Miller, Dana, Nicole and David Maietta, Thomas, Matthew, Christian and Teresa Miller, Tasha and Elizabeth Wistuk and Sarah Miller. Mel was lucky to know his eight great-grandchildren: Christopher, Joshua, Andrew, Lauren, Nicholas, Noah, Jacob and Samantha.

Mel's devotion to New Brighton and the education of its youth led him to transition from teaching to counseling-then went on to become principal of New Brighton High School, Riverside High School and Superintendent of the New Brighton Schools where he did much to improve the quality of education. His crowning accomplishment as Superintendent was to secure the architectural plans and funding for the new (currently existing) high school complex on the hill.

Always eager to improve himself and expand his educational experience, Mel took a sabbatical and pursued a Doctorate in Education from the University of Pittsburgh. A perennial historian and educator, Mel wrote his doctoral dissertation on the educational practices of the Harmonite Society in Ambridge, Pa. He admired their ability to integrate religious belief and education. Dr. Miller eventually took a faculty position at Geneva College where he taught a variety of education classes and supervised the student teachers. Nothing pleased him more than mentoring young, aspiring teachers. He held his position as Superintendent of the Blackhawk Schools for a number of years until he eventually retired with a part-time faculty position at Geneva. Travel with his wife and family and summer learning at the Jamestown, N.Y. Chattagua campus filled his retirement years.

Mel loved his family and enjoyed being a grandfather. He loved sporting activities and was an avid participant in golf, horseshoes and volleyball. The Beaver County Hall of Fame honored him in 1999 for his multifaceted athletic accomplishments. Dr. Miller maintained active memberships in a number of professional and social organizations. He was a Member Emeritus of the American Association of School Administrators, and was a member of the Pennsylvania Association of School Retirees. Locally, he was a member of the Beaver Valley Club of Retired Persons, the Methodist Men and the Association for the Blind. Melvin Miller was very involved in church; he loved teaching Sunday school and helped as both trustee and deacon in the Westminster United Presbyterian Church of New Brighton and then Park Gate Baptist Church in Ellwood City.

Mel is survived by his wife, Roberta, and their children and grandchildren. A private service officiated by Sam Blair, spiritual care coordinator of Gateway Hospice, was held Thursday in the J&J SPRATT FUNERAL HOME, 1612 Third Ave., New Brighton, www.jjsprattfh.com. The committal service immediately followed at Grove Cemetery.

The family asks that you make a donation to the hospice of your choice in his memory.

More About Melvin R. Miller:
Residence: 1983, Chicago, IL[6767,6768]
SSN issued: Pittsburgh, Allegheny Co., PA[6769]

Children of Roberta Christner and Melvin Miller are:

4136	i.	Janice[9] Miller. She married McCrea.
4137	ii.	Marilyn Miller. She married Duane Maietta.
4138	iii.	Jr. Melvin E. Miller. He married Loren.
4139	iv.	Thomas Miller.
4140	v.	Nancy Miller.

2145. Elizabeth[8] Christner (Barton Roy[7], Amos Dickey[6], Gabriel[5], Joseph "Zep"[4], Johannes John Hans[3], Christian[2], Christen[1]) was born 28 Oct 1925 in Rochester, Beaver Co., PA[6770], and died 15 Oct 2005 in Donegal[6770]. She married **Merle Harry Gerhart** 10 Jun 1945 in New Brighton, Beaver Co., PA, son of Lawrence Gerhart and Harriet Ulery. He was born 28 Nov 1918 in Donegal, PA, and died 27 Jul 1995 in Donegal, PA.

Notes for Elizabeth Christner:
Cause of death - cancer

Buried in the Donegal Cemetery, Donegal, PA

Diploma from New Brighton High School, New Brighton, PA 1939 - 1943

Postmaster (part-time), US Postal Service, Donegal, PA 1949 - 1963

Mortgage Specialist, greensburg Savings & Loan Bank, Greensburg, PA 1964 - 1972

Floor Manager/Sales Representative Woolworth Department Store, Mt. Pleasant, PA 1972 - 1982

Receptionist/Desk Manager Days Inn Motel, Donegal, PA 1982 - 2002

Tax Collector, Donegal Boro, PA 1975 - 2002

Wrote Special Event Articles, Mt. Pleasant Journal, Mt. Pleasant, PA

Served 2 four year terms as School Director, Mt. Pleasant School District, Mt. Pleasant, PA

She enjoyed gardening.

More About Elizabeth Christner:
Race: White[6771]
Residence: 1930, Age: 4; Marital Status: Single; Relation to Head of House: Daughter/Rochester, Beaver, Pennsylvania[6771]

Notes for Merle Harry Gerhart:
Belonged to Mt. Zion Lutheran Church, Donegal, PA.

Diploma, Mt. Pleasant High School, Mt. Pleasant, PA 1932- 1936

Mayor of Donegal, PA 1957 - 1969

Farmer/Cattleman, Gerhart Farm - 400 acres, Donegal, PA

Meat Packing Specialist/Butcher for Glicks Packing Company, Mt. Pleasant Alfrey Meats, Mt. Pleasant, PA

Activities:

Enjoyed Hunting and supporting childrens programs

Children of Elizabeth Christner and Merle Gerhart are:

+   4141   i.   Rodney Merle[9] Gerhart, born 13 Nov 1946 in Connellsville, Fayette Co., PA.
     4142   ii.   Lynn Thayer Gerhart, born 01 Apr 1948 in Connellsville, Fayette Co., PA. He married (1) Sharon A. Agar[6772] 03 Jun 1972; born Abt. 1944[6772]. He married (2) Nancyann Eiko Blackburn[6773] 10 Nov 1979[6774]; born 09 May 1951 in Sacramento, California[6775,6776].

               Notes for Lynn Thayer Gerhart:
               Ramsey High School, Mt. Pleasant, PA - Diploma

               Construction/Interior Finisher

               US Army - 2 years

               More About Lynn Thayer Gerhart:
               Residence: Cuyahoga, Ohio, United States[6777]

               More About Sharon A. Agar:
               Residence: Cuyahoga, Ohio, United States[6778]

               More About Nancyann Eiko Blackburn:
               Residence: Cuyahoga, Ohio, United States[6779]

     4143   iii. Timothy Eugene Gerhart, born 14 Oct 1958 in Greensburg, Westmoreland Co., PA.

               Notes for Timothy Eugene Gerhart:
               Mt. Pleasant High School - 1972 - 1976

               Lafayette College, Easton, Pa - BS
               Football Scholarship 1976 - 1980
               All American Defense Linebacker

               Professional Football Payer
               Denver Broncos
               Oakland Raiders
               Washington Federals

               Gerhart Construction 1980
               Civil Engineer

2146. LaReine Mary[8] Christner (Gabriel Dickey "Milton"[7], Nelson Brown[6], Gabriel[5], Joseph "Zep"[4], Johannes John Hans[3], Christian[2], Christen[1]) was born 21 Jul 1901. She married **D.D.S. Vankirk S. Fehr.**

More About LaReine Mary Christner:
Residence: 1910, McKeesport Ward 8, Allegheny, PA[6780]

Child of LaReine Christner and Vankirk Fehr is:
     4144   i.   Vankirk S.[9] Fehr Jr..

2147. Alan Shirley[8] Christner (Gabriel Dickey "Milton"[7], Nelson Brown[6], Gabriel[5], Joseph "Zep"[4], Johannes John Hans[3], Christian[2], Christen[1])[6781,6782,6783,6784,6785] was born 11 Jun 1906 in McKeesport, Allegheny Co., PA[6786,6787,6788,6789,6790], and died 04 Aug 1994 in Holmes Beach, Manatee Co., FL[6791,6792,6793]. He married **Alice Eleanor Crist**[6794,6795,6796], daughter of Ira Crist and Mary Hughes. She was born 22 May 1906 in Pittsburgh, Allegheny Co., PA[6797,6798], and died 12 Dec 2000 in Holmes Beach, Manatee Co., FL[6799,6800,6801].

Notes for Alan Shirley Christner:
SS# 178-12-4496   Iss. PA

More About Alan Shirley Christner:
Occupation: Vice President of Mellon Bank/Pittsburg, Allegheny Co., PA[6802,6803]
Residence: 1930, McKeesport, Allegheny, Pennsylvania[6803,6804,6805]
Social Security Number: 178-12-4496/[6806]
SSN issued: Connellsville, Fayette Co., PA[6806]

More About Alice Eleanor Crist:
Residence: 1920, Thornburg, Allegheny Co., PA[6807,6808]
Social Security Number: 209-38-7603/[6809]

Children of Alan Christner and Alice Crist are:
      4145   i.   Alan Shirley[9] Christner Jr.[6810] He married Jane Randolph Hurd[6810,6811].
      4146   ii.   Ellen Chaney Christner.
      4147   iii. Mary Carol Christner.
      4148   iv.   Richard Sloan Christner.

2148. Lois Frances[8] Christner (Gabriel Dickey "Milton"[7], Nelson Brown[6], Gabriel[5], Joseph "Zep"[4], Johannes John Hans[3], Christian[2], Christen[1]) was born 28 Sep 1912. She married **James Manely Thorn**.

Child of Lois Christner and James Thorn is:
      4149   i.   Alice Jane[9] Thorn.

2149. Goldie Fern[8] Raffensparger (Amanda[7] Miller, Elizabeth[6] Christner, Joseph[5], Joseph "Zep"[4], Johannes John Hans[3], Christian[2], Christen[1]) was born 28 Dec 1883 in Spencer, IA, and died 28 Sep 1973 in Orange Co., CA. She married **Charles Christner**[6812] 20 Jun 1901 in Belleville, Republic Co., IA, son of Jonas Christner and Rebecca Mankemeyer. He was born 08 Dec 1876 in Garrett, Somerset Co., PA[6812], and died 07 Jun 1934 in Lincoln, Lancaster Co., NE.

Notes for Goldie Fern Raffensparger:
B.Hochstedler book 13356 C. Stutzman--------Goldie Raffensparger mother Amanda Miller had a mother Elizabeth Christner married to Henry Miller
Elizabeth Christner Miller is the daughter of Joseph Christner, Jr. and Mary Keim.

Notes for Charles Christner:
Charles & his son Dale plus another man went hunting. They got out of their Ford model T automobile. The auto came out of parking gear and started to roll down a hill. Charles tried to stop the auto from rolling down the Mountain side with all the strength he could muster up and in doing so ruptured something in his stomach. Being a Christner he didn't go to the doctor because he will just tough it out by himself, well he got gangrene and died.

More About Charles Christner:
Burial: Wyuka Cemetery (free ground space 334) Lincoln NE.
Cause of Death: Gangrene
Christened: Presbyterian

Children are listed above under (267) Charles Christner.

2170. Sylvester Francis[8] Christner (Clyde Evans[7], Samuel J. "Matlick Sam"[6], Joseph[5], Joseph "Zep"[4], Johannes John Hans[3], Christian[2], Christen[1])[6813,6814,6815,6816] was born 25 Dec 1920 in Connellsville, Fayette Co., PA[6817,6818,6819,6820], and died 25 May 1995 in Lorain, Lorain Co., OH[6821,6822]. He married **Lucille R. Baer**[6823,6824,6825]. She was born 02 Jun 1925 in Greenville Twp., Somerset Co., PA[6826,6827,6828], and died 18 Mar 1986 in Barberton, Summit Co., OH[6829,6830].

Notes for Sylvester Francis Christner:
SS#185-14-8607 ISS PA   last address 44053 Lorain OH

Birth: 1920
Death: 1995

Burial: Hillcrest Memorial Gardens, Seville, Medina Co., OH

More About Sylvester Francis Christner:
Military service: 12 Oct 1942, Altoona, Blair Co., PA[6831]
Residence: 1930, Johnstown, Cambria, PA[6832,6833]
Social Security Number: 185-14-8607/[6834]
SSN issued: Pittsburgh, Allegheny Co., PA[6834]

Notes for Lucille R. Baer:
Birth: 1925
Death: 1986

Burial: Hillcrest Memorial Gardens, Seville, Medina Co., OH

More About Lucille R. Baer:
Burial: 21 Mar 1986, Hillcrest Cemetery, Norton, Summit Co., OH[6835]
Residence: 1930, Greenville, Somerset, PA[6836]
Social Security Number: 188-22-3640/[6837]
SSN issued: Pittsburgh, Allegheny Co., PA[6837]

Children of Sylvester Christner and Lucille Baer are:
    4150   i.   James[9] Christner.
    4151   ii.   Kenneth Christner.
    4152   iii. Diane Christner. She married Albright.

2172. Flowella[8] Argenbright (Florence Ruth[7] Christner, Henry J.[6], Joseph[5], Joseph "Zep"[4], Johannes John Hans[3], Christian[2], Christen[1]) was born 20 Aug 1903 in W.Salisbury, PA, and died 16 Nov 1983 in Oxnard CA.. She married **Howard Edgar Carpenter** 24 Oct 1925. He was born 12 Oct 1901, and died 14 Feb 1938 in Chicago IL..

Notes for Flowella Argenbright:

More About Flowella Argenbright:
Burial: Cremated
Residence: 1920, Elk Lick, Somerset Co., PA[6838]

More About Howard Edgar Carpenter:
Burial: Cremated

Children of Flowella Argenbright and Howard Carpenter are:
    4153   i.   William Edgar[9] Carpenter, born 11 Sep 1926.
    4154   ii.   Robert Howard Carpenter, born 02 Jul 1929.

2173. Mary Gertrude[8] **Argenbright** (Florence Ruth[7] Christner, Henry J.[6], Joseph[5], Joseph "Zep"[4], Johannes John Hans[3], Christian[2], Christen[1]) was born 30 Apr 1905 in W.Salisbury, PA, and died 09 Aug 1999 in York Co., PA. She married **(1) Chester Clair Bowman** 21 Jun 1927 in Cleveland OH. He was born 09 Sep 1900 in Grapeville West Moreland Co. PA, and died 23 Jun 1953. She married **(2) Carl Alexander Kennedy** 1954.

Notes for Mary Gertrude Argenbright:

More About Mary Gertrude Argenbright:
Burial: 28 Aug 1999, Greenlawn Cemetery Butler Co. PA.
Residence: 1920, Elk Lick, Somerset Co., PA[6838]

More About Chester Clair Bowman:
Burial: Greenlawn Cemetery Butler Co. PA.

Children of Mary Argenbright and Chester Bowman are:
+   4155   i.   Mary Helen[9] Bowman, born 29 Mar 1928 in Butler City, PA; died 09 Jun 2002 in York Co., PA.
+   4156   ii.   Clara Jean Bowman, born 19 Mar 1930 in Butler City, PA.
+   4157   iii.   Ruth Anne Bowman, born 11 Jan 1932 in Butler PA..
+   4158   iv.   Ronald McNeal Bowman, born 15 May 1938.

2174. Annabelle[8] **Argenbright** (Florence Ruth[7] Christner, Henry J.[6], Joseph[5], Joseph "Zep"[4], Johannes John Hans[3], Christian[2], Christen[1])[6838] was born 20 Dec 1908 in W.Salisbury, PA, and died Jun 1999 in Huntingdon Co. PA.. She married **Raymond Coulter** 06 Aug 1930.

Notes for Annabelle Argenbright:

More About Annabelle Argenbright:
Residence: 1930, Huntingdon, Huntingdon, PA[6838]

Children of Annabelle Argenbright and Raymond Coulter are:
   4159   i.   Jack[9] Coulter, born Sep 1931 in Huntingdon Co. PA.; died 2001 in Huntingdon Co. PA..
   4160   ii.   Sandra Coulter, born 04 Jul 1937 in Huntingdon Co. PA..
   4161   iii.   Bonnie Bell Coulter, born 1939 in Huntingdon Co. PA..
   4162   iv.   Raymond Coulter Jr., born 1942 in Huntingdon Co. PA..

2175. Esther Mildred[8] **Argenbright** (Florence Ruth[7] Christner, Henry J.[6], Joseph[5], Joseph "Zep"[4], Johannes John Hans[3], Christian[2], Christen[1]) was born 24 Mar 1910 in W.Salisbury, PA, and died Nov 1999 in Jackson Co., MI.

More About Esther Mildred Argenbright:
Residence: 1930, Huntingdon, Huntingdon, PA[6838]

Children of Esther Mildred Argenbright are:
   4163   i.   Charles[9] Christner, died 1999 in Jackson Co., MI.
   4164   ii.   Jerry Christner, born in Jackson Co., MI.
   4165   iii.   Charles Christner.

2177. Joe Franklin[8] **Argenbright** (Florence Ruth[7] Christner, Henry J.[6], Joseph[5], Joseph "Zep"[4], Johannes John Hans[3], Christian[2], Christen[1]) was born 25 May 1923 in Boyton PA or W.Salisbury, PA. He married **Viginia Baker** in Altoona PA.

Notes for Joe Franklin Argenbright:
Lives in Boswell, PA near Johnstown, PA.

Children of Joe Argenbright and Viginia Baker are:
4166   i.   David[9] Argenbright.
4167   ii. James Argenbright.

2180. Paul Jay[8] Christner (Hubert Eugene[7], Henry J.[6], Joseph[5], Joseph "Zep"[4], Johannes John Hans[3], Christian[2], Christen[1]) was born 30 Jun 1920 in Elk Lick Twp., Somerset Co., PA, and died 09 Jul 1967 in Meyersdale, Somerset Co., PA. He married **Mary Edna Combs** 24 Jul 1939 in Oakland, MD. She was born 03 Apr 1921 in Meyersdale, Somerset Co., PA, and died 14 Nov 1995 in Johnstown, Cambria Co., PA.

Notes for Paul Jay Christner:
SS#175-16-8459 ISS PA   Wounded in action in WWII. He worked in Highway construction as a cement finisher. He died suddenly of a heart attack at age 47.

OBIT: Paul Jay CHRISTNER, 1967, Meyersdale, Somerset Co., PA

PAUL CHRISTNER

Paul Jay Christner, 47, Meyersdale, died July 9 at his home. Born June 30, 1920, in Elk Lick Twp., he was a son of Hubert and Florence (Brown) Christner. He is survived by his parents of Boynton; his wife, the former Mary Edna Combs; two daughters, Mrs. John Brown, Salisbury, and Miss Edna Pauline, at home; two grandchildren; two brothers: Earl of Baltimore and Everett of
Boynton; two sisters: Mrs. Harry Ludy, Glencoe, and Mrs. Ray Wahl, Boynton. Funeral service will be held this (Thursday) morning in Konhaus Funeral Home, Meyersdale, with Rev. Charles E. Staub officiating. Interment will be made in Union cemetery.

Meyersdale Republican, July 13, 1967

More About Paul Jay Christner:
Burial: Union Cemetery, Meyersdale, Somerset Co., PA
Cause of Death: Heart Attack

Notes for Mary Edna Combs:
OBIT: Mary Edna (COMBS) CHRISTNER, 1995, Salisbury, Somerset County, PA - Daily American, November 16, 1995

Mary Edna Christner, 74, of Salisbury, formerly of Meyersdale, died Nov 14, 1995, at Good Samaritan Medical Center, Johnstown. She was born April 3, 1921, in Meyersdale, a daughter of the late Eddie and Emma (Meyers) Combs. She was preceded in death by her husband, Paul J., and a daughter, Edna "Polly." She is survived by a daughter, Irene, married to Jon Brown of Salisbury; three grandchildren: Mike Brown, Pamara Bernard and Eddie Christner, and three great-grandchildren. Member of Zion Lutheran Church, Meyersdale VFW and American Legion auxiliaries, and Salisbury Fire Department. Friends will be received from 2 to 4 and 7 to 9 p.m. Thursday in the Leckemby Funeral Home, Meyersdale, where services will be held at 11 a.m. Friday, with the Rev. Randall Marburger officiating. Interment in Union Cemetery.

More About Mary Edna Combs:
Burial: Union Cemetery, Meyersdale, Somerset Co., PA

Children of Paul Christner and Mary Combs are:
4168   i.   Florence Irene[9] Christner, born 06 Feb 1941. She married Jon D. Brown 04 Sep 1959 in Cumberland, Alleganey Co., MD.
4169   ii. Edna Pauline Christner, born 17 Jun 1944 in Meyersdale, Somerset Co., PA[6839]; died 17 Nov 1992 in Cumberland, Allegany Co., MD.

Notes for Edna Pauline Christner:
She never Married.   She died of cancer two weeks after she was diagnosed.

More About Edna Pauline Christner:
Burial: Union Cemetery, Meyersdale, Somerset Co., PA
Cause of Death: Cancer
Social Security Number: 211-38-7081/[6839]
SSN issued: PA[6839]

2181. Earl Ray[8] Christner (Hubert Eugene[7], Henry J.[6], Joseph[5], Joseph "Zep"[4], Johannes John Hans[3], Christian[2], Christen[1])[6840] was born 18 May 1922 in Boynton, Somerset Co., PA[6840], and died 06 Apr 1985 in Cumberland, Allegany Co., MD[6840]. He married **Blanche Emogen Thomas** 03 Jul 1947 in Cumberland, Allegaey Co., MD. She was born 10 Sep 1930 in Midlothian, MD.

Notes for Earl Ray Christner:
Wounded in action in WWII. Was reported missing in action for quite some time as he became seperated from his company, his family worried for a long time. He died of a heart attack at age 62, survived two weeks on a machine. He was a coal miner and a custodian. He liked fishing and playing cards.

Obituary: Earl R. Christner, 1985, Salisbury, Somerset Co., PA - Daily American, April 8, 1985
Earl R. Christner, 62, Salisbury RD 1, died April 6, 1985, Cumberland Memorial Hospital. Born May 18, 1922, in Boynton, son of the late Hubert Christner and Florence (Brown) Christner of Boynton. Besides his father, also preceded in death by two brothers, Paul J. and Everett F. Also survived by his wife, the former Emogen Thomas; one son, Thomas E. Christner, Baltimore, Md.; a daughter, Mrs. Gloria A. Morrell of Pylesville, Md.; four Grandchildren; and three sisters: Mrs. Kathleen Gutowski of Moscow, Pa.; Mrs. Irene Ludy, Glencoe; and Mrs. Janet Wahl, Salisbury. He was a retired employee of Baltimore City Transit and Traffic. A veteran of World War II. Friends will be received Monday (today) 2 to 4 and 7 to 9 p.m. at the Thomas Funeral Home, Salisbury, where funeral services will be held Tuesday 2 p.m. with the Rev. DeWayne Johnson officiating. Interment, Salisbury Cemetery.

SS# 185-14-8576 Iss.PA Last zip 15558

More About Earl Ray Christner:
Burial: Salisbury Cemetery Salisbury PA
Cause of Death: Heart Attack
Military: 31 Oct 1942, Altoona, Blair Co., PA[6840]
Residence: PA, Somerset, PA[6840]

Children of Earl Christner and Blanche Thomas are:
+   4170   i.   Thomas Eugene[9] Christner, born 21 Aug 1948 in Salisbury, Somerset Co., PA.
+   4171   ii. Gloria Ann Christner, born 27 Sep 1950 in Salisbury, Somerset Co., PA.

2182. Kathleen May[8] Christner (Hubert Eugene[7], Henry J.[6], Joseph[5], Joseph "Zep"[4], Johannes John Hans[3], Christian[2], Christen[1]) was born 27 May 1923 in Boynton, Somerset Co., PA, and died 04 Aug 2009 in Moscow, Lackawanna Co., PA[6841]. She married **(1) Ernest Butler** 17 Jun 1956 in Las Vegas, NV. He was born 24 Aug 1917 in Mt. Cobb PA, and died 13 Nov 1999 in Greenville SC. She married **(2) William Gutowski** 27 Jun 1980 in Dunmore PA. He was born 18 Apr 1919.

Notes for Kathleen May Christner:
She was known as a very hard worker in the factory or on the farm plus the nursing home. She was known to her family and friends around Somerset Co. PA as (sis).

More About Ernest Butler:
Burial: Mt. Cobb Cemetery

Child of Kathleen Christner and Ernest Butler is:

4172   i.   Tonya K.[9] Butler, born 22 Jun 1959 in Piqua, OH. She married Jeffrey Alan Zehner 17 Jul 1979 in Dunmore PA.

2183. Everett Fay[8] Christner (Hubert Eugene[7], Henry J.[6], Joseph[5], Joseph "Zep"[4], Johannes John Hans[3], Christian[2], Christen[1])[6842] was born 08 Jun 1924 in Boynton, Somerset Co., PA[6843], and died 16 Feb 1973 in Meyersdale, Somerset Co., PA. He married **Kathleen Hilda Hotchkiss** 08 Jan 1943 in Cumberland, Alleganey Co., MD. She was born 25 Feb 1924 in Coal Run, Somerset Co., PA, and died 09 Aug 2004 in Confluence, Somerset Co., PA.

Notes for Everett Fay Christner:
SS#;196-18-1503 Worked in the coal mines. He did not pass his physical for the military service. He died suddenly of a heart attack at age 48.

OBIT: Everett F. CHRISTNER, 1973, Boynton, Somerset County, PA - Meyersdale Republican, February 22, 1973

Everett F. Christner, 48 of Boynton, died Feb. 16, 1973, in Elk Lick Township. Born June 8, 1924, in Boynton, he was the son of Florence (Brown) Christner and the late Hubert Christner.

Also surviving are his wife, the former Kathleen Hotchkiss; three sons, Roger of Muncie, Ind.; David of Birdsboro; and Randy, at home; a daughter, Mrs. Sherry Ross, Meyersdale; five grandchildren; a brother, Earl Christner, Baltimore, Md.; and three sisters, Mrs. Kathleen Butler, Lake Ariel; Mrs. Irene Ludy of Glencoe; and Mrs. Janet Wahl, Salisbury.

Funeral service was conducted Tuesday afternoon in Thomas Funeral Home, Salisbury, with Rev. Paul H. Yoder and Rev. Ronald Grossglass officiating. Interment in Salisbury Cemetery.

More About Everett Fay Christner:
Burial: I.O.O.F Cemetery in Salisbury PA
Cause of Death: Heart Attack
Residence: 1930, Elk Lick, Somerset Co., PA[6844]
Social Security Number: 196-18-1503/[6845]
SSN issued: PA[6845]

Notes for Kathleen Hilda Hotchkiss:
Obituary: Kathleen Hilda CHRISTNER, 2004, Salisbury, Somerset County, PA - Daily American Newspaper 10 August 2004

Kathleen Hilda Christner, 80, 70 Grant St., Salisbury, died Aug. 9, 2004, at the Resh home in Confluence. Born Feb. 25, 1924, in Coal Run, she is the daughter of the late Andrew and Elizabeth (Hinebaugh) Hotchkiss. She is preceded in death by her husband, Everett Fay Christner; son, Roger; four brothers: Leroy, Harold, Bill and Fay; two sisters: Ethel Hotchkiss and Shirley Engle; and a granddaughter, Lisa. She is survived by two sons, David, Birdsboro; and Randy, Meyersdale; one daughter, Sherry Ross, Somerset; one sister, Elaine Franklin, Meyersdale; 11 grandchildren and 10 great-grandchildren. Mrs. Christner was a homemaker. Friends will be received 2 to 4 and 7 to 9 p.m. Tuesday at the Newman Funeral Home Inc., 9168 Mason-Dixon Highway, Salisbury where funeral service will be conducted 1 p.m. Wednesday. The Rev. Paul H. Yoder officiating. Interment, Salisbury Cemetery.

Children of Everett Christner and Kathleen Hotchkiss are:
4173   i.   David Eugene[9] Christner, born 09 Mar 1942 in Somerset, Somerset Co., PA. He married Deloris Shuck 03 May 1966.
4174   ii.   Roger Lee Christner, born 29 Feb 1944 in Boynton, Somerset Co., PA[6846]; died 24 Aug 1986 in Muncie, Delaware Co., IN[6847]. He married (1) Elizabeth Anne Ray 25 Sep 1965 in Pittsburgh, Allegheny Co., PA. He married (2) Mickie Tighe Aft. 1966.

       Notes for Roger Lee Christner:
       Died suddenly of a heart attack at age 42. He was a Navy veteran. He worked over 20 years for Mid-

West Metal Co. Muncie Indiana.

Obituary: Roger Christner 1986, native of Boynton, Somerset County, PA - The Republic, August 28, 1986

Roger Christner, 42, died early Sunday morning, Aug. 24, 1986, in Muncie, IN after a sudden illness. He was born in Boynton and had moved to Indiana after serving in the Navy in the early 60's, and had worked over 20 years for the Mid-West Metal Co. in Muncie.

Survivors include his wife, Mickie (Tighe), two sons, Steven and Mark Christner, both of Muncie, a daughter Nova Lee Christner, of Muncie, his mother Kathleen Christner, of Meyersdale, two brothers Dave and Randy Christner, of Meyersdale; a sister Sherry Ross, of Somerset, his grandmother Florence Christner, of Meyersdale; and seven nieces and nephews. He was preceded in death by his father Everett. Services were held at 2 p.m. Tuesday in the Parson Mortuary, 801 West Adams, Muncie, Ind. Burial in Elm Ridge Cemetery.

More About Roger Lee Christner:
Burial: Elm Ridge Cemetery, Muncie, Deleware Co., IN
Cause of Death: Heart Attack
Social Security Number: 159-36-4399/*6848*
SSN issued: PA*6848*

4175   iii.   Sherry Elaine Christner, born 09 Jul 1953 in Meyersdale, Somerset Co., PA. She married Frank Ross 26 Apr 1971.

4176   iv.   Randy Lynn Christner, born 05 Sep 1962 in Meyersdale, Somerset Co., PA. He married Lisa Marie Shaffer 09 Nov 1996 in Meyersdale, Somerset Co., PA.

Notes for Randy Lynn Christner:
Over the road semi truck driver.

2184. Anna Irene[8] Christner (Hubert Eugene[7], Henry J.[6], Joseph[5], Joseph "Zep"[4], Johannes John Hans[3], Christian[2], Christen[1]) was born 26 May 1928 in Boynton, Somerset Co., PA. She married **Harry Freeman Ludy** 07 Sep 1946 in Cumberland, Alleganey Co., MD. He was born 25 May 1922 in Northampton Twp., Somerset Co., PA.

Notes for Harry Freeman Ludy:
Also known as Bunn. He and his wife owned and operated a diary farm. They recently celebrated their 57 wedding anniversary.

Children of Anna Christner and Harry Ludy are:
4177   i.   Bonnie Lee[9] Ludy, born 19 Jul 1947. She married Melvin S. Baughman 08 Feb 1964 in Berlin, Somerset Co., PA.

Notes for Bonnie Lee Ludy:
He and his wife owned and operated a diary farm.

4178   ii.   Karen Diane Ludy, born 11 Jul 1951 in Meyersdale, Somerset Co., PA; died 21 Feb 1982 in MacDonaldton, PA. She married James Joseph Woytek 08 Jun 1974 in MacDonaldton, PA.

Notes for Karen Diane Ludy:
Nurse = L.P.N.

More About Karen Diane Ludy:
Burial: Mt Lebanon Cemetery Northampton Twp. Somereset Co. PA

4179   iii.   Deborah Louise Ludy, born 09 Oct 1953 in Northampton Twp., Somerset Co., PA. She married John Imhoff 27 Sep 1993.

Notes for Deborah Louise Ludy:
Nurse = L.P.N.

4180   iv.   Beverly Ann Ludy, born 24 May 1958 in Northampton Twp., Somerset Co., PA.

           Notes for Beverly Ann Ludy:
           Nurse RN

4181   v.   Daniel Ray Ludy, born 30 Jan 1960 in Meyersdale, Somerset Co., PA. He married Cathy Ann Rohrs 14 Aug 1982 in Northampton Twp., Somerset Co., PA.

           Notes for Daniel Ray Ludy:
           He and his wife own a farm. They love horses.

2187. Clair Glines[8] Bender (Arthur Grover[7] Christner, Harvey[6], Joseph[5], Joseph "Zep"[4], Johannes John Hans[3], Christian[2], Christen[1]) died 1987.

Child of Clair Glines Bender is:
    4182   i.   Norman[9] Bender.

2192. Hilda Marie[8] Christner (Karl J.[7], Urias Jonas[6], Jonas Yone[5], Joseph "Zep"[4], Johannes John Hans[3], Christian[2], Christen[1])[6849] was born 24 Nov 1922 in Summit Twp.Somerset Co., PA, and died Jul 2009 in Johnstown, Cambria Co., PA[6849]. She married **Ray Stanley Fink** 27 Oct 1943 in Somerset PA Old Trinity Luteran by Rev.I.Hess Wagner. He was born 27 Feb 1922 in Somerset, Somerset Co., PA[6850,6851], and died 25 Apr 2006 in Johnstown, Cambria Co., PA[6852].

Notes for Hilda Marie Christner:
Quilter & Seamstress last known address 331 Penn Ave. Johnstown PA 15905 Made her own Clothing. Her Quilts were displayed at the Johnstown Art Center.

Notes for Ray Stanley Fink:
He was a Machinist & Electrician 1945 to 1986 in Somerset PA. After returning from WWII, Ray entered into business with his father in Fink's Electric & Machine Works At 220 Ankney Ave., Somerset PA. Herbert & Selma lived in an apartment above the electrical or front shop, while Ray,Hilda and family lived above the machine or back shop. Herbert repaired electric motors and generators while Ray did repair work on a variety of mechanical parts. When Herbert died in 1978, the name changed to Fink Electric & Machine Works and Ray took over both parts of the business. He retired in December 1986. In retirement he continues to do woodworking, some small motor repairs and miscellaneous house-hold repairs for friends and neighbors.

More About Ray Stanley Fink:
Military service: 05 Jun 1943, Pittsburgh, Alleghaney Co., PA[6853]
Residence: Allegheny Co. PA[6853]
SSN issued: PA[6854]

Children of Hilda Christner and Ray Fink are:
+   4183   i.   Drake C.[9] Fink, born 01 Jan 1948 in Somerset, Somerset Co., PA.
    4184   ii.   Sally C. Fink, born 07 May 1951 in Somerset Co., PA. She married George R. Paczolt 09 Feb 1980 in Johnstown, Cambria Co., PA; born 09 Jul 1950 in Johnstown, Cambria Co., PA.

           Notes for Sally C. Fink:
           Johnstown, PA   artist///Costume Designer & writer. She divorced George R. Paczolt in Johnstown PA. In 1998 she was elected Barroness of her shrine.

           More About Sally C. Fink:
           Hobby: Costume designer & writer
           Occupation: Art Director for Johnstown Tribune/Democrat in PA

2193. Bette Lucile[8] Christner (Karl J.[7], Urias Jonas[6], Jonas Yone[5], Joseph "Zep"[4], Johannes John Hans[3], Christian[2], Christen[1])[6855] was born 25 Oct 1926 in Meyersdale, Somerset Co., PA[6855]. She married **William Herbert Firl**[6856] 21 Jun 1947 in Cumberland, Allegany Co., MD. He was born 27 Jun 1928 in Meyerdale,

Somerset Co., PA, and died 27 May 2008 in Meyersdale, Somerset Co., PA[6856].

Notes for Bette Lucile Christner:
She was a housewife & nursery school aide.

More About Bette Lucile Christner:
Residence: 1930, Summit, Somerset Co., PA[6857]

Notes for William Herbert Firl:
Truck Driver Meyersdale PA 15552

More About William Herbert Firl:
Occupation: Truck Driver/
Residence: 1930, Summit, Somerset Co., PA[6858]

Children of Bette Christner and William Firl are:

+   4185   i.   Danny C.[9] Firl, born 24 Mar 1949 in Meyersdale, Somerset Co., PA.
      4186   ii.   Robyn Ann Firl, born 10 Mar 1955 in Meyersdale, Somerset Co., PA. She married Jack F. Gauntz; born 08 Feb 1955.

2194. Anna Bertha[8] Christner (Karl J.[7], Urias Jonas[6], Jonas Yone[5], Joseph "Zep"[4], Johannes John Hans[3], Christian[2], Christen[1]) was born 20 Jul 1936 in Meyerdale, Somerset Co., PA. She married **Ira Richard Adams** 06 Apr 1958 in Lutheran Church, Berlin, Somerset Co., PA. He was born 22 May 1937 in Jennerstown, PA.

Notes for Anna Bertha Christner:
She was a bookkeeper.

More About Anna Bertha Christner:
Occupation: Secretary//Bookkeeper

Notes for Ira Richard Adams:
Radio Station Owner at 373 High St., Somerset, PA 15501.

Children of Anna Christner and Ira Adams are:

+   4187   i.   Amy Jo[9] Adams, born 10 Jul 1963.
+   4188   ii.   Cristine Lynn Adams, born 25 Apr 1965.

2195. Stewart Norman[8] Christner (Stewart A.[7], Urias Jonas[6], Jonas Yone[5], Joseph "Zep"[4], Johannes John Hans[3], Christian[2], Christen[1]) was born 27 Dec 1930 in McMurray, PA, and died 04 Oct 2012 in SC. He married **Virginia Albright Murphy** 14 Feb 1953 in Mount Lebanon, PA. She was born 02 Dec 1930 in Dormont, PA[6859].

Notes for Stewart Norman Christner:
Gina and I raced in our 22 foot Pearson Ensign sailboat for over 15 years in upstate New York. I wore out 2 pair of sailing gloves in 12 weeks; she is the Skipper. I graduated from college with a degree in Automotive Engineering. After 2 years as a design engineer with ALCOA in Pittsburgh, I was drafted and after Basic Training, was assigned as a Project Engineer for the new Army Ford Jeep testing program. After 2 years, I was discharged and went to work for Ford in new engine development - that lasted 18 months, we did not care for Detroit and Ford was not interested in aluminum engines. On to GE in jet engine development in Evendale, Ohio for 3 years; then to Schenectady, New York for 30+ years in nuclear power. Retired in 1991 and moved to Seneca, Oconee County, SC and built our dream home on the lake. The Ensign is at the dock along with a 22 foot deck boat (so the kids and grand kids can water ski). We have a 12 foot Zuma sailboat in the garage for the grand kids.

What is it with Christner's and water? I was in the Sea Scouts when I was in high school, and we sailed almost every weekend.   Stewart

Stewart N. Christner
Born in McMurray, PA
Departed on Oct. 4, 2012 and resided in Seneca, SC.

Visitation: Monday, Oct. 8, 2012
Service: Monday, Oct. 8, 2012
Funeral Home: Sandifer Funeral Home
Please click on the links above for locations, times, maps, and directions.

STEWART CHRISTNER

Seneca - Stewart N. Christner, 81, loving husband of 63 years to Virginia M. Christner, 800 Keowee School Road, left this earth Thursday, October 04, 2012 at his residence.

Born in McMurray, PA, he was the son of the late Stewart and Francis Barnum Christner. Mr. Christner was a graduate of Carnegie Mellon University of Pittsburgh, PA where he earned his Engineering Degree. He was a Nuclear Engineer at General Electric for 30 years. He was a Veteran of the United States Army, an avid sailor, and avid water conservationist.

Survivors in addition to his wife, Virginia, include his sons, Scott, Alan, and Dean Christner; 5 grandsons, 1 granddaughter, and 2 great-grandchildren.

A memorial service will be held 2 PM, Monday, October 8, 2012 from the Chapel of Sandifer Funeral Home. Visitation will follow the service. Flowers are accepted or memorials in his memory may be made to Hospice of the Foothills, Attn: Foundation Office, 298 Memorial Drive, Seneca, SC 29672

More About Stewart Norman Christner:
Residence: 01 Apr 1940, Peters, Washington Co., PA[6860]

More About Virginia Albright Murphy:
Residence: Seneca, SC[6861]

Children of Stewart Christner and Virginia Murphy are:
+ 4189   i.   Scott Norman^9 Christner, born 28 Apr 1962 in Schenectady, NY.
+ 4190   ii.   Alan Stewart Christner, born 02 Dec 1964 in Schenectady, NY.
+ 4191   iii.   Dean William Christner, born 15 May 1968 in Schenectady, NY.

2208. Trudy Kay^8 Christner (Paul Jacob^7, Urias Jonas^6, Jonas Yone^5, Joseph "Zep"^{4}, Johannes John Hans^3, Christian^2, Christen^1) was born 03 Jul 1943 in Meyersdale, Somerset Co., PA. She married **Marvin K. Hetrick** 21 Nov 1964 in Meyersdale, Somerset Co., PA. He was born 10 Apr 1943 in Grantsville MD.

Notes for Trudy Kay Christner:
Trudy is a registered nurse.

Children of Trudy Christner and Marvin Hetrick are:
+ 4192   i.   David Paul^9 Hetrick, born 04 Aug 1964 in Canton, OH.
+ 4193   ii.   Ronald Lee Hetrick, born 06 Jun 1968 in Newark, OH.

2211. Ronald Dale^8 Christner (Dale Wilber^7, Charles^6, Jonas Yone^5, Joseph "Zep"^{4}, Johannes John Hans^3, Christian^2, Christen^1) was born 18 Apr 1938 in Lincoln, Lancaster Co., NE. He married **Janice Lee Simons** 05 Jul 1957 in Downey, Los Angeles Co., CA. She was born 20 Jun 1937 in Los Angeles, Los Angeles Co., CA.

Children of Ronald Christner and Janice Simons are:
+ 4194   i.   Ronald Craig^9 Christner, born 18 May 1961 in Downey, Los Angeles Co., CA.

4195   ii.   Karin D. Christner, born Apr 1964 in Downey, Los Angeles Co., CA. She married Rick Poster.

2222. Lewis Calvin[8] Christner (Clarence Cadalso[7], Calvin M.[6], Jonas Yone[5], Joseph "Zep"[4], Johannes John Hans[3], Christian[2], Christen[1]) was born 26 Aug 1918 in Meyersdale, Somerset Co., PA[6862], and died 05 May 1967 in Morgantown, Monongalia Co., WV[6862]. He married **Annabelle Walker**. She was born 16 Dec 1924 in Boynton, and died 14 Sep 2004 in Morgantown, Monongalia Co., WV.

Notes for Lewis Calvin Christner:
SS#705-12-8036 ISS RR

OBIT: Lewis C. CHRISTNER, 1967, native of Meyersdale, Somerset County, PA - Meyersdale Republican, May 11, 1967

Lewis C. Christner, 48, Frostburg RD 2, died May 5 at University Medical Center, Morgantown. Born Aug. 26, 1918, on Meyersdale RD 4, he was a son of Clarence and Mary (Knepp) Christner, who survive.   Also surviving are his wife, the former Annabelle Walker, and three children, Paris L., Bonnie Lou and Cheryl Ann, all at home: also two brothers, Lester L., Frostburg RD 2; C. Eugene, Cumberland; and a sister, Mrs. Wayne Stone, Meyersdale RD 4.

An employee of Kelly-Springfield Tire Company, Cumberland, for 21 years, he was a veteran of World War II, and a member of White Oak Lutheran Church. Funeral service was held at Price Funeral Home, Meyersdale, on Monday afternoon, with Rev. Charles E. Staub officiating. Interment was made in White Oak Cemetery.

Birth: Aug. 26, 1918
Meyersdale, Somerset Co., PA
Death: May 5, 1967
Morgantown, Monongalia Co., WV

Parents:
Clarence C. Christner (1891 - 1971)
Mary Leona Knepp Christner (1899 - 1994)

Burial: White Oak Cemetery, Wittenberg, Somerset Co., PA

More About Lewis Calvin Christner:
Burial: White Oak Cemetery, Wittenberg, Somerset Co., PA
Social Security Number: 705-12-8036[6862]
SSN issued: Railroad Board (Issued Through)[6862]

Notes for Annabelle Walker:
She was a member of the Boynton Church of God and woman of the Moose in Frostburg, MD.

More About Annabelle Walker:
Burial: White Oak Cemetery Meyersdale PA

Children of Lewis Christner and Annabelle Walker are:
    4196   i.   Cheryl Ann[9] Christner. She married Edward Winner.

                  Notes for Cheryl Ann Christner:
                  Lives in Frostburg, MD.

    4197   ii.   Paris L. Christner. He married Deb.

                  Notes for Paris L. Christner:
                  Lives at Frostburg

+   4198   iii.   Bonnie Lou Christner, born 25 Apr 1889 in Asheville, Buncombe Co., NC; died 16 Nov 1932 in Asheville, Buncombe Co., NC.

2225. Norma Alberta[8] **Christner** (Walter C.[7], Calvin M.[6], Jonas Yone[5], Joseph "Zep"[4], Johannes John Hans[3], Christian[2], Christen[1]) was born 29 Mar 1924 in Wittenberg, Somerset Co., PA[6863], and died 18 Feb 1983 in Cumberland, Allegany Co., MD[6863]. She married **(1) Bernard Allen Murray**. He was born 13 Nov 1925 in Corriganville, Allegany Co., MD[6863], and died 18 Apr 1986 in Pittsburgh, Allegheny Co., PA[6863]. She married **(2) Hetz**.

Notes for Norma Alberta Christner:
Birth: Mar. 24, 1924
Wittenberg, Somerset Co., PA
Death: Feb. 18, 1983
Cumberland, Allegany Co., MD

Spouse: Bernard Allen Murray (1925 - 1986)

Burial: White Oak Cemetery, Wittenberg, Somerset Co., PA

Notes for Bernard Allen Murray:
Birth: Nov 13, 1925 - Corriganville, Allegany Co., MD
Death: Apr 18, 1986 - Pittsburgh, Allegheny Co., PA

Spouse: Norma Alberta Christner Murray (1924 - 1983)

Burial: White Oak Cemetery, Wittenberg, Somerset Co., PA

Child of Norma Christner and Hetz is:
+   4199   i.   Lisa Ann[9] Hetz.

2226. JoAnn[8] **Christner** (Walter C.[7], Calvin M.[6], Jonas Yone[5], Joseph "Zep"[4], Johannes John Hans[3], Christian[2], Christen[1]) was born 06 May 1931 in Wittenburg, PA. She married **James F. Kubowski** 30 Dec 1950 in Alexandria, VA. He was born 24 May 1930 in LaCrosse, WI.

Children of JoAnn Christner and James Kubowski are:
    4200   i.   Barry Walter[9] Kubowski, born 14 Aug 1951. He married Shireen Hampton.
    4201   ii. Amy Jo Kubowski, born 04 Jun 1952.
    4202   iii. Paula Sue Kubowski, born 18 Aug 1957. She married Kimberly L. Cantor.

2229. Ray Sandow[8] **Christner Sr.** (Ralph[7], Rufus J.[6], Jonas Yone[5], Joseph "Zep"[4], Johannes John Hans[3], Christian[2], Christen[1]) was born 20 Jan 1929 in Somerset Co., PA[6864,6865], and died 11 Oct 2004 in Akron, Summit Co., OH[6866]. He married **Mary Jane Hotchkiss** 04 Jul 1952 in Morgantown, Monongalia Co., WV, daughter of William Hoctchkiss and Clara Staub. She was born 02 Dec 1935 in Pittsburgh, Allegheny Co., PA[6867,6868], and died 13 Dec 2006 in Akron, Summi Co., OH[6868].

Notes for Ray Sandow Christner Sr.:
Ray S. Christner, 75, passed away Oct. 11, 2004. Ray was born Jan. 20, 1929, in Somerset County, Pa., to the late Ralph and Sadie Christner. Ray entered the U.S. Army on Sept. 9, 1947, and served dur ing the Korean Conflict. He was discharged on Aug. 31, 1951, and married Mary Hotchkiss on July 4, 1952, in Frostburg, Md. They moved to Akron, where Ray was employed at B.F. Goodrich for over 32 years. He was preceded in death by his sisters, Betty and Eva, and granddaughter, Angie. He is survived by his wife, Mary; children, Ray "Butch" Jr. (Sherry), Margie (Bill) Simmons, Glenn (Pam), William (Joyce), and Wendy (Jerry) Hatcher; siblings, Jack (Alice), Janet (Grady) Gil pin, and Jim (Shirley); grand children, Staci (Mike) Martin, Ed, Chris, Terry, and Brandin Christner; great-grandson, Ty Christner. Friends and family may call TODAY from 5 to 8 p.m. at NEWCOMER-FARLEY FUNERAL HOME, 131 N. Canton Rd., where funeral services will be held Wednesday at 11 a.m., with Pastor Jim Jensen officiat ing. Visitation for one hour prior to service. Interment at Hillside

Memorial Park, with military honors provided by Mogadore V.F.W. 8487. In lieu of flowers, memorials may be made to Sawyerwood United Methodist Church or Hospice Visiting Nurses Service. (NEWCOMER-FARLEY FUNERAL HOME, 330- 784-3334.) Published in the Akron Beacon Journal on 10/12/2004.

OBIT: Ray S. CHRISTNER, 2004 from Somerset County, PA - New Republic - 14 Oct 2004

Ray S. Christner, 75, of Akron, OH passed away Monday, October 11, 2004. Ray was born January 20, 1929, in Somerset County, PA, to the late Ralph and Sadie Christner. He is survived by his wife, Mary; children: Ray ñButchî, Jr. (Sherry); Margie (Bill) Simmons; Glenn (Pam); William (Joyce); and Wendy (Jerry) Hatcher; siblings: Jack (Alice); Janet (Grady) Gilpin; and Jim (Shirley); five grandchildren; one great-grandson. All services were handled by Newcomer-Farley Funeral Home in Akron, OH.

U.S. Veterans Gravesites, ca.1775-2006
Name: Ray S Christner
Service Info.: CPL US ARMY KOREA
Birth Date: 20 Jan 1929
Death Date: 11 Oct 2004
Cemetery: Hillside Memorial Park, 1025 Canton Rd., Akron, OH 44312

More About Ray Sandow Christner Sr.:
Burial: Hillside Memorial Park
Residence: Summit, Summit, Ohio, United States[6869]
SSN issued: PA[6870]

Notes for Mary Jane Hotchkiss:
Obituary: Mary Jane (Hotchkiss) CHRISTNER, 2006, native of Somerset County, PA

CHRISTNER, Mary Jane 12/21/2006 - The New Republic - December 13, 2006

Mary Jane Christner, 71, died peacefully at home, surrounded by her much loved family, on December 13, 2006. Born in Somerset County but resided in Akron, OH for most of her life. Preceded in death by her parents William and Clara Hotchkiss; husband Ray of 52 years; brothers: Bobby, William, Jr., David, Donald; sister Margaret; and granddaughter Angie. She is survived by her children: Ray (Butch) Jr. (Sherry); Margie Simmons (Bill); Glenn (Pam); William (Joyce) and Wendy Hatcher (Jerry); brother Larry Hotchkiss (Jeannie); grandchildren: Staci Martin (Mike); Eddie (Tasha); Christopher, Terry, Brandin; great-grandson Ty; and also a large group of extended family and friends. She retired from Summit Grinding after 25 years of service. Her loving and unselfish acts touched many lives, often times anonymously. Even nearing death, her family was still her main priority. She was dearly loved and will be greatly missed. If she had a boat filled with love, hers would surely sink. Friends and family were received at Newcomer Funeral Home, 131 N. Canton Rd., Akron, OH 44305. Funeral service was held at the funeral home, Pastor Jim Jensen officiating. In lieu of flowers, memorials may be made to Sawyerwood United Methodist Church or Hospice of VNS.

Mary was the daughter of William and Clara Staub Hotchkiss.

More About Mary Jane Hotchkiss:
SSN issued: OH[6871]

Children of Ray Christner and Mary Hotchkiss are:

+   4203   i.   Ray Sandow[9] Christner Jr., born 21 Sep 1953.

      4204   ii.   Margie Louise Christner[6872,6872], born 04 Apr 1955[6872,6872]. She married (1) Theodor G Burkey[6872] 14 Jun 1974[6872]. She married (2) William P. Simmons[6872] 19 Sep 1981[6872].

                More About Margie Louise Christner:
                Residence: Summit, Somerset Co., PA[6872]

+   4205   iii.   Glenn Lee Christner, born 17 Dec 1957.

      4206   iv.   William Ralph Christner, born 23 Apr 1961. He married Joyce.

4207   v.   Wendy Sue Christner, born 30 Nov 1965. She married Jerry Hatcher 16 Dec 1984[6873].

More About Wendy Sue Christner:
Residence: Summit Co., OH[6873]

2230. Betty Dean[8] Christner (Ralph[7], Rufus J.[6], Jonas Yone[5], Joseph "Zep"[4], Johannes John Hans[3], Christian[2], Christen[1])[6874,6875] was born 02 Jun 1930 in Summitt Twp., Somerset Co., PA[6876], and died 30 Oct 1975 in Cumberland, Cumberland Co., MD[6876]. She married **Leroy Emerson Christner** 01 May 1954 in Morgantown, Monongalia Co., WV, son of Harry Christner and Edith Grew. He was born 07 Jun 1921 in Garrett, Somerset Co., PA[6877], and died 16 Jan 2005 in Meyersdale, Somerset Co., PA.

Notes for Betty Dean Christner:
Betty is the daughter of Ralph Christner and Sadie Alma Yoder Christner   SS# 208-22-9867 Iss.PA Last zip 15552.

Obituary - Mrs. Leroy Christner - Meyersdale Republic, November 13, 1975

Mrs. Betty D. Christner, 45, of Meyersdale RD 1, died Oct. 30, 1975, in
Sacred Heart Hospital, Cumberland, Md. Born June 2, 1930, in Summit
Twp., she was a daughter of Ralph and the late Sadie (Yoder) Christner.
Surviving are her father and husband, Leroy Christner; and three children,
Roger, Terry and Kim, all at home; three brothers and two sisters, Ray,
Jack and James Christner, and Mrs. Janet Gilpin, all of Akron, OH; and
Mrs. Eva Hotchkiss, of Mogadore, OH.

She was an employee of Meyersdale Manufacturing, Inc., for more than 20 years. Funeral service was conducted Saturday afternoon in Price Funeral Home, Meyersdale, with Rev. Richard duPont officiating. Interment in St. Paul Cemetery.

More About Betty Dean Christner:
Christened: Luthern, Garrett, PA
Residence: 1920, Garrett, Somerset, PA[6878]

Notes for Leroy Emerson Christner:
Obituary: Meyersdale, Somerset County, PA - 16 Jan 2005 - The New Republic - June 7, 1921 - January 16, 2005

Leroy E. Christner, 83, of Meyersdale, died Sunday, January 16, 2005, at
Beverly Healthcare Meyersdale. Born June 7, 1921 in Garrett, he was a son of the late Harry and Edith (Grew) Christner.

He was also preceded in death by his wife, Betty D. Christner, October 30,
975. He is survived by three children: Roger L. Christner, Meyersdale; Terry A. Christner, Winchester, VA; and Kim Corbet, Buffalo, NY; also three grandchildren and two great-grandchildren. He was a sister of Odette Dneaster and June Miller, both of Garrett.

Leroy was a veteran of the U.S. Army WWII. Friends were received Monday at the Price Funeral Home, Meyersdale, where service was conducted at 11 a.m. Tuesday, with the Rev. Albert Valentine officiating. Interment, St. Paul's (Wilhelm) Cemetery, Meyersdale. Arrangements by the William Rowe Price Funeral Home, Inc., Meyersdale.

More About Leroy Emerson Christner:
Burial: St. Paul's (Wilhelm) Cemetery, Meyersdale, Somerset Co., PA
Military service: Army World War II/

Children of Betty Christner and Leroy Christner are:
4208   i.   Roger Leroy[9] Christner, born 22 Aug 1954.

4209   ii.   Kim Michelle Christner, born 30 May 1965. She married Corbet.
4210   iii. Terry A. Christner, born 24 Dec 1969.

2231. Jack Allen⁸ Christner (Ralph⁷, Rufus J.⁶, Jonas Yone⁵, Joseph "Zep"⁴, Johannes John Hans³, Christian², Christen¹) was born 28 Jul 1934 in Meyersdale, Somerset Co., PA. He married **Alice Jane Hersh** 24 Dec 1955 in Morgantown, Monongalia Co., WV. She was born 22 Aug 1939 in Meyersdale, Somerset Co., PA.

Notes for Alice Jane Hersh:
Alice is the daughter of Walter and Catherine Hotchkiss Hersh.

Children of Jack Christner and Alice Hersh are:
4211   i.   Dale Allen⁹ Christner, born 31 May 1957 in Meyersdale, Somerset Co., PA; died 14 Mar 1974 in Springfield Twp., OH.

              Notes for Dale Allen Christner:
              Obituary: Dale Allen Christner 1974, native of Meyersdale, Somerset County, PA - Somerset American, March 21, 1974

              Dale Allen Christner, 16, of Springfield Twp., OH died Mar 14 as the result of an automobile accident. Born May 31, 1957 in Meyersdale, the son of Jack and Alice Hersh Christner. Survived by parents; a brother James at home; paternal grandfather, Ralph Christner of Meyersdale RD 1 and maternal grandmother, Mrs. Catherine Hersh also of Meyersdale RD 1. He was a member of the junior class of Springfield High School and a member of Boy Scout Troop 35 of Lakemore, OH. Friends will be received after 2 p.m. Saturday at the Thomas Funeral Home, Salisbury, where services will be held Sunday at 2 p.m. with the Rev. Paul H. Yoder officiating. Interment to follow in the St. Paul's Cemetery.

4212   ii.   James Randall Christner, born 01 Jun 1960[6879]. He married Gloria D. Christner[6879,6880]; born 24 Jun 1969[6880,6881].

              More About James Randall Christner:
              Residence: Lakewood, Cuyahoga Co., OH[6881]

              More About Gloria D. Christner:
              Residence: Cleveland, Cuyahoga Co., OH[6881]

2232. Eva Marie⁸ Christner (Ralph⁷, Rufus J.⁶, Jonas Yone⁵, Joseph "Zep"⁴, Johannes John Hans³, Christian², Christen¹)[6882] was born 14 Jun 1936 in Meyersdale, Somerset Co., PA[6882,6883], and died 22 Apr 2003 in Grand Rapids, Kent Co., MI[6884]. She married **David Earl Hotchkiss** in Morgantown, Monongalia Co., WV, son of William Hoctchkiss and Clara Staub. He was born 09 Aug 1932 in Jerome PA[6885], and died 02 Mar 2000 in Mogadore, Summit Co., OH[6885].

More About Eva Marie Christner:
Social Security Number: 287-48-2230[6886]

Notes for David Earl Hotchkiss:
U.S. Veterans Gravesites, ca.1775-2006

Name: David E Hotchkiss
Service Info.: SGT US ARMY KOREA
Birth Date: 9 Aug 1932
Death Date: 2 Mar 2000
Cemetery: Greenwood Cemetery, 135 South Cleveland Ave Mogadore, OH 44260

More About David Earl Hotchkiss:
Social Security Number: 200-24-4851[6887]

Children of Eva Christner and David Hotchkiss are:

4213   i.   Donna Marie[9] Hotchkiss, born 09 Mar 1953. She married Walter Jenkins.

4214   ii.   Jeanne Sue Hotchkiss, born 10 Apr 1955.

4215   iii.   Richard Wayne Hotchkiss, born 07 Nov 1956. He married Vicki.

4216   iv.   Ruth Ann Hotchkiss, born 09 Jul 1960.

4217   v.   Ronnie Lynn Hotchkiss, born 23 Feb 1965[6888]. He married (1) Marilyn Hotchkiss[6888]; born 1964[6888]. He married (2) Maria L. Curren[6889,6890] 28 Feb 2003 in Stark Co., OH[6891]; born 06 Feb 1969[6892].

Notes for Ronnie Lynn Hotchkiss:
Ohio Marriage Index, 1970, 1972-2007
Name: Ronnie L. Hotchkiss
Age: 38
Birth Year: abt 1965
Residence County: Stark
Times Married: 1
Spouse's Name: Maria L. Curren
Spouse's Age: 34
Spouse's Birth Year:abt 1969
Spouse's Residence County: Stark
Marriage Date: 28 Feb 2003
Marriage License County: Stark
Cerificate Number: 14294
Volume Number: 19753
Source Citation: Ohio Department of Health; Columbus, Ohio; Ohio Marriage Index, 1970 and 1972-2007.

More About Ronnie Lynn Hotchkiss:
Residence: Summit, Ohio, United States[6893]

More About Marilyn Hotchkiss:
Residence: Akron, Summit[6893]

Notes for Maria L. Curren:
Ohio Marriage Index, 1970, 1972-2007

Name: Ronnie L Hotchkiss
Age: 38
Birth Year: abt 1965
Residence County: Stark
Times Married: 1
Spouse's Name: Maria L. Curren
Spouse's Age: 34
Spouse's Birth Year: abt 1969
Spouse's Residence County: Stark
Marriage Date: 28 Feb 2003
Marriage License County: Stark
Cerificate Number: 14294
Volume Number: 19753
Source Citation: Ohio Department of Health; Columbus, Ohio; Ohio Marriage Index, 1970 and 1972-2007.

More About Maria L. Curren:
Residence: Stark, Ohio, United States[6894]

2233. Janet Ruth[8] Christner (Ralph[7], Rufus J.[6], Jonas Yone[5], Joseph "Zep"[4], Johannes John Hans[3], Christian[2], Christen[1]) was born 17 Apr 1943 in Meyersdale, Somerset Co., PA. She married **Grady Gilpin Jr.** 26 May 1960 in Grantsville, Garret Co., MD. He was born 24 Apr 1940 in Grantsville MD.

Notes for Grady Gilpin Jr.:
Grady is the son of Ira and Celesta Myers Gilpin

Children of Janet Christner and Grady Gilpin are:
　　4218　　i.　Dwayne Edward[9] Gilfin, born 13 Aug 1961.
　　4219　　ii.　Ronda Lee Gilfin, born 31 Mar 1963.

2234. James Cornett[8] Christner (Ralph[7], Rufus J.[6], Jonas Yone[5], Joseph "Zep"[4], Johannes John Hans[3], Christian[2], Christen[1]) was born 29 Aug 1945 in Meyersdale, Somerset Co., PA. He married **Shirley Marie Ebel** 19 Aug 1967 in Grantsville, Garret Co., MD, daughter of Clyde Ebel and Evelyn Angle. She was born 03 Aug 1949.

Notes for Shirley Marie Ebel:

Children of James Christner and Shirley Ebel are:
　　4220　　i.　Jennifer[9] Christner. She married Ed Grubb.
　　4221　　ii.　Michael James Christner, born 15 Jun 1968[6895,6896]. He married Erin M. Dreyer[6897] 21 Dec 2002[6897]; born 1977[6898].

　　　　　　More About Michael James Christner:
　　　　　　Residence: DE[6899,6900]

　　　　　　More About Erin M. Dreyer:
　　　　　　Residence: Delaware[6900]

2235. Charles A. "Cappy"[8] Pritts (Harrison Simon[7], Mary Ann[6] Christner, Moses C.[5], Joseph "Zep"[4], Johannes John Hans[3], Christian[2], Christen[1])[6901] was born 10 Aug 1884 in Black Twp., Somerset Co., PA[6901,6902], and died 26 Aug 1966 in Meyersdale Community Hospital, Somerset Co., PA[6903]. He married **Amanda Mary "Mandy" Weimer** 21 Oct 1904 in Somerset Co., PA[6904]. She was born 28 Dec 1889 in Pittsburgh, Allegheny Co., PA[6904], and died 02 Feb 1969 in Black Twp., Somerset Co., PA[6904].

Notes for Charles A. "Cappy" Pritts:
Birth: Aug 10, 1884 - Garrett, Somerset Co., PA
Death: Aug 26, 1966 - Meyersdale, Somerset Co., PA

Charles is the son of Harrison and Barbara E.(Romesburg) Pritts. Married to Amanda M. Weimer on August 17, 1904. Parents to Florence M.(Miller),Edna B.(Schrock),Orville H.,Carl R.,Julia G.(Kaloduka) He was a brother of George, Elmer, James and Nellie (Mullen). Charlie was coal miner and also worked for the Black Township road department. They lived at the intersection of Wilson & Hauger Road.

Spouse: Amanda M. Weimer Pritts (1887 - 1969)

Burial: Somerset County Memorial Park, Somerset, Somerset Co., PA
Find A Grave Memorial# 101510739

More About Charles A. "Cappy" Pritts:
Burial: Memorial Park Cemetery, Somerset, Somerset Co., PA[6905]
Residence: 1920, Black Twp., Somerset Co., PA[6905]
Social Security Number: 191-07-2064/[6906]
SSN issued: Pittsburgh, Allegheny Co., PA[6906]

Notes for Amanda Mary "Mandy" Weimer:
Birth: Dec. 28, 1887 - Brothersvalley Twp., Somerset Co., PA
Death: Feb. 2, 1969 - Black Twp., Somerset Co., PA

Amanda is the daughter of Cyrus and Lucilla Weimer. Married to Charles Pritts on August 17, 1904. Parents to Florence M.,Edna B.,Orville H.,Carl R.,Julia G. They lived at the interection of Wilson & Hauger Roads.

Spouse: Charles E. Pritts (1884 - 1966)

Burial: Somerset County Memorial Park, Somerset, Somerset Co., PA
Find A Grave Memorial# 101511398

More About Amanda Mary "Mandy" Weimer:
Residence: 1930, Black Twp., Somerset Co., PA[6907]

Children of Charles Pritts and Amanda Weimer are:

4222   i.   Florence M.[9] Pritts[6907], born Abt. 1905 in Pittsburgh, Allegheny Co., PA[6907].

More About Florence M. Pritts:
Residence: 1930, Shade, Somerset, PA USA[6907]

4223   ii.   Edna Blanche Pritts[6907], born 01 Dec 1906 in Pittsburgh, Allegheny Co., PA[6907]; died Oct 1992 in Rockwood, Somerset Co., PA[6907].

More About Edna Blanche Pritts:
Residence: 1930, Black Twp., Somerset Co., PA[6907]

4224   iii.   Orville Harrison Pritts[6907], born 04 Sep 1908 in Pittsburgh, Allegheny Co., PA[6907]; died 03 Jul 1994 in Fishkill, Dutchess Co., NY[6907].

More About Orville Harrison Pritts:
Residence: 1920, Black Twp., Somerset Co., PA[6907]

4225   iv.   Carl R. Pritts[6907], born 16 Jan 1911 in Pittsburgh, Allegheny Co., PA[6907]; died Jan 1991[6907].

More About Carl R. Pritts:
Residence: 1930, Black Twp., Somerset Co., PA[6907]

2238. Irene "Grace"[8] Pritts (Harrison Simon[7], Mary Ann[6] Christner, Moses C.[5], Joseph "Zep"[4], Johannes John Hans[3], Christian[2], Christen[1])[6908] was born 19 Mar 1889 in Black Twp., Somerset Co., PA[6908], and died 13 Mar 1986 in Rockwood, Somerset Co., PA[6908]. She married **James Ephraim Weimer**[6909,6910] 30 Jun 1904[6911]. He was born 01 Jul 1880 in Wilson Creek, Somerset Co., PA[6911], and died 17 Apr 1932[6911,6912].

More About Irene "Grace" Pritts:
Burial: Rockwood IOOF Cemetery, Somerset Co., PA[6913]
Residence: 1920, Black Twp., Somerset Co., PA[6914]

More About James Ephraim Weimer:
Residence: 1900, Black Twp., Somerset Co., PA[6914]

Children of Irene Pritts and James Weimer are:

+   4226   i.   Melvine Ray[9] Weimer, born 29 Jan 1905 in Black Twp., Somerset Co., PA; died 06 Oct 1988 in Somerset Community Hospital, Somerset, Somerset Co., PA.
    4227   ii.   Elwell C. Weimer[6914], born 13 Sep 1906 in Black, Somerset, PA[6914]; died 06 Apr 2001 in Saint Petersburg, Pinellas, Florida, United States of America[6914].

More About Elwell C. Weimer:
Social Security Number: 170-26-6021/[6914]
SSN issued: Pittsburgh, Allegheny Co., PA[6914]

    4228   iii.   Elsie Weimer[6914], born 15 Nov 1907[6914].
    4229   iv.   Kathryn Weimer[6914], born 16 May 1917[6914]; died 27 Jun 2004[6914].
    4230   v.   E. James Bus Weimer[6914], born 29 Sep 1922[6914]; died 30 Dec 1998[6914].

2241. Elmer Isreal[8] Pritts (Harrison Simon[7], Mary Ann[6] Christner, Moses C.[5], Joseph "Zep"[4], Johannes

John Hans[3], Christian[2], Christen[1])[6915,6916] was born 02 Oct 1894 in Black Twp., Somerset Co., PA[6917,6918], and died 22 Nov 1983 in Somerset, Somerset Co, PA[6919]. He married **(1) Margaret Pritts Wright**[6920]. She was born 12 Feb 1902 in Somerset Co., PA[6920], and died 23 Jul 1982 in Meyersdale Community Hospital, Meyersdale, Somerset Co., PA[6920]. He married **(2) Minnie E. Kimmel**[6920] 29 Apr 1914[6920]. She was born 31 Oct 1896 in Pittsburgh, Allegheny Co., PA[6920], and died 10 Nov 1969 in Somerset Co., PA[6920].

Notes for Elmer Isreal Pritts:
Birth: Oct. 2, 1894
Death: Nov. 22, 1983

Obituary: PRITTS - Daily American, November 23, 1983

Elmer Pritts, 89, of Rockwood, died Nov 22, 1983, in the Somerset Community Hospital. He was born Oct 2, 1894, in Black Township, a son of the late Harrison and Barbara (Romesberg) Pritts. He is survived by one son, Floyd of Rockwood; two daughters, Mrs. Ernest(Peggy) Enos and Mrs. Charles (Zola) Wiltrout, both of Rockwood RD 3; two sisters, Mrs. Grace Weimer of Rockwood and Mrs. Nellie Mullen of Somerset; six grandchildren, nine great-grandchildren. He was preceded in death by his first wife, Minnie (Kimmel) Pritts, Nov 10, 1969; also by his second wife, Margaret, July 23, 1982; two daughters, Violet and June; five brothers and one sister. He was a member of the UMWA Local 1742, Jennerstown. He was a lifelong member of St. John's (Sanner) Lutheran Church of Rockwood, and presently a member of the Messiah Lutheran Church of New Centerville. Friends will be received at the William J. Wood Funeral Home in Rockwood, Wednesday 7-9 p.m., 2-4 and 7-9 p.m. Thursday, and up until 10 a.m. Friday, when the remains will be removed to the Messiah Lutheran Church for services at 11 a.m., the Rev. Gregory Pile and the Rev. James Roth officiating. Interment to follow in Somerset County Memorial Park.

Burial: Somerset County Memorial Park, Somerset, Somerset Co., PA
Find A Grave Memorial# 90273652

More About Elmer Isreal Pritts:
Burial: Somerset Co Memorial Pk Cem, Somerset, PA[6921]
Residence: 01 Apr 1940, Black, Somerset, PA, United States[6922]
Social Security Number: 206-03-1159/[6923,6924]
SSN issued: Pittsburgh, Allegheny Co., PA[6925]

More About Margaret Pritts Wright:
Burial: St. John Cem, Somerset, PA[6926]
Residence: 1910, Middle Creek, Somerset Co., PA[6926]

More About Minnie E. Kimmel:
Burial: Memorial Park Cemetery, Somerset, Somerset Co., PA[6926]
Residence: 01 Apr 1940, Black, Somerset, PA, United States[6927]

Children of Elmer Pritts and Margaret Wright are:
    4231   i.   Violet[9] Pritts.
    4232   ii.   June Pritts[6928], born 05 Jun 1916[6928]; died 31 Aug 1916[6928].

Children of Elmer Pritts and Minnie Kimmel are:
    4233   i.   Zola Pauline[9] Pritts[6929], born 16 Sep 1917 in Pittsburgh, Allegheny Co., PA[6929]; died 12 Jan 2008 in Pittsburgh, Allegheny Co., PA[6929]. She married Charles Wiltrout; born 11 Aug 1914[6929]; died 11 Jun 2001 in Rockwood, Somerset Co., PA[6929].

        More About Zola Pauline Pritts:
        Residence: 1920, Black Twp., Somerset Co., PA[6929]

        More About Charles Wiltrout:
        Residence: 1930, Rockwood, Somerset Co., PA[6929]
        Social Security Number: 206-07-7247/[6929]

SSN issued: Pittsburgh, Allegheny Co., PA[6929]

4234   ii.   Floyd Pritts[6930], born 12 Aug 1919 in Pittsburgh, Allegheny Co., PA[6930]; died 15 Jan 2006 in Somerset, Somerset Co., PA[6930].

              More About Floyd Pritts:
              Residence: 1930, Black Twp., Somerset Co., PA[6930]

4235   iii.   Peggy Pritts, born 1933 in Pittsburgh, Allegheny Co., PA[6931]. She married Ernest Enos.

              More About Peggy Pritts:
              Residence: 01 Apr 1940, Black, Somerset, PA, United States[6931]

2256. Israel Harmon "Jumbo"[8] Pritts (Irvin Franklin[7], Mary Ann[6] Christner, Moses C.[5], Joseph "Zep"[4], Johannes John Hans[3], Christian[2], Christen[1]) was born 26 Apr 1898[6932,6933], and died 30 May 1971 in Rockwood, Somerset Co., PA[6934]. He married **Fannie Viola Phillippi**[6935], daughter of Jeremiah Phillippi and Tena Hoover. She was born 20 Feb 1902[6935], and died 02 Jan 1979.

Notes for Israel Harmon "Jumbo" Pritts:
Birth: Apr. 26, 1898 - Wilson Creek, Somerset Co., PA
Death: May 30, 1971 - Black Twp., Somerset Co., PA

Obituary: Daily American, June 3, 1971

Israel "Jumbo" Pritts, 73, RD 1, Rockwood, died May 30, 1971, in the Somerset Community Hospital. He was born April 26, 1898 in Rockwood, a son of Irvin and Eliza (Shaffer) Pritts. He is survived by his wife Fannie (Phillippi) Pritts, RD 1, Rockwood. Four sons, Earl, Norval (Gene), Richard, all of RD 1, Rockwood, also James, Ohio. Four daughters, Mrs. Mary Metz, Rockwood; Mrs. Ellouise Barndt, RD 1, Rockwood; Mrs. Ethel Murray, RD 1, Rockwood, and Mrs. Audrey Kubis, Aliquippa, Pa. One brother, Luther, Kent, Ohio. One sister, Mrs. Martha Kendall, RD 1, Rockwood. Sixteen grandchildren and four great grandchildren. He was preceded in death by five brothers and three sisters. He was a retired United Mine Worker.

Parents:
Irvin Franklin Pritts (1871 - 1950)
Eliza Shaffer Pritts (1878 - 1936)

Spouse: Fannie Viola Phillippi Pritts (1902 - 1979)

Children: Mary Elizabeth Pritts Metz (1928 - 1996)

Burial: Rockwood IOOF Cemetery, Rockwood, Somerset Co., PA

More About Israel Harmon "Jumbo" Pritts:
Social Security Number: 209-09-7736/[6936]
SSN issued: Connellsville, Fayette Co., PA[6936]

Notes for Fannie Viola Phillippi:
Birth: Feb. 20, 1902
Death: Jan. 2, 1979

Obituary: The Republic, January 11, 1979
Fannie (Phillippi) Pritts, 76, of Rockwood RD 1, died Jan 2, 1979 in the Somerset Community Hospital. She was born Feb 20, 1902 in Rockwood, a daughter of Jermiah and Tina (Hoover) Phillippi. She is survived by four sons: Earl, Norval, and Richard, all of Rockwood RD 1, and James of Somerset; also by four daughters: Mrs. Mary Metz of Somerset; Mrs. Elloise Barndt of Rockwood RD 1; Mrs. Ethel Murray, with whom she resided at Rockwood RD 1; and Mrs. Audrey Kubis of Alliquippa; one sister, Mrs. Etta Handwork of Osterburg; 19 grandchildren and 11 great-grandchildren. She was preceded in death by husband, Israel "Jumbo" Pritts, May 30,

1971. She was a member of the Christian Gospel Tabernacle of Rockwood and senior citizens' group. Friends were received in the William J. Wood Funeral Home, Rockwood, where services were conducted with the Rev. Arnold Ansell officiating; Interment, Rockwood I.O.O.F. Cemetery.

Parents:
Jeremiah B. Phillippi (1864 - 1939)
Tena Hoover Phillippi (1867 - 1950)

Spouse: Israel Harmon Pritts (1898 - 1971)

Children: Mary Elizabeth Pritts Metz (1928 - 1996)

Burial: Rockwood IOOF Cemetery, Rockwood, Somerset Co., PA

Child is listed above under (2123) Fannie Viola Phillippi.

2273. Boyd[8] **Christner** (Laura Virginia[7], Jacob M.[6], Moses C.[5], Joseph "Zep"[4], Johannes John Hans[3], Christian[2], Christen[1])[6937] was born 31 Aug 1890 in NE, and died 1914. He married **Ethel Daughtery**.

Notes for Boyd Christner:
How can we know who Boyd's father was, see his mothers notes. Boyd married Ethel Daughtery and had one child (Lida) who his mother raised because Boyd abandoned his family.

More About Boyd Christner:
Burial: Willard, Colorado
Residence: 1900, Davenport, Thayer Co., NE[6937]

Children of Boyd Christner and Ethel Daughtery are:
    4236   i.   Infant[9] Christner.
    4237   ii.   Lida Christner.

2277. Arthur Benjamin[8] **Muckel** (Geneive Rebecca[7] Christner, Jacob M.[6], Moses C.[5], Joseph "Zep"[4], Johannes John Hans[3], Christian[2], Christen[1])[6938] was born 11 Jun 1893 in Hebron, Thayer Co., NE[6938], and died 05 Apr 1976 in Bloomington, Franklin Co., NE. He married **Florence Dunn** 1916. She was born 18 Feb 1897[6939,6940], and died 11 Apr 1989 in Bloomington, Franklin Co., NE[6941].

More About Arthur Benjamin Muckel:
Burial: Maple Grove Cemetery, Bloomington, Franklin Co., NE
Residence: 1930, Bloomington, Franklin Co., NE[6942]

More About Florence Dunn:
Residence: 1930, Bloomington, Franklin Co., NE[6942]
Social Security Number: 505-60-3841/[6943]

Children of Arthur Muckel and Florence Dunn are:
    4238   i.   Raymond A.[9] Muckel[6944,6945], born 18 Mar 1919[6945,6946]; died 02 Jun 2009 in Apache Junction, Pinal Co., AZ[6947]. He married Florence Dunn; born 11 Feb 1897; died 11 Apr 1989 in Holdredge, Phelps Co., NE[6948].

            Notes for Raymond A. Muckel:
            Obituary: Lincoln Journal Star on 5 Jun 2009

            Raymond A. Muckel 90, went to be with the Lord on Tuesday (6/2/09). He was born on March 18, 1919 in Bloomington, NE. Memorial service 10 a.m. Saturday (6/6/09). Internment at a later date in Bloomington, NE. Donations may be made to Wesley Methodist Church or charity of choice.

            More About Raymond A. Muckel:

Residence: 1930, Bloomington, Franklin Co., NE[6949]

Notes for Florence Dunn:
Birth: Feb. 11, 1897
Death: Apr. 11, 1989

Parents:
William Marion Dunn (1857 - 1930)
Catherine Amanda Garbison Dunn (1863 - 1935)

Spouse: Arthur Muckel (1893 - 1976)

Children: Raymond Muckel (1919 - 2009)

Burial: Maple Grove Cemetery, Bloomington, Franklin Co., NE
Find A Grave Memorial# 60999861

4239   ii.   Francis L. Muckel[6949], born 19 Oct 1924[6950]; died 12 Feb 1997 in Franklin, Franklin Co., NE[6950].

More About Francis L. Muckel:
Residence: 1930, Bloomington, Franklin Co., NE[6951]
Social Security Number: 508-18-9388/[6952]

2286. Jack[8] Christner (Warren Jacob (Grant)[7], Jacob M.[6], Moses C.[5], Joseph "Zep"[4], Johannes John Hans[3], Christian[2], Christen[1]) was born 11 Apr 1918 in Willard, Logan Co., CO[6953,6954], and died 14 Sep 2003 in Carson City, Carson Co., NV[6954]. He married **Shirley Stoops** 14 Jul 1941.

Notes for Jack Christner:
This info came from Dora Lue and is very incomplete.

More About Jack Christner:
Military service: 23 Jan 1942[6955]
SSN issued: CO[6956]

Children of Jack Christner and Shirley Stoops are:
    4240   i.   Jere[9] Christner.
    4241   ii.   Kurt Christner.

2308. Ruby Alice[8] Wright (Mary[7] Christner, Joseph M.[6], Moses C.[5], Joseph "Zep"[4], Johannes John Hans[3], Christian[2], Christen[1])[6957,6958] was born 05 Aug 1912 in Billings, Yellowstone Co., MT[6958,6959,6960], and died 24 Feb 1992 in Fayetteville, AR[6961]. She married **Thelbert W. Miller**[6962], son of Donald Miller and Althea Wolcott. He was born 02 Jun 1907 in Cheyenne, Wells Co., CO[6962], and died 24 Feb 1992 in Erie Co., CO[6962].

Notes for Ruby Alice Wright:

More About Ruby Alice Wright:
Residence: 01 Apr 1940, Marshall, Saline Co., MO[6963,6964]

More About Thelbert W. Miller:
Residence: 1930, Erie, Weld Co., CO[6964]

Children of Ruby Wright and Thelbert Miller are:
    4242   i.   Charles[9] Miller[6964], born 20 Jun 1931[6964]; died Abt. 2005 in Boulder, CO[6964].
    4243   ii.   Gillard Gene Miller[6964], born 07 Jul 1932 in CO[6964]; died 22 May 2003 in Berthoud, Larimer Co.,
            CO[6964].

More About Gillard Gene Miller:
Residence: Bet. 1935 - 1993, Longmont, Boulder Co., CO[6964]

4244   iii.   Leonard Dean Miller[6964], born 27 Oct 1937[6964]; died 29 Nov 1937 in Erie, Weld, Co., CO[6964].

2310. Ethel Marie[8] Wright (Mary[7] Christner, Joseph M.[6], Moses C.[5], Joseph "Zep"[4], Johannes John Hans[3], Christian[2], Christen[1])[6965,6966] was born 16 Oct 1914 in Miles City, Custer Co., MT[6966], and died 03 Sep 2004 in Montrose, Montrose Co., CO[6966]. She married **Otis Karl Millard**[6966] 1932 in Firestone, CO[6966], son of Millard. He was born 15 Apr 1907 in CO[6966], and died 18 May 1986 in Montrose, Montrose Co., CO[6966].

Notes for Ethel Marie Wright:

More About Ethel Marie Wright:
Residence: 1930, Frederick, Weld Co., CO[6967]
Social Security Number: 523-40-7110/[6968]
SSN issued: CO[6968]

More About Otis Karl Millard:
Occupation: 07 Apr 1930, Electrician Western Electric/[6968]
Residence: 07 Apr 1930, Los Angeles, Los Angeles County, California[6968]
Social Security Number: 524-10-1240/[6968]
SSN issued: CO[6968]

Children of Ethel Wright and Otis Millard are:
4245   i.   Eulalia Mae[9] Millard[6968], born 26 Aug 1934 in Denver, CO[6968]; died 16 Jul 2000 in Rifle, CO[6968].
4246   ii.   William Leroy Millard[6968], born 14 Jun 1941 in Montrose, Montrose Co., CO[6968]; died 21 May 1990 in Montrose, Montrose Co., CO[6968].

2314. Laura Jane[8] Wright (Mary[7] Christner, Joseph M.[6], Moses C.[5], Joseph "Zep"[4], Johannes John Hans[3], Christian[2], Christen[1])[6969,6970] was born 25 Apr 1921 in CO[6971,6972], and died 28 May 1995 in Lakewood, Jefferson Co., CO[6973,6974]. She married **Joseph Edward Pauletick** 23 Dec 1946 in Sidney, Cheyenne Co., NE[6974], son of John Pauletich and Mary Leiler. He was born 27 Apr 1918 in Cedar Hill Coal Camp, Las Animas Co., CO[6974,6975,6976], and died 05 Apr 1997 in Lakewood, Jefferson Co., CO[6977,6978,6979].

Notes for Laura Jane Wright:
Laura married Joseph Pauletick born April 27, 1918. We have gotten large amounts of info from Laura.

More About Laura Jane Wright:
Residence: 01 Apr 1940, Age: 18; Marital Status: Single; Relation to Head of House: Daughter/Frederick, Weld, Colorado, United States[6980]

More About Joseph Edward Pauletick:
Burial: 11 Apr 1997, Age: 78/CO[6981]
Military service: 04 Jun 1942, Age: 24; : 09/11/1945/[6981]
Residence: 1930, Trinidad, Las Animas Co., CO[6982]
Social Security Number: 523-01-0565/[6983]

Children of Laura Wright and Joseph Pauletick are:
4247   i.   Robert Delbert[9] Pauletick[6984], born 22 Jul 1942 in Frederick, Weld Co., CO[6984]; died 24 Jul 2008 in Denver, Denver Co., CO[6984].

        More About Robert Delbert Pauletick:
        Residence: 1995, Lakewood, CO[6984]

4248   ii.   Joseph Edward Pauletich Jr.[6984], born 24 May 1947 in Denver Co., CO[6984]; died 24 Aug 2010 in Lakewood, Jefferson Co., CO[6984].

More About Joseph Edward Pauletich Jr.:
Residence: 1994, Marion, OH[6984]

2316. Violet Lauretta[8] Christner (Jacob J.[7], Joseph M.[6], Moses C.[5], Joseph "Zep"[4], Johannes John Hans[3], Christian[2], Christen[1])[6985] was born 03 Jan 1913 in Davenport, Nuckolls, NE[6985], and died 26 Dec 1977 in Bellevue, Sarpy Co., NE[6985]. She married **(1) Frank E. Roller**. She married **(2) Roy A. Fry**.

Children of Violet Christner and Frank Roller are:
4249   i.   Frank E.[9] Roller Jr., born 06 Sep 1929. He married Josephine Quintana.
4250   ii.   Phyllis Roller, born 10 Aug 1937. She married Ronald Lee Langheine[6986]; born 14 Aug 1928[6986]; died 03 Dec 1988[6986].

2320. Wesley Edward[8] Burright (Kate[7] Christner, Joseph M.[6], Moses C.[5], Joseph "Zep"[4], Johannes John Hans[3], Christian[2], Christen[1])[6987,6988] was born 02 Mar 1919 in Guthrie, Logan Co., OK[6989], and died 29 Jan 1994 in Ponca, Kay Co., OK[6989]. He married **Rosamond Aileen Summers**. She was born 18 Aug 1922[6990,6991], and died 02 Jun 2006 in Ponca City, Kay Co., OK[6991,6992].

Notes for Wesley Edward Burright:
Birth: Mar. 2, 1919 - Guthrie, Logan Co., OK
Death: Jan. 29, 1994 - Ponca City, Kay Co., OK

Parents:
Clyde Charles Burright (1879 - 1951)
Kate Christner Burright (1890 - 1974)

Spouse: Rosamond Aileen Summers Burright (1922 - 2006)

Children: Terry Wesley Burright (1944 - ____)

Burial: Christner Cemetery, Oklahoma Co., OK

More About Wesley Edward Burright:
Residence: 1930, Kildare, Kay Co., OK[6993,6994]

More About Rosamond Aileen Summers:
Residence: 1987, Ponca City, OK[6994]
SSN issued: OK[6995]

Child of Wesley Burright and Rosamond Summers is:
4251   i.   Terry Wesley[9] Burright, born 28 Apr 1944 in Ponca City, Kay Co., OK[6996]; died 28 Apr 1944[6996].

Notes for Terry Wesley Burright:
Birth: Apr. 28, 1944 - Ponca City, Kay Co., OK
Death: Apr. 28, 1944 - OK

Parents:
Wesley Edward Burright (1919 - 1994)
Rosamond Aileen Summers Burright (1922 - 2006)

Burial: Christner Cemetery, Oklahoma Co., OK

More About Terry Wesley Burright:
Burial: Oklahoma Co., OK[6996]

2324. William Eugene[8] **Christner** (Archie B.[7], Joseph M.[6], Moses C.[5], Joseph "Zep"[4], Johannes John Hans[3], Christian[2], Christen[1])[6997] was born 16 Jul 1928 in CA[6997], and died Jan 1982 in Sunset Beach, Orange Co., CA[6997]. He married **Ellen Elizabeth Theriot**. She was born 18 Jul 1928.

Notes for William Eugene Christner:
William married Ellen Elizabeth Theriot. She was born July 18 1928.

SS#573-28-5959 ISS CA   Last address 90742 CA

Children of William Christner and Ellen Theriot are:
| 4252 | i. | David William[9] Christner[6998], born 03 Sep 1949 in Los Angeles Co., CA[6998]. |
| 4253 | ii. | Jon Eric Christner, born 23 Oct 1957 in Los Angeles Co., CA[6999]. |

2332. Robert Eugene[8] **Moore** (Lauretta[7] Christner, Joseph M.[6], Moses C.[5], Joseph "Zep"[4], Johannes John Hans[3], Christian[2], Christen[1])[7000] was born 24 Aug 1927 in Denver, Denver, CO[7000], and died 17 Feb 2004 in Denver, Denver, CO[7000]. He married **(1) Leona Marie Wymer**. She was born 22 Mar 1928, and died 21 Jul 1969.

Notes for Robert Eugene Moore:

Notes for Leona Marie Wymer:
Birth: Mar 22, 1928
Death: Jul 21, 1969

Burial: Fort Logan National Cemetery, Denver, Denver Co., CO
Plot: P, 2785
Find A Grave Memorial# 3362109

Children of Robert Eugene Moore are:
4254	i.	Lauretta[9] Moore[7000], born Abt. 1950 in Denver, CO[7000]; died Abt. 1950 in Denver, CO[7000].
4255	ii.	Gary Moore[7000], born Abt. 1953 in Denver, Denver, CO[7000]; died Abt. 1953 in Denver, Denver, CO[7000].
4256	iii.	Robert Moore[7000], born Abt. 1954 in Denver, Denver, CO[7000]; died Abt. 1954 in Denver, Denver, CO[7000].
4257	iv.	Debra Dawn Moore[7000], born 05 Jan 1962 in Denver, Denver, CO[7000]; died 05 Mar 1997 in Littleton, Arapahoe, Colorado, United States of America[7000].

2338. George B.[8] **Surber** (Annie[7] Christner, Joseph M.[6], Moses C.[5], Joseph "Zep"[4], Johannes John Hans[3], Christian[2], Christen[1]) was born 29 Jul 1921 in Guthrie, Logan Co., OK[7001]. He married **Mary Hinkle**[7001]. She was born 11 Nov 1925.

Child of George Surber and Mary Hinkle is:
| 4258 | i. | Sandra[97001]. |

2348. Bessie Marie[8] **Christner** (Sidney Lewis[7], Nelson "Nels"[6], Moses C.[5], Joseph "Zep"[4], Johannes John Hans[3], Christian[2], Christen[1])[7002] was born 21 Oct 1916 in OK[7002,7003], and died 29 Jan 1999 in Kingfisher, Kingfisher Co., OK[7004]. She married **Allen W. Kordis** 09 Jun 1937. He was born 09 Jul 1915 in Okarche, Kingfisher Co., OK[7005], and died 30 Apr 2012 in Oklahoma City, Oklahoma Co., OK[7005].

Notes for Bessie Marie Christner:
Birth: Oct 21, 1916 - Logan Co., OK
Death: Jan 29, 1999 - Kingfisher, Kingfisher Co., OK

Parents:
Sidney Lewis Christner (1890 - 1970)
Lydia Ruth Burright Christner (1896 - 1986)

Spouse: Allen Willard Kordis (1915 - 2012)

Burial: Kingfisher Cemetery, Kingfisher, Kingfisher Co., OK
Find A Grave Memorial# 75639873

More About Bessie Marie Christner:
Residence: 1930, Deer Creek, Oklahoma Co., OK[7006]
Social Security Number: 447-70-3838/[7007]
SSN issued: OK[7007]

Notes for Allen W. Kordis:
Obituary - The Enid News and Eagle, Enid, OK - May 2, 2012

ENID - Funeral for Allen Kordis, 96, will be 2 p.m. Friday, May 4, 2012, at Cashion Christian Church. Enternment will follow in Kingfisher Cemetery. Arrangements by Sanders Funeral Service Inc., Kingfisher.

Allen was born July 9, 1915, in Okarche to William Allen and Hettie Mabel Hansen Kordis and died Monday, April 30, 2012, in Oklahoma City.

Surviving are children, Herbert Allen Kordis, Kenneth Randal Kordis, Ellen Marie Richards and Ruth Mabel Blasius; 10 grandchildren; 13 great-grandchildren; four great-great-grandchildren; five stepgrandchildren; five stepgreat-grandchildren; and seven stepgreat-great-grandchildren.

Preceded in death by his wife and two grandchildren.

Birth: Jul. 9, 1915 - Okarche, Kingfisher Co., OK
Death: Apr. 30, 2012 - Oklahoma City, Oklahoma Co., OK

Spouse: Bessie Marie Christner Kordis (1916 - 1999)

Burial: Kingfisher Cemetery, Kingfisher, Kingfisher Co., OK
Find A Grave Memorial# 90852304

Children of Bessie Christner and Allen Kordis are:
    4259   i.   Ellen Marie⁹ Kordis, born 23 Sep 1938.

                  Notes for Ellen Marie Kordis:
                  Ellen married Charles F. Gillett. Charles born Sept 1, 1932.

    4260   ii.   Ruth Mabel Kordis, born 20 Mar 1940. She married Roy Allen Blasius; born 19 Nov 1934.

                  Notes for Ruth Mabel Kordis:
                  Ruth married Roy Allen Blasius
                  Roy born Nov 19 1934

    4261   iii.   Herbert Allen Kordis, born 07 Nov 1942.

                  Notes for Herbert Allen Kordis:
                  Herbert married Maureen Johnson
                  Maureen born Nov 18 1942

    4262   iv.   Kenneth Randel Kordis, born 22 Jan 1952.

2349. Beryl Mabel[8] Christner (Sidney Lewis[7], Nelson "Nels"[6], Moses C.[5], Joseph "Zep"[4], Johannes John Hans[3], Christian[2], Christen[1])[7008] was born 15 Aug 1920 in Lockridge, Logan Co., OK[7008], and died 1973 in Oklahoma City, Oklahoma Co., OK[7008]. She married **John Orville Deaton**[7008,7009] Abt. 1941[7010]. He was born 09 Jun 1903 in Topaz, Douglas Co., OK[7010], and died 25 Nov 1971 in Edmond, Oklahoma Co., OK[7010].

Notes for Beryl Mabel Christner:
Birth: Aug. 15, 1920 - Logan Co., OK
Death: Mar. 5, 1973 - Oklahoma City, Oklahoma Co., OK

Parents:
Sidney Lewis Christner (1890 - 1970)
Lydia Ruth Burright Christner (1896 - 1986)

Spouses:
John Orville Deaton (1903 - 1971)
Oscar Harold Perry (1918 - 1949)

Children: Harold Dean Perry (1940 - 1940)

Burial: Christner Cemetery, Oklahoma Co., OK
Find A Grave Memorial# 89158528

More About Beryl Mabel Christner:
Burial: Christer Cemetery, Deer Creek, OK[7010]
Residence: 1930, Deer Creek, Oklahoma Co., OK[7010]

Notes for John Orville Deaton:
Birth: Jun 9, 1903 - Topaz, Douglas Co., MO
Death: Nov 25, 1971 - Edmond, Oklahoma Co., OK

Spouse: Beryl Mable Christner Deaton (1920 - 1973)

Burial: Christner Cemetery, Oklahoma Co., OK
Find A Grave Memorial# 89162865

More About John Orville Deaton:
Burial: Christner Cem, Oklahoma
Social Security Number: 500-09-7325/[7011]
SSN issued: MO[7011]

Children of Beryl Christner and John Deaton are:
    4263   i.   James[9] Deaton, born 08 Mar 1942. He married Charlene Dillard; born Jul 1944.
    4264   ii.   Harolyn Jean Deaton, born 29 Aug 1944. She married Don Hoelscher; born 19 Oct 1943.
    4265   iii. Sharon Lea Deaton, born 05 Sep 1946. She married Fredrick E. Knight 18 Apr 1972; born 25 Jun 1944.

        Notes for Sharon Lea Deaton:
        Texas, Divorce Index, 1968-2011

        Name: Sharon L. Deaton
        Estimated Birth Year: abt 1946
        Age: 27
        Spouse's Name: Frederick E. Deaton
        Spouse's Age: 29
        Marriage Date: 18 Apr 1972
        Divorce Date: 28 Sep 1973
        Divorce Place: Tarrant Co., TX

+ 4266 iv. John Sidney Deaton, born 27 Oct 1949 in Edmond, Oklahoma Co., OK; died 02 Dec 1910 in Edmond, Oklahoma Co., OK.

2350. Betty Ruth[8] Christner (Sidney Lewis[7], Nelson "Nels"[6], Moses C.[5], Joseph "Zep"[4], Johannes John Hans[3], Christian[2], Christen[1]) was born 07 Jul 1926 in Edmond, OK[7012], and died 23 Jan 2003 in Le Claire, Scott Co., IA[7013]. She married **G.C. Hopper Jr** in Edmond, OK. He was born 16 Oct 1925 in Floydada, TX, and died 03 Aug 1994.

Notes for Betty Ruth Christner:
We have lived in Dallas, TX since Jan 1978. My husband passed away Aug 3, 1994. My youngest son lives with me. I keep very busy with my church which is Spring Valley United Methodist. I am a Stephen Minister- United Math Women- now as president I'm in a large S.S. Class of 130 & I'm in charge of arts & crafts. I have two new puppies. 9 mos. old. Got them when they were 7 weeks old. Peter & Pacha - Boston Terrier. I love to read, enjoy my computer so much, like to attend movies, concerts, plays, & etc. I travel some with my son Tommy. Hope this will help you so keep in touch. Betty Christner Hopper

More About Betty Ruth Christner:
Residence: 1930, Deer Creek, Oklahoma Co., OK[7014]
SSN issued: IA[7015]

More About G.C. Hopper Jr:
Burial: Dallas Texas Restland Cem.

Children of Betty Christner and G.C. Hopper are:
4267 i. Gary Charles[9] Hopper, born 27 Sep 1950 in Oklahoma City, Oklahoma Co., OK. He married Jacquelinann Carter 19 Mar 1976 in Oklahoma City, Oklahoma Co., OK.
4268 ii. Betty Sue Hopper, born 07 Jan 1954 in Oklahoma City, Oklahoma Co., OK. She married Dennis Leo Bruehl 31 Mar 1984 in Oklahoma City, Oklahoma Co., OK.
4269 iii. Tommy Scott Hopper, born 05 Sep 1955 in Oklahoma City, Oklahoma Co., OK.
4270 iv. Rocky Lynn Hopper, born 15 Mar 1959 in Oklahoma City, Oklahoma Co., OK.

2352. Gladys Opal[8] Christner (Earl Harrison[7], Nelson "Nels"[6], Moses C.[5], Joseph "Zep"[4], Johannes John Hans[3], Christian[2], Christen[1])[7016] was born 25 Nov 1925 in NE[7016], and died 24 May 2007 in Orange, Orange Co., CA[7016]. She married **(1) Robert Boatright**. She married **(2) Frank Eberly**.

Child of Gladys Christner and Robert Boatright is:
4271 i. Daniel Lee[9] Boatright, born 30 Aug 1938.

Children of Gladys Christner and Frank Eberly are:
4272 i. Sue Ann[9] Eberly, born 30 Aug 1953.
4273 ii. Beth Ann Eberly, born 26 Oct 1965 in Orange Co., CA[7017].

2353. Roy Marvin[8] Christner (Earl Harrison[7], Nelson "Nels"[6], Moses C.[5], Joseph "Zep"[4], Johannes John Hans[3], Christian[2], Christen[1])[7018] was born 25 Jan 1928 in NE[7018], and died 03 Aug 1994[7018]. He married **Lila May Burch**[7019]. She was born 12 Dec 1930[7019], and died 19 Feb 2007[7019].

Notes for Roy Marvin Christner:
SS#506-26-7505 ISS NE

More About Roy Marvin Christner:
Burial: 08 Aug 1994, Ft. McPherson , Nat'l Cemetery, Mexwell, NE[7020]

Children of Roy Christner and Lila Burch are:
4274 i. Michael Lee[9] Christner, born 30 Jan 1950[7021].

More About Michael Lee Christner:
Residence: 1993, North Platte, Lincoln Co., NE[7021]

4275   ii.   Sandra Kay Christner, born 14 Jun 1951.
4276   iii.   Carolyn Theresa Christner, born 08 Sep 1955.

2354. Theodore Eugene[8] Christner (Earl Harrison[7], Nelson "Nels"[6], Moses C.[5], Joseph "Zep"[4], Johannes John Hans[3], Christian[2], Christen[1])[7022] was born 08 Jul 1932 in North Platte, Lincoln Co., NE[7022], and died 19 Apr 2007 in Sacramento, Sacramento Co., CA[7022]. He married **Barbara Jean Hocquell** 05 Apr 1953 in North Platte, Lincoln Co., NE. She was born 18 Jan 1935[7023], and died 16 Jul 2011 in Elk Grove, Sacramento Co., CA[7023].

Notes for Theodore Eugene Christner:
Obituary: Christner, Theodore Eugene - Sacramento Bee on 21 Apr 2007

Of Elk Grove, CA, died of cancer on April 19, 2007 at the age of 74, with his beloved wife and two sons by his side at Sutter General Hospital in Sacramento, CA.

Ted was born one of six children on July 8, 1932 in North Platte, NE. He graduated from North Platte High School in 1950. It was there that he met his childhood sweetheart, Barbara Jean Hocquell. Ted and Jean were fortunate enough to celebrate their 54th anniversary on April 5th, before he passed.
In his younger years, Ted was an avid fisherman, hunter, and camper. He loved the outdoors. He enjoyed planting large vegetable gardens and sharing the fruit of his efforts with his friends and neighbors. He always kept busy making home improvements, and usually had a project of some kind underway.

Ted joined the United States Army in 1952 where he served honorably for 5 years, including a tour of duty in the Korean War. He and Jean were married in 1953 after he completed basic training, before being sent overseas. After the war, they relocated to Northern California where they spent most of their lives together, including 37 years in the Elk Grove community. During the 1970's they relocated to Holdrege, NE to raise the boys, returning to the pleasant climate of Northern California in 1980, where they have remained ever since.

Ted was employed by Proctor & Gamble for 10 years before moving to Holdrege, NE where he worked for the Tri County Irrigation District. After returning to California, he joined J.H. Kleinfelder & Associates as a Construction Inspector, where he retired after many years of service. He then decided to start his own construction inspection business. During that time he served as President of the Construction Inspectors Association, and head of the local American Inspectors Association, respectively. Ted inspected many of the modular school buildings still in use today, in the Elk Grove and San Joaquin School Districts.
Ted is survived by his wife Jean of 54 years, his sons Tom Christner of Lenexa, KS and Scott and Tawny Christner of Marysville, CA and his three grandchildren, Rehana, Alicia and Kile, and two great grandchildren, Amaya and Aiden, his sister Gladyce Eberly of Orange, CA, and Conrad and Stephanie Christner of Aurora, CO. Preceding him in death were his brothers Donald, Roy and Richard.

Ted, being the humble man he was, requested that no service be held on his behalf. The family will take his ashes to their final resting place at Fort McPherson National Cemetery in Maxwell, NE.

More About Barbara Jean Hocquell:
SSN issued: NE[7023]

Children of Theodore Christner and Barbara Hocquell are:
     4277   i.   Tawny[9] Christner.
     4278   ii.   Scott Christner, born 24 Apr.
     4279   iii.   Thomas Earl Christner, born 22 Jan 1959.

2355. Richard[8] Christner (Earl Harrison[7], Nelson "Nels"[6], Moses C.[5], Joseph "Zep"[4], Johannes John Hans[3], Christian[2], Christen[1])[7024,7025] was born 16 Jan 1937[7026], and died 20 Feb 2003 in North Platt, Lincoln Co., NE[7026]. He married **Marilyn Gooden**. She was born 09 Jan.

More About Richard Christner:
SSN issued: NE[7027]

Children of Richard Christner and Marilyn Gooden are:

4280   i.   Kim[9] Christner, born 01 Aug.
4281   ii.   Trudy Lynn Christner, born 17 Nov 1964. She married Dean A. Brauer[7028] 30 Jan 1984 in Grimes, TX[7028]; born Abt. 1963[7028].

Notes for Trudy Lynn Christner:
Texas, Marriage Collection, 1814-1909 and 1966-2011

Name: Trudy L. Christner
Gender: Female
Birth Year: abt 1965
Age: 19
Marriage Date: 30 Jan 1984
Marriage Place: Grimes, TX
Spouse: Dean A. Brauer
Spouse Gender: Male
Spouse Age: 21
Source: Texas Marriage Index, 1966-2002

Notes for Dean A. Brauer:
Texas, Marriage Collection, 1814-1909 and 1966-2011

Name: Trudy L. Christner
Gender: Female
Birth Year: abt 1965
Age: 19
Marriage Date: 30 Jan 1984
Marriage Place: Grimes, TX
Spouse: Dean A. Brauer
Spouse Gender: Male
Spouse Age: 21
Source: Texas Marriage Index, 1966-2002

2356. Conrad[8] Christner (Earl Harrison[7], Nelson "Nels"[6], Moses C.[5], Joseph "Zep"[4], Johannes John Hans[3], Christian[2], Christen[1]) was born 23 Apr 1939. He married **Stephanie**. She was born 20 Aug.

Children of Conrad Christner and Stephanie are:

4282   i.   Danny[9] Christner, born 26 Jun.
4283   ii.   Diane Christner, born 31 Aug.

2359. Lloyd Nelson[8] Souders (Jeanette "Nettie"[7] Christner, Nelson "Nels"[6], Moses C.[5], Joseph "Zep"[4], Johannes John Hans[3], Christian[2], Christen[1])[7029] was born 21 Sep 1921[7029], and died 19 Sep 2008 in Sterling, Logan Co., CO[7029]. He married **Betty Jean Griess** 10 Mar 1951.

Notes for Lloyd Nelson Souders:
Birth: Sep. 21, 1921
Death: Sep. 19, 2008

Lloyd Nelson Souders, a long time resident of Sterling, passed away on Friday, September 19th surrounded by family members. Lloyd was born on September 21, 1921 in Willard, Colorado to Frank Souders and Nettie Christner. Lloyd was married to Betty (Griess) Souders in Fort Collins, Colorado on March 10, 1951. His wife Betty, elder son Jerry Souders, his wife Deborah and son Adam, all of Sterling and also his youngest son, Rick Souders of Lakewood, Colorado, survive Lloyd. His youngest brother Dale Souders and wife Bea, of Fort Collins and three half sisters Mary Ann Miller, Viana Linnebur and Rosalee Hoffman, also survive him. His honorary son Steve Heimbegner and wife Cher of Greeley, Colorado also survive him. Lloyd's brothers Cecil, Marvin, Ray, Wayne, sister Dorothy, half sister Linda Lou and stepmother Edna Souders are all deceased. He is survived by many nieces and nephews.

Lloyd worked at the Welce Elevator as well as Iowa Electric Light and Power Company for over 20 years. He also worked with the Colorado Department of Transportation from 1968 - 1986. Lloyd was inducted into the US Navy in July of 1942 and served with the USS Pasadena for two years. He then Joined the third fleet of the USS Saint Paul. The Saint Paul was credited with fireing the last shot on Japan. Lloyd was awarded the Asiatic - Pacific Campaign Ribbon with one Star and the American Area Carrier Ribbon. Lloyd was a lifetime member of the VFW Post 3541. He received a Bronze Coyote Award for his years of Service with the Boy Scouts of America Troop 15 in Sterling. Lloyd received his Private Pilot License for single engine aircraft in 1951. He was the recipient of the Indoor Archery State Champion Award. Lloyd taught leather craft at the Northeastern Junior College. His hobbies included leather craft, woodcarving, arrowhead hunting, making bird shovels, fishing, and watching baseball.

The Celebration of Life Memorial Service will be held Friday morning at 11:00 a.m. at the Chaney - Reager Funeral Home at 443 South second street in Sterling. The memorial service will be followed by a luncheon at the Sterling Masonic Temple at 198 Springdale Road in Sterling. A memorial fund was set up in honor of Lloyd and his mother Nettie. Donations will be made to the Salvation Army in their honor. Donations can be sent to Souders, 1301 Ulysses St., Golden, CO 80401.

Burial: Sunset Memorial Gardens, Sterling, Logan Co., CO
Find A Grave Memorial# 47142808

Children of Lloyd Souders and Betty Griess are:
4284   i.   Jerry Lee[9] Souders.
4285   ii.   Ricky Allen Souders.

2360. Cecil Ermit[8] Souders (Jeanette "Nettie"[7] Christner, Nelson "Nels"[6], Moses C.[5], Joseph "Zep"[4], Johannes John Hans[3], Christian[2], Christen[1]) was born 25 Apr 1923[7030], and died 09 Jan 2008 in Sterling, Logan Co., CO[7030]. He married **Alberta Mae Franklin** 02 May 1947. She was born Abt. 1920 in TX.

Notes for Cecil Ermit Souders:
Obituary: Cecil Ermit Souders, Sterling, CO
1923 - 2008

Cecil Ermit Souders, 84 of Sterling, passed away Wednesday, Jan. 9, 2008 in Sterling. A memorial service will be held at 11 a.m. Saturday, Jan. 12, at Chaney-Reager Funeral Home with services concluding at the funeral home. The Rev. Derek DeToni-Hill will officiate. Military rites will be performed by the Veterans of Foreign Wars Post No. 3541.

Cecil was born April 25, 1923 to Frank Dave and Nettie (Christner) Souders in Cashion, Okla. He graduated from high school and served in the U.S. Navy during World War II as a Baker Second Class on the USS White Plains. He later worked at the grain elevator as a feedmill operator.

He married Alberta Mae Franklin May 2, 1947 in Sterling.

Cecil was a lifetime member of VFW Post No. 3541, and a member of Cooties, Disabled American Veterans No. 34, Senior Citizens and Royal Neighbors.

He will be forever loved an greatly missed by us all.
Cecil is survived by his wife, Alberta of Sterling; sons, Cecil Edward Souders and wife Helen of Sterling, and Dennis Souders and wife Jean of Hutchinson, Kan.; daughter, Louise Jones of Sterling; brothers, Lloyd Souders of Sterling, and Dale Souders of Fort Collins; sisters, Vianna Linnebur of Roggen, Rosalie Hoffman of Rozel, Kan., and Mary Miller of Greeley; grandchildren, Kendra Walter and family of Model, Jenette Hofer and family

of Fort Collins, Jeremy Souders of Walden, Jonathon Jones and family of Sterling, and Joshua Souders of Hutchinson, Kan.; great-grandchildren, Ashley, Kimmie, Jacob and Robert Walter of Model, Anna Jones and Dante Kohl of Sterling, and Kylie Hofer of Fort Collins.

He was preceded in death by his parents; son David Souders, brothers Marvin, Wayne and Ray Souders; sisters Dorothy Williams and Linda Baumgartner; and grandson Scott Souders.
Memorial contributions may be made to the Hospice of the Plains.

Children of Cecil Souders and Alberta Franklin are:

4286   i.   Cecil Ermit[9] Souders Jr..
4287   ii.   Louise Souders.
4288   iii.   Dennis Souders.
4289   iv.   David Souders, born 11 Nov 1948 in Sterling, Logan Co., CO[7031,7032]; died 07 Dec 1998 in Denver, Adams Co., CO[7033].

         More About David Souders:
         Residence: 1994, Denver, CO[7033]
         Social Security Number: 523-62-4734/[7034]

2361. Marvin L[8] Souders Sr. (Jeanette "Nettie"[7] Christner, Nelson "Nels"[6], Moses C.[5], Joseph "Zep"[4], Johannes John Hans[3], Christian[2], Christen[1])[7035,7036] was born 29 Apr 1925[7036,7037], and died 25 Apr 1994 in Fort Collins, Larimer Co., CO[7038]. He married **Leona Ruth Grauberger**[7039] Feb 1954[7039], daughter of John Grauberger and Rachel Wagner. She was born 21 Feb 1932 in Logan Co., CO[7039], and died 21 Nov 2000 in Resthaven Memory Gardens Fort Collins, Larimer, Colorado, USA/Greensboro, Guilford Co., NC[7039].

More About Leona Ruth Grauberger:
Residence: 01 Apr 1940, Atwood, Logan, Colorado, USA[7039]

Child of Marvin Souders and Leona Grauberger is:

4290   i.   Rodney Wayne[9] Souders[7039,7040], born 19 Oct 1962 in Fort Collins, Larimer Co., CO[7040,7041]; died 12 Apr 1965 in Fort Collins, Larimer Co., CO[7042].

2362. Raymond[8] Souders (Jeanette "Nettie"[7] Christner, Nelson "Nels"[6], Moses C.[5], Joseph "Zep"[4], Johannes John Hans[3], Christian[2], Christen[1]) was born 26 Feb 1927. He married **Marlene Fay Biehm.**

Notes for Raymond Souders:
Raymond served in the US Navy.

Children of Raymond Souders and Marlene Biehm are:

4291   i.   Anthony[9] Souders.
4292   ii.   Steven Souders.
4293   iii.   Teresa Souders.

2363. Dorothy[8] Souders (Jeanette "Nettie"[7] Christner, Nelson "Nels"[6], Moses C.[5], Joseph "Zep"[4], Johannes John Hans[3], Christian[2], Christen[1]) was born 16 Mar 1930. She married **Joseph Williams.**

Children of Dorothy Souders and Joseph Williams are:

4294   i.   Daniel[9] Williams.
4295   ii.   Charles Jeffrey Williams.

2364. Wayne[8] Souders (Jeanette "Nettie"[7] Christner, Nelson "Nels"[6], Moses C.[5], Joseph "Zep"[4], Johannes John Hans[3], Christian[2], Christen[1])[7043] was born 28 Dec 1931 in Sterling, Logan Co., CO[7043], and died 03 Jun 1996 in Ft Collins, Larimer Co., CO[7043]. He married **Mimi Sue Glessey.** She was born 23 Jun 1940[7044].

Notes for Wayne Souders:
Wayne married Mimi Sue Glessey.

More About Mimi Sue Glessey:
Residence: 1993, Age: 53/Fort Collins, CO[7044]

Children of Wayne Souders and Mimi Glessey are:
4296	i.	Julia[9] Souders.
4297	ii.	Daniel Souders.
4298	iii.	Timothy Souders.
4299	iv.	Joel Souders.

2365. Dale[8] Souders (Jeanette "Nettie"[7] Christner, Nelson "Nels"[6], Moses C.[5], Joseph "Zep"[4], Johannes John Hans[3], Christian[2], Christen[1]) was born 01 Jan 1935. He married **Beatrice Miller**.

Children of Dale Souders and Beatrice Miller are:
4300	i.	Kenneth[9] Souders.
4301	ii.	Douglas Souders.

2367. Imogine Pauline[8] Christner (Ermit Theodore "Erm"[7], Nelson "Nels"[6], Moses C.[5], Joseph "Zep"[4], Johannes John Hans[3], Christian[2], Christen[1])[7045,7046,7047] was born 23 Apr 1925 in Lockridge, Logan Co., OK[7048], and died 09 Sep 2012 in Everett, Snohomish Co., WA[7049]. She married **Mabry James Carter Jr.**[7050] 27 Jul 1947[7050]. He was born 29 Jan 1925 in Fearns Springs, Winston Co., MS, and died 25 Nov 1996 in Vian, Sequoyah Co., OK.

Notes for Imogine Pauline Christner:
Birth: Apr 23, 1925 - Logan Co., OK
Death: Sep 9, 2012 - Everett, Snohomish Co., WA

Parents:
Ermit Theodore Christner (1900 - 1979)
Nora Pauline Burright Christner (1904 - 1985)

Spouse: Mabry James Carter (1925 - 1996)

Children: Mark Ermit Carter (1953 - 1971)

Burial: Chapel Hill Memorial Gardens Cemetery, Oklahoma City, Oklahoma Co., OK
Find A Grave Memorial# 96958223

More About Imogine Pauline Christner:
Burial: 15 Sep 2012, Chapel Hill Funeral Home, Oklahoma City, Oklahoma, Oklahoma USA/[7051]
Residence: 1930, Spring Creek, Logan Co., OK[7052]

Notes for Mabry James Carter Jr.:
Birth: Jan 29, 1925 - Fearns Springs, Winston Co., MS
Death: Nov 25, 1996 - Vian, Sequoyah Co., OK

Spouse: Imogene Pauline Christner Carter (1925 - 2012)

Children: Mark Ermit Carter (1953 - 1971)

Burial: Chapel Hill Memorial Gardens Cemetery, Oklahoma City, Oklahoma Co., OK
Find A Grave Memorial# 86823857

More About Mabry James Carter Jr.:
Arrival: 05 Mar 1945, Age: 20/New York, NY[7053]
Burial: Oklahoma City, Oklahoma Co., OK[7053]
Departure: Southampton, England[7053]
Residence: 01 Apr 1940, Age: 15; Marital Status: Single; Relation to Head of House: Son/Oklahoma City, Oklahoma, Co., OK[7053]

Children of Imogine Christner and Mabry Carter are:
4302   i.   Barry James[9] Carter, born 11 Jul 1948.
4303   ii.   Mark Ermit Carter[7054], born 06 Nov 1953 in Williston, Williams Co., ND[7054,7055]; died 09 Oct 1971 in Ft. Collins, Larimer Co., CO[7055].

Notes for Mark Ermit Carter:
Birth: Nov. 6, 1953 - Williston, Williams Co., ND
Death: Oct. 8, 1971 - Fort Collins, Larimer Co., CO

Parents:
Mabry James Carter (1925 - 1996)
Imogene Pauline Christner Carter (1925 - 2012)

Burial: Chapel Hill Memorial Gardens Cemetery, Oklahoma City, Oklahoma Co., OK
Find A Grave Memorial# 86760317

More About Mark Ermit Carter:
Burial: Minco Cem

4304   iii. Bart David Carter, born 15 Sep 1956.

2372. Valda Elaine[8] Perry (Alma[7] Christner, Nelson "Nels"[6], Moses C.[5], Joseph "Zep"[4], Johannes John Hans[3], Christian[2], Christen[1]) was born 26 Dec 1924 in Cashion, Logan Co., OK. She married **Sylvester Moses Rodgers**, son of James Rodgers and Flora Butler. He was born 15 Jan 1915[7056,7056], and died Sep 1983 in Gutherie, Logan Co., OK[7056].

Notes for Valda Elaine Perry:

More About Sylvester Moses Rodgers:
Residence: Bet. 1935 - 1993, Guthrie, OK[7056]

Children of Valda Perry and Sylvester Rodgers are:
4305   i.   Virgil Ray[9] Rodgers.
4306   ii.   Allen Lee Rodgers.
4307   iii. Roy James Rodgers[7056], born 22 Jun 1941[7056]; died Mar 1971[7056].

2373. Floyd Wayne "Moe"[8] Perry (Alma[7] Christner, Nelson "Nels"[6], Moses C.[5], Joseph "Zep"[4], Johannes John Hans[3], Christian[2], Christen[1])[7057] was born 22 Mar 1927 in Seward, Logan Co., OK[7057], and died 12 May 1985[7057]. He married **Volna Lou Woodrel**. She was born 10 Feb 1933[7058], and died 19 Feb 2001 in Age at Death: 68/Edmond, Oklahoma Co., OK[7058].

Notes for Floyd Wayne "Moe" Perry:
Floyd worked for Mustang Fuel. He loved helping people and loved a good joke. He died in a motorcycle accident near the Christner Cemetery.

Birth: Mar. 22, 1927
Death: May 12, 1983

Burial: Christner Cemetery, Oklahoma Co., OK

Find A Grave Memorial# 37027508

More About Floyd Wayne "Moe" Perry:
Burial: Christer Cemetery, Deer Creek, OK[7059]

Notes for Volna Lou Woodrel:
Birth: Feb. 10, 1933
Death: Feb. 19, 2001

Burial: Christner Cemetery, Oklahoma Co., OK
Find A Grave Memorial# 37027521

More About Volna Lou Woodrel:
Social Security Number: 445-32-7874/[7060]

Children of Floyd Perry and Volna Woodrel are:
    4308   i.   Ricky Joe[9] Perry.
    4309   ii.   Jana Lou Perry.
    4310   iii.   Timothy Lynn Perry.

2374. Eunice Irene[8] Perry (Alma[7] Christner, Nelson "Nels"[6], Moses C.[5], Joseph "Zep"[4], Johannes John Hans[3], Christian[2], Christen[1])[7061] was born 03 Apr 1929 in Seward, Logan Co., OK[7061], and died 30 Apr 2001 in Guthrie, Logan Co., OK[7061]. She married **(1) Roy Darrell Lacy**. She married **(2) Lee Russell Clay** Abt. 1950[7061]. He was born 29 May 1920 in Logan Co., OK[7061], and died 30 Apr 1967 in Guthrie, Logan Co., OK[7061].

Notes for Eunice Irene Perry:
Eunice married Lee Russell Clay
Lee died April 30 1967 in Logan Co Oklahoma
Eunice married Roy Darrell Lacy

Notes for Lee Russell Clay:
U.S., Social Security Death Index, 1935-Current

Name: Lee Clay
SSN: 442-12-4853

Last Residence:
73044 Guthrie, Logan Co., OK
Born: 29 May 1920
Died: 30 Apr 1967
State (Year) SSN issued: OK

More About Lee Russell Clay:
Burial: May 1967, Summit View Cemetery/Guthrie, Logan Co., OK[7061]
Residence: 01 Oct 1942, U. S. World War II Army Enlistment/Oklahoma City, Oklahoma Co., OK[7061]

Child of Eunice Perry and Lee Clay is:
    4311   i.   Cleopatra May[9] Clay[7061,7062], born 26 Oct 1946[7063,7064,7065]; died 28 Jul 2011 in Guthrie, Logan Co., OK[7065,7066].

        Notes for Cleopatra May Clay:
        Birth   26 October 1946
        Death   28 July 2011

        Buried: Christner Cemetery, Edmond, OK

        More About Cleopatra May Clay:

Burial: Edmond, Oklahoma, Oklahoma, United States[7066]

2376. Delbert Jerald⁸ Perry (Alma⁷ Christner, Nelson "Nels"⁶, Moses C.⁵, Joseph "Zep"⁴, Johannes John Hans³, Christian², Christen¹) was born 12 Nov 1939 in Seward, Logan Co., OK. He married **Mary Warren**.

Children of Delbert Perry and Mary Warren are:

4312	i.	Delbert Jerald⁹ Perry Jr..
4313	ii.	Karen Ann Perry.
4314	iii.	Jerald Dean Perry.

2378. Leon George⁸ Perry (Verdell⁷ Christner, Nelson "Nels"⁶, Moses C.⁵, Joseph "Zep"⁴, Johannes John Hans³, Christian², Christen¹)[7067] was born 12 Jan 1925 in OK[7067], and died 26 Feb 1987 in Edmond, Logan Co., OK[7067]. He married **Erma Jean Dunlap**.

Notes for Leon George Perry:
Birth: Jan 12, 1925
Death: Feb 26, 1987

Spouse: Erma Jean Perry (1927 - ____)

Burial: Christner Cemetery, Oklahoma Co., OK
Find A Grave Memorial# 37027290

More About Leon George Perry:
Residence: OK[7067]

Child of Leon Perry and Erma Dunlap is:

4315	i.	Jimmy⁹ Perry[7067], born 28 Mar 1947 in Edmond, Oklahoma County, Oklahoma, USA[7067]; died 07 May 1994 in Oklahoma City, Oklahoma County, Oklahoma, USA[7067].

> More About Jimmy Perry:
> Residence: 1993, Oklahoma City, OK[7067]

2381. Roberta Sue⁸ Davis (Gladys Irene⁷ Christner, Nelson "Nels"⁶, Moses C.⁵, Joseph "Zep"⁴, Johannes John Hans³, Christian², Christen¹) was born 27 Dec 1943 in Edmond, Oklahoma Co., OK. She married **Richard Forbes Williams** 08 Jun 1962 in Cashion, Kingfisher Co., OK, son of Ennis Williams and Kathleen Hill. He was born 09 Oct 1941 in Oklahoma City, Oklahoma Co., OK.

Notes for Roberta Sue Davis:
Roberta Davis grew up on the Christner family homestead, attended twelve years at Cashion School in Kingfisher Co., OK, and was valedictorian of her class at Cashion High School. She married Richard Williams in 1962. She earned a B.S. degree in Special Education from University of Central Oklahoma, a Master of Visual Impairment degree from Northeastern Oklahoma State University and a Master of School Administration from Southwestern Oklahoma State University.

She and Richard moved their family to Mangum, Oklahoma in 1977 where Roberta started new programs for junior high and high school special education students, teaching in those programs for fifteen years. She served as Federal Programs Director and Special Education Director for the Mangum School District for seventeen years before her retirement in 2009. Roberta enjoys gardening, traveling, camping, reading, writing, and the theatre. She is a charter member of the Southwest Oklahoma Community Theatre and enjoys acting and working in its productions. She loves working with children and teaching at church Sunday mornings at the First United Methodist Church in Mangum and is active in the women's programs and mission work.

Children of Roberta Davis and Richard Williams are:

+ 4316	i.	Shari Sue⁹ Williams, born 30 May 1964 in Edmond, Oklahoma Co., OK.

+ 4317   ii. Brian Forbes Williams, born 17 Mar 1967 in Midwest City, Oklahoma Co., OK.

2382. Iris[8] Davis (Gladys Irene[7] Christner, Nelson "Nels"[6], Moses C.[5], Joseph "Zep"[4], Johannes John Hans[3], Christian[2], Christen[1]) was born 13 Apr 1948 in Edmond, Oklahoma Co., OK. She married **Richard Dean Deurmyer** 11 Jul 1973 in Midwest City, Oklahoma Co., OK, son of Wayne Deurmyer and Rozella Finto. He was born 17 Mar 1947.

Children of Iris Davis and Richard Deurmyer are:
    4318   i. Christopher[9] Deurmyer, born 26 Sep 1974 in Oklahoma City, Oklahoma Co., OK. He married Alice Ann Brendle[7068] 01 Jun 2002 in Mangum, Greer Co., OK; born 24 Dec 1979 in Lubbock, Lubbock Co., TX[7068].
    4319   ii. David Dean Deurmyer, born 26 Aug 1980 in Springfield, OR; died 03 Jan 1981 in Las Vegas, NV.
    4320   iii. Jeremy Lynn Deurmyer, born 28 Jan 1982 in Springfield, OR.

2383. Carol Ann[8] Christner (Roy M.[7], Nelson "Nels"[6], Moses C.[5], Joseph "Zep"[4], Johannes John Hans[3], Christian[2], Christen[1]) She married **Warren Walkup**.

Children of Carol Christner and Warren Walkup are:
    4321   i. Donetta[9] Walkup.
    4322   ii. Shannon Walkup.

2387. Florence Louise[8] Stewart (Josephine[7] Christner, Alexander[6], Moses C.[5], Joseph "Zep"[4], Johannes John Hans[3], Christian[2], Christen[1])[7069,7070] was born 06 Jun 1901 in Hennessey, Kingfisher Co., OK[7071,7072], and died 11 Mar 1996 in Woodland Yolo, CA[7073]. She married **(1) Lester Sanders**.   She married **(2) Clark Harold Hinson**[7074,7075,7076] Aft. 1958[7077]. He was born 04 Jul 1893 in Oklahoma Co., OK[7078,7079], and died 11 Apr 1958 in Yuba, CA[7079,7080,7081].

Notes for Florence Louise Stewart:
Florence married Harold Hinson and 2nd marriage to Lester Sanders.

More About Florence Louise Stewart:
Residence: 1920, Age: 18; Marital Status: Single; Relation to Head of House: Daughter/Waconda, Caddo Co., OK[7082]
Social Security Number: 527-01-8580/[7083]
SSN issued: AZ[7083]

More About Clark Harold Hinson:
Residence: 1930, Canton, Blaine Co., OK[7084]

Children of Florence Stewart and Clark Hinson are:
+ 4323   i. Hazel[9] Hinson, born 07 Aug 1923; died 28 Oct 1993 in Hennepin, MN.
+ 4324   ii. Josephine Florence Hinson, born 03 Jun 1925 in OK; died 15 Oct 2011 in Lodi, CA.

2397. Gilbert Leroy[8] Christner (Philo Leroy (Roy P)[7], Alexander[6], Moses C.[5], Joseph "Zep"[4], Johannes John Hans[3], Christian[2], Christen[1])[7085,7086] was born 31 Jul 1912 in Estes Park, Larimer Co., CO[7086,7087], and died 13 Dec 1981 in Aurora, Arapahoe Co., CO[7087]. He married **(1) Esther Marie Heitfield** 14 Nov 1927 in Trinity Lutheran Church, Ft. Morgan, CO. She was born in Lawton, OK. He married **(2) Maude Bernice "Bunny" Jones** 1952 in Georgetown, CO. She was born 11 Mar 1918, and died 29 Oct 1992 in Denver, Arapahoe Co., CO.

Notes for Gilbert Leroy Christner:
SS#;522-05-1792 Iss CO Last address Aurora CO near Denver CO 80012

He was 37 years old when he tried several times to get in the Navy but he had a growth on his back and the Navy refused to take him so he had it removed and retried, this time they accepted him. He was in training to be a Pharmacist. The Navy put him on the submarine tender "USS Protius" as a medic. He was involved in capturing the first Japanese submarine and helped take it into Tokyo Bay at the end of the war. He went back to be a full fledged pharmacist by testing out, he was the first person to do this in the state of Colorado.

Dear Family,
My oldest brother Gilbert Leroy Christner, Sr. was in the Navy during World War II. He served on submarines and sub tenders as a pharmacist's Mate First Class He was on active duty from May 19, 1943 to May 8, 1946. He served in the Pacific in a Sub-division 202 then was transferred to Sub-division 22 by confidential dispatch of Sept 26, 1945 (whatever that means) He participated in the surrender, seizure, and occupation of Japan in Tokyo Bay. I remember him telling about being put on the first Japanese Sub that surrendered as one of the crew of Americans to hold it captive and sail it into Tokyo Bay, since he had not had much to do with guns the machine gun he had to handle was really a new experience for him since he had only been a medic. Attached is his picture if you are interested . He was a very nice guy had no enemies was always thoughtful of his family after my Dad died in 1954 Gilbert became head of the whole family as well as his own family. When he got home from the war his then wife wanted a divorce she had met someone new and wanted to marry this guy. Since she was the daughter of a Lutheran minister she did not want to file so he did and I guess the church really looked down on divorce at that time. He quit going for awhile then came back to another church but was never a steady church goer after that He married again had two boys and Gil Christner is his oldest son and you all know him from our Christner family group.

Donna Christner Reese

More About Gilbert Leroy Christner:
Burial: Hampton Memorial Gardens Denver CO.
Social Security Number: 522-05-1792/^{7087}
SSN issued: CO^{7087}

Notes for Esther Marie Heitfield:
CHRISTNER Heirfeld
Marriage Solemized

A pretty wedding. Sunday was the climax to the farewell given for Rev. H. Heitfield who is leaving for orlahoma. The marriage was that of his daughter Esther to Gilbert L. Christner of this city.

The ceremony was performed at Trinity Lutheran Church at 1:20, the bride's father officiating.

To the strains of Lobengrin'sWedding March, played by Miss Lenora Goecker, the couple marched down the asile, attended by Miss Marie Heitfeld sister of the bride as maid of honor and Mr. and Mrs. Marlin Cordin of Strassburg, Colo.

Mr. walter Sohl of Enid, Okla. cousin of the bride and Mr. Marvin Mitchell sang "Our Father, thou in heaven Above."

The bride was lovely in a gown of rich wine velvet with matching accessories and a gold metallic Juliet cap with short veil. Her corsage was of yellow tallsman roses and sweet peas. The gold bracelet which she wore was her mother's who had worn it at her wedding.

Notes for Maude Bernice "Bunny" Jones:
Birth: Mar. 11, 1918
Death: Oct. 29, 1992

Burial: Hampden Memorial Estates, Denver, Denver Co., CO
Find A Grave Memorial# 66090843

More About Maude Bernice "Bunny" Jones:
Burial: Hampton Gardens Denver CO.

Children of Gilbert Christner and Maude Jones are:

4325   i.   Gilbert Leroy[9] Christner Jr., born 06 Jun 1953 in Denver, Arapahoe Co., CO. He married Sheila Schwartz 27 May 1984 in San Francisco, San Francisco Co., CA; born 26 Oct 1948 in Bronx, New York Co., NY.

Notes for Gilbert Leroy Christner Jr.:
GIL Christner - Actor   Height: 5' 10" Weight: 180 Hair: Brown Eyes: Blue Telephone: (310) 475-2010
TELEVISION
RENO 911 - Guest Star - Hilarious Prods.
THE WEST WING - Co-star - John Wells Prods.
THE BERNIE MAC SHOW - Co-star - Regency Television
DISNEY'S THAT'S SO RAVEN - Co-Star - Brookwell McNamara Prods.
BUFFY THE VAMPIRE SLAYER - Co star - Mutant Enemy Prods.
PROVIDENCE - Co-star - NBC Productions
3rd ROCK FROM THE SUN - Also Starring - Carsey/Werner Prods.
SABRINA THE TEENAGE WITCH - Co-Star - Viacom Prods.
CHICAGO HOPE - Co-Star - Twentieth Century Fox
FAMILY MATTERS - Co-Star - Miller/Boyet Prods
COACH - Guest Star - Universal TV
MEN BEHAVING BADLY - Also Starring - Carsey/Werner Prods.
LOVE & WAR - Guest Star - SEE Prods.
WEIRD TV - Starring Role - UPN Network.
THE 4TH FLOOR SHOW - Co-Star - E! Entertainment TV Prods.
CINEMAX COMEDY EXPERIMENT - Starring Role - ShadoeVision, Inc.
TIME/LIFE INDUSTRIAL - Starring Role - HBO Productions
ADAM 12 - THE 90'S - Guest Star - The Arthur Co.
SAFE AT HOME - Guest Star - The Arthur Co.
A PERFECT LITTLE MURDER - Feature Role Saban Co.
MATHNET - Feature Role - Webb Productions
SUPERIOR COURT - Principle - Ralph Edwards Prod.
JONATHAN WINTERS - Ensemble Player - Windsor Prods.
SHOWTIME PLAYBOY COMEDY HOUSE - Starring Role - Playboy Prod

FILM
MYSTERY MEN - Feature Role - Universal
BOB'S VIDEO - Also Starring - Andrade/Bergman Prods.
MIND GAMES - Co-Star - Purloined Prods.
MAXIMUM REVENGE - Co-Star - Royal Oaks Prods.
FAMILY VALUES - Co-Star - Family Values Prods.
DEADLY DELUSIONS - Feature Role - Matovich Producitons
THE DRIFTER - Feature Role - Concorde
OVEREXPOSED - Feature Role - Concorde
MASQUE OF THE RED DEATH - Feature Role - Concorde
MORE AMERICAN GRAFITTI - Feature Role - Universal
SUBURBIA - Feature Role - New World

STAGE
MURIETTA & KASSIN SHOW - Writer - Masquer's Café
ETCH A SKETCH - Writer - Theatre/Theatre
THE BUZZ BELMONDO SHOWS - Writer/Performer - Various Theatres
COMEDY STORE PLAYERS - Writer/Performer - Comedy Store
JOHN ROARKE INDUSTRIALS - Contributing Writer - Roarke Prods.
JOEL LEDER STAND UP - Contributing Writer - Various Clubs
STAND-UP COMEDY - Original Material - Various Clubs
ANDI'S ACT - West Coast Ensemble Theatre -
MURIETTA & KASSIN: THE EARLY YEARS - Masquers' Cafe
COMEDY STORE PLAYERS - Comedy Store
OFF THE WALL - The Improvisation
FUNNY YOU SHOULD ASK - Coronet Theatre -

SAN FRANCISCO COMEDY COMPETITION (Winner) - San Francisco
GOLDEN HORSESHOE REVIEW - Disneyland
PONTIAC INDUSTRIAL - starring LESLIE UGGAMS - National Tour

LEAD ROLES - C.S.U.:   CAT ON A HOT TIN ROOF   PIRATES of PENZANCE
SCHOOL for SCANDAL   REAL INSPECTOR HOUND   LITTLE MURDERS
CYRANO   MARAT/SADE   OKLAHOMA   DIE FLEDERMAUS BOYS in the BAND
FANTASTICKS   COUNTRY WIFE

COMMERCIALS   LIST UPON REQUEST

PUBLICATIONS
YOU KNOW YOU'RE ANONYMOUS - Contributing Writer - St. Martin's Press
LAFF LINES - Contributing Writer - Los Angeles Times
MADHATTER GREETING CARDS - Contributing Writer - Paper Rainbow Press

MISCELLANEOUS
SHOCKFORCE - Script Doctor - WhiteBridge Prods.
LITTLE FOX RECORDS - Staff - Lauber Prod.
COMEDY WRITING JUDGE - Ace Awards - Cable Academy

TRAINING
Dee Wallace Stone, Joe Regalbuto, Arlene Golonka, Scene Study, Carolyn Barry, Beverly Long,
Commercial Acting, Jim Cranna, Dee Marcus, Del Close, Improv Acting, Colorado State University,
B.A. Theatre Arts

SPECIAL SKILLS
Stand-up Comedy, Improvisational Comedy, Clarinet, Guitar, Stick Shift, Bowling, Golf, Balloon
Animals, Producer/Head Writer: Syndicated Radio Comedy - Premiere Radio Productions

4326   ii.   Michael Douglas Christner, born 22 Apr 1955 in Denver, Arapahoe Co., CO.

2398. Eva Lucile[8] Christner (Philo Leroy (Roy P)[7], Alexander[6], Moses C.[5], Joseph "Zep"[4], Johannes John Hans[3], Christian[2], Christen[1]) was born 22 Dec 1914 in Estes Park, CO[7088], and died 12 Dec 1994 in Denver, Arapahoe Co., CO. She married **(1) Merlin "Barney' George Cardin**[7089] 1941. He was born 1909 in Denver, Arapahoe Co., CO, and died Sep 1978 in Colorado Springs, El Paso Co., CO[7089]. She married **(2) Verle Lloyd George** 19 Jan 1947 in Strasburg, Colorado[7090]. He was born 12 Dec 1916, and died 27 Feb 1990 in Denver, Arapahoe Co., CO[7090].

More About Eva Lucile Christner:
Burial: Montveiw Cemetery, Bennett, Adams Co., CO[7090]
Social Security Number: 521-18-7588/[7091]
SSN issued: CO[7091]

More About Merlin "Barney' George Cardin:
Social Security Number: 487-03-5151/[7092]
SSN issued: MO[7092]

More About Verle Lloyd George:
Burial: 02 Mar 1990, Montveiw Cemetery, Bennett, Adams Co., CO[7093]
Social Security Number: 521-26-3402/[7094]
SSN issued: CO[7094]

Child of Eva Christner and Merlin Cardin is:
+   4327   i.   Gary Bernard Cardin[9] George, born 06 Jun 1942 in Penrose Hospital, Colorado Springs, NJ.

Children of Eva Christner and Verle George are:
+   4328   i.   Nancy Jean[9] George, born 10 Jul 1949 in Denver, Arapahoe Co., CO.

4329   ii.   Laurel Ann George, born 07 Nov 1951 in Denver, Arapahoe Co., CO.

2400. Richard Robert[8] Christner (Philo Leroy (Roy P)[7], Alexander[6], Moses C.[5], Joseph "Zep"[4], Johannes John Hans[3], Christian[2], Christen[1])[7095] was born 29 Sep 1923 in North of Strasburg, CO[7096], and died 26 Mar 2002 in Afton, Ottawa Co., OK. He married **(1) DePhone Cook**[7097]. She was born 06 Nov 1915 in Lake Creek Iow, IA[7097], and died 24 Mar 1986 in Fairfield, CA[7097]. He married **(2) Emma Jean Olson**.   He married **(3) Betty Jeanette McLaughlin** 02 Jun 1946 in Christner Homestead Straburg, CO.. She was born 23 Nov 1921 in Beatrice, NE, and died 19 Oct 1992 in Ceres, Stanislaus Co., CA[7098].

Notes for Richard Robert Christner:
Served in the Marine Corp in the South Pacific in World war II, he was wounded in Tarawa Island.

My other older brother Richard R. (Dick) was in the marines. He enlisted he was on active duty from Feb.13, 1943 to November 28, 1945 he was so different from my two other brothers he liked to party etc. he was wounded on the island of Tarawa going in on th beach he had a broken leg and some shrapnel, He also was discovered to have a bad heart which followed him the rest of his life turned out he had holes in his heart and had to have surgery when he was 38 years old nobody knows how he lived that long and did all the things he did. He married and had 4 children I cannot get his service records because so many were destroyed in a fire the only information I have is when he first went in he was in the 162 Platoon US Marine Corp in San Diego, CA. 1943. He was a Buck Private His picture appeared in the Life magazine in July of 1945 on Guam dancing with the Governor's daughter also the same pictures appeared in the Leatherneck magazine about the same time I have both.
Donna Christner Reese

Birth: Sep. 29, 1923
Death: Mar. 26, 2002

Burial: Mount View Cemetery, Bennett, Adams Co., CO
Find A Grave Memorial# 35274777

More About Richard Robert Christner:
Burial: 30 May 2002, Montview Cemetery, Bennett, Adams Co., CO
Fact 1: 29 Sep 1923, Born on homestead farm No.Strasburg, co.[7099]
Fact 2: missed a year of school because of illness[7099]
Fact 3: went to high school in Strasburg, Co[7099]
Fact 4: 1942, entered the US Marine Corp.[7099]
Medical Information: [7099]
Social Security Number: 522-26-4091/[7100]
SSN issued: CO[7100]

More About Betty Jeanette McLaughlin:
Social Security Number: 530-38-4449/[7101]
SSN issued: NV[7101]

Children of Richard Christner and Betty McLaughlin are:
+   4330   i.   Linda Gayle[9] Christner, born 30 May 1948.
+   4331   ii.   Patricia Lee Christner, born 13 Aug 1950.
     4332   iii.   Richard Robert Christner Jr., born 16 Apr 1952. He married Camille.
+   4333   iv.   Mark Eric Christner, born 03 Jan 1959; died 2008 in CA.

2401. Donna Lee[8] Christner (Philo Leroy (Roy P)[7], Alexander[6], Moses C.[5], Joseph "Zep"[4], Johannes John Hans[3], Christian[2], Christen[1]) was born 10 May 1932 in Strasburg, Arapaho Co., CO. She married **Charles Edward Reese**[7102] 05 Mar 1949 in Raton, Colfax Co., NM. He was born 23 Nov 1926 in North Braddock, Fayette Co., PA, and died 31 Mar 2013 in Home 14022 Hwy. 86 Kiowa, CO[7102].

Notes for Charles Edward Reese:
Obituary: April 2013

Charles Edward Reese Sr. (Sweet Water Charley) passed away March 31, 2013 at his home near Kiowa, Colorado with his family at his side. He was born November 23, 1926 in Braddock, Pennsylvania and was the eldest son of Neil Robison Reese and Clara Felder Reese. Charles graduated from William Smith High School in Aurora, Colorado in 1945. He served honorably in the U.S. Army during World War II in the Headquarters Battery, 309th Field Artillery Battalion. Upon returning home from serving in the Army, Charles attended Colorado State University in Fort Collins for one year. Charles met his loving wife of 64 years, Donna Lee Christener after leaving CSU and they were married March 5, 1949 in Raton, New Mexico. Their first home was in Grand Lake, Colorado where Charles worked on the construction of the Shadow Mountain Dam. Charles and Donna then moved to California where he worked for Firestone in Oakland California for two years. Charles and Donna returned to Colorado in 1952 where Charles would start his career as a Firefighter for the City of Aurora, Colorado in 1957. Charles served 30 years on the Aurora Fire Department, retiring December 6, 1986. Charles' service as an Aurora Firefighter was a career in which he served proudly and often spoke about fondly. He also worked part time as Journeyman Electrician during his time with Aurora Fire and after retirement. Charles and Donna moved for the final time to their retirement home East of Kiowa, Colorado in January 1983 where he and Donna lived for the past 30 years surrounded by family and a great many friends, until his passing.

Charles had many interests but especially enjoyed his cattle, gardening, arrowhead hunting, model airplanes, golf, big game hunting, fishing, Pony Express racing, and most of all his dogs. He was a member of the NRA, American Legion Elbert County Post, Colorado Cattlemen's Association, Douglas-Elbert County Livestock Association, Kiowa Lions Club, and the Elbert County Republican and Tea Parties. Charles was honored and thrilled to be selected to carry the Olympic Torch in the 2002 relay at Buena Vista, Colorado for the Salt Lake City Winter Olympics.

Charles was a beloved husband and is survived by his loving wife, Donna Lee Christener Reese; son, Charles Edward Reese Jr. (Lynette) of Simla; daughter, Carollyn Reese Hall (Bruce) of Ordway; daughter, Charlene Reese Gee of Parachute; as well as grandchildren; Stetson Tapp (Teri) of Riverton, Wyoming; Tiffany Guynn (Scott) of Kiowa; Mandy Taylor (Jimmy) of Kiowa; Gabrielle Perryman (Shawn) of Kanorado, Kansas; Crystal Lenard of Elbert; Kenneth "Keg" Gee (Raquel) of Calhan; and Matt Reese of Simla, Charles is also survived by 14 great grandchildren, one brother, Neil Robison Reese Jr. of Golden; and one sister Mary Cecil Reese Slade of Kiowa as well as many nieces and nephews.

Charles' legacy lives on in his children, grandchildren, great grandchildren and all who knew and loved him. He was a man of integrity, high energy and compassion which he demonstrated in his service to others throughout his life. His family loved him deeply and will miss him greatly forever.

Funeral Services will be held with Aurora Fire Department honors on April 6, 2013 at the Kiowa Creek Community Church in Kiowa, Colorado. www.OlingerAndrews.com is the web site for his Memorial. In Lieu of flowers, memorial contributions may be made to Kiowa Creek Community Church.

More About Charles Edward Reese:
50th annv.: 05 Mar 1999, St Mark Presbyterian Church, Kiowa, Colorado, USA[7102]

Children of Donna Christner and Charles Reese are:
+ 4334   i.   Carollyn Jean[9] Reese, born 09 Nov 1949 in Kremmling, Grand Co., CO.
+ 4335   ii. Charlene Reese, born 29 Dec 1950 in Kremmling, Grand Co., CO.
+ 4336   iii. Charles Edward Reese IV, born 19 Aug 1954 in Rose Memorial Hospital, Denver, Arapaho Co., CO.

2402. Neil Wesley[8] Christner (Philo Leroy (Roy P)[7], Alexander[6], Moses C.[5], Joseph "Zep"[4], Johannes John Hans[3], Christian[2], Christen[1]) was born 07 Aug 1934 in Strasburg Co., CO. He married **(1) Stacey Diane Wilson** in Faith Presbyterian Church, Denver, CO. She was born 04 May 1941. He married **(2) Nancy Ann Pericy** 30 Mar 1985. She was born 11 Jul 1943 in Baton Rouge, LA.

Notes for Neil Wesley Christner:
Served in the Army 1957 to 1960. Served in Greenland one year and Ft. Carson, Colorado one year. He reenlisted for two years to serve in the Niki missile program at Chatsfield, California and then the Niki Hercules

at Ft. Worth TX. He was discharged at Brandywine, Maryland as a specialist 3rd class. He is a photographer and has a store called Fair Hill Gallery in Maryland.

My younger brother Neil Wesley Christner who lives in Maryland now was in the Army he enlisted in Oct. 1957 of he came out of tthe Army with a rank of 1957 SP4-E4 (T) I have no idea what this means but it is good he ended up going to Ft. Bliss, Texas where he took Mike Hercules course other training was Mil Justice, Geneva Conv. Battle INdoc ATP 21-114, Code of good conduct. When he came out he went to work for Xerox Corp. and was classified for work on certain bases that required classification. His last duty assignment in the Army was Btry C 3d Msl Bn (N-H) 562d Arty Waldorf Maryland. Honorable dicharge Oct. 1960.
Donna Christner Reese

Notes for Stacey Diane Wilson:
Maybe Tracy or Tracey

Children of Neil Christner and Stacey Wilson are:

4337	i.	Michyl Roy[9] Christner, born 23 May 1958 in Los Angeles Co., CA[7103]. He married Denise Fiorine; born 01 Oct 1957.
+ 4338	ii.	Morris Todd Christner, born 09 Dec 1960.
+ 4339	iii.	Monty Ernest Christner, born 04 Jun 1964 in Albuquerque, NM.

2408. Virginia Wynona[8] Christner (Irvin Gibert[7], George Washington[6], Moses C.[5], Joseph "Zep"[4], Johannes John Hans[3], Christian[2], Christen[1])[7104] was born 25 Dec 1915, and died 17 Aug 1976 in Sterling, Logan Co., CO[7104]. She married **(1) James Lou Kintz**. He was born 08 Dec 1918. She married **(2) Carl L. Cutler** Abt. 1936[7104]. He was born 25 May 1905, and died Abt. 1962 in Denver, Denver, CO[7104].

Notes for Carl L. Cutler:
U.S. Veterans Gravesites, ca.1775-2006

Name: Carl Leland Cutler
Service Info.: M/SGT US ARMY WORLD WAR II
Birth Date: 25 May 1905
Death Date: 9 Jun 1964
Service Start Date: 7 May 1942
Interment Date: 12 Jun 1964
Cemetery: Ft. Logan National Cemetery
Cemetery Address: 4400 West Kenyon Avenue Denver, CO 80236
Buried At: Section Q Site 1071

Children of Virginia Christner and Carl Cutler are:

4340	i.	Virginia[9] Cutler, born 12 Oct 1937. She married Ronald Galios.
4341	ii.	Lynda Kay Cutler, born 20 Mar 1947. She married Victor Rboertson.

Notes for Lynda Kay Cutler:
Lynda married Victor Rboertson

2409. Irvin[8] Christner Jr. (Irvin Gibert[7], George Washington[6], Moses C.[5], Joseph "Zep"[4], Johannes John Hans[3], Christian[2], Christen[1]) was born 12 Jun 1917 in Garrett, Somerset Co., PA[7105], and died 15 Apr 1995 in Sterling, Logan Co., CO. He married **(1) Delores Smith**. He married **(2) Delores Irene Fender**[7106] 19 Aug 1962 in Sterling, Logan Co., CO[7106]. She was born 25 Jan 1931 in Ovid, Sedgwick Co., CO[7106], and died 25 Dec 1997 in Sterling, Logan Co., CO[7106]. He married **(3) Ruby Otzenberger** 19 Aug 1962 in Sterling, Logan Cty., CO[7107]. She was born 28 Mar 1917, and died 25 Dec 1997 in Cancer/Sterling, Logan Cty., CO[7107].

Notes for Irvin Christner Jr.:

SS#;524-12-6202 Iss CO

More About Irvin Christner Jr.:
Burial: 19 Apr 1995, Tennant Funeral Home/Sunset Memorial Gardens[7107]
Residence: 1930, Willard, Logan Co., CO[7108,7109]

Notes for Delores Irene Fender:
Birth: Jan. 25, 1931
Death: Dec. 25, 1997

Delores J. Christner, 66, of Sterling, died Dec. 25, 1997, in Denver. Visitation and viewing will be held from 10 am. to 3 p.m. Wednesday, Dec. 31, and from 10 am to 7 p.m. Thursday, Jan. 1, at the Tennant Funeral Home. The funeral will be at 11 a.m. Friday, Jan. 2, at the Tennant Funeral Home with the Rev. John Roberts officiating. Burial will follow at Sunset Memorial Gardens.

Mrs. Christner was born Jan 25, 1931 to Russell and Isabelle (Herfert) Fender in Ovid. She grew up in the Ovid area and graduated from Ovid High School in 1948 and from Sterling Junior College in 1950. She worked for the McCoy Co. for awhile.

She married Len Smith in January, 1952. They lived in the Iliff and Padroni areas. He died in 1959 and the family moved to Sterling. Delores went to work for Drs. Tennant and Carter in the radiology department at the Logan County Hospital.

She married Irvin Christner on Aug 19, 1962 in Sterling. She then worked at Sterling Truck and Equipment until retiring in the mid-1980s.
She was a member of the American Legion Auxiliary, the VFW Auxiliary, Order of Eastern Star, White Shrine of Jerusalem, League of Women Voters, the Logan County Genealogy Society, BetaSigma Phi, and the First Baptist Church.

Mrs. Christner is survived by two daughters, Linda Smith of Anchorage, Alaska, and Janet Smith Parker and husband Dan of Lakewood; one son, Kevin Christner and wife Chantell of Sterling; two brothers, Donald Fender and wife Delma of Sterling and James Fender and wife Marilyn of Ovid; and four grand-children.
She was preceded in death by her first husband Len in 1959, her second husband Irvin in 1995, an infant Smith son, and a daughter, Marsha Ann Christner.

Memorial contributions may be made to the American Cancer Society or to a charity of the donor's choice.

Spouse: Irvin Gilbert Christner (1917 - 1995)

Burial: Sunset Memorial Gardens, Sterling, Logan Co., CO

Notes for Ruby Otzenberger:
Not sure if Irvin Jr. son Daniel mother was Ruby or Irvins second wife was Delores.

More About Ruby Otzenberger:
Burial: Riverside Cemetry Sterling< CO[7110]
CauseOfDeath: Cancer/[7110]
Residence: 1930, Sterling, Logan Co., CO[7111]

Child of Irvin Christner and Delores Smith is:
    4342   i.   Daniel[9] Christner, born 11 Jan 1951.

2410. George N.[8] Christner (Irvin Gibert[7], George Washington[6], Moses C.[5], Joseph "Zep"[4], Johannes John Hans[3], Christian[2], Christen[1]) was born 15 May 1919[7112], and died Aug 1981 in Sterling, Logan Co., CO[7112]. He married **Eleanor E.**

Notes for George N. Christner:
Birth: May 15, 1919
Death: Aug. 29, 1981

Parents:
Irvin Gilbert Christner (1889 - 1961)
Fannie Emma Lenhart Christner (1895 - 1968)

Burial: Riverside Cemetery, Sterling, Logan Co., CO

SS#;522-20-6317 Iss CO Last address Sterling, CO 80751

More About George N. Christner:
Social Security Number: 522-20-6317/[7112]
SSN issued: CO[7112]

Children of George Christner and Eleanor E are:
4343	i.	Darlene[9] Christner.
4344	ii.	Raymond Christner.
4345	iii.	Elmer Christner.
4346	iv.	George Christner, born 15 Jan 1965.
4347	v.	Georgia Christner, born 15 Jan 1965.

2411. Marie Arlene[8] Christner (Irvin Gibert[7], George Washington[6], Moses C.[5], Joseph "Zep"[4], Johannes John Hans[3], Christian[2], Christen[1]) was born 21 Aug 1927, and died 14 Feb 2006. She married **Robert Alonzo Pettys** 21 Feb 1955 in Sterling, Logan Co., CO. He was born 03 Jun 1922, and died 29 Jun 2009 in Sterling, Logan Co., CO[7113].

Notes for Marie Arlene Christner:
Birth: Aug 21, 1927
Death: Feb 14, 2006

Parents:
Irvin Gilbert Christner (1889 - 1961)
Fannie Emma Lenhart Christner (1895 - 1968)

Spouse: Robert A. "Bob" Pettys (1922 - 2009)

Children: Scott Robert Pettys (1959 - 1979)

Burial: Brush Memorial Cemetery, Brush, Morgan Co., CO

Notes for Robert Alonzo Pettys:
Birth: Jun. 3, 1922
Brush, Morgan Co., CO
Death: Jun. 29, 2009

Parents Alonzo and Anna C. Pettys
Married Marie A. "Chris" Christner - Sterling, CO
Feb 21, 1955

Spouse: Marie A Christner Pettys (1927 - 2006)

Children: Scott Robert Pettys (1959 - 1979)

Burial: Brush Memorial Cemetery, Brush, Morgan Co., CO

More About Robert Alonzo Pettys:
SSN issued: CO[7113]

Children of Marie Christner and Robert Pettys are:

4348   i.   Merrie Leslie[9] Pettys, born 03 Jan 1950.

4349   ii.   Scott Robert Pettys, born 14 Mar 1959; died 30 Nov 1979 in Boulder, Boulder Co., CO.

> Notes for Scott Robert Pettys:
> Birth: Mar. 14, 1959
> Death: Nov. 30, 1979
>
> Memorial services will be Tuesday morning for Scott R. Petteys, 20, who died Friday in a Boulder hospital. The services will be at 10 a.m. at the First United Presbyterian Church with Rev. Keith Watson officiating.
>
> Mr. Petteys was a student at the University of Colorado. He was born March 14, 1959 in Denver, a son of Robert A. and Marie A. Christner Petteys. He was reared in Sterling, graduating from Sterling High School in 1976, where he was active in music and ten nis. He received awards at local and state levels in piano and trombone performance. At the University, he was a junior, majoring in economics. He was a member of Christ United Methodist Church.
> Survivors include his parents, Mr. and Mrs. Robert Petteys, 309 Delmar; a sister, Leslie Petteys, Kansas City, Mo., and a brother, Tom Petteys, Sterling.
>
> The Hettinger Funeral Home is in charge of arrangements.
>
> Parents:
> Robert A. "Bob" Petteys (1922 - 2009)
> Marie A Christner Petteys (1927 - 2006)
>
> Burial: Brush Memorial Cemetery, Brush, Morgan Co., CO

4350   iii. Thomas Alonzo Pettys, born 20 Jul 1963.

2412. Allen B.[8] Christner Sr. (Irvin Gibert[7], George Washington[6], Moses C.[5], Joseph "Zep"[4], Johannes John Hans[3], Christian[2], Christen[1])[7114] was born 03 Feb 1935 in CO[7114]. He married **Carole Rae Greco**[7115]. She was born 28 Dec 1937[7115].

Notes for Allen B. Christner Sr.:
This information is from Dora Lue Gilliam.

More About Allen B. Christner Sr.:
Residence: 1993, Colorado Springs, El Paso Co., CO[7116]

More About Carole Rae Greco:
Residence: 1964, Colorado Springs, El Paso Co., CO[7117]

Children of Allen Christner and Carole Greco are:

4351   i.   Michael Allen[9] Christner, born 25 Jun 1958.

4352   ii.   Timothy Allen Christner, born 12 Nov 1959.

4353   iii. Lori Rae Christner, born 29 Mar 1964[7118].

> More About Lori Rae Christner:
> Residence: 1995, Littleton, CO[7118]

4354   iv. Susan Rae Christner, born 21 Dec 1967.

2414. Elizabeth Vera[8] Cobb (Bessie Vera[7] Christner, George Washington[6], Moses C.[5], Joseph "Zep"[4],

Johannes John Hans[3], Christian[2], Christen[1]) was born 13 Feb 1920, and died 23 Mar 2002. She married **Paul William McKee**[7119], son of Alonzo McKee and Mary Davis. He was born 18 Aug 1917 in OK[7119,7120], and died 08 Jul 1983 in Cashion, Kingfisher Co., OK[7121].

Notes for Elizabeth Vera Cobb:
Buried in Cashion Cemetery, Cashion, Kingfisher Co., OK

Notes for Paul William McKee:
Birth: Aug 18, 1917 - OK
Death: Jul 8, 1983 - Cashion, Kingfisher Co., OK

Spouse: Elizabeth V. McKee (1920 - 2002)

Burial: Cashion Cemetery, Cashion, Kingfisher Co., OK
Find A Grave Memorial# 7883216

More About Paul William McKee:
Burial: Cashion, Kingfisher County, Oklahoma, USA[7122]
Residence: 01 Apr 1940, Tulsa, Tulsa, Oklahoma, United States[7123]

Child of Elizabeth Cobb and Paul McKee is:
    4355   i.   Dianne Adele[9] Mckee[7123], born 20 Apr 1945[7123]; died 1945 in Cashion, Kingfisher Co., OK[7123].

2419. Harry[8] Ray (Bertha Idella "Della"[7] Judy, Cornelius[6], Eve[5] Christner, Joseph "Zep"[4], Johannes John Hans[3], Christian[2], Christen[1]) He married **Mabel Hoover**.

Child of Harry Ray and Mabel Hoover is:
+   4356   i.   Harry[9] Ray Jr.

2453. Charles LeRoy[8] Merrill (William John[7], Jane Elizabeth[6] Christner, Solomon McKenzie[5], Benjamin[4], Johannes John Hans[3], Christian[2], Christen[1]) was born 1887.

Notes for Charles LeRoy Merrill:
Lived in Lincoln, NE.

Child of Charles LeRoy Merrill is:
+   4357   i.   Hazel Alice[9] Merrill, born 1916.

2454. Martha Marcella "Marcella"[8] Merrill (Benjamin Christner[7], Mary Ann[6] Christner, Solomon McKenzie[5], Benjamin[4], Johannes John Hans[3], Christian[2], Christen[1])[7124] was born 02 Feb 1894 in NE[7124], and died Jul 1981 in Elsie, Perkins Co., NE[7124]. She married **(1) William Chichester**. He was born 1855 in NY, and died 1921 in CO. She married **(2) Henry M. Bressie**. He was born 1861, and died 1934.

Notes for Martha Marcella "Marcella" Merrill:
Birth: 1867
Death: 1955

Parents:
William H. Merrill (1837 - 1917)
Mary Ann Christner Merrill (1841 - 1914)

Spouses:
William Chichester (1855 - 1921)
Henry M. Bressie (1861 - 1934)

Children: Alice A Chichester (1902 - 1946)

Burial: Riverside Cemetery, Wauneta, Chase Co., NE
Find A Grave Memorial# 37819206

More About Martha Marcella "Marcella" Merrill:
Residence: 1920, Deerfield, Hayes, Nebraska[7124]

Notes for William Chichester:
Birth: Feb 1855 - NY
Death: 1921 - CO

Spouse: - Martha Marcella Merrill Bressie (1867 - 1955)

Children: Alice A. Chichester (1902 - 1946)

Burial: Riverside Cemetery, Wauneta, Chase Co., NE
Find A Grave Memorial# 37224258

Notes for Henry M. Bressie:
Birth: 1861
Death: 1934

Spouses:
Eliza J. Bressie (1859 - 1925)
Martha Marcella Merrill Bressie (1867 - 1955)

Children:
Infant Bressie (1886 - 1886)
Infant Bressie (1888 - 1888)
Norman Edker Bressie (1891 - 1918)
Infant Bressie (1895 - 1895)

Burial: Mount Zion Cemetery, Benkelman, Dundy Co., NE
Find A Grave Memorial# 76127044

Child of Martha Merrill and William Chichester is:
     4358   i.   Alice A.[9] Chichester, born 1902; died 1946.

          Notes for Alice A. Chichester:
          Birth: 1902
          Death: 1946

          Parents:
          William Chichester (1855 - 1921)
          Martha Marcella Merrill Bressie (1867 - 1955)

          Burial: Riverside Cemetery, Wauneta, Chase Co., NE
          Plot: 42-4-3
          Find A Grave Memorial# 37224267

2457.   John Theron[8] Merrill (Benjamin Christner[7], Mary Ann[6] Christner, Solomon McKenzie[5], Benjamin[4], Johannes John Hans[3], Christian[2], Christen[1])[7124,7125] was born 02 Jan 1908 in NE[7126,7127], and died Aug 1978 in Wauneta, Chase Co., NE[7128,7129]. He married **Della Decker**, daughter of Elsie M. Englehart. She was born 05 Apr 1913 in KS[7130,7131], and died 21 Dec 2005 in Wauneta, Chase Co., NE[7132,7133].

More About John Theron Merrill:
Burial: Riverside Cemetery, Wauneta, Chase, Nebraska[7134,7135]
Residence: 1920, Antelope, Hayes, Nebraska[7135,7135,7136]

Notes for Della Decker:
Obituary:

Della Merrill Saturday, December 24, 2005

WAUNETA -- Della Merrill, 92, died Tuesday (Dec. 20, 2005) at the Heritage of Wauneta Nursing Home.

Services will be Tuesday, 10 a.m., at the Wauneta Church of Christ with Randy Hayes officiating. Interment will follow at Riverside Cemetery in Wauneta. Visitation will be Tuesday, before services, at the church. Memorials are being accepted in her name. Liewer Funeral Home of Imperial is in charge of arrangements.

More About Della Decker:
Burial: Riverside Cemetery, Wauneta, Chase, Nebraska[7137]
Residence: 1920, Beaver, Decatur, Kansas[7137]

Child of John Merrill and Della Decker is:
  4359   i.   Elsie Christina[9] Merrill[7137], born 20 Jan 1941[7137]; died 11 Dec 1999 in Iowa City, Wright Co., IA[7137]. She married Kershal 08 Jun 1958.

           More About Elsie Christina Merrill:
           Burial: Riverside Cemetery, Wauneta, Chase, Nebraska[7137]
           Residence: 1993, Wauneta, Chase Co., NE[7137]

2470. Mary Jane[8] Knapp (May Adelaide[7] Irvine, James[6], Mary Jane[5] Christner, Benjamin[4], Johannes John Hans[3], Christian[2], Christen[1]) was born 06 Nov 1933. She married **Kenneth M. Asselstine** 18 Jun 1955 in Toronto, Canada. He was born 20 Jan 1931 in Wallaceburg, Ontario, Canada.

Children of Mary Knapp and Kenneth Asselstine are:
  + 4360   i.   John William[9] Asselstine, born 19 Dec 1956 in Toronto, Canada.
  + 4361   ii. Katherine A. Asselstine, born 24 Nov 1960 in Toronto, Canada.
  + 4362   iii. Peter Knapp Asselstine, born 23 Jan 1965 in Northbay Ontario Canada.

2474. Katherine "Katie" Ann[8] Christner (Christian C "Chris"[7], Peter C.[6], Christian[5], Peter[4], Christian[3], Christian[2], Christen[1]) was born 14 Dec 1882 in Wayland, Henry Co., IA[7138], and died 25 Sep 1980 in Parkview Home Wayland, Henry Co., IA. She married **John R. Wenger**[7139] 19 Sep 1904. He was born 31 Oct 1879 in Wayland, Henry Co., IA[7139], and died 28 Jan 1940[7139].

Notes for Katherine "Katie" Ann Christner:
Wenger, Katie Ann daughter of Christian C. and Barbara (Guden) Christner, was born in Wayland, IA Dec 14, 1882; died at Parkview Home, Wayland, IA Sep 25, 1980; aged 97 y. On Sep 19, 1904, she was married to John R. Wenger, who died on Jan 28, 1940. Surviving are 3 sons (Ira, Raymond, an Harold Wenger), one daughter (Barbara-Mrs. Unternahrer), 20 grandchildren, and 31 great-grandchildren. She was a member of Bethel Mennonite Church, where funeral services were held on Sep 27 in charge of Oliver Yutzy; interment in Sugar Creek Cemetery.
Glenora Pedan 1900--1954 came to live with the family at age 11

Birth: Dec 14, 1882 - Wayland, Henry Co., IA
Death: Sep 25, 1980 - Wayland, Henry Co., IA

Parents:
Christian C. Christner (1849 - 1926)

Barbara S. Gunden Christner (1848 - 1929)

Spouse: John R. Wenger (1879 - 1940)

Children:
Raymond Wenger (1907 - 1989)
Barbara Elizabeth Wenger Unternahrer (1920 - 2010)

Burial: Sugar Creek Cemetery, Wayland, Henry Co., IA

More About Katherine "Katie" Ann Christner:
Burial: 27 Sep 1980, Sugarcreek Cemetery, Wayland Iowa
Religion: Bethel Mennonite Church Wayland, Iowa/
Residence: 1930, Marion, Washington Co., IA[7140,7141]
Social Security Number: 481-58-7178/[7142]
SSN issued: IA[7142]

Notes for John R. Wenger:
Birth: Oct 31, 1879 - Wayland, Henry Co., IA
Death: Jun 28, 1940 - Wayland, Henry Co., IA

Spouse: Katie Ann Christner Wenger (1882 - 1980)

Children:
Raymond Wenger (1907 - 1989)
Barbara Elizabeth Wenger Unternahrer (1920 - 2010)

Burial: Sugar Creek Cemetery, Wayland, Henry Co., IA

More About John R. Wenger:
Residence: 1930, Marion, Washington Co., IA[7143,7144]

Children of Katherine Christner and John Wenger are:
    4363   i.   Joseph[9] Wenger[7145], born 03 Oct 1905 in IL[7146,7147]; died 06 Nov 1975 in Wayland, Henry Co., IA[7148,7149].

            More About Joseph Wenger:
            Residence: 1930, Marion, Washington Co., IA[7150,7151]
            Social Security Number: 481-42-2560/[7152]
            SSN issued: IA[7152]

    4364   ii.   Raymond Wenger, born 1907; died 29 May 1989 in Mt. Pleasant, Henry Co., IA[7153].

            Notes for Raymond Wenger:
            Birth: Aug. 23, 1907 - Washington Co., IA
            Death: May 29, 1989 - Wayland, Henry Co., IA

            Parents:
            John R. Wenger (1879 - 1940)
            Katie Ann Christner Wenger (1882 - 1980)

            Burial: Sugar Creek Cemetery, Wayland, Henry Co., IA
            Plot: Row 1

            More About Raymond Wenger:
            Residence: 1987, Wayland, IA[7153]

+   4365   iii.   Ira Wenger, born 02 Sep 1911 in Wayland, Henry Co., IA; died 23 Oct 1991.
    4366   iv.   Harold Wenger, born 1915.

+ 4367   v.   Barbara Wenger, born 11 Nov 1920 in Wayland, Henry Co., IA; died 16 Dec 2010 in Wayland, Henry Co., IA.

2475. John G.[8] **Christner** (Christian C "Chris"[7], Peter C.[6], Christian[5], Peter[4], Christian[3], Christian[2], Christen[1])[7154,7155,7156] was born 03 Jan 1885 in Jefferson Twp., Henry Co., IA[7157,7158,7159], and died 24 Nov 1962 in Mount Pleasant, Henry Co., IA[7160,7161,7162]. He married **Della Elizabeth "Delia" McNabb**[7162] Abt. 1906 in Iowa[7162]. She was born 20 Apr 1887 in Keokuk County, Iowa, USA[7162], and died 28 Feb 1963 in Winfield, Henry County, Iowa, USA[7162].

More About John G. Christner:
Residence: 01 Jan 1925[7162,7163]
Social Security Number: 481-26-6389/[7164]

More About Della Elizabeth "Delia" McNabb:
Residence: 1915[7165]

Child of John Christner and Della McNabb is:
    4368   i.   Ruth May[9] Christner[7165], born 11 May 1909 in Jefferson, Henry County, Iowa, USA[7165]; died 04 Nov 1987 in Washington, Washington County, Iowa, USA[7165].

            More About Ruth May Christner:
            Residence: 1930, Crawford, Washington County, Iowa[7165]

2477. Jacob C.[8] **Troyer** (Susanna[7] Christner, Jacob[6], Christian[5], Peter[4], Christian[3], Christian[2], Christen[1]) was born 23 Apr 1871 in Goshen, Elkhart Co., IN, and died 26 Feb 1929 in Goshen, Elkhart Co., IN[7166]. He married **Sarah E. Miller** 05 Feb 1894. She was born 08 Aug 1874.

Notes for Jacob C. Troyer:
Sarah is the daughter of Eli J. and Mary Yoder Miller. He was Old Order Amish and a farmer.

Buried Nisley Cemetery, Elkhart Co., IN.

More About Jacob C. Troyer:
Residence: 1920, Clinton, Elkhart Co., IN[7166]

Children of Jacob Troyer and Sarah Miller are:
    4369   i.   Christian[9] Troyer.
    4370   ii.   Jacob Troyer.
    4371   iii. Sarah Troyer.
    4372   iv.   Jephtha Troyer.
    4373   v.   Lydia Troyer.
    4374   vi.   Mary Ann Troyer, born 26 Apr 1894. She married Moses Borkholder; born 07 Feb 1894.

            Notes for Mary Ann Troyer:
            They were Amish.

+ 4375   vii. Eli J. Troyer, born 04 Sep 1904 in Brown Co., IN; died 12 Dec 1997 in Lagrange Co., IN.

2478. Elizabeth[8] **Troyer** (Susanna[7] Christner, Jacob[6], Christian[5], Peter[4], Christian[3], Christian[2], Christen[1]) was born 09 Dec 1872, and died 18 Mar 1935 in Bremen, Marshall Co., IN[7166]. She married **John J. Yoder** 09 Apr 1893 in Goshen, Elkhart Co., IN. He was born 12 Dec 1871.

Notes for Elizabeth Troyer:
Elizabeth married John J Yoder on April 9 1893
John born Dec 12 1871 son of Jonas and Anna Kauffman Yoder
O.O.Amish/farmer

More About Elizabeth Troyer:
Residence: 1930, German, Marshall Co., Indiana[7166]

Notes for John J. Yoder:
John is the son of Jonas and Anna Kauffman Yoder. He is Old Order Amish and a farmer.

Children of Elizabeth Troyer and John Yoder are:

4376	i.	Cephus[9] Yoder.
4377	ii.	Mary Yoder.
4378	iii.	Millie Yoder.
4379	iv.	Ellen Yoder.
4380	v.	Mahlon Yoder.
4381	vi.	Sarah Yoder, born 09 May 1897. She married Levi S. Schrock 1918; born 08 Aug 1896.

> Notes for Sarah Yoder:
> Amish

2479. Magdalena Mattie[8] Troyer (Susanna[7] Christner, Jacob[6], Christian[5], Peter[4], Christian[3], Christian[2], Christen[1])[7167,7168,7169] was born 31 Mar 1874 in Goshen, Elkhart Co., IN[7170,7171,7172], and died 24 Nov 1947 in Goshen, Elkhart Co., IN[7173,7174]. She married **Samuel D. Hochstetler**[7175,7176,7177] 26 Mar 1893 in Goshen, Elkhart Co., IN[7177], son of David Hochstetler and Magdalena Hochstetler. He was born 25 Aug 1872 in Elkhart, Elkhart Co., IN[7178,7179,7180], and died 17 Feb 1954 in Goshen, Elkhart Co., IN[7181,7182].

More About Magdalena Mattie Troyer:
Residence: 1930, Clinton, Elkhart Co., IN[7183]

Notes for Samuel D. Hochstetler:
Samuel was an ordained bishop in the Old Order Amish on Nov 23, 1923.

More About Samuel D. Hochstetler:
Residence: 1930, Clinton, Elkhart Co., IN[7183]

Children of Magdalena Troyer and Samuel Hochstetler are:

4382	i.	Mary[9] Hochstetler.
4383	ii.	Elmer S. Hochstetler, born 09 May 1895 in Goshen, Elkhart Co., IN[7184]; died 07 Dec 1963 in Goshen, Elkhart Co., IN[7184].
4384	iii.	Sarah Ella Hochstetler[7184], born 17 Dec 1896 in Goshen, Elkhart Co., IN[7184]; died 05 May 1976 in Goshen, Elkhart Co., IN[7184].
4385	iv.	Mary Hochstetler[7184], born 29 Sep 1898 in Ninevah, Brown Co., IN[7184]; died 04 Sep 1990 in Goshen, Elkhart Co., IN[7184].
4386	v.	Jeptha Hochstetler[7184], born 18 Apr 1900 in Ninevah, Brown Co., IN[7184]; died 30 Dec 1900 in Nineveh, Johnson Co., IN[7184].
4387	vi.	Samuel Hochstetler, born 02 Dec 1901 in Nineveh, Johnson Co., IN[7184]; died 11 Dec 1901 in Nineveh, Johnson Co., IN[7184].
4388	vii.	Elam Hochstetler[7184], born 27 Dec 1902 in Nineveh, Johnson Co., IN[7184]; died 10 Nov 1994 in Middlebury, Elkhart Co., IN[7184].

> More About Elam Hochstetler:
> Social Security Number: 312-40-7752/[7184]
> SSN issued: IN[7184]

4389	viii.	Fanny Hochstetler[7184], born 03 Dec 1904 in Hamblen, Brown Co., IN[7184]; died 13 Jun 1959[7184].
4390	ix.	Lucy Edna Hochstetler[7185,7186,7187,7188], born 10 Feb 1906 in Hamblen, Brown Co., IN[7189,7190,7191,7192]; died 17 Jan 1978 in Middlebury, Elkhart Co., IN[7192].

> More About Lucy Edna Hochstetler:
> Residence: 1920, Clinton, Elkhart Co., IN[7193]

Social Security Number: 311-62-5612/[7194,7195]

SSN issued: IN[7196,7197]

4391   x.   Susie Hochstetler[7197], born 1908 in Hamblen, Brown Co., IN[7197].

2481. Jeptha[8] Troyer (Susanna[7] Christner, Jacob[6], Christian[5], Peter[4], Christian[3], Christian[2], Christen[1]) was born 17 Jul 1878, and died 03 Nov 1956 in Lagrange Co., IN[7198]. He married **Ada May Yoder**. She was born 12 Apr 1879 in Goshen, Elkhart Co., IN[7199], and died 17 Aug 1948 in Topeka, Lagrange Co., IN.

Notes for Jeptha Troyer:
Amish Minister

More About Jeptha Troyer:
Residence: 1942, Lagrange Co., IN[7200]

Notes for Ada May Yoder:
Gospel Herald - Volume XLI, Number 39 - September 28, 1948 - pages 918, 919

Troyer - Ada May Yoder was born April 12, 1879; passed away at her home in Topeka, IN, Aug 17, 1948; aged 69 y. 4 m. 5 d. At the age of fourteen she accepted Christ and was a member of the Shore Mennonite Church at the time of her death. On July 23, 1899, he was united in marriage to Jephtha S. Troyer. Two infant children preceded her in death. Surviving are her husband and 9 children (Mahlon, Lockport, N.Y.; Arthur, Ligonier, Ind.; Edwin, Wawaka, Ind.; Nora - Mrs. Ernest Bender, Milford, Ind.; Elva - Mrs. Abner Stutzman, Ligonier, Ind.; Christ, Syracuse, Ind.; Ruby - Mrs. Noah Leighty, Grabill, Ind.; Elsie - Mrs. Orville Birkey, Kouts, Ind.; and Erma, at home). Most of her early life was spent in the Jonathan Troyer home. Funeral services were held at the home and at the Shore Church, Shipshewana, by the local ministers and Edwin Yoder.

Children of Jeptha Troyer and Ada Yoder are:
    4392   i.   Elona[9] Troyer.
    4393   ii.   Jonathan Troyer.
    4394   iii.   Mahlon Troyer.
    4395   iv.   Nora Troyer.
    4396   v.   Edwin Troyer.

2483. Fannie E.[8] Yoder (Elizabeth[7] Christner, Jacob[6], Christian[5], Peter[4], Christian[3], Christian[2], Christen[1]) was born 03 Dec 1875 in Elkhart Co., IN, and died 30 Apr 1964 in Yoder, KS. She married **John M. Bontrager** 17 Feb 1898 in Haven, KS, son of Daniel E. Bontrager. He was born 17 Feb 1877 in Elkhart Co., IN, and died 20 Aug 1946 in Yoder, KS.

Notes for Fannie E. Yoder:
He was a Mennonite.

Notes for John M. Bontrager:
Obituary: Gospel Herald - Vol. XXXIX, No . 25 - September 17, 1946--Pages 542-43

Bontrager.--John M., son of Daniel E. and Mary (Nissley) Bontrager, was born near Lagrange, Ind., Feb. 17, 1877; died Aug. 20, 1946; aged 69y 6m 3d. His death was the result of an automobile accident which occurred when he was returning from a trip to Indiana. On Feb. 17, 1898, he was united in marriage to Fanny Yoder, of Haven, Kans., who survives. Also surviving are one daughter (Elizabeth Yoder), 4 sons (Jerry J., Mahlon, Simon, and Emery), 15 grandchildren, one great-grandson, 3 brothers and 3 sisters (Jake T., Topeka, Ind.; Fanny Miller, Hutchinson, Kans.; Barbara Miller, also of Topeka; Harry D., Haven, Kans.; Dan M., Scott City, Kans.; and Mary Plank, Arthur, Ill.), and many other relatives and friends. Two daughters, one brother (Rudy), and one sister (Anna Miller) preceded him in death. He was a faithful member of the Yoder Kans. Mennonite Church and will be greatly missed by family, church, and community. Funeral services were conducted at the Yoder Church, Aug. 23, in charge of Harry A. Diener, assisted by L. J. Miller. Text, I Thess. 4:13-16. Interment was made in the adjoining cemetery.

Children of Fannie Yoder and John Bontrager are:
+ 4397   i.   Jerry J.[9] Bontrager.
+ 4398   ii. Emery Bontrager, born 13 Mar 1909 in Yoder, Reno Co., KS; died 08 Dec 1992 in Hutchinson, Reno Co., KS.

2484. Jacob E.[8] Yoder (Elizabeth[7] Christner, Jacob[6], Christian[5], Peter[4], Christian[3], Christian[2], Christen[1])[7201] was born 23 Aug 1877 in Middlebury, Elkhart Co., IN[7201], and died 20 Apr 1954 in Age at Death: 76/[7201]. He married **Anna C. Miller**[7201] 10 Feb 1904 in Reno Co., KS[7201]. She was born 14 Sep 1878 in Shelby, IL[7201], and died 16 Nov 1969 in Age at Death: 89/Hutchinson, Reno Co., KS[7201].

Notes for Jacob E. Yoder:
Anna is the daughter Nov 16, 1969 daughter of Christian and Polly Plank Miller.

More About Jacob E. Yoder:
Burial: Yoder, Reno County, Kansas, USA[7201]
Residence: 1930, Yoder, Reno Co., KS[7201]

More About Anna C. Miller:
Burial: Yoder, Reno County, Kansas, USA[7201]
Residence: 1930, Yoder, Reno Co., KS[7201]

Children of Jacob Yoder and Anna Miller are:
4399   i.   Tobias C[9] Yoder[7201], born 04 Jan 1900 in KS[7201]; died 20 Jul 1979 in Yoder, Reno Co., KS[7201].

          More About Tobias C Yoder:
          Residence: 1920, Yoder, Reno Co., KS[7201]

4400   ii. Edwin J Yoder[7201], born 12 Nov 1904 in KS[7201]; died 15 Dec 1996 in Kempner, Lampasas Co., TX[7201].

          More About Edwin J Yoder:
          Residence: 1925, Yoder, Reno Co., KS[7201]

4401   iii. Polly Suzanne Yoder[7201], born 21 Jul 1906 in Haven, Reno Co., KS[7201]; died 09 Oct 1994 in Hutchinson, Reno Co., KS[7201].

          More About Polly Suzanne Yoder:
          Burial: Yoder, Reno County, Kansas, USA[7201]
          Residence: 1935, Castleton, Reno, Kansas[7201]

4402   iv. Elizabeth Yoder[7201], born Abt. 1909 in KS[7201].

          More About Elizabeth Yoder:
          Residence: 1910, Haven, Reno Co., KS[7201]

4403   v. Lizzie Yoder[7201], born 07 Feb 1909 in Haven, Reno Co., KS[7201].

          More About Lizzie Yoder:
          Residence: 1930, Yoder, Reno Co., KS[7201]

4404   vi. Moses J. Yoder[7201], born Abt. 1913 in KS[7201]; died 29 Jul 2003 in Wooster, Wayne Co., OH[7201].

          More About Moses J. Yoder:
          Residence: 1930, Yoder, Reno Co., KS[7201]

2485. David J.[8] Yoder (Elizabeth[7] Christner, Jacob[6], Christian[5], Peter[4], Christian[3], Christian[2], Christen[1])[7202] was born 26 Feb 1880 in Middlebury, Elkhart Co., IN[7202], and died 28 Jul 1970 in Hutchinson, Reno Co., KS[7202]. He married **(1) Kate Ramer**. She was born 10 Aug 1884, and died 1980. He married **(2) Mary Lucinda**

Kauffman[7202] 22 Dec 1903 in Reno, Reno Co., KS[7202]. She was born 05 Jan 1879 in Amish, Johnson Co., IA[7202], and died 01 Apr 1947 in Kansas City, Wyandotte Co., KS[7202].

Notes for David J. Yoder:
David married Lucinda Kauffman. Lucinda born Jan 5 1879 died April 1 1947
2nd marriage Kate Ramer born Aug 10 1884 died 1980.

More About David J. Yoder:
Residence: 1910, Haven, Reno Co., KS[7202]

More About Mary Lucinda Kauffman:
Residence: 01 Mar 1905, Haven, Reno Co., KS[7202]

Children of David Yoder and Mary Kauffman are:

4405   i.   Reuben[9] Yoder[7202], born 22 Sep 1904 in Yoder, Reno Co., KS[7202]; died 25 Nov 1968 in Yoder, Reno Co., KS[7202].

    More About Reuben Yoder:
    Residence: 1910, Haven, Reno Co., KS[7202]

4406   ii.   Rubin Yoder[7202], born Abt. 1905 in KS[7202].

    More About Rubin Yoder:
    Arrival: 26 Mar 1905, New York, New York Co., NY[7202]
    Departure: Liverpool, England[7202]
    Residence: 1910, Haven, Reno Co., KS[7202]

4407   iii.   Ruth Yoder[7202], born 22 Sep 1905 in Yoder, Reno Co., KS[7202]; died 1910 in Yoder, Reno Co., KS[7202].

    More About Ruth Yoder:
    Residence: 1910, Haven, Reno Co., KS[7202]

4408   iv.   Barbara Yoder[7202], born 28 Nov 1906 in Yoder, Reno Co., KS[7202]; died 25 Nov 1968[7202].

    More About Barbara Yoder:
    Residence: 1910, Haven, Reno Co., KS[7202]

4409   v.   Elizabeth D. "Lizzy" Yoder[7202], born 16 May 1908 in Yoder, Reno Co., KS[7202]; died 16 Mar 2001 in Haven, Reno Co., KS[7202].

    More About Elizabeth D. "Lizzy" Yoder:
    Residence: 1915, Yoder, Reno Co., KS[7202]

4410   vi.   Henry D. Yoder[7202], born 17 Jan 1910 in Haven, Reno Co., KS[7202]; died 10 Jun 1989 in Hutchinson, Reno Co., KS[7202].

    More About Henry D. Yoder:
    Residence: 1910, Haven, Reno Co., KS[7202]

4411   vii.   Ida D. Yoder[7202], born 23 Aug 1911 in Yoder, Reno Co., KS[7202]; died 15 Mar 1995 in South Hutchinson, Reno, Kansas, United States[7202].

    More About Ida D. Yoder:
    Residence: 1930, Yoder, Reno Co., KS[7202]

4412   viii.   Levi L. Yoder[7202], born 28 Jan 1918 in Yoder, Reno Co., KS[7202]; died Apr 1967 in Newton Co., IN[7202].

    More About Levi L. Yoder:
    Residence: 1920, Yoder, Reno Co., KS[7202]

2488. Susan[8] Yoder (Elizabeth[7] Christner, Jacob[6], Christian[5], Peter[4], Christian[3], Christian[2], Christen[1])[7203] was born 01 May 1887 in Middlebury, Elkhart Co., IN[7203], and died 29 Jul 1981 in Schowalter Villa, Hesston Co., KS[7203]. She married **Daniel J. Headings**[7203] 07 Feb 1907 in KS[7203], son of John Headings. He was born 21 Apr 1885 in New Castle, Lawrence Co., PA[7203], and died 01 May 1951 in Hutchinson, KS[7203].

Notes for Susan Yoder:
Susan married Daniel Headings on Feb 7 1907. Daniel born April 21 1885 died May 1 1951. Daniel is the son of John Headings

Child of Susan Yoder and Daniel Headings is:
    4413   i.   Alpha Jerry[9] Kauffman[7203], born 10 Jan 1910 in Haven, Reno, Kansas[7203]; died 06 Jan 2001 in Hutchinson, Reno, Kansas[7203].

2490. Daniel J.[8] Christner (Samuel[7], Jacob[6], Christian[5], Peter[4], Christian[3], Christian[2], Christen[1])[7204] was born 06 Mar 1879 in Elkhart Co., IN[7205], and died 03 Apr 1943 in Buried Pigeon River Mennonite Church Cemetery, Pigeon, Huron Co., Michigan/Huron Co., MI[7205]. He married **Katie Zehr**[7205] 1913. She was born 01 Oct 1890 in Baden, Ontario, Canada[7205], and died 15 Mar 1956 in Pigeon, Huron Co., MI.

Notes for Daniel J. Christner:
Christner - Daniel of Pigeon, MI was born Mar 6, 1879, near Elkhart, IN died Apr 3, 1943. He was united in marriage to Katie Zehr. To this union 7 children were born (Orie and Emma of Pigeon; Walter and Viola, Mrs. Emery Seaman, of Detroit, MI; Clayton and Floyd in the Army; and Bertha who died in infancy). He left to mourn his departure his bereaved companion, 4 sons, 2 daughters, 6 grandchildren, and one brother Jacob of near Pigeon. The funeral was held at the Pigeon River A.M. Church, Apr 6, 1943. Services at the house were held by Bro. M.S. Zehr, at the church by Bro. Emil Swartzendruber (text, II Cor. 5:10) and Bro Earl Maust (text, Job 14:14).

More About Daniel J. Christner:
Residence: 1900, West Albany Precinct (Excl. Albany City), Linn Co., Oregon[7205]

Notes for Katie Zehr:
Christner, Katie daughter of the late Daniel and Anna Zehr was born Oct. 1, 1890 at Baden, Ontario passed away at her home in Pigeon, MI on March 15, 1956, after a long illness aged 65 y. 5 m. 14 d. Her husband, Daniel J. Christner, preceded her in death in April 1943. Surviving are 2 daughters, Mrs. Viola Seaman of Bay City, MI and Mrs. Emma Heintz of Pigeon; 4 sons, Clayton, of Detroit, MI; Walter of Washington, MI; Floyd of Muskegon, MI and Orrie of Pigeon; and 3 brothers, Noah, Baden, Ont.; Abraham, Keota, IA and David, Bad Axe, MI. Funeral services were held March 18 at the Pigeon River Mennonite Church with Willard Mayer and Emanuel Swartzendruber officiating. Burial was made in the adjoining cemetery.

More About Katie Zehr:
Arrival: 1904[7205]
Burial: 18 Mar 1956, Pigeon River Mennonite Church Cemetery Pigeon Mi.
Residence: 01 Apr 1940, Pigeon, Huron Co., MI[7205]

Children of Daniel Christner and Katie Zehr are:
    4414   i.   Clayton[9] Christner[7206,7207,7208], born 30 Dec 1913 in Huron Co., MI[7208]; died 14 Aug 1979 in Pigeon, Huron Co., MI[7209].

                    Notes for Clayton Christner:
                    SS# 374-14-5893 Iss.MI Last zip 48720

                    More About Clayton Christner:
                    Military service: 27 Jul 1942, Service 27 July 1942 until 2 January 1946/Served in US Army during World War II[7210]
                    Other-Begin: Pigeon, Huron, Michigan, United States of America[7211]
                    Residence: 1920, Winsor, Huron Co., MI[7212]

Social Security Number: 374-14-5893/[7213]
SSN issued: MI[7213]

+ 4415   ii.   Orrie John Christner, born 22 Jul 1915 in Huron Co., MI; died 04 Dec 1959 in Huron Co., MI.

   4416   iii.   Bertha Ellen Christner, born 10 Oct 1916. She married Charles John Adam Cook 10 Jun 1932; born 15 Mar 1910; died 20 Sep 1966 in Burial in Dresden Cem. under the name Christner.

Notes for Bertha Ellen Christner:
Bertha, daughter of Dan and Katie Christner, was born Jan 24, 1921, at Pigeon, MI; died May 1, 1921. She leaves father, mother, 1 sister, and 3 brothers. Funeral services were conducted at the Pigeon River Church by Bro. Sol. Swartzendruber. Text, Mark 10:14.
"A little bud to us was given,
To claim a portion of our love,
It left us soon and went to heaven,
There to dwell in that home above."

Notes for Charles John Adam Cook:
Burial in Dresden Cemetery under the name Christner in Ontario, Canada His father was Charles. His Grandfather was Jabez. His Great Grandfather was Jonathan.

More About Charles John Adam Cook:
Burial: Burial in Dresden Cem. under the name Christner in Canada

+ 4417   iv.   Walter J. Christner, born 29 Jan 1917 in Huron Co., MI; died 03 May 1969 in Washington, Macomb Co., MI.

+ 4418   v.   Viola Christner, born 22 Feb 1919; died 17 Apr 1973 in Belleville, Wayne Co., MI.

+ 4419   vi.   Emma Christner, born 08 May 1922 in Pigeon, Huron Co., MI; died 05 Feb 2006.

+ 4420   vii.   Floyd Christner, born 01 Sep 1924 in Huron Co., MI; died 20 Mar 1992 in Brooks, Newaygo Co., MI.

2491. John Adam[8] Christner (Samuel[7], Jacob[6], Christian[5], Peter[4], Christian[3], Christian[2], Christen[1]) was born 05 Sep 1880 in Middlebury, Elkhart Co., IN, and died 09 Sep 1920 in Pigeon, Huron Co., MI. He married **Lydia Boshart**[7214] 01 Jan 1900. She was born 08 Jan 1879 in Baden, Ontario, Canada, and died 07 Dec 1961 in Bad Ax, MI.

Notes for John Adam Christner:
Christner - John Christner was born near Middlebury, Indiana, Sept. 5, 1880; died near Pigeon, MI Sep 9, 1920; aged 40 y. 4 d. He leaves a sorrowing wife, three sons, four daughters, father, and two brothers. Funeral services were held at the Pigeon River Church Sep 12, 1920, conducted by Bros. S. J. Swartzendruber, Peter Ropp, and Alfred Wideman.

Birth: Sep. 5, 1880 - IN
Death: Sep. 9, 1920 - Pigeon, Huron Co., MI

Son of Sam Christner and Elizabeth Mast

Husband of Lydia Christner

Died at his own hand at age 40

Spouse: Lydia Boshart Christner (1879 - 1961)

Children: Baby Boy Christner (1918 - 1918)

Burial: Pigeon River Mennonite Church Cemetery, Pigeon, Huron Co., MI

More About John Adam Christner:
Burial: 12 Sep 1920
Residence: 1920, Oliver, Huron Co., MI[7214]

Notes for Lydia Boshart:
Christner, Lydia, daughter of Menno Bosharts, was born at Baden, Ontario, Canada Jan 8, 1879; died at the Health Center near Bad Axe, MI Dec. 7, 1961; aged 82 y. 10 m. 29 d. On Jan 1, 1900, she was married to John Christner, who died Sept. 5, 1920. Surviving are 3 daughters (Mrs. Elizabeth Erickson, Upland, Calif.; Mrs. Sadie Zimmer, Traverse City, MI; and Mrs. Anne Miller, Saginaw, MI), 3 sons (John, Pigeon; Solomon, Bad Axe; and William, Pontiac), 12 grandchildren, 15 great-grandchildren, one sister (Mrs. Jacob Christner, Pigeon), one half sister (Lillian Fowler, Watertown, NY), one brother (Eli), and 3 half brothers (Allen, Harvey, and Jay, all of Rome, NY). One daughter preceded her in death. She was a member of the Conservative Mennonite Church, where funeral services were held Dec. 10, in charge of Willard Mayer and Earl J. Maust.

Birth: 1879, Canada
Death: 1961

Spouse: John A Christner (1880 - 1920)

Children: Baby Boy Christner (1918 - 1918)

Burial: Pigeon River Mennonite Church Cemetery, Pigeon, Huron Co., MI

More About Lydia Boshart:
Residence: 1920, Oliver, Huron Co., MI[7214]

Children of John Christner and Lydia Boshart are:
+   4421   i.   Martha[9] Christner, born 28 Aug 1902; died 19 Jul 1960.
+   4422   ii.   Elizabeth Christner, born 26 Oct 1903 in Wilmout, MN; died 26 Oct 1984 in Whittier Hospital Whittier, CA.
+   4423   iii.   John Christner, born 06 Jan 1905; died 18 Dec 1999 in Pigeon, Huron Co., MI.
+   4424   iv.   Sadie Christner, born 21 Oct 1907; died Jan 1987.
     4425   v.   David Christner, born 10 Dec 1908; died 06 Mar 1909.

         Notes for David Christner:
         Christner - David, infant son of John and Lydia Christner, was born Dec. 10, 1908; died near Pigeon, Mich., Mar. 6, 1909; aged 2 m. 24 d. He leaves his father, mother, one brother and three sisters to mourn their loss. Funeral services were held March 8, by S. J. Swartzendruber and M. S. Zehr. "The Lord hath given, the Lord has taken; blessed be the name of the Lord."

     4426   vi.   Infant Christner, born Jun 1909; died Jun 1909.
     4427   vii.   Anne Christner, born 15 Apr 1911. She married Warren Miller 21 Nov 1930; born 10 Mar 1910.
     4428   viii.   Katie Christner[7215], born 08 Jun 1914; died 13 Jun 1914.

         Notes for Katie Christner:
         Birth: Jun 8, 1914
         Death: Jun 13, 1914

         Burial: Pigeon River Mennonite Church Cemetery, Pigeon, Huron Co., MI
         Find A Grave Memorial# 74350979

         More About Katie Christner:
         Residence: MI[7215]

     4429   ix.   Solomon Christner, born 08 Jun 1914 in MI; died 25 Feb 1979 in MI. He married Doris Cutler 12 Jan 1957; born 21 Aug 1915.

         Notes for Solomon Christner:
         SS#372-16-7239 ISS MI   Last address 48735

         Birth: 1914
         Death: 1979

         Burial: Grand Lawn Cemetery, Pigeon, Huron Co., MI

4430   x.   William Christner[7216], born 10 May 1916 in Pigeon, Huron Co., MI; died 08 Aug 1994 in Bad Axe, Huron Co., MI[7216].

Notes for William Christner:
Burial at Pigeon River Mennonite Church Cemetery, Pigeon, MI.

Christner, William, 78. Born: May 10, 1916, Pigeon, Mich., to John A. and Lydia Boshart Christner. Died: Aug. 8, 1994, Cass City, Mich. Survivors - brother and sisters: John, Martha Hiebel, Elizabeth Erikson, Sadie Zimmer, Ann Miller. Funeral: Aug. 10, Meyersieck-Bussema Funeral Home, by Tom Beachy. Burial: Pigeon River Mennonite Church Cemetery.

Birth: May 10, 1916
Pigeon, Huron Co., MI
Death: Aug. 8, 1994
Cass City, Tuscola Co., MI

Survivors included brother and sisters: John Christner, Martha Hiebel, Elizabeth Erikson, Sadie Zimmer, Ann Miller.

Meyersieck-Bussema Funeral Home

Burial: Pigeon River Mennonite Church Cemetery, Pigeon, Huron Co., MI

More About William Christner:
Burial: 10 Aug 1994, Pigeon River Mennonite Church Cemetery
Social Security Number: 378-24-7092/[7216]
SSN issued: MI[7216]

4431   xi.   Infant Christner, born 12 Jun 1918; died 12 Jun 1918.

2492. Barbara[8] Christner (Samuel[7], Jacob[6], Christian[5], Peter[4], Christian[3], Christian[2], Christen[1])[7217] was born 14 Sep 1882 in IN[7217], and died 22 Mar 1915 in Hubbard, Marion Co., OR. She married **Noah E. Berkey**[7217] 24 Sep 1907. He was born 15 Apr 1879 in Nashville, Davidson Co., TN[7217], and died Mar 1963 in Scotts Mills, Marion Co., OR[7217].

Notes for Barbara Christner:
Berkey - Barbara (Christner) Berkey was born in Indiana, Sept. 14, 1882; died near Hubbard, OR, March 22, 1915; aged 32 y. 6 m. 8 d. She was a daughter of Samuel and Elizabeth Christner, and united in matrimony to Noah E. Berkey Sept. 24, 1907. To this union were born 4 sons and 1 daughter who remain with the husband, to mourn her early departure; also 3 brothers of Pigeon, Mich., and a host of friends. She accepted her Savior in youth and remained faithful until death. Funeral services at the Zion A. M. Church by the brethren, A. P. Troyer and E. Z. Yoder. Text, Jno. 11:25. The remains laid to rest within the cemetery near by.

More About Barbara Christner:
Burial: Near Zion A.M. Church by the Brethren Hubbard Oregon
Residence: 1910, Aurora, Marion Co., OR[7217,7218]

More About Noah E. Berkey:
Residence: 1910, Aurora, Marion Co., OR[7219]

Children of Barbara Christner and Noah Berkey are:
+   4432   i.   Earl[9] Berkey, born 01 Jul 1908.
+   4433   ii.   Lawerence Berkey, born 25 Jul 1909 in OR; died 05 Jun 2000 in Sheridan, Yamhill Co., OR.
    4434   iii.   William Berkey, born 1910.
+   4435   iv.   Ivan Berkey, born 08 May 1912.
    4436   v.   Florence Berkey, born 1913; died 1922.
    4437   vi.   Daughter Berkey, born 22 Mar 1915; died 22 Mar 1915.

2493. Jacob[8] Christner (Samuel[7], Jacob[6], Christian[5], Peter[4], Christian[3], Christian[2], Christen[1])[7220,7221,7222,7223,7224] was born 11 Jun 1884 in Goshen, Elkhart Co., IN[7225], and died 06 Dec 1960 in Pigeon, Huron Co., MI[7226,7227]. He married **Mary Boshart**[7227,7228,7229] 17 Aug 1905. She was born 21 Feb 1882 in Baden, Ontario, Canada[7230,7231], and died 07 Aug 1962 in Wauseon, Fulton Co., OH[7232].

Notes for Jacob Christner:
Christner, Jacob, son of Samuel and Elizabeth (Mast) Christner, was born June 17, 1884, Elkhart, IN; died at Pigeon, MI, on Dec. 6, 1960; aged 76 y. 5 m. 19 d. In 1905 he was married to Mary Boshart, who survives. Also surviving are 5 daughters (Alta-Mrs. Lloyd Piehl, Pontiac; Elizabeth-Mrs. Vernon Swartzendruber, Sebewaing; Marion-Mrs. Freeman Nofziger, Archbold, Ohio; Margaret-Mrs. Maurice Nofziger, Pettisville, Ohio), 4 sons (Jess and Louis, Pigeon; Alvin, Phoenix, AZ; and Ervin, Detroit), 27 grandchildren, and one great-grandchild. One son and 3 infant children preceded him in death. He was a member of the Pigeon River Church, where funeral services were held Dec. 9, in charge of Emanuel Swartzendruber and Earl J. Maust.

More About Jacob Christner:
Burial: Pigeon River Mennonite Church Cemetery, Pigeon, Huron Co., MI
Residence: 1910, Oliver, Huron Co., MI[7233]

Notes for Mary Boshart:
Source: Gospel Herald - Vol LV, No 36, September 11, 1962 - pages 814

Birth: Feb. 21, 1882 - Baden, Ontario, Canada
Death: Aug. 7, 1962 - Wauseon, Fulton Co., OH

Mary Christner, daughter of Menno Boshart and Catherine (Swartzendruber) Boshart, was born at Baden, Ont., Feb. 21, 1882; died at Wauseon, Ohio, Aug. 7, 1962; aged 80 y. 5 m. 17 d.

On Aug. 17, 1905, Mary Boshart was married to Jacob Christner, who died Dec. 6, 1960. Four children also preceded her in death.

Surviving are 9 children (Alta-Mrs. Lloyd Piehl, Pontiac, Mich.; Elizabeth-Mrs. Vernon Swartzendruber, Sebewaing, Mich.; Marian-Mrs. Freeman Nafziger, Archbold, Ohio; Margaret-Mrs. Glen King. Sarasota, Fla.; Dorothy-Mrs. Morris Nafziger, Pettisville, Ohio: Jesse, Elkton, Mich.; Alvin, Phoenix, Ariz.; Ervin, Detroit, Mich.; and Louis, Pigeon, Mich.), 27 grandchildren, 2 great-grandchildren, one brother (Eli, Rome, N.Y.; 3 half brothers and one half sister (Harvey and Allen, Syracuse, N.Y.; Jay, Rome, N.Y.; and Lillian Fowler, Watertown, N.Y.).

She was a member of the Pigeon River Conservative Church, where funeral services were held Aug. 11, in charge of Roy Sauder, Earl J. Maust, and Willard Mayer.

Spouse: Jacob Christner (1884 - 1960)

Children:
Elizabeth Viola Christner Swartzentruber (1916 - 2006)
Emanuel Christner (1918 - 1918)
Louis Lee Christner (1920 - 1989)

Burial: Pigeon River Mennonite Church Cemetery, Pigeon, Huron Co., MI

More About Mary Boshart:
Arrival: 1883[7233]
Residence: 1930, Oliver, Huron Co., MI[7234]

Children of Jacob Christner and Mary Boshart are:
 4438 i. Bertha[9] Christner[7235], born 03 Feb 1906; died 10 Feb 1906.

More About Bertha Christner:
Residence: MI[7235]

4439 ii. Alta Christner[7236,7236], born 05 Jan 1907 in Huron Co., MI[7236,7237]; died 04 May 1999 in Troy, Oakland Co., MI[7238]. She married Lloyd Phiel 12 Jun 1940; born 12 Oct 1903 in Oxford, Ontario, Canada[7238]; died Jul 1966 in Troy, Oakland Co., MI[7238].

Notes for Alta Christner:
Birth: 1907
Death: 1987

Burial: Alden Union Free Cemetery, Alden, Erie Co., NY

More About Alta Christner:
Residence: 1910, Oliver, Huron Co., MI[7238]
Social Security Number: 370-16-7451/[7239]
SSN issued: MI[7239]

+ 4440 iii. Jesse Christner, born 12 Jul 1908; died 27 Nov 1981 in Elkton, Huron Co., MI.
+ 4441 iv. William P. Christner Sr., born 28 Sep 1909 in Elkton, Huron Co., MI; died 28 Sep 1944 in Mars, Butler Co., PA.
+ 4442 v. Alvin Christner, born 30 Aug 1911 in Elkton, Huron Co., MI; died 31 Jul 1994 in Phoenix, Maricopa Co., AZ.
+ 4443 vi. Ervin Christner, born 02 Mar 1915; died 21 Nov 2004 in SelfDeathAge: 89/Palm Harbor, Pinellas Co., FL.
+ 4444 vii. Elizabeth Viola Christner, born 08 Oct 1916 in Elkton, MI; died 12 Dec 2006 in Pigeon, Huron Co., MI.
4445 viii. Emanuel Christner[7240], born 04 Aug 1918 in MI; died 18 Oct 1918 in Huron Co., MI.

Notes for Emanuel Christner:
Birth: Aug. 4, 1918 - MI
Death: Oct. 18, 1918 - Huron Co., MI

Infant son of Jacob Christner (b. IN) and Mary Boshart Christner (b. Canada)

Parents:
Jacob Christner (1884 - 1960)
Mary Boshart Christner (1882 - 1962)

Burial: Pigeon River Mennonite Church Cemetery, Pigeon, Huron Co., MI

+ 4446 ix. Louis Lee Christner, born 09 Jun 1920 in Elkton, Huron Co., MI; died 27 Oct 1989 in Pigeon, Huron Co., MI.
+ 4447 x. Marion Christner, born 31 Mar 1922.
+ 4448 xi. Margaret Christner, born 04 Nov 1923.
+ 4449 xii. Dorothy Alice Christner, born 07 Jan 1926 in MI; died 17 Jan 2009 in Archbold, Fulton Co., OH.

2494. Elizabeth Lizzie[8] Schlabaugh (Frances Frany[7] Christner, Jacob[6], Christian[5], Peter[4], Christian[3], Christian[2], Christen[1]) was born 18 Oct 1883 in Goshen, Elkhart Co., IN, and died 05 Jul 1973 in Goshen, Elkhart Co., IN. She married **(1) Edward J. Stutzman** 05 Feb 1907. He was born 11 Nov 1883, and died 21 Feb 1912. She married **(2) Noah S Miller** 05 Feb 1918. He was born 25 Jul 1882, and died 14 Dec 1967.

Notes for Elizabeth Lizzie Schlabaugh:
Lizzie married Edward J Stutzman on Feb 5, 1907.
Edward born Nov 11, 1883 died Feb 21, 1912.
Edward so of Joseph and Rachel Yoder Stutzman
O.O.Amish/farmer
2nd marriage Noah S. Miller on Feb 5, 1918.
Noah born July 25, 1882 died Dec 14, 1967.
Noah son of Stephen I. and Catherine Yoder Miller
O.O.Amish/farmer

More About Elizabeth Lizzie Schlabaugh:
Occupation: Farmer/
Religion: Old Order Amish/

More About Edward J. Stutzman:
Occupation: Farmer/
Religion: Old Order Amish/

More About Noah S Miller:
Occupation: Farmer/
Religion: Old Order Amish/

Children of Elizabeth Schlabaugh and Noah Miller are:
    4450   i.   Dora[9] Miller, born 16 Feb 1922; died 26 Feb 1923.

> Notes for Dora Miller:
> Birth: Feb 16, 1922
> Death: Feb 26, 1923
>
> Parents:
> Noah N. Miller (1882 - 1967)
> Elizabeth Schlabach Miller (1883 - 1973)
>
> Inscription:Dau of Noah & Lizzie
>
> Burial: Nisley Cemetery, Goshen, Elkhart Co., IN
> Plot: Row 9 #23

    4451   ii.   Clara F. Miller, born 30 Mar 1927; died 16 Oct 1947.

> Notes for Clara F. Miller:
> Birth: Mar 30, 1927
> Death: Oct 16, 1947
>
> Parents:
> Noah N. Miller (1882 - 1967)
> Elizabeth Schlabach Miller (1883 - 1973)
>
> Inscription: Dau of Noah N. and Lizzie
>
> Burial: Nisley Cemetery, Goshen, Elkhart Co., IN
> Plot: Row 9 #22

2496. Osa[8] Schlabaugh (Frances Frany[7] Christner, Jacob[6], Christian[5], Peter[4], Christian[3], Christian[2], Christen[1]) was born 16 Dec 1887 in Goshen, Elkhart Co., IN, and died 09 Apr 1977 in Goshen, Elkhart Co., IN. He married **Mary Ann Stutzman** 10 Jan 1918. She was born 01 Sep 1890 in Walnut Creek, Holmes Co., OH, and died 16 Mar 1967.

Notes for Osa Schlabaugh:
Mary Ann daughter of Joseph Stutzman. He is Old Order Amish/farmer.

More About Osa Schlabaugh:
Occupation: Farmer/
Religion: Old Order Amish/

Children of Osa Schlabaugh and Mary Stutzman are:

4452   i.   Alpha^9 Schlabach, born 25 Oct 1921; died 27 May 1940.

          Notes for Alpha Schlabach:
          Birth: Oct. 25, 1921
          Death: May 27, 1940

          Parents:
          Osa Schlabach (1887 - 1977)
          MaryAnn Stutzman Schlabach (1890 - 1967)

          Burial: Nisley Cemetery, Goshen, Elkhart Co., IN
          Plot: Row 9 #24

4453   ii.   Henry J. Schlabaugh, born 04 Aug 1923; died 14 Oct 1985.

          Notes for Henry J. Schlabaugh:
          Birth: Aug 4, 1923
          Death: Oct 14, 1985

          Parents:
          Osa Schlabach (1887 - 1977)
          MaryAnn Stutzman Schlabach (1890 - 1967)

          Burial: Nisley Cemetery, Goshen, Elkhart Co., IN

4454   iii.   Infant Schlabaugh, born 21 Nov 1924; died 21 Nov 1924.

          Notes for Infant Schlabaugh:
          Birth: Nov. 21, 1924
          Death: Nov. 21, 1924

          Parents:
          Osa Schlabach (1887 - 1977)
          MaryAnn Stutzman Schlabach (1890 - 1967)

          Note: Son of Osa and Mary Ann Schlabach

          Burial: Nisley Cemetery, Goshen, Elkhart Co., IN
          Plot: Row 9 #26

4455   iv.   Dorothy Schlabaugh, born 22 Jul 1928 in OH; died 25 Dec 1928.

          Notes for Dorothy Schlabaugh:
          Birth: Jul 22, 1928 - OH
          Death: Dec 25, 1928

          Parents:
          Osa Schlabach (1887 - 1977)
          MaryAnn Stutzman Schlabach (1890 - 1967)

          Burial: Nisley Cemetery, Goshen, Elkhart Co., IN
          Plot: Row 9 #28

4456   v.   Osa Schlabaugh Jr., born 06 Sep 1930; died 30 Mar 1931.

          Notes for Osa Schlabaugh Jr.:
          Birth: Sep 6, 1930
          Death: Mar 30, 1931

          Parents:
          Osa Schlabach (1887 - 1977)
          MaryAnn Stutzman Schlabach (1890 - 1967)

Burial: Nisley Cemetery, Goshen, Elkhart Co., IN
Plot: Row 9 #26

2499. David J.C.[8] Miller (Mary[7] Christner, Jacob[6], Christian[5], Peter[4], Christian[3], Christian[2], Christen[1]) was born 04 Dec 1878 in Goshen, Elkhart Co., IN[7241], and died 15 Oct 1945 in Goshen, Elkhart Co., IN[7241]. He married **Elizabeth B. Jantzi**[7241] 04 Aug 1900 in Wilmont, Nobles, Minnesota[7241], daughter of Joseph Jantzi and Mattie Boshart. She was born 08 Oct 1883 in Waterloo Co., Ontario, Canada[7241], and died 29 Oct 1958 in Goshen, Elkhart Co., IN[7241].

Children of David Miller and Elizabeth Jantzi are:

4457   i.   Noah D.[9] Miller[7241], born 26 Oct 1900[7241,7242]; died 21 Oct 1965 in Goshen, Elkhart Co., IN[7242,7243]. He married Fannie Miller; born 21 Mar 1912; died 17 Jan 2003.

Notes for Noah D. Miller:
Birth: Oct. 26, 1900
Death: Oct. 21, 1965

Spouse: Fannie Miller (1912 - 2003)

Burial: Thomas Cemetery, Goshen, Elkhart Co., IN
Find A Grave Memorial# 61696154

More About Noah D. Miller:
Burial: Thomas Cemetery at Fair Haven Amish-Mennonite Church on State Road 4 between Goshen and[7243]
Social Security Number: 308-05-4910/[7244]

Notes for Fannie Miller:
Birth: Mar. 21, 1912
Death: Jan. 17, 2003

Spouse: Noah D. Miller (1900 - 1965)

Burial: Thomas Cemetery, Goshen, Elkhart Co., IN
Find A Grave Memorial# 61696207

4458   ii.   David D Miller[7245], born 28 Apr 1902[7245]; died 02 May 1903[7245].
4459   iii.   Nancy Miller[7245], born 08 Mar 1904 in Nobles, IN[7245].
4460   iv.   Mattie Miller[7245], born 14 Sep 1906 in IN[7245]; died 08 Oct 1987[7245].
4461   v.   Laura Kaufman[7245], born 15 Jan 1909 in Goshen, Elkhart Co., IN[7245].
4462   vi.   Clarence Miller[7245], born 01 Oct 1911[7245]; died 25 Jul 1939[7245].
4463   vii.   Alma Miller[7245], born 02 May 1914[7245]; died 02 Dec 1951[7245].

2500. Levi J.[8] Miller (Mary[7] Christner, Jacob[6], Christian[5], Peter[4], Christian[3], Christian[2], Christen[1]) was born 25 Sep 1881 in Elkhart Co., IN, and died 04 Jan 1959. He married **Mary Schrock** 07 Mar 1907. She was born 09 Feb 1889 in Elkhart Co, and died 25 Nov 1965.

Notes for Levi J. Miller:
The Descendants of John J. Christner, privately published February 1961, p. 11.

Levi is Old Order Amish.

Child of Levi Miller and Mary Schrock is:

+   4464   i.   Annon[9] Miller, born 28 Jan 1912 in Elkhart Co., IN; died 04 Mar 1996.

2502. Jacob J. C.[8] Miller (Mary[7] Christner, Jacob[6], Christian[5], Peter[4], Christian[3], Christian[2], Christen[1]) was born 01 Nov 1885 in Elkhart Co., IN, and died 07 Nov 1959[7246]. He married **Ada C. Miller** 02 Jan 1908 in

Lagrange, Lagrange Co., IN[7246], daughter of Christian Miller and Mary Bender Miller. She was born 19 Jul 1886 in Lagrange, Lagrange Co., IN[7246], and died 18 Feb 1963[7246].

Notes for Jacob J. C. Miller:
Ada is the daughter of Christian C. and Mary Bender Miller. He was Old Order Amish. Row 11 Plot 16.

More About Jacob J. C. Miller:
Burial: Clinton Union Cemetery Co Rd. 34 Elkhart Co Indiana
Residence: 01 Jun 1925, Age: 37; Relationship: Head/Rensselaer Ward 07, Rensselaer, NY[7246]

More About Ada C. Miller:
Burial: Millersburg, Elkhart Co., IN[7246]
Residence: 1930, Clinton, Elkhart, Indiana[7246]

Children of Jacob Miller and Ada Miller are:

4465   i.   Janet[9] Miller[7246], born Abt. 1905 in United States[7246].

More About Janet Miller:
Residence: 01 Jun 1925, Age: 20; Relationship: Stepdaughter/Rensselaer Ward 07, Rensselaer, NY[7246]

4466   ii.   Oba Miller[7246], born 11 May 1908 in Goshen, Elkhart Co., IN[7246]; died Jul 1972[7246].

More About Oba Miller:
Residence: 1910, Age in 1910: 1; Marital Status: Single; Relation to Head of House: Son/Clearspring, Lagrange Co., IN[7246]

4467   iii.   Clarence Jay Miller[7246], born 03 Aug 1909 in Lagrange, Lagrange Co., IN[7246]; died 29 Jun 1973 in Age: 64/Elkhart, Elkhart Co., IN[7246].

More About Clarence Jay Miller:
Burial: Cranberry (Venango County), Venango County, Pennsylvania, USA[7246]
Civil: IN[7246]
Residence: Bet. 1935 - 1993, Age: 26/Johnstown, NY[7246]

4468   iv.   Barbara J Miller Hochstedler[7246], born 31 May 1911 in Lagrange, Lagrange Co., IN[7246]; died 18 Jun 2004 in Age at Death: 93/Kokomo, Howard Co., IN[7246].

More About Barbara J Miller Hochstedler:
Burial: Plevna, Howard County, Indiana, USA[7246]
Residence: 1935, Liberty Township, Howard, Indiana[7246]

4469   v.   Mattie J. Miller[7246], born 15 Feb 1914 in Goshen, Elkhart Co., IN[7246]; died 20 Aug 1980 in Goshen, Elkhart Co., IN[7246].

More About Mattie J. Miller:
Residence: 1930, Age: 16; Marital Status: Single; Relation to Head of House: Daughter/Clinton, Elkhart, Indiana[7246]

4470   vi.   Olen Jacob Miller[7246], born 30 May 1918 in Goshen, Elkhart Co., IN[7246]; died 01 Sep 1993 in Goshen, Elkhart Co., IN[7246].

More About Olen Jacob Miller:
Residence: 1930, Age: 12; Marital Status: Single; Relation to Head of House: Son/Clinton, Elkhart, Indiana[7246]

4471   vii.   Nancy Alta Miller[7246], born 08 Mar 1922 in Elkhart, Elkhart Co., IN[7246]; died 28 Sep 2007[7246].

More About Nancy Alta Miller:
Residence: 1930, Age: 8; Marital Status: Single; Relation to Head of House: Daughter/Clinton, Elkhart, Indiana[7246]

4472   viii.   Lester J Miller[7246], born 07 Nov 1925 in Goshen, Elkhart Co., IN[7246]; died 23 Jan 2012 in Parkview

Lagrange Hospital/Lagrange, Lagrange, Indiana, USA[7246].

More About Lester J Miller:
Residence: 1930, Age: 4; Marital Status: Single; Relation to Head of House: Son/Clinton, Elkhart, Indiana[7246]

2504. Mary J.[8] Miller (Mary[7] Christner, Jacob[6], Christian[5], Peter[4], Christian[3], Christian[2], Christen[1]) was born 30 Jun 1889 in Goshen, Elkhart Co., IN[7247], and died 13 Mar 1926 in Lagrange Co., IN[7247]. She married **Samuel J. Kaufman**[7247] 21 Nov 1912 in Elkhart Co., IN[7247]. He was born 26 May 1884 in Newbury, Lagrange Co., IN[7247], and died 02 Dec 1969 in Kosciusko Co., IN[7247].

Children of Mary Miller and Samuel Kaufman are:

> 4473   i.   Elnora[9] Kaufman[7247], born 20 Sep 1902 in Shipshewana, Lagrange Co., IN[7247]; died 20 May 1986 in Elkhart Co., IN[7247].
>
> More About Elnora Kaufman:
> Social Security Number: 267-52-6298/[7247]
> SSN issued: Florida[7247]

> 4474   ii.   Ora Kaufman[7247], born 15 Oct 1904 in Shipshewana, Lagrange Co., IN[7247]; died 09 Jul 1905 in Shipshewana, Lagrange Co., IN[7247].
>
> 4475   iii.   Lizzie May Kaufman[7247], born 24 Mar 1906 in Shipshewana, Lagrange Co., IN[7247].
>
> 4476   iv.   Ida Irene Kaufman[7247], born 30 Apr 1909 in Shipshewana, Lagrange Co., IN[7247]; died 17 Feb 1984 in Goshen, Elkhart Co., IN[7247].
>
> More About Ida Irene Kaufman:
> Social Security Number: 303-40-5284/[7247]
> SSN issued: IN[7247]

> 4477   v.   Edward Kaufman[7247], born 13 Feb 1913 in Shipshewana, Lagrange Co., IN[7247]; died Dec 1913 in Shipshewana, Lagrange Co., IN[7247].
>
> 4478   vi.   Kaufman[7247], born 28 Mar 1914 in Shipshewana, Lagrange Co., IN[7247]; died 28 Mar 1914 in Shipshewana, Lagrange Co., IN[7247].
>
> 4479   vii.   Katie S. Kaufman[7247], born 30 Oct 1915 in Shipshewana, Lagrange Co., IN[7247]; died 30 Oct 1915 in Shipshewana, Lagrange Co., IN[7247].
>
> 4480   viii.   John S. Kaufman[7247], born 24 Jun 1917 in Shipshewana, Lagrange Co., IN[7247]; died 07 Mar 1946[7247].
>
> 4481   ix.   Kaufman[7247], born 13 Jan 1919 in Elkhart Co., IN[7247]; died 1919 in Elkhart Co., IN[7247].
>
> 4482   x.   Boy Kaufman[7247], born 11 Apr 1920[7247]; died in Elkhart Co., IN[7247].
>
> 4483   xi.   Fannie S. Kaufman[7247], born 29 Jul 1922[7247]; died 14 Feb 1923 in Elkhart Co., IN[7247].
>
> 4484   xii.   Kaufman[7247], born 23 Apr 1925[7247]; died 23 Apr 1925 in Elkhart Co., IN[7247].

2506. Mattie J.[8] Miller (Mary[7] Christner, Jacob[6], Christian[5], Peter[4], Christian[3], Christian[2], Christen[1]) was born 01 Jan 1896 in Reno Co., KS[7248], and died 17 Jul 1985 in Goshen, Elkhart Co., IN[7248]. She married **Andrew Yoder** 15 Jan 1914 in Reno Co., KS[7248], son of Joseph Yoder and Anna Hershberger. He was born 28 Aug 1892 in Lagrange Co., IN[7248], and died 09 May 1985 in Goshen, Elkhart Co., IN[7248].

Notes for Mattie J. Miller:
Andrew is the son of Joseph A. and Anna Hershberger Yoder.
Andrew born Aug 28, 1892 in Lagrange Co., IN and was Old Order Amish.

More About Mattie J. Miller:
Residence: 1930, Eden, Lagrange, Indiana, USA[7248]

More About Andrew Yoder:
Residence: 1930, Eden, Lagrange, Indiana, USA[7248]
Social Security Number: 308-40-0244/[7248]
SSN issued: Indiana, USA[7248]

Children of Mattie Miller and Andrew Yoder are:

4485   i.   Elmina A[9] Yoder[7248], born 16 Aug 1916 in Lagrange Co., IN[7248]; died 22 Jul 1982 in Congestive heart failure/Goshen, Elkhart Co., IN[7248].

        More About Elmina A Yoder:
        CauseOfDeath: Congestive heart failure/[7248]
        Residence: 1930, Eden, Lagrange, Indiana, USA[7248]

4486   ii. Katie Ann Yoder[7248], born 27 Oct 1918 in Lagrange Co., IN[7248]; died 01 Nov 1998 in Parkinson's and Massive Stroke/heart failure/Goshen, Elkhart Co., IN[7248].

        More About Katie Ann Yoder:
        CauseOfDeath: Parkinson's and Massive Stroke/heart failure/[7248]
        Residence: 1930, Eden, Lagrange, Indiana, USA[7248]
        Social Security Number: 312-56-5703/[7248]
        SSN issued: Indiana, USA[7248]

4487   iii. Freeman A Yoder[7248], born 19 Jul 1920 in Lagrange Co., IN[7248]; died 07 May 1993 in Heart Attack/Goshen, Elkhart Co., IN[7248].

        More About Freeman A Yoder:
        CauseOfDeath: Heart Attack/[7248]
        Residence: 1930, Eden, Lagrange, Indiana, USA[7248]
        Social Security Number: 306-20-5236/[7248]
        SSN issued: Indiana, USA[7248]

4488   iv. Truman A Yoder[7248], born 11 Nov 1922 in Lagrange Co., IN[7248]; died 30 Jan 1996 in Sarasota, Sarasota, Florida, USA[7248].

        More About Truman A Yoder:
        Residence: 1930, Eden, Lagrange, Indiana, USA[7248]

4489   v.   Alvin Yoder[7248], born 27 Jul 1926 in Lagrange Co., IN[7248]; died 06 Dec 1926 in Lagrange Co., IN[7248].

2515. Abner Ozias[8] Christner (Jacob J.[7], Jacob[6], Christian[5], Peter[4], Christian[3], Christian[2], Christen[1])[7249,7250] was born 09 May 1890 in Kalona, Washington Co., IA[7250], and died 11 Dec 1977 in Kalona, Washington Co., IA[7251]. He married **Charlotte Brenneman**[7251,7252,7253] 13 Nov 1921 in Kalona, Washington Co., IA[7254]. She was born 15 Mar 1888 in Kalona, Washington Co., IA[7254], and died 07 Nov 1960 in Kalona, Washington Co., IA[7255].

Notes for Abner Ozias Christner:
Conservative Mennonite. Abner died of a heart attack.

Birth: 1890
Death: 1977

Shares stone with Lottie; Parents of George, Alvin, Esther, Joseph

Parents:
Jacob Christner (1862 - 1939)
Fannie A. Yoder Christner (1861 - 1929)

Spouse: Lottie Christner (1888 - 1960)

Burial: Eash Cemetery, Johnson Co., IA

More About Abner Ozias Christner:
Burial: Eash Cemetery, Sharon Center, Johnson Co., IA
Residence: 01 Jan 1925, Sharon, Johnson Co., IA[7256]

Notes for Charlotte Brenneman:

Birth: 1888
Death: 1960

Shares stone with Abner; Parents of George, Alvin, Esther, Joseph

Spouse: Abner O. Christner (1890 - 1977)

Burial: Eash Cemetery, Johnson Co., IA

Charlotte, daughter of Joseph and Susan (Plank) Brenneman, was born Mar 15, 1888, in Johnson Co., IA; died of a heart attack at her farm home near Iowa City, IA Nov 7, 1960; aged 72 y. 7 m. 23 d. On Nov 13, 1921, she was married to Abner Christner, who survives. Also surviving are 3 sons and one daughter (George, Millersburg, OH; Alvin, IA City; Mrs. Esther Fuller, Crookston, MN; and Joseph, Iowa City), 22 grandchildren and 2 sisters (Sarah-Mrs. Eli Miller, Hicksville, OH; and Lizzie-Mrs. Monroe Miller, Sugarcreek, OH). She was a member of the Fairview Conservative Mennonite Church, where funeral services were held Nov 10, in charge of Morris Yoder and Mose Gingerich; interment in East Cemetery.

More About Charlotte Brenneman:
Burial: 10 Nov 1960, Eash Cemetery, Sharon Center, Johnson Co., IA
Residence: 1900, Hagarstown, Fayette, Illinois[7256]

Children of Abner Christner and Charlotte Brenneman are:
+   4490   i.   George[9] Christner, born 06 Dec 1922 in Iowa City Johnson Co., IA; died 18 Feb 2006 in New Philadelphia, Tuscarawas, OH.
+   4491   ii.   Alvin Christner, born 18 Apr 1924 in Kalona, Washington Co., IA; died 22 Nov 2003 in Abilene, Taylor Co., TX.
+   4492   iii.   Esther Christner, born 11 Sep 1925.
+   4493   iv.   Joseph Christner, born 24 Sep 1928 in Kalona, Washington Co., IA.

2516. Elam Josiah[8] Christner (Jacob J.[7], Jacob[6], Christian[5], Peter[4], Christian[3], Christian[2], Christen[1]) was born 16 Jan 1892 in Near Middlebury, Elkhart Co., IN[7257], and died 06 Sep 1969 in Kalona, Washington Co., IA. He married **Nettie E. Swartzendruber** 24 Jun 1926. She was born 14 May 1897 in Kalona, Johnson Co., IA[7258], and died 23 Apr 1988 in Kalona, Washington Co., IA[7258].

Notes for Elam Josiah Christner:
He had 2 foster children Helen married Lloyd Swartzendruber and Verna married William Diltz they had a son Billie Diltz. He was a member of the Lower Deer Creek Church with Robert K. Yoder and John Y. Swartzendruber Officiating.

Gospel Herald - Volume LXIII, Number 10 - March 10, 1970, page 239, 240

Christner.- Elam Josiah, son of Jacob J. and Fannie (Yoder) Christner, was born near Middiebury, Ind., Jan. 16, 1892; died at his home in Kalona, Iowa, Sept. 6, 1969; aged 77 y. 7 m. 21 d. On June 24, 1926, he was married to Nettie E. Swartzendruber, who survives. Also surviving are 4 children (Cecil, Eudora-Mrs. Henry Mullet, John, and Leo), 2 foster daughters (Helen-Mrs. Lloyd Swartzendruber and Verna-Mrs. William Diltz), 16 grandchildren, and 2 brothers (Abner and Gid). He was preceded in death by his parents, 3 brothers (Simon, Jess, and Anon), one sister (Lizzie-Mrs. Reuben Mast), and one grandson. He was a member of the Lower Deer Creek Church, where funeral services were held Sept. 9, with Robert K. Yoder and John Y. Swartzendruber officiating.

More About Elam Josiah Christner:
Burial: Lower Deer Creek Church Conservative Mennonite Church Cemetery, IA
Social Security Number: 479-18-9557/[7259]
SSN issued: IA[7259]

Notes for Nettie E. Swartzendruber:
Christner.- Nettie Ellen Swartzendruber, daughter of Simon C. and Mary (Kauffman) Swartzendruber, was born in Johnson Co., IA May 14, 1897; died at University Hospital, Iowa City, IA Apr. 23, 1988; aged 90 y. On June

24, 1926, she was married to Elam J. Christner, who died on Sept. 6, 1969. Surviving are 3 sons (Cecil, John, and Leo) and 3 daughters (Eudora Mullet, Helen Swartzendruber, and Verna Diltz). She was a member of Lower Deer Creek Mennonite Church, where funeral services were held on Apr. 27, in charge of Dean Swartzendruber and Orie Wenger; interment in Lower Deer Creek Cemetery.

More About Nettie E. Swartzendruber:
Burial: 27 Apr 1988, Lower Deer Creek Mennonite Church Cemetery
Social Security Number: 484-48-5215/[7260]
SSN issued: IA[7260]

Children of Elam Christner and Nettie Swartzendruber are:

	4494	i.	Verna[9] Christner, born in IA. She married Dietz.
	4495	ii.	Helen Christner. She married Swartzendruber.
+	4496	iii.	Cecil Edward Christner, born 26 Mar 1927 in Kalona, Washington Co., IA.
+	4497	iv.	Eudora Ann Christner, born 19 Aug 1929 in Kalona, Washington Co., IA.
+	4498	v.	John Lewis Christner, born 20 Apr 1932 in Kalona, Washington Co., IA.
+	4499	vi.	Leo Ray Christner, born 19 Jan 1937 in Wellman, IA.

2519. Gideon Andrew[8] Christner (Jacob J.[7], Jacob[6], Christian[5], Peter[4], Christian[3], Christian[2], Christen[1])[7261,7262] was born 25 Nov 1897 in Parnell, Iowa Co., IA[7263,7264], and died 26 Jul 1978 in Wellman, Washington Co., IA[7265]. He married **Hester K. Hochstedler**[7265,7266] 25 Oct 1922 in Washington Co., IA[7267], daughter of William Hochstedler and Susan Knepp. She was born 16 Oct 1900 in Kalona, Washington Co., IA[7267], and died 17 Mar 1981 in Wellman, Washington Co., IA[7267,7268].

Notes for Gideon Andrew Christner:
Gideon is a mennonite and a farmer near Wellman Iowa/// SS#427-14-9923 ISS MS

More About Gideon Andrew Christner:
Burial: Upper Deer Creek Conservative Mennonite Church Cemetery, Wellman, Washington Co., IA

Notes for Hester K. Hochstedler:

More About Hester K. Hochstedler:
Burial: Upper Deer Creek Mennonite Cemetery, Wellman, Washington Co., IA[7269]

Children of Gideon Christner and Hester Hochstedler are:

+	4500	i.	Susan Jean[9] Christner, born 24 Mar 1924 in Iowa City, Wright Co., IA.
	4501	ii.	Willard Leroy Christner, born 28 Aug 1925 in Wellman, Washington Co., IA[7270,7271]; died 06 Feb 2004 in Wellman, Washington Co., IA.

Notes for Willard Leroy Christner:
Willard is single.

The Mennonite, April 6, 2004, pages 25-27, Vol. 7, No. 7.

Christner, Willard 78, Wellman, Iowa, died Feb. 6. Parents: Gideon A. and Hester Hochstedler Christner. Funeral: Feb. 9 at Lower Deer Creek Mennonite Church, Kalona, IA.

More About Willard Leroy Christner:
Burial: Upper Deer Creek Mennonite Cemetery, Wellman, Washington Co., IA[7271]
SSN issued: IA[7272]

+	4502	iii.	Ada Marie Christner, born 06 Jan 1928 in Kalona, Washington Co., IA.
	4503	iv.	Anna Bell Christner, born 14 Jun 1931 in Kalona, Washington Co., IA. She married Richard Hoogenboon.
+	4504	v.	James Edward Christner, born 07 Jan 1936 in Wellman, IA.

2520. Simon Peter⁸ Christner (Jacob J.⁷, Jacob⁶, Christian⁵, Peter⁴, Christian³, Christian², Christen¹) was born 25 Mar 1900 in Wellman, IA, and died 15 Jun 1943. He married **Dorothy Adaline Visser**⁷²⁷³ 30 Oct 1925 in South Bend, IN. She was born 15 Apr 1906 in Holland, MI⁷²⁷³, and died 16 Jan 1995 in Age at Death: 88/Granger, St Joseph Co., IN⁷²⁷³.

Notes for Simon Peter Christner:
Buried:
80 feet south of the Bell Tower and 20 feet west. White flat stone and military marker.

More About Simon Peter Christner:
Burial: Silver Brook Cemetery off 31 Niles Michigan

Notes for Dorothy Adaline Visser:
Dorothy is the daughter of Arthur Lenard and Anna Sena VanDenBorsch Visser.

Web: Indiana and Michigan, Michiana Genealogical Cemetery Index, 1800-2010

Death Date: 16 Jan 1995
Birth Date: 15 Apr 1906

Buried: Silverbrook Cemetery, New, Nile Twp., Berrien Co., MI

More About Dorothy Adaline Visser:
Social Security Number: 312-20-6047/⁷²⁷³

Children of Simon Christner and Dorothy Visser are:

+ 4505   i.   Eugene Richard⁹ Christner, born 29 Jul 1927 in Mishawaka, St. Joseph Co., IN; died 27 Jun 2004 in Watervliet, Berrien Co., MI.
   4506   ii.   Fanny Christner, born 06 Jan 1928.
+ 4507   iii.   Marlene Grace Christner, born 19 Jan 1937 in Niles, Berrien Co., MI.
+ 4508   iv.   JoAnne Darlene Christner, born 02 Feb 1939 in Niles, Berrien Co., MI.
+ 4509   v.   Jack Leonard Christner, born 07 Oct 1940.

2521. Mary Elizabeth⁸ Christner (Jacob J.⁷, Jacob⁶, Christian⁵, Peter⁴, Christian³, Christian², Christen¹) was born 17 Aug 1902 in Iowa City, Wright Co., IA, and died 19 Mar 1926. She married **Reuben Mast**. He was born 11 Jul 1902, and died 25 Mar 1926.

More About Mary Elizabeth Christner:
Burial: Eash Cemetery, Sharon Center, Johnson Co., IA

Notes for Reuben Mast:
Reuben is the son of Elias N and Lucy Ann Weaver Mast. Reuben died after surgery for an appendectomy.

More About Reuben Mast:
Burial: Eash Cemetery, Sharon Center, Johnson Co., IA

Child of Mary Christner and Reuben Mast is:
   4510   i.   Fannie Edith⁹ Mast, born 17 Nov 1925.

         Notes for Fannie Edith Mast:
         Fannie was adopted by her uncle Anan Christner and her name was changed to Christner.

2523. Fanny Mae⁸ Christner (David J.⁷, Jacob⁶, Christian⁵, Peter⁴, Christian³, Christian², Christen¹) was born 12 Feb 1891 in Goshen, Elkhart Co., IN, and died 15 Jan 1921 in Age: 29/Shelbyville, Shelby Co., IL[7274]. She married **Menno M. Kauffman** 08 Dec 1918 in Shelbyville, Shelby Co., IL. He was born 02 Sep 1893, and died 10 Apr 1986[7275].

Notes for Fanny Mae Christner:
Birth: Feb 12, 1891
Death: Jan 15, 1921 - IL

Burial: Mount Hermon Cemetery, Shelbyville, Shelby Co., IL
Find A Grave Memorial# 75100123

More About Fanny Mae Christner:
Burial: 18 Jan 1921, Mt. Hermon A.M. Church Cemetery, Clarksville RD. off Route 66 near Shelbyville IL.
Occupation: Housewife/[7276]
Race: White/[7276]

Notes for Menno M. Kauffman:
Menno is the son of Moses M. and Susan Troyer Kauffman. He was a farmer.

More About Menno M. Kauffman:
Other-Begin: Elkhart Co.[7277]
Residence: Elkhart Co., IN[7277]

Child of Fanny Christner and Menno Kauffman is:
+   4511   i.   Freida[9] Kauffman, born 08 Nov 1920 in Shelbyville, Shelby Co., IL; died 07 Sep 1961.

2524. Daniel D.[8] Christner (David J.[7], Jacob[6], Christian[5], Peter[4], Christian[3], Christian[2], Christen[1]) was born 11 Jul 1892 in Goshen, Elkhart Co., IN[7278], and died 04 Feb 1979 in Alden, NY or Batavia, NY. He married **Alta Meyer** 18 Nov 1924 in Rapids, NY. She was born 09 Feb 1907 in Shipshewana, Elkhart Co., IN[7279], and died 06 Mar 1987 in Genesee Memorial Hospital Alden, New York.

Notes for Daniel D. Christner:
Daniel was a farmer SS# 051-24-1102 Iss. NY Last zip 14004 Mennonite

Gospel Herald - Volume 72, Number 10 - March 6, 1979, page 206.

Christner.- Daniel D., son of David and Lavina (Raber) Christner, was born in Goshen, Ind., July 11, 1892; died at Batavia, N.Y., Feb. 4, 1979; aged 86 y. On Nov. 18, 1923, he was married to Alta Meyers. Surviving are 2 sons Walter and Daniel Jr.), 5 daughters (Virginia-Mrs. Joseph Erb, Betty-Mrs. Paul Miller, Martha-Mrs. Clair Albrecht, Shirley-Mrs. Joseph Frey, and June-Mrs. Donald Risser), 24 grandchildren, 4 great-grandchildren, and 2 sisters (Mrs. Anna Brenneman and Lula-Mrs. Willis Guengerich). He was preceded in death by 3 sons (Theodore, Leo, and James). He was a member of Alden Mennonite Church, where funeral services were held on Feb. 7, in charge of Titus Kauffman and Richard Bender.

More About Daniel D. Christner:
Burial: Co. Line Union Cemetery, Alden., NY
Residence: Shelby Co., IL[7280]
Social Security Number: 051-24-1102/[7281]
SSN issued: NY[7281]

Notes for Alta Meyer:
Alta is the daughter of Samuel S and Emma Hooley Meyer.

Gospel Herald - Volume 80, Number 13 - March 31, 1987 - page 230

Christner, Alta Meyer, daughter of Samuel and Emma (Hooly) Meyer, was born in Indiana on Feb. 9, 1907; died in the Genesee Memorial Hospital on Mar. 6, 1987; aged 80 y. On Nov. 18, 1923, she was married to Daniel D. Christner, who died on Feb. 4, 1979. Surviving are 2 sons (Walter and Daniel, Jr.), 5 daughters (Virginia Erb, Betty Miller, Martha Albrecht, Shirley Frey, and June Risser), 23 grandchildren, 22 great-grandchildren, 2 sisters (Martha Leichti and Jenny Walker), and one brother (Nathan Meyer). She was preceded in death by 3 sons (Theodore, Leo, and James), one brother (Paul Meyer), and one grandson.

More About Alta Meyer:
Burial: Co. Line Union Cemetery, Alden., NY
Social Security Number: 099-38-6762/[7282]
SSN issued: NY[7282]

Children of Daniel Christner and Alta Meyer are:

	4512	i.	Theodore[9] Christner, born 13 Feb 1925 in Akron, NY; died 20 Feb 1925 in Akron, NY.
+	4513	ii.	Homer Walter Christner, born 16 Jan 1926 in Royalton, NY.
+	4514	iii.	Daniel Christner Jr., born 17 Jun 1927 in Clarence, NY; died 09 Aug 2010 in Naples, Collier Co., FL.
	4515	iv.	Leo David Christner, born 11 Nov 1928 in Pembroke, NY; died 07 Feb 1946.

Notes for Leo David Christner:
Developed Rickets making his back rounded, but then at the age of 17 he was the tallest in the family when he got extra teeth, the doctors gave him a spinal injection and he had a fatal reaction due to his enlarged thyroid glands.

More About Leo David Christner:
Burial: Co. Line Union Cemetery, Alden., NY

+	4516	v.	Virginia Aldean Christner, born 24 Dec 1929 in Pembroke, NY.
+	4517	vi.	Betty Lou Christner, born 26 Dec 1935 in Akron, NY.
+	4518	vii.	Martha Jane Christner, born 07 Jun 1937 in Akron, NY.
	4519	viii.	James Samuel Christner, born 03 Mar 1939 in Akron, NY; died 25 Jan 1947 in Akron, NY.

Notes for James Samuel Christner:
At the age of 7 he was struck by a car walking home from school and died. He died in his fathers arm's.

You can read more of this story in H. Walters book.

Homer Walter Christner is the author of the book, Our Immigrants, Christian and Elizabeth Christner's family Published by H. Walter Christner 2912 E. Forest Lake Drive Sarasota, FL 34232. Well written Many stories & pictures about family of Christian (2) brother of John Han's Christner.

The book can be seen at Goshen College, Goshen, Indiana.

More About James Samuel Christner:
Burial: Co. Line Union Cemetery, Alden., NY

| + | 4520 | ix. | Emma Shirley Christner, born 23 Nov 1940 in Akron, NY. |
| + | 4521 | x. | Vera June Christner, born 04 Aug 1943 in Akron, NY. |

2525. Anna Faye[8] Christner (David J.[7], Jacob[6], Christian[5], Peter[4], Christian[3], Christian[2], Christen[1]) was born 08 Jun 1894 in Goshen, Elkhart Co., IN[7283,7284,7285,7286,7287], and died 12 Jun 1983 in Kolona, Washington Co., IA[7288]. She married **Ephriam E. Brenneman**[7289] 14 Jun 1921 in Shelbyville, Shelby Co., IL, son of Benjamin Brenneman and Barbara Kauffman. He was born 25 May 1896 in Kalona, Washington Co., IA[7290], and died 29 Dec 1968 in Kolona, Washington Co., IA.

More About Anna Faye Christner:
Residence: 1900, Clinton, Elkhart Co., IN[7291]
Social Security Number: 480-80-1683/[7292]
SSN issued: Kalona, Washington Co., IA[7292]

Notes for Ephriam E. Brenneman:
Ephriam was a farmer, seed corn dealer and a telephone company director. He was a Mennonite.

More About Ephriam E. Brenneman:
Residence: 01 Jan 1925, Sharon, Johnson Co., IA[7293]

Children of Anna Christner and Ephriam Brenneman are:

4522   i.   David Benjamin[9] Brenneman.

4523   ii.   Virgil John Brenneman, born 27 Nov 1921 in Kolona, Washington Co., IA[7293,7294].

Notes for Virgil John Brenneman:
Virgil married Helen Elizabeth Good Nov 3, 1947. Helen is the daughter of Lewis Christian and Lois Eby Good. Helen born Nov 26, 1925.

More About Virgil John Brenneman:
Residence: 01 Jan 1925, Sharon, Johnson Co., IA[7295]

4524   iii.   Gaylord Henry Brenneman[7296], born 06 Mar 1923 in Kalona, Washington Co., IA[7297,7298,7299]; died 14 Jul 1974 in Tampa, Hillsborough Co., FL. He married Mary Katheryn Hostetler 25 Mar 1951; born 30 May 1931.

Notes for Gaylord Henry Brenneman:
Gaylord is a realtor. Mennonite.

More About Gaylord Henry Brenneman:
Residence: 01 Jan 1925, Sharon, Johnson Co., IA[7300]
Social Security Number: 481-22-5436/[7301]
SSN issued: IA[7301]

4525   iv.   Evan Elmer Brenneman, born 04 Mar 1924 in Kolona, Washington Co., IA[7302,7303]. He married Anna Miller 06 Jun 1948; born 22 Apr 1926.

Notes for Evan Elmer Brenneman:
Evan married Anna Miller June 6 1948. Anna born April 22 1926 daughter of Dan H and Katie Miller Miller.

More About Evan Elmer Brenneman:
Residence: 01 Jan 1925, Sharon, Johnson Co., IA[7304]

4526   v.   David Benjamin Brenneman, born 13 Jun 1925; died 24 Jul 1929.

4527   vi.   Sven G Brenneman[7305], born 1927[7305].

More About Sven G Brenneman:
Residence: 1930, Sharon, Johnson Co., IA[7305]

4528   vii.   Ivan Glenn Brenneman, born 15 Jul 1927 in Kolona, Washington Co., IA. He married Paula M. Zoebel 25 Feb 1948; born 26 Nov 1928.

Notes for Ivan Glenn Brenneman:
He is a city employee of Montrey, CA and a Methodist.

4529   viii.   Mary Magdalene Brenneman, born 11 Aug 1931 in Kolona, Washington Co., IA. She married Leslie Roy Gingerich 18 Mar 1953; born 27 Mar 1931.

Notes for Mary Magdalene Brenneman:
Mennonite.

4530   ix.   Mildred Faye Brenneman, born 16 Oct 1932 in Kalona, Washington Co., IA. She married John Edward Yoder 11 Oct 1953; born 03 Sep 1932.

Notes for Mildred Faye Brenneman:
Mennonite.

4531   x.   Milford Jay Brenneman, born 16 Oct 1932 in Kalona, Washington Co., IA. He married Kay Frances Rives[7306,7307] Dec 1965; born 26 Sep 1944 in Wilson, TX[7307,7308].

Notes for Milford Jay Brenneman:
daughter of James W. and Freddie Lorena Brown Rives.

4532   xi.   Lulu Jane Brenneman, born 01 Nov 1939 in Kalona, Washington Co., IA. She married Vigil Lynn Miller 27 Jun 1964; born 10 Jul 1940.

Notes for Lulu Jane Brenneman:
Virgil is a mail carrier Lulu a secretary.

Notes for Vigil Lynn Miller:
Parents of Virgil are Emery B. Miller & Mary Ellen Shetler.

2526. Joseph Davis[8] Christner (David J.[7], Jacob[6], Christian[5], Peter[4], Christian[3], Christian[2], Christen[1]) was born 08 Dec 1895 in Goshen, Elkhart Co., IN[7309], and died 01 Apr 1972 in Shelbyville, Shelby Co., IL. He married **Emma Eigsti**[7310] 28 Aug 1921 in Shelbyville, Shelby Co., IL. She was born 14 Sep 1900 in Fayette Co., IL[7311], and died 28 May 1980 in Roanoke, IL.

Notes for Joseph Davis Christner:
SS#;343-32-4649 Iss IL

Birth: Dec. 8, 1895
Death: Apr. 1, 1972

Spouse: Emma E. Christner (1900 - 1980)

Burial: Mount Hermon Cemetery, Shelbyville, Shelby Co., IL
Find A Grave Memorial# 75100483

More About Joseph Davis Christner:
Burial: Mt. Hermon A.M. Church Cemetery, Clarksville RD. off Route 66 near Shelbyville IL.
Social Security Number: 343-32-4649/[7312]
SSN issued: IL[7312]

Notes for Emma Eigsti:
Emma is the daughter of Christ and Mary Kennel Eigsti.

Birth: Sep. 14, 1900
Death: May 28, 1980 - IL

Spouse: Joe D. Christner (1895 - 1972)

Burial: Mount Hermon Cemetery, Shelbyville, Shelby Co., IL
Find A Grave Memorial# 75100505

More About Emma Eigsti:
Burial: Mt. Hermon A.M. Church Cemetery, Clarksville RD. off Route 66 near Shelbyville IL.
Residence: 1920, Shelbyville, Shelby Co., IL[7313]
Social Security Number: 322-56-6577/[7314]
SSN issued: IL[7314]

Children of Joseph Christner and Emma Eigsti are:
+   4533   i.   Christy Jean[9] Christner, born 15 May 1922 in Corfu, NY.
+   4534   ii.   Lovina Fern Christner, born 23 Sep 1923 in Pembroke, NY.
     4535   iii.   Mary Marie Christner, born 13 Dec 1924 in Pembroke, NY; died 17 Oct 1926.

More About Mary Marie Christner:
Burial: Old Pioneer Good Mennonite Cemetery, Greiner Rd., Clarence, NY

> 4536 iv. Gloria Ann Christner, born 21 Feb 1926 in Pembroke, NY.

> Notes for Gloria Ann Christner:
> Gloria is a housekeeper for Dr. and Mrs. Leonard Bernstein of San Diego., CA.

+ 4537 v. Luella Christner, born 09 May 1927 in Corfu, NY.
+ 4538 vi. Joseph Davis Christner Jr., born 14 May 1929 in Corfu, NY; died 01 Jul 1995 in Shelbyville, Shelby Co., IL.
+ 4539 vii. Barbara Elizabeth Christner, born 08 Mar 1931 in Shelbyville, IN.
+ 4540 viii. Franklin Delano Christner, born 18 Jun 1932 in Shelbyville, IN.
+ 4541 ix. Emma Josephine Christner, born 29 Sep 1934 in Shelbyville, IN.
+ 4542 x. Jacob Theodore Christner, born 20 Sep 1937 in Shelbyville, IN.

2527. David J.[8] Christner Jr. (David J.[7], Jacob[6], Christian[5], Peter[4], Christian[3], Christian[2], Christen[1]) was born 22 Jan 1899 in Goshen, Elkhart Co., IN[7315], and died 23 Jul 1956 in Goshen, Elkhart Co., IN. He married **Caroline Burkholder** 23 Sep 1928 in Middlebury, Elkhart Co., IN. She was born 11 Aug 1903 in Nappanee, Elkhart Co., IN, and died 03 Dec 1995 in Elkhart Co. IN.

Notes for David J. Christner Jr.:
Some sources have his death as July 27 1956.

Christner, David son of David and Lavine (Raber) Christner was born at Goshen, IN on Jan 22, 1899; departed this life at the Elkhart General Hospital on Jul 23, 1956; aged 57 y. 6 m. 1 d. He was married to Caroline Burkholder at Corfu, NY on Sep 3, 1928. This union was blessed with 3 sons and 3 daughters. One son, Elmer Joseph, preceded him in death on Sept. 18, 1952. Surviving are his wife, 5 children (Jonas, Fort Wayne, Ind.; Edna-Mrs. Floyd Miller, Goshen, IN; Viola Fern, Freda and John David, all at home), 2 grandchildren, 3 sisters and 2 brothers (Laura-Mrs. Daniel Yoder, Mendon, MI; Anna-Mrs. Ephraim Brenneman, Kalona, IA; Lula-Mrs. Willis Guengerich, Greenwood, DE, Daniel, Alden, NY and Joseph, Shelbyville, IL). On Sunday, Jul 15, after returning from church, he went out to investigate an electrical power failure, when he accidentally came in contact with a high voltage wire which left him in a crucial condition for 8 days. During this period of intense suffering, about which he never complained, he was in almost constant prayer. In early youth he accepted Christ as his personal Saviour and united with the Conservative Mennonite Church of which he was a faithful member until his departure. Services were conducted at the Pleasant Grove Church on July 26 with Home Miller and Clarence Yoder in charge. Interment was made at the Clinton union Cemetery at Goshen.

More About David J. Christner Jr.:
Burial: Clinton Union Chapel Cemetery near Goshen Indiana N41°34.072'xW85°44.270'
Residence: Shelby Co., IL[7315]

Notes for Caroline Burkholder:
Caroline (Carolina) is the daughter of Jonas and Amanda Schmucker Burkholder. Married at maybe Corfu NY. She was a homemaker and member of Bethel Conservative Mennonite Church Nappanee IN. Burial at Clinton Union Cemetery Nappanee IN.

More About Caroline Burkholder:
Burial: Clinton Union Chapel Cemetery near Goshen Indiana N41°34.072'xW85°44.270'

Children of David Christner and Caroline Burkholder are:
+ 4543 i. Jonas Edwin[9] Christner, born 27 Jul 1929 in Corfu, NY.
+ 4544 ii. Edna Mae Christner, born 12 Aug 1930 in Corfu, NY.
  4545 iii. Viola Ferne Christner, born 19 Jan 1932 in Pembrook, NY; died 30 Sep 1996 in Wakarusa, IN or Goshen, IN.

Notes for Viola Ferne Christner:
Viola is an elementary school teacher having taught at Middlebury and Clinton Christian Schools for 25 years,plus has a business in computer sales and training.She graduated from Bethany Christian High School, received her bachelor's degree from Goshen College and her Master's degree from Western Michigan University.

Burial in Bethel Cemetery By Bethel Conservative Mennonite Church, Nappanee, IN. She also pieced Quilts for Lolly's in Shipshewana, IN.

More About Viola Ferne Christner:
Burial: Bethel Conservative Mennonite Church Cemetery near Nappanee Indiana

+   4546   iv.   Freida Lavina Christner, born 04 Sep 1934 in Pembrook, NY.
     4547   v.   Elmer Joseph Christner, born 24 Aug 1938 in Corfu, NY; died 18 Sep 1952 in Northern Indiana Childrens Hospital at South Bend, IN.

Notes for Elmer Joseph Christner:
Christner, Elmer Joseph, son of David and Caroline (Burkholder) Christner was born at Corfu, N. Y., Aug. 29, 1938; passed away at the Northern Indiana Children's Hospital, South Bend, Sept. 18, 1952; aged 14 y. 20 d. On the evening of Sept. 14, after having attended church services, he became ill with polio. He is survived by his parents, 2 brothers (Jonas, Fort Wayne, Ind.; and John, at home), 3 sisters (Edna, Viola, and Freida, all at home), one grandmother and a number of other relatives and friends. Funeral services were held at the Griner Church, Middlebury, Ind., Sept. 21, in charge of John J. S. Yoder, Clarence Yoder, and Samuel T. Eash. Burial was made in the Clinton Union Chapel Cemetery, Goshen, IN.

More About Elmer Joseph Christner:
Burial: Row 7 Plot1/Clinton Union Chapel Cemetery, near Goshen, IN
Cause of Death: Polio

     4548   vi.   John David Christner, born 23 Jul 1946 in Goshen, Elkhart Co., IN.

Notes for John David Christner:
John graduated from Goshen college in 1969. Masters degree from Indiana University in 1973. 4th grade school teacher at Fairfield Comm. Schools since 1969. Last address 1255 Camden Ct. Goshen, IN 46526

2528. Lovina Lulu[8] Christner (David J.[7], Jacob[6], Christian[5], Peter[4], Christian[3], Christian[2], Christen[1]) was born 10 Feb 1903 in Goshen, Elkhart Co., IN, and died 28 Aug 1995 in Greenwood, DE. She married **Willis Guengerich** 21 Sep 1924[7316]. He was born 22 May 1900 in Centralia, Audrain Co., MO[7316,7317], and died 04 Jun 1980 in Milford, DE.

Notes for Lovina Lulu Christner:
Guengerich, Lulu Lovina Christner, 92, Sarasota, FL born Feb. 10, 1903, Goshen, IN to David and Lovina Reber Christner. Died: Aug. 28, 1995, Greenwood, DE of a stroke. Survivors-children: Vivian Zehr, Grant, Owen, Inez Embleton; 19 grandchildren, 30 great-grandchildren. Predeceased by: Willis Guengerich (husband). Congregational membership: Sarasota Mennonite Church. Funeral and burial: Aug. 30, Greenwood Mennonite Church by Owen Guengerich and Robert O. Zehr.

More About Lovina Lulu Christner:
Burial: 30 Aug 1995, Greenwood Mennonite Church, Greenwood, DE
Residence: 1930, Pembroke, Genesee Co., NY[7318]

Notes for Willis Guengerich:
Willis is the son of Elmer and Magdalena Guengerich. Willis is a farmer.

More About Willis Guengerich:
Residence: 1930, Pembroke, Genesee Co., NY[7318]

Social Security Number: 078-03-8543/*7319*
SSN issued: NY*7319*

Children of Lovina Christner and Willis Guengerich are:

4549   i.   Infant Son[9] Guengerich*7320*, born 27 Nov 1925 in Kalona, , Iowa*7320*; died 27 Nov 1925 in Kalona, , Iowa*7320*.

4550   ii.   Grant A. Guengerich, born 08 Mar 1929 in Lockport, NY. He married Ella Troyer 28 Nov 1948.

          Notes for Grant A. Guengerich:
          Grant is a contractor appraiser and Ella is a homemaker.

4551   iii.   Vivian M. Guengerich, born 08 Mar 1929 in Lockport, NY. She married Zehr.

          Notes for Vivian M. Guengerich:
          Vivian married Robert O Zehr on Mar 25 1953
          Robert is the son of Vernon and Vera Schrock Zehr
          Vivian is a registered nurse
          Robert is a pastor

4552   iv.   Owen Guengerich, born 09 Aug 1934 in Lockport, NY.

          Notes for Owen Guengerich:
          Owen married Twila Swartzentruber on Dec 28 1954
          Twila born Jan 5 1936 daughter of Eli and Amelia   Swartzentruber
          Owen is a minister
          Twila is owner/manager of a store

4553   v.   Inez Guengerich, born 03 Dec 1935 in Lockport, NY; died 09 Jan 2010 in DE*7320*. She married Merle Embleton 05 Oct 1956; born 06 Mar 1936.

          Notes for Inez Guengerich:
          Inez and Merle own a restaurant and are manufacturers of cultured marble

2530. Laura D.[8] Christner (Joseph[7], Jacob[6], Christian[5], Peter[4], Christian[3], Christian[2], Christen[1])*7321* was born 22 Sep 1887 in Goshen, Elkhart Co., IN*7321*, and died 21 Apr 1961 in Sturgis, St. Joseph Co., MI*7321*. She married **Daniel L. Yoder** 07 Feb 1907 in Goshen, Elkhart Co., IN. He was born 24 Dec 1884 in Arthur, IL.

More About Laura D. Christner:
Residence: 1920, Lowe, Moultrie, Illinois*7321*

Notes for Daniel L. Yoder:

More About Daniel L. Yoder:
Religion: Amish/

Children of Laura Christner and Daniel Yoder are:

4554   i.   David D.[9] Yoder, born 06 Jan 1908 in Arthur, IL. He married Mary D. Yoder; born 13 Apr 1911 in White Cloud, Newaygo Co., MI.

          Notes for David D. Yoder:
          Mary D. Yoder is the daughter of Joe and Susan Hostetler Yoder. He was Old Order Amish and a farmer.

+   4555   ii.   Clara Caroline Yoder, born 04 Jul 1909 in Arthur, IL; died 02 Apr 2000 in Carriage Manor Nursing center Goshen IN..

4556   iii.   Bessie Mae Yoder, born 27 May 1911 in Arthur, IL; died 25 Oct 1966 in Ft.Wayne, IN. She married Raymon Rappe 05 Sep 1946; born 30 May 1909.

Notes for Bessie Mae Yoder:
Bessie died as the result of an auto accident.

\+   4557   iv.   George D. Yoder, born 14 Feb 1913 in Arthur, IL; died 16 Sep 1984.

4558   v.   Not Named Yoder, born 11 Nov 1914 in Arthur, IL; died 11 Nov 1914 in Lagrange Co., IN.

\+   4559   vi.   Virgil D. Yoder, born 11 Nov 1915 in Arthur, IL; died 01 Sep 2002 in 28340 Spring Creek Road Mendon, MI.

\+   4560   vii.   Moses D. Yoder, born 16 Sep 1917.

4561   viii.   Mahlon D. Yoder, born 20 Feb 1919 in Arthur, IL; died 04 Apr 2002 in Sarasota, Sarasota Co., FL. He married Mary J. Yoder 16 Feb 1941; born 28 Feb 1919; died 08 Jun 1984.

Notes for Mahlon D. Yoder:
Mary daughter of Jonas J. and Anna Bontrager Yoder. He is Mennonite.

More About Mahlon D. Yoder:
Burial: Miller Cemetery Goshen.IN

\+   4562   ix.   Mirrell D. Yoder, born 16 Feb 1921 in Arthur, IL; died 20 Jun 2005 in Sarasota, Sarasota Co., FL.

4563   x.   Lloyd D. Yoder, born 29 Jan 1923 in Arthur, IL. He married Mattie Mae Miller 12 Nov 1944; born 06 Jan 1917; died in Lagrange Co., IN.

Notes for Lloyd D. Yoder:
Mattie is the daughter of Emmanuel P. and Elizabeth Miller Miller.

4564   xi.   Jerry D. Yoder, born 30 Sep 1925 in Arthur, IL. He married Alma Hochstetler 17 May 1945; born 03 May 1928.

Notes for Jerry D. Yoder:
Alma is the daughter of Tobias and Martha Troyer Hochstetler. He is a farmer.

Notes for Alma Hochstetler:
The Descendants of John J. Christner, privately published February 1961, pp. 53, 54.

2538. James Blaine[8] Christner (John Hubert[7], Daniel S.[6], Christian[5], Peter[4], Christian[3], Christian[2], Christen[1])[7322] was born 13 Dec 1892 in NE[7322], and died 11 Sep 1976 in Shamrock, Wheeler Co., TX[7322]. He married **Donna Ruby Vaughan**[7322]. She was born 26 Feb 1906 in AR[7322], and died 03 Apr 1988 in Shamrock, Wheeler Co., TX[7322].

Notes for James Blaine Christner:
Birth: Dec 13, 1892
Death: Sep 1976

J.B. graduated from the University of Texas with a Masters Degree in geology.

Parents: John Hubert Christner (1860 - 1941)

Children: MacGregor Vaughan Christner (1933 - 2003)

Spouse: Donna Ruby Vaughan Christner (1906 - 1988)

Burial: Shamrock Cemetery, Shamrock, Wheeler Co., TX
Plot: Blk-G2, Lot 54, Sp 8

More About James Blaine Christner:
Residence: 1930, Lockhart, Caldwell, Texas[7322]

Notes for Donna Ruby Vaughan:
Birth: Jan 6, 1906 - Lockesburg, Sevier Co., AR
Death: Jul 8, 1988 - Shamrock, Wheeler Co., TX

Ruby graduated from the University of Texas with a Bachelors of Science degree in geology. One of the first women to obtain that degree from UT.

Parents:
Hal Hugh Vaughan (1879 - 1966)
Leila Clyde Knox Vaughan (1881 - 1940)

Spouse: James Blaine Christner (1892 - 1976)

Children: MacGregor Vaughan Christner (1933 - 2003)

Burial: Shamrock Cemetery, Shamrock, Wheeler Co., TX
Plot: Blk-G2, Lot 54, Sp 7

More About Donna Ruby Vaughan:
Residence: 1930, Lockhart, Caldwell, Texas[7322]

Child of James Christner and Donna Vaughan is:
    4565   i.   MacGregor Vaughan[9] Christner[7322], born 23 Jan 1933 in Ausitn, Travis Co., TX[7322,7323]; died 11 Oct 2003 in San Antonio, Bexar Co., TX[7324].

        Notes for MacGregor Vaughan Christner:
        Birth: Jan. 23, 1933
        Austin, Travis Co., TX
        Death: Oct. 11, 2003
        San Antonio, Bexar Co., TX

        "Seeing is believing." For many, those words simply represent a motto. But for MacGregor Vaughan Christner, it summarized in every way who he was. He was modest, quiet and observant, taking in everything around him and always thinking before acting. He was a realist, someone who was efficient and practical in everything he did. He was a friendly person who truly cared about those around him.

        Mac was born on 23 January 1933 at Breckinridge Hospital in Austin, Texas. He was the son of James Blaine Christner and Donna Ruby Vaughan Christner. Raised in Shamrock, Texas, he was brought up to be tolerant and trustworthy. His mother named him after his paternal Great Grandfather McGregor DeGarmo. As a child, he learned to be conscientious, responsible and punctual. These were all traits that he would carry with him throughout his life.

        As a young boy, Mac was always aware of how others around him felt and this quality served him well. With a deep capacity to tolerate the feelings of others, Mac was generally able to avoid conflicts. It seemed as if Mac was the family member who was always working to keep stress at bay. Preferring a quiet environment where he could concentrate, Mac also had the ability to relate well with his family and friends. Mac was raised with two siblings. He had one older brother, John Hal, and one younger brother Tom Henry. Mac was constantly involved in activities with his family. Mac and his siblings had the typical rivalries while growing up but they deeply cared for each other and shared many life experiences over the years.

        Growing up, Mac was one of those children who didn't need to be in the center of a whirlwind of activity. He was content to entertain himself. Mac was never pushy when it came to games and other activities, but rather, he was able to enjoy the pure fun these could bring. In just about everything he did as a child, Mac was intent on pleasing both the adults and the other children around him. Mac took part in a number of activities as a child. He took part in working on the family's dairy farm. He was a member of Future Farmers of America. In his spare time he liked hunting and fishing. Mac's memorable achievements included competing in FFA events.

        Mac enjoyed learning. He always had a great memory and was particularly skilled at retaining factual information. Mac was generally quiet in class, learning best through observation. He often showed great concentration and was competent at completing the tasks at hand. Good with details, Mac was painstaking and accurate in his efforts. All of these talents culminated in a successful high school career. He graduated from Shamrock High School in 1951. Mac enjoyed some courses more than others, having favorite subjects and teachers. His favorite class in high school was math.

He attended Texas A&M University in 1951 but left before graduation to join the Army. Mac was a member of the Corp of Cadets.

Most folks would say that Mac was shy until they got to know him. Those who were privileged to know him well learned that he was a solid, good friend. Mac was reluctant to generalize about people, and he based his friendships on his personal experiences. Because of this, Mac best trusted those people that he truly knew. He was concerned about how those around him felt, and he always seemed to uncover the positive side of people. He could relate to others and had the ability to see their point of view, to "walk a mile in their shoes," as the saying goes. The friends that he made, Mac kept. While growing up, some of his best friends were his brothers John Hal and Tom. Later in life, he became friends with Mary Gibson, Mark Frankenberry, Mike Gomez and most of the people in Wheeler, Texas.

Mac was a good father to his children. He had "old fashioned" parental values and could handle typical family conflicts in a fair and calm manner. Because he trusted emotions, Mac was reluctant to force issues and used gentle persuasion to resolve situations. In this way he seemed to radiate an aura of warmth and caring to those around him, always thinking before acting. In addition, Mac was a master planner. No matter how hectic life around him might be, he seemed to know and track everyone's schedule. Mac was blessed with two sons, MacGregor Vaughan Jr. and Jeff. He was also blessed with twelve grandchildren, Lea, Kathryn Azile Vaughan, Kevin, Kate, Darcie, Jeremy MacGregor Faulkner, Darius Charles MacBeth, Quentin George DeGarmeaux, Shaylee Nicole Carson, Chesney, Emily and Katie.

If you gave Mac a deadline, he would meet it. At work, Mac was always on task. Without hesitation, Mac could adhere to any assignment and see it through to its completion. His primary occupation was a cowboy. He was employed with Brainard Cattle Company and Christner Brother's Ranch. He was able to quickly grasp concrete ideas and could organize and plan the best way to accomplish things with remarkable consistency. Mac was good at staying on track and was considerate in listening to what others had to say. In this way, Mac had at true gift for being able to come up with practical resolutions to difficult problems.

Mac was an Army veteran. He seemed to thrive on the routines offered up by the military. Being a literal thinker with a calm exterior helped him handle the rigors of the military. He was stationed in El Paso during the Korean Conflict. Through his hard work and dedication, he achieved the rank of staff sergeant.

Mac liked to experience things first hand, in addition to simply learning about them. This quality influenced Mac's choice of leisure time activities. A methodical and patient worker, Mac preferred to set aside uninterrupted time to work on his hobbies. His favorite pursuits were water skiing, golf, riding motorcycles, fishing and working on cars.

Mac loved music and movies. His favorite artists included Willie Nelson, Ray Price, Waylon Jennings, Hank Williams, Hank Jr., Dean Martin, Frank Sinatra, Johnny Cash, and Jerry Jeff Walker. His favorite actors included John Wayne, Clint Eastwood, and Sophia Loren.

While thorough and measured in his approach to things, Mac often liked to physically do things rather than just think about them. He was like that with sports. Recreational sports included golf, fishing and water skiing. He was an expert mechanic and could fix anything that had a motor. He also enjoyed watching his favorite teams whenever he got the opportunity. Tops on his list were Longhorn football, the Dallas Cowboys, golf (Arnold Palmer and Ben Crenshaw) and auto racing. He enjoyed a cold Coors beer when appropriate and loved to relax in his swimming pool.

Due to his excellent organizational skills, Mac was a welcome addition to the professional and community organizations to which he belonged. Mac could bring established, successful methods to the discussion table, along with a generous helping of common sense. Mac was good at making and keeping schedules and never got bogged down in unnecessary details. In high school, Mac was a member of the Future Farmers of America. In college, Mac joined the Corp of Cadets. Throughout his later years, Mac was an active member of the VFW, American Motorcycle Association, NRA, Texas Exes and the Longhorn Foundation.

Mac was active in the community. He was practical and grounded and based his decisions on first hand experience. He was responsible and liked working to achieve results rather than just chattering about possibilities. Mac was a member of the Wheeler Volunteer Ambulance Service.

Anyone who traveled or went on vacation with Mac had smooth sailing. It was often taken for granted that he was the trip planner. He would start early and examine all of the possibilities, selecting the best and most effective options. Favorite vacations included Lake Travis, Red River, New Mexico, and Colorado.

Mac had His bird dog Ben Bird, who was his best friend for 10 years. Mac was as loyal to his pets as they were to him.

Mac passed away on 11 October 2003 at the Veterans Hospital in San Antonio, TX. Mac fought a brave lonely battle against Alzheimers. He was predeceased by his parents, his brother Tom Henry and a granddaughter Natalie Kate. He was survived by his children MacGregor Vaughan and Jeff, his 11 grandchildren and his brother John Hal. One of his grandsons proudly carries MacGregor as his middle name. Services were held at the McIntire-Christner Ranch in Texas. Mac was laid to rest in McIntire-Christner Cemetery.

It is said that some people can't see the forest for the trees. Mac was able to focus on each individual tree, tending to its needs, thus making the forest stronger as a whole. Mac was a trustworthy, pragmatic and sympathetic person, the kind of man to whom everyone was drawn. He was thorough and practical. Mac Christner was very literal with his words. You always knew where you stood with Mac. He will be missed. MacGregor Vaughan Christner

Parents:
James Blaine Christner (1892 - 1976)
Donna Ruby Vaughan Christner (1906 - 1988)

Burial: McIntire-Christner Cemetery, Miami, Roberts Co., TX

More About MacGregor Vaughan Christner:
SSN issued: TX[7325]

2540. Arthur George[8] **Christner** (Michael M.[7], Daniel S.[6], Christian[5], Peter[4], Christian[3], Christian[2], Christen[1])[7326,7327] was born 19 Feb 1891 in NE[7328,7329], and died 28 Dec 1976 in Wauneta, Chase Co., NE[7330,7331]. He married **Caroline A. "Carrie" Faulkner**[7332,7333]. She was born 24 Jan 1892 in IL[7334,7335], and died 30 Jul 1972[7335].

Notes for Arthur George Christner:
Birth: Feb. 19, 1891
Death: Dec. 28, 1976

Spouse: Caroline A. Faulkner Christner (1892 - 1972)

Burial: Meadow Lawn Cemetery, Hamlet, Hayes Co., NE

More About Arthur George Christner:
Arrival: 1874[7336]
Residence: 1920, Antelope, Hayes, Nebraska[7337,7338,7339]

Notes for Caroline A. "Carrie" Faulkner:
Birth: Jan. 24, 1892
Death: Jul. 30, 1972

Spouse: Arthur George Christner (1891 - 1976)

Burial: Meadow Lawn Cemetery, Hamlet, Hayes Co., NE

More About Caroline A. "Carrie" Faulkner:
Residence: 1930, Antelope, Hayes, Nebraska[7339]

Child of Arthur Christner and Caroline Faulkner is:

4566   i.   Warren Richard[9] Christner[7339], born 24 Feb 1921[7339]; died 03 Nov 1974[7339]. He married Elaine Irene Hoffke[7339] 01 Dec 1950[7339]; born 25 Aug 1928 in Grand Island, Hall Co., NE[7339]; died 27 May 2002 in Wauneta, Chase Co., NE[7339].

Notes for Warren Richard Christner:
Birth: Feb 24, 1921 - Wauneta, Chase Co., NE
Death: Nov 3, 1974

Son of Arthur and Caroline (Faulker) Christner.

Spouse: Elaine Irene Noffke Christner (1928 - 2002)

Burial: Riverside Cemetery, Wauneta, Chase Co., NE
Plot: 133-4-1
Find A Grave Memorial# 37608239

More About Warren Richard Christner:
Residence: 1930, Antelope, Hayes, Nebraska[7339]

Notes for Elaine Irene Hoffke:
Birth: Aug 25, 1928
Death: May 17, 2002

Marriage 2: Lyle Foth

Parents:
Henry Noffke (1897 - 1985)
Meta Quandt Noffke (1900 - 1985)

Spouse: Warren Richard Christner (1921 - 1974)

Burial: Riverside Cemetery, Wauneta, Chase Co., NE
Plot: 133-4-2
Find A Grave Memorial# 37608257

2547. Jason Oliver[8] Christner (Daniel Lincoln[7], Daniel S.[6], Christian[5], Peter[4], Christian[3], Christian[2], Christen[1]) was born 24 Feb 1898, and died 22 May 1990 in Hayes Co., NE[7340]. He married **Anna Jane Barnett**[7340]. She was born 30 Nov 1901, and died 10 Apr 1971 in Hamlet, NE[7340].

Notes for Jason Oliver Christner:
Birth: Feb 24, 1898
Death: May 22, 1990

Children: David Christner (1930 - 1930)

Spouse: Anna Jane Barnett Christner (1901 - 1971)

Burial: Meadow Lawn Cemetery, Hamlet, Hayes Co., NE

More About Jason Oliver Christner:
Residence: 1900, Hayes Center, Hayes Co., NE[7340]

Notes for Anna Jane Barnett:
Birth: Nov 30, 1901

Death: Apr 7, 1971

Children: David Christner (1930 - 1930)

Spouse: Jason Oliver Christner (1898 - 1990)

Burial: Meadow Lawn Cemetery, Hamlet, Hayes Co., NE

More About Anna Jane Barnett:
Residence: 1930, Swan Lake, Hayes Co., NE[7340]

Child of Jason Christner and Anna Barnett is:

4567   i.   David[9] Christner, born 05 Jul 1930 in Hayes Co., NE[7340]; died 09 Jul 1930 in Hayes Co., NE[7340].

> Notes for David Christner:
> Birth: Jul. 6, 1930
> Death: Jul. 9, 1930
>
> Parents:
> Jason Oliver Christner (1898 - 1990)
> Anna Jane Barnett Christner (1901 - 1971)
>
> Burial: Meadow Lawn Cemetery, Hamlet, Hayes Co., NE

2548. Clarence Herbert[8] Christner (Daniel Lincoln[7], Daniel S.[6], Christian[5], Peter[4], Christian[3], Christian[2], Christen[1])[7341,7342,7343] was born 30 Jan 1900 in NE[7344], and died 27 Jun 1977 in Wauneta, Chase Co., NE[7344]. He married **Frieda Maud Ochs**[7345]. She was born 1904 in NE[7345], and died 1970 in Chase County Hospital/Imperial, NE[7345].

Notes for Clarence Herbert Christner:
Birth: Jan. 30, 1900
Death: Jun. 27, 1970

Spouse: Frieda Maud Ochs Christner (1903 - 1970)

Burial: Riverside Cemetery, Wauneta, Chase Co., NE
Find A Grave Memorial# 37414855

More About Clarence Herbert Christner:
Residence: 1910, Government, Hayes Co., NE[7345,7346]

Notes for Frieda Maud Ochs:
Birth: Aug. 4, 1903
Death: Jun. 27, 1970

Spouse: Clarence Christner (1900 - 1970)

Burial: Riverside Cemetery, Wauneta, Chase Co., NE
Find A Grave Memorial# 37414905

More About Frieda Maud Ochs:
Residence: 1930, Ough, Dundy Co., NE[7347]

Children of Clarence Christner and Frieda Ochs are:

+   4568   i.   Dean L.[9] Christner, born 17 Mar 1926 in NE; died 12 Mar 1991 in Carbondale, Garfield Co., CO.
    4569   ii.   La Rue N. Christner[7348], born 19 Mar 1926 in NE[7348]; died 19 Nov 1997 in Carbondale, Garfield Co., CO[7348]. She married Harry Gunderson[7349] 22 Dec 1944[7349]; born 05 Apr 1915; died 19 Jun 1950 in buried Wauneta, NE/[7349].

Notes for La Rue N. Christner:
Birth: Mar 19, 1926
Death: Nov 19, 1997

Spouse: Harry John Gunderson (1915 - 1950)

Burial: Riverside Cemetery, Wauneta, Chase Co., NE
Find A Grave Memorial# 50151643

More About La Rue N. Christner:
Residence: 1993, Carbondale, CO[7350]

Notes for Harry Gunderson:
Birth: Apr 5, 1915
Death: Jun 19, 1950

Spouse: LaRue N. Christner Gunderson (1926 - 1997)

Burial: Riverside Cemetery, Wauneta, Chase Co., NE
Find A Grave Memorial# 50151644

2550. Richard Earl[8] Christner (Daniel Lincoln[7], Daniel S.[6], Christian[5], Peter[4], Christian[3], Christian[2], Christen[1])[7351,7352] was born 29 Sep 1902[7353], and died 15 Apr 1985 in McCook, Red Willow Co., NE[7354]. He married **Myrtle Lavern Polly**[7354] 05 Aug 1925 in Chase Co., NE[7354]. She was born 01 Sep 1905 in Wauneta, Chase Co., NE[7354], and died 13 Aug 1929 in Rochester, Olmsted Co., MN[7354].

More About Richard Earl Christner:
Residence: 1930, Swan Lake, Hayes Co., NE[7354]
Social Security Number: 522-50-0028/[7355]
SSN issued: CO[7355]

Child of Richard Christner and Myrtle Polly is:
    4570   i.   Donna[9] Christner, born 1926.

2565. Ava[8] Christner (Joseph J.[7], Daniel S.[6], Christian[5], Peter[4], Christian[3], Christian[2], Christen[1]) was born 29 Sep 1893 in NE[7356], and died 11 Oct 1935 in North Platte, Lincoln Co., NE[7356]. She married **Samuel Smith Stinnette**[7356]. He was born 25 Dec 1876 in Osceola, St. Clair, MO[7356].

More About Ava Christner:
Residence: 1930, Wauneta, Chase Co., NE[7356]

More About Samuel Smith Stinnette:
Residence: 1930, Wauneta, Chase Co., NE[7356]

Child of Ava Christner and Samuel Stinnette is:
    4571   i.   Lola Marie[9] Stinnette[7356], born 23 Oct 1916 in Wauneta, Chase Co., NE, United States[7356]; died 05 Apr 1996 in Wauneta, Chase Co., NE, United States[7356].

                More About Lola Marie Stinnette:
                Residence: 1920, Frenchman, Hayes Co., NE[7356]

2586. Elizabeth J.[8] Christner (Joseph B. "Just"[7], John B.[6], Peter[5], Peter[4], Christian[3], Christian[2], Christen[1]) was born 01 Oct 1879 in Elkhart Co., IN[7357], and died 05 Mar 1937 in Kent Co., DE[7357]. She married **David Y. Miller** 02 Oct 1898 in McMinnvile, Yamhill Co., OR[7357]. He was born 29 Aug 1874 in Arthur, Douglas Co., IL[7357], and died 05 Apr 1939 in Kent Co., DE[7357].

More About Elizabeth J. Christner:
Residence: 1920, Precinct 15, Yamhill Co., OR[7357]

Notes for David Y. Miller:
Davis is the son of Jacob K. and Lizzie Yoder Miller. He was Old Order Amish and a farmer.

More About David Y. Miller:
Residence: 1920, Precinct 15, Yamhill Co., OR[7357]

Children of Elizabeth Christner and David Miller are:

4572   i.   Eli[9] Miller, born 21 Aug 1899; died 25 Oct 1974 in Greenwood, Sussex Co., DE[7357]. He married Anna D. Schrock 11 Dec 1923; born 10 Feb 1892; died 01 Nov 1977.

Notes for Eli Miller:
Anna was the daughter of Daniel and Mary M. Yoder Schrock.

More About Eli Miller:
Residence: Dawson, Montana[7357]

4573   ii.   Edna Schlabuagh Miller[7358], born 30 Sep 1901 in McMinnville, Yamhill Co., OR[7358,7358]; died 25 Mar 1987 in Elklick Twp., Somerset Co., PA[7358]. She married (1) Amos Slabaugh. She married (2) Levi D. Christner[7359,7360,7361,7362,7363,7363] Feb 1967[7363]; born 20 Aug 1897 in Topeka, Lagrange Co., IN[7364,7365,7366,7367,7368,7368]; died 08 Nov 1985 in Elklick Twp., Bedford (now Somerset) Co., PA[7369,7370,7371,7372].

Notes for Edna Schlabuagh Miller:
Edna was married to Amos Schlabaugh. She was the daughter of David Y. Miller and Elizabeth Christner Miller. Edna's grandfather was Joseph Christner and her Great Grandfather was John B. Christner.

Joseph's nickname was Just Christner.

OBIT: Edna (MILLER) CHRISTNER, 1987 of interest in Somerset Coo., PA - The Republic, April 2, 1987

EDNA CHRISTNER

Edna Christner, 85, died March 26, 1987 at her home in Elk Lick Township. She was born Sept. 30, 1901 at McMinnville, Oregon a daughter of the late David Y. and Elizabeth (Christner) Miller. Also preceded in death by husbands Amos Slabaugh and Levi Christner.

She is survived by sons, Rufus Slabaugh of Guthrie, KY; Joseph Slabaugh of Grantsville, MD; daughters Mrs. Ida (Joseph) Beer of
Cattlet, VA; Mrs. Annie (Amos) Zook of Meyersdale; Mrs. Elizabeth (Wilmer) Yoder of Salisbury. She was the sister of Jacob Miller of Stuarts Draft, VA; Enos Miller of Mifflinburg; Mrs. Susannah Yoder of Meyersdale. Also survived by 32 grandchildren, 54 great-grandchildren and ten stepchildren.

She was a member of the Old Order Amish Church, of Summit Mills. Services were held Friday at 10 a.m. at the Old Order Amish Church with Noah J. Yoder officiating. Interment, Summit Mills Amish Cemetery.

More About Edna Schlabuagh Miller:
Residence: 1930, District 4, Kent, Delaware[7373]

Notes for Levi D. Christner:
The Descendants of John J. Christner, privately published February 1961, p. 25.

Levi and Goldie moved to Willington, Delaware from IN Dec 1928 and returned home about 1 year later. They went by train along with all the livestock and the farm implements. He was very affluent in reading and writing high German. He built 11 grandfather clocks. He owned and operated a Farm and sheet metal shop north of Topeka, IN. (N41°34.800 x W85°31.250) for many years. He got too successful in the sheet metal venture so the Bishop's forced him to curtail the sales. They upset him to the point of selling all the equipment to Christian Hochstetler who started Honeyville Metal, Inc. which became a large enterprise. He also had a peppermint distillery on his land. He spent over 20 years of his life working on the Christner genealogy. If it were not for his small scraps of paper with notes, the work that has been accomplished would of been nearly impossible. He had so many little tid bits of info that it took several years just to connect them all, but it was well worth the time.

He bought a farm along the west side of Messick Lake and Mud Lake in Lagrange Co., IN when he retired. His hobbies were fishing and reading. He moved to Elklick Twp., Somerset Co., PA with his second wife Edna Christner Schlabaugh in 1977. The farm on Messick lake was the entire west side from river to dam. He was a very organized man and planned more to do in a day than most men could accomplish, but he could get it done. He had a very bright personality and an extra ordinary drive for knowledge. He had a buggy horse "NELLIE" that he kept for many many years and Nellie knew which Sunday was church Sunday and would have herself backed into the buggy when he got to the barn. Hans Christner wife Frany Johns brought the 1548 Froschauer Bible with her. The bible is at Goshen College Goshen, Indiana. The Bible was given to the College by Levi D. Christner (born 8/20/1897) this is Frany's 3rd. great grandson. Levi got the Bible at an auction in Lagrange Co. Indiana about 1960 to 1965. Monroe Yoder ask him if he (Levi) wanted to buy a bible for $20.00 as it has Christner family infomation in it. Levi said NO as he knew he knew Monroe didn't pay that much for it and he (Levi) didn't want him to make a profit on selling this bible. Later he (Monroe Yoder) came to him and ask him (Levi) if he can pay him just what he paid for it and Levi agreed to pay him the $17.00. This was the 1548 Froschauer Bible.

When Jonathon Miller died Levi bought his suit.

Obituary: Levi D. CHRISTNER, 1984, Salisbury, Somerset County, PA - The Republic, November 22, 1984

Levi D. Christner, 87, of Salisbury RD 1, died November 8, 1984 at Meyersdale Community Hospital.

He was born August 20, 1897, at Lagrange, IN. He was the son of David and Elizabeth (Burlingcourt) Christner. Besides his parents, he was preceded in death by his first wife, Goldie O'Neal.

He is survived by his wife Edna (Miller) Christner and sons: Menno of Wawaka, IN David, of Lagrange, Indiana; Christian, of Shipshewana, IN Amos of Huntsville, AL; Samuel of Nappanee, Indiana; John of Stockton, California; Levi, of Goshen, IN; Arthur, of Topeko, IN, Also daughters: Mrs. Lizzie Ann Miller of Goshen, IN; Mrs. Sue Christner of Millersburg, IN; Mrs. Mary Ann Fereva, of Manteca, CA; Mrs. Edith Lyons of Lagrange, IN. Stepsons: Joseph Slabaugh, Grantsville RD 1, Maryland; Ruffs Slabaugh, Trenton, KY.

Stepdaughters: Mrs. Anna Zook, Meyersdale RD 1; Mrs. Lizzie. Yoder, Salisbury RD 1: Mrs. Ida Bender, Catlett, VA; also 37 grandchildren, 51 great-grandchildren and one great-great grandson.

He was a member of the Old Order Amish Church of Summit Mills. Services were held November 9, at the Summit Mills Amish Church with the Rev. Noah J. Yoder officiating and on November 11, at Lagrange, IN.
Interment, Clear Spring Amish Cemetery, Lagrange Co., IN.

More About Levi D. Christner:
Burial: Miller Cem, Lagrange Co, IN. N41°35.339'xW85°28.937'Row 12 Plot 19--21
Cause of Death: Stroke
Christened: Amish
Residence: 1910, Clearspring, Lagrange Co., IN[7374,7375,7376]

4574   iii.   Susanna Miller, born 19 Dec 1903; died 23 Dec 1995 in Meyersdale, Somerset Co., PA. She married (1) Albert J. Yoder. She married (2) Albert J. Yoder 11 Feb 1930 in Dover, DE; born 30 Nov 1906.

Notes for Susanna Miller:
Albert is the son of Joseph J. and Elizabeth D. Schrock Yoder. He is Old Order Amish.

More About Susanna Miller:
Residence: 1930, Summit, Somerset Co., PA

4575   iv.   Jacob Miller, born 30 May 1905. He married Sarah N. Yoder 24 Nov 1927 in Dover, DE; born 25 Sep 1903.

Notes for Jacob Miller:
Sarah born Sept 25 1903 daughter of Noah M and Amanda Tice Yoder.
2nd married Nancy D. Schrock on Mar 28, 1940.
Nancy born Feb 16, 1908 daughter of Daniel and Mary Yoder Schrock.

More About Jacob Miller:
Residence: 1920, Precinct 15, Yamhill Co., OR[7377]

4576   v.   Noah D. Miller, born 07 Oct 1907 in Mcminnville, Yamhill Co., OR[7377]; died 19 Jan 1985 in Union City, Union Co., PA[7377]. He married Mattie Byler 29 Dec 1927; born 17 May 1910.

Notes for Noah D. Miller:
Mattie is the daughter of William and Marianne Yoder Byler. Noah is an electrician and Bishop.

More About Noah D. Miller:
Residence: 1920, Precinct 15, Yamhill Co., OR[7377]

4577   vi.   Joseph D. Miller, born 22 Oct 1913; died Jun 1983 in Mill Creek, Huntingdon Co., PA[7377]. He married Melinda D. Mast 25 Nov 1937; born 05 Jan 1919.

Notes for Joseph D. Miller:
Melinda was the daughter of Yost and Amanda Byler Mast. They owned and operate a restraunt at Mill Creek, PA.

More About Joseph D. Miller:
Residence: 1930, District 4, Kent, Delaware[7377]

4578   vii.   Enos D. Miller, born 02 Jul 1915; died 11 May 2008 in Mifflinburg, Union Co., PA[7377]. He married Sadie Y. Mast[7378] 17 Sep 1935; born 22 Nov 1915 in New Wilmington, Lawrence Co., PA[7378,7379]; died 26 Oct 1986 in Mifflinburg, Union Co., PA[7380,7381].

Notes for Enos D. Miller:
Sadie born Nov 22, 1915 daughter of Yost and Amanda Byler Mast Beechy.

More About Enos D. Miller:
Residence: 1930, District 4, Kent, Delaware[7382]

More About Sadie Y. Mast:
Social Security Number: 194-60-4134/[7383]

2587. Mary[8] **Christner** (Joseph B. "Just"[7], John B.[6], Peter[5], Peter[4], Christian[3], Christian[2], Christen[1])[7384] was born 02 Dec 1880 in IN[7384], and died 11 Aug 1956. She married **Alvin M. Beachy**[7384] 13 Sep 1900 in McMinnville, Yamhill Co., OR[7384]. He was born 25 Jan 1876 in Salisbury, Somerset Co., PA[7384].

Notes for Mary Christner:
Birth: Dec. 2, 1880
Death: Aug. 11, 1956

Burial: Hawpatch Cemetery, Topeka, Lagrange Co., IN

Notes for Alvin M. Beachy:
Alvin is the son of Manasses J. and Elizabeth Heading Beachy Plain City, OH.

Birth: Jan. 25, 1876
Death: Oct. 21, 1956

Burial: Hawpatch Cemetery, Topeka, Lagrange Co., IN

Children of Mary Christner and Alvin Beachy are:

4579   i.   Anna A[9] Beachy[7384,7385], born 12 Jul 1901 in McMinnville, Yamhill Co., OR[7386]; died 26 Jan 1998 in McMinnville, Yamhill Co., OR[7386]. She married William Weirich[7387] 17 Jun 1927 in Connellsville, Fayette Co., PA; born 13 Apr 1902 in Whiteson, Yamhill Co., OR[7387]; died 29 Mar 1960 in Yamhill Co., OR[7387].

        More About Anna A Beachy:
        Burial: Whiteson Cemetery McMinnville Oregon
        Residence: 1930, Eden, Lagrange Co., IN[7388]
        Social Security Number: 543-12-4892/[7388]
        SSN issued: OR[7388]

+ 4580   ii.   Samuel A. Beachy, born 26 Jun 1903 in Plain City, Madison Co., OH; died Jul 1984 in Salisbury, Somerset Co., PA.

4581   iii.   Jonas A. Beachy[7388], born 22 Aug 1905 in Plain City, Madison Co., OH[7388]; died Nov 1973 in Goshen, Elkhart Co., IN[7388]. He married Mary Miller 12 Nov 1931; born 22 Aug 1905.

        Notes for Jonas A. Beachy:
        Jonas marreid Mary Miller Nov 12 1931
        Mary born Aug 22 1905 daughter of Jonas M and Mattie Miller Miller
        North Goshen Mennonite Goshen Elkhart Co In

        More About Jonas A. Beachy:
        Social Security Number: 313-24-7498/[7388]
        SSN issued: IN[7388]

4582   iv.   Elizabeth Beachy[7388], born 10 Apr 1908 in McMinnville, Yamhill Co., OR[7388]. She married John Erb 16 Oct 1932; born 20 Apr 1908.

        Notes for Elizabeth Beachy:
        Elizabeth married John Erb Oct 16 1932 Goshen In
        John born April 20 1908 son of Peter and Fannie Miller Erb

+ 4583   v.   Susanna Beachy, born 26 Nov 1915.
+ 4584   vi.   Mary Beachy, born 24 May 1918.

2588. Rachel J.[8] Christner (Joseph B. "Just"[7], John B.[6], Peter[5], Peter[4], Christian[3], Christian[2], Christen[1])[7389] was born 14 Dec 1882 in Goshen, Elkhart Co., IN[7389], and died 05 Aug 1971 in Blair Co., WI[7389]. She married **Joseph Schrock** 29 Sep 1901. He was born 22 Oct 1881, and died 02 Dec 1962.

Notes for Joseph Schrock:
Joseph is the son of David and Madgalena Nisley Schrock. He is Old Order Amish.

Children of Rachel Christner and Joseph Schrock are:

4585   i.   David[9] Schrock, born 06 Mar 1902; died 24 Mar 1973. He married Edna Miller 29 May 1927 in Bedford, WI; born 31 Mar 1903; died 25 Aug 1977.

        Notes for David Schrock:
        Edna is the daughter of William and Sarah Miller Miller.

+ 4586   ii.   Susie Schrock, born 02 Jul 1903 in Middlefield, OH; died 07 Jan 1987 in Rome City, Noble Co., IN.
4587   iii.   Joseph Schrock Jr., born 14 Jan 1905 in Geauga Co., OH[7390]; died 03 May 1995 in Medford, Taylor Co., WI[7390]. He married Rosa Miller 20 Dec 1928 in Medford, Taylor Co., WI; born 27 Sep 1900 in Reno Co., KS[7390]; died 18 Sep 1981 in Medford, Taylor Co., WI[7390].

Notes for Joseph Schrock Jr.:
Rosa born Sept 27 1900 daughter of William and Sarah Miller Miller
O.O.Amish farmer

More About Joseph Schrock Jr.:
Religion: Old Order Amish/Medford, Taylor Co., WI[7390]
Residence: 1930, Little Black, Taylor, Wisconsin[7390]

More About Rosa Miller:
Religion: Old Order Amish/Medford, Taylor Co., WI[7390]
Residence: 1930, Little Black, Taylor, Wisconsin[7390]

+ 4588   iv.   Anna Schrock, born 31 Jan 1907 in McMinnville, Yamhill Co., OR; died 14 Apr 1985 in Meyersdale, Somerset Co., PA.

+ 4589   v.   Fannie J Schrock, born 28 Aug 1908 in Mcminnville, Yamhill Co., OR; died 20 Aug 1997 in Augusta, Eau Claire Co., WI.

+ 4590   vi.   Urias J. Schrock, born 12 Dec 1909 in McMinnville, Yamhill Co., OR; died 18 May 1999 in Wolcottville, Lagrange Co., IN.

4591   vii.   Mahlon J. Schrock, born 02 Oct 1911. He married Maryanne Petersheim; born 1908 in Haven, Reno Co., KS[7391]; died 1998[7391].

Notes for Mahlon J. Schrock:
Mahlon married Maryanne Petersheim Feb 4_____ Curtiss Wis
Maryanne born Oct 9 1908 daughter of David and Lizzie Ann Hostetler Petersheim
O.O.Amish   Farmer

4592   viii.   Lawerence J. Schrock, born 22 May 1913. He married Anna Coblentz 02 Nov in Dover, DE; born 01 Jan 1923.

Notes for Lawerence J. Schrock:
Anna is the daughter of Issac and Mary Slabaugh Coblentz.

4593   ix.   Phoebe Schrock, born 31 Dec 1915. She married Stanley Bartosiak Jun 1939; born 06 Aug 1912.

Notes for Phoebe Schrock:
Stanley is the son of Anton and Mary Grajek Bartosiak, He is a farmer and a member of the United Church of Christ.

4594   x.   Phineas J. Schrock, born 19 Apr 1919. He married Anna Schrock 30 Mar 1950; born 15 Feb 1927 in IL.

Notes for Phineas J. Schrock:
Anna is the daughter of Joe B and Eleanora Helmuth Schrock. He is an Elevator operator and is Old Order Amish.

4595   xi.   Emma Schrock, born 20 Dec 1920. She married John Schmiedeke 19 Dec 1947 in Debuque, IA; born 22 Jul 1923.

Notes for Emma Schrock:
John was the son of John and Ida Nobe Schmiedeke.

4596   xii.   Harley J. Schrock[7392], born 10 Jul 1923[7392]; died 16 Apr 1999 in Age at Death: 75/Arcola, Douglas, Illinois, USA[7392]. He married Fannie J. Otto 22 Jan 1948 in Arcola, IL; born 29 Oct 1919[7393]; died 01 Nov 2010 in Cerro Gordo, Piatt Co., IL[7393].

Notes for Harley J. Schrock:
Fannie born Oct 29 1919 daughter of Jacob M and Katie Helmuth Otto

More About Harley J. Schrock:
Social Security Number: 323-28-7482/[7394]

Notes for Fannie J. Otto:
Birth: Oct. 29, 1919
Death: Nov. 1, 2010

Obituary: Decatur Herald & Review on November 2, 2010

ARTHUR - Fannie J. Schrock, 91, of Arthur, IL formerly of Cerro Gordo, IL and Arcola, IL passed away at 4:35 A.M. on Monday, November 1, 2010 at the Arthur Home. Fannie was born on October 29, 1919 in Douglas County, IL. She was a daughter of Jacob and Katie (Helmuth) Otto. She married Harley J. Schrock on January 22, 1948 in Arcola, IL. He passed away on April 16, 1999. She is survived by one son Lawrence Schrock and his wife Cheryl of Arcola, IL; one daughter Rachel Ghere and her husband Ken of Cerro Gordo, IL; seven grandchildren; fourteen great-grandchildren; one sister Amanda Kemp of Arcola, IL; one brother Elmer Otto and his wife Nancy of Sullivan, IL and a sister-in-law, Nancy Otto Arthur, IL. She was preceded in death by her parents, her husband, one brother Noah Otto, one sister, Elizabeth Schrock, one granddaughter, Lisa Schrock, and three great-grandchildren, Carmon Schrock, and Cody and Cameron Schrock.

Burial: Pleasant View Church Cemetery, Chesterville, Douglas Co., IL
Find A Grave Memorial# 61148649

4597   xiii. Henry Schrock, born 10 May 1925. He married Elizabeth Miller 08 Jun 1952 in Hutchinson, KS; born 09 Sep 1927.

Notes for Henry Schrock:
Elizabeth is the daughter of William A and Rebecca Nisley Miller.

2589. Samuel S.[8] Christner (Joseph B. "Just"[7], John B.[6], Peter[5], Peter[4], Christian[3], Christian[2], Christen[1]) was born 02 Apr 1884 in Lagrange Co., IN[7395], and died 09 Mar 1951 in Orrville, OH. He married **Mary Schrock** 19 Feb 1914. She was born 08 Sep 1894, and died 11 May 1962 in Orrville, OH.

Notes for Samuel S. Christner:
Christner, Samuel S., son of Joseph and Susanna (Weirich) Christner, was born April 2, 1884, in Lagrange Co., IN; died March 9, 1951, at Orrville, OH; aged 66 y. 11 m. 7 d. He was married to Mary Schrock in Lagrange Co., IN. To this union were born 2 children (Mae Bucher, of the home and Harley L., Massillon, OH). He was a member of the Orrville Mennonite Church. He was preceded in death by one grandson and 3 sisters. Besides his wife, Mary, and son and daughter, he leaves 3 grandchildren, 7 sisters (Mary-Mrs. Alvin Beachy, Topeka, Ind.; Rachel-Mrs. Joe D. Schrock, Curtis, Wis.; Malinda-Mrs. Andy S. Yoder, McMinnville, Oreg.; Mrs. Fannie Beachy, Bareville, PA; Mrs. Ollie Miller, Lancaster, Pa.; Ada-Mrs. Howard Kreider, Willow Street, PA; and Elva-Mrs. Aaron Kauffman, Lancaster, PA), and 1 brother (Benjamin J. Christner, Greenwood, DE). Funeral services were held at the home and the Orrville Mennonite Church, with Harold Bauman, Stanford Mumaw, and I. W. Royer in charge. Burial was made in the Martins Church Cemetery.

More About Samuel S. Christner:
Burial: Martins Church Cemetery
Religion: Mennonite/
Residence: 1930, Orrville, Wayne Co., OH[7396]

Notes for Mary Schrock:
Obituary:

Christner, Mary, daughter of John and Pauline (Kandel) Schrock, was born in Lagrange Co., Ind., Sept. 8, 1894; died at Orrville, Ohio, May 11, 1962; aged 67 y. 8 m. 3 d. On Feb. 19, 1914, she was married to Samuel S. Christner, who died in 1951. Surviving are one son and one daughter (Mae-Mrs. George Herald, Orrville, Ohio; and Harley, Massillon, Ohio), 2 sisters (Lydia-Mrs. Elvin Bender and Katie-Mrs. Dan R. Miller), and 5 brothers (Noah, Daniel, Levi, John, and Henry). She was a member of the Orrville Church, where funeral services were held May 14, in charge of J. Lester Graybill and O. N. Johns; interment in Martins Church Cemetery.

More About Mary Schrock:
Burial: 14 May 1962, Martins Church Cemetery

Residence: 1930, Orrville, Wayne Co., OH[7396]

Children of Samuel Christner and Mary Schrock are:

    4598   i.   Rosa Mae[9] Christner[7396], born 15 Mar 1916 in Orrville, OH; died 01 Jul 1988 in Orrville, Wayne Co.,
                    OH[7396]. She married George R. Harold; born 10 Aug 1915.

                    More About Rosa Mae Christner:
                    Religion: Methodist/
                    Residence: 1930, Orrville, Wayne Co., OH[7396]

                    Notes for George R. Harold:
                    George is the son of Stephen Harold and _____.
                    Rosa and George have an adopted daughter Kathy.

+   4599   ii.   Harley L. Christner, born 20 Aug 1920 in Van Buren, Lagrange Co., IN; died 18 Dec 2006 in Massillon,
                    Stark Co., OH.

2591. Benedict J.[8] Christner (Joseph B. "Just"[7], John B.[6], Peter[5], Peter[4], Christian[3], Christian[2],
Christen[1])[7397,7398,7399] was born 29 Feb 1888 in Reno, Reno Co., KS[7399,7400,7401], and died 13 Jun 1957[7402,7403].
He married **Anna Miller**[7404] 25 Feb 1915 in Berlin, Holmes Co., OH[7404]. She was born 13 Dec 1889 in Holmes
Co., OH[7404,7405], and died 31 May 1975 in Salem, Polk Co., OR[7406].

Notes for Benedict J. Christner:
Birth: 1888
Death: 1957

Spouse: Anna M. Christner (1889 - 1975)

Burial: Greenwood Mennonite Cemetery, Greenwood, Sussex Co., DE

More About Benedict J. Christner:
Residence: 1900, Whiteson, Yamhill Co., OR[7407]

Notes for Anna Miller:
Anna is the daughter of Noah B and Mary M Kauffman Miller.

Birth: 1889
Death: 1975

Spouse: Benedict J. Christner (1888 - 1957)

Burial: Greenwood Mennonite Cemetery, Greenwood, Sussex Co., DE

More About Anna Miller:
Residence: 1930, Paint, Holmes Co., OH[7408]

Children of Benedict Christner and Anna Miller are:

+   4600   i.   Mary[9] Christner, born 28 Apr 1916.
+   4601   ii.   Owen Christner, born 09 Jun 1918; died 27 Jul 1998 in Salem, Marion Co., OR.
+   4602   iii.   Melvin B. Christner, born 10 Aug 1919 in Berlin, Holmes Co., OH; died 23 Jul 2006 in Hamshire,
                    Jefferson Co., TX.

2592. Malinda[8] Christner (Joseph B. "Just"[7], John B.[6], Peter[5], Peter[4], Christian[3], Christian[2], Christen[1]) was
born 14 Mar 1891. She married **Andrew S. Yoder** 17 Oct 1909. He was born 29 Mar 1887.

Notes for Andrew S. Yoder:
Andrew is a Mennonite and a farmer near McMinnville, OR.

More About Andrew S. Yoder:
Occupation: Farmer/
Religion: Mennonite/

Children of Malinda Christner and Andrew Yoder are:
    4603   i.   Alvin[9] Yoder, born 02 Dec 1910; died 24 Dec 1910.
    4604   ii.   Ada Yoder, born 06 Jul 1912. She married Lewis Swartzentruber Aug 1932; born 18 Jan 1906.

                    Notes for Ada Yoder:
                    Lewis is the son of Joe P. Swartzentruber born Jan 18, 1906. Lewis was a fur dealer in Sheridan, OR. and a Mennonite.

+   4605   iii.   Ammon A. Yoder, born 30 Jul 1914; died Oct 1985 in Carlton, Yamhill Co., OR.
    4606   iv.   Elmer A. Yoder, born 20 Apr 1917; died 10 Oct 1972.

                    Notes for Elmer A. Yoder:
                    Elmer is a sawmill employee. Elmer married Fannie D. Miller Jan 24 1939
                    Fannie born Aug 16 1923 the daughter of Dan and Susie Stutzman Miller

    4607   v.   Clara Yoder, born 05 Feb 1921.

                    Notes for Clara Yoder:
                    Single sewing machine operator. He was a Mennonite in McMinnville, OR.

    4608   vi.   Henry A. Yoder, born 01 Jun 1925. He married Ruth Gault 01 Jun 1946; born 28 Sep 1923 in Mcminnville, Yamhill Co., OR.

                    Notes for Henry A. Yoder:
                    Henry is a farmer and Mennonite.

2594. Ollie[8] Christner (Joseph B. "Just"[7], John B.[6], Peter[5], Peter[4], Christian[3], Christian[2], Christen[1]) was born 11 Mar 1897 in Hubbard, Marion Co., OR[7409], and died 26 Apr 1988 in Lancaster Co., PA[7409]. She married **Rudolph A. Miller** 16 Apr 1916 in McMinnville, Yamhill Co., OR. He was born 19 Jun 1897, and died 05 Feb 1946.

More About Ollie Christner:
Residence: 1900, Whiteson, Yamhill Co., OR[7409]

Notes for Rudolph A. Miller:
Rudolph is the son of Abram and Lizzie _____ Miller.

Birth: 1897
Death: 1946

Spouse: Ollie Miller (1897 - 1988)

Burial: Mellinger Mennonite Cemetery, Lancaster, Lancaster Co., PA
Plot: Section H
Find A Grave Memorial# 79490503

Children of Ollie Christner and Rudolph Miller are:
    4609   i.   Benedict[9] Miller, born 28 Apr 1917.
+   4610   ii.   Elva Miller, born 25 Oct 1918.

2595. Ada A.[8] Christner (Joseph B. "Just"[7], John B.[6], Peter[5], Peter[4], Christian[3], Christian[2], Christen[1])[7410] was born 03 Aug 1900 in Yamhill Co., OR[7411,7412], and died 17 Mar 1988 in Lancaster, Lancaster Co., PA[7412]. She married **Howard Bowers Kreider**[7413] 10 Sep 1932 in Lancaster Co., PA. He was born 15 Jan 1896 in Connellsville, Fayette Co., PA[7414,7415], and died 08 Sep 1964 in Lancaster, Lancaster Co., PA[7416,7417].

More About Ada A. Christner:
Residence: 1920, Precinct 29, Yamhill Co., OR[7418]
Social Security Number: 179-05-6761/[7419]
SSN issued: Connellsville, Fayette Co., PA[7419]

Notes for Howard Bowers Kreider:
Howard is the son of Jacob and Mary Bowers Kreider. He was a Mennonite and a farmer in New Providence, PA.

More About Howard Bowers Kreider:
Residence: 01 Apr 1940, Providence, Lancaster Co., PA[7420]
Social Security Number: 186-07-2609/[7421]
SSN issued: Pittsburgh, Allegheny Co., PA[7421]

Children of Ada Christner and Howard Kreider are:
+ 4611   i.   Howard[9] Kreider Jr.[7422,7423], born 1923 in Pittsburgh, Allegheny Co., PA[7424].

             More About Howard Kreider Jr.:
             Residence: 01 Apr 1940, Providence, Lancaster Co., PA[7424]

+ 4612   ii. Minnie E. Kreider[7424], born 1924 in Pittsburgh, Allegheny Co., PA[7424].

             More About Minnie E. Kreider:
             Residence: 01 Apr 1940, Providence, Lancaster Co., PA[7424]

2598. Anna S.[8] Miller (John E.[7] Christner, John B.[6], Peter[5], Peter[4], Christian[3], Christian[2], Christen[1])[7425] was born 26 Jan 1899 in Lagrange Co., IN[7425], and died 21 Jun 1973. She married **Levi S. Miller**[7426] 20 Jan 1921, son of Simon Miller and Magdalena Lantz. He was born 23 Jun 1896 in Topeka, Lagrange Co., IN[7427], and died 12 Nov 1989[7428].

Notes for Levi S. Miller:
The Descendants of John J. Christner, privately published February 1961, p. 102.

More About Levi S. Miller:
Burial: Amish Cemetery/Saling, Audrain, Missouri, USA[7428]
Find A Grave Link: Memorial# 27751113/[7428]
Residence: 1910, Wilcox, Newaygo Co., MI[7429]

Children are listed above under (444) Levi S. Miller.

2599. Emma J.[8] Christner (John E.[7], John B.[6], Peter[5], Peter[4], Christian[3], Christian[2], Christen[1])[7430,7431,7432] was born 02 Mar 1901 in Topeka, Lagrange Co., IN[7433,7434], and died 09 Jul 1969. She married **Jacob H. Mast**[7435,7436] 02 Dec 1919 in Shipshewana, Lagrange Co., IN. He was born 05 Mar 1896 in Douglas Co., IL[7437], and died 18 Apr 1986 in Lagrange Co., IN.

Notes for Emma J. Christner:
The Descendants of John J. Christner, privately published February 1961, p. 51.

Emma was raised by her aunt Mary - Mrs. Tobias Kemp. She was only two weeks old when her mother died.

Birth: Mar. 2, 1901
Death: Jul. 9, 1969

68 yrs., wife of Jacob Mast

Burial: Yoder Cemetery, Shipshewana, Lagrange Co., IN

More About Emma J. Christner:
Religion: Old Order Amish/
Residence: 1930, Eden, Lagrange Co., IN[7438]

Notes for Jacob H. Mast:
The Descendants of John J. Christner, privately published February 1961, p. 51.

Jacob is the son of Henry and Emma Eash Mast. He was a minister
10303 Hochstedler/Stutzman. He was Old Order Amish.

More About Jacob H. Mast:
Burial: Miller Cemetery, Lagrange Co., IN.
Occupation: Farmer/[7439]
Religion: Old Order Amish/
Residence: 1930, Eden, Lagrange Co., IN[7440]

Children of Emma Christner and Jacob Mast are:

    4613   i.   Amos J.[9] Mast, born 26 Jan 1921 in Lagrange Co., IN; died 21 Nov 1996 in Centerville, MI.

              Notes for Amos J. Mast:
              The Descendants of John J. Christner, privately published February 1961, p. 51.

              Amos had Parkinson's Disease for 25 years. Burial at Yoder Cemetery, Shipshewana, IN.   Last address
              3475 North 425 West LagGrange. He assisted in farming and worked at ARC,LaGrange for 12 years.

+   4614   ii.   Anna J. Mast, born 23 Sep 1923 in Lagrange Co., IN; died Jun 1970.
+   4615   iii.   Melvin J. Mast, born 20 Dec 1925 in Topeka, Lagrange Co., IN.
+   4616   iv.   Henry J. Mast, born 03 Nov 1931 in Topeka, Lagrange Co., IN.
    4617   v.   Ora J. Mast, born 27 Oct 1932. He married Effie Swartz 16 Oct 1953 in By Bishop Jacob P Miller; born
              20 Mar 1934.

              Notes for Ora J. Mast:
              The Descendants of John J. Christner, privately published February 1961, p. 52.

              Amish and a factory worker.

              More About Ora J. Mast:
              Occupation: Factory Worker/
              Religion: Old Order Amish/

              Notes for Effie Swartz:
              The Descendants of John J. Christner, privately published February 1961, p. 52.

              More About Effie Swartz:
              Religion: Old Order Amish/

+   4618   vi.   Ervin J. Mast, born 29 Jun 1937; died 10 Jun 2006 in Grovespring, Wright Co., MO.
+   4619   vii.   Esther J. Mast, born 29 Jul 1939 in Centerville, MI.
    4620   viii.   Ella Mast, born 28 Oct 1942; died Sep 1979 in Benton IN south of Goshen IN.

              Notes for Ella Mast:
              The Descendants of John J. Christner, privately published February 1961, p. 51.

              Ella married Henry L. Miller July 29, 1961. Ella and her husband were critically injured in an explosion
              near Benton, IN in 1979. Benton is south of Goshen, IN.

2600. Cletus S.⁸ Christner (John E.⁷, John B.⁶, Peter⁵, Peter⁴, Christian³, Christian², Christen¹) was born 18 Oct 1911 in Topeka, Lagrange Co., IN⁷⁴⁴¹, and died 08 Nov 1990 in Geneva, Adams Co., IN⁷⁴⁴²,⁷⁴⁴³. He married **Rebecca D. Wickey** 10 Nov 1938 in Berne, Adams Co., IN⁷⁴⁴³. She was born 13 Jul 1916 in Berne, Adams Co., IN⁷⁴⁴³, and died 26 Jan 2006 in Adams Co., IN⁷⁴⁴³.

Notes for Cletus S. Christner:
The Descendants of John J. Christner, privately published February 1961, p. 47.

More About Cletus S. Christner:
Burial: Adams Co., IN
Residence: 1930, Scott, Kosciusko Co., IN⁷⁴⁴⁴

Notes for Rebecca D. Wickey:
The Descendants of John J. Christner, privately published February 1961, p. 47.

Children of Cletus Christner and Rebecca Wickey are:

+   4621   i.   Mary C.⁹ Christner, born 28 Jul 1939 in Berne, Adams Co., IN; died 01 Mar 2002 in Berne, Adams Co., IN.
+   4622   ii.   Levi C. Christner, born 16 Aug 1940 in Berne, Adams Co., IN.
     4623   iii. Rebecca C. Christner, born 21 Mar 1942.

             Notes for Rebecca C. Christner:
             The Descendants of John J. Christner, privately published February 1961, p. 47.

+   4624   iv.   Sylvia C. Christner, born 22 May 1944 in Geneva, Adams Co., IN.
+   4625   v.   Katie C. Christner, born 23 Apr 1945 in Berne, Adams Co., IN.
+   4626   vi.   Elizabeth C. Christner, born 18 Mar 1946 in Berne, Adams Co., IN.
+   4627   vii. Esther C. Christner, born 15 Apr 1948 in Berne, Adams Co., IN.
+   4628   viii. David C. Christner, born 08 Nov 1949 in Berne, Adams Co., IN.
     4629   ix.   Kathryn K. Christner, born 30 Dec 1950.

             Notes for Kathryn K. Christner:
             The Descendants of John J. Christner, privately published February 1961, p. 47.

     4630   x.   Samuel C. Christner⁷⁴⁴⁵, born 11 Feb 1951 in Berne, Adams Co., IN⁷⁴⁴⁵; died 11 Feb 1951 in Berne, Adams Co., IN⁷⁴⁴⁵.

             Notes for Samuel C. Christner:
             The Descendants of John J. Christner, privately published February 1961, p. 47.

+   4631   xi.   Cletus C. Christner Jr., born 05 May 1952 in Berne, Adams Co., IN.
     4632   xii. Christner⁷⁴⁴⁵, born 09 Aug 1953 in Adams Co., IN⁷⁴⁴⁵; died 09 Aug 1953 in Adams Co., IN⁷⁴⁴⁵.

             Notes for Christner:
             The Descendants of John J. Christner, privately published February 1961, p. 47.

     4633   xiii. Amos C. Christner⁷⁴⁴⁵, born 05 Sep 1955 in Adams Co., IN⁷⁴⁴⁵; died 05 Sep 1955 in Adams Co., IN⁷⁴⁴⁵.

             Notes for Amos C. Christner:
             The Descendants of John J. Christner, privately published February 1961, p. 47.

     4634   xiv. John C. Christner⁷⁴⁴⁵, born 25 Mar 1958 in Adams Co., IN⁷⁴⁴⁵; died 25 Mar 1958 in Adams Co., IN⁷⁴⁴⁵.

             Notes for John C. Christner:
             The Descendants of John J. Christner, privately published February 1961, p. 47.

2601. Alvin S.⁸ Christner (John E.⁷, John B.⁶, Peter⁵, Peter⁴, Christian³, Christian², Christen¹)⁷⁴⁴⁶,⁷⁴⁴⁷ was born 15 Jul 1914 in Topeka, Lagrange Co., IN[7448,7449], and died 20 Jan 2012 in Berne, Adams Co., IN. He married **Caroline E. Schwartz**[7450] 28 May 1939 in Adams Co., IN. She was born 21 Jun 1920 in Berne, Adams Co., IN[7450], and died 14 Mar 1992[7450].

Notes for Alvin S. Christner:
Birth: Jun. 15, 1917
Lagrange Co., IN
Death: Jan. 20, 2012
Berne, Adams Co., IN

Alvin S. Christner, 94,of Berne, IN, passed away at 2:30 AM, on Friday, January 20, 2012 at his residence in Berne, IN. He was born on Sunday, July 15, 1917, in Lagrange County, IN. Alvin was a member of the Old Order Amish.

He married Carline E. (Schwartz) Christner in Adams County. Carline E. (Schwartz) Christner passed away on March 14, 1992.

He was the son of the late Sam Christner and the late Elzabeth Ann (Miller) Christner.

Survivors include: sons-Ervin C. (wife, Lizzie) Christner of Berne, Ind., Jacob C. (wife, Barbare) Christner of Berne, Ind., Sam C. (wife, Anna) Christner of Berne, Ind., Alvin C. (wife, Clara) Christner of Bryant, Ind., Harvey C. (wife, Mary) Christner of Berne, IN, Enos C. (wife, Rebecca) Christner of Bryant, IN, Ben C. (wife, Josaphine) Christner of Bryant, IN, Rudy C. (wife, Elizabeth) Christner of Oweningsville, KY and Reuben C. (wife, Lizzie) Christner of Canaan, IN; daughters-Emily (husband, John K.) Schwartz of Berne, Ind., Elizabeth (husband, David K.) Schwartz of Campbellsburg, KY, Rusina (husband, Jerry) Geriod of Carlisle, KY, Ida (husband, Sam) Troyer of Richards, MO and Caraline (husband, Jerry) Troyer of Campbellsburg, KY; sisters-Edna Schwartz of Hamilton, IN, Sylvia Eicher of Geneva, IN and Ida Lengaeher of Grabill, IN.

He was preceded in Death by: wife-Carline E. (Schwartz) Christner; parents-Sam Christner & Elzabeth Ann (Miller) Christner; 2 deceased daughter; sister-Emma Girod; brothers-Cletus Christner & Levi Christner

Arrangements are being handled by Downing & Glancy Funeral Home, 100 N. Washington Street, Geneva, IN, where Family and Friends May Gather from 12:00 PM to 8:00 PM Saturday, January 21, 2012 and from 8:00 AM to 8:00 PM Sunday, January 22, 2012 at the John K. Schwartz Residence at 8463 S. - 600 E . A service will be at 8463 S. - 600 E.-Berne, IN at 9:00 AM Monday, January 23, 2012 with Bishop Pete Eicher officiating. Internment in Bunker Hill Cemetery, Geneva, Adams Co., IN.

Burial: Bunker Hill Cemetery, Geneva, Adams Co., IN

More About Alvin S. Christner:
Residence: 1920, Scott, Kosciusko Co., IN[7451]

More About Caroline E. Schwartz:
Burial: Adams Co., IN[7452]

Children of Alvin Christner and Caroline Schwartz are:
+   4635   i.   Emily (Emma) C.[9] Christner, born 13 Mar 1940 in Berne, Adams Co., IN.
+   4636   ii.   Elizabeth C. Christner, born 17 Apr 1941 in Berne, Adams Co., IN.
+   4637   iii.   Ervin C. Christner, born 25 May 1942 in Geneva, Adams Co., IN.
+   4638   iv.   Jacob C. Christner, born 23 Jan 1944 in Berne, Adams Co., IN.
+   4639   v.   Samuel A. Christner, born 13 Apr 1945 in Berne, Adams Co., IN.
    4640   vi.   Alvin C. Christner, born 09 Jul 1946.

        Notes for Alvin C. Christner:
        The Descendants of John J. Christner, privately published February 1961, p. 47.

+   4641   vii.   Harvey C. Christner, born 29 Oct 1947 in Berne, Adams Co., IN.
+   4642   viii.   Rosina Christner, born 18 Nov 1948 in Berne, Adams Co., IN.

4643   ix.   Edna C. Christner, born 27 Nov 1949.

Notes for Edna C. Christner:
The Descendants of John J. Christner, privately published February 1961, p. 47.

4644   x.   Amanda C. Christner, born 01 Jan 1951.

Notes for Amanda C. Christner:
The Descendants of John J. Christner, privately published February 1961, p. 47.

+   4645   xi.   Ida C. Christner, born 13 Feb 1952 in Adams Co., IN.
+   4646   xii.   Enos C. Christner, born 17 Jan 1954 in Adams Co., IN.
+   4647   xiii.   Caroline C. Christner, born 14 Feb 1955 in Adams Co., IN.
+   4648   xiv.   Benjamin C. Christner, born 13 Apr 1956 in Adams Co., IN.
+   4649   xv.   Rudy C. Christner, born 18 Feb 1958 in Adams Co., IN.
+   4650   xvi.   Reuben C. Christner, born 09 Mar 1962 in Adams Co., IN.

2602. Elmina J.[8] Christner (John E.[7], John B.[6], Peter[5], Peter[4], Christian[3], Christian[2], Christen[1]) was born 13 Jun 1919, and died 17 Jan 1970. She married **Amos J. Miller** 18 Jan 1940 in By Mose M Miller, son of Joseph Miller and Sarah Troyer. He was born 12 May 1917 in Shipshewana, Elkhart Co., IN, and died 27 Oct 2006 in Shipshewana, Lagrange Co., IN[7453].

Notes for Elmina J. Christner:
The Descendants of John J. Christner, privately published February 1961, p. 64.

Notes for Amos J. Miller:
The Descendants of John J. Christner, privately published February 1961, p. 62.

Children of Elmina Christner and Amos Miller are:
4651   i.   Infant[9] Miller, born 27 Feb 1941; died 27 Feb 1941.

Notes for Infant Miller:
The Descendants of John J. Christner, privately published February 1961, p. 64.

4652   ii.   Infant Miller, born 13 Feb 1942; died 13 Feb 1942.

Notes for Infant Miller:
The Descendants of John J. Christner, privately published February 1961, p. 64.

4653   iii.   Daniel A. Miller, born 11 Aug 1943; died 15 Jun 1969.

Notes for Daniel A. Miller:
The Descendants of John J. Christner, privately published February 1961, p. 64.

4654   iv.   Mary A. Miller, born 27 Oct 1944. She married Andrew C. Troyer 25 May 1965; born 04 Mar 1939.

Notes for Mary A. Miller:
The Descendants of John J. Christner, privately published February 1961, p. 64.

Notes for Andrew C. Troyer:
The Descendants of John J. Christner, privately published February 1961, p. 64.

4655   v.   Katie A. Miller, born 25 Jun 1946.

Notes for Katie A. Miller:
The Descendants of John J. Christner, privately published February 1961, p. 64.

2603. Edna[8] Christner (John E.[7], John B.[6], Peter[5], Peter[4], Christian[3], Christian[2], Christen[1]) was born 21 Jul 1922. She married **Ura I. Yoder**[7454] 18 Nov 1941 in Middlebury, Elkhart Co., IN. He was born 28 Aug 1917[7454,7455], and died 28 Feb 2008 in Philadelphia, Marion Co., MO[7455,7456].

Notes for Ura I. Yoder:
Ura is the son of Isaac and Mattie Mullet Yoder. Ura is a Bishop, Old Order Amish near Bowling Green, MO.

Birth: Aug. 28, 1917
Death: Feb. 28, 2008

Obituary: Ura I. Yoder

Ura I. Yoder, 90, Of Philadelphia, Missouri, Passed Away 5:45 A.M. Thursday At The Maple Lawn Nursing Home In Palmyra. Ura Was Born August 28, 1917 At Napponee, Indiana To Isaac D. And Mattie Mullett Yoder. Ura Was Married To Edna Christner November 18, 1941 At Middlebury, Indiana. She Survives at The Home. Survivors Include:Sons: Ivan Yoder Of Union, Mo.; Glen Yoder & Wife Ida Of Maywood, Mo.; Levi Yoder & Wife Miriam Of Mansfield, Oh; Daughter, Mrs. Mattie Bontrager & Husband John Of Philadelphia, Mo.; Brother, Herman Yoder Of Nappanee, In; Sisters: Mrs. Fanny Graber Of Branson, Mi; Mrs. Edna Yoder & Husband Elmer Of Fredericktown, OH. Also surviving are 30 Grandchildren and many great grandchildren. He Was Preceded In Death By A Daughter, Laura Mae Yoder; 4 Brothers And 5 Sisters. Mr. Yoder Was A Self-Employed Farmer. Mr. Yoder Loved To Play The Guitar And Sing Gospel Music. He Was A Well Known Musician At Hannibal Arts Festivals As Well As Other Musical Events In Marion County. He Was A Volunteer At Maple Lawn Nursing Home In Palmyra Where He Shared In His Special Ministry Of Scripture & Music. Ura Never Met A Stranger, And Loved To Visit With All Those He Met. He Was A Member Of The Community Baptist Church In Emden, Missouri. Mr. Yoder loved the Lord and put his faith and trust in Jesus Christ for the forgiveness of his sins and the hope of eternal life. Funeral Services Will Be Held At 10:30 A.M. Monday At The Community Baptist Church In Emden. Pastor Glen Yoder, Pastor David Yoder And Pastor Orlie Yoder Will Officiate. Burial Will Be At The Philadelphia Cemetery In Philadelphia, Missouri. Visitation Will Be Form 4-7:00 Pm Sunday At The Lewis Brothers Funeral Chapel In Palmyra. Memorial Contributions May Be Made To Community Baptist Church, Emden, Missouri . Casket Bearers Isaac I. Yoder, Ivan G. Yoder, Isaac L. Yoder, David L. Yoder, Samuel L. Yoder, Orlie G. Yoder, Herman G. Yoder, Joas L. Yoder, Floyd G. Yoder, Glen L. Yoder, Marvin J. Bontrager, Kevin R. Bontrager, Honorary Bearers, Earl Michaels Kent, Carroll Sam Wilson, Joe Schrock

Burial: Philadelphia Cemetery, Philadelphia, Marion Co., MO
Find A Grave Memorial# 25050488

More About Ura I. Yoder:
Burial: Philadelphia, Marion Co., MO[7456]

Children of Edna Christner and Ura Yoder are:
4656	i.	Laura Mae[9] Yoder, born 06 Sep 1942. She married Simon Gingerich Jr.; born 25 Apr 1941.
4657	ii.	Ivan U. Yoder, born 28 Mar 1944. He married Marry Miller 04 Nov 1966; born 23 Feb 1945.
4658	iii.	Glen U. Yoder, born 20 Jan 1950. He married (1) Ida Bontrager 05 Jun 1973. He married (2) Ida Bontrager 05 Jun 1973; born 24 Aug 1950.
4659	iv.	Levi U. Yoder, born 16 Jun 1951. He married Miriam Mullet 30 Sep 1973; born 22 Apr 1947.
4660	v.	Mattie U. Yoder, born 30 May 1961.

2606. John Foster[8] Schrock (Margaret[7] Christner, John B.[6], Peter[5], Peter[4], Christian[3], Christian[2], Christen[1])[7457,7458,7459,7460] was born 03 Oct 1887 in Lagrange Co., IN[7461], and died 10 Jan 1940 in Huntington, IN[7461]. He married **Ruth Ella Swartzendruber**[7461] 11 Nov 1910[7461]. She was born 26 Jul 1890 in IA[7461,7462], and died Jun 1963 in IN[7463].

Notes for John Foster Schrock:
He was killed in a car Accident near Fort Wayne, IN.

Birth: Oct. 3, 1887
Death: Jan. 10, 1940

Spouse: Ella Ruth Swartzendruber Schrock (1890 - 1963)

Burial: Shore Cemetery, Shipshewana, Lagrange Co., IN

More About John Foster Schrock:
Burial: Shore Church Cemetery, Shipshewana, IN
Residence: 1920, Greene, Iowa Co., IA[7464,7465,7466]

Notes for Ruth Ella Swartzendruber:
Birth: Jul 26, 1890 - Johnson Co., IA
Death: Jun 1963 - IN

Parents: Christena Elizabeth Gunden Swartzendruber (1856 - 1929)

Spouse: John F. Schrock (1887 - 1940)

Burial: Shore Cemetery, Shipshewana, Lagrange Co., IN

More About Ruth Ella Swartzendruber:
Residence: 1920, Greene, Iowa Co., IA[7467]

Child of John Schrock and Ruth Swartzendruber is:
    4661   i.   Catherine[9] Schrock[7467], born 1915 in TX[7467].

                  More About Catherine Schrock:
                  Residence: 1920, Greene, Iowa Co., IA[7467]

2608. Edna Sarah[8] Schrock (Margaret[7] Christner, John B.[6], Peter[5], Peter[4], Christian[3], Christian[2], Christen[1]) was born 06 May 1892 in Lagrange Co., IN[7468], and died 16 Jan 1974 in Sarasota, Manatee Co., FL[7468]. She married **Levi M. Detwiler** 17 Oct 1909[7468]. He was born 04 Nov 1887 in Iowa[7468], and died 15 Feb 1966 in Sarasota, Manatee Co., FL[7468].

Notes for Edna Sarah Schrock:
Edna was married to Levi M. Detwiler and later divorced him.

More About Edna Sarah Schrock:
Residence: 1930, Clarence, Erie Co., NY[7468]

More About Levi M. Detwiler:
Residence: 1930, Clarence, Erie Co., NY[7468]

Children of Edna Schrock and Levi Detwiler are:
    4662   i.   Mary Elizabeth[9] Detwiler[7468], born 06 Apr 1912 in Corpus Christi, Kleberg Co., TX[7468]; died 28 Apr 2002 in Clarence, Erie Co., NY[7468].

                  More About Mary Elizabeth Detwiler:
                  Residence: 1930, Elizabeth, Union Co., NJ[7468]

    4663   ii.   Lee Detwiler[7468], born 23 Aug 1915 in MI[7468]; died Jun 1965 in Norfolk, Princess Ann Co., VA[7468].

                  More About Lee Detwiler:
                  Residence: 1930, Clarence, Erie Co., NY[7468]

    4664   iii.   John Detwiler[7468], born 02 Sep 1919 in Pigeon, Huron Co., MI[7468]; died 28 Jul 2009 in Inverness, Citrus Co., FL[7468].

                  More About John Detwiler:
                  Residence: Inverness, FL[7468]

2620. Sarah Ann⁸ Christner (Samuel J.⁷, John B.⁶, Peter⁵, Peter⁴, Christian³, Christian², Christen¹) was born 16 Jan 1902 in Shipshewana Lagrange Co., IN⁷⁴⁶⁹, and died 06 Feb 1994. She married **Albert D. Miller** 24 Nov 1927 in Lagrange Co., IN. He was born 08 Apr 1905 in Howard Co., IN, and died 12 Sep 1982.

Notes for Sarah Ann Christner:
Died at 8:30 a.m. Sunday in Century Villa Health Care Center, Greentown, IN. Member of Howard - Miami Mennonite Church. Burial at Christner Cemetery, Kokomo, IN by Laird Funeral Home in Amboy, IN.

Miller, Sarah Ann Christner, 92, Greentown, IN Born Jan. 16, 1902, Shipshewana, IN to Samuel and Fannie Miller Christner. Died Feb. 6, 1994, Greentown, Ind. Survivors- sons: Wilbur, Daniel, Olen; sister: Ida Eash; 11 grandchildren, 28 great-grandchildren. Predeceased by: Albert D. Miller (husband). Funeral: Feb. 9, Howard, Miami Mennonite Church, by Lee Miller. Burial: Christner Cemetery. Christner Cemetery, Greentown, IN 10 miles north of Kokomo, IN.

More About Sarah Ann Christner:
Residence: 1910, Newbury, Lagrange Co., IN⁷⁴⁷⁰
Social Security Number: 304-70-8669/⁷⁴⁷¹
SSN issued: IN⁷⁴⁷¹

Notes for Albert D. Miller:
Albert is the son of Daniel M and Mary Ann Beachy Miller. Albert is a farmer and Old Order Amish near Kokomo, IN. He is buried in the Christner Cemetery Kokomo, IN Howard-Miami Mennonite Church.

Died of Cancer at Dukes Memorial Hospital, Peru, IN.

More About Albert D. Miller:
Burial: 15 Sep 1982, Christner Cem. Greentown In. 10 miles north of Kokomo IN.
Cause of Death: Cancer

Children of Sarah Christner and Albert Miller are:
+ 4665   i.   Olen⁹ Miller.
  4666   ii.   Wilbur A. Miller, born 09 Oct 1929.
  4667   iii.   Daniel A. Miller, born 28 Nov 1932.

2621. John S.⁸ Christner (Samuel J.⁷, John B.⁶, Peter⁵, Peter⁴, Christian³, Christian², Christen¹) was born 03 Sep 1905 in Shipshewana, Elkhart Co., IN, and died 07 Mar 1983 in Shipshewana, Elkhart Co., IN. He married **Gertrude M. Yoder** 10 Mar 1927 in Shipshewana, Elkhart Co., IN. She was born 13 Jan 1905 in Topeka, Lagrange Co., IN, and died 07 Mar 1983 in Shipshewana, Elkhart Co., IN.

Notes for John S. Christner:
John was a farmer and Old Order Amish near Shipshewana, IN. A double funeral was held on this couples 56 wedding anniversary. The couple died from carbon monoxide poisoning. Their daughter Mary Jane checked on her folks every day and found them. There automobile was still running in the attached garage at 9:30 AM. SS#;306-38-4419 Iss IN

Birth: Sep 3, 1905
Death: Mar 7, 1983
Shipshewana, Lagrange Co., IN

Gospel Herald Obituaries - June, 1983

Christner, John was born Sept 3, 1905 he died of carbon monoxide poisoning at his home in Shipshewana, IN Mar 7, 1983; aged 77 y. On Mar. 10, 1927 he was married to Gertie Yoder. Surviving are one daughter (Mary Jane-Mrs. Roy Yoder), one son (Vernon), 6 grandchildren, 2 sisters (Mrs. Sarah Miller and Ida-Mrs. Ora Eash), and one brother (Glen). He was a member of Marion Mennonite Church. Funeral services were held on Mar 10 in charge of Tim Lichti; interment at Shore Cemetery.

Spouse: Gertrude Yoder Christner (1905 - 1983)

Burial: Shore Cemetery, Shipshewana, Lagrange Co., IN

More About John S. Christner:
Burial: Shoremennonite Cemetery, Shipshewana, Lagrange Co., IN
Religion: Marion Mennonite Church/
Residence: 1910, Newbury, Lagrange Co., IN[7472]

Notes for Gertrude M. Yoder:
Christner, Gertie daughter of Mose and Mary (Yoder) Yoder, was born near Topeka, IN Jan 13, 1905; died of carbon monoxide poisoning at her home in Shipshewana, IN Mar 7, 1983; aged 78 y. On Mar. 10, 1927 she was married to John S. Christner. Surviving is one daughter (Mary Jane-Mrs. Roy Yoder), one son (Vernon), 6 grandchildren, one sister (Mrs. Sarah Kropf), and 2 brothers (Ernest Yoder and Orva Yoder). She was a member of Marion Mennonite Church. Funeral services were held at Shore Mennonite Church on Mar. 10, in charge of Tim Lichti; interment at Shore Cemetery.

Birth: Jan 13, 1905 - Topeka, Lagrange Co., IN
Death: Mar 7, 1983 - Shipshewana, Lagrange Co., IN

Spouse: John Christner (1905 - 1983)

Burial: Shore Cemetery, Shipshewana, Lagrange Co., IN

More About Gertrude M. Yoder:
Burial: Shoremennonite Cemetery, Shipshewana, Lagrange Co., IN

Children of John Christner and Gertrude Yoder are:
+   4668   i.   Vernon Jay[9] Christner, born 17 Apr 1929 in Lagrange Co., IN; died 23 Oct 2005 in Lagrange Co., IN.
+   4669   ii.   Mary Jane Christner, born 15 Sep 1937; died Jan 1984 in Age at Death: 46/Shipshewana, Lagrange Co., IN.

2622. Olen S.[8] Christner (Samuel J.[7], John B.[6], Peter[5], Peter[4], Christian[3], Christian[2], Christen[1])[7473] was born 23 Sep 1909 in Lagrange Co., IN[7474], and died 02 May 1992 in Lagrange Co., IN. He married **Polly C. Miller** 02 Apr 1931 in Lagrange Co., IN. She was born 01 Jan 1907 in Hutchison, Reno Co., KS[7474], and died 15 Jan 1997 in Shipshewana, Elkhart Co., IN.

Notes for Olen S. Christner:
Olen was O.O.Amish and a farmer near Shipshewana, Lagrange Co., IN
SS#313-76-7026 - ISS IN

More About Olen S. Christner:
Burial: 04 May 1992, East Barren Cemetery, Shipshewana, Lagrange Co., IN
Race: White/[7474]
Residence: 1910, Newbury, Lagrange Co., IN[7475]
Social Security Number: 313-76-7026/[7476]
SSN issued: IN[7476]

Notes for Polly C. Miller:
Polly is the daughter of Christian M. and Lydiann C. Miller. Burial at East Barrens Cemetery.

More About Polly C. Miller:

Burial: East Barren Cemetery, Shipshewana, Lagrange Co., IN
Race: White[7477]
Residence: 01 Apr 1940, Age: 33; Marital Status: Married; Relation to Head of House: Wife/Newbury, Lagrange, Indiana, United States[7477]

Children of Olen Christner and Polly Miller are:

+	4670	i.	Orvil H.[9] Christner, born 15 Jun 1933.
+	4671	ii.	Wayne O. Christner, born Abt. 1938 in IN.
+	4672	iii.	Dean O. Christner, born 02 Jan 1940 in Lagrange Co., IN.
+	4673	iv.	Olen Christner Jr., born 23 Sep 1941 in Lagrange Co., IN.
+	4674	v.	Marlene Christner, born 05 Feb 1945 in Lagrange Co., IN.

2623. Ida[8] Christner (Samuel J.[7], John B.[6], Peter[5], Peter[4], Christian[3], Christian[2], Christen[1]) was born 16 May 1912 in Shipshewana, Elkhart Co., IN[7478], and died 19 Dec 1996 in Shipshewana, Lagrange Co., IN[7478]. She married **Ora W. Eash**[7479] 28 Nov 1935 in Shipshewana, Elkhart Co., IN, son of William Eash and Lydia Yoder. He was born 11 Sep 1912, and died 21 May 1995 in Shipshewana, Lagrange Co., IN[7479].

Notes for Ida Christner:
Last address 3530 North -- 675 West of LaGrange IN She was a homemaker. Burial at East Barren Cemetery, Shipshewana, IN.

More About Ida Christner:
Burial: East Barren Cemetery, Shipshewana, IN
Social Security Number: 312-76-8166/[7480]
SSN issued: IN[7480]

Notes for Ora W. Eash:
Old Order Amish and a farmer near Shipshewana LaGrange Co., IN.

More About Ora W. Eash:
Burial: East Barren Cemetery, Shipshewana, IN
Social Security Number: 311-44-3879/[7481]
SSN issued: IN[7481]

Children of Ida Christner and Ora Eash are:

4675   i.   Fannie Mae[9] Eash, born 18 Apr 1938. She married William Langacher.

Notes for Fannie Mae Eash:
Fannie married William Langacher in Shipshewana
Fannie Frannie Freny Frany Freni are all nicknames for Veronica as the german pronunciation uses an F sound instead of a V as in Furronica. (roll the R's) so like many languages if you add a Y sound to the end of a name you have a nickname. Example Johnny, Dickie or Dicky, Bobby, Maggie, Lizzie.

Last names had the same problem, Schantz became Johns as you can play with the word in german it will sound like (chaunts) the a is ah.

4676   ii.   Perry Eash, born 20 Jan 1942. He married Edna Yoder.

Notes for Perry Eash:
Old Order Amish in Shipshewana, IN.

4677   iii.   Orla Eash, born 02 Sep 1945. He married Lydia Mae Yoder; born 19 Dec 1945 in Shipehewana, Lagrange Co., IN.

4678   iv.   Gladys Eash, born 16 Dec 1948. She married William Ray Yoder.

Notes for Gladys Eash:

2633. Barbara[8] **Schmucker** (Catherine[7] Christner, Peter[6], Peter[5], Peter[4], Christian[3], Christian[2], Christen[1])[7482,7483] was born 13 Jul 1878 in Greentown, Howard Co., IN[7484,7485], and died 01 Apr 1940 in Greentown, Howard, Indiana, United States[7485,7486]. She married **Emanuel C. Hochstedler** 11 Jan 1900 in Kokomo, Howard Co., IN. He was born 19 Jul 1875.

More About Barbara Schmucker:
Residence: 1880, Liberty, Howard, Indiana, United States[7487]

Children of Barbara Schmucker and Emanuel Hochstedler are:

+	4679	i.	Savillo[9] Hochstedler, born 31 Jan 1901 in Kokomo, Howard Co., IN.
+	4680	ii.	Polly Hochstedler, born 27 Jan 1902 in Kokomo, Howard Co., IN.
+	4681	iii.	John E. Hochstedler, born 20 Nov 1903 in Kokomo, Howard Co., IN.
+	4682	iv.	William E. Hochstedler, born 04 Aug 1907 in Kokomo, Howard Co., IN.
+	4683	v.	Victor Hochstedler, born 21 Mar 1910 in Kokomo, Howard Co., IN.
+	4684	vi.	Harvey Hochstedler, born 26 Sep 1913 in Kokomo, Howard Co., IN.

2634. John C.[8] **Schmucker** (Catherine[7] Christner, Peter[6], Peter[5], Peter[4], Christian[3], Christian[2], Christen[1])[7488,7489] was born 08 Dec 1879 in Greentown, Howard Co., IN[7490,7491], and died 28 Dec 1950[7492,7493]. He married **Anna Hershberger** 22 Oct 1903. She was born 16 Apr 1885.

Notes for John C. Schmucker:
Lived at Hartville, OH.

More About John C. Schmucker:
Residence: 1900, Howard Township, Howard, Indiana[7493]

Children of John Schmucker and Anna Hershberger are:

+	4685	i.	Mary J.[9] Schmucker, born 12 Apr 1905.
	4686	ii.	Rebecca J. Schmucker, born 16 Jan 1907.
	4687	iii.	Christian J. Schmucker, born 06 Sep 1908. He married Vinnie Estella Caris 24 Jan 1931; born 04 Jun 1904.
+	4688	iv.	Daniel J. Schmucker, born 04 Jul 1912.
+	4689	v.	Robert J. Schmucker, born 18 Nov 1921.

2635. Joseph P.[8] **Schmucker** (Catherine[7] Christner, Peter[6], Peter[5], Peter[4], Christian[3], Christian[2], Christen[1])[7494] was born 18 Apr 1881 in Greentown, Howard Co., IN[7494,7495], and died 04 May 1948[7496,7497]. He married **Amy Slabaugh** 30 Jan 1901 in Midland MI. She was born 02 Jan 1881.

More About Joseph P. Schmucker:
Residence: 1900, Howard Township, Howard, Indiana[7497]

Children of Joseph Schmucker and Amy Slabaugh are:

+	4690	i.	Malenda[9] Schmucker, born 28 Apr 1902.
+	4691	ii.	Mary Schmucker, born 08 Jul 1904.
	4692	iii.	Sarah Schmucker, born 29 Nov 1907; died 17 Feb 1934.
	4693	iv.	Leona Schmucker, born 04 Feb 1913; died 02 May 1913.

2636. Jacob[8] **Schmucker** (Catherine[7] Christner, Peter[6], Peter[5], Peter[4], Christian[3], Christian[2], Christen[1])[7498] was born 07 Jan 1883 in Greentown, Howard Co., IN[7498]. He married **Lydia Yoder** 07 Feb 1907 in Goshen, IN. She was born 03 Jul 1888, and died 16 May 1939.

Notes for Jacob Schmucker:
Lived around Topeka, IN.

Children of Jacob Schmucker and Lydia Yoder are:
+   4694   i.   Anna[9] Schmucker, born 04 Sep 1908.
+   4695   ii.   Noah J. Schmucker, born 29 Dec 1914 in Lagrange Co., IN; died 26 Jan 2003.

2638. Noah C.[8] **Schmucker** (Catherine[7] Christner, Peter[6], Peter[5], Peter[4], Christian[3], Christian[2], Christen[1])[7498] was born 17 Mar 1891 in Greentown, Howard Co., IN[7498,7499], and died 05 Jun 1975 in Middlebury, Elkhart Co., IN[7500,7501]. He married **Ida P. Miller** 24 Nov 1910 in Goshen, Elkhart Co., IN. She was born 09 Apr 1890 in Elkhart Co., IN, and died 12 Jan 1989 in Elkhart Co., IN.

Notes for Noah C. Schmucker:
Lived around Millersburg, IN.

More About Noah C. Schmucker:
Residence: 1930, Benton, Elkhart, Indiana[7501]
Social Security Number: 308-40-0181/[7502]
SSN issued: IN[7502]

Children of Noah Schmucker and Ida Miller are:
    4696   i.   Infant Son[9] Schmucker.
    4697   ii.   William Schmucker.
+   4698   iii.   Kathryn S. Schmucker, born 29 Oct 1911 in Lagrange Co., IN; died 08 Jan 2000 in Elkhart Co., IN.
    4699   iv.   William Schmucker, born 19 Oct 1912; died 21 Oct 1912.
+   4700   v.   Rosa Schmucker, born 04 Sep 1914.
+   4701   vi.   Edna Schmucker, born 07 Sep 1916.
    4702   vii.   Infant Son Schmucker, born 12 Oct 1919.
    4703   viii.   Infant Son Schmucker, born 02 Aug 1922.
+   4704   ix.   Willard Schmucker, born 12 Jun 1924.
+   4705   x.   Esther Schmucker, born 02 Oct 1928.

2639. Levi[8] **Christner** (Jacob[7], Peter[6], Peter[5], Peter[4], Christian[3], Christian[2], Christen[1]) was born 12 Dec 1884 in Hubbard, Marion Co., OR, and died 15 May 1953 in Clackamas Co., OR[7503]. He married **Barbara Ellen Hostetler** 02 Oct 1910, daughter of Moses Hostetler and Elizabeth Eash. She was born 16 Feb 1891 in Cass Co., MO.

Notes for Levi Christner:
Christner, Levi son of Jacob and Fannie (Miller) Christner was born near Hubbard, OR Dec. 12, 1884; met his death when he was accidently stuck down by an auto May 15, 1953; aged 68 y. 5 m. 3 d. All of his life was spent in the Willamette Valley. For the past ten years he had been employed at the Dronbecker Sawmill at Oregon City. In his youth he accepted Christ as his personal Saviour and united with the Zion Mennonite Church, Hubbard, OR where he was a member at the time of his death. In 1910 he was married to Ella Hostetler. To this union were born 5 sons and 3 daughters (Roy, Hubbard, OR; Etta Beer, Wickensburg, AZ; Roscoe, Barlow, OR; Fred, Hubbard, OR; Harold, Troutdale, OR; Rovena Kallstrom, Canby, OR; and 13 grandchildren, and one stepsister (Etta Watzig, Orchard, WA). One brother preceded him in death. Funeral services were in charge of Edward Kenagy with burial in the Zion Mennonite Church Cemetery.

More About Levi Christner:
Burial: Zion Mennonite Church Cemetery

Children of Levi Christner and Barbara Hostetler are:
    4706   i.   Titus Leroy[9] Christner, born 02 Sep 1911 in Hubbard, Marion Co., OR; died 30 Jun 1999 in Hubbard, Marion Co., OR.
    4707   ii.   Etta Elizabeth Christner, born 07 Dec 1912.
    4708   iii.   Henry Roscoe Christner, born 17 Sep 1914 in Molalla, Clackamas Co., OR[7503]; died 01 Dec 2001 in Canby, Clackamas Co., OR[7504,7505].

               More About Henry Roscoe Christner:
               Military: 06 May 1942, Portland, Multnomah Co., OR[7506]
               Social Security Number: 541-14-4440/[7507,7508]

SSN issued: OR[7509,7510]

4709 iv. Alice Berdina Christner[7511], born 18 Jul 1916 in Molalla, Clackamas Co., OR[7511]; died 06 Mar 2005 in Oregon City, Clackamas Co., OR[7511]. She married Roy Lawrence Brown[7511] 1934[7511]; born 1914[7511]; died 24 May 1987[7511].

Notes for Alice Berdina Christner:
Birth: 1917
Death: Mar. 6, 2005

Burial: Mountain View Cemetery, Oregon City, Clackamas Co., OR
Plot: Section I, Block 7, Lot 12, Grave E
Find A Grave Memorial# 93261549

More About Alice Berdina Christner:
Residence: 1920, Molalla, Clackamas Co., OR[7511]
Social Security Number: 543-42-0714[7511]

Notes for Roy Lawrence Brown:
Birth: 1914
Death: May 24, 1987

Burial: Mountain View Cemetery, Oregon City, Clackamas Co., OR
Plot: Section I,Block 7,Lot 12,Grave D
Find A Grave Memorial# 93261610

4710 v. Fred Jacob Christner, born 23 Oct 1917; died 11 Mar 2008 in Hubbard, Marion Co., OR[7512].

More About Fred Jacob Christner:
Residence: OR[7513]
SSN issued: OR[7514]

4711 vi. Harold Clinton Christner[7515], born 15 Mar 1919 in Molalla, Clackamas Co., OR[7515]; died 24 Mar 1955 in Whisky Hill 30 miles south of Portland OR/Bridal Veil, Multnomah Co., OR[7515].

4712 vii. Rovena Faith Christner, born 19 Mar 1923. She married Wailan M. Kallistrom[7516] 31 Dec 1942 in Clark, Washington[7516].

4713 viii. Leonard Arnold Christner[7517,7518], born 12 Mar 1926[7519,7520]; died 08 Apr 2008 in Canby, Clackamas Co., OR[7521,7522].

More About Leonard Arnold Christner:
Social Security Number: 543-26-8571/[7523]
SSN issued: OR[7523]

2642. Barbara Delilah "Lila"[8] Miller (Magdalena "Mattie"[7] Christner, Peter[6], Peter[5], Peter[4], Christian[3], Christian[2], Christen[1])[7524,7525] was born 02 Apr 1881 in Woodburn, Marion Co., OR[7526], and died 03 Apr 1982 in Woodburn, Marion Co., OR. She married **(1) Amos Kauffman**[7526] 01 Oct 1899[7526], son of Daniel Kauffman and Susanna Yoder. He was born 02 Aug 1878 in Arthur, Douglas Co., IL[7526], and died 02 Dec 1934 in Woodburn, Marion Co., OR[7526]. She married **(2) Clarence Isaac Kropf**[7527] May 1938[7527], son of John Kropf and Charity King. He was born 24 Nov 1885 in Garden City, Cass Co., MO[7527], and died 09 Sep 1969 in Woodburn, Marion Co., OR[7527].

Notes for Barbara Delilah "Lila" Miller:
Birth: Apr. 2, 1881 - Woodburn, Marion Co., OR
Death: Apr. 3, 1982 - Woodburn, Marion Co., OR

Woodburn Independent, April 5, 1962, page 2

Mrs. Delila Kropf
Funeral services for Mrs. Delila Kropf, 81, wife of Bishop Clarence I. Kropf, will be held at 2 p.m. Friday, April 6, at Zion Mennonite church east of Hubbard with Bishop Nick Birky of Albany officiating. Interment will be in

the church cemetery with Ringo-Cornwell Funeral Chapel making arrangements.

Mrs. Kropf died at her home on Boone's Ferry road just north of Woodburn Tuesday morning following a long illness. She was born near Woodburn April 2, 1881, and lived in the area all her life. She was married to Clarence Kropf in 1938 and was a member of Zion Mennonite church. Her first husband Amos Kauffman died in 1934.

Survivors in addition to the widower are six sons, Lawrence Kauffman of Waldport, Roy Kauffman of Hubbard, Marion Kauffman of Mt. Rainier, Wash., Lewis Kauffman of Eastside, Charles Kauffman of Waldport, and Morris Kauffman of Wecoma Beach; one daughter, Mrs. Lucille King of Wecoma Beach; a brother, Sam Miller of Hubbard; a sister, Mrs. Abe (Tillie) Jones of Hubbard; 23 grandchildren and 25 great grandchildren. There also are six step-children, Mrs. John Hershberger of Woodburn, Herman Kropf of Harrisburg, Milo Kropf of Woodburn, Leland and Lawrence Kropf of Waldport, and Delbert Kropf of Molalla.

Parents:
Solomon L. Miller (1857 - 1941)
Mattie Christner Miller (1862 - 1929)

Spouses:
Amos Kauffman (1878 - 1934)
Clarence Isaac Kropf (1885 - 1969)

Children:
Harley Amos Kauffman (1905 - 1975)
Marion E. Kauffman (1909 - 1962)
Mary Alice Kauffman (1910 - 1913)
Pearl Lorene Kauffman (1912 - 1913)
Baby Kauffman (1914 - 1914)
Charles Kauffman (1917 - 1967)
Morris E. Kauffman (1919 - 2008)

Burial: Zion Mennonite Cemetery, Ninety-one, Clackamas Co., OR
Plot: 6S-2

More About Barbara Delilah "Lila" Miller:
Burial: Apr 1962, Zion Menn. Cem., Needy, Clackamas Co., OR[7528]
Residence: 01 Apr 1940, McKee, Marion Co., OR[7529]

More About Amos Kauffman:
Burial: Dec 1934, Zion Menn. Cem., Needy, Clackamas Co., OR[7530]

Notes for Clarence Isaac Kropf:
Birth: Nov 24, 1885 - Garden City, Cass Co., MO
Death: Sep 9, 1969 - Albany, Linn Co., OR

Gospel Herald - Volume LXII, Number 44 - November 11, 1969, page 1000.

Kropf - Clarence Isaac, son of John and Charity (King) Kropf, was born at Garden City, Mo., Nov. 24, 1885; died at Albany, Ore., Sept. 9, 1969; aged 83 y. 9 m. 16 d. In 1908, he was married to Mary Ann Miller, who died in 1936. In 1938, he was married to Delila Miller Kauffman, who died in April 1962. On July 12, 1923, he was ordained to the office of deacon, and on July 1, 1936, to the office of bishop, serving the Zion congregation. Surviving are 6 children (Herman S., Milo E., Leland E., Lawrence M., Delbert E., and Etta-Mrs. John Hershberger), 5 stepchildren (Lawrence, Roy, Lewis, and Morris Kauffman, and Lucille King), and 3 brothers (Harvey, Chauncey, and Roy). He was preceded in death by one daughter (Gladys Lorene) in 1938. He was a member of the Zion Church, where funeral services were held Sept. 12, with Paul Brunner and Edward Kenagy officiating.

Parents:

John Kropf (1850 - 1912)
Charity Ann King Kropf (1856 - 1940)

Spouses:
Mary Ann Miller Kropf (1887 - 1936)
Barbara Delila Miller Kauffman Kropf (1881 - 1982)

Children:
Etta Pearl Kropf Hershberger (1911 - 2003)
Gladys Lorene Kropf (1917 - 1938)

Burial: Zion Mennonite Cemetery, Ninety-one, Clackamas Co., OR
Plot: 5S-6
Find A Grave Memorial# 5456751

More About Clarence Isaac Kropf:
Residence: Woodburn, Oregon, United States[7531]

Children of Barbara Miller and Amos Kauffman are:

4714	i.	Samuel Melvin[9] Kauffman[7532], born 18 Jun 1900 in Oregon, USA[7532]; died in Y/[7532].
4715	ii.	Lawrence Reuben Kauffman[7532], born 17 Aug 1902[7532]; died in Y/[7532].
4716	iii.	Harley Amos Kauffman[7532], born 09 Jan 1905 in Hubbard, Marion Co., OR[7532]; died 08 May 1942 in Portland, Multnomah Co., OR[7532].

More About Harley Amos Kauffman:
Burial: May 1942, Zion Menn. Cem., Needy, Clackamas Co., OR[7532]

4717	iv.	Roy Monroe Kauffman[7532], born 04 Apr 1907[7532]; died in Y/[7532].
4718	v.	Marion E. Kauffman[7532], born 11 Feb 1909 in Aurora, Marion Co., OR[7532]; died 16 Oct 1962 in Carson, Skamania Co., WA[7532].

More About Marion E. Kauffman:
Burial: Oct 1962, Zion Menn. Cem., Needy, Clackamas Co., OR[7532]

4719	vi.	Mary Alice Kauffman[7532], born 21 Aug 1910[7532]; died 21 Apr 1913[7532].

More About Mary Alice Kauffman:
Burial: Apr 1913, Zion Menn. Cem., Needy, Clackamas Co., OR[7532]

4720	vii.	Pearl Lorene Kauffman[7532], born 09 Mar 1912[7532]; died 21 Apr 1913[7532].

More About Pearl Lorene Kauffman:
Burial: Apr 1913, Zion Menn. Cem., Needy, Clackamas Co., OR[7532]

4721	viii.	Infant Kauffman[7532], born 17 Feb 1914 in U/[7532]; died 17 Feb 1914[7532].

More About Infant Kauffman:
Burial: Feb 1914, Zion Menn. Cem., Needy, Clackamas Co., OR[7532]

4722	ix.	Charles Kauffman[7532], born 23 Apr 1917 in Oregon, USA[7532]; died 16 Oct 1967 in Molalla, Clackamas Co., OR[7532].

More About Charles Kauffman:
Burial: Oct 1967, Zion Menn. Cem., Needy, Clackamas Co., OR[7532]

4723	x.	Morris Kauffman[7532], born Apr 1919 in Oregon, USA[7532]; died Aft. 09 Sep 1969[7532].

2643. Samuel Serious[8] Miller (Magdalena "Mattie"[7] Christner, Peter[6], Peter[5], Peter[4], Christian[3], Christian[2], Christen[1]) was born 04 Apr 1883 in Hubbard, Marion Co., OR, and died 22 Jul 1967 in Salem, Marion Co., OR. He married **(1) Mary Ann Egli**. She was born 07 Mar 1888 in Wayland, Henry Co., IA, and died 12 Aug 1970 in Albany, Linn Co., OR. He married **(2) Nellie Catherine Hooley**. She was born 05 Dec 1889 in Garden City, Cass Co., OR, and died 09 Sep 1950 in Oregon City, Clackamas Co., OR.

Notes for Samuel Serious Miller:
Birth: Apr 4, 1883 - Hubbard, Marion Co., OR
Death: Jul 22, 1967 - Salem, Marion Co., OR

Miller - Samuel S. son of Solomon and Mattie (Christner) Miller was born at Hubbard, OR Apr 4, 1883 died at Salem Memorial Hospital, Salem, OR Jul 22, 1967 from injuries sustained in an automobile accident; aged 84 y. 3 m. 18 d. In Dec 1908. He was married to Nellie Hooley who preceded him in death. On May 8, 1954 he was married to Mamie Egli Bauman Miller, who survives. Also surviving are 4 children (Velma-Mrs. Roy Evers, Irene-Mrs. Jim Evans, Leonard, and Ralph), one sister (Tillie Jones), and 3 stepsons (Hershel Hooley, Ed Hooley, and Virgil Hostettler). Two daughters (Florence and Sophia) preceded him in death. He was a member of Zion Church, where funeral services were held July 26, with Paul Brunner officiating.
~ Gospel Herald

Parents:
Solomon L. Miller (1857 - 1941)
Mattie Christner Miller (1862 - 1929)

Children: Sophia Ardell Miller Schrock (1931 - 1959)

Spouses:
Nellie Catherine Hooley Miller (1889 - 1950)
Mary Ann Egli Hooley Hostetler Bauman Miller (1889 - 1970)

Burial: Zion Mennonite Cemetery, Clackamas Co., OR
Plot: row 17 plot 1 sec 1 n

Notes for Mary Ann Egli:
Birth: Nov. 21, 1889 - Wayland, Henry Co., IA
Death: Aug. 12, 1970 - Albany, Linn Co., OR

Miller, Mary Ann (Mamie), daughter of John and Lena Egli was born at Wayland, IA Nov. 21, 1889; died at the Albany Old People's Home, Aug. 12, 1970; aged 80 y. 8 m. 22 d. She was married to Edwin Hooley, who died in 1914, to Amasa Hostetler, who died in 1939, to Sam Bauman, who died in 1948, and on May 8, 1954, she was married to Sam Miller, who died on July 22, 1967. Surviving are 3 sons (Hershal and Edwin Hooley, and Virgil Hostetler), 6 stepchildren, 16 grandchildren, and 9 great-grandchildren. She was preceded in death by 2 sons (Wayne Hooley and Raymond Hostetler). She was a member of the Zion Church, where funeral services were held Aug. 16, with Paul D. Brunner officiating; interment in the Zion Cemetery.

Parents:
John Egli (1852 - 1924)
Magdalena Rich Egli (1858 - 1926)

Spouses:
Samuel Serious Miller (1883 - 1967)
Amasa Hostetler (1888 - 1939)
Joseph Edwin Hooley (1887 - 1914)

Burial: Zion Mennonite Cemetery, Clackamas Co., OR
Plot: row 16 plot 2 sec 1 n

Notes for Nellie Catherine Hooley:
Birth: Dec. 5, 1889 - Garden City, Cass Co., MO
Death: Sep. 9, 1950 - Oregon City, Clackamas Co., OR

Miller. - Nellie Catherine, daughter of M. S. and Fanny Hooley was born at Garden City, MO Dec. 5, 1889; died at the Hutchinson Hospital, Oregon City, OR, Sep 9, 1950; aged 60 y. 9 m. 4 d. On Dec 12, 1908, she was married to Samuel S. Miller, who survives. Also surviving are 2 sons and 3 daughters (Velma-Mrs. Roy Evers, Elmira, OR; Irene-Mrs. Frances Evans, Brooks, OR; Leonard, Hubbard, OR; Ralph, Sweet Home, OR; Sophia-Mrs. Perry Schrock, Albany, OR), 14 grandchildren, 2 brothers, and 3 sisters. One daughter (Florence Edna) preceded her in death. She moved with her parents from Garden City, MO to Hubbard, OR in 1906. There she lived until her death. She accepted Christ as her Saviour early in life and united with the Mennonite Church. She was a faithful, willing worker in Sunday school and church and will be greatly missed in her home. Always healthy, she had been a hard worker until the last two weeks of her life when she was ailing. Funeral services were held at the Zion Mennonite Church near Hubbard, OR by Chester Kauffman. Text: John 11: 35. Her body was laid to rest in the Zion Cemetery.
~ Gospel Herald

Parents:
Menno Simon Hooley (1857 - 1934)
Veronica Frances Hostetler Hooley (1857 - 1942)

Spouse:
Samuel Serious Miller (1883 - 1967)

Children: Sophia Ardell Miller Schrock (1931 - 1959)

Burial: Zion Mennonite Cemetery, Ninety-one, Clackamas Co., OR
Plot: row 17 plot 2 sec 1 n

Child of Samuel Miller and Mary Egli is:
4724   i.   Sophia Ardell[9] Miller, born 04 Apr 1883 in Hubbard, Marion Co., OR; died 14 Sep 1959 in Lebanon, Linn Co., OR. She married Perry Galen Schrock.

Notes for Sophia Ardell Miller:
Birth: Jan.16, 1931 - Hubbard, Marion Co., OR
Death: Sep 14, 1959 - Lebanon, Linn Co., OR

Schrock, Sophia Ardell daughter of Samuel S. and Nellie Miller was born Jan. 16, 1931; died at the Lebanon (Oreg.) Community Hospital at Sept. 14, 1959; aged 28 y. 7 m. 29 d. On June 26, 1949, she was married to Perry Galen Schrock, who survives. Also surviving are 4 daughters and 2 sons (Patricia Joann, Myrna Kathryn, Lavonne Marie, Carolyn Ardell, Raymond Eugene, Stanley Galen, all living at the family home near Lebanon), her father and stepmother (Samuel S. and Mamie Miller, Hubbard, OR), 2 sisters (Velma-Mrs. Roy Evers, Elmira, OR and Irene-Mrs. Jim Evans, Tidewater, Oreg.), and 2 brothers (Leonard, Ukiah, CA; and Ralph, North Pole, Alaska). Her mother and one sister preceded her in death. She had been a member of the Zion Church until her marriage when she transferred to the Fairview Church. At the time of her death she was a charter member of the Plainview Church which was organized in June 1959. Services were held at the Fairview Church, in charge of Louis Landis, N. M. Birky, and Ivan Headings.
~ Gospel Herald

Parents:
Samuel Serious Miller (1883 - 1967)
Nellie Catherine Hooley Miller (1889 - 1950)

Burial: Fairview Mennonite Cemetery, Albany, Linn Co., OR

2644. Polly[8] Miller (Magdalena "Mattie"[7] Christner, Peter[6], Peter[5], Peter[4], Christian[3], Christian[2], Christen[1]) was born 20 Mar 1885 in Brooks, Marion Co., OR, and died 14 Sep 1952 in Silverton, Marion Co., OR[7533]. She married **Harvey Elmer Kropf**. He was born 01 Dec 1883 in Cass, MO[7533], and died 14 Apr 1971[7533].

Notes for Polly Miller:

Birth: Mar. 20, 1885 - Brooks, Marion Co., OR
Death: Sep. 14, 1952 - Silverton, Marion Co., OR

Parents:
Solomon L. Miller (1857 - 1941)
Mattie Christner Miller (1862 - 1929)

Spouse: Harvey Elmer Kropf (1883 - 1971)

Children:
Mabel Alice Kropf Roth (1908 - 2002)
Allen E. Kropf (1918 - 1992)

Burial: Zion Mennonite Cemetery, Ninety-one, Clackamas Co., OR
Plot: 7N-2

Notes for Harvey Elmer Kropf:
Birth: Dec. 1, 1883
Death: Apr. 14, 1971

GOSPEL HERALD - Volume LXIV, Number 19 - May 11, 1971 - pp 435, 436

Kropf, Harvey Elmer, son of John and Charity (King) Kropf, was born in Garden City, Mo., Dec. 1, 1883; died at Lebanon Community Hospital, Lebanon, Ore., Apr. 14, 1971; aged 87 y. 4 m. 13 d. On Jan. 14, 1906, he was married to Polly Miller, who preceded him in death in 1952. Surviving are 3 sons (Ivan, Allen, and Calvin), 3 daughters (Mabel - Mrs. Uriah Roth, Charity Kropf, and Pauline - Mrs. Emmanuel Gerig), and 2 brothers (Chauncey and Roy). He was a member of the Zion Mennonite Church, where funeral services were held Apr. 17, in charge of Paul D. Brunner; interment in the Zion Cemetery.

Parents:
John Kropf (1850 - 1912)
Charity Ann King Kropf (1856 - 1940)

Spouse: Polly Miller Kropf (1885 - 1952)

Children:
Mabel Alice Kropf Roth (1908 - 2002)
Allen E Kropf (1918 - 1992)

Burial: Zion Mennonite Cemetery, Ninety-one, Clackamas Co., OR
Plot: 7N-1

Child of Polly Miller and Harvey Kropf is:
4725 i. Mabel Alice[9] Kropf[7533], born 07 Oct 1908 in Woodburn, Marion Co., OR; died 08 Oct 2002 in Canby, Clackamas Co., OR. She married Uriah Amos Roth; born 27 Jan 1907 in Woodburn, Marion Co., OR; died 03 May 1971 in Canby, Clackamas Co., OR.

  Notes for Mabel Alice Kropf:
  Birth: Oct. 7, 1908 - Woodburn, Marion Co., OR
  Death: Oct. 8, 2002 - Canby, Clackamas Co., OR

  The Mennonite, November 19, 2002, pages 26-27, Vol. 5, No. 22.

  Roth - Mabel Kropf, 94, Canby, Ore., died Oct. 8. Spouse: Uriah Roth (deceased). Parents: Harvey and Polly Miller Kropf (both deceased). Survivors: children Doris South, Don, Ken; six grandchildren; 14 great-grandchildren. Funeral: Oct. 13 at Zion Mennonite Church, Canby.

  Parents:

Harvey Elmer Kropf (1883 - 1971)
Polly Miller Kropf (1885 - 1952)

Spouse: Uriah Amos Roth (1907 - 1971)

Inscription: In all thy ways acknowledge Him.
Prov. 3:6

Burial: Zion Mennonite Cemetery, Ninety-one, Clackamas Co., OR
Plot: 13N-6

Notes for Uriah Amos Roth:
Birth: Jan 27, 1907 - Woodburn, Marion Co., OR
Death: May 3, 1971 - Canby, Clackamas Co., OR

GOSPEL HERALD - Volume LXIV, Number 21 - May 25, 1971 - pp 483, 484

Roth, Uriah Amos, son of Daniel and Amanda (Kauffman) Roth, was born at Woodburn, Ore., Jan. 27, 1907; died at his home near Canby, Ore., May 3, 1971; aged 63 y. 3 m. 6 d. On June 14, 1931, he was married to Mabel Kropf, who survives. Also surviving are one daughter (Doris Roth), 2 sons (Donovan and Kenneth), 3 sisters (Mary - Mrs. Chris Hofstetter, Sadie Roth, and Beulah - Mrs. John Fretz), and 3 brothers (Joel, Noah, and Nathan). He was a member of the Zion Mennonite Church, where funeral services were held May 6, in charge of Paul D. Brunner; interment in the Zion Church Cemetery.

Parents:
Daniel Roth (1868 - 1923)
Amanda Kauffman Roth (1876 - 1955)

Spouse: Mabel Alice Kropf Roth (1908 - 2002)

Inscription: For I know whom I have believed. II Tim. 1:12

Burial: Zion Mennonite Cemetery, Ninety-one, Clackamas Co., OR
Plot: 13N-5

2645. Inez Katherine[8] Christner (Christian S.[7], Peter[6], Peter[5], Peter[4], Christian[3], Christian[2], Christen[1])[7534,7534] was born 01 Jun 1899 in Lane Co., OR[7534], and died 24 Sep 1979 in Molalla, Clackamas Co., OR[7534]. She married **(2) Arthur Lincoln Lantz**[7534] 29 May 1918[7534]. He was born 08 Oct 1896 in Clackamas Co., OR[7534], and died 30 Dec 1971 in Goverment Camp/Clackamas Co., OR[7534].

More About Inez Katherine Christner:
Occupation: Housewife/[7534]
Residence: 1930, Molalla, Clackamas Co., OR[7534]
Social Security Number: [7534]

More About Arthur Lincoln Lantz:
Occupation: Woodcutter(1920)/[7534]

Children of Inez Katherine Christner are:
4726　　i.　Duane Arthur[9] Lantz[7534], born 11 Apr 1921 in Clackamas Co, Oregon[7534]; died 31 Oct 1987 in Lincoln, Placer, California[7534].

　　　　　More About Duane Arthur Lantz:
　　　　　Residence: 1930, Molalla, Clackamas Co., OR[7534]
　　　　　Social Security Number: 541 18 5297 issued Oregon/[7534]

4727　　ii.　Elton Loyd Lantz[7534], born 16 Mar 1926 in Clackamas Co, Oregon[7534]; died 17 Jul 1989 in Molalla, Clackamas Co., OR[7534].

　　　　　More About Elton Loyd Lantz:
　　　　　Residence: 1930, Molalla, Clackamas Co., OR[7534]

Social Security Number: Washington/[7534]

2646. Clinton Chris[8] Christner (Christian S.[7], Peter[6], Peter[5], Peter[4], Christian[3], Christian[2], Christen[1]) was born 29 Jan 1901 in Needy, Clackamas Co., OR[7535], and died 22 Dec 1987 in Molalla, Clackamas Co., OR[7536]. He married **Esther Koch**[7536] 22 May 1926[7536]. She was born 22 Jul 1908 in NE[7536], and died 06 Nov 2000 in Molalla, Clackamas Co., OR[7536].

Notes for Clinton Chris Christner:
Birth: Jan. 29, 1901
Death: Dec. 22, 1987

Parents:
Christian C. Christner (1871 - 1945)
Adaline Roth Christner (1875 - 1943)

Spouse: Esther Helena Koch Christner (1908 - 2000)

Children: Gale L. Christner (1929 - 2012)

Burial: Zion Mennonite Cemetery, Ninety-one, Clackamas Co., OR
Plot: 10N-3

More About Clinton Chris Christner:
Burial: Zion Mennonite Cemetery, Hubbard Co., OR/[7536]
Residence: 1930, Molalla, Clackamas Co., OR[7536]

Notes for Esther Koch:
Birth: 1908
Death: 2000

Spouse: Clinton C. Christner (1901 - 1987)

Children: Gale L. Christner (1929 - 2012)

Inscription: Married May 22, 1926

Burial: Zion Mennonite Cemetery, Ninety-one, Clackamas Co., OR
Plot: 10 N-4

Child of Clinton Christner and Esther Koch is:
  4728   i.   Gale L.[9] Christner, born 14 Dec 1929 in Molalla, Clackamas Co., OR; died 11 Jan 2012 in Molalla, Clackamas Co., OR.

            Notes for Gale L. Christner:
            Birth: Dec 14, 1929 - Molalla, Clackamas Co., OR
            Death: Jan 11, 2012 - Molalla, Clackamas Co., OR

            Oregonian, Portland, OR
            January 13, 2012, page A7, column 3

            Gale L. Christner
            Dec. 14, 1929 - Jan. 11, 2012

            Resident of Molalla, Gale died of brain cancer. Survivors are his wife of 60 years, Shirley; children, Pam, Terry and Timothy; seven grandchildren; and two great-grand-children.

            Graveside services on Saturday, Jan 14 at 11 a.m. at Zion Memorial Park Canby. Memorials to Macksburg Lutheran Church, Canby.

Parents:
Clinton C. Christner (1901 - 1987)
Esther Helena Koch Christner (1908 - 2000)

Burial: Zion Memorial Park, Canby, Clackamas Co., OR

2650. Harley Simon[8] Christner (Christian S.[7], Peter[6], Peter[5], Peter[4], Christian[3], Christian[2], Christen[1]) was born 02 Feb 1914 in Molalla, Clackamas Co., OR[7537], and died 17 May 1984 in Estacada, Clackamas Co., OR[7537]. He married **Clara E. LaValley** 1944 in Tacoma, Pierce Co., WA[7538]. She was born 06 May 1916 in Great Falls, Cascade Co., MT[7538], and died 30 Oct 2007 in Estacada, Clackamas Co., OR[7538].

More About Harley Simon Christner:
Residence: 1930, Needy, Clackamas Co., OR[7539,7540]

Notes for Clara E. LaValley:
Birth: May 6, 1916 - Great Falls, Cascade Co., MT
Death: Oct. 30, 2007 - OR

Obituary: Oregonian, Nov 1, 2007

A graveside service will be at 2 p.m. Friday, Nov. 2, 2007 in Estacada Funeral Chapel for Clara E. Christner, who died Oct. 30 at age 91.

Clara LaValley was born May 6, 1916, in Great Falls, Mont., and raised in Salem. She moved in 1949 to Estacada, where she was a homemaker. In the early 1930s, she married John Rutherford; they divorced. She married Harley "Dutch" Christner in 1944; he died in 1984.

Survivors include her sons, Stan Rutherford and Ken Rutherford; stepson, William; 10 grandchildren; and great-grandchildren.

Remembrances to Estacada Garden Club.

Spouse: Harley Christner (1914 - 1984

Inscription: Clara E. Christner
1916 - 2007

Burial: Redland Pioneer Cemetery, Redland, Clackamas Co., OR
Plot: Section 5, Row 7, Plot 23

More About Clara E. LaValley:
Residence: 1920, Salem Ward 1, Marion, OR[7540]

Child of Harley Christner and Clara LaValley is:
    4729   i.   Sally Ann[9] Christner[7540], born 27 Aug 1933 in Clackamas Co., OR[7540]; died 31 Aug 1986 in Washington Co., OR[7540].

2657. Bertha[8] Christner (Jacob E.[7], Jacob[6], Peter[5], Peter[4], Christian[3], Christian[2], Christen[1])[7541,7542,7543,7544] was born 23 Jan 1889 in Wayland, Henry Co., IA[7545,7546,7547], and died 12 Dec 1977 in Mt. Pleasant, Henry Co., IA[7548]. She married **John William Hill**[7549,7550]. He was born 20 Aug 1888 in Trenton, Henry Co., IA[7551], and died 23 Feb 1962 in Henry Co., IA[7551,7552].

Notes for Bertha Christner:
Birth: Jan. 23, 1889 - Henry Co., IA

Death: Dec. 12, 1977 - Henry Co., IA

Parents:
Jacob E. Christner (1863 - 1933)
Fannie Rich Christner (1868 - 1947)

Spouse: John William Hill (1888 - 1962)

Burial: Green Mound Cemetery, Henry Co., IA
Plot: Section 4, Row 25

More About Bertha Christner:
Burial: Green Mound-Trenton Cemetery Henry Co. Iowa[7552]
Residence: 1910, Jefferson, Henry Co., IA[7553]
Social Security Number: 478-80-1117/[7554]
SSN issued: IA[7554]

Notes for John William Hill:
Birth: Aug. 20, 1888
Death: Feb. 23, 1962

Parents:
Robert Irvin Hill (1860 - 1937)
Litisha Margaret Hinkle Hill (1870 - 1934)

Spouse: Bertha Christner Hill (1889 - 1977)

Burial: Green Mound Cemetery, Henry Co., IA
Plot: Section 4, Row 25

More About John William Hill:
Burial: Green Mound-Trenton Cemetery Henry Co. Iowa[7555,7556]
Residence: 01 Jan 1925, Trenton, Henry Co., IA[7557,7558]

Children of Bertha Christner and John Hill are:
   4730   i.   Lester Allen[9] Hill[7558], born 01 Apr 1911 in IA[7558]; died 04 Jul 1993 in Wayland, Henry Co., IA[7558]. He married Mary L; born 12 Apr 1910; died 26 Mar 1990.

               Notes for Lester Allen Hill:
               Birth: Apr. 1, 1911
               Death: Jul. 4, 1993

               Parents:
               John William Hill (1888 - 1962)
               Bertha Christner Hill (1889 - 1977)

               Spouse: Mary L. Hill (1910 - 1990)

               Burial: Green Mound Cemetery, Henry Co., IA

               More About Lester Allen Hill:
               Burial: Greenmound Cemetery, Henry Co., IA[7558]
               Residence: 1920, Trenton, Henry Co., IA[7558]
               Social Security Number: 485-38-1975/[7558]

               Notes for Mary L:
               Birth: Apr. 12, 1910
               Death: Mar. 26, 1990

               Spouse: Lester Allen Hill (1911 - 1993)

Burial: Green Mound Cemetery, Henry Co., IA

+ 4731 ii. Max Dillian Hill, born 18 Apr 1920 in Trenton, Henry Co., IA; died 05 Jan 2004 in Washington, Washington Co., IA.

2658. Nicholas[8] Christner (Jacob E.[7], Jacob[6], Peter[5], Peter[4], Christian[3], Christian[2], Christen[1])[7559,7560,7561,7562,7563,7564] was born 13 Jan 1891 in Washington Co., IA[7565,7566], and died 05 May 1977 in Mt. Pleasant, Henry Co., IA[7567]. He married **Jessie Mae Hill**[7568] 24 Jan 1912[7569,7570]. She was born 20 Jul 1892 in Henry Co., IA[7570], and died 09 Aug 1942[7570,7571,7572].

Notes for Nicholas Christner:
Birth: Jan. 13, 1891
Henry Co., IA
Death: May 5, 1977
Henry Co., IA

Parents:
Jacob E. Christner (1863 - 1933)
Fannie Rich Christner (1868 - 1947)

Spouse: Jessie Hill Christner (1892 - 1942)

Burial: White Oak Cemetery, Trenton, Henry Co., IA

More About Nicholas Christner:
Residence: 1920, Lockridge, Jefferson Co., IA[7573]
Social Security Number: 485-44-8100/[7574]
SSN issued: IA[7574]

Notes for Jessie Mae Hill:
Birth: Jul 20, 1892 - Henry Co., IA
Death: Aug 9, 1942 - Henry Co., IA

Parents:
Robert Irvin Hill (1860 - 1937)
Litisha Margaret Hinkle Hill (1870 - 1934)

Spouse: Nicholas Christner (1891 - 1977)

Burial: White Oak Cemetery, Trenton, Henry Co., IA

More About Jessie Mae Hill:
Residence: 1905, Trenton, Henry Co., IA[7575]

Children of Nicholas Christner and Jessie Hill are:
4732 i. Archie Melvin[9] Christner[7576,7577], born 04 Mar 1913 in IA[7578,7579]; died 21 Nov 2003 in Washington, Washington Co., IA[7580]. He married Marie V; born 19 Nov 1915[7581]; died 29 Jul 2002 in Mount Pleasant, Henry Co., IA[7581].

Notes for Archie Melvin Christner:
Birth: Mar. 4, 1913
Death: Nov. 21, 2003

Spouse: Marie V. Christner (1915 - 2002)

Burial: White Oak Cemetery, Trenton, Henry Co., IA

More About Archie Melvin Christner:
Residence: 1915, Walnut, Jefferson Co., IA[7582,7583]

Notes for Marie V:
Birth: Nov. 19, 1915
Death: Jul. 29, 2002

Spouse: Archie M. Christner (1913 - 2003)

Burial: White Oak Cemetery, Trenton, Henry Co., IA

More About Marie V:
Social Security Number: 480-54-2760/[7584]
SSN issued: IA[7584]

4733 ii. Dale Christner[7585,7586], born 20 Mar 1919 in IA[7587,7588]; died 29 Dec 1992 in Mount Pleasant, Henry Co., IA[7589]. He married Darlene M; born 28 Dec 1922.

   Notes for Dale Christner:
   Birth: Mar 20, 1919
   Death: Dec 29, 1992

   Burial: White Oak Cemetery, Trenton, Henry Co., IA

   More About Dale Christner:
   Residence: 1930, Lockridge, Jefferson Co., IA[7589,7590]

   Notes for Darlene M:
   Burial: White Oak Cemetery, Trenton, Henry Co., IA

4734 iii. Alta Ruth Christner[7590,7591], born 27 Dec 1923 in Henry Co., IA[7592,7593]; died 25 Oct 2001 in Mount Pleasant, Henry Co., IA[7594].

   More About Alta Ruth Christner:
   Residence: 1930, Lockridge, Jefferson Co., IA[7594,7595]

2659. Jacob[8] Christner (Jacob E.[7], Jacob[6], Peter[5], Peter[4], Christian[3], Christian[2], Christen[1])[7596,7597,7598] was born 04 Jan 1893 in Henry Cty., IA[7599,7600], and died 28 Apr 1974 in Buried: North Hill Cemetery/[7601]. He married **Goldie Mae Schroll**[7602] 20 Dec 1922[7602]. She was born 03 May 1901 in Marion, Henry Co., IA[7603], and died 18 May 1987 in North Hill, Henry Co., IA[7604].

Notes for Jacob Christner:
Buried: North Hill Cemetery

More About Jacob Christner:
Residence: 1910, Jefferson, Henry Co., IA[7605]

More About Goldie Mae Schroll:
Residence: 1930, Coppack, Washington Co., IA[7606]
Social Security Number: 481-28-1986/[7607]
SSN issued: IA[7607]

Child of Jacob Christner and Goldie Schroll is:
4735 i. Harold J.[9] Christner[7608,7609], born 19 May 1926[7610,7611,7612]; died 06 Jul 1993 in Eustis, Lake Co., FL[7613].

   More About Harold J. Christner:
   Residence: 1930, Coppack, Washington Co., IA[7613]
   Social Security Number: 483-24-8008/[7614]
   SSN issued: IA[7614]

2668. Florence Anna[8] Christner (Christian E.[7], Jacob[6], Peter[5], Peter[4], Christian[3], Christian[2], Christen[1])[7615,7616] was born 28 Jan 1905 in Henry Co., IA[7617], and died 05 May 1994 in Wayland, Henry Co., IA. She married **Herman Lleichty** 10 Sep 1933. He was born 1902, and died 1978.

More About Florence Anna Christner:
Residence: 1930, Wayne, Henry Co., IA[7617]

Notes for Herman Lleichty:
Leichty

Children of Florence Christner and Herman Lleichty are:

4736	i.	Alice Louise[9] Lleichty.
4737	ii.	Clarence John Lleichty.
4738	iii.	James Herman Lleichty.
4739	iv.	Jeanne Carol Lleichty.
4740	v.	Ronald Wayne Lleichty.
4741	vi.	Vernon Chris Lleichty.

2669. Erna Barbara[8] Christner (Christian E.[7], Jacob[6], Peter[5], Peter[4], Christian[3], Christian[2], Christen[1])[7618] was born 19 May 1908 in Henry Co., IA[7618,7619], and died 18 Jan 2001 in Wayland, Henry Co., IA[7620]. She married **Jesse R. Roth** 19 Jun 1928. He was born 26 Feb 1892, and died 1981.

Notes for Erna Barbara Christner:
Roth - Erna Christner, 92, Wayland, Iowa, died Jan. 18. Spouse: Jesse Roth (deceased). Parents: Christian and Emma Conrad Roth (deceased). Survivors: children Arnold, Charles, Arline Neff Roth, Ruth Ridenour, Mary; 23 grandchildren; 45 great-grandchildren. Funeral: Jan. 22 at Sugar Creek Mennonite Church, Wayland.

More About Erna Barbara Christner:
Burial: 22 Jan 2001, Sugarcreek Mennonite Church, Wayland, Henry Co., IA
Residence: 1930, Jefferson, Henry Co., IA[7620]
Social Security Number: 480-40-7304/[7621]

Children of Erna Christner and Jesse Roth are:

4742	i.	Aldine Emma[9] Roth. She married Donald Joseph Roth.
4743	ii.	Arnold Chrestian Roth. He married Lucille Mae Schultz.
4744	iii.	Charles Jesse Roth.
4745	iv.	Mary Elane Roth.
4746	v.	Mildred Eileen Roth. She married Davis Herman Freeman.
4747	vi.	Ruth Marie Roth.
4748	vii.	Arlene Emma Roth. She married David Ralph Neff.

2671. Verda Emma[8] Christner (Christian E.[7], Jacob[6], Peter[5], Peter[4], Christian[3], Christian[2], Christen[1])[7622,7623] was born 21 Nov 1915 in Henry Co., IA[7624], and died 04 Aug 1999 in Wayland, Henry Co., IA[7625]. She married **Glen Reschly**[7625] 28 Feb 1935[7625]. He was born 25 Jul 1911 in Jefferson Twp., Henry Co., IA[7625], and died 31 Oct 1978 in Iowa City, Johnson Co., IA[7625].

Notes for Verda Emma Christner:
Reschly, Verda Christner, 83, Wayland, IA died Aug. 4 of complications of a stroke and pneumonia. Spouse: Glen Reschly (deceased). Parents: Christian and Emma Conrad Christner (deceased). Survivors: Marilyn Manley, Edwin, Daniel, Janice Miller, Steven; 11 grandchildren; seven great-grandchildren. Funeral: Aug. 8 at Sugar Creek Mennonite Church, Wayland.

Birth: Nov. 21, 1915
IA
Death: Aug. 4, 1999
Wayland, Henry Co., IA

Daughter of Christian Christner & Emma Conrad

Mother of five children;
2 daughters & 3 sons

Obituary
Reschly, Verda Christner, 83, Wayland, IA died Aug. 4 of complications of a stroke and pneumonia.
Spouse: Glen Reschly (deceased).
Parents: Christian and Emma Conrad Christner (deceased). Children: Marilyn Manley, Edwin, Daniel, Janice Miller, Steven;
11 grandchildren; seven great-grandchildren.
Funeral: Aug. 8 at Sugar Creek Mennonite Church, Wayland.

Spouse: Glen Reschly (1911 - 1978)

Burial: Sugar Creek Cemetery, Wayland, Henry Co., IA

More About Verda Emma Christner:
Burial: 08 Aug 1999, Sugarcreek Mennonite Church, Wayland, Henry Co., IA
Cause of Death: Stroke & Pneumonia
Residence: 1920, Wayne Twp., Henry Co., IA[7625]

Notes for Glen Reschly:
Birth: Jul. 25, 1911
Death: Oct. 31, 1978

Family links:
Spouse:
Verda Christner Reschly (1915 - 1999)

Burial:
Sugar Creek Cemetery, Wayland, Henry Co., IA
Plot: Row 14

More About Glen Reschly:
Residence: 1920, Jefferson Twp., Henry Co., IA[7625]

Children of Verda Christner and Glen Reschly are:
4749	i.	Daniel[9] Reschly.
4750	ii.	Edwin Reschly.
4751	iii.	Janice Reschly.
4752	iv.	Marilyn Reschly.
4753	v.	Steven Reschly.
4754	vi.	Edwin Glen Reschly[7625], born 08 Dec 1938 in Wayland, Henry Co., IA[7625]; died 28 Jan 2006 in Escondido, San Diego Co., CA[7625].

More About Edwin Glen Reschly:
Burial: 31 Jan 2006, North Hill Cem., Henry Co., IA[7625]
Residence: 1993, Escondido, San Diego Co., CA[7625]

2672. John Thomas[8] Christner (Benjamin E.[7], Jacob[6], Peter[5], Peter[4], Christian[3], Christian[2], Christen[1])[7626,7627,7628] was born 31 Dec 1907 in Wayne, Henry Co., IA[7629], and died 27 May 1956 in Iowa City, Johnson Co., IA[7629,7630]. He married **Agnes Dolly Pickard**[7630,7631,7632] 20 May 1927[7633,7634]. She was born 28 Sep 1907 in Cedar, Lee Co., IA[7634], and died 15 Apr 1995 in Sunrise Terrace, Winfield, Henry Co., IA[7634].

Notes for John Thomas Christner:
Birth: Dec. 31, 1907 - Wayland, Henry Co., IA

Death: May 27, 1956 - Iowa City, Johnson Co., IA

John T. Christner Dies At Iowa City - Mount Pleasant News - Monday, 28 May 1956

John T. Christner, 48, died at the University hospital, Iowa City, Sunday night after an illness of several months. The son of Benjamin and Della May (Messer) Christner he was born in Henry county. He had been a resident of Mt. Pleasant the last four years. On May 20, 1927, he and Agnes Pickard were married. She and their ten children survive. The children are: Mrs, Virginia Richenberger, Wayland, Basil and Homer, Mt. Pleasant, Howard, Ft, Hood, Texas, Richard, Downey, Calif., Mrs. Doris Peppel, Mt. Pleasant, Darlene, Patty, Bonnie and Loretta at home. Also surviving are his mother, Mrs. Della Christner of Washington, four brothers,three sisters and seven grandchildren. His father and a sister predeceased him.

Services will be held at the Crane Funeral Home Tuesday afternoon at two o'clock with the Rev. C. R. DeJaynes of the Open Bible church officiating. burial will be at Green Mound.

Parents:
Benjamin E. Christner (1877 - 1919)
Della May Messer Christner (1883 - 1968)

Spouse: Agnes Dolly Pickard Christner (1907 - 1995)

Burial: Green Mound Cemetery, Henry Co., IA

More About John Thomas Christner:
Burial: 29 May 1956, Green Mound Cemetery, Henry Co., IA[7635]
Race: White/[7636,7636,7636]
Residence: 1935, Mount Pleasant, Henry Co., IA[7636]

More About Agnes Dolly Pickard:
Burial: 19 Apr 1995, Green Mound Cemetery, Henry Co., IA[7637]
Race: White/[7638,7638,7638]
Residence: 1935, Mount Pleasant, Henry Co., IA[7638]

Children of John Christner and Agnes Pickard are:

4755	i.	Patty[9] Christner.
4756	ii.	Bonnie Christner.
4757	iii.	Virginia Christner[7638], born Abt. 1928 in IA[7638]. She married Soto.

More About Virginia Christner:
Race: White/[7638]
Residence: 01 Apr 1940, Mount Pleasant, Henry Co., IA[7638]

4758	iv.	Basil Kenneth Christner[7639,7640], born 12 Sep 1929 in IA[7641]; died 27 Nov 2008 in Ventura, Ventura Co., CA[7641]. He married Tina.

More About Basil Kenneth Christner:
Residence: 1930, Canaan, Henry Co., IA[7641,7642]

4759	v.	Howard Christner[7643], born Abt. 1931 in Iowa[7643].

More About Howard Christner:
Residence: 01 Apr 1940, Age: 9/Mount Pleasant, Henry Co., IA[7643]

4760	vi.	Homer Christner[7643], born Abt. 1931 in IA[7643]. He married Brenda.

More About Homer Christner:
Race: White/[7643]
Residence: 01 Apr 1940, Age: 9; Marital Status: Single; Relation to Head of House: Son/Mount Pleasant, Henry Co., IA[7643]

4761 vii. Richard Christner[7643], born Abt. 1934 in IA[7643]. He married Leota.

More About Richard Christner:
Race: White/[7643]
Residence: 01 Apr 1940, Mount Pleasant, Henry Co., IA[7643]

4762 viii. Doris Christner[7643], born Abt. 1935 in Iowa[7643]. She married William Timmerman.

More About Doris Christner:
Race: White/[7643]
Residence: 01 Apr 1940, Age: 5; Marital Status: Single; Relation to Head of House: Daughter/Mount Pleasant, Henry Co., IA[7643]

+ 4763 ix. Darlene M. Christner, born 25 Feb 1937 in Mount Pleasant, Henry Co., IA; died 10 Aug 2004 in Muscatine Care Center, Muscatine, Muscatine Co., IA.

2675. Emery Levi[8] Good (Jacob[7], Christian[6] Guth, Barbara[5] Christner, John Johann[4], Christian[3], Christian[2], Christen[1]) was born 18 May 1892 in Hopedale, IL, and died 15 Nov 1961 in Hopedale, IL. He married **Leah Nafziger**. She was born 13 Nov 1893 in Hopedale, IL, and died 25 May 1989 in Hopedale, IL.

Child of Emery Good and Leah Nafziger is:
+ 4764 i. Elva Lydia[9] Good, born 15 Jan 1918 in Hopedale, IL.

2689. Howard Franklin[8] Christner (John Melvin[7], Aaron[6], Peter L.[5], John Johann[4], Christian[3], Christian[2], Christen[1]) was born 14 Aug 1897 in Elkhart Co., IN[7644], and died 19 Nov 1986 in St Petersburg, Pinellas Co., FL[7645]. He married **Florence Viola Miller**[7646] 21 Mar 1921. She was born 17 Feb 1894.

Notes for Howard Franklin Christner:
Accountant & Bookkeeper for the City Treasurer of Elkhart, IN.

More About Howard Franklin Christner:
Occupation: Accountant and book-keeper, served as City Treasurer of Elkhart./[7647]
Social Security Number: 308-03-5989/[7648]
SSN issued: IN[7648]

Child of Howard Christner and Florence Miller is:
+ 4765 i. Howard Franklin[9] Christner Jr., born 13 Nov 1921 in Elkhart Co., IN; died 02 Jun 2002 in Leesburg, Lake Co., FL.

2690. Paul G.[8] Christner (Charles Franklin[7], Aaron[6], Peter L.[5], John Johann[4], Christian[3], Christian[2], Christen[1]) was born 05 Feb 1902 in Elkhart Co., IN, and died 13 Apr 1996 in Goshen, Elkhart Co., IN[7649]. He married **Helen M. Todd** 18 Aug 1926. She was born 30 Oct 1904 in Elkhart Co., IN[7649], and died 09 May 1996 in Goshen, Elkhart Co., IN[7649].

Notes for Paul G. Christner:
Paul was a farmer and developed a gravel pit (Christner Gravel Co.) on his farm at 24065 County Road 40 in Eklhart Co., Indiana. He died at 3:10 p.m. on a Saturday in Elkhart General Hospital. He was a 32nd Degree Mason and a member of the Scottish Rite Valley of South Bend, The Elks and Moose Lodges in Goshen, Indiana and Maple Crest Country Club in Goshen.

More About Paul G. Christner:
Burial: Apr 1996, Riverview Add. Block E, Row 2, lots 10 & 11/Violett Cemetery, Goshen, Elkhart Co., IN
Residence: 1920, Harrison, Elkhart Co., IN[7649]

Notes for Helen M. Todd:

Helen was a 1949 graduate of Goshen College, she taught at Jefferson, Harrison, Union and Vistula Township Schools and in the Wakarusa school system. In 1988 she received the Outstanding Alumnus Award from the Wakarusa Alumni Association. Helen was active as a volunteer front dest receptionist for Goshen Hospital for many years. She enjoyed golf at Maplecrest Country Club. She enjoyed Bowling for teams in Goshen & Wakarusa. She was a member of the Nappanee Eastern Star and the Delphians of Goshen. On her 91st birthday the book "Froggy" Bottom was dedicated to the memories of Helens early teaching days.

More About Helen M. Todd:
Burial: Riverview Add, Block E, Row 2, lots 10 & 11/Violett Cemetery, Goshen, Elkhart Co., IN
Religion: Wakarusa United Methodist Church/
Residence: 1930, Union, Elkhart Co., IN[7649]

Children of Paul Christner and Helen Todd are:
    4766   i.   Nancy J.^{9} Christner. She married Eduardo Targioni; born in Marbella, Spain.
+   4767   ii. Phyllis Christner, born 21 Jul 1930 in Elkhart Co., IN; died 27 Mar 1998 in Goshen, Elkhart Co., IN.

2693. Ralph O.^{8} Christner (Henry Edward[7], Aaron[6], Peter L.[5], John Johann[4], Christian[3], Christian[2], Christen[1]) was born Aug 1897 in IN[7650], and died 1947. He married **Hattie F. Wagner**. She was born 25 Apr 1900[7651], and died 11 Jan 1987 in Elkhart, Elkhart Co., IN[7651].

Notes for Ralph O. Christner:
Birth: 1898
Death: 1947

Spouse: Hattie F. Christner (1900 - 1987)

Burial: Plum Grove Cemetery, Union, Cass Co., MI
Find A Grave Memorial# 97668082

More About Ralph O. Christner:
Residence: 1900, Harrison, Elkhart Co., IN[7652]

Notes for Hattie F. Wagner:
Birth: 1900
Death: 1987

Spouse: Ralph O. Christner (1898 - 1947)

Burial: Plum Grove Cemetery, Union, Cass Co., MI
Find A Grave Memorial# 97668096

More About Hattie F. Wagner:
Residence: 1920, Mason, Cass Co., MI[7653]
Social Security Number: 308-30-8856/[7654]
SSN issued: IN[7654]

Children of Ralph Christner and Hattie Wagner are:
+   4768   i.   Donald C.^{9} Christner, born 10 Jun 1920 in Cassopolis Co., MI; died 05 May 1987 in Cassopolis Co., MI.
+   4769   ii. Duane Edward Christner, born 25 Aug 1922 in Cassopolis, MI; died 04 Apr 1993 in Edwardsburg, MI.

2694. Ora A.^{8} Christner (Henry Edward[7], Aaron[6], Peter L.[5], John Johann[4], Christian[3], Christian[2], Christen[1]) was born 27 Jan 1900 in Wakarusa, Elkhart Co., IN[7655], and died 01 Feb 1973 in Edwardsburg, MI. He married **(1) Helen Konneck**. She was born 1899 in South Bend, St. Joseph Co., IN, and died 1933. He married **(2) Emily Vanecek** 31 Mar 1934 in Elkhart Co., IN. She died 01 Mar 1976.

Notes for Ora A. Christner:

Birth: Nov. 22, 1923
Death: Nov. 11, 1984

Spouse: Betty J. Christner (1926 - ____)

Burial: Union Cemetery, Berrien Co., MI
Plot: Block D, Lot 64, Grave 5

More About Ora A. Christner:
Burial: Plum Grove Cemetery, Union Co., MI
Occupation: Brick Mason/
Residence: 1930, Elkhart, Elkhart Co., IN[7656]
Social Security Number: 304-01-7766--IN/
SSN issued: IN[7657]

More About Helen Konneck:
Burial: Plum Grove Cemetery, Union Co., MI
Cause of death (Facts Pg): Cancer

Children of Ora Christner and Helen Konneck are:

| | 4770 | i. | Henry[9] Christner. He married Betty Young; born 11 Nov 1920 in Buchanan, MI; died 06 Dec 2004 in Conway, Faulkner Co., AR[7658]. |

> More About Betty Young:
> Occupation: School Teacher/
> SSN issued: AR[7658]

+	4771	ii.	Henry Christner, born 19 Dec 1921 in Elkhart Co., IN.
+	4772	iii.	Ora Christner Jr., born 22 Nov 1923 in Elkhart Co., IN or Vandalia MI; died 11 Nov 1984 in Berrien, Berrien Co., MI.
+	4773	iv.	Willis (Bill) Dean Christner, born 19 Feb 1928 in Elkhart Co., IN; died 23 Jan 2004 in Erlanger, Kenton Co., KY.

Children of Ora Christner and Emily Vanecek are:

| | 4774 | i. | Harold[9] Christner. |
| | 4775 | ii. | Kenneth Christner. |

2695. Beulah[8] Christner (Henry Edward[7], Aaron[6], Peter L.[5], John Johann[4], Christian[3], Christian[2], Christen[1]) was born 29 Jul 1903[7659,7660], and died 20 Oct 1991 in Jefferson, Cass Co., MI[7660,7661]. She married **Paul Otto Konneck** 16 Sep 1919 in St Joseph Co., MI. He was born 23 Jun 1895, and died 20 Nov 1975 in Cassopolis Co., MI.

More About Beulah Christner:
Residence: Porter, Cass, Michigan[7662]
Social Security Number: 308-42-9560/[7663]
SSN issued: IN[7663]

More About Paul Otto Konneck:
Burial: Kessington Cemetery near Union MI
Military service: 1917, WWI Army Rainbow Div. in Germany/
Occupation: Landscaping/

Children of Beulah Christner and Paul Konneck are:

	4776	i.	Kenneth B.[9] Konneck, born 1920; died 1924 in Auto Accident.
+	4777	ii.	Pauline Konneck, born 13 Dec 1923.
+	4778	iii.	Robert Konneck, born 01 Jun 1925.
+	4779	iv.	Charlotte Irene Konneck, born 1927.

+   4780   v.   Paul Bud Konneck, born 29 May 1929.
+   4781   vi.   Donna Elizabeth Konneck, born 01 Apr 1932.
+   4782   vii. Dallas Keith Konneck, born 1935.
     4783   viii. Victor Konneck, born 14 Apr 1937.
+   4784   ix.   Charles Barton Konneck, born 28 Oct 1946.

2697. Charles E.[8] **Christner** (Henry Edward[7], Aaron[6], Peter L.[5], John Johann[4], Christian[3], Christian[2], Christen[1]) was born 19 Jul 1914 in MI[7664,7665], and died 02 Feb 1980 in Union, Cass Co., MI[7666]. He married **Thelma M. Hall** 11 Apr 1936 in Goshen, Elkhart Co., IN[7666]. She was born 24 Oct 1913 in Cassopolis, MI[7666], and died 02 Jan 2003 in Union, Cass Co., MI.

More About Charles E. Christner:
Residence: 01 Apr 1940, Mason, Cass Co., MI[7666]
Social Security Number: 316-14-6457/[7667]
SSN issued: IN[7667]

More About Thelma M. Hall:
Burial: Kessington Cemetery, IN[7668]
Religion: Mason Township Baptist Church/
Residence: 01 Apr 1940, Mason, Cass Co., MI[7668]

Child of Charles Christner and Thelma Hall is:
     4785   i.   Phyllis[9] Christner, born in Jones, MI. She married James Russell.

2700. Jaunita Fern[8] **Christner** (Sarah Mandella[7], Aaron[6], Peter L.[5], John Johann[4], Christian[3], Christian[2], Christen[1]) was born 08 Mar 1911 in Elkhart Co., IN[7669], and died 18 Mar 2003 in Age: 92/Miller's Merry Manor, Wakarusa, Elkhart Co., IN[7669]. She married **Noble M. Detwiler** 15 Oct 1927 in Warsaw, Kosciusko Co., IN. He died 07 Sep 1996.

More About Jaunita Fern Christner:
Burial: Yellow Creek Cemetery, Elkhart Co., IN
Religion: Southwest Bible Church/
Residence: 1958, Elkhart Co., IN[7669]

More About Noble M. Detwiler:
Occupation: retired 1971 after 22 years at Tecumseh Products, Elkhart IN/

Children of Jaunita Christner and Noble Detwiler are:
     4786   i.   Carol[9] Detwiler. She married Roy Martin.
     4787   ii.   Dale Eugene Detwiler.
     4788   iii. Donald Dean Detwiler.
     4789   iv.   Eunice Detwiler. She married Keith Miller.
     4790   v.   Noble Detwiler Jr..
     4791   vi.   Phyllis Detwiler. She married Arthur Valentine.

2701. William Dale[8] **Christner** (Orange Vandever Eugene[7], Aaron[6], Peter L.[5], John Johann[4], Christian[3], Christian[2], Christen[1])[7670] was born 11 Dec 1916 in Elkhart Co., IN[7670], and died 08 Jan 2009 in Nappanee, Elkhart Co., IN[7670,7671]. He married **Catherine "Kate" Alice Slabaugh**[7672] 13 Jul 1940 in Evangelical Church in Mishawaka, IN by Rev. H. Berger. She was born 11 Oct 1917 in Nappanee, Elkhart Co., IN[7672,7673], and died 13 Dec 2009 in Middlebury, Elkhart Co., IN[7674].

Notes for William Dale Christner:
His name is William Dale Christner but always went by Dale W. Christner he Owned Christner Oil which consisted of many stores that sold Gasoline for automobile's plus food kind of like an old country store. At 90 years old he is still very active in running his stores and enjoying it. He provided much of the info for his side of the family.

Obituary:

W. DALE CHRISTNER
Dec. 11, 1916 - Jan. 8, 2009
Published: 1/10/2009 12:00:00 AM

NAPPANEE -- W. Dale Christner, 92, of Nappanee, died at 10:20 a.m. Thursday (Jan. 8, 2009) at Elkhart General Hospital.

He was born Dec. 11, 1916, in Elkhart County to Orange Eugene and Leona (Wagner) Christner. On July 13, 1940, he married Cathern Slabaugh.

She survives, along with one son, John (Judy) Christner of Middlebury; two grandsons; two step-grandchildren; four great-grandchildren; and one step-great-grandchild.

He was preceded in death by one sister, Evelyn Clouse.

Friends may call from 4 to 8 p.m. Sunday at Thompson-Lengacher & Yoder Funeral Home, 950 N. Main St., Nappanee, and one hour prior to the 2:30 p.m. service Monday at First Presbyterian Church, Nappanee. The Rev. Terry Tyler of First Presbyterian Church will officiate. Burial will be at Hepton Union Cemetery.

Mr. Christner was a Mason, a former Wa-Nee School Board member, and a member of First Presbyterian Church, Kiwanis and Nappanee American Legion Post 154. He was a graduate of Nappanee High School and a U.S. Army veteran of World War II.

He retired from Christner Oil Company.

Memorials may be given to First Presbyterian Church.

More About William Dale Christner:
Elected: Nappanee and Wa-Nee school boards/
Religion: Presbyterian Church/
Residence: 1993, Nappanee, IN[7674]
SSN issued: IN[7675]

Notes for Catherine "Kate" Alice Slabaugh:
Cathern said her birth cirtificate is WRONG it shows Oct.11, 1917 but real date was Oct. 18, 1917.

Birth: Oct. 11, 1917
Death: Dec. 13, 2009

NAPPANEE -- Cathern "Kate" Christner, 92, of 952 W. Walnut St., died at 9:35 p.m. Sunday (Dec. 13, 2009) in Luann Nursing Home.

She was born Oct. 11, 1917, in Nappanee to Frank and Eva (Kring) Slabaugh. On July 13, 1940, she married William Dale Christner. He died Jan. 8, 2009.

Mrs. Christner is survived by one son, John (Judy) Christner of Middlebury; two grandsons; two stepgrandchildren; five great-grandchildren; two stepgreat-grandchildren; and one sister, Mary E. Watkins of Nappanee.

She was preceded in death by five siblings, Wilson and George Slabaugh, Lola Hahn, Dorothy Klotzbach and Mona Heckaman.

Mrs. Christner was co-owner of Christner Oil Co., Nappanee, for many years. She was an active member at Grace

Point Presbyterian Church, Nappanee, and a member of Nappanee Order of the Eastern Star and the Thursday Club.

Friends may call one hour prior to Saturday's 11 a.m. funeral service at Grace Point Presbyterian Church. The Rev. Terry Tyler will officiate. Burial will be in Hepton Union Cemetery, Nappanee.

Memorials may be given to the church.

Parents:
Franklin E. Slabaugh (1884 - 1952)
Mary Eva Kring Slabaugh (1887 - 1968)

Spouse: W. Dale Christner (1916 - 2009)

Burial: Hepton Union Cemetery, Kosciusko Co., IN

More About Catherine "Kate" Alice Slabaugh:
SSN issued: IN[7676]

Child of William Christner and Catherine Slabaugh is:
+ 4792   i.   John Howard[9] Christner, born 24 Jan 1949.

2702. Elizabeth Evelyn[8] Christner (Orange Vandever Eugene[7], Aaron[6], Peter L.[5], John Johann[4], Christian[3], Christian[2], Christen[1]) was born 09 Nov 1918 in Union Twp. Elkhart Co., IN[7677], and died 31 Mar 2006 in Hubbard Hill Retirement Home Elkhart, IN. She married **J. Maxwell Clouse**[7678] 17 Oct 1948 in Nappanee, Elkhart Co., IN. He was born 31 Aug 1913[7678], and died 01 Apr 1979 in Nappanee, Elkhart Co., IN[7678].

Notes for Elizabeth Evelyn Christner:
Member of Eastern Star, Nappanee Thursday Club, Nappenee Ladies Rural Club, Nappanee Heritage & Historic Preservation efforts with the Nappanee Public Library.

More About Elizabeth Evelyn Christner:
Burial: South Union Cemetery Elkhart Co. Indiana Cr 50 -Cr 11 N41°28.210xW86°03.187
Graduation: 1936, Nappanee High School
Occupation: National Bank of Nappanee/
Religion: Nappanee First Presbyterian Church/
SSN issued: IN[7679]

More About J. Maxwell Clouse:
Other-Begin: Nappanee, Elkhart Co., IN[7680]
Social Security Number: 304-38-7306/[7680]
SSN issued: IN[7680]

Children of Elizabeth Christner and J. Clouse are:
    4793   i.   Ray[9] Clouse, born in Elkhart Co., IN.
    4794   ii.   Ann Clouse, born 20 Jul 1949 in Elkhart Co., IN; died in Indianapolis, Marion Co., IN. She married Moberly.

Generation No. 9

2715. Edna Mae[9] Hershberger (Malinda[8] Mishler, Andrew S.[7], Sarah[6] Sipe, Elizabeth[5] Christner, Christian J.[4], Johannes John Hans[3], Christian[2], Christen[1])[7681,7682] was born 15 Aug 1911 in Near Honeyville, Lagrange Co., IN[7682], and died 01 May 2001 in Topeka, Lagrange Co., IN[7683,7684]. She married **Monroe D. Christner**[7685,7686] 08 Dec 1931 in Maple Grove Menn, Topeka, Lagrange Co., IN, son of Daniel Christner and

Amelia Schrock. He was born 21 Oct 1911 in Newbury, Lagrange Co., IN[7687,7688], and died 29 Jan 1986 in Topeka, Lagrange Co., IN[7689,7690].

Notes for Edna Mae Hershberger:
The Descendants of John J. Christner, privately published February 1961, p. 31.

Edna is the daughter of William Henry Hershberger and Malinda Mishler. She Enjoyed Quilting and gardening selling her produce around LaGrange & Wolcottville Indiana She also enjoyed Woodworking even Furniture. She lived at 18274 Eleven Mile Road and died at 1:40 a.m. Her Specialty was her Strawberries. Her grandson Pastor Marvin Christner officiated the Funeral.

More About Edna Mae Hershberger:
Burial: N41°39.320xW85°33.919/Shoremennonite Cemetery, Shipshewana, Lagrange Co., IN
Marriage: Married by Rev. Edwin Yoder in Home of Edwin Yoder./[7691]
Social Security Number: 513-16-8873/[7692]

Notes for Monroe D. Christner:
The Descendants of John J. Christner, privately published February 1961, p. 31.
Monroe was mennonite . He retired from Ross Laboratories Sturgis, MI in
1973. SS#383-32-5133 ISS MI Lived near Plato, IN for many years.

More About Monroe D. Christner:
Burial: Shoremennonite Cemetery, Shipshewana, Lagrange Co., IN
Social Security Number: 383-32-5133/[7693]
SSN issued: MI[7693]

Children of Edna Hershberger and Monroe Christner are:

+   4795   i.   Arnold Eugene[10] Christner, born 27 May 1932 in Topeka, Lagrange Co., IN; died 28 Dec 2010 in Sturgis, Saint Joseph Co., MI.
     4796   ii.   Agnes Marie Christner, born 16 Sep 1933 in Topeka, Lagrange Co., IN; died 05 Apr 1954 in IN.

                   Notes for Agnes Marie Christner:
                   The Descendants of John J. Christner, privately published February 1961, p., 31.

                   Birth: 1933
                   Death: 1954

                   Burial: Shore Cemetery, Shipshewana, Lagrange Co., IN

                   Obituary:
                   Christner, Agnes Marie, daughter of Monroe and Edna (Hershberger) Christner was born in Topeka, Ind., Sept. 16, 1933; passed away at her home near Lagrange, IN April 4, 1954; aged 20 y. 6 m. 20 d. She leaves her parents, one sister (Esther), 5 brothers (Arnold, Plymouth, MI; Allen, Adrian, Gerald, and Larry, at home) 4 grandparents, 7 uncles, 4 aunts and many other relatives and friends. Marie entered the Lagrange Co. Hospital on Feb. 27, where she was a patient for 29 days. Eight days before her death she was taken to her home. Death came as a result of broncho-pneumonia. At the age of ten Marie accepted Christ as her Saviour and became a member of the Maple Grove Mennonite Church. Later the family moved to their present home near Plato, Lagrange, Ind., where she served faithfully. Funeral services were held at the Plato Mennonite Church, April 8, in charge of Edwin Yoder and Willis C. Troyer, with burial in the Shore Mennonite Cemetery.

                   More About Agnes Marie Christner:
                   Burial: Shore Mennonite Cemetery, US 20 east of Shipshewana, Lagrange Co., IN

+   4797   iii. Allen Ray Christner, born 05 Apr 1935 in Topeka, Lagrange Co., IN.
+   4798   iv.   Adrian Orva "Chris" Christner, born 16 Sep 1937 in Topeka, Lagrange Co., IN; died 03 Aug 1987 in Indianapolis, Marion Co., IN.
     4799   v.   Gerald M. Christner, born 11 Jan 1939 in Topeka, Lagrange Co., IN; died 03 Jun 2009. He married Shirley Derringer 27 Sep 1976; born 23 Dec 1935 in Indianapolis, Marion Co., IN.

                   Notes for Gerald M. Christner:

The Descendants of John J. Christner, privately published February 1961, p. 31.

85 Christner Lane State Road 144, Mooresville, IN 46158

Birth: Mar 8, 1939
Death: Jun 3, 2009

Pvt U.S. Army

Burial: White Oak Cemetery, Trenton, Henry Co., IA

Notes for Shirley Derringer:
Gerald is in landscaping. Gerald's step children are1. Mike; 2. Debbie, 3. Brenda, 4. Jason;

+   4800   vi.   Esther Ellen Christner, born 13 May 1940 in Topeka, Lagrange Co., IN; died 10 May 2006 in Battle Creek, MI.
+   4801   vii.   Larry Wayne Christner, born 22 Jun 1945 in Topeka, Lagrange Co., IN.

2716. Wesley C.[9] **Stutzman** (Amanda[8] Christner, Joseph J.[7], John J.[6], Joseph C.[5], Christian J.[4], Johannes John Hans[3], Christian[2], Christen[1])[7694,7695] was born 31 May 1882 in Milford, Seward Co., NE[7696], and died 26 Oct 1948 in Chappell, Deuel Co., NE[7696]. He married **Emma Yoder**[7697,7698] 01 Sep 1910 in Chappell, Deuel Co., NE[7698]. She was born 01 Oct 1891 in Kalona, Washington Co., IA[7699], and died 20 Jul 1997 in Heston, Harvey Co., NE.

Notes for Wesley C. Stutzman:
Birth: May 31, 1883
Death: Oct. 26, 1948

Stutzman - Wesley C., son of Adam and Amanda (Christner) Stutzman was born at Milford, NE May 31, 1883; passed away at his home in Chappell, Nebr., Oct. 26, 1948; aged 65 y. 4 m. 26 d. At the age of two he moved with his parents to Deuel Co., near Chappell. On Sept. 1, 1910, he was united in marriage to Emma Yoder, who survives. Also surviving are one son (Paul, Chappell, NE), 3 daughters (Lela-Mrs. Perry Stutzman, Thelma-Mrs. Ray Stutzman, both of Chappell; and Cora - Mrs. Wilton Stauffer, Milford, Nebr.), 10 grandchildren, one brother (Frank, of Chappell), 3 sisters (Clara, Chappell; Minerva-Mrs. Ezra Yoder, Oshkosh, NE; and Belva-Mrs. Joe Yoder, Wellman, IA), and a large number of other relatives and friends. One infant son, his parents, and one brother (Joe) preceded him in death. He was a mem-ber of the Mennonite Church from the time of his youth and attended services as long as his health permitted. He was a lover of music and took an active part in leading the singing at church services. In 1942 he was forced by ill health to retire from active farming. He suffered greatly the last two weeks of his life, but did not complain, being resigned to the Lord's will. He was a kind and loving husband and father, deeply concerned about the welfare of his family and the church. Funeral services were held at the Chappell Mennonite Church, in charge of Edward Diener and Fred Gingerich. Interment was made in the adjoining cemetery.

Parents:
Adam Stutzman (1861 - 1921)
Amanda Christner Stutzman (1861 - 1947)

Spouse: Emma Yoder Stutzman (1891 - 1997)

Children:
Lela Mae Stutzman (1911 - 2005)
Paul E. Stutzman (1912 - 1993)
Infant Son Stutzman (1916 - 1916)
Thelma B. Stutzman (1919 - 2006)

Burial: Mennonite Cemetery, Chappell, Deuel Co., NE
Find A Grave Memorial# 20843906

More About Wesley C. Stutzman:
DBH Book: 10819/[7700]
Residence: 1930, Swan, Deuel Co., NE[7701]

Notes for Emma Yoder:
Birth: Oct 1, 1891 - Kalona, Washington Co., IA
Death: Jul 20, 1997 - Hesston, Harvey Co., KS

Parents:
Christian Stephen Yoder (1853 - 1930)
Anna Swartzendruber Yoder (1858 - 1949)

Spouse: Wesley C. Stutzman (1883 - 1948)

Children:
Lela Mae Stutzman (1911 - 2005)
Paul E. Stutzman (1912 - 1993)
Infant Son Stutzman (1916 - 1916)
Thelma B. Stutzman (1919 - 2006)

Burial: Mennonite Cemetery, Chappell, Deuel Co., NE
Find A Grave Memorial# 58118603

More About Emma Yoder:
Residence: 1930, Swan, Deuel Co., NE[7701]

Children of Wesley Stutzman and Emma Yoder are:

4802   i.   Lela Mae[10] Stutzman[7702,7703], born 01 Jul 1911 in Chappell, Deuel Co., NE[7704,7705]; died 02 Dec 2005 in Hesston, Harvey Co., KS[7705,7706]. She married Perry R. Stutzman[7706] 19 Apr 1938 in Chappell, Deuel Co., NE[7706]; born 06 Sep 1913 in Wood River, Hall Co., NE[7706]; died 12 Jan 1982 in Hesston, Harvey Co., KS[7706].

Notes for Lela Mae Stutzman:
Birth: Jul. 1, 1911
Death: Dec. 2, 2005

Lela M. Stutzman, 94, died on Friday, Dec. 2, 2005, at Schowalter Villa in Hesston. Burial was Monday, Dec. 5, at the Eastlawn Cemetery. The funeral service was on Monday, Dec. 5, at Hesston Mennonite Church, with the Revs. Cheryl Hershberger and Beverly Baumgartner officiating.

She was born on July 1, 1911, in Chappell, Neb., to Wesley C. and Emma (Yoder) Stutzman. On April 19, 1938, she married Perry R. Stutzman in Chappell. He preceded her in death in 1982.
She was a schoolteacher and a homemaker. Survivors include two daughters, Delores and Sanford Headings of Hutchinson, and Marva and Jim Blough of Hesston; two sisters, Cora Stauffer of Richardson, Texas, and Thelma Stutzman of Hesston; six grandchildren; eight great-grandchildren; and many nieces and nephews. A memorial fund has been established with the Good Samaritan Fund at Schowalter Villa.

Sibling to: Paul Stutzman and Thelma B. Stutzman. (bio by: Tom Crago)

Parents:
Wesley C. Stutzman (1883 - 1948)
Emma Yoder Stutzman (1891 - 1997)

Burial: Eastlawn Cemetery, Zimmerdale, Harvey Co., KS
Find A Grave Memorial# 15999815

More About Lela Mae Stutzman:
Other-Begin: Hesston, Harvey Co., KS[7707]

Residence: 1930, Swan, Deuel Co., NE[7708]
Social Security Number: 507-40-6435/[7709]
SSN issued: NE[7710,7711]

More About Perry R. Stutzman:
Social Security Number: 508-28-4862/[7711]
SSN issued: NE[7711]

4803   ii.   Paul Eldon Stutzman[7712], born 28 Nov 1912 in Chappell, Deuel Co., NE[7713]; died 11 Apr 1993 in Kearney, Buffalo Co., NE[7713].

More About Paul Eldon Stutzman:
Residence: 1930, Swan, Deuel Co., NE[7714]
Social Security Number: 524-28-2975/[7715]
SSN issued: CO[7715]

4804   iii. Infant Son Stutzman[7716], born 29 Aug 1916 in Chappell, Deuel Co., NE[7716]; died 29 Aug 1916 in Chappell, Deuel Co., NE[7716].

Notes for Infant Son Stutzman:
Birth: Aug. 29, 1916 - Deuel Co., NE
Death: Aug. 29, 1916 - Deuel Co., NE

Infant son of Wesley & Emma (Yoder) Stutzman.

Parents:
Wesley C. Stutzman (1883 - 1948)
Emma Yoder Stutzman (1891 - 1997)

Burial: Mennonite Cemetery, Chappell, Deuel Co., NE
Find A Grave Memorial# 74552604

More About Infant Son Stutzman:
Residence: 1930, Swan, Deuel Co., NE[7716]

+   4805   iv.   Thelma Byrnece Stutzman, born 15 Oct 1919 in Chappell, Deuel Co., NE; died 28 Jan 2006 in Hesston, Harvey Co., KS.

2717. Frank[9] **Stutzman** (Amanda[8] Christner, Joseph J.[7], John J.[6], Joseph C.[5], Christian J.[4], Johannes John Hans[3], Christian[2], Christen[1])[7717] was born 31 Jan 1885 in Milford, Seward Co., NE[7717], and died 15 Jan 1972 in Chappell, Deuel Co., NE[7717]. He married **Elizabeth "Bess" Yoder**[7718] 18 Dec 1912. She was born 11 Apr 1894[7718,7719], and died Jul 1990[7719].

Notes for Frank Stutzman:
Birth: Jan. 31, 1885
Death: Jan. 15, 1972

Stutzman, Frank, son of Adam and Amanda (Christner) Stutzman, was born at Milford, Neb., Jan. 31, 1885; died at a Rest Home in Chappell, Neb., Jan. 15, 1972; aged 86 y. 11 m. 15 d. On Dec. 18, 1912, he was married to Bess Yoder, who survives. Also surviving are 2 sons (Donald and Russell), one daughter (Mary - Mrs. Warren Oswald), 10 grandchildren, 6 great-grandchildren, and one sister (Minerva - Mrs. Ezra Yoder). He was preceded in death by one daughter (Dorothy - Mrs. Walter White), two brothers, and two sisters. He was a member of the Chappell Mennonite Church, where funeral services were held Jan. 18, in charge of Arthur Roth and Paul White; interment in the church cemetery.

Parents:
Adam Stutzman (1861 - 1921)
Amanda Christner Stutzman (1861 - 1947)

Spouse: Elizabeth Yoder Stutzman (1894 - 1990)

Children: Dorothy Irene Stutzman White (1913 - 1959)

Burial: Mennonite Cemetery, Chappell, Deuel Co., NE
Find A Grave Memorial# 20843227

More About Frank Stutzman:
Burial: 18 Jan 1972, Chappell Mennonite Church Cemetery/Chappell, Deuel Co., NE[7720]

Notes for Elizabeth "Bess" Yoder:
Birth: Apr 11, 1894 - Wright Co., IA
Death: Jul 1990 - NE

Daughter of Christian S. & Anna (Swartzendruber) Yoder.

Wife of Frank Stutzman, married 18 Dec. 1912 in Chappell, NE. Mother of known children: Dorothy, Donald, Mary and Russell.

Spouse: Frank Stutzman (1885 - 1972)

Children: Dorothy Irene Stutzman White (1913 - 1959)

Burial: Mennonite Cemetery, Chappell, Deuel Co., NE
Find A Grave Memorial# 72936688

More About Elizabeth "Bess" Yoder:
Social Security Number: 507-52-2867/[7721]
SSN issued: NE[7721]

Child of Frank Stutzman and Elizabeth Yoder is:

4806 i. Dorothy Irene[10] Stutzman[7722], born 16 Nov 1913 in Chappell, Deuel Co., NE[7722]; died 12 Apr 1959 in Chappell, Deuel Co., NE[7722]. She married Walter Henry White[7723] 12 Nov 1935 in Chappell, Deuel Co., NE; born 23 Nov 1910 in Hydro, Blaine Co., OK[7723]; died 21 Aug 1975 in Englewood, Arapahoe Co., CO[7723].

Notes for Dorothy Irene Stutzman:
Birth: Nov. 16, 1913 - Deuel Co., NE
Death: Apr 1959

Daughter of Frank & Elizabeth (Yoder) Stutzman. Married Walter Henry White November 12, 1935 in Chappell, NE.

Parents:
Frank Stutzman (1885 - 1972)
Elizabeth Yoder Stutzman (1894 - 1990)

Spouse: Walter Henry White (1910 - 1975)

Burial: Mennonite Cemetery, Chappell, Deuel Co., NE
Find A Grave Memorial# 72937451

Notes for Walter Henry White:
Birth: Nov. 28, 1910 - OK
Death: Aug. 21, 1975 - Englewood, Arapahoe Co., CO

Son of William Robert & Magdalena (Miller) White.

Married Dorothy Irene Stutzman on 12 Nov. 1935 in Chappell, NE.

Spouse: Dorothy Irene Stutzman White (1913 - 1959)

Burial: Mennonite Cemetery, Chappell, Deuel Co., NE
Find A Grave Memorial# 72937714

More About Walter Henry White:
Burial: Chappell, Deuel Co., NE[7723]

2718. Belva[9] **Stutzman** (Amanda[8] Christner, Joseph J.[7], John J.[6], Joseph C.[5], Christian J.[4], Johannes John Hans[3], Christian[2], Christen[1])[7724] was born 07 Apr 1888 in Chappell, Deuel Co., NE[7724], and died 23 Jul 1963 in Goshen, Elkhart Co., IN[7724]. She married **Joe F. Yoder**. He was born 03 Nov 1889 in Kalona, Washington Co., IA, and died 05 Jul 1963 in Goshen, Elkhart Co., IN.

Notes for Belva Stutzman:
Birth: Apr 7, 1888 - Chappell, Deuel Co., NE
Death: Jul 23, 1963 - Goshen, Elkhart Co., IN

Yoder, Belva, daughter of Adam and Amanda (Christner) Stutzman, was born at Chappell, Nebr., April 7, 1888; died at the Goshen (Ind.) General Hospital, July 23, 1963; aged 75 y. 3 m. 16 d. On Nov. 26, 1912, she was married to Joe F. Yoder, who died 18 days before her death, on July 5, 1953. Two daughters and 2 sons lost their lives in a tornado on Aug. 10, 1924, at Thurman, Colo. Surviving are 2 daughters (Florence and Erma Lou), one brother (Frank), and one sister (Minerva-Mrs. Ezra Yoder). She was a member of the Wellman (Iowa) Mennonite Church. Funeral services were held at the Yoder-Culp Funeral Home on July 26, in charge of Robert Detweiler and John Mosemann; interment in the Violett Cemetery.

Spouse: Joe F. Yoder (1889 - 1963)

Children:
Blanche Yoder (1913 - 1924)
Vera Ruth Yoder (1915 - 1924)
Robert Stanley Yoder (1917 - 1924)
Ray Vernon Yoder (1923 - 1924)

Burial: Violett Cemetery, Goshen, Elkhart Co., IN
Find A Grave Memorial# 18560429

Notes for Joe F. Yoder:
Birth: Nov 3, 1889 - Kalona, Washington Co., IA
Death: Jul 5, 1963 - Goshen, Elkhart Co., IN

Yoder, Joe F. son of Christian S. and Anna (Swartzendruber) Yoder, was born at Kalona, IA Nov. 3, 1889; died at Goshen, IN, July 5, 1963; aged 73 y. 7 m. 2 d. On Nov. 26, 1912, he was married to Belva Stutzman, who survives. Also surviving are 2 daughters (Florence and Erma), 4 brothers (Sanford C., Elmer, Ezra, and Harry), and 4 sisters (Mrs. Emma Stutzman, Bess - Mrs. Frank Stutzman, Mrs. Cora Stutzman, and Mrs. Sade Albin). Two sons and 2 daughters were killed in a tornado at Thurman, Colo., in 1924. He was a member of the Wellman (Iowa) Church. Funeral services were held at the Yoder-Culp Funeral Home, Goshen, July 7, in charge of John Mosemann and Robert Detweiler; interment in Violett Cemetery.

Spouse: Belva Stutzman Yoder (1888 - 1963)

Children:
Blanche Yoder (1913 - 1924)
Vera Ruth Yoder (1915 - 1924)
Robert Stanley Yoder (1917 - 1924)
Ray Vernon Yoder (1923 - 1924)

Burial: Violett Cemetery, Goshen, Elkhart Co., IN

Find A Grave Memorial# 18560547

Children of Belva Stutzman and Joe Yoder are:

4807   i.   Florence[10] Yoder.

4808   ii.   Emma Lou Yoder.

4809   iii.   Blanche Yoder, born 21 Nov 1913; died 10 Aug 1924 in Washington Co., CO.

Notes for Blanche Yoder:
Birth: Nov 21, 1913
Death: Aug 10, 1924 - Washington Co., CO

Yoder - Blanche Yoder and Vera Ruth Yoder, daughters of Bro. Joe and Sister Belva Yoder, were born respectively Nov 21, 1913 and July 12, 1915; aged 10 y. 8 m. 19 d., and 9 y. 28 d.

Yoder -- Robert Stanley Yoder and Ray Vernon Yoder, sons of Bro. Joe and Sister Belva Yoder, were born at Thurman, Colo., Jan. 24, 1917, and Aug. 4, 1923; aged 7 y. 6 m. 16 d., and 1 y. 6 d., respectively. All four met their death in the tornado that wrecked the home of Bro. Henry Kuhns on Aug. 10, 1924. They leave their heartbroken parents and many relatives and friends to mourn their untimely demise. All the above were laid to rest in the Mennonite Cemetery near Thurman, CO. Funeral services were held on Aug 13, conducted by Bro. John Roth of Chappell, Nebr., Mr. MaGill, minister of the Baptist Church, Bro. L. C. Miller of Limon, CO and N. M. Birky, the home minister. Testimonies were given by several others.
(Mennobits)

Parents:
Joe F. Yoder (1889 - 1963)
Belva Stutzman Yoder (1888 - 1963)

Burial: Thurman Cemetery, Washington Co., CO
Plot: Row F, Plot 11
Find A Grave Memorial# 18573320

4810   iv.   Vera Ruth Yoder, born 12 Jul 1915; died 10 Jun 1924.

Notes for Vera Ruth Yoder:
Birth: Jul. 12, 1915
Death: Jun. 10, 1924

Yoder - Blanche Yoder and Vera Ruth Yoder, daughters of Bro. Joe and Sister Belva Yoder, were born respectively Nov. 21, 1913, and July 12, 1915; aged 10 y. 8 m. 19 d., and 9 y. 28 d.

Yoder - Robert Stanley Yoder and Ray Vernon Yoder, sons of Bro. Joe and Sister Belva Yoder, were born at Thurman, Colo., Jan. 24, 1917, and Aug. 4, 1923; aged 7 y. 6 m. 16 d., and 1 y. 6 d., respectively. All four met their death in the tornado that wrecked the home of Bro. Henry Kuhns on Aug. 10, 1924. They leave their heartbroken parents and many relatives and friends to mourn their untimely demise. All the above were laid to rest in the Mennonite Cemetery near Thurman, Colo. Funeral services were held on Aug. 13, conducted by Bro. John Roth of Chappell, Nebr., Mr. MaGill, minister of the Baptist Church, Bro. L. C. Miller of Limon, Colo., and N. M. Birky, the home minister. Testimonies were given by several others. (Mennobits)

Parents:
Joe F. Yoder (1889 - 1963)
Belva Stutzman Yoder (1888 - 1963)

Inscription: Dau of Joe & Belva Yoder

Burial: Thurman Cemetery, Washington Co., CO
Plot: Plot: Row F, Plot 11
Find A Grave Memorial# 40811058

4811   v.   Robert Stanley Yoder, born 24 Jan 1917; died 10 Jun 1924 in Washington Co., CO.

2722. Joseph⁹ Stutzman (Amanda⁸ Christner, Joseph J.⁷, John J.⁶, Joseph C.⁵, Christian J.⁴, Johannes John Hans³, Christian², Christen¹)⁷⁷²⁴,⁷⁷²⁵ was born 24 Oct 1895 in Chappell, Deuel Co., NE⁷⁷²⁶, and died 07 Sep 1948⁷⁷²⁶,⁷⁷²⁷. He married **Cora Ann Yoder**⁷⁷²⁷ 07 Apr 1919 in Chappell, Deuel Co., NE⁷⁷²⁷. She was born 28 Mar 1899 in Clarion, Wright Co., IA⁷⁷²⁸, and died 21 Sep 2001 in Omaha, Douglas Co., NE⁷⁷²⁸,⁷⁷²⁹.

Notes for Joseph Stutzman:
Birth: Oct. 24, 1895
Death: Sep. 7, 1948

Stutzman - Joe, son of Adam and Amanda (Christner) Stutzman was born near Chappell, NE Oct. 24, 1895; died of acute leukemia at the Oshkosh Community Hospital, Sep 7, 1948; aged 52 y. 10 m. 13 d. On April 7, 1919, be was married to Cora Yoder, of Chappell, who survives. Also surviving are 4 sons (Harold, Wellman, IA; Duane, Mt. Pleasant, IA; Robert, at present employed in Omaha; and Cecil, at home), one grandson, 2 brothers (Wesley and Frank, of Chappell), 3 sisters (Minerva-Mrs. Ezra Yoder, Oshkosh, NE; Belva - Mrs. Joe Yoder, Wellman, IA and Clara, of Chappell) and one (Joe Christenham) who lived in their home from the age of eight. An infant daughter preceded him in death. In youth be confessed Christ as his Saviour and united with the Chappell Mennonite Church, of which he re-mained a member until death. His entire life was spent in the Chappell community, where he farmed for a few years, served as caretaker of the Deuel County Courthouse for a number of years, and at the time of his illness was em-ployed as caretaker of the Deuel County High School. He was well known and highly respected as a quiet, sincere, honest man, and a kind husband and father. He bore his several-month illness very patiently, often expressing his desire to go home to his Lord. Funeral services were held Sept. 10 at the Chappell Mennonite Church by E. M. Yost and Fred Gingerich.

Parents:
Adam Stutzman (1861 - 1921)
Amanda Christner Stutzman (1861 - 1947)

Spouse: Cora Yoder Stutzman (1899 - 2001)

Children: Infant Daughter Stutzman (1933 - 1933)

Burial: Mennonite Cemetery, Chappell, Deuel Co., NE
Find A Grave Memorial# 20843623

More About Joseph Stutzman:
Burial: Chappell Mennonite Church Cemetery/Chappell, Deuel Co., NE⁷⁷²⁹

Notes for Cora Ann Yoder:
Birth: Apr 7, 1899 - Deuel Co., NE
Death: Sep 21, 2001 - Deuel Co., NE

Daughter of Christian S & Anna (Swartzendruber) Yoder, married Joe Stutzman on 7 April 1919 in Chappell, NE. Mother of sons: Harold, Duane, Robert and Cecil.

Parents:
Christian Stephen Yoder (1853 - 1930)
Anna Swartzendruber Yoder (1858 - 1949)

Spouse: Joe Stutzman (1895 - 1948)

Children: Infant Daughter Stutzman (1933 - 1933)

Burial: Mennonite Cemetery, Chappell, Deuel Co., NE

More About Cora Ann Yoder:
Burial: Chappell Mennonite Church Cemetery/Chappell, Deuel Co., NE⁷⁷²⁹
Social Security Number: 507-40-5078/⁷⁷³⁰

SSN issued: NE[7730]

Children of Joseph Stutzman and Cora Yoder are:

4812   i.   Robert[10] Stutzman.

4813   ii.   Harold J Stutzman[7731], born 12 Dec 1919 in Chappell, Deuel Co., NE[7731]; died 10 May 1978[7731].

More About Harold J Stutzman:
Burial: Wellman Cemetery (North Side)/Wellman, Washington, Iowa, USA[7731]

4814   iii. Duane Henry Stutzman[7731], born 18 Feb 1922[7731]; died 10 Feb 1952[7731].

2723. Oscar Ira[9] Christner (John D.[8], Joseph J.[7], John J.[6], Joseph C.[5], Christian J.[4], Johannes John Hans[3], Christian[2], Christen[1]) was born 08 Mar 1901 in Eden, Lagrange Co., IN[7732], and died 15 Nov 1970 in Lagrange, Lagrange Co., IN. He married **Mary Velda Howard** 28 Mar 1924 in Parents Home, Shipshewana, Lagrange Co, IN, daughter of Walter Howard and Nancy Young. She was born 18 Dec 1902 in Clearspring Twp, Lagrange Co, IN, and died Mar 1987 in Lagrange, Lagrange Co., IN[7732].

Notes for Oscar Ira Christner:
Oscar rented Perry Huff farm (80 acres) 1924. The next year he rented the Haggerty farm (200 acres) on State road 120. He also operated a grain thrashing rigg. He served AAA committie chairman for the Lagrange Co. program. This job payed 50 cents per hour and he worked 8 hours a day. Oscar rented Perry Huff farm (80 acres) 1924.
SS#308-40-0225 ISS IN

Obituary:
Oscar Christner, 69, of LaGrange, route 1, died Sunday (11-15-1970) at 8:30 a.m. at his home following an illness of two and one-half years.

He was born near Topeka (IN) March 3, 1901, the son of John D. and Lucrettia (Renner) Christner. Christner, a farmer, moved in 1944 from Scott, north of Shipshewana, to his present home. He was married March 28, 1924, to Mary Howard, who survives. Also surviving are two daughters, Mrs. C. Gene (Velma) Sherck of Lagrange and Mrs. Keith (Ruby) Notestine of Elkhart; three sons, Rollin of Syracuse, Lawrence of Fort Wayne and Duaine of Goshen; 15 grandchildren; one great-grandchild; a brother, Dana of LaGrange, and three sisters, Mrs. Glen (Luella) S. Troyer of LaGrange, Mrs. Everett (Verona) Barness of Scott and Mrs. Lloyd (Beulah) Mockler of Middlebury.

Funeral services were held yesterday (11-18-1970) at 10:30 a.m. in the Fruip Funeral Home in Lagrange with the Rev. Ted Rigdon of Mooresville and the Rev. Robert Fields, pastor of the Lagrange Church of God, officiating.

Burial was in the Woodruff Cemetery, northeast of Wolcottville, Lagrange Co., IN.

The Descendants of John J. Christner, privately published February 1961, p. 5.

More About Oscar Ira Christner:
Burial: Row 4 Plot 4/Woodruff Cemetery, Lagrange Co., IN
Social Security Number: 308-40-0225 issued in IN/
SSN issued: IN[7733,7734]

Notes for Mary Velda Howard:
Her parents lived N. of Shipshewana, Lagrange Co., IN.

The Descendants of John J. Christner, privately published February 1961, p. 5.

More About Mary Velda Howard:
Social Security Number: 312-54-9175/[7735,7736]
SSN issued: IN[7737,7738]

Children of Oscar Christner and Mary Howard are:

+ 4815   i.   Rollin Floyd[10] Christner, born 25 Mar 1925 in Lagrange Co., IN; died 30 Apr 2005 in Syracuse, Kosciusko Co., IN.

+ 4816   ii.   Lawerence Everett Christner, born 28 Jul 1926 in Elkhart Co., IN; died 08 May 2000 in Golden Eagle Years Homestead Nursing Home, IN.

   4817   iii.   Duaine Edward Christner, born 16 Apr 1929 in Lagrange Co., IN; died 11 Jun 1996 in Goshen, Elkhart Co., IN. He married Phyllis J. (Ainsworth) Johnson 31 Aug 1968.

         Notes for Duaine Edward Christner:
         Newspaper clipping Friday June 21, 1991

         Duaine "Chris" Christner retired his truck,Old #7 after 38 years of delivering petroleum products for G&R Transport. Chris never had an accident in the 37 years that he drove. He drove a 1971 tractor 550,000 miles before he traded it in and never touched the engine. He also had a 1985 truck with 700,000 miles without any engine work, not even replacing a clutch. He was drafted in the Army and served during the Korean war. He was a horse harness racer and trainer. He was a member of the Indiana Trotting and Pacing Association and Trotting Association. He was Barn Manager for the Elkhart County Fairgrounds.

         The Descendants of John J. Christner, privately published February 1961, p. 5.

         Notes for Phyllis J. (Ainsworth) Johnson:
         The Descendants of John J. Christner, privately published, February 1961, p. 5.

+ 4818   iv.   Velma Lucretia Christner, born 20 May 1934 in Lagrange Co., IN; died 08 Nov 2000.

+ 4819   v.   Ruby Ellen Christner, born 19 Feb 1940 in Lagrange Co., IN.

2724. Beulah V.[9] Christner (John D.[8], Joseph J.[7], John J.[6], Joseph C.[5], Christian J.[4], Johannes John Hans[3], Christian[2], Christen[1])[7739] was born 16 Mar 1905 in Middlebury, Elkhart Co., IN, and died 24 Sep 1996 in Goshen, Elkhart Co., IN. She married **Henry Lloyd Mockler**[7740] 12 Jun 1926 in Middlebury, Elkhart Co., IN[7740]. He was born 18 Nov 1904 in Kouts, IN[7740], and died Dec 1968 in Middlebury, Elkhart Co., IN[7740].

Notes for Beulah V. Christner:
She worked at Krider Nursery and Middlebury Creamery Burial at Forest Grove Cemetery.She worked at Krider Nursery and Middlebury Creamery Burial at Forest Grove Cemetery.

The Descendants of John J. Christner, privately published, February 1961, p. 5.

More About Beulah V. Christner:
Social Security Number: 304-36-9708/[7740]
SSN issued: IN[7740]

Notes for Henry Lloyd Mockler:
The Descendants of John J. Christner, privately published, February 1961, p. 5.

Children of Beulah Christner and Henry Mockler are:

   4820   i.   Robert Devon[10] Mockler, born 15 Sep 1929 in Middlebury, Elkhart Co., IN; died 15 Sep 1929 in Middlebury, Elkhart Co., IN.

         Notes for Robert Devon Mockler:
         The Descendants of John J. Christner, privately published February 1961, p. 5.

+ 4821   ii.   Donald Elroy Mockler, born 28 Apr 1931 in Middlebury, Elkhart Co., IN.

+ 4822   iii.   Merlin Ray Mockler, born 08 Feb 1934 in Middlebury, Elkhart Co., IN.

+ 4823   iv.   Joyce Ellen Mockler, born 03 May 1937 in Middlebury, Elkhart Co., IN.

2725. Venona L.[9] Christner (John D.[8], Joseph J.[7], John J.[6], Joseph C.[5], Christian J.[4], Johannes John Hans[3], Christian[2], Christen[1])[7741] was born 06 May 1907 in White Pigeon, St. Joseph Co., MI, and died 27 Dec 2002 in Sturgis, St Joseph Co., MI. She married **Everett Barnell** 14 Jan 1928 in Howe, Lagrange Co., IN[7741]. He was born 10 Jul 1909, and died 27 Mar 1992 in or 12 / 27/Shipshewana, Elkhart Co., IN.

Notes for Venona L. Christner:
The Descendants of John J. Christner, privately published February 1961, p. 6.

More About Venona L. Christner:
Burial: Oak Lawn Cemetery in Sturgis, St Joseph Co., MI

Notes for Everett Barnell:
He retired as a truck driver for Hagen Cement Co., White, Pigeon Co., MI and was a member of Scott United Methodist Church Burial at Oak Lawn Cemetery, Sturgis Co., MI.

The Descendants of John J. Christner, privately published, February 1961, p. 6.

Children of Venona Christner and Everett Barnell are:
    4824   i.   Robert Lamar[10] Barnell, born 10 May 1933; died 1999.

                  Notes for Robert Lamar Barnell:
                  The Descendants of John J. Christner, privately published, February 1961, p. 6.

    4825   ii.   Keith Elwin Barnell, born 10 Sep 1937. He married Patricia Ardell Fergison 24 Jan 1960.

                  Notes for Keith Elwin Barnell:
                  Keith married Patricia A. Fargison Jan 24 1960.

                  The Descendants of John J. Christner, privately published, February 1961, p. 6.

                  Notes for Patricia Ardell Fergison:
                  The Descendants of John J. Christner, privately published February 1961, p. 6.

    4826   iii.   Stanley Wayne Barnell[7742], born 26 Aug 1939[7742]. He married Carol Lee Marks 21 Dec 1958; born 08 Dec 1939.

                  Notes for Stanley Wayne Barnell:
                  The Descendants of John J. Christner, privately published February 1961, p. 6.

                  More About Stanley Wayne Barnell:
                  Residence: 1993, Sturgis, MI[7742]

2726. Dana R.[9] Christner (John D.[8], Joseph J.[7], John J.[6], Joseph C.[5], Christian J.[4], Johannes John Hans[3], Christian[2], Christen[1])[7743,7743] was born 11 Jul 1909 in Topeka, Lagrange Co., IN[7743,7743], and died 14 Jan 2000 in Mesa, Maricopa Co., AZ[7743,7743]. He married **Mary Emily Kauffman**[7743] 29 Nov 1933 in Goshen, Elkhart Co., IN[7743]. She was born 06 Mar 1906 in Kalona, Washington Co., IA[7743], and died 23 Jan 1996 in Lagrange Co., IN[7743].

Notes for Dana R. Christner:
Dana was a feed salesman and owner of the Topeka Roller Mill (N 41°32.150' W 85°32.650')-- (a grain milling plant that milled by pressing grain between two steel rollers).

Birth: 1909
Death: 2000

Burial: Greenwood Cemetery, Lagrange, Lagrange Co., IN
Plot: Section C

More About Dana R. Christner:
Burial: Greenwood Cemetery, Lagrange Co., IN
Social Security Number: 306-16-6903/[7743,7743]
SSN issued: IN[7743,7743]

Notes for Mary Emily Kauffman:
Emily is the daughter of Bendict J. Kauffman and Barbara Miller. Burial Greenwood Cemetery, Lagrange, IN She retired as a food service supervisor at Lagrange Hospital in 1977. Member of the First United Methodist Church.

Child of Dana Christner and Mary Kauffman is:
+   4827   i.   John B.[10] Christner, born 15 Nov 1939.

2727. Luella Mae[9] Christner (John D.[8], Joseph J.[7], John J.[6], Joseph C.[5], Christian J.[4], Johannes John Hans[3], Christian[2], Christen[1])[7744] was born 31 May 1917 in Van Buren, Lagrange Co., IN[7744], and died 09 Oct 2008 in Shipshewana, Lagrange Co., IN[7744]. She married **Glen S. Troyer** 02 Jun 1935 in Lagrange Co., IN[7744]. He was born 28 Jul 1914 in Lagrange Co., IN[7744], and died 12 Jun 1984 in Lagrange, Lagrange Co., IN[7744].

Notes for Luella Mae Christner:
Luella enjoyed her 90 th birthday party at Shore Menonite Church. The church is Southeast of Shipshewana, Indiana on US 20 one mile east of State road 5.

The Descendants of John J. Christner published Feb. 1961, p. 6.

More About Luella Mae Christner:
Social Security Number: 308-60-8139/[7744]
SSN issued: IN[7744]

Notes for Glen S. Troyer:
The Descendants of John J. Christner published February 1961, p. 6.

Glen was bedridden from a stroke.

Children of Luella Christner and Glen Troyer are:
     4828   i.   Roberta Jane[10] Troyer, born 20 Dec 1935. She married Richard Steider 29 Mar 1959; born 23 Dec 1937.

                    Notes for Roberta Jane Troyer:
                    Roberta married Richard Steider Mar 29, 1959.

                    The Descendants of John J. Christner published Feb. 1961, p. 6.

                    Notes for Richard Steider:
                    The Descendants of John J. Christner published February 1961, p. 6.

+   4829   ii.   Gerald Lavon Troyer, born 06 Dec 1936 in Elkhart Co., IN.
     4830   iii.   Janet Elaine Troyer, born 01 Oct 1938. She married William Weaver.

                    Notes for Janet Elaine Troyer:
                    The Descendants of John J. Christner published February 1961, p. 6.

     4831   iv.   James Leroy Troyer, born 02 Nov 1939.

                    Notes for James Leroy Troyer:
                    The Descendants of John J. Christner published February 1961, p. 6.

     4832   v.   Dorothy Jean Troyer, born 15 Aug 1941.

                    Notes for Dorothy Jean Troyer:
                    The Descendants of John J. Christner published February 1961, p. 6.

     4833   vi.   David Wayne Troyer[7745], born 06 Mar 1943[7745]; died 07 Apr 2011 in Age at Death: 68/LaGrange, LaGrange, Indiana[7745].

Notes for David Wayne Troyer:
Davids wife was killed in a farm tractor accident.

The Descendants of John J. Christner published February 1961, p. 6.

Birth: Mar. 6, 1943
Death: Apr. 7, 2011

Burial: Shore Cemetery, Shipshewana, Lagrange Co., IN
Find A Grave Memorial# 96903365

4834   vii.   Nancy Joan Troyer, born 18 Feb 1944.

Notes for Nancy Joan Troyer:
The Descendants of John J. Christner published February 1961, p. 6.

4835   viii.   Carol June Troyer, born 28 Jun 1949.
4836   ix.   Dennis Richard Troyer, born 28 Jan 1952.

Notes for Dennis Richard Troyer:
The Descendants of John J. Christner published February 1961, p. 6.

Dennis worked at Shipshewana State Bank as a loan officer.

2728. Edna Mae[9] Miller (Annie J.[8] Christner, Joseph J.[7], John J.[6], Joseph C.[5], Christian J.[4], Johannes John Hans[3], Christian[2], Christen[1])[7746] was born 11 Sep 1897 in Shipshewana, Lagrange Co., IN[7746], and died 23 Jun 1976[7746]. She married **William S. Miller**[7747,7748] 13 Feb 1919 in Shipshewana, Lagrange Co., IN[7748], son of Samuel Miller and Elizabeth Miller. He was born 23 Jan 1897 in White Cloud, Newaygo Co., MI[7749,7750,7751], and died 11 May 1985[7751,7752].

Notes for Edna Mae Miller:
The Descendants of John J. Christner, privately published February 1961, p. 6.

Notes for William S. Miller:
The Descendants of John J. Christner, privately published February1961, p. 6.

He was Old Order Amish and a farmer.

More About William S. Miller:
Occupation: Farmer/
Religion: Old Order Amish/

Children of Edna Miller and William Miller are:
+   4837   i.   Ella W.[10] Miller, born 24 Feb 1920 in Lagrange Co., IN.
     4838   ii.   Elva W. Miller[7752], born 16 Jul 1922 in Shipshewana, Lagrange Co., IN[7752]; died 19 Dec 1926 in IN[7752].

Notes for Elva W. Miller:
The Descendants of John J. Christner, privately published February 1961, p. 7.

+   4839   iii.   Ora W. Miller, born 13 May 1924 in Lagrange Co., IN; died 13 Feb 1979.
+   4840   iv.   Mary Elizabeth Miller, born 07 Sep 1926 in Lagrange Co., IN; died 21 Dec 1990.
+   4841   v.   Ida Mae Miller, born 04 Dec 1928 in Lagrange Co., IN.
+   4842   vi.   Howard W. Miller, born 28 Jul 1931 in Lagrange Co., IN; died 30 Jun 1999.
     4843   vii.   Emma Miller, born 19 Feb 1934.

Notes for Emma Miller:

The Descendants of John J. Christner, privately published February 1961, p. 7.

+   4844   viii.   Ervin E. Miller, born 17 Sep 1936 in Lagrange Co., IN.

     4845   ix.   Amos Miller[7752], born 02 Aug 1939 in Shipshewana, Lagrange Co., IN[7752]; died 12 Mar 1940 in Lagrange Co., IN[7752].

Notes for Amos Miller:
The Descendants of John J. Christner, privately published February 1961, p. 7.

2729. Willis E.[9] Miller (Annie J.[8] Christner, Joseph J.[7], John J.[6], Joseph C.[5], Christian J.[4], Johannes John Hans[3], Christian[2], Christen[1])[7753] was born 29 Jan 1899 in Shipshewana, Lagrange Co., IN[7754], and died 14 Sep 1980 in Shipshewana, Lagrange Co., IN[7754]. He married **(1) Fannie Brenneman**. He married **(2) Fannie Elmina Miller**[7755,7756] 20 Feb 1921, daughter of Simon Miller and Magdalena Lantz. She was born 30 Mar 1900 in White Cloud, Newaygo Co., MI[7756], and died 11 Oct 1968[7756]. He married **(3) Elizabeth D. Bontrager** 21 Dec 1969[7756]. She was born 12 Jun 1905 in Lagrange Co., IN, and died 25 Jul 1983 in Goshen, Elkhart Co., IN.

Notes for Willis E. Miller:
Willis married Fannie Elmina Miller Feb 20, 1921.

Willis married a 2nd time to Elizabeth Bontrager Christner 1969
Elizabeth died July 25 1983

Elizabeth born June 12 1905 and her 1st husband was Amos J. Christner.

Notes for Fannie Elmina Miller:
The Descendants of John J. Christner, privately published February 1961, pp. 7, 102.

More About Fannie Elmina Miller:
Residence: 1910, Wilcox, Newaygo Co., MI[7757]

Notes for Elizabeth D. Bontrager:
The Descendants of John J. Christner, privately published February 1961, p. 50.

Birth: 1905
Death: 1983

Burial: Forks Yoder Cemetery, Lagrange Co., IN

Elizabeth is the daughter of Dan R. Bontrager and Amelia Wingard Elizabeth married the 2nd time to Willis E. Miller son of Eza and Annie Christner Miller.

More About Elizabeth D. Bontrager:
Burial: Yoder Cemetery, Lagrange Co., IN
Religion: Old Order Amish/
Residence: 1930, Middlebury, Elkhart Co., IN[7758]

Child of Willis Miller and Fannie Brenneman is:

     4846   i.   Russell James[10] Miller, born 15 Feb 1949. He married Janice Lavonne Kauffman 22 Jun 1968; born 19 Dec 1947.

Children are listed above under (445) Fannie Elmina Miller.

2730. Mary E.[9] Miller (Annie J.[8] Christner, Joseph J.[7], John J.[6], Joseph C.[5], Christian J.[4], Johannes John Hans[3], Christian[2], Christen[1]) was born 01 Oct 1900 in Honeyville, Eden Twp., Lagrange Co., IN, and died 29 Dec 1998 in Goshen, Elkhart Co., IN. She married **Ezra S. Troyer** 29 Mar 1923 in Lagrange Co., IN. He was born 23 Apr 1899 in Clinton Twp. Elkhart Co. IN, and died 22 Mar 1969 in Sarasota, Sarasota Co., FL.

Notes for Mary E. Miller:
Mary worked 9 seasons for Pine Manor Dressing Farm (turkeys) & was a member of the Mount Joy Conservative Church.

The Descendants of John J. Christner, privately published February 1961, p. 8.

More About Mary E. Miller:
Burial: Thomas Cemetery Rural Goshen Area

Notes for Ezra S. Troyer:
Ezra owned a feed grinding mill & tree log sawing mill for many years. He smoked tobacco and it made him cough so bad he would go down on all fours for several minutes then sometimes fall over, after he would recover he would get up and light another cigarette. He smoked cigarette's in a method they call chain smoking, as in chain has links , one right after another. He had several sons and grandsons with the same affliction. The author of this history (Steven Carl Christner) had this same problem for 35 years, (80 cigarette's per day) quitting at age 50. That's 1,022,000 cigarette's , that's $51,100 in 1970 dollars. They were Conservative/Amish, thats almost Amish but not quite Mennonite.

The Descendants of John J. Christner, privately published February 1961, p. 8.

More About Ezra S. Troyer:
Burial: Thomas Cem, ELKHART CO, GOSHEN, IN. N41°36.182byW85°43.380
Religion: Conservative/Amish

Children of Mary Miller and Ezra Troyer are:

4847   i.   Infant Dau.[10] Troyer, born 04 Feb 1924 in Clinton Twp. Elkhart Co. IN; died 04 Feb 1924 in Clinton Twp. Elkhart Co. IN.

             Notes for Infant Dau. Troyer:
             The Descendants of John J. Christner, privately published February 1961, p. 8.

+ 4848   ii.   Omer E. Troyer, born 29 Dec 1924 in Clinton Twp. Elkhart Co. IN; died 22 Nov 2009 in Goshen, Elkhart Co., IN.
+ 4849   iii. Edna Ellen Troyer, born 12 Feb 1927 in Lagrange Co., IN.
+ 4850   iv.   Melvin E. Troyer, born 10 Dec 1928 in Lagrange Co., IN; died 13 Dec 2003 in Goshen, Elkhart Co., IN.
+ 4851   v.   Marion E. Troyer, born 28 May 1930 in Clinton Twp. Elkhart Co. IN.
+ 4852   vi.   Elmer E. Troyer, born 08 Nov 1932 in Clinton Twp. Elkhart Co. IN.
+ 4853   vii. Mervin Ezra Troyer, born 09 Feb 1936 in Clinton Twp. Elkhart Co. IN.
   4854   viii. Luella Mae Troyer, born 13 Dec 1937 in Clinton Twp. Elkhart Co. IN; died 19 Jul 1938 in Clinton Twp. Elkhart Co. IN.

             Notes for Luella Mae Troyer:
             The Descendants of John J. Christner, privately published February 1961, p. 9.

+ 4855   ix.   Gladys Marie Troyer, born 06 Aug 1939 in Goshen, Elkhart Co., IN.

2731. Enos E.[9] Miller (Annie J.[8] Christner, Joseph J.[7], John J.[6], Joseph C.[5], Christian J.[4], Johannes John Hans[3], Christian[2], Christen[1])[7759,7760] was born 12 Mar 1903 in Shipshewana, Lagrange Co., IN[7760], and died 15 Feb 1988 in IN[7760]. He married **Ida J. Yoder**[7760] 15 Jan 1925[7761]. She was born 19 Oct 1904 in Shipshewana, Lagrange Co., IN[7762].

Notes for Enos E. Miller:
Enos married Ida J. Yoder Jan 15, 1925. Ida died Jan 21, 1970 and then Enos married Fannie Miller. Enos died of a heart attack at home Shipshewana, Lagrange Co., IN. Enos was O.O.Amish and a farmer.

The Descendants of John J. Christner, privately published February 1961, p. 9.

More About Enos E. Miller:
Burial: Yoder Cemetery, Forks, Lagrange Co., IN
Occupation: Farmer/
Religion: Old Order Amish/

Notes for Ida J. Yoder:
The Descendants of John J. Christner, privately published February 1961, p. 9.

Children of Enos Miller and Ida Yoder are:

+	4856	i.	Wilma E.[10] Miller, born 22 Sep 1926 in Shipshewana, Elkhart Co., IN; died 22 Apr 1995.
+	4857	ii.	Harley E. Miller, born 23 May 1928 in Shipshewana, Elkhart Co., IN.
+	4858	iii.	Ezra E. Miller, born 27 Dec 1929 in Lagrange Co., IN.
+	4859	iv.	Jerry E. Miller, born 29 Jul 1932; died 10 Dec 1990.
	4860	v.	Amanda Miller, born 03 Jun 1934.

Notes for Amanda Miller:
The Descendants of John J. Christner, privately published February 1961, p. 9.

+	4861	vi.	Alma E. Miller, born 30 Jun 1936 in Topeka, Lagrange Co., IN.
	4862	vii.	Ida Mae Miller, born 26 Oct 1940 in Shipshewana, Elkhart Co., IN. She married Ervin S Bontrager 19 Nov 1959; born 01 Mar 1938.

Notes for Ida Mae Miller:
The Descendants of John J. Christner, privately published February 1961, p. 9, 10.

Notes for Ervin S Bontrager:
The Descendants of John J. Christner, privately published February 1961, pp. 10, 22.

More About Ervin S Bontrager:
Religion: Old Order Amish/

	4863	viii.	Anna Miller, born 08 Nov 1942.

Notes for Anna Miller:
The Descendants of John J. Christner, privately published February 1961, p. 9.

	4864	ix.	Vernon Miller, born 25 Jun 1948; died 04 Sep 1952.

Notes for Vernon Miller:
The Descendants of John J. Christner, privately published February 1961, p. 9.

2732. Ada E.[9] Miller (Annie J.[8] Christner, Joseph J.[7], John J.[6], Joseph C.[5], Christian J.[4], Johannes John Hans[3], Christian[2], Christen[1]) was born 31 Jul 1906 in Lagrange Co., IN, and died 06 Jul 1994 in Lagrange Co., IN. She married **William J. Bontrager**[7763] 22 Dec 1925 in Lagrange Co., IN. He was born 03 Feb 1904 in Lagrange Co., IN[7764,7765], and died 10 Dec 1991 in Lagrange Co., IN[7766,7767,7768].

Notes for Ada E. Miller:
Ada married William J. Bontrager Dec. 22 1925 in Lagrange. He died Dec 10, 1991. Last address 7045 west 50 south Lagrange Co.IN burial at Yoder Cemetery 850 west 100 south Shipshewana IN.

The Descendants of John J. Christner, privately published February 1961, p. 10.

Notes for William J. Bontrager:
The Descendants of John J. Christner, privately published February 1961, p. 10.

More About William J. Bontrager:

Religion: Old Order Amish/
Residence: 1930, Newbury, Lagrange Co., IN[7769]
Social Security Number: 305-22-5570/[7770,7771]
SSN issued: IN[7771,7772]

Children of Ada Miller and William Bontrager are:

+   4865   i.   Elmer W.[10] Bontrager, born 15 May 1927 in Topeka, Lagrange Co., IN.
+   4866   ii.   Amos W. Bontrager, born 11 Aug 1929 in Lagrange Co., IN.
     4867   iii.   Ervin W Bontrager, born 27 Aug 1932 in Lagrange Co., IN. He married Martha Miller 20 Oct 1955; born 12 Jan 1932.

         Notes for Ervin W Bontrager:
         The Descendants of John J. Christner, privately published February 1961, p. 10.

         More About Ervin W Bontrager:
         Religion: Old Order Amish/

         Notes for Martha Miller:
         The Descendants of John J. Christner, privately published February 1961, p. 10.

+   4868   iv.   Anna W. Bontrager, born 09 Dec 1934 in Lagrange Co., IN.
     4869   v.   Mattie Bontrager, born 26 Dec 1936.

         Notes for Mattie Bontrager:
         The Descendants of John J. Christner, privately published February 1961, p. 10.

     4870   vi.   Emma Bontrager, born 05 Jun 1939.

         Notes for Emma Bontrager:
         The Descendants of John J. Christner, privately published February 1961, p. 10.

     4871   vii.   Ada Bontrager, born 10 Jan 1942.

         Notes for Ada Bontrager:
         The Descendants of John J. Christner, privately published February 1961, p. 10.

     4872   viii.   Daniel Bontrager, born 08 May 1945.

         Notes for Daniel Bontrager:
         The Descendants of John J. Christner, privately published February 1961, p. 10.

     4873   ix.   Enos Bontrager, born 26 Jun 1948.

         Notes for Enos Bontrager:
         The Descendants of John J. Christner, privately published February 1961, p. 10.

2733. Sylvia E.[9] **Miller** (Annie J.[8] Christner, Joseph J.[7], John J.[6], Joseph C.[5], Christian J.[4], Johannes John Hans[3], Christian[2], Christen[1])[7773] was born 10 May 1909 in Lagrange Co., IN, and died 30 Dec 2002 in Lagrange Co., IN. She married **(2) Jonas A. Hostetler** 20 Oct 1932 in Shipshewana, Elkhart Co., IN. He was born 11 Apr 1910 in Bucklin, Ford Co., KS, and died 15 Aug 1986 in at his home N40° 39' by W85° 29.867' Lagrange IN..

Notes for Sylvia E. Miller:
The Descendants of John J. Christner, privately published February 1961, p. 11.

Old Order Amish 3765w x 50n LaGrange Co., IN

Sylvia died at 5:45 am at her home N40° 39' by W85° 29.867' Lagrange Co., IN.

More About Sylvia E. Miller:

Burial: 02 Jan 2003, Mast Cemetery   Lagrange Co.
Religion: Old Order Amish/

Notes for Jonas A. Hostetler:
The Descendants of John J. Christner, privately published February 1961, p. 11.

More About Jonas A. Hostetler:
Burial: Mast Cemetery Lagrange Co. Indiana
Occupation: Farmer/
Religion: Old Order Amish/

Children of Sylvia Miller and Jonas Hostetler are:
+   4874   i.   Anna Mae[10] Hostetler, born 02 Feb 1934 in Shipshewana, Elkhart Co., IN.
+   4875   ii.   Willis J. Hostetler, born 18 Feb 1937 in Lagrange Co., IN.
     4876   iii.   Harley Hostetler, born 28 Mar 1939 in Lagrange Co., IN; died 05 Mar 1942 in Howe, IN.

              Notes for Harley Hostetler:
              The Descendants of John J. Christner, privately published February 1961, p. 11.

              More About Harley Hostetler:
              Burial: Yoder Cemetery

+   4877   iv.   Edward J. Hostetler, born 11 Jul 1941 in Howe, IN.
+   4878   v.   Elsie Hostetler, born 08 Apr 1945 in Lagrange Co., IN.
+   4879   vi.   Vernon J Hostetler, born 29 Nov 1947 in Lagrange Co., IN.

2734. Emma E.[9] Miller (Annie J.[8] Christner, Joseph J.[7], John J.[6], Joseph C.[5], Christian J.[4], Johannes John Hans[3], Christian[2], Christen[1]) was born 08 Sep 1911 in Shipshewana, Lagrange Co., IN, and died 12 Jan 2004 in 0330 South Indiana State Road 5 at 12:30 AM. She married **(2) Henry F. Graber**[7774] 18 Nov 1937 in Shipshewana, Elkhart Co., IN. He was born 21 Dec 1914[7774], and died 16 Jul 1998[7774].

Notes for Emma E. Miller:
The Descendants of John J. Christner, privately published February 1961, p. 12.

Emma married Henry Graber. He was Old Order Amish.

More About Emma E. Miller:
Burial: Yoder Cemetery Shipshewana IN.

Notes for Henry F. Graber:
The Descendants of John J. Christner, privately published February 1961, p. 12.

He was Old Order Amish.

More About Henry F. Graber:
Religion: Old Order Amish/
Social Security Number: 217-54-8567/[7774]
SSN issued: MD[7774]

Children of Emma Miller and Henry Graber are:
+   4880   i.   Anna Ruth[10] Graber, born 22 Feb 1939.
     4881   ii.   Elsie Graber, born 24 Dec 1940.

              Notes for Elsie Graber:
              The Descendants of John J. Christner, privately published February 1961, p. 12.

     4882   iii.   Elmer Graber, born 02 Aug 1942.

              Notes for Elmer Graber:

The Descendants of John J. Christner, privately published February 1961, p. 12.

4883   iv.   Amos Graber, born 14 Jul 1944.

Notes for Amos Graber:
The Descendants of John J. Christner, privately published February 1961, p. 12.

4884   v.   Ruby Graber, born 06 Dec 1946.

Notes for Ruby Graber:
The Descendants of John J. Christner, privately published February 1961, p. 12.

4885   vi.   Harley Graber, born 13 Sep 1948.

Notes for Harley Graber:
The Descendants of John J. Christner, privately published February 1961, p. 12.

4886   vii.   Fannie Graber, born 28 May 1950.

Notes for Fannie Graber:
The Descendants of John J. Christner, privately published February 1961, p. 12.

4887   viii.   Ernest Graber, born 06 Jul 1952.

Notes for Ernest Graber:
The Descendants of John J. Christner, privately published February 1961, p. 12.

4888   ix.   Edna Graber, born 22 Feb 1955.

Notes for Edna Graber:
The Descendants of John J. Christner, privately published February 1961, p. 12.

4889   x.   Orva Graber, born 03 Jan 1957.

Notes for Orva Graber:
The Descendants of John J. Christner, privately published February 1961, p. 12.

2735. Alma E.[9] **Miller** (Annie J.[8] Christner, Joseph J.[7], John J.[6], Joseph C.[5], Christian J.[4], Johannes John Hans[3], Christian[2], Christen[1])[7775] was born 12 Dec 1912 in Middlebury, Elkhart Co., IN, and died 06 Jun 1942. She married **(3) Annon Miller** 30 Nov 1933[7776], son of Levi Miller and Mary Schrock. He was born 28 Jan 1912 in Elkhart Co., IN[7776], and died 04 Mar 1996[7776].

Notes for Alma E. Miller:
The Descendants of John J. Christner, privately published February 1961, p. 11.

Alma is a twin to Amos.

Notes for Annon Miller:
The Descendants of John J. Christner, privately published February 1961, pp. 11, 72.

Children of Alma Miller and Annon Miller are:
+   4890   i.   Edna Mae[10] Miller, born 08 Mar 1935.
+   4891   ii.   Amos Eldon Miller, born 10 Mar 1938.
     4892   iii.   Amy Ellen Miller, born 10 Mar 1938. She married Marvin Ray Beachy 10 Apr 1960.

Notes for Amy Ellen Miller:

The Descendants of John J. Christner, privately published February 1961, p. 12.

Notes for Marvin Ray Beachy:
The Descendants of John J. Christner, privately published February 1961, p. 12.

4893   iv.   Elva Dean Miller, born 24 Feb 1941.
4894   v.   Willis Miller, born 05 Jun 1942.
4895   vi.   Willis Miller, born 19 Apr 1949.

Notes for Willis Miller:
The Descendants of John J. Christner, privately published February 1961, p. 74.

2736.   Amos E.[9] **Miller** (Annie J.[8] Christner, Joseph J.[7], John J.[6], Joseph C.[5], Christian J.[4], Johannes John Hans[3], Christian[2], Christen[1]) was born 12 Dec 1912 in Lagrange Co., IN, and died 22 Aug 1969 in Home, Middlebury, IN. He married **Susie S. Riegsecker** 24 Nov 1940. She was born 01 Feb 1920 in Middlebury, Elkhart Co., IN, and died 31 Dec 2000 in Middlebury, Elkhart Co., IN.

Notes for Amos E. Miller:
The Descendants of John J. Christner, privately published February 1961, p. 11.

More About Amos E. Miller:
Burial: Miller Cemetery Goshen Indiana

Notes for Susie S. Riegsecker:
The Descendants of John J. Christner, privately published February 1961, p. 11.

Baked pie's for sale at Goshen Sale Barn and served meals in here home for over 30 years. Griner Mennonite Church south of Middlebury Indiana.

More About Susie S. Riegsecker:
Burial: Miller Cemetery Goshen Indiana

Children of Amos Miller and Susie Riegsecker are:
4896   i.   Omer[10] Miller, born 18 Oct 1941.

Notes for Omer Miller:
The Descendants of John J. Christner, privately published February 1961, p. 11.

4897   ii.   Fannie Ellen Miller, born 01 Oct 1943.

Notes for Fannie Ellen Miller:
The Descendants of John J. Christner, privately published February 1961, p. 11.

4898   iii.   Marvin Jay Miller, born 27 Nov 1946.

Notes for Marvin Jay Miller:
The Descendants of John J. Christner, privately published February 1961, p. 11.

4899   iv.   David Devon Miller, born 15 Jan 1953.

Notes for David Devon Miller:
The Descendants of John J. Christner, privately published February 1961, p. 11.

2737.   Alma D.[9] **Eash** (Lydia J.[8] Christner, Joseph J.[7], John J.[6], Joseph C.[5], Christian J.[4], Johannes John Hans[3], Christian[2], Christen[1]) was born 10 Mar 1904 in Topeka, Lagrange Co., IN, and died 22 Aug 1994 in Topeka, Lagrange Co., IN. She married **(2) Christ L. Miller** 27 Feb 1923. He was born 15 Dec 1902, and died 30 Apr 1980.

Notes for Alma D. Eash:
The Descendants of John J. Christner, privately published February 1961, p. 12.

More About Alma D. Eash:
Residence: 01 Apr 1940, Newbury, Lagrange Co., IN[7777]

Notes for Christ L. Miller:
The Descendants of John J. Christner, privately published February 1961, p. 12.

He was Old Order Amish and a farmer.

More About Christ L. Miller:
Occupation: Farmer/
Religion: Old Order Amish/
Residence: 01 Apr 1940, Newbury, Lagrange Co., IN[7777]

Children of Alma Eash and Christ Miller are:
+ 4900 i. Mary Alice[10] Miller, born 05 May 1925.
  4901 ii. Ida Mae Miller, born 10 Oct 1926; died 21 May 1928.

    Notes for Ida Mae Miller:
    The Descendants of John J. Christner, privately published February 1961, p. 12.

+ 4902 iii. Nettie Jean Miller, born 06 Oct 1929 in Ligoiner, IN.
  4903 iv. Wilma Louise Miller, born 01 Mar 1931. She married Floyd Bontrager 20 Nov 1951; born 18 Jun 1931.

    Notes for Wilma Louise Miller:
    The Descendants of John J. Christner, privately published February 1961, p. 12.

    Notes for Floyd Bontrager:
    The Descendants of John J. Christner, privately published February 1961, p. 27.

+ 4904 v. Ruby Miller, born 03 Mar 1934.
  4905 vi. Cletus LeRoy Miller, born Jul 1936. He married Frieda Hostetler 25 Jun 1960; born 07 Aug 1937.

    Notes for Cletus LeRoy Miller:
    The Descendants of John J. Christner, privately published February 1961, p. 12.

    Notes for Frieda Hostetler:
    The Descendants of John J. Christner, privately published February 1961, p. 12.

+ 4906 vii. Katie Miller, born 12 Mar 1938.
  4907 viii. Leanna Miller, born 21 May 1939; died 04 May 1944.
  4908 ix. Perry Miller, born 12 Apr 1945.
  4909 x. Elvon Lee Miller, born 02 Aug 1948.

2738. Levi D.[9] Eash (Lydia J.[8] Christner, Joseph J.[7], John J.[6], Joseph C.[5], Christian J.[4], Johannes John Hans[3], Christian[2], Christen[1]) was born 14 Dec 1913 in Topeka, Lagrange Co., IN, and died 31 Mar 1954. He married **Violet Whirledge** 28 Sep 1935. She was born 23 Oct 1916.

Notes for Levi D. Eash:
The Descendants of John J. Christner, privately published February 1961, pp. 12,13.

Levi married Violet Whirledge Sept 28 1935 He owned the Honeyville General Store for many years. It was a typical country store. I enjoyed eating hand dipped ice cream local made while the men played checkers on a hand painted counter. You could buy most things by the pound but dynamite sold by the stick to anyone, no license needed. My uncle bought a case to help my grandfather blow some tree stumps out of the ground. He told me (as a little kid I was always hanging around with the wild guys, More fun) anyway he told me dynamite makes his nerves jumpy but if he has a few beers his nerves are smooth. He drank enough to get his nerves really smooth. The first two tree stumps blew so high in the air when they came back to earth the got caught in the other tree limbs. My grandfather made him quit because the stumps can fall out of the tree later and kill a cow or him.

More About Levi D. Eash:
Cause of Death: heart ailment

Notes for Violet Whirledge:
The Descendants of John J. Christner, privately published February 1961, p. 13.

Children of Levi Eash and Violet Whirledge are:
+   4910   i.   Theodore Marlin[10] Eash, born 10 Dec 1936 in Honeyville, Lagrange Co., IN.
+   4911   ii.   Janet Elizabeth Eash, born 13 Oct 1939 in Honeyville, Lagrange Co., IN.
+   4912   iii. Gerald Lee Eash, born 12 Aug 1941.
     4913   iv.   Thomas Allen Eash, born 02 Aug 1952.

         Notes for Thomas Allen Eash:
         The Descendants of John J. Christner, privately published February 1961, p. 13.

2739. Erma[9] Eash (Lydia J.[8] Christner, Joseph J.[7], John J.[6], Joseph C.[5], Christian J.[4], Johannes John Hans[3], Christian[2], Christen[1]) was born 29 Jul 1915 in Topeka, Lagrange Co., IN. She married **Tobias Bontrager** 16 Feb 1939. He was born 30 Apr 1913 in Middlebury, Elkhart Co., IN.

Notes for Erma Eash:
The Descendants of John J. Christner, privately published February 1961, p. 13.

Notes for Tobias Bontrager:
The Descendants of John J. Christner, privately published February 1961, p. 13.

Children of Erma Eash and Tobias Bontrager are:
     4914   i.   Merle Dean[10] Bontrager, born 16 Mar 1943.

         Notes for Merle Dean Bontrager:
         The Descendants of John J. Christner, privately published February 1961, p. 13.

     4915   ii.   Julianna Bontrager, born 13 Jun 1948.

         Notes for Julianna Bontrager:
         The Descendants of John J. Christner, privately published February 1961, p. 13.

     4916   iii. Sharon Kay Bontrager, born 28 Aug 1950.

         Notes for Sharon Kay Bontrager:
         The Descendants of John J. Christner, privately published February 1961, p.13.

2741. Wilma[9] Eash (Lydia J.[8] Christner, Joseph J.[7], John J.[6], Joseph C.[5], Christian J.[4], Johannes John Hans[3], Christian[2], Christen[1]) was born 27 Jun 1922 in Topeka, Lagrange Co., IN. She married **Ernest D. Miller**[7778]. He was born 10 Nov 1920 in Eden, Lagrange Co., IN[7778], and died 18 Sep 1989 in Goshen, Elkhart Co., IN[7778].

Notes for Wilma Eash:
The Descendants of John J. Christner, privately published February 1961, p. 13.

More About Ernest D. Miller:

Social Security Number: 306-20-7422/[7778]
SSN issued: IN[7778]

Children of Wilma Eash and Ernest Miller are:

4917   i.   Ronald Lee[10] Miller, born 20 May 1946.

        Notes for Ronald Lee Miller:
        The Descendants of John J. Christner, privately published February 1961, p. 13.

4918   ii. Virginia Elaine Miller, born 21 May 1957.

        Notes for Virginia Elaine Miller:
        The Descendants of John J. Christner, privately published February 1961, p. 13.

        She was adopted.

2743. Elva[9] Eash (Lydia J.[8] Christner, Joseph J.[7], John J.[6], Joseph C.[5], Christian J.[4], Johannes John Hans[3], Christian[2], Christen[1]) was born 13 Dec 1909 in Topeka, Lagrange Co., IN. He married **(1) Audrey Shedka** 19 Dec 1946.   He married **(2) Evylnn Kline** 19 Dec 1946. She was born 08 Nov 1917.

Notes for Elva Eash:
The Descendants of John J. Christner, privately published February 1961, pp. 12, 13.

Elva married Evylnn Kline Dec 19 1946. This may have been a 2nd marriage.

Notes for Audrey Shedka:
Source:
The Descendants of John J. Christner, privately published February 1961, p. 13.

Notes for Evylnn Kline:
Source:
The Descendants of John J. Christner, privately published February 1961, p. 13.

Child of Elva Eash and Evylnn Kline is:

4919   i.   James[10] Eash, born 18 Mar 1948.

        Notes for James Eash:
        The Descendants of John J. Christner, privately published February 1961, p. 13.

2745. Joseph Mahlon[9] Christner (Noah J.[8], Joseph J.[7], John J.[6], Joseph C.[5], Christian J.[4], Johannes John Hans[3], Christian[2], Christen[1]) was born 22 Dec 1909 in Plain City, Madison Co., OH[7779], and died 07 Jan 1989 in Columbus., OH. He married **Verbal Stutzman** 04 Nov 1929. She was born 29 Jan 1908 in Pedro, OH.

Notes for Joseph Mahlon Christner:
The Descendants of John J. Christner, privately published February 1961, p. 13.

SS#;291-05-3660 Iss OH   Last address 43224

Christner - Joe son of Noah and Martha Christner was born in Plain City, OH Dec. 22, 1909; died at Columbus, OH Jan. 7, 1989; aged 79 y. On Nov. 4, 1929, he was married to Verbal Stutzman, who survives. Also surviving are one son (Kenneth Dale), 2 daughters (Joann Kindske and Mary Christner), 6 grandchildren, 5 great-grandchildren, 2 brothers (Glen and Willis) and 3 sisters (Lula Frey, Edna Hreshberger, and Mary Borntrager). He was a member of Sharon Mennonite Church, where funeral services were held on Jan. 11, in charge of Elvin Sommers and Bob Lemon; internment in the church cemetery.

More About Joseph Mahlon Christner:
Burial: 11 Jan 1989, Sharon Mennonite Church Cemetery
Social Security Number: 291-05-3660/[7779]
SSN issued: OH[7779]

Children of Joseph Christner and Verbal Stutzman are:
+ 4920   i.   Oren Lee[10] Christner, born 09 Jan 1931 in Plain City, Madison Co., OH; died 19 May 1963 in Wellston, Jackson Co., OH.
+ 4921   ii. Martha Joann Christner, born 29 Aug 1932 in Plain City, Madison Co., OH.
  4922   iii. Mary Elizabeth Christner, born 03 Jul 1935 in Plain City, Madison Co., OH.
+ 4923   iv. Kenneth Dale Christner, born 18 May 1937 in Plain City, Madison Co., OH.

2746. Ollie N.[9] Christner (Noah J.[8], Joseph J.[7], John J.[6], Joseph C.[5], Christian J.[4], Johannes John Hans[3], Christian[2], Christen[1]) was born 08 Feb 1912 in Honeyville, Lagrange Co., IN[7780], and died 13 Apr 1987 in Plain City, Madison Co., OH. He married **Katie Miller** 04 Feb 1932. She was born 30 Jun 1912 in Ford Co., KS.

Notes for Ollie N. Christner:
The Descendants of John J. Christner, privately published February 1961, p. 14.
Ollie was active in the Pleasent Valley Senior Citizens
SS#300-16-8254 ISS OH

More About Ollie N. Christner:
Burial: 15 Apr 1987, Plain City United Bethel Conserv., Mennonite Church Cemetery, Plain City, Madison Co., OH
Christened: Beechy Amish
Social Security Number: 300-16-8254/[7780]
SSN issued: OH[7780]

Notes for Katie Miller:
The Descendants of John J. Christner, privately published February 1961, p. 14.

Katie is the daughter of Dan A. and Mattie Schrock Miller.

Children of Ollie Christner and Katie Miller are:
  4924   i.   Paul Edward[10] Christner[7781], born 21 Aug 1935 in Madison Co., OH[7782,7783]; died 29 May 1992 in Plain City, Madison Co., OH[7784].

           Notes for Paul Edward Christner:
           The Descendants of John J. Christner, privately published February 1961, p. 14.

           More About Paul Edward Christner:
           Burial: Forrest Grove Cemetery, Plain City, OH
           Social Security Number: 290-32-9221/[7784]
           SSN issued: OH[7784]

+ 4925   ii. Martha Ellen Christner, born 13 Jun 1937.

2747. Edna Mae[9] Christner (Noah J.[8], Joseph J.[7], John J.[6], Joseph C.[5], Christian J.[4], Johannes John Hans[3], Christian[2], Christen[1])[7785,7786,7787] was born 24 Mar 1913 in Honeyville, Lagrange Co., IN[7788,7789,7790], and died 13 Aug 1992 in Plain City, Madison Co., OH[7790]. She married **Emanuel S. Hershberger**[7791] 08 Dec 1931[7791], son of Simon Hershberger and Anna Troyer. He was born 04 May 1908 in Dundee, Tuscarawas Co., OH[7791], and died 19 May 1965[7791].

Notes for Edna Mae Christner:
The Descendants of John J. Christner, privately published February 1961, p. 13.

More About Edna Mae Christner:
Burial: United Bethel Mennonite Church, Plain City, Madison Co., OH
Publication: 21 Aug 1992[7791]
Residence: 1920, Canaan, Madison, OH[7792]
Social Security Number: 295-42-9755/[7793]
SSN issued: Union Co., OH[7793]

Notes for Emanuel S. Hershberger:
Emanuel is the son of Simon P and Anna Troyer Hershberger

Children of Edna Christner and Emanuel Hershberger are:

4926   i.   Susan Ellen[10] Hershberger, born 02 Mar 1932; died 26 Dec 1997 in Plain City, Madison Co., OH.

     Notes for Susan Ellen Hershberger:
     The Descendants of John J. Christner, privately published February 1961, p. 15.

4927   ii.   Hershberger, born 26 Oct 1939; died 26 Oct 1939.

     Notes for Hershberger:
     The Descendants of John J. Christner, privately published February 1961, p.15.

4928   iii.   Willis Andrew Hershberger, born 02 Jul 1941.

     Notes for Willis Andrew Hershberger:
     The Descendants of John J. Christner, privately published February 1961, p. 15.

4929   iv.   Mary Naomi Hershberger, born 02 Jul 1942; died 01 Nov 1993 in Plain City, Madison Co., OH.

     Notes for Mary Naomi Hershberger:
     The Descendants of John J. Christner, privately published February 1961, p. 15.

4930   v.   Emma Jean Hershberger, born 03 Jan 1944. She married Robert Depew 01 Jan 1966; born 01 May 1943.

     Notes for Emma Jean Hershberger:
     The Descendants of John J. Christner, privately published February 1961, p. 15.

4931   vi.   Esther Anne Hershberger, born 06 Feb 1946; died 03 Mar 1946.

     Notes for Esther Anne Hershberger:
     The Descendants of John J. Christner, privately published February 1961, p. 15.

4932   vii.   Rebecca Hershberger, born 08 Jan 1947. She married Alvin Headings 01 Jul 1967; born 22 Nov 1944.

     Notes for Rebecca Hershberger:
     The Descendants of John J. Christner, privately published February 1961, p. 15.

     Alvin born Nov 22 1944 son of Robert Henry and Edna Mae Beachy Marner.
     Alvin adopted by Raymond Headings of Hutchinson, KS in 1948.

4933   viii.   Glen Eldon Hershberger, born 08 Jun 1948. He married Melvina Sue Butz 28 Sep 1966; born 08 May 1948.

     Notes for Glen Eldon Hershberger:
     The Descendants of John J. Christner, privately published February 1961, p. 15.

     Divorced

4934   ix.   Joseph Ray Hershberger, born 06 Mar 1950. He married Sandra Kay Haude 06 Jun 1970; born 02 Sep

1952.

Notes for Joseph Ray Hershberger:
The Descendants of John J. Christner, privately published February 1961, p. 15.

4935   x.   Nila Kay Hershberger, born 21 Oct 1953.

Notes for Nila Kay Hershberger:
The Descendants of John J. Christner, privately published February 1961, p. 15.

2748. Eli N.[9] **Christner** (Noah J.[8], Joseph J.[7], John J.[6], Joseph C.[5], Christian J.[4], Johannes John Hans[3], Christian[2], Christen[1])[7794] was born 30 Mar 1915 in Plain City, Madison Co., OH[7794], and died 08 Jan 1982 in New Philadelphia, Tuscarawas Co., OH[7794]. He married **Ruth Melhorn** 25 Jun 1948 in York, PA. She was born 20 Apr 1924 in York, PA.

Notes for Eli N. Christner:
The Descendants of John J. Christner, privately published February 1961, pp. 13, 15.

Birth: Mar. 31, 1915
Death: Jan. 8, 1982

Burial: East Avenue Cemetery, New Philadelphia, Tuscarawas Co., OH
Plot: Section 23

Address as of March 1980 - 413 St. Clair Ave. New Philadelphia, OH 44663 - SS# 272-18-7881 Iss.OH

More About Eli N. Christner:
Burial: 11 Jan 1982, East Avenue Cemetery, New Philadelphia, Tuscarawas Co., OH
Social Security Number: 272-18-7881/[7794]
SSN issued: Union Co., OH[7794]

Notes for Ruth Melhorn:
The Descendants of John J. Christner, privately published February 1961, p. 15.

Children of Eli Christner and Ruth Melhorn are:
+ 4936   i.   Joseph Lee[10] Christner, born 21 Dec 1950 in Campbellsville, KY.
+ 4937   ii. Dennis Ray Christner, born 02 Jul 1952 in Taylor, Kentucky.
+ 4938   iii. William Gerald Christner, born 24 Aug 1953 in Dover, Tuscarawas Co., OH.
+ 4939   iv. Philip Andrew Christner, born 06 Feb 1957 in Coshocton, Coshocton Co., OH.
+ 4940   v. Priscilla Rose Christner, born 19 Jun 1959 in Coshocton, Coshocton Co., OH.
+ 4941   vi. Donald Eugene Christner, born 02 Aug 1963 in Coshocton, Coshocton Co., OH.

2749. Lula Hellen[9] **Christner** (Noah J.[8], Joseph J.[7], John J.[6], Joseph C.[5], Christian J.[4], Johannes John Hans[3], Christian[2], Christen[1]) was born 13 Jan 1918 in Plain City, Madison Co., OH[7795], and died 20 Jan 1993 in Plain City, Madison Co., OH. She married **Jonas Marvin Frey** 24 Feb 1942. He was born 05 Sep 1918 in Plain City, Madison Co., OH.

Notes for Lula Hellen Christner:
The Descendants of John J. Christner, privately published February 1961, pp. 13, 15.

More About Lula Hellen Christner:
Burial: United Bethel Mennonite Church, Plain City, Madison Co., OH
Social Security Number: 279-36-6618/[7795]
SSN issued: OH[7795]

Notes for Jonas Marvin Frey:

Jonas is the son of Eli B. and Susanna J. Yoder Frey.

Children of Lula Christner and Jonas Frey are:

4942   i.   Gerald Lloyd[10] Frey, born 15 Nov 1942. He married Karolyn Cantor 10 Sep 1067; born 25 Jan 1948.

            Notes for Gerald Lloyd Frey:
            The Descendants of John J. Christner, privately published February 1961, p. 15.

4943   ii.   John Allen Frey, born 07 Feb 1944. He married Nancy Cordaro 17 Sep 1966; born 21 Aug 1949.

            Notes for John Allen Frey:
            The Descendants of John J. Christner, privately published February 1961, p. 15.

4944   iii.   Linda Christina Frey, born 15 Aug 1945. She married Larry Miller 18 Dec 1965; born 23 Jul 1946.

            Notes for Linda Christina Frey:
            The Descendants of John J. Christner, privately published February 1961, p. 15.

4945   iv.   Fredrick Eli Frey, born 20 Jul 1947. He married Judy Ann Smith 24 Sep 1966.

            Notes for Fredrick Eli Frey:
            The Descendants of John J. Christner, privately published February 1961, p. 15.

4946   v.   Edna Pauline Frey, born 21 Feb 1950.

            Notes for Edna Pauline Frey:
            The Descendants of John J. Christner, privately published February 1961, p. 15.

4947   vi.   Mariam Sue Frey, born 21 Oct 1951. She married James Earl Wise 11 Nov 1969; born 13 Feb 1948.

            Notes for Mariam Sue Frey:
            The Descendants of John J. Christner, privately published February 1961, p. 15.

            Divorced.

4948   vii.   Steven Carl Frey, born 25 Sep 1953.

            Notes for Steven Carl Frey:
            The Descendants of John J. Christner, privately published February 1961, p. 15.

4949   viii.   Philip Jonas Frey, born 25 Jun 1955.

            Notes for Philip Jonas Frey:
            The Descendants of John J. Christner, privately published February 1961, p. 15.

2750. Mary Janet[9] **Christner** (Noah J.[8], Joseph J.[7], John J.[6], Joseph C.[5], Christian J.[4], Johannes John Hans[3], Christian[2], Christen[1]) was born 27 Mar 1921 in Plain City, Madison Co., OH, and died 09 Dec 2002 in Cantpn, Stark Co., OH. She married **John T. Borntrager** 27 Jun 1940. He was born 28 Aug 1920[7796], and died Aug 1987 in Canton, Stark Co., OH[7796].

Notes for Mary Janet Christner:
The Descendants of John J. Christner, privately published February 1961, pp. 13, 15.

Author of many Amish books including: Ellie's People, Mandy, Annie , Sarah, Polly, Andy, Ruben, Daniel, Rachel, Rebecca, Ellie publication by Herald Press.

Birth: Mar. 27, 1921
Plain City, Madison Co., OH

Death: Dec. 9, 2002
Canton, Stark Co., OH

Daughter of Noah & Martha (Yoder) Christner. Married John T. Borntrager on 27 June 1940. Mrs. Borntrager was the author of the "Ellies People Series" of books and enjoyed public speaking. She taught at Lake Center School from 1958 to 1965. From 1966 to 1979 she was a house parent for the Summit County Children Services.

Spouse: John T. Borntrager (1920 - 1987)

Burial: Hartville Mennonite Church Cemetery, Hartville, Stark Co., OH
Find A Grave Memorial# 55581494

More About Mary Janet Christner:
Occupation: author/
Religion: Hartville Mennonite Church/

Notes for John T. Borntrager:
Birth: Aug. 28, 1920 - Hutchinson, Reno Co., KS
Death: Aug. 18, 1987 - Canton, Stark Co., OH

Son of Tobias & Nettie (Knepp) Borntrager. Married Mary J. Christner on 27 June 1940.

Spouse: Mary J. Christner Borntrager (1921 - 2002)

Burial: Hartville Mennonite Church Cemetery, Hartville, Stark Co., OH
Find A Grave Memorial# 55581488

More About John T. Borntrager:
Social Security Number: 515-10-7432/[7796]
SSN issued: KS[7796]

Children of Mary Christner and John Borntrager are:

4950   i.   Noah[10] Bontrager, born 01 Nov 1940. He married Nancy Ethridge 06 Jun 1965; born 03 Oct.

           Notes for Noah Bontrager:
           The Descendants of John J. Christner, privately published February 1961, p. 15.

4951   ii.   Edna Kathryn Bontrager, born 18 May 1942. She married Benjamin Keim 27 May 1961.

           Notes for Edna Kathryn Bontrager:
           The Descendants of John J. Christner, privately published February 1961, p. 15.

4952   iii.   John Tobias Bontrager, born 29 Feb 1944. He married Rowene Stoltzfus 07 Sep 1963.

           Notes for John Tobias Bontrager:
           The Descendants of John J. Christner, privately published February 1961, p. 15.

4953   iv.   Geneva Ann Bontrager, born 25 May 1945. She married Mervin Miller 16 Mar 1963.

           Notes for Geneva Ann Bontrager:
           The Descendants of John J. Christner, privately published February 1961, p. 15.

           Divorced.

2751. Willis N.[9] Christner (Noah J.[8], Joseph J.[7], John J.[6], Joseph C.[5], Christian J.[4], Johannes John Hans[3],

Christian², Christen¹) was born 24 Dec 1922 in Plain City, Madison Co., OH⁷⁷⁹⁷, and died 07 Sep 2006 in Glendale, Maricopa Co., AZ. He married **Anna Beachy**⁷⁷⁹⁸ 04 Nov 1944. She was born 30 Oct 1926 in Plain City, Madison Co., OH⁷⁷⁹⁸.

Notes for Willis N. Christner:
The Descendants of John J. Christner, privately published February 1961, pp. 13, 15.
Willis was a mennonite and a farmer   Last Address was Phoenix.

More About Willis N. Christner:
Social Security Number: 292-24-0658/⁷⁷⁹⁹
SSN issued: OH⁷⁷⁹⁹

Notes for Anna Beachy:
Last Address was Phoenix, AZ.

Children of Willis Christner and Anna Beachy are:
+   4954   i.   Richard Dale¹⁰ Christner, born 07 Jan 1946 in Plain City, Madison Co., OH.
+   4955   ii.   Robert Eli Christner, born 10 Dec 1946 in Plain City, Madison Co., OH.
+   4956   iii. Mary Lucille Christner, born 20 Aug 1949 in Plain City, Madison Co., OH.
+   4957   iv.   James Michael Christner, born 09 Sep 1951 in Plain City, Madison Co., OH.
     4958   v.   Thomas Lee Christner, born 13 Mar 1956 in Plain City, Madison Co., OH⁷⁸⁰⁰; died 04 Oct 1972 in Columbus (Pt), Franklin Co., OH⁷⁸⁰⁰.

               Notes for Thomas Lee Christner:
               The Descendants of John J. Christner, privately published February 1961, p. 15.
               Thomas died in an automobile accident. He was single.

     4959   vi.   Teddy Wayne Christner, born 09 Nov 1958 in Plain City, Madison Co., OH. He married Cindy Lou Swartz 07 Nov 1981; born 09 Dec 1961.

               Notes for Teddy Wayne Christner:
               The Descendants of John J. Christner, privately published February 1961, p. 15.

               Notes for Cindy Lou Swartz:
               Cindy is the daughter of Ronald Swartz and Bonnie Schrock Swartz
               Cindy and Teddy are mennonite. They live in Arizona. He is a carpenter and she is a secretary.

2753. Paul N.⁹ Christner (Noah J.⁸, Joseph J.⁷, John J.⁶, Joseph C.⁵, Christian J.⁴, Johannes John Hans³, Christian², Christen¹) was born 07 Oct 1930 in Plain City, Madison Co., OH, and died 20 May 1987 in Dayton, OH. He married **Esther Hilty** 02 Jun 1956. She was born 05 Aug 1927.

Notes for Paul N. Christner:
The Descendants of John J. Christner, privately published February 1961, pp. 13 - 15.

SS#289-30-4121 ISS OH Last address Medway near Dayton, OH.

More About Paul N. Christner:
Burial: 23 May 1987, Huber Mennonite, Cem, OH

Notes for Esther Hilty:
The Descendants of John J. Christner, privately published February 1961, p. 13.

Children of Paul Christner and Esther Hilty are:
     4960   i.   Gayle Lynette¹⁰ Christner, born 22 May 1957⁷⁸⁰¹. She married Peterson 26 Jul 1986⁷⁸⁰¹.

               Notes for Gayle Lynette Christner:
               The Descendants of John J. Christner, privately published February 1961, pp. 13, 15.

More About Gayle Lynette Christner:
Residence: Clark, Holmes Co., OH[7801]

+ 4961   ii.   Faith Lowleen/Louine Christner, born 02 Sep 1958 in Xenia, Greene Co., OH.
    4962   iii.   Jewell Christner, born 31 Dec 1959. She married Truxel.
    4963   iv.   Rachel Christner, born 01 Dec 1962.

2754. Carrie[9] **Christner** (Noah J.[8], Joseph J.[7], John J.[6], Joseph C.[5], Christian J.[4], Johannes John Hans[3], Christian[2], Christen[1])[7802,7803,7804] was born 22 Oct 1907 in Topeka, Lagrange Co., IN[7805,7806,7807,7808], and died 29 Oct 1984 in Plain City, Madison Co., OH. She married **Joseph J. Stutzman** 04 Dec 1934. He was born 26 Sep 1904, and died 23 Mar 1987 in Sarasota, Sarasota Co., FL.

Notes for Carrie Christner:

More About Carrie Christner:
Burial: Palms Memorial Park Plain City, OH
Residence: 1910, Canaan, Madison, OH[7809]

Notes for Joseph J. Stutzman:
The Descendants of John J. Christner, privately published February 1961, pp. 13, 14.

Joe is a roofer and a lot of his sons are roofers. Joe is the son of Joseph J. and Elizabeth Troyer Stutzman.

Children of Carrie Christner and Joseph Stutzman are:
+ 4964   i.   Eli J.[10] Stutzman, born 11 Oct 1935.
    4965   ii.   Harvey J. Stutzman, born 21 Mar 1937. He married Renate Staudenecker 02 Mar 1969; born 01 Dec 1940.

       Notes for Harvey J. Stutzman:
       The Descendants of John J. Christner, privately published February 1961, p. 14.

+ 4966   iii.   Noah J. Stutzman, born 14 Oct 1938 in Plain City, Madison Co., OH.
+ 4967   iv.   Martha Lou Stutzman, born 06 Feb 1940 in Plain City, Madison Co., OH.
    4968   v.   Ollie Jonas Stutzman, born 05 May 1941 in Plain City, Madison Co., OH. He married Inell Pitts 08 Jul 1959; born 28 Oct 1941.

       Notes for Ollie Jonas Stutzman:
       The Descendants of John J. Christner, privately published February 1961, p.14.

    4969   vi.   Mary Elizabeth Stutzman, born 19 Nov 1944. She married Amos Weber 13 Dec 1968; born 09 Jul 1948.

       Notes for Mary Elizabeth Stutzman:

    4970   vii.   David Eugene Stutzman, born 03 Jun 1946. He married Sharon Marini 20 Jul 1968; born 16 May 1950.
    4971   viii.   Ruth Ann Stutzman, born 08 Feb 1948. She married Raymond Weaver 25 Jan 1969; born 14 Aug 1943.

       Notes for Ruth Ann Stutzman:
       Raymond is the son of Abe J. and Sarah Miller Weaver.

    4972   ix.   Sarah Marie Stutzman, born 06 Sep 1949.
    4973   x.   Glen Allen Stutzman, born 12 Nov 1951. He married Rita Ann Knepp 12 Sep 1973.

Notes for Glen Allen Stutzman:

2757. Wilbur E.⁹ Christner (Eli J.⁸, Joseph J.⁷, John J.⁶, Joseph C.⁵, Christian J.⁴, Johannes John Hans³, Christian², Christen¹) was born 02 Dec 1919 in Topeka, Lagrange Co., IN, and died 12 Jun 1987 in Goshen, Elkhart Co., IN. He married **Mary Irene Borntrager**⁷⁸¹⁰ 22 Nov 1944 in Ligonier, Noble Co., IN, daughter of Daniel Borntrager and Polly Stutzman. She was born 09 Sep 1923 in Gladstone, Union Co., NM⁷⁸¹⁰, and died 19 Apr 2000 in Goshen, Elkhart Co., IN⁷⁸¹⁰.

Notes for Wilbur E. Christner:
The Descendants of John J. Christner, privately published February 1961, p. 16.
Wilbur operated the Honeyville Feed Mill with his brother Freeman for many years. He is buried at Maple Grove Cemetery, Topeka, IN.
SS#305-34-8017 ISS IN

More About Wilbur E. Christner:
Burial: 15 Jun 1987, Maple Grove Cem., TOPEKA, Lagrange Co., In.

Notes for Mary Irene Borntrager:
The Descendants of John J. Christner, privately published February 1961, p. 16.

Mary is the daughter of Dan C. Borntrager and Polly Stutzman Borntrager Retired from Lyell Electric in Topeka IN in 1973 as a superviser. She attended First Church of God Goshen, IN and a volunteer for World Missionary Press & Goshen General Hospital.

More About Mary Irene Borntrager:
Burial: Maple Grove Cemetary / 1 mile south & 1 1/2 mile west of Topeka⁷⁸¹⁰
Christened: Mennonite
Civil: IN⁷⁸¹⁰
Residence: 1930, Age: 6; Marital Status: Single; Relation to Head of House: Daughter/Topeka, Lagrange, Indiana⁷⁸¹⁰
Unspecified: Topeka, Lagrange Co., IN⁷⁸¹⁰

Children of Wilbur Christner and Mary Borntrager are:
+   4974   i.   Ferman Eugene¹⁰ Christner, born 23 Mar 1947 in Goshen, Elkhart Co., IN.
+   4975   ii.   Kenneth Duane Christner, born 19 Aug 1949 in Goshen, Elkhart Co., IN.
+   4976   iii. Richard Lee Christner, born 08 Feb 1951 in Lagrange, Lagrange Co., IN.
     4977   iv.   Darlene Kay Christner, born 19 Aug 1954 in Lagrange Co., IN. She married (1) Ellwood Kauffman. She married (2) Melvin Bontrager Jr. 18 Oct 1975; born 12 Feb 1951 in Goshen, Elkhart Co., IN.

          Notes for Darlene Kay Christner:
          The Descendants of John J. Christner, privately published February 1961, p. 16.
          Works at Farm Bureau Credit Union Bank.

          More About Darlene Kay Christner:
          Christened: Mennonite

          Notes for Melvin Bontrager Jr.:
          Melvin J. Sr. and Mary Stump Bontrager. Mel is a Realty salesman. Mel has a daughter Deana Michelle born Oct 11 1970 in Goshen Hospital Goshen In. by a previous marriage.

          More About Melvin Bontrager Jr.:
          Christened: Mennonite

2758. Freeman E.⁹ Christner (Eli J.⁸, Joseph J.⁷, John J.⁶, Joseph C.⁵, Christian J.⁴, Johannes John Hans³, Christian², Christen¹)⁷⁸¹¹,⁷⁸¹²,⁷⁸¹² was born 28 Jan 1924 in Topeka, Lagrange Co., IN⁷⁸¹²,⁷⁸¹², and died 04 Aug

2012 in IN. He married **(1) LaVerta Gerber**. He married **(2) Waneta Mae Miller**[7813] 01 Feb 1946. She was born 31 Oct 1925 in Kokomo, Howard Co., IN[7813], and died 09 May 1980 in Elkhart, Elkhart Co., IN[7813]. He married **(3) Arlene Hartzler Keim** 1990 in Eighth Street Mennonite Church in Goshen IN.

Notes for Freeman E. Christner:
The Descendants of John J. Christner, privately published February 1961, p. 16.

Told in Freemans own words. We began in a small way. Before 1937, Dad (Eli J. Christner) hed a small mill on our farm west of Honeyville. Then in 1937 he built a larger mill and granary and installed a hammer mill for custom grinding. We stared with Hubbard Sunshine Concentrates. Hubbard Milling was noted for its Mother Hubbard Pancake Flour. During World War II we had to quit because we couldn't buy concentrate. But by the end of 1947, Hubbard's concentrates became available again, so we stated up the mill again.

Wolfe Grain Co. then sold us the mill "uptown". It was located south of the present mill and originally was a blacksmith shop. Dad and I owned the mill 50/50. In 1950, my brother Wilbur bought Dad's share and it became Christner Feed Mill, Inc.

We bought the old Honeyville School from the township for $900.00 to store feed. Andy Eash, an Amish carpenter, Help us add a new part for the mill. The concrete work was done with old-fashioned cement mixers. Then we moved our operation across the road.

We first used gas and diesel fuel to power our hammermill. By 1961, three-phase power became available. In 1967, we constructed a new office and installed a big platform scale for trucks. befor that we had only a smaller wagon scale.

One day someone stole the snow tires and wheels off our bulk delivery truck and our semi-tractor and took tools worth $1200. We never found out who robbed us. Then someone set a fire in our truck shed. I got the fir out before Stan Miller, Topeka fire chief and his crew arrived; there was no real damage.

DeWayne Bontrager, now town clerk at Topeka, was our first employee. He worked in the mill and delivered feed. Lester Miller,Sam Mast,and Perry J. Lehman also helped in the mill. Several young men in the neighborhood helped at various times.

Also driving truck for us were Levi Bontrager,Carl Christner, and our brother Vernon Christner. Manasses Bontrager worked in the office and Rudy Borntrager was our salesman for a time.

In addition to grinding, we sold feed,fence,fertilizer,seed corn,small grains,and water softener salt. Most of our customers were very loyal local people. However one man drove from Cromwell to buy our lamb and calf feed.

When we sold the mill in 1980, Wilber and I realized our Christner Feed Mills had served four generations of at least two families. One family was Joni Bontrager, his son Manasses, Manasses son and their sons. The other was John J. Christner, his daughter Mary's husband, Manas C.Hochstetler; their daughter Edna's husband,Roy J. Miller; and Roy and Edna's son, Wilber R. Miller.

We enjoyed our 30-plus years of doing business in the Honeyville community. When we left,only a single $30. bill was uncollected. From Topeka Area Historical Society Topeka, IN Celebrating a Century 1893-1993. Goshen News - August 7, 2012

Birth: Jan. 28, 1924
Middlebury, Elkhart Co., IN
Death: Aug. 4, 2012
IN

Freeman E. Christner, 88, died of natural causes Saturday at 9:30 p.m. at his home. Freeman was born Jan. 28, 1924 in Middlebury, to Eli J. and Polly (Yoder) Christner.

In 1947, he married Waneta Miller. Following her death, he married LaVerta Gerber. After her death, he married

Arlene Hartzler Keim in 1990.

He is survived by his wife Arlene; brother Vernon; children, Shirleen (Ron) Weaver, Gary (Nedra) Christner, Connie (Seth) Kauffman; six stepchildren, Kay (Randy) Nusbaum, Becky (Jeff) Bryan, Tom (Debbie) Gerber, Carolyn Sprunger, Darlene (Mike) Affolder and Gary (Verna) Gerber; four grandchildren, Jennifer (Heath) Miller, Kris (Rob) Henschen, Adrian (Chris) Fisher and Emily (Jeff Moore) Christner; 13 stepgrandchildren; and a number of great grandchildren.

Freeman was preceded in death by his first two wives, Waneta and LaVerta; a brother, Wilbur Christner; and his parents, Eli and Polly Christner.

After his retirement, Freeman had a variety of interesting jobs, which he enjoyed because he liked having new experiences and enjoyed staying active and busy. Freeman volunteered for numerous organizations such as Mennonite Central Committee in Akron, Pa,; doing maintenance at Wilderness Wind, a spiritual retreat in northern Minnesota and at Children's Bible Mission in Florida; and working at Camp Friedswald in southern Michigan. He and Arlene spent a number of winters at their home in Florida and then moved to Greencroft in 2008.

Visitation will take place at Evergreen Place, 1300 Greencroft Drive, at Greencroft in Goshen from 2 to 4 and 6 to 8 p.m. Aug. 24.

Cremation has taken place. Private burial will be at Maple Grove Cemetery in Topeka.

Friends and family are invited to a memorial service to celebrate the life of Freeman at 11 a.m. Aug. 25 at Eighth Street Mennonite Church, 602 S. Eighth St. in Goshen. Officiating will be Pastors Kevin Farmwald and Brenda Sawatzky Paetkau.

Parents:
Eli I. Christner (1894 - 1972)
Polly D. Christner (1895 - 1979)

Spouse: Waneta Christner (1925 - 1980)

Burial: Maple Grove Cemetery, Topeka, Lagrange Co., IN

The Mennonite, November 2012, pages 47 - 49, Vol. 15, No. 11.
Christner.- Freeman E., 88, Goshen, Ind., died Aug. 4. Spouse: Arlene Hartzler Keim Christner. Spouse: Waneta Miller Christner (deceased). Spouse: LaVerta Gerber Christner (deceased). Parents: Eli J. and Polly Yoder Christner. Children: Shirleen Weaver, Gary Christner, Connie Kauffman; four grandchildren; step-children: Kay Nusbaum, Becky Bryan, Tom Gerber, Carolyn Springer, Darlene Affolder, Gary Gerber; 13 step-grandchildren; numerous great-grandchildren. Funeral: Aug. 25 at Eighth Street Mennonite Church, Goshen.

More About Freeman E. Christner:
Residence: 1930, Eden, Lagrange Co., IN[7814]

Notes for Waneta Mae Miller:
The Descendants of John J. Christner, privately published February 1961, p. 16.

Waneta died of cancer.

Birth: 1925
Death: 1980

Waneta married Freeman Christner on 1 Feb 1946

Spouse: Freeman E Christner (1924 - 2012)

Burial: Maple Grove Cemetery, Topeka, Lagrange Co., IN

More About Waneta Mae Miller:
Burial: 12 May 1980, Maple Grove Cem., Lagrange Co., / 1 mile south & 1 1/2 mile west of Topeka
Social Security Number: 313-28-6948/[7815]
SSN issued: IN[7815]

Children of Freeman Christner and Waneta Miller are:
+   4978   i.   Shirlene Kay[10] Christner, born 28 Dec 1949.
+   4979   ii.   Gary Lamar Christner, born 20 Apr 1952.
      4980   iii.   Connie Lou Christner, born 09 Jul 1953.

> Notes for Connie Lou Christner:
> The Descendants of John J. Christner, privately published February 1961, p. 16.

2759. Vernon E. Shorty[9] Christner (Eli J.[8], Joseph J.[7], John J.[6], Joseph C.[5], Christian J.[4], Johannes John Hans[3], Christian[2], Christen[1]) was born 01 Apr 1929 in Topeka, Lagrange Co., IN. He married **Lila Joan Chupp** 04 Jan 1951. She was born 21 Nov 1933.

Notes for Vernon E. Shorty Christner:
The Descendants of John J. Christner, privately published February 1961, p. 16.

Notes for Lila Joan Chupp:
The Descendants of John J. Christner, privately published February 1961, p. 16.

Lila is the daughter of Sylvester Chupp and Sylvia Miller Chupp.

Children of Vernon Christner and Lila Chupp are:
+   4981   i.   Doris Elaine[10] Christner, born 28 Jan 1952; died 04 Feb 2010 in Elkhart, Elkhart Co., IN.
+   4982   ii.   Charlotte Kay Christner, born 23 Dec 1954 in Goshen, Elkhart Co., IN.
      4983   iii.   Cheryl Jean Christner, born 18 Jul 1957 in Goshen, Elkhart Co., IN. She married Corky James Warren McBride 11 May 1991 in Bristol, IN; born 29 Nov 1962 in Detroit, Wayne Co., MI.

> Notes for Cheryl Jean Christner:
> The Descendants of John J. Christner, privately published February 1961, p. 16.

> Notes for Corky James Warren McBride:

2760. Carl I.[9] Christner (Ira J.[8], Joseph J.[7], John J.[6], Joseph C.[5], Christian J.[4], Johannes John Hans[3], Christian[2], Christen[1])[7816] was born 24 Mar 1921 in Honeyville, Lagrange Co., IN[7816], and died 09 Apr 2005 in Goshen, Elkhart Co., IN. He married **Susanna L. Christner**[7817] 25 Apr 1942 in Goshen, Elkhart Co., IN, daughter of Levi Christner and Goldie Eash. She was born 05 Aug 1919 in Topeka, Lagrange Co., IN[7817,7818], and died 12 Nov 2010 in Topeka, Lagrange Co., IN[7819].

Notes for Carl I. Christner:
Carl farmed for his father until 1943 Hhe went to South Dakota & worked on Deerfield Dam-Hill city, SD for his conscientious objector obligation. Returned in 1944 & farmed again for his father. He hauled milk from Topeka, IN. to Cleveland, OH 7 days a week for 5 & 1/2 half years. He also was a lumberjack for 5 years. He worked for the Indiana State Highway for 15 years. Raised hogs & farmed his own 40 acres in Honeyville IN. Hobbies Fishing, Carl was always an extremist in everything. #1 Ate a large meal then on a bet ate a gallon of ice cream at the Honeyvill Store won the bet then ate an ice cream cone.#2 Fed hogs so well with protein they got sick& the vet.had to give them shots & told Carl not to be so nice to them. #3 He dieted to extremes weighing from 270 lbs,to 160 lbs. He ate only grapefruit for 3 months. He was a lot of fun & was loved by everyone. He had a rare gift for making friends with old & young people. Hard worker One person you can truly say was a good

father,husband & grandfather.

Carl was burning weeds along his fence line Sep 19, 1995 on his farm with a jug of gasoline when he spilled some on his leg and it caught fire, burning his leg. He was in the hospital for 2 months and got a lung infection. This problem led to his heart enlarging and being on oxygen for the rest of his life. He could not sleep laying down so he slept in a recliner for over 40 years.

When Carl & Sue were older (in their late 70's) they had company 7 days a week. The Amish neighbors brought prepared food three days a week and cleaned the house, mowed the lawn. Relatives, neighbors, church members, their son's, and friends were there. Some days there would be 4 or 5 different couples visiting.

Memories of Carl by Jerry Wittrig
I first met Carl Christner in 1968, the year Ruth Ann and I started attending North Goshen Mennonite Church.

I still remember the first time I shook hands with Carl. My hand was totally enveloped by his and I felt a grip that could surely have crushed my hand with ease.

My first thoughts were of my grandfather. He was the only other person I had known who had forearms and hands the size of Carl's.

It was some 20 years later I became aware there was a reason Carl's hands and arms were similar to my grandfather's. They were related. I found that Carl and I have several common ancestors who lived in the Amish-Mennonite settlements in the Alsase.

There is a story told about one of our ancestors in that Alsase that was reputed to have been very strong. One day he was going to the village on the back of his donkey. The donkey refused to cross a small stream that had been swollen by the Spring rains. Our ancestor is said to have picked up the donkey and carried it across the stream and continued on his way. When Carl was a young man, I could see him doing something like that!
Carl inherited the strong work ethic of his ancestors. He particularly loved the soil and enjoyed working with his hands. He enjoyed telling me stories about the field of mint he grew many years ago.

Carl loved all of God's creation, great or small. He loved the sight of his neighbors with a team of horses preparing the ground in the Spring of the year for the planting of corn or beans.

He loved the fish God had created to inhabit the lakes and streams of Northern Indiana.

He loved the birds, especially the purple martins that he fed and cared for in his yard.

Carl always had a hearty appetite and many conversations would include talking about food. When I would visit him during the last few years of his live he would often comment about the wonderful food that his neighbor had brought to share with Sue and himself.

He would put "way too much pepper" on his hamburger just to get a comment from his grand daughters.

My favorite food story took place when Carl was in the Goshen Hospital about two years ago. I was visiting him one day and he commented, "Jerry, they just don't feed me enough here in the hospital. And the food they give me just isn't very good."

I replied, "Carl, what are you really hungry for?
He said, "Onion rings, I would really like some good onion rings."
I said, "Carl, I'll be back in 15 minutes." I went to Dairy Queen and brought back an order of onion rings. Carl's hands were not very steady, so I fed him the order of onion rings which he enjoyed to the very last bite.
Just as he finished, the nurse came into the room. There was Carl with a big grin on his face and crumbs from the onion rings all over the front of his shirt. The nurse just smiled, shook her heard and said, Carl, I won't tell a soul!

To know Carl was to have a friend. Whether you were young or old, Carl had a way of making you feel at home and a part of the family.

Argus and Nancy Myers were friends of Carl and Sue from the North Goshen Church. Argus was 90- years old and Nancy was 92. One day when Ruth Ann and I were visiting them, Argus mentioned how much he missed visiting with Carl and Sue.

We said, "Well let's go over and visit them. Ruth Ann and I will pick you up and take you over to Honeyville. We set up the arrangements and picked them up at their home in New Paris. On the way, Argus reminded us, " I can't stay long, I have to keep my feet up because of my circulation problems in my legs. About 15 minutes is about all I can handle."

More than an hour later we finally got Argus back in the car for the trip back to New Paris. This special visit was all he could talk about for the next several weeks. He had visited with his friend Carl one last time.
Carl knew just about everyone that lived in the Honeyville area and nearly everyone knew Carl. He was affectionately called "The Mayor of Honeyville", a title I think he rather enjoyed.

Carl had a quiet confident faith that the promises God made in this book were true and they applied to him. He believed in Jesus as his personal Savior and that relationship became more real with each passing year. He knew when the struggles of this life were over, there was something better ahead.

He summed it up so well last week when he said, "Mom, I think it's time to move to God's house."

I can imagine Carl today, free for the first time in years from the limits of declining health and the length of the oxygen tube, renewing friendships and praising his Lord and Savior.

And Sue, there is one more reunion he is waiting for. Nearly 63 years you and Carl were married. What a wonderful testimony! Someday soon he will "meet you in the morning just inside the Eastern Gate." And I think Carl will probably say, "Mom, what took you so long?"

Birth: Mar. 24, 1921
Death: Apr. 9, 2005

Carl I. Christner, 84, died Saturday, April 9th 2005 at Goshen General Hospital.

He was born March 24, 1921, in Honeyville, to Ira and Sylvia (Swartzentruber) Christner.

Spouse: Sue L Christner Christner (1919 - 2010)

Burial: Town Line Cemetery, Topeka, Lagrange Co., IN

The Mennonite, May 3, 2005, pages 25-26, Vol. 8, No. 9.
Christner.- Carl I., 84, Millersburg, Ind., died April 9. Spouse: Sue Christner. Parents: Ira and Sylvia Swartzentruber Christner. Children: Steven C., Larry; four grandchildren; six great-grandchildren. Funeral: April 12 at Maple Grove Mennonite Church, Topeka, IN.

The Descendants of John J. Christner, privately published February 1961, p. 16.

More About Carl I. Christner:
Burial: Pallbears=Chuck/Todd/Dean/Don Christner-Jackson Roe-Dick Graber
Funeral Service: 12 Apr 2005, Rev. Jerry Wittrig & Rev. Art Smoker of North Goshen Mennonite Church
Religion: Mennonite/
Social Security Number: 315-20-6366/[7820]
SSN issued: IN[7820]

Notes for Susanna L. Christner:
Sue sold Dutchmaid* clothing from 1967 to 1972. Sue started her own quilt business in 1975. She sold old and new quilts all over the USA.She has had a number of quilts put into the national quilt registry and her mothers quilt called "jonny round the corner" has been featured on the cover of a number of national magazines. The Quilt

Show has held it's 33rd year in 2007.

Sue and Carl were 2nd cousins.

She loved flowers and plants and always had a great interest in genealogy. She attended a one room school with only an outside toilet, called Wortinger School which was a one mile walk from her home. She thinks it was one mile up hill both ways. In the winter the wind blew in her face going to school and back home. The school was located at the southeast corner of W300S and S500W Lagrange Co. Indiana N41°35.8413' by W85°31.2186

Home of Carl & Sue Christner Located at Honeyville, LaGrange Co., Indiana.N41°34.183-W85°36.474 - on County Road 950W - just north of 500S or ¾ mile south of the Honeyville store. Abe Christner & Mary Yoder lived here when they got married in 1914; they planted the Yucca & Poppies that are still growing there. The home was torn down about 1986 to make way for a new home. Sue's father was Levi D. Christner born 8/20/1897 & Carl's father was Ira J. Christner born 3/27/1897 his father was Joseph J. Christner born 2/19/1851 his father was John J. Christner born 11/24/1827. John J Christner was the first Christner to own the home in the photo. The home had a tin roof & as I (Steven Carl Christner) was born in the northwest corner of this home, I remember it getting hit with lightning often. I remember when I was about 12 years old, my brother (Larry) & me were in our bedroom upstairs when lightning hit. Larry was standing in front of the window & I could only see his skeleton. I screamed like a little girl & made it down the stairs only touching 2 steps. Once it blow the Telephone right off the wall in pieces. I can't remember every having a roof leak except around the chimney in all those years.
I remember when we got hot & cold running water inside the house but the biggest deal was when we got a toilet in the house. This I thought was really great as it was my job to empty the pot in the morning. My grandfather Ira tried to explain how this toilet was going to work, I was still puzzled but hopeful this could be possible. For those that don't know what a POT is, it is a container to go into in the middle of the night so you don't have to go to the OUT house, OH, you don't know what a outhouse is, well we had small one holer.

Obituary: Aug. 5, 1919-Nov. 12, 2010
MILLERSBURG - Sue L. Christner, formerly of 4860S. 950 West, died Friday at 12:15 a.m. at the home of her sister-inlaw, Gladys Christner, 5380 W. 400 South, Topeka. She had been in declining health and was seriously ill the past three weeks. She was born Aug. 5; 1919 in Topeka, to Levi D. and Goldie (O'Neil Eash) Christner She was a homemaker and a lifelong resident of the Topeka and Millersburg areas. She was a longtime member of North Goshen Mennonite Church. Sue sold Dutchmaid clothing from 1967 until 1972 and started her own quilt business in 1975, selling old and new quilts all over the United States. She had a number of quilts put into the National Quilt Registry. Her mother's quilt, called "Jonnie Round the Corner" was displayed at the Indiana State Museum, Indianapolis, and appeared on the cover of the Indiana Historical Society magazine, "Traces." She loved flowers and plants and always had a great interest in genealogy. she married Carl I Christner April 25, 1942. He died April 9, 2005. She is survived by her two sons, Steve (Tracey) Christner, Goshen, and Larry (Anita) Christner, Topeka; four grandchildren; six great-grandchildren; and a brother, Samuel Christner, Leesburg. She was preceded in death by five sisters, Lizzie Ann Miller, Emma Hostetler, Edith Lyon, Goldie L. Christner and Mary Fereva; and seven brothers, Menno L., Christian L., Amos L., John Levi, David A., Levi Lee and Arthur L. Christner. Friends may call Sunday from 2 to 4 and 6 to 8 p.m. at Maple Grove Church, Topeka, where a funeral service will take place Monday at 2:30 p.m. The Rev. Dean Linsenmeyer of North Goshen Mennonite Church will officiate. Burial will be in Town Line Cemetery, Topeka. Pallbearers will be John Kozinski, Kevin Christner, Allen Reiling, Dean Christner, Chuck Christner and Cletus Schwartz. Memorial donations can be made to North Goshen Mennonite Church. Yoder-Culp Funeral Home, Goshen, is assisting the family with arrangements.

Birth: Aug. 5, 1919
Topeka, Lagrange Co., IN
Death: Nov. 12, 2010
Elkhart Co., IN

Obituary:
Sue L. Christner, 91, died at home early Friday morning, November 12, 2010.
She was born August 5, 1919, in Topeka to Levi D. and Goldie (O'niel Eash) Christner. She married Carl Christner on April 25, 1942, in Goshen. He died April 9, 2005.
She is survived by two sons, Steve (Tracey) Christner of Goshen, and Larry (Anita) Christner of Topeka; four grandchildren; six great-grandchildren; and a brother Samuel Christner of Leesburg.
She was preceded in death by sisters, Lizzie Ann Miller, Emma Hostetler, Edith Lyon, Goldie L. Christner, and

Mary Fereva; and brothers, Menno L., Christian L., Amos L., John Levi, David A., Levi Lee and Arthur L. Christner.

A homemaker and lifelong resident of the Topeka/Millersburg area, Mrs. Christner was a longtime member of North Goshen Mennonite Church. Mrs. Christner sold Dutchmaid clothing from 1967-1972. In 1975 she started her own quilt business, selling old and new quilts all over the USA. She has had a number number of quilts put into the national quilt registry and her mother's quilt called "Jonnie Round the Corner" was displayed at the Indiana State Museum, Indianapolis, and appeared on the cover of the Indiana Historical Society Magazine "Traces". She loved flowers and plants and had a great interest in genealogy.

Friends may call 2 to 4 and 6 to 8 p.m., Sunday, November 14, at Maple Grove Mennonite Church, Topeka.

A 2:30 p.m., funeral service will be conducted on Monday, November 15, 2010, at the Maple Grove Mennonite Church, Topeka. Pastor Dean Linsenmeyer of North Goshen Mennonite Church will officiate.

Burial will follow in Town Line Cemetery, Topeka. Memorials may be made to North Goshen Mennonite Church.

Spouse: Carl I. Christner (1921 - 2005)

Burial: Town Line Cemetery, Topeka, Lagrange Co., IN

Obituary - Mennonite Obits
Christner, Sue L. Christner, 91, of Millersburg, IN died November 12, 2010 at the same place. She was born August 5, 1919 at Topeka, IN to Levi D. and Goldie (O'Niel Eash) Christner. On April 25, 1942 at Goshen, IN she was married to Carl I. Christner, who died April 9, 2005.

Surviving are two sons, Steve (Tracey) Christner and Larry (Anita) Christner,
4 grandchildren, 6 great-grandchildren, and a brother, Samuel Christner.

Her brothers and sisters, Lizzie Ann Miller, Emma Hostetler, Edith Lyon, Goldie L. Christner, Mary Fereva, Menno L. Christner, Christian L. Christner, Amos L. Christner, John Levi Christner, David A. Christner, Levi Lee Christner, and Arthur L. Christner preceded her in death.

A homemaker and lifelong resident of the Topeka/Millersburg area, Mrs. Christner was a longtime member of North Goshen Mennonite Church. Mrs. Christner sold Dutchmaid clothing from 1967 to 1972. In 1975, she started her own quilt business, selling old and new quilts all over the U.S.A. She had a number of quilts put into the national quilt registry, and her mother's quilt called "Jonnie Round the Corner" was displayed at the Indiana State Museum, Indianapolis, and appeared on the cover of the Indiana Historical Society magazine "Traces." She loved flowers and plants and had a great interest in genealogy.

Memorials may be given to North Goshen Mennonite Church.

Memorial services were held November 15, 2010 at Maple Grove Church, Topeka IN with burial in Town Line Cemetary, Topeka, IN.

The Descendants of John J. Christner, privately published February 1961, p. 16.

More About Susanna L. Christner:
Residence: 1930, Clearspring, Lagrange Co., IN[7821]
SSN issued: IN[7822]

Children of Carl Christner and Susanna Christner are:
+   4984   i.   Steven Carl[10] Christner, born 15 Aug 1945 in Honeyville, Lagrange Co., IN.
+   4985   ii. Larry Lee Christner, born 10 Mar 1950 in Kendalville, IN.

2761. Freda[9] Christner (Ira J.[8], Joseph J.[7], John J.[6], Joseph C.[5], Christian J.[4], Johannes John Hans[3],

Christian[2], Christen[1])[7823] was born 03 Jul 1927 in Goshen, Elkhart Co., IN[7824,7825], and died 16 Jul 1997 in Sarasota, Sarasota Co., FL. She married **Mirrell D. Yoder** 18 Jul 1946, son of Daniel Yoder and Laura Christner. He was born 16 Feb 1921 in Arthur, IL[7826], and died 20 Jun 2005 in Sarasota, Sarasota Co., FL.

Notes for Freda Christner:
Frieda was always healthy and did everything to stay that way. She met her untimely death in very good health while riding a bicycle to work. A pickup truck hit her.

Yoder, Frieda Christner, 70, Sarasota, FL born: July 3, 1927, Topeka, IN to Ira and Sylvia Christner. Died: July 16, 1997, Sarasota, FL in a bicycle accident. Survivors - husband: Merrill Yoder; children: Phyllis Aboulfadl, Thomas J., Paul R.; brother: Carl Christner; 10 grandchildren, one great-grandchild. Funeral: July 20, Bahia Vista Mennonite Church, by Barry Loop. Burial: Palms Memorial Park.

The Descendants of John J. Christner, privately published February 1961, p. 16.

More About Freda Christner:
Burial: 20 Jul 1997, Palms Memorial Cemetery/Sarasota, Sarasota Co., FL
Social Security Number: 313-28-6701/[7827]
SSN issued: IN[7827]

Notes for Mirrell D. Yoder:
Mirrell had his own automobile sales lot selling cars on weekly payments was a very good business man. He could sell cars in four languages. He became very wealthy had the ability to know what other people would think about anything or any subject. It was amazing to watch this thought process. He did a lot of things that were radical, extreme, wacky, peculiar, weird and just plain bizarre. He had so much fun watching everyones reaction to, what he called, "setting the stage". I, (Steven C. Christner) was a witness to many of these. Mirrell and I were on our way to Flint, MI to an auto auction. We stopped at a Big Boy restaurant, he ordered 100 Big Boy Burgers and 100 1/2 pints of milk to go. We drove down the eating all we could then he said what you can't eat throw out the car window, at 85 miles per hour. We went to O Hare airport after an auto auction in Chicago. Mirrell bought a ticket to Puerto Rico. He had an hour to wait for his flight so he went to a ticket counter and had himself paged on the public address system while running up the down escalator and down the up escalator. Yes, with people on the escalator. Mirrell told me to tell his wife where he had gone but wait till 11:00 am the next day. Mirrell got to Puerto Rico, went out on the beach and fell asleep. When he awoke he was a cooked Lobster. He got back on the plane to Chicago, they had an ambulance waiting to take him to the closest hospital. Three days later he hired an ambulance to transfer him to his home town hospital for three more days. Next story = We bought a convertible at the auto auction, we drove past a bakery advertising day old bread sale, Mirrell backed the car against traffic back to the bakery, cars were honking, people were yelling, but we made it alive. Mirrell bought bread until the back seat was so full the loaves were rounded up and falling off the car. We drove down the road throwing loaves of bread at people on the sidewalks. The most fascinating part of all this is while these things are going on he could articulate pearls of wisdom few people could grasp. I was always ready for them because they were very valuable to me and a Goshen business man (Paul Presler) made many trips to Florida to get more pearls of wisdom and Paul built a successful business out of it.. Next story = We went to Flint Michigan to an auto auction and left late (like always) and Mirrell was driving over 100 miles per hour except in the towns we went through, in town we went 50 in a 30 MPH speed limit. When we got to the auction a fellow auto dealer ask Mirrell if he had a good trip to the auction, I think he ask Mirrell just trying to make small talk and be courteous. Mirrell was not a guy for mindless small talk, like asking, how do you like this weather or how have you been? Mirrell's response to the gentleman was, all I saw on the trip was the back of cars coming toward us, as Mirrell spoke the last word Mirrell was walking away. The gentleman was insulted at the lack of small talk and completely missed what kind of a trip we had. Next story = Me and Mirrell walk into a restaurant and Mirrell orders one of everything in the menu for the two of us, we had 15 drinks, 12 dinners, 33 sandwiches, two salads, all the sides, but he said we would restrain ourselves from having desert. If that story had any meaning I missed it, but the look on the peoples faces in the restaurant was really funny. The waitress had a storm in her brain trying to understand what he wanted to order. Next story = Mirrell had a character wanting odd jobs to do. His name was Bill Fox. Mirrell would make stories up to rhyme with Bill's last name of Fox, like Bill Fox fixes clocks in his socks while sitting on docks. He would do this to watch Bill's reactions to this and learn how to read his way of thinking as Mirrell had any normal thinking person figured out, but people like Bill Fox were a inviting challenge to him.

More About Mirrell D. Yoder:
Burial: 22 Jun 2005, Palms Memorial Park, Sarasota, Sarasota Co., FL
Religion: Bahia Vista Mennonite, 4041 Bahia Vista St. Sarasota, Florida 34232/
SSN issued: MI[7828]

Children of Freda Christner and Mirrell Yoder are:
+ 4986   i.   Phyllis Ann[10] Yoder, born 02 Nov 1955 in Goshen, Elkhart Co., IN.
+ 4987   ii.   Thomas Jefferson Yoder, born 26 Jun 1962 in Goshen, Elkhart Co., IN.
+ 4988   iii.   Paul Revere Yoder, born 06 Dec 1965 in Goshen, Elkhart Co., IN.

2762. Lloyd J.[9] Harshberger (Bessie Amanda[8] Christner, Joseph J.[7], John J.[6], Joseph C.[5], Christian J.[4], Johannes John Hans[3], Christian[2], Christen[1])[7829,7830] was born 21 Mar 1927 in Goshen, Elkhart Co., IN[7831,7832,7833], and died 14 Aug 1992 in Elkhart Co., IN[7834,7835]. He married **Lydia Miller** 17 Apr 1949. She was born 15 Jul 1926 in Geauga Co., OH[7836], and died 06 Aug 1980 in Goshen, Elkhart Co., IN[7836].

Notes for Lloyd J. Harshberger:
The Descendants of John J. Christner, privately published February 1961, p. 17.

Burial Thomas Cemetery, Goshen, IN.

More About Lloyd J. Harshberger:
Social Security Number: 303-40-4628/[7837,7838,7839]
SSN issued: IN[7840,7841]

Notes for Lydia Miller:
The Descendants of John J. Christner, privately published February 1961, p. 17.

More About Lydia Miller:
Alt. Birth: 15 Jul 1926[7842]

Children of Lloyd Harshberger and Lydia Miller are:
  4989   i.   Glen Ray[10] Harshberger, born 15 Aug 1954.

      Notes for Glen Ray Harshberger:
      The Descendants of John J. Christner, privately published February 1961, p 17.

  4990   ii.   Marion Lee Harshberger, born 15 Aug 1956.

      Notes for Marion Lee Harshberger:
      The Descendants of John J. Christner, privately published February 1961, p. 17.

  4991   iii.   Ivan LeRoy Harshberger, born May 1959.

      Notes for Ivan LeRoy Harshberger:
      The Descendants of John J. Christner, privately published February 1961, p. 17.

2764. Eli J.[9] Harshberger (Bessie Amanda[8] Christner, Joseph J.[7], John J.[6], Joseph C.[5], Christian J.[4], Johannes John Hans[3], Christian[2], Christen[1])[7843,7844] was born 18 Aug 1929 in Goshen, Elkhart Co., IN[7845,7846], and died 10 Oct 1970 in St Joe River, Berrien Springs, MI[7846]. He married **Sylvia Ileen Simons** 02 Aug 1957. She was born 21 May 1925[7847], and died 13 Sep 2009 in Lagrange, Lagrange Co., IN[7847].

Notes for Eli J. Harshberger:
The Descendants of John J. Christner, privately published February 1961, p 17.

Eli and Freeman R. Miller of Bristol In were fishing on the river and their boat capsized in turbulent water as they were trying to bail out the boat. Miller managed to get to shore. Eli was found down river about 2 miles.

More About Eli J. Harshberger:
Burial: Clinton Community Cemetery, Goshen, Elkhart Co., IN
Social Security Number: 303-32-3527/[7848,7849]
SSN issued: IN[7850,7851]

Notes for Sylvia Ileen Simons:
The Descendants of John J. Christner, privately published February 1961, p. 16.

She had 2 Chidren Mitchel William, 8 28 1948 & Nona Ann, 8 26, 1951.

May 21, 1925 - Sept. 13, 2009

Lagrange - S. Ileen Parsons, 84, of LaGrange, died Sunday (Sep 13, 2009) at Miller's Merry Manor.

She was born May 21, 1925, in Delphi to Jacob Anderson and Jessie (Hughes) Simons. In 1955 she married Eli Hershberger in Monticello. He preceded her in death in 1970. In 1974 she married Charles Parsons in Howe. He preceded her in death in 1990.

She is survived by a daughter, Nona A. Chamness of Lagrange; a stepson, Joe Parsons of LaGrange; four grandchildren; two stepgranddaughters; and six great-grandchildren.

She was preceded in death by a daughter, Theresa Hershberger; a son, Michael W. Hershberger; two sisters; and two brothers.

Graveside services will be at 1 p.m. Tuesday at Clinton Brick Cemetery in Goshen. The Rev. Michael Booher will officiate.

Mrs. Parsons worked for United Telephone Company in Monticello and LaGrange as an operator and was of the Mennonite faith.

Memorials may be given to the American Heart Association.

More About Sylvia Ileen Simons:
SSN issued: IN[7852]

Children of Eli Harshberger and Sylvia Simons are:
 4992 i. Mitchel William[10] Harshberger, born 28 Aug 1948.

     Notes for Mitchel William Harshberger:
     The Descendants of John J. Christner, privately published February 1961, p. 17.

 4993 ii. Nona Ann Harshberger, born 26 Aug 1951.

     Notes for Nona Ann Harshberger:
     The Descendants of John J. Christner, privately published February 1961, p. 17.

2770. Ray J.[9] **Harshberger** (Bessie Amanda[8] Christner, Joseph J.[7], John J.[6], Joseph C.[5], Christian J.[4], Johannes John Hans[3], Christian[2], Christen[1])[7853] was born 16 Nov 1941. He married **Lizzie Miller** 23 Jan 1964. She was born 09 Mar 1942.

Notes for Ray J. Harshberger:
The Descendants of John J. Christner, privately published February 1961, p. 17.

He was a factory worker.

Children of Ray Harshberger and Lizzie Miller are:

4994	i.	Orva R.[10] Harshberger, born 03 Mar 1966. He married Naomi A. Yoder.	
4995	ii.	Carolyn R. Harshberger, born 25 Mar 1967. She married Lee Alen Chupp.	
4996	iii.	Ruth Ann Harshberger, born 11 Sep 1969. She married Ronnie Yoder.	
+ 4997	iv.	LaVern R. Harshberger, born 11 Sep 1971.	
4998	v.	Vernon Harshberger, born 20 Sep 1973. He married Clara Mae Yoder.	
4999	vi.	David R. Harshberger, born 05 Apr 1975. He married LeEtta Miller.	
5000	vii.	Ida Ellen Harshberger, born 08 May 1976. She married William Jay Miller.	
5001	viii.	Mervin R. Harshberger, born 07 Sep 1979. He married Ruth Lehman.	

2772. Annie C.[9] Christner (Cornelius D.[8], David J.[7], John J.[6], Joseph C.[5], Christian J.[4], Johannes John Hans[3], Christian[2], Christen[1]) was born 01 Oct 1903 in Lagrange Co., IN, and died 08 Oct 1982. She married **(1) Eli J. Troyer** 30 Nov 1922, son of Jacob Troyer and Sarah Miller. He was born 04 Sep 1904 in Brown Co., IN, and died 12 Dec 1997 in Lagrange Co., IN. She married **(2) Eli J. Troyer** 30 Nov 1922 in Lagrange Co., IN, son of Jacob Troyer and Sarah Miller. He was born 04 Sep 1904 in Brown Co., IN, and died 12 Dec 1997 in Lagrange Co., IN.

Notes for Annie C. Christner:
The Descendants of John J. Christner, privately published 1961, p. 17.
Old Order Amish.

Birth: 1903
Death: 1982

Burial: Yoder Cemetery, Shipshewana, Lagrange Co., IN

More About Annie C. Christner:
Burial: Mast Cemetery, Clay Twp., Lagrange Co., IN
Residence: 1920, Clearspring, Lagrange Co., IN[7854]

Notes for Eli J. Troyer:
The Descendants of John J. Christner, privately published February1961, p. 17.

Eli and Annie lived 1 mile N and 1 mile W of Lagrange, IN. Eli is a farmer and a preacher Old Order Amish. He was ordained to the ministry Oct. 29, 1951.

Died at his home at 0365W by 200 N, Lagrange Co., IN.

More About Eli J. Troyer:
Burial: Mast Cemetery, Clay Twp., Lagrange Co., IN
Ordination: 20 Oct 1951, Old Order Amish Ordained Minister
Residence: 01 Apr 1940, Clay Twp., Lagrange Co., IN[7855]

Notes for Eli J. Troyer:
The Descendants of John J. Christner, privately published February1961, p. 17.

Eli and Annie lived 1 mile N and 1 mile W of Lagrange, IN. Eli is a farmer and a preacher Old Order Amish. He was ordained to the ministry Oct. 29, 1951.

Died at his home at 0365W by 200 N, Lagrange Co., IN.

More About Eli J. Troyer:
Burial: Mast Cemetery, Clay Twp., Lagrange Co., IN
Ordination: 20 Oct 1951, Old Order Amish Ordained Minister
Residence: 01 Apr 1940, Clay Twp., Lagrange Co., IN[7855]

Children of Annie Christner and Eli Troyer are:
+ 5002   i.   Daniel E.[10] Troyer, born 25 Aug 1923.
   5003   ii.   Mary E. Troyer, born 16 Mar 1930.

        Notes for Mary E. Troyer:
        The Descendants of John J. Christner, privately published February 1961, p. 17.

+ 5004   iii.   Annie E. Troyer, born 15 Oct 1931.
   5005   iv.   Joseph Troyer, born 17 Feb 1940 in Lagrange Co., IN.
   5006   v.   Samuel E. Troyer, born 16 Oct 1942.

        Notes for Samuel E. Troyer:
        The Descendants of John J. Christner, privately published February 1961, p. 17.

Children of Annie Christner and Eli Troyer are:
+ 5007   i.   Felty E.[10] Troyer, born 19 Mar 1927 in Kenton, OH.
+ 5008   ii.   Sarah E. Troyer, born 24 Oct 1928.
+ 5009   iii.   Lena E. Troyer, born 18 Feb 1933.
   5010   iv.   No Name Troyer, born 29 Jan 1935; died 29 Jan 1935.

        Notes for No Name Troyer:
        The Descendants of John J. Christner, privately published February 1961, p. 17.

   5011   v.   Susie E. Troyer, born 04 Apr 1936.

        Notes for Susie E. Troyer:
        The Descendants of John J. Christner, privately published February 1961, p. 17.

+ 5012   vi.   Joseph E. Troyer, born 31 Mar 1938 in Lagrange Co., IN.
   5013   vii.   John E. Troyer, born 17 Feb 1940.

        Notes for John E. Troyer:
        The Descendants of John J. Christner, privately published February 1961, p. 17.

   5014   viii.   Ella E. Troyer, born 12 Mar 1945.

        Notes for Ella E. Troyer:
        The Descendants of John J. Christner, privately published February 1961, p. 17.

   5015   ix.   Jacob E. Troyer, born 21 May 1947.

        Notes for Jacob E. Troyer:
        The Descendants of John J. Christner, privately published February 1961, p. 17.

2775. Glen E.[9] **Christner** (Eddranis D.[8], David J.[7], John J.[6], Joseph C.[5], Christian J.[4], Johannes John Hans[3], Christian[2], Christen[1])[7856] was born 23 Sep 1909 in Topeka, Lagrange Co., IN[7856,7857], and died 11 Jun 1980 in Goshen, Elkhart Co., IN[7858]. He married **Maxine Klase** 01 Sep 1944. She was born 15 Jun 1921 in Goshen, Elkhart Co., IN.

Notes for Glen E. Christner:
The Descendants of John J. Christner, privately published 1961, p. 18.

Nickname Hawkshaw---worked & retired from Goshen Rubber Co., Goshen IN.
SS#;702-10-9448 Iss RR

More About Glen E. Christner:
Burial: 13 Jun 1980, Violet Cemetery, Goshen, Elkhart Co., IN

Social Security Number: 702-10-9448/[7858]
SSN issued: Railroad Board (Issued Through)[7858]

Notes for Maxine Klase:
The Descendants of John J. Christner, privately published 1961, p. 18.

Maxine is the daughter of Roy and Abbie Klase from Goshen In. Maxine had Harold before she married Glen. Harold tried to discipline a child by putting pepper in its mouth. The child died.

Children of Glen Christner and Maxine Klase are:

+   5016   i.   Harold Smith[10] Christner.
    5017   ii.   Leon Harvey Christner, born 09 Dec 1944 in Goshen, Elkhart Co., IN; died 15 Aug 2003 in 7:05am at his brother Chuck's home on Dewart Lake.

           Notes for Leon Harvey Christner:
           The Descendants of John J. Christner, privately published 1961, p. 18.

           Leon was liked by everyone how knew him. He worked at Starcraft Marine in Topeka Indiana for 38 years. In 38 years he was never late for work even one day. He was so insistent on being there on time he would park beside the front gate of the factory at 11:00 PM and tell the gate guard to wake him at 6:30AM. He was never married. He enjoyed fishing at his brothers (Chuck) house on Dewart lake between Syracuse and Milford, IN. He also enjoyed finding coins with a electronic metal detector.

           More About Leon Harvey Christner:
           Burial: 19 Aug 2003, Violett Cemetery, Goshen, Elkhart Co., IN
           SSN issued: IN[7859]

+   5018   iii.   Betty Christner, born 04 Nov 1949 in Goshen, Elkhart Co., IN.
+   5019   iv.   Charles D. Christner, born 15 May 1952 in Goshen, Elkhart Co., IN.

2777. George E.[9] Christner (Eddranis D.[8], David J.[7], John J.[6], Joseph C.[5], Christian J.[4], Johannes John Hans[3], Christian[2], Christen[1]) was born 25 Apr 1914 in Topeka, Lagrange Co., IN[7860], and died 27 Apr 1985 in Elkhart Co., IN[7860]. He married **Thelma Molebash** 06 Nov 1937 in Topeka, Lagrange Co., IN. She was born 15 Jul 1917 in Wakarusa, Elkhart Co., IN, and died 27 Jul 2012 in Elkhart, Elkhart Co., IN.

Notes for George E. Christner:
The Descendants of John J. Christner, privately published 1961, pp. 18, 19.

He is retired from Ira C. Mast Construction Co after 32 years. Methodist.
SS#;308-03-9150 Iss IN

Birth: 1914
Death: Apr. 25, 1985

Spouse: Thelma M. Molebash Christner (1917 - 2012)

Burial: Chapel Hill Memorial Gardens, Osceola, St. Joseph Co., IN
Find A Grave Memorial# 103021321

More About George E. Christner:
Burial: Chapel Hill, Memorial Gardens, ELKHART CO, IN
Social Security Number: 308-03-9150/[7860]
SSN issued: IN[7860]

Notes for Thelma Molebash:
She was a kind woman doing volunteer work in retiement homes for many years.

Birth: Jul. 15, 1917 - Wakarusa, Elkhart Co., IN

Death: Jul. 27, 2012 - Elkhart, Elkhart Co., IN

Obituary: Thelma M. Christner
July 15, 1917 - July 27, 2012

Thelma M. Christner, 95 of Elkhart, passed away July 27, 2012 at Riverside Village, Elkhart.

She was born July 15, 1917 in Wakarusa to Reuben M. and Lulu (Myers) Molebash and married Geroge E. Christner on November 6, 1937 in Topeka, IN. He died April 27, 1985. Surviving are 2 daughters, Nancy (Robert) Firestone of Goshen and Peggy Golightly of Elkhart; 1 son, Thomas G. (Victoria) Christner of Atlanta, GA; 6 grandchildren and 6 great-grandchildren. She was preceded in death by a son-in-law, Ray Golightly and a brother, Doyle Molebash.

Thelma was a homemaker and a member of Bethel United Methodist Church. She also was a member of the Willowdale Homemakers Club and enjoyed sewing, crocheting, and knitting.

Visitation will be from 4-8 pm Tuesday at Stemm-Lawson-Peterson Funeral Home, Elkhart and one hour prior to services that will be held at 10 am Wednesday. Pastor Ron Bowman will officiate. Burial will follow at Chapel Hill Memorial Gardens.

Spouse: George E. Christner (1914 - 1985)

Burial: Chapel Hill Memorial Gardens, Osceola, St. Joseph Co., IN
Find A Grave Memorial# 94448799

Children of George Christner and Thelma Molebash are:

5020   i. Nancy[10] Christner, born 31 May 1939. She married John Reed; born 06 Nov 1939.

Notes for Nancy Christner:
The Descendants of John J. Christner, privately published February 1961, p. 19.

Notes for John Reed:
The Descendants of John J. Christner, privately published February 1961, p. 19.

+ 5021   ii. Peggy Jo Christner, born 01 Jan 1946.
    5022   iii. Thomas Christner, born 02 Jun 1947.

Notes for Thomas Christner:
The Descendants of John J. Christner, privately published February 1961, p. 19.

2778. Verlo[9] Christner (Eddranis D.[8], David J.[7], John J.[6], Joseph C.[5], Christian J.[4], Johannes John Hans[3], Christian[2], Christen[1])[7860] was born 29 Jun 1916 in Topeka, Lagrange Co., IN[7860], and died 04 Jul 1971 in Topeka, Lagrange Co., IN[7860]. He married **Veda Elizabeth Wemple** 19 Apr 1941. She was born 12 Jun 1918 in Lagrange Co., IN.

Notes for Verlo Christner:
The Descendants of John J. Christner, privately published 1961, p. 18.

Verlo was a vetern of WWII
SS#566-10-1124 ISS CA
He helped his brother LeRoy in the furniture and undertaking business in Topeka In 1953. Verlo became postmaster for Topeka in 1958 and discontiued the undertaking business. LeRoy managed Christner Furniture until 1973 Larimer Furniture of Goshen and Wakarusa bought the business.

Verlo died of a heart attack while setting off the fire works for the town of Topeka.

Birth: 1916
Death: 1971

Parents:
Eddranis D Christner (1886 - 1963)
Harriet E Renner Christner (1889 - 1950)

Children: Mary Ruth Christner Mickem (1942 - 2001)

Burial: Eden Cemetery, Topeka, Lagrange Co., IN

More About Verlo Christner:
Burial: Eden Cemetery, IN
Military: 02 Mar 1944, Fort Benjamin Harrison, Indiana[7860]
Residence: Elkhart Co., IN[7860]
Social Security Number: 566-10-1124/[7860]
SSN issued: CA[7860]

Notes for Veda Elizabeth Wemple:
The Descendants of John J. Christner, privately published February 1961, p. 19.

Elizabeth is the daughter of "Pink" Wemple.

More About Veda Elizabeth Wemple:
Burial: N41°32.392xW85°33.948/Eden Cemetery, IN

Children of Verlo Christner and Veda Wemple are:
+   5023   i.   Mary Ruth[10] Christner, born 04 Dec 1942 in Elkhart Co., IN; died 05 Dec 2001 in Goshen General Hospital, Elkhart Co., IN.
     5024   ii.   Vicky Christner, born 27 Feb 1953.

         Notes for Vicky Christner:
         The Descendants of John J. Christner, privately published February 1961, p. 19.

2781. Elias Jay[9] Frye (Mary Ann[8] Christner, David J.[7], John J.[6], Joseph C.[5], Christian J.[4], Johannes John Hans[3], Christian[2], Christen[1])[7861] was born 27 Oct 1914 in Topeka, Lagrange Co., IN[7861], and died 08 Oct 1998 in Wakarusa, Elkhart Co., IN. He married **(1) Naomi Jean Hurst** 22 Aug 1946 in Princeton. She was born 05 Feb 1918, and died 10 Feb 1984. He married **(2) Erma Drake** 26 Jan 1991.

Notes for Elias Jay Frye:
The Descendants of John J. Christner, privately published February 1961, p. 19.

Elias lived at 104 South Washington Street, Wakarusa, IN. He graduated from Topeka High School. He served in the Army during WWII and was awarded 5 battle stars and the French and Luxembourg Croix De Guerre. Following his retirement from Domore Office Furniture as an engineer he worked for Indiana Chair Frame until 1997. He was a member of Wakarusa United Methodist Church and the American Legion Post 30, Goshen.

More About Elias Jay Frye:
Burial: Violett Cemetery Goshen IN.
Military: 12 Oct 1942, Toledo, Ohio[7861]
Residence: Elkhart Co., IN[7861]
Social Security Number: 310-09-3826/[7861]
SSN issued: IN[7861]

Notes for Naomi Jean Hurst:
The Descendants of John J. Christner, privately published February 1961, p. 19.

Child of Elias Frye and Naomi Hurst is:
     5025   i.   Bethanie Jean[10] Frye, born 10 Jan 1954.

Notes for Bethanie Jean Frye:
The Descendants of John J. Christner, privately published February 1961, p. 19.

2783. Ernest R.[9] **Frye** (Mary Ann[8] Christner, David J.[7], John J.[6], Joseph C.[5], Christian J.[4], Johannes John Hans[3], Christian[2], Christen[1]) was born 18 Jul 1919 in South Bend, St. Joseph Co., IN, and died 03 Oct 1996 in South Bend, St Joseph Co., IN[7861]. He married **Norma Jean Evans** 09 Apr 1955. She was born 14 May 1928.

Notes for Ernest R. Frye:
The Descendants of John J. Christner, privately published February 1961, p. 19.

More About Ernest R. Frye:
Social Security Number: 314-05-3751/[7861]
SSN issued: IN[7861]

Notes for Norma Jean Evans:
The Descendants of John J. Christner, privately published February 1961, p. 19.

Child of Ernest Frye and Norma Evans is:
    5026   i.   Lester Charles[10] Frye, born 20 Sep 1944.

                    Notes for Lester Charles Frye:
                    The Descendants of John J. Christner, privately published February 1961, p. 19.

                    Ernest adopted Norma's son Lester.

                    More About Lester Charles Frye:
                    Adopted: Ernest adopted his wife Norma Jean's son.

2787. Dorothy June[9] **Frye** (Mary Ann[8] Christner, David J.[7], John J.[6], Joseph C.[5], Christian J.[4], Johannes John Hans[3], Christian[2], Christen[1]) was born 03 Jun 1928, and died 23 Oct 2010 in Tonawanda, Erie Co., NY[7862]. She married **Jack Roe**[7863] 10 Oct 1953. He was born 12 Jan 1923, and died 08 Apr 1988[7863].

Notes for Dorothy June Frye:
The Descendants of John J. Christner, privately published February 1961, p. 19.

She had a son Jackson Zell that married Diane Fay Christner Daughter of Arthur and Gladys Christner.

More About Dorothy June Frye:
Other-Begin: Tonawanda, Erie Co., NY[7864]
SSN issued: NY[7864]

Notes for Jack Roe:
The Descendants of John J. Christner, privately published February 1961, p. 19.

More About Jack Roe:
Social Security Number: 317-12-8487/[7865]
SSN issued: IN[7865]

Children of Dorothy Frye and Jack Roe are:
    5027   i.   Ronald Jay[10] Roe, born 05 Feb 1948.

                    Notes for Ronald Jay Roe:
                    The Descendants of John J. Christner, privately published February 1961, p. 19.

+   5028   ii.   Jackson Zell Roe, born 30 May 1955 in Goshen, Elkhart Co., IN.

2789. Soloma[9] Christner (David D.[8], David J.[7], John J.[6], Joseph C.[5], Christian J.[4], Johannes John Hans[3], Christian[2], Christen[1]) was born 10 Dec 1910 in Lagrange Co., IN[7866], and died 07 Nov 1997 in 11322 Co.Rd.34 Goshen, Elkhart Co., IN. She married **Joseph B. Bontrager** 16 Nov 1933 in Topeka, Lagrange Co., IN, son of Benjamin Bontrager and Elizabeth Miller. He was born 05 Jan 1910, and died 17 Nov 1984 in Lagrange, Lagrange Co., IN.

Notes for Soloma Christner:
The Descendants of John J. Christner, privately published 1961, p. 19.
Old Order Amish Homemaker.

More About Soloma Christner:
Burial: Miller Cemetery, Lagrange Co., IN
Religion: Old Order Amish/
Residence: 1920, Clearspring, Lagrange Co., IN[7866]

Notes for Joseph B. Bontrager:
The Descendants of John J. Christner, privately published February 1961, p. 19.

More About Joseph B. Bontrager:
Burial: Miller Cemetery, Lagrange Co., IN
Occupation: Farmer/
Religion: Old Order Amish/

Children of Soloma Christner and Joseph Bontrager are:
+   5029   i.   Wilma[10] Bontrager, born 08 Sep 1934 in Lagrange Co., IN.
     5030   ii.   Mary Ellen Bontrager, born 06 Apr 1936. She married Larry Jones 09 Jun 1960; born 22 Nov 1938.

        Notes for Mary Ellen Bontrager:
        The Descendants of John J. Christner, privately published February 1961, p. 20.

        More About Mary Ellen Bontrager:
        Religion: Old Order Amish/

        Notes for Larry Jones:
        The Descendants of John J. Christner, privately published February 1961, p. 20.

     5031   iii.   Melvin Bontrager, born 16 Jan 1938. He married Mary Miller.

        Notes for Melvin Bontrager:
        The Descendants of John J. Christner, privately published February 1961, p. 20.

        More About Melvin Bontrager:
        Religion: Old Order Amish/

     5032   iv.   Katie Bontrager, born 27 Jan 1940. She married Mose Elmer Miller 30 Mar 1961; born 06 Jan 1941.

        More About Katie Bontrager:
        Religion: Old Order Amish/

     5033   v.   Uriah Bontrager, born 23 Jul 1941. He married Reenie Maple in Indianapolis, Marion Co., IN.

        Notes for Uriah Bontrager:

     5034   vi.   Josey Bontrager, born 17 Aug 1943. He married Judy Jones.

Notes for Josey Bontrager:
Josey married Judy Jones

5035   vii.   Elizabeth Bontrager, born 08 Jun 1946. She married Wayne Carpenter.
5036   viii.   Mattie Bontrager, born 23 Jun 1948. She married Vernon R. Chupp 02 May 1968; born 02 Feb 1942.

Notes for Mattie Bontrager:

5037   ix.   Edna Bontrager, born 09 Sep 1950.

Notes for Edna Bontrager:
Edna married Edwin Miller
Edna and Ed Miller owned the gas station in Topeka In that was purchased by
Steve Christner (compiler of the history book).This is the location that Steve
opened Topeka Radiator.
Edna married Edwin Miller
Edna and Ed Miller owned the gas station in Topeka In that was purchased by
Steve Christner (compiler of the history book).This is the location that Steve
opened Topeka Radiator.
Edna married Edwin Miller
Edna and Ed Miller owned the gas station in Topeka In that was purchased by
Steve Christner (compiler of the history book).This is the location that Steve
opened Topeka Radiator.

5038   x.   Barbara Bontrager, born 25 Feb 1952.
5039   xi.   Freeman Bontrager, born 25 Feb 1959; died 31 Aug 1959.

2791. Wilma L.[9] Christner (David D.[8], David J.[7], John J.[6], Joseph C.[5], Christian J.[4], Johannes John Hans[3], Christian[2], Christen[1])[7866] was born 25 May 1913 in Lagrange Co., IN[7866], and died 15 Apr 1977 in Lagrange Co., IN[7867]. She married **Christian C. Hochstetler**[7867] 16 Nov 1933 in IN[7867]. He was born 30 Dec 1912 in Lagrange Co., IN[7867], and died 15 May 1991 in Lagrange Co., IN[7867].

Notes for Wilma L. Christner:
The Descendants of John J. Christner, privately published February 1961, p., 19.

Birth: May 25, 1913
Death: Apr. 15, 1977

Wife of C.C.

Spouse: Chris C. Hochstetler (1912 - 1991)

Burial: Miller Amish Cemetery, Lagrange, Lagrange Co., IN
Find A Grave Memorial# 66593232

More About Wilma L. Christner:
Religion: Old Order Amish/
Residence: 1920, Clearspring, Lagrange Co., IN[7868]

Notes for Christian C. Hochstetler:
Chris is the son of Christian D. and Katie Bontrager Hochstetler
Chris was Old Order Amish and a farmer.

Birth: Dec. 30, 1912
Death: May 15, 1991

Spouse: Wilma L. Hochstetler (1913 - 1977)

Burial: Miller Amish Cemetery, Lagrange, Lagrange Co., IN
Find A Grave Memorial# 98720165

More About Christian C. Hochstetler:
Occupation: Farmer/
Religion: Old Order Amish/

Children of Wilma Christner and Christian Hochstetler are:

5040   i.   Rosie C.[10] Hochstetler, born 17 Jan 1935 in Lagrange Co., IN; died 31 Mar 1988 in Goshen, Elkhart Co., IN. She married Jesse O. Schlabaach 30 Nov 1961; born 02 Jun 1933.

Notes for Rosie C. Hochstetler:
The Descendants of John J. Christner, privately published February 1961, p. 20.

More About Rosie C. Hochstetler:
Burial: Nisley Cem, CR #35, GOSHEN, IN

Notes for Jesse O. Schlabaach:
Jesse was a farmer and a bishop of the Old Order Amish.

+ 5041   ii.   Ida C. Hochstetler, born 07 Jun 1936 in Topeka, Lagrange Co., IN; died 31 Mar 1988 in Goshen, Elkhart Co., IN.

+ 5042   iii.   Lester C. Hochstetler, born 11 Feb 1938 in Wolcottville, Lagrange Co., IN.

5043   iv.   Mattie C. Hochstetler, born 25 Jan 1940. She married Levi E. Miller 16 Mar 1961; born 27 Apr 1941.

Notes for Mattie C. Hochstetler:
The Descendants of John J. Christner, privately published February 1961, p. 20.

Levi is a farmer and factory employee.

5044   v.   Katie C. Hochstetler, born 17 May 1942. She married Elmer Eugene Mast 17 Oct 1963; born 18 Oct 1943.

Notes for Katie C. Hochstetler:
The Descendants of John J. Christner, privately published February 1961, p. 20.

Elmer is the son of Mose M. and Anna Mae Miller Mast Jr.
Elmer is a farmer and a Deacon Old Order Amish.

5045   vi.   David C. Hochstetler, born 03 Jan 1944.

Notes for David C. Hochstetler:
The Descendants of John J. Christner, privately published February 1961, p. 20.

5046   vii.   Harvey C. Hochstetler, born 30 Mar 1946. He married Lizzie Marie Bontrager 14 Nov 1968; born 16 Sep 1947.

Notes for Harvey C. Hochstetler:
The Descendants of John J. Christner, privately published February 1961, p., 20.

Lizzie is the daughter of Harley E.and Orpha Lambright Bontrager.
Harvey is a farmer.

5047   viii.   Christy C. Hochstetler, born 06 May 1948. He married Leanna D. Miller 25 Dec 1969; born 31 Aug

1949.

Notes for Christy C. Hochstetler:
The Descendants of John J. Christner, privately published February 1961, p. 20.

Christy is a factory employee.

5048   ix.   Anna Mae C. Hochstetler, born 13 May 1950. She married Ernest L. Schrock 14 Dec 1972; born 11 Jan 1949.

Notes for Anna Mae C. Hochstetler:
The Descendants of John J. Christner, privately published February 1961, p. 20.

Ernest is the son of Levi J. and Martha Miller Schrock.
Ernest builds custom made furniture and is a duck farmer.

5049   x.   Elsie C. Hochstetler, born 02 Dec 1952.

Notes for Elsie C. Hochstetler:
The Descendants of John J. Christner, privately published February 1961, p. 20.

5050   xi.   Mary C. Hochstetler, born 25 Dec 1954. She married Elmer J. Miller.

Notes for Mary C. Hochstetler:
The Descendants of John J. Christner, privately published February 1961, p. 20.

Mary married Elmer J. Miller Nov 8 1973
Elmer is the son of Joni J. and Susie A. Bontrager Miller
Elmer born Aug 7 1953
Elmer is a farmer.

5051   xii.   John C. Hochstetler, born 02 Nov 1955. He married Annabelle Mast 03 Jun 1976; born 27 Sep 1956.

Notes for John C. Hochstetler:
The Descendants of John J. Christner, privately published February 1961, p. 20.

Annabelle is the daughter of Joe U. and Josephine Slabach Mast
John is a factory employee.

5052   xiii.   Mervin C. Hochstetler, born 10 Mar 1959. He married Clara Fern Nissley 16 Oct 1980; born 16 Sep 1960.

Notes for Mervin C. Hochstetler:
Mervin is a farmer.

2793. Uriah D.[9] **Christner** (David D.[8], David J.[7], John J.[6], Joseph C.[5], Christian J.[4], Johannes John Hans[3], Christian[2], Christen[1])[7868,7869] was born 16 Sep 1915 in Clearspring Twp., Lagrange Co., IN[7870], and died 31 Oct 2003 in Lagrange Hospital Lived at 5615 W--500 S//N41°34.128xW85°31.962. He married **(1) Verna Elizabeth Miller**[7871] 11 Mar 1937 in Topeka, Lagrange Co., IN, daughter of Henry Miller and Susanna Schrock. She was born 04 Sep 1915 in Lagrange Co., IN[7871], and died 22 Dec 1968 in Lagrange Co., IN[7871]. He married **(2) Amanda M. Yoder** 04 Jan 1970 in Topeka, Lagrange Co., IN, daughter of Martin Yoder and Lovina Yoder. She was born 26 Apr 1924.

Notes for Uriah D. Christner:
The Descendants of John J. Christner, privately published February 1961, pp., 19, 20.

Old Order Amish Farmer He lived at 5615 West -- 500 South in Lagrange Co. Indiana N41°34.128xW85°31.962

Burial at Miller Cem, LaGrange Co, IN. N41°35.339'xW85°28.937' Row 13 Plot 3, Short row north of the south entrance, between rows 7 & 8. This cemetery is located at County Roads 300S and 300W -- 3 miles south & 3 miles west of the Lagrange Co. Court House.

More About Uriah D. Christner:
Burial: 03 Nov 2003, Miller Cemetery, Lagrange Co., IN. N41°35.316'xW85°28.937 row 13 plot 3
Occupation: Farmer/[7871,7871]
Religion: Old Order Amish/[7871]
Residence: 1920, Clearspring, Lagrange Co., IN[7872]
Social Security Number: 312-54-8860/[7873,7873]
SSN issued: IN[7874,7875]

Notes for Verna Elizabeth Miller:
The Descendants of John J. Christner, privately published February 1961, pp. 19, 20, 39.

Burial at Miller Cemetery, Lagrange Co, IN. N41°35.316'xW85°28.937' Row 13 Plot 3, Short row north of the south entrance, between rows 7 & 8. This cemetery is located at County Roads 300S and 300W -- 3 miles south & 3 miles west of the Lagrange County Court House.

More About Verna Elizabeth Miller:
Burial: Miller Cemetery, Lagrange Co., IN. N41°35.316'xW85°28.937'Row13 plot 3

Notes for Amanda M. Yoder:
Amanda is the daughter of Martin and Lovina Yoder Yoder.

Child of Uriah Christner and Verna Miller is:
+   5053   i.   Wilma U.[10] Christner, born 02 Dec 1946 in Kendallville, IN.

   2795. Mattie L.[9] Christner (David D.[8], David J.[7], John J.[6], Joseph C.[5], Christian J.[4], Johannes John Hans[3], Christian[2], Christen[1]) was born 09 Oct 1918 in Topeka, Lagrange Co., IN[7876,7877], and died 26 Feb 1999 in Lagrange Co., IN. She married **Amos F. Mishler** 02 Feb 1939 in Lagrange Co., IN, son of Frederick Mishler and Mary Schrock. He was born 20 Sep 1917 in Lagrange, Lagrange Co., IN[7878], and died 09 May 1982 in Home.

Notes for Mattie L. Christner:
The Descendants of John J. Christner, privately published February 1961, pp. 19, 20.
He was Old Order Amish and is buried in the Miller Cemetery, Lagrange, IN.

More About Mattie L. Christner:
Burial: Miller Cemetery, Lagrange Co., IN
Residence: 1920, Clearspring, Lagrange Co., IN[7879]
Social Security Number: 309-64-6598/[7880]
SSN issued: IN[7880]

Notes for Amos F. Mishler:
The Descendants of John J. Christner, privately published February 1961, pp. 20, 42.
Amos was an Old Order Amish farmer & the son of Fred and Mary Schrock Mishler. When he was 15 years old he lost his right hand while filling the silo (corn storage) at his family farm. About a year before he died he had brain tumor surgery & later suffered a stroke.

More About Amos F. Mishler:
Burial: Miller Cemetery, Lagrange Co., IN
Occupation: Farmer/
Religion: Old Order Amish/
Residence: 28 Apr 1930, Clearspring Township, Lagrange Co., IN[7881]

Children of Mattie Christner and Amos Mishler are:

5054 i. Lydia Mae[10] Mishler, born 15 Aug 1943. She married Paul W. Brubaker 28 May 1994; born 08 Nov 1928.

   Notes for Lydia Mae Mishler:
   The Descendants of John J. Christner, privately published February 1961, p. 21.

   More About Lydia Mae Mishler:
   Occupation: Sales Associate/
   Religion: Old Order Amish/

5055 ii. Orva Mishler, born 20 Jan 1951.

   Notes for Orva Mishler:
   The Descendants of John J. Christner, privately published February 1961, p. 21.

   He has Downs Syndrome.

+ 5056 iii. Alvin Mishler, born 24 Apr 1953.
+ 5057 iv. Mary Mishler, born 27 Nov 1955.
+ 5058 v. Wilma Mishler, born 23 Jan 1958.
+ 5059 vi. Melvin Mishler, born 04 Nov 1961.
+ 5060 vii. Ervin Mishler, born 27 Nov 1962.

2800. Milo William[9] Christner (David D.[8], David J.[7], John J.[6], Joseph C.[5], Christian J.[4], Johannes John Hans[3], Christian[2], Christen[1])[7882] was born 04 Jul 1928 in Elkhart, Elkhart Co., IN[7882], and died 27 Jun 1965 in Elkhart, Elkhart Co., IN[7882]. He married **Betty Joe Davis** 08 Sep 1956 in Elkhart Co., IN. She was born 22 Mar 1931.

Notes for Milo William Christner:
The Descendants of John J. Christner, privately published February 1961, p. 21.
Died at his home from injuries Suffered in a automobile crash three weeks earlier. He was a veteran of World War II and a member of the Moose Lodge in Elkhart, IN. Burial at Rice Cemetery, Elkhart, IN.

Notes for Betty Joe Davis:
The Descendants of John J. Christner, privately published February 1961, p. 21.

Child of Milo Christner and Betty Davis is:

5061 i. Michael William[10] Christner, born 04 Jul 1958[7883]; died 08 Feb 2007 in Goshen, Elkhart Co., IN[7884]. He married Lou Ann 22 Sep 1979; born 02 Jan 1959.

   Notes for Michael William Christner:
   The Descendants of John J. Christner, privately published February 1961, p. 21.

   Birth: Jul. 4, 1958
   Death: Feb. 8, 2007

   GOSHEN -- Michael W. Christner, 48, of U.S. 20, died at 1:21 a.m. Thursday (Feb. 8, 2007) in Elkhart General Hospital after an illness.

   He was born Aug. 4, 1958, in Elkhart to Milo W. and Betty Jo (Yonkers) Christner. On Sept. 22, 1979, in Edwardsburg, Mich., he married Lou Ann Windbigler.

   She survives, along with two daughters, Samantha Jo and Courtney Ann Christner, both of Goshen; and two brothers, Benny (Donna) and James (Debra) Wheeler, both of Elkhart.

   Friends may call from 5 to 8 p.m. Sunday and one hour prior to the 1 p.m. Monday funeral service, all at Paul E. Mayhew Funeral Home, 26863 W. Main St., Edwardsburg. Pastor Chris Garner of Crystal Valley Missionary Church, Middlebury, will officiate. Burial will be in Edwardsburg Cemetery.

   Mr. Christner was a manager at Jason Industries, a maker of truck caps, in Elkhart. He had lived in the

Edwardsburg and Elkhart area all of his life and was a former member of the Road House Band.

Memorials may be given to United Cancer Services of Elkhart County, 23971 U.S. 33, Elkhart, IN 46517.

Inscription: Married Sept. 22, 1979

Burial: Edwardsburg Cemetery, Edwardsburg, Cass Co., MI

More About Michael William Christner:
Burial: IN[7885]
SSN issued: MI[7886]

2809. Susan J.[9] Miller (Katie D.[8] Christner, David J.[7], John J.[6], Joseph C.[5], Christian J.[4], Johannes John Hans[3], Christian[2], Christen[1]) was born 17 Mar, and died 10 Oct 1968 in Lagrange Co., IN[7887]. She married **Samuel R. Bontrager** 13 Dec 1934 in By Cornelius Christner[7887]. He was born 02 Apr 1914 in Lagrange Co., IN, and died 09 Mar 2000.

Notes for Susan J. Miller:
The Descendants of John J. Christner, privately published February 1961, pp., 21, 22.

Notes for Samuel R. Bontrager:
The Descendants of John J. Christner, privately published February 1961, p. 22.

He died at his home at 10:33 p.m. Thursday. He was a Old Order Amish Farmer.

More About Samuel R. Bontrager:
Burial: Miller Cemetery, Lagrange Co., IN
Occupation: Farmer/
Religion: Old Order Amish/
Social Security Number: 303-40-5244/
SSN issued: IN

Children of Susan Miller and Samuel Bontrager are:
+   5062   i.   Mary Ellen[10] Bontrager, born 27 Jun 1936.
     5063   ii.   Ervin S Bontrager, born 01 Mar 1938. He married Ida Mae Miller 19 Nov 1959; born 26 Oct 1940 in Shipshewana, Elkhart Co., IN.

                    Notes for Ervin S Bontrager:
                    The Descendants of John J. Christner, privately published February 1961, pp. 10, 22.

                    More About Ervin S Bontrager:
                    Religion: Old Order Amish/

                    Notes for Ida Mae Miller:
                    The Descendants of John J. Christner, privately published February 1961, p. 9, 10.

     5064   iii.   Orva Bontrager, born 13 Jul 1943.

                    Notes for Orva Bontrager:
                    The Descendants of John J. Christner, privately published February 1961, p. 21.

     5065   iv.   Samuel Bontrager Jr, born 27 Sep 1953.

                    Notes for Samuel Bontrager Jr:
                    The Descendants of John J. Christner, privately published February 1961, p. 21.

2810. Mary Ann[9] Miller (Katie D.[8] Christner, David J.[7], John J.[6], Joseph C.[5], Christian J.[4], Johannes John Hans[3], Christian[2], Christen[1]) was born 26 Jul 1909 in Topeka, Lagrange Co., IN, and died 24 Jul 1930. She married **Irvin Weaver**[7888] 13 Jan 1930. He was born 1912 in IN[7888].

Notes for Mary Ann Miller:
The Descendants of John J. Christner, privately published February 1961, p. 21.

May have died giving birth to her son Mahlon J. Weaver,. Some have her death as July 17, 2001.

Notes for Irvin Weaver:
The Descendants of John J. Christner, privately published February 1961, p. 21.

More About Irvin Weaver:
Residence: 1920, Elkhart, Elkhart Co., IN[7888]

Children of Mary Miller and Irvin Weaver are:
  5066   i.   Clarence[10] Weaver.
  5067   ii.   Edwin Weaver. He married Martha.
  5068   iii. Irene Weaver.
  5069   iv.   Katie A. Weaver. She married Lloyd Miller.
  5070   v.   Mary A. Weaver. She married Jack Lennon.
  5071   vi.   Vernon Weaver.
  5072   vii. William Weaver. He married Susan.
  5073   viii. Wilmer Weaver. He married Dorothy.
  5074   ix.   Mahlon J. Weaver[7889], born 24 Jul 1930 in Topeka, Lagrange Co., IN; died 06 Jan 2003 in 770 N. by 75 E. Lagrange Co., IN. He married Verna E. Miller 27 Oct 1955 in Goshen, Elkhart Co., IN; died 10 Feb 2001.

            Notes for Mahlon J. Weaver:
            The Descendants of John J. Christner, privately published February 1961, p. 21.

            He was a butcher at Yoder's Butchering.

            More About Mahlon J. Weaver:
            Burial: 08 Jan 2003, Townline Cemetery, Lagrange Co., IN
            Other-Begin: Wolcottville, Lagrange, Indiana, United States of America[7889]
            SSN issued: VA[7889]

            Notes for Verna E. Miller:
            The Descendants of John J. Christner, privately published February 1961, p. 21.

2811. Alice J.[9] Miller (Katie D.[8] Christner, David J.[7], John J.[6], Joseph C.[5], Christian J.[4], Johannes John Hans[3], Christian[2], Christen[1])[7890] was born 10 May 1911 in Topeka, Lagrange Co., IN, and died 17 Jul 2001 in Middlebury, Elkhart Co., IN[7890]. She married **Levi W. Miller** 22 Feb 1934 in Topeka, Lagrange Co., IN. He was born 23 Nov 1911, and died 14 Feb 1967.

Notes for Alice J. Miller:
The Descendants of John J. Christner, privately published February 1961, p. 21.

More About Alice J. Miller:
Burial: 20 Jul 2001, Grace Lawn Cemetery   Middlebury IN.
Occupation: Homemaker/
Religion: First Mennonite Church/
Social Security Number: 312-54-7635/[7890]
SSN issued: IN[7890]

Children of Alice Miller and Levi Miller are:
  + 5075   i.   Louella Marie[10] Miller, born 19 Mar 1936.

5076   ii.   Orla L. Miller, born 29 Sep 1937; died 07 Jan 1993. He married Betty Stutzman; born 23 Jul 1942.

Notes for Orla L. Miller:
The Descendants of John J. Christner, privately published February 1961, p. 21.

Middle name may be Vernon and may have died 7 Jan 1993.

5077   iii.   Elva Jay Miller, born 16 Jan 1939.

Notes for Elva Jay Miller:
The Descendants of John J. Christner, privately published February 1961, p. 21.

5078   iv.   Ernest Leroy Miller, born 10 Sep 1941.

Notes for Ernest Leroy Miller:
The Descendants of John J. Christner, privately published February 1961, p. 21.

5079   v.   Wilbur Lee Miller, born 10 Dec 1946; died 01 Oct 1983.

Notes for Wilbur Lee Miller:
The Descendants of John J. Christner, privately published February 1961, p. 21.

5080   vi.   Sharon Diana Miller, born 07 Aug 1954. She married Hank Hanna.

Notes for Sharon Diana Miller:
The Descendants of John J. Christner, privately published February 1961, p. 21.

2812. Tobias J.[9] Miller (Katie D.[8] Christner, David J.[7], John J.[6], Joseph C.[5], Christian J.[4], Johannes John Hans[3], Christian[2], Christen[1]) was born 02 Feb 1913 in Topeka, Lagrange Co., IN. He married **Elizabeth Yoder** 01 Nov 1934. She was born 18 Mar 1916 in White Cloud, Newaygo Co., MI[7891], and died 14 Sep 2008 in Goshen, Elkhart Co., IN[7891].

Notes for Tobias J. Miller:
The Descendants of John J. Christner, privately published February 1961, p. 21.

Tobias married Elizabeth Yoder Nov 1, 1934.

Notes for Elizabeth Yoder:
The Descendants of John J. Christner, privately published February 1961, p. 21.

Children of Tobias Miller and Elizabeth Yoder are:
+   5081   i.   Lasetta Mae[10] Miller, born 13 Dec 1935.
+   5082   ii.   Lloyd Eugene Miller, born 29 May 1938.
     5083   iii.   Mary Ellen Miller, born 06 Jun 1941.

Notes for Mary Ellen Miller:
The Descendants of John J. Christner, privately published February 1961, p. 21.

5084   iv.   Ernest LeRoy Miller, born 22 Feb 1944.

Notes for Ernest LeRoy Miller:
The Descendants of John J. Christner, privately published February 1961, p. 21.

5085   v.   Danny Jay Miller, born 23 Aug 1955.

Notes for Danny Jay Miller:
The Descendants of John J. Christner, privately published February 1961, p. 21.

2813. Amos J.[9] **Miller** (Katie D.[8] Christner, David J.[7], John J.[6], Joseph C.[5], Christian J.[4], Johannes John Hans[3], Christian[2], Christen[1])[7892,7893,7894] was born 19 Oct 1915 in Lagrange Co., IN[7895,7896,7897], and died 04 Apr 1987 in Sarasota, Sarasota Co., FL[7897,7898,7899]. He married **(1) Anna G. Helmuth** 19 Oct 1939.   He married **(2) Katie L. Borntrager**[7900,7901] 09 Jun 1984 in Lagrange Co., IN[7901]. She was born 04 Oct 1918 in Reno, Reno Co., KS[7902,7903,7904], and died 07 Aug 2010 in Sarasota, Sarasota Co., FL[7905].

Notes for Amos J. Miller:
The Descendants of John J. Christner, privately published February 1961, pp. 21, 22.

Amos married Anna G. Helmuth.

More About Amos J. Miller:
Occupation: Farmer & Carpenter/
Religion: Old Order Amish/
Social Security Number: 307-16-1827/[7906]
SSN issued: IN[7906]

Notes for Anna G. Helmuth:
The Descendants of John J. Christner, privately published February 1961, p. 22.

More About Katie L. Borntrager:
SSN issued: IN[7907]

Children of Amos Miller and Anna Helmuth are:
+   5086   i.   Mary Edna[10] Miller, born 27 Jul 1905.
    5087   ii.   Susie Carolyn Miller, born 04 Jul 1940.

>   Notes for Susie Carolyn Miller:
>   The Descendants of John J. Christner, privately published February 1961, p. 22.

    5088   iii.   Glen Miller, born 17 Jun 1941.

>   Notes for Glen Miller:
>   The Descendants of John J. Christner, privately published February 1961, p. 22.

    5089   iv.   Harley Miller, born 20 May 1943.

>   Notes for Harley Miller:
>   The Descendants of John J. Christner, privately published February 1961, p. 22.

    5090   v.   Ada Mae Miller, born 10 Mar 1945.

>   Notes for Ada Mae Miller:
>   The Descendants of John J. Christner, privately published February 1961, p. 22.

    5091   vi.   Katie Anna Miller, born 13 Apr 1949.

>   Notes for Katie Anna Miller:
>   The Descendants of John J. Christner, privately published February 1961, p. 22.

    5092   vii.   Jacob Miller, born 12 Apr 1951.

>   Notes for Jacob Miller:
>   The Descendants of John J. Christner, privately published February 1961, p. 22.

    5093   viii.   Amos Miller Jr, born 11 Mar 1952.

>   Notes for Amos Miller Jr:
>   The Descendants of John J. Christner, privately published February 1961, p. 22.

    5094   ix.   Delbert Miller, born 11 May 1953.

Notes for Delbert Miller:
The Descendants of John J. Christner, privately published February 1961, p. 22.

5095   x.   Lydia Ellen Miller, born 03 Jan 1956; died 26 Jan 1956.

Notes for Lydia Ellen Miller:
The Descendants of John J. Christner, privately published February 1961, p. 22.

5096   xi.   Mary Edna Miller, born 10 Jun 1957.

Notes for Mary Edna Miller:
The Descendants of John J. Christner, privately published February 1961, p. 22.

2814. Eli J.[9] Miller (Katie D.[8] Christner, David J.[7], John J.[6], Joseph C.[5], Christian J.[4], Johannes John Hans[3], Christian[2], Christen[1]) was born 02 Apr 1919 in Shipshewana, Lagrange Co., IN, and died 26 Nov 2004 in Montezuma, GA. He married **Katie Lehman** 23 Nov 1939 in by David Nissley/. She was born 31 Jul 1918.

Notes for Eli J. Miller:
The Descendants of John J. Christner, privately published February 1961, pp. 21, 22.

His funeral was held at Clearview Mennonite Church Montezuma, GA.
He was a carpenter and Old Order Amish.

More About Eli J. Miller:
Occupation: Farmer/
Religion: Old Order Amish/

Children of Eli Miller and Katie Lehman are:
5097   i.   Ervin[10] Miller.
5098   ii.   Christian Jay Miller, born 01 Mar 1941.

Notes for Christian Jay Miller:
The Descendants of John J. Christner, privately published February 1961, p. 22.

5099   iii.   Richard Miller, born 06 Jul 1942.

Notes for Richard Miller:
The Descendants of John J. Christner, privately published February 1961, p. 22.

5100   iv.   LeAnna Miller, born 07 Mar 1944.

Notes for LeAnna Miller:
The Descendants of John J. Christner, privately published February 1961, p. 22.

5101   v.   Ervin Miller, born 25 Apr 1946.

Notes for Ervin Miller:
The Descendants of John J. Christner, privately published February 1961, p. 22.

5102   vi.   Marvin Miller, born 14 Sep 1948. He married Clara G. Yoder; born 22 Mar 1945.

Notes for Marvin Miller:
The Descendants of John J. Christner, privately published February 1961, p. 22.

5103   vii.   Edna Ellen Miller, born 01 Dec 1952.

Notes for Edna Ellen Miller:
The Descendants of John J. Christner, privately published February 1961, p. 22.

5104   viii.   Vera Sue Miller, born 01 Aug 1955. She married Norman Yoder.

2816. Jacob Willis⁹ Miller (Katie D.⁸ Christner, David J.⁷, John J.⁶, Joseph C.⁵, Christian J.⁴, Johannes John Hans³, Christian², Christen¹) was born 28 Dec 1923 in Topeka, Lagrange Co., IN, and died in This is triple Jake as his dad was called Jake Jake. He married **Anna Pauline Schrock** 26 Feb 1948 in By Jacob P Miller, daughter of John Schrock and Elizabeth Wingard. She was born 16 Jun 1927.

Notes for Jacob Willis Miller:
The Descendants of John J. Christner, privately published February 1961, pp. 21, 22.

Old Order Amish and a Farmer. People Called him Triple Jake. This is triple Jake as his dad was called Jake Jake, because his father was called Jake.

More About Jacob Willis Miller:
Occupation: Farmer/
Religion: Old Order Amish/

Notes for Anna Pauline Schrock:
The Descendants of John J. Christner, privately published February 1961, pp. 22, 42.

Children of Jacob Miller and Anna Schrock are:

5105   i.   Leroy Ray¹⁰ Miller, born 29 Jun 1949.

        Notes for Leroy Ray Miller:
        The Descendants of John J. Christner, privately published February 1961, p. 22.

5106   ii.   Homer Lee Miller, born 11 Nov 1950.

        Notes for Homer Lee Miller:
        The Descendants of John J. Christner, privately published February 1961, p. 22.

5107   iii. Glen Jay Miller, born 16 Feb 1953.

        Notes for Glen Jay Miller:
        The Descendants of John J. Christner, privately published February 1961, p. 22.

5108   iv.   Jonny Ray Miller, born 31 Jul 1954.

        Notes for Jonny Ray Miller:
        The Descendants of John J. Christner, privately published February 1961, p. 22.

5109   v.   Elizabeth Mae Miller, born 07 Jun 1956.

        Notes for Elizabeth Mae Miller:
        The Descendants of John J. Christner, privately published February 1961, p. 22.

5110   vi.   Mary Kathryn Miller, born 04 Mar 1958.

        Notes for Mary Kathryn Miller:
        The Descendants of John J. Christner, privately published February 1961, p. 22.

2817. Amzie J.⁹ Miller (Katie D.⁸ Christner, David J.⁷, John J.⁶, Joseph C.⁵, Christian J.⁴, Johannes John Hans³, Christian², Christen¹) was born 22 Sep 1926 in Goshen, Elkhart Co., IN. He married **Anna Mae Beechy**[7908] 03 Dec 1946 in married by David Nissley/, daughter of William Beechy and Amanda Schrock. She was born 15 Nov 1927 in Topeka, Lagrange Co., IN[7908,7909,7910], and died 18 Aug 2005 in Goshen, Elkhart Co., IN[7911,7912].

Notes for Amzie J. Miller:
The Descendants of John J. Christner, privately published February 1961, pp. 21, 23.

He was Old Order Amish and a farmer.

More About Amzie J. Miller:
Occupation: Farmer/
Religion: Old Order Amish/

Notes for Anna Mae Beechy:
The Descendants of John J. Christner, privately published February 1961, p. 44.

More About Anna Mae Beechy:
Fact 1: Homemaker/[7912]
Fact 4: Beachy Amish Mennonite/[7912]
Fact 10: The Descendants of John J. Christner by Mr. & Mrs. David R. Bontrager... 1961/[7912]
Fact 11: Descendants of Daniel J. Hochstetler & Barbara C. Miller 1842-1990 by Dan A. Hoc/[7912]
Fact 12: Family Record of Daniel J. Hochstetler, 1842-1968, by Alvin & Susie Bontrager/[7912]
Fact 13: The Descendants of Peter C. Nisley, June, 1969 by Mr. & Mrs. Harley A. Bontrager/[7912]
Marriage Fact: 0/married by David Nisley[7912]
SSN issued: IN[7913]

Children of Amzie Miller and Anna Beechy are:
> 5111   i.   Homer Ray[10] Miller, born 01 Mar 1948.
>
>   Notes for Homer Ray Miller:
>   The Descendants of John J. Christner, privately published February 1961, p. 23.
>
> 5112   ii.   Jacob Eugene Miller, born 22 Feb 1949.
>
>   Notes for Jacob Eugene Miller:
>   The Descendants of John J. Christner, privately published February 1961, p. 23.
>
> 5113   iii.   Mary Alice Miller, born 09 Aug 1950.
>
>   Notes for Mary Alice Miller:
>   The Descendants of John J. Christner, privately published February 1961, p. 23.
>
> 5114   iv.   Freeman Wayne Miller, born 01 Sep 1952.
>
>   Notes for Freeman Wayne Miller:
>   The Descendants of John J. Christner, privately published February 1961, p. 23.
>
> 5115   v.   Amanda Carolyn Miller, born 29 Sep 1953.
>
>   Notes for Amanda Carolyn Miller:
>   The Descendants of John J. Christner, privately published February 1961, p. 23.
>
> 5116   vi.   William Ray Miller, born 22 Aug 1958.
>
>   Notes for William Ray Miller:
>   The Descendants of John J. Christner, privately published February 1961, p. 23.

2818. Obie J.[9] **Miller** (Katie D.[8] Christner, David J.[7], John J.[6], Joseph C.[5], Christian J.[4], Johannes John Hans[3], Christian[2], Christen[1]) was born 03 Jul 1928 in Topeka, Lagrange Co., IN. He married **Ruby Mae Miller** 18 Mar 1948 in married by David Nissley/. She was born 30 Jan 1930 in Milford, and died 19 Nov 2006 in home--60812 Co. Road 35 Elkhart Co. Indiana--N41°36.758 x W85°44.034.

Notes for Obie J. Miller:

The Descendants of John J. Christner, privately published February 1961, pp. 21, 23.

More About Obie J. Miller:
Occupation: Farmer/
Religion: Old Order Amish/

Notes for Ruby Mae Miller:
The Descendants of John J. Christner, privately published February 1961, p. 23.

She lived at 60812 County Road 35 Elkhart Co., IN.

More About Ruby Mae Miller:
Burial: 22 Nov 2006, Miller Cemetery Goshen, Elkhart Co. Indiana
Occupation: Homemaker/
Religion: Old Order Amish/
Residence: N41°36.758 x W85°44.034--60812 Co. Road 35 Elkhart Co. Indiana

Children of Obie Miller and Ruby Miller are:

5117   i.   LaVern[10] Miller.

            Notes for LaVern Miller:
            The Descendants of John J. Christner, privately published February 1961, p. 23.

5118   ii.   Calvin Jay Miller, born 10 Mar 1950.

            Notes for Calvin Jay Miller:
            The Descendants of John J. Christner, privately published February 1961, p. 23.

5119   iii.   Floyd Miller, born 03 Aug 1952.

            Notes for Floyd Miller:
            The Descendants of John J. Christner, privately published February 1961, p. 23.

5120   iv.   Lloyd Miller, born 03 Aug 1952.

            Notes for Lloyd Miller:
            The Descendants of John J. Christner, privately published February 1961, p. 23.

5121   v.   Richard Ray Miller, born 18 Jun 1956.

            Notes for Richard Ray Miller:
            The Descendants of John J. Christner, privately published February 1961, p. 23.

2819. Wanetia Katie[9] Miller (Katie D.[8] Christner, David J.[7], John J.[6], Joseph C.[5], Christian J.[4], Johannes John Hans[3], Christian[2], Christen[1]) was born 09 Mar 1931 in Shipshewana, Lagrange Co., IN. She married **Freeman D. Eash** 23 Nov 1951 in by David Nissley/. He was born 14 Dec 1930[7914], and died Jun 1990[7914].

Notes for Wanetia Katie Miller:
The Descendants of John J. Christner, privately published February 1961, pp., 21, 23.

Freeman was Old Order Amish. Freeman operated an international cattle trading business with a partner Paul Neely. This business was located on State Road 5 south of Shipshewana, IN. Calves were purchased from Canada. Cows were sold to Saudia Arabia, California,Texas, etc.

Notes for Freeman D. Eash:
The Descendants of John J. Christner, privately published February 1961, p. 23.

More About Freeman D. Eash:
Occupation: Farmer/
Religion: Old Order Amish/
Social Security Number: 312-30-5241/[7914]
SSN issued: IN[7914]

Children of Wanetia Miller and Freeman Eash are:
    5122   i.   Wilbur Lee[10] Eash, born 23 Aug 1952.

                    Notes for Wilbur Lee Eash:
                    The Descendants of John J. Christner, privately published February 1961, p. 23.

    5123   ii.   Kathryn Eash, born 19 Oct 1953.

                    Notes for Kathryn Eash:
                    The Descendants of John J. Christner, privately published February 1961, p. 23.

    5124   iii. Loretta Mae Eash, born 30 Dec 1955.

                    Notes for Loretta Mae Eash:
                    The Descendants of John J. Christner, privately published February 1961, p. 23.

    5125   iv. Jerry Wayne Eash, born 19 Feb 1958.

                    Notes for Jerry Wayne Eash:
                    The Descendants of John J. Christner, privately published February 1961, p. 23.

    5126   v.   Orla Eash, born 16 Feb 1959.

                    Notes for Orla Eash:
                    The Descendants of John J. Christner, privately published February 1961, p. 23.

2820. Edna Ellen[9] Miller (Katie D.[8] Christner, David J.[7], John J.[6], Joseph C.[5], Christian J.[4], Johannes John Hans[3], Christian[2], Christen[1]) was born 08 Mar 1935 in Topeka, Lagrange Co., IN. She married **William D. Miller** 03 Dec 1953 in by David Nissley/Lagrange Co., IN. He was born 08 Aug 1934 in Lagrange Co., IN, and died 26 Apr 2004 in Middlebury, Elkhart Co., IN.

Notes for Edna Ellen Miller:
The Descendants of John J. Christner, privately published February 1961, pp. 21, 23.

Notes for William D. Miller:
Farmer and Livestock Hauler or farm animal trucker. Ordained May 8 1966 as a Deacon Fairhaven Amish Mennonite Church at Goshen, Indiana. Funeral Service at Woodlawn Amish Mennonite Church at Goshen, Indiana with Bishop Wilber Yoder, Revs. Dan B. Miller, Neal Beachy and Dale Hochstetler Officiating.

More About William D. Miller:
Burial: 29 Apr 2004, Thomas Cemetery   Goshen, Indiana
Occupation: Farmer/
Religion: Old Order Amish/

Children of Edna Miller and William Miller are:
    5127   i.   Maynard[10] Miller. He married Rhoda.

                    Notes for Maynard Miller:
                    The Descendants of John J. Christner, privately published February 1961, p. 23.

    5128   ii.   Glen Wayne Miller, born 20 Apr 1955. He married Esther.

                    Notes for Glen Wayne Miller:
                    The Descendants of John J. Christner, privately published February 1961, p. 23.

5129   iii.   Wilbur Dean Miller, born 21 Oct 1957. He married Marilyn.

        Notes for Wilbur Dean Miller:
        The Descendants of John J. Christner, privately published February 1961, p. 23.

2821. Leo M.[9] **Yoder** (Emma D.[8] Christner, David J.[7], John J.[6], Joseph C.[5], Christian J.[4], Johannes John Hans[3], Christian[2], Christen[1]) was born 13 Oct 1911 in Topeka, Lagrange Co., IN, and died 19 Apr 1997 in at his home Lagrange Co, IN   N41°37.750' by W85°28.375'. He married **Mima Luella Miller** 30 Nov 1933. She was born 20 Mar 1914, and died 18 Apr 1991.

Notes for Leo M. Yoder:
The Descendants of John J. Christner, privately published February 1961, pp. 23, 92.

Lived at 0890 South & 250 West LaGrange Co., IN. He was old order Amish & a farmer. He Died at his home at 4:50 P.M. Saturday.

More About Leo M. Yoder:
Burial: Miller Cemetery, Lagrange Co., IN
Occupation: Farmer/
Religion: Old Order Amish/

Notes for Mima Luella Miller:
The Descendants of John J. Christner, privately published February 1961, pp. 23, 92.

Children of Leo Yoder and Mima Miller are:
+   5130   i.   John Jay[10] Yoder, born 24 Feb 1935 in Lagrange Co., IN.
+   5131   ii.   Susie Elizabeth Yoder, born 02 Apr 1938 in Lagrange Co., IN.
+   5132   iii.   Edna Mae Yoder, born 06 Feb 1940.
    5133   iv.   Mary Ellen Yoder, born 24 Oct 1942.

        Notes for Mary Ellen Yoder:
        The Descendants of John J. Christner, privately published February 1961, p. 23.

    5134   v.   Alta Marie Yoder, born 06 Oct 1947.

        Notes for Alta Marie Yoder:
        The Descendants of John J. Christner, privately published February 1961, p. 23.

    5135   vi.   Katie Irene Yoder, born 26 May 1957.

        Notes for Katie Irene Yoder:
        The Descendants of John J. Christner, privately published February 1961, p. 23.

2822. Susanna M.[9] **Yoder** (Emma D.[8] Christner, David J.[7], John J.[6], Joseph C.[5], Christian J.[4], Johannes John Hans[3], Christian[2], Christen[1]) was born 18 Feb 1913 in Lagrange, Lagrange Co., IN. She married **Joseph J. Miller**[7915] 12 Mar 1936 in By Cornelius D Christner, son of Joseph Miller and Sarah Troyer. He was born 28 Dec 1911 in Lagrange Co., IN[7915], and died Apr 1986 in Luzerne, PA[7915].

Notes for Susanna M. Yoder:
The Descendants of John J. Christner, privately published February 1961, p. 23.

Notes for Joseph J. Miller:
The Descendants of John J. Christner, privately published February 1961, p. 62.

More About Joseph J. Miller:
Occupation: Farmer/

Religion: Old Order Amish/

Child of Susanna Yoder and Joseph Miller is:
+   5136   i.   Edna Ellen[10] Miller, born 20 Feb 1940 in Lagrange Co., IN.

2823.   Edna M.[9] Yoder (Emma D.[8] Christner, David J.[7], John J.[6], Joseph C.[5], Christian J.[4], Johannes John Hans[3], Christian[2], Christen[1]) was born 06 Aug 1914 in Lagrange, Lagrange Co., IN, and died 30 Aug 1982 in Lagrange Co., IN. She married **Menno Schlabach**[7916] 10 Feb 1938 in By Cornelius Christner. He was born 06 Nov 1913 in Lagrange Co., IN[7916,7917], and died 03 Feb 1978[7918,7919].

Notes for Edna M. Yoder:
The Descendants of John J. Christner, privately published February 1961, p. 24.

More About Edna M. Yoder:
Burial: Miller Cemetery, Lagrange Co., IN

Notes for Menno Schlabach:
The Descendants of John J. Christner, privately published February 1961, p. 24.

More About Menno Schlabach:
Occupation: Farmer/
Religion: Old Order Amish/[7919]
Residence: 1930, Clay, Lagrange Co., IN[7920]

Children of Edna Yoder and Menno Schlabach are:
     5137   i.   Susie LuElla[10] Schlabach, born 20 Sep 1940.

               Notes for Susie LuElla Schlabach:
               The Descendants of John J. Christner, privately published February 1961, p. 24.

     5138   ii.   Raymond Schlabach, born 17 Apr 1943.

               Notes for Raymond Schlabach:
               The Descendants of John J. Christner, privately published February 1961, p. 24.

     5139   iii.   Harley Schlabach, born 06 Jun 1947.

               Notes for Harley Schlabach:
               The Descendants of John J. Christner, privately published February 1961, p. 24.

2824.   John M.[9] Yoder (Emma D.[8] Christner, David J.[7], John J.[6], Joseph C.[5], Christian J.[4], Johannes John Hans[3], Christian[2], Christen[1]) was born 21 Jun 1917 in Lagrange, Lagrange Co., IN, and died 12 Dec 1993 in Lagrange Co., IN. He married **Alta Marie Wingard**[7921] 23 Nov 1939, daughter of Levi Wingard and Amanda Christner. She was born 16 Jun 1915 in Lagrange Co., IN[7921], and died 17 Apr 1991 in Goshen General, Hospital, Goshen, Elkhart Co., IN.

Notes for John M. Yoder:
The Descendants of John J. Christner, privately published February 1961, pp. 23, 24.

Burial Miller Cemetery, Lagrange, IN. He is Old Order Amish Farmer.

More About John M. Yoder:
Religion: Old Order Amish/

Notes for Alta Marie Wingard:
The Descendants of John J. Christner, privately published February 1961, pp. 24, 49.

John is the son of Meno J. S. and Emma Christner Yoder.

More About Alta Marie Wingard:
Burial: Miller Cem, Lagrange, IN

Children of John Yoder and Alta Wingard are:

5140   i.   Wilma Amanda[10] Yoder, born 12 Dec 1941.

            Notes for Wilma Amanda Yoder:
            The Descendants of John J. Christner, privately published February 1961, p. 24.

5141   ii.   Edna Marie Yoder, born 25 Dec 1943.

            Notes for Edna Marie Yoder:
            The Descendants of John J. Christner, privately published February 1961, p. 24.

5142   iii.   Anna Mae Yoder, born 01 Jun 1946.

            Notes for Anna Mae Yoder:
            The Descendants of John J. Christner, privately published February 1961, p. 24.

5143   iv.   Ida Carolyn Yoder, born 14 Nov 1954.

            Notes for Ida Carolyn Yoder:
            The Descendants of John J. Christner, privately published February 1961, p. 24.

2825. Levi M.[9] **Yoder** (Emma D.[8] Christner, David J.[7], John J.[6], Joseph C.[5], Christian J.[4], Johannes John Hans[3], Christian[2], Christen[1]) was born 06 Apr 1920 in Topeka, Lagrange Co., IN. He married **Annie L. Schrock** 12 Dec 1940, daughter of Levi Schrock and Mary Schlabach. She was born 19 Jan 1920.

Notes for Levi M. Yoder:
The Descendants of John J. Christner, privately published February 1961, pp. 23, 25.

Anna was the daughter of Levi J. and Mary Schlabaugh Schrock.

More About Levi M. Yoder:
Religion: Old Order Amish/

Notes for Annie L. Schrock:
The Descendants of John J. Christner, privately published February 1961, p. 25.

Children of Levi Yoder and Annie Schrock are:

5144   i.   Ervin Leroy[10] Yoder, born 16 Mar 1941.

            Notes for Ervin Leroy Yoder:
            The Descendants of John J. Christner, privately published February 1961, p. 24.

5145   ii.   Mary Alice Yoder, born 12 Jan 1943.

            Notes for Mary Alice Yoder:
            The Descendants of John J. Christner, privately published February 1961, p. 24.

5146   iii.   Viola Pauline Yoder, born 16 Apr 1944.

5147   iv.   Alton Laverne Yoder, born 25 Aug 1947.

Notes for Alton Laverne Yoder:
The Descendants of John J. Christner, privately published February 1961, p. 24.

5148   v.   Lydia Mae Yoder, born 26 Apr 1950.

Notes for Lydia Mae Yoder:
The Descendants of John J. Christner, privately published February 1961, p. 24.

5149   vi.   Sue Ellen Yoder, born 17 Jan 1953.

Notes for Sue Ellen Yoder:
The Descendants of John J. Christner, privately published February 1961, p. 24.

2826. Cornelius M.[9] Yoder (Emma D.[8] Christner, David J.[7], John J.[6], Joseph C.[5], Christian J.[4], Johannes John Hans[3], Christian[2], Christen[1]) was born 29 Dec 1922 in Topeka, Lagrange Co., IN, and died 03 Oct 2000 in Topeka, Lagrange Co, IN. He married **(1) Katie M. Yoder**[7922] 10 Feb 1944 in Topeka, Lagrange Co., IN. She was born 18 Jan 1922 in Lagrange Co., IN[7922], and died 23 Jul 1990 in Lagrange Co., IN[7922]. He married **(2) Mildred Stutzman** 01 Aug 1993 in Topeka, Lagrange Co., IN.

Notes for Cornelius M. Yoder:
The Descendants of John J. Christner, privately published February 1961, pp. 23, 25.

Cornelius was a farmer and Old Order Amish.

More About Cornelius M. Yoder:
Burial: Miller Cem, Lagrange Co, IN. N41°35.348'xW85°28.937'
Occupation: Farmer/
Religion: Old Order Amish/

Notes for Katie M. Yoder:
The Descendants of John J. Christner, privately published February 1961, p. 25.

More About Katie M. Yoder:
Alt. Birth: 18 Jan 1922[7922]

Children of Cornelius Yoder and Katie Yoder are:
    5150   i.   Elva Jay[10] Yoder, born 08 Nov 1944.

        Notes for Elva Jay Yoder:
        The Descendants of John J. Christner, privately published February 1961, p. 25.

    5151   ii.   Amelia Viola Yoder, born 13 Sep 1947.

        Notes for Amelia Viola Yoder:
        The Descendants of John J. Christner, privately published February 1961, p. 25.

    5152   iii.   Daniel C. Yoder, born 23 Oct 1953; died 26 Oct 1953.

        Notes for Daniel C. Yoder:
        The Descendants of John J. Christner, privately published February 1961, p. 25.

5153   iv.   Perry C. Yoder, born 04 Oct 1955.

Notes for Perry C. Yoder:
The Descendants of John J. Christner, privately published February 1961, p. 25.

5154   v.   Elsie Mae Yoder, born 11 Dec 1956.

Notes for Elsie Mae Yoder:
The Descendants of John J. Christner, privately published February 1961, p. 25.

2828. Menno L.[9] **Christner** (Levi D.[8], David J.[7], John J.[6], Joseph C.[5], Christian J.[4], Johannes John Hans[3], Christian[2], Christen[1])[7923,7923] was born 15 Feb 1917 in Topeka, Lagrange Co., IN[7923,7923,7924], and died 11 Feb 1995 in Moulton, Lawrence Co., AL[7925]. He married **(1) Mary Beachy** 08 Nov 1936 in Lagrange Co., IN Divorced July 1946, daughter of Alvin Beachy and Mary Christner. She was born 24 May 1918. He married **(2) Eva Lee Kennedy** 11 Mar 1950 in Lexington, NC. She was born 05 Apr 1921 in Thomasville, NC[7926], and died 02 Feb 1988 in Home, Wawaka, IN[7926].

Notes for Menno L. Christner:
The Descendants of John J. Christner, privately published February 1961, p.,25.

Menno was a bee keeper and lived in Wawaka, IN. He once said that he had a $500.00 queen bee.

SS#306-16-5407 ISS IN

Mennos 1st wife Mary Beachy was the granddaughter of Just Christner. This Christner is the same man related to Edna Christner Schlabaugh Christner.

Menno Christner died Feb. 11, 1995 at Decatur General Hospital, Decatur, Ala. Born in Topeka, he was a former Wawaka resident. He was a beekeeper and worked for boat manufacturers. He was a WW II U.S. Navy veteran. Surviving are his wife, Lillian; 3 sons, Rick of Elkhart, Lloyd of Walkerton and Alvin of Philadelphia; a daughter, Carol Minier of Ligonier; 4 brothers, Dave of Wolcottville, Sam of Nappanee, Lee of Goshen and Arthur of Topeka; 3 sisters, Lizzie Miller of Goshen, Sue Christner of Millersburg and Mary Fereva of Reno, NV and 13 grandchildren. Graveside services Thursday at Cosperville Cemetery.

More About Menno L. Christner:
Burial: [7927]
Residence: 1930, Clearspring, Lagrange Co., IN[7928]
Social Security Number: 306-16-5407/[7928]
SSN issued: IN[7928]

Notes for Mary Beachy:
The Descendants of John J. Christner, privately published February 1961, p. 25.

Mary Beachy is the daughter of Alvin Beachy and Mary Christner. This Mary Christner may not be related to our line of Christners. Mary Beachy is the granddaughter of Joseph Christner. Most of the notes have a nickname for Joseph as Just Christner.

Divorced in July 1946.

Notes for Eva Lee Kennedy:
The Descendants of John J. Christner, privately published February 1961, p. 25.

Eva was the daughter of Thomas Kennedy and Ida Elizabeth Tesh Stricklin. Eva had a child Thomas Kennedy born May 23, 1937 in Thomasville, NC. This child was raised by Menno but he never was adopted and he never carried the Christner name. Thomas died Mar 28, 1974 carbon monxide poisioning.

Eva worked at Essex Wire in Ligonier and Topeka IN she made wire harness for automobiles Eva lived in Wawaka for 25 years. Burial at Cosperville Cemetary She had a sister Bertha Lackey.

Birth: Apr. 5, 1921 - Thomasville, Davidson Co., NC
Death: 1988 - Wawaka, Noble Co., IN

Eva Christner died Tuesday at her residence. She was born April 5, 1921 in Thomasville, NC the daughter of Thomas and Ida Kennedy. On March 11, 1905 in Lexington, NC she married Menno L. Christner. A Wawaka resident since 1963, she was a former employee of Essex Wire, Ligonier. Surviving are her husband; a daughter, Carol Minier of Ligonier; two sons, Rick of Elkhart and Lloyd of LaPorte; a stepson, Dale Chistner of Philadelphia; a sister, Bertha Lackey of Thomasville; and eight grandchildren. One son preceded her in death. Services Friday in Ulrey-Renner Funeral Home, Ligonier. Burial Cosperville Cemetery

Spouse: Menno Christner (1917 - 1995)

Burial: Cosperville Cemetery, Wawaka, Noble Co., IN
Plot: 2-10

More About Eva Lee Kennedy:
Burial: 05 Feb 1988, Cosperville Cemetery, Wawaka, Noble Co., IN
Social Security Number: 238-30-0083/[7929]
SSN issued: NC[7929]

Child of Menno Christner and Mary Beachy is:
+ 5155   i.   Alvin Dale[10] Christner, born 21 Aug 1943 in Sturgis, St. Joseph Co., MI; died 14 Dec 2006 in Philadelphia, Philadelphia Co., PA.

Children of Menno Christner and Eva Kennedy are:
+ 5156   i.   Carolyn Sue[10] Christner, born 24 Mar 1953 in New Castle, Henry Co., IN.
   5157   ii.   Rickie Joe Christner, born 22 Nov 1955 in Lagrange, Lagrange Co., IN.

       Notes for Rickie Joe Christner:
       The Descendants of John J. Christner, privately published February 1961, p. 25.

       More About Rickie Joe Christner:
       Occupation: Welder at Hummer H-2 truck plant/

+ 5158   iii.   Lloyd Wayne Christner, born 07 Jan 1959 in Lagrange, Lagrange Co., IN; died 29 Oct 2004 in Elkhart, Elkhart Co., IN.

2829. Lizzie Ann[9] Christner (Levi D.[8], David J.[7], John J.[6], Joseph C.[5], Christian J.[4], Johannes John Hans[3], Christian[2], Christen[1])[7930] was born 17 Jul 1918 in Topeka, Lagrange Co., IN[7930,7930], and died 22 Dec 1999 in Goshen, Elkhart Co., IN[7930,7930]. She married **Valentine Miller** 24 Dec 1938. He was born 14 Feb 1912 in Kokomo, Howard Co., IN, and died 28 Jan 1974.

Notes for Lizzie Ann Christner:
The Descendants of John J. Christner, privately published February 1961, p. 25.

Miller - Lizzie Ann Christner, 82 Goshen, IN died Dec. 22. Spouse: Valentine Miller (deceased). Parents: Levi and Goldie O'Neil Christner (deceased). Survivors: children Goldie Yoder, Sarah, Arthur, Verlin, Raymond. Funeral: Dec. 27 at Clinton Frame Mennonite Church, Goshen.

More About Lizzie Ann Christner:
Burial: 27 Dec 1999, Bainertown Cemetary Elkhart Co. IN
Occupation: Nurses Aid Goshen Gen.Hospital/
Residence: 01 Apr 1940, Jackson, Elkhart, Indiana, United States[7931]

Notes for Valentine Miller:
The Descendants of John J. Christner, privately published February 1961, p. 25.

Val was the son of Menno J. born May 13, 1868 and Sarah J. Schlabaugh Miller born Dec 5, 1878. Menno J. is the son of Jacob S. and Catherine Troyer Miller. Val was in construction all his life.

More About Valentine Miller:
Burial: 31 Jan 1974, Baintertown Cem, New Paris, ELKHART CO, IN
Residence: 01 Apr 1940, Jackson, Elkhart, Indiana, United States[7931]

Children of Lizzie Christner and Valentine Miller are:

+	5159	i.	Sarah Bernith[10] Miller, born 25 Sep 1939 in Shipshewana, Lagrange Co., IN.
+	5160	ii.	Goldie Edith Miller, born 25 Sep 1939 in Shipshewana, Lagrange Co., IN.
+	5161	iii.	Arthur LaVoid Miller, born 26 Feb 1942 in New Paris, Elkhart Co., IN.
+	5162	iv.	David Leroy Miller, born 26 Feb 1942 in New Paris, Elkhart Co., IN; died 06 Mar 1987 in Home.
+	5163	v.	Verlin Lamar Miller, born 07 Dec 1943 in New Paris, Elkhart Co., IN.
+	5164	vi.	Raymond Lavon Miller, born 24 Nov 1944 in Elkhart, Elkhart Co., IN.

2830. Susanna L.[9] Christner (Levi D.[8], David J.[7], John J.[6], Joseph C.[5], Christian J.[4], Johannes John Hans[3], Christian[2], Christen[1])[7932] was born 05 Aug 1919 in Topeka, Lagrange Co., IN[7932,7933], and died 12 Nov 2010 in Topeka, Lagrange Co., IN[7934]. She married **Carl I. Christner**[7935] 25 Apr 1942 in Goshen, Elkhart Co., IN, son of Ira Christner and Sylvia Swartzentruber. He was born 24 Mar 1921 in Honeyville, Lagrange Co., IN[7935], and died 09 Apr 2005 in Goshen, Elkhart Co., IN.

Notes for Susanna L. Christner:
Sue sold Dutchmaid* clothing from 1967 to 1972. Sue started her own quilt business in 1975. She sold old and new quilts all over the USA. She has had a number of quilts put into the national quilt registry and her mothers quilt called "jonny round the corner" has been featured on the cover of a number of national magazines. The Quilt Show has held it's 33rd year in 2007.
Sue and Carl were 2nd cousins.
She loved flowers and plants and always had a great interest in genealogy. She attended a one room school with only an outside toilet, called Wortinger School which was a one mile walk from her home. She thinks it was one mile up hill both ways. In the winter the wind blew in her face going to school and back home. The school was located at the southeast corner of W300S and S500W Lagrange Co. Indiana N41°35.8413' by W85°31.2186

Home of Carl & Sue Christner Located at Honeyville, LaGrange Co., Indiana.N41°34.183-W85°36.474 - on County Road 950W - just north of 500S or ¾ mile south of the Honeyville store. Abe Christner & Mary Yoder lived here when they got married in 1914; they planted the Yucca & Poppies that are still growing there. The home was torn down about 1986 to make way for a new home. Sue's father was Levi D. Christner born 8/20/1897 & Carl's father was Ira J. Christner born 3/27/1897 his father was Joseph J. Christner born 2/19/1851 his father was John J. Christner born 11/24/1827. John J Christner was the first Christner to own the home in the photo. The home had a tin roof & as I (Steven Carl Christner) was born in the northwest corner of this home, I remember it getting hit with lightning often. I remember when I was about 12 years old, my brother (Larry) & me were in our bedroom upstairs when lightning hit. Larry was standing in front of the window & I could only see his skeleton. I screamed like a little girl & made it down the stairs only touching 2 steps. Once it blow the Telephone right off the wall in pieces. I can't remember every having a roof leak except around the chimney in all those years.
I remember when we got hot & cold running water inside the house but the biggest deal was when we got a toilet in the house. This I thought was really great as it was my job to empty the pot in the morning. My grandfather Ira tried to explain how this toilet was going to work, I was still puzzled but hopeful this could be possible. For those that don't know what a POT is, it is a container to go into in the middle of the night so you don't have to go to the OUT house, OH, you don't know what a outhouse is, well we had small one holer.

Obituary: Aug. 5, 1919-Nov. 12, 2010
MILLERSBURG - Sue L. Christner, formerly of 4860S. 950 West, died Friday at 12:15 a.m. at the home of her sister-inlaw, Gladys Christner, 5380 W. 400 South, Topeka. She had been in declining health and was seriously ill the past three weeks. She was born Aug. 5; 1919 in Topeka, to Levi D. and Goldie (O'Neil Eash) Christner She was a homemaker and a lifelong resident of the Topeka and Millersburg areas. She was a longtime member

of North Goshen Mennonite Church. Sue sold Dutchmaid clothing from 1967 until 1972 and started her own quilt business in 1975, selling old and new quilts all over the United States. She had a number ofquilts put into the National Quilt Registry. Her mother's quilt, called "Jonnie Round the Corner" was displayed at the Indiana State Museum, Indianapolis, and appeared on the cover of the Indiana Historical Society magazine, "Traces." She loved flowers and plants and always had a great interest in genealogy. she married Carl I Christner April 25, 1942. He died April 9, 2005. She is survived by her two sons, Steve (Tracey) Christner, Goshen, and Larry (Anita) Christner, Topeka; four grandchildren; six great-grandchildren; and a brother, Samuel Christner, Leesburg. She was preceded in death by five sisters, Lizzie Ann Miller, Emma Hostetler, Edith Lyon, Goldie L. Christner and Mary Fereva; and seven brothers, Menno L., Christian L., Amos L., John Levi, David A., Levi Lee and Arthur L. Christner. Friends may call Sunday from 2 to 4 and 6 to 8 p.m. at Maple Grove Church, Topeka, where a funeral service will take place Monday at 2:30 p.m. The Rev. Dean Linsenmeyer of North Goshen Mennonite Church will officiate. Burial will be in Town Line Cemetery, Topeka. Pallbearers will be John Kozinski, Kevin Christner, Allen Reiling, Dean Christner, Chuck Christner and Cletus Schwartz. Memorial donations can be made to North Goshen Mennonite Church. Yoder-Culp Funeral Home, Goshen, is assisting the family with arrangements.

Birth: Aug. 5, 1919
Topeka, Lagrange Co., IN
Death: Nov. 12, 2010
Elkhart Co., IN

Obituary:
Sue L. Christner, 91, died at home early Friday morning, November 12, 2010.
She was born August 5, 1919, in Topeka to Levi D. and Goldie (O'niel Eash) Christner. She married Carl Christner on April 25, 1942, in Goshen. He died April 9, 2005.
She is survived by two sons, Steve (Tracey) Christner of Goshen, and Larry (Anita) Christner of Topeka; four grandchildren; six great-grandchildren; and a brother Samuel Christner of Leesburg.
She was preceded in death by sisters, Lizzie Ann Miller, Emma Hostetler, Edith Lyon, Goldie L. Christner, and Mary Fereva; and brothers, Menno L., Christian L., Amos L., John Levi, David A., Levi Lee and Arthur L. Christner.
A homemaker and lifelong resident of the Topeka/Millersburg area, Mrs. Christner was a longtime member of North Goshen Mennonite Church. Mrs. Christner sold Dutchmaid clothing from 1967-1972. In 1975 she started her own quilt business, selling old and new quilts all over the USA. She has had a number number of quilts put into the national quilt registry and her mother's quilt called "Jonnie Round the Corner" was displayed at the Indiana State Museum, Indianapolis, and appeared on the cover of the Indiana Historical Society Magazine "Traces". She loved flowers and plants and had a great interest in genealogy.

Friends may call 2 to 4 and 6 to 8 p.m., Sunday, November 14, at Maple Grove Mennonite Church, Topeka.

A 2:30 p.m., funeral service will be conducted on Monday, November 15, 2010, at the Maple Grove Mennonite Church, Topeka. Pastor Dean Linsenmeyer of North Goshen Mennonite Church will officiate.

Burial will follow in Town Line Cemetery, Topeka. Memorials may be made to North Goshen Mennonite Church.

Spouse: Carl I. Christner (1921 - 2005)

Burial: Town Line Cemetery, Topeka, Lagrange Co., IN

Obituary - Mennonite Obits
Christner, Sue L. Christner, 91, of Millersburg, IN died November 12, 2010 at the same place. She was born August 5, 1919 at Topeka, IN to Levi D. and Goldie (O'Niel Eash) Christner. On April 25, 1942 at Goshen, IN she was married to Carl I. Christner, who died April 9, 2005.

Surviving are two sons, Steve (Tracey) Christner and Larry (Anita) Christner,
4 grandchildren, 6 great-grandchildren, and a brother, Samuel Christner.

Her brothers and sisters, Lizzie Ann Miller, Emma Hostetler, Edith Lyon, Goldie L. Christner, Mary Fereva, Menno L. Christner, Christian L. Christner, Amos L. Christner, John Levi Christner, David A. Christner, Levi Lee Christner, and Arthur L. Christner preceded her in death.

A homemaker and lifelong resident of the Topeka/Millersburg area, Mrs. Christner was a longtime member of North Goshen Mennonite Church. Mrs. Christner sold Dutchmaid clothing from 1967 to 1972. In 1975, she started her own quilt business, selling old and new quilts all over the U.S.A. She had a number of quilts put into the national quilt registry, and her mother's quilt called "Jonnie Round the Corner" was displayed at the Indiana State Museum, Indianapolis, and appeared on the cover of the Indiana Historical Society magazine "Traces." She loved flowers and plants and had a great interest in genealogy.

Memorials may be given to North Goshen Mennonite Church.

Memorial services were held November 15, 2010 at Maple Grove Church, Topeka IN with burial in Town Line Cemetary, Topeka, IN.

The Descendants of John J. Christner, privately published February 1961, p. 16.

More About Susanna L. Christner:
Residence: 1930, Clearspring, Lagrange Co., IN[7936]
SSN issued: IN[7937]

Notes for Carl I. Christner:
Carl farmed for his father until 1943 Hhe went to South Dakota & worked on Deerfield Dam-Hill city, SD for his conscientious objector obligation. Returned in 1944 & farmed again for his father. He hauled milk from Topeka, IN. to Cleveland, OH 7 days a week for 5 & 1/2 half years. He also was a lumberjack for 5 years. He worked for the Indiana State Highway for 15 years. Raised hogs & farmed his own 40 acres in Honeyville IN. Hobbies Fishing, Carl was always an extremist in everything. #1 Ate a large meal then on a bet ate a gallon of ice cream at the Honeyvill Store won the bet then ate an ice cream cone.#2 Fed hogs so well with protein they got sick& the vet.had to give them shots & told Carl not to be so nice to them. #3 He dieted to extremes weighing from 270 lbs,to 160 lbs. He ate only grapefruit for 3 months. He was a lot of fun & was loved by everyone. He had a rare gift for making friends with old & young people. Hard worker One person you can truly say was a good father,husband & grandfather.

Carl was burning weeds along his fence line Sep 19, 1995 on his farm with a jug of gasoline when he spilled some on his leg and it caught fire, burning his leg. He was in the hospital for 2 months and got a lung infection. This problem led to his heart enlarging and being on oxygen for the rest of his life. He could not sleep laying down so he slept in a recliner for over 40 years.

When Carl & Sue were older (in their late 70's) they had company 7 days a week. The Amish neighbors brought prepared food three days a week and cleaned the house, mowed the lawn. Relatives, neighbors, church members, their son's, and friends were there. Some days there would be 4 or 5 different couples visiting.

Memories of Carl by Jerry Wittrig
I first met Carl Christner in 1968, the year Ruth Ann and I started attending North Goshen Mennonite Church.

I still remember the first time I shook hands with Carl. My hand was totally enveloped by his and I felt a grip that could surely have crushed my hand with ease.

My first thoughts were of my grandfather. He was the only other person I had known who had forearms and hands the size of Carl's.

It was some 20 years later I became aware there was a reason Carl's hands and arms were similar to my grandfather's. They were related. I found that Carl and I have several common ancestors who lived in the Amish-Mennonite settlements in the Alsase.

There is a story told about one of our ancestors in that Alsase that was reputed to have been very strong. One day

he was going to the village on the back of his donkey. The donkey refused to cross a small stream that had been swollen by the Spring rains. Our ancestor is said to have picked up the donkey and carried it across the stream and continued on his way. When Carl was a young man, I could see him doing something like that!
Carl inherited the strong work ethic of his ancestors. He particularly loved the soil and enjoyed working with his hands. He enjoyed telling me stories about the field of mint he grew many years ago.

Carl loved all of God's creation, great or small. He loved the sight of his neighbors with a team of horses preparing the ground in the Spring of the year for the planting of corn or beans.

He loved the fish God had created to inhabit the lakes and streams of Northern Indiana.

He loved the birds, especially the purple martins that he fed and cared for in his yard.

Carl always had a hearty appetite and many conversations would include talking about food. When I would visit him during the last few years of his live he would often comment about the wonderful food that his neighbor had brought to share with Sue and himself.

He would put "way too much pepper" on his hamburger just to get a comment from his grand daughters.

My favorite food story took place when Carl was in the Goshen Hospital about two years ago. I was visiting him one day and he commented, "Jerry, they just don't feed me enough here in the hospital. And the food they give me just isn't very good."

I replied, "Carl, what are you really hungry for?
He said, "Onion rings, I would really like some good onion rings."
I said, "Carl, I'll be back in 15 minutes." I went to Dairy Queen and brought back an order of onion rings. Carl's hands were not very steady, so I fed him the order of onion rings which he enjoyed to the very last bite.
Just as he finished, the nurse came into the room. There was Carl with a big grin on his face and crumbs from the onion rings all over the front of his shirt. The nurse just smiled, shook her heard and said, Carl, I won't tell a soul!

To know Carl was to have a friend. Whether you were young or old, Carl had a way of making you feel at home and a part of the family.
Argus and Nancy Myers were friends of Carl and Sue from the North Goshen Church. Argus was 90- years old and Nancy was 92. One day when Ruth Ann and I were visiting them, Argus mentioned how much he missed visiting with Carl and Sue.

We said, "Well let's go over and visit them. Ruth Ann and I will pick you up and take you over to Honeyville. We set up the arrangements and picked them up at their home in New Paris. On the way, Argus reminded us, " I can't stay long, I have to keep my feet up because of my circulation problems in my legs. About 15 minutes is about all I can handle."

More than an hour later we finally got Argus back in the car for the trip back to New Paris. This special visit was all he could talk about for the next several weeks. He had visited with his friend Carl one last time.
Carl knew just about everyone that lived in the Honeyville area and nearly everyone knew Carl. He was affectionately called "The Mayor of Honeyville", a title I think he rather enjoyed.

Carl had a quiet confident faith that the promises God made in this book were true and they applied to him. He believed in Jesus as his personal Savior and that relationship became more real with each passing year. He knew when the struggles of this life were over, there was something better ahead.

He summed it up so well last week when he said, "Mom, I think it's time to move to God's house."

I can imagine Carl today, free for the first time in years from the limits of declining health and the length of the oxygen tube, renewing friendships and praising his Lord and Savior.

And Sue, there is one more reunion he is waiting for. Nearly 63 years you and Carl were married. What a wonderful testimony! Someday soon he will "meet you in the morning just inside the Eastern Gate." And I think

Carl will probably say, "Mom, what took you so long?"

Birth: Mar. 24, 1921
Death: Apr. 9, 2005

Carl I. Christner, 84, died Saturday, April 9th 2005 at Goshen General Hospital.

He was born March 24, 1921, in Honeyville, to Ira and Sylvia (Swartzentruber) Christner.

Spouse: Sue L Christner Christner (1919 - 2010)

Burial: Town Line Cemetery, Topeka, Lagrange Co., IN

The Mennonite, May 3, 2005, pages 25-26, Vol. 8, No. 9.
Christner.- Carl I., 84, Millersburg, Ind., died April 9. Spouse: Sue Christner. Parents: Ira and Sylvia Swartzentruber Christner. Children: Steven C., Larry; four grandchildren; six great-grandchildren. Funeral: April 12 at Maple Grove Mennonite Church, Topeka, IN.

The Descendants of John J. Christner, privately published February 1961, p. 16.

More About Carl I. Christner:
Burial: Pallbears=Chuck/Todd/Dean/Don Christner-Jackson Roe-Dick Graber
Funeral Service: 12 Apr 2005, Rev. Jerry Wittrig & Rev. Art Smoker of North Goshen Mennonite Church
Religion: Mennonite/
Social Security Number: 315-20-6366/[7938]
SSN issued: IN[7938]

Children are listed above under (2760) Carl I. Christner.

2831. David L.[9] Christner (Levi D.[8], David J.[7], John J.[6], Joseph C.[5], Christian J.[4], Johannes John Hans[3], Christian[2], Christen[1])[7939,7940,7941] was born 29 Mar 1921 in Lagrange Co., IN[7942,7943], and died 10 Nov 2010 in Wolcottville, Lagrange Co., IN[7944]. He married **Lois Lucille Heilman** 19 Mar 1947 in Old Fort, OH, daughter of Norman Heilman and Irene Henretty. She was born 21 Dec 1926 in Old Fort, OH.

Notes for David L. Christner:
The Descendants of John J. Christner, privately published February 1961, p., 25.

David & Lois had a long career or occupation as dairy milk testers. Testing was for numerous criteria. The volume of mathamatics was quite extensive, this nessesitated the purchase of many mecanical calculating machines as electric calculators were not yet availible.

Wolcottville LaGrange Co. IN resident David L. Christner said he has been "just doing the Lord's work" by leading worship services for more than 20 years.

Mr. Christner was named the 1997 Lagrange Co. Citizen of the year during Corn School festivites.

A member of Shipshewana Church of the Nazarene, Mr. Christner has been quietly volunteering his time in numerous areas over the years. At the Shipshe wana church Mr Christner used his wood working skills to create bulletin boards, storage cabinets and cupboards. He has traveled within the United States and abroad under the Church of the Nazarene Work and Witness Program to assist in building programs. He has also served with the Gideons and distributed New Testaments in schools and Bibles in various nursing homes throughout the community. Mr Christner served his country in WWII.

Birth: Mar. 28, 1921 - IN
Death: Nov. 10, 2010 - IN

David L. Christner, 89 of Wolcottville transferred to Heaven Wednesday, November 10, 2010, from his home on Messick Lake.

He was born March 28, 1921, in Topeka to Levi D. and Goldie O'Neil (Eash) Christner. On March 19, 1946, in Old Fort, Ohio, he married Lois Heilman.

He had lived in the Wolcottville area for the past 52 years. He retired from Duo-Therm in LaGrange where he did general repair and maintenance.

He was a member of the Shipshewana Church of the Nazarene. He was named Lagrange County Citizen of the Year in 1997 for conducting worship services for 25 years at Miller's Merry Manor in Lagrange.

He was a member of the Gideon's, and enjoyed fishing and woodworking. He was a veteran of the U.S. Army.

David is survived by his wife of 64 years, Lois; two sons, Michael E. Christner, Kalamazoo, Michigan, and D. John Christner and wife, Trudy of Noblesville; five grandchildren, Candy, Mindy, Michelle, Chad, and Jaime; nine great grandchildren; brother, Sam Christner; and sister, Sue Christner.

He was preceded in death by his parents, an infant daughter, Betty Lee Christner; sisters, Lizzie Miller, Mary Fereva, Edith Lyon, Emma Hostetler; and brothers, Menno Christner, Christian Christner, Amos Christner, Levi Christner, Arthur Christner, and John Christner.

Funeral services will be Saturday, November 13, 2010, at 10 a.m. in Young Family Funeral Home, Wolcottville Chapel, State Road 9 North, Wolcottville with Pastor Andy Dayton of the Shipshewana Church of the Nazarene officiating. Burial will be in Shore Cemetery, Shipshewana.

Calling is Friday, November 12, 2010, from 4 to 8 p.m. in the funeral home and one hour prior to services on Saturday.

Preferred memorials are to the Shipshewana Church of the Nazarene.

Burial: Shore Cemetery, Shipshewana, Lagrange Co., IN
Find A Grave Memorial# 61553230

More About David L. Christner:
Military service: 20 Jul 1942, Toledo, OH[7945]
Residence: 1930, Clearspring, Lagrange Co., IN[7946,7947]
SSN issued: OH[7948]

Notes for Lois Lucille Heilman:
The Descendants of John J. Christner, privately published February 1961, p. 25.

Children of David Christner and Lois Heilman are:

    5165   i.   Betty Lee[10] Christner[7949,7950], born 02 Jun 1947 in Bellevue, Seneca Co., OH[7950]; died 16 Oct 1947 in MT Carmel[7951].

                 Notes for Betty Lee Christner:
                 The Descendants of John J. Christner, privately published February 1961, p., 26.

                 More About Betty Lee Christner:
                 Burial: Shoremennonite Cemetery, Shipshewana, Lagrange Co., IN

+   5166   ii.   David John Christner, born 01 Jul 1948.
+   5167   iii.   Michael Eugene Christner, born 15 Nov 1952 in Bellevue, Seneca Co., OH.

2832. Christian L.[9] Christner (Levi D.[8], David J.[7], John J.[6], Joseph C.[5], Christian J.[4], Johannes John Hans[3], Christian[2], Christen[1])[7952] was born 10 Jun 1922 in Topeka, Lagrange Co., IN[7952,7952], and died 01 Sep 1994 in Shipshewana, Lagrange Co., IN[7952,752]. He married **Fannie Schlabach** 31 Oct 1946 in Topeka IN. by David Nissley. She was born 25 Dec 1918[7953].

Notes for Christian L. Christner:
The Descendants of John J. Christner, privately published February 1961, p. 26.

Avid checker & game player energetic & enterprising farmer who lived in Lagrange Co., IN. Close to Messick lake retired in Shipshewana, IN. Never a dull Moment with Christain L. around. He had a plumbing business that he ran from his home. When his nephew Steve Christner home burned Christ did 99% of the plumbing work for just the cost of materials. He donated his labor. Him and his sister Sue (Steves Mom) worked at this plumbing job for many days and they were a laugh a minute as he tried to teach her the plumbing parts and how they fit together.Old Order Amish.

SS#317-18-1821 Iss.IN

More About Christian L. Christner:
Cause of Death: Cancer
Military: 28 Dec 1942, Toledo, OH[7954]
Religion: Old Order Amish/
Residence: 1942, WWII Army Enlistment Record/Toledo, OH[7954]
Social Security Number: 317-18-1821/[7954]
SSN issued: IN[7954]

Notes for Fannie Schlabach:
The Descendants of John J. Christner, privately published February 1961, p. 26.

She works at garden produce and chicken raising for Lambright Hatchery. He is Old Order Amish.

More About Fannie Schlabach:
Residence: 1930, Clearspring, Lagrange Co., IN[7955]

Children of Christian Christner and Fannie Schlabach are:
+   5168   i.   Edna[10] Christner, born 02 Sep 1947 in Wolcottville, Lagrange Co., IN.
+   5169   ii.   Amos C. Christner, born 30 Aug 1949 in Wolcottville, Lagrange Co., IN.
+   5170   iii.   William C. Christner, born 04 Nov 1951 in Lagrange Co., IN.
+   5171   iv.   Mary Blanch Christner, born 09 Sep 1953 in Lagrange Co., IN.

2833. Emma L.[9] Christner (Levi D.[8], David J.[7], John J.[6], Joseph C.[5], Christian J.[4], Johannes John Hans[3], Christian[2], Christen[1])[7956,7956] was born 06 Dec 1923 in Topeka, Lagrange Co., IN[7956,7956], and died 20 Oct 1955 in Dhamtari, Chhattisgarh, India[7956,7956]. She married **Alvin D. Hostetler** 13 Jun 1942 in Goshen, Elkhart Co., IN. He was born 28 Feb 1921 in Honeyville, Lagrange Co., IN, and died 29 Jan 2003 in 20761 Co. Road 38 Goshen, IN.

Notes for Emma L. Christner:
Hostetler, Emma Helen (Christner) was born near Topeka, IN Dec 6,1923, the daughter of Mr. and Mrs. Levi D. Christner. She passed on to be with her Lord, in India, on Oct 20, 1955, at the age of 31 y. 10 m. 14 d. Sister Hostetler died of complications which developed following surgery. She was married to Alvin Hostetler on Jun 13, 1942. To this union were born two daughters: Gloria Joyce and Carrol Jewel, both of whom are living. Surviving in addition to her family and parents are the following brothers and sisters, Menno Christner, Lagrange; Lizzie-Mrs. Valentine Miller, Milford; Sue-Mrs. Carl Christner, Topeka; David and Christian Christner, both of Wolcottville; Amos Christner, Huntsville, Ala; Mary-Mrs. Jack Fereva, Stockton, CA; Sam Christner, Rome City, IN; John Christner, Stockton, CA; Edith-Mrs. Bill Lyon, Howe; and Levi and Arthur Christner, both at home. A sister Goldie, preceded her in death. In March 1952, Bro. and Sister Hostetler volunteered to go to India as MRSC workers for a five-year term. Since Sister Hostetler's death Bro. Hostetler and daughters are living in the Doctor Paul Conrad home in Dhamtari, India. Sister Hostetler joined the Clinton Brick Mennonite Church as a

young woman. She later became a member of the North Goshen Mennonite Church. A few Years ago both she and her husband transferred their membership to the church in India, where she was a faithful member until the time of her death. Funeral services were held for Sister Hostetler and she was buried up in the hills of India near the Presbyterian Hospital where she died. A memorial service was held at Dhamtari Nov. 6, 1955. Memorial services were also held at the North Goshen Mennonite Church on Dec. 18, 1955, with J. D. Graber and John C. Wenger as speakers. Missionaries on furlough, Jonathan Hostetler and Sam King, also spoke a word of tribute. She named herself Helen.

Emma and her husband Alvin were missionaries and went to Dhamtari India March of 1952. He was a maintenance man and she was a nurse. They worked five years before her demise. She died from an infection she contracted after surgery for a ruptured disk. She is buried on a hill in Dhamtari, Madyah, Pradesh, India.

More About Emma L. Christner:
Burial: Dhamtari, Chhattisgarh, India
Residence: 1930, Clearspring, Lagrange Co., IN[7956]

Notes for Alvin D. Hostetler:
Alvin is the son of David and Mary Ann Yoder Hostetler Alvin is a photographer and does many of the photos you see on your weekly church bulletin for Mennonite Central Commitee Alvin was a missionary in India with his wife Emma. After Emma's death he married Goldie Hummel on Oct.27, 1956. He spent 7 years as a missionary in Dhamtari, Madyah, Pradesh, India. He was a very talented mechanical movement engineer. He owned his own welding and machining shop. He was a member of Berkey Ave. Mennonite Church in Goshen, IN. He served as a member of the 5th Air Force during WWII as a radio operator.

More About Alvin D. Hostetler:
Burial: Townline Cemetery North End out by Road N41°35.5600' x W85°37.00'
Christened: Mennonite

Children of Emma Christner and Alvin Hostetler are:

5172   i.   Gloria Joyce[10] Hostetler, born 15 Aug 1947 in Goshen, Elkhart Co., IN; died 29 May 2005 in Goshen, Elkhart Co., IN.

    Notes for Gloria Joyce Hostetler:
    Gloria worked in the nursing field for 30 years. She lived in a mobile home park in Mishawaka IN. She and her neighbors did not know the water in there homes was contaminated. She was totally incapacitated. She never married.

    May 27, 2005   Just a quick note to let you know that if you were planning to visit Joy she may not know you are there. They have unhooked the bubblers and have begun giving her morphine when she seems to be in pain. She hallucinates and is not in her right mind more times than not. When she and I discussed what she wanted at the end she requested that family and friends not hang around and wait for her to die. She didn't want to put us through
    that and she didn't want to die "on display". Prayers for a peaceful transition would be the most helpful at this time.
    Thank you, her sister Caroll

    More About Gloria Joyce Hostetler:
    Burial: Town Line

+   5173   ii.   Caroll Jewell Hostetler, born 25 Dec 1952 in Dhamtari, M.P. India.

2835. Mary Ann[9] Christner (Levi D.[8], David J.[7], John J.[6], Joseph C.[5], Christian J.[4], Johannes John Hans[3], Christian[2], Christen[1]) was born 31 Dec 1926 in Topeka, Lagrange Co., IN. She married **Jack Raymond Fereva** 31 May 1950 in Reno, NV, son of Alpha Fereva and Ruth Dimmick. He was born 02 Jun 1917 in New Castle, CA[7957], and died 12 Oct 1986 in Manteca, San Joaquin Co., CA[7957].

Notes for Mary Ann Christner:
The Descendants of John J. Christner, privately published February 1961, p. 26.

Mary lived many years in California then Reno NV at N39°39.00 by W119°52.66. She renamed herself MaryAnn. Later she re-renamed herself Ann.

Notes for Jack Raymond Fereva:
The Descendants of John J. Christner, privately published February 1961, p. 26.

More About Jack Raymond Fereva:
Burial: 17 Oct 1986, New Castle Cem, New Castle, California
Social Security Number: 572-01-7663/[7957]
SSN issued: CA[7957]

Children of Mary Christner and Jack Fereva are:

5174 i. Danny Jay[10] Fereva, born 15 Jul 1954 in Stockton, San Joaquin Co., CA; died 19 Feb 1987 in Car accident.

   Notes for Danny Jay Fereva:
   The Descendants of John J. Christner, privately published February 1961, p. 26.

5175 ii. Peggy Kathleen Fereva, born 24 Jul 1956 in Stockton, San Joaquin Co., CA. She married Kenneth Allen Cleveland 18 Jul 1987 in Reno, NV; born 21 Jul 1953 in San Jose, CA.

   Notes for Peggy Kathleen Fereva:
   The Descendants of John J. Christner, privately published February 1961, p. 26.

   Peggy married Kenneth Allen Cleveland July 16 1987. Kenneth is the son of John and Olga Berryessa Cleveland. Kenneth born July 21, 1953 San Jose, CA.
   Kenneth works in a sawmill. Peggy is an accountant

5176 iii. Paul David Fereva, born 02 Nov 1958 in Stockton, San Joaquin Co., CA.

   Notes for Paul David Fereva:
   The Descendants of John J. Christner, privately published February 1961, p. 26.

2837. John Levi[9] Christner (Levi D.[8], David J.[7], John J.[6], Joseph C.[5], Christian J.[4], Johannes John Hans[3], Christian[2], Christen[1])[7958,7958] was born 09 Dec 1929 in Topeka, Lagrange Co., IN[7958,7958], and died 31 May 1990 in Stockton, San Joaquin Co., CA[7958,7958]. He married **Bernice Elaine Looney** 10 Aug 1962 in Manteca, St.Paulmethodist, California. She was born 12 Sep 1935 in Bakerfields, CA, and died 26 Oct 1986.

Notes for John Levi Christner:
John worked in shipyard construction He was a member of the Port Stockton Boaters and the Vagabondos Boat Club. SS#;313-28-6628 Iss IN

More About John Levi Christner:
Burial: Westwoods Hills Memorial Park Placerville CA
Christened: Methodist
Residence: 1930, Clearspring, Lagrange Co., IN[7958]
Social Security Number: 313-28-6628/[7958]
SSN issued: IN[7958]

Notes for Bernice Elaine Looney:
Bernice was the daughter of Lenard Looney and Ethel Galloway. She was a housewife all her life.

More About Bernice Elaine Looney:
Christened: Methodist

Child of John Christner and Bernice Looney is:

5177　　i.　John Lee[10] Christner, born 22 Jul 1971 in French Camp, San Joanquin Co., CA.

2838. Levi Lee[9] Christner (Levi D.[8], David J.[7], John J.[6], Joseph C.[5], Christian J.[4], Johannes John Hans[3], Christian[2], Christen[1])[7958,7958] was born 12 Sep 1931 in Topeka, Lagrange Co., IN[7958,7958], and died 22 Jul 2001 in Goshen, Elkhart Co., IN[7958]. He married **Martha Pauline Leichty** 13 Oct 1956 in Wolcottville, Lagrange Co., IN. She was born 14 Oct 1928 in Goshen, Elkhart Co., IN.

Notes for Levi Lee Christner:
The Descendants of John J. Christner, privately published February 1961, p. 26.

Lee was raised Amish but he served in the army He had a stroke & died at 2:45 p.m. Sunday July 22, 2001 He lived in the Goshen, IN area for 44 years. He retired from Marque Ambulance Manufacturing in May 1997, where he did small tool repair. He worked for Carriage and managed the auto van conversion assembly line from 1977 to 1990 and prior to that he worked for Smoker Craft from 1950 to 1977 as shop foreman in the aluminum boat plant. He was a member of Clinton Frame Mennonite Church where he served as church trustee. Miller Cemetery is at N41°-37.240 -- W85°- 44.260 in Elkhart Co., IN County Road 126 just west of Co. Rd. 35. Their home was at N41°33.154 x W85°44.053.

More About Levi Lee Christner:
Burial: 25 Jul 2001, Miller Cemetery
Cause of Death: Stroke
Military service: Army Cook/
Social Security Number: 315-32-9041/[7958]
SSN issued: IN[7958]

Notes for Martha Pauline Leichty:
The Descendants of John J. Christner, privately published February 1961, p. 26.

Martha was the daughter of Sam Leighty and Clara Alma Harshberger. Martha was an excellant cook. She and Lee had a very large home and they held many of the Christner reunions at there home just east of Goshen, IN. Their home was at N41°33.154 x W85°44.053

Divorced from Levi.

Children of Levi Christner and Martha Leichty are:

+　　5178　　i.　James Lee[10] Christner, born 23 May 1957 in Goshen, Elkhart Co., IN.
+　　5179　　ii.　Mary Lou Christner, born 18 Feb 1959 in Goshen, Elkhart Co., IN.
　　　5180　　iii.　Bonnie Sue Christner, born 09 Sep 1960 in Goshen, Elkhart Co., IN. She married (1) Steven Eugene Kauffman 17 Dec 1985 in Goshen, Elkhart Co., IN; born 15 May 1963 in Lagrange Co., IN. She married (2) Dusty J. Petre 09 Apr 1990.

　　　　　　Notes for Bonnie Sue Christner:
　　　　　　Bonnie had her own beauty shop in Millersburg for several Years.

+　　5181　　iv.　Carol Ann Christner, born 11 Dec 1962 in Goshen, Elkhart Co., IN.
+　　5182　　v.　Ronald George Christner, born 17 Aug 1964 in Goshen, Elkhart Co., IN.

2840. Edith L.[9] Christner (Levi D.[8], David J.[7], John J.[6], Joseph C.[5], Christian J.[4], Johannes John Hans[3], Christian[2], Christen[1])[7959,7960,7960] was born 23 Jun 1935 in Topeka, Lagrange Co., IN[7961,7962,7962], and died 18 Mar 1987 in Howe, Lagrange Co., IN[7962]. She married **Henry William Lyon**[7963] 09 Jan 1954 in Lagrange Co., IN[7963]. He was born 01 Jan 1932 in Sturgis, St. Joseph Co., MI[7963], and died 24 Jan 1999 in Howe, Lagrange Co., IN[7963].

Notes for Edith L. Christner:
The Descendants of John J. Christner, privately published February 1961, p. 26.
Edith raised tropical fish (for sale) for many years. She also was a Artex (liquid tube paints) dealer. She was a very large women with red hair. She lived all her married life in Lagrange Co., IN.

More About Edith L. Christner:
Burial: Riverside Cemetery, Howe, Lagrange Co., IN
Social Security Number: 304-36-9579/[7963,7964]
SSN issued: IN[7965,7966]

Notes for Henry William Lyon:
The Descendants of John J. Christner, privately published February 1961, p., 26.

Bill is the son Walter Rubert and Augeste Anna Charlotte Elizabeth Vaupel Lyon. Bill and Edith were married by Larwence Beaver and they took their dog to the wedding as a witness. Died at Parkview Hospital, Fort Wayne, IN at 5:50 P.M. Sunday 24 Jan 1999.

More About Henry William Lyon:
Burial: Riverside Cemetery, Howe, Lagrange Co., IN
Cause of Death: Cancer

Child of Edith Christner and Henry Lyon is:
+   5183   i.   Goldie Ann[10] Lyon, born 04 May 1954 in Lagrange Co., IN.

2841. Arthur L.[9] Christner (Levi D.[8], David J.[7], John J.[6], Joseph C.[5], Christian J.[4], Johannes John Hans[3], Christian[2], Christen[1])[7967,7968,7968,7969] was born 13 Jun 1939 in Topeka, Lagrange Co., IN[7970,7971,7971], and died 07 Oct 2000 in Topeka, Lagrange Co., IN[7972,7973,7973]. He married **Gladys Marie Troyer** 17 Aug 1958 in Maple Grove Mennonite, Topeka, Lagrange Co., IN, daughter of Ezra Troyer and Mary Miller. She was born 06 Aug 1939 in Goshen, Elkhart Co., IN.

Notes for Arthur L. Christner:
Art bought the home place at RR#1 Topeka. He was farmer, semi driver and in later years operated Topeka Stone. The gravel pit was dug on the farm. He was a leader in his church, started a bus ministry program. He had an accident while changing a semi truck tire on July 26, 1988. He has been in several hospitals and is mostly confined to bed. He led a life of helping others and working for the church.

The Descendants of John J. Christner, privately published February 1961, p. 9.

More About Arthur L. Christner:
Burial: 09 Oct 2000, Maple Grove Cemetary Topeka IN.N41°31.497xW85°34.432
Social Security Number: 314-40-5851/[7974,7975]
SSN issued: IN[7976,7977]

Notes for Gladys Marie Troyer:
The Descendants of John J. Christner, privately published February 1961, p. 9.

Gladys is the daughter of Ezra S. Troyer and Mary E. Miller. Gladys drove a school bus for many years. She was willing to help anyone at anytime without asking if they deserve help.

Children of Arthur Christner and Gladys Troyer are:
+   5184   i.   Diane Fay[10] Christner, born 06 Oct 1959 in Goshen, Elkhart Co., IN.
+   5185   ii.   Gary Gene Christner, born 08 Dec 1960 in Lagrange Co., IN; died 07 Apr 1989 in Home Farm, Lagrange Co., In.N41°34.800 x W85°31.250.

+ 5186   iii.   Charles Jay Christner, born 13 Jul 1962 in Lagrange Co., IN.
+ 5187   iv.   Donna Kay Christner, born 09 Sep 1966 in Lagrange Co., IN.
   5188   v.   Arthur Dean Christner, born 02 Nov 1968 in Lagrange Co., IN. He married Tammy Jo Miller 17 Aug 1991 in Maple Grove Mennonite Church, Topeka, IN; born 22 Nov 1970 in Goshen, Elkhart Co., IN.

     Notes for Arthur Dean Christner:
     Arthur Dean goes by Dean is studying to be an Xray tech.

     More About Arthur Dean Christner:
     Occupation: Radiologist/

     Notes for Tammy Jo Miller:
     Tammy is the daughter of Floyd Eugene Miller and Linda Jo Phillips Miller. Tammy is a bank teller at Farmers State Bank, Topeka, IN.

     More About Tammy Jo Miller:
     Christened: Mennonite, Clinton Frame
     Occupation: Medical Transcriber/

+ 5189   vi.   Donnie Lynn Christner, born 25 Nov 1974 in Lagrange Co., IN.

2842. Adopted Mary F.[9] Yoder (Katherine[8] Christner, John J.[7], John J.[6], Joseph C.[5], Christian J.[4], Johannes John Hans[3], Christian[2], Christen[1]) was born 26 Sep 1914 in Millersburg, Elkhart Co., IN, and died 02 May 2005 in at 4:45 PM   Row 2 plot 4. She married **Joseph J. Byler** 30 Mar 1939 in Her home farm south of Honeyville IN. He was born 18 Mar 1919, and died 12 Jan 1994 in Row 2 plot 3.

Notes for Adopted Mary F. Yoder:
The Descendants of John J. Christner, privately published February 1961, p. 26.

She was adopted by Katie-------Marys parents are Jonathon S. Yoder & Fannie Miller-----She had two brothers Leo & William Yoder.

She lived all her life at the home farm, south of the Honeyville store 1 mile at the end of the road. N41°33.900 x W85°36.400 --------- 9520W----500South LaGrange Co., IN. She was a gentle, intelligent and a hard working person, nice to be around. When she came into a room people went to her instead of running out the back door. She was a faithful servant to her Lord Jesus Christ. She was very good at using different methods to preserve food.

More About Adopted Mary F. Yoder:
Burial: Christner Cemetery, Honeyville, Lagrange Co., IN
Religion: Old Order Amish/

Notes for Joseph J. Byler:
The Descendants of John J. Christner, privately published February 1961, p. 26.

Old order Amish son of John B. Byler & Lovina Borkholder   He was a farmer and had a construction company building grain storage facilities. He had a millwright buisiness with Harold Lantz. They build & repair feed mills. anything that moves food products like corn or wheat from storage bin to anywhere else. I (Steven Carl Christner) owned 5 % of this Corp. in the 1970s.

More About Joseph J. Byler:
Burial: Christner Cemetery, Honeyville, Lagrange Co., IN

Children of Mary Yoder and Joseph Byler are:
   5190   i.   Elmer[10] Byler, born 08 Apr 1943 in Honeyville, Lagrange Co., IN. He married Ruby.

     Notes for Elmer Byler:
     The Descendants of John J. Christner, privately published February 1961, p. 27.

5191   ii.   Wilma Byler, born 22 Feb 1947 in Honeyville, Lagrange Co., IN. She married Calvin Yoder.

Notes for Wilma Byler:
The Descendants of John J. Christner, privately published February 1961, p. 27.

5192   iii.   Orvan Byler, born 16 Aug 1949 in Honeyville, Lagrange Co., IN. He married Reyna.

Notes for Orvan Byler:
The Descendants of John J. Christner, privately published February 1961, p. 27.

5193   iv.   Perry Byler, born 22 Dec 1953 in Honeyville, Lagrange Co., IN; died 23 Dec 1953 in Row 2 plot 5.

Notes for Perry Byler:
The Descendants of John J. Christner, privately published February 1961, p. 27.

More About Perry Byler:
Burial: Christner Cemetery, Honeyville, Lagrange Co., IN

5194   v.   Katie Byler, born 03 Dec 1955 in Honeyville, Lagrange Co., IN. She married Joas Schlabach.

Notes for Katie Byler:
The Descendants of John J. Christner, privately published February 1961, p. 27.

2843. Amanda Mae[9] Bontrager (Lydia M.[8] Christner, John J.[7], John J.[6], Joseph C.[5], Christian J.[4], Johannes John Hans[3], Christian[2], Christen[1]) was born 25 Nov 1909 in Millersburg, Elkhart Co., IN, and died 05 Mar 1936 in Elkhart, Elkhart Co., IN. She married **Noah J. Raber** 15 Jan 1931. He was born 10 Nov 1906, and died 13 Feb 1934.

Notes for Amanda Mae Bontrager:
The Descendants of John J. Christner, privately published February 1961, p. 27.

Notes for Noah J. Raber:
The Descendants of John J. Christner, privately published February 1961, p. 27.

Child of Amanda Bontrager and Noah Raber is:
+   5195   i.   Lydia N.[10] Raber, born 08 Apr 1932 in Topeka, Lagrange Co., IN.

2844. Levi D.[9] Bontrager (Lydia M.[8] Christner, John J.[7], John J.[6], Joseph C.[5], Christian J.[4], Johannes John Hans[3], Christian[2], Christen[1]) was born 01 Jan 1914 in Millersburg, Elkhart Co., IN, and died 20 Nov 2004 in Honeyville, Lagrange Co., IN. He married **Elizabeth Schlabach** 23 Feb 1939 in By Cornelius Christner, daughter of Andrew Schlabach and Barbara Miller. She was born 06 Mar 1915, and died 24 Aug 1989.

Notes for Levi D. Bontrager:
The Descendants of John J. Christner, privately published February 1961, p. 27.

Levi is a cabinet maker and farmer. Levi did all the cabinet work in our (Steven Carl Christner) new home after our fire in 1980. The craftmanship and quality was some of the best work we had done. He showed his children by example how to work smart & careful and do good work which they followed his example.

He was Old Order Amish. He was known & called Levi D. & lived at 10455W on 500S north side of the road where the south road tee's in. N41°34.091' W85°37.605'.

More About Levi D. Bontrager:
Burial: 23 Nov 2004, Hawpatch Cemetery at Topeka Indiana
Occupation: Farmer/
Religion: Old Order Amish/[7978]

Social Security Number: 316-09-9704/*7978*
SSN issued: IN*7978*

Notes for Elizabeth Schlabach:
The Descendants of John J. Christner, privately published February 1961, p. 27.

Children of Levi Bontrager and Elizabeth Schlabach are:

5196   i.   Floyd[10] Bontrager, born 18 Jun 1931. He married Wilma Louise Miller 20 Nov 1951; born 01 Mar 1931.

Notes for Floyd Bontrager:
The Descendants of John J. Christner, privately published February 1961, p. 27.

Notes for Wilma Louise Miller:
The Descendants of John J. Christner, privately published February 1961, p. 12.

+   5197   ii.   Esther Bontrager, born 09 Feb 1940 in Shipehewana, Lagrange Co., IN.
+   5198   iii.   Orpha Bontrager, born 24 Apr 1941 in Millersburg, Elkhart Co., IN.
    5199   iv.   John Bontrager, born 29 May 1942.

Notes for John Bontrager:
The Descendants of John J. Christner, privately published February 1961, p. 27.

5200   v.   Floyd Bontrager, born 14 Mar 1944.

Notes for Floyd Bontrager:
The Descendants of John J. Christner, privately published February 1961, p. 27.

5201   vi.   Alice Bontrager, born 23 Apr 1945.

Notes for Alice Bontrager:
The Descendants of John J. Christner, privately published February 1961, p. 27.

5202   vii.   Alvin Bontrager, born 23 Apr 1945.

Notes for Alvin Bontrager:
The Descendants of John J. Christner, privately published February 1961, p. 27.

5203   viii.   Mabel Bontrager, born 20 Apr 1946.

Notes for Mabel Bontrager:
The Descendants of John J. Christner, privately published February 1961, p. 27.

5204   ix.   David Bontrager, born 08 Nov 1947.

Notes for David Bontrager:
The Descendants of John J. Christner, privately published February 1961, p. 27.

5205   x.   Harley Bontrager, born 10 May 1951.

Notes for Harley Bontrager:
The Descendants of John J. Christner, privately published February 1961, p. 27.

5206   xi.   Edna Bontrager, born 22 Oct 1953.

Notes for Edna Bontrager:
The Descendants of John J. Christner, privately published February 1961, p. 27.

5207   xii.   Ernest Bontrager, born 31 Aug 1956.

Notes for Ernest Bontrager:
The Descendants of John J. Christner, privately published February 1961, p. 27.

Index of Individuals

"Joy" -
  Joanne B.: 610
A -
  Peggy: 1173
Abbott -
  Kenneth Francis: 1204
Able -
  Christine: 1126
  Jr Guy: 1126
  Sharon: 1126
Aboulfad -
  Ahmed Jr.: 1287
Aboulfadl -
  Ahmed: 1287
  Miriam: 1287
  Racid: 1287
  Sliman D.: 1287
Acker -
  Purney: 259
Ackerman -
  Dennis: 159
  Eva Geneva Idella: 159, 396
  Harry: 159
  Irving C.: 159
  Mahlon P.: 159
  Paul: 159
  Roy: 685
  Samuel: 159
Ackles -
  Bertha Lorene: 308
Adams -
  Amy Jo: 712, 1171
  Bridgette: 1486, 1496
  Charles E. Jr.: 379
  Cristine Lynn: 712, 1171, 1172
  Donald Raymond: 1486
  Ira Richard: 712
  Karen Lee: 1486, 1496
  Larry: 1486
Addleman -
  Pauline Nicola: 689, 690
Adkinson -
  Nancy: 1486
Agar -
  Sharon A.: 703
Aiken -
  Barbara: 456
Akins -
  Rachael Copeland: 288, 289
  Robert: 288
Albrecht -
  Amos R.: 1235
  Bobby Joe Sr: 1236
  Clair J.: 1203, 1204
  Clifford D.: 1204
  Jay Clair: 1204
  John: 1203
  Mary E.: 1235
  Pamela Lee: 1204
  Tamara L.: 1204
  Virginia Sue: 1204

Albricht -
  Betty: 1235
  Elenanor: 1235
  Kenneth: 1236
Albright -
  Unnamed: 705
  Donald: 267
  Margaret: 267
  Melvin C.: 266, 267
  Patricia: 267
  Robert: 267
  William: 267
Aldrich -
  Crystal: 1311
  Jeanette Evelyn: 1372
Alice -
  Unnamed: 660
  Mary: 1187
Allen -
  Barbra Carol: 1172
  Charlette: 934
  Frances Jean: 1095
Alta -
  Unnamed: 68, 69
Alverta -
  Unnamed: 337
Alwine -
  Lois: 924
Amanda -
  Unnamed: 435
  Unnamed: 161, 162
  Wanda ??: 120
Amichaux -
  Roxanne: 1152
Amy -
  (name: Amanda Mae Christner): 1246
Andereson -
  Esther: 313
Andersen -
  Allen S.: 1325
  Michael Allen: 1325
Anderson -
  Clyde: 632
  Elizabeth: 230
  James Franklin: 602
  Joseph: 49
  Josephine B.: 1357, 1358
Angle -
  Evelyn: 720
Anglea -
  Abigal Marie: 1443
  Hannah Louise: 1443
  Luke Christner: 1443
  Robert Benjamin: 1443
  Robert Terry: 1443
Anglemyer -
  Kelly Richard: 1308
Ankeny -
  David Wayne: 1148
Anliker -
  Lisa Kristine: 1421

Ruth: 688, 689

Balhiser -
Blake Alexander: 1414
Justin: 1414

Bame -
David: 1490
Jacob Eli: 1491
Julia Noelle: 1491

Banghart -
Gary D.: 1308
Hershal: 1308

Barbara -
Unnamed: 1406
Unnamed: 42

Barker -
Laura: 285

Barnell -
Everett: 838, 839
Keith Elwin: 839
Robert Lamar: 839
Stanley Wayne: 839

Barnett -
Anna Jane: 785, 786

Barney -
(name: Herman Christner): 36, 115, 116, 318-321, 323,
    661-664, 666-681, 1138-1142, 1144-1157, 1159,
    1410-1418, 1487-1489
(name: Merlin "Barney' George Cardin): 743

Barnum -
Francis Margaret: 352

Barron -
David Lynn: 1136, 1409, 1410
Michael David: 1410
Orlin: 659
Sandra L.: 1136, 1409
Sherry S.: 1136, 1409
William Miller: 659, 1136, 1409
William Miller Jr.: 1136

Barry -
Jane: 1436

Barstow -
Unnamed: 1191
Thomas: 1191

Bartik -
Unnamed: 326

Bartlett -
Mary Kathryn: 1105
Robert L.: 1105
Robert Thomas: 1105

Bartolotta -
Debbie: 1487

Bartosiak -
Stanley: 792

Basinger -
Bryan Lee: 1413
Rodger Wayne: 1413

Bassett -
Florence: 347, 348
Jane E.: 1273

Bast -
Nancy: 1202

Bates -
Berdine: 1011

Battenfield -

Elizabeth: 637, 638

Battler -
Christian Thomas: 448
Christina: 448
Clarence Arthur: 448
George Wesley: 448
Howard David: 448, 449

Baughman -
Lelia Lucille: 684, 685
Melvin S.: 710

Baumgardner -
John: 178, 179

Beachey -
Alvin D.: 1336
Carissa A.: 1334
Mary Alice: 1336
Susannna: 1337
Wilbur: 1337

Beachley -
Generva Minerva "MO": 334, 335

Beachy -
Alvin Jay: 1265
Alvin M.: 790, 791, 895, 935
Alvin S.: 1214
Amanda Sue: 1265
Amanda W.: 513, 968
Ammon W.: 513, 964, 965
Anna: 857
Anna A: 791
Anna Sue: 1073
Annie Marie: 965
Daniel: 1265
Daniel D.: 1264, 1265
Daniel David: 1016
Edwin Eugene: 966
Elizabeth: 433
Elizabeth: 791
Elva: 513, 965
Ernest: 1265
Esther Mae: 965
Fannie: 1214
Fannie Irene: 1265
Frieda: 966
Galen: 575
Grace: 1202
Harley: 1265
Harley: 966
Ida: 911
Ida Mae: 1265
Irene: 965
Irma: 1265
Jonas A.: 791
Margaret Mary: 966
Marianna: 575
Martha: 1265
Marvin Ray: 847, 848
Mary: 1265
Mary: 791, 895, 896, 1214
Mary Elizabeth: 513, 966, 967
Mel: 575
Menno S.: 1214
Nora Tresia: 966
Rachel: 1214
Rebecca Jean: 1016
Robert Laverne: 965

Sam A. Jr.: 1214
Samuel A.: 791, 1213, 1214
Samuel J.: 1202
Sue Ann: 965
Susan Elizabeth: 1016
Susanna: 791, 935, 936, 1214
Vera: 1265
Vernon: 1265
Vernon: 1016
Vernon: 965
Vernon John: 966
Vernon W.: 513, 966
Veronica: 966
William: 966
William Ray: 1016
Wilma: 965

Beal -
Unnamed: 269
Albert: 135
Chauncey F.: 135
Christiana: 135
Dahlgren: 135
Ezra: 136
George: 29
Richard L.: 1308
Savilla: 135, 341

Beall -
Christian William: 1484
Emma Shannon: 1484
Isaiah Shannon: 1484
Joel Jahdal: 1308, 1484
Kearstin Danae: 1484
Shannon Dewayne: 1308, 1484
Wayne L.: 1308

Beam -
Alexander: 400, 401
Edith: 401
Ethyl May: 401
Grace: 401
Herbert Rollin: 401
Victoria Marie: 401
William: 401

Beaner -
Mary Katherine: 309

Bear -
Jeremy: 1452

Beard -
Amber Sue: 1334
Arthur L.: 610, 611
Dennis A.: 1334
Frank: 1334
Keri Ann: 1414
Ronald: 1414
Scott Allen: 1334
Stephine Marie: 1334

Beattie -
Helen Lohr: 680, 681

Bechtel -
Allan: 197, 462
Catharine (Catharina?): 60
Christian: 60
Esther Hettie: 60
Isaac: 60
John Wilfred: 462
Leah: 197

Leah: 59
Lora: 197
Lydia: 60
Maranda: 197
Marguerite: 1054
Mary Maria: 59
Menno: 59, 196, 197, 462
Milton: 197
Moses: 59
Noah (Nohale): 60
Noah Shoemaker: 58, 59
Veronica "Fanny" Christner: 60, 198
Winney: 198

Bechtold -
Lydia: 204

Beck -
Betty: 1444

Beckner -
Elizabeth: 188, 189
Louisa: 55

Beechy -
Aaron D.: 914
Aaron Leroy: 546, 1073, 1301
Abbie: 1070
Alvin Jay: 546, 1071, 1072
Alvin Jay: 1072
Amos: 916
Amos D.: 914
Anna: 1071
Anna: 1070
Anna Mae: 513, 887, 888, 967
Anna Mae: 546, 1073, 1453
Barbara J.: 546, 1066, 1067
Barbara Mae: 1069
Calvin: 1069
Clemence: 1073
Dan M.: 913
Daniel: 916
Daniel: 1073
Daniel J.: 546, 1069, 1345
Daniel Jr.: 913
David D.: 913
Edna: 1069
Edna Ellen: 1072
Edna Mae: 1070
Eli: 913
Elizabeth J.: 546, 1068
Elmer: 916
Ervin D.: 914
Floyd: 1069
Glen Ray: 1072
Ida M.: 1345
John A.: 545, 546, 1301, 1345, 1453
John D.: 914
John Henry: 1070
John M.: 916
John W.: 546, 1070, 1071
Joseph J.: 546, 1070
Katie J.: 546, 1067
Levi D.: 914
Lydia: 914
Lydia J.: 546, 1071
Mable D.: 914
Marie: 1069
Mary: 1069
Mary: 1071

Eli: 912
Elizabeth: 1358
Elizabeth: 877
Elizabeth: 1090
Elizabeth Ann: 960
Elizabeth D.: 522, 842
Elizabeth D.: 493, 912, 1060, 1061
Elizabeth Mae: 1006, 1364
Ella: 1266
Ella: 1266
Ellis O.: 1035
Elma: 517
Elmer: 1266
Elmer Dean: 978
Elmer S.: 515
Elmer W.: 845, 1265
Elroy: 1035
Elsie Mae: 978
Elvie: 1035
Emanuel: 1233
Emery: 757, 1181, 1182, 1428, 1492
Emma: 845
Emma: 1091
Emma: 1265
Enos: 845
Enos: 1037
Erma: 517
Ernest: 960
Ernest: 910
Ernest Dean: 978
Ernie R.: 553, 554
Ervin: 912
Ervin: 1262
Ervin M.: 984
Ervin S: 844, 882
Ervin W: 845
Esther: 910, 1312, 1313
Esther: 1265
Fannie: 582
Fannie: 912
Fannie Marie: 964, 1006, 1365
Fanny Irene: 517
Fanny Mae: 1348
Floyd: 849, 910
Floyd: 910
Floyd Douglas: 1010, 1011
Freeman: 877
Freeman Jay: 978
Freman: 960
Geneva Ann: 856
Gerald: 554
Glen: 1472
Glenda Fern: 562
Gloria "Nan": 1182, 1428, 1492
Grace Estella: 1181, 1428, 1492
Harley: 910
Harley: 960
Harley: 1266
Harley A.: 519
Harold Lee: 1034
Harvey: 1091
Helen Jean: 565, 1096
Helen Vivian: 1077
Ida: 801
Ida: 653
Ida: 1343

Ida: 912
Ida: 801
Ida: 1091
Ida Ellen: 984
Ida Mae: 515
Ida Mae: 1262
Ida W.: 1265
Inah: 994, 995
Irene D.: 1366
Iva Jean: 1010
J. Willis: 1010
Jane Marie: 1034
Jasmine Marie: 1481
Jeffra Lee: 1386
Jerry J.: 757, 1181, 1428, 1492
Jerry Lavern: 1010
Jill: 1386
Joe C.: 1090
John: 910
John: 1265
John Henry: 1006
John M.: 756, 757
John Richard: 1010
John Tobias: 856
Jonas: 1037
Joseph: 531, 1005, 1359, 1363
Joseph B.: 531, 876, 1007, 1294
Josey: 876, 877
Judith Ann: 564
Julianna: 850
Karen: 1452
Katie: 876
Katie: 912
Katie Mae: 493, 913
Katie Marie: 977
Katy: 1037
Keturah Marie: 1470
Kevin Dean: 1470
Larry Eugene: 564
Larry Eugene: 562
Lena: 1091
Leota Fay: 1034
Lester: 1006
Levi: 912
Levi D.: 493, 909, 910, 1312, 1313
Levi D.: 984
Levi E.: 1298
Levi Jr.: 583
Levi R.: 652, 653
Levi W.: 582
Lila Jean: 1034
Lizzie Ann: 1262
Lizzie Marie: 878
Lloyd: 960
Lola Grace: 1181
Lonita Eveylin: 563, 1095
Luella: 1006, 1007
Lydia: 531, 1007, 1008
Lydia S.: 1289
Mabel: 910
Malinda: 1030, 1031
Manas A.: 984
Manas B.: 531, 964, 1005, 1006, 1364, 1365
Marcus Lynn: 1470
Marilyn Louise: 563, 1094
Marlin: 1036

Martha: 1471
Martha Edna: 233
Martha Sue: 949
Marvin: 949
Mary: 1368, 1369, 1474
Mary: 493, 914, 915
Mary: 1006, 1366
Mary: 1035
Mary: 1265
Mary A.: 911
Mary Alice: 984
Mary Edna: 1471
Mary Edna: 1472
Mary Ellen: 1045
Mary Ellen: 876
Mary Ellen: 882, 1298
Mary Ellen: 1006, 1365
Mary Etta: 949
Mary Etta: 979
Mary J.: 541
Mary Janell: 1386
Mary Katherine: 562
Mary Rose: 1470
Mary S.: 515
Marylin Mae: 1034, 1386, 1387
Mattie: 1454
Mattie: 845
Mattie: 877
Mattie: 1265
Melvin: 876
Melvin Jr.: 859
Menno Lavern: 979
Merle Dean: 850
Michael Christian: 1481
Mildred: 554
Milo: 1233
Miriam Kay: 1034
Monroe E.: 959, 960
Moses: 1090
Nedra Fern: 1034, 1283, 1387
Nettie: 515, 970, 971
Noah: 856
Noah B.: 531, 1006, 1365, 1366
Norma: 554
Norman: 1472
Obadiah J.: 565
Ola: 1035
Ola J.: 1027, 1028
Ora: 1266
Ora J.: 1034
Ora Jay: 1006
Orla: 949, 950
Orpha: 910, 1313
Orpha Marie: 949
Orva: 882
Orva D.: 984
Orva Jay: 977
Orvan: 1472
Paige Marie: 1311
Parker Reed: 1311
Perry: 563
Perry: 1006
Perry: 582
Perry: 1262
Perry: 960
Perry D.: 984

Phineas: 1091
Polly: 1037
Quenlin Ray: 1031
Ray Edwin: 1181
Raymond: 990
Rebecca Joann: 1010
Regina: 1472
Reuben E.: 519
Richard Dwaine: 563
Robert Dale: 565
Ruby S.: 1035
Ruby S.: 517
Rudy M.: 1036
Ruthie: 1471
Ruthie: 1472
Saloma: 531
Samuel: 1006
Samuel J.: 513, 515, 1263
Samuel Jr: 882
Samuel R.: 882
Sara Ann: 1031, 1386
Sarah: 1341
Sharon Kay: 850
Sondra Sue: 1011
Sue Ann: 1472
Susanna: 1372
Susie Ellen: 978
Terry Lynn: 1359
Tobias: 850
Todd Reed: 1311
Uriah: 876
Velda Dorene: 1034, 1231, 1387
Velma: 1035
Velma Marie: 1197
Velva Lee: 565
Vera Louise: 1010
Verlo: 1035
Vernon: 1471
Vernon: 1037
Vernon: 960
Vernon: 1472
Vernon Jr.: 1472
Viola: 515, 517
Wanda: 1296
Wayne D.: 1366
William: 1233
William: 582, 583
William: 950
William: 1481
William A.: 551
William J.: 844, 845
Wilma: 515, 968
Wilma: 1092, 1093, 1262
Wilma: 876, 1294
Wilma: 1266
Wilma E.: 1038
Wilma Ellen: 977
Wilma Jean: 984
Book -
    Allen Royce: 1432
    Mahlon Royce: 1432
Booker -
    Helen V.: 525
Booth -
    Alfred H.: 305
    Bernice E.: 305

Clarence O.: 304
Harry F.: 304
Helen: 305
Kenneth D.: 305

Borell -
Una K.: 1121

Boren -
Mina Ethel: 395, 396

Borkholder -
Linda Sue: 1480
Moses: 754

Borman -
Sarah (Bechtel): 197

Borntrager -
Unnamed: 550
Ada: 551, 1092
Ada: 1086
Albert C.: 549, 1081
Alma: 1087
Alma S.: 550, 1085
Amos: 1087
Andrew: 548
Barbara: 549
Barbara: 1085
Bertha: 1087
Christian: 1083
Clemens: 1083
Clemens R.: 219, 551, 552, 1092, 1093
Dallas Jay: 1077
Daniel: 1084
Daniel: 1085
Daniel C.: 859
Daniel R.: 218, 548, 1076-1078
David: 1087
David: 1084
David S.: 550, 1084, 1085, 1390, 1485
Douglas Edward: 1077
Duane Lee: 1082
Edna: 550
Edna: 1086
Edna D.: 548, 1077, 1078
Edwin: 551
Eli: 1086
Elizabeth: 174-176
Elizabeth: 549
Elizabeth: 551, 1091
Elizabeth: 552, 1093
Elizabeth: 1083
Elizabeth: 1088
Elizabeth D.: 548, 1076
Ella: 552
Elnora: 550
Elnora: 1087
Emma: 551, 1090
Ernest: 1088
Esther: 549
Fanny: 1083
Fanny S.: 550, 1086
Felty: 1086
Floyd: 1085
Freddie: 1086
Garie Lee: 1082
Gregory Wayne: 1082
Gwyn Allen: 1082
Harvey: 552

Harvey C.: 549, 1082
Harvey R.: 218, 551, 1090-1092
Helen Diana: 1077
Henry R.: 218, 549, 1081, 1082
Ida Mae: 548, 1078, 1079
Infant: 219
Infant Dau.: 552
Infant Son: 218
Jeanine Ann: 1082
John T.: 855, 856
Jonas: 549
Jonathan: 1087
Joseph F.: 1085
Judy Kay: 1077
Katie: 1083
Katie: 1087
Katie: 1085
Katie Ann: 1079
Katie L.: 885
Katie S.: 550, 1084
Kent L.: 1092
Kevin: 1082
Laura: 551
Laura: 550
Laura: 1088
Leander H.: 551, 1092
Levi: 1086
Levi S.: 550, 1087
Levi V.: 1086
Lizzie: 1085
Lizzie: 1085
Lizzie: 1086
Lloyd: 549, 1082
Lovina: 552
Lydia: 1083
Lydia D.: 548, 1076
Lydia Lorene: 552, 1092, 1093
Magaret: 1088
Mary: 218, 550, 551, 1088
Mary: 552, 1093, 1094
Mary: 1083
Mary D.: 1084, 1085
Mary D.: 548, 1078
Mary Irene: 859
Mary S.: 550, 1083
Mattie: 551, 1090
Moses: 1083
Philip Eugene: 1082
Polly: 1085, 1269, 1390, 1485
Rebecca: 1085
Roger Duana: 1077
Royer: 1092
Ruby: 1083, 1084
Rudolph: 549
Rudolph D.: 218
Rudolph D.: 548, 1077
Rudy: 551
Rudy: 1085
Rudy: 1086
Rudy S.: 550, 1088
Samuel: 1086
Samuel: 1083
Samuel D.: 548, 1077
Samuel R.: 218, 549, 550, 1083-1088, 1390, 1485
Sarah: 550
Sarah: 1087

Shirley Ann: 1077
Susan: 549, 1081
Susan R.: 218, 548, 1079, 1080, 1389
Susie: 552
Truman: 1085
Uriah R.: 218
Verena: 1088
Willard: 1087
Willard S.: 550, 1087, 1088
William C.: 1083

Boshart -
Lydia: 760, 761
Mary: 763
Mattie: 767

Bosse -
Katy Marie: 1446
Lindsey Nicole: 1446
Sarah Grace: 1446
Thomas: 1446

Bostron -
Unnamed: 1399

Boughman -
Lori: 1195

Bourke -
Doris: 409

Bouser -
Beatrice: 619

Bowman -
Chester Clair: 706
Clara Jean: 706, 1169, 1424
Georgia Anita: 369
Kelly Lynne: 1170
Mary Helen: 706, 1169, 1424
Megan Elizabeth: 1170
Montey: 962
Paul Daniel: 598
Paul E.: 598
Ronald McNeal: 706, 1170
Ruth Anne: 706, 1169, 1170, 1425
Sally Anne: 1170

Bowser -
Abbie Mae: 293, 641
Hazel V.: 293, 642, 1129, 1406
Jesse Ray: 293
John Elmer: 293
Kathyrn: 1161, 1162
Laura: 293
Mae: 293
Wade: 293

Boyer -
Annie Edith: 309
Ardith Justice: 682
Barry: 1160
Donald: 1160
Donald L.: 682, 1160
Emma Jane: 105
Gene L.: 682
Irene L: 682
Isabelle: 141, 142
Nancy E.: 1231
Ross Emerson: 682

Bradley -
Lisa Ann: 1303
Manila Sarah 'Sally': 169

Bragg -

Mary Ann: 586, 1101
Sherman: 586

Brallier -
Charles Harrison: 669
Charles Husband: 669, 1148, 1412
Craig H.: 1148, 1412, 1413
Heather: 1413
Jessica: 1413
Rebecca Sue: 1148
Stacey: 1413

Brandenberger -
Luella: 972

Brandonberger -
Noah: 69

Brandt -
Walter Edmund: 1145

Brant -
Delores: 668
Donna: 672
Elizabeth: 668
Gay Anne: 672
James: 668
Jarvis: 672
Jim: 672
Louisa "Dillie" Verbena: 161, 162
Louise: 668
Verda: 373
Walter J.: 668
William Lewis: 373

Brash -
Ellen Clyde: 193, 194

Brauer -
Dean A.: 733

Brechbiel -
Beulah Elizabeth: 1122
Joe Cephus: 1122

Brenda -
Unnamed: 822

Brendle -
Alice Ann: 740

Brennan -
Bill: 660

Brenneman -
Benjamin E.: 775
Charlotte (aka: Lottie): 770, 771
David Benjamin: 776
David Benjamin: 776
Ephriam E.: 775, 776
Evan Elmer: 776
Fannie: 842
Gaylord Henry: 776
Ivan Glenn: 776
Lulu Jane: 777
Mary Magdalene: 776
Mildred Faye: 776
Milford Jay: 777
Sven G: 776
Virgil John: 776

Bressie -
Henry M.: 750, 751

Breuy -
Mary: 174

Brewer -
Charles: 238

Buddy or Bud -
    (name: Ervin D. Hostetler): 1311, 1312
Bungard -
    Alice: 94, 286, 287, 635, 1127, 1128
    Alverda M.: 283, 634
    Doris: 637
    Earl: 285
    Edna: 285
    Elizabeth: 1128
    Elizabeth: 94
    Florence: 637
    Gary: 1128
    Hazel: 637
    Henry Jacob: 94
    Irene Bungard: 285
    Isaiah: 94, 285
    Jacob: 92-94
    James H.: 1128
    Janet: 637
    Jerry: 1128
    Josiah C.: 94, 283, 630, 631, 633, 634, 1126
    Kathryn: 637
    Kenneth: 285
    Kevin L.: 1128
    Lucinda: 94
    Lula Blanche: 283, 633, 634
    Malinda: 94, 284, 634
    Mary: 285
    Mary Marie: 283, 630, 631
    Michael: 1128
    Minnie Mahala: 94
    Nancy: 637
    Nancy: 94
    Noah: 94
    Norman: 637
    Ortha: 287
    Paul: 1128
    Priscilla: 94
    Ray: 636
    Richard: 637, 1128
    Robert Sr.: 637
    Ruth Ann: 1128
    Sadie Grace: 283, 631, 632, 1126
    Samuel C.: 94
    Sarah: 94
    Scott: 1128
    Sophia: 94, 285, 286, 634, 635
    Susannah: 92-94, 282
    Walter: 637, 1127, 1128
    Walter Jr.: 1128
    William: 637
    William: 285
    William Earl: 636
    Zella: 637
Bunn -
    (name: Harry Freeman Ludy): 710
Bunny -
    (name: Maude Bernice "Bunny" Jones): 740-742
Bunten -
    Alicia Dawn: 1482
    Brian: 1482
    Kyle Brian: 1482
Burch -
    Lila May: 731
Burian -

Machele: 1116
Burket -
    Aaron Ross: 1409
    Alice: 160
    Angel: 1409
    Baby Boy: 1136
    Keanu: 1409
    Kevin Ross: 1136, 1408, 1409
    Lindsay Rhea: 1409
    Ramon C.: 1135, 1136
Burkett -
    Lillian Iva Dean (aka: Dean): 695
    Nathan: 127
Burkey -
    Mildred: 961
    Theodor G: 716
Burkhard -
    Barbara: 5
    Barbara: 5, 6
Burkhart -
    Diane: 1148
    Wayne: 1148
    Wayne Jr.: 1148
Burkholder -
    Barbara "Peggy" (aka: Peggy): 16, 17
    Barbara Ellen: 165
    Belva R.: 671, 672
    Caroline: 778
    Charles: 329
    Elwood: 685
    Esther: 573
    Harvey W.: 329
    Irvin: 329
    James: 329
    Laura: 329
    Leonard: 329
    Lowell: 1244
    Lydia: 37
    Lydia: 330
    Marjorie: 1244
    Mary: 662
    Nellie Mae: 329, 685
    Susanna: 15
    William: 165
Burright -
    Clyde Charles: 376
    Donald Gene: 377
    Edna Olive: 378
    Irene M.: 377
    James Orville: 376, 377
    Lydia Ruth: 383, 384
    Nora Pauline: 387
    Terry Wesley: 727
    Verlin Clyde: 377
    Wesley Edward: 377, 727
Burris -
    Allen Stuart: 1421, 1422
    Elliott: 1422
    Jessica: 1422
Busch -
    Edmund W.: 1402
    Fred Ludwig Sr: 1402
Bush -
    Cecil H.: 1121
    Karen Ruth: 1442, 1443

lma Grace: 1121
Butch -
    (name: Ray Sandow Christner Jr.): 716, 1174, 1426,
        1491
Butcher -
    Janet: 991
Butler -
    Beulah Rose: 1121, 1122
    Claude: 618
    Debbie: 618
    Ernest: 708
    Flora Elzia: 737
    John M.: 618
    John R.: 618
    Kathy: 618
    Linda Sue: 618
    Mary Ann: 618
    Tonya K.: 709
Butts -
    (name: Sprawls Edward Christner): 667
    James Elmer Otho: 658
    Jane Estelle: 658, 1135, 1136, 1408, 1409
    Joyce Edna: 658, 1135
Butz -
    Melvina Sue: 853
Byler -
    Edna Mae: 1253
    Elmer: 908
    Elsie Ellen: 1204
    Fannie: 568
    Jean: 932, 933
    Joseph J.: 908
    Katie: 909
    Leanna: 1253
    Lester: 1252, 1253
    Luella: 1253
    Mary Arlene: 1253
    Mattie: 790
    Mervin Lester: 1253
    Orvan: 909
    Perry: 909
    Ruth: 1253
    Ruth: 1459
    Velma: 1253
    Wilma: 909
C -
    Mary: 106
Calvin -
    Alta: 541
Camero -
    Franklin: 1486
    Scott: 1486
Cameron -
    Jimmy: 401
    Patrick Foster: 1428
Camille -
    Unnamed: 744
Campbell -
    Glen R.: 1166
    Glenn Jeffrey: 1166, 1422
    Janett Lee: 1166, 1422
    Jeanne Ann: 1166, 1422
    Jenny Lyn: 1166, 1422
    Sean Robert: 1422

Camut -
    Ross: 655
Cannon -
    Adam Jason: 1324
    Amanda Lee: 1324
    David: 1496
    Dennis: 1496
    Johnathan Lynn: 1324
    Rachel: 1496
    Stephen Lynn: 1324
Canton -
    Unnamed: 591
Cantor -
    Karolyn: 855
    Kimberly L.: 715
Cardin -
    Merlin "Barney' George (aka: Barney): 743
Carey -
    Anna Louisa (Annie): 241, 243
    Grover Francis: 248
Caris -
    Vinnie Estella: 806
Carlan -
    Larry: 637
Carman -
    Judy A. Massy: 1462
Carol -
    Unnamed: 1122
Carpenter -
    Chester B.: 659
    Chester B. "Bud" Jr.: 659
    Ellis E.: 406, 407
    Elmer Henry: 405, 406
    Glenda J.: 407
    Howard Edgar: 705
    Keith: 659
    LaWanda: 659, 1136
    Merril: 406
    Robert Howard: 705
    Ruth Alberta: 407, 408
    Theron Virgil Bradford: 405
    Vivian: 659
    Wayne: 877
    William Edgar: 705
Carrie -
    (name: Clara Ann Carrie Christner): 127
    Unnamed: 256, 257
Carroll -
    John: 85
    Patricia Bagley: 1165
Carter -
    Barry James: 737
    Bart David: 737
    Beulah: 686
    Charles Randall: 1101
    Charlotte: 686
    George: 686
    George Jr.: 687
    Isabel: 686
    Jacquelinann: 731
    Jessatine: 687
    Leona: 686
    Mabry James Jr.: 736, 737
    Mark Ermit: 737

Michael: 1101
Randall: 1101
Ruth: 687
Walter: 687
William: 686

Cartwright -
Candance Elaine: 1048
Debra Jo: 1048
Edward Dean: 1048
Michael Edward: 1048

Casey -
Ellen Lenora: 153
Frances: 390
Mary Jane: 153
Terri Jo (Demoret): 1441

Castillo -
Gilbert: 1360

Catelinet -
Barry: 1148

Catherine -
Unnamed: 624

Cavenaugh -
Phineas: 44

Cease -
Luteria (aka: Louie May): 101, 102

Chacken -
Gay: 632

Chamberlin -
Ada Pearl: 344

Champion -
Barbara: 1315, 1316

Chang -
Unnamed: 1166

Chapin -
Clell Marion: 1384
Johnny Lee: 1384

Chappel -
Garol D.: 1047, 1048
Garol Wayne: 1048
Janet: 1429
Janice Kay: 1048
Julia Ann: 1048

Charles -
Connie Sue: 1481

Chason -
Terry Lynn: 617

Cheever -
Bevery June: 1401

Chelsia -
Cyndi: 1412

Cheryl -
Unnamed: 1459

Cheuvrant -
Jessie L.: 237

Chevens -
Elizabeth: 49

Chic -
(name: Charles Theodore Christner): 336, 693, 1164, 1421

Chichester -
Alice A.: 751
William: 750, 751

Chopin -

Erin Elizabeth: 1489
Megan Elizabeth: 1489
Rene Adrian III: 1489
Rerre Adrian IV: 1489
Sarah Elizabeth: 1489

Chris -
Unnamed: 1492
 (name: Cary A. Christner): 672, 1149, 1413
Unnamed: 1492

Chrislop -
Dorthy Louise: 654
Hubert Albert "Bud": 654
Hubert Wesley: 654
Leona Mae: 654
Lewis Wesley: 654

Chrisman -
Shirley Irene: 1359, 1360

Christner -
Unnamed: 326, 682
Unnamed: 798
Aaron: 18
Aaron: 58, 194, 195, 458, 460-462, 823-826, 828, 1239-
1243, 1461-1463, 1493, 1494
Aaron: 49
Abigail M.: 1454
Abner Ozias: 417, 770, 771, 1194-1196, 1438-1442
Abraham: 43
Abraham: 55, 56
Abraham A.: 202, 471, 472
Abraham B.: 1227
Abraham D.: 17, 35, 36, 91, 111-113, 115-120, 317-
321, 323, 325-328, 661-664, 666-684, 1137-
1142, 1144-1157, 1159, 1160, 1410-1418, 1487-
1489
Abraham J.: 63, 207, 208, 494, 496-501, 918-930, 932-
935, 1243-1246, 1314-1327, 1463-1466, 1484
Ada A.: 430, 796
Ada Fanny: 444
Ada Louisa: 186
Ada Marie: 772, 1199
Ada O.: 292, 640, 641
Adam Jeffery: 1458
Addison: 1335
Adeline A.: 1391
Adeline Polly: 47, 151-153, 370-372
Aden E.: 1229
Adrian Ann: 1283
Adrian Orva "Chris": 829, 1244, 1245, 1465, 1466
Agnes Marie: 829
Alan Shirley: 341, 704
Alan Shirley Jr.: 704
Alan Stewart: 713, 1172
Alan William: 1277
Albert: 45
Albert James: 86
Albert Paul Jr.: 320, 672, 673
Albert Paul. Sr.: 116, 320, 669-672, 1148, 1149, 1413
Albert Raymond: 324, 681, 682, 1157, 1159, 1417,
1418, 1489
Aletha: 675
Alexander: 47, 158, 159, 393, 395, 740, 743-745, 1175-
1178, 1426, 1427
Alexander: 186
Alfred: 73, 237, 238, 586, 1101
Alfred Arthur (aka: Fritz): 621, 1118, 1399, 1486
Alfred B: 194

Alfred Hoy: 240, 587, 588
Alfred R. "Boots": 685, 1161, 1162, 1419
Alice: 155
Alice: 629
Alice Ann: 95
Alice Berdina: 808
Alice D.: 89, 275, 623, 624
Alice Mae: 264
Alice Marie: 975
Alice V.: 322
Alicia Marie: 1463
Alisha Dawn: 1464
Allen B. Sr.: 397, 749
Allen Ray: 829, 1244, 1463-1465
Allison Marie: 1319
Allyson: 1335
Alma: 1121, 1402
Alma: 158, 389, 737-739
Almede Iclee: 386
Almon M.: 97
Alpha: 73
Alphus: 518
Alta: 764
Alta Bernice: 472
Alta Ruth: 819
Alvin: 764, 1189, 1190, 1437
Alvin: 771, 1195, 1196, 1439-1441
Alvin B.: 1226
Alvin C.: 799
Alvin Dale: 896, 1302
Alvin E.: 1226, 1392, 1456
Alvin J.: 1229
Alvin M.: 1227
Alvin R.: 1228
Alvin S.: 431, 798, 799, 1225-1230, 1455-1457
Alvin S.: 1227
Alyssa Dawn: 1311
Alyssa Gwenevier: 1446
Amanda: 1462
Amanda: 81
Amanda: 201, 464, 465, 830, 832, 834, 836, 1246
Amanda: 116, 319, 320, 668, 669, 1148, 1412
Amanda: 130
Amanda Ann: 1246
Amanda Anne: 1442
Amanda C.: 800
Amanda E.: 486
Amanda J.: 213, 520, 521, 892, 946, 982-985
Amanda Mae (aka: Amy): 1246
Amanda Rose Eileen: 1450
Amanda Sue: 1449
Amelia: 209
Amos: 183, 447, 448
Amos C.: 903, 1306, 1482, 1483
Amos C.: 798
Amos D.: 96, 290, 638, 1128
Amos Dickey: 42, 130, 337-339, 700, 702, 1167, 1423
Amos J.: 213, 522, 989-992, 1334, 1335, 1484
Amos J.: 1229
Amos M.: 1097
Amos R.: 490, 491
Amy Beth: 1279
Amy C.: 1223
Amy Elizabeth: 1401
Amy Marie: 1282
Amy Veronica: 29

Anan Uriah: 417, 418
Ananias Sipe: 89, 270, 271, 620-622, 1118-1123, 1399-1403, 1486, 1487, 1496
Andrea Michelle: 1246
Andrew: 206, 207
Andrew L.: 975
Andrew L.: 1230
Angela Leigh: 1286, 1477
Angela Rae: 1152, 1414
Anita: 1430, 1492
Anna: 6-8
Anna: 26
Anna: 64, 210, 212, 504-513, 940-944, 946, 947, 949-955, 957-970, 1296-1298, 1328-1331, 1480, 1481
Anna: 173
Anna Bell: 772
Anna Bertha (aka: Bert): 352, 712, 1171
Anna C.: 1225
Anna Faye: 419, 775, 776
Anna Irene: 350, 710
Anna Mae: 444
Anna Maria: 28
Anna Marie: 522, 988
Anna S.: 1227
Anne: 761
Annie: 115
Annie: 56, 189
Annie: 422
Annie: 156, 380, 728
Annie C.: 477, 870, 871, 1180, 1181
Annie Estelle: 134
Annie J.: 201, 234, 466, 467, 841-848, 1099, 1194, 1252-1269, 1466-1475, 1494, 1495
Annie Mae: 308, 652, 653, 1132
Annie S.: 85
Anthony Brian: 922, 1318, 1319
Anthony Wayne: 1206
Archie B.: 155, 377, 728
Archie Melvin: 818, 819
Ariel E.: 144
Arlene (aka: Doll): 667, 1146, 1147, 1412
Arlene: 1218
Arlene Kay: 1307, 1483
Arnold: 301
Arnold Eugene: 829, 1243, 1244, 1463
Arnold Lane: 1207
Arthur: 271, 620, 621, 1118-1122, 1399-1403, 1486, 1496
Arthur Dean: 908
Arthur George: 421, 784, 785
Arthur Grover: 142, 351, 711
Arthur Jacob: 157
Arthur L.: 492, 907, 1261, 1293, 1309-1311
Arthur Leroy: 1118, 1119
Ashley Nicole: 1463
Ashli: 1457, 1493
Audrey Ann: 655, 1133, 1134
Audrey Marciel: 623, 1125
Austin: 1421
Austin George: 127, 330, 686, 687
Austin Wayne: 1459
Authur Broy: 1410
Authur E.: 662, 1138, 1410
Ava: 426, 787
Avalon Mae: 682, 1159, 1418

Baby: 621
Barbara: 5
Barbara: 11
Barbara: 21, 53, 54, 183, 448, 823, 1239
Barbara: 18, 49
Barbara: 24, 65, 66, 219, 552
Barbara: 57, 58
Barbara: 176, 415, 416
Barbara: 56
Barbara: 413, 762, 1187, 1434, 1435
Barbara: 444
Barbara: 667, 1145
Barbara Ann: 496, 923
Barbara B.: 1227
Barbara E.: 1391
Barbara Elizabeth: 778, 1206
Barbara J.: 571, 1099
Barbara L.: 1098
Barbara May: 441
Barbara S.: 1097
Barbe: 12, 19
Barnaby: 1239
Barry James: 1443
Barton Roy: 131, 339, 340, 700, 702, 1167, 1423
Basil Kenneth: 822
Beatrice: 370
Benedict J.: 430, 794, 1217, 1218, 1454
Benjamin: 11, 17, 18, 49, 50, 165-171, 400-405, 408,
        409, 750-752, 1178, 1179, 1427
Benjamin: 49
Benjamin Alvin: 1440
Benjamin Bradley: 169
Benjamin C.: 800, 1229
Benjamin E.: 183, 446, 447, 821, 1238
Benjamin E.: 1226
Benjamin Edward: 1405
Benjamin Franklin: 167
Benjamin Gary: 1311
Benjamin J.: 1229
Benjamin L.: 1230
Benjamin Scott: 1463
Bernard Jay: 1201, 1444
Bernice: 461
Bernice Mae: 346
Bertha: 444, 816, 817, 1237
Bertha: 228, 555
Bertha: 763, 764
Bertha Belle: 133
Bertha Ellen: 760
Bertha Ida: 167, 403
Bertha L.: 1230
Bertha May: 100, 294-296, 642-644, 1129, 1406, 1487
Beryl Mabel: 384, 730, 1174
Bessie Amanda: 202, 475, 868, 869, 1287
Bessie Marie: 384, 728, 729
Bessie Vera: 161, 397, 398, 749
Bessie Virginia: 273
Beth Ann: 1318
Beth Ann: 1440
Beth E.: 629
Bette Lucile: 352, 711, 712, 1171, 1425
Betty: 695, 1167
Betty: 1240
Betty: 872, 1292
Betty Dean: 362, 717, 1141
Betty Delores: 655

Betty Delores: 693, 1163, 1164, 1421, 1491
Betty Lee: 902
Betty Lizzie Ann: 497
Betty Lou: 775, 1203, 1371
Betty Louise: 685, 1161, 1419
Betty Marie: 268
Betty Ruth: 384, 731
Beulah: 460, 825, 1242, 1243
Beulah: 622
Beulah D.: 324, 680, 1157, 1417
Beulah Fern: 225, 554
Beulah V.: 466, 838, 1250-1252
Beverly Jane: 1155, 1415
Beverly Jayne: 1449
Billy: 673
Blanche Beloye: 163, 398, 399
Blanche P.: 333, 334
Bobbie: 1320
Bonnie: 670
Bonnie: 822
Bonnie: 1183, 1430
Bonnie Jo: 1155, 1415, 1488
Bonnie Lou: 714, 1173, 1425
Bonnie Sue: 906
Boyd: 368, 724
Braden Hurst: 100, 297, 645
Bradley Howard: 1243
Brandin: 1426
Brenda Diane: 1449
Brenda Kay: 1399
Brenda Lou: 922, 1319
Brett Allan: 1488
Brian Curtis: 1410
Brian David: 1445
Brian Lee: 1244, 1464
Brian Paul: 1278
Brianna: 1421
Bridget Renae: 1459
Bridgette Marie: 1410
Bruce: 148, 149
Bruce Galen: 1132
Burton: 102
Butch: 1152
Butch: 1432
Cade: 1465
Cain: 29, 89, 90, 275-278, 624, 627
Caleb Christian: 1392
Calvin M.: 45, 144-146, 356, 357, 359, 360, 714, 715,
        1173, 1174, 1425
Candy Christine: 1306
Carah Jean: 1459
Carey: 1419
Carl: 105
Carl Eugene: 650
Carl I.: 475, 862, 864, 866, 897, 899, 901, 1285, 1286,
        1476, 1477
Carl Osborne: 321
Carla Jean: 1244, 1465
Carlee Joyce: 1459
Carley: 1479
Carlson Drew: 665
Carol Ann: 393, 740
Carol Ann: 1242, 1463
Carol Ann: 906, 1309
Carol Jean: 1206
Carol Louise: 655

Diana Lynn: 1446
Diana Rebecca: 1245, 1465, 1466
Diane: 1152
Diane: 705
Diane: 733
Diane E.: 1456
Diane Elizabeth: 1431
Diane Fay: 907, 1293, 1294, 1309
Diane Sue: 925, 1321
Diane VaLeria: 1132
Dianne: 1125
Dianne Kay: 1217
Dinah Christina: 44, 142
Dinah Christina: 29
Dolores: 670
Don Lamar: 1232
Donald: 385
Donald: 104
Donald Allen: 1122
Donald C.: 824, 1240, 1461
Donald Duane: 923
Donald Edgar: 331
Donald Eugene: 854, 1278
Donald Jr.: 1240
Donald Ray: 621, 1122
Donald William: 1189, 1437
Donna: 787
Donna: 1190
Donna Kay: 908, 1311
Donna Lee: 396, 744, 745, 1177, 1426, 1427
Donna Lee: 1202, 1445
Donna Marie: 1151, 1413
Donnie Lynn: 908, 1311
Dora: 155
Doris: 823
Doris: 671, 1148
Doris Elaine: 862, 1283, 1285
Doris Loiuse: 693, 1164, 1165, 1421
Dorotha Minerva: 306, 651, 652
Dorothy: 301, 649
Dorothy: 1430, 1492
Dorothy Alice: 764, 1193, 1194
Dorothy Caroline: 86, 270
Dorothy Fern: 1195
Dorothy Jean: 339
Dorothy Lucille: 678, 1153, 1154
Dorsey N.: 131
Dorthy Elaine: 424
Dorvin Jay: 1196, 1441
Douglas: 1213
Douglas Earl: 924
Douglas Lynn: 1207, 1448
Douglas Ray: 1198
Douglas Truman: 922, 1319
Drew Mitchell: 1172
Duaine Edward: 838
Duane "Hud": 651
Duane Edward: 824, 1240, 1241, 1461, 1462, 1493,
    1494
Dustin Allan: 1429
Dwane: 638
Dwight R.: 307
E. Wayne: 651, 1132, 1407
Earl: 306
Earl: 497, 924, 1320
Earl Harrison: 158, 384, 385, 731-733

Earl Joseph: 441
Earl Ray: 350, 708, 1170
Earl Robert: 289
Earl Weimer: 279, 629
Ebbert Clinton: 288
Eddie S.: 1124, 1405
Eddranis D.: 204, 477, 478, 871-873, 1291-1293, 1478,
    1479
Edgar Haze: 102
Edgar James: 324, 679, 1157, 1417
Edith: 143
Edith Arlene: 279, 629
Edith D.: 1225
Edith L.: 492, 906, 907, 1309
Edith M.: 265
Edith M.: 1097
Edith Mable: 102
Edith May: 289
Edna: 682
Edna: 429
Edna: 325
Edna: 430
Edna: 431, 800, 801
Edna: 1218, 1454
Edna: 903, 1306, 1344
Edna Bell: 318, 662, 663, 1139, 1140
Edna C.: 800
Edna Irene: 310
Edna J.: 1229
Edna L.: 85
Edna Mae: 470, 852, 853
Edna Mae: 306, 652
Edna Mae: 778, 1209, 1451, 1452, 1493
Edna Pauline: 707, 708
Edna Rebecca: 134
Edna S.: 232, 572
Edward: 1174
Edward: 497
Edward: 700
Edward Carl: 318, 664, 665
Edward Dale: 1292, 1478, 1479
Edward J.: 179, 435
Edward T: 292
Edward Twain: 292
Edwin: 310
Edwin B.: 689
Eileen Marie: 1159, 1418, 1489
Elam: 36
Elam Josiah: 417, 771, 772, 1197, 1198, 1442, 1443
Elba May "Eggy": 423
Eldon: 184
Eldon: 1218, 1454, 1455
Eldon Merle: 986
Elenor: 45
Eleve: 675, 1150, 1413
Eli: 179
Eli: 485
Eli: 486
Eli J.: 202, 473, 859, 862, 1281-1283, 1285, 1475
Eli N.: 470, 854, 1276-1278
Elias: 31, 99, 100, 294, 297, 642-645, 1129, 1406, 1487
Elias: 36, 119, 327, 683
Elijah H.: 31, 104, 105, 304, 305, 651, 652, 1132, 1407
Elijah James: 1475
Elisbeth: 5
Elizabeth: 13, 21, 22, 60, 61, 199, 463, 464, 828

Elizabeth: 17, 37, 38, 124, 125, 329
Elizabeth: 51
Elizabeth: 33, 106, 309
Elizabeth: 36
Elizabeth: 24, 68, 227, 409
Elizabeth: 42, 134, 341, 704
Elizabeth: 53
Elizabeth: 34, 35
Elizabeth: 28, 77, 78, 249, 251-253, 256-258, 260, 593, 596-601, 603, 604, 609, 610, 612, 613, 1103-1106, 1108, 1111-1114, 1392-1394, 1397, 1398, 1485
Elizabeth: 36, 118, 326, 683
Elizabeth: 25
Elizabeth: 176, 412, 756, 757, 759, 1181, 1428, 1492
Elizabeth: 58, 189, 190, 450
Elizabeth: 177, 420
Elizabeth: 64
Elizabeth: 81, 261, 613
Elizabeth: 100, 300
Elizabeth: 761, 1185, 1432
Elizabeth: 460
Elizabeth: 340, 702, 703, 1167, 1423
Elizabeth: 647
Elizabeth "Lizzie": 67, 220
Elizabeth A.: 209, 499, 500
Elizabeth Amelia: 166, 400, 401
Elizabeth Anne: 921, 1318
Elizabeth B.: 1227
Elizabeth C.: 799, 1225, 1226
Elizabeth C.: 798, 1224
Elizabeth Deitz: 32
Elizabeth E.: 1226
Elizabeth Evelyn: 461, 828
Elizabeth Grace: 427
Elizabeth J.: 23, 65, 213-218, 523-533, 535-551, 992-1022, 1024-1027, 1029-1034, 1036-1057, 1059-1088, 1090-1093, 1294, 1301, 1313, 1314, 1335-1390, 1482, 1484, 1485
Elizabeth J.: 429, 488, 787, 788
Elizabeth J.: 571
Elizabeth Lynn (aka: Beth): 1420, 1489
Elizabeth M.: 1097, 1391
Elizabeth N.: 1391
Elizabeth S.: 1097
Elizabeth Susanne: 1429
Elizabeth Viola: 764, 1190, 1191, 1437, 1438
Ella Gertrude: 1120, 1400
Ellamae: 1186, 1432, 1433
Ellen: 140, 141
Ellen Chaney: 704
Ellen Mary: 115, 116
Ellis Martin: 972
Elma C.: 1225
Elmer: 748
Elmer: 271, 620, 1118
Elmer: 419
Elmer A.: 523, 991, 1334, 1335, 1484
Elmer D.: 1225
Elmer E.: 100
Elmer J.: 213, 517, 518, 972, 973, 976, 1331-1333
Elmer Joseph: 779
Elmer L.: 1098
Elmer Ray: 486
Elmer Sherman: 273, 623, 1123-1126, 1403-1405, 1487
Elmina Elizabeth: 1191, 1192

Elmina J.: 431, 800, 1005
Elsie Pearl: 324, 678, 1155, 1156, 1416, 1417, 1488
Elva O.: 158, 388
Elvesta M.: 226
Elvina Belle: 31, 103, 304
Elvira: 156
Elvy Elsworth: 306, 651, 1132, 1407
Elwyn: 279, 630
Emanuel: 764
Emanuel M.: 1227
Emery L.: 422, 423
Emily (Emma) C.: 799, 1225
Emily B.: 1227
Emily Jo: 1283
Emily M.: 1097
Emily Rose: 1476
Emma: 29
Emma: 760, 1183, 1184, 1431
Emma B.: 149
Emma Blanch: 109
Emma Catherine: 86, 269, 618-620
Emma D.: 131, 337, 338
Emma D.: 204, 487, 891-894, 951, 982, 1005, 1300, 1301
Emma D.: 163
Emma E.: 486
Emma J.: 64, 212, 213, 231, 430, 431, 1215
Emma J.: 431, 796, 797, 1219-1222
Emma Josephine: 778, 1207, 1208
Emma L.: 321
Emma L. (aka: Helen): 490, 903, 904, 1308, 1484
Emma L.: 1098
Emma Louise: 1449
Emma M.: 1228
Emma Marie: 662, 1138, 1139
Emma P: 291
Emma P.: 291
Emma S.: 232, 570, 1096, 1390
Emma S.: 1097
Emma Shirley: 775, 1204
Enos: 183
Enos A.: 1391
Enos C.: 800, 1228, 1455, 1457
Enos E.: 1226
Enos H.: 55, 185, 186, 449
Enos L.: 1098
Enos R.: 1228
Enos S.: 1227
Equilla: 331
Eric: 1148
Eric: 1479
Eric Brian: 1278
Eric Lee: 922
Erica Faye: 1320
Erma: 104
Erma: 518, 976
Erma: 622, 1122, 1403, 1487
Ermit Theodore "Erm": 158, 387, 736
Erna Barbara: 446, 820
Ernest: 495, 921, 1317, 1318
Ernest D.: 1225
Ernest Dana: 921, 1317
Ernest Duaine: 986
Ernest Emerson: 301
Ernest L.: 1230
Ernie Lyn: 1450

George C.: 33
George Calvin: 137, 342, 343
George Curtis: 318, 661, 662, 1138, 1410
George David: 650
George Deitz: 33, 105, 106, 307, 652, 653, 1132
George E.: 479, 872, 873, 1292
George I.: 343
George Jr.: 342
George L.: 86, 268
George M.: 165
George N.: 397, 747, 748
George Washington: 47, 160, 161, 397, 746-749
George Washington: 127, 331, 332
George Washington: 101, 301, 302, 649
George West: 85, 264, 615
George William: 264
Georgeanna: 302
Georgia: 748
Gerald: 105
Gerald M.: 829
Gerald Max: 557
Geraldine: 918, 1314, 1315
Geraldine Mildred: 1119
Gertie: 523, 990, 991
Gertrude: 101, 300
Gertrude: 83
Gertrude: 336, 695, 696, 1167, 1422, 1423, 1491
Gertrude Francina: 294
Gideon Andrew: 418, 772, 1198, 1199, 1443, 1444
Gilbert Leroy: 396, 740-742
Gilbert Leroy Jr. (aka: Gil): 742
Ginger Roline: 1249
Gladys Irene: 158, 390, 391, 739, 740, 1175
Gladys Opal: 385, 731
Glen Alan: 1186, 1433
Glen Dale: 992
Glen E. (aka: Hawkshaw): 478, 871, 872, 1291, 1292, 1478, 1479
Glen N.: 470, 471
Glenn H.: 320, 669, 670
Glenn L. Sr: 647
Glenn Lee: 716, 1174
Glenn R.: 301, 646, 647
Glennda Sue: 1196
Gloria Ann: 778
Gloria Ann: 708, 1170
Gloria D.: 718
Gloria Grace: 1207, 1449, 1450
Goldie L.: 492
Grace: 155
Grace Alverta: 291, 639
Grace Estelle: 167, 402, 403
Grace Lucille: 323, 674
Gregory Scott: 1244, 1463
Guy E.: 323
Hailee Denese: 1311
Hannah: 18
Hannah: 42
Hannah: 1421
Hannah Bell: 151, 369
Harlan Arthur: 1182, 1428, 1429
Harley: 495, 918, 1314
Harley D.: 484
Harley L.: 794, 1217, 1453, 1454
Harley L. Jr.: 1217
Harley Simon: 442, 816

Harold: 825
Harold Clinton: 808
Harold Dean (Kosh) (aka: Kosh): 667, 1142-1144, 1410, 1411, 1487, 1488
Harold Floyd: 1120, 1401
Harold J.: 819
Harold Maynard: 693, 1164, 1421
Harold S.: 315
Harold Smith: 872, 1291
Harold Wayne: 923, 1320
Harriet: 102, 103
Harriet "Hattie": 35, 110, 111, 317
Harriet Jean: 340
Harry: 109, 315, 316, 660, 1137
Harry Albert: 318, 663, 664, 717, 1140-1142
Harry Buford: 139, 347, 348
Harry C.: 189
Harry Cramer: 105, 305, 306, 651, 652, 1132, 1407
Harry Edison: 144
Harry Edward: 167
Harry Irvin: 228, 556
Harry Jones: 161
Harry Jr.: 655
Harry R.: 290
Harry Robert: 262, 614
Harry Sr.: 311, 654, 655
Harry Urbane: 133
Harvey: 43, 141, 142, 351, 711
Harvey B.: 1227
Harvey C.: 67, 226, 227, 554
Harvey C.: 799, 1227
Harvey M.: 1227
Harvey S.: 1227
Hattie: 137, 343, 344
Hazel: 458
Hazel: 238
Hazel Arlene: 448
Hazel Hughes: 424
Hazel Irene: 628
Hazel M.: 667, 1144
Hazel Marie: 302, 649
Heather Joyce: 1277
Heather Marie: 1172
Heather Renee': 1439
Heidi Jean: 1149
Heidi Jo: 1233
Heidi Marie: 1198, 1443
Helen: 772
Helen: 622
Helen: 682
Helen: 18
Helen: 326
Helen Grate: 923, 1319
Henry: 825
Henry: 122
Henry: 122
Henry: 67
Henry: 97
Henry: 825, 1241, 1462
Henry A.: 36, 117, 118, 326, 682
Henry Edward: 196, 460, 824-826, 1240-1243, 1461-1463, 1493, 1494
Henry J.: 43, 138, 139, 347, 348, 705-710, 1169, 1170, 1424, 1425
Henry Jr.: 1241, 1462
Henry Roscoe: 807

James: 975
James: 1192
James: 925
James Alan: 1207, 1449
James Allen: 85, 264, 265
James Allen: 1401
James Blaine: 421, 781, 782
James Cornett: 362, 720
James Daniel: 1200
James Edgar: 1131
James Edward: 772, 1199
James H.: 166
James Hoy: 74, 238, 239, 586-588
James J.: 1188
James Lambert: 167
James Lee: 906, 1308
James Lewis: 615
James Michael: 857, 1279, 1280, 1475
James R.: 655
James Randall: 718
James Ruffus: 303
James S.: 290
James Samuel: 775
James Scott: 1199
Jamon Dean: 1459
Jan Scott: 924, 1320
Jane: 1240
Jane Elizabeth: 49, 167, 168, 404, 750, 1178, 1427
Janet: 1240
Janet: 1190, 1437
Janet Marie: 350
Janet Ruth: 362, 719, 720
Janet Winifred: 678, 1152
Janice Elaine: 1196, 1439
Janie Kay: 672, 1149, 1150
Jared: 1412
Jason: 1462
Jason: 1402
Jason: 1436
Jason Daryle: 1278
Jason Oliver: 423, 785, 786
Jaunita: 521, 985
Jaunita Fern: 461, 826
Jaunita Rose: 1465
Jay: 271, 621, 622, 1122, 1403, 1487
Jay Carl: 1418
Jay D.: 1232, 1459
Rev. Jay Lewis: 682, 1157, 1159, 1417, 1418, 1489
Jr. Jay Lewis: 1159, 1418
Jay William Jr.: 325
Jean: 20
Jean: 673
Jeanette (aka: Nettie): 130
Jeanette "Nettie": 158, 386, 733-736
Jeff Lloyd: 1200
Jeffery: 1430
Jeffery Allen: 1244, 1463
Jeffery Carl: 1206
Jeffrey: 618
Jeffrey Grant: 1401
Jenna Marie: 1407
Jennie: 127
Jennie: 109
Jennifer: 720
Jennifer: 1411
Jennifer Jean: 1405

Jennifer Nicole: 1445
Jennifer Renee': 1282
Jenny Ann: 1279
Jenny Lynn: 1208
Jere: 725
Jeremiah (aka: Jerry): 43, 140
Jeremiah: 93
Jeremiah: 92
Jeremiah: 419
Jeremiah E.: 1226
Jeremy: 1412
Jeremy: 1320
Jeremy: 1431
Jeremy: 1479
Jeremy Lane: 1208
Jerome: 29
Jerome F.: 1457
Jerry: 706
Jerry: 1125
Jerry Clark: 1206
Jerry Dean: 1232, 1458
Jerry Dennis: 1200
Jerry E.: 1229
Jerry Lee: 1202
Jerry Lee: 1099
Jerusha: 280
Jerusha: 280
Jesse: 107, 310, 311, 654, 655, 1133
Jesse: 764, 1187, 1188, 1435, 1436, 1492
Jesse C.: 651
Jesse Calvin: 109, 314, 315, 659
Jesse Matthias: 418
Jessica Carmen: 1442
Jessica Louise: 1444
Jessie: 16, 34, 108-110, 314-317, 659, 660, 1136, 1137
Jessie Deering: 1462
Jewell: 858
Jill Ann: 1429
Jill Lynn: 1281
Jo Lynn: 1411
Joan: 670
JoAnn: 360, 715
Joanna: 36, 119, 327, 683, 684, 1160
JoAnne Darlene: 773, 1200
Jocelyn Louice: 1325
Jodee Ann: 930, 1325
Joe Logan: 1200
Joel: 1431
Johannes: 5
Johannes John Hans: 6, 8-12, 14-18, 21-27, 29-35, 37, 40-43, 45, 48-50, 60, 61, 65, 66, 68-72, 74, 76, 77, 79, 81-87, 89-101, 103-106, 108-113, 115-121, 123-130, 132, 134-138, 140-142, 144, 146, 149, 151, 154, 156, 158-161, 163-171, 199, 202, 205, 207, 209, 210, 212-224, 226-235, 237, 238, 240, 241, 244, 246-249, 251-253, 256-258, 260-271, 275-288, 290-294, 297-305, 307, 309-321, 323, 325-332, 334, 336-348, 350-357, 359-365, 367-381, 383-390, 392, 393, 395-405, 408, 409, 463-467, 469, 471, 473, 475-477, 479, 481, 486-488, 492-494, 496-502, 504-513, 523-533, 535-554, 557-569, 573-593, 596-601, 603, 604, 609, 610, 612-624, 627, 629-631, 633-635, 637-649, 651-664, 666-688, 690, 692, 693, 695-700, 702-715, 717-721, 723-728, 730-740, 743-752, 828, 830, 832, 834, 836-852, 854-859, 862, 866, 868-

877, 879-897, 901, 903-909, 911-930, 932-944,
946, 947, 949-955, 957-970, 992-1022, 1024-
1027, 1029-1034, 1036-1057, 1059-1088, 1090-
1096, 1099-1106, 1108, 1111-1129, 1131-1142,
1144-1157, 1159-1167, 1169-1179, 1243-1246,
1248-1283, 1285-1287, 1291-1331, 1335-1390,
1392-1394, 1397-1427, 1463-1491, 1494-1496

John: 185

John: 1493

John: 15, 29, 86, 87, 89-97, 116, 270, 271, 275-288, 290-
293, 620-624, 627, 629-631, 633-635, 637, 638,
641, 642, 1118-1129, 1399-1406, 1486, 1487,
1496

John: 35, 109, 314-316, 659, 660, 1136, 1137

John: 43

John: 55

John: 93

John: 107, 309, 310

John: 173, 227, 228, 409, 555-557

John: 67, 224

John: 97

John: 185

John: 761, 1186, 1432, 1433

John: 1192, 1438

John: 1131, 1407

John (Invalid John): 28, 79, 80

John A.: 209, 498, 499, 929, 930, 932, 1324-1327

John Adam: 413, 760, 761, 1185, 1186, 1432-1434

John B.: 52, 178, 212, 429-435, 517-522, 570, 572, 573,
787, 790, 791, 793-796, 798, 800-805, 972, 973,
976, 978-992, 1096-1099, 1213-1233, 1331-
1335, 1390-1392, 1453-1460, 1484, 1493

John B.: 840, 1252

John B.: 1227

John C.: 40, 121, 122, 128, 129, 328, 329, 684, 685,
1160, 1161, 1418, 1419

John C.: 798

John Cheyenne: 129

John D.: 201, 465, 466, 837-840, 1248-1252, 1466

John D.: 485

John David: 779

John E.: 179, 212, 213, 231, 233, 430, 431, 517-522,
570, 572, 573, 796, 798, 800, 972, 973, 976, 978-
992, 1005, 1096-1099, 1215, 1219-1230, 1331-
1335, 1390-1392, 1455-1457, 1484

John Elmer: 423

John Eugene: 1205, 1447

John Frederick: 678, 1154, 1155, 1414, 1415, 1488

John G.: 411, 754

John Howard: 828, 1243

John Hubert: 178, 420, 421, 781

John III: 15, 26, 34, 70-72, 74, 76, 235, 237, 238, 240,
241, 244, 246-248, 585-592, 1100-1103

John J.: 14, 23, 24, 65, 66, 68, 219-224, 226, 227, 552-
554, 1094

John J.: 23, 61-63, 199, 202, 205, 207, 209, 210, 212,
430, 464-467, 469, 471, 473, 475-477, 479, 481,
486-488, 492-494, 496-502, 504-513, 830, 832,
834, 836-852, 854-859, 862, 866, 868-877, 879-
897, 901, 903-909, 911-930, 932-944, 946, 947,
949-955, 957-970, 1099, 1243-1246, 1248-1283,
1285-1287, 1291-1331, 1392, 1463-1484, 1494,
1495

John J.: 63, 205, 206, 492, 493, 908, 909, 911-917,
1311-1313, 1484

John J. Jr.: 11, 14, 15, 26, 27, 34, 70-72, 74, 76, 77, 79,

81-85, 235, 237, 238, 240, 241, 244, 246-249,
251-253, 256-258, 260-270, 585-593, 596-601,
603, 604, 609, 610, 612-620, 1100-1106, 1108,
1111-1118, 1392-1394, 1397, 1398, 1485

John Johann: 12, 20, 21, 53, 54, 56, 58, 183, 185, 187-
190, 193, 194, 196, 198, 448-451, 455, 458, 460-
462, 823-826, 828, 1239-1243, 1461-1463, 1493,
1494

John Lee: 906

John Leland: 975

John Levi: 491, 905, 906

John Lewis: 772, 1197, 1198, 1443

John Manley: 58

John Mark: 1208, 1450, 1451

John Melvin: 195, 458, 823, 1239

John Paul: 1243, 1375

John Ray: 303, 649, 650, 1131

John Riley: 73, 237, 585, 1100

John Robert: 623, 1125

John S.: 434, 803, 804, 1230, 1231, 1457

John Samuel: 638

John Smith: 49, 165

John Steven: 1198, 1443

John Thomas: 447, 821, 822, 1238

John Thomas: 921, 1317, 1318

John Thomas: 677, 1152, 1414

John W.: 86, 268

John Walter: 1122

John William "Bill": 650

Jon Eric: 728

Jon Henry: 1325

Jon Scott: 930, 1325

Jonas: 122

Jonas: 11, 18, 19

Jonas: 14

Jonas: 122

Jonas: 45

Jonas: 497, 923, 924, 1320

Jonas Edwin: 778, 1208, 1450

Jonas H. Jr.: 45, 149

Jonas Jr.: 19

Jonas Yone: 17, 43-45, 142, 144, 146, 149, 351-357,
359-361, 704, 711-715, 717-720, 1170-1174,
1425, 1426, 1491

Jonathan: 16

Jonathan E.: 1229

Jonathan Lynn: 1448

Jonathan Paul: 1420

Joni Sue: 1416

Josef: 20, 53, 183, 448

Josef: 53, 183, 448

Josef: 448

Joseph: 30, 97, 293, 641, 642, 1129, 1406

Joseph: 176

Joseph: 181

Joseph: 177, 419, 420, 780, 1210-1212, 1286, 1287

Joseph: 45

Joseph: 206

Joseph: 771, 1196, 1441, 1442

Joseph "Zep": 11, 16, 17, 35, 37, 40-43, 45, 48, 111-
113, 115-121, 123-130, 132, 134-138, 140-142,
144, 146, 149, 151, 154, 156, 158-161, 163-165,
317-321, 323, 325-332, 334, 336-348, 350-357,
359-365, 367-381, 383-390, 392, 393, 395-400,
639-641, 661-664, 666-688, 690, 692, 693, 695-
700, 702-715, 717-721, 723-728, 730-740, 743-

750, 1137-1142, 1144-1157, 1159-1167, 1169-
    1178, 1410-1427, 1487-1491
Joseph B. "Just": 178, 429, 787, 790, 791, 793-796,
    1213-1218, 1453, 1454
Joseph C.: 13, 22, 23, 61, 65, 199, 202, 205, 207, 209,
    210, 212-218, 464-467, 469, 471, 473, 475-477,
    479, 481, 486-488, 492-494, 496-502, 504-513,
    523-533, 535-551, 830, 832, 834, 836-852, 854-
    859, 862, 866, 868-877, 879-897, 901, 903-909,
    911-930, 932-944, 946, 947, 949-955, 957-970,
    992-1022, 1024-1027, 1029-1034, 1036-1057,
    1059-1088, 1090-1093, 1099, 1243-1246, 1248-
    1283, 1285-1287, 1291-1331, 1335-1390, 1392,
    1463-1485, 1494, 1495
Joseph David: 204
Joseph Davis: 419, 777, 1205-1208, 1446-1450
Joseph Davis Jr.: 778, 1206, 1447, 1448
Joseph Denton: 424
Joseph Dewey: 426, 427
Joseph J.: 24, 66, 67, 220-224, 226, 552-554, 1094
Joseph J.: 63, 199-201, 464-467, 469, 471, 473, 475,
    830, 832, 834, 836-852, 854-859, 862, 866, 868,
    869, 1099, 1246, 1248-1283, 1285-1287, 1466-
    1477, 1494, 1495
Joseph J.: 178, 425, 426, 787
Joseph Joe: 202
Jr. Joseph Jr.: 17, 42, 134-138, 140, 141, 328, 341-348,
    350, 351, 639-641, 704-711, 1169, 1170, 1424,
    1425
Joseph Lee: 854, 1276
Joseph M.: 47, 154, 155, 374-381, 725-728
Joseph Mahlon: 470, 851, 852, 1274, 1275
Joseph Scott: 1202
Joseph Todd: 1440
Josephine (aka: Josie): 159, 393, 740, 1175, 1176
Josephine: 571
Josephine J.: 1229
Josephine L.: 1098
Josephine M.: 1097, 1392
Josephine R.: 1228
Josephine S.: 1097, 1391
Joshua: 1291
Joshua Abraham: 1325
Joshua Adam: 1423
Joshua David: 1421
Joshua G.: 1177
Joshua Joe: 1447
Joshua Scott: 1172
Joyce Collen: 1198, 1443
Joyce Elaine: 1182, 1429, 1430
Joyce Elaine: 1448
Joyce Linda: 1200
Juanita Faye: 1232, 1459
Judy: 586
Julianna: 36, 112
Julie: 1232, 1458
Julie: 1431
Julie Ann: 1437, 1493
June Matilda: 664, 1141, 1142
Justin Joe: 1207, 1448
Kalin Joe: 1449
Karen: 1124, 1405
Karen: 1183, 1431
Karen: 675, 1150, 1413
Karen Fay: 924, 1320, 1321
Karen Lynn: 1274

Karen Michelle: 1278
Karen Wanda: 1281
Kari Ruth: 1276
Karin D.: 714
Karl J.: 143, 351, 352, 711, 712, 1170, 1171, 1425
Karrie: 1432
Karyn Louise: 930
Kate: 155, 376, 727
Katherine: 42, 135, 341
Katherine (aka: Katie): 206, 492, 493, 908, 1484, 1485
Katherine: 1431
Katherine "Katie" Ann: 411, 752, 753, 1179
Katherine Ann: 47, 159, 160
Kathleen May: 350, 708
Kathryn "Katie" Ann: 194, 455, 456
Kathryn Ann: 1410
Kathryn Joan: 1307, 1483
Kathryn K.: 798
Kathryn Sue: 1488
Kathy Ann: 648
Kathy Jane: 1275
Katie: 761
Katie Ann: 208
Katie C.: 798, 1223
Katie D.: 204, 486, 882-890, 959, 967, 1298-1300
Katie D.: 1225, 1455
Katie R.: 1228
Katlen Marie: 1309
Kay Carol: 682, 1159, 1160
Kayla: 1436
Kaylene Jo: 1196, 1442
Keith Edward: 921, 1316, 1317
Kelby Ryan: 1459
Kellie Lynn: 1309
Kelly: 1412
Kelly Beth: 1488
Kelly Lequita: 1149, 1413
Kelsey Nicole: 1311
Kenneth: 825
Kenneth: 705
Kenneth: 238
Kenneth: 521, 986, 1334
Kenneth: 1183, 1430, 1492
Kenneth Charles: 1164
Kenneth Craig: 1430
Kenneth Dale: 852, 1275
Kenneth Duane: 859, 1281, 1282, 1475
Kenneth F.: 267
Kenneth Joe: 1205, 1447
Kenneth La Mar: 435
Kenneth McCoy: 377
Kenneth Raymond: 655
Kent: 1432
Kent David: 1420
Keri M.: 1438
Kerri Lynne: 1149, 1413
Kerry Ann: 1420, 1490
Keturah May: 97, 293, 641, 642, 1129, 1406
Kevin D.: 1173
Kevin Lee: 1275
Kevin Lynn: 1286
Kim: 733
Kim Michelle: 718
Kimberly: 1431
Kimberly Kay: 1435
Kimberly Sue: 1286, 1476

Kirby Ray: 1249
Kohle J.: 1458
Krishelle Sawaka: 1151
Kristie: 1412
Kristine Marie: 1325
Kristoffer John: 1451
Krystal Lynn: 1318
Kurt: 725
Kurt Nelson: 1164
Kurtz Masami: 1151
La Rue N.: 786, 787
Lakretia Lynn: 1447
Lana Sue: 676, 1151, 1414
LaReine Mary: 341, 703
Larry Kevin: 588
Larry Lee: 866, 1286, 1477
Larry Lee: 987
Larry Wayne: 830, 1246
Larry Wayne: 1155, 1416
Larry Wayne: 1146, 1411
Larry Wayne III: 1322
Laura: 1244
Laura: 228
Laura B.: 98
Laura B.: 1227
Laura D.: 420, 780, 867, 1210-1212, 1286, 1287, 1340, 1342
Laura D.: 1225
Laura Ellen: 131, 338
Laura Virginia: 151, 367, 368, 724
Lauretta: 155, 379, 728
Laurie Jo: 1149
Lavenia Deitz: 33
Laverin Lazarus: 19
Lavina: 34
Lavina: 444
Lawerence: 96
Lawerence Everett: 838, 1249
Lawerence William: 323, 675, 676, 1150, 1151, 1413, 1414
Layla Magenta: 1446
Leah: 47, 159, 396
Leah: 56, 187
Leah: 178, 428
Leanne Rhea: 1278
Lee: 1432
Lee Edward: 239, 587
Leland E.: 518, 973, 974
Lelon: 334
Lena: 433
Lena: 282
Lena Belle: 167, 402
Lena Lee May: 1319
Leo: 143
Leo David: 775
Leo Irvin: 346
Leo Ray: 772, 1198, 1443
Leo W.: 310
Leon Harvey: 872
Leona: 433
Leona Arlene: 301
Leona Mae: 1306, 1482, 1483
Leona O.: 334, 690
Leonard Arnold: 808
Leondus: 74
Leota Irene: 336, 696

Leroy: 1120, 1401
Leroy E. Roy: 478, 479
Leroy Emerson: 664, 717, 1140, 1141
Leroy Paul: 1401
Lester: 149
Lester L.: 358
Leta M.: 144, 355
Levi: 431
Levi: 16, 30, 31, 98-101, 103, 104, 294, 297-305, 642-649, 651, 652, 1129, 1131, 1132, 1406, 1407, 1487
Levi: 107
Levi: 93, 281, 282
Levi: 92
Levi: 101
Levi: 438, 807
Levi: 208
Levi: 485, 486
Levi: 1483
Levi C.: 798, 1223
Levi D.: 204, 488-490, 788, 789, 862, 895-897, 901, 903-907, 1214, 1261, 1302-1311, 1392, 1481-1484, 1495
Levi J.: 213, 521, 985-988, 1215, 1334, 1344
Levi J.: 571, 1098
Levi Lee: 491, 906, 1308, 1309
Levi M.: 1097, 1391
Levi S.: 232, 570, 571, 1096-1099, 1390-1392
Levi S.: 1097
Lewis: 116, 323, 324, 677-681, 1152-1157, 1159, 1414-1418, 1488, 1489
Lewis Calvin: 358, 714, 1173, 1425
Libbie J.: 132
Lida: 724
Lilah: 1124
Lilly Mae: 484
Lilly May: 109
Linda: 615
Linda: 1213
Linda (aka: Linnie): 146, 356, 357
Linda Gayle: 744, 1176
Linda Kay: 991, 1334, 1335, 1484
Linda Kay: 925, 1321
Lindsay Taylor: 1416
Lisa Ann: 1278
Lisa Marie: 932, 1327
Living: 620
Lizzie: 107
Lizzie: 1218, 1454
Lizzie Ann: 490, 896, 897, 1303-1305, 1481, 1482, 1495
Lizzie Mae: 499, 930-932, 1325, 1326
Lloyd E.: 336, 693, 694, 1165, 1166, 1422
Lloyd Elwood Jr.: 694, 1165, 1166
Lloyd M.: 131
Lloyd Wayne: 896, 1303
Lodine Marlene: 1399
Lois: 315
Lois Ann: 1209
Lois Frances: 341, 704
Lois Pauline: 655
Lorelei: 1157, 1417
Loren: 1432
Loren P.: 441
Lorene: 226
Loretta: 1099, 1392

Menno L.: 490, 895, 896, 1214, 1215, 1302, 1303
Menno S.: 1097
Merle: 306
Merle: 521, 986, 1344
Merle Jay: 986, 1334
Merle Jay II: 1334
Merle Ray: 1196, 1441, 1442
Mervin Roy: 521, 987, 988
Michael: 1302
Michael: 1183, 1431
Michael: 1440
Michael A.: 1391
Michael Allen: 749
Michael David: 1444
Michael Dean: 987
Michael Dean: 1202, 1445
Michael Douglas: 743
Michael Eugene: 902, 1305, 1306
Michael James: 720
Michael John: 1443
Michael Lee: 731, 732
Michael Lynn: 1232, 1233
Michael M.: 178, 421, 784
Michael Shannon: 1280, 1475
Michael Wayne: 1208, 1450
Michael William: 881, 882
Michele: 1462
Michele Renee': 1411
Michelle: 1432
Michelle Dawn: 1449
Michelle Rena': 1306
Michelle Renee': 1454
Michyl Roy: 746
Mildred: 228
Mildred: 639
Mildred M.: 223
Mildred R.: 289
Mildred Ruth: 294, 642
Mildred Ruth: 321, 673, 674
Mildred Ruth: 623, 1123, 1124, 1404
Miles E: 146, 360, 361
Millard Francis: 323, 676, 677, 1151, 1152, 1414
Millard Francis. Jr.: 677, 1151
Milo William: 486, 881
Milton Earl: 693, 1162, 1163, 1419-1421, 1489, 1490
Mindy Diane: 1305
Minnie: 185
Minnie L.: 105, 304
Minnie Mae: 73
Miriam Ann: 974
Miriam Rose: 1448
Miriam Virginia (aka: Min): 667, 1145
Missouri: 73
Mitchell Gary Dean: 1310
MO: 127, 331
Mon Jay: 1166
Monica Dena: 1442
Monroe D.: 496, 828, 829, 922, 1243-1246, 1463-1466
Monty Ernest: 746, 1178
Morris Dean: 1195
Morris Todd: 746, 1178
Moses: 18
Moses: 155
Moses C.: 17, 45-47, 149, 151, 154, 156, 158-161, 362-
    365, 367-381, 383-390, 392, 393, 395-398, 720,
    721, 723-728, 730-740, 743-749, 1174-1178,

1426, 1427
Moses Isaac: 49, 169, 408
Muriel Edna: 396
Musetta: 158, 385
Musin: 331
Myers Wilson "K.O.": 336, 692, 693, 1162, 1163, 1419-
    1421, 1489-1491
Myrtle Larue: 144
Myrtle Marion: 170
Myrtle Pauline: 315, 659, 660
Nancy: 18
Nancy: 177
Nancy: 667, 1147
Nancy: 873
Nancy: 1241
Nancy Ann: 621, 1119, 1120, 1399, 1400, 1486, 1496
Nancy Dee: 1196, 1442
Nancy J.: 824
Nancy Jane: 975
Nanette Kay: 932, 1327
Nannie: 156, 380
Naomi Ruth: 311, 654
Natalie Ann: 1245, 1466
Natalie Anne: 1173
Nate: 149
Nathan: 209, 494, 495, 918-921, 1314-1319
Nathan Alexander: 1446
Nathan Allen: 1244, 1465
Nathan L.: 1098
Nathan M.: 1228
Nathaniel: 44
Nathaniel: 45
Nathaniel Jacob: 1207
Ned: 105
Nedra Fern: 1230
Neil Wesley: 396, 745, 746, 1178
Nellie M.: 321
Nelson "Nels": 47, 156, 157, 383-390, 392, 728, 730-
    740, 1174, 1175
Reverend Nelson Brown: 42, 132, 340, 703, 704
Nelson D.: 96, 292, 293
Neoma: 308
Nevin Jacob: 638
Nicholas: 444, 818
Nicholas: 1241
Nicholas: 1492
Niki Angelique: 1246
Nina Marie: 446
Niva: 225, 553, 1094
Noah: 63
Noah: 181
Noah J.: 202, 469-471, 851, 852, 854-858, 1274-1281,
    1475
Noah J.: 499, 929, 930, 1325
Nola: 1213
Nora: 83, 262, 614
Nora: 434
Nora: 239, 586
Nora Belle: 307
Nora Delia: 73, 237, 586, 1100
Norma Alberta: 360, 715, 1174
Norma Jean: 555
Norma Jean: 1190, 1437
Norman: 123
Norman: 1433
Norman: 1099, 1392

Norman B.: 137, 291, 341, 342, 639-641
Norman D.: 291
Norman Wissinger: 133
Not Named: 484, 485
Oakie: 98
Odette Lucille: 664, 1142
Olen Jr.: 805, 1232, 1459
Olen S.: 434, 804, 805, 1231-1233, 1387, 1457-1460, 1493
Olive Jean: 306
Olive Mae: 340
Olive R.: 292
Ollie: 430, 795, 1218
Ollie N.: 470, 852, 1275
Opal Arlene: 343
Ora: 143, 351
Ora A.: 460, 824, 825, 1241, 1242, 1462, 1463
Ora Catherine: 651, 1131, 1132
Ora Jr.: 825, 1241, 1242, 1462
Ora Louisa: 297, 298
Ora May: 311
Orange Vandever Eugene: 196, 461, 826, 828, 1243
Oren Lee: 852, 1274
Orlin R.: 143
Orpha Maude: 335, 690, 691, 1162, 1419, 1489
Orrie John: 760, 1182, 1428-1430
Orrin: 196
Orvil H.: 805, 1231, 1457, 1458, 1493
Orville Ermit: 387
Orville R. "Speedy": 685, 1161
Oscar Beno: 421
Oscar Ira: 466, 837, 838, 1248-1250, 1466
Owen: 794, 1217, 1218
Pamela Marie: 1274
Pamela Sue: 1241
Pansy: 140
Paris L.: 714
Patricia: 1188, 1435
Patricia Ann: 1155, 1414, 1415
Patricia Lee: 744, 1176, 1177, 1426
Patty: 822
Paul: 331
Paul Bernard: 1195, 1438, 1439
Paul Clayton "Pont": 677, 678
Paul Edward: 852
Paul G.: 460, 823, 824, 1240
Paul Jacob: 143, 354, 355, 713, 1172, 1173
Paul Jay: 350, 707
Paul M.: 1228
Paul N.: 471, 857, 1280
Paul Ray: 1170
Pauline Elizabeth: 460
Pearl: 156, 381
Pearl Ada: 237, 585, 1100
Pearl May: 227
Peggy Jo: 873, 1292, 1293
Peggy Sue: 1277
Penny: 352
Perry Mark: 1206
Peter: 12, 19, 20, 50, 52, 53, 171, 173, 174, 177, 178, 180, 182, 183, 409, 411-416, 418-422, 424, 425, 428-436, 438, 440, 442, 443, 445-448, 517-522, 555-557, 570, 572, 573, 752, 754-757, 759, 760, 762-765, 767, 769-775, 777-781, 784-787, 790, 791, 793-796, 798, 800-808, 810, 812, 814-816, 818-821, 972, 973, 976, 978-992, 1096-1099,

1179-1238, 1269, 1270, 1286-1291, 1331-1335, 1390-1392, 1428-1461, 1477, 1478, 1484, 1492, 1493
Peter: 11, 15, 29-31, 86, 87, 89-101, 103, 104, 270, 271, 275-288, 290-294, 297-305, 620-624, 627, 629-631, 633-635, 637, 638, 641-649, 651, 652, 1118-1129, 1131, 1132, 1399-1407, 1486, 1487, 1496
Peter: 29, 87-89, 270, 271, 275, 620-624, 1118-1126, 1399-1405, 1486, 1487, 1496
Peter: 181
Peter C.: 51, 173, 174, 227, 409, 411, 555-557, 752, 754, 1179
Peter II: 20, 52, 178, 180, 182, 429-436, 438, 440, 442, 443, 445-447, 517-522, 570, 572, 573, 787, 790, 791, 793-796, 798, 800-808, 810, 812, 814-816, 818-821, 972, 973, 976, 978-992, 1096-1099, 1213-1238, 1331-1335, 1390-1392, 1453-1461, 1484, 1493
Peter III: 53, 180, 181, 436, 438, 440, 806-808, 810, 812, 814-816, 1233-1237, 1460, 1461
Peter J.: 179, 432, 433
Peter L.: 21, 56-58, 189, 190, 193, 194, 450, 451, 455, 458, 460-462, 823-826, 828, 1239-1243, 1461-1463, 1493, 1494
Pheobe Or Philipine: 178, 424
Philip: 1202
Philip: 1138, 1410
Philip: 1202
Philip Andrew: 854, 1277, 1278
Philip Thomas: 1441
Philip Wayne: 1209
Phillip: 1152
Philo Leroy (Roy P) (aka: Roy P.): 159, 395, 396, 740, 743-745, 1176-1178, 1426, 1427
Phineas S.: 1227, 1457
Phoebe: 297, 645
Phyllis: 826
Phyllis: 824, 1240
Phyllis Geraldine: 557
Phyllis Jean: 1196, 1440
Polly: 122
Priscilla: 30, 94, 270
Priscilla: 90, 278
Priscilla Rose: 854, 1278
Rachel: 31
Rachel: 93
Rachel: 858
Rachel: 1335
Rachel Ann: 1280, 1475
Rachel Ann: 1443
Rachel Anne: 1408
Rachel Diane: 1465
Rachel J.: 429, 521, 791, 1215, 1216, 1453
Rachel Pearl: 288
Ralph: 238
Ralph: 682
Ralph: 148, 361, 362, 715, 717-720, 1141, 1174, 1426, 1491
Ralph: 1218
Ralph Harry: 306
Ralph Leroy: 650
Ralph O.: 460, 824, 1240, 1461, 1462, 1493, 1494
Ralph Peter: 446
Ramona: 929, 1324
Randall Craig: 1199
Randall David: 1416, 1488

Randolph: 1183, 1431
Randy: 1431
Randy Lynn: 710
Randy Wayne: 925, 1321
Ray Nelson: 158
Ray Sandow Jr. (aka: Butch): 716, 1174, 1426, 1491
Ray Sandow Sr.: 362, 715, 716, 1174, 1426, 1491
Raymond: 748
Raymond: 622
Raymond: 499, 929, 1324
Raymond Alfred: 306
Raymond John: 449, 450
Raymond Mack: 623, 1125, 1126
Raymond Russell "Friz": 228, 557
Rebecca: 26
Rebecca: 1440
Rebecca: 1436
Rebecca Ann: 929
Rebecca B.: 1226
Rebecca C.: 798
Rebecca D.: 1225
Rebecca Frances: 109
Rebecca J.: 571, 1098
Rebecca M.: 1097
Rebecca R.: 1228, 1457
Rebecca S.: 1097
Rebecca Sue: 1206, 1448
Rebekah Lynn: 1420, 1490
Regan Daneen: 1178
Regina: 587
Regina Lynn: 1455
Regina Sue: 1448
Reginald D.: 1202, 1446
Rena: 47, 154, 373
Reuben C.: 800, 1230
Reuben J.: 1229
Reuben L.: 1230
Reuben S.: 1227
Reuel Stanley: 279, 627, 628
Rex Everett: 303
Richard: 361
Richard: 49, 170
Richard: 823
Richard: 385, 732, 733
Richard Allen: 1465
Richard Dale: 857, 1278
Richard Dean: 1196, 1439
Richard E.: 95, 287, 288
Richard Earl: 423, 787
Richard Henry: 49
Richard Lee: 859, 1282
Richard P.: 1192
Richard Robert: 396, 744, 1176, 1177, 1426
Richard Robert Jr.: 744
Richard Sloan: 704
Richard Sr.: 301, 646
Richard W.: 47, 161, 162, 398
Rick Allen: 1308
Rickie Joe: 896
Ricky: 1188, 1436
Ricky Lynn: 930, 1325
Rita Mae: 655, 1133
Robbie: 83
Robert: 1167
Robert: 637
Robert: 324

Robert: 336
Robert: 340
Robert: 450
Robert: 1184, 1431
Robert: 1189
Robert Allan: 1415, 1488
Robert Burns: 664
Robert C.: 268, 618
Robert C. "Amos": 322, 323
Robert Clare: 1188, 1435, 1492
Robert Donald: 1155, 1415, 1488
Robert Eli: 857, 1278, 1279
Robert Floyd: 1432
Robert Foster: 1410
Robert G.: 354
Robert G.: 189
Robert Harold: 1401
Robert Henry: 614
Robert Jr.: 1410
Robert Jr.: 655
Robert Kenneth: 1334
Foster son Robert Kerry: 1275
Robert L.: 408
Robert Lee: 348
Robert Lee: 1119
Robert Lloyd: 1463
Robert Sr.: 1138, 1410
Robert Sr.: 311, 655, 1133
Robert Wayne: 1197, 1442, 1443
Roberta Samatha: 340, 700-702
Rodger: 1196
Rodney: 1188, 1436
Rodney John: 1252
Roger Dale: 1124
Roger Lee: 709, 710
Roger Leroy: 717
Rollie Herbert: 226
Rollin Floyd: 838, 1248, 1466
Roman F.: 1457
Roman S.: 1227
Ronald: 1138, 1410
Ronald Craig: 713, 1173
Ronald Dale: 356, 713, 1173
Ronald Dean: 1242
Ronald George: 906, 1309
Ronald Ray: 1196, 1441
Ronald Ray Jr.: 1441
Ronda Michelle: 1286, 1476
Roosevelt T.: 422
Rory Mitchyl: 1178
Rosa D.: 1225
Rosa M.: 1097, 1391
Rosa Mae: 167, 402
Rosa Mae: 794
Rosa N.: 1391
Rosanna Marie: 1448
Roselynn: 1152
Rosetta A.: 1307, 1483
Rosina: 799, 1228
Rovena Faith: 808
Roxanne: 1432
Roy: 239
Roy Dimple: 621
Roy E.: 288
Roy Lemoine: 623, 1124, 1405
Roy M.: 158, 392, 393, 740

Roy Marvin: 385, 731
Roy Milton: 330
Ruby: 629
Ruby: 238, 586, 1101
Ruby Ellen: 838, 1250
Rudolph: 122, 328, 329, 684, 1160, 1161, 1418, 1419
Rudy C.: 800, 1229
Rudy E.: 1229
Rudy S.: 1227
Rufus: 31, 104
Rufus: 31, 101, 102, 302, 303, 649, 1131
Rufus: 45
Rufus: 495, 920, 921, 1316
Rufus J.: 45, 146, 147, 361, 715, 717-720, 1174, 1426, 1491
Russell: 268, 269
Russell Wayne: 1170
Ruth: 267
Ruth (aka: Dolly): 147
Ruth: 332
Ruth A.: 1198
Ruth Arlene: 359
Ruth Blanche: 325, 682, 1160
Ruth Edna: 167
Ruth Karen: 1240, 1461
Ruth L.: 331
Ruth M.: 628, 629
Ruth Marie: 293
Ruth May: 754
Ruth Olive: 292, 641
Ryan Allen: 1311
Ryan Douglas: 1319
Ryan James: 1308
Ryan Patrick: 1441
Sadie: 116, 321
Sadie: 101
Sadie: 761, 1186, 1187, 1433, 1434
Sadie Emma: 83
Sadie M.: 292
Sadie Margaret: 292, 641
Sadie Marie: 86, 265, 266, 616, 617, 1114-1118, 1398
Sadie Sarah: 146, 360
Salina: 495, 919, 920, 1316
Sally Ann: 816
Sally Sarah: 36, 119, 136, 328
Saloma: 5
Saloma: 81, 124
Samantha: 1411
Sampson Samuel: 155, 378
Samuel: 15
Samuel: 30, 90, 91, 279, 627, 629, 630
Samuel: 33, 106, 107, 309-311, 654-656, 1133
Samuel: 40
Samuel: 176, 412, 413, 759, 760, 762, 763, 1182-1193, 1428-1438, 1492, 1493
Samuel: 29, 82, 262, 614
Samuel: 93
Samuel: 92
Samuel: 45
Samuel A.: 36, 120, 121
Samuel A.: 523, 992
Samuel A.: 799, 1227, 1457
Samuel A.: 1391
Samuel B.: 1227
Samuel C.: 798
Samuel Deitz: 33

Samuel E.: 96, 288, 289, 637
Samuel H.: 292
Samuel J.: 1229
Samuel J.: 179, 434, 803-805, 1230-1233, 1457-1460, 1493
Samuel J.: 213, 231, 232, 518, 570, 572, 573, 1096-1099, 1390-1392
Samuel J.: 289, 637, 638
Samuel J.: 342
Samuel J.: 289
Samuel J.: 571, 1097, 1390, 1391
Samuel J.: 1229
Samuel J. "Matlick Sam": 43, 136, 137, 291, 328, 341-346, 639-641, 705
Samuel L.: 491
Samuel L.: 1098
Samuel Lawrence: 1405
Samuel Lewis: 678, 1152
Samuel M.: 1097, 1391
Samuel M.: 1228
Samuel Ray: 992, 1438
Samuel Raymond: 85
Samuel S.: 1097
Samuel S.: 430, 793, 794, 1217, 1453, 1454
Samuel S.: 1227
Samuel S.: 1097
Sandi Maxine Whitt: 1321
Sandra: 1430, 1492
Sandra Jay: 991, 1334
Sandra Kay: 732
Sandra Rae: 929, 1324
Sara Ann: 694, 1166, 1422
Sara Elizabeth (aka: Bertha): 271, 622, 1123
Sara Jane: 1144, 1411, 1488
Sara Lynn: 1440
Sarah: 28
Sarah: 43, 137
Sarah: 91
Sarah: 73
Sarah: 179, 433, 434
Sarah: 301, 648, 649
Sarah Ann: 434, 803
Sarah B.: 93
Sarah Ellen "Helena": 26, 74, 75, 240, 241, 244, 246-248, 589-592, 1101-1103
Sarah Etta: 167, 401
Sarah Eva Marie: 1317
Sarah Jane: 921, 1318
Sarah Jean: 1408
Sarah Mandella: 196, 461, 826
Savilla: 121
Savilla E.: 1456
Scott: 732
Scott: 336
Scott: 1320
Scott Alan: 1282, 1475, 1476
Scott Allen: 1277
Scott Allen: 1463
Scott Brian: 1249
Scott J.: 1438
Scott Norman: 713, 1172
Seth Arthur: 1311
Seth James: 1449
Sevilla: 44
Sevilla: 43, 141, 350
Sevilla: 122, 329, 685

Shantra: 1441
Sharon: 986
Sharon Darlene: 1205, 1446, 1447
Sharon Sue: 588
Shaunai Michelle: 1401
Shawda Lynn: 1291
Shawn: 1232
Shawn Alan: 1436
Sheena Renee: 1418
Shelby Rose: 1207, 1449
Sheldon Ray: 1244
Sheri Lynne: 1126
Sherral: 1430
Sherry Elaine: 710
Sherryl Ann: 1230, 1457
Sheryl: 988
Sheryl: 1231, 1457
Shirlene Kay: 862, 1283
Shirley: 1153
Shirley: 1189, 1437
Shirley: 268
Shirley Ann: 1241, 1462, 1494
Shirley Ann: 1197, 1442
Shirley Diann: 1205, 1447
Shirley Irene: 646
Shirley Jean: 1182
Shirlisa Jo: 988
Sidney Lewis: 158, 383, 384, 728, 730, 731, 1174
Silas: 42
Simon: 47
Simon: 47
Simon B.: 1227
Simon Peter: 418, 773, 1199-1201
Simon Sipe (Pete) (aka: Pete): 621, 1120, 1400, 1401
Soloma: 209, 501
Soloma: 484, 876, 1007
Soloman: 19
Soloman: 31
Solomon: 102
Solomon: 761
Solomon McKenzie: 18, 49, 165-170, 400-405, 408,
    750, 751, 1178, 1427
Sonda: 1231, 1458
Sophia: 93, 280
Sourie Grace: 329
Sovilla C.: 1225
Sprawls Edward (aka: Butts): 667
Staci: 1174
Stanley Davis: 1207
Starla Lynette: 1232, 1458
Starr Elizabeth Grace: 1446
Stella M.: 293
Stephanie: 1432
Stephen: 1148
Stephen E.: 1226, 1456
Stephen Jay: 1444
Stephen Marc: 1420
Stephen Owen: 1207
Stephen Sterling: 1155, 1416
Steven: 269
Steven: 1185, 1432
Steven Carl: 866, 1285, 1286, 1476
Steven Curtis: 1157
Steven Dale: 986
Steven Jr.: 1432
Steven Paul: 976

Steven R.: 1173
Steven Wayne: 1231, 1457, 1493
Stewart A.: 143, 352, 712, 1172
Stewart Norman: 352, 712, 713, 1172
Stuart: 131
Susan: 16, 32, 105, 307, 652, 653, 1132
Susan: 18
Susan: 36
Susan: 107
Susan: 81
Susan: 155
Susan: 83, 262, 263
Susan: 586
Susan "Sadie": 81
Susan D.: 1225
Susan E.: 1226
Susan J.: 1229
Susan Jean: 772, 1198, 1443, 1444
Susan M.: 1227
Susan R.: 1228, 1455, 1457
Susan Rae: 749
Susan S.: 1097
Susana Susannah: 90, 277
Susann E.: 1456
Susanna: 429
Susanna: 17
Susanna: 36, 91, 92, 116
Susanna: 31
Susanna: 176, 411, 754-756, 1180, 1288-1291, 1477,
    1478
Susanna: 430
Susanna Deitz: 33, 108, 312, 313, 657-659, 1134-1136,
    1408, 1409, 1487
Susanna L.: 490, 862, 864, 866, 897, 899
Susanna Lucy Anne (aka: Louisa): 40, 127, 128, 336,
    697-699
Susannah: 49
Susannah: 43, 138
Susie J.: 213, 519, 520, 976, 978, 1062
Suzanne B.: 1227
Sylvester: 324, 677, 1152-1155, 1414-1416, 1488
Sylvester Francis: 346, 705
Sylvia: 431
Sylvia C.: 798, 1223
Sylvia E.: 486
Sylvia Florence: 621, 1122
Sylvia Grace: 921, 1318
Sylvia S.: 232, 572, 573
Tabitha Beri: 1310
Tamara Sue: 1198, 1443
Tammy: 1232, 1458
Tara Ellen: 1178
Tawny: 732
Taylor Jean: 1322
Teddy Wayne: 857
Tena Tenia: 28
Teresa Dennell: 1437
Terri Jo: 1278
Terry: 1426
Terry: 1167, 1423
Terry A.: 718
Terry Lee: 1155, 1416
Thayer H.: 340, 700
Theal E.: 163
Theodore: 775
Theodore "Dorrie": 127, 334, 335, 690, 692, 693, 695,

696, 1162-1167, 1419-1423, 1489-1491
Theodore Allen: 1196
Theodore Eugene: 385, 732
Thomas: 873
Thomas Earl: 732
Thomas Eugene: 708, 1170
Thomas G.: 586
Thomas Jacob: 667, 1146, 1411
Thomas Jacob Jr.: 1146, 1411
Thomas L.: 1240
Thomas Lee: 857
Thomas Leroy: 1196, 1440
Thomas W.: 336, 696, 697, 1167, 1423
Tien: 1152
Timothy: 1303
Timothy: 975
Timothy Alan: 924, 1320
Timothy Alan: 1199
Timothy Allen: 932, 1326
Timothy Allen: 749
Timothy Allen: 1147
Timothy Charles: 1282
Timothy E.: 1390
Timothy W.: 1437
Tina: 1430, 1492
Tina Marie: 1292, 1479
Titus Leroy: 807
Tobias D.: 484
Todd: 1410
Todd: 1435, 1492
Todd Allen: 1462, 1493
Todd Anthony: 1201
Todd Michael: 1217
Todd William: 1437
Tom Evans: 346, 347
Tonya: 1402
Tonya Jean: 1149
Tracy Sue: 1462, 1493, 1494
Trent Lynn: 1178
Trever Eugene: 1178
Trey William: 1464
Trina: 1436
Trudy Kay: 355, 713, 1172, 1173
Trudy Lynn: 733
Truman: 495, 921, 922, 1318, 1319
Twin Infants: 143
Ty: 1491
Tyrannus: 36, 113, 114, 317, 661, 1137, 1138
Ula: 143, 353
Ulyses: 157
Unnamed: 306
Unnamed Infant: 204
Uriah: 30, 92, 93, 280-282
Uriah D.: 484, 879, 880, 946, 1295, 1479
Urias: 30, 91, 92, 116
Urias Bud: 143, 353, 354
Urias Jonas: 45, 142, 143, 351-354, 711-713, 1170-
    1173, 1425
Valarie Jean: 1147, 1412
Valerie Ann: 1308
Velma: 225, 553
Velma G.: 331, 688
Velma Lucretia: 838, 1249, 1250
Venona L.: 466, 838, 839
Veoma: 309
Vera: 143

Vera June: 775, 1204, 1205
Verda Emma: 446, 820, 821
Verdell: 158, 390, 739
Verena L.: 1098
Verena S.: 1097
Verena Veronica: 21
Verlo: 479, 873, 874, 1293
Verna: 772
Vernon E. Shorty: 473, 862, 1283, 1285
Vernon Jay: 804, 1230, 1457
Veronica: 36
Veronica: 29
Veronica "Fanny": 52
Veronica "Frany" (aka: Fannie/Fanny): 26, 76, 77
Veronica Fannie: 15, 26, 27
Veronica Fannie: 14, 24, 69, 228-235, 557-569, 573-
    584, 1094-1096
Veronica Fannie: 181, 436
Veronica Frany Fanny: 178
Veronica Luckenbill: 21, 58, 59, 196, 198, 462
Vicki Sue: 1432
Vickie: 1492
Vicky: 874
Victor: 96
Victoria: 49
Victoria Sue: 1399
Viola: 760, 1183, 1431
Viola: 1218
Viola Ferne: 778, 779
Viola Frances: 240
Viola M.: 288
Viola R.: 149
Violet: 162
Violet: 306
Violet Lauretta: 376, 727
Virgil: 458
Virgil Oscar: 311
Virginia: 822
Virginia Aldean: 775, 1202
Virginia Bessie (aka: Bessie): 623, 1126
Virginia Wynona: 397, 746
Walter: 622
Walter: 282
Walter: 401
Walter Akins: 289
Walter C.: 146, 359, 360, 715, 1174
Walter D.: 1225
Walter H.: 324, 680, 681
Walter J.: 760, 1182, 1183, 1430, 1431, 1492
Walter Joseph: 101, 300, 301, 646-649, 1131, 1407
Walter Jr. (aka: Budd): 681
Walter Orville: 621, 1121, 1122, 1403
Warren: 91, 279, 280
Warren Jacob (Grant): 151, 369, 370, 725
Warren Joseph: 677
Warren Richard: 785
Washington (aka: Wash): 127, 331, 688
Washington: 318, 319
Wayne: 497, 924, 925, 1321, 1322
Wayne: 1232, 1459
Wayne B.: 435
Wayne Eugene: 1126
Wayne O.: 805, 1231, 1387, 1458
II Wayne W. II: 925, 1322
Weldon W.: 556, 557
Wendell Lee: 1120, 1401

Wendell Newill: 1129
Wendy Lynn: 1437, 1493
Wendy Sue: 717
Wendy Sue: 1416
Whitney: 1458
Wilbert D.: 325
Wilbur: 690
Wilbur E.: 473, 859, 1281, 1282, 1475
Wilbur Ray: 623, 1124
Willard: 146
Willard Dean: 326
Willard Leroy: 772
William: 1174
William: 19
William: 1303
William: 104
William: 177
William: 1174, 1426, 1491
William: 429
William: 117, 325, 682, 1160
William: 178
William: 108, 109
William: 324
William: 310
William: 762
William Arthur: 170, 408
William C.: 903, 1099, 1307, 1392
William Clayton: 348
William D.: 82
William D.: 1225
William Dale: 461, 826-828, 1243
William Dale: 676, 1150, 1151, 1413
William E.: 264
William Eugene: 378, 728
William Fred: 1119
William Gerald: 854, 1277
William H.: 116, 321, 673
William H.: 100, 101
William Henry: 49, 166, 400-403
William Irvin: 196
William J.: 67, 224, 225, 553, 554, 1094
William J.: 227, 554, 555
William J.: 1229
William L.: 228
William L.: 1098
William Lee: 695, 1166
William Leigh: 1122
William P. Jr.: 1189, 1436, 1437, 1493
William P. Sr.: 764, 1188, 1189, 1436, 1437, 1493
William R.: 133
William Ralph: 716
William S.: 102, 302, 303, 649, 1131
William Thomas: 167
William Wade: 225
Willis (Bill) Dean: 825, 1242, 1463
Willis Earnest: 423
Willis J.: 1457
Willis N.: 470, 856, 857, 1278, 1279, 1475
Wilma: 523
Wilma G.: 378
Wilma Irene: 316, 660, 1137
Wilma L.: 484, 877, 878, 1294, 1295
Wilma U.: 880, 1295, 1479
Wilmer: 282
Wilson: 122
Wilson Clay: 1465

Wilson William: 127, 332, 333, 688, 690
Winfield Scott: 91, 279, 627, 629, 630
Winfield Scott: 89, 271-274, 623, 1123-1126, 1403-
    1405, 1487
Wodrow: 331
Yvonne Diane: 1248, 1466
Zachariah: 40, 126, 127, 330-332, 334, 686-688, 690,
    692, 693, 695, 696, 1162-1167, 1419-1423, 1489-
    1491
Zachary William: 1172
Zachery Lee: 1416

Christophel -
    Eldon Clare: 1245
    James Eldon: 1245
    Kevin Monroe: 1245
    Yvonne Marie: 1245

Chupp -
    Adaline: 533
    Amos: 532, 533
    Andrew I.: 548
    Barbara: 1233
    Christy Jac: 1447
    Clarence L. "J.R." Jr.: 1360
    Clarence LeRoy: 1001, 1359, 1360
    Darlene Joan: 1273
    Dema: 957
    Edna: 532, 1012
    Eli: 532
    Elizabeth J.: 1073, 1216, 1217
    Ella: 1079
    Ellen Renee: 1447
    Ernest: 1079
    Ida J.: 533
    Ida L.: 1079, 1389
    Infant: 548
    Infant: 533
    Jess: 1079, 1080
    John: 1447
    Jonas: 532
    Kim: 1360
    Lamar Dean: 1447
    Lee Alen: 870
    Levi A.: 548, 1079, 1389
    Lila Joan: 862
    Lizzie: 1079
    Lizzie A.: 548, 1079, 1080, 1389
    Mary Edna: 1001
    Mary Ellen: 987, 988
    Mattie A.: 549, 1080
    Nathaniel: 533
    Olen J.: 1446, 1447
    Oleta Mae: 1001, 1359, 1363, 1364
    Richard Lee: 1002
    Robert: 1360
    Rudolph: 548
    Samuel N.: 1001, 1363
    Sharon: 1360
    Treva Elaine: 1447
    Vernon R.: 877
    Wilis: 533
    Wilma: 1079

Churchill -
    Debra Louise: 1441

Cicman -
    Unnamed: 657

Clair -
Ivan: 375
Clark -
Unnamed: 1398
Betty Virginia: 1348
Brian: 1398
Lois: 684
Rachel Florence: 369
Clary -
Louise Thelma: 394
Clay -
Barbara: 1161, 1419
Bryan: 1419
Cleopatra May: 738
Clyde E.: 1161
Edward: 1161, 1419
Heidi: 1419
Kenneth: 1161, 1419
Leah: 1419
Lee Russell: 738
Luke: 1419
Claypool -
Lenore Ellen: 1156, 1157
Cleveland -
Kenneth Allen: 905
Click -
Glenn: 1281
Phyllis Lee: 1281
Clink -
Unnamed: 1214
Close -
?: 316
Jesse: 316
Kenneth J.: 316
Orval Clarence: 316, 660
Orval Ray: 660, 661
Clough -
Jean: 1380
Clouse -
Ann: 828
J. Maxwell: 828
Ray: 828
Cobb -
Clois Cornelius: 398
Debbie: 1101
Elizabeth Vera: 398, 749, 750
Grady: 1101
Jaunita Oleta: 398
William F.: 397, 398
Cober -
Debra: 1114
Donald Glenn III: 1115
Donald Glenn Jr: 1115
Donald Glenn Sr.: 616
Melissa Ann: 1115
Coblentz -
Anna: 792
Dianne Louise: 1279, 1280
Esther: 1468
Jerry Lee: 1076
Katie: 1019
Laverne: 1076
Moses D.: 1076
Moses Jr: 1076

Verton Daniel: 1076
Cochran -
Charlotte: 1412
Eva: 593, 594
Coffman -
Unnamed: 635
Colagrossi -
Anthony: 1009
Phyllis Darlene: 1009
Colbert -
Ellis: 296
Cole -
Betty: 1270
Irene L.: 654, 655
Coleman -
Grace E.: 264
Nancy Ann: 620
Sevilla Catherine: 142, 143
Collins -
Otto Karns: 385
Vera Luella: 385
Colman -
Kim: 1125
Combs -
Mary Edna: 707
Concini -
Dace Shavez: 1140
Daniel Dominic: 1140
David Clarence: 1140
John William: 1140
Robert: 1140
Connie -
Unnamed: 264
Conrad -
Emma Estalena: 445
Maida Joan: 676, 677
Ruth: 624
Contrares -
Javier: 1160
Cook -
Charles John Adam: 760
DePhone: 744
Donald P.: 383
Earl Paul: 1351
Eryn Coleen: 1351
Herbert: 1350, 1351
Kerry Ann: 1351
Mary Margaret: 938
Nadine: 382
Copeland -
Harold Thomas: 612
Corbet -
Unnamed: 718
Corbin -
Arthur: 370
Cordaro -
Nancy: 855
Corely -
Ada: 344
Blair: 344
Clyde: 344
Evelyn: 344
Guy: 344
Corley -

Virginia: 746
D -
    Lovina: 177
Dahl -
    Cathy: 1413
Dahlberg -
    Carolyne F.: 381
Dale -
    Lydia: 82
Daniels -
    Dennis Jake: 1282
Danley -
    Carl: 237, 586, 1100
    Frances: 586, 1100
    Guy: 237
    Jefferson: 73
Darlene -
    Unnamed: 920
Darr -
    Cleo: 932
Datko -
    Julia Irene: 1155
Daughtery -
    Ethel: 724
    Patsy: 1430
Dave -
    Unnamed: 1492
Davis -
    Unnamed: 89
    Benjamin: 390
    Betty Joe: 881
    Carol Lynn: 1282
    Darrel Wayne: 391
    Frances Catherine: 392
    Iris: 392, 740
    Leroy James "Jake": 390, 391
    Mary Melvina: 750
    Michael: 1148
    Roberta Sue: 392, 739, 1175
    Sarah: 96, 341
Dawn -
    Unnamed: 1463
Deach -
    Cecil F.: 192, 193
Deal -
    Beatrice: 1124
Dean -
    (name: Lillian Iva Dean Burkett): 695
    Bertha I.: 258, 259
    Carla: 1410
Deaton -
    Alexandra: 1175
    Harolyn Jean: 730
    James: 730
    John Orville: 730
    John Sidney: 731, 1174, 1175
    Sharon Lea: 730
Deb -
    Unnamed: 714
Debbie -
    Unnamed: 1412
Decker -
    Carol Alice: 1140
    Cheri Lynn: 1140

Clyde Eugene: 1139
Connie Marie: 1140
Dale Allen: 1139
David James: 1115
David James Jr: 1115
Della: 751, 752
Donald Arthur: 1139
Edward Keith: 1140
Ethel Marie: 663
Eugene Mahlon Jeff: 663, 1139
Grace Marie: 1139
Harriet Hattie: 309, 310
James Edward: 1139
Jeremy Lynn: 1115
Jesse Lynn: 1115
Karen Lee: 1140
Larry Dean: 1140
Millard (aka: Mick): 663, 1139, 1140
Millard Martin: 1140
Preston Dean: 663, 1140
Richard L.: 663
Richard William: 1140
Robert Eugene: 1139
Robert Woodrow: 663, 1139
Ruth Lucille: 663, 1140
William Forest: 662, 663
William Walter: 663, 1140
Willis: 662
Deering -
    Katherine Ruth: 1430
    Phyllis: 1430
    Randy Lee: 1430
    Richard Lee: 1430
    Rick John: 1430
    Scott Jacob: 1430
Defreese -
    ?: 316
    ?: 316
    Charles: 316
DeGarmo -
    Augusta Louise "Gussie": 420, 421
Deitz -
    George: 32
Delcamp -
    Robert: 314
Delia -
    (name: Deilia Cordelia Yoder): 477, 478
Delores -
    Unnamed: 1445
Dematteo -
    David Anthony: 1485
Demeret -
    Cherry Lynn: 1328
    Howard: 1328
Demers -
    Janice Ann: 1420
Denton -
    Harriet "Hattie" (Christner) (aka: Hattie): 422
Depew -
    Robert: 853
Depp -
    Toni M: 1276
Derington -
    Charles Hugh: 382

Dillinger -
    Dean Charles: 1368
    Glenn Martin: 1367, 1368
    Martin Glenn: 1368
DiLoreto -
    Arthur: 1417
Dimmick -
    Ruth E.: 904
Dimond -
    James Galvin: 1321
    Junious Galvin: 1321
Dinger -
    Joan: 451
Dintaman -
    Carl E.: 919, 920
    Carl Patrick: 920
    Carol Patricia: 920
    Pamela Rose: 920
    Philip Jay: 920
    Phyllis Kay: 920, 1316
    Stephen Fredrick: 920
Dirks -
    Juatin: 930
Dixon -
    Emily: 170
Dneaster -
    Michael: 1142
    Michael Phillip: 1142
    Samuel: 1142
Doane -
    Karen: 1319
Doble -
    Opal Joyce: 1322
Dobson -
    Renetta Ann: 1478, 1479
Dodd -
    Joshua Robert: 1466
    Rachel Diana: 1466
    Randy: 1466
    Zackery Randol: 1466
Doll -
    (name: Cheryl Ann Christner): 714
    (name: Arlene Christner): 667, 1146, 1147, 1412
Dolly -
    (name: Ruth Christner): 147
Domer -
    Unnamed: 112
Donahue -
    Louella: 664, 665
Donavan -
    Charles Henry: 601, 602
    Laura May Elizabeth: 602
    Rebecca Lois "Becky": 602, 1105, 1106
    Virginia F.: 602
Donna -
    Unnamed: 264
    Unnamed: 1271
Donohoe -
    Anna R.: 661
Dooty -
    Samuel Edward: 528, 529
    Samuella Fern: 529, 1000
    Vera Mae: 529

Dorman -
    Kenneth Frank: 1394-1396
Dorothy -
    Unnamed: 883
Dorthy -
    Teresa Ann: 1467
Doubt -
    Jack: 309
Dowty -
    Esther A.: 1124
Drake -
    Erma: 874
    Harry: 1403
    Robert Randall: 1487
    Sean Michael: 1403, 1487
Drenner -
    Hilda: 1147
Dreyer -
    Erin M.: 720
Driesenga -
    Connie Pearl: 1436
Duby -
    Maria L.: 1360
Duedall -
    Mark: 1396
Duffin -
    Dawni Lynne: 1408
Dunbar -
    Campbell W.: 697, 698
    Kenneth E.: 698
Duncam -
    Clyde R.: 374
Dunithan -
    Daniel Edward: 1273
    Deborah Elaine: 1273
    Iva Viola: 504
    Larry Edward: 1273
Dunlap -
    Erma Jean: 739
Dunn -
    Florence: 724, 725
    Florence: 724
    Kimberly Lynn: 1426
Dupont -
    Debra: 1414
Durian -
    Mary Ann: 1444
Durr -
    Elizabeth Betty: 1259
Durst -
    Lynn: 670
Dustman -
    Charles: 1162
    Donnie: 1162
    Jack Thomas: 1419, 1489
    James Richard: 1419
    John Paul: 1419, 1489
    Richard Thomas: 1489
    Ryan John: 1489
    Tom: 1162, 1419, 1489
Duvall -
    Melinda Sue: 1462
Dyson -

Braiden Reid: 1427
Leanne: 1427

E -
Eleanor: 747, 748
Lela: 228
Mary: 673

Eagle -
Cheryl A.: 1174

Eagy -
Perry Alan: 423

Eales -
Jamie Kay: 1326

Eash -
Ada: 581, 1307
Alma D.: 469, 848, 849, 963, 1263, 1270-1272
Amos S.: 941, 942
Anita Kay: 930
Annette: 1273
Anthony Vou: 1357
Brent Allen: 1273
Carolyn Louise: 1356
Christian S.: 435
Christopher L.: 1273
Cory M.: 1273
Daniel J.: 467-469
Dennis Gene: 1357
Edna: 469
Edna D.: 954
Elizabeth S.: 807
Ella: 181
Ellen J.: 1205
Elsie Elmina: 1033, 1034, 1231, 1283
Elva: 469, 851
Emma: 1236
Enos: 469
Erma: 469, 850
Erma Sue: 1287
Ernest Eugene: 1092
Erwie Michael: 1357
Esther: 911
Esther: 1236
Esther LaVada: 942
Etta Fern: 1356
Fannie Mae: 1059, 1060
Fannie Mae: 805
Freeman D.: 889, 890
Gary Earl: 1329
Gerald Lee: 850, 1273
Gladys: 805
Goldie O'Neil: 488-490, 862, 1214, 1261
Harvey E.: 1356, 1357
Ida: 1236
Ina: 1475
Jacob A.: 1074, 1236
James: 851
James Edward: 1357
Janet Elizabeth: 850, 1273
Jerry Wayne: 890
Jerry Wayne: 1313
John: 1205
John H.: 911
Joyce: 1356
Judy Renea: 930
Kathryn: 890
Katie J.: 1335

Katie Mae: 1074, 1236, 1460
LaVerda: 1313
LaVern: 1313
Lena: 1006
Levi D.: 469, 849, 850, 1272, 1273
Linda: 930
Linda Jo: 1357
Loretta Mae: 890
Lydia: 435
Mable: 926, 927
Martha Lou: 1329
Mary Ellen: 942, 1330
Melvin: 930
Neal Samuel: 1197
Ora E.: 1356
Ora W.: 805
Orla: 805
Orla: 890
Patricia Elaine: 1357
Perry: 805
Perry Edward: 1092
Polly: 1236, 1460
Richard Lee: 1356
Richard Lee: 1357
Ronald Ray: 930
Ruth Ann: 942
Ryan S.: 1273
Steven Jay: 930
Theodore Marlin: 850, 1272, 1273
Thomas Allen: 850
Tyler J.: 1273
Virgil DeWayne: 942, 1329
Wilbur: 1313
Wilbur Lee: 890
William J.: 805
Wilma: 469, 850, 851
Wilma: 1382
Zanetta: 1356

Easter -
Doraine Arlene: 1111, 1394-1396
Jacqueline Lee: 1111, 1397
Jacques Eric: 1397
Jacques Oran: 1108, 1110, 1111
Nicole Antionette Marie: 1397
Sherri Kay: 1111, 1397
Timmie Rae: 1111, 1397, 1398, 1485

Easterly -
Nena Corbin: 1423

Eastwood -
Ethel E.: 408

Ebejer -
Elizabeth: 1430

Ebel -
Clyde: 720
Shirley Marie: 720

Eberly -
Beth Ann: 731
Frank: 731
Sue Ann: 731

Eberstein -
Rachal: 1495

Eby -
Magdalena Amanda: 56, 58

Echard -
Malinda: 86

Samuel: 94

Edenfield -
Ruth: 609

Edith -
Unnamed: 1326

Edlund -
David: 1137
Dawn: 1137
Douglas: 1137
Edward: 1137

Edmiston -
Louise Joann: 1419

Edwards -
Unnamed: 1034
Dustin Joel: 1495
Harley Roy: 1467
Jacob Ray: 1467
Jeremiah Lee: 1467, 1494, 1495
Jonas LaVerne: 1467, 1495
Parker Lee: 1495
Shyloh Matteson: 1495
Tyler Jeremiah: 1495

Eerig -
Karen: 1192

Egle -
Irene Della: 406, 407

Egli -
Barbara: 173, 174
Barbara: 182, 183
Christian: 173
Mary Ann: 810-812

Egoff -
David: 1403
Dixie: 1403
Linda: 1403, 1487
Phillip DeVoe: 1403
Terry: 1403

Ehrismann -
Pheobe (aka: Bena): 183

Eichelberger -
Darlene: 1199
Warren: 1199

Eicher -
Amos: 550
Anna Mae: 1223
Benjamin S.: 573
Caroline N.: 1456
Catherine W.: 1088
Conrad: 113, 114
Edna S.: 573
Elizabeth S.: 573
Ellen Joan: 1329
Elmer E.: 1223
Elmer William: 1223
Jacob N.: 1456
Jerry S.: 573
John E.: 1223
John S.: 573
Joseph J.: 572, 573
Mahlon E.: 1097, 1223
Marie S.: 573
Mark E.: 1223
Mary A.: 1097
Matthew E.: 1223
Nathan N.: 1456

Nathaniel E.: 1456
Phillip E.: 1223
Phoebe K.: 1223
Rachel: 95
Rebecca E.: 1223
Samuel E.: 1223
Samuel N.: 1456
Sylvia E.: 1223
Terry: 270
Verna E.: 1223

Eichner -
Unnamed: 112

Eigsti -
Emma: 777
Esther Elizabeth: 1449
Evelyn Rose: 1449
Janelle Yvonne: 1449
Jerrin Mark: 1449
Jerry Jean: 1449
Jessie Lynn: 1449
John: 1449
John J: 1474
Karmen Rose: 1450
Matthew Marvin: 1449, 1450
Sabrina Dawn: 1474

Ekstein -
Mary Stella: 161

Elam -
Elizabeth Ann: 1323, 1324

Elderman -
Peg: 1125

Eldridge -
Dorothy: 1438

Elizabeth -
Unnamed: 50, 51
Unnamed: 120, 121
-
Elizabeth M.: 133

Ellen -
Unnamed: 1140

Ellenberger -
Effie: 280

Ellenora -
Unnamed: 149

Ellis -
Byron Eric: 1096
Gregory Dean: 1096
John Robert: 1096
Marion: 1095, 1096
Steven Lynn: 1096

Elmer -
Molinda Kay: 1431
Tom: 1431

Elza -
Eva Darlene: 1170

Embleton -
Merle: 780

Emerick -
Roy: 259

Emert -
Roxie Pauline: 1136

Emigh -
JoDonna: 1112

Emily -

Unnamed: 1176

Emma -
Unnamed: 331, 332

Enders -
Jennifer Neil: 1463
Neil: 1463

Engle -
Gavin: 1493
Gertrude E.: 664, 665
John: 664
Nic: 1493

Englehart -
Elsie M.: 751

Enos -
Ernest: 723

Epp -
Jennifer Ann Mariah: 1493
Julianna Laura Paola: 1493
Michael: 1493

Erb -
Clyde: 502
David S.: 501
James C.: 1203
John: 791
Joseph: 1202
Joseph J.: 1203
Lowell Dean: 1181
Marie: 502
Michael: 1202
Mildred: 501
Omer: 502
Sandra Lee: 1202
Seth: 501
Violet Elizabeth: 501

Erbskorn -
Mike: 1194

Erickson -
Carolyne F.: 381
Charles: 1185
Debbie: 1401
Hugo: 1185
Mona: 1185, 1432

Ernsberger -
Matt: 1484
Wyatt Mathew: 1484

Espinosa -
Ana Bertha: 1398

Esther -
Unnamed: 890
Unnamed: 1265
Unnamed: 342, 343
Unnamed: 381
Mary: 1265

Estnick -
Doris: 668

Ethel -
Unnamed I: 1213

Ethridge -
Nancy: 856

Ettline -
June: 558

Eunice -
Unnamed: 650

Eva -

Unnamed: 268

Evans -
Norma Jean: 875
Rosa Day: 271-273
Steven: 1468

Eveline -
Unnamed: 1123

Evelyn -
Unnamed: 1434
Unnamed: 399

Evens -
Barbara: 963

Eyer -
Elise Ingold: 183

Fannie/Fanny -
(name: Veronica "Frany" Christner): 26, 76, 77

Fannin -
Guy Wade: 1121

Farmer -
Mollie Vera: 447, 448

Farmwald -
Barbara: 65
Elizabeth: 235
Jeffry Lynn: 935
Oliver Eugene: 934, 935
Paul Michael: 935
Steven Eugene: 935

Farver -
Mark: 1293

Fassold/Fasshold -
Unnamed: 339

Faulkner -
Caroline A. "Carrie": 784, 785
Minnie G: 1174

Faust -
David: 36

Fawcett -
Robert W.: 645

Faye -
Ruby: 1092

Feather -
Clara Viola: 586

Featherstone -
Paula: 1320

Feeley -
Deanne Lynn: 1422
Eugene J.: 1422
Kimberly Ann: 1422, 1491
Leeanna Marie: 1422, 1491

Fega -
Clarice Marie: 665, 666

Fehr -
D.D.S. Vankirk S.: 703
Vankirk S. Jr.: 703

Feick -
Hannah: 184
Hannah Adeline: 185, 186

Fender -
Delores Irene: 746, 747

Fenton -
Mabel Shirley Hayter: 264

Fereva -
Alpha: 904

Danny Jay: 905
Jack Raymond: 904, 905
Paul David: 905
Peggy Kathleen: 905

Fergison -
Patricia Ardell: 839

Fern -
Unnamed: 1308

Ferris -
David H.: 1204

Fields -
Carl R.: 660
Joan: 660
Paul L.: 660
Robert C.: 659, 660

Fielstra -
Melanie: 1465

Fike -
Barbara: 14
Wilson: 141

Fink -
Drake C.: 711, 1170, 1171
Ellen Marie: 1171
Joshua Evan: 1171
Ray Stanley: 711
Sally C.: 711

Finto -
Rozella: 740

Fiorine -
Denise: 746

Firestone -
John: 277

Firkins -
Jeffery Arthur Joesph: 1199

Firl -
Danny C.: 712, 1171, 1425
Jill Marie: 1171, 1425
Robyn Ann: 712
Stephen James: 1171
William Herbert: 711, 712

Fischbach -
Alvin: 998

Fisher -
Barbara Ann: 1120, 1400, 1486
Christopher Joe: 1283
Frances Florence: 1120, 1400
Herbert August: 1119, 1120
John Edmond: 1400
John Herbert: 1120, 1400, 1486, 1496
Lucille Ruth: 1120, 1399, 1486, 1496
Mary Elizabeth: 1400
Nancy Ann: 1400, 1486, 1496
Rory Edward: 1400
Wayne Edward: 1120, 1400

Fittler -
Gabriele: 1442

Flack -
Albert Painter: 1278
Charles Sisley: 276
Emery C.: 633, 634
Infant: 634
Jean Ann: 1278, 1279

Flanigan -
Jefferson Jackson: 73

Fleck -
Carol Anna: 1350

Fleenor -
Lois: 1351

Fleming -
Joan: 659, 1136
Joel Frederic: 659, 1136, 1409
Mark Alexander: 1136
Matthew: 1409
Michael Fredric: 1136, 1409
Morgan: 1409
Rebecca Mae: 1136
Sarah: 1409
Steven Andrew: 1136, 1409
Susan Rae: 1136
Willard F.: 658, 659

Flesher -
Betty L.: 644
Fern A.: 644
Roy E.: 644

Flick -
Beth: 677

Flinner -
George: 66

Flossie -
(name: Florence "Flossie" Christner): 159

Floyd -
Unnamed: 680

Fogel -
Donald William: 616, 1114, 1398
Doni May: 1114
Esther Ellen: 616, 1115
Gary: 1115
Holli Jean: 1114, 1398
Janet Marie: 616, 1115
Timothy Edward: 616, 1114
William Joseph: 1114
William R.: 616

Fogle -
Anna Pearl: 1146

Folk -
Amanda: 199, 201
Mary A.: 119

Folker -
Anthony Brian: 1137
Ronald Claude: 1137
Tammy Lorraine: 1137
Terry Reid: 1137
Todd Michael: 1137

Foos -
Shirley: 1371

Force -
Georganna: 1164, 1421, 1491
Robert: 1163, 1164

Ford -
Claudia: 1463

Forman -
Theresa: 1414

Forrest -
Delrosa Snyder: 631
Donald: 353
Lloyd: 352, 353
Mary Louise: 353
Ruth Elizabeth: 353

Joseph: 534
Joseph D.: 65, 215, 216, 536-541, 1012-1022, 1024-
         1027, 1029-1034, 1036-1048, 1366-1387, 1485
Joseph D. M.: 218, 547, 1075
Joseph E.: 544, 912, 1060, 1313, 1314
Joseph E.: 532
Joseph J.: 215
Joseph Jacob: 1204
Joseph Jay: 1204
Judith Kay: 535
Katie Irene: 913
Kenneth Dewayne: 1055
Kenneth Jay: 1063
Leonard J.: 1063
Linda Christina: 855
Lizzie: 215
Lizzie E.: 532
Lizzie Ellen: 1063
Lucy Irene: 1060
Lydia Mae: 912, 1313, 1314
Mahlon: 543, 1054, 1055
Mahlon Dan Elias: 1055
Mahlon J.: 1063
Margaret: 1314
Mariam Sue: 855
Mark: 1314
Martha D.: 1064
Mary: 218
Mary D.: 65, 213, 214, 523-528, 992-1000, 1335-1355,
         1482
Mary D.: 1064
Mary Ellen: 544, 978, 1062
Mary Ellen: 912, 1314
Mary Ellen: 534
Mary Jo: 1445
Mayme Maude: 531, 1010
Melvin Jay: 1060, 1298, 1299
Mervin Jay: 912, 1314
Michael Dean: 1011
Noah D.: 65, 217
Philip Jonas: 855
Rachel Ellen: 1204
Randall Edward: 1008
Richard: 913
Robert: 215
Robert Arlen: 1008
Roger Dean: 1008
Rosemary E.: 532
Roy Meyer: 1204
Samuel: 534
Samuel D.: 65, 216, 542, 543, 1049-1054
Samuel J.: 215, 535
Sarah J.: 215, 532, 1012
Sherry Ann: 1009
Simon J.: 215, 531, 1008-1012
Steven Carl: 855
Susan: 1010
Susannah S.: 531, 1009
Susie: 534
Tobias D.: 544, 1059, 1060
Vernon Jay: 531, 1011
Virginia Lee: 1009
Walter Harley: 531, 1009, 1010
Wayne D.: 1064
Wesley E.: 532
Willard: 1445

Willard J.: 215, 535
William: 215
William: 533
William D.: 217
William Owen: 531, 1011
Wilma: 912, 913
Wilmer D.: 1064
Yvonne Elaine: 1011
Fricke -
   Brigitte Hensch: 1441
Frickey -
   Nettie: 328, 329
Friend -
   Jean Christine: 1132
Frisholtz -
   Betty: 1135
Fritcher -
   Jane: 1195
Fritz -
   (name: Alfred Arthur Christner): 621, 1118, 1399, 1486
   (name: Freeman L. Wingard): 521, 985
   Alverta G.: 635
   Evelyn M.: 1139, 1140
   Helen: 635
   Homer: 1139
   Wesley J.: 634, 635
Fry -
   Ada: 540
   Alice: 1036
   Alvin LeRoy: 539, 1032
   Alvin Lloyd: 1031, 1385
   Amos E.: 539, 1036
   Amos J.: 216, 538, 1030-1033, 1384-1386
   Andrea Elizabeth: 1383, 1384
   Andrew Duane: 1383
   Andrew W: 1030
   Andy H.: 1029, 1383
   Anna: 1029
   Anna: 1038
   Barbara: 540
   Barbara A.: 538, 539
   Barbara Ann: 216, 540, 541, 1040-1043
   Barbara Ann: 1053
   Bennie Ray: 1037
   Betty: 1269, 1390, 1485
   Calvin Jay: 1051
   Cassie S.: 217, 543, 1054
   Cheryl Denice: 1045
   Christian A.: 538, 1030, 1031, 1384, 1385
   Christina: 1053
   Dale DeVon: 1045
   Danette: 1049
   Daniel: 538
   Daniel J.: 216, 538, 1027, 1029, 1030, 1382-1384
   Daniel Lee: 1385
   Danny Jay: 1029
   David: 540
   David D.: 538, 1027, 1028, 1382, 1383
   David J.: 216
   David O.: 1028
   David Orven: 1051
   Donna Rae: 1045
   Doris: 1030
   Dorothy: 1382
   Edna: 1038

Elizabeth: 537, 1025, 1378-1381, 1438
Elizabeth: 540, 1039
Elizabeth: 539, 1036
Elizabeth: 1037
Elizabeth J.: 216, 536, 1012-1016, 1300, 1366-1371, 1485
Elmer Lee: 1031, 1385
Emery W.: 1030
Enos A: 539, 1032
Enos J.: 216, 539, 1034, 1036-1038
Erma: 1383
Ervin: 1029
Esther Anna: 1033
Esther Faye: 1026
Ezra N.: 541, 1044, 1045
Fannie D.: 547
Fannie J.: 216, 539, 1033, 1386, 1387
Fay Eugene: 1031
Felty: 540
Felty: 1029
Fred: 217
Freddie: 537, 1026, 1381
Gerald Walton: 1032
Geraldine: 1045
Glen D.: 1028, 1382
Glen David: 1382
Gloria Jean: 1050
Harley: 1029
Harvey: 216
Harvey D.: 538, 1029, 1383
Harvey O.: 1028
Ida: 1038
Ida Carolyn: 1382
Ida D.: 1029
Ira D.: 1028, 1029
Irene: 547
Irene: 1038
Iva: 1029
Ivan Kay: 1032
Jacob D.: 1028
Jacob N.: 541, 1045
James Lee: 1044
Joetta Collenn: 1045
John J.: 216, 537, 1025, 1026, 1378-1381, 1438
Jonas: 217
Joseph: 217
Joseph: 1037
Joseph A.: 539, 1031, 1032
Joseph E.: 540, 1038
Joseph N.: 541, 1043, 1044
Joseph Wayne: 1032
Joyce Ann: 1032, 1033
Karen Louise: 1044
Katie: 539, 1034
Katie: 1030
Katie D.: 547, 1075
Keith: 1054
Keith Deuane: 1044
Kim Eugene: 1044
Lavern G.: 1382
Levi: 1269, 1390
Levi: 1038
Levi E.: 540, 1037
Lloyd Lee: 1032
Lydia: 1030
Manileus J.: 216, 540, 1039

Margaret LaFern: 1031, 1384
Marlene Kay: 1026, 1381
Mary: 540, 1038, 1039
Mary: 1036
Mary: 1053
Mary D.: 547
Mary Ellen: 1385
Mary Esther: 1031, 1384
Mary J.: 216, 536, 537, 1016-1022, 1024, 1371-1378
Mattie: 216, 541, 542, 1045-1048
Mattie A.: 539, 1031, 1385, 1386
Micheal Joe: 1044
Nancy Ellen: 1026
Nelson: 1053
Noah J.: 216, 541, 1043-1045
Norma: 1382
Olen W: 1030
Ora Floyd: 539, 1033
Paul D.: 1028, 1383
Paul D.: 547
Paul Jay: 1382
Perry: 1029
Philip Dean: 1051
Phyllis Diane: 1044
Polly: 1029
Randy Eugene: 1385
Rebecca Lynn: 1385
Rodney Leroy: 1032
Roger Lee: 1050
Rose Mary: 1049
Roy A.: 727
Ruby: 1036
Sadie J.: 538, 1026, 1027
Sara N.: 541, 1044
Sherry Lee: 1033
Susan: 539
Susan Kay: 1053
Susie: 1385
Susie Ellen: 1382
Sylvia: 540
Treva Jo: 1049
Vern D.: 1028, 1382
Wayne: 1382, 1383
Wilbur: 1037
William Ray: 1383
Willie: 1029, 1383
Willie D.: 538, 1030, 1384
Wilma: 1030, 1384

Frye -
Ada Mae: 542, 944, 1049
Bethanie Jean: 874, 875
Calvin: 543
Daniel N.: 542, 1049
Dorothy June: 481, 875, 1293, 1309
Edna: 543, 1054
Edward: 481
Elias Jay: 480, 874
Elizabeth Mae: 480
Ella: 543, 1054
Elvie H.: 543, 1053
Ernest R.: 481, 875
Freeman H.: 481
Harley N.: 542, 1050
Harvey S.: 479, 480
Henry S.: 217, 542, 1050-1054
Ira Frank: 481

Clarence: 1007
Daniel: 574
David: 574
Dora O.: 1087
Douglas Kent: 1046
Dwane Eugene: 1046
Edna: 232, 575
Edna: 964
Edna: 573
Edward: 1483
Eli J.: 542
Eloise Kay: 1258
Emma: 232, 576
Ervin N.: 232, 573
Eugene Ray: 1258
Fannie: 538
Fannie: 232, 576
Fred E.: 542, 1046
Freeman: 1007
John: 1483
John M.: 542, 1046
John William: 1047
Joseph E.: 542, 1045
Kathryn: 1483
Kathryn Faye: 1046
Katie Irene: 1007
Larry: 1007
Leanna: 1483
Leslie Roy: 776
Lovelle Fanny: 542, 1048, 1049
Lyle Dean: 1046
Mahlon: 232, 577
Mahlon: 574
Martha: 574
Mary: 232, 575
Mary: 574
Mary Jo: 1258
Mary Lou: 542, 1047, 1048
Merl M.: 542, 1046, 1047
Merle: 573
Michael Merl: 1047
Moses: 232
Myron: 577
Naomi: 574
Noah M.: 70
Orla: 1007
Orpha: 577
Perry: 1007
Ralph Eugene: 1045, 1046
Raymond: 1258
Raymond: 573, 574
Ronal Lee: 1045
Ronald Jay: 1258
Rosetta: 1483
Ruby: 577
Ruth: 574
Samuel: 1483
Shirley Marie: 1258
Simon Jr.: 801
Velma M.: 542, 1047
Wayne Lamar: 1258
Wilma: 577

Gingery -
Magdaline Martha: 87-89
Gingrich -
Larry: 920

Gint -
Mary: 33
Girod -
Alvin C.: 1228
Anna E.: 1227
August P.: 550
Benjamin C.: 1224, 1455, 1457
Benjamin C.: 1228
Benjamin M.: 1224, 1457
Caroline C.: 1228
Cletus C.: 1224
Daniel E.: 1455
Elizabeth: 570
Elizabeth B.: 1229
Elizabeth C.: 1224
Elizabeth E.: 1229
Elizabeth M.: 1226, 1392
Emanuel M.: 1455
Emma A.: 1456
Emma M.: 1097
Enos E.: 1455
Ernest E.: 1455
Ernest L.: 1455
Ervin E.: 1455
Esther C.: 1224
Fannie R.: 1457
Jeremiah M.: 1228
Jerry C.: 1228
Jesse C.: 1224
John M.: 1392
John R.: 1392
John S.: 570
Josephine: 570
Levi: 570
Lovina: 570, 1096, 1390, 1455
Mahlon E.: 1455
Marcus E.: 1455
Mark: 570
Martha E.: 1098
Mary Ann: 1455
Maryann C.: 1224
Maryann C.: 1228
Matthew C.: 1224
Menno C.: 1228
Menno C.: 1224
Miriam: 570
Neal E.: 1455
Rebecca B.: 1455
Reuben: 570
Rudy C.: 1228
Samuel: 570
Samuel R.: 1229
Simon E.: 1455
Susan E.: 1455
Sylvia C.: 1224
Walter M.: 1392
William C.: 1224
Gish -
Glen: 941
Glenda Ruth: 941
Jeannine: 941
Julia Ann: 941
Kristena Elaine: 941
Gisser -
Unnamed: 183

Arthur Ray: 612
Daniel L.: 612
Ivan: 604
William Ray: 612

Goslin -
Jerolin Jane: 1243

Gould -
Lillian B.: 84

Graber -
Allen Wayne: 990
Amos: 847
Anna Marie: 915
Anna Ruth: 846, 1269
Cassandra Jo: 1285
Edna: 847
Elizabeth: 951, 952
Elizabeth Kay: 990
Elmer: 846
Elsie: 846
Ernest: 847
Ervin: 915
Fannie: 1219, 1220
Fannie: 847
Gary Lee: 1333
Harley: 847
Harry: 915
Henry F.: 846
Ida Mae: 990
Jack Ryan: 1451
Joan: 990
Katie: 916
Lavern J.: 1333
Linda Sue: 1333
Mary Magdalena: 990
Matthew Wayne: 1451
Melvin D.: 915
Naomi: 990
Orva: 847
Randy: 991
Richard: 990, 991
Richard Wayne: 1283, 1285
Rickey: 991
Robert: 991
Ruby: 847
Ruth Ann: 990
Sandra Kay: 1333
Shirley Ann: 991
Timothy Lee: 1451
Tina Marie: 1285
Vernon Lee: 990
Wilmer: 989, 990

Graf -
Mildred R.: 1237, 1238

Grant -
James B.: 25

Grauberger -
John R: 735
Leona Ruth: 735

Gray -
Archibald Thomas: 83
Catherine Nora: 82
Emma Margaret: 82
George Harrison: 82, 261
Ida Susan: 82
John: 81

Margaret: 262
Nora: 262
Thomas: 81
William Harry: 81

Greco -
Carole Rae: 749

Greer -
Jennifer: 1174, 1175

Greeser -
Robert P.: 1217

Gregg -
Charles Elbert: 301

Gretchen -
Unnamed: 1137

Grew -
Edith L.: 663, 664, 717

Grieser -
Carmilla Sue: 1194
Lloyd J.: 226

Griess -
Betty Jean: 733, 734

Griffin -
Myrtle E.: 638

Griffith -
Ebenezer: 29
Elma: 1274
Harry: 319
Susannah: 29, 116, 270, 282

Grim -
Catherine: 125
Susan: 84

Grimes -
Elizabeth: 235
Misti Dawn: 1495, 1496

Grippando -
Addison Sophia: 1424
Robert Thomas: 1423, 1424

Grogg -
Catherine: 624
Earl: 624
Forrest Ivan: 275, 624
Josephine: 624
Malinda: 624
Marylin: 624
Mason H.: 275
Theresa: 275
Theron Defoe: 275, 623, 624
Un-Named: 624
Viginia: 624

Gross -
Ali: 1413
Michael: 1413
Michael Jr: 1413

Grover -
Chase Kassidy: 1118
Cora: 171
Terry: 1117

Grubb -
Ed: 720
Lee: 1462

Grubich -
Drew Edward: 1000
Elraye Eleanor: 1000
Rudy A.: 1000

Rhoda Jean: 613, 1114
Tressa: 256
Hampton -
Shireen: 715
Hamsher -
Andrew: 61, 199, 463
Betty J: 464
Dallas Eugene: 463
Daniel M: 463
DeEtta: 199
Edward D: 463, 464
Iva: 199
James A: 464
John F.: 60
John Henry: 463
Mary E: 463
Melvin: 199
Milo: 199, 463
Paul A.: 199
Reuben Andrew: 463
Robert D: 464
Sadie: 199
Soloman: 60
Thomas Franklin: 463
Tressie: 199
Wallace: 199
Handwerk -
Adam: 111, 112
Lydia: 112
Handwork -
S. A.: 43
Haney -
Martha J.: 1309
Hanks -
Barry Lynn: 1147, 1148
Cathy Lynn: 1148
Vicki Jo: 1148
Hanna -
Edward V.: 374
Hank: 884
Hansbrough -
Patricia: 1136
Hansen -
Francine: 1461
James: 1461
Hansley -
Colleen: 1031
Harbath -
Annelee Margaret: 1491
Mark Alfred: 1491
William Douglas: 1491
Harber -
Mary K.: 1178
Harden -
Benjamin Jr.: 130
Charles E. Jr.: 1106
Charles Edward Sr.: 608, 1106
Charlotte Mae: 1106
Eloise T.: 608
Fred: 604, 606, 608
Judith: 1106
Kenneth: 608
Renee: 1106
Theresa: 1106

Hardig -
Renee: 1420
Harless -
Edna Margret: 996
Harman -
Mary Elizabeth: 285
Harmon -
Evelyn: 1124
Harned -
Crystal Gayle: 1439
David E.: 1439
David Eugene Jr.: 1439
James Alexander: 1439
Scott Worthy: 1439
Harold -
George R.: 794
Harper -
Arlene O.: 636
Harriet -
Unnamed: 270
Harrington -
Harlan H.: 368
Harris -
Kenneth Leslie: 389
Michael J: 1115
Steven R.: 988
Harrison -
Elma: 620
Harshberger -
Alma: 476
Alvin: 475
Carolyn R.: 870
David R.: 870
Edward Herman: 1201
Eli J.: 475, 868, 869
Glen Ray: 868
Ida Ellen: 870
Ida J.: 476
Infant Dau.: 476
Infant Son: 475
Infant Son: 476
Infant Son: 476
Ivan LeRoy: 868
Joseph Eli: 475
Karena Rose: 1287
LaVern R.: 870, 1287
Lloyd J.: 475, 868
Lyndon Eugene: 1287
Lynette Sue: 1287
Marion Lee: 868
Mervin R.: 870
Mitchel William: 869
Nona Ann: 869
Orva R.: 870
Ray J.: 476, 869, 870, 1287
Rexetta Darlene: 1201
Ruth Ann: 870
Vernon: 870
Harshman -
Esther L.: 610
John Lee: 645
Joseph: 644, 645
Joseph Leroy: 609, 610
Josephine: 645

Hart -
    Christina Elizabeth: 89, 90
    Robert: 1268
Hartman -
    Amanda: 1412
    Cheryl: 1412
    Douglas: 1412
    Earl: 1412
Hartzell -
    Elizabeth: 131
Harvey -
    Clyde: 609
    Edward: 49
    Elizabeth Nicole: 1442
    George: 50
    George M.: 609
    Hannah Margaret: 49, 50
    John Franklin: 50
    Jon Richard: 1442
    Peter Benjamin: 50
    Richard: 1442
    Robert: 49
    Shawna Lynn Marie: 1442
    Wiley Stevens: 604, 607-609
Hastings -
    Allan: 185
    Annie: 185
    James: 185
    Jennie: 185
    Oliver: 185
    Roy: 185
Haston -
    Eric Rex: 1350
    Ernest Reed: 1349, 1350
    Gregory Dean: 1350
    Marc Douglas: 1350
    Mary Susan: 1350
Hatcher -
    Jerry: 717
Hatfield -
    Benjamin Franklin: 371
    Clifford Ananias: 372
    Cora Mae: 372
    Francis Marion: 371
    Juanita Elaine: 372
    Mabel Irene: 371
    Rebecca Madge: 372
Hattie -
    (name: Harriet "Hattie" (Christner) Denton): 422
Haude -
    Sandra Kay: 853
Haus/Haas -
    Barbara: 180, 181
Haverfield -
    David W.: 1411
Hawkins -
    Clara Elizabeth: 252, 601, 602, 1105
    Kingery: 1245
    Lemuel J.: 251, 252
    Nancy Ethel: 1244, 1245
Hawkshaw -
    (name: Glen E. Christner): 478, 871, 872, 1291, 1292,
        1478, 1479
Hawn -

Sarah: 117, 118
Hayden -
    Barbara: 1441
Haynes -
    Jerry Lynn: 1454
    Jerry Lynn Jr: 1454
    Roberta Ann: 1454
    Ronda Lee: 1454
Headings -
    Alvin: 853
    Chester: 1281
    Daniel J.: 759
    Darrel Lynn: 1370
    Gary Keith: 1370
    John: 759
    Kathryn Fay: 1370
    Keith: 1013, 1369, 1370
    Levi: 1013
    Linda Mae: 1370
    Lois: 1014
    Marylin Jean: 1370
    Philip: 1013, 1370
    Randy Scott: 1279
    Ricky: 1281
    Ricky Lee: 1279
    Robert: 1013
    Robert E.: 1279
    Roger Lyn: 1279
    Ronald Lynn: 1370
    Sanford: 1013
    Sharon Jay: 1370
Heater -
    Isaac: 425
    Minnie Miranda: 425, 426
Hebrank -
    Unnamed: 1399
    Mark Franklin: 1399
    Mitzie: 1399
Heckman -
    Edna: 1433
    Ruth Olive: 615
Heffelder -
    Joy: 1242
Heffley -
    Sally: 1145, 1146
Heidereich -
    Lisa: 1409
Heidi -
    Unnamed: 1137
Heilman -
    Lois Lucille: 901, 902
    Norman Charles: 901
Heining -
    Mary E: 261
Heintz -
    George: 1183, 1184
    George Jr: 1184
    Keith Duane: 1184
    Michael L.: 1184
    Richard: 1184
    Thomas Gregory: 1184
Heiny -
    Edwin O.: 137
Heitfield -

Esther Marie: 740, 741

Helen -
    Unnamed: 253
    (name: Emma L. Christner): 490, 903, 904, 1308, 1484
    Mary: 1162

Helleim -
    Dolores G.: 609
    Jacguelyn: 609

Hellen -
    Unnamed: 1280

Helmkamp -
    Renee Marie: 1282

Helmuth -
    Anna G.: 885, 1014
    Bertha Mae: 1022
    Cheryl Anna: 583
    Daniel: 583
    David Roy: 1022
    Eldon Lynn: 1022
    Fanny: 415
    Floyd Roger: 1022
    James Daniel: 1022
    John C.: 1022
    John Dale: 1022
    Lena M.: 1210
    Lydia G.: 533, 534
    Norman Ray: 583

Helvey -
    Esther Anne: 997

Hemmings -
    Dallas: 1140
    Margaret Elaine: 1140

Hengst -
    Chris Lee: 1422
    John D.: 1422
    Mark Douglas: 1422

Hennessey -
    Thomas: 79

Henretty -
    Irene: 901

Hepler -
    Nedra Lucille: 1360, 1361

Herboldheimer -
    Mike: 373

Herboldshiemer -
    Michael: 160

Herold -
    Amber Mae: 1445
    Daniel: 1445
    Rebecca Lea: 1445

Herschberger -
    Cheryl Elaine: 1299
    Freeman A.: 990
    Lasla Fay: 1299

Hersey -
    Pearl: 1465

Hersh -
    Alice Jane: 718
    Connie: 1116

Hershbergen -
    Amanda: 219
    Lavina: 219

Hershberger -
    Unnamed: 853

Andrew: 1075
Angie Elizabeth: 1475
Anna: 806
Anna W.: 769
Betty Lou: 1333, 1334
Beulah Cleora: 504
Burdette Curtis: 1199
Catherine M. "Katie" (aka: Katie): 481, 483, 486
Charlotte Faye: 1428, 1492
Cleo Mae: 561
Daniel J.: 178, 179
Daniel N: 219
David: 1002
David Jr.: 1479
David Lee: 1479
Dennis: 1002
Dwight: 1474, 1475
Edna: 1075
Edna: 1483
Edna Mae: 464, 828, 829, 922
Emanuel S.: 852, 853
Emma Jean: 853
Ervin A.: 1075
Esther: 1483
Esther Anne: 853
Fanny: 1483
Geneva Ann: 1428
George Anthony: 1199
Glen Eldon: 853
Infant: 220
Ivan: 1002
Ivan: 1482, 1483
Jacob: 1483
Jeffrey Owen: 1428
John: 1075
John Delbert: 1428
John Douglas: 1199
Joseph: 1483
Joseph Ray: 853, 854
Karen: 1479
Kate: 552
Kay Louise: 1428
Kenneth: 1479
Kristina: 1479
LeAnna: 1002
Leonard: 219
Lloyd George: 220
Lovina: 216
Lydia: 1213, 1214
Magdalena W.: 501
Martha: 1483
Mary: 1483
Mary Ann: 496, 497
Mary Elizabeth: 224, 225
Mary Jill: 1199
Mary Naomi: 853
Meriam M.: 1288
Nathaniel J: 219
Nila Kay: 854
Olivia Grace: 1475
Omer J.: 1299
Orpha: 1075
Ray: 220
Rebecca: 853
Sarah: 199
Sarah: 70, 232, 573-577, 1337

1878

Kathryn Frances: 1234
Lydia Mae: 520
Magdalena: 1210, 1211
Mary Ellen: 137
Merville: 1234
Percy Emanuel: 1234
Polly: 806, 1233
Savillo: 806, 1233
Shirley: 1234
Victor: 806, 1234
William B.: 772
William E.: 806, 1234
William Jr.: 1234

Hochstetler -
Ada: 494, 915
Albert Lee: 1336
Albert M.: 524, 575, 992, 1335-1337
Alice: 993
Allen: 1384
Alma: 781, 993, 1340
Alva Ray: 1344
Amanda: 199
Amos D.: 994, 1343
Amos M.: 524
Amos V.: 994, 1345
Andrew: 980
Anita Joy: 1347
Anna M.: 524, 995, 1348
Anna Mae: 992
Anna Mae: 993
Anna Mae C.: 879
Anna Marie: 995
Annabelle: 1065
Arthur Jay: 993, 1064, 1339
Barbara: 215, 216
Barbara A.: 992, 1336
Barbara D.: 994, 1211, 1342
Barbara Kay: 1335
Calvin: 1065
Carl Dean: 1268
Celesta J.: 520, 979
Christ U.: 994, 1347
Christian C.: 877, 878
Christian M.: 524, 994, 995, 1347
Christy C.: 878, 879, 1004, 1005
Daniel: 1338
Daniel: 993
Daniel: 980
Daniel A.: 992, 1335
Daniel D. Jr.: 994, 1306, 1344, 1482
Daniel Dewayne: 1306
Daniel Lee: 1064
Daniel M.: 524, 986, 993, 994, 1211, 1253, 1306, 1342-
    1344, 1482
David C.: 878
David J.: 755
David Lee: 1341
Debbie Lynn: 1306, 1482
Debrah Jean: 1341
Devon Ray: 1347
Edna: 995
Edna: 494, 917, 918
Edna Mae: 994, 1346
Edna Mae: 986, 994, 1344
Elam: 755
Eli: 980

Eli J.: 520, 981, 982
Elizabeth: 125
Elizabeth: 993, 1339
Elizabeth: 1355
Elizabeth A.: 575, 992, 1337
Elmer: 980, 981
Elmer S.: 755
Elsie: 995
Elsie: 982
Elsie C.: 879
Erma Marie: 1338
Ernest: 995
Ervin D.: 994, 1343
Fannie: 981
Fanny: 755
Frederick: 995
Freeman M.: 1384
Gideon J.: 520, 982
Harley: 1345
Harley J.: 520, 980
Harvey C.: 878
Ida: 981
Ida Anna: 1335
Ida C.: 878, 1294, 1295
Ida Mae: 1063
Ida Mae: 1343
Inez: 1232
Infant: 524
Infant: 524
Irene: 1343
Ivan Jay: 1335
Jacob: 1346
Jacob E.: 520
Jacob H.: 980
Jeptha: 755
Jeremiah: 1480
Joanna: 39
John A.: 992, 1337
John C.: 879
John LeRoy: 994
John Sr: 6-8
Jonathan: 8
Jonathan: 994
Joseph Z.: 22
Karon Kay: 1347
Katie C.: 878
Katie M.: 494, 916
Katie V.: 994, 1069, 1345
Lena Mae: 1336
LeRoy: 993, 1341
Lester C.: 878, 1295
Levi: 980
Loulda Sue: 1341, 1342
Lucy Edna: 755
Luke Andrew: 1480
Lydia Mae: 494, 916, 917
Lydia Mae: 487, 488
Magdalena: 755
Maneleus D.: 523, 524
Manelius C.: 493, 494
Marie: 994
Mark James: 1348
Marlin: 1480
Mary: 755
Mary: 994, 1253, 1342
Mary: 755

William Augustus: 627

Honderich -
Christian: 23
Magdalene: 23, 24

Honsberger -
Nancy Anna: 54, 55

Hoogenboom -
Tim: 1327

Hoogenboon -
Richard: 772

Hook -
Mary: 1146
Patsy Marie: 1249
Ralph: 1249

Hooley -
Barbara Holly: 12, 13
Greg: 1309
Joshua: 1309
Larry: 1309
Nellie Catherine: 811

Hoopingarner -
Cory: 1282

Hoover -
Alfred: 128
Ardith: 1144
Arthur Marion: 1460, 1461
Bessie: 342
Charles Franklin: 154
Cloyd M.: 1144
Jr. Cloyd M. Jr.: 1144
Dale La Vern: 1461
Dinah: 128
Dorothy Jane: 1461
Elizabeth Baker: 120
Ellen: 128
Eva Irene: 1237
Floyd William: 1236
George Edward: 1236
Glenn Richard: 1461
Harvey: 122, 129
Helen Arlene: 1461
Ida Victoria: 154, 373
Issah: 1144
Jefferson: 128
Jerry Alan: 1461
John: 127, 128
John Jr.: 128
John Leroy: 1237
Jonathan: 129
Laura Jean: 1461
Linda Rose: 1461
Lois Kay: 1237
M. William: 1237
Mabel: 750
Magdalene "Maggie": 126, 127
Marie Ann: 1237
Marvin: 1250
Mary (Maria): 35, 36, 91
Melinda: 128
Melvin Lewis: 1236
Roy William: 1145
Ruth Vivian: 1236
Susie: 1137
Tena: 128, 336, 337, 697-699, 723
Thelma Lucile: 1236, 1461

Valerie Anna: 1461
William Lenard: 154

Hopper -
Betty Sue: 731
G.C. Jr: 731
Gary Charles: 731
Rocky Lynn: 731
Tommy Scott: 731

Hopwood -
Henry Thomas: 186

Horn -
Unnamed: 1406

Horner -
Nancy Belle: 693, 694

Horning -
Judith: 1136

Hostetler -
Alvin D.: 903, 904
Amos L.: 1198
Anna Mae: 846, 1267, 1467, 1494, 1495
Anthony Jay: 1470
Arlene E.: 1233
Bailey Dewayne: 1474
Barbara Ellen: 807
Beth Ann: 1470
Bettie K.: 1233
Brady Cole: 1474
Bryan Earl: 1452
Buel G: 125
Caroll Jewell: 904, 1308, 1484
Carolyn: 1269, 1475
Catherine: 125
Christ: 1346
Christina: 1269, 1474, 1475
Conrad: 125
Cora: 125
Cornelius M.: 64
Darlene Fay: 1468, 1495
Darlene Mary: 1448
David Allen: 1312
David Jr: 1471
David Lee: 1268, 1470, 1471
David M.: 583, 584
Delilah: 124
Delores Kay: 1471
Dominic Joseph: 1471
Doris Jean: 1468
Douglas Wade: 1428
Duane John: 1233
Duane Ray: 1471
Dwight Kenneth: 1428
Edna: 1447
Edward J.: 846, 1268, 1470, 1471, 1495
Elijah Lewis: 1475
Elizabeth: 126
Elizabeth Fern: 1268
Elsie: 846, 1268, 1471-1474, 1485
Elsie Marie: 1268, 1469
Emma Jane: 125
Ernest Eugene: 584
Ervin: 1206
Ervin D. (aka: Buddy or Bud): 1311, 1312
Esther: 1346
Floyd Ray: 1268, 1470
Freeman: 1346

Frieda: 849
Gabriel: 38, 124, 329
Gloria Joyce (aka: Joyce): 904
Harley: 846
Harvey: 125
Heidi Salome: 1471
Hiram H: 126
Isaiah Quinn: 1475
Jacob C.: 39
James Wayne: 1468
Jason Lee: 1468
Jay Dean: 1471
Jeffrey Lee: 1452
Jemima: 528
Jennifer Dawn: 1474
Jeremiah: 40, 125, 126
Jeremiah Lee: 1474
Jeremy Ross: 1452
Jerry: 1346
Jethro Jay: 1474
Joan Arlene: 1312
Joanna Kay: 1268, 1469
Jodi Lynnette: 1474
John: 39
John: 125
John: 1347
John E.: 1206
John E.: 1208
John J.: 1206
Jonas A.: 845, 846, 1485
Jonathan: 39, 125
Joshua Jon: 1474
Julie A: 1206
Karen Sue: 1268, 1469
Keith Edward: 939
Kendal Marc: 1452
Kenneth Lee: 1269, 1474
Kristina Lynn: 1452
Lazarus: 37, 38
Lee Anna Marie: 1233
Lester: 1448
Levi J.: 1346
Lisa Nan: 1428, 1492
Lora Mae: 1268
Loretta Kay: 1269, 1474
Loretta Mae: 584
Lucinda: 125
Mae: 552
Marion: 1269, 1475
Marion Duane: 939
Marlin Jay: 1269, 1474
Marvin Gerold: 939
Mary: 126
Mary: 39
Mary: 125
Mary Ann: 217
Mary E.: 415
Mary Ellen: 1268, 1468, 1469
Mary Etta: 1312
Mary Katheryn: 776
Melvin Wayne: 1268, 1471
Mervin Jay: 1268
Michael Bruce: 1428
Moses Henry: 807
Myron Eugene: 1471
Nettie O.: 1295

Nora Jane: 1208
Norman Ray: 1269
Phyllis J.: 1198
Rachel: 417, 418
Rebecca Lynn: 1316, 1317
Richard Lee: 584
Robert: 126
Robert Devon: 1233
Roger Dale: 1208
Rolla G: 125
Ron: 1452
Rosa: 1346
Rosanah: 38, 39
Rose Mary: 1268, 1470
Ruby: 1346
Ruth Ann: 1268, 1470
Ruthie Mae: 1268, 1468
Sally A.: 1195
Samuel: 125
Sarah Ellen: 1468
Shirley Ann: 1140
Shirley Ann: 584
Stanley Stephen: 939
Susan Kay: 1268, 1470, 1495
Timothy Allon: 1471
Vernon J: 846, 1269, 1474, 1475, 1485
Vickie Ann: 939
Victor Floyd: 1233
Wayne Edward: 1268, 1468, 1495
Wesley: 125
William Bittinger: 125
Willis J.: 846, 1267, 1468, 1469, 1495
Zachery Jon: 1452

Hostetter -
    Aaron: 125, 329, 330
    George E.: 330
    Vernel A.: 330
Hotchkiss -
    Barbara A.: 1151
    David Earl: 718, 719
    Donna Marie: 719
    Jeanne Sue: 719
    Kathleen Hilda: 709
    Marilyn: 719
    Mary Jane: 715, 716
    Richard Wayne: 719
    Ronnie Lynn: 719
    Ruth Ann: 719
Hough -
    David Nicholas: 615, 616
    Dorothy Jean: 616
Housel -
    Agnes Marie: 266
    Amy Sue: 620
    Anna Catherine: 266, 617, 1117
    Betty Irene: 266, 616, 617
    Brenda: 269
    Carl Eugene: 617
    Catherine Irene: 269
    Clyde Franklin: 266, 617, 618, 1117, 1118
    Donald Clayton: 269
    Doris Lavern: 266, 617, 1116, 1117
    Eleanor Louise: 266, 616, 1114, 1115, 1398
    Emma Arlene: 269
    Emma Irene: 267
    George Clayton: 269

Veronica Frany (Schantz): 9-11

Johnson -
    Amy: 1136
    Ann: 1136
    Arvid Emmet: 629
    Burton: 78
    Carol Ann: 1112
    Charlotte Ruby: 1476
    Cyril Arvid: 629, 630
    Dahl Melvin: 673, 674
    Eric: 1136
    Esther Jean: 1112, 1398
    Frank: 226
    Gerald: 1149
    Harlan: 629
    Janet Edith: 629
    Jerry: 1112
    Jerry Jr.: 1113
    Katheryn: 1305
    Keith: 1136
    Lance: 1222
    Lloyd Arthur: 674
    Michelle A.: 1179
    Mike: 1479
    Phyllis J. (Ainsworth): 838
    Rhonda: 1113, 1398
    Sarah Jayne Black: 1476
    Terry Lee: 1476
    Wade Henry: 78
    William: 1393

Johnston -
    Anna Marie: 647, 648

Jones -
    Unnamed: 440
    Abe: 503
    Alvin Fredrick: 936
    Amelia: 503, 938
    Betty Jean: 936
    David Eugene: 1327
    David J.: 504, 939, 940
    David Lynn: 938
    Dawn Rene: 940
    Debra Ann: 936
    Devon Eugene: 937
    Dorvin Jay: 937
    Duane Lyle: 937
    Elizabeth: 503
    Eugina Ilaine: 938
    Fred: 503, 935, 936, 1214, 1327
    Glenda Kay: 937
    Glendon N.: 1080
    Ida Mae: 372
    Infant: 1080
    Ivan Jaye: 936, 1327
    Jacob: 502, 503, 1214
    Jacob Jr.: 503, 937
    Jane Desma: 937
    Janet Ellen: 1349
    Joseph Erie: 1349
    Joseph W.: 1349
    Judith Elaine: 1349
    Judy: 876
    Kenneth Eugene: 936
    Larry: 876
    Larry Wayne: 936
    Leroy Jr: 1111

    Levi: 503, 937
    Mabel: 160, 161
    Mary Anna: 503, 939
    Mary Lou: 936
    Mattie N.: 1080, 1389
    Maude Bernice "Bunny" (aka: Bunny): 740-742
    Millie N.: 1080, 1389, 1390
    Nathaniel J.: 503, 936
    Neal: 503
    Neil E.: 1079, 1080
    Nellie: 503
    Pamela: 939
    Perry Allen: 938
    Perry J.: 503, 938
    Randall Linn: 936
    Raymond Jacob: 936, 1327
    Regina Elaine: 937, 938
    Robert: 939
    Robert Daniel: 1349
    Robert Wayne: 1327
    Ronald H.: 1197
    Ronald Jay: 940
    Sharon Diane: 937
    Terry Lee: 936, 937
    Toby: 503
    Vicki: 1122

Joquet -
    Nina: 1276

Joquish -
    Justin Jaquish: 1116

Jorzick -
    Rita: 645

Josephthal -
    David: 1282

Josie -
    (name: Josephine Christner): 159, 393, 740, 1175, 1176

Joyce -
    Unnamed: 716
    Unnamed: 1174, 1426
    (name: Gloria Joyce Hostetler): 904

Jr -
    (name: Paul Murray): 1156, 1416

Jubic -
    Julia: 646

Judy -
    Unnamed: 920
    Albert: 316
    Albert: 668
    Albert Barton: 165, 400
    Albert Devon: 400
    Alice: 164
    Anna B.: 165
    Babe: 164
    Barbara Bevvy: 37, 121, 122, 128, 129
    Bertha Idella "Della": 164, 399, 750, 1178
    Caroline: 48
    Charles H.: 165
    Charlotte Margaret: 400
    Christina Dinah: 37, 123
    Cornelius: 48, 163, 164, 399, 750, 1178
    Delilah: 37
    Deloris Mowrey: 277
    Earl: 165
    Elias F.: 164, 399
    Elizabeth: 38, 124

Ellen Malinda: 48
Emaline R: 400
Florence: 316
Frank Ervin: 165
George: 331
George Arthur: 165
Harry Albert: 165
Hattie B: 164
Henry Wilson: 164
Irene: 316
Ivadene Louise: 400
Jacob: 48
Jerome Henry: 48, 165, 400
John: 48, 164
John C: 164
John W.: 48
Jonathan: 48
Kenneth: 316
Lavina: 38
Leonard: 316
Mable: 316
Maggie B: 164
Mary Anne: 38
Mary Polly: 48
Matthias: 37, 38, 128
Minerva: 37
Minnie M: 164
Nelson: 37
Ofelia M: 331
Paul: 316
Paul Eugene: 399
Pauline Naomi: 400
Ralph Rudolph: 331
Regina B: 400
Richard Thomas: 165
Robert: 316
Roseann: 38
Samuel: 37
Scott: 331
Susanna: 38
Verda M: 165
Verda May: 165
William: 48
William Lewis: 165

Juhde -
Beverly: 1082

Juliana -
Unnamed: 252

Julie -
Unnamed: 1478, 1479
Juliet: 25

Junge -
Julia A.: 381

Juntunen -
Mayme Alina: 347

Justin -
Daphne: 1421

Kalkhorst -
John Jack: 317

Kallistrom -
Wailan M.: 808

Kalp -
Anna "Annie" (aka: Annie): 284
Charles R.: 284
Clyde B.: 284, 634

Daisy H.: 285
Davis C.: 284
Gertrude "Gertie" (aka: Gertie): 285
Harry E.: 284
Hattie: 284
Lloyd J.: 284
Robert: 634
Samuel R.: 285

Kapphan -
Albert Thomas: 353
Carol: 353

Kapustka -
Jan H: 356

Kaser -
Fannie: 215
Ida: 224
Lydia L.: 532

Kathleen -
Unnamed: 1127

Katie -
(name: Katherine Christner): 206, 492, 493, 908, 1484, 1485
(name: Catherine M. "Katie" Hershberger): 481, 483, 486

Katie Ann -
(name: Catherine Ann Christner): 67, 223, 224, 552

Katona -
David Nelson: 1107, 1393
Denise: 1107
Dennis Shawn: 1108
Dianna Lynn: 1107, 1394
Douglas Stephen: 1107
Shannon: 1393
Stephen Peter: 1106, 1107

Kauffman -
Unnamed: 315
Alpha Jerry: 759
Amos: 808-810
Barbara: 775
Brandon Richard: 1444
Brent Jeffery: 1444
Carol Ann: 928
Charles: 810
Cheryl Ann: 928
Daniel: 1267
Daniel J.: 808
Ellwood: 859
Elnora Mae: 1081
Elsie: 1053
Eunice Maxine: 1081
Freida: 774, 1201
Gary Duane: 1078
Harley Amos: 810
Henry J.: 1198
Infant: 810
Isabella O: 1461
Jacob: 436
Jacob J.: 436, 438
Jacob Marion: 1198
James Merlin: 1198
Janet Marie: 1386
Janice Lavonne: 842, 1198
Jeffrey Deon: 1198
Jerrold Jacob: 1198, 1444
Joann Ranae: 1199

John Richard: 1198, 1443
Jorge Eugene: 1199
Joyce Colleen: 1198
Julia Annette: 1199, 1444
Larry Lee: 928
Lawrence Reuben: 810
Mabel: 513
Marion E.: 810
Marvin Ray: 1081
Mary Alice: 810
Mary Emily: 839, 840
Mary Lucinda: 757, 758
Melvin R.: 1078
Menno A.: 928
Menno M.: 774
Morris: 810
Pearl Lorene: 810
Raymond: 1267
Richard Lee: 928
Robert Lee: 928
Roy Monroe: 810
Samuel B.: 1461
Samuel Melvin: 810
Shawn Michael: 1444
Shirley Ann: 928
Steven Eugene: 906
Twyla Mae: 1081
Verl Lamar: 1081
Vernon: 1267
Viola Marie: 1195, 1196
Winifred M: 1461

Kaufman -
Unnamed: 769
Unnamed: 769
Unnamed: 769
Boy: 769
Edward: 769
Elnora: 769
Fannie S.: 769
Ida Irene: 769
John S.: 769
Julia: 462
Katie S.: 769
Laura: 767
Lizzie May: 769
Ora: 769
Samuel J.: 769

Kausner -
Adriene: 1494

Kay -
Unnamed: 1432
Linda: 1265

Kear -
Hanna Elilzabeth: 1490
Kelton Royal: 1490

Keatley -
Lydia A.: 277

Kebar -
Alyssa: 1491
Erica: 1491
Michael: 1491

Keefer -
Bonnie Lou: 1159
Brooks Alexander: 1418
Carl Henry: 1159

Lonnie Wade: 1418
Michael Alen: 1418
Sara Ann: 1159, 1418
Teri Lynn: 1418
Timothy Allen: 1418
Virginia Lee: 1159, 1418

Keeler -
Charissa: 1484
Ivan Michael: 1484

Keffer -
Charles Emerson: 631
Daniel Lee: 631
Daniel M.: 630, 631
Emory Thaddeus: 631
Infant: 631
Josiah Glenn: 631
Ligonier: 631
Margaret Blanche: 650
Meade Wayne: 631
Oscar Lloyd: 631
Ruth Marie: 631
Willa: 631
Wilmer: 631

Keim -
Arlene Hartzler: 860
Benjamin: 856
Carolyn: 1327
Karl Keirn or: 1466
Lena: 551
Mary Salome: 42, 328
Tracy Keirn or: 1466

Kein -
Arlene: 1483
Benjamin: 1483

Keiser -
Clyde Daniel: 959
Clyde E.: 958, 959
Gloria Jean: 959
Gregory Alan: 959
Jerome Edmund: 959

Kellerman -
Beth Ann: 1409
Mary E.: 317
Paula Jane: 1409
Roger: 1409

Kelley -
James Scott: 1421
Richard: 1325

Kelly -
Helen: 654
Jacque: 1150

Kemp -
Bertha: 210, 502, 503, 935-939, 1214, 1327
Not Named: 210
Tobias D.: 209, 210

Kempf -
Lorraine Marie: 1207

Kendall -
Ezra: 263
George: 83, 263
Gertrude: 83
Lorraine: 676
Peirce: 83

Kennedy -
Carl Alexander: 706

Eva Lee: 895, 896
Kennel -
    Anna: 174, 176
Kennell -
    Amanda: 1206, 1208
    Audrey Gail: 1208
    Daniel Clark: 1447
    Darren Kent: 1447
    David Alan: 1208
    Elaine Susan: 1208
    Harlan Rodrick: 1447
    Harold Jr.: 1447
    James Lynn: 1208
    Kenneth D.: 1207, 1208
    Kurt Travis: 1447
    Lori MIchelle: 1208
    Mark Albert: 1447
    Rubin: 1207
Kenny -
    Brenda Lee: 1437
    Cindy Marie: 1437
    Vernon: 1437
Kent -
    Allen James: 1177, 1426
    Allen James II: 1426
    Amy Rachelle: 1177
    Daniel Robert: 1426
    Katelynn Marie: 1426
    Millious Allen: 1176, 1177
Kepner -
    Teresa Ann: 990
Kepple -
    Sarah: 306
Kerlin -
    Harry B.: 135
Kershal -
    Unnamed: 752
Keslar -
    Arden Fay: 633
    Carl Welfred: 632
    Claude Laverne: 633
    David: 1127
    Forrest Iven: 631, 632
    Gilbert Edmond: 632
    Hazel Catherine: 632
    Infant: 632
    Ivan Harold: 632
    Josiah Bungard: 633
    Luella Irene: 632
    Morris Woodrow: 632
    Shelby Otis: 633, 1126, 1127
    Vernon Theodore: 633
Kesler -
    Peter: 112
Kessler -
    Catherine: 112
    Deliah: 112
    Elizabeth: 112
    Emaline Emma: 112
    Herman: 112
    Lydia E.: 112
    Sarah: 112
    Simon: 112
    Wesley: 112
Ketring -

Shirley: 659
Keyes -
    Louis: 655
Kibridge -
    Bill: 356
Kiddy -
    Nancy Jane: 1446
Kilgore -
    David Burrell: 1135, 1136
    Jackson David Jr.: 1409
    John Alexander: 1136, 1409
    Sarah Jane: 1409
Kilpatrick -
    Unnamed: 244
Kimberland -
    Sharon Rose: 1115
Kimmel -
    Minnie E.: 722
    Ruth Ann: 1416
Kincaid -
    George Garman: 365
    William F.: 365
    William L.: 365
Kinder -
    P. M.: 278
King -
    Charity Ann: 808
    David: 1193
    Glen R.: 1193
    Jaynee: 1457
    Kirby: 282
    Lola May: 401
    Mariam Ann: 1193
    Rhonda Sue: 1194
    Rose Mary: 963
    Ruth P.: 288
    Sherill: 1193
Kingery -
    Daniel: 990
Kinik -
    Desiree Chantell: 1407
Kinneer -
    Eliza Jane: 627, 628
    James W.: 94
    Mary: 632
Kinsey -
    Henry Etta: 957
Kinsinger -
    Jacob P.: 112
Kintz -
    James Lou: 746
Kister -
    Candace Jean: 1416
Kitchen -
    Phyllis: 578
Kitson -
    Betty E.: 315
Klaas -
    Bailey Brian: 1116
    Brian Michael: 1116
    Carson Riley: 1116
    Connon Robert: 1116
    Payton Marie: 1116
Klack -

Agnes: 1175
Klase -
    Maxine: 871, 872
Klassen -
    Katherine: 1196
Kleck -
    Bethany: 1491
Klein -
    Frances: 1235
    Paul: 1235
    Robert: 1235
    Shirley: 1235
Kline -
    Bonnie Jean: 1248
    Donald: 670
    Evylnn: 851
    Mayzel Evelyn: 580, 581
    Norman T: 261
Kling -
    Brian Michael: 1118
    Nathan Michael: 1118
    Timothy Shelton: 1118
Klink -
    Cornelius: 28
    Daniel: 81
    Darrell Jr.: 1149
    Gloria Ann: 617
    Pearl E.: 670, 671
    Peter: 81
Kloos -
    Brian Scott: 1175
    Casen James: 1175
    Erin: 1175
    Logan Kathleen: 1175
    Raymond: 1175
Kluck -
    Karen: 1432
Knapp -
    John Bernard: 408, 409
    Marjorie: 409
    Mary Jane: 409, 752, 1178, 1179
Knepp -
    Mary Leona: 357, 358
    Renell: 1232
    Rita Ann: 858
    Sara Sue: 1099
    Susan: 772
Knetich -
    Louie: 538, 539
Knight -
    Fredrick E.: 730
    Mary Ann: 340, 341
Knopsnider -
    William: 277
Knopsnyder -
    Joyce: 619
    Kenneth Earl: 1144
Knox -
    Deborah Sue: 1448
    Laurie/Loria Elizabeth: 1449
    Virginia Mary: 1207
Kobb -
    Mary: 693
Koch -

Esther: 815
Koehler -
    Melanie May: 1200
    Pamela Kay: 1200
    Raymond Lynn: 1200
    Richard Lynn: 1200
Koehn -
    Dorothy Mae: 1385
Koenig -
    Benetta Marie: 1440
    Emily Edna: 1492
    John Charles: 1492
Kolb -
    Nancy: 1418
Kolkhorst -
    Fritz Hienrich Martin "Fred": 317
Konneck -
    Charles Barton: 826, 1243
    Charlotte Irene: 825, 1242
    Cindy: 1243
    Dallas Keith: 826, 1243
    Donna Elizabeth: 826, 1243
    Elaine: 1242
    Helen: 824, 825
    Judy: 1243
    Kenneth B.: 825
    Kevin: 1243
    Linda: 1242
    Nancy: 1243
    Nick: 1242
    Paul Bud: 826, 1242, 1243
    Paul Otto: 825
    Pauline: 825, 1242
    Robert: 825, 1242
    Ronda: 1243
    Shelly: 1243
    Teressa: 1243
    Terry: 1243
    Tim: 1242
    Vickki: 1243
    Victor: 826
Koontz -
    Bernice: 1157
    Edward: 111
    John: 111
Kooser -
    Ella: 98
    Isaac N.: 98
    John Andrew: 98
    Kate: 98
    Marguerite: 98, 294
    William F.: 98
Kordis -
    Allen W.: 728, 729
    Ellen Marie: 729
    Herbert Allen: 729
    Kenneth Randel: 729
    Ruth Mabel: 729
Kosh -
    (name: Harold Dean (Kosh) Christner): 667, 1142-
        1144, 1410, 1411, 1487, 1488
Kozinski -
    John Kenneth: 1477
    John Kenneth Jr.: 1477
    Mac Thomas: 1477

Zoe Rose: 1477
Krabill -
  Teresa: 1453
Krahulik -
  Karen Elaine: 1425
Kralsill -
  Jeanette May: 921, 922
Krass -
  Adena: 1493
Kraushouer -
  Florence Margaret: 614
Krebs -
  Kimberly: 1418
Kreemer -
  Jean: 19
Kreider -
  Howard Bowers: 796
  Howard Jr.: 796
  Lyle: 1193
  Minnie E.: 796
Krell -
  Patricia: 1318
Kresky -
  Dana Lee: 1400
  Robert T.: 1400
  Robert Timothy: 1400
  Stephen Douglas: 1400
Kretchman -
  Elizabeth Ann: 79, 80
Krichbaum -
  Allen Ray: 1126
Krieg -
  Inez Jane: 972
Kristi -
  Unnamed: 1137
Kropf -
  Unnamed: 440
  Clarence Isaac: 808-810
  Harvey Elmer: 812, 813
  John: 808
  Mabel Alice: 813
Krug -
  Viola M.: 681, 682
Kubowski -
  Amy Jo: 715
  Barry Walter: 715
  James F.: 715
  Paula Sue: 715
Kuhns -
  Emma: 1256
  Esther: 561
  Horace Harris A.: 252
  Leon: 252
  May: 252
  Menno M.: 415
Kunkel -
  Don: 991
Kurek -
  Thomas: 85
Kurtz -
  Mary: 911
Kutrz -
  Marion: 259

Kyle -
  Helen: 1009
L -
  Grace: 298
  Mary: 817
La Von Youree -
  Tresea: 1043
Labick -
  Theresa Mildred: 655
LaCount -
  Karen L.: 934
Lacy -
  Laura L.: 683
  Roy Darrell: 738
Lafferty -
  Amy Lea: 1151, 1414
  Kayla Sue: 1414
  Michelle Renee: 1151, 1414
  Roger Eugene: 1151
Laird -
  Betty Jo: 1042
Lakotish -
  John: 255
Lamb -
  Leona Mae: 924
Lambert -
  Ivan Oscar Ben: 310
  Jerlyn: 1303
  Joy: 932
Lambright -
  Ada Mae: 969
  Alvin Lee: 969
  Amos J.: 433, 434
  Betty Fern: 584
  Birdena Loraine: 1039, 1040
  Carolyn Sue: 1348
  Christy: 995, 1348
  Clara J.: 1004
  Cletus: 953
  Daniel J.: 968
  David: 1295
  Devon Jay: 584, 585
  Diana Kay: 584
  Dorothy Marie: 1348
  Elsie Irene: 953
  Elva H.: 1295
  Eugene Ray: 584
  Fannie Alzoa: 434
  Fannie Marie: 969
  Floyd O.: 1063
  Freeman: 995
  Frieda: 968
  Gary Lee: 585
  Gerald Dean: 584
  Harold: 1039
  Harvey J.: 1295
  Irene: 968
  Irene: 969
  Jason Andrew: 1480
  Joas: 969
  Karl Jay: 1040
  Karon Kay: 1040
  LaVern O.: 1062
  LeAnna: 1478
  LeRoy Jay: 1062

Leasa -
    Amanda Pearl: 111
    John W.: 110, 111
Lecallo -
    Eliane Jaclyn: 1400
Lederman -
    Joseph Howard: 455, 456
    Joseph Karl: 456, 458
    Kathryn: 456
Ledyard -
    Amy Lynn: 1495
    Billie Jo: 1468
    Justin Ralph: 1468, 1495
    Luanna Mae: 1468
    William: 1467, 1468
Lee -
    (name: Leonard Leroy Stewart): 394, 395
    C. H.: 91
Lehman -
    Amzie: 1256
    Ben: 314
    Daniel: 915
    Dennis: 1256
    Dennis Manford: 1159
    Edna Ellen: 917
    Edward: 915
    Edward M.: 979
    Elva D.: 1255
    Ernest: 1256
    Ervin M.: 916, 917
    Fannie Mae: 1256
    Freeman: 917
    Glen: 917
    Glen LeRoy: 979
    Ida D.: 1071, 1072
    Ida Mae: 917
    Jacob Lee: 979
    John E.: 914, 915
    John Wayne: 915
    Katie: 886
    Levi M: 915
    Lizzie Mae: 979, 980
    Manas: 917
    Marietta: 979
    Mary: 982
    Mary Ellen: 1255, 1256
    Mary Polly: 1215
    Merlin Jay: 979
    Ora: 1256
    Orva: 917
    Rosanna: 917
    Ruth: 870
    Susie Ellen: 979
Leichty -
    Martha Pauline: 906
Leiler -
    Mary: 726
Leisher -
    Unnamed: 1417
    William: 1417
Lemley -
    Patricia May: 1131
    Robert Raymond: 647
Lemon -
    Billy: 403

Jack: 403
Jinnie: 403
John William: 403
Lena -
    Unnamed: 1448
Lengacher -
    David: 573
    Elizabeth: 573
    John A.: 573
    Joseph: 573
    Nathan: 573
    Paul: 573
Lenhart -
    Adaline: 373
    Ananias: 152, 153
    Bessie: 681
    Billy Joe: 373
    Carl Edward: 370
    Charles Wallace: 153, 371
    Elva Mae: 371
    Emma Elizabeth: 153, 371
    Eugene George: 371
    Everett Casimir: 372
    Fannie Emma: 397
    George Washington: 153
    Hattie Lucelle: 371
    James Blaine: 153, 372
    James Warren "Ike": 373
    John Joseph: 153, 370
    Lola Mae: 373
    Lottie Marie: 372
    Madison Willard (Matt): 153
    Moses Ananias: 153
    Norma Lucy: 373
    Ray Andrew: 373
    Vergel Lucille: 370, 371
    William Harrison: 153
Lennon -
    Jack: 883
Leonard -
    Mary Theona: 631
Leota -
    Unnamed: 823
Lesh -
    Otto L: 317
Leslie -
    Unnamed: 1128
Levelle -
    Margaret Ann: 587
Lewis -
    Amanda Ann: 1423, 1491
    Orval Bruce: 1423
Lichti -
    Abner Leroy: 230
    Alice Marie: 230
    Amos S.: 1234
    Anna Mae: 230
    Anna S.: 1234
    Arlene: 230
    Daniel S.: 1234
    David S.: 1235
    Emanuel S.: 1235
    Jacob S.: 1234
    Kathrine S.: 1235
    Mary S.: 1235

Nancy S.: 1234
Norman S.: 1235
Peter: 230
Rebecca S.: 1235
Ruth S.: 1235
Samuel S.: 1235
Samuel Z.: 1234

Liddle -
Ralph E.: 608

Liechty -
Bradley: 1315
Gregory Ray: 1315
Herbert: 1314, 1315
Jill: 1315
Rodney: 1315

Liedy -
Brian: 1413
Hillary: 1413
Tanner: 1413

Lightcap -
Sarah Belle: 271, 273, 274

Lightwine -
Susan: 1450

Lilley -
Teresa Dawn (aka: Teri): 1426

Linda -
Unnamed: 1189

Lindeman -
Floyd E.: 346
Glenn E.: 346
Mary Ann Elizabeth: 346
Roy: 345, 346
Thomas E.: 346
Viola A.: 346

Linnie -
(name: Linda Christner): 146, 356, 357

Lint -
Hattie M.: 1131
Hazel Neletta: 554, 555
John Calvin: 639
Joseph Jay: 360
Joseph Jesse: 360
Kenneth E.: 640
Mary Leora: 639
Noah: 639
Paul W.: 640
Robert: 640

Litchenwalter -
Russell: 1405

Little Willie -
(name: William Prosper Lowry): 108

Little -
Erlene: 1431
Helen: 1156

Livingston -
Maxine A.: 936

Lizzie -
Unnamed: 1025, 1194

Lleichty -
Alice Louise: 820
Clarence John: 820
Herman: 820
James Herman: 820
Jeanne Carol: 820

Ronald Wayne: 820
Vernon Chris: 820

Lobert -
Geevieve: 1182, 1183

Locke -
Francis Ruthanne: 1304

Lockhart -
Ruth Hope: 355, 356

Lodena -
Unnamed: 1399

Logsdon -
Emma Rosalie: 371
George: 371
Harriet "Hattie": 371

Logson -
John: 28

Logue -
Allen Lee: 1324
Daniel Lee: 1324
Matthew Raymond: 1324

Lohr -
Audrey Jeannette (aka: Sis): 1147
Durdin: 1147
Lydia: 303

Lois -
Unnamed: 1187
Unnamed: 1435
Unnamed: 1459

Long -
Anna: 301, 302
Molly: 1136
Susan: 119

Longacher -
Andrew Joseph: 1492
Joseph Mark: 1492

Looney -
Bernice Elaine: 905, 906
Tabitha M.: 1484

Loquist -
Eric Lee: 1401
Leland George: 1121, 1401
Leola Jane: 1121
Melissa Anne: 1401
Rudolph George (aka: Rudy): 1120, 1121
Sarah J.: 1401
Sylvia JoAnne: 1121, 1401, 1486

Loren -
Unnamed: 702

Lottie -
(name: Charlotte Brenneman): 770, 771

Loucks -
John M.: 461

Louie May -
(name: Luteria Cease): 101, 102

Louisa -
(name: Susanna Lucy Anne Christner): 40, 127, 128, 336, 697-699

Louise -
Mary: 683

Loutner -
Pat: 1432

Lowe -
Clarence: 238
Eva Blanche: 238, 239

Manning -
    Andrea Lee: 1424
    Brian Robert: 1424
    Heather Lyn: 1425
    Kendra Marie: 1425
    Kevin Bowman: 1169, 1424
    Neal Robert: 1169, 1424, 1425
    Robert Frank: 1169
    Vince Robert: 1425
Maple -
    Jesse L: 1277
    Reenie: 876
Marciano -
    Anna: 1198
Marcy -
    David Levi: 1400
    Dianna Lynn: 1400
    Gerald Letcher: 1400
    Marcella Jean: 1400
    Toni Suzanne: 1400
Mardis -
    Charles William: 298
    Grace Beatrice: 299
    Lavernon: 298, 299
    Lew V.: 298
    Ruth T.: 299
    Samuel Adelma: 298
    Theophilus Glenn: 299
    Thomas: 298
Margaret -
    Unnamed: 1134
    Sarah: 165
Marie -
    (name: Mary Ellen Christner): 499
    Dawn: 1232
    Edwina: 1137
    Regina: 1489
    Unnamed V: 818, 819
Marietta -
    (name: Harriet Sipe): 87-89
Marilyn -
    Unnamed: 891
    Unnamed: 1309
Marini -
    Sharon: 858
Marion -
    Unnamed: 1129, 1130
Marker -
    Brian David: 1425
    Eric William: 1425
    Madeline Jane: 1425
    Sauel David: 1425
    Susan: 146, 147
Marks -
    Carol Lee: 839
Marmion -
    Douglas: 1438
    Fred: 1438
    Roger Allen: 1438
Marshal -
    Thelma G.: 378, 379
Marshall -
    John Redman III: 1417
    Nicholas Redman: 1417

Rebecca Adeline: 371
Marteeny -
    Diane Louise: 1157, 1417
    Elaine Kay: 1157, 1417
    Lloyd Glenn: 1157
Marteney -
    Don E: 1412
    Jack: 1412
    Jason: 1412
    Justin: 1412
    Michael Elek: 1412
Martha -
    Unnamed: 935
    Unnamed: 883
Martin -
    Unnamed: 273
    Unnamed: 1174
    Unnamed: 657
    Bonnie Jeanne: 355
    Charles: 680
    Delilah R.: 1484
    Elmer J.: 355
    Elsie Edna: 1207
    Eva Rose: 678
    Evadna JoAnne: 355
    Fitus L.: 1012
    George: 1465
    Grace: 678
    JoEllen: 1125
    John: 678
    Judy: 1125
    Kendall Lane: 1428
    Kent Jay: 1461
    Kirby Ray: 1428
    Larry Richard: 1428
    Lawrence (aka: Larry): 1125
    Mary B.: 678
    Mary Lee: 1041
    Nancy Elaine: 1012
    Ronald Alan: 1204
    Rose: 1451
    Roy: 826
    Rufus S.: 1461
    Susan Irene: 1450
    Sylvia Margaret: 1465
    Terry Steven: 1012
    Tina Dawn: 1461
    Torrie Lynn: 1428
    Virginia Pauline: 929
    William: 115
-
    Marty: 1416
Martz -
    Dorothy Elizabeth: 623
Mary -
    Unnamed: 635
    Unnamed: 16
    Unnamed: 1406
    Unnamed: 105, 106
MaryAnn -
    (name: Mary Ann Christner): 491, 904, 905
Mason -
    Unnamed: 162
    Lois Jane: 560
    William Thomas III: 1148

Mattie -
    (name: Magdalena Miller): 207, 208
    (name: Mary Allen Christner): 271, 620
    (name: Magdalena Yoder): 469-471
Mauk -
    Janet: 1128
Maura -
    Unnamed: 1406
Maust -
    Jacob: 14
    Mary Catherine: 14, 15, 34
May -
    Unnamed: 171
    Marian: 697
Maynard -
    Michael David: 1200
McAninch -
    Ralph Hugh: 622
McArdle -
    Frances Elizabeth "Fannie": 624
    Michael: 624
McAvoy -
    Arlene: 244
    Hilma Mae: 1103
McBride -
    Carolyn Elaine: 1252
    Corky James Warren: 862
McCaffrey -
    Unnamed: 683
    William: 683
McCann -
    Charles "Cub" D: 1106
    Gerald: 1106
    Leslie Lynn: 1106
    Living: 1106
    Paul Eugene Sr.: 1105, 1106
McCavitt -
    Nora: 342
McClain -
    Glen: 634
McClane -
    Roger Gene: 1381
    Roger Patrick: 1381
McCleary -
    Lena Faye: 167
McClure -
    Asa Albert: 593, 1103
    Douglas: 593
    Jerry Lane: 1103
    Kathleen V.: 593
    Leo David: 592, 593
    Linda Sue: 1103
    Merlin Thomas: 593
    Troy Lee: 593
    Victor Ace: 1103
McCoy -
    Buel Lafayette: 1399
    Buel Lafayette: 1399, 1486
    Doyle: 238
    Genevieve: 300
    James Buel: 1486
    James Dennis: 1399
    Nancy Jeanette: 1399, 1486
    Penny Sue: 1399

    Wendy MeiLing: 1486
McCrea -
    Unnamed: 702
McCreary -
    Jessie Eugenia: 642, 643
McCulley -
    Harriet M. "Hattie": 340
McCurtain -
    Imogene: 623
McDaniel -
    Irene: 654
McDonnell -
    Leo Vinson: 394
McElvain -
    Gary Laine: 1151
    Kelly Teresa: 1151
    Kristen Catherine: 1151, 1414
McGee -
    William: 1182
McGinnis -
    Blanche Elizabeth: 634
    Cora Alsetta: 634
    Dorothy Suzannah: 634
    Edwin Albert: 634
    Eugene Alvin: 634
    Gladys Catherine: 634
    Harry: 634
    Ross Franklin: 634
McGlennen -
    Merl: 279
McGoogan -
    Charles Oral: 299
    Edgar: 299
    Harry H.: 299
    Jessie B.: 299
    John McClure: 299
McIntosh -
    William: 1137
McKay -
    Tracy: 1407
McKee -
    Alonzo Rush: 750
    Dianne Adele: 750
    Paul William: 750
McKelvey -
    Joseph: 106
McKenzie -
    Agnes Mae Barbara: 245
    Alice G.: 591
    Anna Jane: 590
    Anne Elizabeth: 77
    B F: 1173
    Beulah L.: 246
    Billy S: 1173
    Catherine: 590
    Cecil Benedict: 249
    Charles Russell (Buzz) Jr.: 1426
    Charles Russell Sr: 1173, 1425, 1426
    Christine: 1103
    Daniel Freeman: 244
    Darren: 1103
    Dorothy: 241, 589, 1101
    Edgar Lewis: 246
    Edith Sarah: 241

Edward Joseph: 241, 589, 590
Elizabeth Cecelia: 241
Elizabeth G.: 76
Emma Theresa: 76, 247
Eulalia Agnes: 76
Francis Leo: 75
Frank Clement Sr: 246
Freda Alta: 245
George: 243
George Thomas: 75, 241, 243, 592, 1103
George W.: 75
Glen Robert Sr Pvt: 246
Grace: 1173
Harry Roy: 247
Helen Delores: 591
Henrietta Anna: 75
Henry Grace: 1173
Irvin E. (Lindy): 590
Jacob Henry: 76, 248, 249
Jacob Patrick: 77
James Francis: 241
James Harris: 75, 244, 245
James Kenneth Sr: 246
Jeanetta Elizabeth: 246
John L.: 74, 75
John Lewis: 241
John Simon: 75
John William: 77
Joseph Alfred: 592, 1101, 1102
Joseph Tecumseh: 76
Lauretta: 75
Lawrence Leo: 246
Leonard Clarence: 241, 591
Leota Beatrice: 245
Lewis Joseph: 240, 241
Lucy: 248, 249
Luella Alice: 249
Mabel F: 245
Margaret: 18
Mary Olive: 75, 240, 241, 589-591, 1101, 1102
Melvin Noah: 244
Meta: 247
Myrtle Catherine: 243
Norma/Nora Mae: 244
Norvell Lee: 244
Patrick: 77
Patrick: 592
Ralph: 592
Randall: 1102
Rhoda Renee: 244
Roger Michael: 592, 1102, 1103
Rose Blanche: 241, 590, 591
Ruby: 243
Ruth: 76, 248
Ruth Gertrude: 241
Samuel Gregory: 75, 246, 247
Sanford Ervin: 247
Sarah Ellen: 249
Scott: 1173
Thomas Patrick: 241, 591, 592, 1101, 1102
Tracey: 1102
Troy: 1102
Ulalia Agnes: 76
Ulela C.: 249
Verna Virginia: 243, 592, 593, 1103
Virginia Agnes: 75

William A.: 590
McLaughlin -
Betty Jeanette: 744
Beverly: 1197
III Charles Emmett: 1159, 1160
IV Charles Emmett IV: 1160
Lisa Ann: 1160
McManus -
Mary A.: 281
McMillan -
Bill: 1435
Rebecca: 1435
McNabb -
Della Elizabeth "Delia": 754
McQuarrie -
Donald: 1137
Meadows -
Gregory Scott: 1248
Meeder -
Doris Jane: 1125, 1126
Meek -
Perry James: 1465, 1466
Meers -
Adeline M.: 375, 376
Meese -
Solomon: 1276
Meier -
Janis Louise: 1122
Walter H.: 1122
-
Melanie: 988
Melhorn -
Ruth: 854
Mellinger -
Chad: 1393
John D.: 1393
John D. III: 1393
Melvina -
Unnamed: 264, 265
Menezes -
Unnamed: 1324
Menges -
David Charles: 1309
David Thain: 1309
Lisa Ann: 1309
William James: 1309
Meroney -
Marylin: 1337
Merrill -
Benjamin Christner: 169, 404, 750, 751
Benjamin W: 405
Charles LeRoy: 404, 750, 1178, 1427
Elsie Christina: 752
Harry Edward: 404
Hazel Alice: 750, 1178, 1427
Herber Franklin: 169
Herbert K.: 405
Jessie Amanda: 169, 405, 406
John Theron: 405, 751, 752
Joseph: 167, 168
Martha Marcella "Marcella": 404, 750, 751
Michael P.: 1398
Michael P. Jr.: 1398
Norman: 169

William Henry: 168, 169
William Henry Jr.: 169, 405
William John: 168, 404, 750, 1178, 1427

Messer -
Della May: 446, 447
Samuel Hiram: 446

Metzger -
Herbert: 1243
Jeffrey: 1455
Sandra Lucille: 1243, 1244

Metzler -
Carl: 1310
Dawn Sue: 1310, 1311

Meyer -
Alexander Noah: 1325
Alta: 774, 775, 1371
Ashley Nichole: 1325
Edna S.: 160
John H.: 681
Joseph: 1325
Mary Jane: 681
Stover C.: 681

Meyers -
Ashley: 1413
Debbie: 1146
Glenn: 1145
Harry: 1145
Paul: 1150
Ronnie: 1145, 1146
Steven: 1150, 1413
Timothy: 1150

Michael -
Martha Lee: 587, 588
Virgil: 988

Michaels -
Mabel A.: 458-460
Nora E.: 458-460

Michalok -
Mary Anna: 1433

Mick -
(name: Millard Decker): 663, 1139, 1140

Mickem -
Mark Douglas: 1293
Melanie Roe: 1293
Melvin Douglas: 1293
Mickey Dale: 1293
Mitzi Renee': 1293

Midge -
(name: Mildred Marie "Midge" Stewart): 394

Mildred -
Unnamed: 1206

Millard -
Unnamed: 726
Eulalia Mae: 726
Otis Karl: 726
William Leroy: 726

Miller -
Unnamed: 416

Miller Hochstedler -
Barbara J: 768

Miller -
Aaron: 1066
Aaron: 1071
Aaron: 1269, 1473

Aaron Dale: 1473
Aaron John: 1285
Abner: 1471
Abner B.: 508, 509
Ada C.: 767, 768
Ada D.: 529, 1001, 1359, 1363
Ada E.: 467, 844, 845, 1265, 1266
Ada Mae: 885
Ada Marie: 235, 584
Alain: 1409
Albert: 87
Albert: 1354
Albert C.: 1018, 1375, 1376
Albert D.: 803
Albert D.: 998, 1352
Albert Lee: 1376
Alexander Clark: 1452
Alice: 1471
Alice: 1471
Alice D.: 536
Alice J.: 486, 883, 1299
Allen: 1471
Allen: 1471
Alma: 767
Alma E.: 467, 847, 1194
Alma E.: 844, 1264, 1265
Alma L.: 234, 580
Alpha H.: 1270, 1271
Alta Marie: 1347
Alvin: 536, 1014, 1203, 1300, 1371
Alvin: 235
Alvin: 1065
Alvin: 1068
Alvin Elias: 231, 564
Alvin Jay: 576
Alvin S.: 1233
Alvin Vincent: 1351
Amanda: 135, 144, 341, 704
Amanda: 844
Amanda: 948
Amanda: 967
Amanda Carolyn: 888
Amelia: 436
Amelia Irene: 952
Ammon H.: 507, 946, 947, 983
Ammon J.: 1071
Ammon Leo: 231, 564
Amos: 234
Amos: 1019
Amos: 842
Amos Christner: 278
Amos E.: 467, 848
Amos Eldon: 847, 1270
Amos H.: 537, 562, 1018, 1372-1375
Amos J.: 486, 885, 1014, 1300
Amos J.: 530, 800, 1005
Amos Jr: 885
Amos L.: 546, 1074
Amos M.: 231
Amos M.: 1067
Amos S.: 70, 232, 577
Amy Ellen: 847
Amy Jo: 1437
Amzie J.: 487, 887, 888, 967, 968
Andrea Beth: 1470
Andrew: 948

Andy S.: 1044
Andy S.: 1025, 1379
Angela Dawn: 1323
Anita F.: 1479, 1480
Anna: 794
Anna: 776
Anna (aka: Polly): 233, 577, 578
Anna: 998
Anna: 844
Anna: 579
Anna C.: 757
Anna Irene: 1066
Anna J.: 575, 992
Anna J.: 994, 1069
Anna L.: 546
Anna Mae: 1377
Anna Mae: 1071
Anna Marie: 947
Anna Marie: 575, 576
Anna Marie: 1372
Anna Marie: 1254
Anna Marie: 1067
Anna S.: 233, 431, 796
Anna W.: 1003, 1004
Annie Ruth: 952
Annie Viola: 507
Annon: 767, 847, 1025, 1194, 1269, 1270, 1438
Arland: 553
Arleen Elizabeth: 1377
Arlene: 234
Arlene: 1330
Arthur LaVoid: 897, 1304
Arthur Scott: 1304
Barbara: 106, 107
Barbara: 537, 1016, 1017
Barbara: 1066
Barbara: 1352
Barbara: 1023
Barbara Ann: 1233
Barbara Ann: 1233
Barbara Ann: 997, 1350, 1351
Barbara Ann: 1075
Barbara Arlene: 1254
Barbara D.: 536
Barbara D.: 529
Barbara Delilah "Lila": 440, 808-810
Barbara Eilene: 558
Barbara S.: 70
Barbara Sue: 1443
Barbara W.: 909
Beatrice: 736
Becky Sue: 1374
Benedict: 214
Benedict: 795
Benjamin: 1023
Benjamin D.: 219
Benjamin L.: 568
Benjamin Thomas: 1451
Bernita Faye: 926, 1323, 1484
Bessie: 278
Beth Ann: 1297
Betty Marie: 1235
Beulah Moda: 507, 947, 948
Bonnie Jean: 1142
Bonnie Jean: 1016
Brendon Lynn: 1470

Brian Timothy: 1304
Bryan Keith: 1275
Calvin: 233
Calvin A.: 581, 582
Calvin Jay: 889
Carl Ray: 1470
Carl Wayne: 1381
Carole Ann: 1114
Carolyn Sue: 1372
Carolynn Sue: 1322
Catherine: 413
Chadwick Evan: 1451
Chalmer Douglas: 998
Charles: 725
Charles LeRoy: 1322
Christ: 1004
Christ L.: 848, 849, 963, 1263
Christian: 576
Christian C: 768
Christian Jay: 886
Christian W.: 1004, 1362
Christie Yavonne: 1305
Christina: 1459
Christopher Paul: 1203
Christopher Todd: 1305
Christy: 1069
Clair Elvin: 564
Clara: 1015
Clara: 1025
Clara: 1295
Clara: 579
Clara: 1353
Clara: 1093
Clara C.: 1018, 1375
Clara Elizabeth: 1330, 1331
Clara F.: 765
Clara J.: 1353, 1354
Clara L.: 568
Clarence: 767
Clarence: 1313, 1314
Clarence: 576
Clarence: 579
Clarence Daniel: 1331
Clarence Jay: 768
Clarence Jr.: 1019
Clarence M.: 537, 1018, 1375-1377
Clem: 1133
Clemen Jr.: 1460
Clemens: 537, 1017, 1371, 1372
Clemens: 1093
Cletus: 233, 577
Cletus: 970
Cletus LeRoy: 849
Clifford LaVern: 1016
Connie Jean: 1361
Cora: 536, 1015, 1016
Cora E.: 1054, 1055
Cynthia Mae: 1374
Dale Lamar: 1437
Dalton S.: 526, 527
Dana L.: 1281
Danial Ray: 1458
Daniel: 1014
Daniel: 1023
Daniel: 953
Daniel: 1268, 1471

Daniel A.: 976
Daniel A.: 803
Daniel A.: 800
Daniel B.: 214, 529, 1000-1002, 1355-1359
Daniel Eugene: 1205
Daniel H.: 567
Daniel J.: 998, 1387
Daniel J.: 1331
Daniel Jay: 1352
Daniel L.: 546, 1073, 1074, 1460
Daniel N.: 536, 1300
Daniel S.: 530, 1004, 1362, 1363, 1484
Danny Jay: 884
David: 553
David: 1014
David: 1027
David: 1262
David: 1269, 1474, 1485
David Allen: 1304, 1482
David C.: 277
David D: 767
David Devon: 848
David G.: 1285
David J.: 557, 558
David J.C.: 415, 767
David Leroy: 897, 1304, 1482
David Leroy: 1371
David Ray: 1351, 1352
David V.: 582
David Y.: 488, 787, 788
Dawn Renee': 1308, 1483, 1484
Debra Jo: 1372
Delbert: 885, 886
Delbert Lee: 1460
Deliah: 86
Delmar Ray: 1314
Denis Ann: 558
Dennis Lee: 1256
Devon: 1271
Devon Jay: 1363
Devon Ray: 1474
Dewayne Ray: 1363
Diana Elaine: 565
Diane Cheryl: 1054
Dianne: 1318, 1319
Donald W: 725
Donna L.: 1149
Donna Marie: 1142
Dora: 765
Dora: 1257
Dora Ann: 1054
Dorcas Mae: 1015
Duane: 1376
Earl: 313
Earl J.: 1274
Edd J.: 486
Edith: 1015
Edna: 791
Edna Ellen: 487, 890
Edna Ellen: 892, 1301, 1302
Edna Ellen: 886
Edna Ellen: 1067
Edna Irene: 1473
Edna Lucy: 233, 578, 579
Edna M.: 537, 1022, 1023
Edna Mae: 467, 841, 1252-1257, 1342, 1466

Edna Mae: 70, 235, 583, 584
Edna Mae: 847, 1269, 1270
Edna Mae: 235
Edna Mae: 1354
Edna Mae: 1255
Edna Schlabuagh: 488, 490, 788
Edward: 1093
Edward C.: 1470
Edwin: 1066
Edwin: 1093
Eileen: 582
Eldora: 1376
Eli: 788
Eli: 918
Eli E.: 1061
Eli H.: 567
Eli J: 543
Eli J.: 486, 886
Elijah W.: 1377
Eliza: 86
Elizabeth: 66
Elizabeth: 1460
Elizabeth: 436
Elizabeth: 277
Elizabeth: 1216
Elizabeth: 1029
Elizabeth: 793
Elizabeth: 546
Elizabeth: 947
Elizabeth: 1354
Elizabeth: 1093
Elizabeth: 558
Elizabeth: 1460
Elizabeth "Lizzie" M.: 233, 430, 431, 841, 1005
Elizabeth Ann: 70, 231, 232, 518
Elizabeth Ann: 1333
Elizabeth Ann: 1024
Elizabeth B.: 214, 530, 531, 876, 1005-1007, 1294,
        1363-1366
Elizabeth J.: 984
Elizabeth J.: 544, 912, 978, 1339
Elizabeth Joan: 1061
Elizabeth Mae: 887
Elizabeth Marie: 1257
Elizabeth Ragvelle: 1451
Ella: 1094
Ella D.: 998, 1354
Ella W.: 841, 1252, 1253
Ellis: 576
Ellis L.: 233, 578
Elmer C.: 577, 578
Elmer J.: 879
Elmer Ray: 1023
Elmina: 529
Elmina C.: 415
Elroy: 1074
Elsie: 1308
Elsie: 948
Elsie: 582
Elsie Mae: 1471
Elsie Mae: 1383
Elsie Mae: 1254
Elsie Mae: 1471
Elton Jr: 1340
Elton S: 1339
Elva: 795, 1218, 1219

Elva: 948
Elva: 1068
Elva: 1264
Elva Dean: 848
Elva Dean: 1255
Elva Jay: 884
Elva Jay: 1061
Elva Jay: 1257
Elva W.: 841
Elvon Lee: 849
Elzina: 315, 316
Emma: 841
Emma: 1093
Emma A.: 980
Emma E.: 231
Emma E.: 467, 846, 1269
Emma H.: 567
Emma L.: 568
Emma Marie: 231, 563, 1094, 1095
Emma Sue: 1027
Enos: 70
Enos: 1018, 1374
Enos C.: 1019, 1377
Enos D.: 790
Enos E.: 467, 843, 844, 969, 1261-1264, 1272
Enos H.: 537
Ephraim Glen: 1025
Ephraim J. S.: 173
Erma Arlene: 1472
Erma D.: 530, 1002
Erma J.: 1070
Ernest: 313
Ernest: 313
Ernest: 993
Ernest: 1003
Ernest: 1068
Ernest: 1352
Ernest: 918
Ernest D.: 850, 851
Ernest Leroy: 884
Ernest LeRoy: 884
Ernest N.: 232, 575, 1337
Ernest V.: 582
Ervin: 886
Ervin: 948
Ervin: 886
Ervin: 1352, 1353
Ervin: 1330
Ervin D.: 576
Ervin E.: 842, 1257
Ervin H: 506, 944, 1049
Ervin H.: 507
Ervin S.: 1025, 1380
Esther: 1392
Esther: 562, 1018, 1373
Esther: 1006
Esther: 1026
Esther: 582, 1099, 1307
Esther: 576
Esther: 1054
Esther: 1262
Esther: 949
Esther Arlene: 1460
Esther L.: 1219
Ethen N.: 634
Etta Marie: 1027

Eva Ruth: 1473
Ezra: 537
Ezra: 1019
Ezra: 1023
Ezra: 579
Ezra E.: 844, 969, 1263
Ezra J.: 234, 466, 467, 1194
Ezra J.: 416
Ezra J.: 578, 579
Ezra M.: 436
Faith Ann: 1209, 1451
Fannie: 767
Fannie: 1018, 1019
Fannie D.: 1306
Fannie Ellen: 848
Fannie Elmina: 70, 234, 580-583, 842
Fannie Irene: 1003
Fannie J.: 415
Fannie Jane: 436
Fannie L.: 233, 579, 580
Fannie Mae: 1004, 1362
Fannie Mae: 547
Fannie Marie: 1230
Fannie S: 531
Farrel Andrew: 926, 1323
Ferman Wayne: 1307, 1308
Florence Viola: 823
Floyd: 1455
Floyd: 234
Floyd: 1014
Floyd: 1025, 1026
Floyd: 948
Floyd: 968
Floyd: 889
Floyd: 918
Floyd: 1264
Floyd: 1069
Floyd E.: 1062
Floyd Wayne: 1209
Floyd William: 926, 1322
Frances: 97
Francis DeWayne: 926, 1322
Frank Allen: 1322
Frank Russell: 527
Franklin Joseph: 926, 1322
Fred Amos S.: 1297, 1481
Freda Irene: 1460
Freddie: 1027
Freddie J.: 1314
Fredrick Eugene: 926
Freeda: 576
Freeman: 947
Freeman: 1004
Freeman: 953
Freeman C.: 86
Freeman D.: 492, 1004, 1363, 1484
Freeman E.: 576
Freeman Jay: 1067
Freeman M.: 567
Freeman S.: 1054
Freeman Wayne: 888
Frieda: 1262
Gabriel Allen: 1460
Gary LaVoid: 1026
Gary Ray: 1392
Gary Verlo: 950

Gene Carlyle: 564
George: 553
George: 364
George F.: 277
Gertrude: 235
Gilbert: 1015
Gillard Gene: 725, 726
Glen: 1271
Glen: 885
Glen: 970
Glen Edvin: 234
Glen Jay: 887
Glen Jay: 1270
Glen Wayne: 890
Glenda Sue: 1469
Glenn: 1054
Gloria Jane: 1209
Goldie Edith: 897, 1303, 1304, 1481, 1482, 1495
Grace: 553, 1094
Grace Elaine: 1209, 1451
Greg Allan: 1275
Hannah: 1473
Harley: 885
Harley Dean: 1074
Harley E.: 844, 1262
Harmon C.: 86
Harold LeRoy: 1068
Harold Marvin: 231, 565
Harold Marvin: 565
Harry: 313
Harry: 313
Harry: 543, 1054
Harvey: 1093
Harvey A.: 1018, 1373
Harvey C.: 536, 537
Harvey C.: 1017, 1371
Harvey H.: 537, 1024
Harvey J.: 415
Hazel: 553
Henry: 134
Henry: 416
Henry: 1093
Henry H. M.: 1093, 1094
Henry L.: 506, 879, 983
Henry L.: 506, 1049
Henry L.: 1219
Henry M.: 537, 1024
Henry M.: 231, 567
Henry O.: 570
Herman: 322
Herman: 1354
Hilda: 1233
Homer Lee: 887
Homer Ray: 888
Howard: 1027
Howard Edward: 1141, 1142
Howard Lee: 1061
Howard Ray: 1332
Howard Vernon: 1257
Howard W.: 841, 1256
Hugo B.: 227
Ida: 965
Ida: 1018, 1373
Ida: 1331
Ida: 1066
Ida Anna: 1340

Ida Bernice: 1181, 1182
Ida Irene: 1061
Ida L.: 233
Ida M.: 231, 568, 569
Ida Mae: 849
Ida Mae: 841, 1255
Ida Mae: 844, 882
Ida O.: 570
Ida P.: 807
Infant: 529
Infant: 529
Infant: 506
Infant: 233
Infant: 233
Infant: 800
Infant: 800
Infant: 577
Infant Dau: 1376
Infant Daughter: 1017
Infant Son: 537
Infant Son: 1019
Infant Son: 1026
Infant Son: 582
Infant Son: 970
Infant Stillborn Son: 1297
Infant Twin Son: 1023
Irene: 939, 940
Irma: 1066
Irvin Jay: 968
Isaac: 86
Isaac Hart: 86
Ivan: 233
J. Virgil: 552
Jacob: 530, 1003, 1004, 1362
Jacob: 790
Jacob: 885
Jacob Atlee: 1269, 1270
Jacob C.: 86
Jacob Eugene: 888
Jacob H.: 275
Jacob J. C.: 415, 767, 768
Jacob J. M. (aka: Jake Jake): 486, 959, 967
Jacob Willis (aka: Triple Jake): 487, 887, 959
James: 1014
James L.: 1197
James R.: 1487
James Ray: 553
James William: 1303
Jamin Lee: 1469
Janeen Carol: 1369
Janelle Ranee: 1480
Janet: 768
Janet Raye: 1054
Janet Rose: 1469
Janetta Faye: 1054
Janice: 702
Jason Roy: 1323
Jay Alan: 1381
Jaylon Lynn: 1392
Jeffrey Lynn: 1372
Jeffrey S.: 1422
Jeffrey Wayne: 1451
Jemima: 1471
Jenette Anna: 1451
Jennifer R.: 1487
Jeremiah: 135

Lizzie: 869, 870
Lizzie Ann: 1236
Lizzie J.: 415
Lloyd: 883
Lloyd: 415, 1272
Lloyd: 1066
Lloyd: 889
Lloyd Eugene: 884, 1299, 1300
Lloyd T.: 990
Lolleta Fern: 926, 1323
Loretta: 1061
Loretta E.: 1295
Lori Ann: 1470
Lorris David: 558
Louella Marie: 883, 1299
Lovina: 1093
Lucinda Joy: 1451
Luke Delbert: 1480
Lydia: 868
Lydia Ellen: 66, 219
Lydia Ellen: 886
Lydia J.: 530
Lydia Mae: 507, 944, 945, 1330, 1331
Lydia Mae: 1065, 1388
Lydian: 537, 1020
Lynda Elaine: 1369
Lynn Oscar: 1205
Madgelina "Mattie" S.: 517, 518
Mae: 574
Magdalena (aka: Mattie): 207, 208
Magdalena H: 537, 1021
Magdalena Mattie: 177
Magdalena Opal: 231, 564, 565, 1095, 1096
Mahala: 537, 1438
Mahlon: 416
Mahlon: 1065
Mahlon: 579
Mahlon E.: 1022, 1023
Mahlon L.: 568
Mahlon M. S.: 231, 566
Malinda: 66
Malinda Fern: 1297
Mamie: 536
Mamie: 1014
Mamie: 1014
Mamie C.: 1019, 1376
Mamie Sue: 1372
Manass D: 1001
Manass D.: 1001, 1002
Marcia: 1251
Marcia: 1472
Marcia Rene: 997
Marcus Wade: 1439
Maretta: 1066
Margaret Ann: 967
Maria Sue: 1460
Marianna: 1067, 1068
Marianna: 1472
Marianne Elizabeth: 564
Marietta: 1339
Marietta T.: 1255, 1297, 1298, 1466, 1467
Marilyn: 702
Marilyn Fern: 1205
Marilyn Fern: 967
Marilyn Gay: 998
Marion: 1271

Marion: 969
Marjorie May: 1201
Mark: 567
Mark: 1023
Mark: 1297
Mark Eugene: 1322
Marlene: 1381
Marlene Susan: 950
Marlin Dennis: 1332
Marlin Lee: 1470
Marry: 801
Martha: 66, 219, 552
Martha: 998, 1351
Martha: 845
Martha: 1379
Martha Kay: 1015
Martha M: 527
Marvin: 567
Marvin: 886, 1210
Marvin: 1379
Marvin E.: 1210
Marvin Jay: 848
Marvin Jr: 1027
Marvin Lavon: 967
Marvin N.: 1026, 1027
Mary: 997, 998
Mary: 416
Mary: 440
Mary: 876
Mary: 214
Mary: 416
Mary: 536, 1013, 1369, 1370
Mary: 791
Mary: 998
Mary: 1019
Mary: 492, 1363
Mary: 1018, 1374
Mary: 1023
Mary: 948
Mary: 1352
Mary: 579
Mary A.: 800
Mary Alice: 849, 1270, 1271
Mary Alice: 1053, 1054
Mary Alice: 888
Mary Alice: 969
Mary Ann: 277
Mary Ann: 135
Mary Ann: 278
Mary Ann: 529
Mary Ann: 486, 883
Mary Ann: 543, 1055, 1355, 1387
Mary Ann: 567
Mary Ann: 1354
Mary Ann: 1268, 1472
Mary Cathrine: 229
Mary Colleen: 1024
Mary D.: 205, 206, 1484
Mary D.: 519, 520
Mary E.: 467, 842, 843, 907, 1257-1261
Mary Edna: 885, 1014, 1203, 1300
Mary Edna: 886
Mary Elizabeth: 1221, 1222
Mary Elizabeth: 841, 1254, 1255, 1297, 1466
Mary Elizabeth: 1256
Mary Ellen: 86

Mary Ellen: 217
Mary Ellen: 527
Mary Ellen: 1030
Mary Ellen: 546, 1075
Mary Ellen: 958
Mary Ellen: 884
Mary Esther: 1027
Mary Etta: 1263
Mary H.: 537, 1022
Mary J.: 415, 769
Mary Kathrine: 1074
Mary Kathryn: 887
Mary Louise: 553
Mary Louise: 1364, 1365
Mary Magdalene: 234, 583
Mary Maria J.: 22, 23
Mary Pauline: 1061
Mary Ruth: 1474
Maryiiln Elizabeth: 944
Matthew: 1409
Matthew: 1472
Matthew James: 1469
Matthew James: 1469
Matthew Jay: 1470
Matthew Jay: 1470
Matthew S.: 1297, 1480
Mattie: 767
Mattie: 1266
Mattie C.: 529
Mattie Elizabeth: 233
Mattie J.: 415, 769
Mattie J.: 768
Mattie M.: 231
Mattie Mae: 781
Mattie Marie: 1019, 1377, 1378
Mattie Marie: 1003, 1361, 1362
May: 999
Maynard: 890
Maynard Ray: 1361
Melissa Ann: 620
Melvin: 235
Melvin: 949
Jr. Melvin E.: 702
Melvin Jay: 1219
Melvin R.: 700-702
Mervin: 856
Mervin: 1068
Mervin: 1380
Mervin: 1264
Mervin Devon: 967
Micah Jon: 1297
Michelle Diana: 1469
Mike: 988
Millie: 1093
Milo: 992
Milo J. K.: 1066, 1067
Milo L.: 568
Milo S.: 70, 231, 566-569
Mima Luella: 891, 1073
Mindy Jo: 1243, 1375
Miriam: 1269, 1473
Miriam Mae: 1209, 1451, 1493
Molly Jo: 1270
Monroe D.: 998
Mose Elmer: 876
Moses P.: 436

Myron: 1297
Nancy: 702
Nancy: 135
Nancy: 767
Nancy Alta: 768
Nancy Jo: 1209
Nathan: 1269, 1473
Nathan Lynn: 1474
Nathan Ryan: 1392
Nathan Wayne: 1469
Nathanal David: 1482
Nathaniel E.: 1065
Nathen Ray: 1015
Nellie: 364
Nelson: 576
Nelson Duana: 1256
Nelson M.: 1470
Neoma: 1472
Nettie Jean: 849, 963, 964, 1271
Nichole Dawn: 1439
Noah: 1019
Noah: 1018
Noah B.: 214, 531
Noah D.: 767
Noah D.: 790
Noah J.: 543
Noah J.: 232, 1337
Noah S: 764, 765
Noah S.: 411, 412
Nora: 536, 1016
Norma: 1472
Norman Eric: 998
Oba: 768
Oba J.: 416
Oba J.: 415
Obie J.: 487, 888, 889
Olen: 803
Olen Jacob: 768
Olen Jay: 1254
Olen S.: 1364
Oleta Mae: 1019
Oleta Pauline: 976
Olive Fay: 1015
Ollie: 463
Omer: 848
Ora: 232
Ora: 1065
Ora Floyd: 1018, 1372
Ora L.: 233
Ora N.: 1330
Ora W.: 841, 1253, 1342
Orla: 1255
Orla D.: 1004, 1363
Orla L.: 884
Orla Vernon: 234, 581, 1099, 1307
Orlen Dean: 1365
Orpha E: 576
Orva: 1068
Orva E: 576
Orva Eldon: 234, 580, 581
Orville Leroy (aka: Roy O.): 925, 926
Owen L.: 568
Owen M.: 231, 569
Owen M.: 566
Pamela Jean: 1371
Pamela Kay: 1054

Patricia Ann: 1371
Patricia Irene: 1361
Patricia Jo: 565
Patti Ann: 1374
Paul: 553
Paul: 1375
Paul: 619
Paul: 1014, 1203, 1371
Paul: 1374, 1375
Paul: 1023
Paul E.: 527, 997, 1350
Paul S.: 1297, 1480
Pauline: 1233
Peggy Joan: 578
Perry: 947
Perry: 849
Perry: 948
Perry: 1264
Peter M.: 436
Phillip: 576
Phillip Lee: 1203
Phineas S.: 70, 230, 563-565, 1094-1096
Phyllis Ann: 578
Polly: 440, 812, 813
Polly: 562, 1018
Polly: 1003
Polly Anna: 1074
Polly Anna S.: 1003, 1361
Polly C.: 804, 805, 1387
Priscilla: 86
Quincy: 277
Rachel: 178, 212
Rachel: 86
Rachel S.: 1297, 1480, 1481
Ralph: 1018
Ramah: 999
Ramon Caryl: 998, 1351
Ramona: 1352
Randall Wayne: 1285
Randell Wade: 1439
Ray: 536, 1015
Ray L.: 546
Rayman J. (Ray): 235
Raymond: 234
Raymond: 1027
Raymond: 1026
Raymond: 1352
Raymond: 569
Raymond D.: 999, 1355, 1387
Raymond Lavon: 897, 1305
Rebecca: 1193
Rebecca: 277
Rebecca: 1473
Rebecca O.: 569
Rebekah: 1471
Regina: 1269, 1473
Rhoda: 1025
Rhoda: 1471
Rhoda Irene: 1372
Rhoda Kay: 1460
Richard: 886
Richard: 1067
Richard D.: 1460
Richard Dean: 581
Richard Edward: 578
Richard Ray: 889

Richard Thomas: 997
Robert: 554
Robert: 1114
Robert Frank: 531
Robert James: 1322
Robert Lee: 1024
Robert S.: 1025, 1381
Roger Allen: 578
Roger R.: 1369
Ronald Lee: 851
Ronald Lee: 1362
Ronald Wayne: 1372
Rosa: 791, 792
Rosa Marie: 1223
Rose Ann: 1473
Rosetta: 577
Rosetta Marie: 1074
Roy: 1018
Roy Allen: 1074
Roy D.: 536
Roy Duane: 1024
Roy J.: 917, 918
Ruby: 1043, 1044
Ruby: 849, 1263, 1271, 1272
Ruby: 1255
Ruby Elizabeth: 231, 565, 566
Ruby Ellen: 234, 582
Ruby J.: 1072
Ruby M.: 992
Ruby Mae: 888, 889
Rudolph A.: 795
Rudy C.: 510
Russell J.: 1198
Russell James: 842, 1198
Ruth: 1199
Ruth Ellen: 1270
Ruthann: 577
Sadie: 1025, 1378, 1379
Sadie Marie: 1025
Salinda Sue: 1020
Sally Jo: 581
Saloma D.: 529, 1000, 1001, 1355-1359
Samuel: 1015, 1016
Samuel: 1027
Samuel A.: 1025, 1194, 1438
Samuel C.: 841
Samuel Earl: 1377
Samuel H.: 537, 1019, 1377
Samuel J.: 416
Samuel J.: 530, 1002, 1003, 1360, 1361
Samuel J.: 1296, 1297
Samuel Lee: 1270
Samuel S.: 1025, 1380, 1381
Samuel Serious: 440, 810-812
Sandra Lee: 564
Sarah: 66
Sarah: 278
Sarah: 1343
Sarah: 1207
Sarah Bernith: 897, 1303
Sarah C.: 135
Sarah E.: 754, 870
Sarah L.: 568
Sarah Mae: 1268, 1471
Sarah Mae: 1270
Sarah Mae: 1268, 1472

William S.: 841, 1342
William S.: 1025, 1380
William Taylor: 1452
Willis: 848
Willis: 848
Willis E.: 234, 467, 842, 1099
Wilma: 235, 583, 584
Wilma: 1004
Wilma: 948
Wilma: 1066
Wilma: 1093
Wilma E.: 844, 1261, 1262
Wilma Ellen: 1377
Wilma Louise: 849, 910
Wilma Mabel: 507, 949
Wilma Viola: 947
Wilmer: 1377
Wyman LeRoy: 967
Yost: 576

Milliman -
Unnamed: 553

Mills -
James: 1250

Milner -
Franklin Holland: 1041
Holland: 1040
Joe Henry: 1041
John Wallace Holland: 1040, 1041

Mimna -
Helen: 679

Min -
(name: Miriam Virginia Christner): 667, 1145

Mineko -
Unnamed: 1165

Minier -
Amiee: 1303
Terry Lee: 1303
Varen Paul (aka: Mouse): 1302

Mirilovich -
Unnamed: 657

Mishler -
Aaron: 1298
Alvin: 881, 1296, 1480
Amanda Ruth: 1452
Amos F.: 509, 880, 881, 955, 1296-1298, 1467, 1480, 1481
Andrew S.: 61, 199, 464, 828
Anna: 61
Anna: 956
Annie: 509
Arlis Keith: 1210, 1453
Brittney Jean: 1453
Bruce Alan: 1209, 1452
Carrie Anita: 1453
Cedric Bruce: 1452
Connie Via: 957
Conrad Jay: 1209
Courtney Marie: 1453
Dalton Kyle: 1452
Daniel: 957
Darnell Brent: 1452
David: 61
David Eugene: 1209, 1452
Dewayne: 1298
Dora Jean: 1296

Doris Jean: 1464
Drusilla: 61
Dustin Eugene: 1452
Elizabeth: 16, 26
Elizabeth: 61
Elvida Jean: 958
Ernest Jay: 1296
Ervin: 1298
Ervin: 881, 1298
Ervin: 1298
Ervin F.: 509, 957
Eugene Alvin: 1480
Fern Elaine: 957
Franklin J: 1251
Frederick A.: 508, 880
Freeman: 956
Frieda Ann: 957, 958
Gloria Jean: 957
Goldie Berniece: 509, 954
Harry F.: 509, 955, 956
Harry Jr.: 956
Jayden Lynn: 1480
Jeremiah: 61
Jewell Kay: 1209, 1452
Joe Devon: 1296
John F.: 509, 957
John Ray: 956
John Ray: 1296, 1480
John William: 1210, 1453
Jonathan: 1298
Juanita Ferne: 1453
Kamilah Sue: 1452
Larisa Kay: 1452
Larry Wayne: 1296
Lavera: 1298
Lawrence Mose: 1452
Leona: 1298
Loranna: 1298
Lydia Ann: 508, 509
Lydia Mae: 881
Malinda: 199, 464, 828, 922
Marion: 1296
Marlene: 1298
Marlene K.: 1251
Martha: 956
Martha Anna: 1296, 1480
Marvin: 956
Mary: 881, 1296, 1297, 1480, 1481
Mary H.: 956
Mary Sue: 1298
Melvin: 881, 1297, 1298, 1466, 1467
Mervin: 956
Michael Jon: 1480
Mose J.: 1209
Naomah: 1473
Naomi: 1298
Natalie Kay: 1453
Noah: 509
Ora Jay: 956
Orva: 881
Orva Lee: 1298
Ramona Joanna: 1453
Rosemary: 1296
Ruth: 1298
Samuel: 61
Sharon Kay: 957

Susan Kay: 1296
Twila Joy: 1210, 1453
Wilma: 881, 1297, 1481
Mitchell -
Dyer: 317
Robert: 670
Moberly -
Unnamed: 828
Mochizuki -
Asami: 1151
Mockler -
Cynthia Josephine: 1251
David: 1251
Debra Roe: 1251
Denise: 1251
Dennis: 1251
Donald Elroy: 838, 1250, 1251
Henry Lloyd: 838
Joyce Ellen: 838, 1252
Merlin Ray: 838, 1251
Randol Keith: 1251, 1252
Robert Devon: 838
Stephen Donald: 1251
Victoria Louise: 1251
Moehing -
Grace Jean: 234
Molchany -
Agnes: 260
Molebash -
Thelma: 872, 873
Molner -
Joseph: 1054
Melody Marie: 1054
Monaghan -
Margaret Theresa: 260, 261
Monce -
Unnamed: 1125
Monohan -
Joan: 645
Moon -
Unnamed: 297
Moore -
Unnamed: 557
Adam Lee: 1397
Amanda Kay: 1397
Betty Jean: 380
Clarence Miller: 379
Debra Dawn: 728
Donald Edward: 380
Dorothy Fern: 379
Gary: 728
Gary Lee: 1397
Gladys: 428
Harold Celland: 379
Hazel Faye: 429
Helen Marie: 429
Henry Ensign: 428
James Miller: 379
Lauretta: 728
Maria: 1425
Marvin Kenneth: 380
Raymond Victor: 429
Robert: 728
Robert Eugene: 380, 728

Thomas James: 379, 380
Vernon Leroy: 380
Vivian Richard: 380
Wesley Andrew: 429
Morello -
Elisa: 1488
Morgan -
William: 115, 116
Mori -
Anna: 238
Moriera -
Anthony Jr.: 1113
Anthony Steven Sr.: 1113
Derrick: 1114
Morocco -
Carol Ann: 1416
Morrell -
Patrick Ian: 1170
Ralph Gary: 1170
Tiffany Lauren: 1170
Morris -
Dwight: 930-932
Sheena Lynn: 932, 1325, 1326
Sheri Lynn: 932, 1326
Moser -
Diana Rose: 1281, 1282
George: 1281
Moses -
Lawrence: 401
Mosgraves -
Beverly: 1419
Mossman -
Ronald F.: 409
Most -
Harold: 1418
James Edward: 1418
Mostoller -
Lori: 1411
Telford Leland: 679
Motivor -
Betty: 1434
Mouse -
(name: Varen Paul Minier): 1302
Moyer -
Gail: 1410
Muckel -
Arthur Benjamin: 368, 724
Dean Christner: 368, 369
Don Cecil: 368
Florence M.: 368
Francis L.: 725
Harold Warren: 368
Harry W.: 368
Hazel Marguerite: 368
Lena May: 368
Obedia Stark: 368
Raymond A.: 724
Mueller -
Barbara: 19
Michael: 19
Michel: 19
Pierre: 19
Mulchay -
Mary: 1135

Bramalette Jean: 1426
Colby Jett: 1426
Logan Lee: 1426
Shawn Tom: 1426
Pertty -
Florence: 926
Pete -
(name: Simon Sipe (Pete) Christner): 621, 1120, 1400, 1401
(name: Devon G. "Pete" Christner): 274, 275
Peterman -
Glenna: 619
Peters -
Gary D.: 1249
Petersheim -
Maryanne: 792
Melvin: 1294, 1295
Rosa Anna: 1295
Peterson -
Unnamed: 857
Elizabeth: 41
Petre -
Dusty J.: 906
Petty -
Ethel Frances: 192
Pettys -
Merrie Leslie: 749
Robert Alonzo: 748, 749
Scott Robert: 749
Thomas Alonzo: 749
Pezzuolo -
Dominic A.: 1493
Nickolas A.: 1493
Phelps -
Brian: 1403
Gary: 1403
Shawn: 1403
Phiel -
Lloyd: 764
Phillipi -
Stephanie: 1147
Phillippi -
Bertha Alice: 337
Calvin B.: 337
Charles Earl: 337
Elizabeth May: 337, 697, 698
Etta Louella: 337
Fannie Viola: 337, 699, 700, 723
James Irwin: 337
Jennie Marie: 337, 698
Jeremiah B.: 336, 337, 723
Martin V.: 337
Ralph Raymond: 337
Sylvester (Jim): 337
Zachariah Henry: 337
Phillips -
Blair: 338
Dorothy: 338
Lawerence M.: 338
Louise: 338
Margaret (aka: Peggy): 18, 19
Marion: 338
Pickard -
Agnes Dolly: 821, 822

Bessie Mae: 342, 343
Pidcock -
Heather: 1287
Pierce -
Denny: 1303
Pifer -
Louisa Pleiffer: 117
Pike -
Charley: 1328
Charlie Eugene: 1328
Pile -
Samantha C.: 130
Pineda -
Leo: 1230
Pipkin -
Ann: 586
Judy: 587
Robert E.: 586
Pipper -
Unnamed: 975
Pitts -
Inell: 858
Pizarro -
Unnamed: 1245
Plank -
Florence Genevieve: 1251
Melva Betsy: 1445
Platter -
Anna Ruth: 614
Margaret Elizabeth: 614
Nellie Mae: 614
William Clayton Jr.: 614
William Clayton Sr.: 613, 614
Pletcher -
Anna Elizabetha: 194, 195
Ida B.: 284
Jacob: 38, 39
Margaret Mae "Maggie": 85, 86
Marling Allen: 264
Poitras -
Valmore: 428
Poleman -
Albetty: 71
Charles Henry: 71
Floyd A.: 71
Frederick: 71
Henry: 71
Jacob: 71
Jerome G.: 71
Richard Thomas: 71
Polgar -
Christopher Scott: 1422, 1491
Gary Eugene: 1167, 1422, 1491
Jason Andrew: 1423
Noah Christopher: 1491
Pam: 1167, 1423, 1491
Ralph Eugene: 1167
Reed Delmar: 1491
Tracy Lynn: 1423
Pollard -
Betty Joan: 924, 925
Tom: 127
Pollie -
(name: Mary Pollie Lowry): 114

Adeline: 440, 441
Aldine Emma: 820
Arlene Emma: 820
Arnold Chrestian: 820
Barbara: 174
Benedict: 174
Charles Jesse: 820
Christian: 174
Christian G.: 50
Daniel: 174
Donald Joseph: 820
Edward: 554
George III: 388
Jacob: 174
Jesse R.: 820
John C.: 174
Joseph: 53
Joseph: 174
Karen Sue: 1438
Katherine: 174
Kyle Michael: 1443
Laura: 1192
Mary Elane: 820
Michael Eldon: 1443
Mildred Eileen: 820
Nicholas: 51, 174
Nicholas Jr.: 174
Norman: 1303
Ruth Marie: 820
Uriah Amos: 813, 814

Rowe -
William: 253
Rowntree -
Elizabeth: 171
Roy O. -
(name: Orville Leroy Miller): 925, 926
Roy P. -
(name: Philo Leroy (Roy P) Christner): 159, 395, 396,
740, 743-745, 1176-1178, 1426, 1427
Roy -
Debra Kay: 1243
Jeff: 1243
Robert: 1243
Robert Jr: 1243
Rozyehic -
Barbara: 564
Ruby -
Unnamed: 1122
Unnamed: 908
Margaret Belle "Maggie": 1277
Ruck -
Amanda Elizabeth: 1491
Hannah Renee: 1491
Roberto: 1491
Rucker -
Adam: 1117, 1118
Haley Nicole: 1118
Savannah Leigh: 1118
Rudy -
(name: Rudolph George Loquist): 1120, 1121
Rugg -
Ada Viola: 698
Peter: 698
Ruiz -
Gloria: 1111

Rumbaugh -
Betty Jane: 339
Cyrus Luther: 339
Rumiser -
Elizabeth: 35, 36
Julia: 27, 28, 129
Ruppert -
Marsena: 1468
Rusbason -
Elizabeth: 344
Rush -
Carlene: 1101, 1102
Gary: 1393
Russell -
James: 826
Ryan -
June: 379
S -
Blanche: 84
Sadie -
Unnamed: 283
Sailor -
Ernest D.: 506
Saine -
Twila: 1277
Salazar -
Anthony James: 1486, 1496
Jonathan James: 1496
Richard Alexis: 1486
Richard Anthony: 1486
Salisbury -
Frankie Jo: 1320
Saloma -
Unnamed: 1449
Salter -
Gregory Scott: 1428
Samples -
Brian Scott: 566
David Nolan: 566
Dennis Patrick: 566
Dewey: 565, 566
Donna Elizabeth: 566
James Jeffrey: 566
Sanchez -
Unnamed: 1415
Sandefer -
Byron: 1160
Sanders -
Florence L.: 306
Lester: 740
Sandra -
Unnamed: 1435
-
Sandra: 728
Sandusky -
Julie Ann: 1488
Sanner -
Amanda: 126
Anthony Adams: 1172
Bennett Lee: 1144
Celia: 280
David C.: 281
Deborah Lou: 281

Elvin: 675
Emma Lou: 281
Evan Banks: 1172
George E.: 281
John: 280
John Skelie: 281
Joseph: 280
Joseph: 281
Michael McKinley: 281
Minerva Edith: 1174
Ralph C.: 281
Samuel H.: 280
Samuel Richard: 1172
Samuel Rue: 1171, 1172
Tillman Henry: 282

Sapp -
John: 1146

Sarah -
Unnamed: 117
Unnamed: 330

Sark -
Connie Renee: 1316
Dana Dwight: 919, 1316
Dean Lavon: 919, 1315, 1316
Dorothy Viginia: 919, 1315
Howard: 918, 919
Rebecca: 1316

Sarver -
Bonnie Kay: 1439

Saylor -
Annie: 39
Civilla: 351

Scaar -
Phoebe: 67

Schaffer -
Elmer H.: 285

Schantz -
David R.: 653, 654
Edward R: 308
Rex C: 654
Verda Maxine: 654
Veronica: 34
Viola May: 654

Scheck -
Agnes: 5, 6

Schegg -
Julia: 368

Scherack -
Lisa Marie: 1416

Schermuly -
Kathryn: 1400

Schiffbauer -
William: 305

Schiller -
Bill: 401

Schlabaach -
Jesse O.: 878

Schlabach -
Albert: 503
Albert J.: 524, 996
Alpha: 766
Amos Clifford: 524, 996, 1348-1350
Andrew J.: 909
Anna J.: 214, 527, 528, 998, 999, 1352-1355

Barbara J.: 214, 526, 527, 997, 1350, 1351
Beth Anne: 1350
Betty Jo: 996, 1349, 1350
Beulah J.: 525
Brian Douglas: 1350
Cathleen Annette: 1348
Charlotte Anne: 996, 1349
Constance Susan: 1348
Corinne: 999, 1000
Crystal: 1468
Daniel J.: 214, 526
David Gregory: 996
David J.: 413
Dennis Marvin: 1348
Donal Keith: 996, 997
Eleanora: 214, 528, 529, 1000
Elizabeth: 909, 910
Elizabeth Lizzie: 214, 523, 524, 992-995, 1335-1348, 1482
Ervin Jr: 235
Esther: 1217
Eugene Clarence: 1222
Ezra J.: 214, 528, 999, 1000
Fannie: 903, 1099, 1344
Gerald: 528, 999
Glen: 526
Gretshen: 528, 1000
Harley: 892
Infant Son: 526
Ira Leonard: 526
Irene: 1217
Jacob J.: 214, 525
Janice Lynne: 996
Joas: 909
Jon Lynden: 996
Jonathan: 213, 214
Joseph J.: 214, 524, 996, 1348-1350
Joyce Marie: 525
Lawrence J.: 526
Lila Gene: 996, 1349
Lula J: 525
Mable Grace: 525
Mahlon E.: 1217
Mary C.: 507, 893
Menno: 892
Neva: 528, 1000
Opal Fern: 526
Paul Terry: 996
Raymond: 892
Richard Amos: 996, 1348
Ronald Duane: 996, 1350
Ruthann: 1000
Simon D. (aka: Simeon): 413, 414
Simon J.: 525
Steven Eugene: 1222
Steven Ray: 1348
Susie LuElla: 892
William: 1000
William Ernest: 525

Schlabaugh -
Catherine Katie: 414
Dora: 414
Dorothy: 766
Elizabeth Lizzie: 414, 764, 765
Henry J.: 766
Infant: 766

Emma E.: 1181
Enos K.: 1058
Ernest K.: 1058
Ervin C.: 1456
Esther N.: 1057
Esther U.: 1059
Fannie A.: 572
Infant: 1226
Jacob: 1378
Jacob A.: 572
Jacob C.: 1456
Jacob D.: 544, 1059
Jacob J.: 1456
Jacob K.: 1058
Jacob N.: 1057
Jacqueline Jane: 1494
James M.: 1224
Jason Edward: 1467, 1494
Jesse James: 1494
Joe N.: 1056
John J.: 1225
John K.: 1225
John LaMar: 1481
John N.: 1057
Jonathan M.: 1223
Jordan James: 1494
Joseph K: 1058
Joseph U.: 1059
Josephine F.: 1098
Josephine M.: 571
Josephine T.: 1229
Katherine K.: 1058, 1224, 1225, 1388, 1390
Kathryn J.: 1225
Kathy M.: 1223
Katy: 1056
Lance James: 1467, 1494
Laura C.: 1456
Laura J.: 1225
Laura U.: 1059
Leslie Ann: 1176
Levi F.: 1098
Levi N.: 1057
Magdalena D.: 1227
Mahlon: 1057
Marianna C.: 1456
Marie J.: 1225
Martha A.: 572
Martha J.: 1457
Martha J.: 1225
Martin K.: 571
Mary A.: 572
Mary Ann: 544
Mary Esther: 1481
Mary F.: 1098
Mary T.: 1227
Mary U: 1059
Melvin J.: 1225
Menno D.: 544, 1056, 1388
Menno F.: 1098
Menno F.: 1098
Menno G.: 1223
Menno G. Jr.: 1223
Menno N.: 1057
Menno N.: 1097, 1098, 1456
Mervin F.: 1098
Mervin J.: 1225

Michael F.: 1098
Michael Joe: 1481
Nathan F.: 1098
Noah C.: 1456
Philip M.: 1224
Phineas M.: 1223
Rachel M.: 1223
Raymond K.: 1058
Rebecca A.: 572
Rebecca T.: 1228, 1455
Rhoda W.: 1456
Rosella: 1378
Rosina J.: 1225
Rosina K.: 1058
Samuel: 1057
Samuel B.: 1226
Samuel E.: 1226
Samuel J.: 1457
Sharen Sue: 1480
Shashana Diane: 1494
Shaunna Elaine: 1467, 1494
Sheila (aka: Sira Windwer): 742
Stephen C.: 1456
Stephen F.: 1098
Susan E.: 1226
Susan Mae: 1378
Susan R.: 1457
Suzy N.: 1057
Syliva A.: 572
Uriah: 1377, 1378
Verda Mae: 1481
Verena F.: 1098
William M.: 1223
Wilma M.: 1223

Schweitzer -
Idella May (aka: Ida): 186
Schwenk -
Alton: 407
Schwerzer -
Anna: 76
Schwetzer -
Kay: 1435
Scott -
Kristia: 1421
Macy Grippen: 462
Margarete Elizabeth: 921
Marie D.: 1239
Phyles: 462
Seafert -
Margaret Josephine: 950
Seagley -
Michael: 1000
Waldo: 1000
Seaman -
David Lee: 1183
Emory: 1183
Emory Jr.: 1183
James: 1183
John J.: 1183
Kathryn: 1183
Nancy Kay: 1183
Sandra Mae: 1183
Sybil Jane: 1183, 1431
Sechler -
Edward R.: 329

Jeffrey Hunter: 1396

Sherck -
Carol Gene: 1249, 1250
Cynthia Velgene: 1250
Dennis Lester: 1250
Kathy Ann: 1250
Richard Marson: 1250
Steven Oscar: 1250

Sherri -
Unnamed: 1291

Shetler -
Mary: 1483

Shields -
Faith Marie: 1172

Shilling -
Unnamed: 22

Shinderling -
Brian: 1408
Jaq: 1408

Shipley -
Chad Michael: 1422
Tanner David: 1422
Thomas E.: 1422
Thomas Logan: 1422

Shirey -
Marie Edna: 394

Shirk -
Isabella: 196, 197

Shively -
Grace E.: 556

Shock -
Arden: 588, 589
Mark Edward: 589
Richard Lee: 589

Shoecraft -
Beverly: 985

Shoemaker -
Abraham: 120
Anthony A.: 119, 136
Barbara: 16, 26, 34
Jacob: 119
Jonas Anthony: 120
Lydia: 119
Lydia: 119
Mary: 43
Mary A.: 119, 136, 137, 291, 328
Samuel A. (aka: Big Sam): 120
Susannah: 120

Shook -
Jerry: 1468

Showalter -
Phyllis: 1310

Showman -
William S.: 612, 613

Shrock -
Mattie: 68

Shrug -
Connie: 618
Julie: 618
Kenneth: 618
Mike: 618
Richard: 618

Shuck -
Unnamed: 269

Ada: 357
Carl: 357
Deloris: 709
Jaunita: 357
Millen: 357
Pauline: 357

Shultz -
Berttia: 325
Jan: 1171

Shumaker -
Anna Elizabeth: 118
Christour: 118
Elizabeth: 326
Leon M.: 683
Merle W.: 327, 683
Soloman: 118
Vincent M.: 683
William: 326
William Howard: 118
Wilson Milton: 118, 326, 683

Shurburn -
Dorothy: 285

Siebarth -
Lorraine Louise: 1199, 1200

Silva -
Unnamed: 1324
Celeste: 1108
John Augustine: 1324, 1325
Kacie Lynn: 1325
Lindsay Raye: 1325

Simeon -
(name: Simon D. Schlabach): 413, 414

Simmons -
William P.: 716

Simons -
Janice Lee: 713
Sylvia Ileen: 868, 869

Singleton -
Mary: 1428, 1429

Singmaster -
Darrell Dean: 1177

Sipe -
Andrew: 21, 22
Anna: 22
Barbara: 22
Benjamin: 22
Elizabeth "Betsy": 22, 60, 199, 463
Harriet (aka: Marietta): 87-89
Leah: 22
Mary: 22
Sarah: 22, 61, 199, 464, 828
Veronica Fanny: 22
William Levi: 22

Sira Windwer -
(name: Sheila Schwartz): 742

Sis -
(name: Audrey Jeannette Lohr): 1147

Skelton -
Janet: 170

Slabach -
Esther Anna: 1297
Jayson: 1481
Katie: 1002, 1003
Margaret Marie: 1297

Mary Kathryn: 1297, 1481
Nathan Allen: 1297
Nathaniel A.: 1297
Rhoda Darlene: 1297
Sharon Kay: 1297, 1481
Steven Ray: 1297

Slabaugh -
Amanda: 1234
Amos: 788
Amy: 806
Catherine "Kate" Alice: 826-828
Edward: 911
Sharon: 1454, 1455

Slabuagh -
Kathryn: 1202

Slatter -
Benjamin C: 172

Slouter -
Emma: 432

Sluis -
Judith Marie: 1304

Slusher -
Charles Earl: 938
Jimmy Lee: 938
Marvin LeRoy Jr.: 938

Smallwood -
Jay Conrad: 1326
Jeremy Jay: 1326
Shawn Lee: 1326
Tiffany Laynette: 1326

Smathers -
Jolayne Arelene: 1325

Smiley -
Landry Dee: 1308

Smith -
Alonzo: 314
Bonnelle Louise: 683
Charlene F.: 683
Charles: 1180
Charles F.: 327, 683, 1160
Charles W. III: 1321
Cinnamon Brooke: 1321
Danny: 1405
Dean: 1405
Deborah: 684
Delores: 746, 747
Delores O.: 327
Dixie: 1419
Donna: 1164
Dorothy I.: 327
Edna Elizabeth: 591
Ella Mefford: 297
Fanny Beatrice: 1187
Forrest H.: 1031
Francis M.: 119, 327, 683, 684, 1160
Grace F.: 327
Harry: 684
Harry J W: 434
Howard E.: 327, 684
Irvin Pete: 314
James: 684
James: 1405
Janice Kay: 1422
Jess Herman: 119
John: 314

John J.: 166
Judy Ann: 855
Linda: 684
Lloyd: 1404, 1405
Lucinda: 683, 1160
Lurenia Isabella "Rea": 370
Lydia: 359, 360
Mae: 1371
Marie "Minnie": 458
Mary Agnes Aggie: 669, 670
May: 314, 659, 1136
Michelle D.: 1113
Mildred: 327
Minnie: 314
Nancy: 314
Nellie: 167
Patricia A.: 656
Ray: 314
Scott: 1434
Sharon: 684
Stephen: 1434
Terry: 684
Tracy Ann: 1204
Vicki: 1434
William G. S.: 433, 434
William Harrison: 119, 327
William Harrison Jr.: 327

Smock -
David Alan: 1447, 1448
David Ryan: 1448

Smoker -
Amanda S.: 1450

Smothers -
Charles L.: 380
Charles Louis: 380

Smucker -
Bonnie C.: 1481, 1482

Snavely -
Jack: 1124

Snellings -
Margret: 347

Snider -
Patricia J.: 1317
Vickie: 1246

Snively -
Albert Charles: 130, 131

Snyder -
Connie: 652
Grant: 652
Jane: 108
Joyce M.: 1302
Lynette Kay: 1177
Marvin: 652
Mary: 117
Mary Ane: 652

Socha -
Barbara Ellen: 1384
Billie J. Sr.: 1384
Billie Jr: 1384

Sodine -
Peggy: 1184, 1185

Soisson -
Adelia: 635

Somerville -

William Robert: 1406

Sommers -
Chris: 1482

Son -
Infant: 546

Sonnenbury -
Alice Amelia: 1008

Sorenson -
B. Leon: 1401
Christopher: 1487
Kent: 1401, 1486
Tara: 1486

Soreson -
Bonnie: 1183

Soto -
Unnamed: 822

Souders -
Anthony: 735
Catherine: 387
Cecil Ermit: 386, 734, 735
Cecil Ermit Jr.: 735
Dale: 387, 736
Daniel: 736
David: 735
Dennis: 735
Dorothy: 386, 735
Douglas: 736
Frank D.: 386
Jerry Lee: 734
Joel: 736
Julia: 736
Kenneth: 736
Lloyd Nelson: 386, 733, 734
Louise: 735
Marvin L Sr.: 386, 735
Raymond: 386, 735
Ricky Allen: 734
Rodney Wayne: 735
Steven: 735
Teresa: 735
Timothy: 736
Wayne: 387, 735, 736

Spangler -
Alicia Anne Clair: 1424
David Walker: 1424
Faith: 1424
George Rudolph: 1169
Laurie Jean: 1169
Lynne Bowman: 1169
Michael George: 1169, 1424
Noah Riley: 1424
Steven Ronald: 1169, 1424

Sparks -
Samuel Hammond: 89

Spezzapria -
Leo: 1475
Vanson Michael: 1475

Spicer -
Rebecca Sue: 935

Spickler -
Unnamed: 1138
Glenn: 1138

Spring -
Robert: 1137

Springer -
Leni: 448

Sprocklen -
Janice Kay: 1408

Sprouse -
Gary: 1101
Paul: 1100
Paula: 1101

Sredy -
Steven: 1149

Staats -
Tamilee: 1421

Stabile -
Susan: 1412, 1413

Stacey -
Jan: 356

Stahley -
Catherine: 173
Saloma: 60

Stantz -
Martha 'Mary' Jane: 222, 223

Stark -
Ruth: 1196

Starkey -
Ruby: 239

Staub -
Clara: 715, 718

Staudenecker -
Klara: 1280
Renate: 858

Stautz -
Mary Jane: 67

Stayer -
Annie: 312

Stayrock -
Unnamed: 1174

Steel -
Elliott: 943
Elliott Laverne: 943

Steele -
Joseph Alexander: 602
Mary Jane: 288

Steely -
Gertrude I.: 1120

Stefl -
Gregory: 1406
Jeffrey: 1406
John: 1406
Timothy: 1406

Steider -
Richard: 840

Stein -
George Herbert III: 1393
George Herbert IV: 1393
Kellie: 1393

Steinberg -
Rebekah: 1244

Steiner -
Carol: 1094
Dan: 1094
Keith: 1094
Living: 648
Marlin: 1094

Gary Glen: 1400, 1486
Linburn Wayne: 1400
Richard Lynn: 1400, 1486
Scott: 1486

Stults -
Aaron Christopher: 1160
Aimee Elizabeth: 1160
Donald LeRoy: 1160

Stump -
Jama Lynne: 1100
James Roy: 1100
Rose: 1292

Stutsman -
Regina: 1452

Stutzman -
Adam: 464, 465
Alexander: 66
Belva: 465, 834, 835
Benjamin: 1316
Betty: 884
Cecelia: 1434
Cecil: 1434
Cheryl: 1280, 1281
Clara: 465
Curtis: 1247
Dallas: 1247
David Eugene: 858
Donald: 1435
Donna: 1434
Dorothy Irene: 833
Duane Henry: 837
Edward J.: 764, 765
Eli J.: 858, 1280
Elizabeth Bessy: 465
Enos: 1090
Eric Jeffery: 1280
Ervin E.: 1060
Frank: 465, 832, 833
George: 221
Glen: 1090
Glen Allen: 858, 859
Hannah: 1316
Harold J: 837
Harry W: 220
Harvey J.: 858
Infant Son: 832
Irwin: 220
Jake J.: 1090
Joseph: 465, 836, 837
Joseph J.: 858
Katie: 221
Laura: 1090
Lela Mae: 831
Lena L.: 1031, 1032
Martha Lou: 858, 1281
Mary Ann: 1198
Mary Ann: 765, 766
Mary Elizabeth: 858
Mildred: 894
Minerva: 465
Minnie: 220
Noah J.: 858, 1280
Ollie Jonas: 858
Paul Eldon: 832
Peggy Lee: 1435
Perry R.: 831, 832

Polly A: 859
Ralph: 1012
Ray: 221
Ray: 1012
Raymon: 1246, 1247
Rebekah: 1316
Robert: 837
Ronald: 1316
Ruth Ann: 858
Sarah: 221
Sarah Marie: 858
Susan: 1268
Susanna: 61, 63
Thelma Byrnece: 832, 1246, 1247
Thomas Ray: 1247
Timothy: 1247
Velma: 961
Verbal: 851, 852
Veronica: 1435
Viola: 1090
Wandy Ann: 1281
Wesley C.: 465, 830, 831, 1246
William J.: 220

Sue -
Unnamed: 1462
Debora: 1489
Dewayne: 1272
Karon: 1272
Marlin: 1272

Sullenberger -
Margaret Elizabeth: 649, 650

Summers -
Rosamond Aileen: 727

Sumpter -
Dorothy: 1237

Sundheimer -
Jeniffer Lynn: 1438, 1439

Surber -
Emmert Joseph: 381
Emmett George: 380
George B.: 381, 728
Robert Calvin: 381

Surkosky -
Adam Edward: 1138
Edward T.: 1138
Kathleen: 1138

Surls -
Lavona: 1401

Surrency -
Myrtice: 486, 487

Susan -
Unnamed: 883
Unnamed: 552
Unnamed: 97

Susanna -
Unnamed: 30

Swank -
Maxine Dale: 1131
William David: 1131

Swarner -
Eliza J: 164

Swartz -
Aaron P.: 1477
Anna: 1477

Edwin: 756
Elaine Ruth: 1260
Eli J.: 754, 870, 871, 1180, 1181, 1288-1291, 1477, 1478
Eli Jacob: 1288
Elizabeth: 411, 754, 755
Elizabeth E.: 1288, 1477
Elizabeth J.: 1229
Elizabeth N.: 1391
Elizabeth S.: 1228
Ella: 780
Ella: 1290
Ella E.: 871
Elmer E.: 843, 1260
Elona: 756
Enos S.: 1228
Esther: 577
Ezra S.: 842, 843, 907
Felty E.: 871, 1289
Floyd: 1478
Gerald Lavon: 840, 1252
Gladys Marie: 843, 907, 1261, 1293
Glen S.: 840
Gregory Ray: 1299
Hannah: 1478
Heidi: 1478
Henry: 1288
Ida J.: 1222
Ida J.: 1229
Ina Marie: 229
Infant: 1089
Infant Dau.: 843
Irene: 1050, 1051
Jacob: 754
Jacob C.: 411, 754, 870, 1180, 1288-1291, 1477, 1478
Jacob E.: 871
James Leroy: 840
Janet Elaine: 840
Jephtha: 754
Jeptha: 412, 756
Jeremiah E.: 1229
Jeremiah J.: 1229
Jerome J.: 1229
Jessie: 1478
John E.: 871
Jonathan: 756
Joseph: 871
Joseph E.: 871, 1291, 1478
Joseph E.: 1222
Joseph J.: 1229
Kathryn J.: 1223
Katie: 567
Kenny Roy: 1299
Kevin Michael: 1261
Lena E.: 871, 1290
Linda Louise: 1089
Lizzie J.: 214, 215
Lloyd S.: 1299
Lonnie Gee: 1259
Luella Mae: 843
Lydia: 754
Lydia: 1291
Lydia Ann: 542
Lydia C.: 1226
Magdalena Mattie: 411, 755
Mahlon: 756

Margaret Loraine: 1257
Maria: 1478
Marion E.: 843, 1259
Martha: 993, 1064
Mary: 412
Mary: 1291
Mary Ann: 754
Mary E.: 871
Melissa Joy: 1469
Melvin E.: 843, 1258, 1259
Mervin Ezra: 843, 1260, 1261
Michael Lynn: 1260
Mose: 1469
Moses: 1288
Nancy Joan: 841
Neil J.: 1229
No Name: 871
Nora: 756
Omer E.: 843, 1257
Otis: 1478
Panela Kay: 1299
Patrick Scott: 1261
Perry: 1478
Ralph Eugene: 1260
Rebecca J.: 1223
Robert Dean: 1257
Robert Ray: 1089
Roberta Jane: 840
Ronald Dee: 1259
Ronald Jay: 1089
Rosemary Elizabeth: 1089
Rufus J.: 1223
Samuel E.: 871
Samuel S.: 1228
Samuel S. Jr.: 1228
Sarah: 754
Sarah: 173, 227
Sarah E.: 530, 800, 891
Sarah E.: 871, 1290
Sarah J.: 1223
Sharon Mae: 1089
Simon J.: 1229
Simon S.: 1228
Stephen Marian: 1259
Steven: 1478
Steven Kay: 1089
Sue Ann: 1478
Susanna: 1288
Susanne J.: 1223
Susie: 1289, 1290
Susie E.: 871
Susie M.: 1267
Sylvia J.: 1223
Tamera Ann: 1252
Teresa Elizabeth: 1260
Veronica Fannie: 411
Vickie Sue: 1260
Viola: 1290
Wayne Mark: 1469
Wilbur Jay: 1088, 1089
Willard LeRoy: 1089
William: 1289
Wilma: 1290

Truffin -
Joy Renee: 1417
Trump -

Eugene Arthur Sr.: 398, 399
Glenda: 1125
Liz: 1404
Olive: 153
Richard: 270
Robert: 1124, 1404
Susan: 13, 14
Susanna: 40, 81, 121
Susie Caroline: 124

Ward -
Unnamed: 273

Wargo -
Dorothy Mae: 1155

Warner -
Gale A.: 1123
James: 1429

Warnes -
Karl Edward: 223

Warnick -
Donald Ray: 1413
Shawn Charles: 1413

Warren -
Mary: 739

Warrick -
Mary: 30, 31
Micheal Anthony: 1132

Wash -
(name: Washington Christner): 127, 331, 688

Washabaugh -
Sallie Nellie: 292, 293

Wass -
Amanda Nicole: 1326
Joseph J.: 1326

Waste -
Helen Lucille: 368, 369

Waters -
Nancy: 1476

Watkins -
Tracey JoAnne: 1285, 1286

Watson -
Unnamed: 1230
Vella Vernice: 395

Waugh -
Marvie Ruth: 377

Weary -
Eleanor: 1157, 1159

Weaver -
Ada: 1039
Anita: 1495
Carla: 1453
Cheryl Renea: 1468
Chris: 1468
Christopher Jadon: 1468
Clarence: 883
Daniel J.: 1039
Daniel Jr.: 1133
Daniel L.: 1132, 1133
David Lee: 1133
David Ray: 1468
Debert: 1039
Edwin: 883
Ervin Ray: 1133
Florence: 1322
Freeman J: 1039

Irene: 883
Irvin: 883
Jennifer Lynn: 1283
John: 1133
Jonas L.: 1038, 1039
Karen Louis: 1416
Katie: 1039
Katie A.: 883
Kimberly Kae: 1458
Kris Lynette: 1283
Levi J.: 1132
Levi J.: 1039
Levi Jay: 1133
Mahlon J.: 883
Mary: 1133
Mary A.: 883
Mary L.: 68
Matthew Jay: 1468
Moses N.: 414
Pearl Edith: 505
Rachel Ann: 1416
Raymond: 858
Ronald Lamar: 1283
Sharon Kay: 1468
Susan: 416
Susie: 1039
Timothy Wayne: 1468
Vera J.: 1039
Vernon: 883
Waneta: 1474
William: 883
William: 840
William Herbert: 1416
Wilmer: 883

Webber -
Jennie Lynn: 314, 315

Weber -
Amos: 858
Babette: 448
Jenny: 1199

Weeden -
Lisa Nadine: 1172

Weedewn -
Cindy: 1137

Weichart -
Donald: 238

Weichler -
Barbara Jean: 1487

Weidbrauk -
Diane Lynn: 1434
Myron: 1434
Tony Lee: 1434

Weigel -
Evelyn: 1126

Weight -
Howard: 105

Weimer -
Unnamed: 624
Albert John: 626
Amanda Mary "Mandy": 720, 721
Andrea Jo: 1171
Cain C.: 276, 624-626
Charles Earl: 1174
Daniel Richard: 1171
David: 276

Walter Henry: 833, 834
Whitney -
  Alice: 1190
Whorrel -
  Patricia: 1148
Whysong -
  Rosa Marie: 535
Whyte -
  Lancelot A.: 656
Wickey -
  Allen: 1338
  Amanda J.: 1099
  Amos A.: 1099
  Amos E.: 1099
  Amos T.: 1097
  Anna S.: 986, 993, 994, 1211, 1253, 1306
  Barbara: 1340, 1341
  Barbara A.: 1099
  Barbara J.: 1098
  Benjamin J.: 1455
  David E.: 1096, 1455
  Edna A.: 1099
  Edna D.: 1096, 1390, 1455
  Edna J.: 1098
  Elizabeth B.: 1230
  Elizabeth J.: 1098
  Elizabeth T.: 1097, 1223
  Emma T.: 1097
  Ernest E.: 1391
  Esther: 1339
  Henry: 1338
  Irene J.: 1099
  Jacob A.: 1099
  Jacob J.: 1098
  Jacob L.: 1098
  Jonas B.: 1455
  Jonathan A.: 1099
  Joseph J.: 1098
  Josephine T.: 1097
  Katie: 1058
  Lavern J.: 1098
  Leland: 1338
  Loraine: 1338
  Marcus J.: 1099
  Margaret T.: 1097
  Martha: 1338
  Martin J.: 1098
  Marvin: 1339
  Marvin E.: 1391
  Matthew J.: 1099
  Menno J.: 1098
  Mervin E.: 1391
  Michael A.: 1099
  Michael J.: 1098
  Monroe T.: 1097
  Rebecca D.: 798, 1388
  Rebecca J.: 1098
  Ruby A.: 1099
  Tobias E.: 1096, 1097
  Wilbur: 1338, 1339
Wiederstein -
  Evelyn: 1334
Wilcox -
  Alex: 1179
  Cameron: 1179

Hannah: 1179
James A. S.: 1179
Wilhelm -
  Elijah Wolfgang: 1487
  Peter: 1487
Wilker -
  Richard: 1219
Wilkins -
  Lillian (Noch): 631
Willford -
  Lionel DeLoy: 386
Willhite -
  Kathleen: 1046
William -
  Esther: 999
Williams -
  Barbara June: 1047
  Brian Forbes: 740, 1175
  Charles Jeffrey: 735
  Crystal LaJoyce: 1446
  Daniel: 735
  Ennis Forbes: 739
  Helen Susan: 651
  Ina Lee: 339
  Janis Irene: 1095
  Joni Lonise: 1095
  Joseph: 735
  June Violet: 1164
  Marcie Ann: 1095
  Milton: 433
  Piper Morgan: 1175
  Richard Forbes: 739
  Richard Harris: 1095
  Richard Harris Jr.: 1095
  Shari Sue: 739, 1175
Willis -
  Randy: 1466
Willtrout -
  Alford C.: 32
Wilma -
  Unnamed: 975
Wilson -
  Culver Glenn: 425
  Deborah Jean: 1486
  Dick: 1123
  Effie Grace: 424
  Eka E: 420
  Eska E: 424
  Eunice M: 425
  George: 401
  Harold Ross "Barney": 642, 1129, 1406
  James Myrl: 642
  Jr. Johnny L. Jr.: 159
  June Elaine: 1129, 1406
  Margaret Elizabeth: 1242
  Richard R.: 425
  Roy A: 424
  Ruby R: 425
  Scott: 1492
  Stacey Diane: 745, 746
  William Culver: 424
Wilt -
  Kenneth Edward: 618
Wiltrout -

1941

Yoak -
    Jean: 1164
Yocke -
    Nile Joseph: 1417, 1418
    Thomas L.: 1417
Yoder -
    Aaron D.: 569
    Abraham T.: 498
    Ada: 795
    Ada May: 756
    Adam: 1324
    Aicha I.: 1287
    Albert J.: 789
    Albert J.: 789
    Alta Marie: 891
    Alton Laverne: 894
    Alvin: 1289
    Alvin: 795
    Alvin: 770
    Alvin: 945
    Alvin: 1289
    Alvin: 1331
    Alvin D.: 569
    Alvin Jay: 498, 926, 927, 1323
    Alvin L.: 1055, 1355
    Amanda: 1211
    Amanda M.: 879, 880
    Amelia Viola: 894
    Ammon A.: 795, 1218
    Amos E.: 560
    Amos J.: 1303, 1304
    Amos N.: 528, 999
    Andrew: 412
    Andrew: 769
    Andrew S.: 794, 795
    Angela: 1287
    Anna: 412
    Anna: 1382
    Anna Bontrager: 537
    Anna Ellen: 1020
    Anna Mae: 893
    Anna Mae: 1212
    Anna V.: 538
    Annie D.: 976
    Annie Mae: 945
    Ashli Scot: 1482
    Barbara: 8
    Barbara: 758
    Barbara M.: 1224
    Barbara Sue: 1053
    Becky M.: 1224
    Benedict Ray: 1294
    Benjamin: 1340
    Benjamin Lynn: 1020
    Benjamin Lynn: 1020
    Bertha: 911
    Bertha: 1381
    Bessie Mae: 781
    Bessie Mildred: 999
    Betsy: 1383
    Beulah: 945
    Blanche: 835
    Bradi Korin: 1459
    Brant Jason: 1458
    Brien: 1287
    Brooke Kalyn: 1459

Calvin: 909
Carl David: 1481, 1495, 1496
Carl Jay: 1290
Carl Wayne: 1304, 1481, 1495
Carol Ann: 1211
Carol Jean: 1218
Carrin Ann: 1481
Catharine Jane: 1055
Cephus: 755
Cheryl June: 1303
Christian D.: 1210
Christine: 1470
Christopher G.: 1210
Christy: 945
Clara: 69
Clara: 795
Clara Caroline: 780, 1210
Clara G.: 886, 1210
Clara Mae: 870
Clara V.: 524
Cletus Dewayne: 1303
Cora Ann: 836, 837
Cora D.: 569
Cornelius M.: 487, 894
Daniel: 1375
Daniel C.: 894
Daniel J.: 1388
Daniel L.: 780, 867, 1340, 1342
Daniel M: 520
Daniel M.: 487
Daniel M.: 1211
Daniel N.: 231, 568, 569
Daniel Ray: 1300
Daniel Richard: 1467
Danielle: 1482
Daryl Ray: 927
David: 1287
David: 1388
David: 1287
David A.: 529
David Allen: 951
David D.: 780
David Deshon: 1467
David J.: 412, 757, 758
David M.: 1224
David Ray: 1304, 1482
Dean Roger: 560
Deborah Elizabeth: 1324
Deidra: 1482
Deilia Cordelia (aka: Delia): 477, 478
Dennis LaMar: 928
Doris Kay: 1231
Edith: 498
Edna: 805
Edna: 232
Edna: 1014
Edna Ellen: 498, 928, 929
Edna Ellen: 1052
Edna M.: 487, 892
Edna Mae: 891, 1073, 1301
Edna Marie: 893
Edwin J: 757
Eldon Lee: 928
Elenora: 528
Elizabeth: 519
Elizabeth: 757

Loretta: 971
Lou Ann: 1267, 1467, 1468, 1495
Lou Ida: 1472
Lovina: 879, 986
Lowayne: 1340
Luella: 229, 230, 1373
Lulu G.: 1210
Lydia: 805
Lydia: 806, 807
Lydia Ann T.: 481-484, 946, 955, 1007
Lydia Kathryn: 1051
Lydia Mae: 805
Lydia Mae: 894
Lydiann D.: 525
Mable Marie: 498, 928
Magdalena (aka: Mattie): 469-471
Magdalena: 1218
Mahlon: 755
Mahlon D.: 781
Mahlon M.: 1224
Malinda M.: 1224
Marcia Ann: 1367
Margaret: 1322
Margery: 1340
Maridan: 1367
Marilyn: 1211
Mark M.: 1224
Marlene: 1480
Marlene Kay: 1267, 1467, 1494, 1495
Marlin Ray: 1218
Martin: 879, 986
Marvin Jay: 927
Mary: 755
Mary: 412
Mary Alice: 893
Mary D.: 214, 215
Mary D.: 471, 472
Mary D.: 780
Mary Edna: 1020
Mary Ellen: 974
Mary Ellen: 891
Mary Ellen: 1211
Mary Etta: 1049
Adopted Mary F.: 493, 908
Mary J.: 781
Mary Jane: 498, 927
Mary Kathryn: 1294
Mary Kay: 1056
Mary Lou: 1290
Mary Lou: 951
Mary V.: 1375, 1376
Mattie: 981, 982
Mattie D.: 539
Mattie U.: 801
Mattie W.: 1291
Maud: 1005, 1359
Melvin A.: 1301
Melvin E.: 1210
Menno J. S.: 487, 519, 520, 951, 982, 1005
Menno S.: 1378
Merle W.: 1303
Mervin M. Jr.: 1224
Mervin R.: 1224
Millie: 755
Milo: 945, 946
Mirrell D.: 781, 867, 868, 1212, 1286, 1287

Moses D.: 781, 1211, 1342, 1343
Moses J.: 757
Moses M. Jr.: 1211
Naomi A.: 870
Nelson Dean: 1208
Noah: 999
Norman: 886
Not Named: 781
Olen A.: 1056
Olympia: 1287
Orlis: 1211
Orpha: 945, 1330
Orpha: 1291
Orval Dean: 1056
Paul Revere: 868, 1287
Pauline: 992
Perry C.: 895
Perry Jay: 1055
Perry Jay: 1300
Perry T.: 945
Philip Leroy: 1020, 1378
Phillip: 1211
Phyllis Ann: 868, 1286, 1287
Phyllis Joan: 1056
Polly: 1033
Polly Anna: 1300
Polly D.: 473
Polly Suzanne: 757
Ralph Eugene: 1304, 1481, 1482
Ralph LaVerne: 1267
Raymond M.: 1211
Rebecca: 1291
Reuben: 758
Rhoda: 1210
Rhoda M.: 1224
Richard: 1340
Richard: 971
Richard: 1052
Richard Dewayne: 1055
Richard LaVern: 1267, 1467
Rick: 1458
Robert Dean: 1459
Robert E.: 1459
Robert Stanley: 835
Ronnie: 870
Rosa: 945
Rosanna: 1375
Rose M.: 1224
Rose Mary: 971
Roy: 1231
Rubin: 758
Ruby: 1052
Rudy M.: 1224
Ruth: 758
Ruth: 1052, 1053
Sadie Alma: 361, 362, 1141
Salinda: 1024
Salinda H.: 1278
Sally Ann: 569
Samuel: 575
Samuel D.: 569
Sarah: 755
Sarah Ann: 538
Sarah Jane: 1290
Sarah N.: 790
Sharon Diane: 1267, 1467, 1494

Sheroldine: 1340
Sol Jr.: 1210
Solomon: 1020
Stanley Eugene: 1052
Stanley Eugene: 927
Sue Ellen: 894
Susan: 412, 759
Susanna D.: 808
Susanna M.: 487, 891, 892, 1005
Susanne M.: 1224
Susannna V.: 476, 477, 1180
Susie: 1289
Susie: 999
Susie: 945
Susie: 1289
Susie Elizabeth: 891, 1300, 1301
Thomas Jefferson: 868, 1287
Tiffany: 1287
Tobias C: 757
Tobias E. (aka: Poor Toby): 497, 498
Tobias L.: 945
Tobie: 945
Treva Mae: 1052
Truman A: 770
Truman G.: 1210
Ura I.: 800, 801
Uriah: 999
Urias V.: 527, 528
Velma: 1210
Vera: 1051
Vera Marie: 1260
Vera Ruth: 835
Verna: 946
Verna M.: 1224
Vernon LaMar: 1056
Veronica A.: 416, 417
Viola G.: 1210
Viola Pauline: 893, 894
Virgil D.: 781, 1210, 1211
Virgil Eugene: 1055
Virgil Jr.: 1211
Vivian Elaine: 1367
Wayne Dale: 928
Wilbur LeRoy: 1055
William: 1210
William: 999
William E.: 970, 971
William L.: 1052
William Ray: 805
Wilma: 1289
Wilma: 1289
Wilma Amanda: 893
Wilma Jean: 1331
Wilma M.: 1224
Wilma Mae: 946

Yodis -
MIchelle Suzanna: 1450, 1451
York -
Carleen Anne: 1407
Yost -
Clara Anna: 237, 238
Lois Marie: 1134, 1135
Yothers -
Chester Eugene: 651, 652
Melvin Ray: 652

Youman -
David: 1176
Young -
Betty: 825, 1241
Karen: 1487
Nancy Amelia: 837
Stella: 622
Sue: 1408
Younkin -
Bernard C.: 247
Eileen: 247
Henry Clay: 291, 292
Katherine: 30, 31
Milton: 247
Rozella: 247
Youree -
Arnard Armstage: 1043
Diana Faye: 1043
Yutzy -
Adin G.: 579, 580
Clare Denise: 1276
Estella: 1370
Kenneth Darryle: 1276
Lutrell Marcus: 1276
Mary Arlene: 580
Myron Eugene: 1276
Norman G.: 233
Olive Kay: 1276
Paul: 580
Paul E.: 1275, 1276
Steven Ray: 1276
Vernon: 580
Zander -
Unnamed: 1393
Zehner -
Jeffrey Alan: 709
Zehr -
Unnamed: 780
Katie: 759
Zeigler -
Dean: 679, 680
Zeller -
Darrell Gustav: 686
Ziegler -
Jack: 368
Patricia Marie: 1201
Zimmel -
Audra Jane: 1425
Kirby: 1425
Matthew: 1425
Zimmer -
Brian Edward: 1434
Danny: 1187
Dennis: 1433
Floyd: 1186, 1187
John Eric: 1434
John Michael: 1187, 1433
Kevin Thomas: 1434
Kurt Joseph: 1434
Laurel Ann: 1434
Leo: 1187, 1434
Michael: 1433
Michael Wayne: 1434
Patricia: 1187, 1434

1945